Principles
of
Business Law

eleventh edition

ROBERT N. CORLEY
Distinguished Professor of Legal Studies
University of Georgia

WILLIAM J. ROBERT
Professor of Business Law
University of Oregon

PRINCIPLES
of
BUSINESS LAW

PRENTICE-HALL, INC., Englewood Cliffs, New Jersey 07632

Library of Congress Cataloging in Publication Data

CORLEY, ROBERT NEIL.
   Principles of business law.

   Includes bibliographical references and index.
   1. Commercial law—United States—Cases.
2. Commercial law—United States. I. Robert,
William J., joint author. II. Title.
KF888.C63 1979   346'.73'07   78-16156
ISBN 0-13-701318-3

© 1979, 1975, 1971, 1967, 1962, 1957, 1952, 1948, 1940
by Prentice-Hall, Inc., Englewood Cliffs, N.J. 07632

Printed in the United States of America
10 9 8 7 6 5 4

PRENTICE-HALL INTERNATIONAL, INC., *London*
PRENTICE-HALL OF AUSTRALIA PTY. LIMITED, *Sydney*
PRENTICE-HALL OF CANADA, LTD., *Toronto*
PRENTICE-HALL OF INDIA PRIVATE LIMITED, *New Delhi*
PRENTICE-HALL OF JAPAN, INC., *Tokyo*
PRENTICE-HALL OF SOUTHEAST ASIA PTE. LTD., *Singapore*
WHITEHALL BOOKS LIMITED, *Wellington, New Zealand*

Contents

v

BOOK II: CONTRACTS

BOOK III: UCC — *Uniform Commercial Code*

superficial

Preface

As we enter the decade of the 1980's, most business law courses are concerned with the legal environment in which business is conducted. This legal environment includes not only the legal principles of such important subjects as contracts but also encompasses such topics as the court system and consumerism. This eleventh edition continues our effort to environmentalize business law.

This edition is divided into eight "books." Each book, except the first and last, contain cases. Book I discusses the various sources of law and our legal system. It traces a lawsuit from the pleadings through the appellate process. It also contains a detailed discussion of arbitration as an alternative to litigation.

Because of the growing impact of the criminal law on contemporary society and the business community, Book I contains a special chapter on that subject. Another example of the environmentalization of the material is found in the discussion of the law of torts, including the trend toward no-fault in auto accident litigation. The chapter on torts contains a discussion of the liability of accountants because of the importance of this subject, especially for C.P.A. candidates.

As in the past, Books II through VII have cases at the end of each chapter. There are 232 such cases or an average of six per chapter. Of the 232 cases, 121 are new to this edition. Many of these new cases were decided in 1976 and 1977. As the courts in recent years have tended toward more "social engineering" and have developed new theories and new approaches to old problems, we believe that it is very important for the students to study the most recent cases. Moreover, we believe that students "relate" more to modern cases than to old cases however sound and well-written they may be.

The eleventh edition expands its coverage of consumer and debtor protection. In addition to the new Federal Trade Commission rule on holders in due course, Chapter 27 contains material on the Magnuson-Moss Warranty Act and the FTC rule on home solicitation sales. The 1977 statute on fair debt collection practices is also discussed.

Throughout the text, we have attempted to illustrate to the student that the law is in a constant state of change and that the dynamic quality of the law is its ability to adapt to changing conditions. Such a trend as the granting of greater protection to debtors in mortgage foreclosures by prohibiting deficiency judgments is illustrative of this attempt. The trend toward greater government regulation of business decisions is highlighted in Chapter 40. This chapter encompasses the application of the Sherman Act to the service sector in its discussion of price-fixing by lawyers. It also covers such subjects as sex discrimination and OSHA.

This edition continues the format of the preceding edition. The Uniform Commercial Code is included as supplementary material. The appropriate sections of the Code are referenced in the body of the text by use of section numbers. We have also included the Revised Article 9 of the Code which has now been adopted by some states and which the others are considering for adoption.

New to this edition is the inclusion in the appendix of the Uniform Partnership Act, the Uniform Limited Partnership Act, the Revised Uniform Limited Partnership Act, and the Model Business Corporation Act. These Acts are not footnoted in the text but are available for those students and professors who may wish to use them.

In the preparation of this manuscript, we continue to recognize the difference in the educational needs of lawyers and of business persons. We have attempted to meet the needs of business persons in the years ahead by stressing those aspects of law that are essential to the decision-making process. We believe the material will make a valuable contribution to the education of tomorrow's business leaders, who must be familiar with the legal aspects of business problems. However, we have deleted most of the procedural issues from the cases and have deleted case references and footnotes as well. Since we believe that students should be required to study the language and reasoning of the courts on substantive issues, we have attempted to include those portions of the cases which show the arguments of each party and the court's resolution of the issues raised. We have attempted to avoid long cases, but at the same time, we believe that case study makes a substantial contribution to the student's education and that the cases should be long enough to provide a good vehicle for class discussion.

As supplementary aids, there are review questions and problems at the end of each chapter. Approximately one-half of these are new for this eleventh edition. They were prepared by Professor Jan Henkel of the University of Georgia, and we are grateful to him for them. In addition, Professor Barbara George has prepared a student workbook to accompany the text, and we are grateful to her for it.

We also wish to express our deep appreciation to Professor Frank S. Forbes, Chairman, Department of Law and Society, University of Nebraska, Omaha, for his detailed and perceptive reviews.

Finally, we wish to thank Donna Weber for preparation of the manuscript.

Robert N. Corley
William J. Robert

book one

LAW,
ITS
SOURCES
AND
PROCEDURES

1

Law and Its Sources

1. Introduction

The subject matter of this text is business law. Before starting the study of business law, one should have an understanding of our legal system—where our laws come from, how they are applied, how they may be changed, and the role of law in our society. Also, if the business-related portion of the subject is to be understood, it is essential that certain terms be defined and classifications be established in advance. Thus, the first six chapters of this text will be devoted to a study of sources of law, the legal system and its procedures. In addition, there will be chapters on criminal law and torts that have a direct impact on the business community.

Now more than ever before in our nation's history, the direct relationship between law and the problems facing our society has a direct and substantial impact upon business and its decision-making processes. Solutions to many of society's problems are found in laws regulating business activity. For example, the basic approach to solving the problems of air and water pollution is found in the law. In the area of employment, legislation now affects the hiring of employees as well as their pay and promotion, especially with regard to minority groups and women. In the field of consumer protection, new laws have been enacted regulating the debtor–creditor relationship and other matters of consumer interest. Many of the laws regulating business activity are included with the materials throughout the text.

3

2.   Definitions of Law

In everyday conversation, people use the word *law* in many different ways. Actually, the word *law* is very difficult to define. In its broad context it expresses a variety of concepts. Law has been defined as those rules and regulations established by government and applied to people in order for civilization to exist. Law and legal theory, however, are far too complex for such a simple definition to suffice; thus, other definitions must be examined if the connotations of the word *law* are to be effectively understood.

In attempting to define *law,* it is helpful to look at its purposes or functions. It is fundamental that a basic purpose of law in a civilized society is to maintain order. This is the prime function of that body of law known as the *criminal law.* Another role of law is to resolve disputes that arise between individuals and to impose responsibility if one person has a valid legal claim against another. Suits for breach of contract would be an example of the latter. It is important to bear in mind that the law is not simply a statement of rules of conduct but is also the means whereby remedies are afforded when one person has wronged another.

Many legal scholars have defined law in relation to the sovereign. For example, Blackstone, the great legal scholar of the eighteenth century, defined law as "that rule of action which is prescribed by some superior and which the inferior is bound to obey." This concept of law as a command from a superior to an inferior is operative in many areas. For example, the tax laws command that taxes shall be paid to the sovereign.

Law has also been defined as the product of the legal system. For example, Justice Oliver Wendell Holmes in one case said, "Law is a statement of the circumstances in which the public force will be brought to bear through courts." In this definition, Holmes used the word *law* in its broad sense and took cognizance of the fact that in our society, all issues and disputes—political, social, religious, economic, or otherwise—ultimately become legal issues to be resolved by courts. Law, according to this definition, is simply what the courts determine it to be as an expression of the public will.

Law has also been defined as a scheme of social control. This definition acknowledges the role of law in governing and regulating a civilized society. Implied in this definition is the dynamic role of law as an instrument of social, political, and economic change. The law is both an instrument of change and a result of change. It is often difficult to determine whether the law brings about changes in society or whether changes in society bring about a change in the law. In our legal system, both are often true. The law—responding to the goals, desires, needs, and aspirations of society—is in a constant state of change. In some areas, it changes more rapidly than does the attitude of a majority of society. In these areas, the law and our legal system provide leadership in bringing about desirable changes. In some areas, most of society is ahead of the law in moving in new directions; other institutions then assume leadership, with the law cast in the role of follower. In either case, the legal system is an integral part of any change in society.

The definition of law as a scheme of social control recognizes that law exists for the protection of social interests, both those between government and individual and those between individuals. In a sense, law as a means of social control influences people in their actions because the control sought may be obtained by state action if necessary.

Law has also been defined as the body of principles, standards, and rules that the courts apply in the decision of controversies brought before them. By this definition, law consists of three elements: (1) formulated legislation, including constitutions, statutes, and treaties; (2) case law, or the common law created by judicial decision; and (3) procedural rules, which determine how lawsuits are handled in the courts and include such matters as the rules of evidence and related issues. The first two elements provide the rules of substantive law that are applied by the courts to decide controversies. The third provides the machinery whereby these rules of substantive law are given effect and applied to resolve controversies.

3. Forces That Shape the Law

Throughout history, legal scholars have written about the nature and origin of law, its purposes, and the factors that influence its development. Legal philosophers have generally acknowledged that logic, history, custom, religion, and social utility are among the major influences and forces that have shaped and directed the law. But there has been disagreement as to the relative importance of these forces, and the influence of each has varied throughout history.

Logic. Judicial reasoning often involves the use of prior decisions as precedents. The use of the analogy is of prime importance to the judicial process because of the need for certainty in the law. Logic may involve deductive reasoning or inductive reasoning. Deductive reasoning takes the form of a syllogism in which a conclusion concerning a particular circumstance (minor premise) is drawn from a general principle (major premise). Inductive reasoning involves the process of using specific cases to reach a general conclusion. It is often said that application of the doctrine of *stare decisis* by basing a decision on precedents announced in prior cases is inductive in nature, while applying a statute to a given set of facts is an example of deductive reasoning, but these examples are open to some criticism. In addition, the development of the law using logic would require that the law consist of a set of known rules. Since it does not, pure logic cannot always be used to decide cases. However, reasoning by example is at the heart of our judicial system.

In any case, "The life of the law has not been logic; it has been experience" (Justice O.W. Holmes). In this statement and in his definition of law as a prediction of what courts will decide, Justice Holmes stressed the empirical and pragmatic aspects of the law with primary reliance on facts to dictate what the law is. Yet he recognized that law is actually unpredictable and uncertain.

History and Custom.   History and custom play a significant role in the development of the law in many areas. The law tends to evolve as we learn from history. As customs and practices gain popular acceptance and approval, they become formalized into rules of conduct. Law was found in the rules and evolved from them. Custom results from repeated approved usage, and when such usage by common adoption and acquiescence justifies each member of society in assuming that every other member of society will conform thereto, a rule of conduct has been formulated. When such a rule is adopted by a court as controlling in a particular case or is enacted into legislation, law has been made.

Religion.   Throughout history, religious principles have played a major role in the development of the law. Many legal theorists have argued that there exists a natural law, based on divine principles established by the Creator, which mortal man is bound to follow.

This natural-law theory softened the rigid common law of England, became the basis of courts of equity, and, finding its way to America, is expressed in the Declaration of Independence in the words "certain unalienable Rights, . . . Life, Liberty, and the Pursuit of Happiness."

Social Utility.   Law was previously defined as a scheme of social control. Social utility is perhaps the most significant force influencing the development of the law today. Social utility involves the use of economic, political, and social considerations as factors in formulating the law. Under the pressure of conflicting interests, legislators and courts make law. Thus, law, when enacted by legislatures or pronounced by courts, is in the end the result of finding an equilibrium between conflicting interests.

Law is not only generalization deduced from a set of facts, a recognized tradition, a prescribed formula for determining natural justice, but it also consists of rules for social control growing out of the experiences of mankind. Current social mores, political ideologies, international situations and conditions, and economic and business interests are all elements to be investigated and evaluated in making the law and in determining how it operates.

4.   Classifications of Law

It is not possible to classify accurately the various legal subjects, because so many are overlapping and interrelated. However, one common classification distinguishes substantive law from procedural law. The rules of law that are used to actually decide disputes may be classified as *substantive* law. On the other hand, the legal procedures that provide how a lawsuit is begun, how the trial is conducted, how appeals are taken, and how a judgment is enforced are called *procedural* law. Substantive law is the part of the law that defines rights, and procedural law establishes the procedures whereby rights are enforced and protected. For example, A and B have entered into an agreement, and A claims that B has breached the agreement. The rules that provide for bringing B into court and for the conduct of the trial are rather mechanical, and they constitute procedural law. Whether the agreement was enforceable and whether A is entitled to damages are matters of substance and would be determined on the basis of the substantive law of contracts.

Law is also frequently classified into areas of *public* and *private* law. Public law includes those bodies of law that affect the public generally; private law includes the areas of the law that are concerned with the relationship between individuals.

Public law may be divided into three general categories: (1) *constitutional law,* which concerns itself with the rights, powers, and duties of federal and state governments under the U.S. Constitution and the constitutions of the various states; ((2) *administrative law,* which is concerned with the multitude of administrative agencies, such as the Interstate Commerce Commission, the Federal Trade Commission, and the National Labor Relations Board; and (3) *criminal law,* which consists of statutes that forbid certain conduct as being detrimental to the welfare of the state or the people generally and provides punishment for their violation. These public-law subjects will be discussed later in this and subsequent chapters.

Private law is that body of law pertaining to the relationships between individuals in an organized society. Private law encompasses the subjects of contracts, torts, and property. Each of these subjects includes several bodies of law. For example, the law of contracts may be subdivided into the subjects of sales, commercial paper, agency, and business organizations. The major portion of this text covers these subjects, which constitute the body of law usually referred to as business law.

The law of torts is the primary source of litigation in this country and is also a part of the total body of law in such areas as agency and sales. It is concerned with wrongful acts against a person or his property and is predicated upon the premise that in a civilized society, people who injure other persons or their property must compensate them for their loss.

The law of property may be thought of as a branch of the law of contracts, but in many ways our concept of private property contains much more than the contract characteristics. Property is the basic ingredient in our economic system, and the subject matter may be subdivided into several areas, such as wills, trusts, estates in land, personal property, bailments, and many more.

Any attempt at classification of subject matter, particularly in the private law, is difficult, because the law is indeed a "seamless web." For example, assume that an agent or a servant acting on behalf of his employer commits a tort. The law of agency, although a subdivision of the law of contracts, must of necessity contain a body of law to resolve the issues of tort liability of the employer and employee. Likewise, assume that a person is injured by a product he has purchased. The law of sales, even though a part of the law of contracts, contains several aspects that could best be labeled a branch of the law of torts. Therefore it is apparent that even the general classifications of contract and tort are not accurate in describing the subject matter of various bodies of law.

SOURCES OF LAW

5.   Introduction

The phrase *sources of law* is used here to describe those methods and procedures by which law is created and developed. The unique characteristic of American law is that a very substantial part of it is not to be found in statutes enacted by legislatures but rather in cases decided by our courts. This concept of decided cases as a source of law comes to us from England. It is generally referred to as the *common law.* Our common law system of heavy reliance on case precedent as a source of law must be contrasted with civil law systems, which developed on the European continent. The civil law countries have codified their laws—reduced them to statutes—so that the main source of law in those countries is to be found in the statutes rather than in the cases. Under the common law system, of course, we have a large number of statutes, but these are only a part of our law. In the United States, common law has been the predominant influence. Since most of the colonists were of English origin, they naturally were controlled by the laws and customs of their mother country. But in Louisiana, and to some extent Texas and California, the civil law has influenced the legal systems, because these states were founded by French and Spanish peoples. It must not be overlooked, however, that much of the law in every state of the United States is statutory, and statutes are becoming increasingly important. Case law, or common law, remains an important source of law because of the extreme difficulty in reducing all law to writing in advance of an issue being raised. In our system, statutes must be in keeping with the constitutions—federal and state—and the courts can declare void a statute that is found to violate constitutional provisions. Statutes and constitutions are sometimes described as "written law." Also included under this heading are treaties, which by the federal Constitution are the supreme law of the land.

Case law, as opposed to written law, is not set forth formally but is derived from an analysis of each case that uncovers what legal propositions the case stands for. It is not proper to call this "unwritten" law, because it is in fact in writing. However, it must be distinguished from statutory law in that it is not the product of the legislature but rather the product of the courts. When a court decides a case, particularly upon an appeal from a lower-court decision, the court writes an opinion setting forth, among other things, the reasons for its decision. From these written opinions, rules of law can be deduced, and these make up the body of what is called case law or common law. The basic characteristic of the common law is that a case once decided establishes a precedent that will be followed by the courts when similar issues arise later.

A third source of law is administrative law. Federal, state, and local administrative agencies make law by promulgating rules and regulations as well as by making decisions concerning matters under their jurisdiction.

In summary, our law comes from written laws such as constitutions, statutes, ordinances, and treaties; from case law, which is based on judicial decisions; and from the rules and decisions of administrative agencies.

6. Constitutions

The federal Constitution is a grant of power by the states to the federal government, whereas the constitutions of the various states basically limit the powers of state government. In other words, the federal government possesses those powers *granted* to it by the states, and state governments possess reserved powers, all powers not taken away in the state constitution or specifically denied to them by the U.S. Constitution.

The Constitution of the United States and the constitutions of the various states are the fundamental written law in this country. A federal law must not violate the U.S. Constitution. All state laws must conform to or be in harmony with the federal Constitution as well as with the constitution of the state.

Two very important principles of constitutional law are basic to our judicial system. They are closely related to each other and are known as the *doctrine of separation of powers* and the *doctrine of judicial review.*

The doctrine of separation of powers results from the fact that both state and federal constitutions provide for a scheme of government consisting of three branches—the legislative, the executive, and the judicial. Separation of powers ascribes to each branch a separate function and a check on and balance of the functions of the other branches. The doctrine of separation of powers infers that each separate branch will not perform the function of the others and that each branch has limited powers. The system of checks and balances may be briefly summarized as follows:

The legislature or a branch of it retains the power to approve key executive and judicial appointments. The legislative branch also exercises control through its power to appropriate funds. In addition, the legislative branch can limit or expand the authority of the executive branch or the jurisdiction of the judicial branch in most cases. The executive has the power to veto legislation and to appoint judges (in some states, the judiciary is elected). The judiciary has the power to review actions of the executive and to review laws passed by the legislative branch to determine if such laws are constitutional. This is known as the *doctrine of judicial review.*

The doctrine of judicial review and the doctrine of supremacy of the Constitution were established at an early date in our country's history, in the celebrated case of *Marbury v. Madison.* In this case, Chief Justice Marshall literally created for the court a power that the Founding Fathers had refused to include in the Constitution. This was the power of the judiciary to review the actions of the branches of government and to set them aside as null and void if in violation of the Constitution. In creating this power to declare laws unconstitutional, Chief Justice Marshall stated, "Certainly, all those who have framed written constitutions contemplated them as forming the fundamental and paramount law of the nation, and consequently, the theory of every such government must be that an act of the legislature, repugnant to the constitution, is void. This theory is essentially attached to a written constitution and is, consequently, to be considered by this court, as one of the fundamental principles of our society." Justice Marshall then decided that courts have the power to review the action of the legislative and executive branches of government to determine if they are constitutional. This doctrine of judicial review has, to a substantial extent, made the courts the overseer of government and of all aspects of our daily lives.

7. Statutory Law

Legislative bodies at all levels make law by statutory enactment. The term *statute* is generally used to describe the product of the legislative process, but some legislative enactments are called *ordinances* or *codes*. For example, laws enacted by Congress become part of the United States Code, and laws passed by local governments are usually called ordinances.

Legislation at all levels contains general rules for human conduct. Legislation is the result of the political process expressing the public will on an issue. However, the courts also have a significant role to play in the field of statutory law in addition to the power of judicial review. Courts interpret legislation and apply these general rules to specific facts.

Legislative bodies have procedural rules that must be followed if a law is to be valid. Among the typical procedural rules are those relating to the way amendments are added to a proposed law, the way proposed statutes are presented for consideration (reading aloud to the members, etc.), and the manner of voting by the members of the legislative body.

Theoretically, legislation expresses the will or intent of the legislature on a particular subject. This theory suffers in actual practice from certain inherent defects. First of all, in using the English language, it is not possible to express the legislative intent in such a manner that all will agree as to the meaning of the words used. Not only are statutes by their very nature couched in general language, but the words and phrases used are frequently ambiguous as well.

Second, the search for legislative intent is often complicated by the realization that the legislative body in fact had no intent on the issue in question and the law is incomplete. The matter involved is simply one that was not thought about when the law was passed. Therefore, sometimes the question about legislation is not, What did the legislature intend? but, What would it have intended had it considered the problem? Both these inherent problems result in an expanded role for courts in our legal system, because the power of courts over legislation is not limited to the doctrine of judicial review. Courts also interpret legislation by resolving these ambiguities and by filling in these gaps in the statutes. There is no need to interpret a statute that is direct, clear, and precise. However, since legislation is by its very nature general, courts are faced with the problem of finding the meaning of general statutes as applied to specific facts.

One technique of statutory interpretation is to examine the legislative history of an act to determine the purpose of the legislation, or the evil it was designed to correct. Legislative history includes the debates, committee hearings, and events that occurred prior to the enactment of the law in issue.

Several generally accepted rules of statutory interpretation are used by courts in determining legislative intent. For example, it is frequently stated that criminal statutes and taxing laws should be strictly or narrowly construed so that doubts as to the applicability of the law will be resolved in favor of the accused or the taxpayer, as the case may be. Another common rule of statutory interpretation is that remedial statutes (those creating a judicial remedy on behalf of one person at the expense of another) should be liberally construed so that the statute will be effective in correcting the condition sought to be remedied.

The foregoing rules of statutory construction illustrate the principles that courts apply in seeking legislative intent when the intent is not clear. Courts usually construe popular words in their popular sense and technical words in their technical sense, but if a word has both popular and technical meaning, its meaning is ordinarily determined from the context in which it is used. Thus it can be seen that the law is not simply the language of a statute, but the "law" includes the interpretations the court places upon the language. A statute means what the court says it means.

8. Uniform State Laws

Since each state legislature enacts its own laws, substantial diversity in the law of the various states can easily develop. The existence of different state laws on some subjects does not necessarily create problems. For example, the fact that Nevada has a complex legalized-gambling statute creates few, if any, problems for most other states. However, if the laws relating to business transactions vary greatly from state to state, the business community, and especially businesses engaged in interstate commerce, will encounter many difficulties. Uniformity in the statutory enactments of the various states is considered highly desirable in the business-law field.

To achieve this uniformity, a legislative drafting group known as the National Conference of Commissioners on Uniform State Laws has been created. This group is made up of commissioners appointed by the governors of the states, and it endeavors to promote uniformity in state laws on all subjects where uniformity is deemed desirable and practical. This goal is accomplished by the drafting of model acts on suitable subjects in which uniformity will make the law more effective. When approved by the National Conference, proposed uniform acts are recommended to the state legislatures for adoption.

More than 100 uniform laws concerning such subjects as partnerships, sale of goods, conditional sales, warehouse receipts, bills of lading, and stock transfers have been promulgated and presented to the various state legislatures. The response from the state legislatures has varied. Very few of the uniform laws have been adopted by all the states. Some states have adopted the uniform law in principle but have changed some of the provisions to meet local needs or to satisfy lobbying groups, so that the result has often been "nonuniform uniform state laws."

The most significant development for business in the field of uniform state legislation has been the Uniform Commercial Code. Because the Code provides the statutory basis for a substantial portion of this text, the next section will be devoted to the Code, its role, and necessary background information on it.

9. The Uniform Commercial Code

The purposes of the Uniform Commercial Code are to simplify, clarify, and modernize the law governing commercial transactions; to permit the continued expansion of commercial practices through custom, usage, and agreement of the parties; and to make uniform the law among the various jurisdictions (U.C.C. 1-102).[1] The Code purports to deal with all aspects of commercial transactions. It is restricted to transactions involving various aspects of sale, financing, and security in respect to *personal property*. It does not relate to *real property* except in a few isolated circumstances. This limitation must be kept in mind as the detailed provisions of the Code are studied later in this text.

The Code contains nine articles, of which eight deal with specific aspects of commercial transactions in detail, one contains general provisions applicable to the whole body of Code law, and one designates statutes that are repealed by the Code.

Article 1—General Provisions—sets forth certain rules of construction and interpretation. Definitions of generally applicable terms are included.

Article 2—Sales—is restricted to transactions involving the sale of "goods." It does not apply to transactions intended to operate only as security transactions.

Article 3—Commercial Paper—is concerned with drafts, checks, certificates of deposit, and notes. Article 3 does *not* apply to money, documents of title, or investment securities.

Article 4—Bank Deposits and Collections—is related to Article 3 and sets forth the rules for the negotiable instruments specified in Article 3 as they pass through banking channels in the collection process. Article 4 also prescribes the relationship between a bank and its customer.

---

[1] The letters U.C.C. shown in the parenthetical reference stand for "Uniform Commercial Code." These letters will be deleted in all further references. The code provisions are available in the appendix.

Article 5—Letters of Credit—covers a device that has long been used in international trade to facilitate sales of goods between remote buyers and sellers. A letter of credit is an engagement whereby one party, usually a bank, agrees in advance with a prospective buyer of goods to honor a draft (order to pay) drawn upon it by a seller of goods upon compliance with certain conditions. The letter of credit furnishes a financing device that substitutes the financial responsibility of a bank vis-à-vis the seller of goods for that of a buyer of goods.

Article 6—Bulk Transfers—relates to sales or transfers "in bulk and not in the ordinary course of the transferor's business, of a major part of the materials, supplies, merchandise or other inventory of an enterprise."

Article 7—Documents of Title—deals with paper that may be negotiable and represents goods or commodities in storage or transportation. Such paper is to be distinguished from "commercial paper," which represents an obligation to pay *money*—a document of title enables the holder to obtain *goods*. Both have the characteristic of *negotiability,* and holders of either have a degree of protection not available to holders of nonnegotiable instruments.

Article 8—Investment Securities—deals with the transfer of securities such as stock certificates and corporate bonds.

Article 9—Secured Transactions—applies to any transaction that is intended to create *a security interest* in personal property. Article 9 also covers the outright *sale* of accounts receivable and certain other intangibles.

As of now, all states except Louisiana have adopted the Code, and Louisiana has adopted portions of it. However, it should be kept in mind that complete uniformity is lacking, in that (1) the legislatures of some of the states have altered certain sections of the Code in line with local economic and financial factors; (2) the Code provides certain alternative sections wherein the legislatures make a choice as to the alternative best suited to the state; (3) the Code has purposely left certain areas open to further development by the courts and has left room for continued expansion as new methods of doing business and new media of communication come into use; (4) some areas were deemed better suited to local regulation in keeping with social problems and other conditions that can best be handled at the individual state level; and (5) it is possible that the courts, in interpreting the various sections of the Code and applying them to factual situations, may reach somewhat varying conclusions. This is especially true of some sections that courts have criticized as being ambiguous. A revised Article 9 has been prepared and has been adopted by 16 states. The revised Article 9 is included in the appendix to this text.

LAW FROM JUDICIAL DECISIONS

10. *Stare Decisis*

Notwithstanding the trend toward reducing law to statutory form, a substantial portion of our law finds its source in decided cases. This case law, or common law, is based on the concept of precedent and the doctrine of *stare decisis,* which means "to stand by decisions and not to disturb what is settled." The doctrine of *stare decisis* must be contrasted with the concept of *res adjudicata,* or *res judicata,* which means "the thing has been decided." *Res adjudicata* applies when, between the parties themselves, the matter is closed at the conclusion of the lawsuit. *Stare decisis* means that when a court of competent jurisdiction has decided a controversy and has, in a written opinion, set forth the rule or principle that formed the basis for its decision, that rule or principle will be followed by the court in deciding subsequent similar cases. Likewise, subordinate courts in the same judisdiction will be bound by the rule of law set forth in the decision. *Stare decisis,* then, affects persons who are not parties to the lawsuit, while *res adjudicata* applies only to the parties.

Stare decisis provides both certainty and predictability to the law. It is also expedient. Through reliance upon precedent established in prior cases, the common law has resolved many legal issues and brought stability into many areas of the law, such as the law of contracts. The doctrine of *stare decisis* provides a system wherein a businessman may act in a certain way with confidence that his action will have a certain legal effect. People can rely on prior decisions and, knowing the legal significance of their action, act accordingly. There is reasonable certainty as to the results of conduct. Courts usually hesitate to renounce precedent and generally assume that if a principle or rule of law announced in a former judicial decision is unfair or contrary to public policy, it will be changed by legislation. Precedent has more force on trial courts than on courts of review; the latter have the power to make precedent in the first instance.

11.   Problems Inherent in Case Law

The common law system as used in the United States has several inherent difficulties. First of all, the unbelievably large volume of judicial decisions, each possibly creating precedent, places "the law" beyond the comprehension of lawyers, let alone laymen. Large law firms employ lawyers whose sole task is to search the case reports for "the law" to be used in lawsuits and in advising their clients. Today, computers are being used to assist in the search for precedent. Legal research involves the examination of cases in hundreds of volumes. Since the total body of ruling case law is beyond the grasp of lawyers, it is obvious that laymen who are supposed to know the law and govern their conduct accordingly do not know the law and cannot always follow it, even with the advice of legal counsel.

Another major problem involving case law arises because conflicting precedents are frequently presented by the parties to an action. One of the major tasks of the courts in such cases is to determine which precedent is applicable to the case at bar and which precedent is correct. In addition, even today, many questions of law arise on which there has been no prior decision or in areas where the only authority is by implication. In such situations, the judicial process is "legislative" in character and involves the creation of law, not merely its discovery.

It should also be noted that there is a distinction between precedent and mere dicta. As authority for future cases, a judicial decision is coextensive only with the facts upon which it is founded and the rules of law upon which the decision is actually predicated. Frequently courts make comments on matters not necessary to the decision reached. Such expressions, called "dicta," lack the force of an adjudication and, strictly speaking, are not precedent courts will be required to follow within the rule of *stare decisis.* However, dicta or implication in prior cases may be followed if sound and just, and dicta that have been repeated frequently are often given the force of precedent.

Finally, our system of each state's having its own body of case law creates serious legal problems in matters that have legal implications in more than one state. This problem will be discussed in more detail in Section 13, under the heading "Conflict of Laws."

12. Rejection of Precedent

The doctrine of *stare decisis* has not been applied in such a fashion as to render the law rigid and inflexible. If a court, and especially a reviewing court, should find that the prior decision was "palpably wrong," it may overrule it and decline to follow the rule enunciated by that case. By the same token, if the court should find that a rule of law established by a prior decision is no longer sound because of changing conditions, it may consider the rule not to be a binding precedent. The strength and genius of the common law is that no decision is *stare decisis* when it has lost its usefulness or the reasons for it no longer exist. The doctrine does not require courts to multiply their errors by using former mistakes as authority and support for new errors. Thus, just as legislatures change the law by new legislation, so also do courts change the law, from time to time, by overruling former precedents. Judges are subject to social forces and changing circumstances just as legislatures are. The personnel of courts change, and each new generation of judges deems it a responsibility to reexamine precedents and to adapt them to the world of the times.

It should be noted, also, that in many cases, a precedent created by a decision will not be a popular one and may be "out of step" with the times. The effect of the decision as a precedent can be nullified by the passage of a statute providing for a different result than that reached by the courts as to future cases involving the same general issue.

Stare decisis may not be ignored by mere whim or caprice. It must be followed rather rigidly in the daily affairs of people. In the whole area of private law, uniformity and continuity are necessary. It is obvious that the same rules of tort and contract law must be applied in the afternoon as in the morning. *Stare decisis* must serve to take the capricious element out of law and to give stability to a society and to business.

However, in the area of public law, and especially constitutional law, precedent is frequently reexamined and often changed. Justice Douglas, speaking before the Association of the Bar of the City of New York at the Eighth Annual Benjamin N. Cardozo Lectures, explained the reasons for less-rigid adherence to precedent in constitutional issue cases:

> A judge looking at a constitutional decision may have compulsions to revere past history and accept what was once written. But he remembers above all else that it is the Constitution which he swore to support and defend, not the gloss which his predecessors may have put on it. So he comes to formulate his own views, rejecting some earlier ones as false and embracing others. He cannot do otherwise unless he lets men long dead and unaware of the problems of the age in which he lives do his thinking for him.

> This reexamination of precedent in constitutional law is a personal matter for each judge who comes along. When only one new judge is appointed during a short period, the unsettling effect in constitutional law may not be great. But when a majority of a Court is suddenly reconstituted, there is likely to be substantial unsettlement. There will be unsettlement until the new judges have taken their positions on constitutional doctrine. During that time—which may extend a decade or more—constitutional law will be in flux. That is the necessary consequence of our system and to my mind a healthy one. The alternative is to let the Constitution freeze in the pattern which one generation gave it. But the Constitution was designed for the vicissitudes of time. It must never become a code which carries the overtones of one period that may be hostile to another.

> So far as constitutional law is concerned *stare decisis* must give way before the dynamic component of history. Once it does, the cycle starts again. Today's new and startling decision quickly becomes a coveted anchorage for new vested interests. The former proponents of change acquire an acute conservatism in their new *status quo*. It will then take an oncoming group from a new generation to catch the broader vision which may require an undoing of the work of our present and their past. . . .

> From age to age the problem of constitutional adjudication is the same. It is to keep the power of government unrestrained by the social or economic theories that one set of judges may entertain. It is to keep one age unfettered by the fears or limited vision of another. There is in that connection one tenet of faith which has crystallized more and more as a result of our long experience as a nation. It is this: If the social and economic problems of state and nation can be kept under political management of the people, there is likely to be long-run stability. It is when a judiciary with life tenure seeks to write its social and economic creed into the Charter that instability is created. For then the nation lacks the adaptability to master the sudden storms of an era. It must be remembered that the process of constitutional amendment is a long and slow one.

> That philosophy is reflected in what Thomas Jefferson wrote about the Constitution, "Some men look at constitutions with sanctimonius reverence, and deem them like the ark of the covenant, too sacred to be touched. They ascribe to the men of the preceding age a wisdom more than human, and suppose what they did to be beyond amendment. I knew that age well; I belonged to it, and labored with it. It deserved well of its country. It was

very like the present, but without the experience of the present; and forty years of experience in government is worth a century of book-reading; and this they would say themselves, were they to rise from the dead."

13. Conflict of Laws

Certain basic facts about our legal system must be recognized. First of all, statutes and precedents, in all legal areas, vary from state to state. For example, in most states the plaintiff in an automobile accident case must be completely free of fault in order to recover judgment, but in some states the doctrine of comparative negligence is used, so that a plaintiff found to be 20 percent at fault could recover 80 percent of his injuries. Second, the doctrine of *stare decisis* does not require that one state recognize the precedent or rules of law of other states. Each state is free to decide for itself questions concerning its common law and interpretation of its own constitution and statutes. (However, courts will often follow decisions of other states if they are found to be sound. They are considered persuasive authority. This is particularly true in cases involving the construction of statutes such as the uniform acts, where each state has adopted the same statute.) Third, many legal issues arise out of acts or transactions that have contact with more than one state. For example, a contract may be executed in one state, performed in another, and the parties may live in still others; or an automobile accident occurring in one state may involve citizens of different states.

These hypothetical situations raise the following fundamental question: Which state's *substantive* laws are applicable in a multiple-state case where the law in one of the states differs from the law in the other? (The court in which the case is tried uses its own rules of procedure.)

The body of law known as *conflict of laws* answers this question. It provides the court or forum with the applicable substantive law in the multistate transaction or occurrence. For example, the law applicable to a tort is generally said to be the law of the state of place of injury. Thus, a court sitting in state X would follow its own rules of procedure, but it would use the tort law of state Y if the injury occurred in Y. There are several rules that are used by courts on issues involving the law of contracts. These include the law of the state where the contract was made; the law of the place of performance; and the "grouping of contacts" or "center of gravity" theory, which uses the law of the state with the most substantial contact with the contract. Many contracts contain provisions which designate the applicable substantive law. For example, a contract may provide "This contract shall be governed by the law of the State of New York." Such a provision will be enforced if New York has at least minimal connection with the contract.

It is not the purpose of this text to teach conflict of laws, but the student should be aware that such a body of law exists and should recognize those situations in which conflict-of-law principles will be used. The trend toward uniform statutes and codes has tended to decrease these conflicts, but many of them still exist. So long as we have a federal system and fifty separate state bodies of substantive law, the area of conflicts of law will continue to be of substantial importance in the application of the doctrine of *stare decisis*.

14. Full Faith and Credit

One further aspect of the scope of precedent must be noted. Article IV, Section 1, of the U.S. Constitution provides, "Full faith and credit shall be given in each State to the public acts, records, and judicial proceedings of every other State. . . ." This does not mean that the precedent in one state is binding in other states, but only that the final decisions or judgments rendered in any given state by a court with jurisdiction shall be enforced as between the original parties in other states. "Full faith and credit" is applicable to the result of a specific decision as it affects the rights of the parties, and not to the reasons or principles upon which it was based. Full faith and credit requires that a suit be brought on the judgment in the other state.

CHAPTER 1
REVIEW QUESTIONS AND PROBLEMS

1. What are the primary sources of the laws in the United States?

2. Determine whether the following areas of law are categorized as private or public law:
    a. Criminal law
    b. Property law
    c. Tort law
    d. Labor law
    e. Contract law

3. In August 1961, Earl Miller of Harrison, New York, went to Brunswick, Maine, where his brother resided and they had mutual business interests. Two days later, while riding with his brother in an automobile owned by his sister-in-law, Earl was killed in an accident. Three months later, the brother and sister-in-law moved to New York. Maine has a statute limiting damages for wrongful death to $20,000. New York has no such statute. In a suit against the brother and sister-in-law, should this limitation on the amount of recovery be imposed? Why?

4. What is the function of the body of law known as *conflict of laws?*

5. What is meant by the term *full faith and credit?*

6. Why is it misleading to refer to case law as "unwritten" law? Explain.

7.   When a court writes an opinion, it sometimes makes comments that are not considered to be precedent. Explain.

8.   The basic characteristic of the common law is that a case once decided establishes a precedent that will be followed by the courts when similar issues arise later. Do courts always follow precedent? Explain.

9.   Explain the relationship of the doctrine of separation of powers to the doctrine of judicial review.

10.   A state statute limits the amount of interest that may be charged upon borrowed money to $8 per year per $100. Is this law an example of substantive or procedural law? Explain.

11.   P brought suit against D, claiming damages in the amount of $50,000. The jury returned a $12,000 verdict in favor of P. P now files a second suit to recover additional damages, and D feels that a proper defense would be the doctrine of *stare decisis*. Is D correct? Why?

12.   What are the purposes of the Uniform Commercial Code?

13.   What is the basic distinction between the common law system and the civil law system?

14.   *Stare decisis* is less likely to be followed in the area of public law than in the area of private law. Explain.

2

The Judicial System

1. Introduction

It is essential for the functioning of an ordered society that institutions for re-solving conflicts be established and maintained. Our system of government has selected courts as the primary means to accomplish this purpose. Courts settle controversies between persons, and between persons and the state. The court is the judge and the judge is the court. The terms are used interchangeably.

The basic function of the court is to apply the law to the facts. The facts are determined by a jury, if one is used. If a jury is not used, the court also serves as the finder of the facts. (Those cases in which the parties are entitled to a jury will be noted later.) The rule of law applied to the facts produces a decision that settles the controversy. Although there are obviously other agencies of government that resolve controversies and use other techniques (see Chapter 4), it is peculiar to our system that for final decision, all contro-versies may ultimately end up in court. Whether the issue is the busing of schoolchildren, the legality of abortions, the enforceability of a contract, or the liability of a wrongdoer, the dispute, if not otherwise resolved, goes to the courts for a final decision.

The preceding chapter noted the following three great powers of the judiciary, which come into play as it performs its functions of deciding cases and controversies: (1) the power of judicial review, (2) the power to interpret and apply statutes, and (3) the power to create law through precedent. The extent to which these powers come into play varies from case to case, but it should be recognized that all three are frequently involved in a single case.

2. State Court Systems

The judicial system of the United States is a dual system consisting of state courts and federal courts. The courts of the states, although not subject to uniform classification, may be grouped as follows: supreme courts, intermediate courts of appeal (in the more populous states), and trial courts. Some trial courts have general jurisdiction, and others have a limited jurisdiction. For example, a justice of the peace has power to hear civil and criminal cases only if the amount in controversy does not exceed a certain sum or the penalty for the crime is restricted.

Lawsuits are instituted in one of the trial courts. Even a court of general judisdiction has geographical limitations. In many states, the trial court of general jurisdiction is called a circuit court, because in early times a single judge sitting as a court traveled the circuit from one county to another. In other states, it is called the superior court or the district court. Each area has a trial court of general jurisdiction.

Each state also has courts of limited jurisdiction. They may be limited as to subject matter, amount in controversy, or area in which the parties live. For example, courts with jurisdiction limited to a city are often called municipal courts. Courts limited as to the amount of money involved in the controversy, frequently called small-claims courts, provide a forum for deciding controversies quickly and inexpensively. These courts are discussed more fully in the next section.

Courts may also be named according to the subject matter with which they deal. Probate courts deal with wills and the estates of deceased persons; family courts with divorces, family relations, juveniles, and dependent children; criminal and police courts with violators of state laws and municipal ordinances; and traffic courts with traffic violations. For an accurate classification of the courts of any state, the statutes of that state should be examined. The chart at the top of p. 22 illustrates the jurisdiction and organization of reviewing and trial courts in a typical state.

3. Small-claims Courts

Small-claims courts are of great importance today. They are an attempt to provide a prompt and inexpensive means of settling the thousands of minor disputes that arise in our society. Such cases often involve suits by consumers against merchants for lost or damaged goods or for services poorly performed. Landlord–tenant disputes and collection suits are also quite common in small-claims courts. In these courts, the usual court costs are greatly reduced. The procedures are simplified so that the services of a lawyer are usually not required. Most of the states have authorized such courts and have imposed a limit on the jurisdiction of such courts. Some states have the amount as low as $500, while others may be as high as $5000. $1000 would be a typical limit.

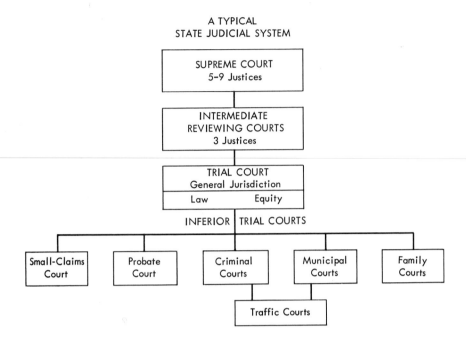

As small-claims courts have grown in number and their case loads have expanded, numerous problems have arisen. In large cities, there is often a need for a bilingual court. In addition, easy accessibility to the courts frequently requires night sessions so that the litigants need not miss work. As a practical matter, the judge often serves as a mediator of the dispute, and most cases are settled by agreement with the court. One continuing problem, however, is that many successful litigants are unable to collect their judgments because the decision of the small-claims court are not self-enforcing. A recent study in New York City found that 44 percent of the successful litigants in small-claims court did not collect any money.

THE FEDERAL COURT SYSTEM

4. Introduction

The courts of the United States are created by Congress under the authority of the Constitution, and their jurisdiction is limited by the grant of power given to the federal government by the states through the Constitution. They are thus courts of limited jurisdiction, as will be discussed more fully later. The Constitution creates the Supreme Court and authorizes such inferior courts as the Congress may from time to time ordain and establish. Congress, pursuant to this authority, has created eleven U.S. courts of appeal, the U.S. district courts (at least one in each state), and others, such as the Court of

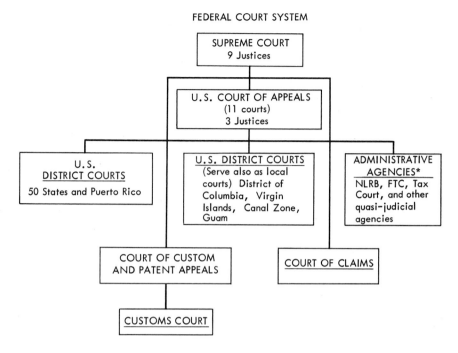

FEDERAL COURT SYSTEM

* The federal administrative agencies are not officially part of the federal court system but are included in this chart because their rulings can be appealed to a federal court.

Customs and Patent Appeals, the Court of Claims, and the Tax Court, which handle special subject matter as indicated by the name of the court. The chart above illustrates the federal court system.

5. Federal District Courts

The district courts are the trial courts of the federal judicial system. They have original jurisdiction, exclusive of the courts of the states, over all federal crimes—that is, all offenses against the laws of the United States. The accused is entitled to a trial by a jury in the state and district where the crime was committed. The same facts may constitute a crime against both state and federal authority. For example, robbery of a bank is a crime against both sovereigns.

In civil actions, the district courts have jurisdiction only when the matter in controversy exceeds the sum or value of $10,000, exclusive of costs and interest, and is based on either diversity of citizenship or a federal question. Diversity of citizenship exists in suits between (1) citizens of different states, (2) a citizen of a state and a citizen of a foreign country, and (3) a state and citizens of another state. The plaintiff or all plaintiffs, if more than one, must be citizens of a different state from that of any one of the defendants for diversity of citizenship to exist. Diversity of citizenship does not prevent the plaintiff from bringing his suit in a state court, but if the defendant is a citizen of another state, the defendant has the right to have the case removed to a federal court. A defendant, by having the case removed to the federal court, has an opportunity of having a jury selected from a larger area than the county where the cause arose, in the hope of avoiding the possibility of jurors prejudicial to the plaintiff.

For the purpose of suit in a federal court, a corporation is considered a "citizen" of the state where it is incorporated and of the state in which it has its principal place of business. As a result, there is no federal jurisdiction in many cases in which one of the parties is a corporation. If any one of the parties on the other side of the case is a citizen of the state in which the corporation is either chartered or doing its principal business, there is no diversity of citizenship and thus no federal jurisdiction.

Federal jurisdiction based on a federal question exists if the controversy arises out of rights granted by the Constitution, laws, or treaties of the United States. If the federal-question case involves a suit for money, the federal jurisdictional amount of $10,000 must be met. However, many federal-question cases are not basically suits for dollar damages, and the federal courts have jurisdiction of such cases without reference to money value of the controversy. For example, the amount of the controversy is not a jurisdictional question when the suit is brought by the United States or a federal officer and arises under the Constitution or federal laws and treaties. These civil actions may involve matters such as bankruptcy or setting aside orders of administrative agencies such as the Interstate Commerce Commission. Other federal-question cases that do not require that $10,000 be involved are suits based on patents, copyrights, trademarks, taxes, elections, the rights guaranteed by the Bill of Rights, and those rights secured to individual citizens by the Fourteenth Amendment. In addition, by statute the district courts now have original jurisdiction to try tort cases involving damages to citizens caused by officers or agents of the federal government, and the power to issue writs of *habeas corpus* and to grant injunctions in a variety of cases. In cases where injunctions are sought, three judges must hear the case.

6. Federal Reviewing Courts

Direct appeals from the decisions of the district courts to the U.S. Supreme Court may be made in several situations, such as (1) in criminal cases when the decision of the lower court is based upon the invalidity or construction of a statute upon which the indictment or information was founded; (2) when the lower court has held an act of Congress unconstitutional, and when an agency of the government is a party; (3) when the lower court consisting of three judges has either granted or denied after notice an interlocutory or permanent injunction. However, in most cases, an appeal is taken from a U.S. district court to the court of appeals.

The intermediate courts of appeal from the U.S. district courts are called the U.S. courts of appeals. In 1891, because of the heavy burden placed upon the Supreme Court, Congress established the courts of appeals. The federal judicial districts are divided into eleven circuits, and a court of appeals has been established for each circuit. These courts are not trial courts and are limited to appellate jurisdiction. After a case has been decided by a district court, a dissatisfied party may appeal to the court of appeals of the circuit in which the district court lies.

In most cases, the decisions of the courts of appeals are final. The jurisdiction of the court is determined by Congress and may be changed from time to time. Cases in the courts of appeals may be reviewed by the Supreme Court by a writ of certiorari granted upon a petition of any party to any civil or criminal case before or after a judgment or decree in the courts of appeals. The writ of certiorari to review a judgment of the courts of appeals is within the discretion of the Supreme Court. The writ will be issued when necessary to secure uniformity of decision or to bring cases of grave public concern to the court of last resort for decision.

Court of appeals decisions may also be reviewed by the Supreme Court in cases in which a state statute has been held unconstitutional and a federal question is presented. In addition, the courts of appeals may by certification seek instructions from the Supreme Court on any question of law in any civil or criminal case.

The U.S. district courts and the courts of appeals cannot review, retry, or correct the judicial errors charged against a state court. Final judgments or decrees rendered by the highest court of a state are reviewed only by the Supreme Court of the United States. State cases appealed to the U.S. Supreme Court must concern the validity of a treaty or statute of the United States or must present a question involving the validity of a state statute on the grounds that the statute is repugnant to the Constitution, treaties, or laws of the United States and that the state decision is in favor of the statute's validity. When a case involves the constitutionality of a state statute or treaty, or when a citizen's rights, privileges, or immunities under the Constitution or laws are impaired, the case may be brought to the U.S. Supreme Court by writ of certiorari. In all other cases, the decision of the highest state court is not subject to review.

7. The Law in the Federal Courts

Our dual system of federal and state courts creates a unique problem. The federal courts use their own body of procedural law and their own body of substantive law in federal-question cases. Decisions of the U.S. Supreme Court on questions involving the U.S. Constitution, treaties, federal statutes, and matters of interstate commerce are binding on state courts. However, as previously noted, the federal courts also have jurisdiction based on diversity of citizenship. Since there is no body of federal common law, in suits based on diversity of citizenship to determine the rights and duties of the parties, federal courts use the substantive law, including conflict of laws principles, of the state in which they are sitting. As in all cases, the federal courts do use their own rules of procedure, however. Thus, just as the state courts are bound by federal precedent in diversity cases involving federal law and federally protected rights, so also are federal courts bound by state precedent when state rights and duties are involved in diversity of citizenship cases.

8.   Law and Equity

Historically, the trial courts in the United States have been divided into two parts—a court of law and a court of equity or chancery. The term *equity* arose because the English law courts were not equipped with remedies for many wrongs. In early English law, the courts could not give remedies for injuries received unless the king's original writs covered the particular remedy sought. Consequently, the proceedings at law were so limited that it was often impossible to obtain justice in the king's courts.

In order that justice might be done, the person seeking a remedy sought redress from the king in person. Since the appeal was to the king's conscience, he referred such matters to his spiritual advisor, the chancellor. Such an individual was usually a church official, and in giving a remedy he usually favored the ecclesiastical law.

By such method there developed a new system of procedure and new rules. Actions involving these rules were said to be brought "in chancery" or "in equity," in contradistinction to a suit "at law" in the king's courts. Courts of equity were courts of conscience and recognized many rights that were not recognized by common law courts. For example, trusts in lands were recognized; rescission was allowed on contracts created through fraud; injunction and specific performance were developed.

In a few states, courts of equity are still separate and distinct from courts of law. In most states, the equity and law courts are organized under a single judge who has two dockets—one in law, the other in equity. (The court will usually have a separate criminal docket as well.) Whether the case is in equity or in law is determined by the remedy desired. Modern Civil Practice Acts have abolished the common law names heretofore used to distinguish different forms of actions at law and in equity, but pleadings usually must denote whether the action is legal or equitable because as a general rule there is no right to a jury trial of an equitable action. The constitutional guarantee to a trial by jury applies only to actions at law.

By statute in some states, a jury may hear the evidence in equity cases, but the determination of the jury in these cases is usually advisory only and is not binding on the court. The judge passes upon questions of both law and fact, and he may decide the case upon the pleadings without the introduction of oral testimony. If the facts are voluminous and complicated, the judge may refer the case to another person, called a master in chancery, to take the testimony. This is the usual procedure when a complicated accounting is required. The master hears the evidence and reports back to the judge his conclusions of fact and law. Sometimes the master's duty is confined to only the hearing and reporting of testimony.

Courts of equity frequently use maxims instead of strict rules of law as the basis for their decisions. There are no legal rights in equity, for the decision is based on moral rights and natural justice.

Some of the typical maxims of equity are:

1. "Equity will not suffer a right to exist without a remedy."
2. "Equity regards as done that which ought to be done."
3. "Where there is equal equity, the law must prevail."
4. "He who comes into equity must do so with clean hands."
5. "He who seeks equity must do equity."
6. "Equity aids the vigilant."
7. "Equality is equity."

These maxims serve as guides to the chancellor to use in exercising his discretion. For example, the clean-hands doctrine (No. 4) prohibits a party who is guilty of misconduct in the matter in litigation from receiving the aid of the court.

The decision of the court in equity is called a decree. A judgment in a court of law is measured in damages, whereas a decree of a court of equity is said to be *in personam;* that is, it is directed to the defendant, who is to do or not to do some specific thing.

Decrees are either final or interlocutory. A decree is final when it disposes of the issues in the case, reserving no question to be decided in the future. A decree quieting title to real estate, granting a divorce, or ordering specific performance is usually final. A decree is interlocutory when it reserves some question to be determined in the future. A decree granting a temporary injunction, appointing a receiver, and ordering property to be delivered to such a receiver would be interlocutory.

Failure upon the part of the defendant to obey a decree of a court of equity is contempt of court because the decree is *in personam.* Any person in contempt of court may be placed in jail or fined by order of the court.

Equity jurisprudence plays an ever-increasing role in our legal system. The movement toward social justice requires more reliance on the equitable maxims and less reliance on rigid rules of law. This also contributes to the further decay of the doctrine of *stare decisis.*

THE LAWSUIT CAST

9. Introduction

The judicial system is not a computer into which facts are fed with a result automatically appearing on a printout. It requires many people with special education and training for its operation. First and foremost are the judges and justices of reviewing courts. Second are the attorneys-at-law who appear and represent the interests of their clients. Finally, laymen who serve as jurors play an extremely important role in the judicial process. The sections that follow briefly discuss the roles of these persons in the judicial system.

10. Judges and Justices

"Judges ought to be more learned than witty, more reverent than plausible, more advised than confident. Above all things, integrity is their portion and proper virtue" (Francis Bacon).

The judge, by virtue of the office, owes very high duties to the state, its people, the litigants, the law, the witnesses, and the jury. The court is the protection of constitutional limitations and guarantees. A judge should be temperate, attentive, patient, impartial, studious, diligent, industrious, and prompt in ascertaining the facts and applying the law. Judges should be courteous, civil, and considerate of jurors, witnesses, and others in attendance upon the court, but should criticize and correct unprofessional conduct of attorneys.

A judge must avoid any appearance of impropriety and should not act in a controversy in which he or a near relative has an interest. He should not be swayed by public clamor or consideration of personal popularity, or be apprehensive of unjust criticism.

The trial judge renders his decisions at a level that deals directly with the people. It is in the trial courts that the law is made alive and its words are given meaning. Since he represents the only contact that most people have with the law, it is apparent that the effective function of the law must depend largely upon the character and training of the trial judge. Members of reviewing courts are usually called *justices* to distinguish them from trial-court judges. The roles of the justice and the judge are substantially different. For example, the trial judge has direct contact with the litigation and the litigants, whereas the justice rarely has any contact with litigants. In many cases he does not even have direct contact with the attorneys, because when oral argument is not requested, the case is submitted for review solely in writing in the form of briefs and records of proceedings. Oral argument is presented in most cases, however.

Justices must do much more than simply decide a case—they are required to give the reasons for their decision in written form so that anyone who desires to do so may examine it and comment on its merits. Each decision will become precedent to some degree and will become a part of our body of law.

Thus, the legal opinion of the justice, unlike that of the trial judge, whose decision has direct effect only upon the litigants, affects society as a whole. The justice, in deciding the case before him, must consider not only the result between the parties involved but the total effect of his decision on the law. In this sense, his role is that of a "legislator."

Because of this difference in roles, the personal qualities required for a justice are somewhat different from those for a trial judge. The duties of a justice bring him into the area of legal scholarship. He is required to be articulate in presenting his ideas in writing and to use the written word as the primary source of his decision. Whereas the trial judge, being a part of the trial arena, observes the witnesses and essentially uses knowledge gained from his participation for his decision, the justice spends hours studying briefs, the record of proceedings, and the law, before preparing and handing down his decisions.

11. The Jury

In Anglo-American law, the right of trial by jury, particularly in criminal cases, is traced to the famous Magna Charta issued by King John of England in 1215, wherein it is stated:

> . . . that no freeman shall be taken or imprisoned or disseised or outlawed or exiled . . . without the judgment of his peers or by the law of the land. . . .

In early English legal history, the juror was a witness; that is, he was called to tell what he knew, not to listen to others testify. The word *jury* comes from the French word *juré,* which means "sworn." The jury gradually developed into an institution to determine facts. The function of the jury today is to ascertain the facts just as the function of the court is to ascertain the law.

A juror must come to a trial with an open mind; otherwise, his previous knowledge might prejudice him in evaluating the testimony presented at the trial. The jury system as brought to the colonies from England was adopted as a matter of right in the Constitution of the United States. The Sixth and Seventh Amendments to the U.S. Constitution guarantee the right of trial by jury in both criminal and civil cases; in addition, the Fifth Amendment provides for indictment by a grand jury for capital offenses and infamous crimes. In civil cases, the right to trial by jury is preserved in suits at common law when the amount in controversy exceeds $20. State constitutions have like provisions guaranteeing the right of trial by jury in state courts.

The persons who are selected to serve on trial juries are drawn at random from lists of qualified voters in the county or city where the trial court sits. Most states by statute have listed certain occupations and professions—such as doctors, dentists, pharmacists, embalmers, policemen, firemen, lawyers, and newspapermen—whose members are exempt from jury duty. When a case is called for trial, those selected as noted above will appear as the jury panel and, unless excused by the judge for personal reasons, will be available to serve as jurors. Twelve persons, or less if the law so provides, will be selected by drawing, and *voir dire* examination will be conducted to select the jury in a particular case. Serving on the jury is an important civic duty. It is one significant way in which a citizen can take part in his government and participate in the administration of justice.

In most states, the decision of the jury, except in particular situations prescribed by constitution or statute, must be unanimous. It operates in "the native way of deciding an issue"—that is, "to discuss it until there is unanimity opinion or until the opposition feels it is no longer worthwhile to argue its point of view." Statutes and constitutions provide the number of jurors who must concur for a verdict. In some states, the concurrence of only three-fourths of the jurors is required in civil cases.

12.   The Lawyer

English law not only gave us the common law, it gave us the profession of attorney-at-law. Attorneys-at-law are also known as lawyers, solicitors, or counselors-at-law. An attorney-at-law is a person qualified in character and by training to serve as an officer of courts in representing and advising people in regard to the law.

The practice of law may be divided into several categories, or types of practice. Some types of practice may be described as trial practice, and trial lawyers as a group are subdivided into plaintiff's counsel and defense counsel because of the different aspects of these activities. Office practice is another type and is concerned with such matters as preparing documents, advising businesses, settling estates, etc. Many office-practice lawyers never participate in a lawsuit but leave the trial arena to the specialist in trial work. Large law firms have lawyers practicing in all areas, but small law firms or sole practitioners often refer matters out of their area of expertise to other lawyers. Of course, the general practitioner, especially in the smaller community, will handle practically every matter that is brought to his office. The term "house counsel" is used to describe another large group of attorneys. House counsel is employed by business to assist in the internal operations of the business by preventing and solving legal problems. Unsolved problems that result in litigation are usually referred to outside counsel for trial.

Whatever the area or location of a lawyer's practice, he will be engaged in certain activities that are of primary significance to society. First of all, he is an advisor. A lawyer's product is advice—advice on an infinite variety of subjects. Much of the advice requested and given is not strictly legal but may involve such matters as business decisions or family affairs. Of course, most of his advice will be connected with the law.

Second, every lawyer is an advocate for his client. The office lawyer negotiating a contract is an advocate just as is the trial lawyer. His advocacy is directed at other attorneys and their clients rather than to judges and juries.

Third, every lawyer is a negotiator of compromise. He seeks to avoid litigation and to find a mutually satisfactory alternative to the expense and difficulties of litigation. These three roles—advisor, advocate, and negotiator—provide insight into the background required for the practice of law.

Hundreds of thousands of words have been written about the personal qualities required for the practice of law. It is generally conceded that a lawyer must be cultured, in the sense of appreciating the historical relevance of our fundamental freedoms and the role of law in our society. He must be keenly aware of the world in which he lives, what is right about it and what is wrong, so that he can fulfill his role as an instrument of change. He must be compassionate and sensitive to human problems and weaknesses, because the practice of law is a very personal matter.

Lawyers must be courageous and willing to represent unpopular causes, because the right to counsel exists as a necessity. They must be willing not only to defend such causes, but to defend the system that requires such representation.

A lawyer's duties are diverse, in that his responsibilities are by the very nature of the profession fourfold. His first duty is to the state as a licensed official and a citizen. Second, he is an officer of the court, and an aid in the administration of justice; third, he is a trustee and fiduciary for his client; and fourth, he is obligated to deal honestly and fairly with other lawyers and the public in maintaining the honesty and integrity of the profession.

THE JUDICIAL PROCESS

13. Introduction

Before studying the next chapter, on litigation, it is helpful to have some understanding of the nature of the judicial process and how the powers of the judicial system are exercised. Recognizing that a court may declare a law unconstitutional, when and why will it do so? Why does a court announce one rule of law, or follow one precedent, rather than another? What factors influence the courts in their decisions?

The judicial system has a rather obvious priority of sources. Constitutions prevail over statutes, and statutes prevail over case law. Precedent prevails over dicta, and dicta would usually be persuasive over mere argument. However, it should be acknowledged that in spite of our almost 200 years as a nation, many legal issues are not directly covered by a statute or case precedent. Litigation is frequently brought to challenge the validity of a statute or to seek to change a precedent that does exist. Frequently the decided cases are in conflict, or the case involves issues of conflicting social policies.

Thus, the law is not a system of known rules applied by a judge. When many legal issues are presented to a court, the law applicable to those issues is made and not merely found by the court in some statute or case. In the sense that the law is made and not found, the role of the courts is legislative in character.

Law is also changed from time to time to meet changing conditions. Thus, courts are an instrument of social, political, and economic change. The law changes as it is applied to new cases. It may expand or contract its application or take off in a new direction, but it is seldom static. Whole new legal principles that change society may also be created by courts.

14. Judicial Philosophy

Courts at different times play different roles in bringing about changes in our society. Some judges and courts adopt what is usually described as the philosophy of "judicial restraint." This philosophy admonishes courts to change only those rules of law that they must change and to decide only those matters that they must decide. According to this view, change for the most part should be left to the political processes and to the legislative and executive branches, which are responsive to the political process.

The other philosophy of many courts and judges has often been referred to as the "activist" philosophy. According to activist judges, the political processes and the other branches of government either may fail to bring about necessary changes in society or may do so too slowly. They view the law and the courts as being leaders of social, political, and economic change. To them, the Constitution and many statutes must be interpreted in the light of the times and our experience as a people, and not merely by what was said. This view of the court's role as an instrument of social change was graphically illustrated in the school desegregation case of *Brown* v. *Board of Education,* 347 U.S. 497 (1954), in which Chief Justice Warren said in part, while discussing the meaning of the Fourteenth Amendment to the U.S. Constitution:

> In approaching this problem, we cannot turn the clock back to 1868 when the Amendment was adopted. . . . We must consider public education in the light of its full development and its present place in American life throughout the Nation. Only in this way can it be determined if segregation in public schools deprives these plaintiffs of the equal protection of the laws.

Throughout our history, the Supreme Court has at least to some degree followed the activist theory. Some Supreme Courts have been more activist than others. The era of the Warren court, from 1954 to 1969, was generally known for its activist majority, but the Supreme Courts of the early thirties were generally labeled as conservative or judicial-restraint-oriented. The majority of the Court of the 1970s has given clear signs of a judicial-restraint orientation. The extent to which the Court is an instrument of change will vary from time to time, depending upon the makeup of the Court. However, the Court will always be an instrument of change to some degree. For example, the Supreme Court in 1973 held that state laws prohibiting abortions were unconstitutional. In 1972 the same Court held the death penalty to be unconstitutional, but in 1976—with a change of only one in the makeup of the Court—it held that capital punishment may be constitutional. Thus, our Court with considerable bent toward judicial restraint has activist tendencies.

15. The Court System's Major Problem—Delay

"Justice delayed is justice denied" sums up the most obvious problem in our court system—court congestion and the delay that results therefrom. In many areas, the backlog of civil cases is so great that a period of several years elapses between the event in question and a jury trial. Such delays cause serious problems for the parties and adversely affect the search for truth. The volume of criminal cases that are awaiting trial or are pending on appeal raise many serious consequences for society, not the least of which is that anyone out of jail on bond is free to commit more crimes while the case is pending.

Chief Justice Burger is seeking to speed up the litigation process in both civil and criminal cases. Among the changes being instituted are (1) reducing the number of written opinions at the appellate level, (2) requiring attorneys to be prepared when the case is first called for trial, and (3) making use of such modern technology as data-processing equipment and computer transcribers to speed up the paperwork of courts.

Many other changes designed to eliminate and reduce court congestion and the backlog of court cases have been proposed. The changes that have had partial acceptance to date include (1) requiring only six-person juries instead of twelve, (2) requiring only majority verdicts instead of unanimous ones, (3) eliminating oral argument on appeal whenever possible, and (4) eliminating jury trials in certain types of cases. In addition, the number of judges has been expanded in many states.

There have been several suggestions made to reduce the case load of the federal courts. Perhaps the most radical idea is to abolish diversity of citizenship jurisdiction. It is argued that there is no rational basis for putting an automobile accident case in a federal court simply because the parties are citizens of different states. The chief justice has also advocated the elimination of three-judge federal district courts with the right of direct appeal to the Supreme Court.

It has also been proposed that a special court be created to hear petitions for writs of certiorari. This would free the Supreme Court to spend its time deciding the cases before it rather than requiring it to spend a significant portion of its time deciding which cases it wants to hear. Each year the Supreme Court must review more than 2,000 petitions for writs of certiorari. This new court would consist of courts-of-appeals justices on a rotating basis.

Other possible changes in the future are (1) the creation of some special courts to handle specialized areas of the law, such as antitrust and consumer protection, (2) the creation of administrative processes to handle complaints of persons in prison, and (3) the use of electronic data-processing techniques to speed up the preparation of transcripts for review purposes, as well as the retrieval of precedent. In regard to the last suggestion, it seems clear that legal research needs to be brought out of the dark past into the last quarter of the twentieth century.

Our system of law is as an adversary system. The courtroom is a place of strife. The modern lawsuit is a substitute for the ancient physical combat; the lawyer today is in a sense a "combatant" for his client. Instead of using physical force, a lawyer represents his client in litigation by the use of words. Through pleadings, persuasion, psychology, and argument, he represents his client in a forum called a courtroom.

Contesting lawyers as partisan advocates, operating within the rules of procedure and evidence, and supervised by the court, make possible the exploration of every aspect of the case. A single arbiter acting as judge, advocate, and jury would by the very nature of the method used find himself prematurely reaching a fixed opinion. Such preconceived judgments will not prevail under the adversary system. The narrowing of issues by the rules of procedure, preparation, and presentation of the case to the jury by partisan advocates; examination and cross-examination of the witnesses; argument by counsel; and the control, supervision, and instruction by the judge make premature conclusions impossible. During the process of a trial, the court and jury have the benefit of seeing both sides of the issue, clearly defined, and they are able to arrive at a just conclusion. Settling private contentions by a public adversary system, manipulated by intelligent advocates, operating under an orderly process supervised by a neutral third party—the judge—is believed to be one of the most important institutions of American democracy.

However, there are many critics of the adversary process. That such a system is best able to find the truth and render justice has been questioned. It is argued by many that the adversary system permits lawyers to overreach witnesses, mislead the jury, and use rules of evidence to cover up facts rather than disclose the truth, and that it makes it possible for a clever, experienced lawyer to dominate the proceedings to such an extent that the other, less experienced party has "not had his day in court."

While these objections may be valid in some cases, it nevertheless must be recognized that the adversary system is the best method yet devised to search for truth. Lawyers are an indispensable part of this search.

CHAPTER 2
REVIEW QUESTIONS AND PROBLEMS

1. What is the advantage of having a small-claims court?

2. Does a citizen always have a right to have his case reviewed by the U.S. Supreme Court?

3.   If X, a citizen of Illinois, sues Y, a citizen of Indiana, and Z, a citizen of Illinois, for $20,000, does a federal court have jurisdiction if the subject matter of the suit is not a federal question? Why?

4.   What is the basis for decisions in equity?

5.   What are three major duties of lawyers?

6.   A and B are discussing a matter and disagree on the legality of the proposed action. A suggests that a suit be filed to determine the legality of the proposed conduct. Will a court settle their dispute?

7.   X, a citizen of Alabama, sues Y, a citizen of Mississippi, in the Alabama State Court for $7,500. Jurisdiction is obtained by service of process in Mississippi. Can Y have the case removed to the federal courts? Why?

8.   The length of time required to get a case to trial is one of the most serious problems facing the court system. What are the proposed solutions?

9.   The United States has an adversary system of justice. Explain.

10.   The "Warren Court" generally followed the philosophy of "judicial activism," whereas the "Burger Court" generally follows the philosophy of "judicial restraint." Explain the differences in these two philosophies.

11.   P, a citizen of New York, was involved in an automobile accident in New York City involving D, a citizen of Virginia. P sues D in the federal district court in New York City, claiming damages in the amount of $40,000. What substantive law and procedural law will the courts use? Explain.

12.   P was fined for being in violation of a state statute. P brought suit challenging the constitutionality of the statute, but the trial court ruled against him. This decision is upheld by the highest court in the state. P now decides to appeal to the federal district court. Should P succeed? Why?

13.   S listed property for sale with A, a real estate agent. It was agreed that A would receive a commission if the property was sold prior to June 1. In April, B entered into a contract to purchase the property from S. B agreed to date the contract June 2, so that S could avoid paying the commission. S, however, later refused to sell the property to B. B now sues in a court of equity claiming that S should be compelled to turn the land over to him. Is B entitled to relief? Why?

14.   P, a citizen of Georgia, was crossing the street in New Orleans when he was struck by a car driven by D, a citizen of Mississippi. The car was owned by D's employer, X Company, which is an Alabama corporation with its principal place of business in Atlanta, Georgia. P sues both D and X Company in the federal district court in New Orleans, claiming damages in the amount of $100,000. Does the court have jurisdiction? Why?

Litigation

1. Introduction

As previously noted, law may be classified as *substantive law* or *procedural law*. Substantive law defines the rights and duties of citizens and is the result of legislative action or judicial action. Procedural law specifies the method and means by which the substantive law is made, enforced, and administered. Procedural rules prescribe the methods by which courts apply substantive law to resolve conflicts. Substantive rights have no value unless there are procedures that provide a means for establishing and enforcing them.

Judicial procedure is concerned with the rules by which a lawsuit is conducted. One common method of classifying judicial procedure is to divide it into two parts—*criminal* and *civil*. Criminal procedure prescribes the rules of law for the apprehension, prosecution, and fixing of punishment of persons who have committed crimes. Civil procedure prescribes the rules by which parties to civil lawsuits use the courts to settle their disputes.

In most cases there are three basic questions to be answered: (1) What are the facts? (2) What evidence is relevant and proper to prove the facts? (3) What rules of law apply to the facts? It is the function of the jury to answer the first question; the court furnishes the answer to the second; and the court provides the answer to the third by instructing the jury as to the law to be applied to the facts as found by the jury.

The sections that follow will discuss the various stages of litigation. They will illustrate the role of procedure in deciding substantive issues.

THE PLACE OF LITIGATION

2. Jurisdiction

The first requirement in any lawsuit is that it must be brought before a court that has the power to hear the case. This power to hear the case is known as *jurisdiction*. Jurisdiction has two aspects—jurisdiction over the subject matter, and jurisdiction over the parties. Jurisdiction over the subject matter means that the lawsuit is of the type that the court was created to decide. For example, probate courts have jurisdiction of probate matters such as the settlement of estates of deceased persons. A probate court would not have jurisdiction to hear a criminal case. Likewise, a criminal court would have no jurisdiction in a divorce matter.

Sometimes the subject-matter jurisdiction of a court is exclusive. This means that no other court has the *power* to hear such cases. For example, the Supreme Court of the United States has exclusive jurisdiction in all controversies between two or more states; all proceedings against ambassadors, public Ministers and Consuls and; all controversies between the United States and a state; and all actions by a state against citizens of another state or country.

Jurisdiction over the person refers to jurisdiction over the parties—the plaintiff and defendant. Jurisdiction over the plaintiff is obtained by the filing of the lawsuit. A plaintiff voluntarily submits to the jurisdiction of the court when he files his complaint.

Jurisdiction over the defendant is accomplished by the service of a summons that issues out of the court in which the case is to be tried. It is delivered to a sheriff or other person to be served upon the defendant. Jurisdiction over a defendant in some cases is obtained by publishing a notice in a newspaper. This latter is possible in a limited number of cases involving status, such as a suit for divorce or a case involving real estate, in which the "thing" involved is of sufficient importance that notice by publication is deemed sufficient to be constructive notice. Publication may also be accompanied by proper attachment proceedings. In such cases, service by publication brings under the court's jurisdiction all attached property of a nonresident that lies within the territorial limits of the court. When this technique is used, the attached property may be used to satisfy the judgment. Most cases, however, require the actual service of a summons on the defendant in order to give him notice of the suit.

Many states allow a summons to be served at the defendant's home upon any member of the family above a specified age, such as 10 years. In such cases, a copy is also mailed to the defendant.

3. Long-Arm Statutes

Historically, the jurisdiction of courts to enter judgment against a person required actual personal service of the summons on the defendant in the state in which the suit was brought. This was necessary in order to give the defendant notice of the suit and an opportunity to defend. Because the jurisdiction of courts was limited to geographical areas such as a state or a county, power to issue and serve a summons beyond the borders of the state or county did not exist. Extending judicial jurisdiction across a state boundary for the purpose of acquiring jurisdiction over the person of a nonresident was considered a denial of due process of law. Requiring a person to go from his own state or county for trial imposed undue burdens on the defendant and was a denial of the right to a fair trial.

Such reasoning limiting the jurisdiction of courts is no longer accepted. Personal jurisdiction over nonresidents has been expanded because modern transportation and communication facilities have minimized the inconveniences to a nonresident defendant who must defend himself in courts beyond his home state. There is no longer any logical reason to deny a local citizen a remedy in local courts for an injury caused by a nonresident temporarily present in the state. The first extension of jurisdiction over nonresidents occurred in auto accident cases. This was done by creating a "legal fiction" that resulted in the summons's being served within the state whose court issued the summons. This legal fiction was created by the enactment of statutes that provided that a nonresident, by using the state highways, automatically appointed a designated state official, usually the secretary of state, as his agent to accept service of process. The summons would be served on the secretary of state, who would notify the defendant of the suit, and the defendant was then subject to the power of the court.

These nonresident-motorist statutes opened the door for adoption of other statutes, called "long-arm" statutes, which further extend the jurisdiction of courts over nonresidents, whether they be individuals or corporations. Long-arm statutes typically extend the jurisdiction of courts to cases in which a tort injury has been caused by a nonresident "doing business" in the state.

They also usually extend jurisdiction to cases arising out of the ownership of property located within the state. Of course, the conduct of business such as entering into contracts confers jurisdiction. Thus, a nonresident individual or corporation may be subject to a suit for injuries if either has certain "minimal contacts" within the state, so long as the maintenance of the suit does not offend traditional notions of fair play and substantial justice.

What "minimal contacts" and activities are necessary to bring the defendant into a state is a fact question depending upon each particular case. Whatever the basis for the action may be, either in contract or in tort, the court can acquire jurisdiction over the defendant if these minimal contacts are present.

4.   Venue

As previously discussed, the term *jurisdiction* defines the power of the court to hear and adjudicate the case. Jurisdiction includes the court's power to inquire into the facts, apply the law to the facts, make a decision, and declare and enforce a judgment. *Venue* relates to and defines the particular territorial area within the state, county, or district in which the civil case or criminal prosecution should be filed and tried. Matters of venue are usually determined by statute. In a few states, the subject of venue is covered in the state constitution. Venue statutes usually provide that actions concerning interests in land must be commenced and tried in the county or district in which the land is located. Actions for the recovery of penalties imposed by statute against public officers must be commenced and tried in the county or district in which the cause of action arose. Suits for divorce must be commenced and tried in the county in which one of the parties resides. All other suits or actions must be commenced and tried in the county in which one or all of the defendants reside, or in the county in which the transaction took place or where the wrong was committed. For example, a tort action may be commenced and tried either in the county or district where the tort was committed, or where the defendant resides or may be found. If the defendants are nonresidents, and assuming that proper service can be made upon them under a "long-arm" statute, the suit may be commenced and tried in any county the plaintiff designates in his complaint.

The judge may change the place of trial at the request of either party when it appears from an affidavit of either party that the action was not commenced in the proper venue. A change of venue may also be requested on the ground that the judge has an interest in the suit or is related to any parties to the action or has manifested a prejudice so that he cannot be expected to conduct a fair and impartial trial. A change of venue is often requested in criminal trials when the inhabitants of the county are allegedly so prejudiced against the defendant that a fair trial is not possible. The convenience of witnesses and the parties may also justify a change of venue.

PROCEEDINGS PRIOR TO TRIAL

5. Pleadings

A *pleading* is a legal document, prepared by a lawyer and filed with the court, which sets forth the position and contentions of a party. The purpose of pleadings in civil actions is to define the issues of the lawsuit. This is accomplished by each party's making allegations of fact and the other party's either admitting the allegations or denying them. The procedure is as follows: The plaintiff files with the clerk of the court a pleading usually called a *complaint*. In some types of cases, this initial pleading is called a *declaration* or a *petition*. The clerk then issues a summons, which, together with a copy of the complaint, is served on the defendant. The summons notifies him of the date by which he is required to either file a pleading in answer to the allegations of the complaint, or file some other pleading attacking the complaint.

If the defendant has no legal basis to attack the sufficiency of the complaint, he may simply file an entry of appearance, or he may file an answer either admitting or denying each material allegation of the complaint. This answer will put in issue all allegations of the complaint that are denied. A simple entry of appearance is an admission of the truth of all the allegations of the complaint.

In addition to the admissions and denials, an answer may contain affirmative defenses, which if proved will defeat the plaintiff's claim. The answer may also contain causes of action the defendant has against the plaintiff, called *counterclaims*. Upon receipt of the defendant's answer, the plaintiff will, unless the applicable rules of procedure do not so require, file a reply that specifically admits or denies each new allegation in the defendant's answer. These new allegations are those found in the affirmative defense and counterclaims. Thus, the allegations of each party are admitted or denied in the pleadings. Allegations of fact by either party that are denied by the other become the issues to be decided at the trial.

If a defendant subject to the jurisdiction of the court fails to file an answer either originally or after his motions have been overruled, he is in default, and a court of law may enter a default judgment against him. A court of equity would enter a similar order, known as a decree *pro confesso*.

6. Motions Attacking Pleadings

The first pleading (complaint), in order to be legally sufficient, must allege facts sufficient to set forth a right of action or right to legal relief in the plaintiff. The defendant's attorney, after studying the complaint, may (instead of answering) choose one of several different ways to challenge its legal sufficiency. For example, by motion to the court, the defendant may object to the complaint, pointing out specifically its defects. The defendant, through such motion, admits for purposes of argument all the facts alleged in the complaint. His position is that those facts are not legally sufficient to give the plaintiff the relief sought. Such motion, called a *demurrer* at common law, raises questions of law, not questions of fact. If the court finds that the complaint does set forth facts sufficient to give the plaintiff the relief sought, it will deny the motion. The defendant will then be granted leave to answer the complaint; should he fail to do so within the time limit set by the court, a judgment by default will be entered for the plaintiff. If the court finds, however, that the complaint fails to state facts sufficient to give the plaintiff the relief sought against the defendant, the court will allow the motion, dismiss the suit, and grant leave to the plaintiff to file an amended complaint. The plaintiff will thus be given an opportunity to restate his facts so that he may be able to set forth a right to some relief. If he fails to do so, the order of dismissal becomes final.

A defendant may also move to dismiss the suit for reasons that as a matter of law would prevent the plaintiff from winning his suit. Such matters as a discharge in bankruptcy, lack of jurisdiction of the court to hear the suit, or expiration of the time limit during which the defendant is subject to suit may be raised by such a motion. These are matters of a technical nature that raise questions of law for the court's decision.

7. Summary Judgment Procedures

Many lawsuits are decided without a trial even though the pleadings create issues of fact. These decisions result from the use of a procedure known as a summary judgment. This procedure was created to avoid trials when there is no genuine issue as to any material fact in dispute. If there are no facts in dispute, the only issue before the court is the legal effect of those facts. This can be decided without a trial.

Either party may ask the court for a summary judgment by filing a motion, usually with supporting affidavits. The usual procedure is to attach supporting affidavits to the motion setting forth the facts and to supplement these affidavits with depositions taken during the discovery process. The opposing party is also permitted to file affidavits and depositions with the court. These affidavits and depositions in effect supply the court with sworn testimony. The court then examines this sworn testimony to see whether or not there is a genuine issue as to any material fact. If there is no factual issue, the litigation should be decided on the facts presented to the court.

If the court finds that there is no genuine issue of fact, it will grant a summary judgment for one party or the other. In most states, it may render a summary judgment on the issue of liability alone and leave the issue as to the amount of damages to the trial. Many of the cases set forth in the latter chapters of this text were decided by the summary judgment procedure. It should be kept in mind that a summary judgment will not be granted when there is a disputed question of any material fact.

8. Discovery Procedures

During the pleading stage and in the interval before the trial, the law provides for procedures called *discovery* procedures, which are designed to take the "sporting aspect" out of litigation and to ensure that the results of lawsuits are based on the merits of the controversy and less on the ability, skill, or cunning of counsel. Without these procedures, an attorney with no case on the facts or law might win a lawsuit through surprise—by keeping silent about a fact or by concealing his true case until the trial. Lawsuits should not be based on the skill or lack thereof of counsel, but on the relative merits of the controversy. Discovery practice is designed to ensure that each side is fully aware of all the facts involved in the case and of the contentions of the parties, prior to trial. Another of its avowed purposes is to encourage settlement of suits and avoid actual trial.

Discovery practices include the taking of the deposition of other parties and witnesses, the serving of written questions to be answered under oath by the opposite party, compulsory physical examinations in personal injury cases by doctors chosen by the other party, orders requiring the production of statements, exhibits, documents, maps, photographs, and so forth, and the serving by one party on the other of demands to admit facts under oath. Some court procedures even allow the discovery of the amount of insurance coverage possessed by the defendant in a personal injury case. The Federal Rules of Civil Procedure illustrate the trend and scope of discovery procedures. They allow discovery of:

> . . . any matter, not privileged, which is relevant to the subject matter involved in the pending action, whether it relates to the claim or defense of the examining party, including the existence, description, nature, custody, condition and location of any books, documents, or other tangible things and the identity and location of persons having knowledge of relevant facts. It is not ground for objection that the testimony will be inadmissible at the trial if the testimony sought appears reasonably calculated to lead to the discovery of evidence. . . .

Just prior to the trial, a pretrial conference between the lawyers and the judge will be held in states with modern rules of procedure. At this conference, the pleadings, results of the discovery process, and probable evidence are reviewed in an attempt to settle the suit. The issues may be further narrowed and the judge may even give his prediction of the outcome in order to encourage settlement. It is significant that a very substantial number of all lawsuits that are filed are settled sometime prior to trial. Discovery procedures contribute significantly to these settlements.

THE TRIAL

9. Jury Selection

Not every case can be settled even under modern procedures. Some must go to trial on the issues of fact raised by the pleadings that remain after the pretrial conference. If the only issues are questions of law, the court will decide the case without a trial by a ruling on one of the motions previously mentioned. If the case is at law and either party has demanded a jury trial, the cause will be set for trial and a jury empaneled. If the case is in equity or if no jury demand has been made, it will be set down for trial before the court or possibly a *master in chancery*. For purposes of discussion, the following assumes trial before a jury.

The first step of the trial is to select the jury. Prior to the calling of the case, the clerk of the court will have summoned potential jurors known as the *venire.* They will be selected at random from lists of eligible citizens, and twelve of them will be called into the jury box for the conduct of *voir dire* examination. *Voir dire* examination is a method by which the court and the attorneys for each party examine the jurors as to their qualifications to be fair and impartial. Each side in the lawsuit may challenge or excuse a juror for cause; e.g., for bias, prejudice, or relation to one of the parties. In addition, each side will be given a certain number of challenges known as "preemptory challenges" for which no cause need be given. Each side is given an opportunity to question the prospective jurors and to either accept them or reject them until his challenges are exhausted. The prospective jurors are sworn to give truthful answers to the questions on *voir dire.* The process continues until the full jury is selected.

10. The Introduction of Proof

After selecting the jurors, the attorneys make opening statements. An opening statement is not evidence, but is used only to familiarize the jury with the essential facts in the case that each side expects to prove, in order that the jury may understand the overall picture of the case and the relevancy of each piece of evidence as presented. After the opening statements, the plaintiff presents his evidence.

Evidence is presented in open court by means of examination of witnesses and the production of documents and other exhibits. The party calling a witness questions him to establish the facts about the case. As a general rule, a party calling a witness is not permitted to ask "leading questions," questions in which the desired answer is indicated by the form of the question. After the party calling the witness has completed his direct examination, the other party is given the opportunity to cross-examine the witness. Matters inquired into on cross-examination are limited to those matters that were raised on direct examination. After cross-examination, the party calling the witness again has the opportunity of examining the witness, and this examination is called redirect examination. It is limited to the scope of those matters covered on cross-examination and is used to clarify matters raised on cross-examination. After redirect examination, the opposing party is allowed re-cross-examination, with the corresponding limitation as to scope of the questions. Witnesses may be asked to identify exhibits. Expert witnesses may be asked to give their opinion, within certain limitations, about the case, and sometimes experts are allowed to answer hypothetical questions.

In the conduct of a trial, the rules of evidence govern the admissibility of testimony and exhibits and establish which facts may be presented to the jury and which facts may not. Each rule of evidence is based on some policy consideration and the desire to give each party an opportunity to present his evidence and contentions without unduly taking advantage of the other party.

Rules of evidence were not created to serve as a stumbling block to meritorious litigants or to create unwarranted roadblocks to justice. On the contrary, the rules of evidence were created and should be applied to ensure fair play and to aid in the goal of having controversies determined on their merits. Modern rules of evidence are liberal in the sense that they allow the introduction of most evidence that may contribute to the search for truth.

To illustrate the policy considerations that form the basis of the rules of evidence, an examination of the rules relating to privileged communications is helpful.

The policy behind the Fifth Amendment's privilege against self-incrimination is obvious. There are other communications, such as between husband and wife, doctor and patient, clergy and penitent, and attorney and client, that are also considered privileged by the law in order that these communications can be made without fear of their subsequent use against the parties involved. Fair play requires that an attorney not be required to testify as to matters told him in confidence by his client. The preservation of the home requires that a spouse not be required to testify against the other spouse regarding confidential communications. The existence of insurance coverage for a party is privileged because of the impact that knowledge of the existence of insurance would have on a jury. Jurors might award damages or increase the amount simply because of the ability of an insurance company to pay. By these rules of fair play, privileged matters should not be admitted into evidence. Similar policy considerations support all rules of evidence. Each rule is designed to assist in the search for truth.

11. Motions During Trial

A basic rule of evidence is that a party cannot introduce evidence unless it is competent and relevant to the issues raised by the pleadings. A connection between the pleadings and the trial stage of the lawsuit is also present in certain motions made during the trial. For example, after the plaintiff has presented his evidence, the defendant will often make a motion for a directed verdict. This motion asks the court to rule as a matter of law that the plaintiff has failed to establish a right against the defendant and that judgment should be given to the latter. The court can only direct a verdict if the evidence taken in the light most favorable to the party resisting the motion establishes as a matter of law that the moving party is entitled to a verdict. The defendant argues that the plaintiff has failed to prove each allegation of his complaint. Just as a plaintiff must *allege* certain facts or have his complaint dismissed by motion to dismiss, he must have some *proof* of each essential allegation or lose his case on a motion for a directed verdict. If he has some proof of each allegation, the motion will be overruled.

In cases tried without a jury, either party may move for a finding in his favor. Such a motion will be allowed during the course of the trial if the result is not in doubt. The judge, in ruling on such motions, weighs the evidence, but he may end the trial only if there is no room for a fair difference of opinion as to the result.

If the defendant's motion for a directed verdict is overruled, the defendant then presents his evidence. After the defendant has presented all his evidence, the plaintiff may bring in rebuttal evidence. When neither party has any additional evidence, the attorneys and the judge retire for a conference to consider the instructions of law to be given the jury.

12. Jury Instructions

The purpose of the jury instructions is to acquaint the jury with the law applicable to the case. Since the function of the jury is to find the facts and the function of the court is to determine the applicable law, there must be a method to bring them together in an orderly manner that will result in a decision. At the conference, each attorney submits to the court the instructions he feels should be given to the jury. The court examines these instructions and allows each side to object to the other's instructions. A party that fails to submit an instruction on a point of law cannot later object to the failure to instruct on that point. Similarly, the failure to object to an instruction is a waiver of the objection. The court then rules on which instructions will be given to the jury so that it may apply the law to the facts.

After the conference on jury instructions, the attorneys argue the case to the jury. The party with the burden of proof, usually the plaintiff, is given an opportunity to open the argument and to close it. The defendant's attorney is allowed to argue only after the plaintiff's argument and is allowed to argue only once. After the arguments are completed, the court reads the instructions to the jury.

In the federal courts and in some state courts, the judge may comment on the evidence while giving instructions. He may indicate the importance of certain portions of evidence and the inferences that might be drawn therefrom, point out the conflicts, and indicate what statements are more likely to be true than others and state why. The court, however, is duty bound to make clear to the jury that it is not obligated to follow his evaluation of the evidence and that it is its duty to determine the facts of the case. The jury then retires to deliberate upon its verdict.

13. Verdicts and Judgments

Upon reaching a verdict, the jury returns from the jury room and announces its verdict. There are two kinds of verdicts—general and special. A general verdict is one in which the jury makes a complete finding and single conclusion on all issues presented to it. First it finds the facts, as proven by the evidence, then applies the law as instructed by the court and returns a verdict in one conclusion that settles the case. Such verdict is reported as follows: "We the jury find the issues for the plaintiff (or defendant, as the case may be) and assess his damages at One Thousand Dollars." The jury usually does not make separate findings of fact, or report what law is applied.

In a special verdict, the jury only makes findings of fact. It is the duty of the court to apply the law to the facts as found by the jury. A special verdict is not a decision of the case; it resolves only the questions of fact. Since the jury finds only the facts, it receives no instructions from the court as to the law. The duty of applying the law to the fact is left to the court. The circumstances under which a general or a special verdict may be used are controlled by statute.

After the verdict is announced, judgment is entered. Judgments are either *in rem* or *in personam*. A judgment *in rem* is an adjudication entered against a thing—property, real or personal. The judgment is a determination of the status of the subject matter. Thus, a judgment of forfeiture of goods for the violation of a revenue law is a judgment *in rem*. Although a judgment *in rem* is limited to the subject matter, it nevertheless affects the rights and duties of persons. For example, while a decree dissolving a marriage seriously affects persons, it is nevertheless a decision *in rem* because it affects a "status," the marriage relation. A judgment *in rem* is binding not only on the persons previously concerned with the status or thing but on all other persons.

A judgment against a particular person is a judgment *in personam*. It is limited in its application to such person only, whereas a judgment *in rem* is conclusive on all persons.

PROCEEDINGS AFTER THE TRIAL

14. Posttrial Motions

After judgment is entered, the losing party starts the procedure of posttrial motions, which raises questions of law concerning the conduct of the lawsuit. These motions seek such relief as a new trial or a judgment notwithstanding the verdict of the jury. A motion seeking a new trial may be granted if the judge feels that the verdict of the jury is contrary to the manifest weight of the evidence. The court may enter a judgment opposite to that of the verdict of the jury if the judge finds that the verdict is, as a matter of law, erroneous. To reach such a conclusion, the court must find that reasonable men viewing the evidence could not reach the verdict returned. For example, a verdict for the plaintiff may be based on sympathy instead of evidence.

From the ruling on the posttrial motion, the losing party may appeal. It should be noted that lawsuits usually end by a ruling on a motion, either before trial, during the trial, or after the trial. Motions raise questions of law that are decided by the court. The right to appeal, which is discussed in the next section, is absolute if perfected within the prescribed time.

15. Appeals

A dissatisfied party, plaintiff or defendant, has a right to appeal the decision of the trial court to a higher court, provided that he proceeds promptly and in the proper manner. It should be noted that the cases collected and abstracted in this text are with a few exceptions decisions of a reviewing court. Whether he is plaintiff or defendant, the person who appeals is called the appellant, and the opposite party is called the appellee, or respondent. The appellant is often named first in the title of the case on appeal, although in the trial court he may have been the defendant. Therefore, care must be used in reading reported cases in order to properly identify each party as a plaintiff or a defendant.

Appellate procedures are not uniform among the states, and the appellant must comply with the appropriate statute and rules of the particular court. Appeals are usually perfected by the appellant's giving "notice of appeal" to the trial court and opposing parties. Statutes provide that appeals must be taken within a certain number of days from the entry of the judgment.

Most states require that within at least ten days after giving notice of appeal, the appellant must file an appeal bond, which, in effect, guarantees that the appellant will pay costs that may be charged against him on the appeal. This is to protect the respondent so that he may collect his costs if the appellant loses on appeal.

The statutes usually require that within a specified time after the appeal is perfected, the appellant shall file with the clerk of the appellate court what is known as a *transcript*. The transcript consists of a copy of the judgment, decree, or order appealed from, the notice of appeal, the appeal bond, the pertinent portions of the stenographic transcript of the evidence, and such other papers as are required by the rules of the court. The appellee may file an additional transcript if he believes that essential matters have been omitted.

The transcript alone is not enough to present the case to the appellate court. The appellant must prepare and file a "brief," which contains a statement of the case, a list of the assignment of errors upon which the appellant has based his appeal, his legal authorities, and argument. The brief contains the arguments on both fact and law by which the attorney attempts to show how the court below committed the errors alleged.

The appellee (respondent) files a brief of like character setting out his side of the case with points, authorities, and arguments. By such procedure, the case on the issues raised gets to the appellate court for decision.

The appellate court, upon receipt of the appeal, will place it on the calendar for hearing. The attorneys will be notified of the time and will be given an opportunity for oral argument. After the oral argument, there is deliberation by members of the court, and an opinion will be written stating the law involved and giving the court's reasons for its decision. The court by its decision may affirm or reverse the court below, or the court may send the case back for a new trial. At the end of each published opinion found in the reports, there will appear in a few words the result of the court's decision. Such words may be "affirmed," "reversed," "reversed and remanded," and so forth, as the case requires.

16.   Enforcement of Judgments and Decrees

A decision of a court becomes final when the time provided for a review of the decision has expired. In cases in the trial court, it is the expiration of the time for appeal. In cases in a reviewing court, it is the expiration of the time to request a rehearing or to request a further review of the case. After the decision has become final, judicial action may be required to enforce the decision. In most cases, the losing party will voluntarily comply with the decision and satisfy the judgment or otherwise do what the decree requires, but the assistance of the court is sometimes required to enforce the final decision of the court.

If a judgment for dollar damages is not paid, the judgment creditor may apply for a *writ of execution*. This writ directs the sheriff to seize property of the judgment debtor and to sell enough thereof to satisfy the judgment and to cover the costs and expenses of the sale. A judgment creditor with an unsatisfied writ of execution not only has a lien on real property owned by the judgment debtor at the time the judgment becomes final; he also has a judicial lien on any real property acquired by the judgment debtor during the life of the judgment. The life of a judgment is prescribed by statute. The time period is usually several years, and there are provisions for renewal of the judgment. A judgment debtor cannot convey clear title to real estate as long as the judicial lien is unsatisfied. The writ of execution is not the only method of enforcing a judgment, but it is almost always used to ensure that there will be a judicial lien on any real estate owned by the judgment debtor.

Another important method used by judgment creditors to collect a judgment is known as *garnishment*. A judgment creditor can "garnish" the wages of the judgment debtor, or his bank account, or any other obligation owing to him from a third party. In the process of garnishment, the person owing the money to the judgment debtor—the employer, bank of deposit, third party—will be directed to pay the money into court rather than to the judgment debtor, and such money will be applied against the judgment debt.

In connection with writs of execution and garnishment proceedings, it is extremely significant that the laws of the various states have statutory provisions that exempt certain property from writs of execution and garnishment. The state laws limit the amount of wages that can be garnished and usually provide for both real property and personal property exemptions. This will be discussed with the materials on bankruptcy in Chapter 28.

In recent years, many states have adopted a procedure known as a *citation proceeding,* which greatly assists the creditor in collecting a judgment. The citation procedure is commenced by the service of a "citation" on the judgment debtor to appear in court at a stated time for the purpose of examination under oath about his financial affairs. It also prohibits the judgment debtor from making any transfer of property until after the examination in court. At the hearing, the judgment creditor or his attorney questions the judgment debtor about his income, property, and affairs. Any nonexempt property that is discovered during the questioning may be ordered sold by the judge, with the proceeds applied to the judgment. The court may also order that weekly or monthly payments be made by the judgment debtor. Such payments must not violate the laws relating to garnishment. In those states that have adopted the citation proceedings, the difficulties in collecting a judgment have been substantially reduced.

In spite of the remedies the creditor may use, it frequently develops that the judgment is of little value because of the lack of assets that can be reached or because of other judgments. It must be remembered that a judgment standing alone has little value. In many cases, the debtor may file a voluntary petition in bankruptcy or his creditors may file a petition in involuntary bankruptcy against him. In other cases, the creditor recognizes the futility of attempting to use additional legal process to collect, and the matter simply lies dormant until it dies a "natural death" by the expiration of the time allowed to collect the claim or judgment. Everyone should be aware that some people are judgment-proof and that in such cases, the law has no means of collecting a judgment. Debtors are not sent to prison simply because of their inability to pay debts or judgments.

CHAPTER 3
REVIEW QUESTIONS AND PROBLEMS

1. Distinguish between a judgment *in rem* and one *in personam*.

2. How is a lawsuit formally commenced?

3. What is a counterclaim? When is it usually filed?

4. What is the purpose of the pleadings?

5. Who is an appellant; an appellee?

6. What is a *voir dire* examination, and what is its purpose?

7. Trace the steps of a trial once it has commenced.

8. Distinguish between a trial court and an appellate court.

9. What are the purposes of discovery procedures? Explain.

10. What is a motion for summary judgment, and when is it granted? Explain.

11. Distinguish between jurisdiction and venue.

12. What are jury instructions, and what purpose do they serve? Explain.

13. What are three methods for enforcing a judgment for dollar damages? Explain.

14. P was awarded a judgment against D in the trial court. Upon appeal, D claims that because the service of the summons was defective, the trial court lacked the jurisdiction over the subject matter. Is D correct? Why?

15. X was riding in a camper box attached to a truck, when the truck collided with a bus. The impact caused X to be thrown against the camper-box door, which opened and allowed X to fall, resulting in his death. X's widow brought suit in West Virginia state court against Y, a West Virginia company that manufactured the camper box, and also against Z Company, the manufacturer of the door used in the camper box. Z is a New Jersey corporation with its principal place of business in New Jersey. Process had been served on Z under West Virginia's long-arm statute. Z's contact with West Virginia occurred when its product came into the state as a component part of Y's product. Does the court have jurisdiction over Z Company? Why?

16. What are "long-arm" statutes?

17. Explain the differences between general verdicts and special verdicts.

18. Distinguish direct examination from cross-examination.

Additional Methods
for Resolving Disputes

1. Introduction

Litigation is not the only method for resolving disputes in our society. It is not even the primary method, and there is a definite trend away from litigation toward other dispute-resolution techniques. Litigation is too expensive and too time-consuming to be used in most controversies. Therefore, lawyers and others seek voluntary settlements of most matters, and some are resolved by administrative agencies. Arbitration as a means of resolving disputes has never been more important, and its use is expanding daily. Arbitration is the submission of a controversy to a nonjudicial body for a binding decision. The legal principles applicable to compromise agreements, to the administrative process, and to arbitration will be discussed in this chapter.

2. Compromises and Settlements

Most disputes are resolved by the parties involved, without resort to litigation or to arbitration. Only a small fraction of the disputes in our society end up in court, or even in a lawyer's office. There are a multitude of reasons why compromise is so prevalent a technique for settling disputes. Some of the reasons may be described as personal and others as economic.

The desire to compromise is part of human nature, at least for most of us. Most people have a fundamental dislike of trouble and a fear of "going to court." The moral and ethical values of a majority of society encourage compromise and settlement. The opinion of persons other than the parties to the dispute is often influential and is a motivating force in many compromises. Thus, both internal and external forces exist that encourage people to settle their differences amicably.

Compromise and settlement of disputes are also encouraged by the economics of many situations. Lawsuits are expensive to both parties. As a general rule, each party must pay his own attorney's fees, and the losing party must pay the court costs. As a matter of practical economics, the winning party in a lawsuit is a loser to the extent of the fees paid to the attorney.

At least two additional facts of economic life encourage business to settle disputes. First, business must be concerned with its public image and the goodwill of its customers. While the motto "the customer is always right" is not universally applicable today, the influence of the philosophy it represents cannot be underestimated. Second, juries are frequently sympathetic to individuals who have suits against large corporations or "target" defendants who are covered by insurance. Close questions of liability, as well as the size of verdicts, are more often than not resolved against business concerns because of their presumed ability to pay. As a result, business often seeks to settle disputes rather than submit them to a jury for decision.

The duty of lawyers to seek compromise and to achieve it where possible should be understood by laymen. In providing services to a client, a lawyer will devote a substantial amount of time, energy, and talent to seeking a compromise solution of the dispute. Attempts at compromise will be made before resort to the courts in most cases, and most attempts will be successful. Of those that do result in litigation, the great majority are settled without benefit of a final judicial decision. Literally, the attempt of the lawyers to resolve the dispute never ends. It occurs before suit, before and during the trial, after verdict, during appeal, and even after appeal. As long as there is a controversy, it is the function of lawyers to attempt to resolve it.

Lawyers on both sides of a controversy seek compromise for a variety of reasons. A lawyer may view his client's case as weak, either on the law or on the facts. The amount involved, the necessity for a speedy decision, the nature of the contest, the uncertainty of a legal remedy, the unfavorable publicity, and the expense entailed are some other reasons for avoiding a court trial. Each attorney must evaluate the cause of his client and seek a satisfactory—although not necessarily the most desirable—settlement of the controversy. The settlement of disputes is perhaps the most significant contribution of lawyers to our society.

3. Mediation

The term *mediation* describes the process by which a third party assists the parties to a controversy in seeking a compromise. Although a mediator cannot impose a binding solution on the parties, a disinterested and objective mediator is often able to bring about a compromise that is satisfactory to the parties.

The mediation of labor disputes is the function of the National Mediation and Conciliation Service. This government agency, staffed with skilled negotiators, has assisted in the settlement of countless labor disputes. Mediation is playing an expanding role in the relationship between the business community and the consuming public. Better Business Bureaus and others are serving as mediators of consumer complaints and also as arbitrators under arbitration agreements on occasion. Their efforts have been successful in resolving thousands of consumer complaints, in part because they provide a disinterested third party to whom both parties can turn for resolution of their dispute.

The recent amendments to the Federal Trade Commission Act, which were designed to aid consumers, have given added impetus to mediation as a means of resolving consumer complaints. This law provides that if a business adopts an informal dispute-resolution system to handle complaints about its product warranties, then a customer cannot sue the manufacturer or seller for breach of warranty without going through the informal procedures. This law does not deny consumers the right to sue, nor does it compel a compromise solution. It simply favors mediation by requiring an attempt at settlement before litigation.

ADMINISTRATIVE AGENCIES

4. Introduction

In a complex industrial society, social and economic problems are so numerous that courts and legislative bodies cannot possibly resolve all of them. Legislation must be general in character and cannot possibly cover all the problems and situations that may arise in connection with the problem or evil the law seeks to control or correct. There must be a method of filling in the gaps in legislation and for adding meat to the bones of legislative policy. Not only are there too many problems for traditional methods of solution, but interrelationships and conflicting social goals, as well as advances in technology, require constant changes. Administrative agencies are necessary in order to lighten the burdens that otherwise must be borne by the executive branch, legislative bodies, and courts. The multitude of administrative agencies performing governmental functions today encompasses almost every aspect of business operation and, indeed, almost every aspect of our daily lives. These agencies provide flexibility in the law and adaptability to changing conditions.

The functions of administrative bodies generally are described as (1) rule making, (2) adjudicating, (3) prosecuting, (4) advising, (5) supervising, and (6) investigating. These functions are not the concern of all administrative agencies to the same degree. Some agencies are primarily adjudicating bodies, such as the industrial commissions that rule on workmen's compensation claims. Others, such as the Federal Power Commission, are concerned primarily with a special industry, and still others, such as the Federal Trade Commission, with a particular phase of business. Others are primarily supervisory, such as the Securities and Exchange Commission, which supervises the issue and sale of investment securities. Most agencies perform all the foregoing functions to some degree in carrying out their responsibilities.

5. The Quasi-Legislative Function

The legislative function in the administrative process is to make rules and regulations. The rule-making function is based on the authority delegated to the agency by the legislature. This delegation of authority is usually stated in broad, general language. For example, a delegation "to make such rules, regulations, and decisions as the public interest, convenience, and necessity may require" is a typical statement of the authority of an agency.

It is the usual practice for administrative agencies in performing their quasi-legislative functions to hold hearings on proposed rules and regulations. At such hearings, the agency receives testimony as to the need for or the desirability of proposed rules and regulations. Notice of such hearings is usually given to the public, and all interested parties are allowed to present evidence for consideration by the agency. Assuming that the adopted rule is within the delegated authority, the rule cannot be set aside by a court simply because the court does not agree with the rule or because the court believes that a different rule should have been adopted. Courts cannot substitute their judgment for that of the agency, since the legislative body has determined that the agency is the expert in the area and has directed that the agency should make the decision. However, an agency rule that is arbitrary, capricious, and unreasonable will be set aside as being unconstitutional.

6. The Quasi-Judicial Function

Administrative agencies also decide cases or disputes between private parties. These decisions result from hearings conducted by the agency. The purpose of the hearing may be to find if a rule of the agency or an applicable statute has been violated. For example, the National Labor Relations Board conducts hearings to determine if an unfair labor practice has been committed. Other quasi-judicial hearings may be for the purpose of fixing liability, as in the case of workmen's compensation, which provides employer liability for employee deaths, sicknesses, and injury arising out of and in the course of employment. The quasi-judicial hearings receive detailed evidence and determine the rights and duties of the parties subject to the jurisdiction of the agency. The rules of procedure used in these quasi-judicial hearings are usually more informal in character than court trials, but on the whole they follow the general pattern set by courts.

The agency usually appoints a person to conduct the hearing. Such person is an administrative judge. They are sometimes called a hearing examiner or trial examiner. This person receives the evidence, submits findings of facts, and makes recommendations to the board or commission regarding the disposition to be made in the case. The agency studies the report and issues such orders as the law in the case appears to demand. The agency may hear objections to the hearing officer's finding, and sometimes it will hear arguments on the issues.

The quasi-judicial function of administrative agencies is the subject of substantial controversy. A frequent complaint is that administrative agencies make a law; investigate to see if it has been violated; serve as prosecutor, judge, and jury; and then act in the manner of an appellate court in reviewing the decision.

7. Judicial Review of Administrative Agencies

Perhaps the most important question for businessmen in the field of administrative law is, Under what circumstances will the rulings and decisions of an administrative agency be changed or reversed by a court? First of all, one must have "standing to sue" before he or she may challenge the decision of an agency. Standing to sue requires a direct financial or property interest in the decision. A local citizen who likes a particular TV program could not challenge an FCC decision on a TV station license renewal.

Second, it must be recognized that courts will review the findings and rulings of the agency only after the remedies and review provided within the agency have been exhausted. For example, a property owner who wishes to challenge the zoning classification made by his local zoning board must appeal to the appropriate city council or zoning board of appeals as the law may provide before a court challenge is possible. It should be remembered that review of the decisions of federal administrative agencies takes place in the circuit courts of appeal. These courts do not want to become involved until all the proceedings in the various agencies are completely concluded.

Finally, a court will not reverse the decision of the agency if there is substantial evidence on the record as a whole to support the decision of the agency. If a reasonable result was obtained, the decision will not be changed even though the court on the same evidence would have reached a different conclusion.

ARBITRATION

8. Introduction

Arbitration is a procedure whereby a controversy is submitted for a final and binding decision to a person or persons other than the courts. Arbitration may be required in certain cases by statute. However, such cases are rare, and the right to arbitrate usually arises from a contract. Since the right is based on a contract, the parties are obligated to arbitrate only those issues that they have agreed to arbitrate.

There are several advantages to using arbitration as a substitute for litigation. For one thing, it is much quicker and far less expensive. An issue can be submitted to arbitration and decided in less time than it takes to complete the pleading phase of a lawsuit. Then, too, arbitration creates less hostility than does litigation, and it allows the parties to continue their business relationship somewhat more peacefully while the dispute is being decided. Finally, under the arbitration process, complex issues can be submitted to an expert for decision. For example, if an issue arises concerning construction of a building, in arbitration it can be submitted to an architect for decision. Besides lawyers, other specialists frequently serve as arbitrators; physicians decide issues relating to physical disabilities, certified public accountants on those regarding the book value of stock, and engineers decide issues relating to industrial production. Of course, a substantial amount of arbitration is also conducted by the academic community, especially in the area of labor relations.

For the foregoing reasons, arbitration as a substitute for litigation is becoming increasingly important to business. Commercial arbitration clauses are being added to many business contracts. The American Arbitration Association will furnish experienced arbitrators for parties in a dispute; many standard contract clauses provide for submission to this group. Arbitration costs are deductible business expenses, and this speedy, inexpensive solution to conflicts should be carefully considered by business and legal counsel in all possible areas of dispute.

9. The Submission

The term *submission* is used to describe the act of referring an issue or issues to the arbitration process. The submitted issues may be factual, legal, or both; they may include questions concerning the interpretation of the arbitration agreement. The scope of the arbitrator's powers is controlled by the language of the submission. Doubts concerning the arbitrability of the subject matter of a dispute are usually resolved in favor of arbitration.

Submission may occur under two circumstances. First, the parties may enter into an agreement to arbitrate an existing dispute. The arbitration agreement serves as the "submission" in this case. Second, the parties may contractually agree to submit all issues that *may* arise to arbitration, or they may agree that either party *may* demand arbitration of any issue that arises. Submission to arbitration under the second circumstance occurs when a demand to arbitrate is served on the other party. This may take the form of a notice that a matter is being referred to the arbitrator agreed upon by the parties, or a demand that the matter be referred to arbitration. Merely informing the other party that a controversy exists is not an act of submission or a demand for arbitration.

10. Procedures

The usual arbitration procedure is as follows: The parties to the dispute are given notice of the time and place of the hearing; a hearing is held, at which testimony is received; the arbitrator or arbitrators deliberate and render a decision. There are no formal pleadings or motions, and the strict rules of evidence used in trials are frequently not followed. Most often the decision is given without the reasons for it.

Arbitrators have the power to fashion remedies appropriate to the resolution of the dispute. The function of the arbitrators is to find a just solution to the controversy, and to that end, they have the power to fashion the remedy appropriate to the wrong. Arbitrators are not bound by principles of substantive law or the rules of evidence, unless the submission so provides. As a result, errors of law or fact do not justify a court in setting aside the decision of the arbitration process. The arbitrator is the sole and final judge of the evidence and the weight to be given it.

Once an issue is submitted for arbitration, questions of law are for the arbitrator. They are no longer open to judicial intervention or to judicial review. Unless the submission is to the contrary, the means by which arbitrators reach their decision is superfluous. However, there is an obligation to act fairly and impartially and to decide on the basis of the evidence before them. Therefore, it is misconduct for arbitrators to seek outside evidence by independent investigation without the consent of the parties.

11. The Award

The term *award* describes the decision of the arbitrator. An award is binding on all issues submitted and may be judicially enforced. Every presumption is in favor of the validity of an arbitration award, and doubts are resolved in its favor. The scope of judicial review of an award is limited in most states by statute as well as by the agreement to arbitrate. As previously noted, the scope of judicial review is quite limited.

Where the arbitrators are not restricted by the submission to decide according to principles of law, they may make an award according to their own notion of justice without regard to the law. The scope of judicial review is whether or not the issues contained in the submission have been decided. An allegation that there is insufficient evidence to support an award or that it is contrary to the evidence does not constitute a ground for vacating an award. Only clear, precise, and indubitable evidence of fraud, misconduct, or other grave irregularity will suffice to vacate an arbitration award.

Submissions to arbitration are for determinations based on the ad hoc application of broad principles of justice and fairness in the particular instance. Reliance is not placed on the continuity of the tribunal personnel or operation, and predictability is not an objective. Awards do not have, nor is it intended that they should have, the precedential value that attaches to judicial determinations.

12. Common Law Arbitration

Arbitration was recognized by the common law, and it has been the subject of legislation in many states and by the federal government. Arbitration at common law was not a matter of right but was based on an agreement to arbitrate. The agreement to arbitrate was revocable until the time of the final award, because it required continued consent of the parties. Thus, a party who felt that the proceeding was not going favorably would frequently withdraw by repudiating the agreement. When this occurred, the other party could sue for breach of contract, but any recovery was limited to the expenses incurred to date in the proceedings.

A distinction existed at common law between an agreement to arbitrate an existing dispute and an agreement to submit future disputes to arbitration. In the latter case, the agreement was unenforceable, and a party who refused to arbitrate when a dispute arose had no liability.

At common law, a party was bound by the award of the arbitrator. The award was enforceable in court by an action brought for that purpose. Since litigation to enforce the award was necessary, many of the advantages of arbitration over litigation did not exist.

13. Types of Arbitration Systems

The various states have taken four distinct approaches to arbitration. A few have not enacted arbitration legislation. In these states, the principles of the common law are applicable. An agreement to arbitrate is revocable, but a final award is enforceable. Other states have enacted statutes that cover only the method of enforcing awards. These states have taken advantage of the cost-savings and time-reduction aspects of arbitration by eliminating the necessity for a suit on an award. In these states, an agreement to arbitrate is revocable, but there is a quick and inexpensive method for enforcing the award, if rendered.

The majority of states fall into a third category. They have enacted comprehensive arbitration statutes that cover all aspects of submission, the award, and its enforcement. They also recognize common law arbitration. In these states, an arbitration agreement is revocable if common law arbitration is being used but is not revocable if the statutory method is being used. If a question arises as to which method the parties are using, this matter is resolved by reference to the statute. If all the statutory requirements are met in the submission agreement, the arbitration agreement is irrevocable. If any of the statutory requirements for a submission are not met, the arbitration is subject to the common-law principles and the agreement to arbitrate is revocable.

The fourth and final approach to arbitration that has been followed by some states in their legislation is to make the statutory method exclusive. In these states, the statutory requirements for submission must be met, and all proceedings must comply with the statute. Failure to comply with any portion of the statute renders the agreement and the award, if any, a nullity. Statutory compliance makes the agreement irrevocable and the award enforceable.

14. General Aspects of Arbitration Statutes

The Commissioners on Uniform State Laws have prepared a Uniform Arbitration Act. There is also a Federal Arbitration Act, which covers businesses engaged in maritime and interstate commerce. Both these statutes authorize voluntary arbitration.

Most statutes authorizing voluntary arbitration require a written agreement to arbitrate. Written agreements are required as a corollary of the provision that makes the agreement to arbitrate irrevocable. It should be remembered, however, that in many states, failure to follow the statute is not completely fatal because common law arbitration is a concurrent method of proceeding.

Most statutes also contain provisions requiring submission within a stated time after the dispute arises—usually six months. These provisions are consistent with the goal of arbitration to obtain a quick resolution of disputes. These statutes recognize too that arbitration contracts can be rescinded on the same grounds as any other contract. For example, fraud, mutual mistake, or lack of capacity would be grounds for voiding arbitration contracts. Revocation by operation of law is provided for also. Such revocation occurs on the death, bankruptcy, or insanity of a party, or by destruction of the subject matter of the agreement.

15. Judicial Procedures in Arbitration

One purpose of arbitration is to avoid the time and expense of litigation. Judicial action may be necessary, however, if either party refuses to submit the dispute to arbitration or refuses to carry out the terms of the award. Statutes usually contemplate the following as the procedures to be followed when a party to an arbitration contract refuses to submit the dispute to arbitration as agreed:

    1. The aggrieved party may petition the court for an order directing that the arbitration be carried out according to the terms of the agreement. Upon hearing, if the court finds that making the contract to arbitrate or submission to arbitrate is not an issue, the court directs the parties to proceed to arbitrate according to the terms of the agreement.

    2. If, however, there is disagreement as to the making of the contract or submission, the court will try that issue, either with or without a jury. If it is found that no contract was made, the petition is dismissed. If it is found that a contract to arbitrate or to submit was made, and there was a default, the court will issue an order directing the parties to proceed with arbitration according to the contract.

If the parties do submit the issues to arbitration as agreed, or if arbitration is conducted pursuant to a court order, certain judicial proceedings may be necessary in order to enforce the award. These procedures, as prescribed by most statutes, are:

1. After the award is made, it is filed with the clerk of the court. After twenty days, if no exceptions are filed, it becomes a judgment upon which a writ of execution may issue in the same manner as if a judgment had been entered in a civil action.

2. A dissatisfied party may file exceptions to the award for such reasons as (1) the award covered matters beyond the issues submitted, (2) the arbitrators failed to follow the statutory requirements, and (3) fraud or corruption permeated the decision. The court does *not* review the *merits* of the decision.

3. Appeals from the judgment may be taken as in any legal action, and such appeals cannot be denied by contractual provisions.

4. If it appears that the award should be vacated, the court may refer it back to the arbitrators, with instructions for correction and rehearing.

CHAPTER 4
REVIEW QUESTIONS AND PROBLEMS

1. Distinguish between arbitration and mediation.

2. Discuss the advantages of arbitration over "going to court."

3. What are the general functions of administrative agencies?

4. What is the principal distinction between common law arbitration and statutory arbitration?

5. Define *submission* and *award*.

6. What are three requirements that must be met before a court will change the decision of an administrative agency? Explain.

7. What are the reasons for the growth of administrative agencies in the United States? Explain.

8. A is involved in a dispute related to his business. He feels certain that he is right and is considering legal action. List the reasons why it may be financially advantageous to A's business to avoid court and make a compromise and settlement at less money than what he claims is owed to him.

9.   P entered into an agreement whereby D would handle his investment account. The contract provided that all controversies that might arise between the parties should be determined by arbitration, as provided for by state statute. Subsequently, a dispute arose concerning the handling of the account, and P brought suit against D, claiming that the agreement to arbitrate disputes that might arise in the future is void. Is P correct? Why?

10.   The city and the police patrolmen's union reached an impasse on two issues in collective-bargaining negotiations and selected A as arbitrator. A issued an award that made a separate determination for each issue. Two days later, R, the representative of the union, telephoned A, informed him that a mistake had been made, and confirmed this by a review of the appropriate state statute. A stated that he would issue an amended award if both parties so agreed. The city and the union did agree, and the amended award decided both issues in favor of the union. The city brings suit to set aside the award, claiming that the telephone contact between A and R after the first award constituted fraud and misconduct. Is the city correct? Why?

11.   Under what circumstances may a court reverse the decision of an administrative agency?

12.   The Federal Trade Commission is authorized to issue rules declaring certain acts to be unlawful based upon an Act of Congress, which provides: "Unfair methods of competition in commerce are hereby declared unlawful." Is this a valid delegation of authority? Explain.

The Law of Torts

1. Introduction

The term *tort* has been traditionally defined as a wrongful act against a person or against his property, other than a breach of contract, for which a civil action may be brought for the injury sustained. A civil action for damages is allowed the victim, because the wrongdoer was "at fault." A tort is a private wrong or injury, as contrasted with a crime, which is a public wrong or injury.

Torts may be classified as *personal torts* or *property torts*. Personal torts comprise all injuries to the person, whether to reputation, feelings, or body. Property torts comprise all injuries to property, real or personal.

The same act may be both a crime and a tort. For example, an assault and battery is both a wrong against society and a wrong against the person who was the victim of the assault and battery. Society may punish the guilty party, and the injured party may bring a civil action in tort for his injuries. It must be recognized that the criminal action does not benefit the victim of the crime or compensate him for his injury. Such compensation is left to the civil law of torts.

2. Theories of Tort Liability

Tort liability is predicated on two premises: (1) that in a civilized society, one person will not intentionally injure another person or his property, and (2) that all persons will exercise reasonable care and caution in the conduct of their affairs. The first premise has resulted in a group of torts usually labeled *intentional torts.* Intentional torts may also be explained by another basic assumption of a civilized society—that each member of society is entitled to have certain interests protected. If a member of society invades the protected interests of another (violates the duty), the injured party should have a right to seek damages for the intentional wrong committed by bringing a lawsuit for dollar damages using the appropriate intentional tort theory.

Some of these protected interests are (1) freedom from bodily harm or apprehension of bodily harm, or from impairment of movement (invasions of these interests include assault, battery, and false imprisonment); (2) freedom from injury to property (invasions of this interest include trespass to goods, conversion of chattels, trespass to land, and nuisances); (3) freedom from disparagement of reputation (invasions of this interest may be written [libel] or oral [slander]); (4) freedom from wrongful interference with the right of privacy; and (5) freedom from interference with business relationships (invasions of this interest include fraud, inducement of breach of contract, and slander of title and trade name). Some of these intentional torts will be discussed more fully in later sections of this chapter. It should be noted that all of them have certain elements or legal requirements that a plaintiff must allege and prove before there is a right of recovery from the defendant.

In recent years, the courts have expanded the area of intentional torts. Among the new torts of significance to business is one called "outrageous conduct." This tort creates liability when one person by extreme and outrageous conduct causes severe emotional distress to another. Outrageous conduct is more than mere bad manners; it is conduct that goes beyond the bounds of decency in a civilized community. The tort has been used against collection practices by some businesses that were deemed to be extremely harassing.

Intentional torts as a group are given special treatment by other branches of the law. For most intentional torts, a complaining party is entitled to exemplary or punitive damages in addition to the actual damages sustained. Thus, intentional torts have a punitive aspect in order to discourage people from committing them. While there are exceptions, one must keep in mind that recoveries on a theory of intentional wrongdoing are in part designed as a deterrent. Furthermore, judgments obtained on a theory of intentional wrongdoing cannot usually be discharged in bankruptcy. This is another punitive aspect of the law as it relates to intentional wrongs against a person or his property.

The second premise previously discussed is the basis for the general field of tort liability known as *negligence.* Liability based on a theory of negligence is liability based on fault, just as in the case of an intentional tort. However, since the wrong is of a lesser degree, the theory of damages does not include any punishment aspect as a general rule. For simple negligence, a person is entitled to collect from the wrongdoer such sum of money as will make him whole. He is not entitled to collect money to discourage the wrongdoer from repeating his wrong. In addition, simple negligence claims are dischargeable in bankruptcy.

A third theory of tort liability is called *strict liability*. Strict liability is not based on wrongful conduct in the usual sense. It is based on the peculiar factual situation and the relationship of the parties. To the extent that an activity by one party causes injury, there is liability in cases that come within this theory. While one party is not at fault in the sense of wrongdoing, he is at fault in that his actions caused the injuries. For example, the theory of strict liability is imposed in situations where harm is caused by dangerous or trespassing animals, blasting operations, or fire.

3. Elements of Tort Liability

While the actual elements of the various torts vary considerably, most torts have the following elements in common: (1) a duty owed to the injured party by the person whose conduct causes the injury, (2) conversely, a legal right in the injured party that has been affected by the conduct of the other, (3) a breach of the duty or a violation of the right, (4) an act or omission that is the proximate cause of the injury, and (5) the injury itself.

The first two elements of all torts are described as the right–duty relationship. The duty one party owes the other is imposed by law. Moral obligation does not impose a duty or create a right. The duty must be owed to the person claiming injury. For example, an airline owes a duty to its passengers, and the passengers have the right to safe transportation. Assume that this duty is breached and the plane crashes, killing all on board. Assume also that X was the employer of Y, a passenger on the plane, and that Y was a key employee of X. X has no claim or tort action against the airline because the right–duty relationship did not exist. Duties vary with the relationship of the parties.

A tort may consist of either an act or an omission—failure to act. The act or the omission must be wrongful in the sense that another's legal right has been violated, but acts or omissions need not involve moral turpitude. Moreover, an act or an omission that does not invade another's rights is not tortious, even though the actor's motive is bad or malicious. Wrongful intent is not required for unintentional torts.

Perhaps the most difficult of the elements of a tort to understand is the one known as *proximate cause*. Proximate cause means that the act or the omission complained of is the proximate cause of the injury. Problems in applying the rule of proximate cause arise because events sometimes break the direct sequence between an act and the injury. In other words, the chain of events sometimes establishes that the injury is remote from the wrongful act. For example, assume that a customer slips on the floor of a store and breaks his leg. While en route to the hospital in an ambulance, there is a collision in which the customer is killed. The store would not be liable for wrongful death, because its negligence was not the proximate cause of the death, even though it was one event in the chain of causation of the death.

The issue of proximate cause must be decided on a case-by-case basis. Proximate cause requires that the injury be the natural and probable consequence of the wrong. Proximate cause means that the injury was foreseeable from the wrong, and without the wrong, the injury would not have occurred. Issues of foreseeability are often difficult. In one recent case, a plaintiff's daughter and granddaughter were killed in an auto accident. The plaintiff suffered a heart attack when informed of the deaths. The court held that he could not collect from the party at fault in the auto accident. His injury was not foreseeable and predictable. He was too remote for there to be proximate cause.

Proximate cause need not be the sole cause or the one nearest in time. Where several causes contribute together to an injury, they each may constitute proximate cause. For example, if two autos, each with a negligent driver, collide and injure some third party, both drivers are liable. The negligence of each is a proximate cause of the injury.

4. Persons Liable

Every person legally responsible is liable for his or her own torts. It is no defense that the wrongdoer is working under the direction of another. Such a fact may create liability on the part of the other person, but it is no defense to the wrongdoer.

Where two or more persons jointly commit a tort, all may be held liable for the total injury. The liability is said to be *joint and several*. All are liable, and each is liable for the entire damage.

In general, an infant has tort liability. However, an infant's tort liability depends on the age of the infant, the nature of the tort involved, and whether the tort is intentional or based on a theory of negligence. In most states, a child under the age of 7 is conclusively presumed to be incapable of negligence; and from ages 7 to 10, a child is presumed to be incapable, but the presumption may be rebutted. A child older than 10 is treated as any other person insofar as tort liability is concerned. Some states use the age 14 instead of 10 for these rules. A minor above the minimum age is held to the same standard as an adult. For example, a minor driving an automobile owes the same duty of due care as does an adult.

Another area of substantial misunderstanding of the law is concerned with parents' liability for the torts of their children. As a general rule, a parent is not responsible for such torts. Parents are liable if the child is acting as an agent of the parent, or if the parents are themselves at fault. In addition, some states have adopted the "family-purpose" doctrine, which provides that when an automobile is maintained by a parent for the pleasure and convenience of the family, any member of the family, including an infant, who uses it is presumed the owner's agent, and the owner is responsible for the negligence of the family member. The presumption may be rebutted, however. Other states have gone further and provided that anyone driving a car with the permission of the owner is the owner's agent, and the owner has vicarious liability to persons injured by the driver.

PARTICULAR INTENTIONAL TORTS

5.   Trespass

The tort of *trespass* is a common one and affects both real and personal property. A trespass to personal property—goods and the like—is the unlawful interference by one person with the control and possession of the goods of another. A theft of goods constitutes the tort of trespass to personal property. An owner is entitled to have exclusive possession and control of personal property and may recover for any physical harm to goods by reason of the wrongful conduct of another. Closely allied to trespass is the tort of *conversion*. Conversion is the wrongful disposition or detention of goods of one person by another. It may occur by theft, but most conversions occur when a party who legally has possession of goods fails to return them as agreed. The failure to return them converts the lawful possession to one that is unlawful, and thus it is tortious.

The one in exclusive possession of land is entitled to enjoy the use of the land free from interference of others. Entry upon the land of another is a trespass, even though the one who enters is under the mistaken belief that he is the owner or has a right, license, or privilege to enter thereon. It is still an intentional wrong, because a person intends the natural and probable consequences of his acts.

6.   Nuisances

Tort liability may also be predicated upon the unreasonable use of property. Any improper or indecent activity that causes harm to another's person, to his property, or to the public generally is tortious. Such conduct is usually described as a *nuisance*.

For example, the operation of a hog feedlot close to a residential area would constitute a nuisance because of the smell. The operation of a drag strip could be found to be a nuisance if it were located close to a residential area because of the noise.

Nuisances may be either *private* or *public*. A private nuisance is one that disturbs only the interest of some private individual, whereas the public nuisance disturbs or interferes with the public in general. The legal theory supporting tort liability in these areas is that an owner of property, although conducting a lawful business, is subject to reasonable limitations and must not unreasonably interfere with the health and comfort of his neighbors, or with their right to the enjoyment of their property. Liability is imposed for nuisances as a matter of policy and not because of any negligence.

In addition to tort liability, the remedy of an injunction is used to abate a nuisance. This remedy is used when dollar damages would not be an adequate remedy. In such cases, a business activity that is otherwise lawful is declared to be unlawful because of its effect on others.

7. The Right of Privacy

In recent years, the law has developed a tort known as *invasion of the right of privacy* or the right to be left alone. A person's right to privacy may be invaded in numerous ways.

First of all, the right is breached by an intrusion upon a person's physical and mental solitude or seclusion. Second, wrongful public disclosure of private facts is an invasion of one's privacy, as is the publication of purported facts that places a person in a false light in the public eye. Finally, an appropriation of one person's name or likeness for the benefit of another is an actionable invasion of privacy.

8. Business Torts

Interference with another's contracts or business relationships is a tort of growing importance. The actionable wrong here is the inducement to break a contract or to sever a relationship. The contract may be oral or written, and it need not actually be enforceable. The fact that a prospective economic relationship has not attained the dignity of a legally enforceable agreement does not permit third persons to interfere with the relationship.

Many of the cases finding liability for interference with a business relationship involve the employer–employee relationship. One business may attempt to induce an employee of a competitor to quit the competition and go to work for it. Such pirating of employees constitutes an actionable tort. Similarly, if a person encourages an employer to discharge an employee, tort liability may result.

For example, assume that X is employed by a bank as a cashier. Y, a depositor of the bank, tells the bank president that he believes X to be dishonest and suggests that X be discharged. Y has committed a tort. Here, the policy of protecting employees from wrongful interference with their employment contracts must be weighed against the desirability of ensuring that bank employees are honest. The trend of cases is to allow recovery for all wrongful interferences with the rights of others unless there is just cause for the interference.

Another business tort is the wrongful appropriation of another's goodwill or business value. For example, it is a tort to infringe on another's patent, trademark, or copyright. In addition, a trade name, such as Holiday Inn or Coca-Cola, is entitled to protection from theft or appropriation by another. Many cases involving the appropriation of another's business values involve words or actions that are deceptively similar to those of another. It is a tort to use a name or take an action that is deceptively similar to the protected interests of another. Just how similar the mark, name, or trade dress must appear before a wrong has been committed presents an interesting problem.

In general, it can be said that whenever the casual observer, as distinct from the careful buyer, tends to be misled into purchasing the wrong article, an injunction as well as a tort action is available to the injured party.

The remedy of injunction is perhaps more important than the tort action when there is infringement of a patent, copyright, or trademark. The injunction that prohibits the continued appropriation protects not only the owner of the right but the consuming public as well.

Trade secrets are also protected by the law of torts and courts of equity. Information about one's trade, customers, processes, or manufacture is confidential. If a competitor can discover this information fairly through research, study, or observation, he may use it freely in the absence of a patent or a copyright. However, if he obtains such information by bribery of an employee of the first concern or by engaging an employee of the first concern with the understanding that he will use this information, the second party may be enjoined from making use of it.

In this connection, it should be emphasized that an idea once exposed to the public may thereafter be used by anyone. The forward march of civilization is dependent upon the freedom with which new ideas are adopted. A book or a magazine article containing new ideas may be copyrighted, but the ideas set forth therein may be used by anyone so long as the language used is not published by another. One who unfolds to an interested party a plan for financing his product or for merging several industries may discover later that the interested party has made use of these ideas without compensating the originator of them. To forestall such a possibility, the originator of the idea should, before explaining his idea, obtain a promise of payment in case his plan is adopted.

NEGLIGENCE

9. Introduction

The second premise of tort liability previously noted was that people should exercise reasonable care and caution in the conduct of their affairs. Failure to do so is negligence, and people who negligently injure others have liability. Reasonable care and caution is that which a reasonable man, guided by circumstances that ordinarily regulate the conduct of human beings, would exercise under the circumstances.

There are degrees of negligence. These may be described as slight negligence, ordinary negligence, and gross negligence. The last item is rejected by most courts, which prefer the term *willful and wanton misconduct* to describe conduct that is less than intentional but more wrong than ordinary or simple negligence. Willful and wanton misconduct is a conscious disregard of the rights of others.

For example, A recklessly and knowingly drives through a stoplight at a high rate of speed. B is injured. A is guilty of willful and wanton misconduct.

10. Elements of Negligence

now not true in most States

A person seeking damages under the theory of negligence is usually required to establish that (1) he was injured without fault of his own (freedom from contributory negligence), (2) conduct of the defendant was the proximate cause of his injuries, and (3) the defendant's conduct was contrary to a duty owed to the injured party. This duty is usually expressed in terms of the degree of care and caution that the wrongdoer was bound to exercise for the other party by reason of the factual situation and their relationship. For example, an owner of property would owe a higher standard of care and caution to a business visitor than to a trespasser. Therefore, conduct that might be considered negligent to a business visitor might not be so to a trespasser. Negligence, then, is based on a violation of a duty owed that is the proximate cause of an injury to another. Generally, the greater the duty, the higher the standard of conduct.

There are a variety of standards used to describe the duty that one person owes to another. Generally, the greater the duty, the higher the standard of conduct.

The various duties owed under the various theories of fault may be summarized as follows:

Theory of Fault	Duty	Degree of Fault for Liability
1. Slight negligence	To use extreme or high degree of care	Failure to use extreme or high degree of care
2. Ordinary negligence	To use ordinary care	Failure to use ordinary care
3. Willful and wanton misconduct	To use slight care	Actions with a conscious disregard for the safety of others (gross recklessness)
4. Intentional tort	Not to intentionally injure another	Actions with intent to harm
5. Strict liability	Not to injure	None

The nature of the duty owed by one person to another is a question of law for the courts. The issue as to whether or not there has been a breach of the duty owed is almost always a question of fact for the jury. Only when reasonable minds could not differ is the latter issue one of law for a court.

11.   Malpractice Suits Generally

Among the more significant trends in the law of negligence is the substantial increase in malpractice suits against professional persons, such as doctors or accountants, by their patients and clients. Although a malpractice suit may be predicated on a theory of breach of contract, the usual theory is negligence —failure to exercise the degree of care and caution that the professional calling requires. While professional persons do not guarantee that they will make no mistakes, they are required to meet the standards of their profession. Such suits do involve standards of professional conduct, but the issue of negligence is nevertheless submitted to a jury for a decision. In many cases, juries find that liability exists even though members of the profession contend and testify that the services performed were all that could be reasonably expected under the circumstances.

Most negligence actions against professional persons are brought by their patients or clients, but some suits are brought by third persons who are injured. This is especially true in suits against accountants since frequently their services are for the benefit of the public as well as the party who retains them.

12.   The Liability of Accountants

In suits against an accountant by third parties on a theory of negligence, it is necessary to distinguish between third parties that the accountant knew would rely on his work and third parties that may be described as unforeseen. While there is some conflict between various jurisdictions, the majority and better-reasoned rule is that an accountant is liable for negligence in the performance of his services to those persons whose reliance on the financial representations was actually foreseen by the accountant. The Restatement of Torts (second) extends the liability of the accountant to those persons known to the accountant to whom his client intends to supply the product of the accountant's services. For example, if an accountant knows that his financial statements are to be furnished banks as a part of the process of obtaining a loan, the negligent accountant has liability to a lending bank for negligence in the preparation of the financial statements relied upon by the bank.

The liability of the accountant for negligence is limited to the class of third persons who come within the description "actually foreseen." The fact that the accountant knows that someone *may* use the product of his services does not make such people "actually foreseen." An accountant is not liable on a theory of general negligence to "unforeseen" third persons, because there is no contractual connection with the third party. Third persons can sue for fraudulent acts of accountants without a contractual connection but not for mere negligence.

It should be noted that an accountant may also be liable to third persons under the federal securities laws. This statutory liability, which will be discussed later with the materials on corporations, may involve issues of negligence. Under the Securities Act of 1933, an accountant is liable to any purchaser of a security upon proof that the portion of a registration statement attributable to the accountant contains an untrue statement of a material fact or omits to state a material fact necessary to prevent the statements made from being misleading.

However, it is a defense for the accountant that he had, after reasonable investigation, reasonable grounds to believe and did believe that the statements contained in the registration statement were true and that there was no omission to state a material fact required or necessary to make the statements not misleading. In other words, "due diligence" or "lack of negligence" is a defense to an allegation of a 1933 Securities Act violation. In determining whether or not an accountant has made a reasonable investigation, the law provides that the standard of reasonableness is that required of a prudent man in the management of his own property.

13. Problems of the Fault System

In recent years, the fault system has been widely criticized, and major changes in it have been suggested. The criticism and proposed changes have been primarily directed at automobile accident litigation, whether on a theory of negligence or of willful and wanton misconduct. However, there is also substantial criticism of the tort system in the problem areas of malpractice and product liability. Professional persons and businesses are being sued for staggering amounts of money for injuries caused by negligent practitioners and defective products. The cost of this litigation and the sums awarded the plaintiffs are causing drastic increases in insurance rates, professional fees, and the price of every product. Insurance as a means of spreading these risks is becoming unaffordable by almost everyone.

Among the problems inherent in the fault system are (1) court congestion and the inevitable delays caused thereby, (2) the overcompensation of minor claims and the undercompensation of major claims, (3) the high cost of liability insurance, (4) inaccurate testimony and unreliable evidence, (5) inconsistency of juries, and (6) the high cost of operating the system.

Of the criticism directed at automobile accident litigation, perhaps none is more significant than the high cost involved in operating under the fault theory. This high cost is readily apparent in automobile insurance premiums. Verdicts and settlements in auto accident cases are frequently in the hundreds of thousands of dollars. Payments in excess of a million dollars are often demanded and sometimes paid. As a result, the cost of automobile liability insurance has skyrocketed. Many insurance companies have become insolvent owing to the number and extent of recoveries against their insureds and because of the lag time in rate increases. The cost of liability insurance has risen to the extent that many auto owners cannot realistically afford to pay the premiums. There are substantial additional high costs to the victim of the automobile accident, to the alleged wrongdoer, and to society as a whole.

Most victims must utilize the services of an attorney in order to collect their damages. The usual fee for such services is contingent on the total amount collected. The contingent-fee system means that the attorney is paid a percentage of the recovery. Usual contingent fees are 33⅓ percent if a trial is held, and 40 to 50 percent if the case is appealed. Contingent fees eliminate the risk of high attorney's fees if the case is lost and make equal access to the courts a reality for the rich and poor alike. However, if the injuries are very substantial and liability is easily established, the fees of the attorney may be unfair and unreasonable. Assume a $900,000 verdict is given for the loss of two legs by a plaintiff. It is difficult to see how the $300,000 fee could have been earned. In addition, the chance of earning large fees has encouraged "ambulance chasing" of potentially big cases, especially in large cities.

The alleged wrongdoer in most tort litigation is usually defended by an insurance company. A substantial portion of the insurance premium dollar is spent on investigations and in trying to prevent payment to the person seeking the damages. Thus, both parties to the occurrence are spending considerable sums attempting to determine what, if anything, one must pay the other. Moreover, society must operate an extensive court system and pay judges, court personnel, and jurors to try these cases and to settle these controversies. It is readily apparent that the fault system is a very expensive system to operate.

Studies have been conducted attempting to show that the great majority of automobile accident victims are not appropriately compensated. The theory of damages tells us that the victim of a tort should receive a sum of money that will compensate him for the damages he has sustained. The damages paid should make him "whole." In other words, dollar damages are supposed to place the victim of the tort in as good a position as he would have been in had the tort not been committed. This, of course, is impossible, because no amount of money can replace an arm, a leg, or an eye, let alone a life. Therefore, in the very serious cases, especially those that involve substantial pain and suffering, any amount of money damages is probably inadequate.

However, in the very minor cases, many plaintiffs are overcompensated. A person with little or no personal injury who brings suit will frequently be overcompensated for his injuries because of the nuisance value of the case. Because it will cost money to investigate and defend the case and because the amount of jury verdicts are highly unpredictable, insurance companies frequently pay some amount to obtain a settlement of a claim even though the claimant is probably not entitled to the amount paid.

In many auto accident cases, litigation aimed at finding the truth is quite unrealistic. Witnesses usually do not remember exactly what happened, and so they testify as to what they thought and sometimes hoped had happened.

Witnesses with faulty memories have their memories refreshed and tend not to testify about what actually happened but about what somebody said happened.

Moreover, witnesses frequently do not know what happened in the split second of the automobile accident. As a result, many factors influence verdicts in these negligence cases. One very important factor is sympathy for the plaintiff or animosity toward the defendant. A very seriously injured person or the next of kin of a deceased is frequently the obvious beneficiary of sympathy. When the testimony is conflicting and the memory of witnesses questionable, sympathy may play a major role. Animosity is frequently just as important. For example, assume that a teenager runs a stop sign and kills an innocent bystander. The jury in such case is likely to award higher damages, especially if they believe an insurance company for the teenager may be required to pay them.

Finally, the fault system in auto accident litigation has traditionally proceeded on the premise that the accident was the defendant's fault and that negligence on the part of the plaintiff did not contribute to the plaintiff's injuries. In other words, the plaintiff has been required to be free from *contributory negligence.* The law has required that the defendant be 100 percent at fault and the plaintiff 0 percent at fault. This all-or-nothing requirement, of course, built an element into any case that encouraged settlement. Today the legislature in some states and the courts in others are abandoning the doctrine of contributory negligence and substituting for it a doctrine known as *comparative negligence.* Under the doctrine of comparative negligence, liability is assessed in proportion to the fault of each party. In some states using comparative negligence, a plaintiff can collect even if equally at fault or more at fault than the other party, but in other states, when the degree of fault reaches 50 percent, a plaintiff is barred from recovery. Thus, the fault system varies greatly from state to state in its theories and their application.

14. The Trend toward No-Fault

In recent years, there have been numerous proposals to eliminate the fault system in auto accident cases. These proposals have taken various forms. Some have recommended that auto accident cases be turned over to an administrative agency for decision. Others have recommended that the fault system be replaced by a no-fault system, or a system of first-party insurance.

Although the approaches to no-fault vary from state to state, most have elements in common. First of all, a party injured in an auto accident collects from his own insurance company just as he would if he were collecting on his own health insurance. Payment is made irrespective of fault. Just as health insurance would pay the hospital bill of a person attempting suicide, so also would no-fault insurance pay the hospital bill of a person injured in an automobile accident even if he were at fault. Second, claimants are entitled to collect their medical bills, lost earnings, and out-of-pocket expenses up to a stated amount. Third, most no-fault laws contain a formula for computing the amount to be paid for pain and suffering. For example, a person may be paid an amount equal to his medical bills for pain and suffering. If the total doctor bill is $500, then he would be paid an additional $500 for pain and suffering. Fourth, tort claims may still be filed in serious cases. The approach of no-fault to date has been to keep the fault system for serious cases, such as permanent disability, disfigurement, and death. Only the minor cases are usually covered by no-fault legislation. This is accomplished by the law's setting a threshold above which the fault system is retained. Finally, claimants cannot collect their medical bills under no-fault if the medical bills are paid by any other form of health insurance or by workmen's compensation. This eliminates duplicate payment of medical expenses.

The experience to date under state no-fault laws has been quite varied. In some states, such as Massachusetts and Florida, the experience has been that there is a reduction in the cost of automobile insurance and a substantial reduction in the number of lawsuits being filed. Cost savings are present because of the elimination or reduction of investigative costs and attorneys' fees. Savings have also come from the reduced payments for pain and suffering and from the elimination of duplicate payments of medical expenses. In other states, there has been no reduction in auto insurance rates. No-fault laws in some states have been declared unconstitutional on the ground that they denied injured parties the right to a trial by jury. Low thresholds have encouraged some persons to incur additional medical expenses so that the case is back within the fault system.

Critics of no-fault have been able to delay its enactment in many states and have kept the threshold quite low in others. Among the most-often cited objections are (1) that the victims of automobile accidents are receiving substantially less for their injuries under no-fault than they would receive under the fault system, and (2) that the elimination of the jury system from auto accident litigation deprives a plaintiff of his very important fundamental right —the right to a trial by jury. Thus, it is apparent that no-fault has not been universally accepted and is still in the process of development. It appears that some form of no-fault for auto accident litigation will be enacted in most states in this decade, if not at the federal level. The very serious weaknesses of the fault system previously noted will undoubtedly be fatal to that system as it has heretofore existed.

CHAPTER 5
REVIEW QUESTIONS AND PROBLEMS

1. P owned and possessed Blackacres, a small farm on which he operated a chicken and dairy business. Every day, D took off in his airplane from and landed on his airfield, which abutted P's farm, flying his plane within 100 feet of the surface of P's land. The noise and vibration of the air caused by D's plane frightened P's chickens and cows, and their production of eggs and milk became so low that P's business was ruined. P sued D for trespassing on his land. May he recover? Why?

2. P family had been held prisoner in its home for a period of time by three escaped convicts. D, a national magazine, fictionalized the ordeal of the family in its report on the event. P sued for invasion of privacy. What was the result? Why? *act not made public*

could have libel a slander

3. P has been selling hair products bearing the label "Mode de Paris, France" since January 31, 1967. In January 1970, P learned that D was marketing a similar product bearing a label "Mode de France." P sued D, alleging that D has fraudulently encroached upon its business by marketing a similar product with a similar trademark. Is P correct? Why? *no unless can prove infringement*

without patent or Trademark — probably not have infringement

4. D drove his automobile negligently and P drove his automobile negligently in the opposite direction. Through the combined negligence of D and P, they collided and damaged each auto. D's negligence caused 90 percent of the damage and P's negligence caused only 10 percent of the damage. Is D liable to P? Why? *yes, because he is more liable than P* *by comparable Neglig a new*

b) comparable Neg. no

5. X Corporation sought financing from P. P required X to furnish certified financial statements to evaluate X's financial condition. Thus, X retained A, an accountant, to prepare such financial statements. The statements prepared by A represented X to be quite solvent, and in reliance thereupon, P granted the loan to X. In fact, X was insolvent, causing P to lose a substantial sum of money. May P recover such losses from A? Why? *A is liable for the total loss + interest*

6. P was injured while gathering pine cones, without permission, on D Company's land at an area where timber-cutting operations were in progress. A falling pine tree, cut by loggers, hit an oak tree, which struck P. P brings suit contending that he was injured owing to the negligence of D Company. Is D Company liable? Why? *Negligence by Logging Company.*

7. D constructed a continuation of an existing road across a portion of state premises that had been leased to P. P brought suit for trespass. D contends that he had talked to a state land agent and was under the impression that he had obtained oral permission from him. Testimony of the land agent indicated that permission had not been granted. Is D liable for trespass? Why? *yes, even if he thought had permission to do so.*

8. D started and raced the diesel engines of his two semitrailer trucks at all hours of the day and night on his property, which was immediately adjacent to P's property and in close proximity to P's bedroom. This resulted in P's being unable to sleep at night. P brings suit for an injunction to prohibit D from revving the diesel engines between the hours of 8:00 P.M and 7:00 A.M.

[handwritten: court Notice for him to stop]

[handwritten: new]

D contends that noise that interferes with sleep does not constitute a nuisance. Should an injunction be issued? Why?   *[handwritten: yes]*

9.   P, while on his deathbed in his hospital room, was photographed by D, his physician. When D lifted P's head and placed blue toweling thereunder to obtain a color contrast, P protested by raising a clenched fist and moving his head away from the camera. P's wife told D before he entered the room that P did not want his picture taken. P's widow sues D for invasion of privacy of her late husband. Is D liable? Why?   *[handwritten: yes + possibly her pain]*

10.   On a day when it was raining, P entered D's grocery store to shop. When P stepped off a cloth mat at the entrance and onto the terrazzo floor, she slipped and fell. Water had accumulated on the floor from other customers' feet and from grocery carts coming back into the store. The store had been mopped and cleaned periodically throughout the morning, and the area in which P fell had been mopped and cleaned ten minutes prior to the accident. Is D liable to P for her injuries? Why?

[handwritten: negligence and fault]

11.   D operated an adult bookstore. The local board of health sued for an injunction, contending that the bookstore affects the public health and is a public nuisance. Should an injunction be granted? Why?

6

Criminal Law

1. Criminal Law and Business

Much of the law is concerned with wrongful conduct. Conduct that is wrongful against society is a crime. Of course, criminal conduct usually affects individual persons, but this effect is by definition tortious. In this chapter, we will briefly discuss some of the general principles of the criminal law.

The criminal law is of great significance to the business community. American businesses of all sizes and in all sections of the country face a soaring crime wave. Cash and inventory are being stolen at the rate of at least $40 billion per year. This amounts to 17 percent of total business income before taxes. White-collar crime, such as kickbacks, theft by computer, embezzlement, and fraud, is increasing at an alarming rate. Arson and the fire insurance losses that result from it are also a billion-dollar problem today.

Theft from business is both an internal and an external problem. Employees from the lowest-paid to the executive suites are stealing from their employers. It is estimated that 9–10 percent of all employees steal from their employers on a regular basis. Many of these crimes go undetected, and many that are discovered go unreported. However, it has been estimated that 30 percent of all business failures are the result of internal theft. In addition, it is estimated that many retail outlets lose at least 50 percent of their profits to unaccountable "inventory shrinkage." Many stores mark up goods an extra 15 percent to cover such losses, which means that the consuming public actually pays the bill for theft.

White-collar crimes such as bribery, kickbacks, and payoffs have become so common that the Securities and Exchange Commission demands that the amounts so paid be included in the reports filed by major corporations. One reason for the massive amount of white-collar crime is that in the past, the risk of being caught and sent to prison was slight. White-collar crime has often been considered a legitimate cost of doing business, especially overseas. A business is usually hesitant to prosecute its employees because of the adverse effect on the image of the business. In addition, the sentences have been minimal in the light of the economic consequences of the crimes, even when there have been successful prosecutions.

Now that the relation of crime to business has reached crisis proportions, many people are advocating new approaches in an attempt to alter criminal conduct. Perhaps the most common suggestion is to impose stiff penalties, especially for white-collar crime. Another is to greatly improve the internal controls of businesses so that internal theft and wrongdoing are more likely to be discovered. Finally, there is a trend toward punishing corporate officials who commit crimes in behalf of their corporations. For example, a corporate official who fixes prices with competitors in violation of the Sherman Antitrust Act is more likely to go to jail than in the past, and the fine for such conduct has been greatly increased. Knowledge about the criminal law, as well as its prevention and enforcement, is a key element in business decision making. This chapter will introduce the student to some of the problems involved in the criminal law and its enforcement.

2.   Classes of Crimes

Since a crime is a public wrong against society, criminal actions are prosecuted by the government on behalf of the people. Historically, upon a person's conviction of a crime, one of the following punishments has been imposed by society: (1) death, (2) imprisonment, (3) fine, (4) removal from office, or (5) disqualification to hold and enjoy any office or to vote. Among the purposes of punishments and of the criminal law are the protection of the public and the deterrence of crime. Punishment is also imposed simply for the sake of punishment, as well as the isolation and suppression of the criminal element of society.

Crimes are traditionally classified as treason, felonies, and misdemeanors. *Treason* against the United States consists of levying war against them, or in adhering to their enemies, giving them aid and comfort. *Felonies* are offenses usually defined by statute to include all crimes punishable by incarceration in a penitentiary. Examples are murder, grand larceny, arson, and rape. Crimes of lesser importance than felonies, such as petty larceny, trespass, and disorderly conduct, are called *misdemeanors,* usually defined as any crimes not punishable by imprisonment, but punishable by fine or confinement in the local jail.

Violation of traffic ordinances, building codes, and similar municipal ordinances, where prosecution takes place before a city magistrate, are sometimes termed *petty offenses* or *public torts* instead of being classified as crimes. The distinction is insignificant because, whether they are called crimes or public torts, the result is the same—the party charged may be fined or put in jail or both.

3. Terminology

The criminal law has developed some terminology separate and distinct from that of civil-law cases. The word *prosecution* is used to describe criminal proceedings, and *prosecutor* is the name usually given to the attorney who represents the people. Although the proceedings are brought on behalf of the people of a given state or of the United States, the people are generally not called the plaintiff as in a civil case. Rather, the case is titled *U.S.* v. *John Doe,* or *State of Ohio* v. *John Doe.*

In felony cases, the usual procedure is for a court to conduct a preliminary hearing to determine if there is sufficient evidence that the accused committed the crime charged to justify submission of the case to the grand jury. If the court finds this probable cause, the accused is *bound over* to the grand jury. The function of the grand jury is to go over the evidence against the accused and to determine if the evidence is sufficient to cause a reasonable person to believe that the accused probably committed the offense. If this *probable cause* exists, the grand jury *indicts* the accused by returning to the court what is called a *true bill*. If it is the opinion of the grand jury that the evidence is insufficient to indict, then a *no true bill* is returned to the court. Indictment by the grand jury will be discussed further as a part of the Fifth Amendment discussion, later in this chapter.

If the crime involved is a misdemeanor or if the accused waives the presentment of the case to the grand jury, the prosecution may proceed by filing the charges in a document known as an *information*. Both an indictment and an information serve to notify and to inform the accused of the nature of the charges so that a defense may be prepared.

The technical aspects of the various crimes are beyond the scope of this text. However, it should be recognized that every crime has elements that distinguish it from other crimes. To illustrate, larceny, robbery, and burglary are crimes with many common characteristics. Yet they are legally distinct. Robbery is theft with force, while larceny implies no force. Burglary is breaking and entering with intent to commit a felony (usually larceny). One act may be more than one crime, and it is possible to be convicted of more than one crime for any particular act. Many crimes are actually a part of another crime. Such crimes are known as *lesser included offenses*. For example, an assault would be a lesser included offense of forcible rape.

Criminal cases differ from civil cases in the amount of proof required to convict. In a civil case, the plaintiff is entitled to a verdict if the evidence preponderates in his favor. In other words, if, when weighing the evidence, the scales tip ever so slightly in favor of a plaintiff, the plaintiff wins. However, in a criminal case, the people or prosecution must prove the defendant's guilt beyond a reasonable doubt. Note that the law does not require proof "beyond the shadow of a doubt," or proof that is susceptible of only one conclusion. It does require such a quantity of proof that a reasonable man viewing the evidence would have no reasonable doubt about the guilt of the defendant.

4. Act and Intent

As a general rule, a crime involves a combination of *act* and *criminal intent*. Criminal intent without an overt act to carry it out is not criminal. If X says to himself, "I am going to rob the First National Bank," no crime has been committed. Some act toward carrying out this intent is necessary. It should be noted that if X communicates his desire to Y who agrees to assist X, then a crime has been committed. This crime is known as *conspiracy*. The criminal act was the communication between X and Y.

Just as a crime requires an act, most crimes also require criminal intent. A legislature may declare an act to be a crime without intent, but crimes that do not require intent are rare. A wrongful act committed without the requisite criminal intent is not a crime. Criminal intent may be supplied by negligence to the degree that it equals intent. For example, if a person drives a car so recklessly that another is killed, his criminal intent may be supplied by the negligent act.

Criminal intent is not synonymous with motive. Motive is not an element of a crime. Proof of motive may hold in establishing guilt, but it is not an essential element of a prosecution.

Some crimes are known as *specific intent* crimes. When a crime has a specific intent as a part of its definition, that specific intent must be proved beyond a reasonable doubt. For example, in a burglary prosecution, there must be proof of intent to commit some felony, such as larceny, rape, or murder. Also, if a crime is defined in part "with intent to defraud," this specific intent must be proved just like any other element of the crime.

There is a presumption of intent in crimes that do not require a specific intent. The intent in such crimes may be implied from the facts. In other words, the doing of the criminal act implies the criminal intent. The accused may rebut this presumption, however. The accused is presumed to intend the natural and probable consequences of his acts. Thus if one performs an act that causes a result that the criminal law is designed to prevent, he is legally responsible even though the actual result was not intended. For example, assume that X dynamites a safe. A passerby, Y, is killed in the explosion. X is guilty of homicide even though he did not actually intend to kill Y, since X intended the natural and probable consequences of his act.

5. Defenses to Criminal Prosecutions

A defendant in a criminal case may avail himself of a variety of defenses. Of course, he may contend that he did not commit the act of which he is accused. He may present an abili—proof that he was at another place when the crime was committed. He may also contend that if he did the act, it was not done with the requisite intent. There are also many technical defenses used on behalf of persons accused of crimes. Some of them are:

Entrapment. This is a defense commonly raised in certain crimes, such as the illegal sale of drugs. Entrapment means that the criminal intent originated with the police. When a criminal act is committed at the instigation of the police, fundamental fairness would seem to dictate that the people should not be able to contend that the accused is guilty of a crime. To illustrate, assume that a police officer asked X to obtain some marijuana. X could not be found guilty of illegal possession, because the criminal intent originated with the police officer. Entrapment is sometimes described as a positive defense, because the accused must, as a basis for the defense, admit that the act was committed.

Immunity from Prosecution. This is another technical defense. The prosecution may grant immunity in order to obtain a "state's witness." When immunity is granted, the person receiving it can no longer be prosecuted, and thus he no longer has the privilege against compulsory self-incrimination. When several persons have committed a crime together, it is common practice for one to be given immunity so that evidence is available against the others. The one granted immunity has a complete defense.

Insanity. A person cannot be guilty of a crime if he or she lacks the mental capacity to have the required criminal intent. Likewise, a person who is insane cannot properly defend the suit, so insanity at the time of trial is also a defense. This was recently used in the famous "Son of Sam" murder case in New York.

The defense of insanity poses many difficult problems for courts and for juries. Many criminal acts are committed in fits of anger or passion. Others by their very nature are committed by persons whose mental state is other than normal. Therefore, a major difficulty exists in defining insanity. In the early criminal law, the usually accepted test of insanity was the "right-from-wrong" test. If the accused understood the nature and consequences of the act and had the ability to distinguish right from wrong at the time of the act involved, the accused was sane. If he or she did not know right from wrong or did not understand the consequences of the act, insanity was a defense.

Subsequently, the courts of some states, feeling that the right-and-wrong test did not go far enough, adopted a test known as "irresistible impulse." Under this test, it was not enough that the accused knew right from wrong. If the accused was possessed of an irresistible impulse to do what was wrong and this impulse was so strong that it compelled him or her to do what was wrong, insanity was a defense.

As psychiatry and psychology began to play a greater role in the criminal law and in the rehabilitation of criminals, many courts became dissatisfied with both the "right-and-wrong" and "irresistible-impulse" tests of insanity. A new test known as the "Durham rule" was developed. Under the Durham rule, an accused is not criminally responsible if his act was the product of a mental disease or defect. This new test has not received universal acceptance —perpetrators of some crimes almost always have some mental abnormality, and the Durham rule thus makes their conduct unpunishable. For example, the crime of sexual assault on a child is probably committed only by one with some mental depravity. The Durham rule would make prosecution of such cases more difficult and might result in freeing many accuseds who have in fact committed the act alleged. Today there is a wide disparity among the states as to which test of insanity will be followed. All three tests have had significant acceptance. In the years ahead, additional developments in the law of insanity are likely.

Intoxication.   This defense is quite similar to insanity, but its application is much more restricted. Voluntarily becoming intoxicated is generally no defense to a crime. It is simply no excuse for wrongful conduct. However, if the crime charged is one of specific intent and the accused was so intoxicated that he could not form the specific intent required, then intoxication is a defense of sorts. It can be used to establish lack of the required specific intent. For example, in a prosecution for an assault with intent to rape, intoxication sufficient to negate the intent would be a defense.

Other Defenses.   Return of property stolen, payment for damages caused, and forgiveness by the victim of a crime are not defenses. If a person shoplifts some goods and is caught, it is no defense that the goods were returned or that the store owner has forgiven him. Since the wrong is against society as a whole, the attitude of the actual victim is technically immaterial. However, as a practical matter, many prosecutors do not prosecute cases that the victims are willing to abandon.

Ignorance of the law is not a defense to a criminal prosecution. Everyone is presumed to know the law and to follow it. No other system would be workable.

Various constitutional protections and guarantees are available to a defendant. These constitutional guarantees may prohibit or impede prosecution of a case. As a practical matter, they may make it impossible for the prosecution to obtain a conviction. For example, if evidence of the crime is illegally obtained, that evidence is inadmissible. By preventing the admission of the evidence, the accused may obtain an acquittal. These constitutional and procedural aspects of the criminal law are discussed in the sections that follow.

CRIMINAL LAW AND THE CONSTITUTION

6. In General

The Constitution of the United States is a major source of the law as it relates to crimes. Constitutional protections and guarantees govern the procedural aspects of criminal cases. The Bill of Rights, and especially the Fourth, Fifth, Sixth, and Eighth Amendments, contain these constitutional guarantees. The Fourteenth Amendment "picks up" the constitutional protections of the Bill of Rights and makes them applicable to the states.

As these constitutional guarantees are studied, two aspects of constitutional law should be kept in mind. First, constitutional guarantees are not absolutes. Every one of them is limited in its application. Just as freedom of speech under the First Amendment does not allow one to cry "Fire!" in a crowded theater, the Fourth Amendment constitutional protection against illegal search and seizure is not absolute. Both are limited protections. Second, in determining the extent of the limitations on constitutional guarantees, the courts are balancing the constitutional protections against some other legitimate legal or social policy of society. For example, a state enacted a so-called hit-and-run statute. This law required the driver of a motor vehicle involved in an accident to stop at the scene and give his name and address. Such action may obviously be self-incriminating, in that the person is admitting the identity of the driver of the vehicle involved. Thus, the law created a conflict between the state's demand for disclosures and the protection of the right against self-incrimination. The Supreme Court, in resolving this conflict, noted that the mere possibility of incrimination is insufficient to defeat the strong policies in favor of a disclosure and held that the law did not violate the Constitution.

7. The Fourth Amendment

 *unreasonable*

The Fourth Amendment prohibits illegal search and seizure. Several procedural issues may arise as a result of the protection against illegal search and seizure. Among the more common Fourth Amendment issues in criminal cases are (1) the validity of searches incident to an arrest without a warrant, (2) the validity of search warrants—the presence of probable cause, (3) the validity of consents to searches by persons other than the suspect, and (4) the extent of the protection afforded.

To illustrate the first issue, assume that a student is arrested for speeding. Is it a violation of the Fourth Amendment if the police officer searches the trunk of the car without a search warrant and finds heroin? The answer is yes, and the student could not be convicted of illegal possession of drugs because the evidence was unconstitutionally obtained.

A search may be illegal even if it is conducted pursuant to a search warrant. The Constitution provides that a search warrant may be issued only if there is probable cause for its issue presented to the court.

The validity of a consent to search premises without a search warrant is frequently an issue in a criminal case. For example, assume that a parent consents to a police search of a child's room in the family home. Is this a valid waiver of the constitutional protection of the Fourth Amendment? The decision depends on many factors, including the age of the child, the extent of emancipation, and the amount of control the parents have over the total premises. Similar issues are raised when a landlord consents to the search of premises leased to a tenant. As a general rule, such consents are not sufficient to eliminate the need for a search warrant.

The protection afforded by the Fourth Amendment is not limited to premises. It prohibits the use of electronic surveillance equipment to obtain information. For example, in one case, evidence of gambling was obtained by listening in on telephone conversations. Such evidence was inadmissible, since it was illegally obtained.

Fourth Amendment issues frequently have an effect on the civil law as well as the criminal law. The protection has been extended to prohibit such activities as inspection of premises by a fire inspector without a search warrant. Criminal charges for violating building codes cannot be based on a warrantless inspection of the premises if the owner objects. However, the Supreme Court has held that a search by a caseworker of premises of a welfare recipient is not a violation of the Fourth Amendment. The need of government to know how its welfare funds for a child were being spent by its mother exceeded the need to give additional protection to the Fourth Amendment guarantees.

In recent years, the protection of the Fourth Amendment has been narrowed somewhat by court decisions. For example, in order to protect police officers, it has been held that officers may search someone being arrested and the immediate area around the person for weapons. In addition, police officers have been allowed to take paint samples and tire impressions from autos parked on a public street. Officers searching an automobile are given far more latitude than police who are searching a person, a home, or a building. Today, persons lawfully arrested may be convicted of other crimes with evidence obtained as the result of such searches.

8. The Fifth Amendment

The Fifth Amendment is well known for its provision prohibiting compulsory self-incrimination. Almost everyone understands that a person "pleading the

Fifth Amendment" is exercising the right against compulsory self-incrimination. In addition, the Fifth Amendment contains a due process clause, which requires that all court procedures in criminal cases be fundamentally fair. The Fifth Amendment also requires indictment by a grand jury for a capital offense or infamous crime and prohibits double jeopardy.

A grand jury has the function of deciding if there is sufficient evidence of guilt to justify the accused's standing trial. It is contrasted with a petit jury, which actually decides guilt or innocence. Grand juries are usually made up of twenty-three persons, and it takes a majority vote to indict a defendant. It takes less proof to indict a person and to require him to stand trial than it does to convict. The grand-jury provision contains an exception for court-martial proceedings.

The grand-jury provision is limited to capital offenses and infamous crimes. *Infamous crimes* are those that involve moral turpitude. The term indicates that one convicted of such a crime will suffer infamy. Most felonies are infamous crimes.

The prohibition against double jeopardy means that a person cannot be tried twice for the same offense. A defendant who is acquitted in a criminal case cannot be retried on the same offense. However, a defendant who on appeal obtains a reversal of a conviction may be tried again. The reversal in effect means that the defendant was not in jeopardy.

Notwithstanding the foregoing provisions of the Fifth Amendment, the protection against compulsory self-incrimination is still its most important constitutional protection. The prohibition against being compelled to be a witness against oneself extends both to oral testimony of an accused before and during his trial and to documents and to statements before grand juries, legislative investigation committees, and judicial bodies in civil and criminal proceedings.

A statement or a document does not have to be a confession of crime in order to qualify under the privilege. Both are protected if they might serve as a "link in the chain of evidence" that could lead to prosecution. The protection of the Fifth Amendment is the right to remain silent and to suffer no penalty for silence.

To illustrate the extent of the protection provided by the Fifth Amendment, the Supreme Court has held that (1) a prosecutor may not comment on the failure of a defendant to explain evidence within his knowledge, (2) a court may not tell the jury that silence may be evidence of guilt, (3) an attorney may not be disbarred for claiming his privilege at a judicial inquiry into his activities, just as a policeman may not be fired for claiming the privilege before the grand jury, and (4) the privilege protects a state witness against incrimination under federal as well as state law, and a federal witness against incrimination under state law as well as federal law. To illustrate this latter concept, assume that a person is granted immunity from state prosecution in order to compel him to testify. He cannot be compelled to testify if it is possible that his testimony will lead to a conviction under federal law. The granting of immunity must be complete.

Limitations on the protections afforded by the Fifth Amendment are also readily apparent. The hit-and-run-driver law case previously discussed is one example. In another situation, it was held that the prosecution can use as evidence in a drunken-driving case the analysis of a blood sample taken without consent of the accused. Such evidence is admissible even though the accused, on the advice of counsel, objected to the extraction of blood. The Fifth Amendment reaches an accused's communications, whatever form they might take, but compulsion that makes a suspect the source of "real or physical evidence" does not violate it. In addition, the protection is personal and does not prevent the production of incriminating evidence by others. For example, the tax records of a potential defendant were in the hands of an accountant, and the IRS sought to subpoena them. The defendant could not use the Fifth Amendment to prevent the accountant from complying with the subpoena.

9. The Sixth Amendment

The Sixth Amendment contains several provisions relating to criminal cases. It guarantees to a defendant the right (1) to a speedy and public trial, (2) to a trial by jury, (3) to be informed of the charge against him, (4) to confront his accuser, (5) to subpoena witnesses in his favor, and (6) to have the assistance of an attorney.

The right to a speedy trial is of great concern today. Most states require that a defendant in jail be tried within a minimum period of time—such as four months. This limits the punishment of those not convicted of a crime.

The right to a jury trial does not extend to state juvenile-court delinquency proceedings, as they are not criminal prosecutions. However, juveniles do have the right to counsel, to confront the witnesses against them, and to cross-examine them. Thus it can be seen that there are many technical aspects to the Sixth Amendment.

Perhaps no provision of the Sixth Amendment has been given a broader interpretation in recent years than the right to counsel. During this period, the Supreme Court, in a series of decisions, has been confronted with two fundamental questions: (1) At what stage of the proceedings does the right to counsel attach? and (2) To what types of cases is it applicable?

For many years, it was thought that the right to counsel existed only during the trial and that it did not exist during the investigation of the crime. During the 1960s, the Supreme Court extended the right to counsel to events before the trial.

In *Massiah* v. *United States,* 377 U.S. 201, the Court observed that "a Constitution which guarantees a defendant the aid of counsel at . . . trial could surely vouchsafe no less to an indicted defendant under interrogation by the police in a completely extrajudicial proceeding. Anything less . . . might deny a defendant 'effective representation by counsel at the only stage when legal aid and advice would help him.' " In *Escobedo* v. *Illinois,* 378 U.S. 478, the Court extended the right to an accused under arrest but not under indictment at the time he asked for a lawyer. The Court in that case said that the "guiding hand of counsel was essential when the police were seeking to obtain a confession from the accused." This was the stage when legal aid and advice were most critical. What happened at the interrogation could certainly affect the whole trial, since rights "may be as irretrievably lost, if not then and there asserted, as they are when an accused represented by counsel waives a right for strategic purposes."

Subsequent to *Escobedo,* other decisions expanded and clarified the Sixth Amendment protection. Perhaps the best known of these cases is *Miranda v. State of Arizona,* 86 S.Ct. 1602, which resulted in the development of what has become known as the "*Miranda* warning." This warning notifies the accused that he has the right to remain silent, that anything he says may be used against him in court, that he has the right to the presence of an attorney and to have an attorney appointed before questioning if he cannot afford one. The *Miranda* case recognized that a defendant may waive the right to counsel, provided the waiver is made voluntarily, knowingly, and intelligently.

Other decisions have required that the *Miranda* warning be given to an accused who was not in custody at a police station but on whom the investigation was centering, if the accused was being deprived of his freedom of action in any significant way. Today the right to counsel has been extended to postindictment lineups, because the Sixth Amendment protection extends the right to counsel whenever necessary to ensure a meaningful defense. An accused is guaranteed that he need not stand alone against the state at any stage of the prosecution, formal or informal, in court or out, where counsel's absence might derogate the accused's right to a fair trial.

In the 1970s, the Supreme Court in a series of decisions has tended to limit the effect of the *Miranda* decision. For example, the Court held that a confession obtained without the requisite warning being given could nevertheless be used to impeach a defendant who denied under oath committing the crime. The law relative to the *Miranda* warning is still developing, and more limitations may be imposed.

The courts have also extended the types of cases to which the right to counsel attaches. Historically, the right existed only in felony cases. Today, it extends to any case, felony or misdemeanor, in which the accused may be incarcerated. In addition, the right to counsel extends to juveniles in juvenile proceedings. It also extends to investigations by the Internal Revenue Service. Thus, any person charged with any crime for which he may be put in jail or prison has the right to counsel at all stages of the proceedings, from the time the investigations center upon him as the accused, through his last appeal.

10. The Eighth Amendment

The Eighth Amendment provides that "excessive bail shall not be required, nor excessive fines imposed, nor cruel and unusual punishments inflicted." Bail is excessive if greater than necessary to guarantee the presence of the accused in court at the appointed time. The function of bail is not to restrict the freedom of the accused prior to trial, because of the presumption of innocence. Most states today require that only a small percentage of the actual bail be posted. For example, the law may require that 10 percent of the total bail be deposited with the court. If the defendant fails to appear, the persons signing the bail bond then owe the other 90 percent.

At one time, the Eighth Amendment was used as the basis for declaring the death penalty to be unconstitutional. However, many legislative bodies reinstated the death penalty, and some of these laws were later held to be constitutional.

11. The Fourteenth Amendment

The Fourteenth Amendment is quite general in its language; to the extent relevant here, it provides, "No State shall make or enforce any law which shall abridge the privileges or immunities of citizens of the United States; nor shall any State deprive any person of life, liberty, or property, without due process of law; nor deny to any person within its jurisdiction the equal protection of the laws." The three major provisions are known as the "privileges and immunities" clause, the "due process" clause and the "equal protection" clause. Although all three clauses play a significant role in constitutional law, the due-process clause and the equal-protection clause have been involved in more significant criminal law litigation than has the privileges-and-immunities clause.

The term *due process of law* cannot be narrowly defined. The term is used to describe fundamental principles of liberty and justice. Simply stated, due process means "fundamental fairness and decency." It means that government may not act in a manner that is arbitrary, capricious, or unreasonable.

The issues in due process cases are usually divided into questions of *procedural* due process and *substantive* due process. Substantive due process issues arise when property or other rights are directly affected by governmental action. Procedural due process cases are often concerned with whether proper notice has been given and a proper hearing has been conducted. Such cases frequently involve procedures established by state statute. Due process has been used to strike down such varied state action in criminal cases as forced pleas and trials held with excess publicity. Many of the cases decided by the Supreme Court relating to the Fourteenth Amendment have simply ruled that the federal standard on a given issue was to be the minimum state standard. These cases use the due process clause to "pick up" or to "incorporate" the federal standards of criminal jurisprudence and to make them applicable to the states.

The equal protection clause is used more often in civil litigation, such as school desegregation cases. It is used to prevent all types of invidious discrimination, such as discrimination based on race, creed, color, sex, or national origin. It has been used in the criminal law where discriminating laws or practices were involved.

12. Contemporary Problems

The criminal law system has failed to accomplish most of its assumed goals. It has generally failed to act as a deterrent to criminal conduct. Society is faced with an ever-increasing crime rate, especially in larger communities. Crimes of violence as well as the so-called white-collar crimes are constantly in the news. Our penal system has not found the means to rehabilitate convicted offenders, and a significant portion of all crimes are committed by repeat offenders.

Many people believe that the failure of the criminal law results from its failure to provide swift and sure punishment for those committing wrongs against society. Delay in all steps of criminal procedure is quite common. Most delays are probably the result of defense tactics, as time favors the accused. Court congestion also contributes to delay, and vice versa. Recent decisions such as those expanding the right to counsel have contributed to court congestion also.

One of the more controversial procedures used in the criminal law is commonly referred to as *plea bargaining.* This term describes the technique by which an accused pleads guilty to a lesser offense than that which is charged, or when there is an agreement as to punishment less than normal in return for a plea of guilty. Plea bargaining is essential, because the case load is too great to try all cases. However, plea bargaining has many adverse side effects. For example, persons who have committed serious crimes are often almost immediately back on the streets to commit more crimes after only paying a fine or serving a much shorter sentence than would have been imposed if they had been convicted of the crime originally charged.

The increased criminal law case load has had a great impact on the work of reviewing courts. Today, approximately 75 percent of those convicted of crimes appeal their convictions. This increase is largely due to the fact that the indigent defendant is now entitled to a free appeal. We do not have enough judges to handle this case load properly, and delay is inevitable.

Another inherent problem in our criminal law system arises from the fact that many recent law-school graduates join the staff of either the prosecutor or the public defender. Criminal cases are thus frequently tried by lawyers with little experience and a minimum of training. After gaining experience, they leave for private practice. The criminal law has to a significant degree become an internship for training lawyers for private practice.

The free legal services provided to indigents also create some problems. Many people close to the situation believe that the free public defender, who is frequently underpaid by the state and is overworked because of the volume of cases, often does not do an adequate job in defending his or her clients. In addition, these attorneys are to all intents and purposes on the court payroll, which may affect the vigor of their representation of defendants. As a result, an adequate legal defense is a goal that is yet to be achieved for many defendants.

Many other problems have arisen as a result of the failures of our criminal-law system. Overcrowded jails, unworkable probation systems, unequal sentences, plea bargaining that tends to favor the wealthy, and the failure of sentencing laws to deter crime are but a few of the obvious ills. Most legal scholars agree that the criminal law system needs a drastic overhaul. In fact, the Supreme Court, in its process of reviewing convictions, is bringing about many changes. It is requiring prompt trials or the dismissal of charges. Other decisions have reduced the number of appeals that are available to a convicted defendant. Finally, the Court is reconsidering many of the highly technical aspects of the Bill of Rights as they affect criminal prosecutions. In many of these cases, the Court is balancing the competing and conflicting policies more heavily in favor of the police and the victims of crimes than in favor of the accused.

CHAPTER 6
REVIEW QUESTIONS AND PROBLEMS

1. D drove his automobile on the public highway while voluntarily intoxicated and ran into the rear end of X's truck, causing the truck to overturn and kill X. The state tried D for involuntary manslaughter. D's defense was that his drunkenness prevented his being able to foresee the consequences of his act and therefore he was not guilty. Was the defense legally sufficient if proven? Why?

2. D, an Oriental, was suspected by immigration officers of having information concerning the smuggling into the United States of other Chinese. The immigration officers went to D and suggested that he bring Chinese into the United States illegally. D refused. The officers finally induced D to violate the immigration laws and then arrested him. Does D have a valid defense to the charges? Why?

3. D was arrested for "driving under the influence." Part of the evidence admitted against him was a blood sample taken from D while he was unconscious and under hospital supervision. Did the use of the blood sample violate D's constitutional rights? Why?

4. When police entered his home without a warrant, D swallowed two morphine capsules he had in his possession. The capsules were recovered by the police with the use of a stomach pump. Was the evidence lawfully obtained? Why?

5.   What is the purpose of a bail?

6.   D was arrested for stealing hubcaps from a car parked on Main Street in his hometown. D's attorney has told him that if he is convicted, the maximum sentence would be six months in the city jail. D has been accused of what type of crime? Why?

7.   What is the basic distinction between the degree of proof required of a plaintiff in a civil case and that of the prosecution in a criminal case? Explain.

8.   D, who had previously been convicted of gambling, was called to testify before a state investigation of gambling activities. D refused to answer any questions on the ground that it might tend to incriminate him. The state court held that the privilege of refusing self-incrimination is not available to a witness in a state proceeding and sentenced D to jail for contempt. Upon appeal, should D's conviction be reversed? Why?

9.   What is the purpose of the grand jury? petit jury?

10.   D was arrested and tried for burglary. The jury deliberated for three days and then informed the judge that it was hopelessly deadlocked and could not return a verdict. A new trial was scheduled for D. D objected, contending that a second trial constituted double jeopardy. Is D correct? Why?

book two

CONTRACTS

Introduction to Contracts

1. Nature and Importance of the Contractual Relationship

The law of contracts is concerned with the creation, transfer, and disposition of property rights through promises. The Restatement of Contracts defines *promise* as an undertaking "however expressed, either that something shall happen, or that something shall not happen, in the future." A *contract* is a promise or a set of promises for the breach of which the law gives a remedy or the performance of which the law recognizes as a duty. In other words, a contract obligation is a legally enforceable promise.

When they enter into a contract, the parties, by mutual assent, "fix their own terms and set bounds upon their liabilities." In a very real sense, the parties create for themselves their own rights and duties, leaving it only to the state to set up the machinery for the interpretation of the contract and the enforcement of the promises.

Although the parties to a contract fix their own terms and set their liabilities, they are subject to limitations. To create a valid contract, the expression of the terms of the contract must be in compliance with rules of law. Many factors enter into the determination of whether or not a promise is in compliance with the law. What is the status of the person who made the promise? How was the promise expressed? Was the promise made orally or was it in writing? Are the necessary contractual requirements and elements present: offer and acceptance, consideration, legal capacity of the parties, and a legal purpose in the light of the rules of law and of sound public policy? Is the contract covered by the Code or is it subject to common law principles?

In regard to this last, the limited application of the Code as discussed in Chapter 1 should be constantly kept in mind during the study of contracts. The Code governs contracts for the sale of personal property. The material in this and subsequent chapters will discuss the general principles of contract law. In addition, the special rule of the Code applicable to contracts for the sale of goods will be discussed. The reason for these special rules is that ordinary and general contract principles do not always produce a satisfactory result in a commercial transaction. Accordingly, the Code contract rules have been "tailored" to fit the sale-of-goods transaction.

Although the Code provides definite rules that govern commercial transactions, the parties may, by mutual agreement, provide for a different result. To a large degree, the Code provides for those situations that have not been covered by the parties in their contract. Therefore, the parties to a transaction can, within limits, tailor their agreement to suit their needs. The Code supplies the rules and principles that will apply if the parties have not otherwise agreed. Code sections are referenced where appropriate.

Since the law of contracts furnishes the foundation for other branches of commercial law, a study of the general rules applicable to contract law logically comes first in the study of business law. The special rules of law pertaining to agency, sales, commercial paper, corporations, partnerships, and secured transactions are all based upon general principles of contract law. These special areas are discussed in the books that follow this one.

2. Classification of Contracts

For certain purposes, it is desirable to classify contracts according to the characteristics they possess. They may be classified as follows:

1. Valid, voidable, or unenforceable
2. Executed or executory
3. Bilateral or unilateral
4. Express or implied (in fact or in law)

A *valid* contract is one that is in all respects in accordance with legal requirements and will be enforced by the courts. A *voidable* contract is one that will be enforced unless and until one of the parties who has the right to do so elects to disaffirm the contract. For example, a contract entered into by one who is under legal age is voidable and can be disaffirmed or set aside by the underage party. An *unenforceable* contract is one that will not be recognized by the courts if an action is brought to enforce it. For example, the law requires that some contracts, such as contracts for the sale of land, be in writing, and they are not enforceable in court if made orally.

An *executed* contract is one that has been fully carried out by the contracting parties. An *executory* contract is one that is yet to be performed. An agreement may be executed on the part of one party and executory on the part of the other. For example, a contract for the purchase of a suit of clothes on credit, followed by the delivery of the suit, is executed on the part of the merchant and executory on the part of the purchaser.

Contracts ordinarily result from an offer made by one party to another and accepted by the latter. A *bilateral* contract involves two promises, one made by each of the parties to the agreement. To illustrate: A offers to sell to B certain merchandise at an established price. B, after receiving the offer, communicates his acceptance to A by promising to buy the merchandise and to pay the price set forth in the offer. After the promises are exchanged, it becomes the legal duty of each party to carry out the terms of the agreement. Most contracts are bilateral in character.

A *unilateral* contract consists of a promise for an *act*. The acceptance by the offeree is the performance of the act requested rather than the promise to perform it. The Restatement of Contracts, in defining a unilateral contract and in differentiating it from a bilateral contract, states:

> A unilateral contract is one in which no promisor receives a promise as consideration for his promise. A bilateral contract is one in which there are mutual promises between two parties to the contract; each party being both a promisor and a promisee.

IMPLIED CONTRACTS

3. Implied-in-Fact Contracts

A contract may result from an oral or a written agreement, in which event it is said to be an *express* contract. On the other hand, a contract may result as an inference from facts and circumstances. It is derived from the presumed intent as indicated by conduct and the acts of the parties. This is called a contract *implied in fact*.[1] In other instances, the contract may be, and often is, partially expressed and partially implied. The intention of the parties to contract is clear from the facts and the specific circumstances.

A contract may be implied in fact whenever one person knowingly accepts a benefit from another person and the circumstances make it clear that the benefit was not intended as a gift. The person who accepts the benefit impliedly promises to pay the fair value of the benefit that he receives. However, no implied promise to pay arises when the person who receives a benefit is unaware that such a benefit is being conferred. It is the acceptance of benefits at a time when it is possible to reject them that raises the implied promise to pay for them. To illustrate: A, during the absence of B and without B's knowledge, made certain repairs to B's house. B was under no duty to

---

[1] *Newman v. City of Indianola*, page 105.

pay for the repairs, although he of necessity made use of them in connection with his occupancy of the property. The use of the house created no implied promise to pay for the repairs, because B had never had the opportunity to reject them. However, if B had been present and had watched the repairs being made, his silence might well obligate him to pay the reasonable value of the improvement.

Historically, a typical implied-in-fact contract arose when a seller mailed goods to a buyer who had not requested them, with instructions that the buyer should either pay for the merchandise or return it to the seller. This was a common method of selling religious bookmarks, neckties, and even records. At common law, a buyer was not obligated to go to any expense to return the goods and was not obligated to pay for the goods unless he used them as his own. However, use of the goods created an implied-in-fact contract and liability.

To stop this method of selling, the Federal Trade Commission, pursuant to its power to eliminate deceptive practices and unfair methods of competition, has enacted a rule that changes the common law of implied-in-fact contracts. This regulation provides that if a business mails goods to a consumer who has not ordered them, the consumer need not pay for them and need not return them. Many states have enacted similar consumer protection legislation. These laws have almost eliminated the practice by mail-order businesses of sending out unsolicited goods. It should be noted that they do not apply to cases where goods are mailed by mistake.

4. Quasi Contract

A contract implied in fact must be distinguished from a contract implied in law, generally known as *quasi contract*. An implied-in-fact contract is a true contract, created by inference from facts and circumstances that show the assent and intention of the parties. Quasi contract is not a contract in the technical sense; it is a remedy used by courts to do justice and to avoid unjust enrichment. Quasi contract imposes a duty upon a party and considers the duty as arising from a contract. It is a legal fiction dictated by reason, justice, and equity to prevent fraud, wrongdoing, or the unjust enrichment of one person at the expense of another.[2] The law in effect infers a promise by a party to do what in equity and good conscience he ought to do, even though he does not in actuality want or intend to do it. To be entitled to the remedy of quasi contract, the plaintiff must prove that a benefit has been conferred on the defendant, that the defendant has accepted and retained the benefit, and that the circumstances are such that to allow the defendant to keep the benefits without paying for them would be inequitable.

Quasi contract, as a remedy, is used in a variety of situations when one person, unofficiously and without fault or misconduct, confers upon another a

[2] *County of Champaign* v. *Hanks,* page 106.

benefit for which the latter in equity and good conscience ought to pay. Among such situations are those in which property is wrongfully appropriated or converted; money or property is obtained by trespass, fraud, mistake, or duress; or necessities of life are furnished a person who is under legal disability. For example, if a third person provides a minor child with food, clothing, medical care, or other necessities of life, the parent of the child has liability in quasi contract for the reasonable value of these necessaries actually furnished. In each of these situations, no contract exists, but the quasi-contract remedy is given because one person would be unjustly enriched if he were not required to pay for the benefits received.

5. Requirements of a Valid Contract

The basic requirements for a valid contract are:

1. An *agreement,* which consists of an *offer* by one party and its *acceptance* by the other.

2. *Consideration,* which is the price paid by each party to the other, or what each party receives or gives up in the agreement.

3. *Competent parties,* which means that the parties must possess legal capacity to contract (be of legal age and sane) or the contract may be avoided by the party lacking capacity.

4. A *legal purpose* consistent with law and sound policy.

These requirements will be considered in detail in the chapters that follow. The remedies used in contract litigation are discussed in the sections that follow.

6. Judicial Remedies for Breach of Contract

Three basic remedies are afforded for breach of contract: dollar damages, specific performance, and rescission. In general, these remedies are exclusive, and a party is required to elect one to the exclusion of others. The Code is much more flexible in the matter of remedies and allows an "aggrieved party" the privilege of recovering damages *in addition* to one of the other remedies.

Money damages are recoverable in a court of law; specific performance and rescission are equitable remedies. Although damages are always recoverable for a loss sustained as the result of a breach, the equitable remedies are not so readily available and will be allowed only if the remedy at law by way of damages is not an adequate one under the circumstances of the case. Specific performance is a remedy that requires that the party who has breached actually do what he had agreed to do under the contract. Rescission is the disaffirmance of a contract and a return of the parties to the position each occupied prior to entering into the contract.

7. Rescission

The equitable remedy of rescission is available in a variety of circumstances. It may be granted by a court of equity where a transaction has been induced by fraud or mistake. Rescission will also be granted to a minor in order that he may exercise his privilege of withdrawing from a contract. It is also used as a remedy where one party's breach of a contract is so substantial that the other party should not be required to perform either.

A party who discovers facts that warrant rescission of a contract has a duty to act promptly, and if he elects to rescind, to notify the other party within reasonable time so that rescission may be accomplished at a time when parties may still be restored, as nearly as possible, to their original positions. A party entitled to rescission may either avoid the contract or affirm it. Once he makes his choice, he may not change it. Failure to rescind within a reasonable time is tantamount to affirming the contract. The party who seeks rescission must return what he has received in substantially as good a condition as when he received it. Since this remedy is an equitable one, it is subject to the usual maxims of courts of equity.

8. Specific Performance

The legal remedy of dollar damages or the equitable remedy of rescission may not be adequate to provide a proper remedy to a party injured by a breach of contract. The only adequate remedy may be to require the party in breach to perform the contract.

Specific performance is granted in cases when the court in the exercise of its discretion determines that dollar damages would not be an adequate remedy. Specific performance is not a matter of right but rests in the sound discretion of the court. To warrant specific performance, the contract must be clear, definite, complete, and free from any suspicion of fraud or unfairness. Dollar damages are considered inadequate and specific performance the proper remedy when the subject matter of the contract is unique. Since each parcel of real estate differs from every other parcel of real estate, all land is unique, and courts of equity will therefore specifically enforce contracts to sell real estate. Examples of unique personal property are antiques, racehorses, heirlooms, and the stock of a closely held corporation. The last is unique because each share of stock has significance in the power to control the corporation.

The Code takes a liberal view of the remedy of specific performance. In cases under the Code, specific performance will be ordered whenever commercial needs and consideration make it equitable to do so.[3] Contracts that involve personal services or relationships will not be specifically enforced—the only remedy in such cases is money damages. Courts will not usually order

---

[3] *Tower City Grain Co.* v. *Richman,* page 107.

specific performance of employment contracts, because to do so on behalf of the employer would amount to involuntary servitude, and a contract that is not specifically enforceable by one party is not specifically enforceable by the other. The remedies must be mutually available.

DAMAGES

9. Theory of Damages

The purpose and the theory of damages is to make the injured party whole. As a result of the payment of money, the injured party is in the same position he would have occupied had the breach of contract not occurred. Damages give just compensation for the losses that flowed from the breach. In other words, a person is entitled to the benefits of his bargain. If a purchaser receives less than he bargained for, the difference between the actual value and the contract price constitutes the damages. Unusual and unexpected damages resulting from peculiar facts unknown to either party at the time the agreement was entered into are generally not recoverable. In addition, it should be understood that the injured party is not entitled to a profit from the breach of the contract; his recovery is limited to an amount that will place him in the same position in which he would have been had the contract been carried out.

The question as to the amount of damages is usually one of fact for the jury. A jury may not speculate or guess as to the amount of damage. Damages that are uncertain, contingent, remote, or speculative cannot be used. Loss of profits may be included as an element of recoverable damages if they can be computed with reasonable certainty from tangible and competent evidence.

A party suing for breach of contract is not entitled to recover the amount expended for attorney's fees, unless the contract so provides or special legislation permits it. Litigation is expensive, and the party who wins the lawsuit is still "out of pocket," since the legal expenses will usually reduce the net recovery substantially. Court costs, however, which include witness fees and filing costs, are usually assessed against the losing party.

10. Types of Damages

Several terms are used to describe special types of damages. *Nominal damages* are awarded if no measurable actual loss is established. A small and inconsequential sum, usually one dollar, is awarded to the plaintiff to show that a technical breach had occurred.

The term *liquidated damages* or *liquidated damage clause* is used to describe the situation in which the parties provide in their contract for the amount of damages to be awarded in the event of a breach. These provisions will be enforced unless the court considers the stipulation to be a penalty for failure to perform, rather than compensation for damages. Should the court find the term to have been inserted primarily to force actual performance and not to compensate for probable injury, it will be considered to be a penalty and will not be enforced. Doubts are resolved against such clauses.[4] In order to be valid and not regarded as a penalty, the amount of recovery agreed upon must bear a reasonable relation to the probable damage to be sustained by the breach. Recovery is allowed for the amount agreed upon by the parties, although the damages actually suffered may vary somewhat from those agreed upon in the contract.

The Code specifically provides that a contract clause that calls for unreasonably large liquidated damages is void. To be valid under the Code, a liquidated damage clause must be reasonable in the light of the anticipated or actual harm caused by the breach, the difficulties of proof of loss, and the inconvenience or nonfeasibility of otherwise obtaining an adequate remedy (2-718[1]). Another form of liquidation of damages is the forfeiture of goods when a buyer defaults after paying part of the price or making a deposit as security. The Code provides that, absent a liquidated damage clause, a buyer who defaults and does not receive the goods is entitled to recover back from the seller (1) any amount by which his payments exceed 20 percent of the price, or (2) $500, whichever is smaller (2-718[2]). Thus, if the buyer had made a deposit of $500 on the purchase of appliances for a price of $1,500, he would after his breach and return of the goods be entitled to recover $200 from the seller. If the sale contract contained a liquidated damage clause, the buyer would be entitled to recover the excess of the amount by which his deposit exceeds the amount provided for in such clause. Thus, a buyer who has made a part payment will not be unduly penalized by his breach, and the seller will not receive a windfall.

The term *punitive* or *exemplary* damages refers to damages awarded to one party in order to punish the other for his conduct. While it is not the purpose of a civil proceeding to punish a party, punitive damages are allowed in cases of intentional torts such as fraud. These damages are imposed in the interest of society to deter such conduct.

11. Rules Concerning Damages

The injured party is duty bound to mitigate the damages. It is his duty to take reasonable steps to reduce the actual loss to a minimum. He cannot add to his loss or permit the damages to be enhanced when it is reasonably within his power to prevent such occurrence. For example, an employee who has been wrongfully discharged cannot sit idly by and expect to draw his pay. A duty is imposed upon him to seek other work of a substantially similar character in the same community. He is not required to accept employment of a different or an inferior kind.[5]

---

[4] *Southeastern Land Fund* v. *Real Estate World,* page 108.
[5] *Parker* v. *Twentieth Cenutry–Fox Film Corporation,* page 110.

When a contract is willfully and substantially breached after part performance has occurred, there may be some benefit conferred on the nonbreaching party. Furthermore, the benefit may be of such character that the nonbreaching party cannot surrender it to the other. For example, in construction contracts, the benefit received from partial performance cannot be returned. Under these circumstances, the law does not require the person entitled to performance to pay for the benefit conferred upon him if the party conferring it is guilty of a substantial and willful breach. As a result, the party who has refused to complete the job is penalized because of his failure to perform.

A different result obtains when the breach is unintentional—resulting from a mistake or a misunderstanding. In this situation, the party may be required to pay for the net benefit that he has received on a theory of quasi contract. The court may award damages in the amount necessary to complete the performance, in which event the defaulting party is automatically credited for his partial performance.

In those contracts where partial performance confers benefits of such a nature that they can be returned, the recipient must either return the benefits or pay for their reasonable value. This rule is applied to willful breaches as well as unintentional breaches.

The Code provision relating to the obligations of buyers and sellers when there has been a breach after part of the goods has been delivered provides that the buyer may, on notifying the seller of his intention to do so, deduct the damages suffered because of the seller's breach from the price due under the contract (2-717).

While there are exceptions, damages for breach of contract are generally measured as of the date of the breach, with *interest* to the date of trial. Under such a rule, fluctuations in value of the matter or thing contracted for after breach do not affect the recovery allowed—the object of the rule being to place the plaintiff in the same position he would have been in had the contract been performed on the date fixed therein for performance.

12. Construction and Interpretation of Contracts

Just as it is necessary for the courts to interpret legislative enactments and constitutions, they are often called upon to construe or interpret contracts that are drafted by the parties. The basic purpose of construing or interpreting a contract is to determine the intention of the parties. If the language is clear and unambiguous, construction or interpretation is not required, and the intent expressed in the agreement will be followed. When the language of a contract is ambiguous or obscure, courts apply certain established rules of construction in order to ascertain the supposed intent of the parties. For example, writings in longhand in a contract control printed portions of such contract where there is a conflict between the printed and the written portions of the instrument. However, these rules will not be used to make a new contract for the parties or to rewrite the old one, even if the contract is inequitable or harsh. They are applied by the court merely to resolve doubts and ambiguities within the framework of the agreement.

The general standard of interpretation is to use the meaning that the contract language would have to a reasonably intelligent person who is familiar with the circumstances in which the language was used. Thus, language is judged objectively, rather than subjectively, and is given a reasonable meaning. What one party says he meant or thought he was saying or writing is immaterial, since words are given effect in accordance with their meaning to a reasonable man in the circumstances of the parties. In determining the intention of the parties, it is the expressed intention that controls, and this will be given effect unless it conflicts with some rule of law, good morals, or public policy. A person who signs a contract cannot seek to avoid its plain terms on the ground that he did not read it or that he supposed it was different in its terms.

The language is judged with reference to the subject matter of the contract, its nature, objects, and purposes. Language is usually given its ordinary meaning, but technical words are given their technical meaning. Words with an established legal meaning are given that legal meaning. The law of the place where the contract was made is considered a part of the contract. Isolated words or clauses are not considered, but instead the contract is considered as a whole to ascertain the intent of the parties. If one party has prepared the agreement, an ambiguity in the contract language will be construed against him, since he had the chance to eliminate the ambiguity.[6] As an aid to the court in determining the intention of the parties, business custom, usage, and prior dealings between the parties are considered. Under the Code, express terms control over the course of performance, and the latter controls both course of dealing and usage of trade in construing a contract (2-208).

In the interpretation of contracts, the construction that the parties have themselves placed on the agreement is often the most significant source of the intention of the parties. The parties themselves know best what they have meant by their words of agreement, and their action under that agreement is the best indication of what that meaning was. The Code recognizes this principle when it provides:

> Where the contract for sale involves repeated occasions for performance by either party with knowledge of the nature of the performance and opportunity for objection to it by the other, any course of performance accepted or acquiesced in without objection shall be relevant to determine the meaning of the agreement. [2-208]

It should be noted that the foregoing section does not encompass a single occasion of conduct, and the number of repetitive performances required would necessarily vary with differing circumstances. In addition, when it is

---

[6] *Grove* v. *Charbonneau Buick-Pontiac Inc.*, page 111.

not possible to harmonize the course of performance with the actual words of the contract, the express terms control over the course of performance. However, the course of performance of one contract controls both an interpretation based on a prior course of dealing or one based on the usage of the trade in construing a contract (2-208).

INTRODUCTION TO CONTRACTS CASES

Newman v. City of Indianola
232 N.W.2d 568 (Iowa) 1975

The plaintiff owns and operates a trailer court. The defendant owns and operates the municipal electric utility which serves the mobile home park. The plaintiff requested the defendant to serve three new mobile home spaces. In order to do so, the defendant extended its lines approximately 500 feet at a cost of $473.47. The plaintiff seeks a declaratory judgment that he is not obligated to pay the cost of extending the utility lines.

MASON, J. . . . The trial court's decision requiring Newman to pay the reasonable costs of the extension was based on a theory of a contract because there was a request by plaintiff to extend the services and pay the reasonable cost thereof. . . . Plaintiff contends there is not support in the record for this theory. Although plaintiff concedes he requested an extension of the electrical service he points out that the record is void of any evidence he agreed to pay for the work.

The portion of the stipulation apparently relied upon by the trial court reads as follows: "That on or about the 26th day of August, 1971, at the request of the plaintiff, the defendant extended electrical services . . . for the purpose of serving three (3) additional mobile home units with electrical power. . . ."

As indicated, the factual circumstances leading to this lawsuit were stipulated. There is nothing in the stipulation which would support a finding plaintiff had expressly agreed to pay the reasonable costs for the extension in-

volved. Thus, any agreement in order to serve as a basis for the court's theory must be one implied in fact.

A promise may be stated in words either oral or written, or may be inferred wholly or partly from conduct.

This statement of principle quoted in 1 Corbin on Contracts, section 18, n. 42, is relevant:

Contracts may be express or implied. These terms, however, do not denote different kinds of contracts, but have reference to the evidence by which the agreement between the parties is shown. If the agreement is shown by the direct words of the parties, spoken or written, the contract is said to be an express one. But if such agreement can only be shown by the acts and conduct of the parties, interpreted in the light of the subject matter and of the surrounding circumstances, then the contract is an implied one.

It was stipulated Newman requested the City to extend the service a distance of 500 feet in order to serve additional mobile home spaces. His conduct in making such request was effective as a manifestation of his assent to pay the fair and reasonable cost for such service. There was an implied contract.

The court concludes the trial court was correct in holding Newman was to pay the cost of the extension.

The case is therefore affirmed.

County of Champaign v. Hanks
353 N.E.2d 405 (Ill.App.) 1976

The state's attorney of plaintiff county brought suit against the defendant to recover the value of legal services furnished the defendant by the county public defender. Defendant had been charged with burglary. He executed an affidavit of his assets and liabilities which stated that he was indigent. Based on this affidavit, the public defender was appointed and the defendant was furnished extensive free legal counsel. Later it was discovered that the defendant had a net worth in excess of $50,000.

Plaintiff sued on a theory of quasi contract and the trial court awarded plaintiff the sum of $2,000. The defendant appeals.

STENGEL, J. . . . A quasi contract, or contract implied in law, is one which reason and justice dictate and is founded on the equitable doctrine of unjust enrichment. A contract implied in law does not depend on the intention of the parties, but exists where there is a plain duty and a consideration. The essential element is the receipt of a benefit by one party under circumstances where it would be inequitable to retain that benefit without compensation.

The county does not officiously confer the benefits of free legal representation, but furnishes legal services to those criminal defendants who qualify by virtue of their indigency. The undisputed facts reveal that defendant received free legal representation when he clearly was not entitled to such representation and that defendant failed to disclose his assets. Under these circumstances the law will imply a promise by defendant to compensate the county and, accordingly, we find that summary judgment was properly granted. . . .

Defendant's final contention concerns the correct measure of damages. The trial court, having heard testimony from private attorneys that the reasonable value in Champaign County for the type of services furnished to defendant was $3,000, awarded damages of $2,000 after considering the experience of the particular attorneys involved and other factors. Defendant has maintained that the correct measure of damages is the cost to plaintiff, which defendant asserts as being that portion of the defendant's salary attributable to his defense, or $181.

The measure of damages for an implied-in-law contract is the amount by which defendant has been unjustly enriched or the value of the actual benefit received by defendant, and recovery is usually measured by the reasonable value of the services performed by plaintiff. In implied-in-law contracts, involving principles of restitution and the avoidance of unjust enrichment, the proper determination of damages may be difficult and often depends on the peculiar facts of the individual case. The Restatement of Restitution, section 152, provides:

> Where a person is entitled to restitution from another because the other has obtained his services, or services to which he is entitled, by fraud, duress or undue influence, the measure of recovery for the benefit received by the other is the market value of such services irrespective of their benefit to the recipient.

In the instant case, defendant's assertion regarding the proper amount of damages is patently erroneous. Even if plaintiff's recovery were limited to its costs, as opposed to the benefit received by defendant, computation of such an amount would include many factors other than the applicable portion of the attorneys' salaries. Moreover, such an award would not effect substantial justice between the parties, as it ignores defendant's unjust enrichment.

Defendant, by his misrepresentations, received legal services which were found by the trial court to have a reasonable value of $2,000. The services rendered by three different attorneys from the Public Defender's Office were not only competent but lengthy and most thorough. The record reveals that between

March 28, 1972, and July 17, 1972, they appeared in court at least nine days on various matters from preliminary hearing and arraignment to motions to suppress the in-court identification. The jury trial consumed four days from July 17 to July 20, 1972. Motions for mistrial, post-trial motions, probation hearing and finally sentencing hearing were not completed until October 6, 1972. Thus the damage award

does not exceed the extent of defendant's unjust enrichment as it is no more than defendant would have paid for such services had he not misrepresented his assets. This damage award more nearly reflects the value of the benefit received by defendant, and a lesser measure of damages would be tantamount to allowing defendant to profit from his wrongful conduct....

Affirmed.

Tower City Grain Co. v. Richman
232 N.W.2d 61 (N.D.) 1975

Plaintiff sued the defendant for specific performance of an oral contract for the sale of wheat. The lower court ordered specific performance and the defendant appealed. The defendant contested that specific performance was not a proper remedy in this case.

PEDERSON, J. . . . The Uniform Commercial Code is controlling in the instant case and states, in part:

1. Specific performance may be decreed where the goods are unique *or in other proper circumstances.*

2. The decree for specific performance may include such terms and conditions as to payment of the price, damages, *or other relief as the court may deem just.* [Emphasis added.]

While the Richmans' contention that fungible goods were not a proper subject for the remedy of specific relief under prior law is correct, the adoption of the Uniform Commercial Code in 1966 liberalized the discretion of the trial court to grant specific performance in a greater number of situations. The Official Comment to § 2-716, U.C.C., provides in pertinent part:

1. The present section continues in general prior policy as to specific performance and injunction against breach. However, without intending to impair in any way the exercise of the court's sound discretion in the matter,

this Article seeks to further a more liberal attitude than some courts have shown in connection with the specific performance of contracts of sale.

2. In view of this Article's emphasis on the commercial feasibility of replacement, a new concept of what are "unique" goods is introduced under this section. Specific performance is no longer limited to goods which are already specific or ascertained at the time of contracting. The test of uniqueness under this section must be made in terms of the total situation which characterizes the contract.

In addition, [the Code] states that "the remedies provided by this title shall be liberally administered to the end that the aggrieved party may be put in as good a position as if the other party had fully performed. . . ." We cannot presume that an award of damages fails to put an aggrieved party in as good a position as if the other party had fully performed. There was no finding or conclusion to that effect by the trial court in this case.

A complaint which prays for the equitable remedy of specific performance must clearly show that the legal remedy of damages is inadequate. A defendant should not be deprived of a jury trial, to which he would be entitled in an action at law, unless the plaintiff is clearly entitled to the equitable remedy he seeks.

Historically, specific performance, which is an equitable remedy, was applied primarily to contracts relating to goods which were "unique." All real estate was deemed to be unique, and so were goods which had sentimental value as distinguished from market value. Another basis for invoking specific performance was the inadequacy of the remedy at law.

A factual basis for a conclusion that the remedy of specific performance is available should be found by the trier of facts in order that this court, on appeal, may know the basis upon which it arrived at such conclusion.

There is no finding by the trial court in this case that indicates what it believed to be the proper circumstances. Our examination of the record discloses no evidence upon which such finding could be based. The fact that the complaint prayed for specific performance and that the Richmans have in their possession the type and quantity of wheat called for in the contract are not adequate to support such finding.

The buyer may obtain specific performance of the contract for sale when the goods are unique or other proper circumstances are shown. Because the purpose of the section is to liberalize the right to specific performance, it would appear that it is not to be of great significance whether a given situation is regarded as involving "unique goods" or "proper circumstances"; ordinarily, circumstances which are proper will impart uniqueness to the goods. Uniqueness in a reasonable commercial setting is the significant point.

Without holding that specific performance can never be invoked to enforce a contract for grain or other fungible goods, we conclude that it was a manifest abuse of discretion and an error as a matter of law for the trial court to grant such remedy under the circumstances of this case.

Judgment is reversed and remanded with leave to amend.

Southeastern Land Fund v. Real Estate World
227 S.E.2d 340 (Ga.) 1976

The plaintiff and the defendant entered into a contract for the sale of real estate. The defendant-buyer paid $5,000 as earnest money when the contract was signed. He also signed a promissory note for $45,000 representing additional earnest money. When the buyer defaulted at the closing, the seller sued to collect the $45,000 note.

The trial court gave the plaintiff-seller a judgment for $45,000 but this was reversed by the Court of Appeals on the grounds that the earnest money provisions of the contract amounted to a penalty. The contract had provided that the seller could retain the earnest money as liquidated damages and had further barred the remedy of specific performance.

INGRAM, J. . . . If, as the Court of Appeals found, this provision in the contract was a penalty, or is unenforceable as a liquidated damages provision, then the buyer can prevail in asserting a defense to the enforcement of the $45,000 note. If, on the other hand, this is a proper provision for liquidated damages, then the seller can prevail in enforcing the note. Of course, whether a provision represents liquidated damages or a penalty does not depend upon the label the parties place on the payment but rather depends on the effect it was intended to have and whether it was reasonable. Where the parties do not undertake to estimate damages in advance of the breach and instead provide for both a forfeiture [penalty] plus actual damages, the amount, even though called liquidated damages, is instead an unenforceable penalty. . . .

Depending on the language used in the contract and the discernable intent of the parties, the existence of an earnest money provision in a real estate sales contract can have one of three effects in the case of a breach by the buyer. First, the money could be considered as partial payment of any actual damages which can be proven as the result of the buyer's breach. Second, the money could be applied as part payment of the purchase price in the enforcement of the contract in a suit for specific performance by the seller. Third, the money could be liquidated damages for breach of the contract by the buyer. A provision for earnest money cannot, however, under Georgia law, be used for all three results as we shall see.

Of course, if the real estate sales contract is silent on the remedy to be provided, the non-breaching seller is entitled to his proven actual damages. The ordinary measure of damages is the difference between the contract price and the market value of the property at the time of the buyer's breach. If the non-breaching seller sues for actual damages, the earnest money then becomes a fund out of which those damages are partially paid if the proven damages exceed the amount of the earnest money.

Even if the real estate contract is silent as to the remedy of specific performance, it is still available as a remedy unless it is specifically excluded as a remedy. In the cases in which rescission has been used as a remedy the parties are put as nearly as is possible back to the status quo ante.

Of course, Georgia law also recognizes that the parties may agree in their contract to a sum to liquidate their damages. . . .

In deciding whether a contract provision is enforceable as liquidated damages, the court makes a tripartite inquiry to determine if the following factors are present:

> First, the injury caused by the breach must be difficult or impossible of accurate estimation; second, the parties must intend to provide for damages rather than for a penalty; and third, the sum stipulated must be a reasonable pre-estimate of the probable loss.

Another feature implicit in the concept of liquidated damages in addition to the above factors is that both parties are bound by their agreement. A non-breaching party who has agreed to accept liquidated damages cannot elect after a breach to take actual damages should they prove greater than the sum specified. The breaching party cannot complain that the actual damages are less than those specified as liquidated damages. The liquidated damages become the "maximum as well as the minimum sum that can be collected. . . ."

The contract provision that included the retention of the right to elect specific performance as an alternative remedy to damages poses no problem in our analysis as it does not render a valid liquidated damages provision unenforceable. "The law is now well settled that a liquidated damages provision will not in and of itself be construed as barring the remedy of specific performance." To bar specific performance there should be explicit language in the liquidated damages provision that it is to be the sole remedy. Thus the retention of the right to elect specific performance in this contract does not render the purported liquidated damages provision invalid. The answer must be found elsewhere in the construction of these contract provisions.

We think a correct resolution of this issue must be found in the doctrine that "in cases of doubt the courts favor the construction which holds the stipulated sum to be a penalty, and limits the recovery to the amount of damages actually shown, rather than a liquidation of the damages." If the parties intended for the $5,000 and the $45,000 to represent the "maximum as well as the minimum sum that can be collected," from the buyer's breach, the contract should have made it clear that this was the effect intended by these provisions. It is the lingering ambiguity inherent in these provisions of the contract that persuades us to affirm the result reached by the Court of Appeals in construing the contract.

In summary, we hold that these contract provisions are not enforceable under Georgia law as proper liquidated damages provisions in this real estate sales contract. . . .

Affirmed.

Parker v. Twentieth Century–Fox Film Corporation
89 Cal. Rptr. 737 (1970)

Plaintiff, a well-known actress, was engaged by defendant corporation to act in a musical motion picture entitled *Bloomer Girl.* Her compensation to be $750,000. Prior to the date upon which production was to begin, defendant notified plaintiff that production of *Bloomer Girl* had been canceled. The actress was offered a role in a dramatic Western, to be titled *Big Country, Big Man. Bloomer Girl* was to have been filmed in California; *Big Country* was to be produced in Australia at the same compensation. Plaintiff did not accept the new role, but sued instead for payment on the *Bloomer Girl* contract. Defendant asserted as an affirmative defense plaintiff's allegedly deliberate failure to mitigate damages, asserting that her refusal to accept the other role was unreasonable. The lower court found for plaintiff, and defendant appealed.

BURKE, J. . . . The general rule is that the measure of recovery by a wrongfully discharged employee is the amount of salary agreed upon for the period of service, less the amount which the employer affirmatively proves the employee has earned or with reasonable effort might have earned from other employment. However, before projected earnings from other employment opportunities not sought or accepted by the discharged employee can be applied in mitigation, the employer must show that the other employment was comparable, or substantially similar, to that of which the employee has been deprived; the employee's rejection of or failure to seek other available employment of a different or inferior kind may not be resorted to in order to mitigate damages.

In the present case defendant has raised no issue of *reasonableness of efforts* by plaintiff to obtain other employment, the sole issue is whether plaintiff's refusal of defendant's substitute offer of *Big Country* may be used in mitigation. Nor, if the *Big Country* offer was of

employment different or inferior when compared with the original *Bloomer Girl* employment, is there an issue as to whether or not plaintiff acted reasonably in refusing the substitute offer. Despite defendant's arguments to the contrary, no case cited or which our research has discovered holds or suggests that reasonableness is an element of a wrongfully discharged employee's option to reject, or fail to seek, different or inferior employment lest the possible earnings therefrom be charged against him in mitigation of damages.

Applying the foregoing rules to the record in the present case, with all intendments in favor of the party opposing the summary judgment motion—here, defendant—it is clear that the trial court correctly ruled that plaintiff's failure to accept defendant's tendered substitute employment could not be applied in mitigation of damages because the offer of the *Big Country* lead was of employment both different and inferior, and that no factual dispute was presented on that issue. The mere circumstances that *Bloomer Girl* was to be a musical review calling upon plaintiff's talents as a dancer as well as an actress, and was to be produced in the City of Los Angeles, whereas *Big Country* was a straight dramatic role in a "Western Type" story taking place in an opal mine in Australia, demonstrates the difference in kind between the two employments; the female lead as a dramatic actress in a western style motion picture can by no stretch of imagination be considered the equivalent of or substantially similar to the lead in a song-and-dance production.

Additionally, the substitute *Big Country* offer proposed to eliminate or impair the director and screenplay approvals accorded to plaintiff under the original *Bloomer Girl* contract and thus constituted an offer of inferior employment. No expertise or judicial notice is required in order to hold that the deprivation or infringement of an employee's rights held under an original employment contract converts the available "other employment" relied upon by the employer to mitigate damages, into inferior employment which the employee need not seek or accept. . . .

The judgment is affirmed.

Grove v. Charbonneau Buick-Pontiac, Inc.
240 N.W.2d 853 (N.D.) 1976

unilateral contract

As a part of a golf tournament a new 1974 automobile was offered "to the first entry to shoot a hole-in-one on hole No. 8." The golf course on which the golf tournament was played had only nine holes and players played the course twice to complete 18 holes. The first nine holes were marked with blue tee markers, and the second nine holes were marked with red tee markers. As a result, both hole number eight and Hole number 17 were played on the same portion of the golf course. Hole 17 was actually 60 yards longer than hole number eight because of the placement of the tee markers.

The plaintiff scored a hole-in-one while playing from the 17th tee on the eighth hole of the golf course. Plaintiff claimed this satisfied the requirements of the offer but the defendant refused to deliver contending that the hole-in-one had been scored on the wrong hole. The lower court gave the plaintiff damages in the amount of $5,800 and the defendant appealed.

SAND, J. . . . The offer made by Charbonneau Buick stated that a 1974 Pontiac Catalina would be awarded to the "first entry who shoots a hole-in-one on hole No. 8." Grove claims that his performance was an acceptance of this offer and created a binding contract.

Rewards and prizes are governed by the general rules of contract. There must be a genuine offer and an acceptance. To collect a prize, the person must perform all of the requirements of the offer in accordance with the published terms in order to create a valid and binding contract under which he may be entitled to the promised award. . . .

The acceptance or performance may not be a modification of the offer.

Substantial compliance, however, is sufficient.

The general rule of the law of contracts which provides that where an offer or promise for an act is made, the only acceptance of the offer that is necessary is the performance of the act, applies to prizewinning contests. . . .

The . . . burden is upon the contestant in such a case to establish, by a preponderance of the evidence, that the promoter's offer was accepted by substantial performance under (and) in accordance with the terms and conditions of the offer, i.e., the rules of the contest. . . .

If the language of a contract leaves an uncertainty as to its meaning, the legislature has provided for another test to be applied by the court in Section 9-07-19, NDCC, which states:

> In cases of uncertainty not removed by the preceding rules, the language of a contract should be interpreted most strongly against the party who caused the uncertainty to exist. The promisor is presumed to be such party, except in a contract between a public officer or body, as such, and a private party, and in such case it is presumed that all uncertainty was caused by the private party.

Where a contract contains ambiguous terms which are in dispute it is the duty of the court to construe them. The ambiguous terms of a contract will be interpreted most strongly against the party who caused the ambiguity.

In *Schreiner* v. *Weil Furniture Co.*, 68 So. 2d 149 (La.App. 1953), the court stated it is a well settled proposition of law that where there is a dispute over what the terms of a contract are or what the stipulations mean, the document must be interpreted against the one who has prepared it, and applied such rule to an offer of a prize made to the public. The *Schreiner* case involved a "count-the-dots" contest where certificates worth money-off on the purchase of a television were awarded. The plaintiff won and a dispute developed as to what prizes were to be awarded under the rules of the contest. The court held that it was the duty of the defendant to explain the contest so that the public would not be misled.

We believe the rule on ambiguous contracts applies to this case, and therefore any language of this contract which is not clear and definite or in which an uncertainty exists as to its meaning must be interpreted most strongly against Charbonneau.

The offer does not contain any qualifications, restrictions, or limitations as to what is meant by the phrase "on hole No. 8." Neither does the award or offer make any statement restricting or qualifying that the hole-in-one on hole No. 8 may be accomplished only from tee No. 8. If Charbonneau had in mind to impose limitations, restrictions, or qualifications he could have made this in the offer so that a person with ordinary intelligence would have been fully apprised of the offer in every respect. . . .

. . . [W]hen good arguments can be made for either of two contrary positions as to the meaning of a term in a document an ambiguity exists. . . . [W]e are satisfied that the language in question, "hole-in-one on Hole No. 8," in the offer, under this setting is ambiguous.

Having concluded as a matter of law that the offer in this setting is ambiguous, the rule of law providing that the ambiguous terms will be construed and interpreted most strongly against the party who caused the ambiguity applies. . . .

If this rule of law were not applied it would permit the promoter who is so inclined, where there has been a performance, to keep adding requirements or conditions which were not stated in the offer. An example, such as, "must use a certain club; the ball must be of a certain brand; the play must be accomplished by a person playing left-handed," to name only a few.

Both of the constructions and interpretations of the language in the offer as contended by the parties are reasonable and each has some strong convincing points, but that does not constitute legal grounds for not applying the rule of law as to how ambiguities in a contract are to be resolved in a situation or setting we have here.

By interpreting and construing the ambiguous provisions of the offer most strongly against the party who caused them . . . , and as announced in case law developed on this subject, we construe it to mean that an entrant in the golf tournament who had paid the fee and who during regular tournament play drives the ball in one stroke into hole No. 8 from either the 8th or 17th tee has made a hole-in-one on hole No. 8, and has met the conditions of the offer and is entitled to the award or the equivalent in money damages.

Affirmed.

CHAPTER 7
REVIEW QUESTIONS AND PROBLEMS

1. X entered into an express contract with Y, a contractor, to build a house. The contract did not state the amount of compensation, and X refuses to pay. Y contends that an implied contract as to the amount of compensation exists. Does an implied contract exist? Explain. — *must be compensation*

yes, implied in fact *paid*

2. A contracted to build a house for B according to B's plans. After the house was completed, there were several defects that A refused to fix. B hired another contractor to do the repairs at a cost of $8,000. Since A was bonded by another company for faithful performance, B sues for $17,000. How much is B entitled to as damages? Explain. *← because of his actual loss*
$8,000 —

3. X was dismissed from his employment with Y Company for "no good reason." X now seeks reinstatement to his job from the courts. Can X be reinstated to his job if his employment contract was not for a definite period of time? Explain. *if no employment contract he can be released*
no, because no time of employment contract.

4. X and Y were sole shareholders of the Brown Corporation. They signed a written agreement that at the death of either, the other would have the option to buy up the deceased's shares for $1 per share. X died, and now Y seeks specific performance from X's widow. X's widow contends that the stock is worth much more than $1 per share and refuses to sell. Must she sell? Why? *yes en forcible, because of mutual agreement*

is unique property

5. X decided to sell his fruit farm. He contacted a real estate broker but did not give him an exclusive listing. Later, another real estate broker, Y, who had no association with the initial broker, brought a prospective buyer out to X's farm. The prospective buyer purchased the farm, and Y contends that X owes him broker's commissions. Does X owe Y a commission? Why?
yes —

implied contract in fact

6. X contracted to have a house built, and the contractor sublet part of the construction to Y. The contractor did not pay Y for his services. Y now seeks to hold X liable on the basis of quasi contract. Can he collect? Why?
yes

get a lien release from general contract

7. A installed a coin-operated phonograph in O's restaurant. The contract was for a specified period and provided that the damages for breach by O would be the amount of revenue A would have received for the balance of the contract period. O breached the contract and, when sued by A, contended that the provision for liquidated damages was unenforceable. What was the result? Why? *penalty lost revenue*

8. S sold a tractor to B. B could not raise the money to pay for it and returned the tractor after having used it for two weeks. S claims that he should be paid for the rental value of the tractor. Is B liable? Why? *reduced value*
yes for rental — of tractor

9. X Company took over the operation of a nursing home. The nursing home had previously entered into a contract with Y Company by which Y Company was to supply laundry and linen services to it. Y Company continued to furnish services after X Company assumed ownership. X Company contends that it need not pay for the services, since it had not entered into a contract with Y Company. Is Y Company entitled to recover for the contract price? Why? *yes - implied in fact contract*

10. X made reservations through American Express with Y Hotel. The reservations were "confirmed," and American Express guaranteed the first night's payment. Upon arrival, X was refused accommodations because of lack of available space. X sues Y to recover punitive damages in addition to his out-of-pocket loss for breach of contract. Is X entitled to punitive damages? Why?   *not intent   can overbook*

11.   P installed a steam boiler at X University. Subsequently, a leak was discovered. I, the inspector for D, X's insurance company, acknowledged that the loss was covered by an insurance policy issued by D. I directed P to make certain repairs at an agreed price of $8,000. P later informed I that certain additional work would be necessary. I told P to go ahead and complete the additional repairs which P did. D refused to pay for them contending that there was no contract to pay for the additional work. Is the insurance company correct? Explain.   *Implied + in fact Contract*

file
mechanics lien

12.   T leased a restaurant lounge from L. T, with the knowledge and consent of L, extensively remodeled the premises. One year later T did not pay his rent and L evicted him. T sues for reimbursement of the amount spent in remodeling. L claims that he is not liable because he had never agreed to pay for the work. Should T succeed? Why?   *agreement. (Quasi Contract)*
No, improving lease holding agreement

13.   A joined a health club and signed a contract agreeing to pay membership fees for a period of one year whether he used the facilities or not. Shortly afterward, A developed a lung condition and could only make use of a few of the facilities offered by the health club. He now refuses to pay the fee. Must he pay? Why?   *yes, if that what he contracted for.*

8

The Agreement:
Offer and Acceptance

OFFERS

1. Introduction

The first requirement of a valid, enforceable contract is an *agreement* between the parties. The agreement is usually created by one party, the offeror, making an offer and the other party, the offeree, accepting it. Offer and acceptance have been described as the acts by which the parties have a "meeting of minds" or establish a "manifestation of mutual assent."

An *offer* is a conditional promise made by the offeror to the offeree. It is conditional because the offeror will not be bound by his promise unless the offeree responds to it in the proper fashion. The response sought by the offeror is expressed in his offer and will be either (1) that the offeree do something—perform an act; (2) that the offeree refrain from doing something (forbearance); or (3) that the offeree *promise* to do something or refrain from doing something. If the offeree complies with the terms of the offer within the proper time, there is an agreement.

In a unilateral contract, the offeror's promise is conditional upon an act or a forbearance by the offeree. The offeror is promising to do something in return for some performance by the offeree or by the offeree's refraining from doing something (forbearance). To illustrate: A says to B, "I will pay you $500 if you will paint my building." Here, A is not asking for any promise from B, he is simply saying that he will pay B this amount of money if B performs the act of painting the building. To illustrate a forbearance: A promises to pay B $1,000 if B refrains from entering into a business that would compete with a business that B has sold to A. Here, A is asking that B refrain from doing something that he might otherwise do. Note that in the unilateral contract situation, there is only one promise and that the response to the promise is either an act or a forbearance from acting. On the other hand, in an offer for a *bilateral* contract, the offeror is asking for a return *promise* from the offeree. Basically, the offer in either case is a communication of what the offeror is willing to do for a stated price or consideration to be furnished by the offeree.

2. Offers Contrasted with Invitations to Bid

Not all communications that invite future business transactions are worded so as to constitute offers. Many are of a preliminary character, being transmitted primarily for the purpose of inducing the person to whom they are addressed to respond with an offer. Within this class of communications fall most catalogs, circulars, advertisements, estimates, proposals in which major terms are not included, and oral statements of general terms where it is understood that the detailed terms will be reduced to writing and signed before the agreement is to be binding. Such communications may, however, constitute offers, and in a growing number of cases, advertisements are considered to be offers.[1]

The main reason that advertisements do not usually qualify as offers is that the parties making them do not intend to enter into a binding agreement on the basis of the terms expressed. The parties to whom the proposals are directed are expected to realize this. The party making the statement, as the other party should reasonably understand, does not intend that any legal consequences necessarily flow from his action, sometimes because major terms are lacking and sometimes because of the circumstances under which the statements are made.

A typical invitation occurs when bids are solicited for a particular service or other purpose. When one advertises that bids will be received for construction work, it is held that the person calling for bids makes no offer, but that the party who submits a bid is the offeror. The one calling for the bids may reject any or all of them, and in the absence of some statute, the bidder is free at any time to withdraw his bid until it has been accepted. The same is true of public construction. Since the statutes of most states provide only that public work must be let to the lowest responsible bidder, courts have held that all bids may be rejected.

3. An Offer Must Be Definite

Many transactions involve lengthy negotiations between the parties, and often an exchange of numerous letters and proposals, as well as conversations. It is

---

1 *Lefkowitz* v. *Great Minneapolis Surplus Store*, page 129.

frequently difficult to establish the point at which the parties have concluded the negotiation stage and have actually entered into a binding contract. The key question in such situations is whether a definite offer was made and accepted or whether the letters, communications, and proposals were simply part of continuing negotiations. The courts must examine the facts of each case and apply the basic contract rules concerning the requirements of an offer to the facts. An offer must be definite and must be made under such circumstances that the person receiving it has reason to believe that the other party (offeror) is willing to deal on the terms indicated. When material portions are left open for future agreement, there is no contract.

One of the reasons for the requirement of definiteness is that courts may have to determine at a later date whether or not the performance is in compliance with the terms. Consequently, if the terms are vague or impossible to measure with some precision or if major terms are absent, no contract results. Time for performance and the price to be paid are important elements of a contract and would normally be specified and not left open. However, their absence will not preclude enforcement of the contract if the court is satisfied from the evidence that the parties intended to be bound by contract. Without a time clause, the court will imply a "reasonable time" for performance; if no price is specified, the court may rule that a "reasonable price" was intended. However, if neither party has yet performed—that is, the contract is executory as to both parties—an agreement in which the price is not specified will normally not be enforced.

The Uniform Commercial Code recognizes that parties often do not include all the terms of the contract in their negotiations, or even in their contract. It provides that even though one or more terms are left open, a contract for the sale of goods does not fail for indefiniteness if the parties have intended to make a contract and if there is a reasonably certain basis for giving an appropriate remedy (2-204). It further provides that an agreement that is otherwise sufficiently definite to be a contract is not made invalid by the fact that it leaves some of the particulars of performance to be determined by one of the parties. Specification of such particulars must be made in good faith and within limits set by commercial reasonableness (2-311). Unless otherwise agreed, specifications as to the assortment of the goods are at the buyer's option, and those relating to method and mode of shipment are at the seller's option (2-311[2]).

4. The Communication of Offers

An offer is not effective until it has been communicated to the offeree by the offeror. For example, to remain open ten days, an offer mailed on March 1 and received on March 3 would remain open until March 12, or ten days from receipt. But the offeror could have stipulated that the offer would remain open for ten days from the date of the offer, March 1. An offer can be effectively communicated only by the offeror or his duly authorized agent. If the offeree learns of the offeror's intention to make an offer from some outside source, no offer results. To be effective, the offer must be communicated through the medium or channel selected by the offeror.

An offer to the public may be made through the newspapers or the posting of notices. As far as a particular individual is concerned, it is not effective and cannot be accepted until he learns that the offer has been made.

For example, assume that a reward is offered for the arrest of a fugitive. If a person makes the arrest without actual knowledge of the offer of the reward, there is no contract.

An offer is effective even though it is delayed in reaching the offeree. Because the delay normally results from the negligence of the offeror or his chosen means of communication—for example, a telegraph company—he should bear the loss resulting from the delay. However, if the delay is apparent to the offeree, the acceptance will be effective only if it is communicated to the offeror within a reasonable time after the offer would normally have been received. If he knows that there has been a delay in communicating the offer, he cannot take advantage of the delay.

The unexpressed desire to enter into an agreement can never constitute an offer. Thus, writing a letter embodying a definite proposition does not create an offer unless the letter is mailed.

It should be noted that printed material often found on the back of contract forms and occasionally on letterheads, unless embodied in the contract by reference thereto, is not generally considered part of any contract set forth on such a form or letterhead. It is not a part of the contract because it has not been communicated to the offeree by the offeror.

5. Meeting of the Minds

Courts have often stated that unless there is a "meeting of the minds" of the parties on the subject matter and terms of the agreement, no contract is created. To determine whether the minds have met, both the offer and the acceptance must be analyzed. The person making the offer may have had in mind something quite different from that of the person who accepted it.

A classic example of the rule that an uncertain or ambiguous manifestation of intent by either party may preclude formation of a contract is the illustration used in paragraph 71 of the Restatement of Contracts:

> A offers B to sell goods shipped from Bombay ex steamer "Peerless." B expresses assent to the proposition. There are, however, two steamers of the name "Peerless." It may be supposed, firstly, that A knows or has reason to know this fact, and that B neither knows nor has reason to know it; secondly, conversely, that B knows or has reason to know it and that A does not; thirdly, that both know or have reason to know of the ambiguity; or, fourthly, that neither of them knows or has reason to know it at the time when the

communications between them take place. In the case first supposed there is a contract for the goods from the steamer which B has in mind. In the second case there is a contract for the goods from the steamer which A has in mind. In the third and fourth cases there is no contract unless A and B in fact intend the same steamer. In that event there is a contract for goods from that steamer.

The rule that the minds of the parties must be in accord is limited in one important respect: namely, that the intention of the parties is to be determined by their individual conduct—what each leads the other reasonably to believe—rather than by their innermost thoughts, which can be known only to themselves. It is the objective manifestation of intent rather than the subjective that controls.

The minds of the parties are also said to have met when they sign a written agreement. Each person possessing legal capacity to contract who signs a written document with the idea of entering into a contract is presumed to know the contents thereof. Where one who can read signs a contract without reading it, he is bound by the terms thereof unless he can show (1) that an emergency existed at the time of signing that would excuse his failure to read it, (2) that the opposite party misled him by artifice or device, which prevented him from reading it; or (3) that a fiduciary or confidential relationship existed between parties upon which he relied in not reading the contract. Because the act of signing indicates a person's intention to be bound by the terms contained in the writing, he is in no position at a later date to contend effectively that he did not mean to enter into the particular agreement. All contracts should, therefore, be read carefully before they are signed.

Offers clearly made in jest or under the strain or stress of great excitement are usually not enforced because one is not reasonably justified in relying on them. Whether an offer is made in jest can be determined by applying the objective standard. If the jest is not apparent and a reasonable bearer would believe that an offer was being made, a contract is formed.[2]

OFFERS IN SPECIAL SITUATIONS

6. Auctions

When articles are sold at public auction, the offer is said to be made by the bidder and accepted by the seller at the drop of the auctioneer's hammer. Because of this rule, the seller can withdraw his article from sale at any time during the auction. The purchaser may withdraw his bid at any time before the auctioneer has concluded the sale. The withdrawal of a bid does not have the effect of reviving any prior bid. The seller may provide that an auction is "without reserve." This means that the property will be sold to

[2] *Barnes* v. *Treece*, page 130.

the highest bidder and the seller has surrendered his right to withdraw an article put up for sale.

Unless it is otherwise announced before the sale, the seller has no right to bid at his own sale. For him to bid or have an agent do so would amount to fraud, the potential buyers having the right to presume that the sale is held in good faith. If an auctioneer knowingly accepts a bid on the seller's behalf, or if the seller makes or procures such a bid without giving notice of such bidding, the buyer has the alternative of avoiding the sale.

The Code has a separate section that covers sales of goods by auction. It sometimes happens that while the auctioneer's hammer is falling, but before it has struck the table, another bid is made. In this case, the Code provides that the auctioneer can either reopen the bidding or declare the goods sold under the bid on which the hammer was falling (2-328[2]). One who is selling goods at auction cannot bid at his own sale unless notice has been given that he retains this privilege. The Code provides that if the auctioneer knowingly receives a bid that has been made by the seller or on his behalf, and no notice has been given that the seller has the privilege of bidding at his own sale, the buyer has a choice of remedies. If the seller's wrongful bidding has bid up the price, the bidder can refuse to be bound by the sale. If he wishes to do so, he could demand that the goods be sold to him at the price of the last good-faith bid prior to the completion of the sale (2-328[4]). The Code provisions are designed to protect people who bid at auction sales and to prevent them from being defrauded or otherwise taken advantage of.

7.   Options and Firm Offers

An option is a *contract* based upon some consideration whereby the offeror binds himself to hold an offer open for an agreed period of time. It gives the holder of the option the right to accept the continuing offer within a specified time. Quite often, the offeree pays or promises to pay money in order to have the offer remain open. The consideration need not be money—it may be any other thing of value. The significant fact is that the offer has been transformed into a contract of option because of consideration supplied by the offeree. The offer becomes irrevocable for the period of the option. Of course, the offeree in an option contract is under no obligation to accept the offer; he simply has the right to do so during the option period.

Frequently, an option is part of another contract. A lease may contain a clause that gives to the tenant the right to purchase the property within a given period at a stated price, or a sale of merchandise may include a provision that obligates the seller to supply an additional amount at the same price if ordered by the purchaser within a specified time. Such options are enforceable, since the initial promise to pay rent serves as consideration for both the lease and the right to buy, and the original purchase price of goods serves as consideration for the goods purchased and the option to buy additional goods.

The Code contains a provision that creates a limited option, without the requirement of consideration if the offer is made by a merchant. (A merchant is "a person who deals in goods of the kind or otherwise by his occupation holds himself out as having knowledge or skill peculiar to the practices or goods involved in the transaction. . . ." [2-104(1)].) If a merchant states in an offer that the offer will remain open for a stated period, such an offer is called a firm offer, and in such case, the merchant may not withdraw the offer during the stated period provided it does not exceed three months, or for a reasonable length of time not exceeding three months if no period is stated. The firm offer must be a signed, written offer, and in the event the offer is set forth on a form supplied by the offeree, it must be separately signed by the offeror in addition to his signature as a party to the contract. The offeree in a firm offer can rely upon the continuing legal obligation of the offeror and can make other commitments on the strength of it. A firm offer by a merchant is the equivalent of an option.

DURATION OF OFFERS

8. Lapse

An offer that has been properly communicated continues until it lapses or expires, is revoked by the offeror, is rejected by the offeree, or becomes illegal or impossible by operation of law. Of course, an offer ceases to be an offer when it is accepted by the offeree.

An offer does not remain open indefinitely, even though the offeror fails to withdraw it. If the offer stipulates the period during which it is to continue, it automatically lapses or expires at the end of that period. An attempted acceptance after that date can amount to no more than a new offer being made to the original offeror by the original offeree. An offer that provides for no time limit remains open for a reasonable time or for such time as the parties by their conduct treat the offer as continuing. What is a reasonable time is such period as a reasonable person might conclude was intended. Whether an offer has lapsed because of passage of time is usually a question of fact for the jury after it has given proper weight to all related circumstances, one of which is the nature of the property. For example, an offer involving property whose price is constantly fluctuating remains open a relatively short time in comparison with property whose price is more stable. Other factors that should be considered are the circumstances under which the offer is made, the relation of the parties, and the means used in transmitting the offer. For example, an offer made orally usually lapses when the conversation ends unless the offeror clearly indicates that the proposal may be considered further by the offeree.

9. Revocation

Except for options and firm offers by merchants under the Code, an offeror may revoke an offer at any time before it has been accepted. This is true even though the offeror has promised to hold his offer open for a definite period. As long as it is a mere offer and not an option, the offer can be legally withdrawn, even though morally or ethically such action may seem improper.

Under certain circumstances, an offeror cannot withdraw an offer after the offeree, in reliance on it, has substantially changed his position.[3] This result is based on a doctrine of *promissory estoppel,* which is in effect a substitute for consideration. When applied, it is legally sufficient to create a binding obligation to keep an offer open.

The Code reaches somewhat the same result in connection with firm offers by merchants, as does the theory of promissory estoppel in contracts in general. Under the Code, however, the firm offer does not require a material change of position by the offeree in order to have binding effect.

The revocation of an offer becomes effective only when it has been communicated to the offeree. The mere sending of a notice of revocation is insufficient. It must be received by the offeree or have reached a destination where it would have been available to him. But communication of a revocation is effective when actually received, regardless of how or by whom it is conveyed. If the offeree obtains knowledge from any source of the offeror's conduct clearly showing an intent by the latter to revoke, the offer is terminated. To illustrate: An offeree learns that property offered to him for sale has been sold by the offeror to a third party. The offer is considered to be revoked as soon as the offeree learns of the sale, regardless of the source of his information.

An offer made to the public presents a special problem to an offeror who desires to revoke such an offer. It would be impossible to give personal notice of revocation to all persons who may have learned of the offer. Accordingly, the offeror is allowed to withdraw his offer by giving the same general publicity to the revocation that he gave to the offer. A public offer made through the newspapers in a certain locality may be withdrawn through the same medium. While it is thus possible that persons who were made aware of the offer may not actually be aware of its withdrawal, the result is justified on the premise that the offeror is still the master of his offer and that he has taken reasonable means to give notice of revocation.

10. Rejection

Rejection by the offeree causes an offer to terminate. A rejection has this effect, even though the offeror had promised to keep the offer open for a specified time, unless it is the subject of an option. A rejection of an option

---

[3] *Drennan* v. *Star Paving Company,* page 131.

does not terminate the rights of the option holder unless the optionor has materially changed his position prior to the acceptance.[4] After a rejection, the offeree cannot change his mind and accept the offer. An attempt to do so will, at best, amount to a new offer made by him, which must be accepted by the original offeror in order to create a contract.

An attempted acceptance that departs from the terms of the offer is a rejection of the offer and is in effect a counteroffer, since it implies that the terms set forth in the offer are not acceptable. Under the Code, however, it is provided that in some circumstances, a variance between the offer and the acceptance will not prevent the formation of a contract for the sale of goods. This will be discussed more fully later.

It is often difficult to determine whether a communication by an offeree is a rejection or merely an expression of a desire to negotiate further on the terms of the agreement. Thus, it is possible to suggest a counterproposal in such a way as to make it clear that the offer is still being considered—is not being rejected—but that the offeree wishes a reaction by the offeror to the suggested changes. Also, the offeree may, in his acceptance, set forth terms not included in the offer, but the terms may be those that would be implied as ones normally included in such an agreement. The inclusion of such terms will not prevent formation of a contract. A request for further information by an offeree who indicates that he still has the offer under consideration will not constitute a rejection of the offer.

Rejection of an offer is not effective in terminating it until the rejection has been received by the offeror or his agent or is available to him at his usual place of business. Consequently, a rejection that has been sent may be withdrawn at any time prior to delivery to the offeror. Such action does not bar a later acceptance.

11. Termination by Operation of Law

There are several events that will terminate an offer as a matter of law. Notice of the happening of these events need not be given or communicated to the parties, as the offer ends instantaneously upon the happening of the event. Such events include the death or insanity of either party or the destruction of the subject matter of the offer. The occurrence of any one of these events eliminates one of the requisites for a contract, thereby destroying the effectiveness of the acceptance of the offer to create a contract. Thus, if the offeror dies before the offeree has communicated acceptance to him, the offer is terminated, and the acceptance would have no effect. Another event is the promulgation by a lawmaking body of a statute or ordinance making illegal the performance of any contract that would result from acceptance of the offer.

There is a distinct difference between the termination of an offer and the termination of a contract. It should be emphasized that death, for example,

[4] *Ryder* v. *Wescoat*, page 133.

terminates an offer but not a contract. As a general rule, death of either party does not excuse performance of contracts, although it would in contracts for personal service. To illustrate the effect of the death of one of the parties to an offer: Assume that A offers to sell to B a certain electronic computer for $15,000 and that after A's death, B, without knowledge of his decease, mails his acceptance to A and immediately enters into a contract to resell the computer to C for $17,000. The estate of A has no duty to deliver the machine, even though C may have a claim against B for breach of contract if the latter failed to deliver the computer to C. Had B's acceptance become effective before A's death, the executor of A's estate would have been obligated to deliver the computer.

THE LAW AND ACCEPTANCES

12. Introduction

A contract consists of an offer by one party and its acceptance by the person or persons to whom it is made. Figuratively speaking, an offer hangs like a suspended question, and the acceptance should be a positive answer to that question. The offeror says, "I will sell you this article for $200. Will you buy it?" A contract results when the offeree-acceptor answers in the affirmative. An *acceptance* is an indication by the offeree of his willingness to be bound by the terms of the offer. Acceptance may, if the offer permits, take the form of an act (unilateral offer); a return promise, either oral or written, communicated to the offeror (bilateral offer); or the signing and delivery of a written instrument. If a written contract is the agreed method of consummating the transaction, the contract is formed only when it has been signed by both parties and has been delivered. However, delivery of the contract may be conditional upon the happening of some event; then, unless the event occurs, no contract exists even though the written contract has been delivered.

As a general rule, only the person to whom the offer is made can accept it. Offers to the public may be accepted by any member of the public who is aware of the offer. An offeree cannot assign an offer to a third party. Offers contained in option contracts are assignable and may be accepted by the assignee, since they are contracts and not mere offers.

If goods are ordered from a firm that has discontinued business and the goods are shipped by its successor, the offeror-purchaser is under no duty to accept the goods. If he does accept them knowing that they were shipped by the successor, then by implication he agrees to pay the new concern for the goods at the contract price. If he does not know of the change of ownership when he accepts the goods, he is not liable for the contract price—his only liability is in quasi contract for the reasonable value of the goods.

13. Acceptance of a Unilateral Offer

When an offer is unilateral, the offeror does not desire a promise of perform-ance. He seeks actual performance of the act or forbearance requested. As a general rule, substantial performance of the act requested constitutes an acceptance of a unilateral offer. If the offeree ceases performance short of substantial performance, there is no acceptance and no contract.

A difficult question arises when an offeror seeks to withdraw a unilateral offer during the course of the offeree's attempted performance of the act re-quested. In the early common law, many courts allowed the offeror to with-draw the offer prior to substantial performance by the offeree, but the offeror was liable in quasi contract for any benefits received. Today, the generally accepted view is that an offeror of a unilateral offer cannot withdraw during the performance of the offeree. The offeror becomes bound when performance is commenced or tendered, and the offeree has a duty to complete perform-ance. The continuing liability of the offeror is in effect conditioned on the offeree's finishing performance. The underlying theory of this result is that the offer of a unilateral contract includes, by implication, a subsidiary promise that if part of the requested performance is given, the offeror will not revoke his offer. The consideration for this subsidiary promise is the part performance by the offeree. It is the *part performance* by the offeree that gives rise to the obligation of the offeror to keep his offer open. The offeree may incur expense in *preparation* for performance, but this is not the part performance that prevents revocation.

Goods may be ordered by either a unilateral offer or a bilateral one. Un-less otherwise unambiguously indicated, an offer under the Code invites acceptance in any manner and by any medium reasonable under the circum-stances (2-206[1][a]). If a purchase order is signed by a buyer with the order's being subject to approval by the seller's home office, the offer is for a bilateral contract. The seller accepts the offer by sending notice of his approval to the buyer.

On the other hand, if a merchant asks for prompt or current shipment, the offer may either be treated as a unilateral offer and accepted by shipment, or be treated as a bilateral offer and accepted by a promise to ship. The seller is thus afforded an opportunity to bind the bargain prior to the time of shipment (2-206[1][b]). If the seller ships goods that do not conform to the order, he may notify the buyer that the shipment is not an acceptance but is only offered as an accommodation to the buyer. This is, in effect, a counteroffer that the buyer may accept or reject, and the seller may not be charged with having breached the contract because of the nonconformity. Where shipment is a reasonable means of acceptance, an offeror who is not notified of the accept-ance within a reasonable time may treat the offer as having lapsed before acceptance (2-206[2]). Therefore, when an order for goods is treated as unilateral and accepted by shipment, the offeree should notify the offeror of the shipment.

14. Acceptance of a Bilateral Offer

An offer for a bilateral contract is accepted by a promise from the offeree returned in response to the promise of the offeror. The offeree's promise is to perform as stipulated in the offer. The promise of the offeree (acceptance) must be communicated to the offeror or his agent and may consist of any conduct on the part of the offeree that clearly evinces an intention to be bound by the conditions prescribed in the offer. An acceptance must be a manifestation of mutual assent. It cannot be based on mere custom or the usual way of doing business. In construing the language of a purported acceptance, the usual rules of construction, including the principle that ambiguous language is construed against the person using it, are applied. The acceptance may take the form of a signature to a written agreement or of a nod of the head.

Where it is understood that the agreement will be set forth in a written instrument, the acceptance is effective only when the document has been signed and delivered, unless it was clearly the intention of the parties that the earlier verbal agreement be binding and that the writing act merely as a memorandum or evidence of their oral contract.

15. Silence as Assent

As a general rule, the offeror cannot force the offeree to reply to the offer. In most cases, therefore, mere silence by the offeree does not amount to acceptance, even though the offeror in his offer may have stated that a failure to reply would constitute an acceptance. However, a previous course of dealing between the parties or the receipt of goods by the offeree under certain circumstances could impose a duty on the offeree to speak in order to avoid a contractual relationship. This duty to speak arises when the offeree has led the offeror to believe that silence or inaction is intended as a manifestation of intent to accept and the offeree believes that it is. In other words, silence where a duty exists to communicate either an acceptance or rejection is an acceptance.[5]

Under the Code, a buyer has accepted goods when he fails to make an effective rejection or does any act inconsistent with the seller's ownership. However, failure to reject will not be construed as an acceptance unless the buyer has had a reasonable opportunity to examine the goods.

16. Variance Between Offer and Acceptance

As a general rule, to be effective, an acceptance must be the "mirror image" of the offer. If the acceptance contains new terms or conditions or if it other-

---

[5] *Brooks Towers Corp.* v. *Hunkin-Conkey Construction Co.,* page 134.

wise deviates from the terms of the offer, it is a counteroffer and a rejection, unless the offeree explicitly states that it is not to be considered a rejection. Provisions in an offer relating to time, place, or manner of acceptance must be strictly complied with by the offeree.

The Code rejects the mirror-image rule of the law of contracts. Under the Code, a definite expression of acceptance or a written confirmation operates as an acceptance. This is true even though the acceptance states terms additional to or different from those offered or agreed upon, unless acceptance is made conditional upon agreement to the additional or different terms (2-207[1]). This means that the additional terms do not prevent the formation of a contract, unless they are expressed in the form of a counterproposal. The terms in question will otherwise be treated simply as new proposals.

However, when the contract is *between merchants,* such terms become part of the contract unless "(a) the offer expressly limits acceptance to the terms of the offer; (b) they materially alter it; or (c) notification of objection to them has already been given or is given within a reasonable time after notice of them is received" (2-207[2]).[6]

The problem of variance arises in three similar situations: (1) where an acceptance states terms additional to or different from those offered, (2) where a written confirmation of an informal or oral agreement sets forth terms additional to or different from those previously agreed upon, and (3) where the printed forms used by the parties are in conflict, especially in the "fine print." The Code takes the position that in all the situations above, ". . . a proposed deal which in commercial understanding has in fact been closed is recognized as a contract" (2-207).

To illustrate the problem of variance in offer and acceptance, and the Code solution, assume the following: Merchant A sends to Merchant B an offer to sell him 1,000 boxes of select Anjou pears at $10 per box, F.O.B. Medford, Oregon (A's place of business). B replies by wire: "Accept your offer to sell 1,000 boxes of select Anjou pears at $10 per box, F.O.B. Champaign, Illinois. Boxes to be made of wood, and pears individually wrapped." There are two matters to consider here. First, the terms of delivery were changed. A contract had been formed, and A's provision on delivery (Medford, Oregon) prevails. A had effectively objected to B's proposal, since A had stated the terms of delivery in the offer. The law considers the statement of a term as an objection to a change in that term. Second, there were new or additional terms added in the acceptance concerning the boxes and wrapping. As to these additional terms, they would be included *unless* either (1) A objects to these additional terms within a reasonable time, or (2) the additional terms are found to "materially alter" the contract. If A does seasonably object to the additional terms or if a court finds that they constituted a material alteration, they are not included.

[6] *N&D Fashions, Inc.* v. *DHJ Industries, Inc.,* page 134.

It is to be noted that either party could easily have protected himself against the contingencies posed by this example. A, the offeror, could have expressly stipulated in his offer that acceptance was limited to the terms of the offer, or he could have seasonably communicated to B his refusal to include the additional terms. B, the offeree, could have stated in his acceptance that it was to be effective only if A agreed to ship F.O.B. Champaign, Illinois, and to pack in wooden boxes, with each pear separately wrapped. In this event, his acceptance would constitute a *counteroffer*.

In the example, the offeror and the offeree are merchants; if merchants were not involved on both sides, the additional terms would not become a part of the contract unless mutually agreeable. They would simply be proposals for additions to the contract, which A could accept or reject.

17.   Time of Taking Effect

A bilateral offer requires *communication* of the acceptance to the offeror. Is the acceptance effective to create a contract at the moment the communication is deposited in the mail, or is its effectiveness delayed until the offeror actually receives it? It will be recalled that other communications associated with contracts—revocations of offers and rejections of offers—do not have legal effect until they are received. In early English law, the case of *Adams* v. *Lindsell* established the "deposited acceptance rule"—that an acceptance was effective when deposited in the offeror's channel of communication or the one indicated by him to be used by the offeree. If none was indicated, the acceptance was effective when deposited with the post or mails. This rule has been challenged on the ground that there could not actually be a meeting of the minds upon deposit of the acceptance because the offeror would not know that it had been deposited. Notwithstanding this argument, most courts still adhere to the rule of *Adams* v. *Lindsell,* and as a general rule, an acceptance is considered effective when deposited in the offeror's channel of communication or in the mail if no other channel is indicated.[7] If the offeree uses a different means of communication, the acceptance is not effective until received by the offeror.

The Code has adopted and expanded the deposited acceptance rule and provides that, unless otherwise unambiguously indicated by the terms of the offer, "an offer to make a contract shall be construed as inviting acceptance *in any manner* and *by any medium* reasonable in the circumstances." Thus, unless the offeror in the offer stipulates to the contrary, an acceptance is effective when deposited in any channel of communication (2-206[1][a]).

The deposited acceptance rule has the effect of placing on the offeror any possible loss resulting from a failure on the part of the communicating agency to deliver the acceptance. Even though a letter of acceptance is lost in the mails, a contract still exists. The offeror, in such cases, is duty bound to perform, even though he may have entered into other contracts as a result of his

[7] *Morrison* v. *Thoelke,* page 136.

failure to receive a reply. He can avoid this result only by stating in his offer that the acceptance shall be ineffective until it is actually received by him.

OFFER AND ACCEPTANCE CASES

Lefkowitz v. Great Minneapolis Surplus Store
86 N.W.2d 689 (Minn.) 1957

Defendant published the following advertisement in a Minneapolis newspaper:

Saturday 9 A.M.
2 Brand New Pastel
Mink 3-Skin Scarfs
Selling for $89.50
Out they go
Saturday. Each . . . $1.00
1 Black Lapin Stole
Beautiful,
worth $139.50 . . . $1.00
First Come
First Served

Plaintiff was the first person to go to the appropriate counter in defendant's store on the Saturday following publication of the ad. He demanded the stole and indicated his willingness to pay the sale price of $1. Defendant refused to sell the merchandise to plaintiff and stated that by a "house rule" the offer was intended for women only. Plaintiff brought action and was given judgment in the amount of $138.50—the value as stated in the ad less the $1 quoted purchase price. Defendant appealed.

MURPHY, J. . . . The defendant contends . . . that, where an advertiser publishes in a newspaper that he has a certain quantity or quality of goods which he wants to dispose of at certain prices and on certain terms, such advertisements are not offers which become contracts as soon as any person to whose notice they may come signifies his acceptance by notifying the other that he will take a certain quantity of them. Such advertisements have been construed as an invitation for an offer of sale on the terms stated, which offer, when received, may be accepted or rejected and which therefore does not become a contract of sale until accepted by the seller; and until a contract has been so made, the seller may modify or revoke such prices or terms. . . .

. . . On the facts before us we are concerned with whether the advertisement constituted an offer, and, if so, whether the plaintiff's conduct constituted an acceptance.

There are numerous authorities which hold that a particular advertisement in a newspaper or circular letter relating to a sale of articles may be construed by the court as constituting an offer, acceptance of which would complete a contract.

The test of whether a binding obligation may originate in advertisements addressed to the general public is "whether the facts show that some performance was promised in positive terms in return for something requested."

. . . [W]here the offer is clear, definite, and explicit, and leaves nothing open for negotiation, it constitutes an offer, acceptance of which will complete the contract. The most recent case on the subject is *Johnson* v. *Capital City Ford Co.,* in which the court pointed out that a newspaper advertisement relating to the purchase and sale of automobiles may constitute an offer, acceptance of which will consummate a contract and create an obligation in the offeror to perform according to the terms of the published offer.

Whether in any individual instance a newspaper advertisement is an offer rather than an invitation to make an offer depends on the legal intention of the parties and the surrounding circumstances. We are of the view on the facts before us that the offer by the defendant of the sale of the Lapin fur was clear, definite, and explicit, and left nothing open for negotiation. The plaintiff having successfully managed to be the first one to appear at the seller's place of business to be served, as requested by the advertisement, and having offered the stated purchase price of the article, he was entitled to performance on the part of the defendant. We think the trial court was correct in holding that there was in the conduct of the parties a sufficient mutuality of obligation to constitute a contract of sale.

The defendant contends that the offer was modified by a "house rule" to the effect that only women were qualified to receive the bargains advertised. The advertisement contained no such restriction. This objection may be disposed of briefly by stating that, while an advertiser has the right at any time before acceptance to modify his offer, he does not have the right, after acceptance, to impose new or arbitrary conditions not contained in the published offer.

Judgment affirmed for plaintiff.

Barnes v. Treece
549 P.2d 1152 (Wash. App.) 1976

Pacific

The defendant, Vend-A-Win, Inc., is a corporation engaged in the distribution of punchboards. Treece as vice president of the corporation, when speaking before the state gambling commission stated, "I'll put a $100,-000 to anyone that finds a crooked punchboard; if they find it, I'll pay it." The audience laughed. The next morning the plaintiff heard a television (news) report of Treece's statement; he also read about it in the newspaper.

A number of years earlier while employed as a bartender, plaintiff had bought two fraudulent punchboards. After locating his two punchboards, the plaintiff contacted the defendant and inquired if the statement about the $100,-000 had been made seriously. The defendant informed the plaintiff that it had and asked him to bring the punchboards to the company office. The plaintiff took a board to the office and was given a receipt for it. Both Treece and the company refused to pay the $100,000 even though the board was admittedly fraudulent.

The trial court found a contract existed but only with Treece individually since he lacked authority to bind the corporation.

CALLOW, J. . . . The first issue is whether the statement of Treece was the manifestation of an offer which could be accepted to bind the offeror to performance of the promise. Treece contends that no contract was formed.

He maintains that his statement was made in jest and lacks the necessary manifestation of a serious contractual intent.

When expressions are intended as a joke and are understood or would be understood by a reasonable person as being so intended, they cannot be construed as an offer and accepted to form a contract. However, if the jest is not apparent and a reasonable hearer would believe that an offer was being made, then the speaker risks the formation of a contract which was not intended. It is the objective manifestations of the offeror that count and not secret, unexpressed intentions.

> If a party's words or acts, judged by a reasonable standard, manifest an intention to agree in regard to the matter in question, that agreement is established, and it is immaterial what may be the real but unexpressed state of the party's mind on the subject.

The trial court found that there was an objective manifestation of mutual assent to form a contract. This was a matter to be evaluated by the trier of fact. The record includes substantial evidence of the required mutual assent to support the finding of the trial court. Although the original statement of Treece drew laughter from the audience, the subsequent statements, conduct, and the circumstances show an intent to lead any hearer to believe the statements were made seriously. There was testimony, though contradicted, that Treece specifically restated the offer over the telephone in response to an inquiry concerning whether the offer was serious. Treece, when given the opportunity to state that an offer was not intended, not only reaffirmed the offer but also asserted that $100,000 had been placed in escrow and directed Barnes to bring the punchboard to Seattle for inspection. The parties met, Barnes was given a receipt for the board, and he was told that the board would be taken to Chicago for inspection. In present day society it is known that gambling generates a great deal of income and that large sums are spent on its advertising and promotion. In that prevailing atmosphere, it was a credible statement that $100,000 would be paid to promote punch-

boards. The statements of the defendant and the surrounding circumstances reflect an objective manifestation of a contractual intent by Treece and support the finding of the trial court.

The trial court properly categorized Treece's promise of $100,000 as a valid offer for a unilateral contract. The offer made promised that a contract would result upon performance of the act requested. Performance of the act with the intent to accept the offer constituted acceptance. The trial judge entered a specific finding that Barnes performed the requested act of acceptance when he produced a rigged and fraudulent punchboard. We concur with the trial court's holding that a binding unilateral contract was formed between Barnes and Treece and uphold the conclusions of the trial court in that regard. . . .

Affirmed.

Drennan v. Star Paving Company
333 P.2d 757 (Cal.) 1958

Drennan, the plaintiff, was a general contractor, and in preparation for submitting a bid on a school job requested the defendant to submit a bid for certain paving which was involved. Defendant offered to do the work for $7,-131.60, and plaintiff used this subcontractor's offer in making his bid. The contract was awarded to plaintiff, but as he approached defendant, he was notified that it could not perform as it had made an error in its calculations. Plaintiff got another to do the work at a cost of $10,948.60 and sought to recover this difference from defendant. The lower court gave judgment for plaintiff in the amount of $3,817.00.

TRAYNOR, J. . . .There is no evidence that defendant offered to make its bid irrevocable in exchange for plaintiff's use of its figures in computing his bid. Nor is there evidence that would warrant interpreting plaintiff's use of defendant's bid as the acceptance thereof, binding plaintiff, on condition he received the main contract, to award the subcontract to de-

fendant. In sum, there was neither an option supported by consideration nor a bilateral contract binding on both parties.

Plaintiff contends, however, that he relied to his detriment on defendant's offer and that defendant must therefore answer in damages for its refusal to perform. Thus the question is squarely presented: Did plaintiff's reliance make defendant's offer irrevocable?

Section 90 of the Restatement of Contracts states: "A promise which the promisor should reasonably expect to induce action or forbearance of a definite and substantial character on the part of the promisee and which does induce such action or forbearance is binding if injustice can be avoided only by enforcement of the promise." . . .

Defendant's offer constituted a promise to perform on such conditions as were stated expressly or by implication therein or annexed thereto by operation of law. Defendant had reason to expect that if its bid proved the lowest it would be used by plaintiff. It induced "action

. . . of a definite and substantial character on the part of the promisee."

Had defendant's bid expressly stated or clearly implied that it was revocable at any time before acceptance we would treat it accordingly. It was silent on revocation, however, and we must therefore determine whether there are conditions to the right of revocation imposed by law or reasonably inferable in fact. In the analogous problem of an offer for a unilateral contract, the theory is now obsolete that the offer is revocable at any time before complete performance. Thus section 45 of the Restatement of Contracts provides: "If an offer for a unilateral contract is made, and part of the consideration requested in the offer is given or tendered by the offeree in response thereto, the offeror is bound by a contract, the duty of immediate performance of which is conditional on the full consideration being given or tendered within the time stated in the offer, or, if no time is stated therein, within a reasonable time." In explanation, comment *b* states that the "main offer includes as a subsidiary promise, necessarily implied, that if part of the requested performance is given, the offeror will not revoke his offer, and that if tender is made it will be accepted. Part performance or tender may thus furnish consideration for the subsidiary promise. Moreover, merely acting in justifiable reliance on an offer may in some cases serve as sufficient reason for making a promise binding."

Whether implied in fact or law, the subsidiary promise serves to preclude the injustice that would result if the offer could be revoked after the offeree had acted in detrimental reliance thereon. Reasonable reliance resulting in a foreseeable prejudicial change in position affords a compelling basis also for implying a subsidiary promise not to revoke an offer for a bilateral contract.

The absence of consideration is not fatal to the enforcement of such a promise. It is true that in the case of unilateral contracts the Restatement finds consideration for the implied subsidiary promise in the part performance of the bargained-for exchange, but its reference to section 90 makes clear that consideration for such a promise is not always necessary. The very purpose of section 90 is to make a promise binding even though there was no consideration "in the sense of something that is bargained for and given in exchange." Reasonable reliance serves to hold the offeror in lieu of the consideration ordinarily required to make the offer binding. . . .

When plaintiff used defendant's offer in computing his own bid, he bound himself to perform in reliance on defendant's terms. Though defendant did not bargain for this use of its bid neither did defendant make it idly, indifferent to whether it would be used or not. On the contrary it is reasonable to suppose that defendant submitted its bid to obtain the subcontract. It was bound to realize the substantial possibility that its bid would be the lowest, and that it would be included by plaintiff in his bid. It was to its own interest that the contractor be awarded the general contract; the lower the subcontract bid, the lower the general contractor's bid was likely to be and the greater its chance of acceptance and hence the greater defendant's chance of getting the paving subcontract. Defendant had reason not only to expect plaintiff to rely on its bid but to want him to. Clearly defendant had a stake in plaintiff's reliance on its bid. Given this interest and the fact that plaintiff is bound by his own bid, it is only fair that plaintiff should have at least an opportunity to accept defendant's bid after the general contract has been awarded to him.

It bears noting that a general contractor is not free to delay acceptance after he has been awarded the general contract in the hope of getting a better price. Nor can he reopen bargaining with the subcontractor and at the same time claim a continuing right to accept the original offer. In the present case plaintiff promptly informed defendant that plaintiff was being awarded the job and that the subcontract was being awarded to defendant. . . .

Judgment for plaintiff affirmed.

Ryder v. Wescoat
535 S.W.2d 269 (Mo.) 1976

Wescoat gave Ryder an option to purchase a 120-acre farm; the option was to expire September 1. On August 20, Ryder told Wescoat that he was not going to exercise the option. On August 30, Ryder nevertheless attempted to exercise his option, but Wescoat refused to honor the attempted acceptance.

TURNAGE, J. . . . No case has been cited, and diligent research on the part of this court has failed to locate any case involving this precise issue. However, text writers have dealt with the problem. In *Simpson on Contracts,* 2d Ed., § 23, the author states:

> Where an offer is supported by a binding contract that the offeree's power of acceptance shall continue for a stated time, will a communicated rejection terminate the offeree's power to accept within the time? On principle, there is no reason why it should. The offeree has a contract right to accept within the time. At most rejection is a waiver of this right, but waiver not supported by consideration or an estoppel by change of position can have no effect upon subsequent assertion of the right. So an option holder may complete a contract by communicating his acceptance despite the fact that he has previously rejected the offer. Where, however, before the acceptance the offeror has materially changed his position in reliance on the communicated rejection, as by selling or contracting to sell the subject matter of the offer elsewhere, the subsequent acceptance will be inoperative. Here the rejection is a waiver of the offeree's contract right to accept the offer, binding the offeree by estoppel, so his power to accept is gone.

It must be kept in mind Ryder had purchased for a valuable consideration the right to purchase this farm. This removes this case from the rule applied in those cases where an offer has been made, but the offeree has not paid any consideration for the making of the offer. In those cases, it is uniformly held that a rejection of the offer terminates the offer. Likewise, the making of a counter offer terminates the original offer and places it beyond the power of the offeree to thereafter accept the offer.

However, the courts treat options which are purchased for a valuable consideration in a different manner. Thus, in *Sunray Oil Company v. Lewis,* 434 S.W.2d 777 (Mo. App. 1968) this court quoted . . . the rule that a counter-offer does not terminate the power of acceptance when the original offer is an irrevocable offer. . . .

Since an option stands on a different footing from an offer which is made without consideration being paid therefor, and since it has been held that an option is irrevocable for the time stated, and that a counter offer does not effect a rejection, it necessarily follows that a rejection standing alone would not end the rights of the option holder. This court adopts the rule . . . that a rejection of an option which has been purchased for a valuable consideration does not terminate the rights of the option holder unless the optionor has materially changed his position prior to a timely acceptance.

This rule fully protects the rights of both parties. It extends to the optionor the protection he requires in the event a rejection of the option is communicated to him and he thereafter changes his position in reliance thereon to his detriment. At the same time it protects the right of the option holder to have the opportunity to exercise his option for the full period for which he paid, absent the material change in position. . . .

Reversed.

Brooks Towers Corp. v. Hunkin-Conkey Construction Co.
454 F.2d 1203 (1972)

Federal 2nd

Plaintiff, a building owner, sued the construction contractor on the building for damages caused by the delay in completing the building. The contract called for substantial completion by December 8, 1967. The building was actually not completed until November, 1968.

Major changes were made in the building plans during construction. The procedure for changes in the specifications required the architect (Ratner) to prepare a bulletin for changes and to submit it to the contractor for a quotation. The quotation form which was in effect an offer to do the work contained a space for the number of additional days required to complete the contract as a result of the change. The contractor requested a total of 300 days of extensions on 80 formal quotations.

A few of the proposed extensions of time were specifically approved by Ratner, the architect, but most of them were not acted upon. The architect testified that by not acting, he indicated his disapproval. The contractor contended that the lack of express disapproval was a grant of the requests for extensions of time, and that silence was an acceptance of the offer. The lower court found for the contractor and the owner appealed.

BARRETT, J. . . . The trial court found that Ratner was authorized by the owner to act as its architect and agent in supervising the work, in issuing the bulletins for changes, and in approving or disapproving the quotations, including the extensions of time. The trial court found that the extensions of time approved by Ratner totaled 185 calendar days. We agree.

Lacking express disapproval as contemplated on the face of the form, the contractor relied upon Ratner's inaction as approval. Here the silence can be attributed to both Ratner and Paterson, the owner's representatives on the job. When the relations between the parties justify the offeror's expectation of a reply or where a duty exists to communicate either an acceptance or rejection, silence will be regarded as an acceptance. . . .

Affirmed.

N&D Fashions, Inc. v. DHJ Industries, Inc.
548 F.2d 722 (1977)

Fed 2nd

Plaintiff sent the defendant a written purchase order for certain fabric. The defendant in response sent the plaintiff four documents which confirmed the essential terms of the purchase order. The bottom of the forms immediately above the blanks provided for signatures read:

THIS CONTRACT IS SUBJECT TO
ALL THE TERMS AND CONDITIONS
PRINTED ON THE REVERSE SIDE

On the reverse side was a clause requiring arbitration of all controversies arising out of the agreement. Plaintiff's agent signed a copy of the confirmation and returned it to the defendant.

When the fabric was found to be defective, plaintiff sued defendant. The defendant sought to have the case dismissed on the ground that the dispute had to be submitted to arbitration. The district court held that the arbitration provision was an additional term which constituted a material attention of the contract and therefore it was not a part of the agreement. Defendant appeals.

WEBSTER, J. . . . This litigation centers upon the effect to be given to a condition of sale requiring arbitration of disputes that was contained in the seller's acknowledgment of the buyer's written purchase order. It implicates the sometimes murky provisions of Section 2-207 of the Uniform Commercial Code, which was intended to put to rest uncertainty arising from the "battle of the forms. . . ."

I

It is undisputed that the parties reached an agreement with respect to the nature and quantity of the merchandise to be sold and delivered by appellant DHJ, as well as the price to be paid by the buyers. . . . A problem is presented, however, when an acceptance or confirmation contains terms which are "additional to or different from" an offer or prior agreement. Under Uniform Commercial Code § 2-207 if the dealings are between merchants, the additional terms become a part of the agreement provided (1) the original offer did not expressly preclude such additions (the offer here did not), (2) the additions do not materially alter the agreement, and (3) no seasonable notice is given of objections to the additions (none was given here). From this it follows that the provision for arbitration in this case, as a proposed additional term, became a part of the agreement unless, as the district court found, it was a material altera-

tion of the agreement. . . .

A clause will be held to "materially alter" a contract when it would "result in surprise or hardship if incorporated without express awareness by the other party." Official Comments 4 and 5 provide examples of terms which would and would not materially alter a contract, and an arbitration clause is listed under neither. While other cases have held that an arbitration clause would materially alter a contract under § 2-207, the better reasoned position is that the question whether an additional term in a written confirmation constitutes a "material alteration" is a question of fact to be resolved by the circumstances of each particular case.

. . . [W]e cannot say on this record that the district court was clearly erroneous in holding that the arbitration provision in DHJ's acknowledgment form was a "material alteration."

II

The effect of this holding is that we may not presume acceptance from mere failure to object; the arbitration clause in this case will not be considered a part of the agreement unless it was in fact agreed to by N&D.

The test to be applied is found in Uniform Commercial Code § 2-207, Comment 3:

> Whether or not additional or different terms will become part of the agreement depends upon the provisions of subsection (2). If they are such as materially to alter the original bargain, they will not be included *unless expressly agreed to* by the other party.

The only mutually executed documents evidencing the agreement are the acknowledg-

ments which DHJ sent to Nelly Don and which Shriber "accepted" and returned to DHJ. These contracts clearly stated, just above the parties' signatures that they were "subject to all the terms and conditions printed on the reverse side." The arbitration clause was printed on the reverse side and it would thus appear that the clause, although a material alteration to the oral agreement, was "expressly agreed to" by Nelly Don. Appellees contend, however, as the district court found, that Shriber's failure to read the contracts, coupled with the absence of the word "arbitration" on the front of the document to indicate the presence of an arbitration clause on the reverse, precluded actual consent to the inclusion of this clause in the final agreement. We disagree.

The holding of the district court ignores the general rule of contract law that, in the absence of fraud, misrepresentation or deceit, one who executes a contract cannot avoid it on the ground that he did not read it or supposed it to be different in its terms. . . .

We . . . decline to impose in the case of arbitration provisions special and unique requirements which are concededly not applicable to other additional terms and conditions. While a party may not be subjected to a provision which materially alters the contract by failing to object to it, he cannot avoid the effect of his written acceptance of a contract which expressly, above his signature on the face of the contract, incorporates the provisions on the reverse side of the document. There being no evidence of fraud, misrepresentation or deceit in the execution of the acceptance, it follows that the agreement to arbitrate became a part of the agreement and must govern the resolution of the dispute between the parties which produced this litigation. . . .

Reversed.

Morrison v. Thoelke
155 So.2d 889 (Fla.) 1963

Defendants (Morrison) made an offer to buy real property owned by plaintiffs (Thoelke). They executed a contract for sale and purchase and mailed it to plaintiffs for their acceptance and signature. The latter signed the contract and mailed it to defendants. Before it was received by defendants, plaintiffs repudiated the contract by telephone. Nonetheless, when defendants received the contract they recorded it, thereby establishing their interest in the property as a matter of public record. Claiming that no contract existed, plaintiffs brought this suit to "quiet title" to the property—to remove defendants' claim of an interst in it from the record. Defendants counterclaimed, seeking specific performance of the contract. The lower court entered a summary decree for plaintiffs, and defendants appealed.

ALLEN, J. . . . The question is whether a contract is complete and binding when a letter of acceptance is mailed, thus barring repudiation prior to delivery to the offeror, or when the letter of acceptance is received, thus permitting repudiation prior to receipt. Appellants, of course, argue that posting the acceptance creates the contract; appellees contend that only receipt of the acceptance bars repudiation. . . .

The appellant, in arguing that the lower court erred in giving effect to the repudiation of the mailed acceptance, contends that this case is controlled by the general rule that insofar as the mail is an acceptable medium of communication, a contract is complete and binding upon posting of the letter of acceptance.

Appellees, on the other hand, argue that the right to recall mail makes the Post Office Department the agent of the sender, and that such right coupled with communication of a renunciation prior to receipt of the acceptance voids the acceptance. In short, appellees argue that acceptance is complete only upon receipt of the mailed acceptance. . . .

The rule that a contract is complete upon deposit of the acceptance in the mails, hereinbefore referred to as "deposited acceptance rule" and also known as the "rule in *Adams* v. *Lindsell,*" had its origin, insofar as the common law is concerned, in *Adams* v. *Lindsell.* . . .

In support of the rule proponents urge its sanction in tradition and practice. They argue that in the average case the offeree receives an offer and, depositing an acceptance in the post, begins and should be allowed to begin reliance on the contract. They point out that the offeror has, after all, communicated his assent to the terms by extending the offer and has himself chosen the medium of communication. Depreciating the alleged risk to the offeror, proponents argue that having made an offer by post the offeror is seldom injured by a slight delay in knowing it was accepted, whereas the offeree, under any other rule, would have to await both the transmission of the acceptance and notification of its receipt before being able to rely on the contract he unequivocally accepted. Finally, proponents point out that the offeror can always expressly condition the contract on his receipt of an acceptance and, should he fail to do so, the law should not afford him this advantage.

Opponents of the rule argue as forcefully that all of the disadvantages of delay or loss in communication which would potentially harm the offeree are equally harmful to the offeror. Why, they ask, should the offeror be bound by an acceptance of which he has no knowledge? Arguing specific cases, opponents of the rule point to the inequity of forbidding the offeror to withdraw his offer after the acceptance was posted but before he had any knowledge that the offer was accepted; they argue that to forbid the offeree to withdraw his acceptance, as in the instant case, scant hours after it was posted but days before the offeror knew of it, is unjust and indefensible. Too, the opponents argue, the offeree can always prevent the revocation of an offer by providing consideration, by buying an option.

In short, both advocates and critics muster persuasive argument. As . . . indicated, there must be a choice made, and such choice may, by the nature of things, seem unjust in some cases. Weighing the arguments with reference not to specific cases but toward a rule of general application and recognizing the general and traditional acceptance of the rule as well as the modern changes in effective long-distance communication, it would seem that the balance tips, whether heavily or near imperceptibly, to continued adherence to the "rule in *Adams* v. *Lindsell*." This rule, although not entirely compatible with ordered, consistent and sometime artificial principles of contract advanced by some theorists, is, in our view, in accord with the practical considerations and essential concepts of contract law. Outmoded precedents may, on occasion, be discarded and the function of justice should not be the perpetuation of error, but, by the same token, traditional rules and concepts should not be abandoned save on compelling ground.

. . . [W]e are constrained by factors hereinbefore discussed to hold that an acceptance is effective upon mailing and not upon receipt. Necessarily this decision is limited in any prospective application to circumstances involving the mails and does not purport to determine the rule possibly applicable to cases involving other modern means of communication.

In the instant case, an unqualified offer was accepted and the acceptance made manifest. Later, the offerees sought to repudiate their initial assent. Had there been a delay in their determination to repudiate permitting the letter to be delivered to appellant, no question as to the invalidity of the repudiation would have been entertained. As it were, the repudiation antedated receipt of the letter. However, adopting the view that the acceptance was effective when the letter of acceptance was deposited in the mails, the repudiation was equally invalid and cannot alone support the summary decree for appellees.

The summary decree is reversed and the case remanded for further proceedings.

CHAPTER 8
REVIEW QUESTIONS AND PROBLEMS

1. A sustained personal injuries in a fall on B's property. A sought damages against B and mailed a letter to his attorney stating the facts and requesting he handle the case based on a contingent fee. A's attorney received

because no price or method

the letter and replied by mail that he would give the matter his attention as soon as possible. Does a contract exist between A and his attorney? Why?

no

2. X submitted a bid to Y to perform certain work for him. Owing to a clerical error, the bid was considerably lower than X intended. Shortly after opening the bid, Y received a notice from X rescinding the bid. Was the withdrawal valid? Explain.

yes —

3. A agreed to sell B a tract of land with boundaries spelled out in the contract. After A had been paid for the land, he discovered that the tract contained five lots and he had intended to sell only two. A contends that since he made a mistake and had no intention of selling the additional three lots, no contract existed. Can A get his land back? Why?

No, because he sold it

4. A writes to B that he will sell to B between 5,000 and 7,000 tons of steel at $80 per ton. B replies that he accepts the offer for 6,000 tons. Is a contract formed? Why?   *acceptance of between*

yes,

5. A purchased an insurance policy from B for a period of one year. Prior to the expiration of the year, B sent A a renewal policy and a bill for the premium. The bill stated that if A did not want to renew the policy, he should return the policy immediately. A did not renew but kept the policy. B sued for the premium. Did a contract exist? Why?

yes

6. The board of directors of X Company authorized the sale of stock to employees. The employees were informed that if they desire to purchase stock, they should make a written request to the president. Y made a request for 100 shares at $50 each. Y was told that he could not purchase 100 shares because of the large number of subscriptions by other employees, but that he could purchase a lesser amount. Y sues X Company, contending that an offer had been made to him and that he accepted the offer. Is Y correct? Why?

assumed a reasonable price
counter offer

no.

7. S listed his property for sale with R, a realtor, on an exclusive basis. The listing expired, but R continued his efforts to find a buyer and submitted a written offer to buy for $65,000. S rejected this but signed a form containing an offer to sell at $70,000 and agreed to keep that offer open for one day. Before the expiration of one day, S gave notice that the offer was revoked. Does S have the right to revoke his offer to sell before the expiration of the specified time he had agreed to keep it open? Why?

yes only offer

all offers & on Real Estate accept. must be done in writing

8. X, a subcontractor, submitted a bid to Y, a general contractor, that was the low bid. When Y submitted a bid for the general contract, he listed the subcontract bid by X. Y was awarded the contract, but he gave the subcontract bid to another party. X now sues Y, contending that when his bid was listed in the general contractor's bid, this amounted to an acceptance of his offer to perform the work. Should X succeed? Why?

yes — mutuality

assume set price

9. A salesman for X Company solicited an order for a seeding machine from F, a farmer. The order was sent to the home office for approval, but F did not hear any further word from X Company. F contends that there is a contract and that he is entitled to damages for failure to deliver. Is F correct? Why?   *No, no money or method of*

10. B Company ordered from S Company adhesive materials that would be suitable for use in manufacturing cellophane bags for packaging vegetables. B's printed order form specified this intended use. S accepted by mailing its printed order form, which stipulated that the company did not guarantee the results to be obtained from the use of its products and that there were no warranties. The adhesive did not work properly, and B sues for breach of warranty. Can B recover? Why?

yes

11. E terminated his employment with the B Bank to accept a similar position with the C Bank. When E applied for his share of B's Employee Profit Sharing Plan, B returned E's contribution but refused to pay E the amount of money which the bank itself had contributed to E's account. The plan contained a forfeiture-of-contribution clause which provided that an employee forfeited the bank's contribution by engaging in direct competition with the bank. E claims that he did not read the agreement and, therefore, he should be able to recover B's matching contribution. Is B correct? Why?

No – T

12. X, the prime contractor, requested Y, a subcontractor, to submit a bid for work to be used by X in its bid for a prime contract. X received the contract and sent Y a proposed subcontract containing various terms which had not been the basis of any communication between the two. Y refused the contract, and X had to hire someone else at a higher price. X now seeks to recover the difference in price from Y. What result? Why?

No

Consideration

1. Introduction

In addition to offer and acceptance, consideration must be present before there is a valid enforceable contract. *Consideration* is defined as the price bargained for and paid for a promise. It usually takes the form of some benefit to the promisor, but it may also consist of a detriment to the promisee. *Benefit* as used in this context is not limited to tangible benefits but means that the promisor has, in return for his promise, acquired some legal right to which he would otherwise not have been entitled. *Detriment* to the promisee may consist of the promisee's doing something he is not legally bound to do or refraining from doing that which he has a right to do.

Consideration has also been defined as the surrender or promise to surrender a legal right at the request of another. It is what each party to a bargain gives to the other. It is the price paid for a promise. Either the performance of or the promise to perform an act or the surrender of or promise to surrender a right at the request of a promissor is consideration. Without this price paid for the promise, the promisor might be *morally* obligated to carry out his promise, but the law would consider it to be legally unenforceable. For example, a person made a pledge to a general charity fund. The pledge form recited that it was in consideration of and to induce other pledges. The pledge is not legally enforceable. It is a mere gratuitous promise unsupported by consideration.

The Restatement of the Law of Contracts provides that consideration for a promise may be

   a. An act other than a promise, or

   b. A forbearance, or

   c. The creation, modification, or destruction of a legal relation, or

   d. A return promise, bargained for and given in exchange for the promise.

Since consideration is required to make a promise legally binding, a promise to make a gift is unenforceable. The fact that the recipient of a proposed gift must take certain steps to place himself in a position to receive it cannot be substituted for the required consideration. If, however, the promisee of the gift is requested to act in a certain manner, and the action is considered to be the price paid for the promise, the taking of such action as is requested will serve as consideration.

2. Promissory Estoppel

Throughout this chapter, we will assume the basic proposition that consideration is required for a valid contract. A mere moral obligation will not make a promise binding. We will be primarily concerned with what is and what is not "good consideration." Before turning to these issues, it is essential to recognize that there is a significant substitute for consideration commonly known as *promissory estoppel*. This doctrine was mentioned in the preceding chapter in connection with the revocation of offers.

The doctrine of promissory estoppel is an equitable doctrine used where there is in fact no consideration. It allows enforcement of a promise when the promise is such that the promisor should reasonably expect the promisee to take some substantial action or forbearance in reliance on the promise to such an extent that injustice can be avoided only by enforcing the promise. The promise without consideration becomes enforceable because of the reliance upon it. That there would be reliance must have been foreseeable by the promisor, and there must be a change of position. For example, X promises his church $1,000 to be used to construct a new church. The church, in reliance on X's promise and on promises and pledges by others, undertakes the construction project. X's promise may be binding because he induced the church to materially change its position in reliance on his promise. However, if his $1,000 pledge were to be used to discharge an existing mortgage, the promise would probably be unenforceable for lack of consideration. The church did not change its position in reliance on the promise. The doctrine of promissory estoppel is limited in its application and provides only a limited means of enforcing promises that fail to pass the test of consideration.

3. Adequacy of Consideration

Historically, it has not been a function of law to make value or economic judgments concerning contracts voluntarily entered into by the parties.[1] As a

---

[1] *Osborne v. Locke Steel Chain Company,* page 150.

general rule, courts have not attempted to weigh the consideration received by each party to determine if it is fair in light of that which the party gave. It has been sufficient in law if a party receives something of legal value for which he bargained. The law is concerned only with the existence of consideration, not with its value. It does not inquire into the question of whether the bargain was a good one or a bad one for either party. In the usual case, any inadequacy is for the person to judge at the time the contract is created and not for determination by the courts at the time of enforcement. In the absence of fraud, oppression, undue influence, or statutory limitation, a party may make any contract he pleases. The fact that it is onerous or burdensome for one or the other has been unmaterial.

Today, this philosophy is changed to a substantial degree. The Code provides that contracts that are so one-sided as to be unconscionable are unenforceable (2-302). Courts as well as legislative bodies have attempted to protect consumers by changing this historical view of consideration. These matters will be discussed further in subsequent chapters dealing with consumer protection.

There has always been one exception to the general rule on adequacy of consideration. In contracts that call for the exchange of money between the parties, the adequacy of consideration will be scrutinized. A promise to pay $1,000 in one year in return for an immediate $100 loan would not only be usurious, and therefore illegal, but would also be unenforceable because of the inadequacy of consideration. Money has a fixed value, and there is therefore no basis for holding that the payment of $100 is sufficient consideration to support the promise to pay $1,000. Although it could be argued that the borrower may have needed the $100 so badly that it was worth it for him to promise to pay the larger sum, such has not been an acceptable argument to the courts. It is one thing to indulge in the presumption that the parties have provided for a reasonable relationship between the detriment to the promisee and the benefit to the promisor in ordinary contracts, but the basis for the presumption fails when money alone is involved on both sides. Note, however, that if something in addition to money is provided by the promisee, adequacy of consideration is no longer an issue. Thus, for example, if A pays $100 to B and in addition promises to attend a political meeting in return for B's promise to pay him $1,000, the promise would be supported by consideration.

4.   Recitals of Consideration

Most written contracts contain a provision reciting that there is consideration. For example, a contract may state, "For and in consideration of $1 in hand paid, etc." Such a recital of nominal consideration does not conclusively establish the existence of consideration. A recital that consideration exists is not consideration unless it can be proved that the nominal consideration was "bargained for" and the price paid for the promise.

The general rule, therefore, is that a mere recital of consideration may be questioned in an action to enforce the alleged contract. A recital of consideration will stand up in the absence of evidence to contradict the recital, and of course, $1 actually bargained for and paid may be good consideration. Just as a court may examine a contract to determine the presence of consideration, even though consideration is recited, it may also receive evidence of the presence or absence of consideration when the agreement is silent on this score.

5. Forbearance

Consideration, which usually takes the form of a promise or an action, may take the opposite form, forbearance from acting or a promise to forbear.[2] The law considers the waiver of a right or the forbearance to exercise a right to be sufficient consideration for a contract. The right that is waived or not exercised may be one that exists either at law or in equity. It may even be a waiver of a right that one has against someone other than the promisor who bargains for such waiver. A common form of forbearance is a promise not to bring a lawsuit, generally referred to as a release or a covenant not to sue. Such forbearance is good consideration, regardless of the validity of the claim that is surrendered, provided there is a reasonable and sincere belief in its validity. Giving up the right to litigate is something of value and a legal detriment even though it is ultimately discovered that the claim was worthless. However, if the claim is frivolous or vexatious, or if the claimant knows it is not well founded, forbearance to sue would not be good consideration.

SPECIAL ASPECTS OF CONSIDERATION

6. Preexisting Conditions

The performance of a preexisting contractual or statutory duty does not furnish consideration for a promise. If a promisee receives nothing more than he was entitled to without making the promise, he has not received any consideration for the promise. In other words, doing what one is required to do anyway is not valid consideration.

Issues as to the presence of consideration because of the allegation of preexisting obligations arise in a variety of circumstances. A common situation is one in which one party to a contract refuses to continue performance unless and until the terms of the contract are modified. The other party may, in order to ensure continued performance, assent to the demands and agree to terms that are more onerous than those provided in the agreement. He may promise to pay more than the contract price or to accept less in the way of performance. Generally, a promise to pay more than the agreed price is not enforceable. Some exceptions to this general rule are discussed later.

[2] *Grombach* v. *Oerlikon Tool & Arms Corp. of America,* page 151.

Usually, an owner who promises a contractor an additional sum to complete a job already under contract is not legally bound to pay the additional sum. If, however, the promisee-contractor agrees to do anything other than, or different from, that which the original contract required, consideration is provided. The contractor who agrees to complete his work at an earlier date or in a different manner may recover on a promise of the owner to pay an additional amount. It would also be possible for the parties to cancel the original contract and enter into an entirely new agreement, one that includes the new amount.

The requirement of consideration is often a barrier to enforcement of promises, and the Code has made substantial inroads on the consideration element of a contract, especially with regard to authorizing alteration or modification of contracts without requiring consideration to support the changes.

Under the Code, parties to a binding contract for the sale of goods may change the terms, and if such change is mutually agreeable, no consideration is required to make it binding [3] (2-209[1]). This means, for example, that if a buyer agrees with the seller to pay more than the contract price for goods purchased, he will be held to the higher price.

To illustrate: A, an automobile manufacturer, entered into a contract with B, a supplier, to purchase a certain number of wheels at a stated price. Thereafter, B told A that because of higher production and labor costs, he would need to be paid $5 more per wheel in order to carry on with the contract. If A agrees to pay the additional sum, his promise to do so will be binding even though there is no consideration present.

Nevertheless, consideration is very much a part of the framework of modern contract law, and even under the Code it is a viable element. The Code section that sustains modifications of a contract without any additional consideration could, if not limited in some way, permit a party to a contract with a superior bargaining position to take advantage of the other party. Accordingly, the Code provides that the parties must act in good faith, and the exercise of bad faith in order to escape the duty to perform under the original terms is not permitted. The "extortion" of a modification without a legitimate reason therefore is ineffective because it violates the good-faith requirement.

To safeguard against false allegations that oral modifications have been made, it is permissible to include in the contract a provision that modifications are not effective unless they are set forth in a signed writing (2-209[2]). However, if a consumer enters into such a contract, in addition to signing the contract, he must also sign the restrictive provision to assure that he is aware of the limitation—otherwise it is not effective. If it is not signed in this fashion, a consumer is entitled to rely upon oral modifications. The provision is apparently designed to protect the unwary consumer against reliance upon statements made to him that certain provisions of the contract do not apply to him or that others are subject to oral change. He is entitled to be forewarned

---

[3] *J & R Elec. Div., J.O. Mory Stores* v. *Skoog Const. Co.*, page 152.

not to rely upon anything but the printed word, and it is expected that the double signing will bring this message to his attention.

The Code allows necessary and desirable modifications of sales contracts without regard to the technicalities that hamper such adjustments under traditional contract law. The safeguards against improper and unfair use of this freedom are found in the requirements of good faith and the "observance of reasonable commercial standards of fair dealing in the trade." There is recognition of the fact that changes and adjustments in sales contracts are daily occurrences and that the parties do not cancel their old contract and execute an entirely new one each time a change or modification is required.

7. Unforeseen Difficulties

The parties to a contract often make provisions for contingencies that may arise during the course of performance. They are well advised to exercise this foresight. However, they frequently make no provisions at all, or make some that do not encompass all the difficulties that may render performance by either party more burdensome than anticipated. In the absence of an appropriate contract clause, two questions are raised when unanticipated difficulties arise during the course of performance: (1) Will the party whose performance is rendered more difficult be required to complete performance without any adjustment in compensation? (2) Will a promise to pay an additional sum because of the difficulty be enforceable?

Excuses for breach of contract are discussed in Chapter 14. For purposes of this discussion, it must be recognized that additional hardship is not an excuse for breach of contract as a general rule. Therefore, the answer to the first question is usually yes.

The second question therefore assumes that a promisor, although not required to do so, has promised to pay an additional sum because of the difficulty. Such a promise is deemed binding by some courts where *unforeseen* difficulties are encountered after the original agreement is executed and the promise to pay more is made in consideration of this fact. The result is most often justified on the theory that, in effect, the parties rescinded the old agreement because of new circumstances and formed a new one. However, it is prudent for the promisee either to furnish some new consideration or to have the old agreement formally rescinded and a new one executed.

Unforeseen difficulties are those that occur seldom and are extraordinary in nature. Price changes, strikes, inclement weather, and shortage of material occur frequently and are not considered to fall in this category.

8. Discharge of Liquidated Debts and Claims

As previously noted, if the consideration on each side of an agreement involves money, the consideration must be equal. Because of this rule, an agreement between a debtor and his creditor to have a liquidated (fixed in amount) debt discharged upon the payment of a sum less than the amount agreed to be owing is unenforceable. In other words, there is no consideration for the agreement to accept less than the full amount owed. As a result, the unpaid amount is collectible even though the lesser sum has been paid. The payment of the lesser sum is the performance of an existing obligation and cannot serve as consideration for a release of the balance. However, if there is evidence that the creditor made a gift of the balance to the debtor, no recovery of such balance may be had by the creditor. A receipt given to the debtor by the creditor, stating that the payment in full has been received, is evidence that a gift was intended. Furthermore, where the debt is evidenced by a note, the cancellation and return of the note upon receipt of part payment discharges the full debt.

Just as a promise to pay an additional sum for the completion of an existing contract is enforceable if the promisee does something other than, or in addition to, the required performance, a debtor may obtain a discharge of the debt by paying a lesser sum than the amount owing if he gives the creditor something in addition to the money. The settlement at the lower figure will then be binding on the creditor. Since the value of consideration is ordinarily unimportant, the added consideration may take any form. For example, payment in advance of the due date, payment at a place other than that agreed upon, surrender of the privilege of bankruptcy, and the giving of a *secured* note for less than the face of the debt have all been found sufficient to discharge a larger amount than that paid. The mere giving of a note for a lesser sum than the entire debt will not release the debtor of his duty to pay the balance. The note is merely a promise to pay, and consequently, the mere promise to pay less than is due will not discharge the debt.

9. Discharge of Unliquidated Debts and Claims

A promise to forbear from prosecuting a claim is sufficient consideration to support a promise to pay for a release, and the compromise of a claim results in a binding settlement. The parties are surrendering their rights to litigate the dispute, and this detriment serves as consideration. As a result, when one party has a claim against another party and the amount due is disputed, unliquidated (uncertain in amount), a compromise settlement at a figure between the amount claimed or demanded and the amount admitted to be owing is binding on the parties. It does not matter whether the claim is one arising from a dispute that is contractual in nature, such as one involving damaged merchandise, or is tortious in character, such as one arising from an automobile accident. The compromise figure operates as a contract to discharge the claim. Such a settlement contract is known legally as an *accord and satisfaction*.[4] The dispute as to the amount owed by the debtor must be in good faith or the rules for liquidated debts are applicable, and the creditor could pursue

---

[4] *A.G. King Tree Surgeons* v. *Deeb,* page 153.

the debtor for the difference, his agreement to settle for a lesser amount notwithstanding. However, the surrender of even a doubtful claim upon the honest and reasonable belief in its validity is a legal detriment and consideration for a contract.

10. Composition of Creditors

An additional method of satisfying a debt by payment of a lesser sum than the amount claimed or admitted is a "composition of creditors." This is a procedure whereby a person's creditors agree to accept a certain sum of money and/or property in full and complete settlement of the debtor's obligations to them. The creditors prorate the debtor's assets, which are made available to them, and agree with each other and the debtor to accept a percentage of their claims in full satisfaction. The composition is a type of insolvency proceedings enabling a person in debt to satisfy his debts by making most, if not all, of his assets available for distribution to his creditors. Of course, this raises a legal question as to the consideration to support the acceptance of a lesser sum in full satisfaction than the amount admittedly due. The consideration for which each of the assenting creditors bargains may be any one of the following: (1) the promise of each of the other creditors to forego a portion of his claim; (2) the action of the debtor in securing the acquiescence of the other creditors; (3) forbearance or a promise to forbear by the debtor to pay the assenting creditors more than the stipulated proportion. Thus, the law encourages mutual agreements between a debtor and his creditors to the extent of precluding the participating creditors from thereafter collecting the difference between their pro rata share and the amount of the debt.

11. Past Consideration

Past consideration is insufficient to support a present promise. The consideration must consist of some present surrender of a legal right. Some act that has taken place in the past will not suffice. Hence, an express warranty concerning real property, when made after the sale has taken place, is not enforceable,[5] nor is a promise to pay for a gift previously received. Of course, under the Code, a modification does not require consideration. Therefore, a warranty made after a sale of personal property is enforceable.

The past-consideration rule does not apply, for example, to those cases in which one person requests another to perform some work for him without definitely specifying the compensation to be paid, and after the work is completed, the parties agree upon a certain sum to be paid for the work. Although it would appear that the work done in the past furnishes the consideration to support the promise made later to pay a definite sum, such is not really the case. As soon as the work is completed, the party performing it is entitled to

---

[5] *James* v. *Jacobsen,* page 154.

reasonable compensation. His later surrender of this right is consideration for a promise to pay a definite sum. The surrender of the right to receive a reasonable wage is the consideration for the new contract.

There are a few other seeming exceptions to the rules of law concerning past consideration. For example, a new promise to pay a debt that has been discharged in bankruptcy is enforceable without any added consideration. The promise to pay must be clearly expressed. Acknowledgement of the debt or part payment does not import a promise to pay the creditor. Most states by statute require the new promise to be in writing, and provide that the promise may be to pay only a part of the debt or to pay it only when certain conditions are satisfied. Many states have a similar provision for a promise to pay a debt outlawed by the statute of limitations.

A creditor who has given a voluntary and binding release of part of a debt may not enforce a later promise by his debtor to pay the balance. If the release of the unpaid portion is considered in the nature of a gift, the rule relating to a promise to pay for a gift previously received renders such a promise unenforceable.

12. Mutuality of Consideration

Difficult problems in the law of consideration arise in the area of mutuality of consideration or illusory promises. As a general rule, mutual promises furnish a sufficient consideration to support a valid enforceable contract. However, each of these mutual promises must be valuable, certain, and not impossible of performance or they will not suffice as consideration. As a general proposition, if one party is not bound by his promise, neither is bound. A promise is valuable only if it meets the benefit-detriment test previously discussed.

The requirement of mutuality of consideration presents particular problems in unilateral offers. The promisor-offeror is at liberty to withdraw his offer at any time prior to the requested conduct by the offeree; but he loses his power to revoke after the offeree has performed or tendered performance of a part of what was requested. Thus, the offeror is in a sense bound, whereas the offeree can theoretically either continue performance to completion or abandon the act of acceptance. The beginning of performance does not constitute an acceptance, but it does bar the offeror's power of revocation. The Code provides that the beginning of performance can be effective as a bar to revocation only if the offeree gives *notice* within a reasonable time that he accepts the offer. Should the offeror not receive such notice of acceptance within a reasonable time, he may treat the offer as having lapsed before acceptance (2-206[2]). Of course, he also has the option to treat the offer as having been accepted if the offeree does complete performance in response to it.

An agreement that gives to one of the parties the unconditional right to cancel the contract at any time prior to the time for performance is not binding and is illusory. However, if the right to cancel is not absolute but is conditioned upon whether some event happens or does not happen, the contract is such that neither party may avoid it unless the condition occurs and it is not illusory. Mutuality does not require that a contract be definite in all details or that there be reciprocity or a special promise for each obligation. Nor does it require mutuality of remedies between the parties. To determine if mutuality of consideration is present or if the purported promise is illusory, a careful examination of the language of the contract is required.

A contract lacking mutuality becomes binding upon the happening of the event upon which the promise is conditioned. The test of mutuality is at the time of enforcement, not the time when the promise is made.[6] For example, a real estate contract contingent upon the buyer's obtaining a loan becomes mutually binding when the loan is obtained. Mutuality does not require that a contract be definite in all details or that there be reciprocity or a special promise for each obligation. Neither does it require mutuality of remedies between the parties.

Many promises that appear to assure something of value but, when fully understood, do not embody such an assurance are illusory promises, because real mutuality is lacking. Consider the following agreement: B, a trucker, promises to purchase from S all he *wants* of S's gasoline at 50 cents a gallon plus taxes, and S promises to sell all that B *wants* at that price. Careful analysis of this agreement makes it clear that B has not *agreed to buy* any gasoline. He has promised to purchase only in case he wants it, which is equivalent to no promise at all. Since B has thus given S no consideration for his promise, B's promise being illusory, S is at liberty to withdraw, and his withdrawal becomes effective as soon as notice thereof reaches B. Until withdrawn by S, the agreement stands as a continuing offer on his part, and any order received prior to revocation must be filled at the quoted price.

In the case above, if B had agreed to buy his gasoline *needs* or *requirements* from S for a period of one year, the agreement would have been binding. Whenever the buyer is reasonably certain to have needs or requirements, an agreement to purchase all of one's needs or requirements will support the promise to supply them even though the amount to be needed is uncertain. Past experience will, in a general way, aid the seller in estimating the amount required.

The Code provides that a term in a contract that measures the quantity by the output of the seller or by the requirements of the buyer means such actual output or requirements as may occur in good faith (2-306[D]). In addition, no quantity unreasonably disproportionate to any stated estimate, or in the absence of a stated estimate, to any normal or otherwise comparable prior output or requirement may be tendered or demanded. In other words, under the Code, quantity must bear a reasonable relationship to estimates given or to past outputs or requirements (2-306).

[6] *Stone Mountain Properties, Ltd.* v. *Helmer,* page 155.

CONSIDERATION CASES

Osborne v. Locke Steel Chain Company
218 A.2d 526 (Conn.) 1966

COTTER, J. . . . This action was brought by plaintiff to recover damages for breach of contract, alleged to have been caused by the defendant's refusal to make payments to him under a written agreement entered into between the parties under date of November 4, 1960.

The terms of this agreement provided that the defendant pay the plaintiff $20,000 during the year ending September 30, 1961, and thereafter, $15,000 a year for the remainder of the plaintiff's life. The plaintiff agreed to hold himself available for consultation and advice . . . and not to . . . be employed by any business . . . in competition with [defendant]. . . . The defendant made payments in accordance with the terms of the agreement for approximately two and one-half years, following which, after the plaintiff refused to consent to a modification of the agreement, the defendant discontinued further payments. The plaintiff then initiated the present action to recover payments due under the agreement. The defendant, by way of special defenses, alleged that the agreement was invalid and unenforceable, claiming in effect (1) inadequate consideration because the contract was based on past services. . . . The issues were tried to the court, which concluded that the agreement was legally unenforceable. Judgment was rendered for the defendant, and the plaintiff took the present appeal.

The facts necessary to a disposition of the question involved are undisputed. The plaintiff was employed by the defendant from 1912 until November 1961, progressively holding the positions of order clerk, traffic manager, salesman, sales manager, president, and chairman of the board. He was president of the company from 1941 to 1958 and a member of the board of directors from 1941 until 1961. From 1958 until his retirement in November 1961, he served as chairman of the board of directors.

The agreement in suit was approved by the board of directors at a special meeting held in November 1961. . . .

After its approval by the board, the agreement was signed by the plaintiff and by the company acting through its president. . . .

The trial court concluded that there was no consideration for the agreement on the part of the plaintiff. . . .

. . . The doctrine of consideration is of course fundamental in the law of contracts, the general rule being that in the absence of consideration an executory promise is unenforceable. In defining the elements of the rule, we have stated that consideration consists of "a benefit to the party promising, or a loss or detriment to the party to whom the promise is made."

The recited consideration in the present case consists of the plaintiff's promise to hold himself available for consultation with the defendant in connection with the defendant's business and to avoid serving any enterprise in competition with the defendant within a designated area. In essence, what the defendant bargained for, as contained in the terms of the written agreement, was the exclusive right to the plaintiff's knowledge and experience in his chosen field for the remainder of his life.

Absent other infirmities, "bargains . . . moved upon calculated considerations, and, whether provident or improvident, are entitled nevertheless to the sanctions of the law." The defendant cannot now be heard to claim, for its own benefit, that the actual undertaking of the parties was other than that which appears in their written agreement. Even though it might prefer to have the court decide the plain effect of this agreement to be contrary to the expressed intention set forth in the contract between the parties, it is not within the power of the court to make a new or different contract.

Under the facts of this case, the recited consideration constituted a benefit to the defendant, as well as a detriment to the plaintiff, and was therefore sufficient consideration. . . . An exclusive right to the counseling of the plaintiff, who had had almost fifty years of experience in the defendant's business, including some twenty years in positions of ultimate responsibility, and whose capacities are unchallenged, cannot reasonably be held to be valueless. Exactly what value might be placed on such a right is of course irrelevant to this issue. The doctrine of consideration does not require or imply an equal exchange between the contracting parties. "That which is bargained for by the promisor and given in exchange for the promise by the promisee is not made insufficient as a consideration by the fact that its value in the market is not equal to that which is promised. Consideration in fact bargained for is not required to be adequate in the sense of equality in value." The general rule is that, in the absence of fraud or other unconscionable circumstances, a contract will not be rendered unenforceable at the behest of one of the contracting parties merely because of an inadequacy of consideration. . . . The courts do not unmake bargains unwisely made. The contractual obligation of the defendant in the present case, whether wise or unwise, was supported by consideration, in the form of the plaintiff's promise to give advice and not to compete with the defendant, and that obligation cannot now be avoided on this ground.

Reversed.

Grombach v. Oerlikon Tool & Arms Corp. of America
276 F.2d 155 (1960)

Plaintiff and defendant had a written contract by which plaintiff would serve as a public relations representative for defendant. The employer had the right to cancel the contract by giving written notice of cancellation before May 1, 1953. The period of performance extended for several years in the event of no cancellation by that date. On April 27, 1953, the employee agreed to an extension of the cancellation option to June 30, 1953. On June 24, 1953, the employer exercised the option and canceled the contract. Plaintiff-employee sued defendant-employer, contending among other things that the period of cancellation had expired because the extension of the cancellation option was invalid due to lack of consideration.

BARKSDALE, J. . . . Nor can we agree with plaintiff's belated contention that this agreement to extend the time within which the contract of February 10, 1953, might be canceled, was invalid because not supported by a valuable consideration. As set out in paragraph VI(a) of the contract, Buehrle had the right to cancel the contract by giving written notice befor May 1, 1953. By cable, on April 27, 1953, Grombach agreed to an extension of the cancellation option to June 30, 1953. The crux of the situation is that Buehrle requested, and Grombach agreed to, the extension of time in which the option to cancel might be exercised, within the period during which, according to the terms of the written contract, Buehrle had the unquestioned option to cancel. Buehrle's forbearance to cancel at a time when he, by the terms of the contract, had the undoubted right to do so, constituted consideration for the extension of time.

> The waiver of a right or forbearance to exercise the same is a sufficient consideration for a contract, whether the right be legal or equitable, or exists against the promisor or a third person, provided it is not utterly groundless.

In the case of *Millikan* v. *Simmons,* it was held that an agreement to extend an option for the purchase of real estate, made before the expiration of the original option, was valid, the agreement to forego the right to close the transaction at once constituting sufficient consideration to support the agreement to extend the option.

See also *Brown* v. *Taylor,* where the principle is stated as follows:

> There is a consideration if the promisee, in return for the promise, does anything legal which he is not bound to do, or refrains from doing anything which he has the [legal] right to do, whether there is any actual loss or detriment to him or actual benefit to the promissor or not. . . .

Affirmed.

J & R Elec. Div., J.O. Mory Stores v. Skoog Const. Co.
348 N.E.2d 474 (Ill.App.) 1976

GREEN, J. . . . J & R Electric Division of J.O. Mory Stores, Inc. sued defendant Skoog Construction Company, a corporation, . . . for balance due under a construction subcontract. The court . . . found in favor of the plaintiff . . . and awarded damages in the sum of $23,384.11. Defendant appeals.

Community Unit School District No. 1, Coles County, Illinois, decided to undertake a building program known as the Charleston Shop and Ashmore Elementary School project. Plans and specifications were drawn and provided to certain prospective contractors, including defendant, and certain prospective subcontractors, including plaintiff. With reference to the work involved here, these documents provided that "the exterior unit switchgear for the Charleston High School Shop would be purchased by the owner" but that installation and final connection would be performed as part of the contract. Subsequently the project architects issued Addendum G-2, which provided that the contractor would assume the obligation of accepting a purchase order for the exterior unit switchgear at an agreed price of $9,702 and thus furnish that equipment as a part of its obligation.

Defendant was the successful bidder on the project and accepted plaintiff's bid to perform the electric work under the contract. This work included the exterior unit switchgear. . . .

The parties do not now dispute that defendant owes plaintiff at least $12,248.96. Principally in dispute is the sum of $9,702, the purchase price of the exterior unit switchgear. Plaintiff paid the purchase price for the unit and installed it. Plaintiff contends, and the court found, that the subcontract was modified by the parties to provide that defendant would reimburse plaintiff for this purchase by a special payment over and above the amount defendant was otherwise required to pay by the terms of the subcontract. The modification is claimed to have arisen from a promise made in a letter written by defendant, directed and sent to plaintiff during the course of construction. That letter stated:

> We have looked into how the electrical switchgears should be billed and paid for the subject project. On your next billing to us, which should be in our hands no later than October 10, 1972, please include the $9,702 billing for the exterior switchgear.
>
> We shall include it in our request to the Owner which will be approved by the Board of Education on October 18, 1972, and we should receive a check from the School Board for the total request on either Friday, October 20, 1972, or Monday, October 23, 1972. We shall immediately send our check to you for the full amount of your payment request and then you can send your check on to Tepper Electric.
>
> We have been informed by telephone by Mr. John Scaggs of K.E. Unteed & Associates, that there is some cable which attaches to the bus duct and to the switchgear which has not been included by you in your quotation. It is the contention of Mr. Scaggs that this connecting material should have been in your quotation and that it is up to you to install.

His main point in his call was to make sure that the changeover is made on October 7, 8, and 9th and no other time and that there should be no delay in this changeover. Please see that this changeover is made and if there is some question about the connecting material, we can discuss it at a later date.

. . . The court . . . ruled that plaintiff gave no consideration for defendant's promise contained in the letter. Plaintiff disputes this, contending that it gave consideration by making the changeover on the dates requested in the letter, October 7, 8, and 9. Under the subcontract, plaintiff, the subcontractor, agrees that defendant, the contractor, could determine when the work should be done. The performance by an obligor of a duty that it is already required to do is not consideration. The trial court's ruling that plaintiff furnished no consideration for any promise attributed to defendant is amply supported by the evidence and correctly interprets the law.

The court then ruled that consideration was not necessary to make the promise enforceable because of Section 2-209(1) of the Uniform Commercial Code, which provides: "an agreement modifying a contract within this Article needs no consideration to be binding." . . .

No Illinois court of review has determined directly whether a contract or subcontract for the construction of buildings is a "contract for sale" within Article 2. The decisions of other jurisdictions are split. . . .

The enactment of the Uniform Commercial Code provides no indication of any intention to . . . broaden the meaning of the phrase, a "contract to sell goods" to include a construction contract even though goods are thereby furnished and incorporated into a building. We, therefore, hold that the subcontract in question was not governed by Article 2 of the Uniform Commercial Code and could not be modified by a promise for which no consideration was given. The award for $9,702 must be set aside. . . .

Reversed and remanded with directions.

A.G. King Tree Surgeons v. Deeb
356 A.2d 87 (N.J.) 1976

DALTON, J. . . . This is a contract action brought by A.G. King Tree Surgeons for the contract price of $480, plus tax and interest, for tree pruning work performed at the home of defendant George Deeb on or about May 30, 1975.

Plaintiff alleges the work was performed pursuant to an oral contract made by telephone, after an estimate of $480 had been transmitted orally, also by phone, to defendant. The work agreed on and actually performed was, according to plaintiff, the pruning of 15 trees on defendant's property.

Defendant states by way of affirmative defense that . . . an accord and satisfaction was reached before the filing of this lawsuit. . . .

First, it is undisputed that defendant, upon receipt of the invoice for $504 (representing the $480 contract price plus $24 tax), protested to plaintiff by telephone that he had never entered into a contract for this amount and had only authorized an estimate from plaintiff, nor did he ever sign a contract or an acknowledgement of work performed. This is not, therefore, a case of a liquidated sum which is due and owing but rather a genuine dispute between the parties as to what liability, if any, defendant owes to plaintiff for the work performed.

Second, it is undisputed that shortly after this controversy arose defendant's attorney forwarded to plaintiff defendant's check in the amount of $100 with a notation typed on the reverse side (above the space for the indorser's signature) to the effect that this $100 was in full and final settlement of all claims of A.G. King against defendant for work performed in May 1975. Along with the check defendant's attorney sent a letter of transmittal which stated in no uncertain terms that although defendant denied that authorization was ever given to plaintiff to perform work for defendant, nevertheless the $100 check was submitted in good faith in an attempt to amicably settle the claim, and that if plaintiff wished to settle for this amount, he should deposit the check. Plaintiff corporation, through its president A.G. King, did deposit the check but only after he obliterated the notation placed on it by the drawer and substituted in its place a notation that the check was only in partial payment of the amount due. Based on this set of facts defendant argues that an accord and satisfaction was reached between the parties at the time the check was deposited, notwithstanding the fact that the president of plaintiff corporation altered the notation on the reverse side of the check. This court agrees.

The traditional elements of an accord and satisfaction are the following: (1) a dispute as to the amount of money owed; (2) a clear manifestation of intent by the debtor to the creditor that payment is in satisfaction of the disputed amount; (3) acceptance of satisfaction by the creditor.

The president of plaintiff corporation alleges, of course, that there could be no acceptance of any offer of settlement since he deliberately altered the check before depositing it, making it clear that he considered the $100 only a partial payment and not a full settlement of the matter. However, it is clear that plaintiff had no right to alter the check. If the check was unacceptable as a final settlement,

plaintiff's remedy was to return the check to defendant and sue for the full amount claimed due. Plaintiff chose rather to alter the check, accept the $100 "in partial payment" and sue for the difference.

In this case, however, the check did not stand alone; it was accompanied by a letter from defendant's attorney which made it clear that (1) there was a genuine dispute between the parties as to what amount of money, if any, was due plaintiff; (2) defendant intended that the $100 check was to be in full satisfaction of the dispute between the parties, and (3) if, and only if, plaintiff agreed to settle the dispute for this amount, the check was to be deposited.

It is the opinion of this court that the check and letter can, and indeed must, be read together as constituting an offer to settle this dispute for $100, and that the depositing of the check constituted the acceptance of this offer. Once the check was deposited by plaintiff, no matter what alterations the corporation's president personally made on its reverse side, an accord and satisfaction was reached. . . .

The letter of transmittal . . . recites the basis of the genuine dispute between the parties and the intent of defendant to have the enclosed payment totally satisfy the dispute, and this satisfies the first two requirements of an accord and satisfaction. The third requirement of an accord and satisfaction is the acceptance of the offer and, in this case, the deposit of the check by plaintiff operated *ipso facto* as such an acceptance. . . .

Judgment for defendant.

actual in facts?

James v. Jacobsen
91 S.E.2d 527 (Ga.) 1956

Jacobsen brought an action against James, defendant, to recover for alleged breach of warranty to the effect that the property purchased was free of termites. The warranty was given after the contract of sale had been signed.

GARDNER, J. . . . The record reveals that this is an action ex contractu and not ex

delicto. This leads us to consider first whether or not the instrument regarding termite infestation was a legal and binding contract with sufficient consideration to vary the terms of the original contract of sale and contract of purchase. It is our understanding of the law that where the vendor of realty stipulates the terms upon which the property is offered for sale and such offer is accepted by a proposed purchaser, such contract between them is executed within the terms of the agreement. The contract of sale set up certain specifications, all of which were fulfilled by the vendor and the purchaser within the specified time. Before the consummation of the sale there was executed an instrument in which the seller guaranteed to the purchaser, in writing, that the premises in question were free of termite infestation and free of damage due to any previous termite infestation. . . .

The original contract was based on legal consideration and was valid and enforceable.

The original contract of sale here, as the record reveals, was executed on January 14, 1955 and the express warranty with regard to termites was given by the defendant on February 10, 1955. The sale had not taken place and no delivery of the property had been made and the parties had not yet done what the original contract obligated them to do. (See *Woodruff* v. *Graddy & Sons,* 91 Ga. 333, 17 S.E. 264.) Where, as here, the termite instrument is relied upon as a part of the original contract of sale, there are decisions to the effect that such a reliance is not tenable but is *nudum pactum.* . . .

Judgment for defendant.

Stone Mountain Properties, Ltd. v. Helmer
229 S.E.2d 779 (Ga.) 1976

Plaintiff entered into a contract to purchase real estate from the defendant. The contract provided in part: "This contract is made contingent upon Purchaser's being able to obtain approval from the Seaboard Airline Railroad to run a spur rail line into the property *at a location satisfactory to the Purchaser."*

Before plaintiff obtained the approval of the railroad for the spur line, the defendant sold the property to another party. This suit for damages followed. The lower court found for the plaintiff.

WEBB, J. . . . It is well settled that contracts conditioned upon discretionary contingencies lack mutuality. . . . If, in a contract for the sale of real estate, payment of the purchase price is made contingent upon an event which may or may not happen at the pleasure of the buyer, the contract lacks mutuality, and until that contingency has occurred, there is no obligation on the part of the purchaser to purchase or the seller to sell.

Thus where a contract may be terminated by one of the parties should it *"become dissatisfied* with the management and operation of the said bank," the contract lacked mutuality.

The condition here providing for railroad approval for a location "satisfactory to the Purchaser" deprives the contract of mutuality because the purchaser is the sole judge of his satisfaction, regardless of whether there were reasonable and sufficient grounds for such dissatisfaction or not. Where the fancy, taste, sensibility, or judgment of the promisor is involved, there is practical unanimity that if one agrees to accept and pay if he is satisfied with a thing, he cannot be compelled to do so on proof that other people are satisfied with it, or that he ought to be.

Nevertheless, a promise may be nudum pactum when made because the promisee is not bound, but it becomes binding when he subsequently furnishes the consideration contemplated, by doing what he was expected to do. Following this reasoning it has been held that a promise to sell realty becomes binding when the purchaser, although not required to do so, performs the condition precedent to his obligation to buy.

In this case the condition would not be fulfilled until Mitchell was satisfied with the approved location. Where one contracting party agrees to perform services to the satisfaction of or satisfactory to the other party, compliance with the contract is not shown unless it appears that the thing done or the article furnished does in fact satisfy the other party.

It is not sufficient that other people are satisfied with it, or that he ought to be.

Once Mitchell was satisfied with the approved location, however, a binding contract could come into existence, provided Mitchell satisfied the contractual requirement of "notification to Seller by Purchaser that these conditions have been met," and provided this was done before the offer was withdrawn.

. . . The test of mutuality is to be applied, not as of the time when the promises are made, but as of the time when one or the other is sought to be enforced. A promise may be unenforceable for want of mutuality when made, and yet the promisee may render it valid and binding by supplying a consideration on his part *before the promise is withdrawn*. . . .

Mitchell's promise to buy the property, conditioned upon his being able to obtain approval to run a spur line at a location satisfactory to himself, was illusory since no standards were set forth to authorize a determination that, if not satisfied, he nevertheless ought to have been. In these circumstances his discretionary promise to buy was not more effective than if he had promised to buy "provided I decide to do so." Thus at that point the partnership's promise to sell, unsupported by any consideration, was unenforceable and stood as a mere unaccepted offer, creating a power of acceptance in Mitchell, but revocable at any time. . . .

Reversed.

CHAPTER 9
REVIEW QUESTIONS AND PROBLEMS

1. A paid B $250 for a 60-day option to buy B's farm. Nearing the end of the option period, A asked for and was granted a 15-day extension, for which no money was paid. After the original 60-day period but within the 15-day extension, B withdrew the offer. A notified B of his acceptance, but B contended that no option existed for lack of consideration. Was there an option during the extension period? Why?

2. X agreed to supply Y with all his lumber requirements if in turn Y would agree to purchase all his requirements from X for a specified period. Is this an enforceable contract? Why?

3. X agreed to dismiss a paternity suit against Y if he would agree to pay medical expenses and child support until the child became 21 years of age. Y agreed and paid for eighteen months but then discontinued payment. X sues for breach of contract. Y uses the defense that he has undergone blood-grouping tests and has proof that he is not the child's father. What result? Why?

4. A wanted to acquire a franchise from B Corporation for one of its stores. A was informed by B that if he would sell his bakery and purchase a certain tract of land, he would be granted a franchise. A did these things but did not receive a franchise. He now sues for breach of contract, but B contends that there was no consideration for the promise. Should A succeed? Why?

[handwritten: because value consideration.]

5. A paid 25 cents in return for an option to purchase real estate from B for $100,000. B sought to revoke the option. Can B revoke the option? Why? *[handwritten: No — because had valid option]*

6. A agreed to do the testing work on a project that B had completed. The parties agreed upon a price based upon an estimate of the amount of material to be tested. Subsequently, it became obvious that the contract could not be completed within the estimated time, owing to the necessity of moving 1,200,000 tons of material instead of the estimated 600,000 tons. A insisted upon additional payments, and B agreed. However, after the work was completed, B refused to pay the additional amount. Is A entitled to the additional money? Why? *[handwritten: Yes value consideration circumstances changed,]*

7. S sold real estate to B for $4,000, payable in monthly installments. Three years later, S agreed to accept $2,500 in full payment. After B had paid $2,500, she refused to pay more and demanded a deed. S demanded the full amount. Who is correct? Why? *[handwritten: Yes, B because S agreed to $2,500]*

8. B, a grocer, claimed that cheese she had purchased from S was spoiled. S said that B spoiled the cheese trying to force-cure it and, therefore, it could not be returned. After several discussions, the parties could not agree on the amount owed to S. When B paid her account, she withheld 10 cents per pound and sent a check for $746.01, marked, "This pays my account in full to date." S had the check certified by the bank and then sued for the balance of the debt. S established that the cheese was in good condition when received by B. Can S recover the entire amount of the debt? Why? *[handwritten: disputed claim]* *[handwritten: No, because accepted the amt, and negotiated the amt of check,]*

9. S Company entered into a contract to supply valves to B Company. B's purchase order was worded in such a way that B had agreed to purchase only as many valves as it wanted to purchase. S went to considerable expense to tool up for production and now sues for breach of contract. Should S succeed? Why? *[handwritten: no mutuality of performance]*

10. The parents of D, a daughter, transferred land to their son and his wife. The deed recited consideration of $38,400, and the parents were to receive $1,800 annually for the rest of the lives. It was never intended by the parties that the $38,400 would be paid, and the amount was never paid. D sues as guardian of her parents to rescind the sale, contending that the consideration for six quarters of land is inadequate, since her parents were 87 and 83 years old at the time of the sale. Is D correct? Why? *[handwritten: gift]* *[handwritten: competent?]* *[handwritten: contention]* *[handwritten: No, because legal contract, unless fraud]*

10

Voidable Contracts

1. Introduction

The presence of offer, acceptance, and consideration indicates the existence of a contractual relationship. It does not mean that the contract is enforceable or that a party may not legally cause it to be canceled or disaffirmed. This chapter and those that follow will discuss the rights of a party to rescind or disaffirm a contract, and the circumstances under which a contract is unenforceable. This chapter is generally concerned with the various grounds available for the equitable remedy of rescission or cancellation of a contract previously entered into. Such contracts are described by the term *voidable contracts*. A party that avoids a contract will be returned to the position that he occupied before he entered into the contract. If he has paid money and received goods, he will be entitled to return the goods and obtain a return of the money paid. Some allied problems, such as suits for damages as an alternative remedy, are also discussed.

The usual grounds for exercising the right to rescind a contract are (1) lack of capacity to contract, (2) fraud, (3) misrepresentation, (4) mutual mistake, and (5) lack of free will. In addition, a major breach of the contract by one party justifies rescission by the other (see Chapter 14).

158

LACK OF CAPACITY

2. In General

Lack of capacity refers to the mental state of the party to a contract. Minors are presumed to lack the requisite capacity to contract and are thus allowed to disaffirm contracts. Contracts by insane persons are also voidable. The test for insanity for the purpose of avoiding a contract is different from the test for other purposes such as the criminal law, making a will, or commitment to a mental institution. In the law of contracts, the test is whether a person has sufficient mental capacity to understand the nature of the transaction.[1] Insanity may be of a temporary nature, such as that caused by intoxication or drug addiction.

If a contract is disaffirmed by an insane person, the consideration received must be returned if no unfair advantage has been taken of the insane person. If the contract is unreasonable or unfair advantage has been taken, the party without mental capacity is entitled to rescind by returning as much of what he received as he has left.

3. Minors' Contracts Generally

The age of majority and capacity to contract is 18 in most states. However, the statutory law of each state must be examined to determine the age of majority for contracts.

A person below the age of capacity is called an infant or a minor. Minors have the right to disaffirm or to avoid contracts. The law grants minors this right in order to promote justice and to protect them from their presumed immaturity, lack of judgment and experience, limited will power, and imprudence.[2] An adult deals with a minor at his own peril. A contract between an infant and an adult is voidable only by the infant. The right to disaffirm exists irrespective of the fairness or favorability of the contract and whether or not the adult knew he was dealing with a minor.

Legislation in many states has in a limited way altered the right of minors to avoid their contracts. For example, many states provide that a purchase of life insurance or a contract with a college or university is binding. Some statutes take away the minor's right to avoid contracts after marriage, and a few give the courts the right to approve freedom of contract for emancipated minors.

[1] *McPheters* v. *Hapke,* page 169.
[2] *Harvey* v. *Hadfield,* page 171.

4. Disaffirmance and Ratification

Until steps are taken to avoid or to disaffirm, a minor is liable on a contract. The contracts of minors are not illegal—only voidable. A minor can disaffirm a purely executory contract by directly informing the adult of the disaffirmance or by any conduct that clearly indicates an intent to disaffirm. If the contract has been fully or partially performed, the infant also has the right to avoid it and obtain a return of his consideration. If the infant is in possession of consideration that is passed to him, he must return it to the other party. He cannot disaffirm the contract and at the same time retain the benefits.

The courts of the various states are somewhat in conflict as to the judicial treatment of those situations in which an infant has spent or squandered money he received under a contract or in which he either cannot return property he purchased or has damaged such property or allowed it to deteriorate. The majority of the states hold that the infant may disaffirm the contract and demand the return of the consideration with which he has parted, even though he is unable to return that which he received. For example, assume that an infant purchases an automobile and has an accident that demolishes the car. He may obtain a full refund by disaffirming the contract. A few courts, however, hold that if the contract is advantageous to the infant and if the adult has been fair in every respect, the contract cannot be disaffirmed unless the infant returns the consideration he received. These courts also take into account the depreciation of the property while in the possession of the infant.

The minor may avoid both executed and executory contracts at any time during minority and for a reasonable period of time after majority. What constitutes a reasonable time depends on the nature of the property involved and the specific circumstances. Many states establish a maximum period, such as two years, by statute.

A person after reaching majority may ratify a voidable contract entered into while a minor. Conduct which indicates approval of or satisfaction with a contract entered into as a minor is a ratification. Ratification eliminates the right to disaffirm.

Generally, an executed contract is ratified by retention of the consideration received for an unreasonable time after majority. Ratification also results from acceptance of the benefits incidental to ownership, such as rents, dividends, or interest. A sale of the property received or any other act that clearly indicates satisfaction with the bargain made during minority will constitute a ratification. In general, a contract that is fully executory is disaffirmed by continued silence or inaction after reaching legal age. Some of the states hold that ratification is not effective unless the minor knows of his right to disaffirm at the time of the alleged act of ratification, but inaction for an unreasonable length of time will constitute a ratification of an executed contract, irrespective of knowledge of the right to disaffirm. If an infant sells goods to an adult, the latter obtains only a voidable title to the goods. The infant can disaffirm and recover possession from the adult buyer. At common law, even a good-faith purchaser of property *formerly* belonging to an infant cannot retain the property if the infant elects to rescind. This rule has been changed under the Uniform Commercial Code, which provides that a person with voidable title has "power to transfer a good title to a good-faith purchaser for value" (2-403). The common law rule, however, is still applicable to sales of real property by an infant. For example, if a minor sells his farm to Y, who in turn sells it to Z, the minor may disaffirm against Z and obtain the farm back. This is not unfair, since the minor's name appeared in the chain of title.

5. Liability for Necessaries

The law has recognized that certain transactions are clearly for the benefit of an infant and hence are binding. The term *necessaries* is used to describe the subject matter of such contracts. An infant is not liable in *contract* for necessaries, but he is liable in *quasi contract*. The fact that his liability is quasi-contractual has two significant features: (1) He is not liable for the contract price of necessaries furnished to him, but rather for the reasonable value of the necessaries, and (2) he is not liable on executory contracts, but only for necessaries actually furnished to him.

What are necessaries? In general, the term includes whatever is needed for an infant's subsistence as measured by his age, state, condition in life, and so forth. Food and lodging, medical services, education, and clothing are the general classifications of necessaries. It is often a close question as to whether a particular item or service is to be regarded as a necessary.

FRAUD AND MISREPRESENTATION

6. Introduction

A contract is voidable if it has been induced by a misrepresentation of a material fact by one party that is relied on by the party to his injury. The misrepresentation may be intentional, in which case the law considers the misrepresentation to be "fraudulent." It may be unintentional, in which case there has been no fraud but only innocent misrepresentation. In both cases, the victim of the misrepresentation may rescind the contract, because the loss is the same whether the false statements were made innocently or intentionally. In the case of fraudulent misrepresentation, the victim is given the choice of the additional remedy of a suit for dollar damages including punitive damages. Fraud and misrepresentation may be used as a defense to a suit for breach of contract as well as a theory upon which to sue.

A third party, one not a party to the contract, may also be liable for fraudulent misrepresentations. If such a third party makes false statements that he could reasonably expect to be relied on, he can be held liable to the contracting party who relies thereon to his detriment.

While the elements of actionable fraud are stated differently from state to state, the following are those generally required:

1. Scienter, or intention to mislead. This is knowledge of the falsity of statements made with such utter disregard and recklessness for the truth that knowledge is inferred.

2. A false representation or the concealment of a matter of fact material to the transaction.

3. Justifiable reliance on the false statement or concealment.

4. Injury as a consequence of the reliance.

Innocent misrepresentation does not require proof of scienter but does require proof of all the other elements of fraud. The absence of scienter is the reason that a tort action for dollar damages cannot be based on such a theory. However, in cases under the Code, rescission is not a bar to a suit for dollar damages.

Rescission is permitted only in case the defrauded party acts with reasonable promptness after he learns of the falsity of the representation. Undue delay on his part effects a waiver of his right to rescind, thus limiting the defrauded party to an action for recovery of damages. A victim of fraud loses his right to rescind if, after having acquired knowledge of the fraud, he indicates an intention to affirm, or if he exercises dominion over property that he would have to surrender in order to rescind the contract.

7. Scienter

The intent to mislead is often referred to by courts and writers as *scienter*. This Latin word means "knowingly." Scienter is present if the misrepresentation was willfully made. It exists where there has been a concealment of a material fact or a nondisclosure of such a fact. Intent may be and usually is inferred from conduct; of necessity, it must be proved by statements or acts of the person whose act is being scrutinized, and ordinarily it can only be proved by circumstantial evidence. It includes anything calculated to deceive. Moreover, a statement that is partially or even literally true may be fraudulent in law if it was made in order to create a substantially false impression. Intention to mislead may also be established by showing that a statement was made with such reckless disregard as to whether it is true or false that intention to mislead may be inferred. A party who makes a false statement, honestly believing it to be true but without reasonable grounds for such belief, has committed fraud. The negligent misrepresentation is equal to scienter. In other words, culpable ignorance of the truth or falsity will supply the intention to mislead. A false representation made without any belief as to its truth is intentionally false. For example, an accountant who certifies that financial statements accurately reflect the financial condition of a company may be guilty of fraud if he has no basis for the statement. While perhaps he does not actually intend to mislead, his statement is so reckless that the intention is inferred.

8. False Representation

An actual or implied false representation of a past or present fact is the gist of fraud. This misstatement of fact must be material or significant to the extent that it has a moving influence upon the contracting party. It need not be the sole inducing cause for entering into the contract. A fact is material if it is one to which a reasonable person would attach importance in determining his choice of action in the transaction involved.

Statements of fact must be distinguished from statements that are simply promissory in nature. An unfulfilled promise will not support an action for fraud. The failure of the promise only justifies a suit for breach of contract. However, if, at the time the promise is made, the promisor has no intention to perform, the promise may constitute a misrepresentation of a material fact. The false fact is the state of mind or the intention of the promisor and his intent to deceive the promisee.

As a general rule, false statements of opinion as opposed to statements of fact are not actionable. This rule is an oversimplification, because an expression of opinion itself is a fact—the fact being the state of mind of the one expressing the opinion.

If a person has an opinion about something, it is a fact that he has that opinion. If he says his opinion is one thing and in fact it is another, he has misstated a fact—what his opinion actually is. This concept is sometimes used when the person who is allegedly fraudulent is an expert, such as a physician, or when the parties stand in a fiduciary relationship to each other. For example, assume that a doctor, after examining a patient for an insurance-company physical, states that he is of the opinion that the person has no physical disability. If his actual opinion is that the patient has cancer, the doctor is guilty of fraud. He has misstated a fact—his professional opinion. Opinions of persons standing in a fiduciary relationship are actionable because of the high standard of conduct imposed by the relationship.

False opinions regarding the quality of a product or its value may also be considered misrepresentations of fact where the parties do not have equal knowledge of the facts or equal access to them.[3] Whether a particular statement is one of fact or opinion is a matter for the jury to resolve.

The misstatement may in fact be true in part. A half-truth, or partial truth, that has the net effect of misleading may form the basis of fraud just as if it were entirely false. The untruth may be the result of a series of statements, the

---

[3] *Sellers* v. *Looper,* page 172.

net result of which is to mislead. Although each statement taken alone may be true, there is fraud if all of them taken together tend to mislead the party to whom they are made. A partial truth in response to a request for information becomes an untruth whenever it creates a false impression and is designed to do so.

An intentional misrepresentation of existing local or state law affords no basis for rescission, since the law is presumably a matter of common knowledge, open and available to all who desire to explore its mysteries. Moreover, such statements are usually mere opinions.[4]

A misrepresentation may be made by conduct as well as by language. Any physical act that has for its ultimate object the concealment of the true facts relating to the property involved in a contract is, in effect, a misstatement. One who turns back the odometer on a car, fills a motor with heavy grease to keep it from knocking, or paints over an apparent defect—in each case concealing an important fact—asserts an untruth as effectively as if he were speaking. Such conduct, if it misleads the other party, amounts to fraud and makes rescission or an action for damages possible.

9. Silence as Fraud

Historically, the law of contracts has followed *caveat emptor,* especially in real estate transactions. The parties to a contract are required to exercise ordinary business sense in their dealings. As a result, the general rule is that silence in the absence of a duty to speak does not constitute fraud. Where there is a duty to speak, the concealment of a material fact is equivalent to fraudulent misrepresentation.

The law has developed at least three situations in which there is a duty to speak the truth and failure to do so will constitute actionable fraud. First of all, there is a duty to speak when the parties stand in a fiduciary relationship. A fiduciary relationship is one of trust and confidence, such as exists between partners in a partnership or between a director and a corporation or between an agent and a principal. Because such parties do not deal "at arm's length," there is the duty to speak and to make a full disclosure of all facts.

The second exception is based on justice, equity, and fair dealing. This exception occurs when a vital fact is known by one party and not the other and it is such that if known, there would have been no contract. While this concept is difficult to define or describe, it is not difficult to apply on a case-by-case basis, especially when the suit is in equity for rescission. For example, when there is a latent defect in property—one that is not apparent upon inspection —the vendor has a duty to inform the purchaser of the defect. Failure to do so is fraudulent.

The third exception is that a person who has misstated an important fact on

---

[4] *Puckett Paving Company* v. *Carrier Leasing Corporation,* page 173.

some previous occasion is obligated to correct the statement when negotiations are renewed or as soon as he learns about his misstatement.[5] This exception is really not a true exception to the silence rule because there is in fact a positive misstatement.

The gist of these exceptions is that one of the parties has the erroneous impression that certain things are true, whereas the other party is aware that they are not true and also knows of the misunderstanding. It therefore becomes his duty to disclose the truth. And unless he does so, most courts would hold that fraud exists. This does not mean that a potential seller or buyer has to disclose all the factors about the value of property he is selling or buying. It is only when he knows that the other party to the agreement is harboring a misunderstanding on some vital matter that the duty to speak arises.

10. Justifiable Reliance

Before a false statement of fact can be considered fraudulent, the party to whom it has been made must reasonably believe it to be true, must act thereon to his damage, and in so acting must rely on the truth of the statement. If he investigates and the falsity is revealed, no action can be brought for fraud. The cases are somewhat in conflict as to the need to investigate. Some courts have indicated that if all the information is readily available for ascertaining the truth of statements, blind reliance upon the misrepresentation is not justified. In such a case, the party is said to be negligent in not taking advantage of the facilities available for confirming the statement. In determining a person's negligence in relying upon the statements, courts will consider the education, intelligence, and experience of the party. The standard for justifiable reliance is not whether a reasonably prudent man would be justified in so relying, but whether the particular individual had the ability and a right to so rely.

Thus, if a party inspects property or has an opportunity to do so, he is not misled if a reasonable investigation would have revealed untruths with regard to its condition. On the other hand, some courts have stated that one who by misrepresentation has induced another to act to the other's prejudice cannot impute negligence to the other merely because of his reliance on the misrepresentation. He cannot be heard to say, "You should not have believed me." A person has no duty to make inquiries or investigate unless he has knowledge of his own or of facts that should arouse suspicion and cast doubts on the truth of the statement made. Nor can he relieve himself of liability for misrepresentations in advance by a disclaimer. Courts generally agree that reliance is justified when substantial effort or expense is required to determine the true facts. In any case, the issue as to whether or not the reliance is justified is for the jury.

[5] *Bergeron* v. *Dupont,* page 174.

11. Injury or Damage

In order to prevail, the party relying upon the misstatement must offer proof of resulting damage. Normally, such damage is proved by evidence indicating that the property that is the subject of the contract would have been more valuable provided the statements had been true. Injury results when the party is not in as good a position as he would have been had the statements been true.

In an action for damages for fraud, the plaintiff may seek to recover damages on either of two theories. He may use the "benefit of the bargain" theory and seek the difference between the actual market value of what he received and the value if he had received what was represented. A plaintiff may also use the "out of pocket" theory and collect the difference between the actual value and the purchase price.

Perhaps the most significant aspect of a suit for dollar damages is that the victim of fraud is entitled to punitive damages in addition to compensatory damages. If the fraudulent representations are made maliciously, willfully, or wantonly, or so recklessly as to imply a disregard of social obligations, punitive damages as determined by a jury may be awarded. For example, in a recent case where a used car was misrepresented, the jury awarded $500 actual damages and $4,500 punitive damages.

MISTAKE

12. In General

A *mistake* is a state of mind that is not in accord with the facts. There are a variety of possible mistakes in the law of contracts, and they may occur at various stages of a transaction; they may involve errors in arithmetic, in execution of the contract, and in setting forth the terms of the contract, either orally or in writing, to name but a few. The mistake may be bilateral; both parties are mistaken. Or it may be unilateral; only one party is laboring under mistake.

In order that a mistake by one or both of the parties may warrant relief to either of them, the mistake must be a material one. The relief afforded by virtue of the mistake will depend upon a number of factors, including the point of time at which the mistake is discovered; the extent to which performance has already progressed; the extent to which one or the other of the parties has changed his position in reliance on the contract before the mistake was discovered;[6] and the extent to which the parties can be restored to the *status quo*.

The basic remedy for mistake is rescission. The general rule is that one who has made a mistake and wishes to rescind can do so only if he can sub-

---

[6] *Ohio Co.* v. *Rosemeier,* page 175.

stantially return the other party to the *status quo*. No relief will be afforded if the other party has changed his position in reliance on the contract to the extent that he cannot be restored to his former position.

13. Bilateral Mistake

The word *bilateral* as used in this context means two-sided, or mutual, mistakes as contrasted with one-sided, or unilateral, mistakes. Both parties to the contract have made a factual assumption that is false. It is often difficult to classify mistakes as either mutual mistakes or unilateral mistakes, but courts usually hold that no relief can be afforded for the unilateral mistakes.

A bilateral mistake may exist when parties enter into a contract on a mistaken assumption regarding a material fact. This mutual assumption, called *mutual mistake of fact,* arises in two situations. In one, the minds of the parties fail to meet in that they did not agree upon the same thing in the same sense. When this occurs, no contract results. In the other situation, the mistake merely makes the agreement more onerous for one of the contracting parties and therefore renders it voidable at his option. Before a contract can be rescinded for mutual mistake, it must be proven that the parties were both mistaken as to a material fact, that the matter is of such grave consequence that the enforcement of the contract would be unconscionable, that the mistake occurred despite the exercise of reasonable care, and that the other party can be placed in the *status quo.*

Typical of the first type are those cases in which an offer is made in terms that the offeree misunderstands. The offeree accepts in terms that the offeror understands as an assent to the offer that he meant to make. Each party is mistaken as to the meaning of the other, and this is not discovered until important changes have taken place. In such a case, it is very clear that no contract should be held to exist unless one of the parties so negligently expressed himself that the other was caused reasonably to believe that agreement existed.

The second type is illustrated by the sale of floor covering for a certain room at a lump-sum figure on the assumption by both parties that only a certain number of square feet is involved. If the area is greater than both parties thought to be true, the contract is voidable at the instance of the party who would suffer a loss because of the mistake.

In the transaction of business, it is customary in many situations to dispose of property about which the contracting parties willingly admit that all the facts are not known. In such instances, the property is sold without regard to its quality or characteristics. Such agreements may not be rescinded if it later appears that the property has characteristics that neither of the parties had reason to suspect, or if it otherwise differs from their expectations. Under such conditions, the property forms the subject matter of the agreement, regardless of its nature. Thus, A sells B a farm, and shortly thereafter, a valuable deposit of ore is discovered on it. The agreement could not be rescinded by the seller on the ground of mutual mistake.

14. Unilateral Mistake

A contract entered into because of some mistake or error on the part of only one of the contracting parties usually affords no basis for relief to such party. The majority of such mistakes result from carelessness or lack of diligence on the part of the mistaken party and should not, therefore, affect the rights of the other party.

This general rule is subject to certain exceptions. An offeree who has reason to know of a unilateral mistake is not permitted to "snap up" such an offer and profit thereby. For example, if a mistake in a bid on a contract is clearly apparent to the offeree, it cannot be accepted by the offeree. Sometimes the mistake is discovered prior to the bid opening and the offeror seeks to withdraw the bid. Bids are often accompanied by bid bonds, which have the effect of making them irrevocable. Most courts will allow the bidder to withdraw the bid containing the error (1) if the bidder acted in good faith, (2) if he acted without gross negligence, (3) if he was reasonably prompt in giving notice of the error in the bid to the other party, (4) if the bidder will suffer substantial detriment by forfeiture, and (5) if the other party's status has not greatly changed, and relief from forfeiture will work no substantial hardship on him. Courts clearly scrutinize the facts to make sure that all these requirements are met. It should be difficult for low bidders to claim an error in computation as the basis for escaping from a bid noticeably lower than the competition's. This is the "bad-faith" element of the test quoted above.

15. Reformation of Written Contracts

Written agreements sometimes fail to express the intention of the parties at the time of execution of the agreement. This failure often results from a failure of the draftsman to correctly reduce the understandings of the parties to written form. It may also result from a typing or printing error. The failure of the written agreement to accurately set forth the actual contract is a form of mutual mistake of fact. Therefore, courts of equity have the power to reform written agreements notwithstanding the parol-evidence rule.

Reformation is only available where there is clear and positive proof of the drafting error. Courts frequently justify this remedy on the basis that the contract is not being changed—that the written evidence is only being corrected. Reformation relates back to the date of execution of the original agreement, and the courts enforce the agreement as reformed. The fact that one of the parties to a contract denies that a mistake was made does not prevent a finding of mutual mistake or prevent reformation. One party is frequently aware of the mistake in reducing the agreement to written form and often fails to tell the other party. Such a dishonest person is not allowed to take advantage of the other party by denying the existence of the error. However, the proof of the mistake must be clear and convincing.

16. Lack of Free Will

Equity allows a party to rescind an agreement that was not entered into voluntarily. The lack of free will may take the form of duress or undue influence. A person who has obtained property under such circumstances should not in good conscience be allowed to keep it. A person may lose his free will because of duress—some threat to his person, his family, or property—or from a more subtle pressure whereby one person overpowers the will of another by use of moral, social, or domestic force as contrasted with physical or economic force. Cases of undue influence frequently arise in situations involving the elderly. In those cases where free will is lacking, some courts hold that the minds of the parties did not meet.

At early common law, duress would not be present when a courageous man would have possessed a free will in spite of a threat, but modern courts do not require this standard of courage or firmness as a prerequisite for the equitable remedy. If the wrongful pressure applied in fact affected the individual involved to the extent that the contract was not voluntary, there is duress.[7] If a person has a free choice, there is no duress even though some pressure may have been exerted upon him. A threat of a lawsuit is not duress that will allow rescission. Economic pressure may constitute duress if it is wrongful and oppressive.

VOIDABLE CONTRACTS CASES

McPheters v. Hapke
497 P.2d 1045 (Idaho) 1972

SHEPARD, J. . . . This appeal stems from a contract for the purchase and sale of real estate entered into by Virgil McPheters and Joseph W. Fuld, now deceased. Following the death of Fuld, Leon Hapke, the Executor of the Fuld estate, repudiated the contract on the grounds of Fuld's incompetency at the time of his execution of the contract. This action was instituted by McPheters, and following trial to the court, judgment was entered for the defendant. This appeal resulted.

The contract in question was entered into by McPheters and Fuld on February 8, 1966. It provided for the sale of a commercial lot in Hailey, Idaho, upon which was located a service station. The terms of the contract are unusual. Fuld was enabled to retain possession of the property for as long as he desired and the purchase price was not due or payable until thirty days after Fuld might notify McPheters that Fuld wished to transfer the property. No interest was chargeable on the purchase price.

[7] *Shurtleff* v. *Giller,* page 176.

In the event that the possession of the property was not transferred within the lifetime of Fuld it was agreed that the property would be transferred within thirty days after the death of Fuld. The purchase price was $14,000. Fuld's wife had died prior to the execution of the contract and the same property had been appraised in her estate at a sum in excess of $26,700.

At the time of the execution of the contract Fuld was in his late eighties and had recently been widowed. Fuld was unable to care for himself and a niece had been caring for him and his aged sister at Fuld's residence in Hailey for some period of time prior to the contract transaction. . . .

In *Olsen* v. *Hawkins,* 90 Idaho 28 (1965), the test of mental competency to execute a contract is stated:

> The test of mental capacity to contract is whether the person in question possesses sufficient mind to understand, in a reasonable manner, the nature, extent, character, and effect of the act or transaction in which he is engaged; the law does not gauge contractual capacity by the standard of mental capacity possessed by reasonably prudent men. It is not necessary to show that a person was incompetent to transact any kind of business, but to invalidate his contract it is sufficient to show that he was mentally incompetent to deal with the particular contract in issue.

We note that the standard set forth in *Olsen* v. *Hawkins, supra,* differs from and is more stringent than the standard required for the execution of a will and that one may be competent to make a will and still be incompetent to execute a particular contract.

We need only determine herein whether the evidence before the court supports the court's finding of incompetence. We are led to the conclusion that such finding and the judgment entered thereon was and is supported by substantial and competent evidence even though that evidence was in part controverted. Specifically, there was the following evidence which supported the judgment: A medical witness testified that Fuld had a mental disability in 1965 and was very senile by 1968; various witnesses testified that Fuld appeared at times unaware that his wife had died and that he often confused the past and the present; a business associate testified that Fuld had become very confused as to business matters and at times sent the associate moneys which were not owing; it was testified that Fuld was giving away large sums of money to persons to whom he owed no obligation and at one time gave two checks to the same person with the same check number and amount; there was testimony that Fuld's desk was piled high with years' accumulation of bills, letters and other correspondence of which apparently no care had been taken; there was testimony that Fuld had failed to file income tax returns for several years prior to his death; there was testimony that Fuld had been unable to care for his personal needs and had become confused as to how to perform basic personal tasks; there was testimony that although Fuld had been an experienced and very successful business man in the past, the contract herein as well as other contracts entered into at or about the same time were unusual and financially disadvantageous to Fuld; there was testimony that Fuld became easily disoriented as to time and place and actually became lost and wandered in locations that were strange to him; finally, a guardian was appointed for Fuld in July 1967.

There was conflicting evidence regarding Fuld's competence introduced by the plaintiff, which consisted principally of testimony by several witnesses that they thought Fuld was otherwise competent at the time of the contract. However, balancing all of the evidence and determining which of it, if any, was entitled to weight was the function of the trier of the fact and this court will not interfere with that function save where there has been an abuse of discretion by the trial court.

Affirmed.

Harvey v. Hadfield
372 P.2d 985 (Utah) 1962

CROCKETT, J. . . . Plaintiff, a minor, sues by his guardian *ad litem* to recover $1,000 he had advanced defendant under a proposed contract to buy a housetrailer. From adverse judgment he appeals.

Plaintiff, a student attending college at Logan, turned 19 years of age on the 13th day of October, 1959. A few days after his birthday he quit school and got a job. In the latter part of October he went to the defendant's lot and selected a trailer he liked. He told the defendant of the above facts, of his plans to be married and of his desire to buy the trailer. The defendant advised him that he would have to get his father's signature to get financing through the defendant.

Plaintiff responded that he thought he could arrange financing and that he could raise a thousand dollars as a down payment. He paid $500 on November 6 and another $500 on November 13 and applied for financing at the bank. The bank finally refused to accept his application for a loan because of his minority and because his father would not sign with him.

After plaintiff's plans failed to materialize, he asked the defendant to return his money. Defendant refused but finally did agree to a statement which the plaintiff typed up and which both signed. It released the trailer in question for sale and granted plaintiff $1,000 (plus interest) credit on a trailer of his choice the next spring. About February 1, 1960, plaintiff's attorney sent a letter to the defendant disaffirming the contract and demanding the return of his money. Upon refusal, this suit was commenced.

Since time immemorial courts have quite generally recognized the justice and propriety of refusing to enforce contracts against minors, except for necessities. It is fair to assume that because of their immaturity they may lack the judgment, experience, and will power which they should have to bind themselves to what may turn out to be burdensome and long-lasting obligations. Consequently, courts are properly solicitous of their rights and afford them protection from being taken advantage of by designing persons, and from their own imprudent acts, by allowing them to disaffirm contracts entered into during minority which upon more mature reflection they conclude are undesirable. We agree that justice requires that minors have such protection. It is the responsibility of our courts to so safeguard their rights until they have attained their majority and thus presumably have the maturity of judgment necessary to deal with opposing parties on equal terms so that it is fair and equitable to bind them by their acts. Accordingly, adults dealing with minors must be deemed to do so in an awareness of the privilege the law affords the minor of disaffirming his contracts. The rule relating to disaffirmance is codified in our law, Sec. 15-2-2, U.C.A. 1953:

> A minor is bound not only for reasonable value of necessaries but also by his contracts, unless he disaffirms them before or within a reasonable time after he attains his majority and restores to the other party all money or property received by him by virtue of said contracts and remaining within his control at any time after attaining his majority.

Defendant advances the following propositions which he claims exclude this case from the general rule allowing a minor to disaffirm:

. . . That even if the contract is disaffirmed, he is entitled to an offset of the actual damages he has sustained from loss of sale of the trailer from the $1,000.

. . . Defendant urges that from the fact that the plaintiff was "on his own," living away from home, working, and contemplating marriage, he could reasonably regard him as "engaged in business as an adult" and that he was therefore capable of entering into a binding contract. The defendant's position is not sound. . . .

Our statute cannot be construed to support the defendant's contention that the disaffirming minor must compensate him for damages he may have incurred. Sec. 15-2-2, U.C.A. 1953, hereinabove quoted, requries only that the minor restore "to the other party all money or property received by him by virtue of said contracts and remaining within his control at any time after attaining his majority." The trailer was left in the possession of the defendant. That fulfills the requirement of the statute.

The plaintiff minor having disaffirmed the contract is entitled to the return of his money.
The judgment is reversed.

Sellers v. Looper
503 P.2d 692 (Or.) 1972

BRYSON, J. . . . This is an action for damages based on fraudulent misrepresentations pertaining to the well on property plaintiffs purchased from defendants. The jury returned a verdict in favor of plaintiffs. On motion, the trial court granted judgment in favor of defendants notwithstanding the verdict, and the plaintiffs have appealed. . . .

Defendants argue here that the plaintiffs had not submitted evidence sufficient to establish fraudulent representations on the part of defendants to induce plaintiffs to enter into the contract to purchase the property.

The plaintiffs . . . contend: "Statements regarding quality, value or the like may be considered misrepresentations of fact where the parties are not on an equal footing and do not have equal knowledge or means of knowledge" and the "[d]ecision of whether a representation is of fact or of 'opinion' is always left to the jury and therefore the order setting aside the jury's verdict should not have been entered."

Interwoven with defendants' contention that the evidence was insufficient to justify the plaintiffs' verdict is their argument that the representation of a "good well" was "mere inclusion of adjectival words of commendation" or "opinion" and, therefore, not actionable.

In Holland v. Lentz, 239 Or. 332, 345, 397, P.2d 787, 794 (1964), we held:

> . . . It is recognized, however, that statements of opinion regarding quality, value, or the like, may be considered as misrepresentations of fact, that is, of the speaker's state of mind, if a fiduciary relation exists between the parties as, for example, representations of value made by a real estate broker to his principal: or where the parties are not on an equal footing and do not have equal knowledge or means of knowledge.

Prosser treats the matter by stating:

> A statement of opinion is one which either indicates some doubt as to the speaker's belief in the existence of a state of facts, as where he says, "I think this is true, but I am not sure," or merely expresses his judgment on some matter of judgment connected with the facts, such as quality, value, authenticity and the like, as where he says, "This is a very fine picture." It is not, however, the form of the statement which is important or controlling, but the sense in which it is reasonably understood. . . .
>
> It is stated very often as a fundamental rule in connection with all of the various remedies for misrepresentation, that they will not lie for misstatements of opinion, as distinguished from those of fact. . . .
>
> But this explanation is scarcely adequate, since an expression of opinion is itself always a statement of at least one fact—the fact of the belief, the existing state of mind, of the one who asserts

it. . . . [Prosser, Torts (4th ed.) 720–721.]

The evidence discloses that defendants owned a home and acreage located in Illinois Valley near the city of Cave Junction, Josephine County, Oregon. In May of 1969 defendants executed a listing, or employment, agreement to sell their property with Mrs. McLean, a real estate broker. This agreement included information given to realtor by the defendants. Mrs. McLean testified:

I asked the Loopers, "Do you have a good well?" and the comment came back, "Yes, we have a good well. . . ."

On July 28, 1969, plaintiffs contacted Mrs. McLean. They desired to buy a house large enough for plaintiffs and their six children. Mrs. McLean further testified:

Q. . . . At the time you told them that there was a good well on the property, did you tell them that for the purpose of inducing them to buy the Loopers' property?

A. A good well on any property is a tremendous inducement. If you have a good well, that's a selling point. . . .

Q. . . . At the time you represented to Mr. and Mrs. Sellers that there was a, quote, good well on the property, what did you mean to convey by that, what meaning did you mean to get across to prospective buyers?

A. The meaning I've always inferred before, and I inferred at that time, was that it was an adequate well, there was plenty of water.

Q. Plenty of water for what?

A. Well, I told them at the time that you couldn't go out and irrigate the pas-

ture, if they wanted to irrigate pasture they would perhaps have to put down an irrigation well, but there was a good well, and this was understood to be adequate for household, and usually that includes a modest garden. . . .

In the early evening of July 28, 1969, the plaintiffs, with the realtor, met the defendants and inspected the house and "looked at the well and pumphouse." No specifications as to the depth of the well or how many gallons it would pump per hour were given the plaintiffs and the realtor did not have this information. They returned to the realtor's office; she prepared the earnest money agreement; defendants signed the agreement that evening, the plaintiffs signed it and made the down payment. . . .

On August 15, 1969, plaintiffs moved onto the property and on August 22, 1969, the well went dry. Plaintiffs drilled two additional wells but found no water.

We conclude that there was sufficient evidence to submit the case to the jury. A reasonable person, in this day of modern household conveniences, could believe that a "good well" meant a well with adequate water for family household use and the plaintiffs relied on this representation. The evidence shows that defendants knew the water in the well got low in the fall of the year and they had to be careful in flushing the indoor toilet or the well would probably go dry. The plaintiffs were not on equal footing with the defendants and did not have equal knowledge of the adequacy or lack of adequacy of the water in the well. The jury returned a verdict for the plaintiffs and "[T]hese matters are ordinarily for the determination of the jury. . . ."

Reversed with instructions to reinstate the jury's verdict.

Puckett Paving Company v. Carrier Leasing Corporation
225 SE.2d 910 (Ga.) 1976

JORDAN, J. . . . Carrier brought an action to recover four heavy duty trucks from Puckett. The pleadings and the evidence show

that Puckett was in possession of the vehicles under the terms of two certain leases providing for monthly payments in stated sums for 44 months and 35 months respectively; that Puckett had an option to purchase same for a stated price after all monthly payments had been made; that Puckett had made all monthly payments but refused to purchase or return said vehicles. Carrier elected to recover the vehicles rather than damages.

Puckett filed an answer and cross claim alleging that the contracts were induced by fraud in that an agent of Carrier "assured defendant that the lease agreement(s) entered into would be considered a lease by the Internal Revenue Service," but that said IRS considered the same to be a sale and not a lease, resulting in damage to Puckett.

. . . The trial court ordered . . . Puckett to return the vehicles and enjoined Puckett from further use of the property. Puckett appeals from this judgment.

We affirm. Assuming that such statements were made by an agent of Carrier to Puckett, they could only have been the expression of an opinion as to how the IRS had treated such agreements or would treat them in the future. "Where no fiduciary relationship exists, misrepresentations as to a question of law will not constitute remedial fraud, since everyone is presumed to know the law 'and therefore cannot in legal contemplation be deceived by erroneous statements of law, and such representations are ordinarily regarded as mere expressions of opinion. . . .'"

Affirmed.

Bergeron v. Dupont
359 A.2d 627 (N.H.) 1976

GRIFFITH, J. . . . The plaintiff purchased a mobile home park in Belmont from the defendant. Subsequent to the transfer of title, plaintiff brought this action to recover damages allegedly sustained as a result of fraudulent misrepresentations by the defendant Lawrence J. Dupont, Jr., through his agent.

On January 25, 1973, the plaintiff and defendant executed a purchase and sale agreement, which specified a sales price of $89,000. In the course of negotiations leading to the signing of the agreement, the defendant's agent represented to the plaintiff that the septic systems in the park were in satisfactory condition, requiring only an occasional pumping out for proper functioning.

Subsequent to the signing of the agreement but prior to the closing, complaints were lodged in February of 1973 by park tenants with the water supply and pollution control commission to the effect that effluent from some of the systems was emerging above ground. Tests by the State in February were inconclusive because of weather conditions but on March 13 and March 14, tests disclosed that three of the systems had failed.

The defendant Dupont was informed by a sanitary engineer from Concord sometime during this period that they were testing the systems because of emergence of effluent.

The title was transferred on March 14, 1973, and shortly thereafter the plaintiff was informed that three of the septic systems had failed. The plaintiff replaced them and the cost of replacement was the basis of the verdict.

The master found on the issue of defendant's fraud as follows: "At no time did the defendant reveal to the plaintiff that the state was investigating a complaint from the tenants. The defendant's representations to the plaintiff regarding the condition of the septic systems were a material factor in persuading the plaintiff to buy the mobile home park. When the defendant acquired new knowledge regarding the condition of the septic systems by reason of the state's investigation in February 1973, he came under the duty to disclose this additional information to the plaintiff since it was at variance with the representations previously made."

The master correctly ruled that a representation which was true when made could be fraudulent if the maker failed to disclose subsequent information which made the original representation false. While it is true that one who makes a representation believing it to be true and does not disclose its falsity until after the transaction has been consummated has

committed no fraud, both parties herein treat March 14, 1973, the date of closing, as the time at which the rights of the parties became fixed. . . .

Affirmed.

Ohio Co. v. Rosemeier
288 N.E.2d 326 (Ohio) 1972

HESS, J. . . . Plaintiff . . . is a stock brokerage corporaton with branch offices in Cincinnati, Ohio. On April 28, 1969, the defendant . . . presented a stock certificate to the plaintiff's representative for 1,080 shares of Santa Fe International, Inc., a Colorado corporation. This stock was not listed on stock exchanges. At that time this stock was selling for four to eight cents per share. At the same time, stock of the Santa Fe International Corporation, a California corporation, was listed on stock exchanges and selling for $36 to $36.50 per share. The defendant inquired at the plaintiff's office if her stock was selling at $36 per share. After a check of the stocks listed, the plaintiff's representative advised that defendant's stock was selling at $36 per share. Both parties mistakenly believed the defendant's shares to be those listed by Santa Fe International Corporation, the California corporation.

On the same day, a sale of 500 shares of defendant's stock was made at approximately $36.125 per share. Pursuant to this sale, the plaintiff delivered a check to the defendant on May 5, 1969, in the amount of $17,851.30. The defendant subsequently applied the proceeds of the sale to the payment of an existing mortgage on her house and other debts.

Following the sale, plaintiff sent the stock certificate for 1,080 shares to a transfer agent to be split into one certificate of 500 shares and one certificate of 580 shares. In July, 1969, after a series of rejections of the stock certificate by several transfer agents, the plaintiff discovered that it had purchased shares of the unlisted Colorado corporation and not the shares of the Santa Fe International Corpora-

tion of California. The plaintiff notified the defendant of the mistake in July, 1969, and requested a refund of the $17,851.30. Defendant refused to refund the money and plaintiff then commenced this litigation. No fraud or deceit was alleged by either party in the complaint or answer and at trial the parties stipulated that neither fraud nor deceit was present in this litigation.

The trial court awarded judgment to the plaintiff based upon mutual mistake and unjust enrichment. . . . Defendant subsequently filed a motion for a new trial, which was overruled. . . .

. . . Defendant claims the trial court erred in overruling the motion for a new trial because the judgment was against the weight of the evidence. The basis of this contention is that the plaintiff was in a better position to discover the identity of the stock sold and its failure to do so was the sole cause of the payment by mistake to the defendant.

The position of the plaintiff as a stock brokerage firm does not operate to render it solely responsible for a mistake of fact as to the identity of stock to be sold. Even though the mistaken belief by the defendant was innocently induced by the plaintiff, a refund of the amount paid is not barred. . . .

The record is clear that the parties were mutually mistaken as to the identity of defendant's stock when sold. The mutual mistake shown by the record is not modified by a showing that one party could more easily detect the mistake. . . . [T]he defendant claims . . . that a refund by the defendant is barred because she disbursed the money received in good faith to third parties before receiving notice of the mistake.

In the cases concerning the payment of money pursuant to a mistake of fact, the ultimate analysis amounts to this: A payer, even if negligent in making payment under a mistake of fact, may recover if his act has not resulted in a change in the position of the innocent payee to his detriment. . . .

In the instant case, defendant testified that she had redeemed the mortgage on her house and had none of the money paid by the plaintiff left. . . . [T]he defendant merely changed the cash into a paid mortgage and retained the value originally represented by plaintiff's mistaken payment. Since the value of the original payment was retained by the defendant, she has not detrimentally changed her position by liquidating her mortgage.

For the reason that no detrimental change of position by defendant is shown by the record, plaintiff was not barred from recovering the amount paid to the defendant by mutual mistake. . . .

Judgment affirmed.

Shurtleff v. Giller
527 S.W.2d 214 (Tex.) 1975

McDONALD, J. . . . Plaintiff sued defendant on a promissory note dated June 1, 1973, in the amount of $67,136, bearing 9% interest, and payable September 30, 1973. . . .

Defendant answered that he executed the note under duress applied by plaintiff, and but for such duress he never would have executed same.

Trial was to the court without a jury, which rendered judgment plaintiff take nothing. . . . (The trial court filed the following conclusion of law):

Giller executed the note as a result of duress applied by Shurtleff. As a result of such duress, such transaction represented by said note is void and unenforceable, and Giller is not indebted to Shurtleff on the note. . . .

Plaintiff was defendant's superior in the Thorsen Tool Company. Plaintiff and defendant formed a joint venture aside from their duties with Thorsen to construct apartment houses. Plaintiff and defendant signed a note at a bank for $170,000 to get funds for the project. The note was paid down to $60,000 by the project. Plaintiff and defendant dissolved the joint venture, and agreed that all assets of the venture be transferred to defendant and defendant be liable for all indebtedness. Thereafter the bank called on plaintiff to pay the $60,000 due on the $170,000 note plaintiff and defendant had signed. Plaintiff paid such note, and thereafter asked defendant to sign the note here sued on. Defendant testified plaintiff told him that his employment at Thorsen would be terminated unless he signed the note. Plaintiff denied the foregoing. Defendant knew of his covenant not to compete with his employer after termination of employment, and plaintiff knew of the hospitalization of defendant's daughter.

Duress is a question of fact and is the threat to do some act which the party threatening has no legal right to do. Such threat must be of such character as to destroy the free agency of the party to whom it is directed. It must overcome his will and cause him to do that which he would not otherwise do, and which he was not legally bound to do. The restraint caused by such threat must be imminent, and must be such that the person to whom it is directed has no present means of protection.

Plaintiff could have sued defendant on the termination agreement for $60,000 plaintiff paid to the bank, but instead chose to have defendant sign a note. The note is for more than $60,000 and bears 9% interest. Plaintiff did not have the right to threaten to terminate defendant's employment if he did not sign the note.

We think the evidence as a whole is ample and sufficient to establish that plaintiff did threaten to terminate defendant's employment if defendant did not sign the note, that duress has been established, and that the findings and judgment are not against the great weight and preponderance of the evidence.

Affirmed.

CHAPTER 10
REVIEW QUESTIONS AND PROBLEMS

1. X, a minor, bought a car from Y for the purchase price of $750. X paid $600 down on the car. The car, while being operated by X, was involved in a wreck. Its value after the wreck was $50. X now sues to recover $600 from Y. What result? Why?

2. A purchased an automobile from B for $2,000. At the time of purchase, A signed a statement certifying that he was an adult, although he was actually a minor. A few days after the purchase, A seeks to recover his down payment upon return of the car. Does his misrepresentation of age prevent him from disaffirming the contract? Why?

3. X, a 15-year-old boy, was injured in an automobile accident. He received emergency treatment to try to save his life but died shortly afterward. X's estate refuses to pay the hospital expenses on the grounds that X was a minor. Is the estate liable? Why?

4. A purchased a tract of land from B in the belief that it contained 100 acres. After the purchase, A learned that the tract contained only 70 acres. B originally purchased the tract as 100 acres and had no intention of defrauding A. Can A rescind the contract? Why?

5. X, a representative for a data-processing company, negotiated with Y, a salesman for a computer company, to buy a computer. Y falsely assured X that the computer would be adequate for his purposes. X was aware of the specifications of the machine. X purchased the computer and discovered that the printout was too slow for his company's needs. He now seeks to rescind the contract on the basis of fraud. What result? Why?

6. X, an infant, signed a contract with Y employment agency, agreeing to pay a fee if X was able to secure employment through Y's efforts. X obtained a job but refused to pay the $295 fee on the ground that he is a minor. Can Y recover the fee? Why?

7. B purchased a residential lot from S. Subsequently, B learned that the lot had been "filled." The existence of the fill was not mentioned during the negotiations, nor was any inquiry made by B. B sues to rescind the contract. Should he succeed? Why?

8. B, a minor, bought a truck from a used-car dealer and gave a promissory note in payment. The note was transferred to the bank. B made three payments on the note after reaching majority and then attempted to disaffirm his obligation. Can he disaffirm? Why?

9. After making a visual inspection, B purchased property from S and then proceeded with his plans to build a home. The project, however, came to a halt when the possibility of soil slippage became apparent. B sued S to rescind the sale. A soil expert testified that the lot was not suitable for the construction of a residence. S was not aware of the stability hazard of the soil when the sale was transacted. Can B rescind the contract? Why?

10. X borrowed money from the bank and signed a security document as collateral. When the money was not paid on the due date, the bank told X that it would enforce its rights under the security agreement unless a renewal note giving additional collateral was signed. A refusal by X would cause him to default and put the bank in a position to foreclose on his stock in trade, thus putting him out of business. X agreed to the renewal note but was unable to meet the payments on any of the agreements. When sued by the bank, X claimed that the renewal note was voidable due to duress. Is X correct? Why?

11. B purchased a used car from S. The bill of sale showed the car to be a 1972 Oldsmobile when in fact it was a 1971 Oldsmobile. S was aware of the true model year of the car. B brings suit for damages for fraud. Should B succeed? Why?

12. A purchased a bicycle from B. A and B are both minors. A wants to rescind the contract and regain his money. B will not return the money. Is an infant contract with another infant voidable? Why?

11

Illegal Contracts

1. Introduction

An additional requirement for a valid contract is that it have a lawful purpose or object. Contracts that do not have a lawful object are illegal and therefore unenforceable. As a general rule, the status of an illegal contract is that a court will not allow litigation involving it. This means that if the illegal contract is executory, neither party may enforce performance by the other. If it is executed, the court will not order rescission—it will not allow recovery of what was given in performance. An illegal contract cannot be ratified by either party, and the parties can do nothing to make it enforceable. Stated simply, in an illegal-contract situation, the court literally "leaves the parties where it finds them." A party to an illegal contract cannot recover damages for breach of such contract. If one party has performed, he cannot, generally, recover either the value of his performance or any property or goods transferred to the other. As a result of the rule, one wrongdoer may be enriched at the expense of the other wrongdoer, but the courts will not intercede to rectify this because the purpose is to deter illegal bargains.

There are three basic exceptions to the rule that precludes the granting of any relief to a party to an illegal contract. First, if a person falls in the category of those for whose protection the contract was made illegal, he may obtain restitution of what he has paid or parted with or may even obtain enforcement. For example, both federal and state statutes require that a corporation follow certain procedures before securities (stocks and bonds) may be offered for sale to the public. It is illegal to sell such securities without having complied with the legal requirements. Nevertheless, a purchaser is allowed to obtain a refund of the purchase price if he desires to do so. The act of one party (the seller) is more illegal than that of the other party (the buyer). Many statutes are designed to protect one party in an illegal transaction, and when this is the case, the protected is allowed a legal remedy.

A second exception applies when a person is induced by fraud or duress to enter into an illegal agreement. In such cases, the courts do not regard the defrauded or coerced party as being an actual participant in the wrong, and will, therefore, allow restitution of what he has rendered by way of performance. It has been suggested that the same result would obtain if the party were induced by strong economic pressure to enter into an illegal agreement.

Third, there is a doctrine called *locus poenitentiae* that may provide the remedy of restitution to one who has become a party to an illegal contract. Literally, the phrase means "a place for repentance"; by extension, "an opportunity for changing one's mind." As applied to an illegal contract, it means that within very strict limits, a person who repents before actually having performed any illegal part of the contract may rescind it and obtain restitution of his part performance. Thus, wagers are illegal transactions except under certain circumstances. Suppose that A and B wager on the outcome of an election, and each places $100 with C, the stakeholder, who agrees to turn $200 over to the winner. Prior to the election, either A or B could recover his $100 from C by legal action, since the execution of the illegal agreement would not yet have occurred. Actually, the loser could obtain a judgment against C if he gives notice of his demand prior to the time that the stake has been turned over to the winner.

2. Contracts Against Public Policy

A contract or provision of a contract may be declared to be illegal if it is specifically prohibited by statute, contravenes the rule of the common law, or is contrary to public policy. It may be illegal in either its formation or its performance. It is axiomatic that a contract that violates a statute or an ordinance is illegal and void. A contract provision is contrary to public policy if it is injurious to the interests of the public, contravenes some established interest of society, violates the policy or purpose of some statute, or tends to interfere with the public health, safety, morals, or general welfare.[1] Although all agreements are subject to the paramount power of the sovereign and to the judicial power to declare contracts illegal, contracts are not to be lightly set aside on the grounds of public policy, and doubts will usually be resolved in favor of legality.

The term *public policy* is vague and variable and changes as our social,

[1] *Laos* v. *Soble,* page 190.

economic, and political climates change. As society becomes more complex, courts turn more and more to statutory enactments in search of current public policy. A court's own concept of right and wrong, as well as its total philosophy, will frequently come into play in answering complex questions of public policy. Cases involving public policy are often in conflict from jurisdiction to jurisdiction. The economic interests of a state may play a major role in the development of public policy. As the law on illegal contracts is studied, care should be taken to ascertain the reason behind each rule or decision, and the major emphasis should be on indicated trends in the law. It should be kept in mind that matters of illegality will be discussed throughout the text.

3. Violations of License Requirements

A contract that calls for the performance of an act or the rendering of a service may be illegal for one of two reasons. The act or service itself may be illegal, and thus any contract involving this act or service is illegal. For example, prostitution is an illegal activity in most states, and contracts to engage in prostitution are illegal per se in such states. Other personal service contracts are not illegal per se but may be illegal if the party performing or contracting to perform the service is not legally entitled to do so. This refers to the fact that a license is required before a person is entitled to perform certain functions for others. For example, doctors, dentists, pharmacists, architects, lawyers, surveyors, real estate brokers, and others rendering specialized professional services must be licensed by the appropriate body before entering into contracts with the general public.

As a general rule, if the service that is rendered requires a license, the party receiving the benefit of the service can successfully refuse to pay for the service on the ground the contract is illegal because the plaintiff has no license.[2] This is true even if the person is licensed in another jurisdiction but not the one in which the services were rendered. For example, a real estate broker licensed in one state cannot perform services in another state, and if he does so, he cannot collect for the services.

The practice of law by unauthorized persons is a significant problem. A person who practices law without a license is not only denied the right to a fee but is also subject to criminal prosecution in many states, and such activity may also be enjoined. Since the practice of law primarily entails the giving of advice, difficult questions are presented when advice is given by business specialists such as certified public accountants, insurance brokers, bankers, and real estate brokers. Although the line between permissible and impermissible activities of these business specialists is often difficult to draw, it is clear that some of the activities and services that may be performed by the various business specialists do constitute the unauthorized practice of law.

[2] *Markus & Nocka* v. *Julian Goodrich Architects, Inc.*, page 191.

For example, the preparation of a real estate contract of sale by a real estate broker is illegal in most states. Business specialists should be aware that the giving of legal advice and the preparing of legal documents by one not licensed to practice law is illegal. A major danger in doing so is the loss of the right to compensation.

ILLEGALITY BASED ON UNEQUAL BARGAINING POWER

4. Introduction

Many contracts are entered into between parties with unequal bargaining power. In the early law, this factor was generally immaterial. The doctrine of *caveat emptor* was applied, and contracts were enforced according to their terms in the absence of a ground for rescission such as fraud.

Today, the basic philosophy of the law has changed substantially. Courts frequently step in on the side of a party with limited bargaining power and declare provisions to be illegal that would not be agreed to if the bargaining power were equal. Many statutes require such a result also. This is especially true when one of the parties is a consumer or a debtor. Today, when the subject matter of a contract involves items of everyday necessity, courts frequently hold that the party with the superior bargaining power is restricted in what contractual provisions it can enforce. The sections that follow illustrate this trend of the law.

5. Contracts of Adhesion

The term *contract of adhesion* was developed in the French civil law. It has been widely used in international law, and in recent years has become important in our law of contracts. An adhesion contract is a standardized contract entirely prepared by one party. As a result of the disparity or inequality of bargaining power between the draftsman and the second party, the terms are submitted on a take-it-or-leave-it basis. The standardized provisions are such that they are merely "adhered to," with little choice as a practical matter on the part of the "adherer." If the terms are viewed as unsatisfactory, the party cannot obtain the desired product or service. The weaker party in need of the goods or services is usually not in a position to shop around for better terms, either because the author of the standard contract has a monopoly or because all the competitors use the same clause. The opportunity for bargaining and changing terms is usually nonexistent.

Contracts of adhesion are strictly construed against the party drafting them. Such contracts are given special scrutiny by courts to ensure that their terms are not unconscionable. Courts frequently refuse to enforce many of the more onerous or burdensome clauses in contracts of adhesion. They typically find that such clauses are unconscionable. Employment contracts, insurance policies, and leases are frequently held to be contracts of adhesion. In one recent case, a clause in a hospital's admission form providing that any malpractice claim against the hospital would be submitted to arbitration was held to be a contract of adhesion. As such, the court required that for such a clause to be legal, the hospital must call the provision to the attention of the patient, explain it to him, and give the patient an explanation of all available options. Failure to do so made the provision in the admission form ineffective.

Whether the terms of an adhesion contract will be upheld is often analyzed under the doctrine of unconscionability. This is discussed later in this chapter, as Section 8. Unconscionability is a principle of prevention of unfair surprise and oppression, and courts have used that principle as standard for review of adhesion contracts.

6. Contracts Disclaiming Liability

A party to a contract frequently includes a clause that provides that the party has no tort liability even if at fault. Such a clause is commonly called an *exculpatory clause.* These disclaimers of liability are not favored by the law and are strictly construed against the party relying on them. They are frequently declared to be illegal by courts as contrary to public policy.[3] Some states have by statute declared these clauses, in certain types of contracts such as leases, to be illegal and void.

The reasoning behind these statutes and judicial decisions is clear. Absolute freedom of contract exists in a barter situation because of the equal bargaining position of the parties. At the other extreme are the contracts with public utilities, in which there is no equality of bargaining power between the parties because of the existence of a virtual monopoly. The law therefore denies freedom of contract in the monopoly situation. The difficulty is that many contracts involve parties and circumstances that fall between these extremes. Many contracts are entered into between parties with substantially unequal bargaining power. When the subject matter of the contracts involves items of everyday necessity, courts frequently hold that one of the parties is a quasi-public institution and that such institutions are not entitled to complete freedom of contract because freedom of contract is not in the public interest. Thus, contracts or parts of the contracts of such institutions may be held illegal whenever the quasi-public institution has taken advantage of its superior bargaining power and drawn a contract, or included a provision in a contract, that in the eyes of the court excessively favors the quasi-public institution to the detriment of the other party and the public. This is especially true when the contract provision is an exculpatory clause.

---

[3] *Hy-Grade Oil Co.* v. *New Jersey Bank,* page 191.

7. Tickets Disclaiming Liability

Tickets purchased for entrance into places of amusement, as evidence of a contract for transportation, or for a service such as repair or parking a car often contain provisions that attempt to limit or to define the rights of the holder of the ticket. It is generally held that the printed matter on the ticket is a part of an offer that is accepted by the holder of the ticket *if he is aware* of the printed matter even though he does not read it. There are some cases in which the purchaser is presumed to know about the printed matter even though his attention is not called to it at the time the ticket is delivered.

If a ticket is received merely as evidence of ownership and is to be presented later as a means of identification, the provisions on the ticket are not a part of the contract unless the recipient is aware of them or his attention is specifically directed to them at the time the ticket is accepted. Tickets given at checkrooms or repair shops are usually received as a means of identifying the article to be returned rather than as setting forth the terms of a contract. Thus, the fine print on such tickets is usually not a part of the offer and acceptance unless communicated.

However, many terms on tickets may be illegal and will not be enforced in any event. The terms are illegal when public policy, as previously noted, would declare such a provision in a formal contract to be illegal. The equality of the bargaining power of the parties and the nature of the product or service are major factors to be considered in determining legality.

It is also noted that printed material on the back of contract forms, and occasionally on letterheads, is not generally considered part of any contract set forth on such a form or letterhead unless specific reference is made to it in the body of the contract. The law does not favor secret contract provisions.

8. Unconscionable Bargains

People are generally entitled to contract on their own terms without the paternalistic interference of courts. It is not the function of courts to relieve a party from the effects of a bad bargain. The law permits unreasonable contracts, or ones that lead to hardship for one of the parties. However, if a contract is so unconscionable in its effect on one party that no decent, fair-minded person would view the ensuing result without being possessed of a profound sense of injustice, *courts of equity* will deny the use of their good offices in the enforcement of such unconscionability. An unconscionable bargain or contract has been defined as ". . . one which no man in his senses, not under delusion, would make, on the one hand, and which no fair and honest man would accept, on the other." [4]

The Code has a special provision in Article 2—Sales—which provides that if a court as a matter of law finds a contract or any clause of it to have been

---

[4] *Willie* v. *Southwestern Bell Telephone Company*, page 193.

unconscionable at the time it was made, the court may refuse to enforce the contract or unconscionable clause, or it may so limit the application of an unconscionable clause as to avoid any unconscionable result (2-302). Although the Code does not define the term *unconscionable,* the Official Comments include the following:

> The basic test is whether, in the light of the general commercial background and the commercial needs of the particular trade or case, the clauses involved are so one-sided as to be unconscionable under the circumstances existing at the time of the making of the contract. The principle is one of the prevention of oppression and unfair surprise . . . and not of disturbance of allocation of risks because of superior bargaining power. [Official Comment, 2-302]

When parties with unequal bargaining positions enter into contracts, and especially adhesion contracts, that presumably would have been different were the bargaining power equal, courts often declare the contract or a portion of it illegal as against public policy. In doing so, they often use the Uniform Commercial Code provision on unconscionable contracts even though it is technically not applicable because the contract does not involve personal property.

AGREEMENTS IN RESTRAINT OF TRADE

9. Introduction

Several federal laws declare that agreements in restraint of trade are illegal. These laws are discussed in Chapter 39 with other aspects of government regulation of business. In the meantime, it should be recognized that price-fixing and other agreements that tend to eliminate competition are generally illegal. For example, an agreement among lawyers that they would not represent each other's clients for five years is illegal. However, some agreements, such as those between a franchiser and its franchisees, are usually found to be legal. They are legal because their effect on competition is minimal compared with the interests of the franchiser in having similarity in all of its franchised operations. Thus, certain exclusive dealing contracts are legal.

Another form of agreement that may be legal even though it is in partial restraint of trade is an agreement not to compete. An agreement by one person not to compete with another is frequently contained in a contract for the sale of a going business. The seller by such a provision agrees not to compete with the buyer. Agreements not to compete are also commonly found in contracts creating a business or a professional practice. Each partner or shareholder in the closely held corporation agrees not to compete with the firm or practice should he leave the business or professional activity. In addition, as a part of their employment contract, many employees agree that they will not compete with their employer upon termination of their employment.

10. Agreements Not to Compete—General Principles

Agreements not to compete must be a part of another contract. A bare agreement by one party not to compete with another is against public policy. For example, if A threatens to open a business to compete with B, and B offers A $1,000 to agree that he will not do so, such a contract would be illegal.

However, an agreement that is reasonably necessary for the protection of a purchaser, the remaining members of a business, or an employer will be enforced provided the agreement (1) is reasonable in point of time, (2) is reasonable in the area of restraint, (3) is necessary to protect goodwill, or some other legitimate business interest of the covenantee, (4) does not place an undue burden on the convenantor, and (5) does not violate the public interest.[5] Each agreement is examined by the court to see if it is reasonable to both parties and to the general public. Such factors as uniqueness of product, patents, trade secrets, type of service, employee's contact with customers, and other goodwill factors are significant in the reasonableness issue. In the employment situation, whether or not the public is being deprived of the person's skill, and so forth, are factors.

The law will look with more favor on these contracts if they involve the sale of a business interest than it will in the case of such a provision included in an employment contract. In fact, an agreement not to compete may even be presumed in the case of a sale of business and its goodwill, and the seller must not thereafter directly or by circular solicit business from his old customers, although he may advertise generally. The reason courts are more likely to hold the agreements between a buyer and seller or partners valid as contrasted with employer-employee contracts is that in these situations, there is more equality of bargaining power than in the latter. A seller or a former partner could readily refuse to sign an agreement not to compete, whereas an employee seeking a job might feel obliged to sign almost anything in order to gain employment. An employment contract may actually be a contract of adhesion. In addition, it is evident that there is a goodwill factor involved in the sale of almost any going business and that goodwill as an asset deserves protection; whereas in employee-employer situations, it is less evident that the employee is able to create goodwill or take it with him upon termination of his employment.

A few states have by statute or by their constitutions declared agreements

---

[5] *Frederick* v. *Professional Bldg. Main. Indus., Inc.,* page 195.

to restrict an employee's right to seek other employment to be illegal as a matter of public policy. In most states, if the restrictive covenant is unreasonable, it is illegal and the court leaves the parties where it finds them. In other words, the party who agreed not to compete is allowed to do so. However, if the restriction exceeds what is reasonably necessary, a few courts will reform the contract so as to make the restrictions reasonable.

What course of action should the employer follow in those instances in which an employee who had signed a restrictive covenant does nevertheless either compete directly or go to work for a competitor? The employer not desiring the publicity and the inconvenience of a lawsuit may refrain from taking action in the hope that the former employee's new activities will not adversely affect his business. He may ultimately find that the employee's competition is creating an adverse effect and at that time decide to institute suit or action against his former employee. If suit is instituted to enjoin the employee from this competitive activity, the employee may contend that by failing to raise the issue promptly when the breach occurred, the employer has waived his rights. The point may be a good one, since an employer should not allow his former employee to expend money or otherwise materially alter his position by establishing a business or going to work for another firm and then seek to prevent his action by attempting to enforce the contract. The doctrines of estoppel and waiver can thus frequently be used by an employee to prevent the use in equity of the contract rights to which the employer would otherwise have been entitled. Equity does not favor a party who "sleeps on his rights," and the failure to promptly seek enforcement of the agreement may very well preclude its enforcement.

11. Restrictive Covenants—Real Estate Transactions

A situation comparable to that of the employee's agreement not to compete is that of a restrictive provision in a contract for the sale or lease of property. The owner of land may wish to prevent the use of this land for any purpose that would be competitive with his own business. Suppose that A owns an entire block, one-half of which is occupied by his appliance store. He may lease the other half of the property to B with a stipulation that B will not operate an appliance store on the land. As long as the vendor or lessor does not desire to have competition on property that he controls, he may avoid such competition by contract. Since other property in the community may be used for competitive purposes, the agreement is binding, although it does to some extent restrain trade. However, if the restriction is a part of a scheme to create a monopoly or is deemed by the Federal Trade Commission to be an unfair method of competition, the contract may be illegal. This is likely to occur where the lessor is a large and dominant corporation seeking to limit competition.

USURY

12. Introduction

Usury is taking or recovering directly or indirectly a greater rate of interest than is allowed by law for the use or loan of money. The law relating to usury varies greatly from state to state. There are usually criminal penalties in addition to the contract sanctions imposed on usurious agreements.

In most states, the civil penalty for usury is a denial of the right to collect any interest. A few states impose an additional penalty. For example, one state allows the debtor to collect double the interest paid or to collect an amount equal to the interest allegedly due if it is unpaid. A few states prohibit the creditor from collecting the principal as well as the interest. This serves as an additional deterrent to usury.

Usury is usually a defense when a creditor sues to collect a debt. Sometimes, however, a debtor who has paid a creditor and later learns that the loan was usurious sues to recover the interest paid. A few jurisdictions do not allow such suits. The law in these states prohibits a lender from collecting usurious interest, but once it is collected, the matter is closed.

Difficult issues often arise as to what actually constitutes interest. Creditors develop ingenious schemes to charge more than the maximum legal rate of interest. For example, if a creditor requires a debtor to maintain a compensating bank balance on which no interest is paid, such a transaction is usurious. The adjustment of the principal balance for the rate of inflation is in effect charging interest and is usury.[6] The calculation of interest on the basis of 360 days was held to be illegal where the computation produced in a single year more interest than would be produced by applying the maximum legal rate to a calendar year of 365 days.

A lender, in addition to the highest rate of interest, may charge the borrower reasonable fees for services rendered in connection with the loan, or require reimbursement of expenses incurred, such as the examination of title, recordation of papers, and perhaps traveling expenses and other similar expenses. However, such charges must be limited to specific services rendered and expenses incurred, and may not be made a device through which additional interest or profit on the loan may be exacted. A lender may not charge to a borrower the ordinary overhead expenses of his business. In determining which expense items are actually interest, courts look to substances and not to form. A lender cannot make unreasonable charges in addition to lawful interest. In addition, a lender is not entitled to charge interest on interest unless a statute specifically allows it.

[6] *Aztec Prop.* v. *Union Planters Nat. Bank,* page 196.

13. Exceptions

The law against usury is generally not violated if the seller has a cash price different from his credit price. However, a seller cannot disguise interest by calling it something else. If the buyer is charged for making a loan, it is interest regardless of the terminology used.

The laws in usury are not violated in most states by collection of the legal maximum interest in advance or by adding a service fee that is no larger than reasonably necessary to cover the incidental costs of making the loan. It is also allowable for a seller to add a finance or carrying charge on long-term credit transactions in addition to the maximum interest rate. Many of these exceptions are created by statute. Other statutes allow special lenders such as pawnshops, small-loan companies, or credit unions to charge in excess of the otherwise legal limit. In fact, the exceptions to the maximum interest rate in most states far exceed the situations in which the general rule is applicable. The laws relating to usury were designed to protect debtors from excessive interest; this goal has been thwarted by these exceptions so that only modest protection is actually available.

The purchase of a note at a discount greater than the maximum interest is not usurious, unless the maker of the note is the person who is discounting it. Thus if A, who is in need of funds, sells to B a $500 note made by C payable in six months for $100, the sale is not usurious, although the gain to B could be very large. A note is considered the same as any other personal property and may be sold for whatever it will bring upon the market.

As long as one lends the money of others, he may charge a commission in addition to the maximum rate. A commission may not be legally charged when one is lending his own funds, even though he has to borrow the money with which to make the loan and expects to sell the paper shortly thereafter.

Interest rates have increased substantially over the past few years. As a result, most states have raised the legal maximum to 10 or 12 percent. Additional statutory exceptions to the general law have also been created. Perhaps the most common relatively new exception concerns loans to a business. Today, in most states, there is no maximum legal rate of interest when the borrower is a business, whether or not it is incorporated. Some states limit this exception to a fixed sum, such as $10,000, but little protection is afforded by such laws. Historically, loans to corporations were exempt in most states, and the extension of this exemption to all business loans is a recognition of the demands of the money market. If an individual guarantees the loan of a corporation, the fact that the interest rate exceeds the legal limit for an individual is no defense. The law applicable to the corporation is also applicable to the guarantor.

Another new trend in the law of usury is that federal laws supersede state laws with regard to federally guaranteed loans, such as FHA mortgage loans. As a result, interest on such loans can exceed the maximum allowed by the states, and there are legal techniques such as "points" and discounts that would otherwise violate state laws relating to interest.

ILLEGAL CONTRACTS CASES

Laos v. Soble
503 P.2d 978 (Ariz.) 1972

HOWARD, J. . . . This is an appeal from a judgment in favor of defendants in a lawsuit to recover from them a fee purportedly due and owing to the plaintiff.

The plaintiff's claim was predicated upon the following document, written in longhand and signed by attorney Soble:

7–24–70

Paul Laos

Your fee is 1500.00 for appraisal fees for 200,000 or below & 2500.00 for anything over $200,000.

Joseph H. Soble

The case was tried to the court, both Laos and Soble testifying as to the circumstances which gave rise to this writing. The trial court, in ruling in defendants' favor, apparently believed Sobel's version, i.e., that the agreed-upon compensation was for Laos' services as an appraisal witness in an impending condemnation trial. Since, according to him, he did not avail himself of such services, the obligation to pay Laos did not arise.

On appeal, Laos, contends that the document upon which he relied reflects that he was entitled to judgment as a matter of law. We believe that the document reflects the contrary —that, as a matter of public policy, the contract is illegal and therefore void. Although illegality was neither asserted in the trial court nor on appeal, we have a duty to raise such questions *sua sponte* when the face of the record reflects illegality.

An agreement to pay a witness a fee contingent on the success of the litigation is against public policy and void.

Professor Corbin points out that the use of "expert" testimony has been subject to grave abuses and that bargains for obtaining same should be under close supervision by the court. A similar concern was expressed in *Belfonte v. Miller:*

. . . The difficulties and dangers which surround so-called expert testimony are well understood by the profession and it is the manifest duty of our courts to carefully scan all special contracts relating to the employment of experts, providing for the payment of special compensation in addition to the witness fees allowed by the law. . . . The rule applied to such contracts is not to be affected by proof that the behavior of the parties was in fact exemplary, for it is the tendency of such contracts which serves to generate their undesirability. Improper conduct or bias can be predicted easily when the compensation of the witness is directly related to the absolute amount of an award which may in turn be dependent to a great degree on the testimony of that same witness. . . .

We are of the opinion, and so hold, that a contract providing for compensation of a witness contingent on the success of the litigation is subversive of public justice for the reason that his evidence may be improperly influenced. Public policy considerations brand such contract illegal.

Although the trial court's denial of plaintiff's claim was correct, but for a different reason, *we affirm.*

Markus & Nocka v. Julian Goodrich Architects, Inc.
250 A.2d 739 (Vt.) 1969

BARNEY, J. . . . The defendant was the principal architect on a project involving an addition to the DeGoesbriand Hospital in Burlington, Vermont. The hospital directed the defendant to engage the services of the plaintiff firm as consulting architects. The plaintiff is a Massachusetts architectural firm specializing in hospital design. The arrangement was accomplished and evidenced in an exchange of letters between the parties. The project with which the plaintiff was connected involved the development of an outpatient department, emergency department, laboratory and x-ray departments. The duties of the plaintiff included a study of the medical needs to be incorporated into the addition, inspection of the premises, consultation with hospital staff, preparation of construction and equipment estimates, detail drawings of specialized rooms, participation in revision of preliminary sketches, and provision of specifications for cost and bid purposes. The plaintiff's staff made numerous trips to Burlington, consulting with hospital personnel and medical staff, and prepared plans and detailed drawings. As the matter finally wound up, the design recommendations of the plaintiff were not accepted by the hospital staff, and the new expansion was finally put out to bid and constructed on the basis of plans and working drawings of the defendant. The compensation of the plaintiff was to be 1 percent of construction cost plus travel expenses, and this 1 percent figure was the basis of the judgment in favor of the plaintiff awarded below.

It is unquestioned that these activities were carried on in connection with construction to be undertaken within Vermont. The facts show that the plans and sketches were developed on the basis of information obtained from visits to the Vermont site and consultation with the Vermont hospital personnel. Indeed, the acts evidencing performance under the contract, sufficient at law or not, have no other relevance than to this Vermont project on its Vermont site. Thus they are within the ambit of the Vermont architectural registration statute. . . .

Architectural contracts entered into in violation of such registration statutes are held to be illegal, and the provisions for payment of commissions under them are unenforceable. The underlying policy is one of protecting the citizens of the state from untrained, unqualified, and unauthorized practitioners. It has been applied to many professions and special occupations for similar protective purposes. . . .

26 V.S.A. § 121 specifically mentions consultation as one of the activities proscribed for one not registered. This is not to say that any kind of consultation between architects of different states can be contractually valid only with registration. It does mean that when the nonresident architect presumes to consult, advise, and service, in some direct measure, a Vermont client relative to Vermont construction, he is putting himself within the scope of the Vermont architectural registration law. Nothing in that law suggests that the services must be somehow repetitive to be prohibited. No basis for excusing this plaintiff from its express provisions appears here. . . .

Judgment reversed and judgment for the defendants to recover their costs.

Hy-Grade Oil Co. v. New Jersey Bank
350 A.2d 279 (N.J.) 1975

Plaintiff, a customer of the defendant bank, brought suit against the bank when it refused to credit his account with funds allegedly deposited in a night depository box. The plaintiff had signed an agreement with the bank covering such losses. Based upon this agreement, the lower court dismissed plaintiff's complaint.

BISHOFF, J. . . . The resolution of this appeal requires us to determine whether a clause in a "night depository agreement" between a bank and a customer, providing that "the use of the night depository facilities shall be at the sole risk of the customer," is valid and enforceable. . . .

Where they do not adversely affect the public interest, exculpatory clauses in private agreements are generally sustained.

It is clear that where a party to the agreement is under a public duty entailing the exercise of care he may not relieve himself of liability for negligence and unequal bargaining power or the existence of a public interest may call for the rejection of such clauses.

Turning to the factual situation before us, it involves the relationship between a national bank and a depositor. We have held that a "bank has been entrusted with an important franchise to serve the public and has, from time to time, received broad legislative protection."

The Uniform Commercial Code, "Bank Deposits and Collections," contains many provisions protecting banks in their daily operations. We find it significant that the Legislature provided in the same statute, that a bank may not, by agreement, disclaim responsibility for "its own lack of good faith or failure to exercise ordinary care" in the discharge of the duty imposed upon it by that statute.

A review of the cases in other states considering the validity of similar exculpatory clauses in night depository contracts indicates that the majority rule is to give full force and effect to the clauses.

The basic theory underlying these and other similar cases is that the absence of an agent of the bank when the night depository facilities are used creates the possibility of dishonest claims being presented by customers. In New Jersey we have rejected such a thesis in other situations and have held that the possibility of fraudulent or collusive litigation does not justify immunity from liability for negligence.

Other courts have refused to recognize the validity of such clauses. In holding such a clause inimical to the public interest, a [Pennsylvania] court said:

> We find the public need for professional and competent banking services too great and the legitimate and justifiable reliance upon the integrity and safety of financial institutions too strong to permit a bank to contract away its liability for its failure to provide the service and protections its customers justifiably expect, that is, for its failure to exercise due care and good faith. . . .

Banks perform an important and necessary public service. It cannot be seriously argued that they are not affected with a public interest. That this is so is obvious from only a cursory examination of the extensive statutory regulations covering every phase of the banking business, including organization, merger, establishment of branches, investments, insurance of deposits, and others. . . .

We therefore hold that a bank cannot, by contract, exculpate itself from liability of responsibility for negligence in the performance of its functions as they concern the night depository service.

We should not be understood as implying that a bank and a customer may not, by negotiation and agreement, determine the standards by which the responsibility of the bank is to be governed so long as those standards are not unreasonable. The burden of proof of a violation of such a standard and proximate causation would remain on the depositor. However, an agreement such as the one now before us, which exculpates the bank from all responsibility without reference to any standard of care, we hold to be contrary to public policy and invalid.

It follows from what we have said that plaintiff's right to recover herein is based on the usual principles of negligence and proximate cause as they are applied between bailor and bailee. . . .

Reversed and rewarded.

Wille v. Southwestern Bell Telephone Company
549 P.2d 903 (Kan.) 1976

The plaintiff, an operator of a heating and air conditioning business, sued the telephone company to recover damages caused by the omission of his ad from the yellow pages of the telephone directory. The contract for the ad contained a provision limiting the liability of the telephone company to the cost of the ad. The plaintiff contended that this provision was unconscionable. The lower court found for the defendant and the plaintiff appealed.

HARMAN, J. . . . Appellant . . . asserts unconscionability of contract in two respects: the parties' unequal bargaining position and the form of the contract and the circumstances of its execution.

American courts have traditionally taken the view that competent adults may make contracts on their own terms, provided they are neither illegal nor contrary to public policy, and that in the absence of fraud, mistake or duress, a party who has fairly and voluntarily entered into such a contract is bound thereby, notwithstanding it was unwise or disadvantageous to him. Gradually, however, this principle of freedom of contract has been qualified by the courts as they were confronted by contracts so one-sided that no fairminded person would view them as just or tolerable. An early definition of unconscionability was provided by Lord Chancellor Hardwicke, in the case of *Chesterfield (Earl of) v. Janssen,* 2 Ves. Sen. 125, 28 Eng.Rep. 82 (1750):

> . . . [a contract] such as no man in his senses and not under delusion would make on the one hand, and as no honest and fair man would accept on the other; which are unequitable and unconscientious bargains; and of such even the common law has taken notice. . . .

The doctrine . . . received its greatest impetus when it was enacted as a part of the Uniform Commercial Code.

. . . The UCC neither defines the concept of unconscionability nor provides the elements or perimeters of the doctrine. Perhaps this was the real intent of the drafters of the code. To define the doctrine is to limit its application and to limit its application is to defeat its purpose.

The comment to K.S.A. 84-2-302 sheds some light on the drafters' intent. It provides in part:

> . . . The basic test is whether, in the light of the general commercial background and the commercial needs of the particular trade or case, the clauses involved are so one-sided as to be unconscionable under the circumstances existing at the time of the making of the contract. . . . The principle is one of the prevention of oppression and unfair surprise . . . and not of disturbance of allocation of risks because of superior bargaining power. . . .

One commentator has elaborated on the two types of situations which UCC is designed to deal with:

> . . . One type of situation is that involving unfair surprise: where there has actually been no assent to the terms of the contract. Contracts involving unfair surprise are similar to contracts of adhesion. Most often these contracts involve a party whose circumstances, perhaps his inexperience or ignorance, when compared with the circumstances of the other party, make his knowing assent to the fine print terms fictional. Courts have often found in these circumstances an absence of a meaningful bargain.
>
> The other situation is that involving oppression: where, although there has been actual assent, the agreement, surrounding facts, and relative bargaining positions of the parties indicate the possibility of gross overreaching on the part of either party. Oppression and economic duress in a contract seem to be inseparably linked to an inequality of bargaining

power. The economic position of the parties is such that one becomes vulnerable to a grossly unequal bargain.

Although the doctrine of unconscionability is difficult to define precisely courts have identified a number of factors or elements as aids for determining its applicability to a given set of facts. These factors include: (1) the use of printed form or boilerplate contracts drawn skillfully by the party in the strongest economic position, which establish industrywide standards offered on a take it or leave it basis to the party in a weaker economic position; (2) a significant cost-price disparity or excessive price; (3) a denial of basic rights and remedies to a buyer of consumer goods; (4) the inclusion of penalty clauses; (5) the circumstances surrounding the execution of the contract, including its commercial setting, its purpose and actual effect; (6) the hiding of clauses which are disadvantageous to one party in a mass of fine print trivia or in places which are inconspicuous to the party signing the contract; (7) phrasing clauses in language that is incomprehensible to a layman or that divert his attention from the problems raised by them or the rights given up through them; (8) an overall imbalance in the obligations and rights imposed by the bargain; (9) exploitation of the underprivileged, unsophisticated, uneducated and the illiterate; and (10) inequality of bargaining or economic power.

Important to this case is the concept of inequality of bargaining power. The UCC does not require that there be complete equality of bargaining power or that the agreement be equally beneficial to both parties. As has been pointed out:

> [The language of the comment to § 2-302 means] . . . that *mere* disparity of bargaining strength, *without more,* is not enough to make out a case of unconscionability. Just because the contract I signed was proffered to me by Almighty Monopoly Incorporated does not mean that I may subsequently argue exemption from any or all obligation: at the very

least, some element of deception or substantive unfairness must presumably be shown.

The cases seem to support the view that there must be additional factors such as deceptive bargaining conduct as well as unequal bargaining power to render the contract between the parties unconscionable. In summary, the doctrine of unconscionability is used by the courts to police the excesses of certain parties who abuse their right to contract freely. It is directed against one-sided, oppressive and unfairly surprising contracts, and not against the consequences *per se* of uneven bargaining power or even a simple old-fashioned bad bargain. . . .

. . . Williston on Contracts, 3d Ed., [states]

> People should be entitled to contract on their own terms without the indulgence of paternalism by courts in the alleviation of one side or another from the effects of a bad bargain. Also, they should be permitted to enter into contracts that actually may be unreasonable or which may lead to hardship on one side. It is only where it turns out that one side or the other is to be penalized by the enforcement of the terms of a contract so unconscionable that no decent, fairminded person would view the ensuing result without being possessed of a profound sense of injustice, that equity will deny the use of its good offices in the enforcement of such unconscionability. . . .

[The court then reviewed similar cases in other states and noted:]

> The inequality of bargaining power between the telephone company and the businessman desiring to advertise in the yellow pages of the directory is more apparent than real. It is not different from that which exists in any other case in which a potential seller is the only supplier of the particular article or service

desired. There are many other modes of advertising to which the businessman may turn if the contract offered him by the telephone company is not attractive.

We find in this record no basis for a conclusion that the application of the Limitation of Liability Clause could lead to a result so unreasonable as to shock the conscience. . . . The language of the challenged paragraph 4 is not couched in confusing terms designed to capitalize on carelessness but is clear and concise. Appellant . . . was an experienced businessman and for at least thirteen years had used the yellow pages. In his business it is reasonable to assume he as seller and

serviceman had become familiar with printed form contracts that are frequently used in connection with the sale and servicing of heating and air conditioning equipment and their attendant warranties and limitations of liability. . . . Each case of this type must necessarily rest upon its own facts but after examining the terms of the contract, the manner of its execution and the knowledge and experience of appellant we think the contract was neither inequitable nor unconscionable so as to deny its enforcement. . . .

Affirmed.

Frederick v. Professional Bldg. Main. Indus., Inc.
344 N.E.2d 299 (Ind.) 1976

GARRARD, J. . . . In 1967, appellee (PBM) employed appellant Frederick as a management trainee in PBM's contract cleaning and maintenance business. In 1972, Frederick resigned. When he then sought to engage in the contract maintenance business on a part time basis, PBM brought this action to enforce a covenant against competition. The trial court enjoined Frederick, and he appeals. The issue is whether the covenant given by Frederick is enforceable. It reads as follows:

> James Frederick . . . hereby covenants . . . that we will not engage in contract building maintenance business, including, but not limited to, janitorial services, window cleaning, floor cleaning, commercial or residential cleaning, either as a sole proprietor, partner, or agent or employee of a corporation or other business organization in the following localities:
>
> > The counties of Lake, Porter, La Porte and St. Joseph in Indiana; the counties of Will and Cook, in Illinois, except Chicago; and the counties of Berrien and Van Buren in Michigan.
>
> This covenant shall extend for a period of ten years from the date of termination of the undersigned's employment. . . .

Such covenants are in restraint of trade and are not favored by the law. However, they will be enforced if they are reasonable with respect to the covenantee, the covenantor and the public interest. This determination must be made upon the basis of the facts and circumstances surrounding each case. It depends upon a consideration of the legitimate interests of the covenantee which might be protected, and the protection granted by the covenant in terms of time, space, and the types of conduct or activity prohibited.

While the burden of proving the facts and circumstances that may justify relief rests with the party seeking to enforce the covenant, the ultimate determination of whether the covenant is reasonable is a question of law for the courts.

In addition, if the covenant as written is not reasonable, the courts may not enforce a reasonable restriction under the guise of interpretation, since this would amount to the court subjecting the parties to an agreement they had not made.

In the case now before us, the evidence disclosed that Frederick was employed by PBM at a management level. Through his employment, Frederick acquired skills related to the performance of the janitorial services provided by PBM and to the technique of surveying a proposed job and computing a competitive profitable bid. However . . . the potential use by a former employee of merely the skill and ability he has acquired will not justify a restraint.

Frederick also was privy to bidding and cost analysis information which PBM considered confidential. While there was no evidence that this information was novel or unique to PBM so as to constitute a trade secret, it is apparent that it might be utilized in an effort to undercut PBM's bids to its customers. Furthermore, Frederick acquired through his employ the advantage of personal acquaintance with the representatives of PBM's customers in the area where he worked.

. . . [A] restraint [that] is larger than the necessary protection of the party for whose benefit the covenant is given is unreasonable and void. . . . The . . . reasonableness is to be determined upon the totality of the circumstances. It is the interrelation of the considerations of protectible interest, time, space, and proscribed activity that make a particular covenant reasonable or unreasonable. This is true even though in a given case the breadth of a single restriction may appear to dominate the outcome.

Here the proscribed activity was limited to furnishing *contract* maintenance services in any capacity.

The evidence disclosed that PBM conducted its operations in the eight counties enumerated in the covenant. However, it was not established that Frederick worked in all eight counties. Unfortunately no one was questioned as to precisely what counties he worked in although it was generally established that during his training period, he worked in Lake County, Indiana, and thereafter was in charge of operations in Porter County, Indiana. . . . [T]he covenant restraining him from engaging in the contract maintenance business was unreasonable in prohibiting activity in counties where he had not worked to the extent that PBM's protectible interest consisted of having provided Frederick with his acquaintance with its customers and potential customers.

No evidence was introduced bearing directly upon the reasonableness of the covenant's ten year term. Thus, our consideration of the effect of the term is limited to whatever inferences of reasonable duration we may draw from the nature of the protectible interests PBM was shown to possess.

Bringing these factors together, it appears that Frederick was to be restrained from acting not only as a proprietor but also as an employee in furnishing janitorial services by contract. The geographic area of restriction was more broad than the area in which he worked. He was not in possession of any trade secrets, but did have pricing information which in the immediate short term might enable him to undercut PBM. On this basis, he was to be restrained for ten years. Such a restraint is unreasonable, and the covenant is therefore void.

Reversed.

Aztec Prop. v. Union Planters Nat. Bank, etc.
530 S.W.2d 756 (Tenn.) 1975

BROCK, J. . . . This is an action to recover on a promissory note. The facts are stipulated.

On July 12, 1974, Aztec Properties, Inc., executed a promissory note payable to Union Planters National Bank of Memphis in exchange for a $50,000 loan. The promisor agreed to pay the promisee $50,000, "in constant United States Dollars adjusted for inflation (deflation)" with interest at ten percent per annum. The adjusted principal was to be calculated according to a formula contained in the note, to wit:

Amount of principal due shall equal the amount of original principal multiplied by the consumer price index adjustment factor. This adjustment factor shall be computed by dividing the consumer price index at maturity by the consumer price index on date of borrowing. Said consumer price index numbers shall be for the most recent month available preceding borrowing and maturity dates. This consumer price index shall be the index not seasonably adjusted for all items as reported by the United States Department of Labor.

On maturity of the note Aztec Properties repaid to the bank $50,000, with discounted interest at the rate 9.875 percent, in the amount of $419.35 (which is an effective yield of 9.96% per annum), but the borrower refused to pay the additional "indexed principal" of $500, based on the inflation adjustment formula.

Whereupon, the bank sued Aztec Properties in Chancery Court for the "indexed principal" together with interest from maturity at the rate of ten percent per annum. Both parties filed Motions for Summary Judgment, the Chancellor holding in favor of the bank. Aztec Properties now appeals to this Court alleging that the Chancellor erred in granting the bank's Motion and in denying its own.

The first issue to be resolved is whether this note is usurious, i.e., whether it charges interest in excess of the legal rate of ten percent per annum . . . 14-112. Interest includes *all* compensation for the use of money. "Any payment to the lender in addition to the rate of interest legally permissible, whether called by the name of bonus or commission or *by any other name,* is usurious." [Emphasis added.] Compensation is determined not by what the borrower pays but by what the lender receives; thus, if the borrower is the beneficiary of a pay-

ment it will not be interest. Nor are expenses incident to making a loan and furnishing the lender with satisfactory security for its repayment compensation or interest.

The note executed by Aztec Properties bears ten percent interest on its face; that interest has been paid and is not in issue here. The borrower claims that the "indexed principal" constitutes additional interest. The bank argues that the "indexed principal" equals the difference in value between the principal lent and returned, and is not extra compensation.

We have found no case holding that an intentional increase in the face value of the principal to account for inflation does not constitute interest. In practice the lender has long borne the risk of inflation in this state. The interest charged by a lender is not profit, strictly speaking, but compensation for the use of money and for bearing the risk that the borrower might not repay or the principal might depreciate in value. We accordingly hold that the "indexed principal" constitutes usurious interest. . . .

It is recognized, of course, that "indexing" is a current and very legitimate concept in modern business transactions. Nothing in this opinion should be taken to suggest that there is an impropriety in measuring future rentals by a consumer price index, or some comparable standard, in leasing agreements. Nor is there anything improper in computing future wages or salaries by such an index in collective bargaining or employment contracts. As long as there is a national currency, however, which by law is legal tender for the payment of public and private debts, we hold that the indexing device cannot properly be applied to the principal of a debt evidenced by a promissory note payable in that currency. . . .

Reversed.

CHAPTER 11
REVIEW QUESTIONS AND PROBLEMS

1. A purchased a series of different items from B, a furniture dealer, on installment plans. Each installment contract stated that in the event of default of payment on any of the items purchased, all the items purchased could be reclaimed. Is this contract enforceable? Why?

2. A brought action against B, a department store, because B was charging a 1½ percent service charge per month on his revolving charge account. The usury statutes allowed a maximum of 7½ percent per year. Is this usurious? Explain.

3. X contacted a real estate broker, Y, to find a buyer for his property. Y found a buyer and aided X in closing the deal. X found out that Y was not a licensed broker and refused to pay. Would a court of equity force X to pay Y his commission? Why?

4. X, an avid gambler, paid Y a considerable sum of money to prevent X from being prosecuted for gambling. Y had influence with the law-enforcement agencies and assured X of his safety from prosecution. X was prosecuted and now sues Y to recover his money. Will he recover? Why?

5. X sold Y a restaurant, and the contract contained a covenant restricting X from opening a similar business within the city for a period of five years. X later sued, contending that this was unreasonable. Is the covenant enforceable? Why?

6. X rented a trailer and hitch from Y Company. The trailer was improperly attached to X's car by an employee of Y; as a result, the car overturned and X was injured. Y denies liability because the rental agreement contained a clause that relieved it from any liability in case of accident. Is Y liable? Why?

7. W leased a service station from X Oil Company. X's employee was repairing the gas pump when he negligently sprayed gasoline on W; it ignited and caused injury to W. The lease provided that X Company was not liable for its negligence and that W would indemnify X for any damages or loss caused by the oil company on the leased premises. Should W be required to indemnify X? Why?

8. A contracted with B for a directional survey of A's oil and gas well. The contract prohibited B from communicating the results to anyone but A. The report indicated that A's well was slanted and that it was taking oil and gas from neighboring lands. B notified the owners of the adjoining land of the deviation, and they established in court the right to their oil and gas. A now sues B for breach of contract. Should A succeed? Why?

9. A, an experienced veterinarian with an established practice, engaged the services of an associate, B, who was also a veterinarian. The agreement provided that if B left the association, he would not practice his profession for a period of five years within a radius of 30 miles from the place where the two had their practice. The agreement was terminated, but B claims that the restrictive provision is not enforceable. Is B correct? Why?

10. S sold his plant, which manufactured window frames, to B. As part of the sales contract, S agreed to refrain from manufacturing or selling window frames within a 150-mile radius of B's plant as long as B was engaged in that business. Thereafter, S did engage in such manufacture, and B brings suit for an injunction. Should B succeed? Why?

11. E worked for X Company as a welder of precision titanium castings. Titanium is a reactive metal and difficult to weld. E became certified after 20 hours of training. E subsequently went to work for a competitor of X Company, and X sued to enforce a "noncompetition" provision of the employment agreement which provided that E would not go to work for a competitor of X within a stated period. (Assume that the area and time of the restraint are reasonable.) Should X succeed? Why?

12. A contracted to design a house for B. A represented himself as an architect but made no mention of the fact that he was not a licensed architect. B later refused to pay A, contending that A was not licensed. Is the contract enforceable?

Form of the Agreement

1. Introduction

As a general rule, an oral contract is just as valid and enforceable as a written contract. However, there are obvious advantages to written contracts over oral contracts. First, it is much easier to establish the existence and terms of a written contract, since the contract is its own proof of terms. The terms of oral agreements must be established by testimony, and the testimony is often conflicting. Second, the terms of a written contract cannot ordinarily be varied by oral evidence. This rule, known as the *parol-evidence rule,* is discussed in the next section.

By statute it is required that some contracts be evidenced by a writing before they are enforceable. These provisions are contained in legislation known as the *statute of frauds and perjuries.* This statute is based on the recognition that there is a need for written evidence of the existence of certain types of contracts because of their susceptibility to fraudulent proofs and perjured testimony. The various types of contracts covered by the statute of frauds are exceptions to the general rule on the validity of oral contracts.

A few states also have statutes that require that certain types of contracts be executed with special formalities. For example, a statute may require the parties to certain contracts to acknowledge their signatures before a notary public. Some statutes, such as those relating to wage assignments by an employee, require that a contract of assignment be on a sheet of paper that is separate from other contracts to which the assignment is related. The purpose of this type of statute is to protect a wage earner against a blanket assignment of his wages without his being fully aware of the import of his action.

A major issue that frequently arises relating to the form of the agreement involves the situation in which an oral agreement is reached with the understanding that the parties will subsequently execute and sign a formal instrument. The question is whether the informal agreement is binding until the document is prepared and signed. The mere fact that a subsequent formal writing was contemplated does not prevent the informal agreement from being enforceable if the parties have actually reached an agreement. The oral contract will be enforced unless there is clear evidence that the parties intended not to be bound until the written contract was signed and delivered. As a result, if the written contract does not accurately express the agreement, a party may refuse to sign it and may enforce the actual oral agreement. If the parties actually stipulate that there shall be no binding contract until it is reduced to writing and signed, such a stipulation is obviously a condition precedent to a binding contract.

2. The Parol-Evidence Rule

The *parol-evidence rule* prevents the introduction of oral testimony to alter or vary the terms of a written agreement. Thus, a party to a contract or other witness may not testify about matters that are in conflict with the written agreement. Everything that transpires prior to the execution of the written agreement is assumed to be integrated into it. Therefore, the written contract is the only permissible evidence of the agreement. All negotiations and oral understandings are said to have merged in the agreement.

Since the parol-evidence rule is based on the concept that all prior negotiations are integrated or merged into the written agreement, it does not prevent the use of oral evidence to establish modifications agreed upon subsequent to the execution of the written agreement or to establish cancellation of the contract by mutual agreement.

There are several other exceptions to the parol-evidence rule. These find their basis in equity, good conscience, and common sense. For example, evidence of fraudulent misrepresentation, lack of delivery of an instrument when delivery is required to give it effect, and errors in drafting or reducing the contract to writing are admissible under various exceptions to the rule. Also, oral evidence is allowed to clarify the terms of an ambiguous contract.

The Code recognizes that the parol-evidence rule prevents the use of oral evidence to contradict or vary the terms of a written memorandum or of a contract that is intended to be the final expression of the parties. However, the Code substantially reduces the impact of the rule when it provides that a written contract may be explained or supplemented by a prior course of dealing between buyer and seller, by usage of trade, or by the course of performance. It also allows evidence of consistent additional terms to be introduced unless the writing was intended to be not only complete but an exclusive statement of the terms of the agreement (2-202). The provisions allowing such evidence are designed to ascertain the true understanding of the parties as to the agreement and to place the agreement in its proper perspective. The assumption is that prior dealings between the parties and the usages of the trade were taken for granted when the contract was worded. Often a contract for sale involves repetitive performance by both parties over a period of time. The course of performance is indicative of the meaning that the parties by practical construction have given to their agreement and is relevant to its interpretation and thus is admissible evidence.

When oral evidence of a course of dealing, trade usage, or course of performance is introduced under the Code exceptions to the parol-evidence rule, the law recognizes an order of preference in the event of inconsistencies. Express terms will prevail over an interpretation based on the course of performance, and the course of performance will prevail over an interpretation predicated upon either the course of dealing or the usage of trade (2-208).

THE STATUTE OF FRAUDS

3. Introduction

The statute of frauds is of ancient English origin. It is designed to prevent fraud by excluding from the courts legal actions on certain specified contracts unless there is written evidence of the agreement signed by the defendant. The statute was enacted in order to protect people from perjured testimony in connection with contracts.

The statute in effect creates a defense to a suit for breach of contract. Except for some cases under the Code, to be discussed later, the statute may be used as a defense even though there is no factual dispute as to the existence of the contract or to its terms. A contract that requires a writing may come into existence at the time of the oral agreement, but it is not enforceable until written evidence of the agreement is available. The agreement is valid in every respect except for the lack of proper evidence of its existence. The statute creates a defense in suits for the breach of executory oral contracts if such contracts are covered by its provisions. The statute has no effect on contracts that are fully performed.

Historically and in modern times, the statute of frauds requires a writing in connection with the following contracts: (1) contracts to be liable for another person's debts; (2) contracts involving real property; (3) agreements that cannot be performed within one year from the date of making; and (4) contracts for the sale of goods when the price exceeds $500. There are also many special statute-of-frauds provisions. For example, most states require by statute that all life insurance contracts, real estate listing agreements, and promises to pay debts that have been discharged in bankruptcy be in writing. In addition, many statutes provide that any agreement required to be in writing may be modified only by a writing. Such a provision does not bar all oral modifications, but it does bar any modification of an element necessary to satisfy the statute of frauds. If the contract as orally modified would violate the statute, the statute is a defense. The sections that follow discuss the modern version of the major statute-of-frauds provisions.

4. Promise to Pay for the Debt of Another

To be unenforceable because of the statute of frauds, a promise to answer for the "debt, default, or miscarriage" of another must be a *secondary* promise. A primary promise is not within the statute and is enforceable even though oral.[1] For example, B purchases goods on credit from S. X, a friend of B, promises S that he, X, will pay if B fails to do so. X's promise comes within the statute, since it is a promise to be responsible for the debt of another. The primary liability is on B; the liability of X is *secondary*—to pay only in the event that B fails to do so.

Assume that the hypothetical facts are changed so that X says to S, "Sell and deliver goods to B, and I will pay for them." In this situation, X is exclusively assuming primary liability, and S is not extending credit to B. Hence, the oral promise by X is binding, and the statute of frauds is no defense. An original or primary promise can be distinguished from a secondary promise by analyzing the leading object or main purpose of the promisor in making the promise. When the leading object is to become a guarantor of another's debt, the promise is collateral, and it is covered by the statute. When the leading object of the promisor is to subserve interest or purpose of his own, even though it involves the debt of another, the promise is original, and it is not within the statute.

An agreement that has for its object the substitution of one debtor for another does not fall within the statute, and no writing is required. For example, assume that A says to Y, "If you will release B from his liability to you, I will assume and pay it," and Y consents. This contract, although made orally, is binding because it is a primary promise of A and is not secondary to B's promise.

When a third party agrees to become responsible for the default or debt of another because of some pecuniary advantage he may gain from the transaction, no writing is required. Thus, an oral guaranty by a *del credere* agent—a consignee who sells consigned goods on credit, but who guarantees to the consignor that the buyers will pay for the goods purchased—is enforceable. Since the agent obtains a commission for selling the merchandise, his pecuniary interest in the consignment disposes of the necessity of a writing, and if the

---

[1] *Howard, Weil, Labouisse, etc.* v. *Abercrombie,* page 210.

purchaser fails to pay, the consignor may collect from the consignee on the oral guaranty.

5. Contracts Involving Real Property

Contracts involving interests in land have always been considered important by the law; therefore, it is logical that such contracts are covered by the statute of frauds. The statute requires a writing for a contract creating or transferring any interest in land. In addition to contracts involving a sale of an entire interest, the statute is applicable to contracts involving interests for a person's lifetime, called life estates; to mortgages; to easements; and to leases for a period in excess of one year.

The statute requires a writing in contracts for real property—land and those things affixed thereto. The status as real estate of such things as standing timber, minerals, growing crops, and the like depends on the passage of title to them. The general rule is that these items are real property if the title to them is to pass to the buyer before they are severed from the land; they are personal property if title to them passes subsequently. The Code provides that a contract for the sale of timber, minerals, and the like or for a structure or its materials to be removed from realty is a contract for the sale of goods if they are to be severed by the seller (2-107). If the buyer is to sever them, the contract affects and involves land and is subject to real estate provisions of the statute of frauds. The Code also provides that a contract for the sale apart from the land of growing crops or things other than timber or minerals attached to realty and capable of severance without material harm to the land is a contract for the sale of goods, whether the subject matter is to be severed by the buyer or by the seller (2-107[2]).

As previously discussed, the statute of frauds has no effect on fully executed contracts. It is not a grounds for rescission. It serves only as a defense to a suit for breach of an executory contract. This principle creates a special problem in real estate contracts, because many oral contracts involving real estate become partially executed as a result of part payment by the buyer, or surrender of possession to the buyer by the seller, or both. Since the statute of frauds is a complete defense to an executory oral contract involving real estate and is no defense to a fully executed contract, partially executed contracts create problems for courts.

Part performance will satisfy the statute of frauds if two conditions are met in addition to clear proof of the oral agreement. First, the part performance must establish and point unmistakably and exclusively to the existence of the alleged oral agreement. Part performance eliminates the statute of frauds as a defense in such cases because it eliminates any doubt that the contract was made, and thus the reason for the defense does not exist.

Second, the part performance must be substantial enough to warrant specific performance of the oral agreement. In other words, it must be such that returning the parties to the *status quo* is not reasonably possible. To illustrate, assume that a buyer under an oral contract has paid part of the purchase price. The money can be returned and the statute of frauds would still be a defense because there is no equitable reason to enforce the oral agreement. However, when the seller under an oral contract also delivers possession to the buyer, the defense of the statute of frauds becomes more tenuous, because returning the parties to the *status quo* becomes somewhat difficult. When improvements are made by one in possession, a return to the *status quo* becomes quite difficult if not impossible.

As a general rule, part performance will eliminate the statute of frauds as a defense if the part performance is "substantial." It is clear that the part performance is substantial if the buyer has taken possession, paid all or part of the price, and made valuable improvements.[2] However, a lesser part performance may also take the contract out of the statute in many states. If the buyer takes possession and pays part of the price, there is good evidence of a contract. Payment of the price standing alone is not a basis for specific performance and will not satisfy the statute. If the buyer enters into possession and makes valuable improvements without a payment on the purchase price, there is sufficient part performance to make the contract enforceable and to satisfy the statute in many states. A few states require all three—payment, possession, and improvements—however, before the oral agreement is enforceable.

6. Contracts Not to Be Performed within One Year

A promise is within the statute if, by its terms, it cannot be carried out within one year from the time it is made. The period is measured from the time the oral contract is entered into to the time when the promised performance is to be completed. Thus, oral agreements to hire a person for two years, to form and carry on a partnership for ten years, or to grant a three-year extension on the maturity of a debt would not be enforceable.

The decisive factor in determining whether a long-term contract comes within the statute is whether performance is *possible* within a year from the date of making the contract.[3] Even though it is most unlikely or improbable that performance could be rendered within one year, the statute does not apply if there is even a remote possibility that it could. Thus, a promise to pay $10,000 "when cars are no longer polluting the air" would be enforceable even though given orally. There is a split of authority on the question of enforceability of an oral contract that extends for a period of more than a year but contains a provision allowing cancellation by one or both parties within a year. Some courts hold that such an oral contract is not enforceable, whereas

[2] *Louron Industries Inc.* v. *Holman,* page 211.
[3] *Haveg Corporation* v. *Guyer,* page 211.

the majority hold that such a contract is not within the statute because there is possibility of discharge within one year.

A question arises when one party to a bilateral contract has performed completely in less than a year, but the other party's performance is not capable of being completed within a year. Does the complete performance by one take the contract out of the statute? The majority rule is that it does. It must be borne in mind that an *executory* oral contract is not enforceable unless both parties can perform within a year.

7. Nature of the Writing

The statute of frauds does not require a formal written contract signed by both parties. All that is required is a note or memorandum that provides written evidence of the transaction. It must be signed by the party sought to be bound by the agreement (the defendant). The memorandum need contain only the names of the parties, a description of the subject matter, the price, and the general terms of the agreement. A memorandum of sale of real property must describe the real estate with such certainty that a court may order its conveyance.[4]

Under the statute, one party may be bound by an agreement even though the other party is not. Only the party who resists performance need sign. Such a result is predicated on the theory that the agreement is legal in all respects, but proper evidence of such an agreement is lacking, and this is furnished when the person sought to be charged with the contract has signed a writing.

The note or memorandum may consist of several writings, even though the writing containing the requisite terms is unsigned. However, it must appear from an examination of all the writings that the writing signed by the party to be charged was signed with the intention that it refer to the *unsigned writing*. In effect, the writings must be connected by *internal reference* in the signed memorandum to the unsigned one, so that they may be said to constitute one paper relating to the contract. If the signed memorandum makes no reference to the unsigned memorandum, they may not be read together. Parol evidence is inadmissible to connect them.

As to the signature of the party sought to be charged, it may be quite informal and need not necessarily be placed at the close of the document. It may be in the body of the writing or elsewhere, as long as it identifies the writing with the signature of the person sought to be held.

THE CODE

8. Contracts for the Sale of Goods

The Code contains several statute-of-frauds provisions that are far more liberal than the original English statute. The provision applicable to the sale

4 *Cash* v. *Maddox,* page 212.

of goods provides that, as a general rule, a contract for the sale of goods for the price of $500 or more is not enforceable unless there is some writing sufficient to indicate that a contract for sale has been made. The writing must be signed by the defendant or his authorized agent or broker (2-201).

The liberal approach of the Code is seen in the Code provision stipulating that the writing need not contain all material terms of the contract, and errors in stating a term will not affect the fact that the statute of frauds is not a defense. The writing need not indicate which party is the buyer or which is the seller, or include the price or time of payment. The only term that must appear is the quantity term, which need not be accurately stated. However, a contract is not enforceable beyond the quantity stated in the writing. Since the requirement is that it be signed by the party to be charged, it need not be signed by a plaintiff who is seeking to enforce it.

9. Exceptions

The Code also contains several exceptions to the rule requiring a writing. The first exception is limited to transactions between "merchants," and it arises from the business practice of negotiating contracts by oral communication followed by written confirmations. A merchant who contracts orally with another merchant can unilaterally satisfy the requirement by sending a writing to the other confirming the contract. This confirmation is sufficient against the party receiving it, unless written notice of objection to its contents is given within ten days after it is received. To be valid, the confirmation must be sufficient to bind the sender (2-201[2]).

For purposes of this rule, the courts of several states have held that a farmer is a merchant. These decisions are quite important in grain sales. Grain is often sold orally by a farmer to an elevator. The elevator usually sends a written confirmation. In those states holding that a farmer is a merchant, the oral contract becomes enforceable as a result of the confirmation. In those states holding that a farmer is not a merchant, the oral sale of grain is not made enforceable by the written confirmation. Of course, it may be enforceable under one of the other Code provisions.

Other exceptions are based on partial performance of the contract for the sale of goods. An oral contract is enforceable with respect to goods (1) for which payment has been made, or (2) that have been received and accepted. Either of these conditions constitutes an "unambiguous overt admission" by both parties that a contract actually exists. Thus, there is no need for a writing to establish this fact. The effect of this part performance is limited to the payment actually made or the goods actually received (2-201[3c]).

Another exception under the Code relates to specially manufactured goods. If (1) the goods are to be specially manufactured for the buyer (that is, according to the buyer's specifications) and are not suitable for sale to others, (2) the seller has either made a substantial beginning of their manufacturing or commitments for their procurement, and (3) the circumstances reasonably indicate that the goods are for the buyer, the contract is enforceable without a writing (2-201[3a]). This simply means, however, that the statute of frauds has been satisfied—the seller still must establish and prove the terms of the contract.

The final substitute for a writing is predicated upon the fact that the required writing is a formality; a contract may very well exist, but no action can be taken unless and until the necessary proof of its existence is forthcoming—the contract is simply unenforceable pending such proof. The proof may become available at a later date, and its effect will be retroactive. If the party who is resisting the contract admits its existence in the proper circumstances and surroundings, such admission will substitute for a writing. Thus, the Code provides that an oral contract is enforceable ". . . if the party against whom enforcement is sought admits in his pleading, testimony or otherwise *in court* that a contract for sale was made, but the contract is not enforceable under this provision beyond the quantity of goods admitted . . ." (2-201[3b]). This provision is particularly significant in the light of modern judicial procedures such as discovery practices. Under the statute of frauds other than the Code, a party may admit the existence of a contract in court and still rely upon the statute as a defense. If the contract involves goods, however, he will lose his defense.[5]

Since the statute is applicable only to sales where the price is $500 or more, it must be determined whether a transaction involves more than that amount. In determining whether the value of property is such as to cause it to fall within the statute, it often becomes necessary to decide how many contracts have been entered into. Thus, A orders from B $400 worth of one item to be delivered at once and $200 of another item to be delivered ten weeks later. Either item considered alone is worth less than $500; both items total over $500. If the parties intended only one contract, the statute of frauds is applicable; however, if two contracts were entered into, no writing is required. The intention of the parties in these cases is gleaned from such factors as the time and place of the agreement, the nature of the articles involved, and other circumstances.

10. Contracts for the Sale of Personal Property Other Than Goods

The Code has several additional sections that require a writing. A contract for the sale of securities such as stocks and bonds is not enforceable unless (1) there is a signed writing setting forth a stated quantity of described securities at a defined or stated price; (2) delivery of the security has been accepted or payment has been made; (3) within a reasonable time, a writing in confirmation of the sale or purchase has been sent and received, and the party receiving it has failed to object to it within ten days after receipt; or

[5] *Farmers Elevator Co. of Reserve* v. *Anderson,* page 213.

(4) the party against whom enforcement is sought admits in court that such a contract was made. Note that this relates only to contracts for the sale of securities (8-319).

Another section provides for contracts for the sale of personal property *other than* goods or securities. Here, there is a requirement of a writing if the amount involved exceeds $5,000. Included in this coverage are such things as royalty rights, patent rights, and rights under a bilateral contract (1-206).

In addition, the Code requires a signed security agreement in the article on secured transactions. This means that when a person, for example, borrows money and gives the lender an interest in his property as security, the debtor (borrower) must sign a security agreement that describes the transaction (9-203). Such a signed agreement is not required if the secured party (lender) has possession of the property. If he is not in possession, the secured party cannot enforce his security interest unless there is a signed security agreement.

11. Contracts Involving More Than One Section of the Statute of Frauds

One agreement may involve more than one provision of the statute of frauds. A contract for the sale of personal property might not be possible of full performance within a year. If the contract is unenforceable under any provision of the statute of frauds, it is entirely unenforceable. The fact that one provision of the statute of frauds is satisfied will not make it enforceable if some other provision is not satisfied. For example, a written confirmation between merchants will satisfy the Code requirement, but it would not satisfy the requirement of a writing for a contract of long duration. This problem also arises when part performance satisfies one provision but not another.

12. The Doctrine of Estoppel and the Statute of Frauds

The Code specifically incorporates the basic principles of law and equity, including the law relative to the various grounds for rescinding a contract and the principle of estoppel. This equitable concept of estoppel is sometimes used by courts to prevent a party to an oral agreement from using the statute of frauds as a defense.

The elements of proof that invoke an estoppel in such case are three; namely, (1) the oral agreement must be established by satisfactory evidence; (2) the party asserting rights under the agreement must have relied thereon and have indicated such reliance by the performance of acts unequivocally referable to the agreement; and (3) it must appear that because of his change of position in reliance on the agreement, to enforce the statute will subject such party to unconscionable hardship and loss. The term *unconscionable* is quite significant here. In most cases, there is some reliance on the oral agreement; but the doctrine of estoppel will not make it enforceable. In those unusual cases where equity and justice absolutely require it, the doctrine will be used. In such cases, the statute of frauds, if used, would constitute a fraud on the other party—the wrong that the law was adopted to prevent.

FORM OF THE AGREEMENT CASES

Howard, Weil, Labouisse, etc. v. Abercrombie
231 S.E.2d 451 (Ga.) 1976

Plaintiff, a customer of the defendant brokerage firm, sued to recover an amount which the defendant had charged against his account. The amount was due from another customer (Waters), but the plaintiff had orally agreed to "stand behind Waters' account."

The lower court held for the plaintiff and the defendant appealed.

DEEN, J. . . . While it is obvious that the brokerage firm had psychological reasons to believe that any deficit accumulated by Waters in his personal account would be covered by Abercrombie, and it is uncontested that Abercrombie had "backed" Waters by lending him money and covering his deficits, we agree with the court and jury that there was no legal obligation upon him to continue doing so. It is not contended that the oral "guaranty," if made, was for any particular amount of money. Abercrombie did back Waters in the ways stated; this did not bind him to continue making good Waters' losses. Had the defendant wanted an unconditional guaranty to this effect it should of course have had the matter committed to writing. Such a writing would doubtless state the ceiling amount of funds pledged, the time limit, and other general conditions.

A promise to answer for the debt, default, or miscarriage of another must be in writing. There are various exceptions: If the agreement of the third party guarantor is an original undertaking; that is, one furthering his own interests rather than underwriting the debt of another, it is not within the Statute of Frauds. "The promise required by this section to be in writing does not include an original undertaking whereby a new promisor, for valuable consideration, substitutes himself as party who is

to perform, and releases the original promisor." This exclusion does not apply here. There is no scintilla of evidence that the extension of credit to Waters was of benefit to Abercrombie, or that he in any way attempted to substitute himself for Waters as a potential debtor of the brokerage firm. . . . The case is most nearly controlled by *Southern Coal & Coke Co.* v. *Randall,* 141 Ga. 48, 80 S.E. 285. There the debtor company was behind in its payments for shipments of coal. It desired to enter new orders, which the creditor was unwilling to fill. The president of the debtor corporation then orally stated that if they would continue shipping "he would guarantee they were paid." The court held that the promise of future payment was collateral and not an original undertaking, thus within the Statute of Frauds, and that it mattered not whether the promisor be considered a surety or guarantor. In that case as here the promisor undertook to offer himself as a surety for the future debt of another, the other continuing to be the principal debtor. This does not meet what Professor Williston considers the true test of whether the undertaking is original rather than collateral: "If as between them the original debtor still ought to pay, the debt cannot be the promisor's own, and he is undertaking to answer for the debt of another." "When one person tells another to let a third person have goods and that he will see that the debt is paid, in order for the promisor to become bound in the absence of a writing, it is requisite that credit shall be given exclusively to the promisor." Even reliance on the oral promise will not remove it from the statute. . . .

Judgment affirmed.

Louron Industries Inc. v. Holman
502 P.2d 1216 (Wash. App.) 1972

Plaintiffs sued defendants for specific performance of an oral contract to sell land. Plaintiffs had originally leased the land from defendants and had signed a written contract of purchase. Believing that defendants had also signed the agreement, plaintiffs made substantial improvements to the land beyond those permitted by the lease. Defendants asserted the statute of frauds as a defense, but the lower court found sufficient part performance and held for plaintiffs. Defendants appealed.

EDGERTON, J. . . . Appellants . . . contend there was not a sufficient writing or part performance to take this case out of the statute of frauds. . . . [W]e disagree.

In *Miller* v. *McCamish,* 78 Wash.2d 821, 826, 479 P.2d 919, 922 (1971), the court stated:

> [T]his Court has long held that an agreement to convey an estate in real property, though required . . . to be in writing with the formal requisites specified for a deed, may be proved without a writing, given sufficient part performance; and that specific performance will be granted where the acts allegedly constituting the part performance point unmistakably and exclusively to the existence of the claimed agreement.

And in *Richardson* v. *Taylor Land & Livestock Co.,* 25 Wash.2d 518, . . . (1946), the Supreme Court pointed out what are evidences of part performance, saying:

> The principal elements or circumstances involved in determining whether there has been sufficient part performance by a purchaser of real estate under an oral contract otherwise within the statute of frauds, are (1) delivery and assumption of actual and exclusive possession of the land; (2) payment or tender of the consideration, whether in money, other property, or services; and (3) the making of permanent, substantial, and valuable improvements, referable to the contract.

In considering these factors of part performance in relation to the facts of this case, respondent's possession of the real property in and of itself would not be sufficient to take the case out of the statute of frauds because possession had been gained under the terms of the lease rather than by the contract to purchase. That possession alone would not point unequivocally to the existence of a seller-buyer relationship but would be equally consistent with the relationship of landlord and tenant. However, the payment of the $1,000 earnest money to appellants' agent, when the terms of the lease called for $65 per month rental, was consistent with the sale and pointed toward a vendor-vendee relationship and was inconsistent with continuation of the lease. Moreover, the evidence shows that respondent made very substantial permanent improvements to the real property. These were in excess of those allowed by the terms of the lease and so they, too, were consistent with a sale rather than a lease. These factors bring the case within the rule announced above and constitute sufficient evidence of part performance to take the case out of the statute of frauds. . . .

Affirmed.

Haveg Corporation v. Guyer
211 A.2d 910 (Del.) 1965

This is an action by the seller for breach of five alleged oral contracts. Plaintiff, Guyer, agreed to furnish all the requirements for cutting and sewing certain nylon phenolic tape used by defendant corporation in its business. It was agreed that the contracts were exclusive and were not to terminate until defendant had no further requirement for the services involved. Defendant defended by, among other things, stating that the alleged contracts violated the statute of frauds. Defendant moved for a summary judgment, and when the trial court denied the motion, it appealed.

HERRMANN, J. . . . The question for decision in this facet of the case is whether a contract contemplating continued performance for an indefinite period of time comes within the Statute of Frauds.

The majority rule is that an oral promise of a long-extended performance, which the agreement provides shall come to an end upon the happening of a certain condition, is not within the Statute of Frauds if the condition is one that may happen in one year. There is a minority rule to the contrary.

The Superior Court applied the majority rule and held that, since the defendant's requirements for the services to be rendered under the alleged contracts may have actually and finally terminated within a year, the Statute of Frauds does not apply.

We agree with the Superior Court's conclusion on this point. It has been the law in Delaware for many years that the Statute of Frauds does not apply to a contract which may, by any possibility, be performed within a year. In *Devalinger* v. *Maxwell* (4 Pennewill 185, 54 A. 684, 686 (1903)), this court approved the following statement of the rule:

> . . . the statute [of frauds] does not extend to an agreement which may by any

possibility be performed within a year, in accordance with the understanding and intention of the parties at the time when the agreement was entered into. And if the specific time of performance be not determined upon at the time of the making of the contract, yet, if by any possibility it may be performed within a year, the statute does not apply, and such an agreement need not be in writing. And likewise when the performance of the agreement rests upon a contingency which may happen within a year.

And in *Duchatkiewicz* v. *Golumbuski* (12 Del. Ch. 253, 111 A. 430 (1920)), the Chancellor stated:

> In this state the law is settled authoritatively that if any agreement by any possibility may, under the contract, be performed within one year it is valid notwithstanding the statute [of frauds]; or rather, unless it appear that the contract could not possibly be performed within one year from the making thereof, its enforcement is not prohibited by the statute. . . .

We approve and adhere to the rule as thus stated and restated.

Since the defendants were unable to show that the alleged contracts could not possibly be performed within a year, we affirm the conclusion of the Superior Court that the alleged agreement are not within the Statute of Frauds. . . .

Affirmed.

Cash v. Maddox
220 S.E.2d 121 (S.C.) 1975

NESS, J. . . . John and Sue Maddox allegedly contracted to sell Morris and Betty Cash 15 acres of land. The trial court held there was a binding contract and ordered specific performance. The Maddoxes, appellants, contend the memorandum of the alleged contract of sale is too vague and indefinite to

satisfy the Statute of Frauds. We agree and reverse the lower court.

Appellants and respondents are husband and wife respectively. The Cashes lived in Florida. They telephoned the Maddoxes, who live in Georgia, and discussed the purchase of 15 acres of land owned by the Maddoxes. The only written evidence of the contract is a check mailed by the Cashes for Two Hundred ($200) Dollars as part payment. Written on the check was "15 acres in Pickens, S.C., land binder, 30 days from date of check to June 3, 1970." John Maddox endorsed and cashed the check. Subsequently, the Maddoxes advised the Cashes they did not wish to sell as it would cause trouble in the family and returned the Two Hundred ($200) Dollars which the Cashes refused. There was testimony the Maddoxes owned a 76 acre tract of land in Pickens County, of which 15.6 acres was south of the Pickens-Greenville highway, outside of the city limits of the town of Pickens.

The Statute of Frauds does not require any particular form of writing. It may be satisfied entirely by a written correspondence. However, the writings must establish the essential terms of the contract without resort to parol evidence. One of the essential terms of a contract of sale of land is the identification of the land. . . . Parol evidence cannot be relied upon to supplement a vague and uncertain description. . . .

For a contract to meet the requirements of the Statute of Frauds, S.C. Code § 11-101, every essential element of the sale must be expressed therein.

The alleged contract gives no definite location or shape of the 15 acres. The writing does not indicate whether the subject matter of the contract was north or south of the road, or in another area of the county. The fact 15.6 acres of the entire tract may be south of the road is not legally sufficient to satisfy the Statute of Frauds. Parol evidence may be used to explain terms appearing in the description, but the description itself must clearly identify the particular parcel of land.

In the absence of equities removing the case from the operation of the Statute of Frauds, which do not here exist, we hold before a court will decree specific performance of a contract for a sale of land, the writing must contain the essential terms of the contract. They must be expressed with such definiteness, certainty and clarity that it may be understood without recourse to parol evidence to show the intention of the parties. The terms of the contract must be such that neither party can reasonably misunderstand them. It would be inequitable to carry a contract into effect where the court is left to ascertain the intention of the parties by mere guess and conjecture. . . .

There was not a contract between these parties as would satisfy the Statute of Frauds. The land proposed to be sold was not described or designated as would enable a court to render a decree for its conveyance. The words in the check afford no means to adequately identify the property.

The parties should be restored to their original status.

Reversed.

Farmers Elevator Co. of Reserve v. Anderson
552 P.2d 63 (Mont.) 1976

HARRISON, J. . . . This appeal is taken from a judgment entered August 25, 1975, in the district court, Sheridan County. Farmers Elevator Co. of Reserve, a cooperative enterprise, successfully sought damages for breach of a contract made with Dale Anderson, a local farmer in the Dagmar area. . . .

On October 28, 1972, Anderson contracted with the Farmers Elevator Co. for the sale of 18,000 bushels of durum wheat at a price stipulated in the record to be $1.80 per bushel. . . .

The contract was strictly oral, the only written evidence of the agreement being an unsigned notation in a small "book" used by Farmers Elevator Co. to record its purchases in the ordinary course of its business. Testimony and a confirmatory memorandum established that the approximate delivery date contemplated by the parties was February 1973.

Although the contract was oral in nature, we note Anderson has at no time denied the existence of the contract, the quantity contracted for, or the stipulated price. Farmers Elevator Co. normally contracts orally with its patrons and pays by check upon delivery, whether in full or partial satisfaction of its purchase contracts.

Pursuant to his contract, Anderson delivered 8,802 bushels of durum wheat in approximately 36 truckloads between March 27, 1973, and May 30, 1973. . . .

On September 27, 1973, the Board Chairman learned by telephone of Anderson's refusal to deliver further on his contract. The next day plaintiff was forced to cover for the undelivered wheat, and purchased 9,198 bushels at the then current market price, which by that time had risen to $6.50 per bushel. It was established at trial that Anderson sold his wheat to another elevator in North Dakota for $5.35 per bushel. Anderson raised and harvested more wheat in August and September 1973, but he never tendered any of this to plaintiff or made any further effort to honor his contract with it.

Is enforcement of the oral agreement . . . barred by the Statute of Frauds?

In a commercial setting such as here, Montana law provides that no contract for the sale of goods, for the price of $500 or more, is enforceable unless some writing exists sufficient to establish that an agreement between the parties was reached. However, several exceptions are listed in the statute; one is:

> A contract which does not satisfy the requirements of subsection (1) but which is valid in other respects is enforceable. . . . (b) if the party against whom enforcement is sought admits in his pleading, testimony or otherwise in court that a contract for sale was made but the contract is not enforceable under this provision beyond the quantity of goods admitted. . . .

That the agreement, but for the lack of writing, is "valid in other respects" is not contested by the parties. There can be no doubt of Anderson's admissions, in his deposition and at trial, as to the existence of the contract. At trial he testified:

> Q. So your testimony is that there was an agreement for you to sell eighteen thousand bushels of durum? A. Yes.
>
> Q. And that agreement was made in October, October 28th, of 1972, is that correct? A. Yes.

The so-called "judicial admission" exception to the Statute of Frauds . . . prevents a litigant from simultaneously admitting the existence of a contract and claiming the benefits of the statute. . . .

Affirmed.

CHAPTER 12
REVIEW QUESTIONS AND PROBLEMS

1. X went to work for Y and was assured by Z that if Y did not pay X's salary, then Z would. After 2½ years, Y stopped paying X his salary. X sued Y and Z, but Z raised the defense that he was not liable because of the statute of frauds. What result? Why?

2. X orally sold his house to Y. Y made a down payment, sold his old residence, moved to the house, and made substantial improvements thereon. Is X's contract enforceable? Explain.

3. X replied to a newspaper advertisement of an employment agency for a job. X orally agreed with Y, the client, to a two-year contract to work in Venezuela. X was discharged before two years and sued Y for damages. Y asserted the statute of frauds. X contended the newspaper advertisement served as a sufficient memorandum. What result? Why?

4. A entered into an oral contract with B for the purchase of a house trailer for $3,000. B later refused to sell the house trailer, and A sued for breach of contract. Does B have a defense? Explain.

5. A was given the exclusive right to haul goods for B for one year, commencing when A moved into Y's house. A breached the contract and pleaded the statute of frauds as a defense against the enforcement of the contract. Is this a valid defense? Explain.

6. X sold food and other supplies on credit to a restaurant. The restaurant was late in paying its bills, so X contacted Y, who had some financial interest in the corporation that operated the restaurant. Y orally promised to be responsible for the payment for supplies delivered to the restaurant. When sued by X, Y asserted the statute of frauds as a defense. Should X collect? Why?

7. B had a written option to purchase 1.862 acres of land out of a 10-acre tract owned by S. The exact piece of property covered by the option was not specified. When B tried to exercise his option, S refused to sell. B sues for specific performance, and S pleads the statute of frauds as a defense. Who wins? Why?

8. B purchased a mobile home from S. The written contract disclaimed any warranty obligation of S. B experienced problems with the mobile home and brought suit, contending that S orally promised that if problems did arise with the trailer, he would "take care of them." S claims that this oral evidence is inadmissible in court. Is S correct? Why?

9. X and Y had an oral agreement by which X would buy corn on the market and thereafter Y would buy it from X at his cost plus 4 cents per bushel. X purchased a substantial amount of corn and then Y refused to honor the agreement, even though he had made a prepayment to X of $27,882. When sued, Y pleaded the statute of frauds as a defense. Will the statute of frauds bar enforcement of the contract? Why?

10. F, a farmer, entered into an oral contract with G, operator of a grain elevator, for the sale of soybeans for future delivery. Five days later, in confirmation of the oral agreement, G sent F a written contract for his signature. F, however, did not sign or acknowledge the instrument and later refused to deliver the soybeans. When sued, F claimed that he is not liable for breach of contract because the agreement was not in writing. At the trial it was determined that F had been farming for 34 years, had 150 acres in soybeans, and had sold his crops to grain elevators in "cash sales" and "future contracts" for at least five years. Is F liable? Why?

11. X Company hired E as a sales representative. To safeguard its list of customers, X Company entered into an oral contract with E whereby E would be employed for one year and E upon termination of employment would not compete in the same capacity in a similar business for two years.

Five months later E resigned and began work for a competitor of X Company as a sales representative. X sued E for damages and to enjoin E's employment with the competitor. Should X Company succeed? Why?

12. S orally agreed to sell land to B. B then paid $150 for a title search and preparation of a mortgage deed and $2,860 for a preliminary survey and design of a subdivision on the land. S subsequently refused to sell the land, and B brought suit for specific performance. Is the contract enforceable? Why?

13. A entered into a written agreement to sell B certain property on an installment contract. When B failed to make payments on time they entered into a new written agreement, with B orally promising to pay interest on late payments. B was late in making payments and paid the interest, but later sued to recover the interest payments. Can he recover? Explain.

14. X wanted to lease a building from Y. Y sent X a letter promising that after completion of alterations, he would lease X the building. Rent was to be determined at a later date. After completion of alterations, Y refused to rent the building to X, and X sued for breach of contract. Y used the statute of frauds as a defense, but X contended that the letter served as a written contract to satisfy the statute of frauds. Who is correct?

Rights of Third Parties

1. Introduction

The discussion up to this point has dealt with the law of contracts as applied to the contracting parties. Frequently, persons who are not parties may have rights and even duties under the contract. There are two basic situations in which the rights and duties of third parties (persons not involved in the original contract) may come into play: (1) when there is an *assignment* of the contract—a party to a contract (assignor) transfers to a third party (assignee) his rights under the contract; or (2) when there is a *third-party beneficiary* contract—one in which a party contracts with another party for the purpose of conferring a benefit upon a third party (beneficiary). In both these situations, the primary question is whether the third party—assignee or beneficiary—can enforce the contract.

ASSIGNMENTS

2. Terminology and Requirements

A bilateral contract creates *rights* for each party and imposes on each corresponding *duties*. With respect to the duties, each is an obligor (has an obligation to perform); likewise as to rights, each is an obligee (is entitled to receive the performance of the other). Either party may desire to transfer to another his rights or both his rights and his duties. A party *assigns* rights and *delegates* duties. The term *assignment* may mean a transfer of one's rights under a contract, or it may mean a transfer of both the rights and the duties. The person making the transfer is called the *assignor,* and the one receiving the transfer is called the *assignee.*

A person who has duties under a contract cannot relieve himself of those duties by transferring the contract or delegating the duties to another person. An obligor that delegates duties as well as assigning rights is not thereby relieved of liability for proper performance if the assignee fails to perform. An assignor continues to be responsible for the ultimate performance.

No particular formality is essential to an assignment. Consideration, although usually present, is not required. As a general proposition, an assignment may be either oral or written, although it is of course desirable to have a written assignment. Some statutes require a writing in certain assignment situations. For example, an assignment of an interest in real property must be in writing in most states.

3.   Consent—Generally

The rights under most contracts may be assigned if both parties to the agreement are willing to let this be done. Public policy prevents the assignment of some contract rights, however. For example, many states by statute prohibit or severely limit the assignment of wages under an employment contract. In addition, rights created by the law, such as the right to collect for personal injuries, cannot be assigned in most states.

As a general rule, contract rights may be assigned by one party without the consent of the other party. In most contracts, it is immaterial to the party performing who receives the performance. A party has no right to object to most assignments.

There are certain exceptions to these general rules. Some contracts cannot be assigned without consent of the other party. Of the several classes of contracts that may not be transferred without the consent of the other party, the most important are contracts involving personal rights or personal duties. A personal right or duty is one in which personal trust and confidences are involved, or one in which skill, knowledge, or experience of one of the parties is important. In such cases, the personal acts and qualities of one or both of the parties form a material and integral part of the contract. For example, a lease contract where the rent is a percentage of sales is based on the ability of the lessee and would be unassignable without the consent of the lessor. Likewise, an exclusive agency contract would be unassignable.[1]

Some duties that might appear to be personal in nature are not considered so by the courts. For example, unless the contract provides to the contrary,

---

[1] *Wetherell Bros. Co.* v. *United States Steel Co.,* page 225.

a building contractor may delegate responsibility for certain portions of the structure to a subcontractor without consent. Since construction is usually to be done according to specifications, the agreement is assignable. It is presumed that all contractors are able to follow specifications. Of course, the assignee must substantially complete the building according to the plans and specifications. The obligator will not be obligated to pay for it if it is not, and the assignor will be liable in event of default by the assignee.

Another example of a contract that is unassignable without consent is one in which an assignment would place an additional burden or risk upon a party —one not contemplated at the time of the agreement. Such appears to be true of an assignment of the right to purchase merchandise on credit. Most states hold that one who has agreed to purchase goods on credit, and has been given the right to do so, may not assign his right to purchase the goods to a third party (assignee), since the latter's credit may not be as good as that of the original contracting party—the assignor.

This reasoning is questionable because the seller could hold both the assignor and the assignee responsible. However, the inconvenience to the seller in connection with collecting has influenced most courts to this result. But in contracts where the seller has security for payment such as retention of title to the goods, a mortgage on the goods, or a security interest in the goods, the seller has such substantial protection that the courts have held that the right to purchase on credit is assignable.

4. Consent under the Code

The Code contains provisions that generally approve the assignment of rights and delegation of duties by buyers and sellers of goods. The duties of either party may be delegated *unless* the parties have agreed otherwise or the non-delegating party has ". . . a substantial interest in having his original promisor perform or control the acts required by the contract" (2-210[1]). Accordingly, a seller can ordinarily delegate to someone else the duty to perform the seller's obligations under the contract. This would occur when no substantial reason exists why the delegated performance would be less satisfactory than the personal performance of the assignor.

The Code does provide that rights cannot be assigned where the assignment would materially change the duty of the other party, or increase materially the burden or risk imposed on him by his contract, or impair materially his chance of obtaining return performance (2-210[2]). These Code provisions in effect incorporate the personal rights and duties exception previously discussed.

5. Contracts Prohibiting Assignment

Some contracts contain a provision that they are not assignable without consent. Clauses purporting to restrict the power to assign an otherwise assignable contract are ineffective unless the restriction is phrased in express, precise language. Courts usually enforce such a provision, even though it has the effect of restraining transfer of property.[2] Many courts allow an assignment in violation of an agreement. These courts consider the assignment to be a breach of contract for which dollar damages become due. However, many courts in effect specifically enforce the agreement against assignment by holding that an obligor who refuses to perform for the objectionable assignee has no liability. The breach of the clauses prohibiting the assignment is in effect an excuse for breach of contract.

Under the Code, a provision prohibiting assignment only prohibits the delegation of duties; it does not prohibit the assignment of rights (2-210[3]). In addition, a prohibition against the assignment of a contract does not prevent the assignment of a claim for damages for breach of a contract, nor does it prevent assignment of the right to receive money payments that are due or to become due under the contract (2-210[2]).

6. Claims for Money

As a general rule, claims for money, due or to become due under existing contracts, may be assigned. For example, an automobile dealer may assign to a bank the right to receive money due under contracts for the sale of automobiles on installment contracts. Likewise, an employee may assign a portion of his wages to a creditor in order to obtain credit or to satisfy an obligation. There is a trend in the law toward greatly reducing or eliminating the right of employees to assign wages. For example, the Uniform Consumer Credit Code adopted in several states provides that a seller cannot take an assignment of earnings for payment of a debt arising out of a consumer credit sale. Lenders are not allowed to take an assignment of earnings for payment of a debt arising out of a consumer loan. The Consumer Credit Code is a part of the trend toward greater consumer and debtor protection.

When a claim for money is assigned, an issue that frequently arises is the liability of the assignor in case the assignee is unable to collect from the debtor-obligor. If the assignee takes the assignment merely as *security* for a debt owing from the assignor to the assignee, it is clear that, if the assigned claim is not collected, the assignor will still have to pay the debt to the assignee. On the other hand, an assignee that has purchased a claim against a third party from the assignor generally has no recourse against the assignor upon default by the debtor-obligor. However, if the claim is *invalid* for some reason or if the claim is sold expressly "with recourse," the assignor would be required to reimburse the assignee if the debtor-obligor did not pay.

In all cases, an assignor *warrants* that the claim he assigns is a valid legal claim that the debtor-obligor is legally obligated to pay and that there are no valid defenses to the assigned claim. If this warranty is breached—that is, if

---

[2] *Hanigan* v. *Wheeler,* page 227.

there are valid defenses or the claim is otherwise invalid—the assignee has recourse against the assignor.

7. Rights of the Assignee

An assignment is more than a mere authorization or request to the person who owes the money or other duty to pay or to perform for the assignee rather than the assignor. The obligor-debtor *must* pay or perform for the assignee, who now in effect owns the rights under the contract. If there is a valid assignment, the assignee owns the rights and is entitled to receive them. Performance for the original party will not discharge the contract. Unless the contract provides otherwise, the assignee receives the identical rights of the assignor. Since the rights of the assignee are neither better nor worse than those of the assignor, any defense that the third party (obligor) has against the assignor is available against the assignee.[3] For example, part payment, fraud, duress, or incapacity can be used as a defense by the third party (obligor) if an action is brought against him by the assignee, just as the same defense could have been asserted against the assignor had he been the plaintiff. A common expression defining the status of the assignee is that he "stands in the shoes" of the assignor.

Some contracts contain a provision to the effect that "if the seller assigns the contract to a finance company or bank, the buyer agrees that he will not assert against such assignee any defense that he has against the seller-assignor." This clause is an attempt to give the contract a quality usually described as negotiability. Although the concept of negotiability will be discussed in detail in Chapters 19–21, it should be recognized here that if a negotiable instrument is properly negotiated to a party described as a holder in due course, then personal defenses of the original party cannot be asserted against the holder in due course. The purpose of the concept of negotiability is to encourage the free flow of commercial paper. Adding a provision to a contract that gives it the same effect obviously places the assignee in a favored position and makes contracts with such clauses quite marketable.

As a part of the growing movement toward greater consumer protection, the Federal Trade Commission has ruled that such clauses cutting off defenses when a contract is assigned constitute an unfair method of competition, and they are therefore illegal. The commission has also prohibited the use of the holder-in-due-course concept against consumers. This 1976 action by the Federal Trade Commission will be discussed further in Chapter 21.

8. Duties of the Parties

As previously noted, an assignor is not relieved of his obligations by a delegation of them to the assignee. The assignor is still liable if the assignee fails to

[3] *Hudson Supply & Equipment Company* v. *Home Factors Corp.,* page 228.

perform as agreed, in which case the assignor would have a cause of action against the assignee. If a party upon the transfer of a contract to a third person wishes to be released of liability, a legal arrangement known as a novation is required. The requirements for a valid novation are discussed in Chapter 15.

The liability of the assignee to third persons is a much more complicated issue. The liability of the assignee is determined by a careful examination of the transactions to see whether it is an assignment of only the rights under the agreement or whether the duty has also been delegated. This is often difficult to determine when the language used refers only to an "assignment of the contract."

As a general rule, the *mere assignment* of a contract calling for the performance of affirmative duties by the assignor, with nothing more, does not impose those duties upon the assignee. However, there is a decided trend in such cases to hold that an assignment of an entire contract carries an implied assumption of the liabilities. When the assignee undertakes and agrees to perform the duties as a condition precedent to enforcement of the rights, or has assumed the obligation to perform as part of the contract of assignment, he has liability for failure to perform. To illustrate: If a tenant assigns a lease, the assignee is not liable for future rents if he vacates the property prior to expiration of the period of the lease, unless he expressly assumes the burdens of the lease at the time of the assignment. He is obligated simply to pay the rent for the period of his actual occupancy. To the extent that an assignee accepts the benefits of a contract, he becomes obligated to perform the duties that are related to such benefits.

If an "entire contract" has been assigned—that is, if duties have been delegated to the assignee as well as the assignment of the rights—a failure by the assignee to render the required performance gives rise to a cause of action in favor of the third party (obligee). The obligee can elect to sue either the assignor or the assignee.

Under the Code, an assignment of "the contract" or of "all my rights under the contract" or an assignment in similar general terms is an assignment of rights, and unless the language or the circumstances (as in an assignment for security) indicate the contrary, it is also a delegation of performance of the duties of the assignor and an assumption of these duties by the assignee. Its acceptance by the assignee constitutes a promise by him to perform these duties. This promise is enforceable by either the assignor or the other party to the original contract (2-210[4]).

When the assignor delegates his duties, although the assignor remains liable, the obligee may feel insecure as to the ability of the assignee to perform the delegated duties. The obligee may demand that the assignor furnish him with adequate assurance that the assignee will in fact render proper performance (2-210[5]).

9. Notice

Immediately after the assignment, the assignee should notify the third party, obligor, or debtor, of his newly acquired right. This notification is essential for two reasons:

1.   In the absence of any notice of the assignment, the third party is at liberty to perform—pay the debt or do whatever else the contract demands— for the original contracting party, the assignor. In fact, he would have no knowledge of the right of anyone else to require performance or payment. Thus, the right of the assignee to demand performance can be defeated by his failure to give this notice. The assignor who receives performance under such circumstances becomes a trustee of funds or property received from the obligor, and can be compelled to turn them over to the assignee. As soon as notice of the assignment is given to him, the third party *must perform* for the assignee, and his payment or performance to the assignor would not relieve him of his obligation to the assignee.

2.   The notice of assignment is also for the protection of innocent third parties. The assignor has the *power,* although not the *right,* to make a second assignment of the same subject matter. If notice of the assignment has been given to the obligor, it has much the same effect as the recording of a mortgage. It furnishes protection for a party who may later consider taking an assignment of the same right. A person considering an assignment should, therefore, always confirm that the right has not previously been assigned by communicating with the debtor. If the debtor has not been notified of a previous assignment, and if the assignee is aware of none, the latter can, in many states, feel free to take the assignment. He should immediately give notice to the debtor. In other words, the first assignee to give notice to the debtor, provided such assignee has no knowledge of a prior assignment, will prevail over a prior assignee in most states.[4]

In some other states, it is held that the first party to receive an assignment has a prior claim, regardless of which one gave notice first. In these states, the courts act on the theory that the assignor has parted with all his interest by virtue of the original assignment and has nothing left to transfer to the second assignee. In all states, however, the party who is injured by reason of the second assignment has a cause of action against the assignor to recover the damages he has sustained—the assignor has committed a wrongful and dishonest act by making a double assignment.

[4] *Boulevard Nat. Bank of Miami* v. *Air Metals Industry,* page 229.

CONTRACTS FOR BENEFIT OF THIRD PARTIES

10. Nature of Such Contracts

Contracts are often made for the express purpose of benefitting some third party. Such contracts, called *third-party beneficiary contracts,* are of two types—*donee-beneficiary* and *creditor-beneficiary.* Both types of third-party beneficiary contracts are entitled to enforce a contract made in their behalf because the promisee has provided that the performance shall go to the beneficiary rather than to himself.

If the promise was purchased by the promisee in order to make a gift to the third party, such party is a donee-beneficiary. The most typical example of such an agreement is the contract for life insurance in which the beneficiary is someone other than the insured. The insured has made a contract with the life insurance company for the purpose of conferring a benefit upon a third party; namely, the beneficiary named on the policy.

If the promisee has contracted for a promise to pay a debt that he owes to a third party, such third party is a creditor-beneficiary—the debtor has arranged to pay the debt by purchasing the promise of the other contracting party to satisfy his obligation. The promisee obtains a benefit because his obligation to the creditor will presumably be satisfied. To illustrate: A operates a department store. He sells his furniture, fixtures, and inventory to B, who, as part of the bargain, agrees to pay all of A's business debts. A's purpose for making this contract was to have his debts paid, and he obtained B's promise to pay them in order to confer a benefit on his creditors. A's creditors are creditor-beneficiaries and can enforce their claims directly against B. Of course, to the extent that B does not pay them, the creditors still have recourse against A.

11. Legal Requirements

A third-party beneficiary is not entitled to enforce a contract unless he can establish that the parties actually intended to benefit the third party, who must be something more than a mere incidental beneficiary. The intent to benefit the third party must clearly appear from the terms of the contract. The intent is more easily inferred in creditor-beneficiary situations than in donee-beneficiary ones. The third party need not be named as an individual in the contract if he can show that he is a member of a group for whose direct benefit the contract was made.[5] A third-party beneficiary need not have had knowledge of the contract at the time it was made. The fact that the actual contracting party could also sue to enforce the agreement will not bar a suit by the beneficiary if he was intended to directly benefit from the contract. A third-party beneficiary need not be the exclusive beneficiary of the promise.

If the benefit to the third party is only incidental, the beneficiary cannot sue.

[5] *Howell* v. *Worth James Const. Co.,* page 231.

Contracts of guaranty assuring the owner of property that contractors performing construction contracts for him will properly complete the project and pay all bills have been held in many states to benefit the materialmen and laborers. A few states have held otherwise, indicating their belief that the agreement was made primarily to protect the owner and benefits others only incidentally.

In most states, a contract made for the express purpose of benefitting a third party may not be rescinded without the consent of the beneficiary after its terms have been accepted by the beneficiary. The latter has a vested interest in the agreement from the moment it is made and accepted. For example, an insurance company has no right to change the named beneficiary in a life insurance policy without the consent of the beneficiary, unless the contract gives the insured the right to make this change. Until the third-party beneficiary has either accepted or acted upon provisions of a contract for his benefit, the parties to the contract may abrogate the provisions for the third party's benefit and divest him of the benefits that would otherwise have accrued to him under contract. Minors, however, are presumed to accept a favorable contract upon its execution, and such contract may not be changed so as to deprive the minor of its benefits.

One who seeks to take advantage of a contract made for his benefit takes it subject to all legal defenses arising out of contract. Thus, if the obligee has not performed or satisfied the conditions precedent to the other party's obligation, the third party would be denied recovery.

RIGHTS OF THIRD PARTIES CASES

Wetherell Bros. Co. v. United States Steel Co.
105 F.Supp. 81 (1952)

Wetherell Bros. Co., a Massachusetts corporation, had held a contract since 1930 with defendant whereby it had the exclusive right in the New England states to sell cold, rolled steel strips on a 5 percent commission and stainless steel products on a 7 percent commission. The contract was to run indefinitely except as it might be terminated by two years' notice. On March 1, 1950, the Massachusetts corporation liquidated and ceased to function but sold some assets to Penn Seaboard Iron Co., a Pennsylvania corporation, and so far as possible sought to assign to the latter its right to represent United States Steel Co. in New England. The

Pennsylvania corporation changed its name to Wetherell Bros. Co. but refrained from giving notice of the assignment to defendant. Learning of the new arrangement, however, defendant notified the parties of the immediate termination of the sales relationship. Plaintiff, the Pennsylvania corporation, brings suit for breach of contract.

McCARTHY, J. . . . The plaintiff seeks to hold the defendant liable because of its action in terminating the contract between it (defendant) and Wetherell-Massachusetts. Since admittedly no contract was ever entered into between the plaintiff and the defendant, the question of law is whether the duties of Wetherell-Massachusetts under the contract could be effectively assigned to plaintiff without the consent of the defendant. The conclusion is inescapable: The assignment to the plaintiff of the duties of Wetherell-Massachusetts under its sales agency contract without the consent of the defendant was ineffective for the purpose of substituting the plaintiff for the "assignor" corporation with whom the defendant contracted.

This was a contract for a sales agency within a particular geographical area, an exclusive agency in that only the principal could compete with Wetherell-Massachusetts in obtaining customers for the defendant's products.

"In a contract for a sales agency the personal performance of the agent is practically always a condition precedent to the duty of the principal and employer. The performance of the agent's duty cannot be delegated to a substitute. The assignee of the agent's right must fail, therefore, in his attempt to enforce it if he merely tenders a substituted performance." IV Corbin, Contracts (1951), § 865, p. 444.

. . . The claim has been made also that it is only in a technical sense that these two companies could be called distinct entities. They had the same capital stock and practically the same stockholders, officers, and agents; the Maine company had taken over all the assets and assumed all the liabilities of the other, and was carrying on the same business, at the same stand, in the same manner, and under the same management. The master has found that for practical purposes the two companies were the same. Accordingly, the plaintiff claims that an agreement with the one is the same as an agreement with the other, that the defendant's ignorance of their separate identity was immaterial, that the agreement may be treated as made with either company indifferently, was capable of enforcement by either or at least by the Maine company, and is valid in the hands and for the benefit of the plaintiff. But we cannot assent to this reasoning. These are two distinct corporations, created by the laws of two different states. The powers of each corporation are limited and controlled by the statutes of the state which created it, and it is scarcely conceivable that the statutes of the two states are the same or that the franchises and powers of the two corporations are identical. But if this were so, it would remain true that they are the creation of two different governments, the offspring of different parents, and not only distinct legal entities, but having separate and distinct existences. . . .

The contract in this case is one requiring a relationship of particular trust and confidence, and such a contract cannot be assigned effectively without the consent of the other party to the contract. The grant of an exclusive agency to sell one's goods presupposes a reliance upon and confidence in the agent by the principal, even though the agent be what is frequently called a large "impersonal" corporation. It is apparent that the principal in this case must have relied upon the "legal equation" represented by the corporation which it chose as its sole sales representative in a large area; otherwise, the surrender of the right to grant additional agencies is illogical.

The plaintiff has argued that the fact that the assignment is made from one corporation to another alters the rule of nonassignability of the agent's duties under the contract. . . .

The plaintiff was not only technically but substantially a different entity from its predecessor. It is true that in dealing with corporations a party cannot rely on what may be termed the human equation in the company. The personnel of the stockholders and officers of the company may entirely change. But though there is no personal or human equation in the management of a corporation, there is a legal equation which may be of the utmost importance to parties contracting with it. In dealing with natural persons in matters of trust and confidence, personal character is or may be a dominant factor. In similar transactions with a corporation, a substitute for personal character is the charter rights of the corporation, the limits placed on its power, especially to incur debt, the statutory liability of its officers and stockholders. These are matters of great importance when, as at present, many states and territories seem to have entered into the keenest competition in granting charters; each seeking to outbid the other by offering to directors and stockholders the greatest immunity from liability at the lowest cash price. . . .

Judgment must be entered for the defendant.

Hanigan v. Wheeler
504 P.2d 972 (Ariz.) 1972

In August 1962, Hanigan entered into a "Dairy Queen Store Agreement" with LeMoine. The agreement provided that "Second Party shall not assign or transfer this Agreement without the written approval of First Party." On March 7, 1972, LeMoine entered into a contract to sell the Dairy Queen franchise and all its assets to Wheeler. Hanigan refused to approve the sale because he felt that the price ($90,000) was too high and that an inflated sales price was detrimental to the Dairy Queen business. Hanigan also stated that Wheeler was too inexperienced in business and too young to run the business properly. Plaintiff Wheeler then sued Hanigan for a declaratory judgment that the contract provision disallowing the assignment of the franchise was unenforceable as against public policy. The trial court found for plaintiff, and defendant appealed.

HOWARD, J. . . . The primary question dispositive of this appeal is whether the trial court erred in determining that the contract provision precluding the franchise transfer without the area franchise holder's approval is unenforceable as against public policy. A review of the record and the relevant law leads us to answer this question in the affirmative. Given the instant fact situation, the law in this area does not warrant the trial court's order requiring Hanigan to consent to the subject transaction:

As a general rule, a contract is not assignable where the nature or terms of the contract make it nonassignable, unless such provision is waived. . . . The parties may in terms, by a provision in the contract, prohibit an assignment thereof. . . .

Provisions in bilateral contracts which forbid or restrict assignment of the contract without the consent of the obligor have generally been upheld as valid and enforceable when called into question, although the meaning of such terms becomes a matter of interpretation. . . . 6 Am.Jur.2d Assignments § 22 (1963).

These general statements are in accord with the Restatement of the Law of Contracts § 151, which reads as follows:

A right may be the subject of effective assignment unless . . . (c) the assignment is prohibited by the contract creating the right.

The treatises on this subject are likewise in accord.

A leading case, *Allhusen* v. *Caristo Construction Corporation,* 303 N.Y. 446, stated the law as follows:

. . . we think it is reasonably clear that, while the courts have striven to uphold freedom of assignability, they have not failed to recognize the concept of freedom to contract. In large measure they agree that, where appropriate language is used, assignments of money due under contracts may be prohibited. When "clear language" is used, and the "plainest words . . . have been chosen," parties may "limit the freedom of alienation of rights and prohibit the assignment."

Such a holding is not violative of public policy. Professor Williston, in his treatise on Contracts, states (Vol. 2 § 422,

p. 1214): "The question of the free alienation of property does not seem to be involved."

In opposition to the above principles, appellees contend that more than a contract right is involved in the case at bench in that the subject clause restricting assignment without Hanigan's approval serves as an unreasonable and unlawful restraint on the right of alienation of property, since the Store Agreement provides no guidelines by which the area franchise holder is to base his approval or disapproval of potential buyers, and that hypothetically, through the whim or arbitrariness of the holder, the LeMoines could be prevented from ever selling their franchise and the property associated with the franchise.

We accept the fundamental principle that one of the primary incidents inherent in the ownership of property is the right of alienation or disposition. However, this right is not limitless. The right to make an assignment of property can be defeated where there is a clear stipulation to that effect. The current state of the law in this area appears to be that a restraint on the alienation of property may be sustained when the restraint is reasonably de-signed to attain or encourage accepted social or economic ends. . . .

We also perceive that despite the restriction on assignment of the store agreement, the LeMoines are not entirely powerless. Where a contract contains a *promise* to refrain from assigning, an assignment which violates it would not be ineffective. "The promise creates a *duty* in the promisor not to assign. It does not deprive the assignor of the *power* to assign and its breach, therefore, would simply subject the promisor to an action for damages while the assignment would be effective. . . .

In summary, we hold that the law as set forth above demonstrates that the contract limitation against assignment of the Store Agreement without the approval of the area franchise holder is proper and valid. The trial court erred in concluding that the provision limiting assignability was unenforceable as against public policy. The court also erred in ruling that defendants had a duty to consent to the franchise sale, for this is contrary to the manifested intention of the parties to the contract. The general proposition is that "a covenantor is not to be held beyond his undertaking and he may make that as narrow as he likes." . . .

Reversed and remanded.

Hudson Supply & Equipment Company v. Home Factors Corp.
210 A.2d 837 (D.C.) 1965

Plaintiff, Home Factors Corp., was the assignee of two accounts receivable for brick sold to defendant by the Eastern Brick & Tile Co., Inc. The accounts were not paid and plaintiff brought action. Defendant admitted that it had purchased the tile on open account but claimed that Eastern was indebted to it for an amount in excess of the assigned account receivable. Defendant thus claimed that it was entitled to set off against the assigned claims the amount that Eastern owed to defendant on the basis of other transactions. The trial court gave judgment to plaintiff for the full amount of its claim. Defendant appealed.

HOOD, J. . . . Home Factors Corp., to which Eastern Brick & Tile Co., Inc. had assigned two accounts receivable for brick sold and delivered to Hudson Supply & Equipment Company, brought this action against Hudson for the amount due under the accounts, namely, $1,034.25.

Hudson's defense was that Eastern was indebted to it in an amount in excess of that sued for, and that it was entitled to a set-off for the full amount claimed.

At trial Hudson offered testimony that at the time of the assignment of the two accounts by Eastern to Home Factors, Hudson had claims of over $2,200 against Eastern growing out of other purchases.

The trial court ruled that there was a proper assignment from Eastern to Home Factors and that Home Factors was entitled to judgment for the full amount of its claim. However, the trial court stated "that the evidence indicated that the problem was between Hudson and Eastern and that defendant Hudson was entitled to credits of $229.22 and $172.31 from Eastern and in addition had other claims for credits against Eastern—all of which indicated that Eastern and Hudson should litigate separately the issues between them."

The general rule here and elsewhere is that the assignee of a chose in action takes it subject to all defenses, including set-offs, exist-ing at the time of the assignment. Since it is undisputed in this case that the asserted claims of Hudson existed at the time of the assignment, it is apparent that the trial court misconceived the law relating to assignments. When it was found that Hudson was entitled to certain credits, those credits should have been set off against the claim of Home Factors; and Hudson's "other claims for credits against Eastern" should have been determined, and, if established, should also have been set off against Home Factors' claim.

Reversed with instructions to grant a new trial.

Boulevard Nat. Bank of Miami v. Air Metals Industries
176 So.2d 94 (Fla.) 1965

Plaintiff bank sued several defendants including a contractor (Tompkins-Beckwith) on a construction project which had a subcontract with Air Metals Industries, Inc., also a defendant. On January 3, 1962, Air Metals procured performance bonds and as security for said bonds assigned to the bonding company (American Fire) "all monthly, final or other estimates and retained percentages; pertaining to or arising out of or in connection with any contracts performed or being performed or to be performed, such assignment to be in full force and effect as of the date hereof, in the event of default in the performance of . . . any contract as to which the surety has issued, or shall issue, any surety bonds or undertakings."

On November 26, 1962, the bank lent money to Air Metals, and to secure the loans Air Metals purported to assign to the bank certain accounts receivable it had with the contractor which arose out of subcontracts being done for that contractor.

In June 1963, Air Metals defaulted on contracts covered by the performance bonds, and on July 1, 1963, the bonding company notified the contractor of its assignment. On August 12, 1963, the bank notified the contrac-tor of its assignment. On October 9, 1963, the contractor paid all funds due to the bonding company, and the bank filed suit. The trial court found for defendants because the notice of the bonding company preceded the notice by the bank. The district court of appeal affirmed.

WILLIS, J. . . . The "question" is whether the law of Florida requires recognition of the so-called "English" rule or "American" rule of priority between assignees of successive assignments of an account receivable or other similar chose in action. Stated in its simplest form, the American rule would give priority to the assignee first in point of time of assignment, while the English rule would give preference to the assignment of which the debtor was first given notice. Both rules presuppose the absence of any estoppel or other special equities in favor of or against either assignee. The English rule giving priority to the assignee first giving notice to the debtor is specifically qualified as applying "unless he takes a later assignment with notice of a previous one or without a valuable consideration." The American rule giving the first assignee in point of time the preference is applicable only when the equities are equal between the contending assignees, and if a subsequent assignee has a stronger equity than an earlier one, he would prevail.

In the case here there are no special equities and no rights, such as subrogation, which would arise outside of the assignments.

The American rule for which petitioner contends is based upon the reasoning that an account or other chose in action may be assigned at will by the owner; that notice to the debtor is not essential to complete the assignment; and that when such assignment is made the property rights become vested in the assignee so that the assignor no longer has any interest in the account or chose which he may subsequently assign to another.

The English rule [holds] that in the case of a chose in action an assignee must do everything toward having possession which the subject admits and must do that which is tantamount to obtaining possession by placing every person who has an equitable or legal interest in the matter under an obligation to treat it as the assignee's property. It was stated:

> For this purpose you must give notice to the legal holder of the fund; in the case of a debt, for instance, notice tantamount to possession. If you omit to give that notice you are guilty of the same degree and species of neglect as he who leaves a personal chattel, to which he has acquired a title, in the actual possession, and under the absolute control, of another person.

It is undoubted that the creditor of an account receivable or other similar chose in action arising out of contract may assign it to another so that the assignee may sue on it in his own name and make recovery. Formal requisites of such an assignment are not prescribed by statute and it may be accomplished by parol, by instrument in writing, or other mode, such as delivery of evidences of the debt, as may demonstrate an intent to transfer and an acceptance of it. . . .

It seems to be generally agreed that notice to a debtor of an assignment is necessary to impose on the debtor the duty of payment to the assignee, and that if before receiving such notice he pays the debt to the assignor, or to a subsequent assignee, he will be discharged from the debt. To regard the debtor as a total nonparticipant in the assignment by the creditor of his interests to another is to deny the obvious. An account receivable is only the right to receive payment of a debt which ultimately must be done by the act of the debtor. For the assignee to acquire the right to stand in the shoes of the assigning creditor he must acquire some "delivery" or "possession" of the debt constituting a means of clearly establishing his right to collect. The very nature of an account receivable renders "delivery" and "possession" matters very different and more difficult than in the case of tangible personalty and negotiable instruments which are readily capable of physical handling and holding. However, the very principles which render a sale of personal property with possession remaining in the vendor unexplained fraudulent and void as to creditors applies with equal urgency to choses in action which are the subject of assignment. It would seem to follow that the mere private dealing between the creditor and his assignee unaccompanied by any manifestations discernible to others having or considering the acquiring of an interest in the account would not meet the requirement of delivery and acceptance of possession which is essential to the consummation of the assignment. Proper notice to the debtor of the assignment is a manifestation of such delivery. It fixes the accountability of the debtor to the assignee instead of the assignor and enables all involved to deal more safely.

We do not hold that notice to the debtor is the only method of effecting a delivery of possession of the account so as to put subsequent interests on notice of a prior assignment. The English rule itself does not apply to those who have notice of an earlier assignment. The American rule is not in harmony with the concepts expressed. It seems to be based largely upon the doctrine of *caveat emptor* which has a proper field of operation, but has many exceptions based on equitable considerations. It also seems to regard the commercial transfers of accounts as being the exclusive concern of the owner and assignee and that the assignee has no responsibility for the acts of the assignor with whom he leaves all of the indicia of ownership of the account. This view does not find support in the statute or decisional law of this State. . . .

After examining the authorities we conclude . . . that "as between successive assignments of the same right the assignee first giving notice prevails." . . .

We concur in the decision of the district court of appeal in this case.

Howell v. Worth James Const. Co.
535 S.W.2d 826 (Ark.) 1976

HOLT, J. . . . The appellant Tall Timber Development Corporation is the owner and developer of Tall Timber subdivision. In March, 1973, Tall Timber Development Corporation entered into a contract with the appellee Worth James Construction Company. Pursuant to this contract, the appellee constructed water and sewer lines for the subdivision. The appellee was fully paid the contract price of $363,672.22. In October, 1973, the appellant Tall Timber entered into a separate contract with appellant Howell under which Howell did the trenching for the installation of the underground power cables for the subdivision. The appellee brought suit against both appellants for damages . . . which it allegedly suffered as a result of broken water lines in the course of Howell's trenching operations. The trial court, sitting as a jury, awarded judgment against both appellants, in the amount of $7,000. . . .

Appellant Tall Timber first argues for reversal that the trial court erred in holding that it was liable to appellee by virtue of the provisions of its contract with Howell. The contract provides in pertinent part:

> Performance Bond Provisions as set out in paragraph 4 or any other part of this contract is hereby waived provided the owner shall retain 40% of any amounts due contractor until all damages, if any, to other utility lines have been repaired and installation accepted by Arkansas Power & Light Company. Then, owner shall release to contractor all of the re-

> tainage except 10% which shall be retained by the owner until the installation has been accepted by all appropriate governmental and utility agencies, at which time the 10% shall be paid to the contractor.

Appellant Tall Timber asserts that apparently the trial court's holding was based on a third-party beneficiary theory and argues that there is absolutely nothing in the record to indicate that the quoted provision was intended by either party to the contract, Tall Timber or Howell, to benefit the appellee or anyone else other than the contracting parties. . . . Tall Timber argues further that the clear intent of the provision was to protect it, not some third party like the appellee. We cannot agree with appellants' contentions.

It is true, as Tall Timber asserts, the presumption is that the parties contract only for themselves and a contract will not be construed as having been made for the benefit of a third party unless it clearly appears that such was the intention of the parties. In the case at bar, there is substantial evidence that it was the clear intention of the parties to contract for the benefit of appellee and that appellee was a beneficiary of their contract. We have repeatedly held that a contract made for the benefit of a third party is actionable by such third party. . . . In 17 Am.Jur.2d, § 314, it is said:

> It is not essential, in order to enable a third person to recover on a contract made and intended for his benefit, that

he knew of the contract at the time it was made. The fact that he did not act upon the faith of, or the reliance upon, the contract does not defeat his recovery.

In *Carolus* v. *Arkansas L&P Company,* 164 Ark. 507 (1924), we said:

> Where, from the language of the contract itself, or the testimony . . . it could be said that it was the intention of the parties to the contract to confer a direct benefit upon a third person, then such person may sue on the contract. It is not necessary that the person be named in the contract, if he is otherwise sufficiently described or designated, he may be one of a class of persons if the class is sufficiently described or designated.

Here the contract provides that Tall Tim-ber will retain 40% of any amount due Howell until all damages to other utility lines have been repaired. By the terms of the contract, Tall Timber agreed to waive performance bonds for Howell and in effect became the surety for Howell. Clearly, the intent of the retainage provision of the Tall Timber–Howell contract was to provide bonding for Howell for damages he might cause to other utility lines. Therefore, it could logically be found that appellee Worth James is a third-party beneficiary for whom this provision was specifically designed. . . .

[W]e hold the trial court's finding, that Tall Timber is jointly liable to appellee as a third-party beneficiary, is supported by substantial evidence. . . .

Affirmed.

CHAPTER 13
REVIEW QUESTIONS AND PROBLEMS

1. A purchased, on trial, a mechanical water softener from B. B represented that the use of the softener would increase the production at A's dairy-cattle farm and that the increased production could be used to pay for the softener. B then assigned his contract with A to C. The softener did not work and A refused to pay, contending that increased production was a condition precedent to payment. C contended that A could not use this as a defense against him because he only received the rights of collection through the assignment. Who is correct? Explain.

2. X owed money to Y for work performed. Y assigned his claim to Z and notified X of this. Z then demanded payment from X, but X refused and paid Y instead. Can Z collect from X? Why?

3. X purchased a car from a car dealer, Y. Y falsely informed X that the car was in good condition when he knew the car needed extensive repairs. Y assigned the installment contract to a credit corporation, which then sued X for nonpayment. X claims the right to set aside the contract because of fraud. Does he have the right of this defense against the credit company? Why?

4. A had an insurance policy to provide coverage for anyone injured while in his car. B suffered injuries while riding in A's car and was treated by

C, a physician. C then sued the insurance company for payment, claiming the status of a third-party beneficiary. Can he collect? Why?

5. X, a contractor, assigned his claim for work being done to Y, a bonding company. Y did not notify the obligor. X later assigned his claim to Z, who did notify the obligor. To whom should the obligor make payment? Why?

6. A had a contract with the state to build a bridge. The contract provided that A would be responsible for damages caused to third parties during the course of construction. The telephone company's cable, which ran under the river, was cut. Does the telephone company have standing to sue on the contract between A and the state? Why?

7. A entered into a contract with a nonprofit corporation whereby he would receive $200 per month while in medical school provided that he returned to a certain town to practice medicine for ten years after becoming a licensed physician. The residents of the town voted approval of bonds to construct a medical clinic. A practiced medicine in the town for five weeks but then left. Representatives of the medical clinic and the citizens of the town now sue for damages. Do they have standing to sue? Why?

8. A Company entered into a five-year employment contract with X as president of its subsidiary, B Company. A Company decided to sell B Company to C Company. The contract of sale provided for assignment of X's contract of employment to C Company. X was not aware of, nor did he consent to, the assignment. Is X obligated to work for C Company? Why?

9. A real estate broker, seller, and buyer entered into a three-party sales contract in which the seller promised to pay the broker a commission of $3,500 for his services. The prospective buyer defaulted, and the broker sues him. Does the broker have standing to sue? Why?

10. X, an army officer, had an insurance policy on his car with A Insurance Company. X was injured in a car accident and was treated free of personal cost at a government medical facility. The policy required the insurance company to pay reasonable medical expenses, and also provided that the company may pay any person or organization rendering the services for the insured. The government now sues the insurance company. Should the government be allowed reimbursement for reasonable medical expenses rendered to X? Why?

14

Performance of Contracts

1. Introduction

The focus of this chapter is on the problems that arise during the period of the performance of a contract. Such problems come up in a variety of ways. One of the parties may refuse to perform or may perform in an unsatisfactory manner; he may not render complete performance; he may be unable to perform because of circumstances beyond his control; or he may contend that, because of changed conditions, he should be excused from performing. Questions arise as to the order of performance—who must perform first in a bilateral contract? Usually, a default or breach of a contract will occur at or after the time when performance was due, but as will be noted, a contract can be breached prior to the date for performance.

Chapter 7 discussed the three basic remedies in contract litigation—money damages, rescission, and specific performance. This chapter focuses on rescission and money damages and the determination of the circumstances under which a party may rescind or refuse to perform because of the other party's breach.

A party in breach of contract may always be required to pay dollar damages to the other. In addition, the aggrieved party may obtain rescission of the agreement if the breach by one party is so substantial that the other party should not be required to perform.

234

CONDITIONS

2. In General

Those terms of a contract the substantial breach of which justifies rescission are called *conditions.* Terms that constitute conditions are contrasted with those that are mere promises. Conditions are not favored by the law, and when words can be construed as a promise rather than a condition, courts will thus construe them. Although no particular words are necessary for the existence of a condition, such terms as "if," "provided that," "on condition that," and others that condition performance usually connote an intent for a condition rather than a promise. In the absence of such a limiting clause, whether a certain contractual provision is a condition rather than a promise must be gathered from the contract as a whole and from the intent of the parties.

Conditions may be precedent, concurrent, or subsequent. A *concurrent condition* is one that requires the parties to act simultaneously as to certain matters. For example, an agreement calls for a conveyance by A of a certain farm upon payment of $60,000 by B. The deed is to be delivered at the time payment is made. Payment and delivery are concurrent conditions.

A *condition subsequent* is an event whose occurrence takes away rights that would otherwise exist; it may extinguish a duty to make compensation for breach of contract after the breach has occurred. An insurance policy provision that takes away the right to recover for a fire loss unless the insured gives notice of the loss within a stated period is a condition subsequent. Failure to give notice within the prescribed time relieves the company of its obligation to pay for the loss.

The word *condition* means basically an act or event that must take place before a promisor is obligated to render performance. The condition may be one that is under the promisor's control, or it may be an event over which he has no control. The condition may be an *express condition,* specifically provided for in the contract, or it may be a *constructive,* or *implied, condition.* Substantial performance required by one party to a contract is a constructive condition to the duty of performance on the other. Failure to provide substantial performance will discharge the other party from his duty of performance.

3. Conditions Precedent

A condition precedent is a fact that, unless excused, must exist or occur before a duty of immediate performance of a promise arises. It usually takes the form of performance by the other party. Contracts often expressly provide that one party must perform before there is a right to performance by the other party. The first party's performance is a *condition precedent* to the duty of the other party to perform. Since one party must perform before the other is under a duty to do so, the failure of the first party to perform permits the other to refuse to perform and to cancel the contract and sue for damages.

Not all the terms that impose a duty of performance on a person are of sufficient importance to constitute conditions precedent. As a general rule, if a provision is relatively insignificant, its performance is not required before recovery may be obtained from the second party. In such cases, the party who was to receive performance merely deducts the damages caused by the breach. Determining whether the breach of a particular provision is so material as to justify rescission is a construction problem. If the damage caused by the breach can be readily measured in money, or if the nature of the contract has not been so altered as to defeat the justifiable expectations of the party entitled to performance, the clause breached is generally not considered a condition precedent.[1]

4. Express Conditions

An express condition is one that is included in a contract and is designated as a condition that must be strictly performed before the other party's duty to perform arises. The penalty for failure to properly perform such a condition may be the loss of the right to receive payment or to otherwise obtain the return performance. The parties may stipulate that something is a condition precedent even though it would not ordinarily be considered so. In such a case, failure to perform exactly as specified affords ground for rescission, unless the court construes the clause to be a penalty provision and therefore unenforceable.

For example, a contract may provide that "time is of the essence of this agreement." This means that performance on or before the date specified is a condition precedent to the duty of the other party to pay or to perform. Another common condition precedent is found in many construction contracts. Such contracts provide that the duty of the owner to make the final payment on completition of the building is conditional upon the builder's securing an architect's certificate. This is certification by the owner's architect that the construction is satisfactory and in accordance with the plans and specifications. Thus, the condition is to a large degree outside the control of both parties and within the exclusive control of a third party, the architect.

A similar situation arises in a contract that expressly conditions the duty of the promisor on the promisor's "satisfaction" with the promisee's performance. In contracts with this provision, the burden is upon the promisee to prove that the condition has been met.

The term *to the satisfaction of the promisor* is a subjective element. It is usually taken literally. The personal, even if mistaken, judgment of the promisor prevents recovery if the contract involves personal taste on judg-

[1] *Nolan* v. *Williamson Music, Inc.*, page 247.

ment. A promisor is required to act in good faith and to evince an honest dissatisfaction. If the contract involves painting a portrait, for example, the satisfaction is almost entirely subjective.

5. Constructive or Implied Conditions

Most problems involving conditions precedent arise when parties have simply entered into a contract and have not specified which provisions are conditions precedent. In addition to the question as to whether or not a provision is a condition or a promise, other issues arise. One common issue involves the extent of the breach or, conversely, the extent of performance. Another common issue that affects the right of rescission relates to whether the breach was willful or merely inadvertent.

Substantial performance is the basic requirement for the satisfaction of implied conditions. The general principle is that a failure to render full and complete performance will amount to a breach of a condition precedent only if the failure was so significant and important that the other party is deprived of what he bargained for. Stated differently, if the breach is immaterial, there has been substantial performance; if the breach is material, a party is relieved of his obligation to perform.[2] Of course, whether a breach is material or immaterial, damages are recoverable.

Many decisions indicate that a willful breach—one made in bad faith— will more likely be considered material than will one that lacks this element. Since rescission is an equitable remedy, it will be awarded more freely when one party willfully breaches than when the breach is unintentional.

If a breach occurs after a party has partly performed, the courts are less likely to consider the breach material than would be the case if the breach had occurred prior to any performance. The reason for this is that the person who has partly performed stands to forfeit the value of such performance if his deviation is deemed material.

6. Time of Performance as a Condition

A failure to perform on a specified date will not usually be treated as a material breach, especially if there is some justification for the delay. Delays in payment of money or completion of building contracts are regarded as less significant than delays in shipment of goods. Nor is exact compliance with time provisions always required in contracts for the sale of real property.[3] A provision establishing the time for performance of a contract that involves primarily the expenditure of labor and materials or the production of a commodity of little value to anyone other than the contracting party is normally not considered of major significance. Thus, the failure of a contractor to complete a house by the date set in the contract would not justify

---

[2] *Whiteley* v. *O'Dell*, page 248.
[3] *Carsek Corp.* v. *Stephen Schifter, Inc.*, page 249.

rescission by the owner, although he could deduct from the contract price such damages as resulted from the delay.

In a contract for the sale of marketable goods, a clause calling for performance within a certain time is usually held to be a condition precedent. In contracts whereby retailers purchase goods that are normally bought and sold in the market, performance by the seller on the date specified is considered quite important. Sales promotion campaigns and provisions for the normal needs of customers are built around delivery dates. To replace merchandise not received promptly, other sources must be tapped. Failure to comply with the time provisions of such contracts usually justifies the buyer in rejecting an offer to perform at a later date.

Eventually, an extended delay becomes material in the performance of any contract, and ultimately it justifies rescission. Also, if partial performance has not taken place, a relatively short delay may justify rescission; whereas if performance is under way and time is not of the essence, a delay of some time may be required before rescission is justified. If the contract does not provide a specific date for performance, it is implied that performance will take place within a reasonable time—the length of time being dependent upon the nature of the commodity involved and the circumstances. In those contracts in which time for performance is normally deemed not to be a condition precedent, it can be made so by adding a clause that "time is of the essence in this agreement."

7. Tender

A *tender* is an offer to perform one's duties under the contract. It is an attempt to perform by one who is "ready, willing, and able" to perform. The tender is especially significant in those bilateral contracts containing conditions concurrent. Under the terms of such contracts, neither party is placed in default until the other has *offered* to perform. Such an offer on his part is a tender, and actual performance is unnecessary to place the other party in default. Assume again that A agrees to deed a farm to B for $60,000. B could not successfully sue A for failure to deliver the deed until he had offered to make the payment required. Actual payment is not required unless A offers to deliver the deed; tender of payment is sufficient, as is tender of the deed.

The concept of tender is applied not only to concurrent condition situations but also to contract performance in general. The tender may be either an offer to pay or an offer to perform. Suppose that B and S enter into a contract for the sale of goods; that S, the seller, proffers the proper goods at the proper time and place to B, the buyer; and that B refuses to accept the goods. B's refusal of the tender discharges S's obligation, and he can proceed to bring action against B for damages. Also, should B subsequently seek to enforce the contract, S's tender would be a defense.

The results are somewhat different if the tender is an offer to pay money that is due to a creditor. Frequently, one party will tender the money due the other party, and the payment will not be accepted, for any number of reasons. Usually, either there is a dispute as to the amount owing, or a party may feel that his legal rights will be affected by accepting payment. A tender obviously does not pay or discharge the debt. It does, however, have three important legal effects: (1) It extinguishes any security interest such as a mortgage or pledge that secures the debt, (2) it stops interest from accruing thereafter, and (3) in case the creditor later brings suit recovering no more than the amount tendered, he must pay the court costs.

A tender requires that there be a bona fide, unconditional offer of payment of the amount of money due, coupled with an actual production of the money. A tender of payment by check is quite common today; but a check is not a valid tender when objection is made to this medium of payment. However, when a tender is rejected for other reasons, one may not later complain of the medium of tender. A tender before the maturity of an obligation is not a proper tender, and the creditor is under no duty to accept it as would be the case if the obligation was interest-bearing.

There are two aspects to tender under the Uniform Commercial Code. Unless otherwise agreed, *tender of payment* by the buyer is a condition to the seller's duty to tender and complete any delivery (2-511). Such tender may be by any means or in any manner current in the ordinary course of business, unless the seller demands payment in legal tender and gives a reasonable extension of time to procure it. Thus, payment by check is quite customary, but such payment is conditional—it is defeated if the check is dishonored. The Code also provides for the manner of a seller's *tender of delivery*. Basically, the requirement is that the seller put and hold conforming goods at the buyer's disposition and that he give the buyer reasonable notification that the goods are available for him (2-503).

8. Anticipatory Repudiation

There can be no actual breach of contract until the time specified for performance has arrived. However, there may be a breach by anticipatory repudiation. By its very name, an essential element of anticipatory repudiation is that the repudiation occur before performance is due. Anticipatory breach occurs when one of the parties to a bilateral contract repudiates the contract. The repudiation may be express or implied. An express repudiation is a clear, positive, unequivocal refusal to perform. An implied repudiation results from conduct in which the promisor puts it out of his power to perform so as to make substantial performance of his promise impossible. In either case, the repudiation must be positive and unequivocal.[4]

When a promisor repudiates a contract, the injured party faces an election of remedies. He can treat the repudiation as an anticipatory breach and immediately seek damages for breach of contract, thereby terminating the

[4] *McMahon* v. *Fiberglass Fabricators, Inc.*, page 251.

contractual relation between the parties, or he can treat the repudiation as an empty threat, wait until the time for performance arrives, and exercise his remedies for actual breach if a breach does in fact occur at such time. However, if the injured party disregards the repudiation and treats the contract as still in force, then the repudiation is nullified and the injured party is left with his remedies, if any, invocable at the time of performance.

The doctrine of anticipatory breach does not apply to promises to pay money on or before a specified date. For example, if a promissory note matures on June 1, 1983, a statement by the maker in 1979 that he would not pay it when the maturity date arrived would not give rise to a present cause of action by the holder.

The Code provides that after a breach including anticipatory repudiation, the buyer may "cover" by making in good faith and without unreasonable delay any reasonable purchase of or contract to purchase goods in substitution for those due from the seller (2-712). The buyer may recover from the seller as damages the difference between the cost of cover and the contract price together with any incidental or consequential damages. Failure of the buyer to effect cover does not bar him from recovering damages for non-delivery. However, in the latter event, damages will be limited to those that could not have been obviated by proper cover.

A party may retract his repudiation, provided he does so prior to any material change of position by the other party in reliance upon it. The retraction would simply be a notice that he will perform the contract after all. The Code allows a retraction of anticipatory repudiation until the repudiating party's next performance is due, unless the aggrieved party has since the repudiation canceled or materially changed his position or otherwise indicated that he considers the repudiation final (2-611). Retraction may be by any method that clearly indicates to the aggrieved party that the repudiating party intends to perform, but it must include adequate assurance that he will in fact perform if the other party demands it (2-609). Retraction reinstates the repudiating party's rights under the contract, with due excuse and allowance to the aggrieved party for any delay occasioned by the repudiation.

9.   Divisibility—Installment Contracts

Whereas many contracts require a single performance by each party and are completely performed at one point of time, others require or permit performance by one or both parties in installments over a period of time. The rights and obligations of parties during the period when the contract is being performed frequently depend upon whether the contract is "entire" or "divisible." A contract is said to be divisible if performance by each party is divided into two or more parts *and* performance of each part by one party is the agreed exchange for the corresponding part by the other party. It is to be noted that a contract is not divisible simply by virtue of the fact that it is to be performed in installments.

The parties may specify whether a contract is divisible or entire. Thus, a contract may contain a clause stipulating that each delivery is a separate contract, or other language may be used to show the intention of the parties that their agreement is to be treated as if it were a series of contracts.

Where performance of a contract may take place in portions rather than all at one time, several questions arise: (1) Is the contract divisible on both sides, so that the second party is under a duty to perform in part after the first party performs an installment? (2) Does a material breach of any installment justify a rescission of the balance of the agreement? (3) If one party is in default, may he nevertheless recover for the performance rendered prior to default?

The concept of divisibility is applicable to a variety of contracts, including insurance contracts,[5] employment contracts, construction contracts, and sales contracts. As a general proposition, employment contracts are interpreted to be divisible, but construction contracts are usually deemed to be entire. The divisibility of contracts for the sale of goods is the subject of several Code provisions discussed later in this section.

There have been numerous cases involving the question of whether or not a contract is divisible. No general test can be derived from these cases, and the parties seldom provide specifically for this in their contract. The courts are called upon to determine in any given case whether the parties intended that (1) each would accept the part performance of the other in return for his own without regard to subsequent events, or (2) the division of the contract into parts was only for the purpose of providing periodic payments which would apply toward the amount due upon completion of the entire contract. In any event, the party who breaches is liable for damages resulting from his breach.

Under the Code, unless the parties have otherwise agreed, a sales contract is entire—all the goods called for by the contract must be tendered in a single delivery, and payment in full is due upon such tender (2-307). If the contract permits installment deliveries, the seller can demand a proportionate share of the price for each delivery as it is made, provided the price can be apportioned, as is the case when the goods are sold for a certain price per item. If there is a substantial default on an installment, such as when the goods tendered or delivered do not conform to the contract, the buyer may reject the installment (2-307[2]). When an installment breach indicates that the seller will not satisfactorily perform the balance of the contract or that he is unreliable, the buyer can rescind the entire contract. Should the buyer accept a nonconforming installment without giving notice of cancellation or demanding that the seller deliver goods that do conform, he may not use the breach as a basis for rescission (2-612).

---

[5] *First S. & L. Ass'n* v. *American Home Assur. Co.,* page 251.

EXCUSES FOR NONPERFORMANCE

10. In General

Even though the contract is silent on the point, a party may be relieved from performing a contract including conditions precedent, or his liability for breach of contract may be eliminated if he is legally excused from performance of the contract. As noted previously, performance by one party is excused when the other party has failed to perform a condition precedent or when a defense such as fraud or lack of capacity is present. In addition, there is no liability for breach of contract when (1) one party has waived performance by indicating that he does not intend to hold the other party to the terms of the contract, (2) one party has prevented the other party from carrying out the agreement, (3) performance of the contract has been frustrated, or (4) the contract has become impossible of performance, as contrasted with performance merely becoming more burdensome for one of the parties.

In addition, the Code allows substituted performance when the agreed carrier or other facilities have become unavailable, when the agreed manner of delivery becomes commercially impracticable, or when the agreed means or manner of payment fails because of some government regulation (2-614). In such cases, a reasonable substitute or equivalent method of performance will discharge the contract. The Code also gives a seller an excuse if performance has become impracticable by the failure of presupposed conditions. If a seller cannot make delivery because of "unforeseen supervening circumstances not within the contemplation of the parties at the time of contracting" (2-615), he will be relieved of his obligation.

11. Waiver

Waiver has been defined as the passing by of an occasion to enforce a legal right, whereby the legal right is lost. As applied to contract law, it means (1) a promise to forego the benefit of a condition to the promissor's duty, or (2) an election to continue under a contract after the other party has breached. The essence of waiver is conduct that indicates an intention not to enforce certain provisions of the agreement. The waiver may be made either before or after a breach. If it is made before, it constitutes an assurance that performance of the condition will not be insisted upon. For example, a building contract provides for completion on a certain date. If the owner grants an extension of six months, he has waived his right to insist upon completion at the earlier date. The waiver may be retracted unless it is supported by consideration or the promisee has made a substantial change of position in reliance upon it. One who has waived the time for performance may withdraw the waiver if he gives the other party a reasonable opportunity to perform the condition waived.

The Code allows a party who has waived a provision of an executory contract to retract it upon giving reasonable notice that he will require strict performance of it, "unless the retraction would be unjust in view of a material change of position in reliance on the waiver" (2-209[5]). Under the Code, the retention or acceptance of defective goods may constitute a waiver of the defect. A buyer who fails to particularize defects in goods may in fact be waiving his objections based on these defects (2-605).

12. Prevention

One who prevents performance of a condition, or makes it impossible by his own act, will not be permitted to take advantage of the nonperformance. If one party by his conduct makes it impossible for the other to perform, the one failing to perform has no liability. It is an implied condition of every contract that neither party will prevent performance by the other or the carrying out of the contract in the normal course of events.

Prevention often occurs when, by his conduct, one party stops or hinders the occurrence or fulfillment of a condition in the contract. Whenever one party's cooperation is necessary to the agreed performance of the other but is not forthcoming, the Code provides that the other party is excused for any resulting delay in his own performance and may proceed to perform in any reasonable manner.

13. Impossibility of Performance—In General

Actual impossibility of performance is a valid excuse for breach of contract and releases a party from his duty to perform. Impossibility is much more than mere "additional hardship." As a general rule, in the absence of an appropriate contract provision, circumstances that impose additional hardship on one party do not constitute an excuse for breach of contract.[6] The fact that the promised performance of a contractual obligation may be more difficult than expected at the time the promise was made does not discharge the promisor from his duty to perform. Therefore, most contracts provide that manufacturers, suppliers, or builders shall be relieved from performance in case of fire, strikes, difficulty in obtaining raw materials, or other incidents imposing hardship over which they have no control. Without such a provision there would be no excuse, as they do not constitute impossibility of performance.

To have the effect of releasing a party from his duty to perform, the impossibility must render performance "physically and objectively impossible." If objective impossibility is present, the discharge is mutual; that is, the promisor is discharged, and the promisee is also discharged from his corresponding obligation. Many cases state that in order for impossibility to exist, there must be a fortuitous or unavoidable occurrence that was not reasonably foreseeable. The fact that an act of God is involved does not necessarily create an excuse. For example, assume that a house under construction is

---

[6] *Luria Engineering Co. v. Aetna Cas. & Surety Co.,* page 253.

destroyed by fire. The contractor is not excused from his obligation to complete the house. The contractor takes the risk of destruction by fire of the incompleted house unless he protects himself by expressly contracting that he shall not be held liable for an act of God, or other untoward circumstance, against which he is not willing to be bound.

The common law rule is that where the duty is imposed on a party for performance, his nonperformance shall be excused if it be rendered by an act of God, but where by his contract the party engages to do an act, it is deemed to be his own folly and fault that he does not expressly provide against such contingencies and exempt himself in certain events. The party must contract against such contingencies, or abide and suffer the loss entailed by failure to so contract as to relieve himself from liability.

Likewise, if the situation is caused by the promisor or by developments that he could have prevented, avoided, or remedied by corrective measures, there is no excuse. For this reason, the failure of a third party, such as a supplier, to make proper delivery does not create impossibility. Impossibility will not be allowed as a defense when the obstacle was created by the promisor or was within his power to eliminate. It must not exist merely because of the inability or incapacity of the promisor to do it.[7]

14.   Impossibility of Performance—Specific Cases

There are four basic situations in which impossibility of performance is frequently offered as an excuse for nonperformance. In the first of these, performance becomes illegal because of the enactment of some law, or because of some act on the part of the government. Illustrative of this are instances in which a manufacturer or a supplier is prevented from making delivery of merchandise because of government allocations, as in the mandatory allocation of fuel oil and gasoline. Government action that merely makes an agreement more burdensome than was anticipated does not afford a basis for relief.

The second situation is the death or incapacitating illness of one of the contracting parties. This is not deemed to be a form of impossibility unless the nature of the contract is such as to demand the personal services of the disabled or deceased person. Ordinary contracts of production, processing, and sale of property are unaffected by the death or illness of one or both of the parties. In the event of death, it is assumed that the contract will be carried out by the estate of the deceased. However, if a contract is one for personal services or is of such a character as to clearly imply that the continued services of the contracting party are essential to performance, death or illness will excuse nonperformance. In contracts for personal services, the death of the employer also terminates the relation. In such a case, the estate of the employer is not liable to the employee in damages for prematurely terminating the contract.

[7] *White Lakes Shop. Ctr.* v. *Jefferson Stand. L. Ins. Co.,* page 253.

Many agreements involve certain subject matter whose continued existence is essential to the completion of the contract. The third rule is that destruction of any subject matter that is essential to the completion of the contract will operate to relieve the parties of the obligations assumed by their agreement. A different situation arises where property that one of the parties expected to use in his performance is destroyed. If a factory from which the owner expected to deliver certain shoes is destroyed by fire, performance is not excused, inasmuch as performance is still possible even though an undue hardship may result. The shoes needed to fill the order can be obtained from another source. Had the contract stipulated that the shoes were to be delivered from this particular factory, however, its destruction would have operated to excuse a failure to perform. In recent years, there has been a trend toward holding that where both parties understood that delivery was to be made from a certain source, even though it was not expressly so agreed, destruction of the source of supply will relieve the obligor from performing.

The last form of impossibility arises when there is an essential element lacking. This situation has never been satisfactorily defined, but apparently, when some element or property that the parties assumed existed or would exist is in fact lacking, the agreement may be rescinded. Some courts would hold that no contract in fact existed because of mutual mistake. This is said to be a form of impossibility at the time of making the contract, and courts have tended to act as if there had been no meeting of the minds. It must be definitely proved that performance is substantially impossible because of the missing element. For example, A contracts to build an office building at a certain location. Because of the nature of the soil, it is utterly impossible to build the type of building provided for in the agreement; the agreement must therefore be terminated. The missing element is the proper condition of the soil. In other words, from the very beginning, the contract terms could not possibly have been complied with, and in such cases, the courts are prone to excuse the parties.

15. Right to Recovery for Part Performance—Impossibility

Often, impossibility of performance becomes apparent only after the agreement has been partially performed. One coat of paint, for instance, is placed upon a house before the house is destroyed. In such cases, is the loss of the work already completed to fall upon the one doing the work or upon the party who was to have the benefit of the labor? Most states permit the person who has partially performed to recover the value of the benefit the other party would have received had impossibility not arisen. This is simply another way of saying that the recipient of the work must pay for all labor and material expended up to the date of impossibility, provided the labor and material had attached to the property of the one for whom the work was being done. However, there are some states that do not allow any recovery.

Care should be taken in such cases, however, to differentiate between impossibility and mere additional burden. The destruction of a partially completed building does not make recovery for the work done impossible. By starting construction anew, performance is still possible, although the cost will be greater than was anticipated. In the latter case, the additional cost must be borne by the contractor.

16. Frustration

Frequently, an event occurs that does not create actual impossibility but does prevent the achievement of the object or purpose of the contract. In such cases, the courts may find an implied condition that certain developments will excuse performance. *Frustration* has the effect of excusing nonperformance and arises whenever there is an intervening event or change of circumstances that is so fundamental as to be entirely beyond that which was contemplated by the parties. Frustration is not impossibility, but it is more than mere hardship. It is an excuse created by law to eliminate liability when a fortuitous occurrence has defeated the reasonable expectations of the parties. It includes impracticability caused by extreme or unseasonable difficulty or expense when the cause is not foreseeable. If the event was reasonably foreseeable, frustration is not an excuse for nonperformance. If the parties could have reasonably anticipated the event, they are obliged to make provisions in their contract protecting themselves against it. Commercial frustration rests on the basic premise that if a problem develops that a promisor had no reason to anticipate and for the presence of which he is not at fault, then the promisor in equity and good conscience ought to be discharged. Many courts hold that the doctrine is not applicable in the event of only a partial frustration that only increases the cost of performance.[8]

17. Commercial Impracticability

The Code recognizes that without the fault of either party, unexpected developments or government action may cause the promised performance to become impracticable. In some cases, the Code authorizes substituted performance. For example, if the loading or unloading facilities fail on the agreed-upon carrier, causing it to become unavailable, a commercially reasonable substitute must be tendered and accepted if it is available (2-614).

The Code also provides that commercial impracticability is often an excuse for a seller who fails to deliver goods or is delayed in making the delivery. The excuse is limited to cases in which unforeseen supervening circumstances not within the contemplation of the parties arise (2-615[a]). The law does not specify all the contingencies that may justify the application of the doctrine of commercial impracticability. Increased costs will not excuse the seller

[8] *Pete Smith Company, Inc.* v. *City of El Dorado,* page 254.

unless they are due to some unforeseen contingency that alters the basic nature of the contract. For example, one company agreed to sell uranium to several public utilities for use in nuclear reactors. The price of uranium went up dramatically, and it was alleged that the price increase was caused by price-fixing by an international cartel. Based on this tremendous price increase, the supplier sought to be excused from its obligations under the doctrine of commercial impracticability. Another example of a situation giving rise to this excuse is a severe shortage of materials caused by war, embargo, or the shutdown of a major source of supply.

If the excuse affects only part of the seller's capacity to perform, he must allocate his production and make deliveries among his customers in a fair and reasonable manner (2-615[b]). The allocation may include regular customers not then under contract.

In order to use the excuse, the seller is required to notify his customers seasonably of the delay or nondelivery. This is to allow the buyers to take prompt action to find another source of supply. The notice must include an estimate of the buyer's allocation when the seller is able to partially perform and therefore subject to the allocation requirement previously noted (2-615[c]).

Upon receipt of a notice of a material or indefinite delay in delivery or of an allocation, the buyer has two alternative courses of action. The buyer may terminate the contract insofar as that delivery is concerned. He may also terminate and discharge the whole contract where the deficiency substantially impairs the value of the whole contract (2-616[1]). The buyer may also modify the contract by agreeing to take his available quota in substitution. If the buyer fails to modify the contract within a reasonable time not exceeding 30 days, the contract lapses with respect to the deliveries covered by the seller's notice (2-616[2]).

PERFORMANCE OF CONTRACTS CASES

Nolan v. Williamson Music, Inc.
300 F. Supp. 1311 (1969)

Plaintiff, composer of the musical composition "Tumbling Tumbleweed," sought to rescind his publishing agreement with defendant. Plaintiff alleged that defendant had failed to properly account for all royalties and that other breaches of the agreement had occurred.

EDELSTEIN, J. . . . The question to be resolved at this juncture is whether these breaches, when considered together, provide a sufficient basis for rescission.

It is accepted law that not every breach of a contract will justify rescission. Rather, rescission can be permitted only when the complaining party has suffered breaches of so material and substantial a nature that they affect the very essence of the contract and serve to defeat the object of the parties. . . .

Cases which have considered the problem of rescission in situations analogous to the one presented by the case at bar have granted rescission only after finding the equivalent of a total failure in the performance of the contract. In *Raftery* v. *World Film Corp.,* the plaintiff temporarily turned over to the defendant prints from which movies were to be made and then distributed. The contract provided that the defendant was to render weekly accounts of the earnings on the movies and to pay the plaintiff fifty percent thereof. The prints were to be returned at the expiration of the contract term. The court found that the defendant never paid plaintiff the full amount due, deliberately maintained a set of fictitious records, deliberately rendered false accountings, refused to permit inspection of the records as was required by the contract, and failed to return the prints to the plaintiff. Based on all of these factors rescission was granted. . . .

Rescission is not justified in this case. The fact [is] that fraud has not been established. . . . Although defendant has been guilty of divers breaches, these breaches involve a failure to comply fully with the contractual provisions for payment of royalties in various categories, and as to these breaches, it is clear to the court that plaintiff may be rendered whole by an award of monetary damages. Moreover, there seems little danger that Nolan will be deprived of his royalties in the future. This is not a case in which defendant has repudiated his obligations to pay royalties, nor is this a case in which plaintiff's song has not been exploited fully in the past or threatened with not being exploited fully in the future.

Thus, plaintiff is not entitled to rescission.

Whiteley v. O'Dell
548 P.2d 798 (Kan.) 1976

OWSLEY, J. . . . This is an action brought to recover damages for a breach of a real estate purchase contract. Plaintiffs appeal from the trial court's entry of judgment generally in favor of defendant contractor.

On April 16, 1973, plaintiffs Roy L. and Evelyn L. Whiteley entered into a written contract with defendant Clinton E. O'Dell for the purchase of a house in Wichita, Kansas. Under the terms of the contract, O'Dell, doing business as the O'Dell Construction Company, agreed to construct and convey to plaintiffs a house similar to another built by O'Dell. The contract price was listed at $31,040, with $1,000 to be paid as earnest money and the balance due upon closing. The closing date was designated as September 1, 1973, or a "reasonable time thereafter." On the back of the contract, and incorporated therein, were listed certain specifications to be followed by the contractor.

The Whiteleys . . . paid O'Dell $1,000 in earnest money. Shortly thereafter, O'Dell commenced construction of the house, but he did not comply with certain contract specifications hereinafter noted. . . .

In ruling in favor of defendant O'Dell on the plaintiffs' petition, the trial court concluded that "time not being of the essence," the contractor had a reasonable time to complete the house according to specifications, but plaintiffs never gave him an opportunity to do so. The court reasoned that the variances noted by plaintiffs in June could easily have been rectified prior to the completion date of the contract. As a result, the court ruled that plaintiffs were premature in assuming the house had not been built according to specifications. . . .

Plaintiffs contend the trial court erred in finding defendant had not breached the contract. The record reveals that at the time plaintiffs inspected the house in June, 1973, there were variances from the contract specifications in at least three respects. First, the bathroom fixtures were not the color specified in the contract. The trial court determined this was an insignificant difference which could have been resolved rather simply. The fixtures had not been installed at that time. Although O'Dell made no offer to cure the defect we cannot say this alone would entitle the purchaser to rescind the contract. It is not every breach which gives rise to the right to rescind a contract. In order to warrant rescission of a contract the breach must be material and the failure to perform so substantial as to defeat the object of the parties in making the agreement. Obviously, the variance in the appearance of the bathroom fixtures is not so substantial that it would constitute a material breach of contract.

The variances in the shingles and the brick veneer are entirely different matters. While the sealdown shingles used by the builder differed only in appearance from those specified, the contract disclosed that plaintiffs specifically ordered T-lock shingles. Defendant offered no excuse for the variance, nor did he offer to replace them with the proper shingles. From the testimony it is apparent to this court that defendant had no intention of curing this defect. . . .

An even more serious variance of the contract specifications was discovered by plaintiffs when they saw that brick veneer was added only to the front of the house. The contract specified the house was to be all brick. The normal method of adding brick veneer to a house is to extend the foundation so a ledge is formed to support the brick veneer. O'Dell testified his employees had omitted the ledge on three sides of the house by mistake. When plaintiffs discovered the error they immediately notified defendant they were no longer going to buy the house. After learning of the plaintiffs' repudiation of the contract, defendant attempted to remedy the situation by laying cement blocks where the ledge should have been extended. . . . There was considerable testimony indicating it was neither the normal nor the desired method for construction of a brick veneer. . . .

In addition to these defects in construction of the house, O'Dell admitted on cross-examination that he discovered a bow of almost two inches in the foundation. O'Dell attempted to correct the bow by building out the cement blocks at one end of the house. In spite of his efforts there was testimony from other witnesses that by so doing he only increased the amount of weight off center which the footings would have to support.

On the basis of this evidence we are inclined to agree with plaintiffs that there was a material breach of the contract at the time the defects were discovered. If it is clear that one party to a contract is going to be unable to perform it, the other party need not wait for the date when performance is due. He is entitled to treat the contract at an end and pursue his remedies.

Even though O'Dell negotiated with plaintiffs and offered to build them another house, he never offered to correct these variances. . . . As a practical matter, we realize replacement of the shingles and proper construction of the ledge at this stage would be excessively expensive, if not impossible. There is nothing in the record to support the conclusion of the trial court that plaintiffs were premature in their determination that the contract had been breached. After examining the whole of the contract and the expert testimony we are convinced that construction of the house in compliance with the named specifications was of importance to plaintiffs. Substantial variations such as shown herein obviously should entitle the purchaser to rescind the contract. In our opinion, the failure to include a ledge on three sides of the house and the use of the wrong shingles constituted a present material breach of the contract, and the trial court erred in its finding to the contrary. . . .

Reversed.

Carsek Corp. v. Stephen Schifter, Inc.
246 A.2d 365 (Pa.) 1968

Plaintiff (Carsek) entered into a contract to purchase a fifty-seven-acre tract from defendant for the purpose of constructing a housing development thereon. The agreement of sale provided for a price of $200,000—$25,000 in cash on or before settlement and the balance of $175,000 to be paid in four years' time, secured by a purchase-money mortgage. The agreement (Paragraph Seven) stipulated that the buyer would have prepared by the Registered Engineer a statement of the costs to install streets, sidewalks, sewers, etc., and that the seller would absorb the costs in excess of $160,000. Plaintiff was forty-five days late in submitting the statement of costs, and defendant refused to pay the costs in excess of $160,000. Plaintiff sued for the excess. The lower court ruled for defendant. Plaintiff appealed.

O'BRIEN, J. . . . The Chancellor held that Paragraph Seven of the agreement of sale . . . required that the cost estimates be submitted prior to settlement, and that, having failed to submit the estimates prior to settlement, plaintiff was not entitled to any relief. We disagree.

In the first place, we cannot agree with the Chancellor that time was of the essence of this contract. "It is a well-established general principle in equity that time is not ordinarily regarded as of the essence in contracts for the sale of real property unless it is so stipulated by the express terms thereof, or it is necessarily to be so implied."

. . . When it is so easy to insert the commonly-used phrase "time to be of the essence" when that is the desired result, we are loathe to ascribe that result to any other language.

Nor do the circumstances necessarily imply that time is of the essence. On the contrary, they provide a strong indication that time was not to be of the essence. One of those circumstances is the type of performance required. Appellee relies heavily on the language of the agreement providing that the credit for the estimates above $160,000 should be deducted from the consideration being paid by buyer at settlement as indicating that time must be of the essence. Although we have found no Pennsylvania cases directly in point, at least one jurisdiction has decided this precise issue and held that a requirement that a credit be given against a designated payment does not make time of the essence. . . .

Furthermore, appellant's delay really resulted in no harm to appellee. The Chancellor stated that time was of the essence "because, otherwise, final settlement would have been held up and defendant still would have been uncertain as to the net consideration it would ultimately receive for its property." Yet this hardly constitutes harm cognizable by a court of equity. Neither party had the right to rescind the contract regardless of what the estimates totalled. When appellee made the agreement, it left itself open to an uncertain purchase price. A month or two more of uncertainty is scarcely the harm required in order that it be inferred that time is necessarily of the essence. Moreover, the delay resulted in no loss whatsoever of cash in hand, since appellee took a four-year purchase-money mortgage. . . .

Whereas appellee suffered virtually no harm from a slightly delayed performance, it would work a tremendous forfeiture to deny appellant the relief sought. This Court has always sought to avoid forfeitures, and has interpreted contracts in such a way as to effectuate that purpose. Particularly is this so where there has been part performance. The Restatement of Contracts § 276 provides in part, as follows: "In determining the materiality of delay in performance, the following rules are applicable: . . . (c) If delay of one party in rendering a promised performance occurs before any part of his promise has been rendered, less delay discharges the duty of the other party than where there has been part performance of that promise." Here, appellant clearly performed part of its obligation under Paragraph Seven by submitting the cost estimates for Section One. To hold that it forfeited some $45,000 by submitting the remainder approximately forty-five days late would be unconscionable. Time was not stated to be of the essence of this contract, and the circumstances afford absolutely no basis for considering a forty-five day breach to be so material as to discharge appellee from any duty under Paragraph Seven. . . .

The decree is reversed and remanded for proceedings consistent with this opinion.

McMahon v. Fiberglass Fabricators, Inc.
496 P.2d 616 (Ariz.) 1972

Plaintiff filed suit on December 30, 1969, to recover a $1,000 deposit he had made to defendant as partial payment on two campers. The money had been sent on August 4, 1966, with a cover letter confirming the oral purchase agreement. Just before defendant shipped the campers, plaintiff sent defendant a telegram stating:

Do not ship. Letter will follow.

Defendant did not ship the campers. Plaintiff wrote to defendant on January 24, 1967, acknowledging the sending of the telegram, and attempted to explain the reason for sending it. No reference was made to the $1,000, but the letter stated:

Hold the two units I have on order until I have enough for a load. Or, if [you] should have a partial load for the North, then maybe I will have enough cash to lift them.
Please answer as soon as you can.

Defendant's reply to plaintiff's letter included the following:

[W]e can certainly appreciate your position. If you need any additional information or if we can be of any further help to you, please do not hestitate to call on us.

On March 16, 1969, plaintiff demanded the return of his $1,000. He said that he had not asked for it earlier because he thought he would be sending in another order.

Defendant asserted the three-year statute of limitations. The lower court found for defendant, and plaintiff appealed.

HATHAWAY, J. . . . . The [lower] court expressly found that the plaintiff, by his own actions, had prevented the completion of the purchase agreement by sending a telegram in the first week of October, 1966, and that he did not commence his action to recover the down payment within three years from the date the telegram was sent. . . .

. . . We are of the opinion that the trial court's finding that the plaintiff had repudiated the contract in October, 1966, is clearly erroneous. In order to find a breach of contract, there must be a positive and unequivocal manifestation on the part of the repudiating party that he will not render the required performance when it is due. A statement by a party to a contract merely implying that he will not perform is not the equivalent of a positive and unequivocal refusal to perform. We are unable to say that an instruction not to ship, without more, indicates a positive refusal to go through with the purchase of the two campers. Therefore the October, 1966, telegram did not constitute an anticipatory repudiation. Although the letter of January, 1967, sent by the plaintiff to Fiberglass manifests a willingness to perform at a future date, if we were to assume otherwise and treat it as a repudiation, the instant lawsuit filed December 30, 1969, would not be barred by limitation. We hold, therefore, that the action was not barred and plaintiff was entitled to recover against Fiberglass. . . .

Reversed.

First S. & L. Ass'n v. American Home Assur. Co.
277 N.E.2d 638 (N.Y.) 1971

JASEN, J. . . . . The plaintiff . . . holds a mortgage upon certain premises covered by an insurance policy issued by the defendant . . . and asserts its right to insurance proceeds by virtue of the standard mortgage clause contained in the policy. The owner of the premises procured an insurance policy, D7539681, from the defendant insurance company in the amount of $7,000 and paid the premium of $140 for a one-year term commencing on July 19, 1968. Effective October 21, 1968, an endorsement was added to the policy reciting, "This endorsement [is] attached to and forming part of policy numbered below . . . D7539681. . . . In consideration of an additional premium of $119, it is hereby understood and agreed that insurance is increased from $7,000 to $15,000." There is no dispute that the additional premium was never paid and that a written notice of cancellation, dated February 14, 1969, to be effective February 25, 1969, was mailed by the insurance company and duly received by the mortgagee. The cancellation notice stated: "Cancelled for Non-payment of Premium . . . the policy designated below and issued to you, is cancelled . . . D7539681."

A fire occurred on March 13, 1969, causing damage to the premises in the sum of $9,335. Plaintiff instituted this action to recover the sum of $2,563, representing defendant's pro rata share of the original insurance coverage ($7,000) on the premises.

The sole issue presented on this appeal is whether the insurance policy in question was a divisible contract. Put another way, did the February 14, 1969, notice of cancellation affect the entire coverage under the policy, or did it apply, in effect, only to the increased coverage added by the endorsement to the original policy?

We conclude that the policy of insurance in question was not a severable contract and the cancellation of said policy, prior to the loss, terminated the entire contract of insurance. "No formula has been devised which furnishes a test for determining in all cases what contracts of insurance are severable and what are entire. Fundamentally and primarily, the question of divisibility or severability rests upon the question of intention of the parties deducible from the stipulations of the contract and the rules of construction governing the ascertainment of that intention. As a general rule, a contract is entire when by its terms, nature, and purpose, it contemplates and intends that each and all of its parts and the consideration therefor shall be common each to the other and interdependent. On the other hand, the contract is considered severable and divisible when by its terms, nature, and purpose, it is susceptible of division and apportionment."

Williston, referring to divisible contracts, states that: " 'A contract is divisible where by its terms, 1, performance of each party is divided into two or more parts, and, 2, the number of parts due from each party is the same, and, 3, the performance of each part by one party is the agreed exchange for a corresponding part by the other party.' "

Applying these principles, we conclude that the October 21, 1968, endorsement became, as it specifically provided, part of the original insurance contract. The endorsement increased the amount of coverage for the same property and the same risk, namely: damages sustained to the insured premises by fire. Upon the effective date of the endorsement, the insurance company became liable, in the event of a fire, for the full amount of $15,000, even though the additional premium of $119 was not remitted. This added coverage and liability thereunder continued to be in full force and effect for more than four months, ceasing only upon notice of termination for nonpayment of premium. In addition, the cancellation notice specifically referred to policy D7539681 in its entirety. Certainly, under such circumstances, it cannot be said the contract was divisible. The result, of course, would be different if the subsequently added endorsement to the policy extended the scope of the coverage to include a different type of insurance risk than that covered by the original policy. . . .

Affirmed.

Luria Engineering Co. v. Aetna Cas. & Surety Co.
213 A.2d 151 (Pa.) 1965

A general contract to construct a school building was awarded to the plaintiff, who had subcontracts with a number of firms including General Roofing Company, one of the defendants. Aetna, the other defendant, is a bonding company which executed a performance bond on behalf of General Roofing. Work on the school ceased for a period of time as a result of a labor dispute stemming from the fact that one of the subcontractors employed nonunion labor. General Roofing wrote to plaintiff that the delay had prejudiced it and asked to be released from the contract. Plaintiff refused and gave notice that unless General Roofing commenced work within forty-eight hours, it would engage another contractor. Plaintiff brought suit to recover the difference between the contract price agreed to by General Roofing and the price paid to the subsequent roofing contractor. Judgment was awarded to plaintiff, and defendant appealed.

JACOBS, J. . . . We believe the present rule in Pennsylvania to be that acts of a third party making performance impossible or causing a delay resulting in substantial increase in expense to the contracting party do not excuse failure to perform if such acts were foreseeable because it was the duty of the contracting party to provide for that situation in his contract. . . .

In today's union-conscious society, in a job involving the construction of a building of some magnitude, a labor dispute or strike is certainly foreseeable. Especially is this true where, as in our situation, there were at least five different contractors, one of whom employed nonunion labor. Furthermore the parties themselves foresaw the possibility of a strike and provided in Section 8 of the contract for a manner of dealing with claims resulting from "any *damage* which may be caused by strike, fire, flood. . . ." [Emphasis added.] The only relevance of this section of the contract is that here the parties indicated that the possibility of a strike was foreseeable, but they failed to provide that a strike or a delay caused by strike should excuse performance. . . .

Appellants argue that . . . General Roofing's duty to perform was discharged on the basis that the labor dispute created a temporary impossibility which imposed a substantial burden on General Roofing. The argument fails because . . . the duty of the promisor is discharged only if he "had no reason to anticipate" the occurrence making performance impossible. Since we have determined that a labor dispute was foreseeable, General Roofing was not discharged of its duty to perform.

Judgment affirmed.

White Lakes Shop. Ctr. v. Jefferson Stand. L. Ins. Co.
490 P.2d 609 (Kan.) 1971

Plaintiff-borrower brought suit against defendant-lender to recover an advance payment of $77,000 which it had made in connection with a written loan commitment. Plaintiff was building a shopping center, and it arranged with defendant for "end financing" of the final mortgage. Defendant agreed to loan $3,850,-000. The loan commitment contained the following provision:

. . . Upon the loan being closed this $77,000 deposit is to be refunded promptly; but if the loan is not closed in accordance with the terms of this alternate commitment, the $77,000 deposit is to be retained permanently by the Jefferson Standard Life Insurance Company as liquidated damages. . . .

Plaintiff later found that it needed a larger loan, which defendant refused. Plaintiff then found another source and borrowed $4,250,-000. Plaintiff then sued for a return of the $77,000, contending that the contract contained an illegal liquidated damage clause (alleging a penalty) and that defendant's refusal to increase the loan created impossibility of performance, entitling plaintiff to a refund of the $77,000 payment. The lower court found for defendant, and plaintiff appealed.

FROMME, J. . . . Impossibility of performance, recognized in the law as a basis for relief from contractual obligations, is not of the nature contended for by appellant. When one agrees to perform an act possible in itself he will be liable for a breach thereof although contingencies not foreseen by him arise which make it difficult, or even beyond his power, to perform and which might have been foreseen and provided against in the contract.

The impossibility which will, or may, excuse the performance of a contract must exist in the nature of the thing to be done. It must not exist merely because of the inability or incapacity of the promisor or obligor to do it.

Where one agrees to perform an act possible in itself, he will be liable for a breach thereof although contingencies not foreseen by him arise which make it difficult or even beyond his power to perform, and which might have been provided against in the agreement.

The impossibility of performance in this case existed, if at all, by reason of the inability of White Lakes to complete construction at a cost within the loan commitment it had previously secured from Jefferson Standard. This is not the impossibility recognized in the law. . . .

[The court then held that the liquidated damage clause was not a penalty.]

Affirmed.

Pete Smith Company, Inc. v. City of El Dorado
529 S.W.2d 147 (Ark.) 1975

BYRD, J. . . . The appellant Pete Smith Company, Inc., contracted with the appellee, City of El Dorado, Arkansas, to construct an 18-hole golf course for $230,329.88. After appellant had performed all of the clearing and dirt work in accordance with the contract specification, a torrential rainfall of 12.47 inches occurred in a 10-hour period. Substantial erosion resulted from this rainfall. The undisputed testimony is that it will cost in excess of $60,000 to restore the golf course to its condition prior to the rain. Appellant, by way of a declaratory judgment, sought relief under the doctrine of "Commercial Frustration." The trial court denied relief. Appellant appeals raising only the issue of Commercial Frustration.

The commercial frustration doctrine is set forth in *Restatement of Contracts* § 288 (1932), as follows:

Where the assumed possibility of a desired object or effect to be attained by either party to a contract forms the basis on which both parties enter into it, and this object or effect is or surely will be frustrated, a promisor who is without fault in causing the frustration, and who is harmed thereby, is discharged from the duty of performing his promise unless a contrary intention appears. . . .

Judge Riddick stated the doctrine, in *Pacific Trading Co.* v. *Mouton Rice Milling Co.,* 184 F.2d 141 (8th Cir. 1950), as follows:

Under the doctrine of frustration as relieving a party from its contractual obligations, performance remains possible but is excused whenever an event not due to the fault of either party supervenes to cause a failure of consideration or destruction of the expected value of performance. . . .

6 Corbin on Contracts § 1361 points out that a partial frustration by subsequent events is less likely to be held to discharge a contractor from duty than is total frustration. . . .

The contract before us here provides:

Section 1, INSTRUCTIONS TO BID-DERS, § 1-02, *Local Conditions:* Bidders shall *read* and *examine* the Specifications and Plans, and make their own estimates of the existing facilities and difficulties which will attend the execution of the work called for by these Contract Documents, the Specifications and the Plans, including local conditions, uncertainty of the weather, and all other contingencies. Bidders shall satisfy themselves by personal examination of the location of the proposed work, and by such means as they may choose, as to actual conditions and requirements. . . .

Section 2, GENERAL CONDITIONS OF THE SPECIFICATIONS, § 2-06, *The Contractor:* It is understood and agreed that the Contractor has, by careful examination satisfied himself as to the nature and location of the work, the information of the ground, the character, quality and quantity of the materials to be encountered [in] prosecution of the

work, the general location conditions, and all other matters which can in any way affect the work under this Contract. . . .

Section 2, GENERAL CONDITIONS OF THE SPECIFICATIONS. § 2-13, *Protection of Work and Property:* The Contractor shall continuously maintain adequate protection of all his work from damage and shall protect the Contracting Authority's property from injury or loss arising in connection with the Contract. We shall make good any damage, injury, or loss, except such as may be directly due to errors in the Contract Documents or caused by agents or employees of the Contracting Authority. . . .

Thus, from the foregoing it follows that the Chancellor did not err in denying appellant relief under the commercial frustration doctrine whether such denial be placed upon the theory that the contract expressed a contrary intent or the theory that the doctrine is not applicable in the event of only a partial frustration that only increases the cost of performance.

Affirmed.

CHAPTER 14
REVIEW QUESTIONS AND PROBLEMS

1. X gave Y a deposit on the purchase of a house. The contract contained the provision that the agreement was contingent upon X's ability to obtain a mortgage. X was unable to obtain the mortgage, and Y refused to return the deposit. Should X recover the deposit? Why?

Yes – Condit. Precedent

2. A hired B, a mining company, to drill a coal mine. The mine failed because tunneling became too difficult. B claimed the contract was frustrated because of an unforeseeable event. Should A collect damages? Why?

No, frustration not foreseeable.

3. X agreed to take dancing lessons from Y for a specified period at a predetermined price. After only part of the lessons were completed, X became disabled and was unable to fulfill the rest of the contract. Should X be released from the contract? Explain.

Yes, frustration of purpose of contract

4. A and B had a written contract containing a provision that it could not be modified or rescinded except by a signed writing. Later they mutually agreed orally to rescind the contract. Is the contract still enforceable? Why?

Yes, because not done in writing.

5. X sold Y a refrigeration unit in April 1977 with the agreement of a down payment and eighteen installment payments. Y made the down payment but did not make any further payments. In July 1979, X replevied the unit and sold it for its fair market value. X then sued Y to recover the remaining balance. Y defends on the ground that the unit was defective. What result? Why? *wouldn't get defense, since didn't tell on*

6. B purchased a prefabricated house from S, and the agreement specified that the house would be completed on a certain date. On that date, everything was completed except for some grading and paving. B refused to accept the house and demanded the return of his down payment. Is B correct? Why? *No, substantial performance*

7. A leased a building from L with the intent that it would be remodeled into a theater and bookstore. However, A could not obtain building permits, because of fire hazards on the leased premises and also on adjacent premises owned by L. L refused to pay for the cost of bringing his adjacent premises up to the required standards even though A was willing to pay for the cost of repair to the leased premises. Neither party knew that this type of structural change was necessary when the contract was entered. A now sues for the return of his rent deposit. Should A recover the deposit? Why? *Yes - Prevention of Performance*

8. S listed his property for sale with R, a real estate broker. R arranged for B to enter into a contract to buy the property from S, subject to B's selling by October 1 certain other properties he owned. B's property did not sell by October 1, so he did not purchase S's property. S's listing with R expired. Seven months later, B purchased S's property without the services of R. R now sues S for a commission, contending that he obtained B as a purchaser. Should R succeed? Why? *No*

delay-also 6 month

9. X granted a franchise to Y to operate a Mr. Steak restaurant. All franchise agreements contained a clause prohibiting the sale of alcoholic beverages on the restaurant premises. Ten franchise operators in other areas began to sell alcoholic beverages, but X did not have the necessary funds to legally stop them. Y then applied for and received a license to sell alcoholic beverages in his restaurant. X seeks to enjoin Y from selling alcoholic beverages. What result? Why?

separate & divisible contracts

10. X, a professional football player, signed a seven-year contract for $875,000 with Y, a professional football club. X was to receive $50,000 upon signing and another $50,000 at the end of the first year. X did receive $50,000 for signing, but by the end of the first year, Y still owed X $30,000 owing to Y's financial difficulties, which consisted of $1,600,000 indebtedness and an overdraft at the bank of $67,000. X sues for rescission of the contract. Is rescission a proper remedy? Why? *No - money damages is only thing to recover.*

15

Discharge of Contracts

1. Introduction

The rights and duties created by a contract continue in force until the contract is discharged. The usual and intended method of discharge is the complete performance by both parties of their obligations under the agreement. In the preceding chapter, excuses for nonperformance were discussed. A valid excuse is a discharge in the sense that the excused party has no liability for failure to perform. The same may be said of grounds for rescission. A rescinded contract is in effect discharged.

A cancellation of a written contract and the surrender of it by one party to the other will usually discharge the agreement. Such a discharge requires consideration or proof of a gift. If both parties have obligations, there is consideration on the mutual surrender of the rights to performance. If only one party has an obligation, the necessary intent to make a gift and delivery of it may be found in the delivery of the written cancelled contract. However, such evidence is not conclusive, and a jury may find that a gift was not in fact made.

The law makes a distinction between a writing that is merely the *evidence* of the obligation and one that *is* the obligation, such as a promissory note. There is no particular sanctity in the law to the physical evidence of an ordinary contract, and the destruction of this evidence does not destroy the contract. However, if the actual obligation such as a negotiable instrument is

257

surrendered or is intentionally destroyed by the holder of it, the obligation is discharged.

There are other methods of discharge, which are discussed in this chapter. The legal doctrine of *novation* provides for the substitution of one obligor for another and the discharge of the one who is replaced. The legal concept of *accord and satisfaction* allows discharge of a contract by a performance different from that agreed upon in the agreement. Laws sometimes have the effect of discharging obligation by prohibiting lawsuits to enforce them. For example, passage of time without litigation to enforce one's rights will operate to discharge an obligation. A discharge in bankruptcy has the same effect. (This is the subject matter of Chapter 28.)

2. Payment

The obligation of one party to a contract is usually to pay the other for goods sold or services rendered. There are three especially significant issues about payment that affect the matter of discharge: What constitutes payment? What is good evidence that payment has been made and that the obligation has been discharged? When a debtor has several obligations to a creditor, how will a payment be applied?

Certainly, the transfer of money constitutes payment, but this is not necessarily the case when the payment is by a negotiable instrument such as a check or a promissory note. Generally, payment by delivery of a negotiable instrument drawn or endorsed by the debtor to the creditor is a conditional payment and not an absolute discharge of the obligation. If the instrument is paid at maturity, the debt is discharged; if it is not so paid, the debt then exists as it did prior to the conditional payment. In the latter situation, the creditor can either bring an action to recover on the defaulted instrument or pursue his rights under the original agreement.[1]

The parties may agree that payment by a negotiable instrument is an absolute discharge, in which event, if the instrument is not paid at maturity, the only recourse of the creditor is to bring action on the instrument—the original contract is discharged. A similar situation exists when accounts receivable are assigned by a debtor to his creditor. An assignment of accounts is a conditional payment only. If the accounts are not collected, the debtor is still obligated to pay his indebtedness. If the parties intend that the receipt of negotiable instruments or accounts receivable be treated as a discharge of the obligation, they must so specify.

As to what constitutes acceptable evidence of payment and discharge, a receipt given by the creditor will usually suffice. Such receipt should clearly indicate the amount paid and specify the transaction to which it relates. However, the creditor may be able to rebut the receipt by evidence that it was in error or that it was given under mistake. A cancelled check is also evidence

---

[1] *Central Stove Co.* v. *John Ruggiero, Inc.,* page 261.

of payment, but the evidence is more conclusive when the purpose for which it is given is stated on the check. The drawer of a check may specify on the instrument that the payee by endorsing or cashing it acknowledges full satisfaction of an obligation of the drawer. Mutual debts do not extinguish each other, and in order for one to constitute payment of another, in whole or in part, there must be agreement between the creditor and the debtor that the one shall be applied in satisfaction of the other.

Where a debtor owes several obligations to one creditor, the debtor may direct how any payment is to be applied. The creditor who receives such payment is obligated to follow the debtor's instructions. In the absence of any instructions, the creditor may apply the payment against any one of several obligations that are due, or may credit a portion of the payment against each of several obligations. The creditor may apply a payment against a claim that has been outlawed by the statute of limitations, but this will not cause the outlawed claim to revive as to the balance.

If the source of a payment is someone other than the debtor and this fact is known to the creditor, the payment must be applied in such a manner as to protect the third party who makes the payment. Hence, if the money for the payment is supplied by a surety who has guaranteed that a particular obligation will be paid by the debtor, and the creditor knows it, he is bound to apply the payment on the obligation for which the surety was secondarily liable. Finally, if the creditor fails to make a particular application, the payment will be applied by the courts to the obligation oldest in point of time. However, where the creditor holds both secured and unsecured obligations, the courts of most states are inclined to apply it on an unsecured obligation. Similarly, if both principal and interest are due, the court considers the interest to be paid first, any balance being credited on the principal.

3. Accord and Satisfaction

An *accord* is an agreement whereby one of the parties undertakes to give or to perform and the other to accept something different from that which he is or considers himself entitled to. An accord may arise from a disputed claim in either tort or contract. The term *satisfaction* means that the substituted performance is completed.

The doctrine of accord and satisfaction requires that there be a dispute or uncertainty as to amount due and that parties enter into agreement that debtor will pay, and creditor will accept, a lesser amount as a compromise of their differences and in satisfaction of the debt. It must clearly appear that the parties so understood and entered into a new and substitute contract. The surrender of the legal right to litigate the dispute or the settlement agreement often serves as consideration.[2] However, if a debtor at the request of a creditor makes payment in some manner other than what he is obligated to, and this

---

[2] *Farmland Service Coop., Inc.,* v. *Jack,* page 262.

constitutes a detriment, there is consideration for the payment and the debt is discharged.

The usual accord and satisfaction case involves a debtor's sending a creditor a check for less than the amount claimed by the creditor to be due. This check is usually marked "Paid in full." The courts of a few states hold that the cashing of the check constitutes an accord and satisfaction without additional proof. Most states, however, require that the party asserting the accord and satisfaction also prove (1) that the debt or claim was in fact the subject of a bona fide dispute, (2) that the creditor was aware of the dispute, and (3) that the creditor was aware that the check was tendered as full payment. If the creditor cashes the check, this act constitutes the satisfaction of the accord and completes the discharge. The creditor cannot change the language of the check, deposit it, or cash it and still contend that there was no accord and satisfaction.

4. Novation

The term *novation* has two meanings. First of all, it is used to describe the situation in which the parties to a contract substitute a new debt or obligation for an existing one. The substitution of the new agreement operates to release or discharge the old one.

Novation is also used to describe an agreement whereby an original party to a contract is replaced by a new party. A novation is more than a mere assignment and delegation of duties. In order for the substitution to be effective, it must be agreed to by all the parties. The remaining contracting party must agree to accept the new party and at the same time specifically agree to release the withdrawing party.[3] The latter must consent to withdraw and to permit the new party to take his place. The new party must agree to assume the burdens and duties of the retiring party based on consideration. If all these essentials are present, the withdrawing party is discharged from the agreement. A novation is never presumed, and the burden is on the party asserting to prove all its essential requirements.

5. Statute of Limitations

The statute of limitations prescribes a time limit within which suit must be started after a cause of action arises.[4] Failure to file suit within the time prescribed is a complete defense to the suit.

The purpose of a statute of limitations is to prevent actions from being brought long after evidence is lost or important witnesses have died or moved away. An action for breach of any contract for sale of personal property under the Code must be commenced within four years (2-725). The Code

---

[3] *Morning* v. *Miller,* page 263.

[4] *McCroskey* v. *Bryant Air Conditioning Company,* page 264.

further provides that the parties in their agreement may reduce the period of limitation to not less than one year but may not extend it. Contracts that are not controlled by the Code are covered by a variety of limitation periods. Some states distinguish between oral and written contracts, making the period longer for the latter.

Any voluntary part payment made on a money obligation by the debtor with intent to pay the balance tolls the statute, starting it to run anew. Similarly, any voluntary part payment, new promise, or clear acknowledgment of the indebtedness made after the claim has been outlawed reinstates the obligation, and the statute commences to run again.[5] A payment or part payment by a third person or a joint debtor does not operate to interrupt the running of the statute as to other debtors not participating in the payment. No new consideration is required to support the reinstatement promise. If the old obligation has been outlawed, a new promise may be either partial or conditional. Since there is no *duty* to pay the debt, the debtor may attach such conditions to his new promise as he sees fit or may promise to pay only part of the debt. A few states require the new promise or acknowledgement to be in writing. The Code does not alter the law on tolling of the statute of limitations (2-725[4]).

A problem exists when a party is incapacitated by minority or insanity. Most jurisdictions hold that lack of capacity stops the running of the statute and extends the period of filing suit. A minor or an insane person usually has a specified time in which to bring an action—after the minor reaches his majority or the insane person regains capacity—although the full period set by statute has expired earlier.

DISCHARGE OF CONTRACTS CASES

Central Stove Co. v. John Ruggiero, Inc.
268 N.Y.S.2d 172 (N.Y.) 1966

TOMSON, J. . . . The plaintiff seeks to recover for work, labor, and services. The defendant contends that, although the value of the work done was as claimed by the plaintiff, a payment of $2,250 was made by negotiating to the plaintiff a promissory note of a third party in that sum. The defendant's endorsement was "without recourse."

The testimony was sharply conflicting as to the conversation at the time the note was given. The defendant urges that his version of the discussion and the restrictive endorsement, though not conclusive, should result in the inference that there was an agreement between the parties to accept the notes as an unconditional payment. . . .

The Uniform Commercial Code, Sec. 3-802, entitled "Effect of Instrument of Obligation for Which It Is Given," reads:

> (1) *Unless otherwise agreed* where an instrument is taken for an underlying

---

[5] *Whale Harbor Spa, Inc.* v. *Wood*, page 265.

obligation . . . (b) in any other case the obligation is suspended *pro tanto* until the instrument is due or if it is payable on demand until its presentment. *If the instrument is dishonored action may be maintained on either the instrument or the obligation; discharge of the underlying obligor on the instrument also discharges him on the obligation. . . .* [Emphasis supplied.]

See also 43 New York Jur., "Payment," section 42 et seq. where it is stated at page 487:

> Prior to the Uniform Commercial Code the intention of the parties ordinarily prevailed in determining whether the delivery and acceptance of a negotiable instrument drawn by the debtor or by a third person was to be treated as payment in themselves, or as payment conditional on the honoring of the paper by the drawee. But in the absence of a demonstrated intention the general rule was that the acceptance of a commercial paper by a creditor for an antecedent debt did not constitute an absolute payment. . . .

Of some interest is *Herold* v. *Fleming,* 17 Misc. 581, 582, where the court below refused to charge as requested "that the taking of the note of a third person, endorsed 'without recourse,' constitutes a payment, and that the writing must control any oral statements made at the time." The Appellate Court said, "The vice of the proposed charge was that it eliminated the element of an agreement as a constituent of the fact of payment."

On the evidence here it cannot be said, despite the endorsement "without recourse," that the defendant met the burden imposed upon it to prove that it was the intention of the parties to treat the note as absolute rather than conditional payment.

The defendant's indebtedness was not therefore discharged by the delivery of the note; the defendant's obligation was merely suspended *pro tanto* until the instrument became due on September 18, 1964, at which time the plaintiff had the election of maintaining an action either on the instrument or on the obligation.

Accordingly, judgment is directed to be entered in favor of the plaintiff together with costs, disbursements and interest from September 18, 1964.

Farmland Service Coop., Inc. v. Jack
242 N.W.2d 624 (Neb.) 1976

BOSLAUGH, J. . . . This is an action for damages for breach of contracts to sell corn. The plaintiff is a cooperative company which is engaged in the marketing of grain and operates an elevator at Gothenburg, Nebraska. The defendants operate farms in Frontier County, Nebraska.

On May 1, 1973, the defendants agreed to sell 40,000 bushels of No. 2 grade yellow corn to the plaintiff at $1.45 per bushel for delivery between May 1, 1973, and August 31, 1973. On May 2, 1973, the defendants agreed to sell an additional 40,000 bushels of No. 2 grade yellow corn to the plaintiff on the same terms.

During May and June of 1973, the defendants delivered approximately 17,000 bushels of corn to the plaintiff. Late in June the defendants notified the plaintiff they would not deliver any more corn under their contracts. The defendants stated they had received bad advice from the plaintiff's elevator manager and the contract price was too cheap. . . .

On June 26, 1973, there was a meeting at the office of the plaintiff's attorney. The elevator manager and the defendants were present together with the plaintiff's attorney and the defendants' attorney. The defendants offered to deliver the balance of the corn due under the first contract if the plaintiff would agree to a cancellation of the second contract. The plaintiff's attorney requested time to research the legal questions involved.

On June 28, 1973, the elevator manager wrote a letter to the defendants, on the letterhead of the plaintiff's attorney, stating as follows: "The Gothenburg Co-Op elevator will haul 23,000 bushels of your corn for $1.45 a bushel less freight charges from June 29th through the month of July." At the bottom of the letter there was a blank line for the signature of the defendants to acknowledge they had received the letter. Willard Jack acknowledged receipt of the letter and returned a signed copy to the plaintiff.

The defendants delivered an additional 23,000 bushels of corn to the plaintiff in July. On October 9, 1973, the general manager of the plaintiff wrote to the defendants and demanded performance of the second contract. The defendants refused to perform the second contract.

The trial court found there had been an accord and satisfaction between the parties and sustained the defendants' motion for a summary judgment. The plaintiff has appealed.

An accord and satisfaction is an agreement to discharge an existing indebtedness by the rendering of some performance different from that which was claimed due. The acceptance by the claimant of the substituted performance in full satisfaction of the claim discharges the indebtedness. An executed compromise settlement of a good faith controversy is an accord and satisfaction.

The evidence before the trial court in this case showed that the defendants had agreed to sell 80,000 bushels of corn to the plaintiff but a dispute arose after 17,000 bushels had been delivered. At the conference on June 26, 1973, the defendants offered to deliver an additional 23,000 bushels to the plaintiff in full satisfaction of both contracts. The elevator manager claimed that he did not accept the offer on that date, but it is undisputed that the letter stating the plaintiff would haul 23,000 bushels of the defendants' corn at the contract price from June 29 through the month of July and signed by the elevator manager was sent to the defendants several days later. This letter was an acceptance of the defendants' offer made on June 26, 1973. The offer and acceptance followed by performance of the agreement constituted an accord and satisfaction.

The plaintiff suggests there was no consideration for the agreement. The settlement of the dispute between the parties was a sufficient consideration for the agreement. Furthermore, a modification of a sales contract may be made without consideration under the Uniform Commercial Code. . . .

Affirmed.

Morning v. Miller
330 So.2d 93 (Fla. App.) 1976

PER CURIAM. . . . Appellant, plaintiff below, developed a new variety of pecan tree and contracted with Simpson Nursery Company (of which appellee Stuart C. Simpson was a partner) in 1959, whereby Simpson was to obtain and pay for the patent on the plant as well as develop, propagate, produce, and market the variety. Appellant received $500 for the patent right and, by agreement, was to receive 25 cents per tree for each tree sold by appellees during the first 10 years of the term of the patent, and 10 cents per tree royalty for each tree sold during the remainder of the patent term. After the patent was obtained, appellant executed an assignment of the patent rights to Simpson, "for its own use and behoof, and for its legal representatives and assigns." In 1963, Simpson sold its assets, including its contract with appellant, and the patent relating to the pecan tree developed by appellant (the Pensacola Cluster) to A.L. Dickerson, the successor owner of Simpson Nursery, Inc. and Gro-Plant Industries, Inc. After appellant became aware of the assignment, he continued to receive and accept reports concerning the sale of the Pensacola Cluster and royalty payments from the successor assignees. Appellant finally became dissatisfied with the arrangement, feeling that the number of Pensacola Cluster pecan trees actually sold was greater than the number of trees upon which his royalty payments were based; whereupon he filed his complaint in 1967, alleging that appellees had breached their contract with him by failing to properly account for and pay to him the royalties due, and in failing to diligently advertise and promote the sale of nursery stock as required by the contract. . . . In 1974, a jury trial was held on the issue of breach of contract. The final judgment, in which appellant was awarded damages totaling less than $2,000 plus interest, reflected a finding by the trial court that the liability of Stuart C. Simpson should be limited to the period of time prior to October 1, 1963. . . .

[T]he trial court ruled that appellee Stuart C. Simpson would not be liable under his agreement with appellant subsequent to the date of the sale of assets to Alvin L. Dickerson (October 1, 1963). In so ruling, the trial court erred. Whether or not Simpson's contract with appellant was assignable, such assignment did not relieve Simpson of liability under the original contract with appellant. Appellees claim that there was a complete novation when appellant became aware of the assignments of his agreement, and continued to receive and accept reports and royalty payments from the successor assignees. However, the law is well settled that in order to constitute a novation, the parties must agree to a contract which is intended to take the place of a prior obligation. In general terms, mere acceptance of the obligation of the assignee without any intention to relieve the original debtor is not, in and of itself, sufficient to constitute a novation. There is no indication in the record that the parties intended that appellee Simpson be relieved from liability under the original contract. In the absence of such evidence, as a matter of law, there was no novation. . . .

Reversed.

McCroskey v. Bryant Air Conditioning Company
524 S.W.2d 487 (Tenn.) 1975

This products liability action presents the question of when the statute of limitations begins to run. The cause of action for personal injuries and wrongful death is based upon an allegedly defective gas furnace. The gas furnace was manufactured in 1967 and distributed and installed on or about February 9, 1968. The injuries were sustained on May 1, 1971. Suit was filed July 28, 1971. The defendants were granted a judgment upon the ground that the suit was barred by the two-year statute of limitations applicable to torts. It held that the period commenced at the date of installation.

HENRY, J. . . . We approach this analysis from a standpoint of reason, logic and fundamental fairness. These are criteria by which any rule of law should be tested. . . . It is only just for us to decree that in any tort action the cause of action accrues when, and only when, the force wrongfully put in motion produces injury. We cannot embrace or continue any rule of law which charges a litigant with sleeping upon any right which he does not have.

We are challenged by the cogent and colorful language of Judge Jerome Frank's dissenting opinion in *Dincher* v. *Marlin Firearms Co.,* 198 F.2d 821 (2 Cir. 1952):

> Except in topsy-turvey land, you can't die before you are conceived, or be divorced before ever you marry, or harvest a crop never planted, or burn down a house never built, or miss a train running on a non-existent railroad. For substantially similar reasons, it has always heretofore been accepted, as a sort of legal "axiom," that a statute of limitations does not begin to run against a cause of action before that cause of action exists,

i.e., before a judicial remedy is available to the plaintiff.

In *Campbell* v. *Colt Industries, Inc.*, 349 F.Supp. 166 (W.D.VA. 1972), the court in holding that, whether based on negligence or breach of warranty, a cause of action for personal injuries did not accrue until the injury occurred, quoted from a Virginia case as follows:

> Obviously, since the plaintiff had not been injured at the time she purchased the car, she could not then maintain an action for her injuries. To say, then, that her right of action accrued before her injuries were received is to say that she was without remedy to recover damages for her alleged injuries. Such an unjust and inequitable result is not the purpose of statutes of limitation. They are designed to compel the prompt assertion of an accrued right of action; not to bar such a right before it has accrued.
>
> A right of action cannot accrue until there is a cause of action. . . . In the ab-

sence of injury or damage to a plaintiff or his property, he has no cause of action and no right of action can accrue to him. . . . Or, to state the matter another way, a plaintiff's right of action for damages for personal injuries does not accrue until he is hurt. . . .

To hold that a products liability action, which is a recognized legal right is barred by a statute of limitations before any injury is sustained, deprives a person of the opportunity of redress for an injury done him in his goods or person by due process of law, contrary to our Constitution. . . .

We hold that in tort actions, including but not restricted to products liability actions ("conceived in an illicit intercourse of tort and contract") . . . the cause of action accrues and the statute of limitations commences to run when the injury occurs or is discovered, or when in the exercise of reasonable care and diligence, it should have been discovered. . . .

Reversed.

Whale Harbor Spa, Inc. v. Wood
266 F.2d 953 (1959)

JONES, J. . . . The appellant, Whale Harbor Spa, Inc., is a Florida corporation. Its stock was owned in equal shares by Dorothy W. Wood and Al B. Luckey. The corporation was managed by Luckey. The Luckey and Wood families had been close friends over a period of many years. Between May 1, 1946, and October 14, 1948, Mrs. Wood made six open loans aggregating $24,750 to the corporation. These loans were not evidenced by promissory notes or other written obligation. On July 10, 1950, Mrs. Wood loaned the corporation $5,000 upon its demand note. On April 7, 1947, the corporation paid Mrs. Wood $3,000 on account. The amount of the advances unpaid remains at $26,750. The indebtedness was set up on the corporation's books and was carried as a liability of the corporation to Mrs. Wood. On July 10, 1950, the corporation, by

an endorsement on a letter from Mrs. Wood's agent, acknowledged the existence of the indebtedness and the amount of it. From at least as early as November, 1952, and at intervals of never more than six months, the bookkeeper of the corporation, at the direction of Luckey, sent to Mrs. Wood or her agent profit and loss statements and balance sheets of the corporation. The balance sheets showed an indebtedness to Mrs. Wood of $26,750. After the death of both Mrs. Wood and Luckey, the executor of Mrs. Wood brought suit against the corporation for the amount of the unpaid advances. The corporation did not deny that the loans had been made nor did it contend that payment had been made. Its sole defense is that the indebtedness is barred by the Florida statute of limitations. The plaintiff, as executor of Mrs. Wood's estate, contended that the balance sheets were written acknowledgments of the debt sufficient to toll the statute, and further contended that the corporation was equitably estopped to plead the statute of limitations. The court, after a trial without a jury, determined that no part of the debt was barred by the statute of limitations and entered judgment against the corporation. It has appealed.

It is not questioned that the period of limitation has run and that the statute of limitations is a bar to recovery unless the statute has been tolled or the corporation is estopped to assert it. The Florida statute requires that "every acknowledgment of or promise to pay a debt barred by the statute of limitations, must be in writing and signed by the party to be charged." (F.S.A. § 95.04.) This statute does not apply to promises made before the expiration of the period of limitations, and verbal promises made before the cause of action had run will take the cause of action out from the operation of the statute. . . . Where there is a distinct acknowledgment in writing of the debt, a promise to pay it will be inferred. . . .

The precedents of the decided cases point to a rule, which we think is sound in principle, that the requirement of an acknowledgment of an indebtedness which will interrupt the running of the statute of limitations is met by a balance sheet of a corporate debtor where the obligations in question are listed as liabilities of the corporation.

. . . *That judgment is affirmed.*

CHAPTER 15
REVIEW QUESTIONS AND PROBLEMS

1. A made a number of purchases from B. A made a payment on account to B, and the question arose as to how B should apply this payment to the various accounts. How should this question be resolved? Explain.

2. Doctor A operated on B for a gall bladder in 1970. In 1978 an X ray revealed that surgical clamps had been left in B's body during the operation. Does the statute of limitations prevent B from bringing an action against the doctor? Why?

3. M and X were co-makers of a note. After the statute of limitations had expired, M made some payments, and a question arose as to whether the payments extended the period of X's liability. Is the liability of X outlawed, or was it extended by the payments of M? Explain.

4. L & B, a partnership, sued W for services rendered and W urged accord and satisfaction as a defense. W claimed the bill to be excessive and had mailed a check for a lesser amount marked "in full of account." L & B drew a line through the statement and cashed the check. Was this an accord and satisfaction? Explain.

5. A sold a printing machine to B on an installment plan. B sold the machine to C, who agreed to pay the balance of the purchase price. Both parties notified A of the arrangement and A did not object. C failed to make the payments and A sought to hold B. May he do so?

6. P made plumbing modifications on O's house. When P submitted a bill for his services, a dispute in good faith arose between P and O as to the amount owed. O then sent a check to P marked, "Payment of account in full." P crossed out these words, wrote on the check "Paid on account," and deposited it in his account. P now sues O for the difference in the amount of the bill. Should P collect? Why? *no – forged for satisfaction*

7. B Company owed money to S Company for goods purchased. B sold his business to T Company in return for the assumption by T of its obligation to S. T paid $500 on account to S and gave its promissory note for the balance. T became insolvent, and S now sues B for the remaining balance. Is B liable to S? Why?

8. D borrowed from C $1,400 payable in 36 monthly installments. Two years later, D defaulted, but the debt was partially uncollectible because D was unemployed. C then prepared a contract, which D signed, modifying the old contract and requiring D to pay $5 per month to C. D made regular payments, but one year later, C sued on the original contract. Should C succeed? Why? *no, novation*

9. B purchased a franchise from S and gave his promissory note for $8,000 as the purchase price. B later transferred the franchise to T, who agreed to pay B's note to S. T went into bankruptcy, and S now sues B for the balance due. B claims that he is not liable because a novation has occurred. Is B correct? Why? *no, not substituting one for other*

10. A business school hired X to solicit enrollments and agreed to pay him a specified commission on the tuition received. Advances were made to X at the beginning of each month, and this amount was deducted from the commission earned at the end of the month. The school decided to terminate its operations and mailed a check to X for services rendered, marked, "Full and final payment of all obligations." Prior to cashing it, X added, "Endorser in no way agrees." At the time of cashing the check, X was not aware of the exact amount owed to him. When sued by X, the school claimed there had been an accord and satisfaction. Is the school correct? Why?

yes

book three

THE UNIFORM COMMERCIAL CODE

16

The Law of Sales: Basic Concepts

1. Introduction

As discussed in the chapters on contracts, the Code recognizes that many of the principles of general contract law are not desirable in contracts for the sale of goods. Rules and principles of contract law that produce a desirable result in a transaction for the sale or construction of a building, or in a contract between an employer and an employee, do not necessarily produce a good result in a contract for the purchase and sale of goods. Accordingly, many common law contract rules have been changed or modified by the Code in order to achieve a commercially desirable result. Most of the changes are based on common business practice and the customary way of doing business.

The Code provisions on the sale of goods are also based on two additional assumptions: (1) that the parties should be given the maximum latitude in fixing their own terms, and (2) that the parties will act in "good faith." *Good faith* means honesty in fact in the conduct or transaction (1-201[19]). In the case of a merchant, "good faith" also includes the observance of reasonable commercial standards of fair dealing in the trade (2-103[1][b]).

2. Summary of Code Changes

The changes in the law of contracts for the sale of goods were discussed in the chapters on contracts. The chart on the following page contains a summary of these changes and also references to the Code section in which the change is made.

271

SPECIAL RULES FOR CONTRACTS OF SALE OF GOODS

Rule	Code Section

Offer and Acceptance

1. Unilateral offers may be accepted either by a promise to ship or by shipment. — 2-206(1)(b)
2. Firm written offers by *merchants* for three months or less are irrevocable. — 2-205
3. All terms need not be included in negotiations in order for a contract to result. — 2-204
4. Particulars of performance may be left open. — 2-311(1)
5. Failure to reject may constitute an acceptance. — 2-206(1)(b)
6. Variance in terms between offer and acceptance may not be a rejection and may be an acceptance. — 2-207
7. An acceptance may be made by any reasonable means of communication and is effective when deposited. — 2-206(1)(a)
8. Acceptance by performance requires notice within a reasonable time, or the offer may be treated as lapsed. — 2-206(2)
9. For a contract to be valid, the price need not be included. — 2-305

Consideration

1. Consideration is not required to support a modification of a contract for the sale of goods. — 2-209(1)
2. Adding a seal is of no effect. — 2-203

Voidable Contracts

1. A minor may not disaffirm against an innocent third party. — 2-403
2. Rescission is not a bar to a suit for dollar damages. — 2-721

Illegality

1. Unconscionable bargains will not be enforced. — 2-302

Form of the Agreement

1. Statute of Frauds: — 2-201
   a. $500 price for goods.
   b. Written confirmation between merchants.
   c. Memorandum need not include all terms of agreement.
   d. Payment, acceptance, and receipt limited to quantity specified in writing.
   e. Specially manufactured goods.
   f. Admission pleadings or court proceedings that a contract for sale was made.

Rights of Third Parties

1. An assignment of "the contract" or of "rights under the contract" include a delegation of duties. — 2-210(4)

Performance of Contracts

1. Tender of payment is a condition precedent (rather than a condition concurrent) to a tender of delivery. — 2-511
2. Anticipatory breach may not be withdrawn if the other party gives notice that it is final. — 2-610, 2-611
3. Rules on divisible contracts. — 2-307, 2-612
4. Impracticability of performance in certain cases is an excuse for nonperformance. — 2-614
5. Claims and rights may be waived without consideration. — 1-107, 2-209

Discharge

1. The statute of limitations is four years, but parties can reduce by mutual agreement to not less than one year. — 2-725

3. Definitions

Article 2 of the Code is applicable to transactions in "goods" (2-102). It is not applicable to sales of other types of property or to other types of contracts. The term *goods* encompasses all things that are movable; that is, items of personal property (chattels) that are of a tangible, physical nature [1] (2-105[1]). The term is broadly interpreted and even includes such things as electricity.

The definition of *goods* excludes investment securities, such as stocks and bonds and negotiable instruments. The limitation of the coverage to *goods* necessarily excludes sales of real property, contracts for personal services, and those involving intangible personal property. However, the sale of timber, minerals, or a building that is to be removed from the land is a sale of goods if these are to be severed by the seller (2-107). Growing crops are also included within the definition of goods, whether they are to be removed by the buyer or the seller (2-105[1]).

A *sale* consists of the passing of title to goods from the seller to the buyer for a price (2-106[1]). The seller is obligated to transfer and deliver or tender delivery of the goods, and the buyer is obligated to accept and pay in accordance with the contract (2-301). In general, the parties to a contract for sale can agree upon any terms and conditions that are mutually acceptable.

Special provisions of Article 2 relate to transactions involving a *merchant*. A merchant is a person who is in effect a professional businessman and who holds himself out as having knowledge or skill peculiar to the practices or goods involved in the transaction (2-104[1]). This designation is of great importance and is recognition of a professional status for a businessman, justifying the application of different standards to their conduct from those applied to "nonprofessionals." The courts of some states have held that farmers are merchants when selling grain and other items raised by them. Other courts have held that farmers are not merchants. Therefore, the application of the Code to farmers varies from state to state.

Another term used in Article 2 is *future goods*. Future goods are goods that are not in existence at the time of the agreement or that have not been "identified"—designated as the specific goods that will be utilized in the transaction (2-105[2]).

4. Basic Contract Terms

The parties are privileged to specify in detail the terms of their agreement. Most contracts contain terms relating to the price to be paid, the quantity of goods involved, the time and place for delivery, and the time for payment. Sometimes, however, the parties do not specify all the terms; accordingly, the Code sets forth rules that are applicable in the absence of such specific terms.

---

[1] *Lake Wales Pub. Co., Inc.* v. *Florida Visitor, Inc.,* page 283.

The Price Term. The price term of the contract can be left open, with the price to be fixed by later agreement of the parties, or some agreed market standard or other standard may be designated for fixing the price (2-305). It may even be agreed that the buyer or the seller shall fix the price, in which event he is obligated to exercise good faith in doing so. If the contract is silent on price, or if for some reason the price is not set in accordance with the method agreed upon, it will be determined as a reasonable price at the time of delivery. Thus, if it appears that it is their intention to do so, parties can bind themselves even though the price is not actually agreed upon.

The Quantity Term. The Code also allows flexibility in the quantity term of sales contracts.[2] There may be an agreement to purchase the entire output of the seller, or the quantity may be specified as all that is required by the buyer. The Code contains provisions to ensure fair dealing between the parties where the quantity is specified in this manner (2-306). If parties express an estimate as to the quantity involved, no quantity that is unreasonably disproportionate to the estimate will be enforced. If the parties have not agreed upon an estimate, a quantity that is in keeping with normal or other comparable prior output or requirements is implied.

The buyer and the seller may enter into an "exclusive dealing contract," whereby (1) the seller may agree to sell his product only to the buyer, or (2) the buyer may agree that he will exclusively purchase all his requirements from the seller. In either event, the Code requires that each party act in good faith. An exclusive dealing contract may be illegal under certain state or federal antitrust laws.

The Delivery Term. The term *delivery* signifies a transfer of possession of the goods from the seller to the buyer. A seller makes delivery when he physically transfers into the possession of the buyer the actual goods that conform to the requirements of the contract. However, a seller satisfies the requirement that he "transfer and deliver" when he "tenders delivery" (2-507).

A proper tender of delivery requires the seller to make available conforming goods at the buyer's disposition and to give the buyer any notification reasonably necessary to take delivery (2-503[1]). The particulars as to time, place, and manner of tender are to be determined on the basis of the agreement as supplemented by the Code. Each of the parties is required to act "reasonably": (1) The seller's tender must be at a reasonable hour, and he must keep the goods available for a reasonable time to enable the buyer to take possession, and (2) unless there is an agreement to the contrary, the buyer must furnish facilities suited to his receiving the goods.

Unless the contract provides to the contrary, the place for delivery is the seller's place of business. If the seller has no place of business, it is his residence (2-308[a]). In a contract for the sale of identified goods that are known

---

[2] *Pacific Products* v. *Great Western Plywood*, page 284.

to both parties to be at some other place, that place is the place for their delivery (2-308[a][b]).

Goods are frequently in the possession of a bailee such as a warehouseman. In this event, in order to make delivery, the seller is obligated to either (1) tender a negotiable document of title (warehouse receipt) representing the goods, or (2) procure acknowledgment by the bailee (warehouseman) that the buyer is entitled to the goods (2-503[4][a]). In recognition of actual commercial practices, instruments such as delivery orders may be given to the buyer in satisfaction of the seller's delivery obligation unless the buyer objects (2-503[4][b]).

If the goods are stored in a public warehouse and a negotiable warehouse receipt has been issued, the receipt may be negotiated to the buyer in order to transfer ownership of the goods to him. The buyer can take delivery of the goods from the warehouse by surrendering the indorsed warehouse receipt to the warehouseman.

Unless it is otherwise agreed, the seller is required to tender the goods in a single delivery rather than in installments over a period of time. The buyer's obligation to pay is not due until such a tender is made (2-307). In some situations, the seller may not be able to deliver all the goods at once or the buyer may not be able to receive the entire quantity at one time, in which event more than a single delivery is allowed. The time within which the goods are to be delivered is a reasonable time if the parties have not otherwise specified (2-309[1]).

The Time Term.   Where the time for performance has not been agreed upon by the parties, the time for shipment or delivery or any other action under a contract is a *reasonable* time (2-309[1]). What a reasonable time is depends upon what constitutes acceptable commercial conduct under all the circumstances, including the obligation of good faith and reasonable commercial standards of fair dealing in the trade.

A definite time for performance may be found to exist even though the contract did not express it. Such definite time may be implied from a usage of the trade or course of dealing or performance or from the circumstances of the contract. For example, in a given type of business, it may be customary to ship goods within seven days of receipt of an order.

Payment is due at the time and place where the buyer is to receive the goods (2-310). *Receipt of goods* means taking physical possession of them. The buyer is given the opportunity to inspect the goods before paying for them (2-513[1]). The preliminary inspection by the buyer does not require that the seller surrender possession of the goods. However, when the shipment is C.O.D., the buyer is not entitled to inspect the goods before payment of the price (2-513[3][a]).

The term *seasonably* is used throughout the Code to specify the time of doing an act. An action is taken seasonably when it is taken at or within the agreed time or, if no time is agreed, at or within a reasonable time (1-204).

The parties may enter into an open-ended contract that calls for successive performances, such as 1,000 barrels of flour per week. If the contract does not state the duration, it will be valid for a reasonable time, and unless otherwise agreed, either party can terminate it any time.

5. Abbreviations Used in Sales Contracts

As a matter of convenience, a number of contract terms are generally expressed as abbreviations. *F.O.B.* (free on board) is the most commonly used. *F.O.B. the place of shipment* means that the seller is obligated to place the goods in the possession of a carrier so that they may be shipped to the buyer. *F.O.B. the place of destination* means that the seller is obligated to cause the goods to be delivered to the buyer (2-319[1][c]). Thus, "F.O.B. Athens, Georgia," where Athens, Georgia, is the seller's place of business, is a *shipment contract.* "F.O.B. Champaign, Illinois," where Champaign is the place where the buyer is to receive the goods, is a *destination contract.* In such a case, the seller must provide transportation to that place at his own risk and expense. He is responsible for seeing to it that the goods are made available to the buyer at the designated place (2-319[1][b]).

If the terms of the contract specify *F.O.B. vessel, car,* or other vehicle, in addition, the seller must at his own expense and risk load the goods on board. *F.A.S.* (free alongside) *vessel* at a named port requires the seller at his own expense and risk to deliver the goods alongside the vessel in the manner usual in the port, or on a dock designated and provided by the buyer (2-319[2]).

C.I.F. means that the price includes, in a lump sum, the cost of the goods and of the insurance and freight to the named destination (2-320). The seller's obligation is to load the goods, to make provision for payment of the freight, and also to obtain an insurance policy in favor of the buyer. Generally, *C.I.F.* means that the parties will deal in terms of the documents that represent the goods; the seller performs his obligation by tendering to the buyer the proper documents, including a negotiable bill of lading and an invoice of the goods. The buyer is required to make payment against the tender of the required documents (2-320[4]).

6. Returned Goods

The agreement between the buyer and the seller may be such that the buyer has the privilege of returning the goods that have been delivered to him. If the goods are delivered primarily for use, as in a consumer purchase, the transaction is called a *sale on approval.* If the goods are delivered primarily for resale, it is called *sale or return* (2-326[1]). The distinction is an important one, because goods delivered "on approval" are not subject to the claims of the buyer's creditors until the buyer has indicated his acceptance of the goods. Goods delivered on "sale or return," however, are subject to the claims of the buyer's creditors while such goods are in his possession, unless the fact that the goods belong to the seller is known to the buyer's creditors (2-326[2]). A delivery of goods on consignment, such as a transaction in which a manu-facturer or a wholesaler delivers goods to a retailer who has the privilege of returning any unsold goods, is a "sale or return." The goods in possession of the buyer-consignee are subject to the claims of the buyer's creditors, unless (1) the seller complies with the filing provisions of Article 9 dealing with secured transactions (2-326[3]), or (2) it is established that the buyer's creditors had actual knowledge that the title remained with the seller, or (3) it is established that the dealer was generally known by its creditors to be substantially engaged in selling the goods of others.

A characteristic of the sale on approval is that risk of loss in the event of theft or destruction of the goods does not pass to the buyer until he accepts the goods. Failure to seasonably notify the seller of his decision to return the goods will be treated as an acceptance. After notification of election to return, the seller must pay the expenses of the return and bear the risk of loss. In contrast, the buyer in a sale or return transaction has the risk of loss in the event of theft or destruction of the goods (2-327[2]).[3]

7. Adequate Assurance

A concept applicable to both parties in a sales transaction is known as *adequate assurance*. Under certain circumstances, either party may be concerned as to whether or not the other party will *actually render* the performance due. For example, if a buyer is in arrears on payments due to the seller on other con-tracts, the seller will naturally be concerned about making further deliveries to such a buyer. Likewise, a buyer who has contracted to purchase goods may discover that the seller has been delivering faulty goods to other customers. He will be concerned that the goods that he is to receive may also be defective. The law recognizes that no one wants to buy a lawsuit and that merely having the right to sue for breach of contract is a somewhat "hollow" remedy. There is need for some protection to be afforded to the party whose reasonable expectation that he will receive due performance is jeopardized.

The Code grants such protection by providing that the contract for sale im-poses an obligation on each party that the other's expectation of receiving due performance will not be impaired (2-609). A party who has reasonable grounds for insecurity as to the other's performance can demand in writing that the other offer convincing proof that he will in fact perform. Having made

[3] *Harold Klein & Co., Inc.* v. *Lopardo,* page 285.

such demand, he may then suspend his own performance until he receives such assurance. If none is forthcoming within a reasonable time, not to exceed thirty days, he may treat the contract as repudiated (2-609[2]).

Two factual problems are presented: What are reasonable grounds for insecurity? and, What constitutes an adequate assurance of performance? The Code does not particularize but does provide that as between merchants, commercial standards shall be applied to answer these questions (2-609[2]).

THE TRANSFER OF TITLE TO GOODS

8. Introduction

The concept of title to goods is somewhat nebulous, but it is generally equated with ownership. Issues related to the passage of title are important in the field of taxation and in such areas of the law as wills, trusts, and estates. However, the Code has deemphasized the importance of title, and the location of title at any given time is not usually the controlling factor in determining the rights of the parties on a contract of sale. As a general rule, the rights, obligations, and remedies of the seller, the buyer, and the third parties are determined without regard to title (2-401). However, the concept of title is still basic to the sales transaction, since by definition a sale involves the passing of title from the seller to the buyer.

The parties can, with few restrictions, determine by their contract the manner in which title to goods passes from the seller to the buyer. They can specify any conditions that must be fulfilled in order for this to happen. However, since the parties to a contract for a sale seldom indicate any intention regarding title or its passage, the Code sets forth specific provisions as to when title shall pass, if the location of title becomes an issue.

As a general rule, title passes to the buyer at the time and place at which the seller completes his performance with reference to the physical delivery of the goods (2-401). Thus, if the contract is F.O.B. shipping point, title passes to the buyer at the time and place of shipment (2-401[2][a]). If the contract requires delivery at the destination, title passes on tender there (2-401[2][b]).

If delivery is to be made without moving the goods, title passes to identified goods at the time and place of contracting (2-401[3][b]). This assumes that the goods were in existence and that no document of title was to be delivered. If the seller is to deliver a document of title, title passes at the time and place of delivery of the document (2-401[3][a]).

9. Identification to the Contract

Title to goods cannot pass until the goods have been *identified* to the contract (2-401[1]). Identification requires that the seller specify the particular goods involved in the transaction (2-501[1]). For example, A may contract with B to purchase 100 mahogany desks of a certain style. B may have several hundred of these desks in his warehouse. Identification takes place when A or B specifies the particular 100 desks that will be sold to A. There could not, of course, be a present identification of future goods—those not yet in existence or not owned by the seller.

Identification can be made at any time and in any manner "explicitly agreed to" by the parties (2-501[1]). However, the parties usually do not make provision for identification, in which event the Code rules determine when it has occurred. For example, if the goods that are the subject of the contract are in existence and identified at the time the parties entered into the contract, identification occurs at the time and place of contracting (2-501[1][a]).

Contracts to sell future goods and agricultural items raise more difficult identification problems. As to future goods, the seller provides identification when he ships the goods—marks them or otherwise designates them as the goods to which the contract refers (2-501[1][b]).

When there is a sale of a crop to be grown, identification occurs when the crop is planted. If the sale is of the unborn young of animals, identification takes place when they are conceived (2-501[1][c]). The sale of a crop of wool would be included within this framework of identification.

If the buyer rejects the goods when they are tendered to him, title will be revested in the seller. Upon the buyer's refusal to receive or retain the goods, the title automatically returns to the seller, whether the buyer was justified in his action or not. The same result obtains if the buyer has accepted the goods but subsequently revokes his acceptance for a justifiable reason (2-401[4]).

As a means of assurance that the price will be paid before the buyer can obtain title to the goods, a seller may ship or deliver goods to the buyer and reserve title in himself. Under the Code, such an attempted reservation of title does not prevent the title from passing to the buyer. It is limited to the reservation of a security interest in the goods (2-401[1]). To give protection to the seller, the security interest must be perfected under the provisions of Article 9. Accordingly, a seller who simply reserves a security interest will not have availed himself of protection against the claims of third parties.

10. Rights in Identified Goods

The buyer acquires two rights when identification takes place, even if title does not pass. He obtains an "insurable interest" in the identified goods and also a "special property" in them (2-501[1]). This means that the buyer is permitted to carry insurance upon the goods, as he has a sufficient interest in them to justify doing so. The seller may also retain an insurable interest in the goods so long as he has an interest in them. Thus, after identification, each party may have an insurable interest in the goods. If the seller becomes insolvent while he is still in possession of the goods after all or part of the price has been paid, a buyer who has this special property interest is in a favored position. He can recover the goods from the seller if the seller becomes insolvent within ten days after receipt of the first installment on their price (2-502). This may prove a very valuable right to a buyer who might otherwise suffer a substantial loss. Were he not able to claim the goods, they would be subject to the claims of the creditors of the insolvent seller.

Also, a buyer with a special property is entitled to bring suit against a third party whose actions interfere with his rights in the identified goods (2-722). Even though he does not have title, his special property gives him standing in court to recover damages resulting from the improper conduct of a third person.[4] Although the buyer's rights in identified goods are generally superior to those of unsecured creditors of the seller, an identification or a sale may be set aside by the seller's creditors, and they can reach the goods if they can prove that the seller's retention of possession of the goods was fraudulent as to them (2-402[2]). By retaining possession of identified goods, the seller may have created the impression that he still owned them. Creditors may have lent money to him or otherwise extended him credit upon his apparent assets. The matter of fraud is governed by state law, but the Code provides that retention of possession in good faith by a merchant-seller for a commercially reasonable time after identification or sale is not fraudulent.

Identification or delivery made not in the course of trade but rather to satisfy a preexisting debt will not impair the rights of creditors of the seller, if such action is fraudulent or a voidable preference under the Bankruptcy Act as to them (2-402[3][b]).

11. The Title of a Good-Faith Purchaser

Unless the sale is of a limited interest, a purchaser of goods acquires at least as good a title as the seller possessed. Of course, if the seller has no title, the purchaser receives no title. A purchaser from a thief has no property interest in the goods.[5] Moreover, a good-faith purchaser for value may acquire a better title than the seller had if the seller's title was voidable (2-403). For example, assume that X obtains goods by fraud or pays for them with a check that is later dishonored. X has voidable title to the goods. If X should sell the goods to Y, who does not know that X's title was voidable, Y has clear title to the goods. Thus, a good-faith purchaser for value has better title than did X, the seller.

Title issues frequently arise when the same goods are sold to more than one buyer. For example, assume that S sells goods to X. X leaves them at S's store with the intention of picking them up later. Before X takes possession, S sells them to Y, a good-faith purchaser. Under the Code, Y has title to the goods because if possession of goods is entrusted to a merchant who deals in goods of that kind, the merchant has the power to transfer all rights of the entrusting owner to a buyer in the ordinary course of business (2-403[2][3]). A good-

---

4 *Draper* v. *Minneapolis Moline, Inc.*, page 285.
5 *First Nat. Bank & Trust* v. *Ohio Cas. Ins. Co.*, page 286.

faith purchaser from a merchant in the ordinary course of business acquires good title. This rule is applicable to any delivery of possession to a merchant with the understanding that the merchant is to have possession. Thus the rule applies to consignments and bailments as well as to the cash sale situation previously noted. However, the facts of each case must be examined to ensure that the buyer qualified as a good-faith purchaser for value.

RISK OF LOSS

12. In Breach of Contract Cases

The Code sets forth a number of rules for determining which party to a sales contract must bear the risk of loss in the event of theft, destruction, or damage to the goods during the period of the performance of the contract. The approach is contractual rather than title-oriented. Two basic situations are involved: (1) where no breach of contract exists, and (2) where one of the parties is in breach. Of course, the provisions are applicable only where the contract has not allocated the risk of loss (2-303).

If the contract has been breached, the loss will be borne by the party who has breached (2-510[1]). Thus, if the seller has tendered or delivered goods that are "nonconforming" and that the buyer has a right to reject, the seller bears the risk of loss for such goods.[6] He remains responsible until such time as he rectifies the nonconformity or the buyer accepts the goods notwithstanding their defects. A buyer has the privilege of revoking his acceptance of the goods under proper circumstances, and if he does do so for good cause, the risk of loss is on the seller to the extent that the buyer's insurance does not cover the loss. In this situation, the seller has the benefit of any insurance carried by the buyer—the party most likely to carry insurance—but any loss is on the breaching seller.

The loss may occur while the goods are in the seller's control before the risk of loss has passed to the buyer. If the buyer repudiates the sale (breaches the contract) at a time when the seller has identified proper goods to the contract, the seller can impose the risk of loss upon the buyer for a reasonable time, to the extent that the seller's insurance does not cover the loss. The foregoing rules implement the basic concept of the Code that the burden should be that of the party who has failed to perform as required by contract.

13. Where No Breach Exists

There are three distinct situations in risk of loss cases when neither party is in breach. First, the contract may call for shipment of the goods; second, the

---

[6] *Graybar Electric Co.* v. *Shook,* page 287.

goods may be the subject of a bailment; and third, the contract may be silent on shipment, and no bailment exists.

Shipment.   Where the contract between buyer and seller provides for shipment by carrier, the risk of loss passes to the buyer when the goods are delivered to the carrier if it is a shipment contract (F.O.B. shipping point);[7] if it is destination contract (F.O.B. destination), risk of loss does not pass to the buyer until the goods arrive at the destination and are made available to him so that he can take delivery (2-509[1]). A shipment contract is one that requires only that the seller make the necessary arrangements for transport, while a destination contract imposes upon the seller the obligation to deliver at a destination. When the parties do not use such symbols as C.I.F., F.A.S., F.O.B., or otherwise make provision for risk of loss, it is necessary to determine whether a contract does or does not require the seller to deliver at a destination. The presumption is that a contract is one of shipment, not destination, and that the buyer should bear the risk of loss until arrival, unless the seller has either specifically agreed to do so or the circumstances indicate such an obligation.

Bailment.   Often the goods will be in the possession of a bailee such as a warehouse, and the arrangement is for the buyer to take delivery at the warehouse. If the goods are represented by a negotiable document of title—a warehouse receipt, for instance—when the seller tenders such document to the buyer, the risk of loss passes to the buyer. Likewise, risk passes to the buyer upon acknowledgment by the bailee that the buyer is entitled to the goods (2-509[2]). In this situation, it is proper that the buyer assume the risk, as the seller has done all that could be expected to make the goods available to the buyer, who controls the goods at this point. It should be noted that if a nonnegotiable document of title is proffered to the buyer, risk of loss does not pass until the buyer has had a reasonable time to present the document to the bailee (2-503[4][b]). A refusal by the bailee to honor the documents defeats the tender, and the risk of loss remains with the seller. This points up one of the distinctions between a negotiable and a nonnegotiable document of title.

Other Cases.   In all cases other than shipment and bailment as mentioned above, the passage of risk to the buyer depends upon the status of the seller. If the seller is a merchant, risk of loss will not pass to the buyer until he receives the goods, which means takes physical possession of them (2-509[3]). A nonmerchant seller transfers the risk by *tendering* the goods (2-509[3]). A tender of delivery requires that the seller make conforming goods available to the buyer and give him reasonable notice so that he may take delivery. The risk of loss remains with the merchant-seller even though the buyer has paid for the goods in full and has been notified that the goods are at his disposal.

---

[7] *Eberhard Manufacturing Company* v. *Brown*, page 288.

Continuation of the risk in this case is justified on the basis that the merchant would be likely to carry insurance on goods within his control, while a buyer would probably not do so until he had actually received the goods.

THE LAW OF SALES: BASIC CONCEPTS CASES

Lake Wales Pub. Co., Inc. v. Florida Visitor, Inc.
335 So.2d 335 (Fla. App.) 1976

SCHEB, J. . . . This case concerns a contract entered into by the plaintiff/appellant in 1971 to compile, edit and publish certain pamphlets and other printed materials for the defendants/appellees. The issue is whether the contract was subject to the three-year statute of limitations governing unwritten contracts, or the four-year statute under the Uniform Commercial Code. . . .

Appellant filed suit on January 15, 1975. The trial court dismissed the appellant's second amended complaint with prejudice on grounds that its action was barred by the three-year statute of limitations. . . . This appeal ensued. We reverse.

If the 1971 contract was for the sale of "goods," then appellant which filed suit on January 15, 1975, was entitled to the benefit of the four-year U.C.C. statute . . . since the U.C.C. limitation period generally prevails over that contained in a general statute of limitations.

We focus then on whether the printed materials which appellant allegedly furnished to appellee were "goods" under the U.C.C., which defines "goods" as:

> . . . all things (including specially manufactured goods) which are movable at the time of identification to the contract for

sale other than the money in which the price is to be paid, investment securities and things in action.

The specific point has not been passed on by the Florida courts; however, the Official Comment to U.C.C. § 2-105 states that the definition of goods is based upon the concept of their movability. The items allegedly furnished by the appellant were specially produced or manufactured and were movable. Moreover, any services rendered were of necessity directed to production of the items.

While there is a paucity of cases construing the definition of "goods" under the U.C.C., the instant case is somewhat analogous to the situation in *Carpel v. Saget Studios, Inc.,* E.D. Pa. 1971, 326 F.Supp. 1331. There, an action for breach of contract was filed against a photographer for his failure to take pictures of the plaintiff's wedding. In determining the correct measure of damages, the court held that the contract breached by the defendant was one for the sale of "goods."

We conclude that production of printed pamphlets and related materials are goods within the meaning of U.C.C. and that appellant's action was therefore governed by the four-year statute of limitations. . . .

Reversed.

Pacific Products v. Great Western Plywood
528 S.W.2d 286 (Tex.) 1975

Plaintiff, a seller of plywood, brought suit against the defendant buyer for damages arising out of the buyer's refusal to accept delivery of the plywood. The defendant had ordered one carload of ⅜ inch thick plywood. There are three grades of plywood, A-C, B-C and shop grade. The order did not specify the quantity of each grade either by unit or percentage, but it did limit shop grade to 5% of the carload. The price for each grade was specified. The plaintiff's acceptance did not specify the quantity of each grade to be shipped.

Plaintiff's shipment was 85% B-C grade and less than 5% shop grade. The defendant wanted more A-C grade and refused the shipment. The lower court found that the contract was sufficiently definite and gave judgment for the plaintiff. Defendant appeals.

SPURLOCK, J. . . . Pacific's first point of error claims the trial court erred in holding that the exchange of the purchase order from Pacific and the written acknowledgment from Great Western constituted a contract between the parties because such were not sufficiently certain to be enforced, as a matter of law. More specifically, it contends that one cannot determine from the purchase order and acknowledgment the number of units of each grade, price for the total quantity of each grade . . . or the final total price, and therefore the purported contract must fail due to lack of expressed agreement as to certain material terms. . . .

Pacific's primary argument under this point concerns the "uncertainty" of the contract due to the alleged lack of specificity of its terms, as previously mentioned herein. We conclude the agreement is not so uncertain that it is unenforceable; further, even if extrinsic evidence were admitted there is evidenc that Pacific's order was enforceable under industry usage.

The . . . code provides in part:

. . . Section 2.201. Formal Requirements; Statute of Frauds. . . .

(a) A writing is not insufficient because it omits or incorrectly states a term agreed upon but the contract is not enforceable under this paragraph beyond the quantity of goods shown in such writing.

Section 2.204. Formation in General

(a) A contract for sale of goods may be made in any manner sufficient to show agreement, including conduct by both parties which recognizes the existence of such a contract. . . .

(b) Even though one or more terms are left open a contract for sales does not fail for indefiniteness if the parties have intended to make a contract and there is a reasonably certain basis for giving an appropriate remedy.

Section 2.305. Open Price Term

(a) The parties if they so intend can conclude a contract for sale even though the price is not settled. In such a case the price is a reasonable price at the time for delivery if

(1) nothing is said as to price; or

(2) the price is left to be agreed by the parties and they fail to agree; or

(3) the price is to be fixed in terms of some agreed market or other standard as set or recorded by a third person or agency and it is not so set or recorded.

In this case, Mr. Robert Germany, who did the reinspection for Timber Engineering Company, testified to the effect that the reinspection showed Pacific received what it ordered as reflected by the purchase order and acknowledgment; that there is no limitation by "usage" within the industry as to the maximum or minimum quantities of certain grades in a shipment; merchants within the industry do at times order by the carload without specifying quantities by grade. Mr. Harlan Niebling, the manager of the western office of the North American Wholesale Lumber Association (a trade association of wholesale distributors of forest products), testified to the effect that: the carload shipment complied with the purchase order from Pacific; there was nothing in the applicable commercial standards (referred to in the purchase order) which specifies particular percentages of any grade in a shipment mixed with another grade unless specified in the contract between buyer and seller. . . . When the evidence is examined in light of the applicable UCC provisions, we can only conclude there is some evidence from which the trial court could have determined that there was a reasonable good faith meeting of the minds as to the contract and that the shipment in question met the requirements of the contract. There is also some evidence of custom and usage to the effect that it was not unheard of, although perhaps unusual, to order plywood by the carload without specifying the quantities of each grade. We are therefore bound by the trial court's finding that the carload of plywood fully complied with the written contract. . . .

Affirmed.

Harold Klein & Co., Inc. v. Lopardo
308 A.2d 538 (N.H.) 1973

DUNCAN, J. . . . The plaintiff, a wholesale jeweler, seeks to recover from the defendant, a retail jeweler, the wholesale price of two diamonds which were sent to the defendant and never returned. The trial in the superior court resulted in a verdict for the defendant.

There was evidence that the parties had a long standing business relationship whereby plaintiff would deliver jewels to defendant who would in turn sell the jewels to retail customers and pay plaintiff the agreed price. If unable to sell the jewels, defendant would return them to plaintiff. This was a commercial transaction, governed by the Uniform Commercial Code rather than by common law principles of bailment, as suggested by the defendant. Under the code the transaction was a "sale or return" as therein defined. Approximately 10 days after defendant received the diamonds in November 1968, they were stolen from his jewelry store in Exeter. The primary issue before the trial court was whether plaintiff or defendant should bear the loss resulting from the theft.

RSA 382-A:2-327(2) provides that "[u]nder a sale or return unless otherwise agreed . . . (b) the return is at the buyer's risk and expense." Plaintiff contends that the effect of this subsection is to place the risk of loss upon the buyer once the goods are delivered to him. We think this result is consistent with the intent of the U.C.C. draftsmen, and with the general rule allocating risk of loss between parties. When the buyer fails to pay the price as it becomes due, the seller may recover the price of conforming goods lost or damaged within a commercially reasonable time after risk of their loss has passed to the buyer. The plaintiff thus is entitled to the contract price of the two diamonds.

Reversed.

Draper v. Minneapolis Moline, Inc.
241 N.E.2d 342 (Ill.) 1968

Plaintiff entered into a contract to purchase a tractor and plow from a dealer. His old equipment was traded in as part payment. The dealer did not have the items in stock and ordered them from defendant. They were delivered under an agreement in which defendant retained a security interest. Plaintiff refused to take delivery until certain additional equipment was installed. At this point because of the financial condition of the dealer, defendant repossessed all of the inventory including the tractor and plow that had been sold to plaintiff. Plaintiff was deprived of the use of the plow for his spring planting and brought action for damages. Judgment was awarded plaintiff, and defendant appealed.

CULBERTSON, J. . . . The authority for plaintiff's action is found in Section 2-722 of Article 2 of the Uniform Commercial Code (hereinafter referred to as the Code), which, in substance, gives to one having a special property interest in goods a right of action against a third party who "so deals with goods which have been identified to a contract for sale as to cause actionable injury to a party to that contract." The quoted language, we believe, intends that a third party would be liable for conversion, physical damage to the goods, or interference with the rights of a buyer in the goods. Section 2-103(1)(a) of Article 2 states that in such Article: " 'Buyer' means a person who buys *or contracts to buy goods*," and it is thereafter provided in Section 2-501(1) in pertinent part:

> The buyer obtains a special property and an insurable interest in goods by identification of existing goods as goods to which the contract refers *even though the goods so identified are non-conforming* and he has an option to return or reject them. Such identification can be made at any time and in any manner explicitly agreed to by the parties. In the absence of explicit agreement identification occurs . . .
>
> (b) if the contract is for the sale of future goods . . . when goods are shipped, marked or otherwise designated by the seller as goods to which the contract refers. . . .

While defendant makes a mild argument that the tractor did not conform to the contract because the extras had not been installed when it was pointed out by the dealer, we think it manifest from the evidence that there was a complete and sufficient identification of the tractor to the contract within the purview of Section 2-501(1). It is apparent, too, that defendant's conduct made it impossible for the dealer to deliver the tractor to plaintiff, and that defendant so dealt with the goods as to interfere with plaintiff's special property interest. And, without more, it could be said that plaintiff has standing to maintain an action for damages as authorized by Section 2-722. However, there next arises the question of whether plaintiff obtained his special property interest, and its attendant rights, free and clear of defendant's security interest. . . .

. . . The very intent of the commercial papers involved was that the tractor could be sold to a buyer, free and clear of the security interest of the seller's creditor. Accordingly, we hold that plaintiff obtained his special property interest in the tractor free and clear of defendant's security interest, and that such security interest is no bar to the action for damages given to plaintiff by Section 2-722. . . .

Affirmed.

First Nat. Bank & Trust v. Ohio Cas. Ins. Co.
244 N.W.2d 209 (Neb.) 1976

Fernandez owned a 1973 Cadillac insured by the defendant insurance company. On December 10, 1972 it was stolen and on January 9, 1973 the company paid Fernandez $8,400 for the loss of the car. Fernandez assigned his title to the insurance company who obtained a new certificate in its name.

On December 26, 1972 a Nebraska certificate of title was issued on the car based upon a forged Arizona certificate of title. The plaintiff bank loaned money on the car and had its lien shown on the Nebraska certificate of title. Based on information from the F.B.I. the defendant on January 24, 1974 by use of

self help removed the vehicle to California and sold it for $5,500. Plaintiff bank sued the defendant insurance company for the $5,500 and the trial court found for the plaintiff.

BRODKEY, J. . . . The sole issue in this case is whether First National, having noted its lien on the Nebraska certificate of title, acquired rights superior to Ohio Casualty, in view of the fact First National's chain of title originated in a thief. The District Court answered this question in the affirmative. We disagree and reverse. . . .

[A certificate of title] does not . . . create title where none exists, nor does it give a transferee greater title than that of his transferor. . . . A thief with a certificate of title to a stolen automobile does not divest the owner of his right to take it wherever he can find it. A certificate of title is essential to convey the title of an automobile, but it is not conclusive of ownership. It is simply the exclusive method provided by statute for the transfer of title to a motor vehicle. It conveys no greater interest than the grantor actually possesses. . . .

When the property underlying the certificate of title has been obtained by illegal means, a distinction has been made between stolen property and that acquired by fraud. . . . One obtaining property by larceny cannot convey good title even to an innocent purchaser for value, but one obtaining property by fraud has a voidable title, and may convey that title to a bona fide purchaser who is then protected from claims of others. On the other hand, the right of an owner or an assignee of the owner to recover his stolen automobile remains open to him. . . .

In *Hardware Mut. Cas. Co.* v. *Gall,* 15 Ohio St.2d 261 (1968), the court held that a thief could not convey a valid title to a stolen motor vehicle to a bona fide purchaser for value without notice, although the certificate of title used in the purported transfer appeared valid on its face. . . . We agree with the Ohio Supreme Court. . . . That court in making its ruling stated "[W]e apparently must again dispel the erroneous notion that whoever first obtains an apparently valid Ohio certificate of title will be entitled to retain possession of the automobile regardless of whether he is the real owner or a bona fide purchaser without notice, whose title derives from a thief. . . .

We hold that the true owner, and his lawful successors in interest, have rights paramount to those of a subsequent bona fide purchaser of a stolen automobile holding a Nebraska certificate of title on the vehicle based upon a chain of ownership originating with the thief of the car. . . .

Reversed and remanded.

Graybar Electric Co. v. Shook
195 S.E.2d 514 (N.C.) 1973

Defendant, engaged in the business of installing underground telephone lines, ordered three reels of underground cable to be delivered at its construction job. Plaintiff delivered three reels, but only one was underground cable—the other two were aerial cable. Defendant notified plaintiff of its mistake and paid for the one reel. Plaintiff requested that the nonconforming reels be returned. Defendant attempted to comply but was unable to do so because of a strike in the trucking industry. Several months later, the two reels were stolen. Plaintiff brought action to recover the purchase price from defendant. The trial court dismissed the action, and plaintiff appealed.

HIGGINS, J. . . . The plaintiff, having made the error of delivering the nonconforming goods on a moving job in the country, was entitled to notice of the nonconformity sufficient to enable it to repossess the nonconforming goods. The plaintiff was given prompt notice but delayed action for more than three months. The cable was stolen from the defendant's regular storage space where the plaintiff had delivered it. Evidence is lacking that a safer storage space was available. The defendant's workmen moved on, leaving the cable and the responsibility for its safety on the owner.

The plaintiff, failing in its efforts to establish a contract on the part of the defendant to return the shipment, however, contends in the alternative that G.S. § 25-2-602(2) (b) (Uniform Commercial Code) required the defendant to exercise reasonable care in holding the rejected goods pending the plaintiff's repossession and removal and that the defendant failed to exercise the required care in storage.

Actually, the plaintiff made an on the spot delivery at a store and dwelling in the country. The defendant's work force was stringing underground cable along the highway and the crew was in continual movement. Obviously the crew could not be expected to carry with it two thousand pounds of useless cable and was within its rights placing the cable in its regular storage space and notifying the plaintiff of the place of storage. Both parties realized that cable weighing almost a ton would require men and a truck to remove it. Also both parties assumed that the danger of theft from a well lighted store area was a minimal risk. The property itself was a poor candidate for larceny. The cable was permitted to remain where the plaintiff knew it was located for more than three months. The plaintiff, therefore, had ample opportunity to repossess its property.

The Uniform Commercial Code emphasizes promptness and good faith. The prospective purchaser may exercise a valid right to reject and even if he takes possession, responsibility expires after a reasonable time in which the owner has opportunity to repossess. "Where a tender or delivery of goods so fails to conform to the contract as to give a right of rejection the risk of their loss remains on the seller until cure or acceptance." G.S. § 25-2-510(1). The defendant did not accept the aerial cable. According to the evidence and the court's findings, the defendant acted in accordance with the request of the owner in attempting to facilitate the return of that which the defendant rejected. The plaintiff with full notice of the place of storage which was at the place of delivery did nothing but sleep on its rights for more than three months. . . .

Affirmed.

Eberhard Manufacturing Company v. Brown
232 N.W.2d 378 (Mich.) 1975

GILLIS, J. . . . Plaintiff brought action to recover for the price of goods sold and delivered to defendant pursuant to a distributorship agreement. Defendant counterclaimed for damages for breach of the agreement. The . . . Court . . . gave judgment for defendant on his counterclaim in the amount of $6,315.82.

. . . [T]he plaintiff alleges that the court erred in giving defendant a credit of $559.03 for goods which were apparently lost in transit.

At trial, the plaintiff introduced evidence that the goods were sold to defendant F.O.B. plaintiff's factory, and the goods were placed by plaintiff on board a common carrier with instructions to deliver to defendant. This evidence was not controverted by any evidence of defendant's. It is plaintiff's contention that the risk of loss passed to defendant buyer when the goods were put on board the carrier.

On appeal both parties point to M.C.L.A. § 440.2509(1); M.S.A. § 19.2509(1) as controlling. Plaintiff, however, cites subsection (a) and defendant subsection (b). Subsection (a) states the rule where the contract is a "shipment" contract, in which case risk of loss passes to the buyer where the goods are duly delivered to the carrier; subsection (b) states the rule where a contract is a "destination" contract, in which case risk of loss passes to the buyer when the goods are duly tendered at the destination.

An agreement of the parties would control as to who has the risk of loss.

The parties here did not expressly agree on who was to bear the risk of loss. The contract contained no F.O.B. term. There was testimony by plaintiff that its goods are sold F.O.B. place of shipment, plaintiff's factory. That testimony might be evidence of a usage of trade. It was not proof that the parties had agreed, expressly or in fact, as to who had the risk of loss.

Under Article 2 of the Uniform Commercial Code, the "shipment" contract is regarded as the normal one and the "destination" contract as the variant type. The seller is not obligated to deliver at a named destination and bear the concurrent risk of loss until arrival, unless he has specifically agreed so to deliver or the commercial understanding of the terms used by the parties contemplates such delivery.

Thus a contract which contains neither an F.O.B. term nor any other term explicitly allocating loss is a shipment contract.

Defendant argues that since the goods were to be shipped to defendant's place of business in Birmingham, the contract required plaintiff to deliver the goods "at a particular destination." Defendant's position is that "ship to" substitutes for and is equivalent to an F.O.B. term, namely F.O.B. place of destination. But that argument is persuasively refuted by the response that a "ship to" address must be supplied in any case in which carriage is contemplated. Thus a "ship to" term has no significance in determining whether a contract is a shipment or destination contract for risk of loss purposes. . . .

Since the presumption of a shipment contract controls in this case, the trial court should not have given defendant the $559.03 credit for the lost shipment. . . .

Therefore, defendant's recovery is reduced by $559.03, from $6,315.82 to $5,756.79.

So ordered.

CHAPTER 16
REVIEW QUESTIONS AND PROBLEMS

1. A purchased a tractor and plow on a sale and approval agreement from B. A kept the tractor for approximately two months and told B's agent that he would pay for the tractor as soon as a pending deal finalized. Shortly thereafter, the tractor burned, and B sought to recover its value. A contended that the property belonged to B and that he is not liable. Who is correct? Why?

2. X agreed to purchase a truckload of dressed hogs from Y. The hogs were to be shipped C.F., on a shipping-point contract. The meat arrived late, owing to mechanical difficulty of the truck, and X refused to accept the meat. Y then sued for recovery of damages. Should he recover? Why?

3. A ordered goods from X Corp., but there was no agreement between them as to the purchase price of the goods. When the goods were delivered to A, he accepted them. Does this constitute a binding agreement? Explain.

4. A, a fruit grower, entered into a contract to sell fruit to B, a food processor. The contract did not contain a specified price. Is the contract enforceable? Why?

5. B, a Connecticut merchant, ordered goods from S, a supplier in California. The shipment was "F.O.B. Los Angeles," and S delivered the goods to the carrier in Los Angeles. Subsequently, the goods were lost. Which party suffers the loss? Why?

6. X sued Y, an electric utility company, claiming that high voltage had damaged his electrical appliances. The suit was brought more than four years after the incident, and Y Company contended that the claim was barred by the four-year statute of limitations of the Code applicable to goods. X contended the Code was inapplicable because furnishing electrical energy is a service and not a transaction in goods. Who is correct? Why?

7. B Company, a distributor of appliances, had a contract with S Company by which S would supply B's needs for a stated period. The contract provided for termination on 30 days' notice. Upon learning that S intended to terminate, B placed an order for appliances that amounted to nine times the usual monthly order. S refused to fill the order, and B brought suit. Should he recover? Why?

8. X, a car dealer, sold to S, another car dealer, a new Cadillac. In order to protect himself, X retained possession of the certificate of origin (issued by General Motors) and the bill of sale until such time as S paid for the car. S, however, sold the car to B before making payment to X. B was without knowledge of the arrangements between X and S. Should X be allowed to recover the car from B? Why?

9. B Company placed an order with S Company for 288 garments and directed S to "Ship via Stuart." The Stuart Express Company picked up the merchandise but lost the entire shipment en route. Stuart's liability was limited to $1 per garment, per its bill of lading. Should S or B bear the burden of the additional loss? Why?

10. B contracted to buy goods from S. The agreement provided that a representative of B would meet S at a designated place and receive the goods there. Payment for the goods had been made, but there had not yet been a transfer to the representative, when X filed suit for an injunction to the sale. Had title to the goods already passed to B? Why?

17

Performance
of the Sales Contract

1. Introduction

The law recognizes that each party to a contract for the sale of goods has certain rights and obligations unless the contract legally eliminates them. In addition, the Code has several provisions relating to the remedies of buyer and seller in the event of a breach of the contract by the other party.

As a general rule, a seller is obligated to deliver or tender delivery of goods that measure up to the requirements of the contract and to do so at the proper time and at the proper place. The goods and other performance of the seller must "conform" to the contract (2-106[2]).

The seller is required to tender delivery as a condition to the buyer's duty to accept the goods and pay for them (2-507[1]). Thus, the seller has performed when he has made the goods available to the buyer. The buyer in turn must render his performance, which means he must accept the goods and pay for them.

The parties may in their agreement limit or modify the remedies available to each other. The measure of damages may be limited or altered. For example, the agreement may limit the buyer's remedies to return of the goods and repayment of the price or to replacement of the goods or parts.

The parties may limit or exclude consequential damages, and such limitations and exclusions will be enforced if they are not unconscionable (2-719[3]). A limitation of consequential damages for injury to the *person* in the case

291

of *consumer goods* is prima facie unconscionable, but limitations where the loss is commercial are not.

The Code leaves the parties free to shape their own remedies to their specific needs, but it does require that there be a certain minimum of adequate remedies and that the contract not be unconscionable.

THE BUYER'S RIGHTS

2. The Right to Inspect the Goods

The parties may provide in their contract for inspection of the goods by the buyer prior to payment or acceptance. In the absence of such a provision, the buyer has a right before payment or acceptance to inspect the goods at any reasonable time and place and in any reasonable manner (2-513[1]). The place for the inspection would be determined largely by the nature of the contract. If the seller is to send the goods to the buyer, the inspection may be postponed until after arrival of the goods.

If the contract provides for delivery C.O.D., the buyer must pay prior to inspection. Likewise, payment must be made prior to inspection if the contract calls for payment against documents of title (2-513[3]). When goods are being shipped, the documents against which payment is to be made will often be presented to the buyer while the goods are still in transit. In such cases, the buyer will normally have to pay before he has an opportunity to inspect the goods (2-513[3][b]). When the buyer is required to make payment prior to inspection, such payment does not impair his right to pursue remedies if subsequent inspection reveals defects (2-512).

The buyer must pay the expenses of inspection, but he can recover his expenses from the seller if the inspection reveals that the goods are nonconforming and the buyer accordingly rejects them (2-513[2]).

3. The Rights to Reject the Goods

If the goods or the tender of delivery fails to conform to the contract, the buyer has the right to reject it.[1] Several options are available. The buyer may reject the whole, or he may accept either the whole or any commercial unit or units and reject the rest (2-601). A commercial unit is one that is generally regarded as a single whole for purposes of sale, and that would be impaired in value if divided (2-105[6]). Thus the buyer could accept those portions of the goods that were satisfactory to him as long as he did not thereby break up a unit. The buyer, when he accepts nonconforming goods, does not impair his right of recourse against the seller. Provided he notifies the seller of the breach

---

[1] *Zabriskie Chevrolet, Inc.* v. *Smith,* page 302.

within a reasonable time, he may still pursue his remedy for damages for breach of contract.

The right to reject defective or nonconfoming goods is dependent on the buyer's taking action within a reasonable time after the goods are tendered or delivered to him. If the buyer rejects, he must seasonably notify the seller of this fact, and his failing to do so would render the rejection ineffective and constitute an acceptance (2-602[1]). If the buyer continues in possession of defective goods for an unreasonable time, he forfeits his right to reject them.

A buyer who rejects the goods after taking physical possession of them is required to hold the goods with reasonable care, at the seller's disposition, for a time sufficient for the seller to remove them (2-602[2][b]). If the buyer has paid all or part of the purchase price prior to his rejection, he has a security interest in the goods to that extent, and he may resell the goods to satisfy this claim (2-711[3]). The security interest also includes expenses incurred in connection with such items as transportation and care and custody of the goods.

The merchant-buyer has a greater obligation than other buyers with regard to goods he has rightfully rejected and that are in his possession. A merchant-buyer is under a duty to follow any reasonable instructions from the seller with respect to what is to be done with the rejected goods (2-603). This duty arises if the seller does not have an agent or a place of business at the place of rejection. If the seller does not furnish instructions as to the disposition of the rejected goods, the merchant-buyer must make reasonable efforts to sell them for the seller's account if they are perishable or if they threaten to decline in value speedily. When the buyer resells the goods, he is entitled to reimbursement for his expenses in caring for the goods and selling them. For selling the goods, the reselling buyer is entitled to a commission on the basis of what is usual in the trade; otherwise, he will receive a reasonable sum not to exceed 10 percent of the gross proceeds (2-603[2]).

If the seller does not give any instructions to the buyer within a reasonable time after notice of rejection, and if the goods are not perishable, the buyer has three options. He may store the rejected goods for the seller's account; he may reship them to the seller; or he may resell them for the seller's account (2-604). These rights are predicated upon actual nonconformity of the goods and proper notice of rejection to the seller.

The requirement of seasonable notice of rejection is very important. Without such notice, the rejection is ineffective (2-602[1]). As a general rule, a notice of rejection may be simply to the effect that the goods are not conforming, without particular specification of the defects relied upon by the buyer. If, however, the defect could have been corrected by the seller had he been given particularized notice, then the failure to particularize will take away from the buyer the right to rely upon that defect as a breach justifying a rejection (2-605 [1][a]). Therefore, a buyer should always give detailed information relative to the reason for the rejection.

In transactions between merchants, the merchant-seller is entitled to require that he be furnished a full and final written statement of all the defects. If the statement is not forthcoming, the buyer may not rely upon such defects to justify his rejection or to establish that a breach has occurred (2-605[1][b]).

4. Right to Revoke an Acceptance

The buyer has *accepted* goods (1) if, after a reasonable opportunity to inspect them, he indicates to the seller that the goods are conforming or that he will take or retain them in spite of their nonconformity; (2) if he has failed to make an effective rejection of the goods; or (3) if he does any act inconsistent with the seller's ownership (2-606). A buyer who accepts any part of a commercial unit has thereby accepted the entire unit (2-606[1]).

The buyer may revoke his acceptance under certain circumstances. Before nonconformity will justify a revocation of an acceptance, the value of the goods to the accepting party must be substantially impaired. A buyer is not allowed to revoke an acceptance for trivial defects or defects that may be easily corrected. However, the test is whether the value of the goods to the buyer is substantially impaired. To that extent, the test is somewhat subjective. In many instances, the buyer will have accepted nonconforming goods because (1) the defects were not immediately discoverable, or (2) the buyer reasonably assumed that the seller would correct by substituting goods that did conform. In either of these events, the buyer has the privilege of "revoking his acceptance" by notifying the seller of this fact (2-608[1]). Actual notice of the revocation of the acceptance is required (2-607).[2] Such revocation must take place within a reasonable time after the buyer has discovered, or should have discovered, the reason for revocation (2-608[2]). If a buyer revokes his acceptance, he is then placed in the same position with reference to the goods as if he had rejected them in the first instance (2-608[3]); however, he also has a security interest in the goods for the payments made. In addition, the buyer is entitled to damages just as if no acceptance had occurred. Today, many courts treat the right to revoke an acceptance as a special remedy available to buyers and not just a legally enforceable right.

THE BUYER'S REMEDIES

5. In General

When the seller fails to perform properly, a number of remedies are available to the aggrieved buyer. Most of these involve the collection of dollar damages, with the amount being dependent on the remedy used. The basic remedies available to the aggrieved buyer are (1) to cancel the contract, (2) to "cover"

---

2 *Desilets Granite Company* v. *Stone Equalizer Corp., page* 303.

and collect damages, (3) to collect damages for nondelivery of the goods or for delivery of nonconforming goods, and (4) to enforce the contract and obtain the goods from the seller.

The remedy of cancellation does not prevent a suit for damages (2-106[4]). The remedy of cancellation in the sale of goods is the same as in other contracts. A material breach of contract by one party justifies rescission or cancellation by the other.

6. Damages When Buyer Covers

The buyer who has not received the goods he bargained for may *cover*— arrange to purchase the goods he needs from some other source in substitution for those due from the seller (2-712).[3] This is a practical remedy, as the buyer must often proceed without delay in order to obtain goods needed by him for his own use or for resale to others. The only limitation is that he must act reasonably and in good faith in arranging for the cover (2-712[1]).

The buyer may recover from the seller the difference between the cost of cover and the contract price (2-712[2]). In addition, he may recover any incidental and consequential damages sustained, but less expenses saved as a result of the seller's breach. *Incidental damages* include those reasonably incurred in connection with handling rejected goods, commercially reasonable charges, expenses, or commissions in connection with effecting cover, and any other reasonable expense incident to the delay or other breach (2-715[1]). *Consequential damages* include any loss resulting from the buyer's needs of which the seller had reason to know and that could not reasonably be prevented by cover (2-715[2]).

The cover remedy has the advantage of providing certainty as to the amount of the buyer's damages. The difference between the contract price and the price paid by the buyer for substitute goods can be readily determined. While the buyer must act reasonably and in good faith, he need not prove that he obtained the goods at the cheapest price available.

7. Damages When Buyer Does Not Cover

The aggrieved buyer who did not receive any goods from the seller or who received nonconforming goods is not *required* to cover; instead, he may bring an action for damages (2-712[3]). The measure of damages for nondelivery or repudiation is the difference between the *market price at the time the buyer learned of the breach* and the contract price. The buyer is also entitled to any incidental or consequential damages sustained, less expenses saved by the result of the seller's breach (2-713).

The aggrieved buyer's damages are, in effect, determined on the basis of the difference between what the goods would have cost had the buyer elected

[3] *Thorstenson* v. *Mobridge Iron Works Co.,* page 304.

to cover and the contract price. The market price would be that prevailing at the place at which the buyer would have attempted to cover (2-713[2]).

8. Damages for Breach in Regard to Accepted Goods

A buyer who rightfully revokes an acceptance of nonconforming goods is entitled to damages just as if no acceptance had occurred. If the buyer of nonconforming goods fails to revoke his acceptance or loses his right to do so by delay, he is nevertheless entitled to collect damages. However, to avail himself of this right to damages, the buyer must have seasonably notified the seller of the breach. The burden is on the buyer to prove the breach (2-607[4]).

The damages to which a buyer is entitled consist of "the loss resulting in the ordinary course of events from the seller's breach as determined in any manner which is reasonable" (2-714[1]). Nonconformity includes any breach of warranty with regard to the goods. Accordingly, if the goods were not as warranted, the buyer can recover damages measured by the difference between the actual value of the goods and the value they would have had if they had been as warranted (2-714[2]). Also included in the damages are personal injuries or property damage proximately caused by the breach of warranty (2-715[2][b]).

In addition to collecting damages from the seller, an aggrieved buyer may deduct the damages resulting from any breach of contract from any part of the price still due under the same contract (2-717). The buyer may determine what his damages are, and he may withhold this amount when he pays the seller. He is required to give notice to the seller of his intention to deduct. Damages may be deducted only as against the price due under the same contract. Accordingly, a buyer could not deduct damages for goods under one contract from the price due under other contracts from the same seller.

9. Limitations on Damages

The Code adopts the modern view on the legality of liquidated damage clauses. Such a clause is valid only if the amount is reasonable in the light of the anticipated or actual harm caused by the breach. A term fixing unreasonably large liquidated damages is void as a penalty (2-718[1]).

Sellers sometimes justifiably withhold delivery of goods because of the buyer's breach of the contract. This may occur not withstanding the fact that the buyer has made part payment. In such cases, the seller is not permitted to retain all of the buyer's payments. The seller must return to the buyer the amount that is in excess of the liquidated damages term of the contract. If there is no such provision, he must return payments in excess of 20 percent of the value of the total performance for which the buyer is obligated under the contract or $500, whichever is smaller (2-718[2][b]). The seller, however, is entitled to set off against this amount any damages that he can establish against the buyer (2-718[3]).[4] Thus, the seller is allowed to deduct damages resulting from the buyer's breach from the amount that he would otherwise have to return to the buyer.

The provision relating to restitution applies to amounts deposited by the buyer as security for his performance as well as to down payments or part payments. It also covers payments in goods and the proceeds from the resale of such goods (2-718[4]).

10. Right to the Goods

Under proper circumstances, the buyer has rights in and to the goods. The Code makes available the remedy of specific performance when the goods are unique and also when other circumstances make it equitable that the seller render the required performance (2-716[1]). It would appear that to invoke this remedy, the buyer must have been unable to cover. Although the Code does not define "unique," it is fair to assume that it would encompass output and requirement contracts in which the goods were not readily or practically available from other sources.

Another remedy that enables the buyer to reach the goods in the hands of the seller is the statutory remedy of replevin. *Replevin* is an action to recover goods that one person wrongfully withholds from another. A buyer has the right to replevin goods from the seller if the goods have been *identified* to the contract and the buyer is unable to effect cover after making a reasonable effort to do so (2-716[3]). Also, if the seller has shipped the goods under reservation of a security interest and the buyer has tendered satisfaction of the security interest, the buyer can maintain an action of replevin.

A related remedy that also reaches the goods in the hands of the seller is the buyer's right to recover them if the seller becomes insolvent (2-502). The right exists only if (1) the buyer has a "special property" in the goods—that is, existing goods have been identified to the contract, (2) the seller becomes insolvent within ten days after he received the first installment payment from the buyer, and (3) the buyer makes and keeps good a tender of the balance of the purchase price. Absent such factors, the buyer is relegated to the position of a general creditor of the seller.

THE SELLER'S RIGHTS AND REMEDIES

11. Introduction

The Code establishes certain rights and remedies for sellers just as it does for buyers. One of the most significant rights is to "cure" a defective performance.

---

[4] *Neri* v. *Retail Marine Corporation,* page 306.

The Code gives a seller several alternative courses of action when a buyer wrongfully rejects the goods, wrongfully revokes a prior acceptance of the goods, fails to make a payment when due, or wrongfully repudiates the contract. The seller may cancel the contract if the buyer's breach is material.[5] Under certain circumstances, a seller may withhold delivery if it has not been made or may stop delivery if the goods are in transit. The Code also gives a seller the right to resell the goods and recover damages or to simply recover damages for the buyer's failure to accept the goods. Finally, the seller may under certain circumstances file suit to recover the price of the goods. The remedies of the seller are cumulative and not exclusive. The technical aspects of "cure" and of these remedies are discussed in the sections that follow.

12. Cure

If, upon inspecting the goods, the buyer finds that they do not conform to the contract, he may reject them provided he acts fairly in doing so. If the rejection is for a relatively minor deviation from the contract requirements, the seller must be given an opportunity to correct the defective performance. This is called *cure*.[6] The seller may accomplish this by notifying the buyer of his intention to cure and then tendering proper or conforming goods if the time for performance has not expired. If the time for performance has expired, the seller, if he has reasonable grounds to believe that the goods will be acceptable in spite of the nonconformity, will be granted further time to substitute goods that are in accordance with the contract. The main purpose of this rule allowing cure is to protect the seller from being forced into a breach by a surprise rejection at the last moment by the buyer. The seller, in order to take advantage of this privilege, must notify the buyer of his intention to cure and must in fact cure within a reasonable time.

13. Right to Reclaim Goods on Buyer's Insolvency

If a seller discovers that a buyer on credit is insolvent, the seller will want to withhold delivery, or if delivery is in process, to stop it before it is completed. A buyer is insolvent "who either has ceased to pay his debts in the ordinary course of business or cannot pay his debts as they become due or is insolvent within the meaning of the federal bankruptcy law" (1-201[23]).

A seller, upon discovering that the buyer is insolvent, may refuse to make any further deliveries except for cash, and he may demand that payment be made for all goods theretofore delivered under the contract (2-702[1]). If goods are en route to the buyer, they may be stopped in transit and recovered from the carrier (2-705). If they are in a warehouse or other place of storage awaiting delivery to the buyer, the seller may stop delivery by the bailee. Thus,

5 *Mott Equity Elevator* v. *Svihovec,* page 307.
6 See *Zabriskie Chevrolet, Inc.* v. *Smith,* page 302.

the seller can protect his interest by retaining or reclaiming the goods prior to the time they come into the possession of the insolvent buyer.

This right to reclaim the goods on the buyer's insolvency includes situations in which the goods have come into the buyer's possession. If the buyer has received goods on credit while he is insolvent, the seller can reclaim the goods by making a demand for them within ten days after their receipt by the buyer (2-702[2]). He must act within the ten-day period in order to exercise this right.[7] By receiving the goods, the buyer has, in effect, made a representation that he is solvent and able to pay for them. If the buyer has made a written misrepresentation of solvency within the three-month period before the goods were delivered to him, and the seller has justifiably relied on the writing, the ten-day limitation period during which the seller can reclaim the goods from the insolvent buyer does not apply (2-702[2]).

If a seller exercises his right to reclaim the goods from an insolvent buyer, he is not able to collect damages or pursue any other remedy (2-702[3]). This is not too significant, since the buyer is insolvent anyway.

If the buyer has resold the goods to an innocent purchaser before the seller reclaims them, such purchaser will be protected against the claim of the seller that the goods be returned (2-702[3]).

The importance to a seller of the privilege of reclaiming goods or stopping them in transit should be obvious. If the insolvent buyer is adjudicated a bankrupt, the goods will become a part of the bankrupt estate and will be sold by the trustee in bankruptcy for the benefit of *all* the creditors of the buyer. If the seller is able to reclaim the goods, his loss will be kept to a minimum.

14. Right to Reclaim Goods—Buyer Not Insolvent

The right to stop goods in transit or to withhold delivery is not restricted to the insolvency situation. Where the buyer has wrongfully rejected a tender of goods, revoked his acceptance, failed to make a payment due on or before delivery, or repudiated with respect to either a part of the goods or the whole contract, the seller can also reclaim the goods. His right extends to any goods directly affected by the breach, and if the breach is of the whole contract, then also to the whole undelivered balance. If the contract is an installment contract and the breach with respect to one or more installments substantially impairs the value of the whole contract, it will be treated as a breach of the whole.

To exercise his right to stop delivery by a carrier, the seller must give proper and timely notice to such carrier so that there is reasonable time to follow the instructions given (2-705[3]). Once the goods have been received by the buyer, or the bailee has acknowledged that he holds the goods for the buyer, the right of stoppage is at an end. Only in the case of insolvency (2-705[2]) can the seller reclaim the goods after they are in the buyer's possession.

[7] *Stumbo* v. *Paul B. Hult Lumber Co.*, page 309.

The right to stop delivery to a solvent buyer is restricted to carload, truck-load, planeload, or larger shipments. This restriction is designed to ease the burden on carriers that could develop if the right to stop for reasons other than insolvency applied to all small shipments. The seller who is shipping to a buyer of doubtful credit can always send the goods C.O.D. and thus preclude the necessity for stopping in transit. Of course, the seller must exercise care in availing himself of this remedy, as improper stoppage is a breach by the seller and would subject him to an action for damages by the buyer.

15.   The Right to Resell the Goods

The seller who has reclaimed goods, has withheld them, or is otherwise in possession of goods at the time of the buyer's breach or repudiation has the right to resell the goods (2-706). If part of the goods has been delivered, he can resell the undelivered portion. In this way the seller can quickly realize at least some of the amount due from the buyer; he also has a claim against the buyer for the difference between the resale price and the price that the buyer had agreed to pay. To the extent that the seller suffered additional damages, he is also entitled to recover these (2-710). The resale remedy thus affords a practical method and course of action for the seller who has possession of goods that were intended for a breaching buyer.

Frequently, a buyer will breach or repudiate the contract prior to the time that goods have been identified to the contract. Such a factual situation does not defeat the seller's right to resell the goods. The seller may proceed to identify goods to the contract (2-704[1][a]) and then use his remedy of resale. If the goods are unfinished, the seller may use his remedy of resale if he can show that the unfinished goods were intended for the particular contract (2-704[1][b]).

The seller is also given other choices of action when the goods are in process at the time he learns of the breach. He may (1) complete the manufacture and identify the goods to the contract, or (2) resell the unfinished goods for scrap or salvage value, or (3) take any other reasonable action in connection with the goods (2-704[2]). The only requirement is that the seller use reasonable commercial judgment in determining which course of action he will take in order to mitigate his damages. Presumably he would take into consideration such factors as the extent to which the manufacture had been completed and the resalability of the goods if he elected to complete the manufacture. Thus, the law allows the seller to proceed in a commercially reasonable manner in order to protect his interests.

When the seller elects to use his remedy of resale, the resale may be either a private sale or a public (auction) sale (2-706[2]). It must be identified as one relating to the broken contract. If the resale is private, the seller must give the buyer reasonable notification of his intention to resell (2-706[3]). If the resale is public, the seller must give the buyer reasonable notice of the time and place so that he can bid or can obtain the attendance of other bidders. With goods that are perishable or threaten to speedily decline in value, the notice is not required. The seller is permitted to buy at a public sale or resale. The prime requirement is that the sale be conducted in a commercially reasonable manner (2-706[2]).

It is to be noted that the resale could conceivably bring a higher price than that provided for in the contract. In such case, the seller is not accountable to the buyer for any profit (2-706[6]).

16. The Right to Collect Damages

In many situations, resale would not be an appropriate or satisfactory remedy. The seller may elect to bring an action for damages if the buyer refuses to accept the goods or repudiates the contract (2-708). The measure of damages is the difference between the market price at the place for tender and the unpaid contract price, plus incidental damages (2-713). Incidental damages include expenses reasonably incurred as the result of the buyer's breach (2-710). If the market price is for some reason difficult to ascertain, the Code provides reasonable leeway in receiving evidence of prices current in other, comparable markets or at other times comparable to the one in question (2-723).

In most situations, this measure of damages would not be adequate to restore the seller to as good a position as would have been accomplished by performance by the buyer because of the lost sale. Under such circumstances, the measure of damages is the profit that the seller would have made from full performance by the buyer (2-708[2]) as well as incidental damages.[8] In computing profit, the reasonable overhead of the seller may be taken into account. The measure of damages recognizes that a seller suffers a loss, even though he may ultimately resell for the same amount that he would have received from the buyer. He has lost a sale and the profit on the sale.

17. The Right to Collect the Purchase Price

When the buyer fails to pay the price as it becomes due, the seller may sue for the contract price of the goods if (1) the goods were accepted by the buyer; (2) the goods were lost or damaged within a commercially reasonable time after the risk of loss passed to the buyer; or (3) the goods were identified to the contract and the seller was unable to sell them at a reasonable price, or the circumstances indicated that the effort to do so would be unavailing (2-709). Thus, an action for the price is generally limited to those situations in which the buyer has accepted the goods, the goods were destroyed after risk of loss passed to the buyer, or the resale remedy is not practicable. In other cases, the suit for dollar damages would be used (2-709[3]).

If the seller sues for the price, the goods involved are, of course, held by the seller on behalf of the buyer; they become in effect the buyer's goods. After the

---

[8] See *Neri* v. *Retail Marine Corporation,* page 306.

seller obtains a judgment against the buyer, the seller may still resell the goods at any time prior to collection of the judgment, but he must apply the proceeds toward satisfaction of the judgment. Payment of the balance due on the judgment entitles the buyer to any goods not resold (2-709[2]).

The seller may be unsuccessful in his suit for the price, as when the court rules that he has not sustained the burden of proof with regard to the impracticability of resale. But in the same action, the court may award damages for nonacceptance to the seller who is unsuccessful in his suit for the price (2-709[3]).

PERFORMANCE OF THE SALES CONTRACT CASES

Zabriskie Chevrolet, Inc. v. Smith
240 A.2d 195 (N.J.) 1968

DOAN, J. . . . This action arises out of the sale by plaintiff to defendant of a new 1966 Chevrolet automobile. Within a short distance after leaving the showroom the vehicle became almost completely inoperable by reason of mechanical failure. Defendant the same day notified plaintiff that he cancelled the sale and simultaneously stopped payment on the check he had tendered in payment of the balance of the purchase price. Plaintiff sues on the check and the purchase order for the balance of the purchase price plus incidental damages and defendant counterclaims for the return of his deposit and incidental damages. . . .

. . . [T]he . . . issue presented is whether defendant properly rejected under the Code. That he cancelled the sale and rejected the vehicle almost concomitantly with the discovery of the failure of his bargain is clear from the evidence. Code section 2-601 delineates the buyer's rights following nonconforming delivery and reads as follows:

> . . . if the goods or the tender of delivery *fail in any respect to conform* to the contract, the buyer may
> (a) reject the whole; . . . [Italics added.]

Section 2-602 indicates that one can reject after taking possession. Possession, therefore, does not mean acceptance and the corresponding loss of the right or rejection. . . . "Rejection of goods must be within a reasonable time after their delivery or tender. It is ineffective unless the buyer reasonably notifies the seller. . . ."

Section 2-106 defines conforming goods as follows:

> (2) Goods or conduct including any part of a performance are "conforming" or conform to the contract when they are in accordance with the obligations under the contract.

The Uniform Commercial Code Comment to that section states:

> 2. Subsection (2): It is in general intended to continue the policy of requiring *exact performance* by the seller of his obligations as a condition to his right to require acceptance. However, the seller is in part safeguarded against surprise as a result of sudden technicality on the buyer's part by the provisions on seller's cure of improper tender or delivery. . . .

In the present case we are not dealing with a situation such as was present in *Adams* v. *Tramontin Motor Sales.* In that case, brought for breach of implied warranty of merchantability, the court held that minor defects, such as adjustment of the motor, tightening of loose elements, fixing of locks and dome light, and a correction of rumbling noise, were not remarkable defects, and therefore there was no breach. Here the breach was substantial. The new car was practically inoperable and endowed with a defective transmission. This was a "remarkable defect" and justified rejection by the buyer. . . . [P]laintiff urges that under the Code, it had a right to cure the nonconforming delivery. Code Section 2-508 states:

(1) Where any tender or delivery by the seller is rejected because non-conforming, and the *time for performance has not yet expired,* the seller may seasonably notify the buyer of his intention to cure and may then within the contract time make a conforming delivery.

(2) Where the buyer rejects a nonconforming tender which the *seller had reasonable gounds to believe would be acceptable* with or without money allowance the seller may if he seasonably notifies the buyer have a further reasonable time to substitute a conforming tender. . . . [Italics added.]

The Uniform Commercial Code Comment to 2-508 reads:

2. Subsection (2) seeks to avoid injustice to the seller by reason of a surprise rejection by the buyer. However, the seller is not protected unless he had "reasonable grounds to believe" that the tender would be acceptable.

It is clear that in the instant case there was no "forced breach" on the part of the buyer, for he almost immediately began to negotiate for another automobile. The inquiry is as to what is intended by "cure," as used in the Code. This statute makes no attempt to define or specify what a "cure" shall consist of. It would appear, then, that each case must be controlled by its own facts. The "cure" intended under the cited section of the Code does not, in the court's opinion, contemplate the tender of a new vehicle with a substituted transmission, not from the factory and of unknown lineage from another vehicle in plaintiff's possession. It was not the intention of the Legislature that the right to "cure" is a limitless one to be controlled only by the will of the seller. A "cure" which endeavors by substitution to tender a chattel not within the agreement or contemplation of the parties is invalid.

For a majority of people the purchase of a new car is a major investment, rationalized by the peace of mind that flows from its dependability and safety. Once their faith is shaken, the vehicle loses not only its real value in their eyes, but becomes an instrument whose integrity is substantially impaired and whose operation is fraught with apprehension. The attempted cure in the present case was ineffective.

Accordingly, judgment is rendered on the main case in favor of defendant. On the counterclaim judgment is rendered in favor of defendant and against plaintiff. . . .

Desilets Granite Company v. Stone Equalizer Corp.
340 A.2d 65 (Vt.) 1975

DALEY, J. . . . A commercial buyer's attempted revocation of its acceptance of a stone-splitting machine purchased from a seller is at issue in this appeal. After trial, the . . . Court determined that plaintiff Desilets Granite Company had justifiably revoked acceptance of the purchased product under 9A V.S.A. § 2-608. As a consequence, plaintiff was allowed to recover, pursuant to 9A V.S.A. § 2-711, the

amount of the purchase price already paid to defendant Stone Equalizer Corporation, plus escrow monies representing the unpaid balance of the purchase price.

According to the findings, plaintiff is a Vermont corporation manufacturing monuments and other granite products. A foreign corporation, defendant manufacturers machinery used in the granite industry. In 1972, the parties negotiated for and consummated a sale of a stone-splitting machine, after representations as to the superiority of defendant's product. After delivery of the machine in early 1973, problems developed with its operation. By agreement, the machine was returned to defendant for modifications and corrections and on receipt of the renovated stone-splitter, plaintiff was to make the final payment owing.

In August, 1973, defendant notified plaintiff that the corrections were completed. On plaintiff's assurance that payment would be made on delivery, defendant shipped the machine on August 9, but refused to unload it until payment was tendered. On the same day, plaintiff attached the machine and commenced this action below by filing a complaint for breach of warranty. Under order of court, plaintiff was subsequently allowed to operate the refurbished machine, but it again proved to be unsatisfactory and unfit for its purpose.

Acceptance of non-conforming goods under either one of two conditions must occur before a commercial buyer may revoke his acceptance. He may properly revoke (1) when acceptance has occurred on the reasonable assumption that the non-conformity would be cured and it has not so been; or (2) when acceptance has occurred without discovery of the non-conformity if so induced by (a) difficulty of discovery before acceptance or by (b) seller's assurances. And, for the revocation to be effective, it must occur both within a reasonable time after discovery and after buyer has notified the seller of it. We cannot agree with defendant's contention that under the facts of this case neither of the statutory conditions were present to enable plaintiff to revoke his acceptance of the stone-splitting machine. But we do ascribe to the argument that, even granting

plaintiff did properly revoke his acceptance, his failure to give notice thereof renders the revocation ineffective.

Plaintiff gained possession of the refurbished machine on August 9 when, by attachment, it took delivery. Since the non-conformity, if any, contemplated by Section 2-608 (1) could not have been discovered before actual use of the machine, it is clear that the statute allows the plaintiff to revoke its acceptance in such a case when, on eventual use, the machine remains unfit for its purpose. To this extent, the lower court's decision is supportable.

. . . The statute plainly states that revocation of acceptance is not effective until the buyer notifies the seller. . . .

. . . [S]ince . . . an examination of the transcript fails to yield any evidence of notice, plaintiff's attempted revocation of acceptance never became, nor could become, effective. Neither the attachment nor the complaint, in this case, could constitute the required notice. The attachment was merely a means by which buyer was able to obtain control over the machine before payment to determine its workability and fitness. The serving of a complaint for breach of warranty, properly timed, might in some cases constitute notice of revocation, but not here where it was served before plaintiff discovered the non-conformity. If the principal policy behind the rejection notice requirement is to give the seller an opportunity to cure or permit him to assist in minimizing the buyer's losses, that policy has clearly not been met where the complaint was served at the moment of acceptance, before any determination of the conformity of goods could be had. . . .

Reversed and remanded.

Thorstenson v. Mobridge Iron Works Co.
208 N.W.2d 715 (S.Dak.) 1973

Plaintiff and defendant entered into a contract whereby defendant agreed to sell plaintiff a Case 730 farm tractor and a mounted F-11

Farmhand loader at a specific price. Thereafter defendant notified plaintiff that there would be no delivery. Defendant contended that an F-11 could not be mounted on a 730 Case. Plaintiff purchased the equipment from another dealer at a price increase of $1,000. He claimed this amount as "cover" damages. The trial court directed a verdict for defendant, and plaintiff appealed.

DOYLE, J. . . . It is undisputed that the tractor, loader and attachments were not delivered to the plaintiff in accordance with the contract. However, there is considerable dispute between the plaintiff and defendant as to why the equipment was not delivered. The defendant contends that the F-11 Farmhand loader could not be mounted on the 730 Case tractor, that plaintiff refused to accept the tractor and loader unit if mounting required a remodeling or working over of the tractor, and that plaintiff would not accept any other replacement. On the other hand, the plaintiff contends that the loader could be mounted on the 730 Case tractor without remodeling the tractor or loader to the extent that defendant claimed was necessary. He further contends he offered to mount the loader himself and that he later purchased a Case 730 tractor and an F-11 Farmhand mounted as he desired. The plaintiff purchased this equipment in December 1968 from a Case dealer in Aberdeen, South Dakota, at a price increase of $1,000 which the plaintiff claims is a "cover" purchase as provided in SDCL 57-8-31, Uniform Commercial Code (U.L.A.) § 2-712. Plaintiff testified the cover purchase was similar equipment while defendant claims it was an "entirely different tractor" from the one specified in their contract. In our view, these disputed questions of fact should have been submitted to a jury. . . .

When a seller fails to make delivery or repudiates, or the buyer rightfully rejects or justifiably revokes a contract, the buyer has certain remedies available by statute. Uniform Commercial Code (U.L.A.) § 2-711 through § 2-725. In SDCL 57-8-28, it is provided that the buyer may:

> (1) "Cover" and have damages under §§ 57-8-31 to 57-8-33, inclusive . . .

SDCL 57-8-31 provides that:

> . . . the buyer may "cover" by making in good faith and without unreasonable delay any reasonable purchase of or contract to purchase goods in substitution for those due from the seller.

SDCL 57-8-32 provides:

> The buyer may recover from the seller as damages the difference between the cost of cover and the contract price together with any incidental or consequential damages as hereinafter defined . . . but less expenses saved in consequence of the seller's breach.

It is stated in Uniform Commercial Code (U.L.A.) § 2-712, 460:

> This section provides the buyer with a remedy aimed at enabling him to obtain the goods he needs thus meeting his essential need. This remedy is the buyer's equivalent of the seller's right to resell.
>
> The definition of "cover" . . . envisages . . . a single contract or sale; goods not identical with those involved but commercially usable as reasonable substitutes under the circumstances of the particular case. . . . The test of proper cover is whether at the time and place the buyer acted in good faith and in a reasonable manner, and it is immaterial that hindsight may later prove that the method of cover used was not the cheapest or most effective. . . .

From a review of the record it appears there was sufficient evidence of damages to the plaintiff under the statute quoted above to require the question of damages to be submitted to a jury.

Reversed and remanded for trial by jury.

Neri v. Retail Marine Corporation
285 N.E.2d 311 (N.Y.) 1972

Plaintiffs contracted to buy a boat from the defendant for the sum of $12,587.40. Six days later plaintiffs cancelled the contract because of personal problems. Plaintiffs seek to recover their down payment of $4,250 in this suit. Defendant counterclaims for damages in the same amount. The defendant had resold the boat for the same price, but defendant claimed that it had lost the profit on one boat sale which was $2,579. Defendant also established incidental expenses of $674 for storage upkeep, finance charges, and insurance until the resale. Finally defendant sought attorney's fees of $1,250.

The trial court found that the terms of section 2-718, subsection 2(b), of the Uniform Commercial Code are applicable and awarded defendant $500 upon its counterclaim and directed that plaintiffs recover the balance of their deposit, amounting to $3,750. Defendant appeals.

GIBSON, J. . . . The appeal concerns the right of a retail dealer to recover loss of profits and incidental damages upon the buyer's repudiation of a contract governed by the Uniform Commercial Code. This is, indeed, the correct measure of damage in an appropriate case and to this extent the code (§ 2-708, subsection [2]) effected a substantial change from prior law, whereby damages were ordinarily limited to "the difference between the contract price and the market or current price." Upon the record before us, the courts below erred in declining to give effect to the new statute and so the order appealed from must be reversed.

The issue is governed in the first instance by section 2-718 of the Uniform Commercial Code which provides, among other things, that the buyer, despite his breach, may have restitution of the amount by which his payment exceeds: (a) reasonable liquidated damages stipulated by the contractor or (b) absent such stipulation, 20% of the value of the

buyer's total performance or $500, whichever is smaller. As above noted, the trial court awarded defendant an offset in the amount of $500 under paragraph (b) and directed restitution to plaintiffs of the balance. Section 2-718, however, establishes, in paragraph (a) of subsection (3), an alternative right of offset in favor of the seller, as follows "(3) The buyer's right to restitution under subsection (2) is subject to offset to the extent that the seller establishes (a) a right to recover damages under the provisions of this Article other than subsection (1)."

Among "the provisions of this Article other than subsection (1)" are those to be found in section 2-708, which the courts below did not apply. Subsection (1) of that section provides that "the measure of damages for non-acceptance or repudiation by the buyer is the difference between the market price at the time and place for tender and the unpaid contract price together with any incidental damages provided in this Article, but less expenses saved in consequence of the buyer's breach." However, this provision is made expressly subject to subsection (2), providing: "(2) If the measure of damages provided in subsection (1) is inadequate to put the seller in as good a position as performance would have done then the measure of damages is the profit (including reasonable overhead) which the seller would have made from full performance by the buyer, together with any incidental damages. . . .

This section permits the recovery of lost profits in all appropriate cases. . . . Additionally, and "[i]n all cases the seller may recover incidental damages. . . ." The conclusion is clear from the record—indeed with mathematical certainty—that "the measure of damages provided in subsection (1) is inadequate to put the seller in as good a position as performance would have done" and hence that the seller is entitled to its "profit (including reasonable overhead) . . . together with any incidental damages. . . ."

Closely parallel to the factual situation now before us is that hypothesized by Dean Hawkland as illustrative of the operation of the rules: "Thus, if a private party agrees to sell his automobile to a buyer for $2,000, a breach by the buyer would cause the seller no loss (except incidental damages, i.e., expense of a new sale) if the seller was able to sell the automobile to another buyer for $2,000. But the situation is different with dealers having an unlimited supply of standard-priced goods. Thus, if an automobile dealer agrees to sell a car to a buyer at the standard price of $2,000, a breach by the buyer injures the dealer, even though he is able to sell the automobile to another for $2,000. If the dealer has an inexhaustible supply of cars, the resale to replace the breaching buyer costs the dealer a sale, because, had the breaching buyer performed, the dealer would have made two sales instead of one. The buyer's breach, in such a case, depletes the dealer's sales to the extent of one, and the measure of damages should be the dealer's profit on one sale. Section 2-708 recognizes this. . . ."

The record, which in this case establishes defendant's entitlement to damages in the amount of its prospective profit, at the same time confirms defendant's cognate right to "any incidental damages. . . ." From the language employed it is too clear to require discussion that the seller's right to recover loss of profits is not exclusive and that he may recoup his "incidental" expenses as well. . . .

The trial court correctly denied defendant's claim for recovery of attorney's fees incurred by it in this action. Attorney's fees incurred in an action such as this are not in the nature of the protective expenses contemplated by the statute. . . .

It follows that plaintiffs are entitled to restitution of the sum of $4,250 paid by them on account of the contract price less an offset to defendant in the amount of $3,253 on account of its lost profit of $2,579 and its incidental damages of $674. . . .

So ordered.

Mott Equity Elevator v. Svihovec
236 N.W.2d 900 (N.D.) 1975

The plaintiff elevator (buyer) sued the defendant seller for damages for failure of the defendant to deliver 4,000 bushels of grain. The contract provided for March delivery at a price of $1.86 per bushel, but the plaintiff would not accept delivery during that month because of a shortage of railroad boxcars. The defendant attempted to deliver the grain during April and May but this was also refused. However, the plaintiff did accept delivery of the grain of others during these periods. In early June, the defendant sold his grain to another elevator for $2.20 per bushel. In September the plaintiff demanded that the defendant deliver the grain. At this time, the price was $4.00. Plaintiff seeks damages for the price difference in September.

VOGEL, J. . . . [T]he plaintiff elevator breached the agreement by its refusal to accept Svihovec's grain. . . . Under Section § 2-703 of the Uniform Commercial Code:

> Where the buyer wrongfully rejects or revokes acceptance of goods or fails to make a payment due on or before delivery or repudiates with respect to a part or the whole, then with respect to any goods directly affected and, if the breach is of the whole contract, then also with respect to the whole undelivered balance, the aggrieved seller may
>
> 1. withhhold delivery of such goods;
> 2. resell and recover damages as hereinafter provided;

3. recover damages for nonacceptance or in a proper case the price;
4. cancel.

Where the buyer breaches the agreement, the seller is released from his obligation under the contract and may pursue the [aforesaid] remedies. . . . The trial court found that the defendant was within his rights under the Code when he refused to make delivery under the contract and resold the wheat at a private sale. By doing so, he exercised his right under subdivision 6 to cancel the sale.

The elevator strenuously argues that Svihovec was not entitled to resell his grain . . . without giving reasonable notice of his intent to resell. The argument also is made that . . . imposes a duty on Svihovec to give reasonable notice to the other party that he was terminating the contract.

We find these arguments to be without merit. . . . C.C. (UCC § 2-703). Svihovec pursued the remedy of cancellation, as was his right. He thereafter resold his grain to another buyer, as was his right. The parties have confused Svihovec's right to dispose of his grain as he wished under a cancelled contract with the Code remedy allowing a seller to "resell and recover damages. . . ."

The seller's right to resell and recover damages is, of course, available to a seller in addition to his right to cancel. . . .

The only condition precedent to the seller's right to resell is a breach by the buyer. . . . The trial judge found that Svihovec had a right to pursue this remedy when he sold his grain directly to the Grain Terminal Association. We would agree that Svihovec did have such a right if it were necessary to apply this section to the seller's conduct in reselling his grain in this case. But the section does not apply. In a falling market Svihovec would probably have desired to resell and recover damages. To recover damages under this section he would be required to act in good faith, sell in a com-

mercially reasonable manner, and give reasonable notice to the buyer of his intention to resell (if the sale was at private sale). Failure to act properly under this section merely deprives the seller of the measure of damages provided in subsection 1. In any event, the seller is not accountable to the buyer for any profit made on any resale . . . where, as here, the resale occurred in a rising market and the contract had been cancelled. In this case, involving a rising market, Svihovec suffered no damages and thus did not need to resort to this Code remedy.

We hold that the buyer breached the agreement in not accepting delivery within a reasonable time, giving rise to Svihovec's right to cancel. . . . "Cancellation" is defined . . . as follows:

> "Cancellation" occurs when either party puts an end to the contract for breach by the other and its effect is the same as that of "termination" except that the cancelling party also retains any remedy for breach of the whole contract or any unperformed balance.

The elevator's next argument is that Section § 2-309 obligated Svihovec to notify the elevator of his intent to terminate the contract. This section does not apply to the facts of this case. Svihovec did not "terminate" the contract; he pursued the Code remedy of "cancellation" following breach by the buyer. These are two separate things under the Uniform Commercial Code. . . .

> "Termination" occurs when either party pursuant to a power created by agreement or law puts an end to the contract otherwise than for its breach. . . .

In this case, the elevator was in breach, and Section § 2-309 does not apply. The contract was cancelled, not terminated. . . .
Affirmed.

Stumbo v. Paul B. Hult Lumber Co.
444 P.2d 564 (Or.) 1968

Plaintiffs had sold and delivered logs to Keystone Lumber Company. The lumber company suffered a fire which destroyed the mill, and the insurance proceeds were not sufficient to cover its obligations. Plaintiffs, who had not been paid, proceeded to remove logs from Keystones storage area and sold them to Hult, who processed them into lumber. The proceeds of this sale were in question. The holder of a security interest in the logs claimed them, as did plaintiffs. The lawsuit was for a declaratory judgment as to the rights of the various parties. The lower court ruled for plaintiffs, and defendant appealed.

O'CONNELL, J. . . . The Code provides that a seller of goods may, under certain circumstances, recover goods delivered to the buyer. Thus ORS 72.7020(2) permits a reclamation of goods from a buyer who received the goods while insolvent. However, reclamation under this section is conditioned upon a demand made within ten days after the receipt of the goods by the buyer. No such demand was made in the present case.

A seller also may have the right to recover goods from a buyer under ORS 72.5070 (2), which provides as follows:

> (2) Where payment is due and demanded on the delivery to the buyer of goods or documents of title, his right as against the seller to retain or dispose of them is conditional upon his making the payment due.

However, plaintiffs acquired no interest in the logs under the foregoing section for the reason that payment was neither "due" nor "demanded" on the delivery of the logs. . . .

Plaintiffs contend that their removal of the logs constituted a reclamation of goods under ORS 72.7050(1). That section provides as follows:

> (1) The seller may stop delivery of goods in the possession of a carrier or other bailee when he discovers the buyer to be insolvent as provided in ORS 72.7020 and may stop delivery of carload, truckload, planeload or large shipments of express or freight when the buyer repudiates or fails to make a payment due before delivery or if for any other reason the seller has a right to withhold or reclaim the goods.

This section is applicable only when goods are in the process of delivery and before the buyer has acquired possession. It cannot be understood as providing an independent right of recovery of goods in the possession of a buyer. The language "or if for any other reason the seller has a right to withhold or reclaim goods" clearly is intended to indicate only that a seller may stop the delivery of goods in transit or in the possession of a bailee where the conditions of withholding or recovering goods from the buyer himself are otherwise satisfied. In the present case all of the logs had been delivered to Keystone's millpond before plaintiffs attempted to reclaim them. . . .

Consequently, we conclude that plaintiffs had no right to recover the logs from Keystone and were no more than unsecured general creditors without any interest in particular assets of Keystone, including the logs taken from Keystone's millpond. The security interest of M D M was clearly superior to the claim of such a creditor. . . .

Reversed and remanded.

CHAPTER 17
REVIEW QUESTIONS AND PROBLEMS

1. X purchased a color TV from Y. When the set was delivered, the color did not function properly. Y sent a serviceman to check the set. The serviceman informed X that he would have to remove the TV chassis from its cabinet and take it to his shop for inspection. X refused to allow the serviceman to do this and demanded return of the purchase price from Y. Y again offered to repair the set. Should X recover? Explain.

2. X contracted to purchase component parts for his product from Y. Y concedes that certain orders were placed by X and accepted by him, specifying that time was of the essence. Y failed to deliver, and one of X's representatives visited Y's plant to find that X's work had been taken off the machines in favor of other jobs. X then sued for damages for lack of timely delivery by Y. Should he recover? Explain.

3. A ordered a hearing aid from B Company. B Company delivered a newer model than the one ordered, and A refused to accept it. Does B Company have the right to tender the model ordered? Why?

4. A contracted to buy 5,000 bushels of corn from B. Just before harvest, a hailstorm destroyed the crop. Is B still required to perform his obligation of the contract? Why?

5. A entered into a contract to manufacture goods for B, who required them for use in a construction project. A requested delivery instructions but B did not furnish them, and as a result the goods were never delivered. Is A entitled to recover the price of the goods? Why?

6. B purchased a mobile home from S. Shortly after moving in, B discovered water and air leaks as well as other defects. After S's agent had made a series of attempts to repair, B concluded that the attempts were futile and revoked his acceptance. S claimed that revocation was improper because there was no substantial impairment in the value of the mobile home. Is S correct? Why?

7. B purchased a truck from S Company. B requested a certificate of title but was told that it would be given to him at a later date. B took the truck to his shop and proceeded to install a hoist and dump bed, when a fire occurred, destroying the truck. B refused to pay for the truck, contending that since he did not have title, he had no liability. Is B correct? Why?

8. B purchased an irrigation machine from S, and it was installed in January 1968. B notified S that the machine did not function properly, and S tried several times to repair it. On July 27, 1968, B notified S that he was rescinding the contract and demanded a return of the purchase price. S claimed that the attempted revocation was ineffective, since it was not timely. Is S correct? Why?

9. S, a dealer, sold a diesel engine to B, who operated tractor-trailers as a contract carrier. The engine was installed in a tractor, but it did not function properly. S performed repairs at its own expense. However, additional repairs were required, and S billed B for those. When S brought suit for the amount of repairs, B countersued for the loss of the use of the tractor for 27 days as the result of breakdowns. Should B collect? Why?

10. B breached a contract to purchase a bulldozer from S. Fourteen months following the breach, S sold the bulldozer at a private sale. S then brought suit to recover the difference between the resale price and the contract price. Should S succeed? Why?

11. B purchased a mobile home from S. Subsequently, B discovered that the home was infested by beetles. At S's request a pest control company tried on two occasions to rid the home of beetles but was unsuccessful. When B tried to revoke his acceptance S claimed that there had not been a substantial impairment in value to B that would justify the revocation. Is S correct? Why?

12. B contracted to purchase a new Rolls-Royce automobile from S, a dealer for $29,500. B subsequently repudiated the contract. S, without notifying B, sold the car to another dealer for $26,500 and sued B for the difference between the contract price and the resale price. Should S succeed? Why?

13. X sold traffic signal equipment to the city. The city put the equipment in use but contended that the equipment did not meet specifications. However, the city continued to use the equipment and did not claim monetary damages in any amount. Did the notice of failure to meet specifications of the equipment constitute refusal to accept the goods by the city? Explain.

18

Warranties and Products Liability

1. Introduction

The word *warranty* as used in the law of sales of goods describes the obligation of the seller with respect to the goods that have been sold. As a general rule, a seller is responsible for transferring to the buyer a good title and goods that are of the proper quality and free from defects. He may also be responsible for the proper functioning of the article sold and for its suitability to the needs of the buyer. Thus, a warranty may extend not only to the present condition of goods but also to the performance that is to be expected of them.

A seller may make a variety of statements about the goods. It is necessary to evaluate these to determine which statements are warranties and which do not impose legal responsibility because they are merely sales talk.

A warranty made by a seller is an integral part of the contract. If the warranty is breached and the buyer notifies the seller of the breach within a reasonable time, the buyer may bring an action for breach of warranty. The measure of damages is the difference between the value of the goods accepted and the value they would have had if they had been as warranted (2-714). In a proper case, both incidental and consequential damages may also be recovered (2-714[3]). Incidental damages for breach of warranty include expenses reasonably incurred in the care and custody of the goods and any reasonable expense incident to the breach. Consequential damages for breach of warranty include any loss resulting from the general or particular requirements and needs of which the seller at the time of contracting had reason to know and that could not reasonably be prevented by the buyer. A breach of warranty may also result in injuries to the buyer or to third persons. Consequential damages include injuries to persons or property caused by the breach of warranty.

The obligation of a seller of goods to the buyer has been subject to re-evaluation in recent years. In the early law, the parties were usually in fairly equal bargaining positions, and the law did not regard the seller as having any substantial obligation to the buyer. *Caveat emptor* ("let the buyer beware") was the philosophy of the early law of sales.

As the nature of the sales transaction changed over the years, the need for more protection to the buyer was recognized. *Caveat emptor* was gradually replaced by *caveat venditor* ("let the seller beware"). The law generally takes the position that if the goods are defective, the seller should be held responsible. A buyer has the right to justifiably expect that what he purchased is at least sound and of merchantable quality. As the law changed to *caveat venditor,* various tort and contract theories developed that imposed liability on manufacturers, packers, producers, and sellers for injuries caused by defective products. These theories are discussed in this chapter.

The Code has several provisions relating to warranties. It draws a distinction between express warranties made by a seller and those implied from the transaction. The seller may guarantee the product directly, in which case it is an *express* warranty, or the warranty may be *implied* from the transaction and the circumstances. The Code classifies warranties as (1) express warranties, (2) implied warranties, and (3) warranties of title. It should be noted that when the seller is a merchant, special treatment is sometimes afforded to the warranty. This is also true with respect to modifications or exclusions of warranties. A recent federal law on warranties is discussed in Chapter 27 with other aspects of consumer protection.

WARRANTIES

2. Express Warranties

An express warranty is one that is made as a part of the contract for sale and becomes a part of the basis of the bargain between the buyer and the seller (2-313[1][a]). Such a warranty, as distinguished from an implied warranty, is part of the contract because it has been included as part of the individual bargain. To create an express warranty, the seller does not have to use formal words such as "warrant" or "guarantee," nor must he have the specific intention to make a warranty (2-313[3]). For example, a label on a bag of insecticide stated that it was developed especially to control rootworms. This was an express warranty that the insecticide was effective to control the rootworm. The word *guarantee* is often used, however. For example, a contract of sale of automobile tires stated that the tires were guaranteed for 36,000 miles against all road hazards, including blowouts. This constituted an express warranty that the tires would not blow out during the first 36,000 miles of use.

An express warranty comes into existence by virtue of any *affirmation of fact or promise* made by the seller to the buyer that relates to the goods and becomes part of the basis of their bargain (2-313[1][a]). These statements by the seller create an express warranty that the goods will conform to his affirmation or promise. Any statement of fact or even of opinion, if it becomes a part of the basis of the bargain, is an express warranty.

Most statements of opinion such as to the value of the goods do not usually give rise to an express warranty. As a general rule, a buyer is not justified in relying upon mere opinions, and they are not usually a part of the basis of the bargain. However, expressions of opinion by a seller are part of the basis of the bargain in some situations. For example, the opinion of an expert with regard to the value of a gem might be considered to justify the reliance of the buyer, and thus the opinion becomes part of the basis of the bargain.

Statements are warranties if they can properly be considered as terms of the agreement ultimately reached by the parties. The seller makes warranties in order to induce the sale of goods, and for this reason, warranties are regarded as essential parts of the contract. It should be remembered that warranties made after the sale of goods has been consummated are binding without any new consideration (2-209).

An express warranty may be made in a variety of ways. One of these is for the seller to specifically make a factual statement about the goods, such as, "This engine will produce 500 horsepower," or, "This fabric is 100 percent nylon." This factual statement may be on the label to the goods or in a catalog or other sales promotion material. Another is for him to make a direct promise with respect to the goods, such as, "This grass seed is free from weeds." Generally, words that are descriptive of the product are warranties that the goods will conform to the description (2-313[1][b]). Descriptions may also be in the form of diagrams, pictures, blueprints, and the like. Technical specifications of the product would constitute warranties if they were part of the basis for the bargain. An express warranty can also be based on the instructions of the seller on the use of the product.

Just as the seller may describe the goods, he may inform the buyer by showing him a model [1] or a sample of what is being sold. For example, fabrics or clothing might be purchased on the basis of samples shown to the buyer, or a seller might display a working model of an engine. In either event, there would be an express warranty that the goods will conform to the sample or model if the parties have made this a part of their bargain (2-313[1][c]).

---

[1] *Mobile Housing, Inc.* v. *Stone*, page 327.

3. The Implied Warranty of Merchantability

Whereas express warranties come into existence by virtue of the bargaining of the parties, implied warranties come into being as a matter of law, without any bargaining, and as an integral part of the normal sales transaction. Express warranties are negotiated aspects of the bargain between seller and buyer; implied warranties are legally present, unless clearly disclaimed or negated. Implied warranties exist even if a seller is unable to discover the defect involved or unable to cure it if it can be ascertained. Liability for breach of warranty is not based on fault but on the public policy of protecting the buyer of goods.

A warranty that the goods shall be merchantable is implied in a contract for sale if the seller is a merchant who deals in goods of the kind involved in the contract. It is not enough that the defendant sold the goods. The seller-defendant must have been a merchant with respect to the goods. A person making an isolated sale is not a merchant.

For example, a bank when selling a repossessed car is not a merchant and there is no implied warranty of merchantability in such a sale. This important warranty imposes a very substantial obligation upon the merchant-seller. For goods to be merchantable, they must at least be such as

(a)   pass without objective in the trade under the contract description; and

(b)   in the case of fungible goods, are of fair average quality within the description; and

(c)   are fit for the ordinary purposes for which such goods are used; and

(d)   run, within the variations permitted by the agreement, of even kind, quality and quantity within each unit and among all units involved; and

(e)   are adequately contained, packaged, and labeled as the agreement may require; and

(f)   conform to the promises or affirmations of fact made on the container or label if any [2-314].[2]

The foregoing standards provide the basic acceptable standards of merchantability. Fungible goods, (b), are those usually sold by weight or measure, such as grain or flour. The term "fair average quality" generally relates to agricultural bulk commodities and means that they are within the middle range of quality under the description. Fitness for ordinary purposes, (c), is not limited to use by the immediate buyer. If a person is buying for resale, the buyer is entitled to protection, and the goods must be honestly resalable by him. They must be of such nature that they are acceptable in the ordinary

---

[2] *Hauter v. Zogarts,* page 328.

market without objection. Subsection (e) is applicable only if the nature of the goods and of the transaction require a certain type of container, package, or label. Where there is a container or label and there is a representation thereon, the buyer is entitled to protection under (f) so that he will not be in the position of reselling or using goods delivered under false representations appearing on the package or container. He obtains this protection even though the contract did not require either the labeling or the representation.

The implied warranty of merchantability imposes a very broad responsibility upon the merchant-seller to furnish goods that are at least of average quality. In any given line of business, the word *merchantable* may have a meaning somewhat different from the Code definition, and the parties by their course of dealing may indicate a special meaning for the term.

One purpose of this warranty is to require sellers to provide goods that are reasonably safe for their ordinary intended use. Although the law does not require accident-proof products, it does require products that are reasonably safe for the purposes for which they were intended when such products are placed in the stream of commerce.

Liability for breach of the warranty of merchantability extends to direct economic loss as well as to personal injuries and to property damage. (Product liability based on this theory is discussed more fully later in this chapter.) Direct economic loss includes damages based on insufficient product value. In other words, the buyer is entitled to collect the difference in value between what was received and what the product would have had if it had been of merchantable quality. Direct economic loss also includes the cost of replacements goods and the cost of repairs. These damages need not be established with mathematical certainty, but a reasonable degree of certainty and accuracy is required so that the damages are not based on speculation.

4. The Warranty of Fitness for a Particular Purpose

Under the warranty of merchantability, the goods must be fit for the *ordinary purposes* for which such goods are used. An implied warranty of fitness for a particular purpose is created if, at the time of contracting, the seller has reason to know any particular purpose for which the buyer requires the goods and to know that the buyer is relying on the seller's skill or judgment in selecting or furnishing suitable goods (2-315). This means that the seller must in these circumstances select goods that will in fact accomplish the purpose for which they are being purchased.

The implied warranty of fitness applies to both merchants and nonmerchants but would normally apply only to the former, since a nonmerchant would not ordinarily possess the required skill or judgment. The buyer need not specifically state that he has a particular purpose in mind or that he is placing reliance upon the seller's judgment if the circumstances are such that the seller has reason to realize the purpose intended or that the buyer is relying on him. However, the buyer must actually rely upon the seller's skill or judgment in selecting or furnishing suitable goods in order for the warranty to apply. Both issues are questions of fact for a jury.

There is a difference between merchantability and fitness for a particular purpose, although both may be included in the same contract. The particular purpose involves a specific use by the buyer; whereas the ordinary use as expressed in the concept of merchantability means the use that would ordinarily be made of the goods. Thus an appliance such as a dishwasher could be of merchantable quality because it could ordinarily be used to wash dishes but might not be fit for a particular purpose because it would not be suited for the dishwashing needs of a restaurant.

Breach of the warranty of fitness for a particular purpose may result in disaffirmance of the contract. If the product causes an injury including economic loss, it may also result in a suit for dollar damages. This also will be discussed further as a part of products liability later in this chapter.

5. The Warranty of Title

The warranty of title is treated as a separate implied warranty under the Code. Since the concept of title is intangible and is often overlooked by the buyer, the law ensures such a warranty by including it in the sale as a matter of law.

A seller warrants that he is conveying good title to the buyer and that he has the right to sell the goods. He further warrants that there are no encumbrances or liens against the property sold and that no other person can claim a security interest in them (2-312[1]). In effect, the seller impliedly guarantees to the buyer that he will be able to enjoy the use of the goods free from the claims of any third party. Of course, property may be sold to a buyer who has full knowledge of liens or encumbrances, and he may buy such property subject to such claims. In this event, there would not be a breach of warranty of title. The purchase price would, however, reflect that he was obtaining something less than complete title.

Warranty of title can be excluded or modified only by specific language or by circumstances that make it clear that the seller is not vouching for the title (2-312[2]). Judicial sales and sales by executors of estates would not imply that the seller guaranteed the title. Also, a seller could directly inform the buyer that he is selling only the interest that he has and that the buyer takes it subject to all encumbrances.

A seller who is a merchant regularly dealing in goods of the kind that are the subject of the sale makes an additional warranty. He warrants that the goods are free of the rightful claim of any third person by way of infringement of such person's interests—that the goods sold do not, for example, infringe upon a patent (2-312[3]) or a copyright. However, if the buyer furnishes the specifications to the seller, the buyer must hold the seller harmless from any claim arising out of compliance with the specifications (2-312[3]).

6. Disclaimers, Limitations, and Modification of Warranties

A seller will often seek to avoid or restrict warranty liability. The Code provisions on disclaimers of warranties and on the limitation or modification of remedies are designed to protect the buyer from unexpected and unfair disclaimers and limitations.

During the course of the dealings between the buyer and the seller, there may be both statements or conduct relating to the creation of an express warranty and statements or conduct tending to negate or limit a warranty or a remedy. To the extent possible, all statements or conduct are construed as consistent with each other (2-316[1]. However, attempts to negate or limit an express warranty are inoperative if such construction is unreasonable. If an express warranty and the attempt to negate cannot be construed as consistent, there is a warranty. For example, assume that a seller has given the buyer an express warranty and then the written contract includes a provision that purports to exclude "all warranties express or implied." The disclaimer in such a case will not be given effect, and the express warranty will be enforceable.

Implied warranties can be excluded if the seller makes it clear that the buyer will not have the benefit of such warranties. To exclude or modify the implied warranty of merchantability, the word *merchantability* must be used (2-316[2]). If the disclaimer is included in a written contract, it must be set forth in a conspicuous manner. The disclaimer clause of the contract should be in type of a larger size or different color so that it will be brought to the buyer's attention. It has been held that a disclaimer will not be effective if it is set forth in the same type and color as the rest of the contract.

To exclude or modify any implied warranty of fitness for a particular purpose, the exclusion must not only be conspicuous but also be set forth in writing. Such a statement as "there are no warranties which extend beyond the description on the face hereof" is sufficient to exclude the implied warranty of fitness for a particular purpose (2-316[2]). The exclusionary clause should be set forth in type that will set it apart from the balance of the contract.

To remove any doubt that the buyer is aware of the disclaimer of either of the implied warranties, the seller can require the buyer to sign or initial the disclaimer clause in addition to his signature of the entire contract.

The Code also provides for other circumstances in which implied warranties may be wholly or partially excluded. The seller may inform the buyer that he is selling goods "as is," or "with all faults," or use other language that calls the buyer's attention to the exclusion and makes it plain to him that the sale involves no implied warranty (2-316[3][a]) These terms or terms of similar import are ordinarily used in commercial transactions and are understood to mean that the buyer assumes the entire risk as to the quality of the goods involved in the transaction.

The buyer's examination of the goods, or a sample, or a model is also significant in determining the existence of implied warranties. If, before entering into the contract, he has examined the goods, sample, or model as fully as he desired, there is no implied warranty as to defects that an examination ought to have revealed to him (2-316[3][b]). If the seller has demanded that the buyer examine the goods fully and the buyer refuses to do so, there would be no implied warranty as to those defects that a careful examination would have revealed. By making the demand, the seller is giving notice to the buyer that the buyer is assuming the risk with regard to defects that an examination ought to reveal. If the buyer simply fails to make an examination when the goods are available to him for this purpose, the seller will not be protected if a demand has not been made (2-316[3][a]).

A course of dealing between the parties, course of performance, or usage of trade can also be the basis for exclusion or modification of implied warranties. These factors can be important in determining the nature and extent of implied warranties in any given transaction (2-316[3][c]).

The Code also allows the parties to limit the remedies available in the event of a breach of warranty (2-719). The agreement may provide for remedies in addition to or in substitution of those provided by the Code. The parties may also limit or alter the measure of damages. Such provisions usually limit a buyer's damages to the repayment of the price upon return of the goods. Contracts often allow a seller to repair defective goods or replace nonconforming parts without further liability. These provisions in effect eliminate a seller's liability for consequential damages and allow a seller to "cure" a defect or cancel a transaction by refunding the purchase price without further liability.

Clauses limiting the liability of a seller are subject to the Code requirement on unconscionability (2-719). Limitations of consequential damages for personal injury in the case of consumer goods are *prima facie* unconscionable. Limitations of damages where the loss is commercial are presumed to be valid.[3]

Disclaimers of implied warranties are greatly limited by federal law today. As a part of the law relating to consumer protection, Congress passed the Magnuson-Moss warranty law. This law and the Federal Trade Commission rules adopted to carry out its purposes prohibit the disclaimer of implied warranties where an express warranty is given. This law is discussed further in Chapter 26.

7. Third-Party Beneficiaries of Warranties

Historically, suits for breach of warranty required "privity of contract," or a contractual connection between the parties. Lack of privity of contract was a complete defense to the suit.

There are two aspects to privity-of-contract requirements, which are sometimes described as horizontal and vertical. The *horizontal* privity issue is, To

---

[3] *Billings* v. *Joseph Harris Co., Inc.,* page 329.

whom does the warranty extend? Does it run only in favor of the actual purchaser, or does it extend to others who may use or be affected by the product? The *vertical* privity issue is, Against whom can action be brought for breach of warranty? Can the party sue only the seller, or will direct action lie against wholesalers, manufacturers, producers, and growers?

When privity of contract is required, only the actual buyer can collect for breach of warranty, and he can collect only from the actual seller. A seller who is liable may recover from his seller. Thus the requirement of privity of contract not only prevented many suits for breach of warranty where privity did not exist but also encouraged multiple lawsuits over the same product.

It is not surprising that the law has generally abandoned strict privity of contract requirements. It has done so by statute and also on a case-by-case basis.[4]

The drafters of the Code provisions on horizontal privity recognized that there was a great deal of divergence of opinion on the privity issue. Accordingly, the Code contains three alternative provisions that states may adopt (2-318). Alternative A has been adopted by 30 jurisdictions. It provides that a warranty extends to any person who is in the family or household of the buyer or who is a guest in the home, if it is reasonable to expect that such person may consume, or be affected by the goods, and who is injured by them.

Alternative B has been adopted in eight jurisdictions, and alternative C is the law in four states. The remaining states have either omitted the section entirely or have drafted their own version on the extent of the warranties. Alternatives B and C extend warranties to any natural person who may be reasonably expected to use, consume, or be affected by the goods and who is injured by them.

These Code provisions on horizontal privity do not attempt to deal with the vertical privity issue. The Code is neutral on it and leaves the development of the law to the courts on a case-by-case basis. The courts of most states have abandoned the privity of contract requirement, and persons injured by products are allowed to sue all businesses in the chain of distribution without regard to the presence of privity of contract.

The trend of the law on product liability is clearly in the direction of extending greater protection to consumers and to the demise of privity of contract as a defense.

PRODUCTS LIABILITY

8. Introduction

One of the consequences of manufacturing or selling a product is the responsibility to a consumer or user if the product is defective and causes injury

4 *Suvada* v. *White Motor Company,* page 330.

to a person or property. This liability is generally referred to as *products liability*. The subject of products liability involves several legal theories. A suit for dollar damages for injuries caused by a product may be predicated on the theory of (1) negligence, (2) misrepresentation, (3) breach of warranty, either express or implied, or (4) strict liability.

Product liability cases may be brought against manufacturers, sellers, or anyone in the chain of sale. Such cases may be brought by the buyer, by another user of the product, or by some third party whose only connection with the product is the sustaining of an injury caused by it. The sections that follow discuss the four theories previously noted. However, it should be kept in mind that the theory of strict liability has become the dominant theory in most cases.

The trend of the law on products liability is clearly in the direction of extending greater protection to consumers. A manufacturer has an obligation to the public to put on the market a product that is safe to use and free from defects. A manufacturer is presumed to know of the defects in its products and is therefore in bad faith in selling defective products. The consumer is entitled to protection from injuries.

The potential liability under all theories of products liability is usually covered by products liability insurance. In recent years, the cost of products liability insurance has skyrocketed. It has become a significant cost item in many products with a high exposure to products liability suits.

9. Negligence

In order to recover on a negligence theory, a plaintiff has to establish the negligence of the defendant—its failure to exercise reasonable care—and contributory negligence on the part of the plaintiff is a bar to a recovery. The mere fact that an injury occurs from the consumption or use of a product does not ordinarily raise a presumption that the manufacturer was negligent.

In a negligence action, privity of contract is not required, since it is not a contract action. A negligence suit can be brought not only by the person who purchased the defective product but also by any person who suffered an injury on account of a defect in the product if the defect was the proximate cause of his injury.

The Restatement of Torts (Second), Section 395, states the rule as follows:

> A manufacturer who fails to exercise reasonable care in the manufacture of a chattel which, unless carefully made, he should recognize as involving an unreasonable risk of causing physical harm to those who use it for a purpose for which the manufacturer should expect it to be used and to those whom he should expect to be endangered by its probable use, is subject to liability for physical harm caused to them by its lawful use in a manner and for a purpose for which it is supplied.

The plaintiff, of course, must by appropriate evidence prove that the manufacturer was negligent—failed to exercise reasonable care. However, he may be able to rely on the doctrine of *res ipsa loquitur*—"the thing speaks for itself." This doctrine may be used when (1) the instrumentality involved was within the exclusive control of the defendant at the time of the act of negligence, both as to operation and inspection; (2) the injury was not the result of any voluntary action or contribution on the part of the plaintiff; and (3) the accident ordinarily would not have occurred had the defendant used due care. For example, an elevator crashes, killing an occupant. The manufacturer has liability because the very happening of the accident creates a presumption of negligence.

Another method of establishing negligence is to prove that the manufacturer violated some statutory regulation in the production and distribution of his product. Some industries are subject to regulation under state or federal laws with regard to product quality, testing, advertising, and other aspects of production and distribution. Proof of a violation of the statute may be sufficient to establish negligence in the case of a manufacturer in such industries. Negligence established by proof of violation of a statute is called *negligence per se*.

Negligence is frequently based on a failure of a manufacturer to warn of a known danger related to the product. A manufacturer of a product that the manufacturer knows or should know is dangerous owes a duty to exercise reasonable care to prevent injury to those persons who it is foreseeable will come in contact with and consequently be endangered by that product. Therefore, the manufacturer's duty to exercise reasonable care includes the duty to warn of the danger. Negligence is often based on a design defect also. In determining whether a manufacturer exercised reasonable skill and knowledge concerning the design of its product, factors include the cost of safety devices, their use by competitors, their effect on function, and the extent to which the manufacturer conducted tests and kept abreast of scientific development. A manufacturer is not an insurer or required to supply accident-proof merchandise, but the responsibilities for injuries often rest with whoever is in the best position to eliminate the danger inherent in the use of the product.

For example, a manufacturer of a rotary power lawnmower may be liable for negligent design if a user is able to put his hands or feet in contact with the moving blades of the mower.

10.   Misrepresentation

If the seller has advertised the product through newspapers, magazines, television, or otherwise and in so doing made misrepresentations with regard to the character or quality of the product, tort liability for personal injury may be imposed on him. The Restatement of Torts (Second), Section 402B, summarizes the liability of a seller for personal injuries resulting from misrepresentation as follows:

One engaged in the business of selling chattels who, by advertising, labels, or otherwise, makes to the public a misrepresentation of a material fact concerning the character or quality of a chattel sold by him is subject to liability for physical harm to a consumer of the chattel caused by justifiable reliance upon the misrepresentation, even though

(a) it is not made fraudulently or negligently, and

(b) the consumer has not bought the chattel from or entered into any contractual relation with the seller.

The rationale of the Restatement position is that a great deal of what the consumer knows about a product comes to him through the various media, and sellers should be held responsible for injuries caused by misrepresentations made to the public.

For example, a manufacturer may advertise that a certain shampoo contains no harmful ingredients and is perfectly safe to use even by people with tender skin. If someone uses the shampoo and suffers a skin ailment as a result thereof, he would be entitled to recover.

11. Breach of Warranty

An action for personal injuries based upon a defective product can be based on a breach of either an express warranty or an implied warranty. The implied warranty may be either the implied warranty of merchantability or the implied warranty of fitness for a particular purpose. Most cases involve the warranty of merchantability, however.

As previously noted, there has been a gradual elimination of the privity requirement in cases of personal injuries caused by defective products. The early cases that abandoned the privity requirement involved personal injury and sickness caused by food and drugs. The law took the position that as a matter of social policy, a packer, grower, or manufacturer of a product consumed by human beings should be liable if that product caused injury. Liability would be a deterrent to the sale of dangerous foods and drug products, and the loss would be on the party best able to afford it. Privity of contract had never been required for a negligence action, and the elimination of the requirement in breach of warranty actions was a recognition of the similarity of the two theories and of the difficulty of proving negligence of the seller of such products as canned goods. The breach of warranty theory eliminated the need to prove fault, and the elimination of privity of contract made the new theory realistically available and workable. It also avoided multiplicity of suits.

Various courts have used different justifications to eliminate the privity requirement in cases involving products other than food and drugs. Some have employed the dangerous instrumentality theory in nonfood cases. These courts said that privity was not required in such cases because food was inherently dangerous, and therefore if another product was inherently dangerous, the same rationale would be applied, and privity of contract would not be required. The law in effect fed on itself and expanded. Other courts stated that "warranties run with goods" in much the same way that a warranty involving the title to land runs with the land. A warranty is an invisible appendage that is a part of the goods, and as such, it belongs to anyone who is affected by the goods.

Today, in almost every state, the requirement of privity of contract has been relaxed or abolished, and an action can be maintained for breach of implied warranty without privity of contract. An action based upon such breach, being a contract action, does not require proof of negligence on the part of the manufacturer or seller. This is a great advantage to the injured plaintiff, as he must only prove that the product was defective and that such defect was the proximate cause of his injury.

An express warranty may also be the basis of a claim for injuries without privity. It has been held that advertising constitutes an express warranty by the seller and that the affirmations and promises made to the consumer in radio, television, or through the printed media can be relied upon by him and can be the basis for a suit by an injured party with the advertiser.

STRICT LIABILITY

12. Introduction

The latest development in product liability is known as the theory of *strict liability*. This development imposes liability wherever damage or injury is caused by a defective product that is unreasonably dangerous to the user or consumer. It is the logical result of the elimination of the need to prove negligence and of the demise of the privity requirement in breach of warranty actions. In states that have adopted the strict liability theory, the theories of negligence and breach of warranty are becoming less significant.

The theory of strict liability was developed by legal scholars as a part of the Restatement of the Law of Torts. Section 402A of the Restatement (Second) provides:

> 402A. Special Liability of Seller of Product for Physical Harm to User or Consumer.
>
> (1) One who sells any product in a defective condition unreasonably dangerous to the user or consumer, or to his property, is subject to liability for physical harm thereby caused to the ultimate user or consumer, or to his poperty, if
>
> (a) the seller is engaged in the business of selling such a product, and
>
> (b) it is expected to and does reach the user or consumer without substantial change in the condition in which it is sold.
>
> (2) The rule stated in Subsection (1) applies although
>
> (a) the seller has exercised all possible care in the preparation and sale of his product, and
>
> (b) the user or consumer has not bought the product from or entered into any contractual relation with the seller.

The courts have relied heavily upon the foregoing in developing the law of strict liability. Today, it is the law in most states.

13. The Theory of Strict Liability

The law of products liability based on the theory of strict liability has developed in response to changing societal concerns over the relationship between the consumer and the seller of a product. The increasing complexity of the manufacturing and distributional process places upon injured parties a nearly impossible burden of proving negligence where, for policy reasons, it is felt that a seller should be responsible for injuries caused by defects in products. Therefore, the strict liability theory holds that a seller of a product is responsible for injury caused by his defective product even if he had exercised all possible care in its design, manufacture, and distribution. The theory in effect imposes liability without fault, and a seller is effectively the guarantor of his product's safety.

Strict liability is based on the proposition that a manufacturer, by marketing and advertising his product, impliedly represents that it is safe for its intended use. No current societal interest is served by permitting the manufacturer to place a defective article in the stream of commerce and then to avoid responsibility for damages caused by the defect.

Strict liability is limited to products that are unreasonably dangerous.[5] A product that is defective and unreasonably dangerous may be so as the result of its manufacture, or the defect may be the result of design. However, a "defective condition" is not limited to defects in design or manufacture. The seller must provide with the product every element necessary to make it safe for use. One such element may be warnings and/or instructions concerning use of the product. A seller must give such warning and instructions as are required to inform the user or consumer of the possible risks and inherent limitations of his product. If the product is defective absent such warnings, and the defect is a proximate cause of the plaintiff's injury, the seller is liable.[6]

The theory is not applicable to the sale of used goods in most states. The theory imposes liability on manufacturers and designers as well as on the seller of the goods. In almost every state, the liability extends not only to users and consumers but also to bystanders, such as pedestrians.

The theory of strict liability has been applied to leases of goods as well as to sales. The potential liability extends to all commercial suppliers of goods. Strict liability has been applied both to personal injuries and to damage to the property of the user or consumer. Some courts, however, have refused to extend it to property damage. Most courts have refused to extend it to allow recovery for economic loss.

Strict liability may be imposed upon a seller of goods manufactured by a *third person,* if the seller fails to give proper warning that a product is or is

[5] *Byrns v. Riddell, Incorporated,* page 332.
[6] *Hamilton v. Hardy,* page 333.

likely to be dangerous or if he fails to exercise reasonable care to inform buyers of the danger or to otherwise protect them against it. A similar duty to give warning applies to the manufacturer. For example, a warning must be placed on a container or label if a product is explosive, poisonous, and so forth. Some cases extend the liability to the manufacturer of a component part of a product that fails. For example, the manufacturer of the jet engine as well as the manufacturer of the airplane may be liable to the victims of a plane that crashes owing to mechanical failure of the engine.

14. Proof Required

A cause of action in strict liability requires proof that the defendant sold the product in a defective condition unreasonably dangerous to the user or consumer, that it reached the plaintiff without a change of condition, and that the product caused an injury to the plaintiff.[7] The test as to whether or not a defect is unreasonably dangerous depends upon the reasonable expectations of the ordinary consumer. If the average consumer would reasonably anticipate the dangerous condition of a product and fully appreciate the risk, it is not unreasonably dangerous. In strict liability cases, there are no issues on disclaimer of warranties, there is no problem of inconsistency with express warranties, and knowledge of the seller of the defect need not be proved. Of course, privity of contract is not required, and neither is reliance on the warranty by the injured party.

Strict liability requires only two elements of proof: that the product was defective, and that the defect was a proximate cause of the plaintiff's injuries. A plaintiff cannot recover even if he proves injury from a product absent proof of a defect. For example, there is no liability simply because someone becomes intoxicated from drinking whiskey. Neither can a plaintiff recover by proving a defect in the product absent proof of causation between the defect and the injury. In addition, a plaintiff must prove that the defect causing the injury existed at the time the product left the seller's hands; the seller is not liable if a safe product is made unsafe by subsequent changes. All of a plaintiff's proof may be made by circumstantial evidence.

Strict liability is not synonymous with *absolute liability*. There must be proof that some dangerous defect caused the injury. In addition, a plaintiff must prove that the product was being used in the manner reasonably anticipated by the seller or manufacturer.

The crucial difference between strict liability and negligence is that the existence of due care, whether on the part of seller or consumer, is irrelevant. The seller is responsible for injury caused by his defective product even if he has exercised all possible care in the preparation and sale of the product.

In most products liability cases, the injured party sues all those in the

---

[7] *Bellotte v. Zayre Corporation,* page 335.

channel of distribution, including the manufacturer, the wholesaler, the distributor, and the retailer.

In products liability cases involving multiple defendants, the onus of tracing the defect is on the defendant dealers and manufacturer, so that a plaintiff may be compensated while leaving it to the defendants to fight out the question of responsibility among themselves. Anyone who had a hand in putting the defective product in the stream of commerce, whether technically innocent or not, has liability to the injured party.

It is generally held that contributory negligence is not a defense to a suit based on the theory of strict liability. This is somewhat of an oversimplification, however, because misuse of a product is a defense. Moreover, a person who voluntarily encounters a known unreasonable danger is not entitled to recover.

For example, the failure to heed a warning with regard to a product will bar a recovery. This in effect means that "assumption of the risk" is a defense to a strict liability action. Misuse and abnormal use of a product is a defense because the misuse could not reasonably have been foreseen by the manufacturer or seller. For example, if a backwoodsman uses a sharp hunting and fishing knife to shave instead of putting it to its ordinary use and then cuts his throat, it is highly inconceivable that under those circumstances the manufacturer would not be entitled to a defense of misuse of the instrument.

WARRANTIES AND PRODUCTS LIABILITY CASES

Mobile Housing, Inc. v. Stone
490 S.W.2d 611 (Tex.) 1973

Plaintiffs, Mr. and Mrs. Stone, purchased a mobile home from defendant, made a down payment, and agreed to pay the balance in monthly installments. Before purchasing the home they visited defendant's lot on many occasions, and each time were shown a mobile home on the lot as a model of the one that they planned to buy. The mobile home that was delivered to them differed from the model in several respects, and plaintiffs sought to rescind the contract and recover their down payment. The lower court ruled in favor of plaintiffs, and defendant appealed.

BATEMAN, J. . . . The conclusion is inescapable, it seems to us, that appellees' agreement to buy the mobile home was induced by and based upon their numerous in-

spections of Unit No. 103 on appellant's sales lot and the representations of appellant's salesman that the home he was trying to sell them would be precisely like it. There is no evidence that they had ever seen the home they were buying, or even a picture of it, or that the salesman described it in any other manner than by referring to Unit No. 103. The salesman testified that in drawing the contract they took the description from this Unit 103.

Section 2.313 provides:

(a) Express warranties by the seller are created as follows: . . .

(1) Any affirmation of fact or promise made by the seller to the buyer which relates to the goods and becomes part of

the basis of the bargain creates an express warranty that the goods shall conform to the affirmation or promise.

(2) Any description of the goods which is made part of the basis of the bargain creates an express warranty that the goods shall conform to the description.

(3) Any sample or model which is made part of the basis of the bargain creates an express warranty that the whole of the goods shall conform to the sample or model.

(b) It is not necessary to the creation of an express warranty that the seller use formal words such as "warrant" or "guarantee" or that he have a specific intention to make a warranty. . . .

We hold that appellant made express warranties, within the meaning of § 2.313(a) (2), (3), that the mobile home would conform to the description given by the salesman and the model called Unit No. 103. . . .

Affirmed.

Hauter v. Zogarts
534 P.2d 377 (Cal.) 1975

TOBRINER, J. . . . After the jury found for defendants in this products liability case, the trial court granted plaintiffs' motion for judgment notwithstanding the verdict. Defendants appeal, claiming that substantial evidence supports the jury's verdict. . . .

Defendants manufacture and sell the "Golfing Gizmo" (hereinafter Gizmo), a training device designed to aid unskilled golfers improve their games. Defendants' catalogue states that the Gizmo is a "completely equipped backyard driving range." In 1966, Louise Hauter purchased a Gizmo from the catalogue and gave it to Fred Hauter, her 13½-year-old son, as a Christmas present. . . .

The label on the shipping carton and the cover of the instruction booklet urge players to "drive the ball with full power" and further state: "COMPLETELY SAFE BALL WILL NOT HIT PLAYER."

On July 14, 1967, Fred Hauter was seriously injured while using defendants' product. . . .

Fred Hauter had hit underneath the ball and had caught the cord with his golf club, thus drawing the cord upwards and toward him on his follow-through. The ball looped over the club producing a "bolo" effect and struck Fred on the left temple.

The trial court . . . held for plaintiffs on the theory of breach of an implied warranty of merchantability. Unlike express warranties,

which are basically contractual in nature, the implied warranty of merchantability arises by operation of law. Into every mercantile contract of sale the law inserts a warranty that the goods sold are merchantable, the assumption being that the parties themselves, had they thought of it, would specifically have so agreed. Consequently, defendants' liability for an implied warranty does not depend upon any specific conduct or promise on their part, but instead turns upon whether their product is merchantable under the code.

Merchantability has several meanings, two of which are relevant to the instant case: The product must "[c]onform to the promises or affirmations of fact made on the container or label" and must be "fit for the ordinary purposes for which such goods are used." The Gizmo fails in both respects. . . . It does not live up to the statement on the carton that it's "COMPLETELY SAFE BALL WILL NOT HIT PLAYER." Furthermore, as explained below, the evidence shows that the Gizmo is not fit for the ordinary purposes for which such goods are normally used.

The Gizmo is designed and marketed for a particular class of golfers—"duffers"—who desire to improve their technique. Such players rarely hit the ball solidly. When they do, testified the golf pro, "it would be sort of a mistake, really." The safety expert classed the Gizmo as a major safety hazard. Furthermore, defendants *admit* that when a person using the Gizmo hits beneath the ball as Fred Hauter apparently did, he stands a substantial chance of seriously injuring himself. Defense counsel stated to the jury: "It is obvious if you miss the ball and you come along, you touch the cord, that you could possibly get [the ball] either in the head or some other part of your person, and there is no way in the world that I am going to be able to show that couldn't happen to any of us here. . . ."

Affirmed.

Billings v. Joseph Harris Co., Inc.
220 S.E.2d 361 (N.C.) 1975

Plaintiff sued the defendant to recover $50,000 for damages caused by defective cabbage seed sold by the defendant. The purchase order contained a disclaimer of liability in bold type as follows:

NOTICE TO BUYER: Joseph Harris Company, Inc. warrants that seeds and plants it sells will conform to the label description as required under State and Federal Seed Laws. IT MAKES NO WARRANTIES, EXPRESS OR IMPLIED, OF MERCHANTABILITY, FITNESS FOR PURPOSE, OR OTHERWISE, WHICH WOULD EXTEND BEYOND SUCH DESCRIPTIONS, AND IN ANY EVENT ITS LIABILITY FOR BREACH OF ANY WARRANTY OR CONTRACT WITH RESPECT TO SUCH SEEDS OR PLANTS IS LIMITED TO THE PURCHASE PRICE OF SUCH SEEDS OR PLANTS.

Based on this provision, the lower court limited the plaintiff's recovery to the price of the seed and the plaintiff appealed.

BRITT, J. . . . Disclaimers of express and implied warranties are governed by 2-314 and 2-316. Limitation or modification is subject to the provisions of 2-719. A disclaimer of liability serves to limit liability by reducing instances where a seller may be in breach, while a limitation or modification is a restriction on available remedies in event of breach. To be valid . . . a disclaimer provision must be stated in express terms, mention "merchantability" in order to disclaim the implied warranty of merchantability, and be conspicuously displayed. . . .

[The Code] defines "conspicuousness" as that which is "so written that a reasonable person against whom it is to operate ought to have notice of it." Determination of conspicuousness is a question of law for the court. . . . We agree that the proofs establish defendant's compliance with the statute.

Having established the validity of defendant's disclaimer, we next focus our inquiry on the limitation of remedy substituted by defendant. 2-719(1)(a) sanctions such contructual modification and limitation of remedy in event of breach of warranty.

The agreement may provide for remedies in addition to or in substitution for those provided in this article and may limit or alter the measure of damages recoverable under this article, as by *limiting the buyer's remedies to return of the goods and repayment of the price or to repair and replacement of nonconforming goods or parts;* . . . [Emphasis added.]

Taken together, 2-316(2) and 2-719(1)(a) provide for limitation and substitution of remedies. A merchant seller may thereby disclaim all liability . . . stemming from any breach of warranties of merchantability and fitness. . . . We feel that given the inherent element of risk present in all agricultural enterprises, such a cause . . . may operate to limit a buyer's remedy to a return of purchase price. The official commentary to 2-719(3) is instructive:

3. Subsection (3) recognizes the validity of clauses limiting or excluding consequential damages . . . *such terms are*

merely an allocation of unknown or undeterminable risks. The seller in all cases is free to disclaim warranties in the manner provided in Section 2-316.

If a part of the contract, such a clause would serve to limit plaintiff's recovery to $440.00, as determined by the trial judge, and bar further recovery of any consequential damages. The viability of this provision is subject however to the unconscionability provision of 2-719(3):

> Consequential damages may be limited or excluded unless the limitation or exclusion is unconscionable. Limitations of consequential damages for injury to the person in case of consumer goods is prima facie unconscionable but limitation of damages where the loss is commercial is not.

Unconscionability relates to contract terms that are oppressive. It is applicable to onesided provisions, denying the contracting party any opportunity for meaningful choice.

This section gives injured party plaintiffs in personal injury actions a prima facie presumption of unconscionability as to any disclaimer or limitation of liability. No similar presumption is provided in cases of commercial loss, thus putting the burden on plaintiff to show otherwise. Under 2-302(1) determination of unconscionability is a question of law for the court. We . . . hold that the provision in question was not unconscionable. . . .

Thus, we hold that defendant effectively disclaimed liability for breach of warranty and substituted limitations reducing the extent of liability to return of purchase price of the seed. . . .

Affirmed.

Suvada v. White Motor Company
201 N.E.2d 313 (Ill.) 1964

A truck belonging to plaintiffs, partners in a milk-distributing business, collided with a bus as a result of the failure of the brakes on the truck.

In 1957 plaintiffs purchased from White the 1953 motor vehicle for use in plaintiffs' business of distributing milk. White installed a brake system in the reconditioned motor vehicle, which brake system was manufactured and supplied by Bendix. Plaintiffs alleged that the collision was caused by an inherently dangerously made brake system in the tractor-trailer and that the unit was purchased from White and the brake system was manufactured by Bendix; that as a result of the collision the tractor-trailer unit was damaged and numerous persons were injured; that plaintiffs expended money for investigation of the collision and in the defense of lawsuits arising out of the collision; that they made compromise settlements of some of the personal injury claims and property damage claims; and that they expended money in repair of their tractor-trailer. The

complaint alleged that the failure of the braking system to operate was because of an inherently dangerous and defectively made linkage bracket. Plaintiffs sued both the seller, White, and the manufacturer of the brake system, Bendix, for recovery of property damage to their tractor-trailer unit and, additionally, for indemnification of expenditures made by them in settlement, investigation, and defense of claims that arose out of the collision.

BURKE, J. . . . Plaintiffs state that the amounts paid by them for settlement, investigation and defense of personal injuries and property damage claims constitute proper elements of damage for indemnification from defendants; that these expenditures are reasonably probable and foreseeable as a direct result of the sale and manufacturing of an inherently dangerous or defectively made product and that the expenditures under the facts pleaded do not make them volunteers.

In the recent case of *Goldberg* v. *Kollsman Instrument Corp.,* the court said: "A breach of warranty, it is now clear, is not only a violation of the sales contract out of which the warranty arises but is a tortious wrong suable by a noncontracting party whose use of the warranted article is within the reasonable contemplation of the vendor or manufacturer. . . . As we all know, a number of courts . . . have for the best of reasons dispensed with the privity requirement. . . . Very recently the Supreme Court of California imposed 'strict tort liability' (surely a more accurate phrase) regardless of privity on a manufacturer in a case where a power tool threw a piece of wood at a user who was not the purchaser. The California court said that the purpose of such a holding is to see to it that the costs of injuries resulting from defective products are borne by the manufacturers who put the products on the market rather than by injured persons who are powerless to protect themselves and that implicit in putting such articles on the market are representations that they will safely do the job for which they were built." . . .

The cases in Illinois . . . support . . . the proposition that the manufacturer who places in the stream of commerce a product that becomes dangerous to life and limb of the public is liable to a subpurchaser because of the nature of the product and that the liability is not based upon a contractual relationship. In *Lindroth* v. *Walgreen Co., and Knapp-Monarch Co.* (329 Ill. App. 105, 67 N.E.2d 595), the court held that where the product is inherently dangerous a cause of action by the subpurchaser against the manufacturer exists in the absence of privity. Today's manufacturer, selling to distributors or wholesalers, is still interested in the subsequent sales of the product. His advertising is not aimed at his distributors. The historical relative equality of seller and buyer no longer exists. A product that is inherently dangerous or defectively made constitutes an exception to the requirement of privity in an action between the user of the product and its manufacturer. We cannot say from the allegations of the complaint that Bendix is beyond the immediate distributive chain. The complaint alleges that Bendix manufactured an inherently dangerous

or defectively made brake system which was installed by White into a motor vehicle as part of its renovation. Bendix is charged with manufacturing and supplying the brake system. The complaint does not charge that the brake system was reconditioned.

The exception to the privity requirement is not superseded nor is it modified by the provisions of the Uniform Commercial Code. In Comment 3 to Sec. 2-318 of the Code, the drafters state that: "The section is neutral and is not intended to enlarge or restrict the developing case law on whether the seller's warranties, given to his buyer who resells, extend to other persons in the distributive chain." In *Henningsen* v. *Bloomfield Motors, Inc.* (32 N.J. 358, 161 A2d 69, 75 A.L.E.2d 1), the court held that the subpurchaser is entitled to recover from a manufacturer of an automobile that is inherently dangerous or defectively manufactured in the absence of privity. The court said that it could find no distinction between an unwholesome food case and a defective car. This position was taken in *B.F. Goodrich Co.* v. *Hammond* (269 F.2d 501) (10th Circuit, Kansas). In that case the administrator of an estate of a subpurchaser and wife who were occupants of an automobile sued the tire manufacturer for breach of implied warranty. Goodrich sold blowout-proof tires. The mishap resulted because of a defect in the manufacture of a tire that caused a sudden blowout. In deciding that the subpurchaser and his wife had a cause of action against the manufacturer based upon breach of warranty, the court said: "[P]rivity is not essential where an implied warranty is imposed by law on the basis of public policy."

A motor vehicle that is operated on the highways with a braking system that is inoperative is obviously dangerous to life and limb. The State of Illinois recognizes the necessity for a proper braking system in motor vehicles and has declared it to be public policy of the State that all motor vehicles manufactured and sold within the State shall be equipped with brakes adequate to control the movement of the vehicle. The manufacturer of the braking system is in the best position to provide and insure an adequate braking system of motor vehicles that are driven on the public highways. We think that the court erred in striking the counts based on the theory of an implied warranty. . . .

For these reasons the judgment is reversed and the cause is remanded with directions to reinstate the counts that were dismissed and for further proceedings not inconsistent with these views.

Judgment reversed and cause remanded with directions.

Byrns v. Riddell, Incorporated
550 P.2d 1065 (Ariz.) 1976

Plaintiff, a football player who suffered a head injury, brought a products liability action on the theory of strict liability in tort against a football helmet manufacturer. Plaintiff contended that the helmet was inherently dangerous to the user, because it did not absorb a sufficient amount of the energy from blows to the head. The trial court directed a verdict for the defendant and the plaintiff appealed.

HAYS, J. . . . The law of strict liability in tort has followed a steady course of development since its early foundations. . . . This court . . . has adopted the theory of strict liability set forth in Restatement (Second) of Torts § 402A (1965). In view of the steady growth in this area of the law, coupled with the singularity of the facts in this case, a further review and analysis of the law of strict liability in tort is necessary. It is to this analysis that we first turn our attention.

The California Supreme Court in a recent decision . . . rejected the "requirement that a plaintiff also prove that the defect made the product 'unreasonably dangerous' . . ." a standard set forth in Restatement (Second) of Torts § 402A (1965). In *O.S. Stapley*, we specifically adopted Restatement (Second) of Torts § 402A and its concept of an "unreasonably dangerous" defect, and as such rejected the California approach.

The term "unreasonably dangerous" has been considered by many courts in the jurisdictions that have adopted § 402A. A recent survey of cases which considered the concept of an "unreasonably dangerous" defect states that this concept is especially effective as a means of limiting the strict tort liability doctrine "in cases in which the issue is the nature of the duty of a manufacturer with respect to safe design, or in situations in which injury does not follow as a matter of course from the defect, and in which there are serious questions as to the effect to be given harm-producing conduct or misuse on the part of the injured person."

The United States District Court, Eastern District of Pennsylvania, adopted the following test of "unreasonable danger": "whether a reasonable manufacturer would continue to market his product in the same condition as he sold it to the plaintiff *with* knowledge of the potential dangerous consequences the trial just revealed." The court went on to state: "And in measuring the likelihood of harm one may consider the obviousness of the defect since it is reasonable to assume that the user of an obviously defective product will exercise special care in its operation, and consequently the *likelihood* of harm diminishes." Comment (i) Restatement (Second) of Torts § 402A further defines the element of an unreasonably dangerous defect from the viewpoint of the consumer in the following language:

> The article sold must be dangerous to an extent beyond that which would be contemplated by the ordinary consumer who purchases it, with the ordinary knowledge common to the community as to its characteristics. . . .

. . . The obviousness of the defect is only one factor to be considered in the determination of whether the defect is unreasonably dangerous.

The Federal District court in *Dorsey, supra,* subscribed to the following factor analysis prepared by Dean Wade to determine if a defect is unreasonably dangerous:

> (1) the usefulness and desirability of the product, (2) the availability of other and safer proucts to meet the same need, (3) the likelihood of injury and its probable seriousness, (4) the obviousness of the danger, (5) common knowledge and normal public expectation of the danger (particularly for established products), (6) the avoidability of injury by care in use of the product (including the effect of instructions or warnings), and (7) the ability to eliminate the danger without seriously impairing the usefulness of the product or making it unduly expensive.

We must add a note of caution at this point. No all-encompassing rule can be stated with respect to the applicability of strict liability in tort to a given set of facts. Each case must be decided on its own merits. The foregoing analysis is offered as an approach to the question of whether a defect is unreasonably dangerous.

. . . The facts in this case as presented by appellant establish the possibility of a defect in the sling design of the TK-2 suspension system. . . .

"Plaintiff has the burden of proving that the defective condition of the injury producing product was in being at the time it left the hands of the seller. . . . The plaintiff must be permitted to rely upon circumstantial evidence alone." Plaintiff must also prove the relationship between the defect and the injury. "Thus, 'if there is . . . [expert] evidence of the possibility of the existence of the causal relationship together with other evidence or circumstances indicating such relationship, the finding that the accident caused the injury will be sustained.' [Citation omitted.]"

We hold that appellant established the presence of a defect in the helmet at the time it left the hands of the seller to the extent that reasonable minds could reach different conclusions as to that question of fact. Furthermore, we hold that appellant provided sufficient proof that a defect caused appellant's injury. The issue of causation is one fact for the jury to decide. . . .

It was error for the trial court to direct a verdict in favor of appellee.

Reversed and remanded.

Hamilton v. Hardy
549 P.2d 1099 (Colo.App.) 1976

Plaintiff, Hamilton, sued the defendant drug company for damages resulting from a stroke. She alleged that the stroke was caused by the "pill" Ovulen which she was taking as an oral contraceptive. The lower court found for the defendant and the plaintiff appealed. The lower court refused to instruct the jury on the theory of strict liability.

BERMAN, J. . . . Reversal is . . . required because the trial court erred in refusing to instruct the jury on plaintiff's theory of strict liability. She claims that Searle's failure to warn of dangers, hazards, adverse reactions, and side effects which may result from Ovulen renders

the product unreasonably dangerous and provides a basis for the imposition of strict liability pursuant to *Restatement (Second) Torts* § 402A. We agree.

The trial court apparently perceived no difference between a negligence claim based on a failure to warn and a strict liability claim based on a failure to warn, and felt instructing on both theories would be duplicitous and confuse the jury.

Some jurisdictions have held that when the allegation is a failure to warn adequately, there is no difference between the theories of strict liability and negligence. In fact, some courts have found error where the jury is instructed on both theories. The reasoning given by these courts is that the manufacturer can be found strictly liable under § 402A only if it *negligently* failed to warn of the dangerous propensities of its drug, using the test for duty to warn found in *Restatement (Second) Torts* § 388 as being applicable to both strict liability and negligence in the failure to warn context.

Although we agree the evidence which proves a failure to warn is the same under both theories, we disagree that the theories are identical. As the jury was instructed here, in negligence, reasonable care is "that degree of care which a reasonably prudent drug manufacturer would use under the same or similar circumstances," and negligence means "a failure to do an act which a reasonably prudent drug manufacturer would do, or the doing of an act which a reasonably prudent drug manufacturer would not do, under the same or similar circumstances." The jury was then instructed that for plaintiff to prevail they must find that "the Defendant was negligent in marketing of Ovulen by failing to use reasonable care to warn the medical profession on the question of whether Ovulen causes thrombosis."

In strict liability, on the other hand, a manufacturer who sells a product in a defective condition unreasonably dangerous to the consumer is subject to liability for physical harm thereby caused, even though the seller has exercised all possible care in the preparation and sale of the product. And, as plaintiff's tendered instruction stated:

> A product may be in a defective condition unreasonably dangerous to the user without any ascertainable defect or impurity in the product and although the product was precisely what it was intended to be if the manufacturer fails to give adequate and timely warnings as to dangers or hazards which may result from such product. To prevent a product from being unreasonably dangerous, appropriate and timely warnings concerning adverse reactions must be given.

This instruction makes the distinction between the two theories apparent. Under strict liability, the test is whether the failure of Searle to adequately warn of the potentially dangerous propensities of its product rendered that product unreasonably dangerous. It is of no import whether this drug manufacturer's warning comported with the warning a reasonably prudent drug manufacturer would have given. "[S]trict tort liability shifts the focus from the conduct of the manufacturer to the nature of the product."

The distinction between negligence and strict liability based on failure to warn is well stated in *Phillips* v. *Kimwood Machine Co.*, 269 Or. 485, 525 P.2d 1033:

> In a strict liability case we are talking about the condition (dangerousness) of an article which is sold without any warning, while in negligence we are talking about the reasonableness of the manufacturer's action in selling the article without a warning. The article can have a degree of dangerousness because of a lack of warning which the law of strict liability will not tolerate even though the actions of the seller were entirely reasonable in selling the article without a warning considering what he knew or should have known at the time he sold it.

Hence, since plaintiff sought recovery under a strict liability theory as well as a negligence theory, she would be entitled to jury instructions on that theory if the evidence would support a verdict for her on that theory.

In general, for there to be recovery under *Restatement (Second) Torts* § 402A, a plaintiff must demonstrate that the defective condition of a product makes the product unreasonably dangerous. In the case of prescription drugs, such as Ovulen, which may be "unavoidably unsafe" as that term is used in comment k of Section 402A, the requirements of "defective condition" and "unreasonably dangerous" have a different meaning than in the usual 402A sense. Such a drug is made in the way it was intended, contains no impurities, and is in the condition planned, but it proves to be dangerous because it is "incapable of being made safe for (its intended and ordinary use)." *Restatement (Second) Torts* § 402A, comment k. As to such products, *if* the product is accompanied by adequate warning, it is not defective and is not *unreasonably* dangerous. However, when not accompanied by an adequate warning, the product is defective, and thus may be unreasonably dangerous.

The defect is not the dangerous propensities or side effects of the drug, but the failure to warn. Thus the question to be posed to the jury with regard to the strict liability issue is whether the manufacturer's failure to adequately warn rendered the product unreasonably dangerous without regard to the reasonableness of the failure to warn judged by negligence standards. On remand, the jury should be so instructed. . . .

Whether the evidence submitted would warrant a finding for plaintiff on this issue is a question that must be analyzed in light of the following test:

A way to determine the dangerousness of the article, as distinguished from the seller's culpability, is to assume the seller knew of the product's propensity to injury as it did, and then to ask whether, with such knowledge, he would have been [acting unreasonably] in selling it without a warning.

. . . [W]e would also point out that, under a strict liability theory, a manufacturer must warn of dangers and risks, whether or not a causal relationship between use of the product and the various injuries has been definitively established at the time of the warning. . . .

Consequently, in summary, we hold that plaintiff's claim premised on strict liability was separate and distinct from her claim premised on negligence. Further, we hold that plaintiff's evidence relative to Searle's failure to warn adequately concerning the dangers of blood clotting was sufficient to entitle her to an appropriate instruction on a strict liability theory of recovery. . . .

Reversed.

Bellotte v. Zayre Corporation
352 A.2d 723 (N.H.) 1976

GRIMES, J. Certification . . . of a question of law by the United States Court of Appeals for the First Circuit to this court as to the standard for determining whether a product is "unreasonably dangerous to the user or consumer as provided by Restatement of Torts 2d § 402A(1)." . . .

The question certified is as follows: "Where a five-year old child who was playing with matches is seriously burned when his pajama top ignited; where the fabric was not treated with an effective fire-retardant material, but was 100% cotton of a type in general use at the time of the accident for the manufacture of such clothing; and where the question for the jury is whether such fabric is 'unreasonably dangerous to the user or consumer' as provided by Restatement of Torts 2d § 402A(1), should the definition of 'unreasonably dangerous' be

framed in terms of the five-year old child who uses the pajamas or in terms of the child's parent who purchases them?"

On the issue of strict liability, the case was tried and submitted to the jury under the rule of Restatement (Second) of Torts § 402A (1) (1965) as being the law of New Hampshire. . . .

Section 402A(1) provides in relevant part that, "One who sells any product in a defective condition unreasonably dangerous to the user or consumer or to his property is subject to liability for physical harm thereby caused to the ultimate user or consumer. . . ."

The use of the phrase "unreasonably dangerous" by its very terms rules out the imposition of strict liability merely because there is some danger. Sellers are not insurers nor are they subject to absolute liability and the court so instructed the jury in this case. Under the rule of strict liability which governed this trial, liability is imposed only when the danger is unreasonable. Reasonableness in the law is always determined by the objective standard of the ordinary person of average prudence taking into consideration all relevant circumstances including the age and experience of the individual whose conduct is involved. However, it has been held that since children five years of age have no capacity to perceive and appreciate dangers and to exercise judgment, they are incapable of being negligent.

The test for determining whether a product is "unreasonably dangerous" under Restatement (Second) of Torts § 402A(1) (1965) as stated in Comment *i* that it "must be dangerous to an extent beyond that which would be contemplated by the ordinary consumer who purchases it, with the ordinary knowledge common to the community as to its characteristics." The trial court instructed the jury that the basic question for decision was: "Were the pajamas in a defective condition unreasonably dangerous to a child of Jimmy Bellotte's age . . .?" He then instructed them as to the definition of "unreasonably dangerous" as quoted above from Comment *i* and then stated that "the ordinary consumer, for purposes of this case, is the parent of a five-year-old child purchasing the pajamas for such a child." He further stated the question as being, "What knowledge would such a parent have common to the community as to the flammability characteristics, that is the burning characteristics, of children's pajamas?"

Plaintiffs contend that this was error and that the test should be whether they were dangerous to an extent beyond that which would be contemplated by the ordinary five-year-old child. But five-year-old children lack the capacity to contemplate even the unavoidable danger which is inherent in any cotton fabric, whether treated or not. To apply the standard urged by the plaintiffs would, therefore, make the seller an insurer, a path we decline to follow.

Plaintiffs rely heavily on *Jackson* v. *Coast Paint and Lacquer Company*, 499 F.2d 809 (9th Cir. 1974), which involved a painter who was injured when paint fumes ignited while he was painting the inside of a tank car. It was held that the paint was unreasonably dangerous in the absence of adequate warnings as required by Restatement (Second) of Torts § 402A, Comment *j* (1965). Although the court recognized that in some instances, where there was no practical way to give notice to the employee, notice to the employer or supervisor would suffice, it stated that, "At least in the case of paint sold in labeled containers, the adequacy of warnings must be measured according to whatever knowledge and understanding may be common to painters who will actually open the containers and use the paints."

In *Jackson* the court was dealing only with adequacy of warning of a product unreasonably dangerous without warnings, while here we are dealing not with warnings, but with the initial question of whether the product was unreasonably dangerous. Naturally, in the case of warnings, when it is practical to do so the warning should be given to the person who will use the product. Even if warnings were in issue in this case, it would be impractical to give them to the ultimate user—a five-year-old child. The same circumstances which would make it impractical for the seller to give warnings to five-year-old users of the pajamas also make it impractical to use the five-year-old standard in determining the unreasonableness of danger. Children of that age do not contemplate even the unavoidable dangers of cotton pajamas and their flammable characteristics. There would therefore be no base from which to determine unreasonableness and the seller would become an insurer. In *Jackson* the court held with adults who would qualify under § 401A as the "ordinary consumer" having "the ordinary knowledge common to the community."

The answer to the question certified is that the definition of "unreasonably dangerous" should be framed in terms of the parent who purchases the pajamas for the five-year-old child.

Remanded.

CHAPTER 18
REVIEW QUESTIONS AND PROBLEMS

1. X's teeth and gums were injured by a walnut shell while eating walnut ice cream at Y's restaurant. X sued for damages for breach of warranty. Should he recover? Why?

2. X asked Y, a retail paint salesman, to recommend a paint to use on the exterior stucco walls of his house. Y recommended a certain type, and X purchased and used this paint. Shortly thereafter, the paint blistered and peeled off. X sued Y for damages. Should he recover? Why?

3. X purchased a lawn mower from Y. After X had used the mower for approximately a year, one day while X was mowing, an unknown object was hurled out of the grass chute and penetrated the eye of X's five-year-old son. X sued for breach of warranty on behalf of his son. Should he recover? Explain.

4. B purchased an automobile from S. Thereafter, B learned that X had placed a lien on the auto. Does B have any recourse against S? Explain.

5. A, an employee of B, while performing his duties, was injured when a bottle of carbonated soda exploded. The soda was sold to B by XYZ Corp. A sued XYZ Corp. for a breach of warranty. What result? Why?

6. B purchased 2,000 chickens from S. A few weeks after delivery, it was discovered that the chickens had a form of bird cancer. When sued for breach of warranty of merchantability, S claimed no responsibility on the ground that it was impossible to detect this disease in baby chicks. Is S liable for breach of warranty? Why?

7. B was injured when two bottles of soda exploded as he was taking them to the counter at R's self-service store. B sues R for breach of warranty. Should B collect? Why?

8. S, a plumbing supply company, sold pipe to B, a farmer. B purchased the pipe to manufacture harrow attachments (a heavy frame drawn by a tractor for breaking up plowed ground), and B was aware of the intended use of the pipe. In ordering the pipe, B had been shown a sample that had a wall thickness of 0.133 inch. S, however, delivered pipe of less thickness, which proved to be unsatisfactory, and B sued for breach of warranty. Should B succeed? Why?

9. A leased a scaffold from B Company for use in a construction project. The scaffold had been manufactured by C Company. It collapsed, and A sued both B and C for breach of warranty. A had read a brochure published by C that was in the office of B and that had been stamped with B's trade name.

The brochure stated that the scaffold was designed to carry working loads up to 20,000 pounds per panel, but it collapsed under less poundage than that. Can A hold B and C liable for breach of warranty? Why?

10. X was injured when a forklift truck he was operating failed to function properly. The truck had been leased by X's employer from an equipment-handling company. X brought suit, claiming that the manufacturer of the truck should be charged with strict liability. Should X succeed? Why?

11. B purchased a mobile home from S, a seller of mobile homes. The purchase agreement stated "Standard Manufacturer Warranty—OTHER-WISE SOLD AS IS." B subsequently discovered defects in the mobile home and sued S for breach of the implied warranty of merchantability, claiming that there had not been an effective disclaimer because the word "merchantability" was not mentioned, and the disclaimer was not conspicuous. Is B correct? Why?

12. B purchased a cookbook from S, a retail book dealer. Four days later, while following a recipe in the book B ate a small slice of one of the ingredients, commonly known as "elephant ears," and became violently ill. B sues S for breach of the implied warranty of merchantability. Should B succeed? Why?

13. X purchased 2,000 baby chicks from a mail-order house. Shortly thereafter, the chicks appeared sick and when checked by a lab, revealed that they were infected with a type of bird cancer. There was no express warranty concerning the chicks. May X recover?

14. A, a dealer, sold skins to B with knowledge that B would make leather jackets from them. Nothing was said about warranties. Has A made any warranties to B? Explain.

19

Introduction to Commercial Paper

1. Introduction

The term *commercial paper* is used to describe certain types of negotiable instruments. The adjective *negotiable* has long been used to describe special types of written contracts used to represent credit and to function as a substitute for money.

Commercial paper consists of two basic types of instruments—*promissory notes* and *drafts*. A note is a *promise* to pay money; a draft is an *order* directed to another person to pay money to a third party. A *check* is a typical draft—it is an order by the drawer directing the drawee (bank) to pay money to the payee of the check.

Commercial paper serves two basic functions. It is a substitute for money and it is a credit device. For example, if A buys goods from B and pays with a check, the check is a substitute for money. If A pays with a 60-day note, it is a credit device. B may sell the note and receive money for it.

2. The Concept of Negotiability

Negotiable instruments developed because of the commercial need for something that would be readily acceptable in lieu of money and that would accordingly be readily transferable in trade and commerce. This concept requires that substantial protection and assurance of payment be given to any person to whom the paper might be transferred. To accomplish this, it would be necessary to insulate the transferee from most of the defenses that the

339

primary party, such as the maker of a note, might have against the payee. The purpose of the nogotiability trait is to prevent the primary party from asserting defenses to the instrument against the person to whom the paper was transferred.

To achieve the foregoing, Article 3 of the Code provides that a person to whom commercial paper is negotiated take it free of personal defenses of the maker or drawer. This basic theory of negotiability can be further explained by noting the difference between the *assignment* of a contract and the negotiation of a negotiable instrument. For example, assume that A owes B $100 for goods sold by B to A. B assigns to C his right to collect the $100 from A. Assume also that A has a defense against B because the goods sold were defective. The right that C purchased from B would be subject to A's defense of failure of consideration. C, the assignee, would secure no better right against A than the original right held by B, the assignor. C, the assignee, would "stand in the shoes" of B, the assignor. Therefore, C could not collect the $100 from A.

In the example given above, if the evidence of the debt is not a simple contract for money but a negotiable promissory note given by A to B and it is properly negotiated to C, C is in a superior position to that which he occupied when he was an assignee. Assuming that C is a "holder in due course," C has a better title, because he is free of the personal defenses that are available against B, the original party to the paper. Therefore, A cannot use the defense of failure of consideration against C, and C can collect the $100.

Transfer of the instrument free of personal defenses is the very essence of negotiability. Three requirements must be met before a holder is free from personal defenses. First, the instrument must be negotiable; that is, it must comply with the statutory formalities and language requirements. An instrument that does not qualify is nonnegotiable, and any transfer is an assignment subject to defenses. Second, the instrument must be properly *negotiated* to the transferee. Third, the party to whom negotiable commercial paper is negotiated must be a *holder in due course* or have the rights of a holder in due course. Each of these concepts is discussed in the next chapters.

The defenses that cannot be asserted against a holder in due course are called *personal defenses. Real defenses,* on the other hand, may be asserted against anyone, including a holder in due course. Real defenses are matters that go to the very existence of the instruments. Personal defenses such as failure of consideration involve less serious matters and usually relate to the transaction out of which they arose.

3. Type of Instruments

Article 3 of the Code, Commercial Paper, is restricted in its coverage to the draft, the check, the certificate of deposit, and the note. A *draft* is an order upon another person to pay money; a *check* is a draft drawn on a bank. A *certificate of deposit* is a type of savings account wherein the bank agrees to repay the sum with interest at a specified time. A *note* is a promise to pay other than a certificate of deposit (3-104[2]).

A note is two-party paper, as is the certificate of deposit. The parties to a note are the *maker,* who promises to pay, and the *payee,* to whom the promise is made. The draft and the check are three-party instruments. A draft presupposes a debtor-creditor relationship between the *drawer* and the *drawee,* or some other obligation on the part of the drawee in favor of the drawer. The drawee is the debtor; the drawer, the creditor. The drawer-creditor orders the drawee-debtor to pay money to a third party, who is the payee. The mere execution of the draft does not obligate the drawee on the paper. His liability on the paper arises when he formally *accepts* the obligation to pay in writing upon the draft itself, and by so doing becomes primarily liable on the paper (3-410[1]). Thereafter, the drawee is called an *acceptor,* and his liability is similar to the liability of the maker of a promissory note.

A check drawn by a bank upon itself is a *cashier's* check. A *certified* check is a check that has been "accepted" by the drawee bank. *Traveler's* checks are like cashier's checks in that the financial institution issuing such instruments is both the drawer and the drawee. Such instruments are negotiable when they have been completed by the identifying signature. A *bank draft* is a banker's check; that is, it is a check drawn by one bank on another bank, payable on demand. Such drafts are often used in the check collection process and are called "remittance instruments" in this connection.

4. Ambiguous Terms and Rules of Construction

In view of the millions of negotiable instruments that are made and drawn daily, it is to be expected that a certain number of them will be ambiguously worded. Accordingly, the Code provides a number of rules to be applied in interpreting negotiable instruments.

Some instruments are drawn in such a manner that it is doubtful whether an instrument is a draft or a note. For example, it may be directed to a third person but contain a promise to pay rather than an order to pay. The holder may treat it as either a draft or a note and present it for payment to either the person who signed it or the apparent drawee. Where a draft is drawn on the drawer, it is treated as a note (3-118[a]).

An instrument may contain handwritten terms, typewritten terms, or printed terms. Where there are discrepancies in the instrument, handwritten terms control typewritten and printed terms, and typewritten terms control printed terms (3-118[b]). Thus, a printed note form may state that it is payable on demand, but there may be typed or written on the note "payable thirty days from date." Such an instrument would be payable in 30 days.

There may be a conflict between the words and the figures of an instrument. Thus a check may have the words "fifty dollars" and the figures "$500." The words control, and the check would be for fifty dollars. However, if the words are ambiguous, the figures will control (3-118[c]). For example, in a check with the words "Five seventy five dollars" and the figure "$5.75," the figures will control. In some cases, the ambiguity may arise from the context of the words.

If an instrument provides for the payment of interest but does not state the rate, the rate will be at the judgment rate at the place of playment. An unsatisfied money judgment bears interest at a rate specified by statute, and whatever this judgment rate is in a particular state will thus be applicable in this situation. Interest will run from the date of the instrument, or if it is undated, from the date of issue (3-118[d]).

If two or more persons sign an instrument as maker, acceptor, drawer, or indorser as part of the same transaction, they are jointly and severally liable unless the instrument otherwise specifies. This means that the full amount of the obligation could be collected from any one of them or that all of them might be joined in a single action. Joint and several liability is imposed even though the instrument contains such words as "I promise to pay" (3-118[e]).

BANKING TRANSACTIONS

5.   Terminology

The check is the most common form of commercial paper. Article 4 of the Code—Bank Deposits and Collections—provides uniform rules to govern the collection of checks and other instruments for the payment of money. These rules govern the relationship of banks with each other and with depositors in the collection and payment of *items*.

The following terminology of Article 4 is significant, especially with regard to the designation of the various banks in the collection process:

(a)   "Depositary bank" means the first bank to which an item is transferred for collection even though it is also the payor bank;

(b)   "Payor bank" means a bank by which an item is payable as drawn or accepted;

(c)   "Intermediary bank" means any bank to which an item is transferred in course of collection except the depositary or payor bank;

(d)   "Collecting bank" means any bank handling the item for collection except the payor bank;

(e)   "Presenting bank" means any bank presenting an item except a payor bank;

(f)   "Remitting bank" means any payor or intermediary bank remitting for an item. (4-105)

Timing is important in the check collection process. Many of the technical rules of law refer to a *banking day,* which is defined as "that part of any day on which a bank is open to the public for carrying on substantially all of its banking functions" (4-104[1][c]). A bank is permitted to establish a cutoff hour of 2 P.M. or later so that the bank may have an opportunity to process items, prove balances, and make the necessary entries to determine its position for the day. If an item is received after the cutoff hour—if one be fixed—or after the close of the banking day, it may be treated as having been received at the opening of the next banking day (4-107). The term *midnight deadline* with respect to a bank means midnight on its next banking day following the banking day on which the bank receives the check or notice with regard to it (4-104[1][h]).

Another important term is *clearinghouse.* It is an association of banks that engages in the clearing or settling of accounts between banks in connection with checks (4-104[1][d]).

Checks are sometimes payable "through" a bank, rather than by the bank. This is often true of settlement checks issued by insurance companies and dividends paid by corporations.

The words "payable through" do not make the bank the drawee; they do not authorize or order the bank to pay the instrument out of funds in the account of the drawee; nor do they order or require the bank to take the paper for collection (3-120). The bank's authority in this situation is extremely limited; the bank is merely a funnel through which the paper is to be properly presented to the drawee or maker.

A related situation is that in which a note or an acceptance of a draft contains the language "payable at" a designated bank. In recognition of varying banking practices in different sections of the country, the Code provides two alternatives, either of which could be adopted by a state in enacting the Code; namely (1) that a note or an acceptance of a draft "payable at a bank" is like a draft on the bank, and upon its due date the bank is authorized, without consultation, to make the payment out of any available funds of the maker or acceptor; or (2) that such words *are not* an order or authorization, but a mere direction for the bank to request instructions from the maker or acceptor (3-121).

6. Certified Checks

Either the drawer or the holder of a check may present it to the drawee bank for certification. The bank will stamp "certified" on the check, and an official of the bank will sign it and date it. By certifying, the bank assumes responsibility for payment and sets aside funds from its customer's account to cover the check.

Certification may or may not change the legal liability of the parties upon the instrument. When the *drawer* has a check certified, such a certification merely acts as additional security and does not relieve the drawer of any liability. On the other hand, when the *holder* of a check secures certification by the drawee bank, he thereby accepts the bank as the only party liable thereon. Such an act discharges the drawer and all prior indorsers from liability (3-411[1]). The effect of such certification is similar to a payment by the bank and redeposit by the holder.

The refusal of a bank to certify a check at the request of a holder is not a dishonor of the instrument. The bank owes the depositor a duty to pay but not necessarily the duty to certify checks that are drawn on it, unless there is a previous agreement to certify (3-411[2]). A drawer cannot stop payment on a check after the bank has certified it.

7. The Collection Process

The collection process begins when the customer deposits a check to his account. In most banks, the check is encoded so that it may be processed using electronic data-processing equipment. The account is provisionally credited by the bank at that time. The check then passes through the collecting banks, each of which provisionally credits the account of the prior bank. When the check reaches the payor (drawee) bank, that bank debits the drawer's account. The payor bank then credits the account of the presenting bank, remits to it, or, if both belong to the same clearinghouse, includes the check in its balance there. If the payor bank honors the check, the settlement is final. Transactions prior to this final settlement by the payor bank are called "provisional settlements," because it is not known until final settlement whether the check is "good." If the payor bank dishonors the check, each provisional settlement is *revoked,* and the depositary bank which had given its provisional credit to the customer for the deposit cancels it. The dishonored check is then returned to the customer.

When a bank has received a check for collection, it has the duty to use ordinary care in performing its collection operations. These operations include presenting the check to the drawee or forwarding it for presentment, sending notice of nonpayment if it occurs and returning the check after learning that it has not been paid, and settling for the check when it receives final payment. Failure of the collecting bank to use ordinary care in handling a check subjects the bank to liability to the depositor for any loss or damage sustained. And depositary banks have additional responsibilities.

To act seasonably, a bank is generally required to take proper action before the midnight deadline following the receipt of a check, a notice, or a payment. Thus, if a collecting bank receives a check on Monday and presents it or forwards it to the next collecting bank any time prior to midnight Tuesday, it has acted seasonably.

If a check has been dishonored, as in the case of an "N.S.F." (not sufficient funds) check, the presenting bank will revoke its provisional settlement and charge the item back to the account of the next prior collecting bank. Likewise, other banks in the chain of collection will charge back. The final step is a charge-back to the customer's account by the depositary bank. Each of the collecting banks must return the item or send notification of the facts by its midnight deadline. The right to charge back by the depositary bank is not affected by the fact that the depositor may have drawn against the provisional credit.

A depositor does not have the right to draw against uncollected funds. Accordingly, he is not entitled to draw against an item payable by another bank until the provisional settlement his depositary bank has received becomes final (4-213[4][a]). However, many banks allow their customers to do so even though they have no legal right to do so.

Where the deposit is an item *on which the depositary bank is itself the payor* ("on us" items) the credit becomes final on the opening of the second banking day following receipt of the item (4-213[4][b]).

A customer who deposits an item for collection should indorse it, but quite frequently a customer overlooks doing so. The depositary bank may supply the missing indorsement. If the bank states on the item that it was deposited by a customer or credited to his account, such a statement is as effective as the customer's indorsement. This is a practical rule intended to speed up the collection process by making it unnecessary to return to the depositor any items he may have failed to indorse (4-205).

8. Collection from the Payor Bank

An item may be presented to a payor bank for payment *over the counter*,[1] but most items will be presented through a clearinghouse or by mail. If the payor bank makes a provisional settlement for them on the banking day they are received, it has until final payment of the check, but not later than the midnight deadline on the following day, to decide whether or not the item is good. Within this time the bank may revoke the settlement and return the item or, if this is not possible, send written notice of nonpayment. This enables the bank to defer posting until the next day. Where a check drawn by one customer of a bank is *deposited by another customer of the same bank* for credit on its books, the bank may return the item and revoke any credit given at any time on the following day.

Failure of the payor-drawee bank to take action within the prescribed time limits may make it accountable to the person who deposited the check if the check is not paid. This liability is imposed if (1) the bank retains a check presented to it by another bank beyond midnight of the banking day of receipt without settling for it, or (2) the bank does not pay or return the check or send notice of dishonor within the period of its midnight deadline.[2] If the payor bank is also the depositary bank—that is, if the check deposited by the customer is one that is drawn on his bank—settlement on the day of receipt

---

[1] *Kirby* v. *First & Merchants Nat. Bank,* page 350.

[2] *Rock Island Auction Sales* v. *Empire Packing Co.,* page 349.

is not required, but the bank must return the check or send notice of dishonor before its midnight deadline (4-212[3]).

An item is finally paid by a payor bank when the bank (1) pays the item in cash, (2) settles for the item without reserving the right to revoke the settlement, (3) completes the process of posting the item,[3] and (4) makes a provisional settlement and fails to revoke it within the time prescribed (4-213[1]). Upon final payment, the payor bank is accountable for the item.

Another problem relates to the *order of payment of checks*. There is no priority as among checks drawn on a particular account and presented to a bank on any particular day. The checks and other items may be accepted, paid, certified, or charged to the indicated account of its customer in any order convenient to the bank (4-303[2]).

9. Stop Payments

A customer has the right to stop payment on checks drawn on his account. Only the drawer has this right; it does not extend to holders—payees or indorsees. To be effective, a stop-payment order must be received at such time and in such manner as to afford the bank a reasonable opportunity to act on it prior to an action by the bank with respect to the item (4-403). If a check has been certified, the depositor cannot stop payment whether he or the payee procured the certification. An oral stop order is binding on the bank for only fourteen days, unless confirmed in writing within that period. Unless renewed in writing, a written stop order is effective for only six months (4-403).

A bank that honors a check upon which payment has been stopped is liable to the drawer of the check for any loss he has suffered because of the failure to obey the stop order. The burden is on the customer to establish the amount of his loss. It may be that the customer cannot establish any loss. Thus, if the drawer did not have a valid reason to stop payment, he cannot collect from a bank that fails to obey the stop-payment order (4-403[3]). The bank cannot by agreement disclaim its responsibility for its failure to obey stop-payment orders (4-103[1]). Thus, a form signed by a customer agreeing not to hold the bank responsible for failure to pay could not be enforced.

Because of the concept of negotiability previously noted, a stop order on a check gives the drawer only limited protection. If the check is negotiated by the payee to a holder in due course, such person can require payment of the amount of the check by the drawer notwithstanding the stop order.

THE RELATIONSHIP BETWEEN A BANK AND ITS CUSTOMERS

10. Rights and Duties of Banks

The legal relationship between a bank and its depositors is that of debtor and creditor. If the depositor is a borrower of the bank, the reverse relationship

---

[3] *Georgia R.R. Bank & Trust* v. *First Nat. Bank, etc.,* page 351.

(creditor-debtor) also exists between the bank and its customer. This dual relationship is often quite important, because it provides the bank with a prompt and easy method of protecting itself in the event of a depositor's default or insolvency.[4] A bank can "seize" bank deposits under its right of setoff if it becomes necessary to do so to protect its account receivable.

A bank is under a duty to honor checks drawn by its customer when there are sufficient funds in his account to cover the checks. Even if there are insufficient funds, the bank may honor the checks even though this creates an overdraft. The customer is indebted to the bank for the overdraft and impliedly promises to reimburse the bank (4-401[1]).[5]

If a bank wrongfully dishonors a check, it is liable in damages to its customer for damages proximately caused by the wrongful dishonor. When the dishonor occurs by mistake, as distinguished from a malicious or willful dishonor, liability is limited to the *actual damages proved* (4-402). Provision is also made for *consequential damages* proximately caused by the wrongful dishonor and may include damages for arrest or prosecution of the customer. The Code rejects early common law decisions that held that if the dishonored item were drawn by a merchant, he was defamed in his business because of the reflection on his credit. Accordingly, a merchant cannot recover damages on the basis of defamation, and he is limited to actual damages.

If a bank in good faith pays an altered check, it can charge the account of its customer only according to the original tenor of the check. Thus, if a check is raised, the bank can charge its customer's account only with the original amount of the check (4-401[2][a]). However, if a person signs his name to an incomplete check and it is thereafter completed and presented to the drawee bank that pays it, the bank can charge the customer's account for the full amount of such check if it pays in good faith and does not know that the completion was improper (4-401[2][b]).

A bank is not *obligated* to pay a check that is over six months old. The bank, however, is entitled to pay a check that has been outstanding more than six months and may charge it to the customer's account (4-404). Certified checks do not fall within the six months' rule—they are the primary obligation of the certifying bank, and the obligation runs directly to the holder of the check.

As a general proposition, the death or incompetency of a person terminates the authority of others to act on his behalf. If this principle were applied to banks, a tremendous burden would be imposed upon them to verify the continued life and competency of drawers. Accordingly, the death of a customer does not revoke the bank's authority to pay checks drawn by him until the bank knows of the death and has a reasonable opportunity to act on it. The same rule applies to an adjudication of incompetency (4-405).

[4] *Tumarkin* v. *First National State Bank of N.J.*, page 353.
[5] *Continental Bank* v. *Fitting*, page 354.

Even though the bank knows of the death of its customer, it *may* pay or certify checks for a period of ten days after the date of his death. This is intended to permit holders of checks drawn and issued shortly before death to cash them without the necessity of filing a claim in probate. This is subject to the proviso that a stop order may be made by a relative or other person who claims an interest in the account (4-405[2]).

11. Rights and Duties of Depositors

Banks make available to their customers a statement of account. Canceled checks are returned with the bank statements. Within a reasonable time after they are received by the customer, he is under a duty to examine them for forgeries and for raised checks. The bank does not have the right to charge an account with forged checks, but the customer's failure to examine and to notify will prevent him from asserting the forgery (or alteration) against the bank if the bank can establish that it suffered a loss because of this failure. For example, the bank may be able to prove that a prompt notification would have enabled the bank to recover from the forger (4-406[2]).

The Code does not specify the period of time within which the customer must report forgeries or alterations, but it does specify that if the same wrongdoer commits successive forgeries or alterations, the customer's failure to examine and notify within a period not to exceed fourteen days after the first item and statement were available to him will bar him from asserting the forgeries or alterations of subsequent checks by the same person paid by the bank in good faith (4-406[2][b]). This rule is intended to prevent the wrongdoer from having the opportunity to repeat his misdeeds. If the customer can establish that the bank itself was negligent in paying a forged or altered item, the bank cannot avail itself of a defense based upon the customer's failure to promptly examine and report (4-406[3]).[6] The same result occurs when a bank processes an item that has been materially altered or contains an unauthorized indorsement. If a person's negligence contributes to the alteration or unauthorized signature, the bank is not liable for the item paid unless the bank failed to observe reasonable commercial standards. Thus if both parties are "at fault," the bank is liable, because its fault prevents it from asserting the fault of the other party.

A customer is precluded from asserting a forged signature or alteration on a check after one year from the time the check and statement were made available to him, even though the bank was negligent. Forged indorsements must be reported within three years (4-406[4]). If a payor bank, as a matter of policy or public relations, waives its defense of tardy notification by its customer, it cannot thereafter hold the collecting bank or any prior party for the forgery (4-406[5]).

---

[6] *Jackson* v. *First National Bank of Memphis, Inc.*, page 354.

INTRODUCTION TO COMMERCIAL PAPER CASES

Rock Island Auction Sales v. Empire Packing Co.
204 N.E.2d 721 (Ill.) 1965

Plaintiff sold cattle to the Empire Packing Co. and received a check in payment. The check was drawn and deposited on September 24, in plaintiff's bank in Iowa. The check was received by the payor bank on September 27. The payor bank held the check for five days on assurance by Empire that sufficient funds would be deposited to cover it. Finally, on October 2 the bank marked the check "Insufficient Funds" and returned it by mail. The check was never paid, and a petition in bankruptcy was filed against Empire on November 7. Plaintiff filed action against the payor bank (Illinois National Bank and Trust Company). The lower court ruled for plaintiff, and defendant appealed.

SCHAEFER, J. . . . The plaintiff's case against Illinois National Bank and Trust Company of Rockford (hereafter defendant) rests squarely on the ground that as the payor bank it became liable for the amount of the check because it held the check without payment, return or notice of dishonor, beyond the time limit fixed in section 4-302 of the Uniform Commercial Code. . . .

Section 4-302 of the Uniform Commercial Code provides: "In the absence of a valid defense . . . if an item is presented on and received by a payor bank the bank is accountable for the amount of (a) a demand item . . . if the bank . . . retains the item beyond midnight of the banking day of receipt without settling for it or . . . does not pay or return the item or send notice of dishonor until after its midnight deadline. . . ." Section 4-104(1) (h) of the Code defines the "midnight deadline" of a bank as midnight on the banking day following the day on which it received the item.

The important issues in the case involved the construction and validity of section 4-302. The defendant argues that the amount for which it is liable because of its undenied reten-

tion of the check beyond the time permitted by section 4-302 is not to be determined by that section, but rather under section 4-103 (5) which provides that "[t]he measure of damages for failure to exercise ordinary care in handling an item is the amount of the item reduced by an amount which could not have been realized by the use of ordinary care. . . ."

But the statute provides that the bank is accountable for the amount of the item and not for something else. "Accountable" is synonymous with "liable . . . ," and Section 4-302 uses the word in that sense. . . . The circuit court correctly held that the statute imposes liability for the amount of the item.

[Defendant contends] . . . that section 4-302 is invalid because it imposes a liability upon a payor bank for failing to act prior to its midnight deadline that is more severe than the liability which section 4-103(5) imposes upon a depositary bank or a collecting bank for the same default. Of course there are no such separate institutions as depositary, collecting and payor banks. All banks perform all three functions. The argument thus comes down to the proposition that the failure of a bank to meet its deadline must always carry the same consequence, regardless of the function that it is performing.

But the legislature may legitimately have concluded that there are differences in function and in circumstance that justify different consequences. Depositary and collecting banks act primarily as conduits. The steps that they take can only indirectly affect the determination of whether or not a check is to be paid, which is the focal point in the collection process. The legislature could have concluded that the failure of such a bank to meet its deadline would most frequently be the result of negligence, and fixed liability accordingly. The role of a payor bank in the collection process, on the other hand, is crucial. It knows whether or not the drawer has funds available to pay the item. The legislature could have considered that the failure of such a bank to meet its deadline is likely to be due to factors other than negligence, and that the relationship between a payor bank and its customer may so influence its conduct as to cause a conscious disregard of its statutory duty. The present case is illustrative. The defendant, in its position as a payor bank, deliberately aligned itself with its customer in order to protect that customer's credit and consciously disregarded the duty imposed upon it. The statutory scheme emphasizes the importance of speed in the collection process. A legislative sanction designed to prevent conscious disregard of deadlines cannot be characterized as arbitrary or unreasonable, nor can it be said to constitute a legislative encroachment on the functions of the judiciary. . . .

Judgment affirmed.

Kirby v. First & Merchants Nat. Bank
168 S.E.2d 273 (Va.) 1969

The defendant handed a $2,500 check drawn to the order of her and her husband to the teller at the plaintiff bank. The check was drawn on the same bank. The teller handed her $200 and credited her account with the balance. The following day the bank discovered that the check was drawn against insufficient funds. The bank then charged $2,500 to her account leaving an overdraft of $543.47. The bank brought suit for this amount. The trial court gave judgment for plaintiff, and defendant appealed.

GORDON, J. . . . The question is whether the bank had the right to charge Mrs. Kirby's account with $2,500 on January 10 and to recover from Mr. and Mrs. Kirby the overdraft created by that charge ($543.47).

U.C.C. § 4-213 provides:

(1) An item is finally paid by a payor bank when the bank has done any of the following, whichever happens first:

(a) paid the item in cash. . . .

So if First & Merchants paid the Neuse check in cash on December 30, it then made final payment and could not sue Mr. or Mrs. Kirby on the check except for breach of warranty.

When Mrs. Kirby presented the $2,500 Neuse check to the bank on December 30, the bank paid her $200 in cash and accepted a deposit of $2,300. The bank officer said that the bank cashed the check for $2,500, which could mean only that Mrs. Kirby deposited $2,300 in cash.

And the documentary evidence shows that cash was deposited. The deposit of cash is evidenced by the word "currency" before "2,-300.00" on the deposit ticket and by the words "Cash for Dep." on the back of the check. The bank's ledger, which shows a credit of $2,300 to Mrs. Kirby's account rather than a credit of $2,500 and a debit of $200, is consistent with a cashing of the Neuse check and a depositing of part of the proceeds. We must conclude that First & Merchants paid the Neuse check in cash on December 30 and, therefore, had no right thereafter to charge Mrs. Kirby's account with the amount of the check.

The trial court apparently decided that Mr. and Mrs. Kirby were liable to the bank because they had indorsed the Neuse check. But under U.C.C. § 3-414(1) an indorser contracts to pay an instrument only if the instrument is dishonored. And, as we have pointed out, the bank did not dishonor the Neuse check, but paid the check in cash when Mrs. Kirby presented it.

As a practical matter, the contract of an indorser under U.C.C. § 3-414(1) does not run to a drawee bank. That contract can be enforced by a drawee bank only if it dishonors a check; and if the bank dishonors the check, it has suffered no loss.

The warranties that are applicable in this case are set forth in U.C.C. §§ 3-417(1) and 4-207(1): warranties made to a drawee bank by a presenter and prior transferors of a check. Those warranties are applicable because Mrs. Kirby presented the Neuse check to the bank for payment. U.C.C. § 3-504(1). And those warranties do not include a warranty that the drawer of a check has sufficient funds on deposit to cover the check.

The rule that a drawee who mistakenly pays a check has recourse only against the drawer was firmly established before adoption of the Uniform Commercial Code:

> The drawer of a check, and not the holder who receives payment, is primarily responsible for the drawing out of funds from a bank. An overdraft is an act by reason of which the drawer and not the holder obtains money from the bank on his check. The holder therefore in the absence of fraud or express understanding for repayment, has no concern with the question whether the drawer has funds in the bank to meet the check. The bank is estopped, as against him, from claiming that by its acceptance an overdraft occurred. A mere mistake is not sufficient to enable it to recover from him. Banks cannot always guard against fraud, but can guard against mistakes.
>
> It is therefore the general rule, sustained by almost universal authority, that a payment in the ordinary course of business of a check by a bank on which it is drawn under the mistaken belief that the drawer has funds in the bank subject to check is not such a payment under a mistake of fact as will permit the bank to recover the money so paid from the recipient of such payment. To permit the bank to repudiate the payment would destroy the certainty which must pertain to commercial transactions if they are to remain useful to the business public. Otherwise no one would ever know when he can safely receive payment of a check. (*Zollman, The Law of Banks and Banking § 5062 [1936.]*) . . .
>
> *Reversed.*

Georgia R.R. Bank & Trust v. First Nat. Bank, etc.
229 S.E.2d 482 (Ga.) 1976

SMITH, J. . . . Georgia Railroad Bank & Trust Company (plaintiff) brought an action against The First National Bank & Trust Company of Augusta (defendant) to recover $22,500. The defendant filed a third-party complaint against William W. Jones and Bill Jones Dodge City, Inc. . . . The trial court . . . granted defendant's motion for summary judgment against the plaintiff. The plaintiff appeals. . . .

The record shows the following undisputed facts. Both plaintiff and defendant utilize electronic equipment in the handling and processing of checks. When the plaintiff processes a check, it marks the check with magnetic coding ink. The check is subsequently handled by each bank in the chain of collection by electronic equipment which reads the magnetic coding ink. The amount of the check which has been encoded thereon is considered the amount of the check throughout the chain of collection.

On or about September 12, 1974, Charles Freeman deposited into his checking account with plaintiff bank a check in the amount of $25,000.00. The check was drawn on the defendant bank by William W. Jones. The plaintiff under-encoded the check as being $2,500; thus Freeman's account was incorrectly credited with a deposit of $2,500 rather than $25,000.

Jones' check was presented to the defendant through the Augusta Clearing House on or about September 13, 1974. It was processed by the defendant as a $2,500 item. The plaintiff was paid $2,500 as of the date of receipt, and Jones' account was debited in the amount of $2,500 rather than $25,000.

On September 26, 1974, the plaintiff notified Freeman that his account had been overdrawn. Plaintiff's encoding error was then discovered, and the plaintiff credited Freeman's account in the amount of $22,500. On September 27, the plaintiff notified the defendant of its encoding error and requested payment from the defendant in the amount of $22,500. The defendant contacted Mr. Jones and informed him regarding what had happened. Jones' canceled check had already been returned in his monthly statement. Jones told the defendant not to "bother" his account. The defendant then informed plaintiff that it was unable to pay the requested amount even though there were sufficient funds in Jones' account to comply with the demand for payment.

The issue presented is whether the collecting bank can recover the amount of the deficiency from the drawee bank where the latter pays the encoded amount of an under-encoded check. . . .

No particular provision of the Uniform Commercial Code controls the present situation; however, several of its provisions are applicable to the ultimate resolution of the problem. Code § 109A-4-213(1) provides: "An item is finally paid by a payor bank when the bank has done any of the following, whichever happens first: . . . (c) completed the process of posting the item to the indicated account of the drawer, maker or other person to be charged therewith. . . . Upon a final payment under subparagraphs (b), (c) or (d) the payor bank shall be accountable for the amount of the item." The final sentence of the above section would create liability on the part of the drawee bank for the amount of the check when any "final payment" had been made. In the present case, the check had been marked "paid" and returned to the drawer; thus, the item had been posted to the account of the drawer. We find that the posting of the item, although in a smaller amount than the true amount of the item, was sufficient to constitute final payment within the meaning of the statute. Therefore, the item had been "finally paid" under the provision of subparagraph (c) above;

and the payor bank became accountable for the amount of the item.

Further, Code § 109A-4-302 provides in pertinent part: ". . . if an item is presented on and received by a payor bank, the bank is accountable for the amount of (a) a demand item . . . if the bank . . . retains the item beyond midnight of the banking day of receipt without settling for it or . . . does not pay or return the item . . . until after its midnight deadline. . . ." In this case, the payor bank retained the item past the midnight deadline without completely settling for it; thus, under Section 4-302, the payor bank would be accountable for the amount of the retained check.

The payor bank contends that the drawer stopped payment on the check when he told the payor bank not to "touch" his account. The drawer of a check has the right to stop payment of it at any time *before it has been certified or paid by the drawee.* As discussed above, the item had been "finally paid" by the drawee prior to the drawer's attempted revocation. Once the item was finally paid, the right to revoke settlement was lost.

We conclude that the drawer is responsible for the amount of the check according to its tenor. Since only the encoded amount has been paid, the drawee is accountable to the collecting bank for the deficiency. Accordingly, the trial court erred in granting summary judgment for the defendant. Summary judgment should have been granted in favor of the plaintiff against the defendant in the amount of the deficiency.

We are not here concerned with a situation wherein the drawee cannot recover from the drawer the amount of the deficiency. In such a situation there would possibly exist a defense or counterclaim in favor of the drawee bank against the collecting bank which had under-encoded the check. The record in the present case shows that the drawer's account contained sufficient funds, as of the date payment was demanded by plaintiff, to cover the deficiency.

Judgment reversed.

Tumarkin v. First National State Bank of N. J.
361 A.2d 550 (N.J.) 1976

KOLOVSKY, J. . . . On October 18, 1971, Scientific Restaurant Management Corp. (Scientific), a corporation which admittedly was then insolvent, assigned and transferred all its property to plaintiff in trust for the benefit of its creditors. . . .

Scientific had been a depositor in defendant bank (bank). The credit balance in its bank account when the assignment was executed was $21,590.10. On learning of the assignments the bank, on October 18, 1971, debited Scientific's bank deposit account with $21,590.10 and applied that amount as a payment on account of the debt owed it.

In this action, instituted by Scientific's assignee for the benefit of creditors, he alleged that the bank had no right to apply the credit balance in Scientific's bank account in satisfaction of the debt owed it by Scientific and that its doing so constituted an unlawful preference. The trial court agreed and entered judgment in the assignee's favor for $21,590.10 plus interest. Defendant appeals. We reverse.

Plaintiff does not dispute that:

It is a general rule that a bank has the right to set off or apply the deposit of its debtor to the payment of his matured debts, upon the theory that as the depositor is indebted to the bank upon a demand which is due, the funds in its possession may properly and justly be applied in payment of such debt, and it has therefore a right to retain such funds until payment is actually made. . . .

Further, plaintiff concedes that if, by reason of Scientific's insolvency, it had been adjudicated bankrupt or had been adjudicated insolvent under our state Corporation Act, the bank could have applied, as it did here, the corporate funds on deposit with it by way of set-off to the payment of Scientific's indebtedness to the bank without violating the prohibitions against preferences contained in the federal Bankruptcy Law and the Corporation Act.

Plaintiff contends, however, that that right of set-off against trustees in bankruptcy and statutory receivers exists only because the Bankruptcy Act and the Corporation Act contain express provisions authorizing the set-off of mutual debts and credits of an insolvent corporation and its creditors. . . . Plaintiff argues that the absence of a similar statutory provision for set-off in the statutes applicable to assignments for the benefit of creditors establishes that no such right exists and that defendant bank had no right to apply the credit balance of Scientific's bank account in payment of the debt owed by it to the bank.

The argument lacks merit. The right of a debtor of an insolvent corporation to set off a matured debt owed him by the corporation exists irrespective of the forum or the proceedings chosen to wind up the affairs of the corporation—be it bankruptcy, statutory insolvency proceedings or an assignment for the benefit of creditors.

The cited sections of the Bankruptcy Act and the Corporation Act represent "no innovation in the law, and [are] in accord with the principle, generally recognized, that a person against whom a claim is asserted by another may use his own claim against that person in full or partial satisfaction of the asserted claim." . . .

It is uniformly recognized that statutory provisions, such as 11 U.S.C.A. § 108(a) and N.J.S.A. 14A:14-8(1), did not create the debtor's right of set-off; they merely provided a method by which that long recognized right could be dealt with in the bankruptcy or receivership proceeding. . . .

Reversed.

Continental Bank v. Fitting
559 P.2d 218 (Ariz.) 1977

SCHROEDER, J. . . . The appellant, Continental Bank, brought this action to recover the amount of an overdraft which it paid on a check drawn on appellee's account. The appellee, Fitting, resisted the bank's action on the ground that the bank should not have paid the overdraft. . . . The judgment was entered in favor of Fitting . . . and the bank appeals.

The check leading to the overdraft claim was written by Fitting in the amount of $800. After writing the check, she had second thoughts and contacted the bank about the possibility of stopping payment. A bank employee advised that a stop payment order could not be submitted until the bank opened the following morning. Fitting then discussed with the bank employee the possibility of deliberately creating an overdraft situation by withdrawing enough money so that there would remain insufficient funds to cover the check in question. The bank employee indicated that in those circumstances the bank would not pay the check.

Early the next morning, Fitting proceeded to withdraw money from the account, leaving enough money to cover other checks she had written. The bank nevertheless paid the $800 check in question, and sought recovery of the amount of the overdraft from Fitting in this action.

In defense of her judgment below, Fitting's sole reliance is upon evidence . . . showing that under the bank's usual internal procedures and policies, the bank would have known the check represented an overdraft and would not have paid it. . . . Fitting does not contend that her conversations with the bank employees concerning overdraft policies constituted a contractual agreement that the check would be dishonored. . . .

In those circumstances, the sole issue with respect to the overdraft is whether the bank was lawfully entitled to pay it and to seek recourse from Fitting. The matter is governed by A.R.S. § 44-2627 [U.C.C. § 4-401] which clearly gives the bank the option to pay an overdraft and to charge the customer's account for that overdraft when the check is otherwise properly payable.

The bank, therefore, by paying the overdraft and charging the customer's account, was acting in accordance with procedures specifically authorized by law, and violated no claimed contractual agreement with its customer. Fitting offers no support for her theory that the bank's own internal policies may in and of themselves give rise to a duty to follow such policies in every case, despite provisions of the statute authorizing contrary conduct. We perceive no basis for such a holding as a matter of sound policy. As the comment to section 4-401 of the Uniform Commercial Code states:

> It is fundamental that upon proper payment of a draft the drawee may charge the account of the drawer. This is true even though the draft is an overdraft since the draft itself authorizes the payment for the drawer's account and carries an implied promise to reimburse the drawee. . . .

Reversed.

Jackson v. First National Bank of Memphis, Inc.
403 S.W.2d 109 (Tenn.) 1966

This is an action to recover money from a bank, money that had been paid out on forged instruments. The suit was brought by Jackson, trustee of a Church, on behalf of the Church against the Bank. In 1963 the Church opened an account which required two signatures for withdrawal—those of Cleve Jordan, financial secretary, and Jackson. For a period of about one year, Jordan forged Jackson's name on some fifty checks and used the money to gamble at the dog races. The Bank sent monthly statements to Jordan in his capacity as financial secretary. The Church discovered the fraud and brought suit against the Bank for the money. The trial court found for the Church, and the Bank appealed.

BEJACH, J. . . . [A] drawee bank which pays the check on a forged signature is deemed to have made the payment out of its own funds and not the depositor's, provided the depositor has not been guilty of negligence or fault that misled the Bank. . . .

In the instant case, the negligence of the depositor relied on by the Bank is its failure to examine the checks and report the forgery, thus preventing a repetition thereof. The fallacy of this argument is that the checks were mailed to Cleve Jordan, Financial Secretary of the Church, who was the forger. He was an unfaithful servant, and obviously his knowledge and information on the subject would not be reported by him to the Church, nor imputed to it. He had been a faithful and trusted member of the Church and one of its officers for about twenty years, and, consequently, the Church cannot be held guilty of negligence in employing an unfaithful agent. The contention is made, however, that the Church officials, other than Cleve Jordan, himself, should have called on Jordan for an accounting from time to time, and that the Church was negligent in its failure to perform this duty. The proof shows that the Church did from time to time call on Cleve Jordan for production of the checks and records of the Church, but that he made excuses, said he forgot to bring them, or made other excuses. Under these circumstances, in view of his previous good record and reputation, we cannot say that the Bank carried the burden of showing negligence on the part of the Church.

. . . Under the provisions of Section 4-406 of the Uniform Commercial Code subsection 2(b), a depositor is precluded by failure to examine the checks within fourteen days from asserting liability against the bank on ac-count of unauthorized signature or alteration of a check paid by the bank in good faith, but subsection (3) of the same Code section provides: "The preclusion under subsection (2) does not apply if the customer establishes lack of ordinary care on the part of the bank paying the item(s)."

In *Farmers' and Merchants' Bank* v. *Bank of Rutherford* (115 Tenn. 64), the Supreme Court held that, "It is negligence in a drawee bank to pay a forged check drawn on it in the name of its customer, whose signature is well known to it, where the cashier does not examine the signature closely, but relies on the previous endorsements." It is argued on behalf of the Bank that such examination of the signature card, which admittedly was not made in the instant case, is not practical under modern banking methods. Such may be true as a practical matter, but, if so, the Bank, because of that fact, cannot escape the consequences and must, under that decision, be held guilty of negligence.

We think, however, that the Bank must be held to be guilty of negligence in another and much stronger aspect of the instant case. The Bank account here involved was that of a Church, which obviously involved trust funds, and the countersignature of Milton Jackson, Trustee, whose signature has been forged, was required on all checks. In the case of *Fidelity and Deposit Co. of Maryland* v. *Hamilton Nat'l Bank*, 23 Tenn.App.20, . . . [we] . . . held that one who takes paper from a trustee importing upon its face its fiduciary character, is bound to inquire of the transferor the right to dispose of it. . . . Any adequate inquiry made in the instant case by the Bank would have disclosed the situation that Cleve Jordan was forging the name of Milton Jackson, Trustee, and would have prevented a repetition of such forgery.

There is another and a stronger reason why the Bank must be held guilty of negligence and held responsible for the result of the forgery here involved. All of the checks, recovery for which was granted in the instant case, were made payable to Cleve Jordan, personally; and many of them bear the endorsement of the Southland Racing Company, which is the corporation operating the dog racing track in Arkansas across the Mississippi River from Memphis. These circumstances, and especially the one that the checks were made payable to Cleve Jordan, personally, should have put the Bank on inquiry as to whether or not the funds represented by these checks were being withdrawn for unauthorized purposes. Any inquiry would have disclosed the true situation and prevented further depletion of the Church's bank account. The bank account being a trust fund, and the checks withdrawing same being made to one of the authorized signers of checks, was sufficient to put the Bank on notice that the funds were being improperly withdrawn, or should at least have required the Bank to make inquiry as to whether or not the withdrawals involved were authorized. . . .

Affirmed.

CHAPTER 19
REVIEW QUESTIONS AND PROBLEMS

1. A was a depositor in the B Bank. Certain indorsements on checks drawn by him were forged, but he did not call the bank's attention to this until more than three years later. A claimed that he was excused from giving earlier notice. Would the bank be liable for honoring checks with forged indorsements? Why?

2. A's bank wrongfully dishonored two small checks that she had drawn. She brought action against the bank and recovered a judgment of $631.50 as follows: $1.50 for a telephone call to one of the payees; $130.00 for two weeks' lost wages; and $500.00 for illness, embarrassment, and inconvenience. Would this judgment be upheld on appeal? Explain.

3. M made a check payable to the order of P. P then had the check certified. M made a stop-payment order to the bank before the check was presented for payment. Should the bank pay the check to P if M has valid defense to an action on the instrument? Why?

4. A, an attorney, had an account labeled "special account" with B Bank. The purpose of this account was to keep in escrow funds belonging to his clients, one of which was C. A made a withdrawal from this account for his personal use. Does C have grounds for a cause of action against B Bank? Why?

5. A is the holder of a check drawn by M on B Bank. (A also has an account at B Bank.) The check is deposited at the bank on a Monday. On that day, B's account is overdrawn, but B has promised to make a substantial deposit, so the bank holds the check until Thursday. B does not make the deposit, and on Friday the bank returns the check to A marked "Insufficient Funds." Can A require the bank to make good on the check? Why?

6. D signed a promissory note payable to the order of C. The printed figures in the note stated $27,000 as the principal, but in the body of the note the principal was typed as "Two Hundred Twenty-Five Dollars." D made no payments, and C brought suit for $27,000 plus interest. During the trial, evidence was introduced that the note was payable in monthly installments of $225. Is D liable to repay $27,000 or $225? Why?

7. P was the payee of a check drawn by D, which was in repayment of a loan. P took the check to her bank along with a number of other checks and indorsed all the checks except D's. P's bank forwarded D's check to the drawee bank for collection, but it was returned for nonindorsement. P's bank then indorsed the check by stamp and sent it back again for collection. However, during the interim, D's account in the drawee bank had been attached, and the check was returned. P now sues her for negligence in sending her check for collection without an indorsement. Is P correct? Why?

8. X borrowed $4,000 from Y Bank and agreed to repay it on March 17, 1970. X died on February 6, 1970, having $1,610 in a checking account at Y Bank. The bank applied the amount on deposit to the debt and then filed a claim against X's estate for the balance. Did the bank have the right to appropriate X's checking account? Why?

9. A Company employed X as general office manager. X had a personal checking account at the B Bank, but A did not have an account with B. X forged the signature of A Company's president on a letter addressed to B Bank that authorized X to both cash and deposit checks made payable to A Company. Checks deposited were to be credited to X's account. During a two-year period, X either cashed or deposited $18,000 worth of checks that belonged to A Company. A Company sued B. At the trial it was determined that the bank had not acted in accordance with reasonable commercial standards, and also that A Company was negligent in not making a timely inspection of its books. Should A Company be granted a judgment against the bank? Why?

10. A Company drew a check payable to C Company. When C did not receive it in the mail, A placed a stop-payment order in writing with B, the drawee bank. Approximately one year later, B paid on the check to a collecting bank and charged A's account. A had not renewed its stop-payment order. A now sues B to recover the amount of the check. Is B liable? Why?

20

Commercial Paper: Creation and Transfer

1. Introduction

The concept of negotiability was introduced in Chapter 19. It was noted that a holder in due course of a negotiable instrument is not subject to personal defenses that may be asserted by prior parties to the instrument. This chapter and the next one examine this legal principle in detail. They will be concerned with the following four questions (Chapter 20 with questions 1 and 2, Chapter 21 with questions 3 and 4):

1. What legal requirements must be met if an instrument is to qualify for the special treatment afforded negotiable instruments?

2. What distinguishes a transfer by assignment from one by a negotiation?

3. What requirements must be met for a holder to qualify as a holder in due course?

4. Which defenses are personal defenses and which are real defenses?

THE REQUIREMENTS OF NEGOTIABILITY

2. In General

The negotiability of an instrument is determined by the terms written on the face of the instrument. In order for an instrument to be negotiable, it must satisfy four basic requirements. The instrument must (1) be signed by the

358

maker or drawer; (2) contain an unconditional promise or order to pay a sum certain in money; (3) be payable on demand or at a definite time; and (4) be payable to order or to bearer (3-104[1]).

The first requirement is simply that there be a writing signed by the maker or drawer (3-104[1][a]). It is not required that any particular type or kind of writing be used, nor is it necessary that the signature be at any particular place upon the instrument. The instrument may be in any form that includes "printing, typewriting, or any other intentional reduction to tangible form" (1-201[46]). A symbol is a sufficient signature if it was "executed or adopted by a party with present intention to authenticate a writing" (1-201[39]). The use of the word *authenticate* in the definition of *signed* makes it clear that a complete signature is not required. The authentication may be printed or written and may be placed on the instrument by stamp.

3. The Necessity of a Promise or Order

A negotiable note must contain a *promise* to pay. It is not required that the exact word *promise* be used; a word or words expressing an undertaking to pay may be substituted. However, as a practical matter, the word *promise* is used in almost all notes. The promise must be derived from the language of the instrument, not from the fact that a debt exists. A mere acknowledgment of a debt in writing (an IOU) does not contain a promise. Even though such a written memorandum is sufficient to evidence and create a valid enforceable instrument upon which recovery may be had, it is not negotiable.

A draft must contain an *order* to pay. The purpose of the instrument is to order the drawee to pay money to the payee or his order. The drawer must use plain language to show an intention to make an order. The language must signify more than an authorization or request. It must be a direction to pay. Thus, an instrument in the following form would not be negotiable: "To John Doe. I wish you would pay $1,000 to the order of Richard Roe. (Signed) Robert Lee." This would nevertheless be a valid authorization for John Doe to make payment to Richard Roe.

4. The Promise or Order Must Be Unconditional

Negotiable instruments serve as a substitute for money and as a basis for short-term credit. If these purposes are to be served, it is essential that the instruments be readily received in lieu of money and freely transferable. Conditional promises or orders would defeat these purposes, for it would be necessary for every transferee to make a determination with regard to whether or not the condition had been performed prior to his taking the instrument. The instruments would not freely circulate. In recognition of these facts, the law requires that the promise or order be unconditional.

The question of whether or not the promise or order is conditional arises when the instrument contains language in addition to the promise or order to pay money. The promise or order is conditional if the language of the instrument provides that payment is controlled by, or is subject to, the terms of some other agreement (3-105[2][a]). Clearly, a promise or order is conditional if reference to some other agreement is *required* and where payment is *subject to* the terms of another contract.[1] Negotiability is also destroyed if reference to another writing would be necessary to determine the exact nature of the promise or order. However, a mere *reference* to some other contract or agreement does not condition the promise or order and does not impair negotiability. A distinction, then, is to be drawn between additional language that imposes the terms of some other agreement and language that simply gives information as to the transaction that gave rise to the instrument. Thus, the use of the words "subject to contract" conditions the promise or order, while the words "as per contract" would not render the promise or order conditional. The latter is informative rather than restrictive. Implied or constructive conditions, such as the implication that no obligation would arise until an executory promise has been performed, do not render a promise or order conditional (3-105[1][a]).

Statements of the consideration for which the instrument was given and statements of the transaction out of which the instrument arose are simply informative (3-105[1][b]). A draft may have been drawn under a letter of credit, and a reference to this fact does not impose a condition (3-105[1][d]). Notes frequently contain a statement that some sort of security has been given, such as a mortgage on property, or that title to goods has been retained as security for the payment of the note. In either case, the purpose is to make clear to the holder that the promise to pay is secured by something in addition to the general credit of the maker, and as a consequence, a mere reference to the security does not destroy negotiability (3-105[1][e]).

Notes given in payment for property purchased on installment often provide that title to such property shall not pass to the maker of the note until all payments called for have been made. A statement to this effect in a note does not condition the promise to pay.

5. The Particular Fund Concept

A statement that an instrument is to be paid only out of a particular fund imposes a condition (3-105[2][b]). Such an instrument does not carry the general personal credit of the maker or drawer and is contingent upon the sufficiency of the fund on which it is drawn.

There are two exceptions to the foregoing rule with regard to a limitation to payment out of a particular fund. An instrument issued by a government or government agency is not deemed nonnegotiable simply because payment is restricted to a particular fund (3-105[1][g]). Second, an instrument issued by or on behalf of a partnership, unincorporated association, trust, or estate

[1] *Holly Hill Acres, Ltd.* v. *Charter Bk. of Gainesville,* page 369.

may be negotiable even though it is limited to payment out of their entire assets (3-105[1][k]).

A mere *reference* to a particular fund does not impair negotiability (3-105 [1][f]). Such references are often made for purposes of record keeping and accounting, and they do not in any way limit liability to payment out of the fund mentioned. Thus, a check that provides "charge to agent's disbursing account" would not be deemed to contain a conditional order but would simply indicate the account to be debited.

6. Sum Certain in Money

An instrument to be negotiable must be payable in money. Instruments payable in chattels such as wheat or platinum are therefore not negotiable. *Money* means a medium of exchange that is authorized or adopted by a domestic or foreign government as a part of its currency (1-201[24]). The amount payable may be stated in foreign as well as in domestic money (3-107[2]). If the sum payable is stated in foreign currency, payment may be made in the dollar equivalent unless it is specified in the instrument that the foreign currency is the only medium of payment.

The language used in creating commercial paper must be certain with respect to the amount of money promised or ordered to be paid. Otherwise, its value at any period could not be definitely determined. If the principal sum to be paid is definite, negotiability is not affected by the fact that it is to be paid with interest, in installments, with exchange at a fixed or current rate, or with cost of collection and attorney's fees in case payment shall not be made at maturity (3-106).

If at any time during the term of the paper its full value can be ascertained, the requirement that the sum must be certain is satisfied. The obligation to pay costs and attorney's fees is part of the security contract, separate and distinct from the primary promise to pay money and does not, therefore, affect the requirement as to a sum certain. The certainty of amount is not affected if the instrument specifies different rates of interest before and after default; nor is the certainty affected by a provision for a stated discount for early payment or an additional charge if payment is made after the date fixed (3-106[1][c]).

7. The Time of Payment Must Be Certain

As a substitute for money, negotiable instruments would be of little value if the holder were unable to determine at what time he could demand payment. It is necessary, therefore, that there be certainty as to the time of payment. A negotiable instrument must be payable on demand or at a "definite time" (3-104[1][c]).

An instrument is payable on demand when it so states, when payable at sight or on presentation, or *when no time of payment is stated* (3-108). In general, the words "payable on demand" are used in notes and the words "at sight" in drafts. If nothing is said about the due date, the instrument is demand paper.[2] A check is a good illustration of such an instrument. The characteristic of demand paper is that the holder of such paper can require payment at any time by making a demand upon the person who is obligated on the paper.

The requirement of a definite time is in keeping with the necessity for certainty in instruments. It is important that the value of an instrument at any given time be capable of determination. This value will be dependent upon the ultimate maturity date of the instrument. If an instrument is payable only upon an act or event the time of whose occurrence is uncertain, it is not payable at a definite time even though the act or event has occurred (3-109[2]). Thus, an instrument payable "thirty days after my father's death" would not be negotiable.

The requirement of certainty as to the time of payment is satisfied if it is payable on or before a specified date (3-109[1][a]). Thus, an instrument payable "on or before" June 1, 1983, is negotiable. The obligor on the instrument has the privilege of making payment prior to June 1, 1983, but is not required to pay it until the specified date. An instrument payable at a fixed period after a stated date, or at a fixed period after sight, is payable at a definite time (3-109 [1][b]). The expressions "one year after date" or "sixty days after sight" are definite as to time.

8. Acceleration and Extension Clauses

There are two types of provisions appearing on the face of instruments that may affect the definite time requirement. The first is called an *acceleration clause*. An acceleration clause hastens or accelerates the maturity date of an instrument. Accelerating provisions may be of many different kinds. One kind, for example, provides that in case of default in payment, the entire note shall become due and payable. Another kind gives the holder an option to declare the instrument due and payable when he feels insecure with respect to ultimate payment. An instrument payable at a definite time subject to any acceleration is negotiable (3-109[1][c]). If, however, the acceleration provision permits the holder to declare the instrument due when he feels insecure, the holder must act in good faith in the honest belief that the likelihood of payment is impaired.[3] The presumption is that the holder has acted in good faith, placing the burden on the obligor-payor to show that such act was not in good faith (1-208).

The second type of provision affecting time is an *extension clause*. An extension clause is the converse of the acceleration provision. It provides for the extension of the time for payment beyond that specified in the instrument. For example, a note payable in two years might provide that the maker has the right to extend the time of payment six months. An instrument is payable at a

---

[2] *Liberty Aluminum Products Company* v. *John Cortis*, page 370.
[3] *Van Horn* v. *Van De Wol, Inc.*, page 370.

definite time if it is payable "at a definite time subject to extension at the option of the holder, or to extension to a further *definite time* at the option of the maker or acceptor, or automatically upon or after a specified act or event" (3-109[1][d]). If an extension is at the option of the holder, no time limit is required. The holder always has the right to refrain from undertaking collection. However, an extension at the option of the maker or accepter, or an automatic extension, must provide for a definite time for ultimate payment, or negotiability is destroyed.

9. The Words of Negotiability

The words of negotiability express the intention to create negotiable paper. The usual words of negotiability are *order* and *bearer* (3-104[1][d]). When these words are used, the maker or drawer has in effect stated that the instrument may be negotiated to another party. When the word *bearer* is used, it means that payment will be made to anyone who *bears* or possesses it. When the word *order* is used, it means that it will be paid to the designated payee or to anyone that such payee may order or direct.

Other words of equivalent meaning may be used, but to ensure negotiability, it is preferable to use the conventional words. If the instrument is not payable to "order" or to "bearer," it is not negotiable and all defenses are available in suits on the instrument.[4]

10. Order Paper

If the terms of an instrument provide that it is payable to the order or assigns of a person who is specified with reasonable certainty, or to him or his order, the instrument is payable to order (3-110[1]). The expressions "Pay to the order of John Doe," "Pay to John Doe or order," and "Pay to John Doe or assigns" create order paper.

Ordinarily, an instrument will be payable to a payee who is not a maker or drawer or drawee, but an instrument may be drawn payable to order of the maker or drawer or drawee (3-110[1][a][b][c]). A note in which the maker and the payee are the same person will have to be indorsed by the maker as payee before negotiation.

An instrument may be payable to the order of two or more payees together, such as "A and B," or in the alternative, such as "A or B." An instrument payable to "A and B" must be indorsed by both. One payable to the order of "A or B" may be negotiated by either (3-116).

An instrument may be payable to the order of an estate, a trust, or a fund. Such instruments are payable to the order of the representative of such estate, trust, or fund (3-110[1][e]). An instrument payable to the order of a partnership or an unincorporated association such as a labor union is payable to such

---

[4] *Locke v. Aetna Acceptance Corporation*, page 371.

partnership or association. It may be indorsed by any person authorized by the partnership or association (3-110[1][g]).

11. Bearer Paper

The basic characteristic of bearer paper as distinguished from order paper is that it can be negotiated by delivery without indorsement. An instrument is payable to bearer if it is payable (1) to bearer, (2) to the order of bearer (as distinguished from the order of a specified person or bearer), (3) to a specified person or bearer (notice that it is not to *the order of* a specified person or bearer), or (4) to "cash" or "the order of cash," or any other indication that does not purport to designate any specific payee (3-111).

Although bearer paper can be negotiated without indorsement, the person to whom it is transferred will often require an indorsement. The reason for this is that an indorser has a greater liability than one who negotiates without indorsement. Also, the problem of identifying the person who negotiated the paper is much easier. This becomes important if the instrument is dishonored.

12. Terms and Omissions Not Affecting Negotiability

Some additional terms may be included in commercial paper without impairing negotiability. These terms are usually for the benefit of the payee or other holder. For example, many instruments will contain a statement indicating that collateral has been given. Such a statement, including the provisions relating to the rights of the payee or holder in the collateral, does not affect negotiability (3-112[1][b][c]).

The drawer of a check or draft may include a provision that the payee by indorsing or cashing it acknowledges full satisfaction of an obligation of the drawer. Such a provision does not affect negotiability (3-112[f]). Checks or drafts drawn by insurance companies in settlement of claims usually contain such a provision.

Often, the consideration for which an instrument was given is set forth in the instrument, and it is common to include such words as "for value received" or "in payment for services rendered." However, the omission of words stating the consideration for which an instrument was given will not affect its negotiability. Also, the negotiable character of an instrument otherwise negotiable is not impaired by the omission of a statement of the place where the instrument is drawn or payable (3-112[1][a]).

Whether there is no date, a wrong date, an antedate, or a postdate is not important from the standpoint of negotiability (3-114[1]). Any date that does appear on the instrument is presumed correct until evidence is introduced to establish a contrary date (3-114[3]). Any fraud or illegality connected with the date of the instrument does not affect its negotiability, but merely gives a defense.

13. Incomplete Instruments

A person may sign an instrument that is incomplete in that it lacks one or more of the necessary elements of a complete instrument. Thus, a paper signed by the maker or drawer, in which the payee's name or the amount is omitted, is incomplete.

An incomplete instrument cannot be enforced until it is completed (3-115 [1]). If the blanks are subsequently filled in by any person in accordance with the authority or instructions given by the party who signed the incomplete instrument, it is then effective as completed. A person might, for example, leave blank signed checks with an employee with instructions to complete the checks as to amounts and payee in payment of invoices as goods are delivered. When the employee completes the checks in accordance with these instructions, they are perfectly valid.

A date is not required for an instrument to be negotiable. However, if a date is necessary to ascertain maturity ("payable sixty days from date"), an undated instrument is an incomplete instrument. The date, however, may be inserted by the holder. If an instrument is payable on demand or at a fixed period after date, the date that is put on the instrument controls even though it is antedated or postdated (3-114[2]).

If the completion of the blanks is not in conformity with the signer's authority, the unauthorized completion is treated as a material alteration of the instrument (3-115[2]), but a holder in due course can enforce the instrument as completed. The loss is placed upon the person who signed the incomplete paper, because he made wrongful completion possible. A person not a holder in due course is subject to the defense of improper completion.

14. Transfer and Negotiation

The rights that a person has in an instrument may be transferred by either "negotiation" or "assignment." The transfer of an instrument by assignment vests in the transferee such rights as the transferor has. *Negotiation* is defined as a specific type of transfer by means of which the transferee becomes a holder. A *holder* is a person who is in possession of an instrument "drawn, issued, or indorsed to him or to his order or to bearer or in blank" (1-201 [20]). A holder who qualifies as a holder in due course is free of personal defenses of prior parties and thus has rights superior to those of his transferor.

There are two methods of negotiating an instrument so that the transferee will become a holder. If the instrument is payable to bearer, it may be negotiated by delivery alone; if it is order paper, indorsement and delivery are required (3-202[1]). The indorsement must be placed on the instrument itself or on a paper so firmly affixed to it as to become a part thereof. Such paper is called an *allonge*. The indorsement must be made by the holder or by someone who has the authority to do so on behalf of the holder (3-202[2]). If the payee is a corporation, an officer will indorse on its behalf. The indorsement should include the corporate name, but this is not actually required.[5]

The indorsement, to be effective as negotiation, must convey the entire instrument or any unpaid balance due on the instrument. If it purports to be of less, it will be effective only as a partial assignment (3-202[3]). For example, an indorsement "Pay to A one-half of this instrument" would not be a negotiation, and A's position would be that of an assignee.

The indorser may add to his indorsement words of assignment, condition, waiver, guarantee, or limitation or disclaimer of liability and the like. The indorsement is nevertheless effective to negotiate the instrument (3-202[4]). Thus if A, the payee of a negotiable instrument, signs his name on the reverse side with the words, "I hereby assign this instrument to B," he has effectively indorsed the instrument, and a party to whom it is delivered is a holder.

If the name of the payee is misspelled, the payee may negotiate by indorsing either the name appearing on the instrument or in his true name, or both. A person who pays the instrument or gives value for it may require that both names be indorsed (3-203). The desirable practice is to indorse in both names when the name of the payee is misspelled.

It sometimes happens that an order instrument, or one that is specially indorsed, is transferred without indorsement. Thus, a purchaser may pay for an instrument in advance of the time when it is delivered to him, and the seller may either inadvertently or fraudulently fail to indorse the paper. Of course, an indorsement would be necessary for negotiation. If the transferee has given value for the instrument, and if there was no contrary agreement between the parties, the transferee is entitled to an indorsement (3-201[3]). The negotiation is not effective until the indorsement is given. The transferee is not a holder and cannot qualify as a holder in due course until such indorsement is obtained.

INDORSEMENTS

15. Introduction

Indorsements are either special or blank. These are the ordinary indorsements used in negotiating paper. If other terms are added that condition the indorsement, it is also a restrictive indorsement. A restrictive indorsement restricts the indorsee's use of the paper. Also, the indorser may *limit* or qualify his liability as an indorser by adding such words as "without recourse." This qualified indorsement has the effect of relieving the indorser of his contractual liability as an indorser—that he will pay if the primary obligor refuses to do so. A qualified indorsement will also be a blank or a special indorsement. These indorsements are discussed in the sections that follow.

[5] *American National B. & T. Co.* v. *Scenic Stage Lines,* page 372.

16. Blank Indorsements

A blank indorsement consists of the indorser's name written on the instrument. If an instrument drawn payable to order is indorsed in blank, it becomes payable to bearer (3-204[2]). However, if such instrument is thereafter indorsed specially, it reverts to its status as order paper and indorsement is required for further negotiation (3-204[1]). For example, if a check on its face payable to the order of Henry Smith is indorsed, "Henry Smith," it becomes bearer paper. As such, it can be negotiated by mere delivery, and a thief or finder could by such delivery pass title to the instrument.

17. Special Indorsements

A special indorsement specifies the person to whom or to whose order it makes the instrument payable. When an instrument is specially indorsed, it becomes payable to the *order of* the special indorsee and requires his indorsement for further negotiation. Thus an indorsement, "Pay to John Jones," or, "Pay to the order of John Jones," is a special indorsement and requires the further indorsement by John Jones for negotiation. If a bearer instrument is indorsed specially, it requires further indorsement by the indorsee. This is true if the instrument was originally bearer paper or if it became bearer paper as the result of a blank indorsement. In other words, the last indorsement determines whether the instrument is order paper or bearer paper (3-204).

The holder of an instrument may convert a blank indorsement into a special indorsement by writing above the blank indorser's signature any contract consistent with the character of the indorsement (3-204[3]). Thus, Richard Roe, to whom an instrument has been indorsed in blank by John Doe, could write above Doe's signature, "Pay to Richard Roe." The paper would now require Roe's indorsement for further negotiation.

18. Restrictive Indorsements

A person who indorses an instrument may impose certain restrictions upon his indorsement; that is, the indorser may protect or preserve certain rights in the paper and limit the rights of the indorsee. There are four types of restrictive indorsements. A restrictive indorsement may be one that is conditional, such as, "Pay John Doe if Generator XK-711 arrives by June 1, 1982," or it may purport to prohibit further transfer of the instrument, such as, "Pay to John Doe only" (3-205[a][b]). A restrictive indorsement is often used when a check is deposited in a bank for collection. Thus the indorsements, "For Collection," "For Deposit Only," and "Pay any Bank," are restrictive (3-205[c]). The fourth type is an indorsement in which the indorser stipulates that it is for the benefit or use of the indorser or some other person, such as, "Pay John Doe in trust for Richard Roe" (3-205[d]).

A restrictive indorsement does not prevent further transfer or negotiation of the instrument (3-206[1]). Thus, an instrument indorsed, "Pay to John Doe only," could be negotiated by John Doe in the same manner as if it had been indorsed, "Pay to John Doe."

The effect of restrictive indorsements is substantially limited as applied to banks. An intermediary bank or a payor bank that is not a depositary bank can disregard any restrictive indorsement except that of the bank's immediate transferor. This limitation does not affect whatever rights the restrictive indorser may have against the bank of deposit or his rights against parties outside the bank collection process (3-206[2]). Except for an intermediary bank, any transferee under a conditional indorsement, or an indorsement for collection and the like, must pay or apply any value given by him consistently with the indorsement, and to the extent that he does so he becomes a holder for value (3-206[3]).

Where the indorsement is for the benefit of the indorser or another person, such as, "Pay to John Doe in trust for Richard Roe," only the first taker is required to act consistently with the restrictive indorsement (3-206[4]). John Doe has the obligation to use the instrument or the proceeds from it for the benefit of Richard Roe. John Doe could negotiate the instrument to John Smith who could qualify as a holder in due course and ignore the restriction. Of course, if the instrument was transferred in violation of Doe's fiduciary duty, as where Doe transferred it to Roe in payment of a debt that he personally owed to Roe, the latter would not be a holder in due course (3-304[2]).

19. Negotiation Subject to Rescission

Negotiation by an infant or other person lacking in contractual capacity is effective to transfer the instrument notwithstanding the lack of capacity. A transfer is also effective even though it was obtained by fraud, duress, or mistake; in violation of a duty on the part of the transferor; or as part of an illegal transaction (3-207[1]). This reflects the philosophy of negotiability that any person in possession of an instrument that by its terms runs to him is a holder, and that anyone may deal with him as a holder. Thus, the indorsee who has received the instrument under any of the circumstances above is nonetheless a holder and can in turn negotiate the paper. The right to rescind a transaction cannot be exercised against a holder in due course but may be exercised against other parties (3-207[2]).[6]

The Code does not specify which remedies are available when a party is not a holder in due course. These are left to the courts to develop as a part of the common law of each state. The common law remedies are cut off when the instrument is in the hands of a holder in due course.

---

[6] *Snyder* v. *Town Hill Motors, Inc.,* page 373.

COMMERCIAL PAPER: CREATION AND TRANSFER CASES

Holly Hill Acres, Ltd. v. Charter Bk. of Gainesville
314 So.2d 209 (Fla. App.) 1975

SCHEB, J. . . . . Appellant/defendant appeals from a summary judgment in favor of appellee/plaintiff Bank in a suit wherein the appellee sought to foreclose a note and mortgage given by appellant.

The appellee Bank was the assignee from appellees Rogers and Blythe of a promissory note and purchase money mortgage executed and delivered by the appellant. The note, executed April 28, 1972, contains the following stipulation:

> This note with interest is secured by a mortgage on real estate, of even date herewith, made by the maker hereof in favor of the said payee, and shall be construed and enforced according to the laws of the State of Florida. *The terms of said mortgage are by this reference made a part hereof.*

Rogers and Blythe assigned the promissory note and mortgage in question to the appellee to secure their own note. Appellee sued appellant . . . on appellant's note.

Appellant answered incorporating an affirmative defense that fraud on the part of Rogers and Blythe induced the sale which gave rise to the purchase money mortgage. Rogers and Blythe denied the fraud. . . . The trial court held the appellee Bank was a holder in due course of the note executed by appellant and entered a summary final judgment against the appellant.

The note having incorporated the terms of the purchase money mortgage was not negotiable. The appellee Bank was not a holder in due course, therefore, the appellant was entitled to raise against the appellee any defenses which could be raised between the appellant and Rogers and Blythe. Since appellant asserted an affirmative defense of fraud, it was incumbent on the appellee to establish the nonexist-

ence of any genuine issue of any material fact or the legal insufficiency of appellant's affirmative defense. Having failed to do so, appellee was not entitled to a judgment as a matter of law; hence, we reverse.

The note, incorporating by reference the terms of the mortgage, did not contain the unconditional promise to pay required by Fla. Stat. § 673.3-104(1)(b) . . . held that certain bonds which were "to be received and held subject to" a certain. . . .

Appellee Bank relies upon *Scott v. Taylor,* 1912, 63 Fla. 612, 58 So.30, as authority for the proposition that its note is negotiable. *Scott,* however, involved a note which stated: "this note secured by mortgage." Mere reference to a note being secured by mortgage is a common commercial practice and such reference in itself does not impede the negotiability of the note. There is, however, a significant difference in a note stating that it is "secured by a mortgage" from one which provides, "the terms of said mortgage are by this reference made a part hereof." In the former instance the note merely refers to a separate agreement which does not impede its negotiability, while in the latter instance the note is rendered nonnegotiable.

As a general rule the assignee of a mortgage securing a non-negotiable note, even though a bona fide purchaser for value, takes subject to all defenses available as against the mortgagee. Appellant raised the issue of fraud as between himself and other parties to the note, therefore, it was incumbent on the appellee Bank, as movant for a summary judgment, to prove the non-existence of any genuinely triable issue.

Accordingly, the entry of a summary final judgment is reversed and the cause remanded for further proceedings.

Liberty Aluminum Products Company v. John Cortis
14 D.&C.2d 624 (Pa.) 1958

The plaintiff, holder of a note executed by the defendants, obtained a judgment on the note. The defendants filed a motion to have the judgment set aside on the ground that since the note did not contain a schedule of installments and set out no date of maturity, it was not negotiable.

CUMMINS, J. . . . The defendants' motion to strike completely overlooks the Uniform Commercial Code. . . . This Code states categorically that "instruments payable on de-mand include those payable at sight or on presentation and *those in which no time for payment is stated*" [italics added]—that under the Commercial Code this instrument is a demand note by virtue of its tenor. . . .

The parties have the right to use a blank and tailor it to their needs. And the failure to include installment payments simply and clearly means that none were intended. . . .

Affirmed.

Van Horn v. Van De Wol, Inc.
497 P.2d 252 (Wash.) 1972

JAMES, J. Defendant Van De Wol, Inc. operates a golf course. Plaintiff Van Horn, while a stockholder in defendant corporation, made several loans to defendant, totaling $37,-000, and received unsecured demand notes in return. Subsequently, before selling his stock to an investor produced by the corporation, plaintiff entered into an agreement providing, among other things, that he would not accelerate payment of the notes so long as the terms of the agreement were complied with, but that if he should at any time deem himself insecure he would have the right to demand payment of the notes.

Approximately 1 year after liquidating his stock and entering into the agreement, plaintiff, asserting that he deemed himself insecure, demanded payment of the notes. This suit followed when defendant failed to discharge the notes.

The trial judge found that plaintiff, in good faith, deemed himself insecure and granted judgment for the balances due upon the notes. This appeal is from the denial of defendant's motion for a new trial.

Defendant contends that the trial judge erred in holding that plaintiff "in good faith" deemed himself insecure, because plaintiff erroneously believed defendant had been denied a bank loan, when in fact defendant had not been denied a loan.

The trial judge found as a fact that plaintiff knew defendant corporation lost money during the prior business year; that defendant corporation was faced with increasing competition from a newly established public golf course; that the new stockholder refused to hold him harmless on corporate notes which he had signed as a guarantor; and that the corporation refused to refrain from mortgaging the corporate realty until after plaintiff had been paid.

The Uniform Commercial Code, RCW 62A.1-208, provides that the term " 'when he deems himself insecure' " shall be construed "to mean that he shall have power to do so only if he *in good faith* believes that the prospect of payment or performance is impaired." (Italics ours.) RCW 62A.1-201(19) provides that " '[g]ood faith' means *honesty in fact* in the conduct or transaction concerned." (Italics ours.)

The "honesty in fact" standard which the trier of fact must apply has been described as follows:

Section 1-201(19) defines "good faith" as "honesty in fact," and thus follows a number of the uniform commercial acts in making negligence irrelevant to good faith. The adoption of this "subjective" test, sometimes known as the rule of "the pure heart and the empty head," dates back more than a hundred years in the law of negotiable instruments, to the abandonment of the "objective" standard announced in *Gill* v. *Cubitt.* [1824]

Defendant argues that *Hines* v. *Pacific Car Co.,* 110 Wash. 75, 29 (1920) and *Skookum Lbr. Co.* v. *Sacajawea Lbr. & Shingle Co.,* 107 Wash. 356 (1919) require that the alleged facts leading to plaintiff's insecurity be true. We do not agree. Both the *Hines* and *Skookum* cases deal with mortgagees, or *secured* creditors who deemed themselves insecure. A secured creditor must show more compelling facts because he is in a less precarious position than is an unsecured creditor.

Plaintiff, as an unsecured creditor, had to consider the overall financial stability of defendant to determine the likelihood of payment. Anything which adversely affected the corpora-

tion adversely affected plaintiff's prospect of payment.

Even if plaintiff was negligent in not checking to determine whether defendant had in fact been denied a loan, negligence is irrelevant to good faith. The standard is what plaintiff actually knew, or believed he knew, not what he could or should have known. Because plaintiff believed defendant had been denied a loan, and acted in accordance with that belief, he acted in good faith.

Plaintiff's "good faith" is a question of fact. Our review of the record discloses that the trial judge's finding that plaintiff acted in good faith is supported by substantial evidence. The matter of the loan was but one consideration, and even if it were resolved in defendant's favor, that would not eliminate the other substantial bases for plaintiff's insecurity. We may not substitute our judgment for that of the trial judge.

The judgment is affirmed.

Locke v. Aetna Acceptance Corporation
309 So.2d 43 (Fla.App.) 1975

MILLS, J. . . . Defendant appeals from an adverse judgment in a promissory note action. The issue crucial to this appeal is whether the promissory notes were negotiable instruments.

The complaint sought recovery on two promissory notes executed and delivered by defendant to Consumer Food, Inc., who subsequently assigned them to plaintiff. Copies of the notes were attached to the complaint and stated, "Buyer agrees to pay to Seller. . . ." The answer to the complaint denied the material allegations and alleged several affirmative defenses. At the trial, the trial court held, in effect, that the notes were negotiable instruments and that plaintiff was a holder in due course, therefore, not subject to affirmative defenses.

Section 673.104, Florida Statutes, 1973, provides that to be a negotiable instrument, the

writing must be payable to order or to bearer. The notes sued on were payable "to seller" and, therefore, were not negotiable instruments.

Section 673.805, Florida Statutes, 1973, provides that there can be no holder in due course of an instrument which is not payable to order or to bearer.

Under the provisions of Section 673.306, Florida Statutes, 1973, unless a holder in due course, a person takes an instrument subject to all defenses available in an action on a simple contract, as well as the defenses of want or failure of consideration, non-performance of any condition precedent, or non-delivery. Though plaintiff did not qualify as a holder in due course, the trial court refused to consider evidence in support of the defendant's affirmative defenses. This was error. . . .

Reversed.

American National B. & T. Co. v. Scenic Stage Lines
276 N.E.2d 420 (Ill.) 1971

A note was payable to a corporation. It was specially indorsed to the plaintiff by the corporate secretary-treasurer. The indorsement did not include the name of the corporate payee but only included the signature of the corporate officer and his title. Defendant contended that plaintiff could not be a legal holder of the note because the instrument had not been properly negotiated due to improper indorsement.

VAN DEUSEN, J. . . . The initial question here . . . is whether or not a note made payable to a corporation by its corporate name can be legally endorsed by the signature of an individual followed by a description of his position but without reference in the endorsement itself to the entity for which he purports to act. The Illinois Uniform Commercial Code does not deal directly with this issue. Article 3 of the Code dealing with liability of parties does provide in Sec. 3-403—Signature by Authorized Representative—that where the instrument names the person represented and the representative signs in a representative capacity, the representative is not liable. In the Code comment on this section the commentator points out that the unambiguous way to make the representation clear is to sign "Peter Pringle by Arthur Adams, Agent" but that any other definite indication is sufficient as where the instrument reads "Peter Pringle promises to pay" and it is signed "Arthur Adams, Agent." There is a strong inference to be drawn from Sec. 3-403 that where the note names the corporation as payee that an endorsement signed by its agent in his own name, followed by a description of his position, is a sufficient indication that the individual signer is acting as agent for the named payee and that such an endorsement is legally sufficient. To hold otherwise would place the plaintiff Bank in the anomalous position of not being able to bring suit against Scenic Stage Lines, the maker of the note, because the endorsement is legally insufficient to convey any rights to the Bank against the maker, and also to deny the plaintiff Bank any rights against Tarkoff as an individual endorser because of the terms of Sec. 3-403 of U.C.C.A. Such a result would seem to be untenable.

Admittedly, there is not a great deal of case law on this particular form of endorsement, probably because an endorsement is seldom made in this manner, and it obviously is not the recommended method of doing so. Such case law as there is in Illinois would suggest the holding that the endorsement in this case is legally sufficient to pass title to the plaintiff Bank as a holder in due course.

Any doubt, however, would appear to be resolved by the Supreme Court in the case of *Hately* v. *Pike,* 162 Ill. 241, 44 N.E. 441. In this case a corporate note was made payable to its own president in the following manner: "Pay to the order of Adolph Pike, President" and was endorsed, "Pay to the order of Walter C. Hately, (s) Adolph Pike, President." The court rejected the contention that the corporation was the payee and the endorsee and held the word "President" following the name of "Adolph Pike" a mere *descriptio personae.* The court makes clear, however, at page 246, 44 N.E. 441, that if the note were payable to the corporation by its corporate name and then endorsed "Adolph Pike, President" it would be sufficient.

The court cites with approval Daniel on Negotiable Instruments (4th Ed. Vol. 1, Sec. 416):

> Where a note is payable to a corporation by its corporate name, and is then endorsed by an authorized agent or official, with the suffix of his ministerial position, it will be regarded that he acts for his principal who is disclosed on the paper as payee and is therefore the only person who can transfer the legal title. . . .

Affirmed.

Snyder v. Town Hill Motors, Inc.
165 A.2d 293 (Pa.) 1960

A minor (Snyder) entered into a contract with a friend (Rhea) whereby he agreed to trade his 1946 Pontiac plus $1,000 for Rhea's Chrysler. The two thereupon went to the place of business of the defendant (Town Hill Motors) where Rhea negotiated for the purchase of a Lincoln. Rhea instructed Snyder to assign the title of the Pontiac to the Motor Company and to indorse to the company a $1,000 check which was payable to Snyder's order and drawn by a third party, as the down payment by Rhea on the Lincoln. (Snyder had intended to use the check in payment for the Chrysler.) Snyder complied with Rhea's instructions and Rhea gave him a receipt:

"Received of Richard Snyder one-thousand dollars and 1946 Pontiac coupe in exchange for a 1955 Chrysler Windsor."

Snyder accepted delivery of the Chrysler, but a month or so later he returned it to the Motor Company and demanded the return of his Pontiac and the $1,000. He contended that Rhea had misrepresented the amount of the encumbrance against the Chrysler.

The Motor Company which had cashed the check and received the proceeds refused his demand. Snyder then sued the Motor Company for $1,000 on the theory that he had the right to rescind the negotiation of an instrument. The jury returned a verdict for the defendant, and Snyder appealed.

MONTGOMERY, J. . . . Appellant's . . . theory is . . . without merit. The rescission of a negotiable instrument by an infant against a subsequent holder in due course is not permitted by Section 3-207 of the Uniform Commercial Code, on which appellant relies. Having received the instrument by negotiation from Rhea for value, in good faith, and without notice that it was overdue or had been dishonored or that there was any defense against it, the Motor Company was a subsequent holder in due course. The jury has found that there were no dealings between Snyder and the appellees.

Appellant's argument that the Motor Company was not a "subsequent" holder in due course is not supported by the evidence. The fact that the check was not manually transferred from Snyder to Rhea and then to the Motor Company would be immaterial under the definition of "delivery" contained in the Negotiable Instruments Law of 1901 . . . which provides that transfer of possession may be actual or constructive. Although the Uniform Commercial Code repealed the Negotiable Instruments Law, it nevertheless did not prescribe any new definition of the term "delivery." We are of the opinion, therefore, that the established definition should prevail. The generally recognized meaning of "delivery" set forth in Corpus Juris Secundum is as follows: "What constitutes delivery depends largely on the intent of the parties. It is not necessary that delivery should be by manual transfer. A constructive delivery is sufficient if made with the intention of transferring the title, and this rule is recognized by the definition of delivery in Negotiable Instruments Act . . . as the transfer of possession, 'actual or constructive.' "

The facts previously stated show clearly the intention of these parties. Together, Snyder and Rhea took the check to the Motor Company, where it was exhibited and where Rhea exercised dominion over it by directing Snyder to hand it over to the Motor Company. Snyder agreed to this and accepted Rhea's receipt, which acknowledged that Rhea had received the proceeds of the check. This was sufficient to constitute constructive delivery from Snyder to Rhea and "subsequently" from Rhea to the Motor Company.

Orders affirmed. . . .

CHAPTER 20
REVIEW QUESTIONS AND PROBLEMS

1. A indorsed a check as follows: "Pay to the order of any bank, banker, or trust company. All prior endorsements guaranteed." Did A make a special endorsement? Explain.

2. A made and dated a note payable to the order of B. Is the instrument negotiable if it is to be paid "within ten years after date"? Why?

3. D, a customer of B Bank, directed B Bank via a telegram to pay a certain amount to the order of P. The bank complied with D's instructions. Did the bank act properly even though it did not have a printed check made by D to act upon? Explain.

4. When A purchased a new home, A executed a note, which was secured by a mortgage to B. The note contained the following clause: "This note is secured by a mortgage." B sold the note to C. Was the note negotiable? Why?

5. M executed a note to P in the sum of $500. The note did not contain words of negotiability. Can P recover on the note from M? If P transferred the note to X, could X recover from M? (Assume no defense.) Why?

6. A promissory note stated in the lower left-hand corner that it was given "as per contract," which referred to a contract between the maker of the note and the payee. Is the note negotiable? Why?

7. M wrote a letter to her attorney as follows: "I agree to pay your firm as attorneys' fees the sum of $2,760, payable at the rate of $230 per month for twelve (12) months beginning January 1, 1970." It was signed "Very truly yours, Barbara Hall Hodge." Is the letter a negotiable instrument? Why?

8. M signed a promissory note payable to the order of A. A indorsed the note in blank over to B. B then transferred the note to C by delivery. Is C a holder of the instrument? Why?

9. B purchased several items of merchandise from S. As payment, B transferred to S a number of certified checks payable to the order of B. However, B failed to indorse the checks, and S did not notice that the checks required an indorsement. B took the merchandise away. The drawee bank subsequently refused to make payment, but B refused to affix his endorsement, claiming that the merchandise was defective. S now brings suit against B. Can S legally demand an endorsement by B? Why?

10. D signed a contract with C for a loan-origination fee. The contract was titled "Promissory Note" and contained the following language: "The undersigned hereby acknowledges and promises to pay to the order of C at Atlanta, Georgia, or at such other place or to such other party or parties as the holder hereof may from time to time designate, the principal sum of three thousand dollars ($3,000). This amount is due and payable upon evidence of an acceptable permanent loan of $290,000 for D from one of C's investors and upon acceptance of the commitment by the undersigned." Is the note a negotiable instrument? Why?

11. A executed a promissory note which contained the following notation: "with interest at bank rates." Is the note negotiable? Why?

12. M signed a note to the order of B to be paid from "jobs now under construction." Is this note negotiable? Explain.

13. A note provides: "Payable on January 1, 1967, or sooner in the event that the A-B partnership is dissolved." Is the note negotiable? Explain.

14. H, the holder of a check, wishes to protect himself against its loss or theft. It has been indorsed to him in blank. How may he gain this protection? Explain.

Holders in Due Course
and Defenses

1. Definitions

A person in possession of an instrument may be the original party to whom the instrument was issued or drawn. An original owner has the right to transfer the instrument to a third person. A third party in possession may also be a thief or finder—in which case, his rights and powers will be determined by whether the paper is order paper or bearer paper. A thief or finder may negotiate bearer paper, but a thief or finder has no rights or powers in order paper.

If an instrument is rightfully in possession of a third party, the third party may be an *assignee,* a *transferee,* a *holder,* or a *holder in due course.* If the instrument is a simple contract as contrasted with a negotiable instrument, the party in possession is an assignee. Likewise, if the instrument is negotiable but if it has not been properly negotiated (delivery only of order paper), the party in possession is a transferee with the status of an assignee. If an instrument is negotiable and if it has been properly negotiated, the person in possession is a holder. If certain special requirements are met, the holder may qualify as a holder in due course.

A *holder* is a person in possession of a negotiable instrument drawn, issued, or indorsed to him or to his order or to bearer or in blank (1-201[20]). Thus, either an original party or a third party may qualify as a holder. A holder of an instument may transfer or negotiate it. A holder, with certain exceptions, may discharge an instrument and may enforce payment in his own name (3-301). A thief or finder may qualify as a holder of a bearer instrument. A holder who does not qualify as a holder in due course is in a position equivalent to that of an assignee of a simple contract, in that he cannot enforce payment in the event a defense to the instrument legally exists.

A *holder in due course* is a holder who, because he meets certain requirements, is given a special status and a preferred position in the event that there is a claim or a defense to the instrument (3-302). If there is no claim or defense to the instrument, it is immaterial whether the party is a holder or a holder in due course. A holder in due course can enforce payment, notwithstanding the presence of a personal defense to the instrument. (As will be discussed more fully later, defenses fall into two categories—personal and real.) A holder in due course will not be able to enforce the instrument in the event a real defense is asserted. The preferred status of a holder in due course exists only where the defense to the instrument is a personal defense.

Issues as to whether or not a given party is a holder in due course usually arise when the party seeks to collect on the instrument. However, occasionally a party is sued on a negligence theory for losses incurred in transactions involving an instrument. If the defendant in such a negligence case can establish that he is or was a holder in due course, liability can be avoided. Thus, a holder in due course is free of claims as well as not being subject to defenses.

THE REQUIREMENTS TO BE A HOLDER IN DUE COURSE

2. Introduction

To qualify as a holder in due course, a holder must have taken the instrument for value and in good faith. In addition, he must have taken it without notice that the instrument is overdue, that it has been dishonored, or that any other person has a claim to it or a defense against it (3-302[1]).

A payee may be a holder in due course (3-302[1]) if all the requirements are met. Since a holder in due course is only free of personal defenses of parties with whom he has not dealt, any situation that allows a payee to be a holder in due course would be unusual. If the payee deals directly with the maker or drawer, the payee usually will not be a holder in due course.

When an instrument is acquired in a manner other than through the usual channels of negotiation or transfer, the holder will not be a holder in due course. Thus, if an instrument is obtained by an executor in taking over an estate, is purchased at a judicial sale, is obtained through legal process by an attaching creditor, or is acquired as a transaction not in the regular course of business, the party acquiring it is not a holder in due course (3-302[3]).

3. Value

A holder must have given value for an instrument in order to qualify as a holder in due course. Thus, a person to whom an instrument was transferred as a gift would not qualify as a holder in due course. *Value* does not have the same meaning as *consideration* in the law of contracts. A mere promise is consideration, but it is not value. As long as a promise is executory, the value requirement to be a holder in due course has not been met.[1]

Although a mere promise is not value, if the promise to pay is negotiable in form, it does constitute value (3-303[c]). For example, a drawer who issues his check in payment for a negotiable note that he is purchasing from the holder becomes a holder for value even before his check is cashed. Similarly, a holder takes an instrument for value when he makes an irrevocable commitment to a third person (3-303[c]). For example, a bank that issues an irrevocable letter of credit has given value.

A holder who takes an instrument in payment of an existing debt is a holder for value (3-303[b]). Thus, if A owed B $500 on a past-due account and transferred a negotiable instrument to B in payment of such account, B would qualify as a holder for value.

A purchaser of a limited interest in paper can be a holder in due course only to the extent of the interest purchased (3-302[4]). For example, if a negotiable instrument is transferred as collateral for a loan, the transferee may be a holder in due course, but only to the extent of the debt that is secured by the pledge of the instrument.

A person who purchases an instrument for less than its *face value* can be a holder in due course to the full amount of the instrument. For example, A is the payee of a note for $1,000. He may discount the note and indorse it to B for $800. B has nevertheless paid value and is entitled to collect the full $1,000.

4. Good Faith

Good faith is defined as "honesty in fact in the conduct or transaction concerned" (1-201[19]). If a person takes an instrument under circumstances that clearly establish the fact that there is a defense to the instrument, he does not take it in good faith. However, the failure to follow accepted business practices or to act reasonably by commercial standards does not establish lack of good faith.[2] Good faith is determined by looking into the mind of the holder, not into what the state of mind of a prudent man should have been.

A common method of financing consumer purchases is for the purchaser to sign an installment note for the purchase price. In order for the seller to obtain the purchase price to replenish his inventory, the note is sold and negotiated to a finance company or bank. If the finance company or bank is a holder in due course, it would take the paper free of the personal defenses that the consumer has against the seller. This means that the consumer would be required to pay for the goods even if they were defective. The only recourse of the consumer would be against the seller.

---

[1] *Maplewood Bank & Trust Company* v. *F.I.B., Inc.,* page 384.

[2] *Industrial Nat. Bank of R.I.* v. *Leo's Used Car Ex., Inc.,* page 385.

This result has been eliminated for all practical purposes by a 1976 Federal Trade Commission ruling that allows consumers to use all defenses when sued on consumer paper. It is an unfair method of competition to use the holder in due course concept against a consumer.

This FTC rule will be discussed in detail in Chapter 27, which deals with consumer protection. However, it should be kept in mind that as a practical matter, it prevents the use of the holder in due course concept when the maker of a note is a consumer.

5. Without Notice

Closely related to good faith is the requirement that the transferee must not have notice of any claim or defense to the instrument and that he not have notice either that the instrument is overdue or that it has been dishonored (3-304). A person has notice of a fact if he has actual knowledge of it, has received notification of it, or—from the facts and circumstances known to him —has "reason to know" that it exists (1-201[25]). The Code does not define "reason to know." The law generally provides that a person has reason to know a fact if he has information from which a person of ordinary intelligence (or of the intelligence of the person involved, if it is above the ordinary) will conclude that the fact exists, or if there is such a strong probability that it exists that a person exercising reasonable care will assume that it exists. The latter is known as inferable knowledge.[3]

Certain irregularities on the face of an instrument put a purchaser on notice that there may be a claim or defense to the instrument. The presence of these irregularities subjects the purchaser to defenses including those that do not relate to the irregularity. The fact that there are such irregularities is sufficient to place the purchaser on notice that something is wrong and that he should investigate before taking the paper. For example, if there is visible evidence of forgery or alteration, a purchaser is put on notice of a claim or defense (3-304[1][a]). Thus, if the payee of a check in the amount of $50 inexpertly raises the amount to $500 and cashes the check, the holder is not a holder in due course.

If an instrument is incomplete in some important respect at the time it is purchased, notice is imparted and a purchaser is not a holder in due course (3-304[1][a]). Blanks in an instrument that do not relate to material terms do not impart notice. Knowledge that blanks in an instrument have been completed after it was issued does not give notice of a claim or defense. However, if the purchaser has notice that the completion was improper, he is not a holder in due course (3-304[4][d]).

Notice of a claim or defense is given if the purchaser has knowledge that the obligation of any party to the instrument is voidable either in whole or in part (3-304[b]). For example, if the purchaser knows that the payee of a note perpetrated a fraud upon the maker, he is charged with notice of the

---

[3] *Stewart* v. *Thornton,* page 387.

maker's defense. If the purchaser has notice that all the parties to the instrument have been discharged, he has notice of a claim or defense.

A purchaser has notice of a claim against the instrument if he is aware that a fiduciary, such as a trustee or an agent, has negotiated the instrument in payment of, or as security for, his own debt or in any transaction for his own benefit. Thus, if a trustee negotiates a trust instrument in payment of his own personal debt or deposits third-party paper to his personal account, this will give notice of misappropriation of the funds. However, the mere fact that a transferee has knowledge of the fiduciary relation does not prevent him from being a holder in due course (3-304[2]).

A person who purchases an instrument with notice that it has been dishonored cannot become a holder in due course. In the case of a draft, there is a dishonor if the drawee either refuses to accept it or refuses to pay it. A note is presented for payment, and a refusal to pay is a dishonor.

There are other situations in which knowledge of certain facts does *not* of itself give the purchaser notice of a defense or claim. Knowledge that an instrument is antedated or postdated does not prevent a holder from taking in due course (3-304[4][a]). Notice of a defense or claim is not imparted by virtue of knowledge that an instrument was issued or negotiated in return for an executory promise or that the instrument was accompanied by a separate agreement (3-304[4][b]).

Actual notice to prevent a party from being a holder in due course must be received at such time and in such manner as to give a reasonable opportunity to act on it (3-304[6]). For example, a notice received by the president of a bank one minute before the bank's teller cashes a check is not effective to prevent the bank from becoming a holder in due course.

6. Before Overdue

To be a holder in due course, a purchaser of an instrument must take it without notice that it is overdue (3-302[1][c]). A purchaser of overdue paper is charged with knowledge that some defense may exist. The rationale of this rule is that in the ordinary course of events, an instrument will be paid when it is due, and the failure to pay is a factor that would indicate that there was some reason for the nonpayment.

A purchaser has notice that an instrument is overdue if he has reason to know that any part of the principal amount is overdue (3-304[3][a]). However, a past-due interest installment does not impart notice to the holder (3-304[4][f]).

Where the instrument is due upon a fixed date, but subject to an earlier maturity by reason of an accelerating clause, the instrument would not be overdue until the option to mature the paper had been exercised by the holder. If an acceleration of the instrument has been made, the purchaser with notice of such fact is a purchaser of overdue paper (3-304[3][b]). However, a purchaser may take accelerated paper as a holder in due course if he takes without notice of the acceleration.

Demand paper poses a special problem, since it does not have a fixed date of maturity. A purchaser of demand paper cannot be a holder in due course if he has reason to know that he is taking it after a demand has been made, or if he takes it more than a reasonable length of time after its issue (3-304[3][c]). What is a reasonable or an unreasonable time is determined on the basis of a number of factors—the kind of instrument, the customs and usages of the trade or business, and the particular facts and circumstances involved. In the case of a check, a reasonable time is presumed to be 30 days (3-304[3][c]). The 30-day period is a presumption rather than an absolute rule.

7. Holder from a Holder in Due Course

A transferee may have the rights of a holder in due course even though the requirements to be a holder in due course are not met. Because a transferee obtains the rights of the transferor, a person who derives title through a holder in due course has the rights and privileges of a holder in due course (3-201[1]).[4] This is referred to as the "shelter provision." The shelter concept advances the marketability of commercial paper.

The following example illustrates the shelter provision. P fraudulently induces M to execute a note payable to the order of P. P indorses to A, who satisfies the requirements of a holder in due course. A indorses in blank and delivers it to B, who has notice of the fraud but did not participate in it. B makes a gift of the note to C. C sells it to D after the maturity date of the note. While B, C, and D do not qualify as holders in due course because of notice of a defense, lack of value, and taking after maturity respectively, each of them acquired the rights of a holder in due course (A). Therefore, D may collect from M, and B and C could have enforced the note when they owned it.

The shelter provision is subject, however, to the limitation that a person who formerly held the paper cannot improve his position by later reacquiring it from a holder in due course. If a former holder was himself a party to any fraud or illegality affecting the instrument, or if he had notice of a defense or claim against it as a prior holder, he cannot claim the rights of a holder in due course by taking from a later holder in due course.

DEFENSES

8. Introduction

A holder in due course takes commercial paper free from the *personal* defenses (3-305). One who is not a holder in due course or who does not have the

---

[4] *Canyonville Bible Academy* v. *Lobemaster*, page 389.

rights of one under the shelter provision is still subject to all defenses. All transferees, including holders in due course, are subject to what are referred to as *real* defenses.

In general, real defenses are those that relate to the existence of any obligation on the part of the person who asserts them. The most obvious real defense is the forgery of the signature of the maker of a note or the drawer of a check. The person whose signature was forged has not entered into any contract, and he should have an absolute defense even against a holder in due course.

The Code generally specifies which defenses are real and which are personal. A few defenses, however, are real in some states and personal in others; this is true, for example, of the defense of infancy. The following chart indicates various defenses and their usual status. The sections that follow discuss some of the defenses in detail, with special emphasis on the real defenses. The basic aspects of most personal defenses were discussed with the materials on contracts.

COMMERCIAL PAPER: TYPICAL DEFENSES

Personal Defenses	*Real Defenses*
1. Lack or failure of consideration	1. Unauthorized signature
2. Nonperformance of a condition precedent	2. Material alteration
3. Nondelivery, conditional delivery, or delivery for a special purpose	3. Infancy, if it is a defense to a simple contract
4. Payment	4. Lack of capacity
5. Slight duress	5. Extreme duress
6. Fraud in the inducement	6. Fraud in the inception
7. Theft by the holder or one through whom he holds	7. Illegality
8. Violation of a restrictive indorsement	8. Discharge in bankruptcy
9. Unauthorized completion	9. Discharge of which the holder has notice
10. Other defenses to a simple contract	
11. Any real defense where the party was negligent	

9. Real Defenses

As a general rule, a person whose signature is placed upon an instrument without permission or authority is not liable to any holder. The term "unauthorized signature" includes forgeries and signatures by agents without authority (3-404[1]). Unless the person whose signature was placed upon the paper without authority has ratified the signature or is estopped from asserting the lack of authority, this defense is a real defense. A forger or other unauthorized signer has personal liability on an instrument, but the person whose name was used does not.

Material alteration is another real defense. The most common example of a material alteration is the "raising" of a check (3-407). For example, a check drawn in the amount of $50 might be raised by alteration to $500. Such alteration is a real defense to the extent of the alteration. A subsequent holder in due course could enforce the check only in the amount of its original sum, $50. As will be discussed further in the next chapter, a material alteration of an instrument operates to discharge it. Any basic change in the contract without the permission of its creator cancels it.

Infancy or lack of capacity is a real defense in most states. It is a real defense if the state law provides that lack of capacity is a defense to a simple contract (3-305[2][a]). In many states, the use of lack of capacity as a defense is limited by statute. Therefore, state law must be closely examined when this defense is asserted to determine if it is a real or personal defense.

The defense of illegality poses similar problems. If a contract is merely voidable because of some statute or rule of law based on public policy, the illegal aspects of the transaction create only a personal defense. However, if the illegality is such that the law considers the contract to be void, the illegality is a real defense. For example, gambling contracts in most states are void. In these states, gambling creates a real defense. The same view usually holds for usury. However, if the instrument arises out of a transaction that is legal if in conformity with the law, failure to follow the law and the illegality flowing therefrom creates only a personal defense.[5]

A discharge in bankruptcy or other insolvency proceeding is a real defense. Also, a holder in due course takes an instrument subject to any other discharge of which he has notice when he takes the instrument (3-305[2][e]).

10. Personal Defenses

Duress is a defense that may either be real or personal. The effect of duress depends upon the degree of the duress. As a general proposition, an instrument signed at gunpoint would be void even in the hands of a holder in due course because of extreme duress. One signed under threat to prosecute the son of the maker for theft would be merely voidable, because slight duress is a personal defense.

A distinction also exists between fraud in the *inducement* or *consideration* and fraud in the *inception* or *execution*. The former pertains to the consideration for which an instrument is given. The primary party intended to create an instrument but was fraudulently induced to do so. Such a defense is personal and is not available against a holder in due course. Fraud in the *inception* exists where a negotiable instrument is procured from a party when circumstances are such that the party does not know that he is creating a negotiable instrument. Fraud in the inception is a real defense (3-305[2][c]). The theory is that since the party primarily to be bound has no intention of creating an

[5] *New Jersey Mortg. & Inv. Corp.* v. *Berenyi*, page 390.

instrument, none is created. Such fraud is rare because persons are usually charged with knowledge of what they sign.

Bearer paper may be negotiated by a finder or even a thief. Acquisition of title through a thief is only a personal defense. This can always be prevented by converting bearer paper to order paper.

The concept of a material alteration includes the completion of an incomplete instrument otherwise than as it was authorized. A holder in due course is not subject to the defense of unauthorized completion of an incomplete instrument (3-407[3]). In this instance, the defense is personal. The person who left the blank space must bear the risk of wrongful completion as against such a holder.

Negligence of a party will reduce a real defense to a personal defense (3-406).[6] Negligent conduct is frequently present in situations of fraud in the execution and material alteration. Thus, one who writes a check and leaves a large blank space in front of the amount of the check renders it easier for a wrongdoer to raise the check and constitutes negligence, reducing the defense to a personal one.

The reasoning behind the negligence rule is that if commercial paper is to pass as money, the careless creator of paper should suffer the loss as against holders in due course and the innocent drawees and other payors who pay the instrument in good faith. How negligent and careless the drawer must be is a question of fact, but the negligence must be *substantial*.

HOLDERS IN DUE COURSE AND DEFENSES CASES

Maplewood Bank & Trust Company v. F.I.B., Inc.
362 A.2d 44 (N.J.) 1976

PER CURIAM. . . . This is an appeal by F.I.B., Inc., and Robert H. Biscamp, Esq., from a summary judgment entered against them in favor of plaintiff. The judgment directs Biscamp to pay to plaintiff the sum of $7,000 which he is holding in his attorney's trust account for F.I.B. . . .

Defendant Michael Klimashkey made out a $7,000 check to the order of "Robert Biscamp Atty. for F.I.B." The check was drawn on plaintiff bank and represented a deposit on a contract for the purchase of F.I.B.'s restaurant and cocktail lounge and the real property in which the business was conducted.

Attorney Biscamp deposited the check in his trustee account, and when it was presented to plaintiff bank, plaintiff erroneously paid the entire amount because Klimashkey had only $8.50 in his account.

Plaintiff's complaint sought . . . an order directing Biscamp to return the $7,000 proceeds to plaintiff. . . .

The . . . ground of appeal advanced by defendants is that the trial judge erred in granting summary judgment because F.I.B. was a holder in due course of the check and therefore was entitled to keep the proceeds erroneously paid by the bank. We affirm on the merits.

---

6 *Burchett v. Allied Concord Financial Corp.,* page 390.

Defendants claim that N.J.S.A. 12A: 3-418 rendered payment of this check final as to both defendants and prohibited the bank from recovering the proceeds. We do not agree.

N.J.S.A. 12A: 3-418 provides:

> Finality of Payment or Acceptance.
>
> Except for recovery of bank payments as provided in the Chapter on Bank Deposits and Collections (Chapter 4) and except for liability for breach of warranty on presentment under the preceding section, payment or acceptance of any instrument is final in favor of a holder in due course, or a person who has in good faith changed his position in reliance on the payment.

Contrary to defendants' argument on appeal, F.I.B. was not a holder in due course of this check. It was not, in fact, a holder at all. A holder is "a person who is in the possession of . . . an instrument . . . drawn, issued or endorsed to him or his order or to bearer or in blank."

This instrument was not drawn or issued to F.I.B. F.I.B. was not the payee of the check since it was made payable to Biscamp as attorney for F.I.B. . . . Biscamp, not F.I.B., was the payee. Since the check was neither drawn, issued nor endorsed to F.I.B., F.I.B. was never a holder of it and therefore could never have been a holder of the check in due course. . . .

Moreover, the trial judge correctly ruled that there was no proof here that F.I.B. had relied to its detriment upon payment made by the bank. . . . It is clear, then, that F.I.B. did not fall within either category of persons as to whom payment or acceptance is final under N.J.S.A. 12A :3-418.

Similarly, Biscamp, although he was the payee and a holder, was neither a holder in due course nor one who had changed his position in reliance upon payment. . . . One of the prerequisites to attaining the status of a holder in due course of a negotiable instrument is that the holder must take the instrument "for value." A holder takes such instrument for value to the extent that the agreed consideration has been performed or under other circumstances not relevant here. An executory contract is not value nor is the making of a promise to perform in the future within the requirements for the status of a holder in due course. . . .

The record before us does not establish that either defendant gave "value." If no value has been given for the instrument the holder loses nothing by the recovery of the payment . . . and is not entitled to profit at the expense of the drawee. . . .

Affirmed.

Industrial Nat. Bank of R.I. v. Leo's Used Car Ex., Inc.
291 N.E.2d 603 (Mass.) 1973

HENNESSEY, J. . . . This is an action in contract in which the plaintiff seeks to recover on two checks drawn by the defendant on the Security National Bank, one in the amount of $9,650 payable to Villa's Auto Sales, Inc., and the other in the amount of $5,500 payable to Villa's Auto Sales. The District Court judge found for the defendant. . . . The case is before us on appeal by the plaintiff.

We summarize the relevant evidence. On October 9, 1968, an agent of the defendant attended a car auction in the State of Connecticut, and purchased three cars from Frederick Villa, for which he gave the two checks described above. The defendant subsequently resold the cars at a profit.

Frederick Villa was a customer of the plaintiff bank and had a corporate account there under the name of Villa Auto Sales, Inc. The manager of the Centerville Branch of the plaintiff bank in Providence, Rhode Island, was personally acquainted with Frederick Villa. Corporate authority stating that Frederick Villa was the president and treasurer of Villa Auto Sales, Inc., and that he was authorized to sign or indorse any check held by the corporation, was on file with the bank.

Frederick Villa presented both checks to the plaintiff bank on October 10, 1968, and as was his practice, asked the teller to cash them and give him the cash since he was going to another auction and needed it. The checks were cashed and sent through the bank collection process. Meanwhile, the defendant stopped payment on the checks at the Security National Bank in Springfield, Massachusetts, following a telephone call from an officer of the Rhode Island Hospital Trust Company which claimed to hold security interests in the cars he purchased. Consequently, the checks were not honored when presented, and were returned to the plaintiff bank.

There was also evidence of a rule at the plaintiff bank that any corporate checks drawn on another bank must be approved by the manager before being cashed by a teller. In this case, the teller did not obtain the manager's approval before he cashed both checks. However, the manager would cash a check for a corporation if he knew the person cashing the check and knew his business.

The plaintiff requested . . . a ruling that there was no evidence that in cashing both checks it did not act in good faith. The District Court judge . . . denied this request and . . . found that the plaintiff was not a holder in due course of either check. The plaintiff claims an appeal on the basis that there was no evidence to support the District Court judge's finding of lack of good faith. . . .

A holder in due course is a holder who takes the instrument for value, in good faith, and without notice that it is overdue or has been dishonored or of any defence against or claim to it on the part of any person. To the extent that a holder is a holder in due course he takes the instrument free from all claims to it on the part of any person, and all defences of any party to the instrument with whom the holder has not dealt (personal defences) except specifically enumerated "real defences."

The District Court judge found . . . that the checks were not taken in good faith, and

therefore the plaintiff was not a holder in due course. Since the judge also found that a defence existed, he found for the defendant. The only substantive issue before us is whether or not the evidence supports the finding of the judge that the plaintiff did not take the checks in good faith. . . .

The defendant argues that the plaintiff failed to exercise ordinary care in this transaction by violating the plaintiff's own rule of management when its teller cashed these checks without managerial approval. The defendant points to this as evidence of lack of good faith, which would support the judge's finding. Since there is no other evidence in the report which even arguably goes to the issue of good faith, we conclude that there was no evidence to support a finding of lack of good faith, and therefore . . . the District Court judge . . . [was] in error.

"Good faith" . . . is defined . . . as "honesty in fact in the conduct or transaction concerned." Nothing in the definition suggests that in addition to being honest, the holder must exercise due care to be in good faith. Where the Uniform Commercial Code has required more than "honesty in fact" it has explicitly so stated: as in the case of a payor in Article 3—Commercial Paper—who pays on an instrument which has been altered or has an unauthorized signature (good faith and in accordance with the reasonable commercial standards of his business) § 3-406; as in the case of a merchant in Article 2—Sales (honesty in fact and the observance of reasonable commercial standards of fair dealing in the trade) § 2-103(1)(b); as in the case of a bailee in Article 7—Documents of Title (good faith including observance of reasonable commercial standards) § 7-404; and as in the case of an agent or bailee in Article 8—Investment Securities (good faith, including observance of reasonable commercial standards if he is in the business of buying, selling or otherwise dealing with securities) § 8-318. Each word of a statute is presumed to be necessary. Hence, if good faith as defined by § 1-201(19) and applicable to § 3-302(1)(b) included the observance of due care or reasonable commercial standards, the additional words used in the articles cited above would be surplusage.

This conclusion, which is so clear from the Uniform Commercial Code itself, is supported by the legislative history of § 3-302(1)(b). Reference to "reasonable commercial standards" in the definition of a holder in due course of a negotiable instrument in the 1951 Final Text Edition was deleted by the Editorial Board for the Uniform Commercial Code. . . . Our conclusion is also supported by the pre-code case of *Macklin* v. *Macklin,* 315 Mass. 451, 455, where we said, "The rights of a holder of a negotiable instrument are to be determined by the simple test of honesty and good faith, and not by a speculative issue as to his diligence or negligence."

This is not to say that negligence has no role in the determination of a holder's status as a holder in due course under § 3-302. But negligence goes to the notice requirement. . . . Since the District Court judge found that the plaintiff had no notice of dishonor, defence or claim, and the evidence supports this finding, the defendant's argument that the plaintiff failed to exercise due care is inapposite. . . .

Reversed for plaintiff.

Stewart v. Thornton
551 P.2d 95 (Ariz.) 1976

HOWARD, J. . . . Was appellant a holder in due course of a promissory note executed by appellee? The lower court apparently concluded he was not and awarded judgment in favor of appellee in appellant's suit to recover the balance due on the note plus interest thereon.

On May 23, 1971, appellee entered into an agreement with Cochise College Park by the terms of which she agreed to purchase a parcel of realty and to execute a promissory note as part of the purchase price. In accordance with the agreement, she executed a promissory note, dated May 23, 1971, wherein she agreed to pay to the order of Cochise College Park, Inc., the sum of $5,368.44 in 84 monthly installments of $63.91 on the fifteenth day of each and every month beginning July 15, 1971. The note recited that it was executed and delivered in connection with a purchase of a parcel of real property and was secured by a realty mortgage upon said property. A realty mortgage was in fact executed by appellee on May 23, 1971. Two days later on May 25, 1971, Cochise College Park, for a valuable consideration, assigned the note and mortgage to appellant. Also, on May 25, 1971, appellee rescinded her agreement to purchase the property by telephoning Cochise College Park, Inc., and on June 15, 1971, Cochise College Park mailed her a check as a refund of her downpayment. None of the documents executed by her were returned and she made no payments on the note. . . . Appellant had no knowledge of nor actual notice of appellee's rescission of the purchase. . . .

On October 31, 1973, appellant filed suit against appellee to recover the unpaid principal balance plus interest thereon which was due on the promissory note. Appellee's responsive pleading admitted the execution of the note and affirmatively alleged lack of consideration . . . and that pursuant to 15 U.S.C.A. Sec. 1701 et seq., she had voided the purchase contract as well as the note and mortgage. . . .

Appellee's defense to the note was that appellant was not a holder in due course since he had notice of a defense when he purchased the note. . . . A purchaser has notice of a claim or defense if he has notice that "the obligation of any party is voidable in whole or in part." If appellant were not a holder in due course, then he took the promissory note subject to all the defenses appellee could assert against Cochise College Park, Inc.

Appellee's position in the trial court was that appellant was not a holder in due course since he had notice that her obligation under the purchase agreement was voidable under federal law. In 1968, Congress enacted the "Interstate Land Sales Full Disclosure Act." As the title of the Act indicates, it is comprehensive regulation of *interstate land sales*. 15 U.S.C.A. Sec. 1703 provides:

> (a) It shall be unlawful . . . (1) to sell or lease any lot in any subdivision unless . . . a printed property report . . . is furnished to the purchaser in advance of the signing of any contract or agreement for sale or lease by the purchaser. . . .
>
> (b) Any contract or agreement for the purchase or leasing of a lot in a subdivision covered by this chapter, where the property report has not been given the purchaser in advance or at the time of the signing, shall be voidable at the option of the purchaser. *A purchaser may revoke said contract or agreement within forty-eight hours, where he has received the property report less than forty-eight hours before he signed the contract or agreement.* . . .

Appellee testified that she has received no federal property report. . . .

The controlling issue was whether appellant was not a holder in due course and therefore took the note subject to the defenses appellee could have asserted against Cochise College Park, Inc.

The pivotal question was whether appellant had notice of any defense appellee might have had.

Appellee's position in the trial court was that appellant had constructive notice of the federal statute and therefore had notice that her obligation was voidable, thereby giving him notice of a defense. We are of the opinion that appellee was not entitled to prevail for two reasons.

Firstly, whether or not appellee received a federal property report was immaterial as the contract was rescinded by mutual agreement of the parties as a consequence of "buyer's remorse." Our Supreme Court has stated:

> As to notice of a defense or claim, it means, minimally, that from all the facts and circumstances known to him at the time in question one has reason to know a given fact exists.

There is absolutely nothing to show that when appellant purchased the note he would have reason to know that the transaction had been rescinded.

Appellee's reliance upon the voidability provision of the federal statute hinges upon the fortuitous circumstances that the parties agreed to rescission within 48 hours after she signed the contract. However, even assuming *arguendo* that appellee had exercised her option to revoke afforded by the statute, we do not agree that appellant had notice that the note was voidable.

Appellee's reliance upon the voidability the statute but not of the facts constituting the violation of it. The test of "notice" is whether appellant had actual knowledge of appellee's defense or "inferable knowledge," i.e., knowledge of facts from which he could reasonably infer the probable existence of the defense. As the Minnesota Supreme Court stated:

> In applying the test, this court has rather consistently held that having notice by way of the "inferable knowledge" test is something more than failure to make inquiry about an unknown fact. Failure to make such inquiry may be negligence and lack of diligence, but it is not "notice" of what he might discover.

Again, there is nothing in the record to show that appellant had knowledge of any facts and circumstances from which he would have reason to know that appellee would have a statutory right to rescind the contract within 48 hours.

The Interstate Land Sales Act was designed to protect inexperienced unknowledgeable land purchasers from deceptive sales practices. Appellee, however, was not availing herself of the remedy provided thereunder—in fact there was no evidence that she knew about the existence of the Act. Both she and appellant were equally unaware of it. Both of them were relatively innocent but unfortunately appellee, in effecting the rescission, did not procure the return of the promissory note she had executed. The courts of this state have consistently adhered to the principle that where one of two innocent parties must suffer, the loss must be borne by the one whose act caused the loss. . . .

Since appellant was a holder in due course, he was entitled to receive the balance due on the note.

Reversed.

Canyonville Bible Academy v. Lobemaster
247 N.E.2d 623 (Ill.) 1969

Defendants executed an installment note to a trailer sales company in payment for a trailer. The trailer company indorsed the note to a bank. Following a default in payments on the note, the bank assigned all of its interest in the note to the plaintiff. Defendants contended that plaintiff was not a purchaser for value and not a holder in due course and therefore subject to personal defenses of defendants. The lower court rendered judgment for defendants, and plaintiff appealed.

TRAPP, J. . . . Under Section 3-201 of the Uniform Commercial Code (Ill. Rev. Stat. 1963, Ch. 26, § 3-201) transfer is provided for as follows:

> (1) Transfer of an instrument vests in the transferee such rights as the transferor has therein except that a transferee who has himself been a party to any fraud or illegality affecting the instrument or who as a prior holder had notice of a defense or claim against it cannot improve his position by taking from a later holder in due course.

In the Illinois Annotated Statute, the Illinois Code Comment under this section is the following interpretation:

> The first clause of this subsection changes the rule under the first part of § 49 of the Illinois NIL (§ 49 of the NIL with variations), which provided, "where the holder of an instrument payable to his order transfers it *for value* without indorsing it, the transferer vests in the transferee such title as the transferee [transferer] had therein" [emphasis supplied]. This subsection eliminates the requirement of value for purposes of transferring the rights of the holder. It is in accord with Illinois case law indicating that a valid transfer may be made by way of gift.

Additionally, under the Uniform Commercial Code Comment in the Illinois Annotated Statute is the following:

> 2. The transfer of rights is not limited to transfers for value. An instrument may be transferred as a gift, and the donee acquires whatever rights the donor had.

Under Section 3-201 of Ch. 26, Ill.Rev. Stat. (1963), it is quite clear that any transfer of an instrument transfers all rights of the transferor, except in the specific case noted as an exception. Since the Bank was a holder in due course and plaintiff was not a prior holder, the plaintiff by transfer from the Bank acquired the rights of a holder in due course irrespective of the question of value. . . .

We conclude that the transfer of the defendant's note by the Bank to plaintiff gave plaintiff the Bank's status as a holder in due course, and the note is enforceable by plaintiff against defendant.

The cause is reversed and remanded with directions to enter judgment in favor of plaintiff and against the defendants in the amount of $9,674.30 with interest at 7 percent per annum from June 16, 1966, and reasonable attorneys' fees not to exceed 15 percent of the amount due at the time of suit and costs.

Reversed and remanded.

New Jersey Mortg. & Inv. Corp. v. Berenyi
356 A.2d 421 (N.J.) 1976

Plaintiff, the holder of a negotiable promissory note, sued the defendant maker to collect the note. The defendant raised the defense of illegality. The original note was payable to a corporation which had negotiated it for value to the plaintiff prior to maturity.

The note in question was delivered in connection with the sale of carpeting under a sales-referral scheme. Prior to the sale, the Attorney General of the state had obtained an injunction which prohibited the corporate payee from engaging in sales-referral schemes.

PER CURIAM: . . . The trial judge ruled that the fact that the note was obtained as part of a transaction entered into by Kroyden Industries, Inc. (Kroyden) in violation of the injunctive order was not a defense in an action brought by plaintiff, whose status as a holder in due course, with no knowledge or notice of the injunctive order, was admitted.

The controlling issue presented is whether the defense here asserted is a "real" defense or a "personal" defense. Real defenses are available against even a holder in due course of a negotiable instrument; personal defenses are not available against such a holder. We affirm since we are satisfied that the defense presented is not a "real" defense.

Defendant argues that since the transaction which resulted in the execution and delivery of defendant's note was engaged in by Kroyden in violation of the injunctive order, the transaction was "illegal and thus a nullity under N.J.S.A. 12A:3-305," which provides in pertinent part as follows:

> To the extent that a holder is a holder in due course he takes the instru-

ment free from . . . (2) all defenses of any party to the instrument with whom the holder has not dealt except . . . (b) such other incapacity, or duress, or illegality of the transaction, as renders the obligation of the party a nullity; and . . .

However, the fact that it was illegal for Kroyden to enter into the transaction did not by reason of that fact render defendant's obligation under the note she executed a nullity.

On the contrary, as noted in the New Jersey Study Comment on N.J.S.A. 12A:3-305 (2)(b):

> In New Jersey, a holder in due course takes free and clear of the defense of illegality, unless the statute which declares the act illegal also indicates that payment thereunder is void. . . . (See, e.g., N.J.S.A. 2A:40-3 which specifically provides that notes given in payment of a gambling debt "shall be utterly void and of no effect.") . . . where no such statute is involved, it has been held that a negotiable instrument which is rooted in an illegal transaction or stems from a transaction prohibited by statute or public policy is no reason for refusing to enforce the instrument in the hands of a holder in due course.

There being no statute ordaining that a note obtained in violation of an injunction is void and unenforceable, the illegality involved is not a "real" defense; the note is enforceable in the hands of a holder in due course who had no knowledge or notice of the injunction. . . .
Affirmed.

Burchett v Allied Concord Financial Corp.
396 P.2d 186 (N.M.) 1964

Plaintiffs (Burchett and Beevers) purchased an aluminum-siding installation for their home upon the false representation of the salesman that they would receive a one-hundred-dollar credit for every other job contracted in the area. Without reading the forms, they signed notes and mortgages, which were transferred to defendant finance corporation by the siding company. On discovering their predicament, plaintiffs brought suit to have the notes and mortgages canceled. The lower court found for plaintiffs, and defendant appealed.

CARMODY, J. . . . The only real question in the case is whether, under the facts, appellees, by substantial evidence, satisfied the provisions of the statute relating to their claimed defense as against a holder in due course.

. . . The provision of the code applicable . . . is as follows:

To the extent that a holder is a holder in due course he takes the instrument free from . . .

(2) all defenses of any party to the instrument with whom the holder has not dealt except . . .

(c) such misrepresentation as has induced the party to sign the instrument with neither knowledge nor reasonable opportunity to obtain knowledge of its character or its essential terms; and . . .

Although fully realizing that the official comments appearing as part of the Uniform Commercial Code are not direct authority for the construction to be placed upon a section of the code, nevertheless they are persuasive and represent the opinion of the National Conference of Commissioners on Uniform State Laws and the American Law Institute. The purpose of the comments is to explain the provisions of the code itself, in an effort to promote uniformity of interpretation. We believe that the official comments following § 3-305(2)(c), Comment No. 7, provide an excellent guideline for the disposition of the case before us. We quote the same in full:

(7) Paragraph (c) of subsection (2) is new. It follows the great majority of the decisions under the original Act in recognizing the defense of "real" or

"essential" fraud, sometimes called fraud in the essence or fraud in the factum, as effective against a holder in due course. The common illustration is that of the maker who is tricked into signing a note in the belief that it is merely a receipt or some other document. The theory of the defense is that his signature on the instrument is ineffective because he did not intend to sign such an instrument at all. Under this provision the defense extends to an instrument signed with knowledge that it is a negotiable instrument, but without knowledge of its essential terms.

The test of the defense here stated is that of excusable ignorance of the contents of the writing signed. The party must not only have been in ignorance, but must also have had no reasonable opportunity to obtain knowledge. In determining what is a reasonable opportunity all relevant factors are to be taken into account, including the age and sex of the party, his intelligence, education and business experience; his ability to read or to understand English, the representations made to him and his reason to rely on them or to have confidence in the person making them; the presence or absence of any third person who might read or explain the instrument to him, or any other possibility of obtaining independent information; and the apparent necessity, or lack of it, for acting without delay.

Unless the misrepresentation meets this test, the defense is cut off by a holder in due course.

We observe that the inclusion of subsection (2)(c) in § 3-305 of the Uniform Commercial Code was an attempt to codify or make definite the rulings of many jurisdictions on the question as to the liability to a holder in due course of a party who either had knowledge, or a reasonable opportunity to obtain the knowledge, of the essential terms of the instrument, before signing. . . .

The reason for the rule, both as it was applied under the Negotiable Instruments Law and as is warranted under the Uniform Commercial Code, is that when one of two innocent persons must suffer by the act of a third, the loss must be borne by the one who enables the third person to occasion it.

We believe that the test set out in Comment No. 7 above quoted is a proper one and should be adhered to by us. . . . Thus the only question is whether, under the facts of this case, the misrepresentations were such as to be a defense as against a holder in due course. . . .

We recognize that the reasonable opportunity to obtain knowledge may be excused if the maker places reasonable reliance on the representations. The difficulty in the instant case is that the reliance upon the representations of a complete stranger (Kelly) was not reasonable, and all of the parties were of sufficient age, intelligence, education, and business experience to know better. In this connection, it is noted that the contracts clearly stated, on the same page which bore the signatures of the various appellees, the following:

No one is authorized on behalf of this company to represent this job to be "A SAMPLE HOME OR A FREE JOB."

The conduct of the Beevers in signing the additional form some weeks after the initial transaction, without reading it, is a graphic showing of negligence. This, however, is merely an added element and it is obvious that all of the parties were negligent in signing the instruments without first reading them under the surrounding circumstances. . . . In our opinion, the appellees here are barred for the reasons hereinabove stated.

Although we have sympathy with the appellees, we cannot allow it to influence our decision. They were certainly victimized, but because of their failure to exercise ordinary care for their own protection, an innocent party cannot be made to suffer.

Reversed.

CHAPTER 21
REVIEW QUESTIONS AND PROBLEMS

1. X made out several checks to Y. Before these checks were presented to Y, an employee of X stole the checks and forged Y's signature. Z Bank cashed the checks. Is Z a holder in due course? Why?

2. M made a promissory note, and H was the holder of the note. H sued M on the note, and M contended that H could not sue since he was not a holder in due course. Is M correct? Why?

3. M made two notes payable to P. P indorsed the notes to a bank as security for a loan before they were overdue. The bank did not inquire as to the origin of the notes. The notes had been given in payment for stock, and the stock had never been delivered. The bank had no knowledge of this. Is the bank a holder in due course? Why?

4. A was an officer and stockholder of a corporation. He executed a note payable to B Bank and had the proceeds placed in the corporation's account at the bank. The corporation failed, and the bank brought action against A. A contended that there was a failure of consideration. Would this defense be good against the bank? Why?

5.   A drew a check to the order of B. B indorsed it to C in payment of an existing indebtedness that B owed to C. A stopped payment on the check before C deposited it. A seeks to assert his defense of failure of consideration against C. Should he succeed? Why?

6.   M, maker, delivered two promissory notes to Y. Y indorsed them to A, a law firm, as a retainer for legal services to be performed. Y had obtained the promissory note by fraudulent representations from M, but A was unaware of this. When A tried to collect, M asserted the defense of fraud in the inducement. Is this defense effective against A? Why?

7.   On September 28, 1964, B Company purchased goods from S Company. As payment, B transferred two checks payable to the order of S dated December 29, 1964, and January 14, 1965. On October 1, X acquired the checks, and one week later, X discounted the checks to Y. On November 1, B returned the goods and stopped payment on the checks. B claims that Y cannot sue because he is not a holder in due course. Is B correct? Why?

8.   X Company issued a check payable to the order of Y Company. Y indorsed the check and deposited it with B Bank in its checking account. The bank allowed Y to draw on all the credit created by the deposit of the check before it learned that there were defenses to it. When the check was presented to the drawee bank, it was dishonored. When sued, X contended that B Bank was not a holder in due course because it had not given value. Is X correct? Why?

9.   X Company entered into a contract with Y Company by which Y would replace the roof on X's office building. X issued a check to Y because Y told X that it had already purchased certain materials to be used in performing the contract. The same day, Y negotiated the check to Z, who took it as a holder in due course. Soon thereafter, X learned that the materials had not been purchased and stopped payment on the check. Can Z enforce payment of the check from X? Why?

10.   D was indebted to C in the amount of $3,046. X gave D his signed blank check with instructions to cash it for $800 and give the cash to C as partial payment. D, however, wrote out the check for $3,046 and delivered it to C. C negotiated the check to W. X stopped payment on the check. Is W a holder in due course? Why?

The Liability of Parties
in Commercial Paper Transactions

1. Introduction

The preceding chapters were primarily concerned with the rights of holders and holders in due course. In those discussions, it was usually assumed that the party being sued had liability unless there was a valid defense that could be asserted against the plaintiff. In this chapter, the issues arise in the opposite factual situation. It is assumed in most of this chapter that there is no valid defense to be asserted. The issues involved go to the basic issue of the liability of the defendant in the absence of a defense.

The liability of a person in a transaction involving commercial paper may be predicated either on the instrument itself or on the underlying contract. No person is liable on the instrument itself unless his signature appears thereon, but the signature may be affixed by a duly authorized agent (3-401[1]). Persons whose signatures appear on instruments may have different types of liability, depending on their status. This chapter will discuss the liability of various parties to commercial paper transactions. The liability is, unless indicated otherwise, predicated on the instrument itself and on the rules of the Code relating to commercial paper.

2. Liability Based on Signatures

A person's liability on commercial paper results from his signature on the instrument. The signature may be affixed as a maker or drawer on the face of the instrument. It may also be on the back of the instrument as an indorsement.

The general principles of the law of agency are applicable to commercial paper. A principal is bound by the duly authorized acts of his agent. If the agent is not authorized to sign, the principal is not bound. There are two exceptions to the rule that an unauthorized signature does not bind the principal. The principal will be liable if he (1) ratifies it, or (2) is estopped from asserting lack of authority. An agent who fails to bind his principal because of failure to name him or owing to lack of authority will usually be personally liable to third parties.

An agent is also personally liable if he fails to show his representative capacity (3-403[2][a]). This occurs if the agent signs his own name without indicating either the name of his principal or the fact that he is signing in a representative capacity (3-403[2][a]). However, an agent can relieve himself of liability to the person to whom he issued the paper by proving that such party knew that he was acting only as an agent for his principal (3-403[2][b]).[1]

For purposes of internal control, many businesses and other organizations require that instruments be signed by at least two persons or that they be countersigned. When the agreement requires two signatures, the drawee may not pay on only one signature, even if the one signing is authorized. The authority is limited or divided, and both must sign.[2]

Another issue concerning signatures relates to the capacity in which the signature is affixed. The liability of primary parties such as makers of notes is different from the liability of secondary parties such as indorsers. The capacity of a signature may be ambiguous because of its physical location or because of the language used.

The capacity in which a person signs is usually obvious because of the location of the signature. For example, makers and drawers usually sign in the lower right-hand corner of an instrument, and indorsers sign on the back of an instrument. In the case of a drawee, he would normally place his signature of acceptance on the face of the instrument, but his signature on the back would clearly indicate that he was signing as an acceptor unless he could establish otherwise. In those situations in which the signature does not reveal the nature of the obligation or the capacity of the party who signs, the signature is an indorsement (3-402).

3. Liability of Banks in Cases of Forgery

A special problem exists in connection with forgeries insofar as banks are concerned. Checks presented to drawee banks for payment may bear forged signatures of drawers or forged indorsements. If the bank pays on such paper, it incurs liability to the person whose name was forged. If the drawer's signature was forged, the bank that honors the check has not followed the order of the drawer and cannot charge his account (3-418). If charged, it must be re-

---

[1] *Pollin* v. *Mindy Mfg. Co.*, page 406.
[2] *Wolfe* v. *University National Bank*, page 407.

credited. Likewise, the bank will have to make restitution to the party whose name was forged on the check as an indorsement (3-419[1][c]). In either case, the loss is initially that of the bank that pays the instrument bearing the forgery.

In the case of a forged drawer's signature, the drawee bank as a general rule cannot collect the payment back from the party who received it. The bank has the signature of the drawer on file and is charged with knowledge of the forgery. This general rule is subject to the exception that if the party receiving the payment dealt with the forger and was negligent in doing so, the drawee may recover the payment. Thus, if a collecting bank was negligent, the drawee bank that paid on a forged drawer's signature could recover from the collecting bank.

A drawee who pays on a forged indorsement has greater rights in seeking to recover the payment than does the drawee who pays on a forged drawer's signature. In the case of a forged indorsement, the drawee has no way of knowing about the forgery, and thus it can collect from the person to whom payment was made, who in turn can collect from all prior parties back to the forger.

Banks may also cash checks indorsed by agents who lack authority. In such cases, the bank will be held liable to the payee if the bank is charged with knowledge of the lack of authority. Just as in the case of forgery by a stranger, the drawer can insist that the drawee recredit his account with the amount of any unauthorized payment.

4. Impostors: Fictitious Payees

A situation similar to forgery arises when an instrument is made payable to a fictitious person, or to an impostor. The drawer's signature is genuine, but the instrument is indorsed in the fictitious name or the name of the person who is being impersonated. In the impostor situation, one person poses as someone else and induces the drawer to issue a check payable to the order of the person who is being impersonated. The impostor then signs the name of the person being impersonated. In such situations, the indorsement by the impostor is effective, and the loss falls on the drawer rather than on the person who took the check or the bank that honored it (3-405[1][a]).[3]

The loss falls upon the drawer because the check was indorsed by the actual person whom the drawer intended to indorse it. If the check is intended for the party named but is diverted and forged by an employee, the "impostor rule" is not applicable. The impostor rule does not extend to a false representation that the party is the authorized agent of the payee. The maker or drawer who takes the precaution of making the instrument payable to the principal is entitled to have his indorsement.

A typical situation of a fictitious payee is one in which a dishonest employee is either authorized to sign his employer's name to checks or draws checks that

[3] *Fair Park Nat. Bank* v. *Southwestern Inv. Co.*, page 409.

he presents to his employer for the latter's signature. Thus, the employee may draw payroll checks or checks payable to persons with whom the employer would be expected to do business. He either signs the checks or obtains his employer's signature and then cashes the checks, indorsing the name of the payee. If he is in charge of the company's books, he is able to manipulate the books when the canceled checks are returned and may thus avoid detection. The Code imposes this loss on the employer—the dishonest employee can effectively indorse in the payee's name (3-405[1][c]).

LIABILITY BASED ON STATUS

5. Classifications: Primary and Secondary

For the purposes of liability, the Code divides the parties to commercial paper into two groups—primary parties and secondary parties. The primary parties are the makers of notes and the acceptors of drafts. These parties have incurred a definite obligation to pay and are the parties who, in the normal course of events, will *actually* pay the instrument.

The secondary parties are drawers of drafts, drawers of checks, and indorsers of any instrument. These parties do not expect to pay the instrument but assume rather that the primary parties will fulfill their obligations. The drawer and indorsers expect that the acceptor will pay the draft. The indorsers of a note expect that the maker will pay when the note matures. Drawers and indorsers have a responsibility to pay if the primary parties do not, *provided* that certain conditions precedent are satisfied. The drawer and the indorser are, in effect, saying that they will pay if the primary party—acceptor or maker —does not, but only if the party entitled to payment has made proper demand upon the primary party, and due notice of the primary party's dishonor of the instrument has then been given to them (3-413[2]); (3-414[1]).

6. The Liability of Primary Parties

A primary party engages that he will pay the instrument according to its terms. The maker thus assumes an obligation to pay the note as it was worded at the time he executed it. The acceptor assumes responsibility for the draft as it was worded when he gave his acceptance (3-413[1]).

If a maker signs an incomplete note, such note when thereafter completed, even though the completion is unauthorized, can be enforced against him by a holder in due course. On the other hand, if an instrument is materially altered after it is made, the maker has a real defense in the absence of negligence. The maker admits as against all subsequent parties the existence of the payee and his capacity to indorse (3-413[3]).

The drawee of a check or draft is not liable on the instrument until acceptance. Upon acceptance, the acceptor is primarily liable. An acceptance must be in writing on the draft and signed by the drawee-acceptor (3-410[1]). Acceptance is usually made by the drawee's writing or stamping the word "Accepted," with his name and the date, across the face of the instrument. The usual means for accepting a check is to have it certified. The acceptance makes the drawee-acceptor the primary obligor; the drawer and all other parties become secondary parties.

A party presenting a draft for acceptance is entitled to an *unqualified acceptance* by the drawee. Thus, when the drawee offers an acceptance that in any manner varies or changes the direct order to pay or accept, the holder may refuse the acceptance (3-412[1]). The paper is dishonored, and upon notice of dishonor or protest, the holder may hold all prior parties on the paper back to and including the drawer.

THE LIABILITY OF SECONDARY PARTIES

7. Drawers

The drawer engages that upon *dishonor* of the draft and any necessary notice of dishonor or protest, he will pay the amount of the draft to the holder or to any indorser who takes it up (3-413[2]). In effect, the drawer assumes a conditional liability on the instrument—that he will pay if the instrument is dishonored and he is properly notified of this fact. The party who draws a draft or check, like one who makes a note or accepts a draft, admits as against all subsequent parties the existence of the payee and his then capacity to indorse (3-413[3]). In addition, most drawers have liability on the underlying contract or transaction in which they deliver the instrument as drawer.

8. Indorsers

Indorsers of checks, drafts, or notes have two kinds of secondary liability. First, they are liable on their *contract* of indorsement (3-414[1]). If an unqualified indorsement (blank or special) is given, the indorser agrees to pay if the primary party does not. This liability can be disclaimed by a qualified indorsement "without recourse." By indorsing "without recourse," the indorser is in effect saying, "I do not guarantee that the primary party will pay."

The contractual liability of the unqualified indorser is conditional in that the indorser obligates himself to pay only if (1) the instrument is properly presented to the primary party, (2) the instrument is dishonored, and (3) notice of dishonor is given to him. This obligation runs to subsequent parties. It is discussed further later in this chapter.

Second, an indorser has *unconditional* liability. This unconditional liability is based on breach of warranty. An indorser makes warranties with reference to the instrument that is transferred (3-417[2]). He warrants that he has good title to the instrument, that all signatures are genuine or authorized,[4] that the

---

[4] *The Union Bank* v. *Joseph Mobilla,* page 411.

instrument has not been materially altered, and that no defense of any party is good against him. He also warrants that he does not have knowledge of any insolvency proceedings with respect to any of the parties involved (3-417[2][e]).

The warranties are made whether the transfer is by delivery only, by qualified indorsement (without recourse), or by unqualified indorsement. It is important to note that liability is automatic if any of the warranties are breached. The indorser and transferor by delivery must make good without regard to the performance of any conditions precedent, such as presentment or notice of dishonor.

9. Transferors without Indorsement

All secondary parties have unconditional liability, because this liability is based on a theory of breach of warranty. Technically speaking, the party who presents an instrument for payment and signs it is not an indorser. The signature is a receipt for the payment. However, the person who presents the instrument warrants that no indorsements are forged, that so far as he knows the signature of the maker or drawer is genuine, and that it has not been materially altered (3-417[1]). Thus, the person who pays or accepts will have recourse against the presenting party if the warranties are breached. There is no warranty that the drawer has sufficient funds on deposit to cover a check. If a drawee pays a check when the drawer has insufficient funds on deposit, the party presenting the check is not liable for breach of warranty. The warranty with regard to the drawer's signature is not absolute—it is only that the warrantor has no knowledge that such signature is forged or unauthorized.

A transferor without an indorsement (bearer paper) also makes warranties to the transferee. They are the same warranties that a qualified indorser makes. These differ from the warranties of an unqualified indorser in only one particular way. The qualified indorser's warranty about defenses is simply that he has no *knowledge* of any defense (3-417[3]). In the case of delivery of bearer paper without indorsement, the warranties run only to the immediate transferee, whereas the indorser's warranties extend to subsequent holders (3-417[2]).

10. Accommodation Parties and Guarantors

One who signs an instrument for the purpose of lending his name and credit to another party to an instrument is an "accommodation" party (3-415[1]). His function is that of a surety. He may sign as an indorser, maker, or acceptor, or as a comaker or coacceptor. The accommodation party is liable in the capacity in which he signed (3-415[2]). As an indorser, he does not indorse for the purpose of transferring the paper but rather to lend security to it.

There is some significance to the surety status of an accommodation party. In some situations, he is entitled to discharge under the general law and may exercise this right against one who is not a holder in due course (3-415[3]).

He is not liable to the party accommodated, and if he is required to pay he can obtain reimbursement from such party (3-415[5]).

The liability of an accommodation party arises without express words. A guarantor's liability is based on words of guaranty. For example, if the words "Payment guaranteed" or their equivalent are added to a signature, the signer engages that if the instrument is not paid when due, he will pay it *without previous resort by the holder to other parties on the paper* (3-416[1]). If the words "Collection guaranteed" are added to a signature, the signer becomes liable only after the holder has reduced his claim against the maker or acceptor to judgment and execution has been returned unsatisfied, or after the maker or acceptor has become insolvent or it is otherwise apparent that it is useless to proceed against him (3-416[2]). If words of guaranty are used but it is not specified whether of "payment" or "collection," they will be deemed to constitute a guaranty of payment (3-416[3]).

A guarantor waives the conditions precedent of presentment, notice of dishonor, and protest. The words of guarantee do not affect the indorsement as a means of transferring the instrument but impose upon such indorser the liability of a comaker (3-416[5]).

CONDITIONAL LIABILITY

11. Introduction

The term *conditional liability* is used to describe the secondary liability that results from the status of parties as drawers or indorsers. The adjective *conditional* refers to the fact that certain conditions precedent must be fulfilled to establish secondary liability. The conditions precedent are *presentment, dishonor, notice of dishonor,* and, in some instances, *protest.*

The importance of exact compliance with the conditions precedent cannot be overemphasized. Failure to comply will result in either the complete or the partial discharge of the secondary parties unless the performance of the conditions has been waived.

12. Presentment—Generally

Presentment is a demand made upon a maker or drawee (3-504[1]). In the case of a note, it is a demand for payment made by the holder upon the maker. In the case of a draft, it may be either a demand for acceptance or a demand for payment.

The drawee of a draft is not bound upon the instrument as a primary party until acceptance. The holder will usually wait until maturity and present his draft to the drawee for payment, but he may present it to the drawee for acceptance before maturity in order to give credit to the instrument during the period of its term. The drawee is under no legal duty to the holder to accept; but if he refuses, the draft is dishonored by nonacceptance. A right of recourse arises immediately against the drawer and the indorsers, and no presentment for payment is necessary.

In most instances, it is not necessary to present an instrument for *acceptance*. Presentment for *payment* alone is usually sufficient. Failure to make a proper presentment for payment results in the complete discharge of an indorser (3-501[1][b]). A limited discharge is accorded to drawers. They are discharged to the extent that the failure to make a proper presentment caused them a loss.

13. Presentment—How and Where

Presentment may be made by personally contacting the primary party and making a demand for acceptance or payment. Presentment may be made by mail or through a clearinghouse (3-504[2][a][b]). Presentment by mail is effective on the date when the mail is received. If the instrument specifies the place of acceptance or payment, presentment may be made at such place. If no place is specified, presentment may be made at the place of business of the party to accept or pay. Presentment is excused if neither the party to accept or pay nor anyone authorized to act for him is present or accessible at such place (3-504 [2][c]). It is required that a draft accepted or a note made payable at a bank in the United States must be presented at such bank (3-504[4]).

The party to whom presentment is made may without dishonor require the exhibition of the instrument at the proper place. He may also require the reasonable identification of the person making presentment and evidence of authority to make it if made for another. The presenter has the right to a signed receipt on the instrument for any partial or full payment and its surrender upon full payment.

If the primary party does not avail himself of these rights, the presentment is perfectly valid no matter how the presentment is made or where it is made. If he does require that the presentment be made in accordance with the provisions above, the instrument is not dishonored. The requirement of identification of the presenting party applies to bearer paper as well as order paper (3-505).

14. Presentment—When

In general, an instrument must be presented for payment on the day of maturity. The presentment must be made at a reasonable hour, and if at a bank, during banking hours.

When a definite maturity date is not included in the instrument—that is, in sight and demand instruments—the time for presentment is somewhat variable. When an instrument is payable after sight, it must be presented for acceptance or negotiated within a reasonable time after the date on the instrument or the date of issue, whichever is later. In all other situations, it is required, in order to fix liability upon all secondary parties, that presentment for acceptance or payment be made within a reasonable time after such secondary party became liable; for example, after his indorsement (3-503 [1][e]). Thus, in the case of a demand note, an indorser would be discharged if presentment were not made within a reasonable time after he indorsed the note. A reasonable time for presentment is determined by the nature of the instrument, any usage of banking or trade, and the facts of the particular case (3-503[2]).

With respect to the liability of the drawer of a check, a reasonable time within which to present for payment or to initiate bank collection is presumed to be 30 days after date or issue, whichever is later (3-504[2][a]). As to an indorser's liability, the presumed reasonable time is seven days after his indorsement (3-504[2][b]).

Thus, the drawer must "back up" a check for a longer period than an indorser, but the drawer having issued the check is not being imposed upon by the requirement that he keep funds on hand for 30 days to cover it. Thirty days is also the period after which a purchaser has notice of the staleness of a check. But an indorser is in a different position and is entitled to notice promptly, so that he may take adequate steps to protect himself against his transferor and prior parties if the check is dishonored. The drawer of a check is protected as to funds on deposit by Federal Deposit Insurance.

15. Dishonor

The party who presents an instrument is entitled to have the instrument paid or accepted. If the party to whom the instrument is presented refuses to pay or accept, the instrument is dishonored (3-507[1]). The presenting party then has recourse against indorsers or other secondary parties, provided he gives proper notice of such dishonor.

When a draft is presented to the drawee for *acceptance,* the drawee may wish to ascertain some facts from the drawer before he assumes the obligation of an acceptor. As a result, the law allows the drawee to defer acceptance until the close of the next business day following presentment (3-506[1]). If the drawee needs more time within which to obtain information, the holder can give him one additional business day within which to accept. The secondary parties are not discharged by the one-day postponement. The holder who presents the draft for *acceptance* is seeking the drawee's obligation on the paper and will not receive payment until a later date. For this reason, the Code permits a longer period of time within which to accept a draft than is allowed when the draft is presented for payment. When an instrument is presented for payment, the party to whom presentment is made is allowed a reasonable time to examine the instrument to determine whether the instrument is properly payable, but payment must be made in any event on the same day that it is presented and before the close of business on that day (3-506[2]).

16.   Notice of Dishonor

When an instrument has been dishonored on proper presentment, the holder must give prompt notice of the dishonor in order to have a right of recourse against unqualified indorsers (3-507[2]). Failure to give prompt and proper notice of dishonor results in the discharge of indorsers. Notice of dishonor should also be given to the drawer. However, the failure to do so discharges the drawer only to the extent that he has suffered a loss because of the failure of the holder to give proper notice (3-502[1]). This could occur if the bank failed in the interim.

Generally, notice is given to secondary parties by the holder or by an indorser who has himself received such notice. Any party who may be compelled to pay the instrument may notify any party who may be liable on it (3-508[1]).

Except for banks, notice must be given before midnight of the third business day after dishonor (3-508[2]). In the case of a person who has received notice of dishonor and wishes to notify other parties, notice must be given by him before midnight of the third business day after receipt of the notice of dishonor.

In the case of banks, any necessary notice must be given before its "midnight deadline"—before midnight of the next banking day following the day on which a bank receives the item or notice of dishonor (3-508[2]).[5]

Notice may be given in any reasonable manner, which would include oral notice, notice by telephone, and notice by mail. Such notice must identify the dishonored instrument and state that it has been dishonored. The usual practice is to return the instrument bearing a stamp that acceptance or payment has been refused (3-508[3]).

Written notice is effective when sent even though it is not received, assuming proper address and postage (3-508[4]). Note that when *presentment* is made by mail, the time of *presentment* is determined by the time of *receipt* of mail.

Proper notice preceded by any necessary presentment and dishonor imposes liability upon secondary parties to whom such notice of dishonor is given. Proper notice operates for the benefit of all parties who have rights on the instrument against the party notified (3-508[8]). Thus, it is only necessary to notify a party once for his liability to be fixed. For example, assume that A, B, C, and D are indorsers in that order, and the holder gives notice only to A and C. C will not be required to give additional notice to A, and if D is compelled to pay, he would have recourse against A. B and D are discharged if they are not notified by the holder or one of the indorsers. This result follows because indorsers are in general liable in the order of their indorsement. An indorser who is required to pay can recover from an indorser prior to him. But each indorser is entitled to notice of dishonor, in order that he can take appropriate steps to pass the responsibility on to those prior to him on the paper.

[5] *Samples* v. *Trust Co. of Georgia,* page 411.

17.   Protest

Protest is a certificate that sets forth that an instrument was presented for payment or acceptance, that it was dishonored, and the reasons, if any, given for refusal to accept or pay (3-509). It is a formal method for satisfying the conditions precedent. It is required only for drafts that are drawn or payable outside the United States. The protest requirement is in conformity with foreign law in this respect. In other cases, protest is optional with the holder. Protest serves as evidence both that presentment was made and that notice of dishonor was given—it creates a presumption that the conditions precedent were satisfied.

18.   Excuses for Failure to Perform Conditions Precedent

An unexcused delay in making any *necessary* presentment or in giving notice of dishonor discharges parties who are entitled to performance of the conditions precedent. Indorsers are completely discharged by such delay, and drawers, makers of notes payable at a bank, and acceptors of drafts payable at a bank are discharged to the extent of any loss caused by the delay (3-502).

Delay in making presentment, in giving notice of dishonor, or in making protest is excused when the holder has acted with reasonable diligence, and the delay is not due to any fault of the holder. He must, however, comply with these conditions or attempt to do so as soon as the cause of the delay ceases to exist (3-511[1]). Also, a delay in complying with the conditions precedent is excused if the holder did not know that the time for compliance had arrived. Thus, if an instrument has been accelerated, but the holder did not know of this fact, his late presentment would be excused.

The performance of the conditions precedent is entirely excused if the party to be charged has *waived* the condition either before or after it is due.[6] The waiver may be express, as when it is set forth in the instrument or in the indorsement, or it may be by implication. When such waiver is stated on the face of the instrument, it is binding on all parties; when it is written above the signature of the indorser, it binds him only (3-511[6]). Most promissory notes contain such a waiver.

The words "Protest Waived" contained in an instrument mean that presentment and notice of dishonor, as well as technical protest, are waived. This is true even though technical protest is not required (3-511[5]).

The performance of the conditions precedent is also excused if the party to be charged has himself dishonored the instrument, or has countermanded payment, or otherwise has no reason to expect or right to require that the instrument be accepted or paid (3-511[2][b]). For example, if a drawer of a check has stopped payment on the check, the drawer is not in a position to complain about slow presentment or any lack of notice of dishonor.

---

6 *First New Haven National Bank* v. *Clarke,* page 412.

When a draft has been dishonored by *nonacceptance,* a later presentment for payment is excused unless, of course, the drawee has in the meantime accepted the instrument (3-511[4]). This means that a holder who has presented a draft for acceptance is not, if acceptance is refused, required to make a subsequent presentment for payment. The refusal to accept is in itself a dishonor of the instrument.

19. Liability for Conversion

In tort law, a *conversion* is any act in relation to personal property inconsistent with the owner's interest in the goods. There is a conversion of an instrument if (1) a drawee to whom it is delivered for acceptance refuses to return it upon demand, (2) any person to whom it is delivered for payment refuses on demand either to pay it or to return it, or (3) it is paid on a forged indorsement (3-419[1]). The payment over a forged indorsement is a conversion as against the true owner, the party whose indorsement was forged. He can recover from the party who made payment, and the paying party then has recourse against other parties for breach of the presentment warranty. Ordinarily, the measure of damages for conversion will be the face amount of the instrument (3-419[2]).

20. Discharge

The liability of various parties may be discharged in a variety of ways (3-601). Many of these have been previously noted. For example, certification of a check at the request of a holder discharges all prior parties (3-411). Any ground for discharging a simple contract also discharges commercial paper (3-601[2]).

Payment usually discharges a party's liability. This is true even if the payor has knowledge of the claim of another person. Payment does not operate to discharge liability if the payor acts in bad faith and pays one who acquired the instrument by theft. Payment is also no defense if paid in violation of a restrictive indorsement (3-603).

A holder may discharge any party by intentionally canceling the instrument or by striking out or otherwise eliminating a party's signature. The surrender of the instrument to a party will also discharge that party (3-605).

If a holder agrees not to sue one party or agrees to release collateral, then all parties with rights against such party or against the collateral are discharged from liability. This assumes that there is no express reservation of rights by the holder and that the party claiming discharge did not consent to the holder's actions (3-606).

When an instrument is reacquired by a prior party, he may cancel all intervening indorsements. In this event, all parties whose indorsements are canceled are discharged (3-208).

An alteration of an instrument that is both fraudulent and material discharges any party whose liability is affected by the alteration. Of course, this is not true if the alteration is agreed to or if the party seeking to impose liability is a holder in due course (3-407). In fact no discharge is effective against a holder in due course unless he has notice of the discharge when he takes the instrument (3-602).

THE LIABILITY OF PARTIES IN COMMERCIAL PAPER TRANSACTIONS CASES

Pollin v. Mindy Mfg. Co.
236 A.2d 542 (Pa.) 1967

The defendant was the president of Mindy Mfg. Co. In that capacity he signed payroll checks for the company. Some of these checks were cashed by plaintiff, who operated a check-cashing business. Because of insufficient funds in the corporate payroll account, the drawee bank refused to honor the checks. The plaintiff sought to impose personal liability on the president. The name and address of the corporation were printed on the top of each check, along with "Payroll check no. —." The corporate name was also printed at the lower right corner of the checks, above the space for the authorized signature. The lower court held for plaintiff, and defendant appealed

MONTGOMERY, J. . . . Summary judgment against appellant was entered by the lower court on the authority of Section 3-403 of the Uniform Commercial Code . . . which provides, "An authorized representative who signs his name to an instrument . . . (b) except as otherwise established between the immediate parties, is personally obligated if the instrument names the person represented but does not show that the representative signed in a representative capacity . . ." and our decisions thereunder. . . .

The issue before us, therefore, is whether a third party to the original transaction, the endorsee in the present case, may recover against one who affixes his name to a check in the place where a maker usually signs without indicating he is signing in a representative capacity, without giving consideration to other parts of the instrument or extrinsic evidence. This appears to be a novel question under the Uniform Commercial Code.

If this were an action brought by the payee, parol evidence would be permitted to establish the capacity of the person affixing his signature under Section 3-403(b), previously recited. . . .

However, since this is an action brought by a third party our initial inquiry must be for the purpose of determining whether the instrument indicates the capacity of appellant as a signer. Admittedly, the instrument fails to show the office held by appellant. However, we do not think this is a complete answer to our problem, since the Code imposes liability on the individual only ". . . if the instrument . . . does not show that the representative signed in a representative capacity. . . ." This implies that the instrument must be considered in its entirety.

Although Section 3-401(2) of the Uniform Commercial Code provides that "A signature is made by use of any name, including any trade or assumed name, upon an instrument, or by any word or mark used in lieu of a written signature," which would be broad enough to include the printed name of a corporation, we do not believe that a check showing two lines under the imprinted corporate name indicating the signature of one or more corporate officers would be accepted by any reasonably prudent person as a fully executed check of the corporation. It is common to expect that a corporate name placed upon a negotiable instrument in order to bind the corporation as a maker, especially when printed on the instrument, will be accompanied by the signatures of officers authorized by the by-laws to sign the instrument. . . . While we do not rule out the possibility of a printed name being established as an acceptable signature, we hold that such a situation is uncommon, and in the present case the two lines under the printed name dictate against a valid corporate signature. Corporations act through officers.

Next, we must give consideration to the distinction between a check and a note. A check is an order of a depositor on a bank in the nature of a draft drawn on the bank and payable on demand. It is revocable until paid or accepted for payment. A note is an irrevocable promise to pay on the part of the maker. The maker of a check impliedly engages not only that it will be paid, but that he will have sufficient funds in the bank to meet it. In the present instance the checks clearly showed that they were payable from a special account set up by the corporate defendant for the purpose of paying its employees. This information disclosed by the instrument of itself would refute any contention that the appellant intended to make the instrument his own order on the named bank to pay money to the payee. The money was payable from the account of the corporation defendant over which appellant as an individual had no control.

Considering the instrument as a whole, we conclude that it sufficiently discloses that appellant signed it in a representative capacity. . . .

Judgment reversed and entered for appellant-defendant.

Wolfe v. University National Bank
310 A.2d 558 (Md.) 1973

SINGLEY, J. In its simplest form, the question raised by this case is within what period of time may a depositor seek to hold his bank accountable when the bank has honored checks bearing only one signature, drawn on a two-signature account? . . .

The appellant Charles R. Wolfe was one of three general partners of the co-appellant, Watkins Glen Limited Partnership (Watkins Glen). In March, 1969, Watkins Glen opened a checking account with . . . University National Bank (the Bank) in Rockville, Maryland.

Through December, 1969, Watkins Glen's agreement with the Bank required that checks on the Watkins Glen account be signed by any two of its then three general partners: Wolfe, Per Olof Holtze and Wolfgang H. Altmann. From and after 31 December 1969, Watkins Glen's agreement required that checks on its account be signed by either Wolfe and Per Olof Holtze *or* Wolfe and Paul S. Waymoth.

During the period 27 October 1969 through 18 September 1970, 37 checks totalling $235,012.02, each bearing only one signature, were drawn on Watkins Glen's account, and paid by the Bank. Of the 37 checks, 31 were signed by Holtze; five, by Waymoth; and one, by Wolfe. Seven of the checks, six of which were signed by Holtze, in the aggregate amount of $222,900.00, were payable to Holtze Corporation. In August, 1972, Wolfe and Watkins Glen brought suit against the Bank, their declaration sounding in contract and tort.

Although no notice had been given the Bank until March, 1972, it was stipulated that monthly statements, together with the canceled checks, had been sent during the period November, 1969 to September, 1970 to Watkins Glen's office, where they were reconciled by Waymoth's assistant, and were at all times accessible to Wolfe.

In contending that it was entitled to judgment as a matter of law, the Bank relied upon those provisions of the UCC which impose upon a customer the duty to examine statements received from a bank and report an unauthorized signature within one year from date of receipt. The provisions are found in UCC § 4-406(1) and (4).:

> (1) When a bank sends to its customer a statement of account accompanied by items paid in good faith in support of the debit entries or holds the statement and items pursuant to a request or instructions of its customer or otherwise in a reasonable manner makes the statement and items available to the customer, the customer must exercise reasonable care and promptness to examine the statement and items to discover his unauthorized signature or any alteration on an item and must notify the bank promptly after discovery thereof.

> (4) Without regard to care or lack of care of either the customer or the bank a customer who does not within one year from the time the statement and items are made available to the customer (subsection (1)) discover and report his unauthorized signature or any alteration on the face or back of the item or does not within three years from that time discover and report any unauthorized indorsement is precluded from asserting against the bank such unauthorized signature or indorsement or such alteration.

The view which we take of this case, which is markedly different from that taken by the trial court, makes § 4-406(4) only of tangential interest. As we see it, and are prepared to hold, despite the fact that we neither have been referred to, nor have we found a case in point, a single signature on a check drawn against an account on which two signatures are required is not necessarily an *unauthorized* signature.

UCC § 4-401 sets forth the circumstances under which a bank may charge its customer's account:

> (1) As against its customer, a bank may charge against his account any item which is otherwise properly payable from that account. . . .

Here, the Watkins Glen partnership was a "customer" of the Bank. Watkins Glen's signature was comprised of two individual signatures, as provided for in its contract with the Bank. Consequently, since Watkins Glen's signature did not appear on any of the 37 checks in question, the partnership cannot be held liable on them, UCC § 3-401(1), and the Bank may not properly charge them to Watkins Glen's account, in the absence of circumstances which alter the usual rule.

UCC § 4-406 is inapplicable here because it is only concerned with unauthorized signatures and alterations. An "unauthorized signature" "means one made without actual, implied or apparent authority and includes a forgery," UCC § 1-201(43). . . . The signatures of Holtze, Waymoth, and Wolfe were not forged, not made without authority, nor did they constitute an alteration of any kind.

Either Holtze's and Wolfe's signature at all times or Wolfe's signature and Waymoth's after 31 December 1969 was an *authorized* signature. The infirmity lay not in the presence of an unauthorized signature on the check, but in the absence of a second authorized signature, that of either Wolfe or Altmann prior to 31 December 1969, or that of Wolfe thereafter —a second signature which was essential, under the agreement with the Bank.

It naturally follows that the motion for summary judgment should not have been granted, because the one-year period of limitations imposed by § 4-406(4) did not apply, and because Wolfe's claim was asserted by bringing suit in August, 1972, well within the three-year period allowed. . . .

Judgment reversed, case remanded for further proceedings, costs to abide the result.

Fair Park Nat. Bank v. Southwestern Inv. Co.
541 S.W.2d 266 (Tex.) 1976

GUITTARD, J. . . . The "impostor rule" of the Uniform Commercial Code fixes the loss resulting from the fraud of an impostor on the drawer of a check or draft who delivers it to the impostor rather than on a subsequent holder, regardless of the lack of a genuine endorsement by the nominal payee. This case involves applicability of this rule to a draft delivered to one impostor but payable to two payees. We hold that the impostor rule applies so that the drawer cannot recover against the collecting bank on the ground of the lack of genuineness of the endorsement of either of the joint payees. . . .

Plaintiff Southwestern Investment Company agreed to lend $12,000 to James Impson to finance the purchase of a "front loader" machine from persons named by Impson as J. L. Williams and James L. Wilson of Euless, Texas, doing business as Universal Constructors. One of Southwestern's employees inspected the machine pointed out by Impson and approved the security. Southwestern required a bill of sale from the sellers. . . . When the note was signed by Impson . . . Southwestern prepared at Impson's direction a draft for $12,000 payable to J. L. Williams and James L. Wilson. Shortly afterward, a man representing himself to be J. L. Williams appeared at Southwestern's Dallas office with a bill of sale purportedly signed by J. L. Williams and James L. Wilson and tendered it in exchange for the draft. Without requiring any identification, Southwestern accepted the bill of sale and delivered the draft to the supposed J. L. Williams.

Later, Impson, the borrower, appeared at Fair Park National Bank and presented the draft to the teller, Juanita Akins, who knew him as a customer of the bank. She saw that the draft bore the purported endorsements in blank of both payees and accepted it for deposit in Impson's account without requiring

any endorsement by him. The Fair Park Bank stamped its endorsement with the notation "Previous Endorsement Guaranteed," and sent the draft to Amarillo National Bank, which charged Southwestern's account and paid the draft with a cashier's check to Fair Park Bank. Fair Park Bank then issued to Impson its cashier's check for the amount of the draft.

After three payments were made on Impson's note to Southwestern, Impson defaulted. . . . Southwestern undertook an investigation, which revealed that the machine had not been purchased from J. L. Williams and James L. Wilson, but had been stolen. No trace could be found of Williams, Wilson, or of any firm doing business as Universal Constructors. Southwestern then sued . . . both banks for breach of warranty. . . .

The jury found that J. L. Williams and James L. Wilson failed to endorse the draft before it was delivered by Impson to defendant Fair Park Bank, that Fair Park Bank was negligent in not verifying that the named payees had endorsed the draft, and that both J. L. Williams and James L. Wilson were impostors. On this verdict the court rendered judgment . . . against the defendant. . .

Defendant Fair Park Bank . . . has appealed, contending that under the impostor rule, the endorsements on the draft were effective, whether or not they were the genuine signatures of J. L. Williams and James L. Wilson. Southwestern responds that even though the man representing himself to be Williams may have been an impostor, so that the endorsement was effective as respects his purported signature, nevertheless there was no effective endorsement by or on behalf of the other payee, James L. Wilson, because no person representing himself as Wilson had any connection with the issuance of the draft. Southwestern argues that under § 3.116(2) of the Code, when an instrument is payable to two or more persons and not in the alternative, it must be negotiated by both. Consequently, Southwestern asserts that Fair Park Bank is liable for breach of warranty of the Wilson endorsement.

We conclude that Fair Park Bank is not liable for breach of warranty for two reasons. In the first place, the impostor rule applies to the person who signed the bill of sale as James L. Wilson as well as to the person who signed as J. L. Williams. The jury found that Wilson as well as Williams was an impostor. . . . Apparently, Southwestern's position is that there was no imposture with respect to James L. Wilson because no one pretending to bear that name appeared before Southwestern's representative and joined with the purported J. L. Williams in inducing Southwestern to deliver the draft.

This argument erroneously assumes that an "impostor" under § 3.405(a)(1) must meet his victim face to face. That section does not so provide. Rather, it states the rule as follows:

> (a) An indorsement by any person in the name of a named payee is effective if
> 1. an imposter [sic] by use of the mails or otherwise has induced the maker or drawer to issue the instrument to him or his confederate in the name of the payee. . . .

One of the purposes of drafting the rule in this language was to eliminate the requirement of a face-to-face meeting, which had been imposed by some of the pre-Code cases. Under the Code, it is only necessary that "an imposter by use of the mails or otherwise has induced the maker or drawer to issue the instrument to him or his confederate in the name of the payee."

Here the evidence and the verdict established that the person who signed the bill of sale as "James L. Wilson," as well as the person who signed as "J. L. Williams," was an impostor. . . . Although an impostor cannot be a fictitious person, since there must be a real

person who impersonates someone else, an impostor may impersonate a fictitious person. Both of the persons who signed the bill of sale induced Southwestern to issue the draft, since, presumably, Southwestern would not have issued it without a bill of sale bearing both signatures. Consequently, § 3.405(a)(1) makes both endorsements effective to relieve Fair Park Bank of liability for breach of warranty regardless of who wrote them.

In the second place, we conclude that the impostor rule applies even if the "James L. Wilson" named in the bill of sale, or the person who signed the bill in his name, was not an impostor. Southwestern does not challenge the finding that the man who represented himself as J. L. Williams was an impostor. In effect, it concedes that the endorsement of this name on the draft was effective under § 3.405-(a)(1), but it contends that unless Wilson also is shown to be an impostor, the bank is liable for breach of its warranty of his endorsement. We cannot agree. Section 3.405-(a)(1) is not limited to situations in which impostors have impersonated all the joint payees. If an impostor "has induced the maker or drawer to issue the instrument to him or his confederate in the name of the payee," the endorsement of any person "in the name of a named payee is effective." We interpret this language to mean that if an instrument is payable to A and B, and X, by impersonating A, induces the drawer to deliver the instrument to him, then X, or anyone else, can make effective endorsements in the names of both A and B. This interpretation is consistent with the policy of the impostor rule, which is to throw the loss resulting from dealing with an impostor on the person who dealt with the impostor and, presumably, had the best opportunity to take precautions that would have detected the fraud, rather than on a subsequent holder, who had no similar opportunity. A drawer who deals with a person impersonating one of several payees has as good an opportunity to detect the fraud as one who deals with the impersonator of a single payee. Consequently, on this ground also we hold that the endorsement in the name of James L. Wilson was as effective under § 3.401(a)(1) as was the endorsement in the name of J. L. Williams. . . .

Reversed.

The Union Bank v. Joseph Mobilla
43 Erie Co. Leg. J. 45 (Pa.) 1959

LAUB, J. . . . On January 15, 1958, the defendant, a used car dealer, represented to the plaintiff bank that he had sold a used Ford automobile to one Theresa Piotrowski of 650 East 24th Street. For finance purposes, he exhibited an installment sales contract and a judgment note allegedly signed by Theresa Piotrowski as maker. There was nothing on the face of either instrument to indicate that the signatures had not been placed there by the maker or that either had been signed by someone else acting in the maker's behalf. . . . The note which was payable to defendant was endorsed by him "without recourse," and . . . turned over to the bank as part of the finance transaction.

. . . After default the bank importuned both the purported maker and the defendant to discharge the obligation but without avail, the maker having denied executing either document or having bought the vehicle from the defendant. In consequence, plaintiff instituted this action, alleging that defendant is guilty of a breach of an implied warranty of the genuineness of the note.

The defendant in his answer admits that he endorsed the note . . . to the plaintiff. He also admits that the maker did not sign it. It is his defense, however, that . . . he (the defendant) is not liable . . . because his indorsement of the note was "without recourse."

We can see no merit whatever in the defense offered and consider that plaintiff is entitled to the judgment which it seeks. The defendant's conception of the litigation as being a suit against an endorser who signed "without recourse" misses the point. Plaintiff is not suing on the note, but as noted above, is claiming upon a breach of warranty. If it were true that the suit was against the defendant on the sole basis that he was an endorser, there might be some value to the defenses offered, but the pleadings reveal an entirely different situation. As the pleadings now stand . . . the admission that defendant endorsed the note as part of his finance dealings with the plaintiff and that the note was not signed by the maker is clear admission of a breach of the implied warranty which accompanies situations of this character. While no statute is required to establish the common sense conclusion that one who presents a document for discount or otherwise impliedly warrants its genuineness when he accepts a consideration for its transfer, the Uniform Commercial Code has such a provision. In Section 3-417(2)(a) of that Act . . . it is provided that the transferor of an instrument for consideration warrants, among other things, that all signatures are genuine or authorized. This certainly does not imply that a transferor, with knowledge that a signature is not that of the person it purports to belong to and there is no qualifying or descriptive language indicating that the signature was made by someone other than the maker, may remain silent and suppress such knowledge to the detriment of the transferee.

Judgment for the plaintiff.

Samples v. Trust Co. of Georgia
163 S.E.2d 325 (Ga.) 1968

The defendant, Samples, received a check drawn on the plaintiff bank. He indorsed the check and received payment from another bank. The bank sent the check for collection to plaintiff bank and the check was paid. Later, the plaintiff discovered that the drawer of the check did not have an account and that it had mistakenly charged the check to one of its customers. Plaintiff then sought to recover from the defendant indorser. Defendant contended that the check had not been dishonored within the time allowed by law. The lower court gave judgment for plaintiff, and defendant appealed.

BELL, J. . . . "Unless excused . . . notice of any dishonor is necessary to charge any indorser. . . ." Code Ann. § 109A-3-501(2). "Any necessary notice must be given by a bank before its midnight deadline. . . ." Code Ann. § 109A-3-508(2). That is, "midnight on its next banking day following the banking day on which it receives the relevant item." Code Ann. § 109A-4-104(h). "Where without excuse any necessary presentment or notice of dishonor is delayed beyond the time when it is due . . . any indorser is discharged. . . ." Code Ann. § 109A-3-502(1). "Delay by a . . . payor bank beyond time limits prescribed or permitted by this Act or by instructions is excused if caused by interruption of communication facilities, suspension of payments by another bank, war, emergency conditions or other circumstances beyond the control of the bank provided it exercises such diligence as the circumstances require." Code Ann. § 109A-4-108. The plaintiff bank's failure to give notice of dishonor within the prescribed time was not due to "circumstances beyond the control of the bank" and was not excused by any provision of the Code, but was due to the bank's error in mistaking the signature on a check drawn on a fictitious account for the signature of one of its customers with a similar name. A bank is bound to know the signatures of its depositors. . . . § 109A-4-302 also demands a reversal. That section provides: "In the absence of a valid defense such as breach of a presentment warranty . . . settlement effected or the like, if an item is presented on and received by a payor bank the bank is accountable for the amount of . . . a demand item . . . whether properly payable or not if the bank . . . does not pay or return the item or send notice of dishonor until after its midnight deadline. . . ."

The trial court erred in rendering judgment for the plaintiff bank.

Reversed.

First New Haven National Bank v. Clarke
368 A.2d 613 (Conn.) 1976

JACOBS, J. . . . In the complaint the plaintiff alleged that "[b]y a note dated October 23, 1974, Progressive Management Corp. promised to pay to the plaintiff on demand the sum of $9,805.25 plus interest and costs of collection including a reasonable attorney's fee in the event of default." In paragraph two of the complaint the plaintiff further alleged that "the defendants, George B. Clarke, Robert P. Williams and Elder Young, endorsed said note as follows: 'Presentment for payment and notice of nonpayment are hereby waived. Further each endorser consents without notice or further assent (a) to the terms and conditions of this note or any renewal or extension thereof, (b) to the exchange or surrender of the collateral, and (c) to extension of time for payment, or change of interest rate, of this note or of the collateral, and as endorser agrees that upon or after any default in the maker's liability or maker's agreement, holder may exercise, with respect to endorser's personal property at any time in the possession or control of holder in any capacity, the same rights of application to maker's liability and of addition to collateral under the within and foregoing notes as holder thereunder has with respect to maker's personal property.'" In paragraph three of the complaint, the plaintiff alleged that "[s]aid note is in default and there is presently due the sum of $9,805.25 plus interest from November 25, 1974 at the rate of twelve and ¾ (12¾%) per cent per annum accrued at the rate of $3.47 per diem, plus reasonable attorney's fees and costs of collection as the Court may order."

The defendants demurred to the complaint on the ground that the "quoted language in Paragraph 2 . . . does not constitute a guarantee or obligation to pay said promissory note." . . .

Problems arising from surety arrangements are as old as recorded history. "Broadly defined, a surety is a party to a contract who agrees to pay the obligation of another under some circumstances." " 'The term surety is very often used in the broad sense as including both technical surety and guarantor, i.e., all obligations in which the promisor is answering for a loan or extension of credit from the creditor to the principal debtor.' " "More than that of any other party to commercial paper, the endorser's liability is *like* that of a surety." One who signs an instrument without clear indication of capacity or intention automatically becomes an endorser by virtue of § 42a-3-402 of the General Statutes, and such an endorser makes the engagement of General Statutes § 42a-3-414(1) that he will pay if the instrument to which he has subscribed is dishonored by its designated payor. Thus, as pointed out, the concept of the secondary lia-

bility of an endorser finds something of a parallel in the liability of a surety. A surety may appear on a negotiable instrument as an "accommodation party" who, pursuant to § 42a-3-415(1) of the General Statutes, signs "in any capacity for the purpose of lending his name to another party to it."

The endorser's liability, of course, is conditioned on certain formal procedures, such as due presentment and proper notice. Under the provisions of General Statutes § 42a-3-511(2), however, "[p]resentment or notice or protest as the case may be is entirely excused when (a) the party to be charged has waived it expressly or by implication either before or after it is due. . . ."

The endorsements on the reverse side of the note in this case provide that "[p]resentment for payment and notice of nonpayment are hereby waived." Such an endorsement automatically operates as a waiver. The endorsers of the note in question have the major attributes of suretyship. They have endorsed the instrument "without clear indication of capacity or intention. Any such signatory automatically becomes an indorser. . . ." An endorser is bound by the waiver which he endorses.

Demurrer overruled.

CHAPTER 22
REVIEW QUESTIONS AND PROBLEMS

1. A, the holder of a note, transferred the note by a blank endorsement to B. B did not present the note to the maker for payment, nor did he notify A of any dishonor. Can B maintain an action against A as an indorser? Why?

2. M executed a note, and A signed as an accommodation maker. When M had financial problems, A, at the request of the payee, paid the note. The payee then assigned the note to A. If A sues M, can M defend upon the grounds that he was discharged of liability on the note when it was paid by A? Why?

3. D executed a draft on B to pay for livestock purchased from C. B refused to pay the draft. C gave proper notice to D. C then sued D on the draft. D defended on the grounds that (1) he was acting as agent for B, and (2) C understood D should not be personally liable. Is D correct? Why?

4. A indorsed a note. Above all endorsements was printed, "Notice of protest waived." The note was not paid when it came due. H, the holder, sent notice to A. (The notice was sent to A's former address, and consequently, A did not receive it.) Was A properly notified? Why?

5. A was one of two signers of a note. The word "guarantor" followed his signature. The holder of the note brought action against A, and A's only defense was that the holder must sue the other signer before bringing action against A. Is A's contention correct? Why?

6. F, the superintendent of X Construction Company, had the responsibility of verifying bills and approving them for payment. F picked up a number of checks and, instead of delivering them to the payees, forged the endorsements and cashed the checks. X Company demands that the drawee bank reimburse it for the amount paid out on these checks. Is the drawee bank liable? Why?

7. C, the assistant comptroller of Z Company, Inc., drew checks on the corporate bank account payable to "Z Company," omitting the "Inc." The checks were sent to his accomplice, A, who deposited them in the B Bank and then drew checks upon the account. A had previously opened an account in the bank under the name of Z Company and filled out an account card showing himself as the president and the authorized signatory. It was the duty of C to draw checks to be placed in another bank to cover payrolls of Z. Z contends that the B Bank is liable for all funds drawn out of the account. Is the B Bank liable? Why?

8. Two checks drawn upon D, the drawee bank, were deposited at the B Bank. B forwarded the checks through collecting channels to D for payment. D's computer system malfunctioned, and D failed to give notice of dishonor due to insufficient account within the prescribed "midnight deadline." The manufacturer had indicated that repairs would not take too long, but they lasted approximately two days. The D Bank did use a backup computer located 2½ hours away. The B Bank sues the D Bank to collect upon the two checks. Should the B Bank succeed? Why?

9. Robert Smith, president of XYZ, Inc., was sued by the payee of a promissory note that was signed "XYZ, Inc.," and immediately thereunder, "Robert Smith." Is Smith personally liable on the note? Why?

10. The B Bank lent money to X Company in exchange for its promissory note. P, the president of the company, indorsed the note on the back, guaranteeing payment if the corporation defaulted. B sued X and received a judgment, but the company failed to pay the entire amount. B now sues P to recover the unpaid portion. Is P liable? Why?

23

Secured Transactions: Basic Concepts

1. Introduction

A creditor may extend credit to a debtor and simply look to the debtor for payment. Such creditors are called *unsecured creditors.* If the debtor fails to pay, the unsecured creditor may sue the debtor and obtain a judgment. Then, as a *judgment creditor,* he may pursue the enforcement procedures available to a judgment creditor that were discussed in Chapter 3. The lawsuit to obtain the judgment and the enforcement procedures are costly in both time and money. An unsecured creditor usually loses a significant portion of his claim if resort to legal remedies is necessary to collect the amount due.

Unsecured creditors suffer another disadvantage when compared with secured creditors. Many debtors are either insolvent or bankrupt and unable to pay all their debts. When this occurs, some creditors and some debts are either not paid in full or sometimes not paid at all. In this event, the unsecured creditor simply suffers a loss. However, the secured creditor has either someone else or property to turn to for the payment. When the secured creditor has property of the debtor to turn to for payment, the secured creditor is in effect given priority over unsecured creditors.

Debts may be secured by personal property (a secured transaction), real estate (a mortgage or mechanic's lien), or another individual (suretyship). These matters are covered in Chapters 23–26.

415

2. Article 9 of the Code

A *secured transaction* is one in which a borrower or a buyer gives security in the form of personal property to a lender or a seller that an obligation (usually the payment of money) will be satisfied. Secured transactions occur at all levels of commerce. For example, manufacturers finance raw materials, retailers and wholesalers finance inventory, and consumers finance their purchases by giving their creditors security in the form of personal property. These transactions take many forms, but they are all secured transactions under Article 9 of the Code.

The simplest form of secured transaction is a *pledge*. In a pledge transaction, a borrower gives the physical possession of his property—for example, a watch—to a lender as security for a loan. If the loan is not repaid, the lender can sell the watch to satisfy the debt. Stocks and bonds are frequently used as collateral in pledge transactions. In many transactions, the pledge is not satisfactory as a security arrangement because it requires that possession of the personal property be delivered to the creditor. Therefore, security devices that allow the debtor to retain the possession and use of the property have been developed. In the early law, these devices were covered by different statutes and separate rules of law. Among the common terms used to describe such security arrangements were chattel mortgages, conditional sales contracts, trust receipts, factor's liens, and assignment of accounts receivable. These terms continue to be used even though they have been replaced by a single security device under the Code: the *security interest*. Whatever name is used, the purpose of the secured transaction is to give a creditor an interest in the debtor's personal property that the creditor can use to obtain satisfaction of the debt in the event of nonpayment. Such personal property is called *collateral* (9-105[1][c]).

Article 9 as originally written is not the law in very many states today. Nonuniform amendments to 47 of the 54 sections of Article 9 have been adopted by various states. Some sections of Article 9 have been amended by as many as 30 states. As a result, in 1972 a new official text and comments were published. Several states have adopted the Revised Article 9 of the Code and most others are considering it. Therefore, as this chapter and Chapter 24 are studied, it should be kept in mind that the law in this area is in a state of flux. The statutes of each state must be carefully examined not only to see if the revision has been adopted but also to see which of the many amendments to the original Code are applicable. It must be understood that Article 9 is correctly described as the "Un-Uniform Commercial Code."

We will indicate some of the areas of major change in the Revised Article 9 in the sections that follow. Revised Article 9 is included in the appendix, and code section citations in the text refer to it. The Code citations in some cases are to the original Article 9, and thus they may be different.

3. The Scope of Article 9

Although Article 9 deals primarily with secured transactions, it also covers outright sales of certain types of property, such as accounts receivable (9-102 [1][b]). Thus, a sale of the accounts receivable of a business must comply with the Code requirements to the same extent as would be the case if the accounts were used as security for a loan.

Except for sales, such as those of accounts receivable, the main test to be applied in determining whether a given transaction falls within the purview of Article 9 is whether it was intended to have effect as security. Every transaction with such intent is covered (9-102[1][a]). For example, a lease with option to buy may be considered a security transaction rather than a lease if the necessary intent is present.

Certain credit transactions are expressly excluded from Article 9 coverage (9-104). The exclusions in general are transactions that are not basically of a commercial character, such as landlord's liens, wage assignments, or a transfer of an insurance policy. One important exclusion is liens given by state law for services and materials—for example, the artisan's lien given to a person who repairs a car.

4. Terminology

A "security interest" is an interest in personal property or "fixtures" that secures either payment of money or performance of an obligation (1-201 [37]). The reference to "fixtures" is included because personal property is often affixed to real property, in which event it is called a fixture (9-102[1]). The security interest results from the execution by the parties of a "security agreement" covering the debtor's collateral. The parties to the security agreement are the "debtor," who owes the obligation and is giving the security, and the "secured party," lender, seller, or other person in whose favor there is a security interest (9-105[1][d]).

Thus, the typical transaction involves an agreement between a debtor and a secured party (security agreement) whereby the debtor agrees to give the secured party a security interest in the debtor's collateral.

Before a security interest is effective between the parties, it must *attach* to the collateral (9-203); and before it is effective to give priority over the rights of third parties, the security interest must be *perfected* (9-301). Attachment is the means whereby the secured party acquires rights in the collateral; perfection is the method whereby the secured party is given priority over claims of third parties. Perfection usually occurs by the filing of a *financing* statement.

CLASSIFICATIONS OF COLLATERAL

5. Introduction

Collateral may be classified according to its physical makeup into (1) tangible, physical property or goods; (2) purely intangible property, such as an account receivable; and (3) property that has physical existence, such as a negotiable instrument, but is simply representative of a contractual obligation. Each type of collateral presents its own peculiar problems, and the framework of Article 9 is structured on the peculiarities of each type. There may be a security interest not only in the collateral itself but also in the proceeds of the sale of the collateral (9-306[1]). The method of perfecting the security interest depends upon the classification of the collateral.

6. Goods as Collateral

Four classifications of goods are established: consumer goods, equipment, inventory, and farm products. In determining the classification of any particular item of goods, it is necessary to take into account not only the physical attributes but also the status of the debtor who is either buying the property or using it as security for a loan, and the use the debtor will make of the goods. Keep in mind that the classification will determine the place of filing to perfect the security interest against third parties. It may also affect the rights of the debtor on default.

Consumer Goods.   Goods fall into this classification if they are used or bought primarily for personal, family, or household purposes (9-109[1]).

Equipment.   Goods that are used or bought for use primarily in a business, in farming, in a profession, or by a nonprofit organization or government agency fall within this category (9-109[2]). The category is something of a "catchall," so that goods that otherwise defy classification are treated as equipment. Equipment often becomes attached to realty so as to constitute a "fixture," so that the discussion on fixtures later is especially significant for this classification of goods.

Inventory.   Inventory consists of goods that are held by a person for sale or lease or are to be furnished under a contract of service. They may be raw materials, work in process, completed goods, or material used or consumed in a business (9-109[4]). The basic test to be applied in determining whether goods are inventory is whether they are held for immediate or ultimate sale or lease. The reason for the inclusion of materials used or consumed in a business—for example, supplies of fuel, and boxes and other containers to be used in packaging the goods—is that they will soon be used up or consumed in a course of production resulting in an end product that will be sold. A security interest in inventory automatically covers after-acquired inventory.[1]

[1] *In re Fibre Glass Boat Corporation,* page 427.

Farm Products. This category includes crops and livestock, supplies used or produced in farming operations, and the products of crops or live-stock in their unmanufactured state (e.g., ginned cotton, wool, milk, and eggs) —provided that such items are in the possession of a debtor who is engaged in farming operations (9-109[3]). Farm products are *not* equipment or inventory. Note that goods cease to be farm products and must therefore be reclassified when (1) they are no longer in the farmer's possession, or (2) they have been subjected to a manufacturing process. Thus, when the farmer delivers his farm products to a marketing agency for sale or to a frozen-food processor as raw materials, the products in the hands of the other party are inventory. Likewise, if the farmer maintained a canning operation, the canned product would be inventory even though it remained in his possession.

The proper classification of goods is determined on the basis of their nature and the intended use to be made of them by the debtor. For example, a television set in a dealer's warehouse is inventory to the dealer. When the set is sold and delivered to a consumer-customer, it becomes a consumer good. If an identical set were sold on the same terms to the owner of a tavern to be used for entertaining his customers, the set would be equipment in the hands of the tavern owner. The secured party cannot rely on the classification furnished by the debtor. All facts must be analyzed to ensure proper classification and proper filing.[2]

7. "Semi-intangible" Collateral

Three types of property paper are included for convenience under this heading: documents of title, chattel paper, and instruments. They comprise various categories of paper used in commerce that are either negotiable or to some extent dealt with as though negotiable. They are all evidenced by an "indispensable writing" and are representative of obligations and rights.

Documents of Title. Included under this heading are bills of lading, warehouse receipts, and any other document that in the regular course of business or financing is treated as sufficient evidence that the person in possession of it is entitled to receive, hold, and dispose of the document and the goods it covers (1-201[15]).

Chattel Paper. Chattel paper refers to a writing or writings that evidence both (1) an obligation to pay money, and (2) a security interest in or a lease of specific goods (9-105[1][b]). The chattel paper is *itself* a security agreement. A security agreement in the form of a conditional sales contract, for example, is often executed in connection with a negotiable note or a series of notes. The group of writings—the contract plus the note—taken together as a composite constitute "chattel paper." A typical situation involving chattel paper as collateral is one in which a secured party who has obtained it in a transaction with his customer may wish to borrow against it in his own financ-

---

[2] *In re McClain,* page 428.

ing. To illustrate: A dealer sells an electric generator to a customer on a conditional sales contract, and the customer signs a negotiable installment note. At this point, the contract is the security agreement; the dealer is the secured party; the customer is the debtor; and the generator is the collateral–equipment. The dealer, needing funds for working capital, transfers the contract and the note to a finance company as security for a loan. In the transaction between dealer and finance company, the contract and note are the collateral–chattel paper; the finance company is the secured party; the dealer is the debtor; and the customer is now designated as the "account debtor."

Instrument. As distinguished from chattel paper, an *instrument* means (1) a negotiable instrument, (2) a security such as stocks and bonds, or (3) any other writing that evidences a right to the payment of money and is not itself a *security agreement or lease* (9-105[i]). To qualify as an instrument, the "other writing" must also be one that is in ordinary course of business transferred by indorsement or assignment. Thus, the classification includes in addition to negotiable instruments those that are recognized as having some negotiable attributes. Instruments are frequently used as collateral, and they present certain problems in this connection because of their negotiable character.

8. Intangible Collateral

Under this heading are three items: (1) accounts, (2) contract rights, and (3) "general intangibles." They are distinguished from the "semi-intangibles" discussed in the preceding section by virtue of the fact that they are not represented by an indispensable writing.

Account. *Account* means any right to payment arising out of the sale of goods or the rendition of services that is not evidenced by either an instrument or chattel paper (9-106). It is an account receivable and represents a right to payment earned by the seller's performance—the sale of goods or services actually rendered.

Contract Right. This is a right to payment under a contract, which right has not yet been earned, but rather is to be earned by performance under an existing contract (9-106). A contract does exist, and when the party performs his obligations under the contract, his potential account becomes an account receivable. This form of collateral is deleted in the Revised Article 9.

General Intangibles. This heading includes miscellaneous types of intangible personal property that may be used as commercial security and do not fall within any of the preceding five classifications of intangible or semi-intangible property. Examples are goodwill, literary rights, patents, and copyrights (9-106).

CREATION OF THE SECURITY INTEREST

9. The Security Agreement

The creation of a valid security interest as between the parties first of all requires a security agreement. The security agreement must be in writing, unless the security arrangement is a possessory one and the secured party is in possession of the collateral (9-203[1]). The only other formal requirements are that the agreement be signed by the debtor and that it contain a description of the collateral sufficient to reasonably identify it. The security agreement will usually contain many other provisions. The forms in general use include a statement of the amount of the obligation and the terms of repayment; the debtor's duties in respect to the collateral, such as insuring it; and the rights of the secured party on default. In general, the parties can include such terms and provisions as they may deem appropriate to their particular transaction, but there are a few limitations on this freedom to contract in the interest of fairness to the debtor.

10. Attachment

A security interest is not enforceable between the debtor and the secured party until it attaches to the collateral. A security interest attaches to collateral when three events have occurred: when (1) there is an agreement that it attaches, (2) value is given, and (3) the debtor has rights in the collateral (9-204[1]).[3] They may occur in any order. For example, a security agreement may be executed and the secured party may give value—e.g., loan money—to the debtor before the debtor acquires rights in the collateral.

Value for purpose of attachment is defined somewhat differently than it is in commercial paper. Basically, value means that a secured party has furnished to the debtor any consideration sufficient to support a simple contract (1-201 [44]). For example, a bank lends $10,000 to a merchant and takes a security interest in his inventory; the loan of money constitutes the value.

The third requirement for attachment is that the debtor have *rights in the collateral*. A debtor has no rights (1) in crops until they are planted or otherwise become growing crops, or in the young of livestock until they are conceived; (2) in fish until they are caught; (3) in oil, gas, or minerals until they are extracted; (4) in timber until it is cut. A debtor has no rights in an account until it comes into existence—until goods have been sold, there could not be an account receivable. Although a merchant could enter into an agreement to assign future accounts to a secured party, the latter's security interest could not *attach* until the accounts actually came into existence.

The security agreement may provide that property acquired by the debtor at any later time shall also secure the obligation covered by the security agree-

---

[3] *C.I.T. Financial Serv.* v. *First Nat. Bank,* page 429.

ment. This means that if such a clause were included in the security agreement, *after-acquired property* of the debtor would be additional security for the secured party—i.e., as soon as the debtor acquires rights in other property, a security interest would attach to such property in favor of the secured party (9-204). This obviously binds a debtor quite severely, and the Code places a limitation on the effect of after-acquired property clauses in relation to consumer goods on the theory that such clauses are best suited to commercial transactions and might work an undue hardship on a consumer. Thus, no security interest can attach under an after-acquired property clause in consumer goods other than accessions that are given as additional security unless the consumer obtains the goods within ten days after the secured party gives value (9-204). The original Code had a similar provision limiting the security interest in crops to one year. The revised Code eliminated this rule on crops because it did not accomplish its goal of limiting security interests in crops. Lenders avoided the rule by filing a financing statement and then executing a new security agreement each year.

PERFECTION OF THE SECURITY INTEREST

11. In General

The security agreement creates the security interest in the debtor's collateral as between the secured party and the debtor. This is not sufficient, however, to give the secured party priority over other persons who may claim an interest in the collateral. Such claims could arise in a variety of circumstances. The debtor's other creditors might seek to have the collateral sold to satisfy their claims. The debtor might give a security interest in the same collateral to another person, or the debtor might sell the collateral to another person. Finally, the debtor might become bankrupt, and the trustee might seek to include the collateral as an asset of the bankrupt estate. An unperfected security interest is in general subordinate to the claims of others who acquire an interest in the collateral without knowledge of the unperfected security interest, even though it is subsequently perfected.

To have a valid security interest and priority over third persons claiming an interest in the property, the secured party must "perfect" the security interest (9-303[1]). Perfection entails giving notice to third persons that the secured party has a security interest in the debtor's collateral, so that others can take this into account in their dealings with the debtor.

There are three methods for perfecting a security interest: (1) perfection by possession, (2) perfection by attachment, and (3) perfection by filing. Several factors must be taken into account in determining which of the three methods of perfection is appropriate in any given transaction: (1) the kind of collateral in which a security interest was created, (2) the use the debtor intends to make of the collateral, and (3) the status of the debtor in relation to the secured party.

Before discussing these three methods of perfection, it should be kept in mind that even a perfected security interest is subordinate to some third-party rights. For example, a person who repairs or improves the collateral may have an artisan's lien for his services and materials that is superior to the secured party's interest (9-310). In the case of inventory, a buyer from the debtor in the ordinary course of business will obtain title to the goods free of the perfected security interest. There is an exception to this general rule for farm products. A buyer of farm products in the ordinary course of business does not take them free of perfected security interests (9-307).[4]

12. Perfection by Possession

The simplest way to give notice of a security interest is for the secured party to take possession of the collateral (9-305). For example, the delivery of pledged property is the means of perfecting a security interest in it. The possession of the collateral by the secured party gives notice of his security interest—hence no public filing is required. As noted previously, the possessory security interest does not require a written security agreement. Therefore, this is the simplest method of handling a secured transaction. However, its use is quite limited, because most debtors either need or want possession of the collateral.

Possession is the required method of perfection of a security interest in instruments. It is the optional method in the case of collateral consisting of goods, negotiable documents of title, and chattel paper (9-305). However, possession is the only method whereby complete protection in documents and chattel paper can be obtained, since (1) the rights of holders to whom a document has been negotiated by the debtor will prevail over the secured party, even though there has been a filing; and (2) the purchaser of chattel paper from the debtor is given such protection if he takes without *actual notice* of the security interest, gives new value, and takes possession in the ordinary course of his business (9-308).

However, in the case of instruments, the secured party has a perfected security interest for a period of 21 days after the security interest attaches even though he does not take possession. The grace period applies only if the secured party gave new value to the debtor—it would not apply if the security interest in the instrument were given to buttress an existing obligation. Also, for the grace period to apply, it is necessary that there be a *written* security agreement (9-304[4]). The grace period is in keeping with normal commercial necessity, but unless the secured party takes possession of the instrument, his rights will be defeated if the debtor transfers the instrument to a holder in due course during the 21-day period.

---

[4] *United States* v. *McCleskey Mills, Inc.*, page 430.

A 21-day grace period during which the security interest is protected against creditors of the debtor without possession or filing is also provided in the case of *negotiable documents* (9-304[4]). The same risk exists that the documents may be negotiated to a good-faith holder, who, of course, would prevail, and the same requirements of a written security agreement and new value by the secured party apply.

Special considerations are required if a negotiable document of title has been issued covering goods, since there could theoretically be a security interest in both the *goods* and a *document* such as a warehouse receipt or bill of lading that *represents the goods*. This problem is resolved by a provision that no separate security interest can exist in the goods and at the same time in the document, during the period that the goods are in the *possession of the issuer* of a negotiable document (9-304[2]). Therefore, the creditor with a security interest in the document prevails. Possession of goods by a bailee gives notice to any potential financier or purchaser that a document of title may be outstanding and that he should proceed with caution.

A different rule applies if the goods in the hands of a bailee are covered by a *nonnegotiable* document or if no document has been issued. In these circumstances, a security interest in goods in the hands of a bailee may be perfected (1) by issuance of a document in the name of the secured party, (2) by giving the bailee proper notice of the secured party's interest, or (3) by filing as to the goods themselves (9-304[3]).

For a variety of commercial reasons, it may be necessary or desirable that the secured party with a possessory security interest temporarily release possession of the collateral to the debtor. Since the release is of short duration, it would be cumbersome to require a filing. The Code therefore provides that a security interest *remains perfected* for a period of 21 days without filing where a secured party having a *perfected* security interest releases the collateral to the debtor. This grace period applies only to (1) instruments, (2) negotiable documents, and (3) goods in the hands of a bailee not covered by a negotiable document of title. The purposes for which the collateral may be released to the debtor, in the case of *goods* or *documents* representing the goods, are limited to making them available to the debtor (1) for the purpose of ultimate sale or exchange, or (2) for purposes such as loading, unloading, storing, shipping, transshipping, manufacturing, processing, or otherwise dealing with them in a manner preliminary to their sale or exchange (9-304[5]).

In the case of a temporary release of an *instrument* to the debtor, the purpose must be to enable the debtor to make a presentation of it, collect it, renew it, obtain registration of a transfer, or make an ultimate sale or exchange. The risk attendant upon such a release—an improper or unauthorized negotiation to a holder or a sale to a bona fide purchaser by the debtor—is always present.

13. Perfection by Attachment

The second method of perfection is by the attachment of the security interest without further action being required. This method is restricted to transactions involving installment sales to consumers and to sales of farm equipment that have a purchase price of $2,500 or less (9-302). The latter provision on farm equipment is deleted in the Revised Article 9. The Revised Article 9 eliminates farm equipment from perfection by attachment because the effect of the law had been to make farm equipment unacceptable as collateral to many lenders. The transaction must be a purchase-money security interest, one that is related to the purchase of goods. In such transactions, the secured party obtains a perfected security interest without filing a financing statement.[5]

The protection afforded the secured party is limited in perfection by attachment. He is protected against the claims of creditors of the debtor and from others to whom the farmer or consumer debtor may give a security interest in the collateral, but he is *not* protected against the rights of a consumer or farmer (as the case may be) good-faith purchaser from the debtor. For example, if another consumer buys the collateral from the debtor-consumer without knowledge of the security interest, the purchaser will take the collateral free of the security interest (9-307[2]). The secured party can obtain protection against this risk by filing a financing statement if he wishes to do so. The exemption from the filing requirement does not apply if the collateral is a motor vehicle that is required to be licensed.

14. Perfection by Filing—The "Financing Statement"

The most common method of perfecting a security interest is by filing a "financing statement." The financing statement, which is to be distinguished from the *security agreement,* is a document signed by both the debtor and the secured party, which contains a description of the collateral and indicates that debtor and secured party have entered into a security agreement and gives their addresses. Simple forms are available that contain spaces for additional provisions as agreed upon by the parties, but this basic information is all that is required. If crops or fixtures constitute the collateral, then the financing statement must include a description of the real estate concerned (9-402).

A financing statement is not a substitute for a security agreement. A security agreement may be filed as a financing statement if it contains the required information and is signed by both parties, but a financing statement will usually not qualify as a security agreement. However, filing the security agreement would make public information that the parties might prefer to have remain confidential, and for this reason there will usually be a separate financing statement.

[5] *Kimbrell's Furniture Company, Inc.* v. *Friedman,* page 431.

The purpose of filing is to give notice that the secured party who filed it may have a security interest in the described collateral. Potential creditors are charged with the task of going to the recorder's office to check to see if the proposed collateral is already encumbered. A person searching the records therefore obtains minimal information, and further inquiry from the parties to the financing statement is required to obtain more complete information.[6] A procedure is established for such disclosure by the secured party at the request of the debtor.

The financing statement may provide a maturity or expiration date, but more often it is silent on this point, since the statement usually will not mention the debt or obligation. In the absence of such data, the filing is effective for a period of five years, subject to being renewed by the filing of a continuation statement signed by the secured party (9-403[2]). If so renewed, it continues the effectiveness of the original statement for another five years.

The presence in the records of a financing statement constitutes a burden upon the debtor, since it reveals to all persons with whom he may be dealing that his property is or may be subject to the claims of others. Therefore, the Code provides for the filing of a *termination statement* to clear the record when the secured party is no longer entitled to a security interest. Failure of the secured party to send a termination statement within ten days after written demand by the debtor subjects him to a $100 penalty and also renders him liable for any loss occasioned to the debtor (9-404[1]).

Filing a financing statement is *required* in order to perfect a nonpossessory security interest in most secured transactions. As a general rule, filing is required in the case of an assignment of accounts receivable or contract rights. However, an exception exists for certain isolated transactions. If the assignment does not encompass a significant portion of the outstanding accounts or contract rights of the assignor, filing is not required (9-302[1][e]).

The Code allows the various states three alternative methods in regard to the place where the financing statement is to be filed. A state may choose a central filing system, a local filing system, or a combination (9-401). A central filing system means that all filing is in the state capital except for fixtures, which are filed locally. Local filing means that filing is at the county level. Most states have enacted dual filing systems. The usual system requires local filing for fixtures, local filing for farm-related collateral and consumer goods, and central filing for other collateral, such as inventory and equipment.

The Code makes special provisions for goods such as motor vehicles that have a certificate of title. The filing requirements of the Code do not apply, and the usual method of indicating a security interest is to have it noted on the certificate of title (9-302[3]). If the security interest is properly perfected on the certificate of title, the security interest is valid even though a substitute certificate of title fails to disclose the interest of the secured party.[7]

6 *Crete State Bank* v. *Lauhoff Grain Co.*, page 432
7 *Ford Motor Credit Co.* v. *Quality Motors*, page 433.

SECURED TRANSACTIONS: BASIC CONCEPTS CASES

In re Fibre Glass Boat Corporation
324 F.Supp. 1054 (1971)

FULTON, J. . . . Teleflex Industrial Products, Inc. filed a claim in bankruptcy as a secured creditor with a security interest in certain assets of the bankrupt, including "all inventory used in the production of boats." It supported its claim with a financing statement and a letter from the comptroller of the bankrupt, Fibre Glass, to the creditor-claimant, Teleflex, dated February 18, 1969, which provided:

> Pursuant to our telephone conversation, please find a duly executed copy of a financing statement received from your company, wherein the Fibre Glass Boat Corp. agrees to guarantee [sic] all inventory used in the production of boats, limited in the amount of fifteen thousand dollars, in order to cover all merchandise that may be purchased from your company.

By considering both the letter and the financing statement together, the Bankruptcy Court found that claimant Teleflex had a valid security interest in the inventory of Fibre Glass Boat used in the production of boats *as of the date of the bankruptcy.*

Petitioner has presented two issues on review: whether the Referee erred in finding that the letter and the financing statement gave rise to a valid security interest and whether the Referee erred in holding that the creditor-claimant Teleflex was entitled to a security interest in the specific inventory as of the date of the bankruptcy where no after-acquired property clause appeared in either the letter or the financing statement.

Section 9-109 of the Uniform Commercial Code classifies "goods" into four groups. Goods are "inventory if they are held by a person who holds them for sale or lease or to be furnished under contracts of services or if he has so furnished them, or if they are raw materials, work in progress or materials used or consumed in a business. Inventory of a person is not to be classified as his equipment." "Equipment," on the other hand, as defined by § 9-109, includes goods used or purchased for use primarily in business which are not inventory. According to Official Comment 3, U.C.C. § 9-109, goods are equipment when they are fixed assets or have a relatively long use. Inventory, in contrast, is goods used up or consumed in the production of an end product or held or prepared for sale.

It is clear that claimant Teleflex holds a valid security interest in the bankrupt's inventory used in the production of boats. . . . [A] security interest is not enforceable against third parties unless the debtor has signed a security agreement which contains a description of the collateral. Thus, to be a "security agreement" an agreement must be written, contain the debtor's signature, and contain a description of the collateral. An added step is necessary for the agreement to "attach"; value must be given and the debtor must obtain rights in the collateral. To "perfect" the interest, the third step of filing a financing statement must be taken. "Perfected" security interests ordinarily take priority over unperfected but attached interests.

In this case, a financing statement was filed with the proper State authorities in accord with Florida law. Both the creditor and the debtor signed it and it contained a description of the collateral. Additionally, the debtor Fibre Glass sent a signed letter to Teleflex describing the collateral. These two instruments certainly create a perfected security interest. The three formal elements necessary to create a security interest—a writing, the debtor's signature, and a description of the collateral—are present in the letter, and the letter fulfills the requirements of § 9-204, attachment. The financing statement "perfected" this interest.

The second issue presented by the petitioner is whether this security interest creates a lien upon inventory used in the production of boats acquired *after* entry into the agreement. Since neither the letter nor the financing statement contain an after-acquired property clause, it is urged by the petitioner that Teleflex has no rights in inventory acquired afterwards. Section 9-204(3), U.C.C. validates the use of after-acquired property provisions in financing transactions. "A security agreement *may* provide that collateral, whenever acquired, shall secure all obligations covered by the security agreement." A debtor's intent to grant a security interest in after-acquired property must be judged from the language of the agreement. According to *In re Taylor Products, Inc.,* 5 U.C.C. Reporting Service 286 (W.D. Mich. 1968), to permit an interest in property acquired after the execution of the security agreement, the agreement must so provide.

However, the property secured in this case is inventory, goods held for sale and goods consumed in the business. Inventory by its nature and definition changes from day to day. In *Bank of Utica* v. *Smith Richfield Springs, Inc.,* 58 Misc.2d 113, 294 N.Y.2d 797 (1968), it was held that the collateral "motor vehicles" gave the creditor a security interest over after-acquired motor vehicles. Adding the words "after-acquired" to the collateral's description was not necessary because the debtor, an automobile dealer, was obviously buying and selling cars in pursuit of that business. Surely the creditor would not enter into a financing arrangement secured by collateral fixed on a particular date where the collateral by its nature would be constantly changing. It would be straining the normal meaning of the word to imply that inventory meant only that on hand on the particular day the contract was executed, and if a can of paint or the like were used, the collateral would be diminished to that extent. Certainly the parties contemplated that the inventory would be sold or used and replaced; that is what inventory means. Thereupon it is

Ordered and adjudged that the petition for review be and the same is hereby denied.

In re McClain
447 F.2d 241 (1971)

BREITENSTEIN, J. . . . In this voluntary bankruptcy proceeding the question is whether the appellee Utica Square National Bank of Tulsa is a secured or an unsecured creditor. Over the objections of the trustee, the referee held that the bank was a secured creditor and the district court affirmed.

The bankrupt purchased a Chevrolet pickup truck from an automobile dealer in February, 1969, and executed a promissory note and a separate security agreement–financing statement. In that statement he warranted, by checking a box thereon, that the pickup was to be used primarily "In Business." The dealer assigned the note and the purchase-money security interest to the bank for value. In reliance on the "In Business" designation the bank filed the security agreement in Oklahoma County, Oklahoma.

The bankruptcy proceedings were begun in April, 1970. The bank filed a proof of secured claim and the trustee objected thereto on the ground that the security agreement had not been filed in the proper county. The trustee contends that despite the "In Business" designation the pickup had always been used as consumer goods and that the security agreement had to be filed in Tulsa County, the county of the debtor's residence. The trustee offered evidence that the bankrupt never used the pickup for business purposes and, hence, his intent at the time of purchase was not to use it primarily for business purposes. The bank objected. . . . The referee sustained the objection and the district court affirmed.

Oklahoma has adopted the Uniform Commercial Code. An automobile comes within the term "goods" as there defined. Goods are classified into four categories: consumer goods, equipment, farm products, and inventory. The classes are mutually exclusive, and the goods cannot be in two categories at the same time as to the same person.

The perfection of a security interest by filing requires the determination of the proper county in which to file. If the collateral is classified as consumer goods, the proper county in which to file is the county of the debtor's residence, in this case Tulsa County.

If business equipment, the security agreement is to be filed with the county clerk of Oklahoma County. In the case before us the bank filed in Oklahoma County.

The Bankruptcy Act allows the trustee to elect the status of an ideal lien creditor. As such he is in the position of a third-party lien creditor without notice. His priority is determined by the substantive law of the state where the property is located. In Oklahoma an unperfected security interest is subordinate to the rights of a person who becomes a lien creditor without knowledge of the security interest and before it is perfected.

The bank argues that the warranty of use in the security agreement is conclusive. We believe that this is foreclosed by *National Bank of Commerce* v. *First National Bank and Trust*

Company of Tulsa, Okl., 446 P.2d 277, a case involving priority of security interests as affected by the filing requirements of § 9-401. The court there said that the primary issue was "the classification of the [automobile] as equipment, consumer goods or inventory, to determine the proper place of filing." In making the determination the court looked to extrinsic facts and did not give conclusive effect to the warranty in the security agreement. This expression of Oklahoma law is binding on us.

The National Bank of Commerce decision comports with Comment 2 to § 9-109 which says that "the principal use to which the property is put should be considered determinative." Further, in bankruptcy situations involving the Uniform Commercial Code the courts have independently inquired into the classification and filing of collateral. The difficult position in which the bank is placed results from Oklahoma law. The only answer would seem to be that a creditor in doubt about the proper classification of collateral should file in all possible counties where filing might be required. . . .

Reversed and remanded.

C.I.T. Financial Serv. v. First Nat. Bank
344 So.2d 125 (Miss.) 1977

LEE, J. . . . The Circuit Court of the First Judicial District of Hinds County entered a replevin judgment for a mobile home in favor of the First National Bank of Jackson (FNB) and C.I.T. Financial Services Corporation (CIT) appeals. We affirm.

On May 14, 1974, Glenn Duke Mobile Home Sales, Inc. (Duke) received a mobile home from American Way Homes, serial no. 1495, and was issued the manufacturer's statement of origin and invoice which transferred title to it. On June 26, 1974, Duke sold the home to Jeanie E. Holmes, who made a down payment of one thousand dollars ($1,000). FNB financed the balance of seven thousand two hundred thirty-seven dollars twenty-five

cents ($7,237.25), Duke assigned its security instrument to FNB, and the financing statement was recorded in Rankin County where the home was situated. Holmes became dissatisfied with his purchase and declined to make the monthly payments. FNB directed its service agent, Mobile Home Services (MHS), to repossess the home and MHS moved it to Duke's place of business. FNB expected to be paid the balance of the defaulted note by its insurer and, for that purpose, cancelled its filing statement.

CIT began financing mobile homes for Duke in the fall of 1974. On November 15, 1974, it paid forty-three thousand two hundred ninety-nine dollars ninety-seven cents ($43,-

299.97) for eight (8) units. In return, CIT received a manufacturer's statement of origin on the units. Among them was a statement dated November 14, 1974, for one (1) home, serial no. 1495. This manufacturer's statement of origin was identical to the manufacturer's statement of origin issued to Duke May 14, 1974, except it indicated the home was for the year 1975 rather than 1974. CIT filed an inventory financing statement with the Chancery Clerk of Hinds County covering all said units, but did not inspect them upon receipt of the statements of origin. The parties agreed that there is only one mobile home with the serial no. 1495, that the correct year is for 1974, and that the two statements of origin with the serial no. 1495 relate to the mobile home involved in the suit.

Mississippi Code Annotated § 75-9-204(1) (1972) provides the following:

> (1) A security interest cannot attach until there is agreement (subsection (3) of Section 1-201) (§ 75-1-201(3)) that it attach and value is given and the

debtor has rights in the collateral. It attaches as soon as all of the events in the preceding sentence have taken place unless explicit agreement postpones the time of attaching.

In order for CIT to prevail, its security interest in the collateral must have attached. Duke conveyed the home to Jeanie E. Holmes on June 26, 1974, and title remained vested in Holmes. When Duke assigned the security instrument to FNB, title remained in Holmes and the security remained in FNB. Even though a statement of origin was issued to Duke on November 14, 1974, it was not effective to convey any title or interest and no title or interest passed from Duke to CIT. Since Duke had no rights in the collateral, CIT's security interest never attached. . . .

For the reasons stated, we are of the opinion that the trial court was correct in entering judgment for FNB and the case must be and is affirmed.

Affirmed.

United States v. McCleskey Mills, Inc.
409 F.2d 1216 (1969)

McCleskey Mills is in the business of buying and selling farm products including peanuts. The company advances cash to the farmers with whom it deals. In 1963 an advance was made to Steve Smith, a farmer, and there was no security for the advance. The Farmers Home Administration (henceforth called FHA) also loaned money to Smith under the Farm Tenant Act. In February 1964 Smith executed a security agreement to FHA, including his 1964 peanut crop. The agreement was perfected by filing. In October 1964 Smith transferred 12,000 pounds of his crop to McCleskey Mills to be credited against his account. McCleskey Mills did not know of FHA's security interest and had been assured by Smith that the crop was free and clear. McCleskey Mills resold the peanuts, and the government brought this action against McCleskey for conversion

of the peanuts and sought to recover their value. The lower court ruled that McCleskey's undisputed good faith in buying the peanuts precluded recovery by the government. The government appealed from this ruling.

WISDOM, J. . . . Under the scheme imposed by Article Nine of the Code, the United States obtained a perfected security interest in Steve Smith's 1964 peanut crop on February 5, 1964, the day that it filed its financing statement, or whenever the crop was planted thereafter, whichever came last. The perfected security interest would not, it is true, withstand challenge by most "buyer[s] in ordinary course of business." Such buyers . . . take free of previously perfected security interests, for the sake of untrammeled commercial dealing. Section 109A-9-307(1) specifically excepts from that exalted class of buyers in the ordinary course of business, however, "a person buying farm products from a person engaged in farming operations." It can hardly be denied that McCleskey Mills here fits the description of the excluded class of buyers. McCleskey cannot therefore invoke the strong protection afforded a buyer in the ordinary course of business.

. . . [A] security interest continues in collateral notwithstanding sale, exchange, or other disposition by the debtor unless his action was authorized by the secured party in the security agreement or otherwise.

. . . [T]he secured party may in such cases maintain an action for conversion against the subsequent purchaser. This principle underlies the effective operation of any recording system: subsequent transferees, unless they are entitled to special protection, must be on notice of any recorded and hostile interest in the land or chattels they receive. Subjective innocence will not ward off liability. Since the Code makes no exceptions for buyers such as McCleskey Mills, and since the Government had perfected its security interest prior to the purchase from Smith by McCleskey, "the secured party . . . [has] the right to follow collateral into the hands of good faith purchasers for value and to have recovery, by any action in replevin or conversion the law of the relevant state may allow."

The decision of the district court is accordingly reversed and remanded for further proceedings consistent with this opinion.

Kimbrell's Furniture Company, Inc. v. Friedman
198 S.E.2d 803 (S.C.) 1973

The plaintiff furniture company sold a television set and tape player to a customer on a conditional sale contract designated a purchase-money security agreement. On the day of the purchase, the customer pledged the items to Bonded Loan (a pawnbroker) as security for a loan. Kimbrell did not file any financing statement. The lower court ruled that the pawnbroker's lien was prior to the unrecorded purchase security interest of Kimbrell. Kimbrell appealed.

LEWIS, J. The question to be decided is Correctly stated by appellant as follows: Is a conditional seller of consumer goods required to file a financing statement in order to perfect his security interest against a pawnbroker who subsequently takes possession of such goods as security for a loan? . . .

Goods are classified or defined for purposes of secured transactions under Section 10.9-109. Subsection 1 defines "consumer goods" as those "used or bought for use primarily for personal, family or household purposes." The property here involved was a television set and tape player. They are normally used for personal, family or household purposes and the purchasers warranted that such was the intended use. It is undisputed in this case that the collateral involved was consumer goods within the meaning of the foregoing statutory definition.

Kimbrell clearly held a *purchase-money security interest* in the consumer goods sold to the O'Neals and, by them, subsequently pledged to Bonded Loan.

When filing is required to perfect a security interest, the UCC requires that a document designated as a financing statement must be filed. . . . The UCC does not require filing in order to perfect a purchase-money security interest in consumer goods. Pertinent here, Section 10.9-302(1)(d) provides:

(1) A financing statement must be filed to perfect all security interests except the following: . . .

(d) a purchase money security interest in consumer goods; . . .

Since filing was not necessary, the security interest of Kimbrell attached and was perfected when the debtors executed the purchase-money security agreements and took possession of the property. Therefore, Kimbrell's security interest has priority over the security interest of Bonded Loan by virtue of Section 10.9-312(4) which provides:

> (4) A purchase money security interest in collateral other than inventory has priority over a conflicting security interest in the same collateral if the purchase money security interest is perfected at the time the debtor receives possession of the collateral or within ten days thereafter. . . .

Bonded Loan, however, alleges that its interest takes priority over the security interest of Kimbrell by virtue of Section 10.9-307(1) which is as follows:

> (1) A buyer in ordinary course of business other than a person buying farm products from a person engaged in farming operations takes free of a security interest created by his seller even though

the security interest is perfected and even though a buyer knows of its existence.

The above section affords **Bonded Loan** no relief. It was not a buyer in the ordinary course of business so as to take free of the security interest of Kimbrell. A buyer in the ordinary course of business is defined in subsection (9) of Section 10.1-201 as follows:

> "Buyer in ordinary course of business" means a person who in good faith and without knowledge that the sale to him is in violation of the ownership rights or security interest of a third party in the goods buys in ordinary course from a person in the business of selling goods of that kind but does not include a pawnbroker. . . .

Therefore, Bonded Loan could not have been a buyer in the ordinary course of business when O'Neal pledged the property to it, because O'Neal was not "a person in the business of selling goods of that kind."

Reversed.

Crete State Bank v. Lauhoff Grain Co.
239 N.W.2d 789 (Neb.) 1976

NEWTON, J. . . . Norman Hellbusch entered into contracts with Crete Mills on April 14, June 16, October 9, and November 4, 1971. There remains due on these contracts $3,653.69, which sum is claimed by plaintiff and by the State of Nebraska.

Plaintiff holds the promissory note of Norman Hellbusch on which is due $16,780.13. The note is dated August 2, 1971. The State of Nebraska has filed tax liens on which is due the principal sum of $4,164.64 on February 23, 1972, and May 8, 1972. Judgment was entered for the State of Nebraska and plaintiff has appealed. We affirm the judgment of the District Court.

Plaintiff claims it had a perfected security interest in the Crete Mills' contracts to secure indebtedness due the bank. On April 6, 1970,

it filed a financing statement covering "all contracts." A second financing statement was filed on July 28, 1971, covering "All of our contracts and accounts receivable presently owned or hereafter acquired" and proceeds. The statements were signed by both parties. Neither statement specifies any amount. They are short form financing statements which do not themselves purport to create security interests.

Section 9-204, U.C.C., provides that a security interest cannot attach until the debtor has rights in the collateral, or in a contract right until the contract has been made, but "a security agreement may provide that collateral, whenever acquired, shall secure all obligations covered by the security agreement." Section 9-105(h), U.C.C., states that a security agreement means an agreement which creates or provides for a security interest. Section 9-106, U.C.C., defines a contract right as any right to payment under a contract not yet earned by performance.

There had been dealings between the debtor and plaintiff over a considerable period. Early contracts had been assigned to plaintiff and financing statements filed. These earlier contracts had been completed and the proceeds paid to plaintiff. Thereafter debtor entered into four other contracts with Crete Mills. These contracts were fully performed by the debtor and the balance due on them is the subject of this suit. These later contracts were not assigned to plaintiff nor was a separate security agreement entered into in regard to them. Plaintiff simply filed the financing statements of April 6, 1970, and July 28, 1971. The root question appears to be whether the financing statements were sufficient to constitute security agreements required by Section 9-203, U.C.C. That section provides that a security interest in collateral not in the possession of the secured party is not enforceable unless the debtor has signed a security agreement containing a description of the collateral. Section 9-402, U.C.C., provides that a security agreement will suffice as a financing statement if it meets the requirements for a financing statement. It is evident that one instrument may qualify for both purposes and it follows that a financing statement may also constitute a security agreement if it qualifies as such.

Here we have only a promissory note in standard form and the financing statements. There is no other instrument involved. The cases appear to be unanimous in the requirement that to constitute a security agreement there must be a written instrument, signed by the debtor, evidencing that such an agreement existed. There is some variation as to the nature of such instruments. In *American Card Co.* v. *H. M. H. Co.,* 97 R.I. 59, the Rhode Island court held: "The financing statement which the claimants filed clearly fails to qualify also as a security agreement because nowhere in the form is there any evidence of an agreement by the debtor to grant claimants a security interest."

In *Shelton* v. *Erwin,* 472 F.2d 1118 (8th Cir., 1973), it was held: "A 'security agreement' within the Uniform Commercial Code must contain some language actually conveying a security interest. Title application and subsequent certificate of title showing seller of automobile as lien holder were at best financing statements and, as such, were sufficient to perfect a security interest if one existed, but not to create one."

As noted above, the present case reveals only the existence of a promissory note and standard form financing statements. Neither the financing statements nor the note manifest an intent to create or provide for a security interest. We are therefore of the opinion that the statutory requirement for a security agreement has not been complied with and in consequence plaintiff did not acquire a security interest in the contracts entered into between the debtor and Crete Mills. . . .

Affirmed.

Ford Motor Credit Co. v. Quality Motors
541 S.W.2d 119 (Tenn.) 1976

HENRY, J. . . . This is an action for the conversion of an automobile wherein the sole issue is whether a lien perfected by a security agreement in the State of Arkansas is superior to the title of a bona fide purchaser for value without notice of the prior lien.

We respond in the affirmative and reverse a contrary ruling by the Trial Judge.

I

On 30 April 1971, Martin E. Freedman purchased, in the State of Arkansas, a 1971

Mustang automobile, on a retail installment contract with purchase money security interest retained. This contract was assigned by the seller to Ford Motor Credit Company, for full consideration and in the ordinary course of business. Arkansas is a so-called title state and the certificate of title issued in that state showed Ford Motor Credit Company to be the first lien holder.

After purchasing the automobile, Freedman procured a motor tag receipt from the State of Alabama, a non-title state, showing him to be a resident of Montgomery, Alabama, and containing no lien notation.

Thereafter, Freedman appeared at the place of business of Quality Motors in Franklin, Tennessee, presented his Alabama motor tag receipt, and executed a bill of sale to Quality, after advising that he was a veteran just returning from Vietnam and that he desired to sell the automobile in order to continue his education.

Quality Motors purchased the automobile, taking as evidence of the transaction the Alabama tag receipt endorsed by Freedman and a bill of sale. These documents, along with title application, were forwarded to the Motor Vehicle Title Division of the State of Tennessee, and a certificate of title was issued. Thereafter Quality sold the automobile in the course of its business as a used car dealer.

The basic thrust of the defense interposed in the trial court by Quality Motors is that it was a bona fide purchaser for value, without prior notice of any claim by Ford Motor Credit Company; that all documents in its chain of title were complete and regular, and that it had no way of ascertaining any prior liens or encumbrances against the same. . . .

It should be pointed out that Ford Motor Credit Company, according to the pleadings, did not consent to the removal of the property into this state and had no knowledge of its removal here or of its purported registration in the State of Alabama.

II

We recognize it to be a general rule of law that the lien of a mortgage or conditional sale contract, properly recorded or filed according to the law of the state where it was executed and where the property was located at the time, has priority over the rights and claims of other creditors or purchasers from the mortgagor or conditional vendee. This rule continues to prevail even after the removal of the property to another state if that removal is without the knowledge and consent of the mortgagee or conditional vendor.

Tennessee cases have consistently adhered to this general rule of law. . . .

We find nothing in the Uniform Commercial Code that changes this rule of law.

We, therefore, hold that the lien created by the Arkansas retail installment contract was not lost by the removal of the automobile to Tennessee and its subsequent sale to a bona fide purchaser for value without notice of the lien. We recognize that this is a harsh holding which, in isolated instances, could be productive of injustice; however, it is the rule that has been followed consistently in this jurisdiction and which we believe to be necessary in order to give stability to transactions such as these in a mobile society. Caution and prudence are demanded in transactions involving the purchase of automobiles licensed under a state which does not have a title registration law. It is also a harsh result when an owner is permitted to pursue stolen property and recover it in the hands of an innocent purchaser from a thief, but again, legal precedent and the stability of property rights demand that this be permissible. Permitting the holder of a perfected lien to pursue the property and recover it or its value from an innocent purchaser who acquired a semblance of title from a wrongdoer is in essentially the same category. . . .

Reversed.

CHAPTER 23
REVIEW QUESTIONS AND PROBLEMS

1. A gave a note, secured by a ring, to B for a loan. B negotiated the note and ring to C for value. When the note came due, A tendered full payment, but C retained the note and ring for another debt A owed him. A refused to pay the old debt. Does C have a right to keep the note and ring? Why?

2. A, a farmer, obtained fertilizer and other supplies from B and gave B a note, which stated that the note was covered by a security agreement. In fact, no security agreement had been entered into, but the parties had signed and filed a financing statement. Subsequently, A sold his corn crop to C, and B claims the right to the corn by virtue of his security interest. Is B's right in the corn superior to C's? Why?

3. A had a business in Texas and also a mining business in New Mexico. A Texas bank has a security interest in a compressor that was used in the mining operations. How would the bank perfect its security interest? Why?

4. A entered into a security agreement with B. The agreement provided that A was to have a security interest in all of B's inventory and accounts receivable. The financing statement described the collateral as "all inventory" plus proceeds. Does A's security interest include accounts receivable arising from the sale of inventory? Why?

5. A sold a TV set to a dentist for the waiting room in the dentist's office. What should A do to perfect a security interest in the set? Explain.

6. A, an accountant, lent money to X Company, which was already indebted to A for services rendered. As security for the loan and to secure payment for the services, X assigned to A a portion of the expected recovery of a pending lawsuit. A did not file a financing statement with regard to the assignment. Subsequently, Z Company was awarded a judgment against X and, having no knowledge of the assignment to A, had the sheriff levy against X's property. Pursuant to the execution sale, all of X's rights in the pending lawsuit were sold to Z. When the lawsuit was settled, both A and Z claimed rights to the proceeds. Who is entitled to the proceeds? Why?

7. O, a buyer and seller of logs, gave a security interest in 147 walnut logs to the B Bank as collateral for a loan. B filed a financing statement. Thereafter, O sold the logs to X, who in turn sold them to Y Company, which gave X a draft for the purchase price. When X went to the B Bank to cash the draft, the bank withheld the proceeds of the draft. X sues the bank on the draft. Should X succeed? Why?

8. The B Bank agreed to lend money to X Company on a revolving basis. X gave to the bank a security interest in all of its receivables "now existing and hereafter arising." B filed a financing statement describing the collateral as "Accounts Receivable." In a subsequent lawsuit, other creditors of X claimed that B is not a secured creditor because the financing statement did not sufficiently describe the collateral. Is B a secured creditor? Why?

9. The B Bank lent money to a ladies' clothing store. The loan was secured by a security agreement that listed the store's equipment, furniture, and fixtures, but the only reference to inventory, accounts receivable, and contract rights was a check mark in spaces provided for classification of the goods. When D became bankrupt, the trustee contended that B was not a secured creditor on inventory, accounts receivable, and contract rights. Is the trustee correct? Why?

10. A jewelry store sold a diamond ring to B on credit as an engagement present for B's fiancee. The parties entered into a purchase-money security agreement, but this was not filed; nor was a financing statement filed. Does the jewelry store have a perfected security interest in the ring? Why?

11. B approached S, a seller of mobile homes and told him that he was interested in purchasing mobile homes which he could rent to students. S sold nine mobile homes to B on credit, but S did not file a financing statement. What type of goods are the mobile homes? Does S have a perfected security interest in the homes? Why?

Secured Transactions: Technical Aspects

1. Introduction

Many technical aspects in the law of secured transactions result in a substantial amount of Article 9 litigation. The adoption of the Revised Article 9 and its clarifying language will no doubt eliminate much of the confusion that exists relative to some of these technical provisions. However, many highly technical rules of law will remain, and creditors should carefully comply with the statute if the desired security interests are to be obtained.

One of the more important technical aspects of the Code, commonly referred to as the "floating lien," is discussed in this chapter, along with purchase-money security interests, the rules of law that determine priority among conflicting claims, and the rights of the parties upon default. The discussion will be based on the original Article 9 except where the Revised Article 9 is specifically mentioned.

2. The "Floating Lien"

The security agreement may provide that property acquired in the future by the debtor will also constitute collateral.[1] The agreement may also provide that future advances to the debtor will be covered by the collateral in which the secured party has a security interest (9-204). Thus, a secured party may have a security interest in the debtor's future and existing assets even though

---

[1] *Galleon Industries, Inc. v. Lewyn Machinery Co., Inc.*, page 449.

437

the debtor has the freedom to use or dispose of the collateral and even though the debt includes future advances by the creditor. For example, a secured party who is financing a retailer can maintain a security interest in the debtor's constantly changing inventory and also have a security interest in the proceeds of the sale of inventory in the debtor's ordinary course of business. The amount of credit can also vary.

The secured party's security interest is protected against the claims of third parties by virtue of the public notice that such financing arrangement has been made. The amount of the debt and the actual collateral can be constantly changing if the security agreement is so worded as to include after-acquired property and future advances of money. This sort of arrangement has the effect of tying up most of the assets of a debtor by the secured party. This possibility is considered to be acceptable with regard to business financing but is restricted insofar as consumers and farmers are concerned. After-acquired clauses covering farm crops must be limited to crops that become such within one year of the security agreement in states that have not adopted the Revised Article 9. In all states, after-acquired clauses on consumer goods are limited to goods obtained within ten days after the secured party gives value (9-204).

3. Proceeds

The passing of the security interest from goods to the proceeds of the sale is an important part of the "floating lien" concept. A debtor may sell or otherwise dispose of the collateral. In such event, the secured party may have an interest in the "identifiable proceeds." The proceeds may be "cash proceeds" or "non-cash proceeds," such as an account receivable (9-306[1]). Insurance payable to a party to the security agreement is proceeds under Revised Article 9 but not under the original code (9-306[1]).

Two different factual situations may arise. A debtor may have the authority to dispose of the collateral, as in the case of a sale of inventory, or the secured party may consent to the sale. A debtor may also dispose of the collateral without authority to do so. In either situation, the secured party has an interest in the *proceeds*. In the former, he loses his security interest in the *collateral* that is sold in the ordinary course of business or with consent (9-307).[2] In the latter, he retains a security interest in the collateral and thus has a security interest in *both* the collateral *and* the proceeds (9-306[2]).

The financing statement may provide for a security interest in specified types of proceeds, in which event no further filing is required (9-306[1]). If (1) the financing statement did not specifically cover proceeds, or (2) the security interest was perfected by possession or attachment, a perfected security interest in proceeds continues for ten days. At the end of the ten-day period, the interest in the proceeds ends unless the secured party has filed a

---

[2] *Farmers National Bank* v. *Ceres Land Co.*, page 450.

financing statement covering proceeds *within* the ten-day period or has taken possession of the proceeds.

Special provisions relate to the secured party's interest in proceeds if the debtor becomes involved in bankruptcy or other insolvency proceedings. In general, the secured party is entitled to reclaim from the trustee in bankruptcy proceeds that can be identified as relating to the original collateral, including cash proceeds that are identifiable—i.e., have not been commingled with other money or deposited in a bank account prior to the insolvency proceedings. Checks that have not been deposited by the debtor can also be reclaimed. If the cash (money and checks) proceeds are no longer identifiable because they have been commingled or deposited, the secured party nonetheless has a perfected security interest in the debtor's cash or bank account, but subject to the following limitations: (1) It is limited to a maximum of the amount of any cash proceeds received by the debtor within ten days prior to the commencement of the bankruptcy proceedings, (2) less the amount of any cash proceeds that the debtor may have paid to the secured party during the ten-day period, and (3) subject to any existing right of setoff, as where an obligation may be owing from the secured party to the debtor (9-306[4]).

PRIORITIES

4.   Introduction

Collateral is frequently the subject of conflicting claims. Two or more persons may claim a security interest in the same collateral, or a person may claim that he has a better right to the collateral than does the secured party. There are many ways in which conflicting claims to collateral may arise. Some of the more important are (1) when the debtor gives more than one security interest in the same collateral; (2) when a trustee in bankruptcy claims the collateral in connection with bankruptcy proceedings involving the debtor; (3) when the debtor sells the collateral to a good-faith purchaser who is not aware of the security interest; (4) when the collateral becomes attached to real property so that it is a fixture; (5) when it becomes attached to personal property that belongs to another or in which another has security interest; (6) when it has been repaired or improved by the services or materials of another; (7) when it has been processed, as when raw material in which there is security interest is converted into a finished product; and (8) when the government or some other creditor claims a lien on the property. In all the foregoing situations as well as many others, it becomes necessary to sort out the conflicting interests and determine a priority among them.

Generally, a secured party who has not perfected his security interest has only a very limited protection against third parties. He has priority only over persons who acquire the property with *knowledge* of his interest or become lien creditors with such knowledge (9-301).

The Code rules on priorities are based on the nature of the collateral, its intended use, and the relationship of the parties. For example, a buyer in the ordinary course of business takes free of a security interest in the seller's inventory even though the security interest has been perfected (9-307). To illustrate, assume that A, a retailer, has financed his inventory of television sets with X Bank and has given the bank a security interest. He now sells one of the television sets to B, who buys it in the ordinary course of business. B takes the set free of even a perfected security interest on the part of X Bank. This rule does not apply, however, to good-faith purchasers of farm products.

As a general rule, if the conflicting interests in the same collateral are both perfected by filing, the *first to file* will prevail, even though the other interest attached first, and whether it attached before or after filing. Unless both are perfected by filing, the *first to be perfected* will have priority regardless of which one attached first. If neither of the security interests is perfected, priority will be given to the first to attach (9-312[5]).[3]

5. Purchase-Money Security Interest

A purchase-money security interest is one that is either taken or retained by the seller as collateral to secure the price, or taken by one who makes advances that enable the debtor to acquire the collateral (9-107). The secured party who has a purchase-money security interest enjoys a preferred status in some situations (9-312[3]).

This preferred status arises when the debtor has given another secured party a security interest in inventory. To illustrate this preferred status of a purchase-money security interest, assume that X, a retailer, has given the Y Bank a security interest in his inventory. Z, a manufacturer of goods, can defeat the claim of the Y Bank to subsequent inventory purchases from Z if the proper steps are taken. Z, who is going to furnish inventory on a purchase-money basis, can notify the prior secured party that he has or expects to obtain a purchase-money security interest in inventory. The notice must be given prior to the time that X obtains possession of the goods and must describe the collateral by item or type. If such notice is given, Z, the secured party who furnishes the inventory, has priority, provided its interest is perfected at the time the debtor receives possession of the collateral (9-312[3]).

For collateral other than inventory, a purchase-money security interest is superior to conflicting security interests in the same collateral, provided the purchase-money security is perfected at the time the debtor receives the collateral or within ten days thereafter (9-312[4]).[4] Thus, notice to other secured parties is not required in cases of equipment if the security interest is perfected within ten days. The prior-notice requirement is limited to inventory.

A secured party with a purchase-money security interest in collateral other

---

3 *Enterprises Now v. Citizens & Southern Dev.*, page 451.
4 *Brodie Hotel Supply, Inc. v. United States,* page 452.

than inventory is given a special status for ten days after the debtor receives the property. Of course, the secured party must file within the ten-day period. The protection during such period is limited. It gives priority only over the rights of (1) transferees in bulk from the debtor, and (2) lien creditors to the extent that such rights arise between the time the purchase-money security interest attaches and the time of filing (9-301[2]). It is to be noted that the secured party is *not* protected against (1) a sale by the debtor to another party, or (2) a secured transaction wherein the collateral is given as security for a loan during the period prior to filing.

It should be remembered that purchase-money security interests in consumer goods and farm equipment, if the purchase price is under $2,500, may be perfected by attachment. (Farm equipment is eliminated under the revised Code.) As noted, the purchase-money security interest in consumer goods and farm equipment will be inferior to the rights of another consumer or farmer purchaser from the debtor.

6. Priority in Proceeds

More than one interest may exist in the same proceeds. For example, a merchant whose inventory is financed under a security agreement with a secured party may sell items from inventory to a customer on an installment sale contract. Such contract (chattel paper) is now the collateral in place of the item sold, since it is the proceeds derived from the sale. If the secured party does not take possession of the chattel paper, the debtor could sell the paper to a third party, and a question would arise as to the right to the paper as between the secured party and the third party. If the third party gave new value and took the paper in the ordinary course of his business, he will prevail. This is true even though the purchaser of the chattel paper knew that it was subject to a security interest (9-308).

The situation is different if the secured party's interest in the chattel paper is not based upon its status as proceeds of the sale of inventory. If the chattel paper itself was the original collateral, a transferee will not prevail over the secured party if he had knowledge of the prior security interest. Thus, if the secured party under these circumstances entrusts the paper to the debtor for collection purposes, the wrongful disposition by the debtor will not subordinate the interest of the secured party (9-308).

It is to be noted that the secured party who allows the debtor to have possession of the paper could stamp or designate on the paper that it has been assigned or sold. In this way he could impart knowledge of his interest and prevent the conflict from arising.

7. Returned or Repossessed Goods

Conflicting claims to collateral may arise when a debtor who sells an item from inventory receives in return either chattel paper or an account receivable, and the goods are subsequently reacquired. The debtor may have reacquired the goods under several circumstances. The buyer may have returned them because of his dissatisfaction; the seller may have repossessed them because of a default by the buyer; or the seller may have stopped the goods in transit, as allowed under Article 2, upon discovery of the buyer's insolvency. In any event, the goods are now again in the possession of the debtor. There may be a conflict between the inventory secured party and the transferee of the chattel paper or account receivable related to the returned goods.

The original security interest of the inventory secured party attaches to the returned or repossessed goods. The security interest in the goods continues to be perfected provided it has not lapsed or terminated. As between the inventory secured party and the transferee of the chattel paper, the person holding the chattel paper has priority. This is not the result if an account receivable was transferred; then the transferee of the account is subordinate to the party having a security interest in inventory with respect to goods that were returned or repossessed (9-306[5]).

8. Fixtures—Original Article 9

Goods that are collateral for a security agreement may be attached to real property, in which event such goods are fixtures (9-313). This raises a question of priority as between the secured party and one who has a security interest in the real property—e.g., one who has a mortgage upon the real property. An example of a fixture would be a heating system installed in a building. Article 9 does not determine the circumstances under which goods become fixtures, but it does provide rules for determining priorities when a fixture is involved.

A security interest that attaches to goods before they become fixtures will be given priority—if it is *perfected* before they become fixtures—over existing and subsequent interests in the real property (9-313[2]).[5] Even if it is not so perfected, it will have priority over prior mortgages because of the value added to the real estate. It will be inferior to subsequent purchasers or mortgagees because they presumably bought or loaned on the value of the real estate including the fixtures (9-313[3]). It is possible to obtain a security interest in goods after they have become fixtures, in which event the secured party will not prevail over prior claimants to the real property, unless such prior party agrees in writing to the security interest or is willing to state in writing that he disclaims any interest in the goods as fixtures (9-313[3]).

The secured party who has priority is entitled, upon default, to remove the fixtures from the real estate. He is required to reimburse any encumbrancer or owner other than the debtor for the cost of repair of any physical damage caused by the removal (9-313[5]).

---

[5] *Karp Bros., Inc.* v. *West Ward Savings and Loan Ass'n,* page 454.

As noted previously, filing is required to perfect a security interest in fixtures regardless of the classification of the goods as consumer goods, farm equipment, and so forth. The filing should be done in the office where real estate mortgages are filed or recorded.

9. Fixtures—Revised Article 9

No portion of Article 9 has been more criticized than the provisions relating to fixtures. These criticisms arose because the original Code failed to recognize many principles of real estate law relating to competing interests in land and the relative priority of such interests. The Revised Code attempts to correct these errors. The Revised Code recognizes three categories of goods: (1) those that retain their chattel character and are not a part of the real estate, (2) building materials that lose their chattel character entirely and are a part of the real estate, and (3) an intermediate class that becomes a part of the real estate for some purposes but that may be a part of the secured transaction. This latter category is *fixtures* (9-313).

The Revised Code uses the term *fixture filing* to require filing where a mortgage on real estate would be filed. The financing statement for fixture filing must (1) show that it covers fixtures, (2) recite that it is to be filed in the real estate records, (3) describe the real estate, and (4) if the debtor does not own the real estate, show the name of the record owner.

The Revised Code allows a mortgage to describe fixtures in the mortgage and thus treat the mortgage as a financing statement. In such cases, the mortgage is exempt from the five-year limitation on financing statements.

Under the Revised Code, a purchase-money security interest in a fixture prevails over a prior encumbrance on the land if the security interest was perfected by fixture filing before the goods became fixtures, or within ten days thereafter if the debtor had an interest of record or was in possession of the land. However, a security interest in fixtures is subordinate to a construction mortgage or to a "take-out" mortgage replacing it recorded before the goods became fixtures, if the goods became fixtures before completion of the construction. This later provision resolved a major conflict under the original Code and recognized the priority of a construction loan.

The Revised Code continues to give general priority to the first to file. Under this rule, a security interest in fixtures has priority over other interests in the real estate if the security interest was perfected by fixture filing before the other parties' interest in the real estate was filed. The first-to-file priority rule is applicable if the security interest is not a purchase-money security interest or if the conflicting interest arose after the fixture was attached. In such cases, the security interest must be perfected before the conflicting interest becomes a matter of record if it is to have priority.

The Revised Code also has a special rule relating to readily removable fixtures, such as office machines or appliances (9-313[4][c]). A security interest in such fixtures has priority without filing where the security interest is otherwise properly perfected prior to the installation of the fixture. There are other special aspects of the Revised Code relating to fixtures that must be consulted in those states that have enacted it (9-313).

10. Other Priority Issues

Goods, in addition to being affixed to real estate, may become installed in or affixed to other goods. The goods so installed or affixed are called "accessions." In general, a perfected security interest that attaches to goods *before* they become accessions has priority as to such goods over a security interest in the whole and subsequent purchasers of the whole (9-314[1]). A security interest may attach to goods after they have become joined with other goods. The secured party has the same priorities as those stated above, but his security interest will prevail over another security interest in the whole only if the holder of the security interest in the whole has consented in writing to the security interest (9-314[2]). As in the case of fixtures, the secured party can upon default remove his collateral from the whole, but he must make payment for the cost of repair of any physical damage caused by removal (9-314[4]).

In a manufacturing process, several items, including raw materials and components, each of which may be subject to different security interests, combine to make a finished product. The security to which the financing party is entitled will ultimately be the product that results from the combination of the materials in which he has a security interest. If a security interest in the raw materials was perfected, the security interest continues in the product if (1) the identity of the goods is lost, or (2) the original financing statement provided for a security interest that covered the "product" (9-315[1]). In a situation where component parts are assembled into a machine, the secured party would have a choice of either (1) claiming a security interest in the machine, or (2) claiming an interest in a component part as provided for security interests in accessions. If he stipulates "products" in the financing statement, he cannot claim an accession. Where more than one security interest exists in the product, the secured parties share in the product in proportion to the costs of their materials used (9-315[2]).

The common law lien on goods that is allowed for repair, improvement, storage, or transportation is superior to a perfected security interest as long as the lien claimant retains possession of the property.[6] Statutory liens also have such priority unless the statute expressly subordinates them. Even though a lien is second in point of time, it will be granted priority over a perfected security interest in the goods, unless the statute creating the lien provides that it is subordinate (9-310). The reason for this is that the service rendered by the lienholder has added to or protected the value of the property.

---

6 *National Bank of Joliet* v. *Bergeron Cadillac*, page 455.

RIGHTS AND REMEDIES OF THE SECURED PARTY

11. Before Default

As a result of the law and the security agreement, the secured party has certain rights in the collateral. If the secured party is in possession of the collateral, there are also certain duties imposed. For example, the secured party in possession is required to exercise reasonable care of it, and the duty to do so may not be disclaimed by contract.

Unless the security agreement provides otherwise, (1) all reasonable expenses related to the collateral are chargeable to the debtor and are secured by the collateral; (2) the risk of accidental loss or damage is on the debtor to the extent that it is not covered by insurance; (3) the secured party is entitled to hold as additional security any increase or profits, except money, received from the collateral—money so received shall be applied to reduce the secured obligation or remitted to the debtor; (4) the secured party is entitled to repledge—i.e., use the collateral as security in his own financing—but only on such terms as do not impair the debtor's right to redeem it; but (5) the secured party must keep the collateral identifiable, except that fungible goods can be commingled (9-207[2]). Should the secured party fail to meet his obligations in these respects, he is liable for any loss, but he does not thereby lose his security interest (9-207[3]).

In most situations, the collateral will remain in the possession of the debtor, and he may be given wide latitude in using, commingling, or disposing of the property without thereby rendering the security interest invalid or fraudulent against creditors. A security interest is not affected by reason of the failure of the secured party to require the debtor to account for proceeds or replace collateral (9-205).

Usually, the financing statement will state only that a secured party may have a security interest in specified types of collateral owned by the debtor. Nothing is said about either the amount of the secured debt or the particular assets covered. The debtor, for various reasons, may need a detailed statement as to both the present amount of the obligation and the collateral that is covered. The Code provides that the secured party is obligated to furnish such information when so requested by the debtor (9-208).

12. After Default

When the debtor is in default, the secured party is given several remedies. These remedies, as well as the protection afforded the debtor in connection with the default procedures, are determined by the security agreement and the rules set forth in the Code. The Code contains limitations designed to protect not only the defaulting debtor but also other creditors of the debtor. The basic remedies of the secured party on default are to repossess the collateral and to dispose of it (9-504).

If the secured party is already in possession of the collateral, he is of course entitled to retain possession. If he does not have posssesion, he has the right to take possession without any judicial process if he can do so without "breaching the peace" (9-503). If he meets with resistance in his effort to repossess, he can of course obtain judicial assistance in accomplishing it. The security agreement may require the debtor after default to gather the collateral together and voluntarily make it available to the secured party at a place designated by the secured party. In some situations, it is not practical to take possession or remove the collateral, as where it is heavy equipment installed in the debtor's plant. The Code then authorizes the secured party to render the equipment unusuable pending resale or other disposition (9-503).

If the collateral is accounts, chattel paper, contract rights, instruments, or general intangibles, the secured party can simply proceed to collect whatever may become due on the collateral. For example, he may direct the person who owes the account receivable to make payment directly to the secured party. If this type of collateral has been assigned to a secured party as security for a *loan,* then the secured party, upon collection, must account to the debtor for any surplus, and the debtor (absent a contrary provision in the security agreement) is liable for any deficiency if the amount collected is not sufficient to satisfy the obligation (9-502[2]). On the other hand, if the transaction is a *sale* of such items, the assignee can retain any surplus, and the assignor is not liable for any deficiency in the event that the items prove uncollectible. The purchase agreement can, however, provide for a different result.

The secured party has broad powers to dispose of the collateral in order to obtain satisfaction of the obligation (9-504). He may sell the goods at either a public or a private sale, as long as he does so in a commercially reasonable manner (9-504[3]). The requirement of a "commercially reasonable manner" is strictly followed.[7] For example, it has been held that the failure to wash and clean the collateral before the sale established that it was not conducted in a commercially reasonable manner.

In general, the secured party is required to notify the debtor of the time and place of any public sale or of the time after which a private sale is to be made. The notification is not required where (1) the collateral is perishable or threatens to decline speedily in value, or (2) it is a type "customarily sold on a recognized market" (9-504[3]). Notice must also be sent (except in the case of consumer goods) to any other person who has filed a financing statement covering the same collateral and who is known to have a security interest in the collateral. The secured party may buy at the public sale if he so desires. If the sale is private, a secured party has the right to purchase only if the collateral is of a type customarily sold in a recognized market or is of a type that is the subject of widely distributed price quotations. The law imposes these limitations in order to obtain a fair price for the debtor.

---

7 *First National Bank of Bellevue* v. *Rose,* page 456.

The person who buys the collateral at a sale thereof receives it free of the security interest under which the sale was made, and free also of any subordinate security interest (9-504[4]). Thus, the good-faith purchaser at a disposition sale receives substantial assurance that he will be protected in his purchase. After the sale has been made, the proceeds of the sale will be distributed and applied as follows and in this order: (1) the expenses of the secured party in connection with the repossession and sale, including (if provided for in the security agreement) attorney's fees and legal expenses; (2) satisfaction of the debt owing to the secured party; (3) satisfaction of the indebtedness owing to persons who have a subordinate security interest in the collateral (9-504[1]). Finally, if any surplus remains after satisfaction of all the applications above, it belongs to the debtor (9-504[2]). If the security agreement so provides, the debtor is liable for any deficiency, provided the sale is properly conducted.

13.   Acceptance in Discharge

The secured party may prefer to simply keep the collateral in satisfaction of the obligation rather than dispose of it. He is entitled to make such a proposition in writing and send it to the debtor (9-505[2]). Except in the case of consumer goods, the proposal must also be sent to all persons who have filed a financing statement covering the collateral or who are known to have a security interest in it. Within prescribed time limits, the debtor, a secured party entitled to receive notification, or any other secured party can object in writing to the proposal, in which event the collateral would have to be sold. If no such notice is forthcoming, the matter is closed and the secured party can retain the collateral in satisfaction (9-505[2]).

Special provisions relate to consumer transactions. Disposition of the goods is *compulsory,* and a sale must be made within 90 days after possession is taken if (1) in the case of a purchase-money security interest in consumer goods, 60 percent of the cash price has been paid; or (2) in the case of a security interest based upon a loan against consumer goods, 60 percent of the loan has been repaid. The consumer can, however, waive this right by signing a statement to that effect after default (9-505[1]). These rules exist because presumably there will be a surplus as a result of the sale, and the debtor is entitled to it promptly.

14.   The Debtor's Rights

Except for the 90-day period for consumer goods, the secured party is not required to make disposition of the repossessed goods within any time limits. The right to redeem the property by the debtor or another secured party exists until such time as (1) the property has been sold or contracted to be sold, or (2) the obligation has been satisfied by the retention of the property. The redeeming party must, as a condition to redemption, tender the full amount of the obligation secured by the collateral, plus the expenses incurred by the secured party in connection with the collateral and, if so provided in the agreement, attorney's fees and legal expenses (9-506).

If the secured party fails to comply with provisions of the Code relating to default, a court may order disposition or restrain disposition as the situation requires. If the sale has already taken place, the secured party is liable for any loss resulting from his noncompliance. For example, a secured party with a superior claim to the collateral is liable to other secured parties with inferior claims to it if the collateral is sold without notice of the sale to all parties with an interest in it. The liability is for the loss caused by failure of the notification.

A secured party may also lose his right to recover any deficiency that results from the sale. The courts of the various states take different views on the effect of an improper sale or the right to collect a deficiency. Some states deny it altogether. Other courts allow a debtor to deduct any loss resulting from the improper sale. Many courts have followed a middle ground between these extremes. Upon a showing of creditor noncompliance with the Code requirements, the debtor gets the benefit of a presumption that the collateral was worth the amount of the outstanding debt at the time of default. Accordingly, the debtor is freed from any deficiency unless the creditor proves that the collateral had a lower value.

If the collateral is consumer goods, the consumer-debtor is entitled to recover *in any event* an amount not less than (1) the credit service charge plus 10 percent of the principal amount of the debt, or (2) the time-price differential plus 10 percent of the cash price (9-507[1]). The secured party is protected against claims that he did not obtain the best possible price for the goods if he has made the sale in a commercially reasonable manner. Thus, the secured party must closely follow the law in the sale of collateral to satisfy an obligation or the secured party will be liable as noted.

15. Revised Article 9

Some of the provisions contained in the Revised Article 9 have been previously noted. Attachment as a means of perfecting an interest in farm equipment has been eliminated. Fixture filing under Article 9 is a most significant new development. Since this revision is likely to become the law in most states in the near future, its provisions have been included in the appendix containing the Uniform Commercial Code.

Many of the revisions of Article 9 clarify the Code provisions and its relationship with other articles. One of the major clarifications is in the language relating to perfection of interests in multiple-state transactions (9-103). The basic rule is that the controlling law on perfection of security interests is the state where the collateral is when the last event occurs necessary for perfection. The revision also clarifies the consignment situation by providing that a consignor must give notice to prior inventory secured parties the same as if the transaction were a sale (9-114).

Revised Article 9 has clarified and changed the law somewhat relating to termination statements. Under the revision, termination statements must be filed in the case of consumer goods even without a demand for such statements by the consumer. Since many consumers will not realize the significance of the termination statement, the law requires the filing (9-404).

SECURED TRANSACTIONS: TECHNICAL ASPECTS CASES

Galleon Industries, Inc. v. Lewyn Machinery Co., Inc.
279 So.2d 137 (Ala.) 1973

Lewyn contracted to sell some pieces of equipment to Galleon and required payment in cash upon delivery. Lewyn did not have a certain machine in stock and had to order it from a company in Pennsylvania. By mistake the machine was delivered directly to Galleon rather than to Lewyn. Upon learning of this, Lewyn billed Galleon with terms of "net 30 days." In the meantime Galleon had entered into a security agreement with the Central Bank and Trust Company. The agreement covered equipment and inventory and contained an after-acquired property clause. The bank filed a financing statement. The bank later repossessed the equipment, and it was decided by the court that Lewyn had a preferred position over the bank. The bank appealed.

WRIGHT, J. . . . § 9-204 provides for a security agreement covering after-acquired property such as that held by Central. This section also provides the manner in which such security interest shall attach. In the case of the security interest of Central, it attached when the debtor, Galleon, acquired "rights" in the collateral covered by the security agreement. As we have previously stated, the delivery of the machine and the forwarding of the invoice stating "net 30 days" made Galleon a credit buyer. A credit buyer acquires "rights" in the property when possession is received from the seller.

Lewyn, if retaining title until payment, by delivery to a credit buyer reserved only a purchase money security interest, such security interest was never perfected by filing as required by § 9-302. Lewyn could have perfected its purchase money security interest and received priority over the perfected security interest of Central by filing a financing statement at the time of delivery, or within 10 days thereafter. Section 9-312(4). According to the evidence, Lewyn learned of the foreclosure and taking of possession by Central eight days after delivery to Galleon. There still remained two days for perfection of its security interest by filing a financing statement. Such filing would have given it priority over the perfected security interest of Central. Section 9-312(4).

Since sufficient "rights" had passed to Galleon by delivery and the sending of the invoice, the requirements of Section 9-204 were satisfied and the security interest of Central attached to the machine. The failure of Lewyn to perfect its security interest by filing within 10 days after delivery gave Central priority. Thus at the time of the filing of the suit in detinue, Central had a superior right to possession.

We reject the argument of appellee that use of the term "equipment" in the after-acquired property clause of Central's security agreement is insufficient to include the machine involved. Under the evidence there is no question that the machine involved was to be used in the business of Galleon, and was placed within the premises as equipment. The sufficiency of a description in a financing statement is measured in terms of notice. Does the designation of "equipment now owned or hereafter acquired" give notice to a seller of a machine to be installed on the premises of an operating business and used in production that it is subject or likely to be subject to a perfected security interest? We hold it does. . . . *Reversed.*

Farmers National Bank v. Ceres Land Co.
512 P.2d 1174 (Colo.App.) 1973

COYTE, J. Helzer, a tenant farmer on a farm owned by . . . Hoch, financed his operations by borrowing from plaintiff bank. This borrowing was secured by a security agreement on Helzer's interest in crops grown on the farm. A financing statement was duly filed. During the summer of 1969 corn was grown and sold as ensilage. Hoch owned an undivided one-half interest and Helzer owned the other undivided one-half interest in the corn crop subject to the security interest of the bank.

In the fall of 1969 Hoch, with the approval of Helzer and the bank, sold the entire corn crop to defendant Ceres Land Company. The first check was made payable to Hoch, Helzer, and the bank, but the final payment for the corn in the amount of $7,370.55 was made payable only to Hoch, who did not pay the bank. The bank then filed suit against Ceres Land Company for one-half of the amount of the final payment, claiming that Ceres had converted the bank's interest in Helzer's corn crop. Ceres answered, contending that . . . the bank had waived its security interest in the corn crop, and that there was no longer any identifiable proceeds except the purchase price. The trial court entered judgment in favor of the bank against Ceres . . . [and] Ceres appeals. We reverse. . . .

The uncontroverted testimony was that Helzer's obligation to the bank was in excess of one-half the amount of the $7,370.55 check; that Hoch discussed the sale with the president of the bank who authorized him without qualification to sell the ensilage, as did Helzer; that the bank approved of the sale after it had been made; and that Ceres purchased the corn in the form of ensilage and paid Hoch the balance of the purchase price.

C.R.S. 1963, 155-9-306 (The Uniform Commercial Code), provides:

(1) "Proceeds" includes whatever is received when collateral or proceeds is sold, exchanged, collected, or otherwise disposed of. The term also includes the account arising when the right to payment is earned under a contract right. Money, checks, and the like are "cash proceeds." All other proceeds are "noncash proceeds."

(2) Except where this article otherwise provides, a security interest continues in collateral notwithstanding sale, exchange, or other disposition thereof by the debtor unless his action was authorized by the secured party in the security agreement or otherwise, and also continues in any identifiable proceeds including collections received by the debtor.

Under the "Official Comment 3" to the above section is the following:

In many cases a purchaser or other transferee of collateral will take free of a security interest: in such cases the secured party's only right will be to proceeds. The transferee will take free whenever the disposition was authorized; the authorization may be contained in the security agreement or otherwise given.

Although C.R.S. 1963, 155-9-307, limits the situations in which certain purchasers take free of security interests, the last paragraph under "Official Comment 2" to this section provides:

The limitations which this Section imposes on the persons who may take free of a security interest apply of course only to unauthorized sales by the debtor. If the secured party has authorized the sale in the security agreement or otherwise, the buyer takes free without regard to the limitations of this Section. Section 9-306 states the right of a secured party to the proceeds of a sale, authorized or unauthorized.

When the bank consented to the sale of the corn and it was subsequently sold, it lost its lien on the corn. The evidence is clear that Ceres paid Hoch for the corn and, since the sale was authorized by the bank, Ceres would have no obligation or liability to the bank. . . .
Reversed.

Enterprises Now v. Citizens & Southern Dev.
218 S.E.2d 309 (Ga.) 1975

DEEN, J. . . . The record reveals the following facts: Appellee had a long history of financial dealings with the Debtor, and had received a security interest in all of the inventory and equipment of the Debtor. Upon learning that the Debtor was planning to open a new store and fearing that it would be stocked with inventory in which it had a security interest, appellee obtained a financing statement from the Debtor covering inventory and equipment in the new store; the financing statement was filed on June 5, 1972, but no value was given at that time for the statement. Meanwhile, on or about June 1, 1972, appellant agreed to loan Debtor a sum of money taking a security interest in the same collateral covered by appellee's subsequent June 5 filing but appellant did not perfect its interest until June 27, 1972, when its financing statement was filed. On March 5, 1973, appellee and Debtor finally reached a security agreement and a loan was made to Debtor at that time, appellee subsequently filing another financing statement on March 12, 1973. On March 7, 1973, appellant filed a financing statement to secure another loan to Debtor. The Debtor having failed to meet its financial obligations to either appellee or appellant, the question arises: Which party has priority to the inventory and equipment? Appellant argues that the "first to perfect" rule controls and appellee urges that the "first to file" has priority.

Resolution of this issue must begin with Code Ann. § 109A-9-312, dealing with priorities among conflicting security interests in the same collateral. Subsection (5) of this provision provides that: (a) in cases where both interests are perfected by filing, the order of such filing determines priority; (b) in cases where perfection may be made other than by filing, the order of such perfection controls priority; and (c) in cases where no interest is perfected, the order of attachment of the security interest mandates priority. It is therefore clear that under our Uniform Commercial Code determining priority involves a two-prong determination: (1) *how* the security interest is to be perfected and (2) *whether* the security interest has in fact been so perfected. The answer to the first question is easily found in Code Ann. § 109A-9-302—the security interests in the case *sub judice* must be *filed* to be perfected.

The second question—whether the interests were in fact so perfected—is more difficult. As for appellant, we need look only to Code Ann. §§ 109A-9-303 and 109A-9-304. A security interest is perfected when it has attached and when, in this case, a proper filing is made. A security interest "attaches" when there is an agreement to that effect, value is given and the debtor has rights in the collateral. The point in time at which all of these requisites were met was June 27, 1972; after this date appellant was a perfected secured party with regard to Debtor's inventory and equipment. Appellant was the first to "perfect" its security interest.

Under Code Ann. § 109A-9-402 a financing statement may be filed before a security agreement is made or a security interest attaches; such was the case with appellee's filing on June 5, 1972. However, as noted, filing alone does not equal perfection, for Code Ann. § 109A-9-303 also requires "attachment" of the security interest. With regard to appellee, its security interest "attached" (agreement, value, debtor rights in collateral) on March 5, 1973, when the loan was made to Debtor. Code Ann. § 109A-9-303 specifically provides that when filing precedes attachment of the security interest, the interest is perfected at the *time of attachment;* therefore, having filed a financing statement on June 5, 1972, and the interest having attached on March 5, 1973, appellee had a perfected secured interest in Debtor's inventory and equipment as of the latter date, though it was first to file.

Having determined that both appellant and appellee were perfected secured parties, we must turn to Code Ann. § 109A-9-312 to determine priority. Since both were perfected by filing, it is clear Code Ann. § 109A-9-312-(5)(a) applies; the order of such filing de-termining priority. Appellee filed first even though it was perfected at a much later date than appellant, at the time some nine months later when its security interest "attached"; however, the statute specifically provides that priority of filing controls whether the filing *precedes or follows* attachment. Our Uniform Commercial Code gives appellee priority in this situation as the first to file a financing statement covering the inventory and equipment.

The official comments of the Uniform Commercial Code provide that the justification for the rule "lies in the necessity of protecting the filing system—that is, of allowing the secured party who has first filed to make subsequent advances without each time having, as a condition of protection, to check for filings later than his." Official Comment 5 to § 9-312 of the Uniform Commercial Code. See also Example 1. Appellee being entitled to priority as a matter of law, there was no genuine issue as to any material fact. Summary judgment was properly granted to appellee.

Judgment affirmed.

Brodie Hotel Supply, Inc. v. United States
431 F.2d 1316 (1970)

HAMLEY, J. Brodie Hotel Supply, Inc. (Brodie), brought this action against the United States to determine which of the parties had priority, under their respective chattel mortgages, to the proceeds of the sale of certain restaurant equipment. The facts were stipulated and the property was sold and proceeds impounded by agreement. The district court granted summary judgment for Brodie and the United States appeals.

In 1959, Brodie sold the restaurant equipment to Standard Management Company, Inc., for use in a restaurant at Anchorage, Alaska. Standard Management went bankrupt. Brodie repossessed the equipment but left it in the restaurant. With the consent of Brodie, James Lyon took possession of the restaurant and began operating it on June 1, 1964. Throughout the summer of 1964, Brodie and Lyon negotiated over the price and terms under which Lyon was to purchase the equipment.

On November 2, 1964, Lyon borrowed seventeen thousand dollars from the National Bank of Alaska and, as security for the loan, which was evidenced by a promissory note, executed a chattel mortgage covering the restaurant equipment. This equipment consisted of 159 separate types of items, including a refrigerator, a dishwasher, an ice cream cabinet, spoons, forks, cups, ladles, pots, pans, and assorted glassware and chinaware. The bank assigned its mortgage to the Small Business Administration (SBA), represented in this action by the United States. On November 4, 1964, the bank filed a financing statement, showing the SBA as assignee.

On November 12, Brodie delivered to Lyon a bill of sale covering the equipment.

On the same day Lyon executed a chattel mortgage on the equipment, naming Brodie as mortgagee. This mortgage was given to secure the unpaid purchase price of the equipment. Brodie filed a financing statement on November 23, 1964.

Alaska has adopted the Uniform Commercial Code (Code). Under section 9-312-(5)(a) of the Code, the general rule of priority, if both interests are perfected by filing, is that the secured party who first files a financing statement (in this case SBA as assignee of the bank) prevails, regardless of when his security interest attached. However, there is a special exception for purchase-money security interests in collateral other than inventory. Brodie had such an interest. Under this exception, the purchase-money security interest prevails over conflicting interests in non-inventory collateral if "the purchase money security interest is perfected [*i.e.,* here it was perfected by filing a financing statement] at the time the debtor receives possession of the collateral or within 10 days after the debtor receives possession."

On the basis of these stipulated facts Brodie moved for summary judgment. Brodie contended that although Lyon received possession of the restaurant equipment on June 1, 1964, over five months before Brodie's financing statement was filed, Lyon did not become a "debtor," and the equipment did not become "collateral" until November 12, 1964, when Lyon received the bill of sale and executed Brodie's chattel mortgage. Accordingly Brodie contended, it was not until November 12, that "the debtor [Lyon] receive[d] possession of the collateral" within the meaning of the statute referred to above. As already indicated, Brodie's financing statement was filed within ten days of that date. The district court agreed with this analysis in granting summary judgment for Brodie.

If, in A.S. 45.05.754(d), the term "debtor" is given the meaning ascribed to it in A.S. 45.05.698(a)(4), Brodie was entitled to priority. It was not until November 12, 1964, that Lyon purchased the equipment and be-

came obligated to pay the purchase price. Until that obligation came into being, Lyon was not Brodie's debtor with power to mortgage the restaurant equipment as collateral for the unpaid purchase price.

But the United States argues that in the context of this case the priority statute, A.S. 45.05.754(d), is ambiguous as to whether "debtor" is used in the sense defined in A.S. 45.05.698(a)(4), or whether it is used merely to identify an individual in possession, who ultimately becomes indebted to the purchase-money mortgagee. In contending that this "ambiguity" should be resolved in favor of the latter construction, the United States refers to the history and underlying purposes and policies of the Code . . . and the fact that, under A.S. 45.05.770(a) (Code, § 9-402(1)) a financing statement may be filed before a security agreement is made or a security interest otherwise attaches, notwithstanding the fact that this section refers to "debtor," "secured party," and "security interest."

We are not persuaded that either recourse to the history or consideration of the underlying purposes of the Code supports the Government's position. In our view, the term "debtor" as it is used in this particular priority statute, A.S. 45.05.754(d) (Code, § 9-312(4)), means "the person who owes payment or other performance of the obligation secured." Although Lyon might have been liable for the reasonable rental of the equipment or for its return to Brodie, he did not owe performance of an "obligation secured" by the collateral in question until November 12, 1964, and therefore was not a "debtor" for purposes of A.S. 45.05.754(d) (Code, § 9-312(4)). Brodie's filing was therefore within the ten-day period and Brodie has priority over the conflicting security interest held by SBA.

The Government has urged us to look at the policy and the purposes of the Code to resolve what it considers to be the ambiguous meaning of "debtor." The Code has granted a specially favored position to the holder of a purchase-money security interest in non-inventory collateral. The holder of such an interest need not follow the notice procedures which are prescribed for the holders of purchase-money interests in inventory. Such a holder is also given a special priority position. His interest, perfected second, but within the ten-day grace period, will prevail over any previously perfected security interest. This priority exists even though the framers of the Code knew that the holder of the conflicting security interest would be relying on the possession of the collateral and upon the absence of a prior filing. Similarly, the holder of a purchase-money security interest in non-inventory collateral will have priority over a previously perfected security interest which includes the collateral by virtue of an after-acquired property clause. Such a holder therefore is not required to search the files to determine the existence of such a conflicting interest in order to be sure of his priority.

The protection which the Code confers upon a purchase-money interest in non-inventory collateral is not unduly extended by a decision giving priority to Brodie's interest. Although it is true that Brodie could have filed a financing statement as soon as Lyon went into possession and thus protected itself, it is also true that the bank, SBA's assignor, could have protected itself by inquiring into Lyon's interest in the equipment before accepting his chattel mortgage. Due to the favored status given by the Code to the holder of a purchase-money interest in non-inventory collateral, we are not convinced that the trial court erred in refusing to impose this burden on Brodie.

Affirmed.

Karp Bros., Inc. v. West Ward Savings and Loan Ass'n
271 A.2d 493 (Pa.) 1972

Plaintiff, Karp Brothers, Inc. (Karp), brought a replevin action against West Ward Savings and Loan Association (West Ward) for the return of fifty items of property or their value in damages. The lower court found for plaintiff, and West Ward appealed.

The owners of a motel (McCowns) on April 29, 1964, borrowed $24,000 from West Ward and had secured this loan with a real estate mortgage. On January 8, 1965, the McCowns entered into an agreement with the plaintiff by the terms of which plaintiff furnished the McCowns restaurant equipment, utensils, and supplies. On February 10, 1965, Karp filed a financing statement. On March 8, 1965, Karp as lessor and the McCowns as lessees executed a "Bailment Lease" covering the restaurant equipment.

On November 25, 1966, West Ward commenced proceedings to foreclose its mortgage which was in default, as was the "Bailment Lease." A sheriff's sale was held on January 31, 1967, at which West Ward was the purchaser. West Ward claimed the restaurant equipment as a purchaser at the foreclosure sale, contending that Karp had no interest in the equipment.

EAGEN, J. . . . The most important remedy available to a secured party is the right to take possession of the collateral following a debtor's default. In order to clarify any doubt as to what judicial process is available to a secured party in the event he is unable to obtain possession without breaching the peace, the Pennsylvania legislature added a proviso augmenting the official text of the Code which specifically provided that a secured party "may proceed by writ of replevin or otherwise."

Thus, Karp, having established the default, thereby established its right to immediate possession of any collateral covered by its secured agreement with the debtor.

The only interest, which West Ward had, is a real property interest. Therefore, if the property in question remained personal property and never became a part of the realty, West Ward would have gained no interest therein as purchaser at the sheriff's sale. The lower court did not see fit to make any finding as to whether the goods ever became part of the realty, but for the reasons that follow, we deem such a determination is unnecessary to a disposition of the case.

Even if we assume that the goods did, in fact, become affixed to the realty, nevertheless, Karp does have a priority interest in the goods. . . .

Under U.C.C. § 9-313(2): "A security interest which attaches to goods before they become fixtures takes priority as to the goods over the claims of all persons who have an interest in the real estate except as stated in subsection (4)." The only category listed in subsection (4) in which West Ward could hope to be included is that of a "subsequent purchaser for value of any interest in the real estate." However, subsection (4) makes clear that "an encumbrancer purchasing at his own foreclosure sale" [such as West Ward herein] is not deemed to be a "subsequent purchaser" within the meaning of Section 9-313.

Thus, if Karp had a "security interest" and that interest "attached" before the goods became fixtures, its interest takes priority.

A "security interest" is defined as "an interest in personal property or fixtures which secures payment or performance of an obligation. . . . Whether a lease is intended as security is to be determined by the facts of each case; however . . . (b) an agreement that upon compliance with the terms of the lease the lessee shall become or has the option to become the owner of the property for no additional consideration or for a nominal consideration does make the lease one intended for security." U.C.C. § 1-201(37). The "Bailment Lease" in the instant case does so provide. Thus the execution of the "Bailment Lease" did create a "security interest" in Karp.

The question of when a "security interest" "attached" is dealt with in U.C.C. § 9-204(1), which provides: "A security interest cannot attach until there is agreement (subsection (3) of Section 1-201) that it attach and value is given and the debtor has rights in the collateral. It attaches as soon as all of the events in the preceding sentence have taken place unless explicit agreement postpones the time of attaching." When the first "Bailment Lease" was executed on March 8, 1965, there was a manifest agreement that the security interest attach, and value given, in that credit was thereby extended to the bailment lessees. Moreover, the lessee-debtors had rights in the collateral in that the lease gave them a right to possession of the goods. All this occurred before the goods could possibly have become affixed to the realty, since there was testimony found to be true by the court below that none of the goods referred to in the lease were delivered prior to the execution of the first bailment contract. Thus, if the goods became fixtures, this occurred at a time after Karp's "security interest" "attached" under the first "Bailment Lease," and Karp's interest, based on the first security agreement, was superior to that of West Ward, the prior real estate encumbrancer.

Judgment affirmed.

National Bank of Joliet v. Bergeron Cadillac
361 N.E.2d 1116 (Ill.) 1977

WARD, J. . . . In December of 1973, the plaintiff, National Bank of Joliet, brought a replevin action in the circuit court of McLean County against the defendant, Bergeron Cadillac, Inc., seeking to recover a 1971 Cadillac automobile. The trial court entered judgment for the defendant, holding that its common law possessory lien based on repairs it had made on the auto had priority over the plaintiff's prior security interest under Section 9-310 of the Uniform Commercial Code. The appellate court . . . affirmed.

In February of 1973 the plaintiff loaned Gladys Schmidt $4,120 to enable her to purchase the automobile, taking a security interest in the automobile to secure the loan. This security interest was perfected by filing in the office of the Secretary of State. In August of

1973 Schmidt brought the auto to the defendant's shop for repairs. The cost of the materials and service was approximately $2,000, and, when Schmidt failed to pay, the defendant, through an inquiry to the Secretary of State, learned of the plaintiff's security interest. The Defendant exercised its right of lien for the unpaid charges and retained possession of the auto. In September, Schmidt defaulted on her loan payments, and in October the plaintiff ascertained that the Cadillac was in the defendant's possession. The plaintiff's demand on the defendant for the Cadillac under its security interest was refused, and the plaintiff filed the action in replevin.

The plaintiff contends that the right to a common law possessory lien has been superseded in Illinois by two statutes which provide for repairmen's liens.

Section 9-310 of the Uniform Commercial Code, which has been in effect in Illinois since July 1, 1962, provides:

> When a person in the ordinary course of his business furnishes services or materials with respect to goods subject to a security interest, a lien upon goods in the possession of such person given by statute or rule of law for such materials or services takes priority over a perfected security interest unless the lien is statutory and the statute expressly provides otherwise.

The plain language of Section 9-310 gives the lien of persons furnishing services or materials upon goods in their possession priority over a perfected security interest unless the lien is created by statute and the statute expressly provides otherwise.

The comment of Anderson (Anderson Uniform Commercial Code) is:

Code section 9-310 declares the priority of the lien of persons furnishing services or materials with respect to goods in their possession. Such a lien is, basically, the artisan's lien of the common law. Whether such a lien is based upon decision or statute law, Code section 9-310 gives it priority, with one exception, over a pre-existing security interest in the goods.

The single exception relates to a lien created by statute; such a lien does not have such priority if the statute expressly provides otherwise. Accordingly, the lien has priority when it is based upon the common law or decision, or when it is based upon a statute which is silent as to priorities or which gives the lien priority. The lien is subordinated to the security interest only when the lien statute expressly so declares.

The artisan's possessory lien of the common law is recognized in Illinois.

We cannot accept the plaintiff's contention that the General Assembly's enactment of the two statutes creating liens in favor of repairmen with respect to personal property evidenced an intent to supersede the artisan's common law lien. Both of the statutes expressly provide that the liens created shall be in addition to, and shall not exclude, any lien existing by virtue of the common law.

As the defendant had a common law possessory lien for services and materials in connection with the repairs it made, its lien takes priority over the plaintiff's earlier perfected security interest under the provisions of Section 9-310 of the Uniform Commercial Code.

Judgment affirmed.

First National Bank of Bellevue v. Rose
249 N.W.2d 723 (Neb.) 1977

Plaintiff sued the defendant to recover a deficiency judgment for the balance due on a promissory note. Prior to this suit, plaintiff had respossessed and sold certain collateral. The proceeds of the sale had been applied to the note. The defendants on this appeal contend that the sale did not comply with the Uniform Commercial Code.

BRODKEY, J. . . . Defendants raise . . . the issue of whether the plaintiff provided Rose adequate notice of the disposition of the collateral which the plaintiff repossessed and sold. The facts relevant to this issue are as follows. On April 19, 1969, Rose executed a promissory note in favor of the plaintiff, here-inafter referred to as the bank, in the sum of $22,200. . . . The note was secured by equipment. . . .

Rose subsequently defaulted on the loan after three repayments of $2,000 each. The bank notified Rose of his default on September 8, 1969, and initiated a replevin action against Rose in October 1969. The collateral security was then located and repossessed, and in total the bank took possession of 12 items of equipment. One item of collateral equipment was never located.

On November 12, 1969, the bank notified Rose by certified mail that it had obtained bids on the repossessed equipment in an aggregate amount of $10,268.50, and that the collateral would be disposed of "at private sale . . . November 17, 1969." The notice advised Rose to furnish to the bank any bids which he may have on any or all of the equipment. The $10,268.50 bid which the bank had received was from Robert Kouba Construction Company. On November 17, 1969, Rose's attorney brought to the bank another bid from Ernest C. Turley. This bid did not cover all the items of equipment, was much lower than the Kouba bid on the items it did cover, and was therefore rejected.

For some reason not disclosed in the record, the Kouba bid was never consummated, and the bank proceeded to sell the repossessed equipment item by item in a series of private sales. These sales commenced on November 20, 1969, and the last one was completed on June 1, 1970. Three of the items were never actually sold, but the bank credited Rose for the estimated value of these items. In total, the bank credited Rose for $10,268.50.

Rose was not notified of any of these private sales, which were made after the bank contacted 10 to 20 construction firms in the area and requested them to examine the equipment and bid on it. Of the nine items actually sold, two were sold on November 20, 1969; two were sold on November 25, 1969; one was sold on December 16, 1969; three were sold on February 27, 1970; and one was sold on June 1, 1970. Thus there was a total of five separate private sales. Each of the five sales was made to a different purchaser.

The money received from these sales was insufficient to cover the balance due on the promissory note, and the bank brought this action for a deficiency judgment under Section 9-504(2) of the Uniform Commercial Code. There was no dispute that Rose had defaulted on the note. The only evidence adduced at trial as to notice of the sales was that the bank had, on November 12, 1969, notified Rose of the Kouba bid and of its intention to dispose of the collateral at private sale on November 17, 1969. The trial court did not specifically make findings on the issue of whether this was sufficient notice under the provisions of the Uniform Commercial Code.

The trial court found generally that the repossession sales were conducted in good faith and in a commercially reasonable manner. The court, however, did specifically find that one of the sales of three items of equipment was not made in a commercially reasonable manner due to inadequacy of the sale price, and awarded Rose an additional $1,400 credit on these three items. The court also made a minor modification on the credit allowed to Rose on another item of equipment, and awarded Rose a total of $11,720.89 credit on the collateral, as compared to the $10,268.50 credited to Rose by the bank. After allowance for all credits and debits on the promissory note, the trial court found the balance due to be $3,033.82, and awarded the bank this amount, with interest thereon from January 5, 1972.

Section 9-504(3), U.C.C., provides among other things: "Unless collateral is perishable or threatens to decline speedily in value or is of a type customarily sold on a recognized market, *reasonable notification of the time and place of any public sale or reasonable notification of the time after which any private sale or other intended disposition is to be made shall be sent by the secured party to the debtor. . . .* (Emphasis supplied.) It is clear that under this section a secured party has the duty to provide the debtor with reasonable notice of the intended disposition. . . . [The] burden of proof is on the secured party to prove compliance with the statutory requirements of notice and reasonableness of notice. . . . The District Court judgment in the present case must be reversed for the reason that the bank failed to provide Rose with adequate notice of the disposition of collateral.

. . . To constitute reasonable notice of a private sale, the notice should be sent in such time that the debtors would ordinarily have a minimum of three business days to arrange to protect their interest.

. . . The failure to give proper notice of the sales of the collateral is an absolute bar to the recovery of a deficiency judgment.

The notice given in this case did not comply with the (aforesaid) requirements. . . . It is undisputed the bank sent notice to Rose by certified mail on Wednesday, November 12, 1969, that it had received an aggregate bid on the collateral and intended to dispose of it by private sale on Monday, November 17, 1969. Although the record does not show when Rose actually received the notice, it appears that Rose probably had less than three business days to arrange to protect his interests since the notice was not mailed until some time on November 12, 1969. The mailing of notice on Wednesday of a sale to be held the following Monday would appear to make it difficult, if not impossible, for Rose to arrange financing or take other steps to protect his interest in the collateral, particularly if banks were closed on Saturday. In any event, the ordinary 3-day rule . . . is a minimum requirement, and such notice is not necessarily sufficient in all cases. The purpose of giving reasonable notice to a debtor is to insure that he will have sufficient time to take appropriate steps to protect his interest. In this case we do not believe that Rose was given sufficient time to protect his interests, and we find that the notice that was given by the bank was unreasonable.

A deficiency judgment may not be awarded to the bank in this case because it failed to sustain its burden of proof that sufficient notice of the disposition of collateral was given to Rose. . . .

Reversed and remanded.

CHAPTER 24
REVIEW QUESTIONS AND PROBLEMS

1. X sold goods to Y and has a security interest in Y's inventory. The financing statement provides for a security interest in after-acquired property. Y is now negotiating for the purchase of additional inventory items from Z and wishes to give Z a security interest in the new inventory. Z is concerned over the status of his security interest if he sells goods to Y. Advise Z as to the proper course of action.

2. R, a retail automobile dealer, borrowed money at times from the X Company and the Y Company, each of which had filed the necessary statements, X Company being first to file. Thereafter on October 1, R borrowed $10,000 from Y Company and used four cars as security. He later borrowed $8,000 from X Company and used the same cars as security. R is now insolvent, and X Company took possession of the cars. Is this lien superior to that of Y Company? Why?

3. A, a merchant, and the XYZ bank entered into a security agreement which provided XYZ with a security interest in A's inventory. A sold the inventory and deposited the proceeds in a bank account. One week later, A filed a bankruptcy petition. Is XYZ entitled to obtain the amount of the proceeds from the trustee in bankruptcy? Why?

4. A, a furniture dealer, by a valid security agreement retained a security interest in a $750 sofa sold to B on credit. No financing statement was filed. B resold the sofa to C, another consumer. If A is not paid, may he repossess the sofa? Why?

5. K Piano Company consigned pianos to R, a retail dealer. R sold one of the pianos to X for cash but did not account to the K Company for the proceeds of the sale. K Company had filed a financing statement. It claims to be entitled to possession of the piano. Can K Company recover the piano from X? Why?

6. F gave A a security interest in his 1976 potato crop. The crop was destroyed by fire in 1977, but the loss was covered by insurance. B obtained a judgment against F and claimed the insurance money in satisfaction of the judgment. A claimed it as "proceeds" of the collateral. Is the insurance money "proceeds"? (Assume Revised Code) Explain.

7. A contractor assigned his accounts receivable to a bank as security for a loan, but the bank did not file a financing statement. Thereafter, the government filed a tax lien against the contractor for unpaid payroll taxes. The government claimed priority to the receivables. Is the government correct? Why?

8. B purchased a truck on credit from a dealer. The contract was assigned to the F Finance Company, which filed a financing statement. Thereafter, B, without conferring with F, took the truck to R for repairs. B was unable to pay, and R retained possession of the truck and claimed that his lien for repairs is superior to F's security interest. Is R correct? Why?

9. X purchased a car from a dealer and financed the purchase through a bank. After X was in arrears in his payments for two months, the bank repossessed the car by removing it from its parking place on the street. X contends that "self-help" repossession procedures under the Code are unconstitutional. The financing agreement specifically provided for "self-help." Is X correct? Why?

10. R, a furniture retailer, bought various articles of furniture on credit from M, a furniture manufacturing company, and M took a security interest in the furniture. R defaulted, and M repossessed the furniture. M notified R that the furniture would be sold at a private sale within two weeks. M contacted a furniture dealer, who decided that he was not interested. O, the owner of M Company, accepted his own bid and the furniture was sold to him. Have the goods been properly disposed of? Why?

11. C loaned $28,000 to D. D signed a promissory note covering the loan and gave C a security interest in certain trucks owned by him. G signed a separate promissory note as guarantor of the loan. D defaulted and C sold the trucks, giving prior notice of the sale to D but not to G. The amount received from the sale was insufficient and a demand was made upon G. Is G liable for the deficiency? Why?

12. S sold ranch supplies to B, and B gave S a $35,000 promissory note as consideration. S perfected his security interest and when B defaulted, S disposed of the goods at a nonjudicial sale. S and E, a former employee of S, were the only people who attended the sale. S placed the only bid and purchased the collateral for $100. S subsequently sold the collateral for $10,000. Was the sale accomplished in a commercially reasonable manner? Why?

13. The A Bank had a perfected security interest in B's property. C, a creditor of B, obtained a judgment against him. Both A Bank and C are seeking to obtain possession of the property. Who prevails? Explain.

book four

CREDITORS, DEBTORS, AND CONSUMERS

Real Property As Security

MORTGAGES

1. Introduction

A real estate mortgage is an interest in real property that is created for the purpose of securing the performance of an obligation, usually the payment of a debt. A mortgage is not a debt—only security for a debt. The owner of the estate in land that is being used as security for the debt is called the *mortgagor;* the party to whom the security interest in the real estate is conveyed is called the *mortgagee.*

There are three distinct legal theories relating to mortgages. The first of these, known as the *title theory,* was developed at common law. At common law and in those few states following the title theory, a mortgage on land is an absolute conveyance of the title of the land by the owner to the mortgagee, upon condition that the title will revert to the mortgagor when the obligation is performed or the money is repaid. If the mortgagor fails to repay the debt, the property will remain the property of the mortgagee.

The second theory about mortgages is usually known as the *lien theory,* although it is sometimes called the *equitable theory.* Under this theory, a mortgage is not a conveyance of title but only a method of creating a lien on the real estate. The lien or equitable theory avoids the harshness that often results on default in title-theory states when the mortgagee is allowed to keep the real property without any obligation to the former owner. Under the lien theory, a mortgagee does not have title when the mortgagor defaults; he simply has a lien that can be foreclosed. Upon foreclosure of the lien, any proceeds of the sale in excess of the debt and the costs of sale remain the property of the mortgagor. In addition, lien-theory states grant to the mortgagor a right to redeem his property after the default and foreclosure. This right to redeem is known as the mortgagor's *equity of redemption*. The time period during which a mortgagor may redeem is usually prescribed by statute. When it is not, it is fixed by the court in the foreclosure proceedings. If a mortgagor wishes to redeem, he pays the total debt plus the costs of sale. But if the property is not redeemed within the prescribed period, it becomes the absolute property of the purchaser at the foreclosure sale.

Many states do not follow the title theory or the lien theory; they have reached a compromise between the two theories—an *intermediate theory*. By the intermediate theory, a mortgage is a conveyance of title, but the equitable theories are applied to it. Mortgages must be foreclosed and the mortgagor has an equity of redemption, even though the mortgagee has "title." The great majority of states are either lien-theory or intermediate-theory states; the title theory has little support.

2. Types of Mortgages

A mortgage usually states that the property is conveyed to the mortgagee, subject to the conditions set forth in the mortgage. It is executed with all the formalities of a deed. The contract between the parties with respect to the loan need not be included in the mortgage but may be set forth in a separate document.

In order that the mortgagee may give notice to third parties that he has an interest in the real estate, it is necessary that the mortgage be recorded in the recording office of the county where the real estate is situated. Recording serves to notify subsequent parties of the lien or encumbrance of the mortgage.

An instrument known as a *deed of trust,* sometimes called a *trust deed,* may be used as a substitute for a mortgage for the purpose of securing debts. The property is conveyed by the borrower, who executes the deed of trust, to a trustee to hold in trust for the benefit of the noteholders. If the debt is paid at the time required by the contract, the trustee reconveys the property to the borrower, or releases the lien. If there is a default in payment, the trustee forecloses the trust deed and applies the proceeds to the payment of the debt secured.

Deeds of trust are used instead of mortgages when the note is likely to be negotiated and when numerous notes are secured by the same property. A trust deed may also be used to secure bonds held by many different persons. An important feature of the deed of trust is that the note secured by it can be freely negotiated separate and apart from the deed of trust. When the mortgagor pays the note, he surrenders it to the trustee under the trust deed, and the latter makes it a matter of record that the obligation has been satisfied.

Property that one does not own cannot be mortgaged, but a mortgage may be so drawn as to cover property to be acquired in the future. A mortgage of such property creates no lien at the time of its execution; a court of equity, however, will recognize that the lien exists at the time the property is acquired by the mortgagor. If the mortgage is properly recorded, the lien has priority over all rights of others that arise or are created after the recording of the mortgage.

A mortgage may also be given prior to the time when the money is advanced to the mortgagor. Such a mortgage is usually called a *mortgage to secure future advances*. When the mortgagee advances the money, the mortgage is a valid lien as of the date when the mortgage was recorded.

When a mortgage is given as a part or the whole of the purchase price of land, it is known as a *purchase-money mortgage*. In some jurisdictions, a deficiency decree obtained upon the foreclosure of a purchase-money mortgage will not be enforced.

A deed absolute on its face may be shown by parol evidence to be a mortgage if such evidence indicates that the intention of the parties was to make the transfer security for a loan.[1] The grantor of the deed must prove by clear, precise, and positive evidence that it was the intention of the parties to use the deed for the purpose of securing a loan.

3. Rights and Duties of the Parties

The mortgagor is usually personally liable for the mortgage debt, not by reason of the mortgage but because he makes a note, a bond, or other contract that evidences the debt secured by the mortgage. When there is more than one mortgagor, not all of them need sign the note or be liable on the underlying obligation. In such a case, the property is given as security for the debt, but only those signing the note or incurring the obligation have personal liability.

Payment of the mortgage debt terminates the mortgage. Upon payment, the mortgagor is entitled to a release or satisfaction of the mortgage. This release should be recorded in order to clear the title to the land; otherwise, the unreleased mortgage will remain a cloud on the title. If the mortgagee refuses to give a release, he can be compelled to do so in a court of equity.

The mortgagor is entitled to retain possession of the real estate during the period of the mortgage unless a different arrangement is provided for in the mortgage. The mortgagor may not use the property in such a manner as to reduce materially its value. Mining ore, pumping oil, or cutting timber are operations that cannot be conducted by the mortgagor during the period of the the mortgage unless the right to do so is reserved in the mortgage agreement. The rights will be implied when they are being conducted at the time the mortgage is created.

Any parcel of real estate may be subject to more than one encumbrance.

[1] *Kjar* v. *Brimley*, page 472.

For example, the owner may execute more than one mortgage. In addition, mortgaged land may be subject to a lien for property taxes. As a general rule, the first recorded mortgage in point of time has priority over any subsequently recorded mortgage. Taxes usually have priority over mortgages.

A mortgagee has a right to pay off any superior mortgage in order to protect his security, and he can charge the amount so paid to the mortgagor. Likewise, he may pay taxes or special assessments that are a lien on the land and recover the sum so expended. The mortgagor is under a duty to protect the security, but should he fail to do so, the mortgagee has the right to make any reasonable expenditures necessary to protect the security for a debt.

4. Transfer of Mortgaged Property

The mortgagor may sell, will, or give away the mortgaged property, subject, however, to the rights of the mortgagee. A transferee from a mortgagor has no greater rights than the mortgagor. For example, a grantee of the mortgagor's interest may redeem the land by paying off the debt. A grantee of mortgaged property is not personally liable for the mortgage debt, unless he impliedly or expressly assumes and agrees to pay the mortgage. An assumption of a debt secured by a mortgage must be established by clear and convincing evidence. A purchase "subject to" a mortgage is usually considered not to be a legally enforceable assumption. If the grantee assumes the mortgage, he becomes personally liable for the debt, even when the land is worth less than the mortgage.

To illustrate the foregoing, assume that A purchases real estate worth $28,000, which is subject to a mortgage of $20,000. A pays the former owner $8,000 cash. If A assumes and agrees to pay the mortgage, he is personally liable for the $20,000. If the property is sold at a foreclosure sale, A is liable for any deficiency. However, if A merely purchased the property "subject to" the mortgage when he paid the $8,000, A would have no liability for any deficiency on foreclosure.

If the grantee of the mortgaged property assumes and agrees to pay the indebtedness, he thereby becomes the person primarily liable for the debt. As between himself and the mortgagor, by virtue of his promise to the mortgagor to pay the debt, he is the principal debtor and the mortgagor is a surety. This assumption by the grantee, however, does not relieve the mortgagor of his obligation to the mortgagee, and such mortgagor continues liable unless he is released from his indebtedness by the mortgagee. Such a release must comply with all the requirements for a novation.

MORTGAGE FORECLOSURES

5. Introduction

If the mortgagor fails to perform any of his obligations as agreed, the mortgagee may declare the whole debt due and payable, and he may foreclose for the purpose of collecting the indebtedness. The statutes of the various states specify the procedure by which mortgages are foreclosed. The common types of foreclosure proceedings are (1) strict foreclosure, (2) foreclosure by suit in equity, and (3) foreclosure by exercise of the power of sale.

Strict foreclosure gives the mortgagee clear title to the land. A decree of strict foreclosure provides that if the debt is not paid by a certain date, the mortgagor loses the realty and the mortgagee takes it free from the rights of junior mortgagees and lienholders. It is used only where it is clear that the mortgaged property is not worth the mortgage indebtedness, the mortgagor is insolvent, and the mortgagee accepts the property in full satisfaction of the indebtedness.

6. Foreclosure by Suit in Equity

The usual method of foreclosing a mortgage is a proceeding in a court of equity. If the mortgagor is in default, the court will authorize the sale of all the land at public auction. Following the sale, the purchaser receives a deed to the land. The funds received from the sale are used to pay court costs, the mortgage indebtedness, and inferior liens in the order of their priority. If any surplus remains, it is paid to the former owner of the property. Since foreclosure proceedings are in a court of equity, the validity of the proceedings is always subject to the usual equitable principles.[2]

Foreclosure of a second mortgage (one that is second in time to another) is made subject to all superior liens. For example, foreclosure of a second mortgage does not affect a first mortgage. The buyer at the foreclosure sale takes title, and the first mortgage remains a lien on the property. All inferior liens are cut off by foreclosure. For example, a foreclosure of a first mortgage would eliminate the rights of the second.

The statutes in many states provide a period of time after the sale within which the mortgagor or other persons having an interest are entitled to redeem the property. Where such statutes are in force, the purchaser is not entitled to a deed until after the expiration of the period within which redemption may be made. The purchaser may request that the court appoint a receiver and order the mortgagor to pay rent during the redemption period. The purchaser is entitled to the net rent during this period.

7. Foreclosure by Exercise of Power of Sale

The mortgage often provides that upon default by the mortgagor, the mortgagee may sell the land without judicial process. This method of foreclosure can be made only in strict conformity with the terms of the mortgage. The power of sale makes the mortgagee the agent of the mortgagor to sell the land. In many states, however, a power of sale in the mortgage is expressly forbidden by statute, and foreclosures must be effected by judicial proceeding. A power

---

[2] *Garland* v. *Hill,* page 474.

of sale granted in a mortgage or a deed of trust is not revocable, since the agency is coupled with an interest; therefore, the death or insanity of the mortgagor will not revoke the power. In those states where the exercise of power is regulated by statute, the sale must be public after the prescribed notice is given. In the absence of statute or mortgage agreement, however, the sale may be private. Since a mortgagee in selling the land under a power of sale is acting as an agent for the mortgagor, he is not allowed to purchase at the sale, because an agent cannot himself purchase that which he has been given authority by his principal to sell. The purchaser at such a sale secures only such title as the mortgagor had when he made the mortgage.

8. The Mortgagor's Right to Redeem

At any time after default, a mortgagor may exercise his *right to redeem* from the mortgage. The right to redeem from the mortgage means that he has the right to have the lien of the mortgage removed from the land. To do so, he must pay the entire mortgage debt with interest and all other sums, including costs to which the mortgagee may be entitled by reasons of the mortgage. In addition, there are statutory formalities to be complied with.[3]

In most states, a mortgagor may also, within a specified period of time after a foreclosure sale, redeem the real estate so sold. To do so, he must pay to the court for the benefit of the purchaser at the foreclosure sale the sum of money, with interest and costs, for which the premises were sold. The period of time allowed for redemption varies greatly from state to state, and a few states deny this right to redeem. Generally, the redeeming mortgagor is also required to pay, after the foreclosure sale, all costs incurred by the purchaser in protecting and preserving the property during the period from the sale to the redemption. During this period, the purchaser or someone appointed by the court will have possession of the real estate as well as title from the judicial sale. In some states, the redemption price includes the value of any improvements made by the purchaser during the period of his possession.

9. Deficiency Judgments

A person who executes the note or bond secured by the mortgage is personally liable for the debt. If the property that is the security for the debt does not sell for a sum sufficient to pay the indebtedness, the debtor remains liable for the deficiency, and a judgment may be entered for this unpaid balance. This judgment may be collected from the debtor's other property or income.

In order not to impose too great a hardship on mortgagor-debtors, different schemes have been devised to limit the amount of a debtor's liability for deficiencies. Some states have simply outlawed all deficiency judgments. Many other states have statutes that are applicable only to purchase-money mort-

---

[3] *United States* v. *Loosley*, page 475.

gages. Thus, when a mortgage is given to secure payment of the balance of the purchase price of real property, in these states the mortgagee is not entitled to a deficiency judgment. In these states, if the mortgage proceeds are not used to finance the purchase of the real property, deficiency judgments are allowed. The elimination of liability for deficiencies rests on several theories: that the mortgagee loaned his money on the security of the land and not the personal credit of the purchaser-debtor; that a mortgagee-creditor should share with the debtor the risk of declining land value; and that if the land is the limit of the security, fewer inflationary loans, and sounder loans, will be made.

MECHANIC'S LIENS

10. Introduction

Mechanic's lien laws provide for the filing of liens upon real estate where such real estate has been improved.[4] Their purpose is to protect contractors, laborers, and materialmen in the event of nonpayment of their accounts. The laws of the states vary slightly in the protection accorded and the procedure required to obtain it. For this reason, the laws of the state in which the property is located should be consulted.

The persons usually entitled to a lien include those who (1) deliver material, fixtures, apparatus, machinery, forms, or form work to be used in repairing, altering, or constructing a building upon the premises; (2) fill, sod, or do landscape work in connection with the premises; (3) act as architect, engineer, or superintendent during the construction of a building; or (4) furnish labor for repairing, altering, or constructing a building.

Those parties who contract with the owner, whether they furnish labor or material, or agree to construct the building, are known as *contractors*. Thus, practically any contract between the owner and another that has for its purpose the improvement of real estate gives rise to a lien on the premises in favor of those responsible for the improvement.

In addition to contractors, anyone who furnishes labor, materials, or apparatus to contractors, or anyone to whom a distinct part of the contract has been sublet, has a right to a lien. These parties are customarily referred to as *subcontractors*. Their rights differ slightly from those of contractors, and some of these differences will be considered in later sections.

Property that is subject to an existing mortgage is frequently improved. When this occurs, questions may arise as to the priority between the mortgagee and the holder of a mechanic's lien. As a general rule, the mechanic's lien is superior to any mortgage, because presumably the value of the improvements has increased the value of the property to the extent of the liens. Consequently, the value of the property remaining as security under the mortgage after

[4] *United Benefit Life Ins. Co.* v. *Norman Lumber Co.*, page 476.

satisfying the mechanic's lien is as great as it was prior to the improvement that resulted in the lien. However, some states by statute provide that mechanic's liens are subject to prior recorded mortgages because the person furnishing the labor or materials was aware of the existing debt and mortgage.

11.   Perfection of Mechanic's Liens

In some states, a contractor has a lien as soon as the contract to repair or to improve the real estate is entered into. In others, the lien attaches as soon as the work is commenced. A supplier of materials usually has a lien as soon as the materials are furnished. A laborer has a lien when the work is performed. The statutes relating to mechanic's liens provide for the method of perfecting these mechanic's liens and for the time period during which they may be perfected.

The usual procedure is that the party seeking to perfect a mechanic's lien files or records a notice of lien in the office of the county in which deeds to real estate are recorded.[5] A copy of the notice is sent to the owner of record and to the party contracting for the repair or improvement. This notice must be filed within the prescribed statutory period. The law then requires a suit to foreclose the lien and specifies that it be commenced within an additionally prescribed period.

Most mechanic's lien laws provide a relatively long period, such as two or three years, during which time a contractor may file a mechanic's lien and proceed to enforce it against the property interest of the party with whom he contracted. This time period is relatively long because the obligation is known to the owner, and he is in no way prejudiced if the lien is not promptly filed.

However, a much shorter time period is set for subcontractors, laborers, and materialmen to file their mechanic's liens. The owner of the premises may not know the source of materials and may not know the names of all persons performing services on the premises. To this extent, the liens of subcontractors, materialmen, and workers may be secret, and the owner may pay the wrong person. Therefore, the time period in which the statutory procedures must be followed is relatively short, such as 60 to 90 days.

If the property is sold or mortgaged, the existence of any mechanic's lien would often be unknown to the purchaser or mortgagee. For this reason the statutes on mechanic's liens usually specify the same short period of time for the perfection of the mechanic's lien—whether by a contractor, subcontractor, materialman, or laborer, if it is to be effective against good-faith purchasers of the property or subsequent mortgagees. Under these statutory provisions, a mechanic's lien that could be enforced against the property interest of the original contracting owner cannot be enforced against the property interest of the new owner or mortgagee after the expiration of the prescribed statutory period. Thus, during the relatively short statutory period, a mechanic's lien is

[5] *Cone* v. *Jurczyk*, page 477.

good against innocent third parties even though it has not been properly perfected. For this reason, a purchaser of real estate should always ascertain if any repairs or improvements have been made to the premises within the time period for filing mechanic's liens. If it is determined that repairs or improvements have been made, the procedures outlined in the next section should be followed.

If a contractor, subcontractor, supplier of material, or laborer fails to file his notice of lien within the appropriate prescribed time period or fails to commence suit within the additional period, the lien is lost.

Since a person entitled to a mechanic's lien has a prescribed period within which to file his lien, the date on which this time period starts to run is frequently quite important. Most statutes provide that in the case of a supplier, the time period starts to run from the date the materials are delivered; and in the case of a contractor or subcontractor performing services, the time for filing starts to run from the completion of the work. This latter concept requires further clarification, however.

Should a contractor or subcontractor be able to postpone the time for filing by performing additional services at a later date? For example, assume that a contractor has allowed the time for filing his lien to elapse. Should the time period start all over if he makes a minor repair, such as adjusting a doorknob or touching up a paint job? Common sense would say no, and most statutes provide that a contractor or subcontractor cannot extend the statutory period of time by performing minor trifling repairs after the work has been substantially completed. In other words, trivial work done or materials furnished after the contract has been substantially completed will not extend the time in which a lien claim can be filed.[6]

12. Protecting against Mechanic's Liens

Mechanic's lien statutes usually provide that an owner is not liable for more than the contract price if he follows the procedures outlined in the law. These usually require that the owner prior to payment obtain from the contractor a sworn statement setting forth all the creditors and the amounts due, or to become due, to each of them. It is then the duty of the owner to retain sufficient funds at all times to pay the amounts indicated by the sworn statements. In addition, if any liens have been filed by the subcontractors, it is the owner's duty to retain sufficient money to pay them. He is at liberty to pay any balance to the contractor. If the amount owed is insufficient to pay all the creditors, they share proportionately.

An owner has a right to rely upon the truthfulness of the sworn statement of the contractor. If the contractor misstates the facts and obtains a sum greater than that to which he is entitled, the loss falls upon the subcontractors who dealt with him rather than upon the owner. Under such circumstances, the

---

[6] *Mitchell* v. *Flandro,* page 478.

subcontractors may look only to the contractor to make good their deficit. Payments made by the owner, without his first obtaining a sworn statement, may not be used to defeat the claims of subcontractors, materialmen, and laborers. Before making any payment, the owner has the duty to require the sworn statement and to withhold the amount necessary to pay the claims indicated.

The owner may also protect himself by obtaining waivers of the contractor's lien and of the liens of subcontractors, suppliers, and laborers. In a few states, a waiver of the lien by the contractor is also a waiver of the lien of the subcontractors, as they derive their rights through those of the contractor. However, in most states, lien waivers must be obtained from all persons furnishing labor or materials.

REAL PROPERTY AS SECURITY CASES

Kjar v. Brimley
407 P.2d 23 (Utah) 1972

CALLISTER, J. Plaintiffs initiated this action to recover the statutory penalty (three times the amount of interest paid, as provided in Section 15-1-7, U.C.A.1953) on an alleged loan transaction with defendants, wherein an alleged usurious rate of interest was exacted. Defendants moved for summary judgment, which the trial court granted; plaintiffs appealed therefrom. . . .

In July 1966, the plaintiffs were in default on a mortgage on their home. The institutional mortgagee declined to refinance the obligation and referred plaintiffs to defendants. According to plaintiffs, defendants proposed to refinance by means of a security agreement in the form of an absolute deed with an option to repurchase. Plaintiffs contend that the parties intended from its inception that the transaction was a loan, secured by a mortgage on plaintiffs' home. Defendants have urged that the transaction was a conditional sale, i.e., a sale with an option to repurchase at an advanced price; and, therefore, there was no usury.

On July 31, 1966, defendants executed an earnest money agreement to purchase plaintiffs' home for $19,000; they agreed to pay $6,000 down payment and to secure the re-

maining sum with a first mortgage. On August 1, 1966, the parties executed a rental agreement, wherein plaintiffs agreed to pay a monthly rental to defendant Mr. Brimley, in the sum of $118, which the agreement recited was to go to principal and interest, plus an amount equal to the monthly amortization of annual taxes and insurance. The maintenance and upkeep were designated the responsibility of plaintiffs. Plaintiffs were granted an exclusive option to sell or buy the house for a period of three years, with plaintiffs to assume and pay all finance costs incident to the transaction. The agreement provided that an attached amortization chart or schedule of payoffs should determine the price of repurchase. The sales price was designated to be the current mortgage balance, plus all finance costs incident to the transaction, plus the amount indicated on the payoff chart for the current month at the time the repurchase was consummated. The initial payoff was $1,500 and progressed to $4,500, during the thirty-sixth month.

On August 31, 1966, plaintiffs executed a warranty deed to the defendants Brimley. On this same date, Beehive State Bank loaned

Brimley $13,300, which was secured by a mortgage from them on the home; the interest rate was 7 percent per annum. A closing statement was prepared by the bank, which indicated that plaintiffs had received $6,000; in fact, both parties concede that this was a paper figure and that no money was exchanged. The proceeds from the loan from the bank discharged the prior liens on plaintiffs' home.

There were allegations concerning plaintiffs' subsequent default under the rental agreement. Ultimately, the home was sold on November 1968, to a third party. Plaintiffs executed a closing statement and conveyed by quitclaim deed. Defendants received $3,400, in accordance with the payoff schedule in the rental agreement. Plaintiffs' action is predicated on the assertion that this payoff figure together with the portion of monthly payments applied to interest equaled an interest rate in excess of 20 percent, a usurious rate.

In the instant action, there must be an initial determination as to the nature of the transaction, was it a loan or a sale, since only the former would provide a basis to claim usury.

Whether a transaction in the form of a sale with an option to repurchase is in fact a sale, or a loan disguised as a sale to cover up a scheme to collect usurious interest, is an issue for the trier of fact. The controlling question is, what was the intention of the parties as it existed at the time of the execution and delivery of the instrument? A mortgage may exist, although the mortgagee has no right to compel payment. The law may imply a promise to repay a debt under particular circumstances of any case, where it is clear that the lender had relied on the property for his security, being satisfied that he is protected by its high value in relation to the amount loaned. If there be a large margin between the debt or sum advanced and the value of the land conveyed, this represents an assurance of payment stronger than any promise or bond of a necessitous borrower or debtor.

In *Rizo* v. *Macbeth* the court cited circumstances relevant to the determination of whether an instrument was a deed or a security device:

> . . . The adequacy or inadequacy of consideration as compared to the value of the property, which is often stated to be the single most important factor. Retention or nonretention of possession. The conduct of the parties before and after the execution of the instrument. The financial condition of grantor at the time of execution of the instrument. The overall relationship of the parties—financial, business, debtor-creditor, etc. Whether the grantor or grantee paid the taxes. The construction of improvements after the execution of the deed. Whether or not revenue stamps were affixed to the instrument. There are others. Generally it can be said that no one of the circumstances is necessarily controlling, but that all present are to be considered. . . .

. . . [A] warranty deed, absolute in form, is presumed to convey a fee simple title, or at least whatever title the grantor has; but where there is a written agreement between the parties, contemporaneous with the deed, which indicates that the deed has been given for security purposes, the court will look to the real transaction and treat it as a mortgage. If by the terms of the contract the grantor has the right to sell to a third person, such a fact is a clear indication of the intention of the parties that title should not pass to the grantee.

. . . [A]n instrument need not be in any particular form to be a mortgage so long as the intention of the parties is shown, and a mortgage may consist of a warranty deed and a separate contract in writing. In equity, a deed, absolute upon its face, may be shown by parol evidence to have been given for security purposes only; and if such showing be made, equity will give effect to the intention of the parties.

Under the circumstances of the instant case, there is material issue of fact as to whether the parties intended to create a debtor-creditor relationship and whether the alleged sale was intended to be no more than a security transaction, since casting a loan transaction in the form of a sale with an option to repurchase will not insulate the transaction from the usury laws. The judgment of the trial court is re-versed, and this cause is remanded for a trial on the merits.

Reversed and remanded.

Garland v. Hill
357 A.2d 374 (Md.) 1976

SINGLEY, J. . . . This litigation commenced when Thomas A. Garland, trustee, the mortgagor, filed exceptions in the Circuit Court for Charles County to the ratification of a mortgage foreclosure sale. . . . We granted certiorari limited to the question, "whether an inadequate purchase price can be made adequate by the mortgagee's waiver of his right to claim a deficiency degree against the mortgagor."

On 1 November 1972, Mr. Garland, as trustee, had purchased a 359.43 acre farm in Charles County from Francis W. Hill for $359,430.00, or $1,000.00 per acre. Of the total purchase price, $72,000.00 was paid in cash; the balance was secured by a purchase money mortgage in the amount of $287,430.00. By the terms of the mortgage, the principal was to be repaid in 10 annual installments of $28,743.00, plus interest on the unpaid principal balance at the rate of 7%. When a default occurred, Mr. Hill's assignee for purposes of foreclosure instituted foreclosure proceedings on 6 November 1974, in the Circuit Court for Charles County, and the property was sold at auction at the courthouse door on 15 November.

At the time of the sale, the unpaid balance of the mortgage debt was $286,687.00, and the unpaid interest amounted to $22,000.00. There was only one bid, in the amount of $25,000.00, made by Mr. Hill, the mortgagee, and the property was sold to him for that amount.

The sale was reported to the court, which entered an order nisi giving notice that the sale would be ratified unless contrary cause be shown by 24 December 1974, provided that the order be published for three successive calendar weeks commencing 9 December.

Mr. Garland excepted to the ratification of the sale, on the ground, among others, that the purchase price was "shockingly inadequate." The assignee answered, alleging that he intended, in behalf of Mr. Hill, to waive any rights to a deficiency decree against Mr. Garland, with the consequence that if the sale price and the waiver were both taken into account, the sale price would be equivalent to more than $300,000.00.

When the exceptions came on for hearing, Mr. Garland testified that he had purchased the farm for $1,000.00 an acre in 1972, which he regarded as a fair and reasonable price at that time, and that in his opinion, the property had appreciated to a value of $1,200.00 per acre at the time of foreclosure.

The trial court entered a final order ratifying the sale in which it concluded that:

> The purchase price at auction was not shockingly inadequate, in view of the fact that Francis W. Hill, Mortgagee, through his counsel, M. Wayne Munday, also Assignee for the purpose of foreclosure, has waived all rights to a deficiency decree or judgment.

The rule of our cases is that the mere inadequacy of the purchase price at a mortgage foreclosure sale is not enough to prevent the ratification of the sale, unless it is so grossly inadequate as to shock the conscience of the court. . . .

If this had been a sale of the property to anyone other than the mortgagee, the sale of a farm worth $350,000.00 for $25,000.00 might well have been successfully challenged, particularly if $25,000.00 had been the only bid. Here, however, the sale was to Mr. Hill, the holder of the mortgage. Under our practice, Mr. Hill would have been entitled to an *in personam* decree against Mr. Garland for the difference between the sale price of $25,000.00 and the unpaid balance of the mortgage debt, $286,687, plus unpaid interest of $22,000 and the expenses of sale, in an unknown amount, or $283,687. . . .

When Mr. Hill waived his right to the deficiency decree to which he was entitled, the result was exactly that which would have obtained had the property sold for $308,000.00.

At argument before us, and before the Court of Special Appeals, counsel for Mr. Garland conceded that a bid by Mr. Hill in this amount could not have been the subject of a successful challenge.

In short, we agree with the conclusion of the Court of Special Appeals and the trial court that under the circumstances of this case, what was in effect a bid of more than $300,000.00 for the property does not shock the conscience of the court. . . .

Affirmed.

United States v. Loosley
551 P.2d 506 (Utah) 1976

CROCKETT, J. . . . The United States (Small Business Administration) brought a foreclosure action on a service station at Cedar City after the lessors, George and Theodean Loosley, failed to repay a Small Business Administration loan.

Defendants Sterling and Donna Griffiths bid in and purchased the mortgagee's interest in the property at the sheriff's sale held on December 13, 1974. Subsequently, the Loosleys had assigned their interest to the defendants, Marion and Gladys Hammon, and the Hammons thereafter assigned their rights of redemption to defendant, Basic Investment, Inc. (hereinafter referred to as defendants). The latter appeals from a ruling of the district court that its attempt to redeem was invalid.

On June 12, 1975, one day prior to expiration of the six-month redemption period, defendants served a notice of redemption on Michael Park, attorney for the Griffiths, together with a check for $10,706, the correct amount needed to redeem the property. In response to a telephone call, the Griffiths asked Mr. Park if they had to accept the money or if there was any ground for rejecting it. Mr. Park stated, in substance, that he would look into the matter. Eight days later, on June 20, 1975, Mr. Park returned the check to Basic Investment with a letter which included:

Enclosed herewith please find a check for $10,706 made out to Sterling Griffiths with the purchaser listed as Basic Investment Corporation.

My clients have requested that I return that check to you for the reason that a certified copy of the docket of Judgment or a memorandum of record was not presented with the check, nor was an affidavit presented showing the amount actually due on the lien.

Also, my client claims that the check was delivered to the wrong person and should have been delivered to himself or the Sheriff.

The claimed deficiencies referred to in the letter are based upon Rule 69(f)(2), Utah Rules of Civil Procedure:

Redemption—How Made. At the time of redemption the person seeking the same may make payment of the amount required to the person from whom the property is being redeemed, or for him to the officer who made the sale, or his successor in office. At the same time the redemptioner must produce to the officer or person from whom he seeks to redeem, and serve with his notice to the officer: (1) a certified copy of the docket of judgment under which he claims the right to redeem, or, if he redeems upon a mortgage or other lien, a memorandum of the record thereof certified by the recorder; (2) an assignment, properly acknowledged or proved, where the same is necessary to establish his claim; (3) an affidavit by himself or his agent showing the amount then actually due on the lien.

In analyzing the Griffiths' contention that the provisions of the just quoted rule have not been complied with, there are certain principles relating to mortgages and their foreclosure to be considered. The main purpose of a mortgage is to insure the payment of the debt for which it stands as security; and foreclosure is allowed when necessary to carry out that objective. But foreclosure is in the nature of a forfeiture, which the law does not favor. The proceeding is one in equity in which principles of equity should be applied consistent with the above stated purpose; and neither the mortgage nor the foreclosure should be used as an instrument of oppression. Accordingly, the law provides for the six-month redemption period to give the debtor an opportunity to pay his debt and salvage his property.

Consistent with the foregoing, rules and statutes dealing with redemption are regarded as remedial in character and should be given liberal construction and application to permit a property owner who can pay his debts to do so, and thus make his creditor whole, and save his property. Therefore, if a debtor, acting in good faith, has substantially complied with the procedural requirements of the rule in such a manner that the lender mortgagee is not injured or adversely affected, and is getting what he is entitled to, the law will not aid in depriving the mortgagor of his property for mere falling short of exact compliance with technicalities.

Applying the principles just set forth to the facts here, it will be seen that none of the matters relied upon by the Griffiths as stated in the letter of June 20 could have had any adverse effect upon them. It is plainly apparent that they were excuses to justify a preconceived desire to refuse to accept the tender and release the mortgage. They did not then, and do not now, question that the debtor redemptioner's rights had, in fact, been properly assigned to the defendant; nor that the defendant made the tender of the correct amount due for redemption one day before the redemption period expired. When so advised they did not then indicate any ground whatsoever for rejecting the tender. If they had done so, defendants would have had 24 hours to remedy any technical deficiency. Under such circumstances, the law is that if one fails to state his objections to a tender, he is deemed to have waived them.

In view of the undisputed facts as recited herein it is our opinion that the Griffiths were not justified in refusing to accept the tendered payment for redemption; and that upon receipt of that sum they are obliged to release the mortgage.

So ordered.

United Benefit Life Ins. Co. v. Norman Lumber Co.
484 P.2d 527 (Okla.) 1971

HODGES, J. This appeal involves a materialmen's lien foreclosure case tried without a jury. It was held that defendant CAP Interiors had a valid lien upon the carpet and carpet pads in the six homes foreclosed; . . . and that plaintiff in error, United Benefit Life Insurance Co.'s mortgage was inferior to said liens. Judgment affirmed.

The first proposition is whether the carpet and carpet pad furnished by CAP were lienable items. United maintains that these items are personalty not meant to be permanently affixed to the realty and therefore are not lienable items. . . . The parties stipulated as to the facts of the carpeting and pads as follows in the material parts:

That all six of the houses were new and the carpets were installed upon completion of initial construction of the homes and prior to first occupancy; that the ground floors of all houses over which the carpets were laid are concrete and the second story floors over which carpets were laid are rough unfinished plywood; that the carpets and carpet pads are cut to fit the size of the room; that on the concrete floors a product called "Roberts pad cement," which is a long lasting glue, is placed on the concrete between the carpet pad, around the edges of the carpet pad and at various intervals across the room of approximately every 4½' on the rough unfinished plywood, the carpet pad is stapled with ⅜" staples around the edges of the carpet pad and across the pad approximately every 4½'; that after the pad is down, tack strips, which is a piece of wood ¼" thick and 1⅛" wide with ½" tacks sticking up ⅝" approximately every ¼" from the top of the board, are nailed around the edges of the room to the floor with ¾" nails placed approximately every 4" to 5"; that the carpet is attached to the tack strips by means of said ½" tacks and then stretched to the other sides of the room with power stretchers; that the carpet pad, once installed, cannot be removed without destruction of the same as a usable product, but the carpeting itself may be removed without damage to the carpeting.

The test is whether the article or item is permanently affixed to the realty or as set out in 60 O.S.1961, Section 7, ". . . or permanently attached to what is thus permanent, as by means of cement, plaster, nails, bolts or screws." United cites the case of *Hartford Fire Insurance Co.* v. *Balch,* Okl., 350 P.2d 514 (1960), wherein it was held that a carpet was not permanently affixed to the realty and was personal property. This case involved an insurance question. The court in the Hartford case found that the carpet was loosely tacked and glued in place; that the mortgage on the premises did not include the carpet; that the glue was meant to keep it from slipping and it was not the intention of the owners that the carpet was to remain as part of the realty. The courts said, "it appears to us from the above evidence that the small amount of glue used around the edges of the pad, and the small tacks on the edges of the carpet were for the purpose of holding it in place and not for fixing it permanently to the floor." In the present case, if the carpet was removed the ground floor would then be a concrete slab, the second floor an unfinished rough plywood. The glue used to hold down the carpet was a long lasting glue and the tacks were used with great frequency. The carpet was not excepted from the mortgage. The carpet pad would be destroyed if removed. From the circumstances in this case it is apparent that the owner intended that the carpet stay affixed to the realty and as such is a lienable item as the carpet and pads are an improvement upon the property. . . .

Affirmed.

Cone v. Jurczyk
547 S.W.2d 108 (1977)

HICKMAN, J. . . . The Chancery Court of Sharp County dismissed the complaint of Tom Cone, Jr., doing business as Stone Lumber Company, because of a failure to comply with a requirement of the Arkansas Materialmen's law.

The lumber company supplied materials used in the construction of a house owned by Eugene A. Jurczyk and his wife Phyllis, which is located in Sharp County, Arkansas. The company claimed over $5,000.00 was due and gave notice to the Jurczyks that a lien would be filed against their property within ten days from the date of the notice. However, the statement of account or the lien for material was recorded in another county, Fulton

County. Within fifteen months after the statement was filed in Fulton County, a lawsuit was filed in Sharp County, Arkansas, to foreclose the lien. A demurrer was filed asking for a dismissal because the statement of account or lien had been filed in the wrong county. The chancellor sustained the demurrer and dismissed the lawsuit.

Stone Lumber Company argues on appeal that the Jurczyks had notice and the recording of the statement in the wrong county was an inadvertent error which should not result in dismissal of the lawsuit.

We have held that a materialmen's lien is an extraordinary remedy that is not available to most merchants, and there must be substantial compliance with the technicalities of the lien law. The lien law clearly states the account and claim will be filed in the county where the property is located. In this case, the notice stated a claim would be made against the real estate of the Jurczyks, but the claim itself was filed in another county. Therefore, the owner of the real property, or anyone who holds a mortgage on the property, or is interested for any reason, would not have any notice that a claim was being made against the property. It follows that filing the statement of account in another county is not substantial compliance with the lien law. This doesn't mean the materialman has no remedy; it means the land cannot be sold to satisfy the claim. The remedy is a suit against the person or company, or both, who purchased the material.

Affirmed.

Mitchell v. Flandro
506 P.2d 455 (Idaho) 1973

A contractor instituted a suit to foreclose a mechanic's lien. On November 10, 1964, the architect signed a certificate acknowledging the substantial completion of the construction. Thereafter, the contractor continued to do finishing work until January 2, 1965. The lien was filed March 11, 1965. The lower court denied recovery on the ground that the lien was not timely filed, and the contractor appealed.

BAKES, J. . . . Of primary importance in this appeal is the district court's conclusion that respondent's lien was not timely filed as required in I.C. 45-507. At the time that respondent filed his lien, that section provided:

> Every original contractor claiming the benefit of this chapter must, within ninety (90) days . . . after the completion of any building, improvement or structure, or after the completion of the alteration or repair thereof, or in case he cease to labor thereon before the completion thereof, then after he so ceases to labor or after he has ceased to labor thereon for any cause, or after he has ceased to furnish materials therefor . . . file for record with the county recorder for the county in which such property or some part thereof is situated, a claim containing a statement of his demand, after deducting all just credits and offsets, with the name of the owner, or reputed owner, if known, and also the name of the person by whom he was employed or to whom he furnished the materials. . . . I.C. 45-507.

It is respondent's position that due to the fact that he allegedly performed work on the structure up until January 2, 1965, that the lien application filed March 11, 1965, was in fact filed within ninety days of the cessation of work under the contract and hence was timely filed. In finding that the lien was not timely filed, the trial court stated:

> . . . as a matter of fact, that from the November [1964] date through the March [1965] date that plaintiff did not prove services of such a nature as to expand the time for filing his lien and the court

concludes, therefore, as a matter of law, that the lien was not timely filed. . . .

Since there is competent evidence in the record supporting the trial court's factual determination that no substantial work was proven done after November, 1964, we do not disturb it on appeal.

It is undisputed in the record that the certificate of "substantial completion" was submitted by respondent and approved by appellants' architect on November 10, 1964. According to the architect, the certificate issued when the construction was completed to the extent that appellants could assume occupancy. On issuance of the certificate, the respondent-builders were entitled to submit their final estimate for payment. From respondent Mitchell's own testimony it appears that the issuance of the certificate also marked the effective completion of construction under the contract.

It is established that "trivial" work done or materials furnished after the contract has been substantially completed will not extend the time in which a lien claim can be filed under I.C. 45-507. As well articulated in *Gem State Lumber Co.* v. *Whitty*, 37 Idaho 489, 217 P. 1027:

> While the time fixed in the contract for the completion of a building is not controlling against laborers or materialmen, it has a direct bearing upon the time when the building was to be completed under the contract, so that the time for

filing liens for material and labor would begin to run. The statute provides that this time shall be computed from the date of the last item of material furnished, or from the last work performed. *The rule very generally prevails that such time begins to run from a substantial completion of the contract, and that new items thereafter added to the account will not extend the time in which to claim a lien or revive a lien already expired.* The more difficult question is to determine when under this doctrine the contract has been completed. By the weight of authority, this is to be ascertained by the conditions of the contract, the conduct of the parties with reference thereto, and the surrounding facts and circumstances. Ordinarily, *furnishing an article or performing a service trivial in character is not sufficient to extend the time for claiming a lien or to revive an expired lien, where the article is furnished or the service rendered after a substantial completion of the contract, and the article is not expressly required by the terms thereof.*

Since it is undisputed that the contract was substantially completed on November 10, 1964, and since the trial court found inadequate proof that any material or substantial work was performed or supplies furnished after that date which would extend the time for filing a lien, we conclude that the trial court was correct in ruling that the lien was not timely filed. . . .

Affirmed.

CHAPTER 25
REVIEW QUESTIONS AND PROBLEMS

1. X mortgaged certain land to the Federal Land Bank. The mortgage agreement required X to pay the taxes on the land. He failed to do so and the land was sold to pay the taxes. X purchased the land at the tax sale and remained in possession. The mortgage was assigned to Y and Y sued for payment. X contends that the land is now free of the mortgage. Is X correct? Why?

2. A borrowed money from B and gave B a promissory note to evidence the debt. Upon this note A wrote, "This note is secured by a real estate mortgage on" Blackacre. In fact, no mortgage was ever executed. Is B a mortgagee? Why?

3. On May 11, 1962, H and W executed a note to B for the amount of $2,500. At the same time, they executed a mortgage on Blackacre to secure the note. On May 25, 1962, C furnished materials for the construction of the dwelling on Blackacre. On June 1, 1962, B advanced H and W $2,500, for which they executed a note. H and W defaulted on payments to C and he filed a mechanic's lien on Blackacre. Does B have priority over C for his loan on June 1, 1962? Why?

4. A held a mortgage on B's property. B left the state and was in arrears in his payment on the mortgage. A took possession of the property and sold it to C. Nineteen months later, B returned and brought an action for possession of the premises, and for a reasonable rental value during the time C occupied the premises. Should he win? Why?

5. A, desiring to borrow $15,000, gave B an absolute deed as security for a loan of this amount. Upon payment of the debt and interest three years later, B executed an agreement to reconvey the property. Is this a sale or a mortgage? Why?

6. On March 7, O contracted with the C Construction Company for improvements on his home. C ordered all the lumber for the contract from the M Lumber Co. M delivered the lumber to O's home during the period March 14 to April 17. C did not pay M for the lumber, and on August 20, M filed its notice of lien. Is M entitled to a mechanic's lien? Why?

7. A mortgagor redeemed his property, which had been sold at a foreclosure sale. Improvements made by the purchaser amounted to $3,000. Included in that sum was $350 for the value of the purchaser's personal services in supervising and helping in the repairs and improvements. Should the mortgagor be required to pay $3,000 to the purchaser for the value of improvements? Why?

8. O's property was subject to three mortgages. The B Bank, holder of the first mortgage, foreclosed, and the property was sold for $41,000. On the date of the foreclosure sale, the amount owed on the first mortgage was $37,000. O was also indebted to B for $10,000 on a promissory note, which had no reference to the property. Is B entitled to the surplus funds resulting from the sale of the property? Why?

9. O purchased a modular home from M Company. E, an electrical subcontractor, had performed work on the home at the factory, prior to shipment to O's property for final assembly. M did not pay E, and E asserted a mechanic's lien. Should E succeed? Why?

10. O contracted with C Company for the construction of a house on his property. Upon completion, O made a substantial payment to C and instructed C to pay M for the amount of the building material that M had supplied for the house. C delivered a $3,400 check and a $3,400 promissory note to M in exchange for his waiver of lien. Both the check and the note proved to be worthless, and M informed O that the waiver was rescinded. Is M entitled to a mechanic's lien? Why?

11. O Company began building a shopping center upon land which the company owned and entered into a contract with P to do the plumbing work. P performed the work but was not paid by O. P commenced mechanic's lien foreclosure prior recorded mortgage on the property and claimed priority over P. Is O correct? Why?

12. X owed Y money and mortgaged certain real estate as security for the loan. X defaulted on the loan and Y foreclosed. The land was sold at public auction to the highest bidder. The highest bidder was an agent for Y. Y sued X for a deficiency after the foreclosure sale. X contended that Y did not show good faith at the foreclosure sale and purchased the property at an unreasonably low price. Should Y recover the deficiency? Why?

13. A and his minor children owned Blackacre as tenants in common. A ordered from B certain materials and labors. If B files a mechanic's lien, will it attach to the totality of Blackacre? Explain.

26

Laws Assisting Creditors

1. Introduction

Chapters 23 and 24 discussed the use of personal property as security for a debt. Chapter 25 covered the use of real property as security. As was previously noted, creditors also use individuals other than the debtor to guarantee or secure a debt. In early history, these other individuals were hostages. Today, these persons are known as sureties or guarantors. This chapter will discuss the law of suretyship. It will also discuss some other laws that give protection to creditors, such as the law relating to artisan's liens and Article 6 of the Code dealing with transfers of inventory in bulk.

2. Artisan's Liens

An *artisan's lien* is a security interest in personal property in favor of one who has performed services on the personal property, usually in the form of a repair. From a very early date, the common law permitted one who expended labor or material upon the personal property of another to retain possession of such property as security for his compensation.[1] The right arose when the task was completed, and it was not assignable because it was personal. The lien did not arise where the creditor had agreed to extend credit. At common law, the lien also existed in favor of public warehousemen and common carriers of goods entrusted to their care; in almost every state, it has been extended by statute to cover all cases of storage or repair.

The artisan's lien is generally superior to prior liens of record or the claim

[1] *Beck* v. *Nutrodynamics, Inc.,* page 492.

of a party with a security interest in the goods. Because it is based on possession, voluntary surrender of possession terminates the lien, unless the surrender is only temporary, with an agreement that the property will be returned. Even in such case, if the rights of a third party arise while the lienholder is not in possession of the property, the lien is lost. Surrender of part of the goods will not affect the lien on the remaining goods. Surrender of possession will not terminate the lien if a notice of lien is recorded in accordance with state lien and recording statutes.

At common law, the lienholder retained the property until a judgment was obtained, at which time he levied execution on the property. Modern statutes permit the lienholder to foreclose, and the property is sold to satisfy the claim. Such statutes usually require notice to the owner prior to the sale. Any surplus proceeds after the claim is satisfied are paid to the owner of the property.

3. Bulk Transfers—Generally

Article 6 of the Uniform Commercial Code is concerned with bulk transfers. A *bulk transfer* occurs when a major part of the materials, supplies, merchandise, or other inventory is transferred not in the ordinary course of business. The creditors had presumably extended credit on the strength of these assets, and the sale of them could jeopardize the ability of the creditor to collect the debt, since the debtor might fail to pay the debt after receiving the proceeds of the sale. The law attempted to remedy this situation by imposing certain requirements on debtors and those who purchase inventory from them, if the sale is to pass title to the property free of the claims of creditors. As between the parties, a contract of sale is valid without compliance, but if the statutory requirements are not met, the property in the hands of the purchaser is subject to the claim of the seller's creditors. Article 6 of the Code has not only provided uniformity in this area, it has also simplified the procedures to be followed on the sale of a business.

Article 6 covers sales if (1) the sale is in bulk and not in the ordinary course of business; (2) it is of the major part of the materials, supplies, merchandise, or other inventory; and (3) the seller's principal business is the sale of merchandise from stock. Ordinarily, a sale of a manufacturing concern is not subject to the law; it would be if the firm maintained a retail outlet which it was selling. Enterprises that manufacture what they sell—certain bakeries, for example—would be included. Enterprises whose principal business is the sale of services rather than merchandise are not covered.

Article 6 is applicable to transfers of a substantial part of the equipment of an enterprise if they are made in connection with bulk transfers of inventory. A sale of just the equipment of a business is not subject to the law.

4. Article 6 Requirements

Basically, Article 6 imposes two requirements: (1) a scheduling of the property and a listing of the creditors of the seller, and (2) a notification of the proposed sale to the seller's creditors. An optional provision of Article 6 provides for mandatory application of the proceeds of the transfer to the debts of the *transferor*. The states are free to adopt or not to adopt this provision, which gives additional protection to the seller's creditors.

It is the duty of the *transferee* to obtain from the transferor a schedule of the property transferred and a sworn list of the transferor's creditors, including their addresses and the amount owed to each. The transferee can rely on the accuracy of this listing. The transferee must keep this information for six months and have it available for creditors, or, in the alternative, file it at the designated public office.

The transferee must then give notice personally or by registered mail to all persons on the list of creditors and all other persons known to the transferee to assert claims against the transferor. The notice must be given at least ten days before the transferee takes possession of the goods or pays for them (whichever happens first) and must contain the following information: (1) that a bulk transfer is about to be made; (2) the names and business addresses of both transferor and transferee; and (3) whether the debts of the creditors are to be paid in full as a result of the transaction and, if so, the address to which the creditors should send their bills. If no provision is made for payment in full of the creditors, the notice must contain the following additional information: (1) estimated total of transferor's debts; (2) location and description of property to be transferred; (3) address where creditor list and property schedule may be inspected; (4) whether the transfer is in payment of or security for a debt owing to transferee and, if so, the amount of the debt; and (5) whether the transfer is a sale for new consideration and, if so, the amount of the consideration and the time and place of payment.

In states that have adopted the optional provision of Article 6, the transferee is obligated, in effect, to see that creditors are paid in full or pro rata from the "new consideration" paid by the transferee. Failure to do so creates personal liability for the value of the property.

If the required procedures have been followed, the transferor's creditors will have had ample opportunity to take any necessary steps to protect their interests. Such steps might include the levying of execution against the property, or obtaining a writ of attachment or a temporary injunction to stop the sale. If the Code procedures have not been followed, the transfer is ineffective as to the creditors, and they may use any appropriate remedy to collect the debt from the property.[2] The creditors must act within six months after the transferee took possession unless the transfer was concealed, in which case they must act within six months after they learn of the transfer. A purchaser who buys for value and in good faith from the transferee obtains the property free of objection based on noncompliance with the Code.

Article 6 is applicable to bulk sales by auction. The auctioneer is required to obtain a list of creditors and of the property to be sold. (All persons who

[2] *National Bank of Royal Oak* v. *Frydlewicz,* page 493.

direct, control, or are responsible for the auction are collectively called the *auctioneer.*) The auctioneer is also required to give ten days' notice of sale to all persons on the list of creditors. Failure to do so makes the auctioneer liable, up to but not exceeding the proceeds of the auction, to the creditors as a class.

SURETYSHIP

5. Introduction

Suretyship is a method of providing security for a creditor that does not involve an interest in property. In suretyship, the security for the creditor is provided by a third person's promise to be responsible for the debtor's obligation.

In the law of suretyship, the person who borrows money or assumes direct responsibility to perform is called the *principal, principal debtor,* or *obligor.* The party who promises to be liable for the principal's obligation is called the *surety,* or *guarantor.* The party entitled to performance or payment is customarily called the *creditor,* or *obligee.*

The term *surety* has both a broad and a narrow meaning. In the broad sense, it is used to describe those third persons who are liable for the debts or obligations of another person. In this sense, a surety may be primarily, as well as secondarily, liable. The term *surety* in this broad sense includes guarantors. A contract of guaranty is one in which a third party, the guarantor, promises the person who is the creditor that he will pay the debt or fulfill the obligation only *if the debtor does not.* The obligation of a guarantor is secondary to that of the principal debtor. The law relating to commercial paper discussed the distinction between collection guaranteed and payment guaranteed on page 400. It should be reviewed as a part of this discussion.

Surety in the narrow sense of the word does not include a guarantor but is limited to one who is primarily liable. In modern law, the distinction between a surety and a guarantor is of little significance. The Restatement of Security treats suretyship and guaranty as synonymous. Unless otherwise noted, the legal principles of suretyship discussed in this chapter include guaranty contracts.

A contract of suretyship can be distinguished from a contract of indemnity. Both provide security for a promisee, but a surety makes a promise to a person who is *to receive* performance of an act on payment of a debt by another, whereas in a contract of indemnity, the promise is made to one who is promising *to do* an act or *to pay* a debt. Suretyship provides security to creditors, whereas indemnity provides security to debtors. Indemnity is a promise to the debtor, or obligor, to save him harmless from any loss that he may incur as a result of the debt or promise.

Performance bonds and fidelity bonds are also contracts of suretyship. A performance bond provides protection against losses that may result from the failure of a contracting party to perform the contract as agreed. The surety (bonding company) promises the party entitled to performance to pay losses caused by nonperformance by the principal in an amount not to exceed the face of the bond. Fidelity bonds give protection against the dishonest acts of a person. For example, they protect employers from losses caused by embezzlement by an employee—the bonding company promises to repay the employer any loss caused by defalcation of the covered employees not to exceed a stated amount. Thus, bonding companies are sureties in the sense that the term *surety* includes security either for the payment of money or for the faithful performance of some other duty.

6. The Suretyship Contract

Suretyship usually results from an agreement of the parties, but it may also result by operation of law. For example, assume that Jones sells his retail lumber business to Smith. The latter assumes and agrees to pay, as part of the purchase price, all of Jones's outstanding liabilities. As between Smith and Jones, Smith has now become the primary debtor, and Jones is a surety and secondarily liable. As soon as the creditors are notified of the sale, they are obligated to respect the new relationship. However, this does not require that the creditors first attempt to recover from Smith before looking to Jones.

Suretyship most often results from an express contract between the surety and the creditor whereby the surety assumes responsibility for the principal's performance for the creditor. The surety agrees that he may be called upon to pay or to perform in case the principal defaults. The contract of suretyship requires consideration. In most instances, the consideration that supports the surety's promise is the same as that received by the principal.

Contracts of suretyship often require interpretation. If the promise to pay the debt of another does not contain a time or an amount limitation, the courts tend to limit the liability to one transaction and to construe the guaranty as for a single purchase rather than a continuing offer. Where there is a time limitation in the guaranty, the courts tend to construe the guaranty as continuous for the period stated, in a reasonable amount. When there is a limit on amount but not on time, the guaranty is likewise continuous, with the maximum liability being the amount stated.

Some sureties are paid for serving in that capacity, and others are not. Those that are paid are described as compensated sureties. Compensated sureties are usually bonding or insurance corporations. Many cases distinguish between the protection afforded an uncompensated surety and that afforded a compensated surety. It is important that particular attention be paid to the differences in treatment of compensated as opposed to uncompensated sureties in the material that follows.

One major difference in the treatment afforded compensated as contrasted with uncompensated sureties is in the interpretation of the contract. Ambiguous provisions of surety agreements are construed in favor of the unpaid surety and against the creditor. Ambiguous provisions of surety agreements involving compensated sureties are resolved against the surety. This distinction results from the fact that ambiguous language is generally construed against the party using it. In the case of unpaid sureties, the language is usually framed by the creditor and signed by the surety. In the case of compensated sureties, the contract is usually prepared by the surety.

7. Fiduciary Aspects

The suretyship relation is, within limits, fiduciary in character, involving special trust and confidence between the parties. For this reason, a creditor possessing information affecting the risk must communicate such information to the surety before the contract is made. This duty applies only to information that is significant to the risk.

Since the contract is between the surety and the creditor, any misconduct of the principal that induces the surety to become such does not permit the surety to avoid the contract. However, if at the time of the contract the creditor is aware of the principal's misrepresentation, the creditor is obligated to inform the surety of the misrepresentation. For example, an employer who has knowledge of past defalcations of an employee and who seeks a bond ensuring faithful performance by the employee of his duties is obligated to notify the surety at the time the contract is being formed of such misconduct. Similarly, a creditor who learns that the principal has misrepresented his financial condition to a prospective surety is obligated to warn the surety of the unanticipated risk. If the creditor fails to warn the surety, the surety's promise is not enforceable.

An employer who discovers that a bonded employee has been guilty of misappropriation of funds should immediately discharge the employee unless the surety assents to his continued employment. To continue the employee at his task subjects the surety to a risk not contemplated. Rehabilitation of the employee by "giving him a second chance" can be undertaken only with the consent of the surety. If the surety does not consent, and if the employee is guilty of misappropriation a second time, the surety is not liable on the surety bond.

THE LIABILITY OF SURETIES

8. General Principles

A surety is liable to the creditor as soon as the principal defaults. The creditor need not exhaust his remedies against the principal before looking to the surety. Notice of default by the debtor is not a condition precedent to the creditor's right to sue to enforce the promise of the surety, unless the contract of surety requires that notice of default by the debtor be given to the surety.[3]

---

[3] *Lee* v. *Vaughn,* page 494.

When there is more than one surety on an obligation, the liability of the sureties is described as "joint and several." This means that the creditor may sue them jointly for the debt or he may sue each surety separately for the total debt. If the sureties are sued jointly, the entire judgment against them can be collected from one debtor just as if the debtor had been sued separately. The problem of allocating shares of the obligation between the sureties does not concern the creditor, and this matter is left exclusively to the sureties as a result of this joint and several liability.

Whenever two or more sureties become secondarily liable for the same obligation of the principal, they become cosureties. This is true even if one surety does not know of the existence of the other. There is an implied contract between cosureties that they will share any loss equally unless they have agreed otherwise. As long as the balance of a claim remains outstanding and unpaid, a cosurety has no right to contribution unless he has paid more than his share of the claim, and then only to the extent of the excess. This he may recover from any cosurety unless it compels the latter to pay more than his full share.

The liability of a surety may be released and the surety discharged upon the happening of several events. Among these are changes in the contract terms, extension of the time of payment, payment of the obligation, and any other act that materially prejudices the rights of the surety. These matters are discussed in the sections that follow.

9.   The Effect of an Extension of the Time of Payment on Liability

Debtors frequently seek an extension of time for payment from the creditor. In cases where the debt is secured by a promise of a surety, the creditor should be careful not to extend the time for performance without the surety's consent. As a general rule, a binding contract between the principal and the creditor that definitely extends the time within which performance may be demanded releases the unpaid surety absolutely. A similar contract will also release the compensated surety only if the compensated surety can show actual injury as a result of the extension agreement.[4] Injury is shown when the ability of the principal to perform has perceptibly weakened during the period of extension.

A contract of extension releases the unpaid surety because the surety's right to proceed against the principal has been postponed and the financial status of the principal may become less sound during the period of the extension.

To release the surety, the extension agreement must be a binding enforceable contract. As such, it must be for a definite time and must be supported by consideration. Consideration for an extension may take the form of an advance payment of interest, or the giving of a note promising to pay it, or an increase in the interest rate. Merely promising to pay the original debt at a future date will not supply the consideration, because performance of a preexisting contract is not consideration.

4 *Bayer & Mingolia Construction Co.* v. *Deschenes,* page 495.

Mere indulgence upon the part of the creditor, or his passively permitting the debtor to take more time than the contract calls for, does not release the surety. The latter is in no sense injured by such conduct, because he is free at any time to perform and immediately start suit against the principal.

An extension of time by the creditor in which the extension agreement stipulates reservation of rights against the surety does not release the surety. Such an extension binds only the creditor. It does not bind the surety. He is free at any time to complete performance for the principal and immediately to sue him for damages suffered, since to him the arrangement is quite similar to mere indulgence. To illustrate: S becomes surety for P on a note in favor of C. The note falls due on a certain date, and P requests from C an extension of 90 days. The extension is granted with the express stipulation that C reserve all rights against S. S is not released, although he receives no notice of the extension. His right to pay the debt at any time he desires and to turn to P for reimbursement is not impaired.

10. Additional Grounds for Discharge

In addition to an extension of the time for payment, any other material change in terms of the contract between the principal and the creditor, without the consent of the surety, discharges him. Such a change in terms is a novation. A novation without the consent of the surety discharges the surety.[5] Likewise, the creditor's failure to comply with the terms of the contract of suretyship will result in the discharge of the surety.

A discharge of the principal debtor, unless assented to, also releases the surety. This rule is subject to those exceptions existing in the case of an extension of time; that is, the surety is not released if the principal debtor is discharged with reservation of rights against the surety, or if the surety is protected by securities or is a paid surety and is not injured.

Payment of the principal obligation by the debtor or someone in his behalf discharges the surety. A valid tender of payment, by either the principal or the surety, that is rejected by the creditor also releases the surety. In such a case, it is not necessary that the tender be kept good or continuously available in order for the surety to be released. Since the creditor has had an opportunity to receive his money, the surety is no longer liable.

11. The Surety's Defenses

There are numerous defenses available to a surety to avoid liability, in addition to discharge. Some of these defenses are available only to the surety, and others belong to the principal but are also available to the surety. One important defense is that of lack of a principal obligation. In other words, the surety is not bound if the principal is not bound. This may occur when the principal fails to sign the contract although expected to do so. A similar

[5] *Gilbert* v. *Cobb Exchange Bank,* page 496.

defense arises when the signature of a person shown by contract to be a cosurety is missing. Since failure of a cosurety to sign affects the right of contribution, the signature is a condition precedent to liability.

The creditor has a duty to obtain the genuine signature of the principal, and failure to do so is an absolute defense for the surety. The same rule is not used when the cosurety's signature is forged and this fact is unknown to the creditor. The burden is on the surety to ascertain if the cosurety's signature is genuine. Many other defenses available to the principal may be asserted by the surety against the creditor, particularly when the principal is willing to have the defenses so used. Such defenses as mutual mistake, fraud, illegality, lack or failure of consideration, or undue influence, if available to the principal, may be used by the surety.

There are three important exceptions to the general rule that defenses available to the principal may be used by the surety to avoid liability to the creditor. These defenses are infancy, bankruptcy, and the statute of limitations. Infancy and bankruptcy are not available to the surety as a defense because the surety is employed in the first instance to protect the creditor against the inability of the debtor to perform. If a minor avoids a contract and, in so doing, fails to return all of the consideration that he has received, the surety is required to make up any deficiency between the value of the item returned and the amount of the indebtedness.

The statute of limitations available to the principal debtor may not be used by the surety.[6] Each has his own period after which he is no longer liable to the creditor, and the period may be longer for one than for the other. Thus, the debtor may be liable on an oral contract whereas the surety is liable on a written contract, or the debtor may have made a part payment that extends the period of his liability but has no effect upon the liability of the surety.

Setoffs and counterclaims of both the principal and the surety may be used as a defense by the surety under certain circumstances. The surety can set off any claim it has against the creditor and use the setoff to reduce or eliminate the liability. If the debtor is insolvent, if the principal and surety are sued jointly, or if the surety has taken an assignment of the claim of the debtor, the surety is entitled to use as a defense any setoff that could be used by the principal debtor in a suit by the creditor.

RIGHTS OF THE PARTIES

12. Rights of the Surety against the Principal

One who becomes a surety at the request, or with the approval, of the principal is entitled to reimbursement for any loss caused by the principal's default.

---

[6] *Bomud Company* v. *Yockey Oil Company and Osborn*, page 496.

Normally, the surety is not permitted to add any attorney's fees that he has been compelled to pay on his own behalf by way of defense or fees paid to the creditor's attorney. All attorney's fees can be avoided by performance of contract terms; when the principal fails to perform, it becomes the immediate duty of the surety to act. Attorney's fees incurred in a bona fide attempt to reduce the amount of the recovery form an exception to this general rule.

The surety may recover only the amount paid by him. Thus, if he settles a claim for less than the full amount owing to the creditor, his right to recover is limited to the sum paid under the settlement. Furthermore, bankruptcy on the part of the principal, even though it takes place before the surety is called upon to perform, releases the principal from further liability to the surety.

13. Subrogation Rights

Literally, *subrogation* means the substitution of one person in place of another. A creditor has the right to step into the shoes of the surety and to enforce the surety's rights against the principal. For example, assume that the principal delivered corporate stock to the surety in order to protect the surety in the event of the principal's default. The creditor, to the extent of his claim, may substitute his position for that of the surety with reference to the stock. In the event of the return of the stock by the surety to the principal, the creditor is entitled to follow the stock into the hands of the debtor and subject it to a lien. The creditor may also secure an injunction against return of the stock to the principal, thus having it impounded by the court until the principal debt falls due, at which time the stock may be sold for the benefit of the creditor.

The surety who fully performs the obligation of his principal is subrogated to the creditor's rights against the principal. The surety who pays his principal's debt becomes entitled to any security that the principal has placed with the creditor to secure that particular debt. Likewise, if the creditor has obtained a judgment against the principal, the surety receives the benefit of the judgment when he satisfies the principal's debt.

Because of the right of subrogation, a creditor in possession of collateral given to him by the principal is not at liberty to return it without the consent of the surety. Any surrender of security releases the surety to the extent of its value, his loss of subrogation damaging him to that extent. Failure of the creditor to make use of the security, however, does not release the surety, since the latter is free to pay the indebtedness and to obtain the security for his own protection. However, if the creditor loses the benefit of collateral by inactivity—failure to record a mortgage or notify an indorser—the surety is released to the extent that he is injured. In general, if the person who is entitled to protection under the contract of suretyship does anything that will materially prejudice the rights of the surety, the surety will, to that extent at least, be discharged.

LAWS ASSISTING CREDITORS CASES

Beck v. Nutrodynamics, Inc.
186 A.2d 715 (N.J.) 1962

Plaintiff, Beck, procured a writ of attachment and levied upon certain goods owned by defendant, Nutrodynamics, Inc. These goods were in the possession of Ivers-Lee Company. Ivers-Lee filed a motion with the court, claiming a paramount and prior property right in the goods, based on an artisan's lien for materials, labor, and services furnished. The goods involved were 193 cases of pills that Ivers-Lee had packaged for defendant. The sheriff seized the pills, and Ivers-Lee filed the motion to determine the priority of its claim vis-à-vis that of Beck's attachment.

YANCEY, J. . . . In New Jersey there is no statute with reference to an artisan's lien. Such lien stands as at common law. . . .

A common law lien is the right to retain the possession of personal property until some debt due on or secured by such property is paid or satisfied. This lien is one that arises by implication of law and not from express contract. It is founded on the immemorial recognition of the common law of a right to it in particular cases, or it may result from the established usage of a particular trade or from the mode of dealing between the parties.

The right to this common law lien applies to a bailee to whom goods have been delivered. To entitle a bailee to a lien on the article bailed, more is necessary than the mere existence of the bailment relationship. The bailee must, by his labor and skill, contribute to the improvement of the article bailed. The bailee having thus performed, the well-settled rule of the common law is that a bailee (artisan) who receives in bailment personal property under an express or implied contract to improve, better, manufacture or repair it for remuneration, and enhances the value of such property by his skill, labor, or materials employed in such undertaking, has a specific lien on such property. This lien may be enforced against the bailor while the property remains in the bailee's possession, and until the reasonable value of his labor, skill, and expenses is paid.

The first question before the court, therefore, is whether the kind of work done by Ivers-Lee is such as to support its assertion to an artisan's lien. The undisputed facts set forth are that Nutrodynamics, Inc. delivered to the claimant a huge quantity of loose, unpackaged capsules so that the same could be rendered saleable. The agreement required that the claimant prepare, mark and package the capsules and place the packages in cardboard mailing containers suitable for delivery to the customers of Nutrodynamics, Inc. The claimant, Ivers-Lee, agreed to render the service and labor and to supply the materials necessary to accomplish the foregoing. The claimant did in fact supply such labor and packaging materials. This work and materials have become assimilated into the final product, and have enhanced the value of the heretofore loose, unpackaged pills.

In the case of *O'Brien* v. *Buxton*, 9 N.J. Misc. 876, 156 A. 17 (Cir.Ct.1931), the case dealt with a lien on goods for personal services rendered and for repairs to the goods. The court stated:

> A workman who by his skill and labor has enhanced the value of a chattel, under an employment . . . has a lien on the chattel for his reasonable charge. . . .

The lien arises from the rendering of the service, and if such service be not paid for, there is a right to detain. The court further stated:

> . . . It is the natural outcome of the transaction wherein one takes his chattel to another with whom he contracts for the performance by the latter of some service upon it for its betterment.

It is to be concluded from the foregoing that the work done by Ivers-Lee did enhance the value of the product.

As to the contention that the lien was lost when the goods were given over to the sheriff under the writ of attachment, it is to be noted that a lien is lost only by the lienholder's voluntary and unconditional surrender of possession or control of the property. For Ivers-Lee to resist would have placed it in contempt of the order of the court.

For the reasons above stated and in the absence of express language in our lien statute, I find that the work and labor expended by Ivers-Lee did enhance the value of the product, and I further find that Ivers-Lee has a valid common law lien to the goods for the balance now due and owing.

National Bank of Royal Oak v. Frydlewicz
241 N.W.2d 471 (Mich.) 1976

Plaintiff loaned Frydlewicz, who operated a furniture store, $20,020 to pay for inventory and obtained a security agreement covering the inventory. Plaintiff filed its financing statement with the local recorder of deeds rather than with the Secretary of State as the law requires for inventory and, therefore, plaintiff was an unsecured creditor.

Frydlewicz went bankrupt. Prior to filing bankruptcy, Frydlewicz loaned his furniture showroom and sold all of his inventory to National, the defendant, for $13,603.24. Defendant was informed that there were no liens on the furniture, but the bulk sale was not complied with.

Plaintiff served the defendant with a writ of attachment against the inventory. The trial court held for the plaintiff and the defendant appeals.

PER CURIAM. . . . National's status is the dispositive issue in the case. Under the instant facts, one of three legal positions could be ascribed to National: (1) a buyer in ordinary course of business, (2) a buyer not in ordinary course of business or (3) a transferee in bulk. If National is a buyer in the ordinary course of business, UCC § 9-307(1) would give its interest in the disputed merchandise priority over plaintiff's unperfected security interest. As a buyer not in the ordinary course of business, National's interest would be subordinated to plaintiff's interest.

Normally, as a transferee in bulk, National would be entitled to priority over plaintiff's unperfected security interest. Pursuant to UCC § 9-301(1)(c), "an unperfected security interest is subordinate to the rights of in the case of goods . . . a person who is not a secured party and who is a transferee in bulk." However, National failed to satisfy the requirements necessary under the bulk transfer provisions of UCC Art. 6. Therefore it cannot assert a claim of priority as a transferee in bulk. Specifically, UCC § 6-104(1) requires:

> Except as provided with respect to auction sales (section 6-108), a bulk transfer subject to this article is ineffective against *any creditor* of the *transferor* unless:
>
> (a) The *transferee requires the transferor to furnish a list of his existing creditors* prepared as stated in this section; and
>
> (b) The parties prepare a schedule of the property transferred sufficient to identify it; and
>
> (c) The transferee preserves the list and schedule for six months next following the transfer and permits inspection of either or both and copying therefrom at all reasonable hours by any creditor of the transferor, or files the list and schedule in the office of the secretary of state.

It was undisputed at trial that National did not request Frydlewicz to furnish a list of his creditors. . . .

We find from the record that National was, as the trial court held, a transferee in bulk. A bulk transfer is

> any transfer in bulk and not in the ordinary course of the transferor's business of a major part of the materials, supplies, merchandise or other inventory (section 9-109) of an enterprise subject to this article.

The items transferred must be inventory, i.e., held "for sale or lease." Here, the furniture transferred clearly represented the entire inventory held for sale by the King Furniture and Appliance Mart.

The transferor enterprise must have as its "principal business . . . the sale of merchandise from stock." Here, the transferor was a retail furniture store. The transfer must not be in the ordinary course of the transferor's business, and the items transferred must constitute a "major part" of the transferor's inventory. "Major part" has been defined as "meaning something more than 50%. . . ." Ordinary course means day-to-day operation. The bulk sale must be an extraordinary event, one occurring a few times in the life of a merchant. . . .

The closing of a retail store and bulk sale of its stock, both whole and damaged items, constitutes such an extraordinary transaction. Further, the instant case is prototypical of the situation which the bulk sales law was promulgated to remedy. The law attempts to protect a creditor from a "merchant, owing debts, who sells out his stock in trade to anyone for any price, pockets the proceeds, and disappears leaving the creditors unpaid." Here Frydlewicz sold his inventory for less than its value and declared bankruptcy. But for the bulk sales law plaintiff might be without a remedy.

The interaction of the secured transaction and bulk transfer provisions of the MUCC therefore, require that plaintiff be protected against loss of collateral by the coverage of the bulk transfer notice provisions. . . .

Affirmed.

Lee v. Vaughn
534 S.W.2d 221 (Ark.) 1976

HARRIS, J. . . . Appellant, Carl W. Lee, guaranteed the payment of "the first $3,000" of a $4,000 note from Norvile and Rofena Akin, which Lee assigned to appellee, B.J. Vaughn, a resident of Lamesa, Texas; the guaranty agreement was also executed in Texas. The agreement provided that "If any monthly installment is past due more than 15 days, B.J. Vaughn shall promptly mail notice of that fact to the said Lee, P. O. Box 266, Bentonville, Arkansas, 72712." The Akins defaulted on the note, and appellant refused to perform his agreement, contending that appellee failed to give the requisite notice. Appellee instituted suit on the guaranty and the trial court, sitting as a jury, rendered judgment for Vaughn in the amount of $2,921.13. From the judgment so entered, appellant brings this appeal contending that the lack of notice by appellee constituted failure of consideration with a resultant release of appellant from liability under the guaranty.

The record reveals that Lee and Smith executed the assignment and guaranty on August 15, 1968. The note called for monthly payments of $100 by the Akins, and they made seven monthly payments. In April, 1969, no payment at all was made, and only $41.32 was paid in May. Four more payments were made before the Akins missed the payment for October, 1969; likewise, a payment was missed in February, 1970, and no payments were made after March 18, 1970.

Sometime during 1968 or 1969 Vaughn moved to Nashville, Tennessee, apparently leaving the management of his Lamesa interests in the hands of his office manager, and his Lamesa attorney, Robert Snell. The evidence does not reveal that any type of notice was given to either Lee or Smith until "right at the end of 1969 or the early part of 1970." . . .

Lee testified that he was never notified in writing by either Vaughn or his attorney that the Akins were in default; that had he been so notified as the monthly payments became delinquent, he could have, and would have, honored the guaranty agreement.

We are of the opinion that the trial court erred in rendering judgment against Lee. . . .

We have held that a guarantor is entitled to have his undertaking strictly construed and that he cannot be held liable beyond the strict terms of his contract. . . .

A guarantor, like a surety, is a favorite of the law, and his liability is not to be extended by implication beyond the express limits or turns of the instrument, or its plain intent.

However, the instant appeal presents a question of first impression for this court; i.e., apparently no Arkansas case has construed a guaranty contract that contained an express requirement of notice of the principal's default. It seems clear, however, that the great majority of states (all but one, Michigan) that have considered a like situation have reached a conclusion in conformity with the Restatement of Security, § 136, where it is stated:

> Subject to the rules pertaining to negotiable instruments, the surety's obligation to the creditor is not affected by the creditor's failure to notify him of the principal's default *unless such notification is required by the terms of the surety's contract.*

The leading state decision on the point appears to be *Yama* v. *Sigman,* 114 Colo. 323, 165 P.2d 191, in which the debtor was obligated to make biweekly payments, and the guaranty was conditioned upon immediate notice of default. The Colorado Supreme Court held that under such an agreement the guarantor could not be held liable after the debtor's default, when the creditor failed to prove that he had given the necessary notice—"their failure in this respect relieves the defendant of all liability under his guaranty." In a New York decision . . . the rule is summarized as follows:

> Where a contract of guarantee specifically provides for notice of default, the failure to give such notice discharges the guarantor's obligations [citation omitted]. The guarantor may limit his liability as such by whatever conditions he may see fit to impose, and non-compliance with them will preclude recourse to him. As stated above, his undertaking is *strictissimi juris* and cannot be extended beyond the fair import of its language.

Lee was entitled to the protection that he had insisted upon in guaranteeing the note; after all, the note contains an acceleration clause under which the entire indebtedness could have become immediately due and payable following the April, 1969, default. . . .
Reversed.

Bayer & Mingolia Construction Co. v. Deschenes
205 N.E.2d 208 (Mass.) 1965

Plaintiff, Bayer, was the general contractor on a State highway contract, and defendant, Deschenes, was a subcontractor engaged by plaintiff to do certain excavation work as specified in the prime contract. Under the subcontract, all work was to start not later than November 24, 1958, and be completed on or before March 1, 1959. Deschenes was required to furnish a bond of $91,000 for faithful performance. The bond was written by Aetna Insurance Co. Deschenes did not start work until December 1, 1958, and on June 22, 1959, when he quit, he had completed only about half of the work. During this time, Bayer made efforts to get Deschenes to do the work but finally completed the job himself. He brought action against Aetna on the bond, and the lower court rendered judgment for plaintiff. Defendant appealed.

CUTTER, J. . . . Aetna contends that it is discharged as surety by the extensions of time for performance given by Bayer to Deschenes, despite Aetna's knowledge of these extensions, and the absence of any finding of injury to Aetna caused thereby. Aetna, however, "is a compensated surety and is not entitled to invoke the ancient doctrine of *strictissimi juris*. . . ."

In the case of an *accommodation* surety, "where the principal and creditor, without the surety's consent, make a binding agreement to extend . . . time . . . the surety is discharged unless the creditor in the extension agreement reserves his rights against the surety. . . ." The modern rule, however, with respect to a *compensated* surety (see Restate-

ment: *Security,* 129 (2)) is that such a surety "is discharged only to the extent that he is harmed by the extension."

In any event, it is only by a binding, enforceable agreement for new consideration for an extension, which cannot be rescinded or disregarded, that the discharge of a surety will be effected. . . . The auditor's finding concerning the extensions of time for performance is merely that they were made "by mutual agreement of Bayer . . . and Deschenes." This finding does not import to us an enforceable agreement for consideration but merely Bayer's effort to obtain even dilatory performance by Deschenes.

We hold that Aetna, which has not shown itself to have been harmed by the extensions of time, was not thereby discharged as surety.

The order for judgment against Aetna is affirmed.

Gilbert v. Cobb Exchange Bank
231 S.E.2d 508 (Ga.) 1976

BELL, J. . . . This is a suit on a guaranty agreement. The trial court granted plaintiff's motion for directed verdict and a judgment was entered.

Plaintiff's evidence established that defendant's son on July 31, 1970, executed a promissory note to plaintiff in the amount of $3100. The defendant executed an unconditional guaranty of payment of the note and of all extensions or renewals. On October 10, 1971, the note was renewed but an additional $600 cash was added to the principal amount of the original. The defendant argued at trial and here that the addition of the $600 constituted a novation and was accomplished without his consent which operated to discharge him. A novation without the consent of the surety will discharge the surety under

Code § 103-202. This statute has been held to apply to a contract of guaranty. Plaintiff contends that since the guaranty covered all renewals of the note, there was no discharge. While the guaranty did cover extensions or renewals, it could only apply to a renewal of the same obligation and not a new one. The guaranty very clearly guaranteed payment of "that certain note dated July 31, 1970 in the amount of $3,100.00 . . . and all extensions or renewals thereof . . ." and nothing else. The addition of the $600 to principal constituted a material change in the terms of the note. A novation resulted which discharged defendant.

The evidence demands a verdict for the defendant. . . .

Reversed.

Bomud Company v. Yockey Oil Company and Osborn
299 P.2d 72 (Kans.) 1956

Osborn in a letter guaranteed payment by Yockey of oil well supplies which the plaintiff,

Bomud, in reliance on the letter, sold to Yockey on credit. Yockey was no longer liable because of the short statute of limitations for oral agreements, but the five-year statute applying to written accounts had not run. Osborn contended that he was released because Yockey was no longer liable and the lower court awarded judgment in favor of Osborn, against whom the plaintiff had taken this appeal.

FATZER, J. . . . A guarantor, to be relieved from his obligation to pay, must establish one of three facts: (1) the debt has been paid or extinguished; (2) a valid release or discharge or; (3) the bar of the statute of limitations as to himself. It is conceded that the debt has not been paid. The fact that the statute bars recovery against Yockey does not extinguish the debt. . . . It is also conceded that the statute of limitations has not run as to Osborn's individual liability on his written contract if he has not been released or discharged. Did the failure to bring the action upon the open account, until the statute had run in favor of Yockey, release or discharge Osborn from his guarantee to pay under his written contract? We think it did not. . . . The contract of a guarantor is his own separate contract. It is in the nature of a warranty by him that the thing guaranteed to be done by the principal shall be done, and is not an engagement jointly with the principal to do the thing. A guarantor, not being a joint contractor with the principal, is not bound like a surety to do what the principal has contracted to do, but answers only for the consequence of the default of the principal. . . . When default occurs on the part of the principal, the guarantor's liability becomes primary and is absolute. . . .

Osborn's contract with Bomud was based upon a valid consideration. It was a separate undertaking to pay if Yockey defaulted. When Osborn's liability became primary and absolute, the open account was then enforceable against Yockey, and it is of no consequence to Osborn if since that time the statute has run in Yockey's favor. Osborn's liability was fixed and determined by his written guaranty and that obligation has not been discharged. That the statute of limitations had not run in Osborn's favor when suit was filed is conceded. The debt has not been paid. Bomud is entitled to recover from Osborn in accordance with the terms and conditions of his contract.

The judgment is *reversed* with directions to set aside the order entering judgment for execution in satisfaction of plaintiffs' prior accordance with the views expressed in this opinion. It is so ordered.

CHAPTER 26
REVIEW QUESTIONS AND PROBLEMS

1. G held a security interest in a certain automobile. The owner of the car took it to H's garage for repairs. The owner paid neither G nor H, and H is now in possession of the car. G seeks to obtain possession of the car from H. Will he succeed? Why?

2. G, by contract, guaranteed prompt payment of a certain note owing by P to C. The note fell due at a time when the maker was solvent, but C made no attempt to collect and gave G no notice of the default. Later, P became insolvent, and C desires to collect of G. May he do so? Why?

3. Davis was surety for his brother on a $1,152 note in favor of a bank, the brother giving Davis a mortgage on real property to protect him against loss. Davis and his brother are insolvent and are thinking about releasing the mortgage. A court held the bank could have the rights of the mortgage. Why?

4. S was surety upon P's obligation to C. Some time after the debt fell due, P, with the knowledge and consent of S, made a payment on the obligation. Did this payment toll the statute of limitations for S as well as P? Why?

5. X hired Y, a general contractor, to build a house. Y in turn hired Z, a subcontractor, to paint the house. However, knowing Z to be a rather irresponsible person, Y required Z to obtain a bond from an insurance company, the ABC Company, to insure his performance. Z left town, and Y brought an action against the ABC Company alone. May he do so? Why?

6. S, the owner and operator of a gasoline service station, sold the business to B. B immediately began operating the station, but the sheriff served a writ of execution and levied on the personal property and equipment connected with the station on behalf of creditors of S. Even though S paid the creditors within a few days, B sued to rescind the sale on the grounds that S had not complied with the bulk-sales provisions of the Code. Should rescission be granted? Why?

7. S sold a major part of his merchandise to B. B did not require S to furnish a list of existing creditors before the sale was consummated, and B did not give notice to the creditors of S. The creditors of S now sue B. Is B personally liable to the creditors of S? Why?

8. S wrote a letter of guaranty to C on behalf of R, a retailer. The letter stated that S "does guarantee payment of any credit granted by you not to exceed Ten Thousand Dollars ($10,000)." R was involved in a series of individual transactions with C, of which none exceeded $10,000 and the total amount did not exceed $10,000. R failed to pay, and S contends that his total liability is limited to one transaction. Is S correct? Why?

9. D was indebted to C in the amount of $2,200. D agreed to pay in monthly installments of $100. S agreed that if D defaulted in a monthly payment, he would make up the payment, and if D missed three consecutive payments, then he would pay the entire amount due. D made one payment of $100 and two payments of $37.50 and then disappeared. S claims that C's acceptance of partial payment without his knowledge constituted an extension of time, which released him from liability. Is S correct? Why?

10. D purchased drilling equipment from C on credit, and S guaranteed payment. The guaranty agreement required C to submit copies of all invoices to S. One invoice was mailed to S seven months late. S contends that he is discharged from liability. Is S correct? Why?

Debtor and Consumer Protection

1. Introduction

The preceding chapters have discussed several laws that assist creditors in the collection of debts. There are also numerous laws that have as their avowed purpose the protection of debtors and consumers. Many such laws and legal principles have already been discussed. For example, the law relating to usury was covered with the materials on illegal agreements, and the Code provision on unconscionable bargains was discussed as a part of the law as it relates to the sale of goods. This chapter will be concerned with additional efforts to aid debtors and consumers.

This period is sometimes referred to as the era of consumer protection, because so many laws have been enacted at both the state and national levels to aid consumers. Courts have also been active in extending protection to consumers. The demise of privity of contract in the breach of warranty cases is an example of judicial consumer protection.

The law has been aiding the consumer-debtor for several reasons. Consumers and debtors frequently have unequal bargaining power with sellers and creditors. Many of them are financially unsophisticated and easily deceived. Frequently they lack the information to make intelligent decisions. Therefore, much of the consumer movement has been directed at providing all the relevant information to enable borrowers and purchasers to make reasonably intelligent decisions in the marketplace.

2. Exemptions

Typical of state laws protecting debtors are those exempting property from debts. In most states, the exemption statutes include both real and personal property. The real property exemption is usually called the homestead exemption.[1]

It provides that upon the sale of the family home to satisfy a judgment debt, a certain amount of the sale price shall be paid to the judgment debtor to be his property free of the debt. For example, assume a homestead exemption of $5,000 and that the family home sold for $26,000 at public auction to satisfy a judgment for $10,000. Assume also that the house was mortgaged for $15,000 prior to the judgment. The debtor would receive $5,000, the mortgagee $15,-000, and the creditor $6,000, leaving the judgment unsatisfied to the extent of the $4,000. Of course, the judgment creditor could collect the balance from other nonexempt property, if any.

The reason for the homestead exemption is to provide sufficient funds to the debtor for another home. Public policy favors the debtor and his family's having a home rather than the creditor's being able to collect the entire debt. In some states, the homestead exemption is not available to debtors who do not have a family, thus evidencing the policy of protecting the family.

Statutes in most states also exempt a certain amount of personal property. These usually include wearing apparel and other personal possessions, such as family pictures, books, Bible, and a specified dollar value of other items.

3. Limitations on Garnishment

By statute, the various states and the federal government limit the amount of disposable earnings of an employee that may be used to pay judgment creditors (garnishment). For example, the federal law, which is a part of the Consumer Credit Protection Act, provides that for an individual, the maximum part of the total disposable earnings subject to garnishment in any week *may not* exceed the *lesser* of:

1. Twenty-five percent of the disposable earnings for that week, or

2. The amount by which the disposable earnings for that week exceed thirty times the federal minimum hourly wage prescribed by the Fair Labor Standards Act.

Disposable earnings means earnings after deductions for income taxes and Social Security taxes.

The federal law does not preempt the field of garnishment or affect any state law. Many state laws exempt larger amounts than does the federal law, and the net effect of the federal law is to exempt the larger amount that either

---

[1] *Wilkinson* v. *Carpenter,* page 512.

provides. Both the state and the federal law illustrate a public policy against using a wage earner's income to pay judgment debts.

Many employers in the past have discharged employees who were the subject of garnishment proceedings; the federal law has now prohibited this practice in situations involving only one garnishment proceeding. The federal law covers all places of employment.

4. FTC Abolition of Holder in Due Course Doctrine

Historically, the holder in due course concept was predicated on the premise that personal defenses should not be used against a holder in due course because of the need for commercial paper to move freely through the business community as "a courier without luggage" and as the equivalent of money. Today, consumer advocates argue that protection of the consumer is more important than the reasons for the holder in due course concept and that all defenses should always be available to the consumer-debtor. It is felt that the best protection for a consumer is the right to withhold payment if the goods are defective or not delivered.

Before considering the FTC rule relating to the availability of defenses, it should be recognized that defenses may be "cut off" in two basic ways. A holder in due course of a negotiable instrument takes it free of personal defenses. In addition, many contracts specifically provide that if the contract is assigned, the consumer agrees that he will not assert any defense against the assignee. Such provisions not only give the assignee the rights of a holder in due course of a negotiable instrument but purport to eliminate real defenses as well.

A number of states have enacted statutes that prohibit the use of clauses that cut off defenses. If such clauses are used in these states, they will not be enforced. In addition, the courts in many states have held that a holder was not a holder in due course when the finance company was closely connected with the seller. Courts have also strictly construed the application of the holder in due course rule. Doubts about the negotiability of instruments have been resolved against negotiability.[2] Several states have achieved this result by the enactment of the Uniform Consumer Credit Code, whose provisions are applicable to instruments other than checks. This Code offers two alternative approaches to the problem. A state legislature can select the one it considers best suited to the needs of the state.

One alternative simply provides that the consumer can assert all claims and defenses against the assignee of any paper that he signed. This gives maximum protection to the consumer. The other alternative provides that the assignee can give written notice of the assignment to the debtor. The consumer is then given the right to assert defenses for three months. After the three-month period, the assignee is free of any defense and the debtor's only remedy is against the seller.

[2] *Geiger Finance Company* v. *Graham,* page 514.

Some states require by statute that a note given in payment of consumer goods be labeled "consumer paper." The law then provides that consumer paper is not a negotiable instrument. Since the instrument is not a negotiable one, there can be no holder in due course and all defenses are available.

These state efforts have not been universal. Therefore, in 1976, the Federal Trade Commission, acting under its authority to prohibit unfair and deceptive practices, adopted a rule that prohibits the use of the holder in due course concept against consumers. It also provides that a clause purporting to cut off defenses is an unfair method of competition and illegal.

The FTC rule is designed to eliminate substantial abuses that were often inflicted upon the purchaser of consumer goods. Under the holder in due course concept, consumers were often required to pay for defective merchandise and even for merchandise not received. They were also required to pay even though the transaction involved fraud on the part of the seller. Since consumer paper was usually sold to a bank or other financial institution, the purchaser of the paper would qualify as a holder in due course. As such, it would be able to collect, and the consumer was left to fight it out with the seller when a problem arose.

The FTC rule is applicable to any sale or lease of goods or services to consumers in commerce. In such a transaction, it is an unfair or deceptive act or practice for a seller to receive a credit contract that does not contain the following provision in at least 10-point bold type:

NOTICE

ANY HOLDER OF THIS CONSUMER CREDIT CONTRACT IS SUB-
JECT TO ALL CLAIMS AND DEFENSES WHICH THE DEBTOR
COULD ASSERT AGAINST THE SELLER OF GOODS OR SERVICES
OBTAINED PURSUANT HERETO OR WITH THE PROCEEDS
HEREOF. RECOVERY HEREUNDER BY THE DEBTOR SHALL NOT
EXCEED AMOUNTS PAID BY THE DEBTOR HEREUNDER.

Thus, the holder could not be a holder in due course, because the holder agrees to be subject to all defenses.

The FTC rule is not applicable to a direct loan in which the consumer borrows money and makes a cash purchase. Since the lender is dealing directly with the consumer-borrower, the lender is not a holder in due course. Moreover, the lender has no contact with the seller and is not subject to any defense that may arise out of the sales transaction. To prevent sellers from sending buyers directly to the lender and thus circumventing the law by qualifying as a direct loan, the rule has a special provision to prevent circumvention of the law. It declares that it is an unfair or deceptive practice for a seller to accept in payment the proceeds of a purchase-money loan unless the following is included in the consumer credit contract in 10-point bold type:

ANY HOLDER OF THIS CONSUMER CREDIT CONTRACT IS SUB-
JECT TO ALL CLAIMS AND DEFENSES WHICH THE DEBTOR

COULD ASSERT AGAINST THE SELLER OF GOODS OR SER-
VICES OBTAINED WITH THE PROCEEDS HEREOF. RECOVERY
HEREUNDER BY THE DEBTOR SHALL NOT EXCEED AMOUNTS
PAID BY THE DEBTOR HEREUNDER.

For the purpose of the foregoing rule, a purchase-money loan exists if the
seller refers the consumer to the creditor or is affiliated with the creditor by
common control, contract, or business arrangement. This means that if the
lending institution regularly does business with the seller or has an understanding that its customers may obtain financing, the provision must be included in the loan contract. Again, it provides that all defenses are available
to the consumer.

As a result of the FTC rule, if a consumer-purchaser or buyer has any
defense against the seller, it may assert that defense against the bank or other
financial institution that seeks to collect the debt. Thus, banks and other financial institutions must make sure that the seller stands behind the products sold.
The financial institutions become a consumer protection agency to force sellers
to stand behind their products or lose their source of credit. In addition, they
must deal only with responsible parties on a recourse basis if losses are to be
avoided. As a result, many fraudulent firms and businesses with questionable
practices may be forced to close.

The full effect of the FTC rule is not yet known. Many questions remain
unanswered. For example, if the seller suggests various sources of credit to a
customer, is this a referral that brings the rule into play? Sellers of defective
merchandise whose customers constantly complain will probably lose their
source of credit. Credit may tighten and the cost of extending credit may increase. Financial institutions will probably be much more careful in buying
consumer paper. Almost all transfers will be with recourse. Violators of the
rule are subject to a $10,000-per-day fine. In addition, there may be civil
liability to the debtor.

5. Federal Consumer Warranty Act

To provide consumers with adequate information about express warranties
and to prevent deceptive warranties, Congress has enacted a federal law on
warranties (Magnuson-Moss Warranty Act). The law and the Federal Trade
Commission rules adopted under it are applicable to all express warranties if
the product sold for over $15.

The first requirement of the law is that a warrantor of a consumer product
must, by means of a written warranty, fully and conspicuously disclose in
simple and readily understood language the terms and conditions of the
warranty. A consumer product is one normally used for personal, family, or
household purposes. The law and the rules then specify what must be included
in the written warranty. For example, it must include among other things a
statement of what the warrantor will do in the event of a defect or breach of

warranty, at whose expense, and for what period of time. It must also tell the consumer what he must do and what expenses he must bear.

Any exceptions or exclusions from the warranty must be indicated. The warranty must set forth the step-by-step procedure the consumer is to follow in order to obtain performance of the warranty. The law does not require that a warranty be given or that, if given, it be in writing. If one is given, however, it must include the items provided by law and be in simple and readily understood language.

The law also requires that each warranty be labeled "full" or "limited." A full warranty must indicate its duration. Products covered by a full warranty must be repaired or replaced by the seller without charge and within a reasonable time in the event there is a defect, malfunction, or failure to conform to the written warranty. A purchaser of a limited warranty is put on notice to find out its limits.

To assist the consumer in making an intelligent purchase decision, sellers are required to make all information about the warranties available prior to the sale. This information must be clearly and conspicuously displayed in close connection with the warranted product.

A significant aspect of the federal law deals with informal mechanisms for the resolution of consumer disputes. The law does not require such mechanisms, but it strongly encourages sellers to use them. If a seller establishes a procedure for an independent or government entity to resolve disputes with its buyers, the consumer must resort to the procedure before filing suit against the seller. Consumers are given access to these informal dispute procedures free of charge.

Under the federal law, a warrantor may not impose any limitation on the duration of any implied warranty. Any warrantor may not exclude or limit consequential damages for breach of any warranty unless the exclusion or limitation appears conspicuously on the face of the warranty. No supplier may disclaim or modify any implied warranty if there is a written warranty or if, at the time of sale or within 90 days, the supplier enters into a service contract with the buyer. This latter restriction does not prevent a seller from limiting the time period of a written warranty. The time period of the warranty must also be set forth in clear and unmistakable language on the face of the warranty. A warrantor may not condition a warranty on the consumer's using any article or service that is identified by a brand, trade, or corporate name, unless this provision is waived by the Federal Trade Commission. The law also authorizes class-action suits for damages for breach of warranty if at least 100 persons are affected. This could be of substantial help to consumers.

Some persons question whether it is possible to write a warranty in simple and readily understandable language. It will take several years of working with the new law before all its ramifications are known. However, as a result of the new law, warranties are more detailed and their language is changed substantially. Many sellers have opted for the limited warranty, and a few companies, rather than become involved with all the law's requirements, have taken away their warranty in its entirety.

6. Consumer Credit Protection Act

In 1969, the federal Consumer Credit Protection Act was enacted. Its principal provisions were designed to assist debtors, and it is commonly known as the "Truth-in-Lending Act." This law gives protection both to people who buy property on credit and to people who borrow money. Its terms and provisions apply not only to those who lend money or sell on credit in the ordinary course of business but also to anyone who arranges for the extension of credit. It applies only to natural persons who borrow money or obtain credit for personal, family, household, or agricultural purposes. If a purchaser or borrower is other than a natural person (for example, a corporation or partnership), or if the purchase or loan is for business rather than household, etc., use, the law is not applicable. It covers real estate credit transactions as well as personal property transactions. In the latter case, it is not applicable if the loan or purchase exceeds $25,000. It is also not applicable to agricultural credit transactions if the amount financed exceeds $25,000.

The law does not apply to a sale by one consumer to another consumer, since the sale is not in the seller's ordinary course of business. Typical of transactions covered are installment loans and sales, short-term notes, real etate loans, home improvement loans, and farm loans. The act and regulations are liberally construed to protect debtors. Replacing the concept of "Let the buyer beware," the policy of the law is, "Let the seller or creditor disclose." [3]

The Federal Reserve Board was given the responsibility of developing regulations to implement the purpose of the law. For this reason, most of the procedures developed to implement the law are based on the regulations of the Federal Reserve Board, and, like all rules of administrative agencies, they are periodically changed. Because of this, businesses subject to the law should make sure that they comply with the current regulations. These regulations are highly technical. For example, if both sides of a sheet of paper are used, both sides must refer the signer to the other side.[4]

The purpose or goal of the Truth-in-Lending Act is to disclose certain figures to a prospective purchaser or borrower so that he may shop for credit. The theory is that he may then obtain disclosure statements from several dealers or financers, compare them, and determine whether or not he wishes to go ahead with his purchase or loan. But whether this works in practice is subject to debate.

The goals of the Truth-in-Lending Act are expected to be accomplished by the use of disclosure statements. A copy of the disclosure statement is given to the borrower, and the original is retained by the lender for two years or until

[3] *Mourning* v. *Family Publications Service, Inc.,* page 516.
[4] *Southwestern Inv. Co.* v. *Mannix,* page 519.

the debt is paid, whichever is longer. Separate disclosure statements are required for each transaction, including refinancing. These statements inform the borrower of the amount financed, the finance charge, and the annual percentage rate. They also disclose the amount of each payment and the number of payments. It is important to realize that the annual percentage rate will generally not be the same as the interest rate. One important reason for this difference is that the annual percentage rate is based upon the finance charge, and the finance charge includes all charges imposed by the creditor, only one of which is interest. For example, the finance charge may include the cost of credit reports, credit life insurance, health insurance, appraisals, and so forth.

Any creditor subject to the law who fails to make the required disclosure may be sued by the debtor within one year from the date of the violation for his actual damages plus *twice the amount of the finance charge*. This may not be less than $100 or more than $1,000. If the creditor has made an incorrect disclosure, he must, within fifteen days after discovering the error, notify the debtor and make whatever adjustments are necessary to ensure that the debtor will not be required to pay a finance charge in excess of the amount of the percentage rate actually disclosed. If he is to avoid the penalty, the creditor must discover the error and give notice to the debtor before notification by the debtor or before the debtor institutes action against him.

The law makes some distinctions between loans secured by first mortgages and those secured by second mortgages. If the mortgage is a first mortgage in connection with a purchase, the lender is required to state only the annual interest cost; he does not have to state the total interest cost over the life of the loan. If the mortgage is a second mortgage or is a first mortgage not connected with the purchase of the property, the lender must disclose the annual interest and the total interest to be ultimately paid. The law also gives a second mortgagor, and first mortgagors unconnected with a purchase, three days in which to cancel the loan without penalty or obligation. These provisions relating to second mortgages and to borrowing by homeowners are designed to eliminate credit abuses and instinctive borrowing using real estate as security. Prior to the law, people frequently gave second mortgages without realizing it, and the law therefore requires notice that a mortgage is involved. The law also requires that the creditor give the debtor notice of the fact that the transaction may be rescinded.

The Consumer Credit Protection Act also protects borrowers by prohibiting misleading advertising. This misleading advertising often represented lower down payments and lower installment payments than were available under the law. If an advertisement contains any details of a credit plan, it must also include as disclosures any substantial information on finance charges, rates, cash price, down payment, and other information that is included in the specific regulations used to enforce the law.

7. Uniform Consumer Credit Code

The Commissioners on Uniform State Laws have prepared a Uniform Consumer Credit Code designed to accomplish many of the same purposes as the federal Truth-in-Lending Act. The Uniform Consumer Credit Code (U.C.C.C.) also attempts to protect consumers by utilizing the technique of full disclosure of all pertinent facts about the credit transaction to buyers. The U.C.C.C. where enacted is applicable to practically every transaction involving credit. The law contains provisions on retail installment sales, consumer credit, small loans, and usury.

The U.C.C.C. does not fix rates of interest but rather sets maximums that may be charged. For example, when the amount financed is $300 or less, the maximum is 36 percent per year, and when the amount is more than $300 but less than $1,000, it is 21 percent per year. The credit code has detailed provisions covering such matters as delinquency charges, deferral charges, service charges on refinancing or loan consolidation, and revolving charge accounts. It also prohibits deficiency judgments when goods sold as a part of a consumer credit sale are repossessed.[5]

The U.C.C.C. requires a written disclosure that conspicuously sets forth the required facts prior to a sale or loan. Just as in the Truth-in-Lending Act, the annual percentage rate is the key fact that must be disclosed. The difference between the cash price and the credit price is also essential as a part of the disclosure. The provisions on advertising generally require that the ad include the rate of the credit service charge as well as the amount of the charge.

In addition to regulating the cost of credit, the U.C.C.C. prohibits certain types of agreements. As previously noted, it prohibits the rise of the holder in due course concept and outlaws agreements cutting off defenses. It prohibits the use of multiple agreements to obtain higher interest. Since the law authorizes higher charges for smaller purchases, a total higher interest would be possible by use of multiple transactions. It also prohibits "balloon" payments by providing that if any scheduled payment is more than twice as large as the average payment, the buyer has the right to refinance the balloon payment without penalty on terms no less favorable than the original terms. The balloon-payment provision is not applicable to a sale for agricultural purposes or one pursuant to a revolving charge account.

The U.C.C.C. prohibits debtors from assigning their earnings as part of a credit sale. It also prohibits referral sales schemes in which the buyer is given credit on a purchase for furnishing the names of other purchasers.

One major part of the U.C.C.C. deals with home solicitation sales. Its approach is similar to that of the FTC, discussed in the next section.

Violations of the U.C.C.C. may be punished criminally. In addition, debtors are relieved of their obligation to pay the finance charge, and they are entitled

[5] *Central Finance Co., Inc.* v. *Stevens,* page 520.

to recover, from creditors who violate the law, up to three times the finance charge actually paid. Of course, debtors are not obligated to pay charges in excess of those allowable by the act. If a debtor entitled to a refund is refused a refund, the debtor is entitled to recover the total amount of the credit service charge or ten times the excess charge, whichever is greater. If the excess charge was in deliberate violation of the act, the penalty may be recovered even if the excess has been repaid.

8. Home Solicitation

Under its authority to prevent unfair and deceptive business practices, the Federal Trade Commission has regulated door-to-door selling. The FTC rule covers any sale, lease, or rental of consumer goods with a purchase price of $25 or more, at places of business other than the normal place of business of the seller. It does not cover mail order or telephone sales, or sales in which the buyer has requested the seller to visit his home.

The law requires the seller to furnish the buyer with a copy of the contract in the same language—e.g., Spanish—as was used in the oral presentation. The contract must, in 10-point type, notify the buyer that the transaction may be canceled at any time prior to midnight of the third business day after the date of the transaction. The seller is required to furnish the buyer with a form to be used to cancel, so that all the buyer is required to do is to sign the form and send it to the seller. The seller is required to orally inform the buyer of the right to cancel also.

The law requires the seller to honor the notice of cancellation within ten days. This requires a refund of all payments made and of all property traded in, and a return of any instruments signed by the buyer. If the purchase is canceled, all security arrangements are null and void. If the goods have been delivered to the buyer prior to cancellation, the seller must, within ten days, notify the buyer whether the seller intends to repossess or to abandon the goods.

9. Credit Card Protection

Credit cards are often lost or stolen. Lost or stolen credit cards are often used for unauthorized purchases, resulting in a loss to either (1) the business that dealt with the wrong person, (2) the credit card company (which may be the same as number 1, as in the case of an oil company's gasoline credit card), or (3) the actual cardholder. The law seeks to limit the loss of the cardholder and to impose most of the losses on the issuer of the card.

The Truth-in-Lending Law provides that a cardholder is liable only up to $50 for the unauthorized use of a credit card and only if (1) the credit card is an accepted card, (2) the liability is incurred prior to notice to the issuer of the loss or theft, (3) the issuer has warned the cardholder within two years of his liability, and (4) the card issuer has provided the cardholder with a preaddressed notice form that may be mailed in the event of loss or theft of the card. In addition, no cardholder is liable unless the issuer has provided a method whereby the user of the card can be identified as the person authorized to use it. Such identification may be by signature, photograph, or fingerprint on the card. It may be also by electronic or mechanical confirmation.

A cardholder has liability only for an accepted credit card. An accepted card is one that the cardholder has requested. The law also prohibits the issuance of credit cards except upon application therefor, or upon the renewal of an existing card. Thus, no liability for unauthorized purchases is present if the card was issued without being requested.

The warning to the cardholder, which the law requires, may be given by printing it on the card. The notice must state that liability in case of loss or theft shall not exceed $50 and that notice of loss or theft may be given orally or in writing. The notice may contain the name and address of the person to receive the notice.

Most credit card contracts provide that defenses that may be available against the seller cannot be asserted against the credit card company. Such contracts are valid even though the holder in due course concept has been eliminated as applied to consumers. Such firms as American Express, Diner's Club, Carte Blanche, and the various banks with cards cannot operate effectively if subject to a variety of claims and defenses by their cardholders.

CREDIT REPORTING AND COLLECTION PRACTICES

10. Introduction

In recent years, the federal government has enacted several laws relating to the granting of credit. The Fair Credit Reporting Act is aimed at eliminating abuses in the system of credit reporting. The Fair Credit Billing Act imposes duties on creditors when debtors complain about errors in billing. There is also a federal law that prohibits discrimination on the basis of age, race, color, religion, national origin, sex, or marital status in extending credit. In addition, there are numerous federal laws relating to the credit aspects of real estate transactions.

Collection practices are also a concern of the law today. Debt-collection methods that constitute harassment are tortious, and the debtor is entitled to collect damages from the creditor.[6] The damages are for emotional distress.

Congress has enacted a law that attempts to regulate debt-collection practices that amount to high-pressure tactics. Among the collection tactics prohibited by law today are telephone calls late at night, calls to a person's place of employment or to his neighbors and relatives, phony legal documents,

---

[6] *Boudreaux* v. *Allstate Finance Corporation,* page 521.

impersonating lawyers or courts, and threats of action that cannot be legally taken. Several states have passed similar legislation controlling bill collectors.

11.   Fair Credit Reporting Act

This law is not designed to prevent credit reporting. Its purpose is to prevent abuses in the system of credit reports that may result from inaccurate information in a report. It is also designed to prevent the undue invasion of individual privacy in the collection and dissemination of information about a person's credit record. The act is applicable to anyone who prepares or uses a credit report in connection with (1) the extending of credit, (2) the sale of insurance, or (3) the hiring or discharge of an employee. It covers credit reports on consumers but not those on businesses. Violations of the act entitle an injured party to punitive damages as well as actual damages.

The law covers two situations. First of all, it covers cases in which an individual is rejected for credit, insurance, or employment because of an adverse credit report. When this occurs, the person has (1) the right to be told the name of the reporting agency, (2) the right to require the agency to reveal the information given in the report, and (3) the right to correct the information, or at least give the consumer's version of the facts in dispute.

This law has one important limitation. A report containing information solely as to transactions or experiences between the consumer and the person making the report is not a "consumer report." For example, assume that a bank is asked for information about the credit experience of the bank and one of its customers. If it reports only as to its own experiences, the report is not covered by the act. The law only covers credit-reporting agencies that obtain information from several sources, compile it, and furnish it to potential creditors.

Many businesses can avoid being credit-reporting agencies, but most businesses will be subject to the "user" provisions of this law. The "user" provision requires that consumers seeking credit be informed if their application is denied because of an adverse credit report. They must be informed of the source of the report and of the fact that they are entitled to make a written request within 60 days as to the nature of the information received. The information obtained may then be used to challenge the accuracy of the report.

The second situation covered by this law involves "investigative consumer reports." A consumer is entitled to be informed when an "investigative consumer report" is being made. Upon request, he is entitled to be informed as to (1) the nature and scope of the investigation, (2) the kind of information that has been placed in the credit-reporting agency's file, and (3) the name of anyone to whom the report has been sent. He also has the right to require a consumer-reporting agency to reinvestigate any material that he finds to be inaccurate in his file and the right to have removed from his file any inaccurate material or material that cannot be verified by the reporting agency. If there is a dispute as to the accuracy, the consumer has the right to place a

100-word statement in his file setting forth his position with regard to the disputed matter. This statement must be included in all future agency reports that contain the material in dispute.

In addition, the consumer has the right to require that obsolete information included in the consumer report be removed from the file. Included are bankruptcies that occurred more than fourteen years prior to the report; lawsuits and judgments that antedate the report by more than seven years or until the statute of limitations has expired, whichever is longer; and, in general, adverse items of entered information that antedate the report by more than seven years.

12. Fair Credit Billing Act

This 1974 law requires that a creditor must take certain steps if a debtor, within 60 days of the receipt of a bill, complains that the billing is in error. First of all, the creditor is required to acknowledge the notice within 30 days. Second, the creditor, within two billing cycles and within not more than 90 days, must either (1) correct the error, or (2) send a written statement of clarification to the debtor.

The act further provides that a creditor operating an open-end credit plan may not, until explanation of the complaint or its correction, curtail, restrict, or close the debtor's account. In addition, the law prohibits a creditor from reporting or threatening to report the debtor to a credit-rating organization. Violation of either of these provisions results in a forfeiture of the right to collect the amount stated in the billing.

The law also contains several provisions relating to the accounting practices of creditors. For example, prompt posting of all payments is required to prevent the application of additional finance charges. Creditors of revolving charge accounts cannot charge finance charges on a new purchase unless a statement including the billing and finance charge is rendered at least fourteen days prior to the date the finance charge can be avoided by paying the amount of the original bill.

The law also contains some restrictions on credit card issuers and their business practices. For example, issuers of credit cards may not prohibit sellers who honor these cards from offering discounts for cash or immediate payment by check.

13. Other Aspects of Consumer Protection

The preceding sections have discussed several of the important new laws and legal principles that give substantial protection to consumers, and especially to debtor-consumers. There are other proposed laws or changes in existing laws that are designed to give even more protection. Some of these have been enacted in a few states, and others are being developed by courts and legislatures at this time. For example, the Uniform Deceptive Trade Practices Act has been adopted by seven states. This act removes restrictions on common law tort actions for deceptive business practices. It recognizes a cause of action for financial loss as a result of misleading identification of a business or goods or as a result of false or deceptive advertising. It also recognizes common law liability to a competitor because of false or deceptive advertising.

Among the types of conduct considered unfair and deceptive are the following: (1) advertising goods or services without intent to sell them as advertised; (2) misrepresenting the character, extent, volume, or nature of the business; (3) advertising secondhand, used, defective, blemished, or rejected merchandise without disclosure of those facts; (4) selling unassembled items without disclosure of that fact; (5) selling merchandise marked "Made in U.S.A." when it is manufactured elsewhere.

The Uniform Deceptive Trade Practices Act also attempts to prevent one person from passing off his goods or services as those of another. It includes within the concept of deceptive trade practice conduct that causes confusion or misunderstanding about the goods or the seller. In addition to allowing suits for dollar damages, this act authorizes courts to enjoin such conduct.

There is a definite trend in many states toward allowing class-action suits on behalf of consumers. Most consumers cannot afford to sue because their complaints do not involve a sufficient amount of money to warrant the retention of an attorney. However, the class-action suits, which allow one plaintiff to sue on behalf of all persons similarly situated, make such suits worthwhile. Legislation has been introduced in many states authorizing class-action suits on behalf of consumers. In addition, many states have created consumer protection agencies that are authorized to take legal action on behalf of consumers. The Truth-in-Lending Act allows class-action suits subject to a maximum recovery of $500,000 or 1 percent of the net worth of the creditor, whichever is less.

DEBTOR AND CONSUMER PROTECTION CASES

Wilkinson v. Carpenter
561 P.2d 607 (Or.) 1977

HOWELL, J. . . . Plaintiffs filed a motion for an order setting the amount of the homestead exemption claimed by defendants in certain real property which was subject to execution in satisfaction of plaintiffs' prior judgment against defendants. After a hearing, the court set the amount of the homestead exemption at $12,000. Plaintiffs appeal, claiming that the amount of the allowable homestead exemption should have been set at $7,500, as provide in ORS 23.240 as of the date of the prior judgment, rather than at $12,000 as provided by the same statute as amended effective September, 1975. . . .

Plaintiffs contend that the statute increasing the homestead exemption to $12,000 should not be construed to apply to an execution on a judgment entered prior to its effective date, and that if the statute is construed to apply to such a judgment, it would be an unconstitutional impairment of the obligation of contracts under Article I, Section 10, of the United States Constitution.

The applicable part of the statute increasing the homestead exemption provided as follows:

Section 5. ORS 23.240 is amended to read:

23.240. (1) A homestead shall be exempt from sale on execution, from the lien of every judgment and from liability in any form for the debts of the owner to the amount in value of [$7,500] $12,000, except as otherwise provided by law. When two or more members of a household are debtors whose interests in the homestead are subject to sale on execution, the lien of a judgment or liability in any form, their combined exemptions under this section shall not exceed $12,000. The homestead must be the actual abode of, and occupied by the owner, his spouse, parent or child, but such exemption shall not be impaired by:

(a) Temporary removal or temporary absence with the intention to reoccupy the same as a homestead:

(b) Removal or absence from the property;

(c) The sale of the property.

(2) The exemption shall extend to the proceeds derived from such sale to an amount not exceeding [$7,500] $12,000 held, with the intention to procure another homestead therewith, for a period not exceeding one year. Oregon Laws 1975, ch. 208, § 5. [New material underscored; old material in brackets.]

This court has previously noted that the homestead statute should be liberally construed in favor of the debtor's exemption. Under the terms of the statute, the judgment debtor's homestead is "exempt from sale on execution," but the exemption is not automatic and must be affirmatively asserted before the sale or it is lost. Since the exemption applies to the sale on execution and may be asserted at any time prior to such sale, it would appear that the appropriate time to measure the value of the exemption would be the time of the sale on execution.

In this case, the statute increasing the exemption became effective on September 13, 1975. Notice of defendants' homestead exemption claim was filed on January 21, 1976, and the execution sale took place on February 10, 1976. Under the terms of the statute in effect at that time, defendants were entitled to a homestead exemption of $12,000.

Plaintiffs also contend that an application of the increased exemption to an obligation arising under a pre-existing contract would impair the obligation of that contract in violation of Article I, Section 10, of the U.S. Constitution. . . .

In *Home Building & Loan Ass'n* v. *Blaisdell*, 290 U.S. 398 (1934), the Court conducted a complete reexamination of the contract clause and concluded that "the prohibition is not an absolute one and is not to be read with literal exactness like a mathematical formula. . . ."

Therefore, it seems plain that the dictates of the contract clause can no longer be viewed in the same absolute terms which prevailed in earlier times. Modern decisions point out that the prohibition of the contract clause must be balanced against or "harmonized" with the legislative powers reserved to the states.

Under this standard, the real issue is "whether the legislation is addressed to a legitimate end and the measures taken are reasonable and appropriate to that end."

The legislative act in question in this case provided for an increase in the homestead exemption from $7,500 to $12,000. It has been said that the purpose of such exemptions

. . . is to provide a place for the family and its surviving members, where they may reside and enjoy the comforts of home, freed from any anxiety that it may be taken from them against their will, either by reason of their own necessity or improvidence, or from the importunity of their creditors.

If the homestead rule makes any sense at all, it ought to be flexible enough to allow the value of the homestead to keep pace with the times, and thus in reality, and not in mere fiction, grant the debt ridden and poverty stricken the "comforts of home."

The creation of such exemption is certainly a proper subject for legislative action. The purpose is not only to insure indigent individuals the comforts of home, but also to protect the general economic welfare of all citizens, creditors and debtors alike, by promoting the stability and security of our society. Periodic increases in such exemptions reflect similar considerations. . . .

Undoubtedly, any increase in the statutory homestead exemption may impair the value of some pre-existing contracts, at least indirectly, by exempting additional assets from execution and thereby restricting the remedy available for breach. However, if the statutory remedy of sale on execution is to be read into the contract between the plaintiff and the defendant, the reserved power of the state to increase the statutory exemptions for the pro-

tection and welfare of its people must also be included. So long as the increase is reasonable and does not destroy the value of the contract by destroying any meaningful remedy, it does not violate the contract clause. "In all such cases the question becomes, therefore, one of reasonableness, and of that the legislature is primarily the judge.

We conclude that any indirect contractual impairment which may have occurred as a result of the increased homestead exemption is not unconstitutional since the increase was reasonable, and any impairment would not appear to be substantial when balanced against the governmental objective being pursued. . . .

Like the Supreme Court's interpretation of the contract clause, economic conditions have changed substantially since 1878. In our view, the legislature's action in increasing the homestead exemption from $7,500 to $12,000 was not unreasonable in light of current economic conditions, and certainly the increase was not "so large, that . . . it would seriously affect the efficiency of remedies for the collection of debts."

Affirmed.

Geiger Finance Company v. Graham
182 S.E.2d 521 (Ga.) 1971

Plaintiff sued on a note. The defendant pleaded failure of consideration, and the lower court ruled for defendant. Plaintiff appealed.

The evidence showed that on March 12 defendant signed a paper with Economy Exterminating Company entitled "Retail Installment Contract/Including Promissory Note and Security Agreement." It called for a cash price of $250, with a time balance of $300 to be paid in 18 monthly installments. That same day she also signed a "completion ticket" which stated that the agreed services had been satisfactorily performed. Apparently the company made only one spraying under this contract (the same day it was signed) and the description of the service rendered was "treatment for fungus PPB." Defendant testified that when she signed the

contract, this place on the form was blank, and that the agreement she made with Economy's agent was for semi-monthly spraying for roaches over a one year period. Plaintiff purchased the contract from the exterminators either the same day or a few days after its execution. Defendant alleged that Economy failed to treat her premises for roaches with the exception of the one spraying (treatment unknown) for which she stood ready to pay the reasonable cost.

HALL, J. . . . The pleadings showed that a defense existed. Plaintiff therefore had the burden of establishing that it was a holder in due course. . . .

. . . Plaintiff has overlooked one basic factor in the law of commercial paper—the status of "holder in due course" applies only to the holder of a *negotiable* instrument.

Contrary to the rule in many states, Georgia held this type of contract to be a negotiable instrument under the N.I.L. The issue has not been raised since the enactment of the U.C.C., although a footnote in a 1964 case decided under the N.I.L. suggested that conditional-sale contracts would not be Article 3 paper. There has been a wholesale market for these contracts because it has been assumed they were negotiable instruments which, after a quick transfer, were impregnable to most defenses the consumer would have against the purveyor. Under the umbrella labeled "free flow of commercial paper" have flourished not only legitimate businesses but the most pernicious rackets. . . . However, even assuming ordinary commercial ethics, the effect of such a construction is obvious. "Conditional sales contracts are invariably written by sellers and finance companies for sellers and finance companies. They are often printed in unconscionably small type and presented to the buyer as a mere formality. . . . The seller is usually justified in believing either that the buyer will not read the contract at all or will not understand it if he does wade through it. Even were the buyer to read and comprehend the avalanche of legal consequences which would greet any default on his part . . . on the installment plan he must sign one conditional sales contract or another, and they are all pretty much alike. . . . It is against this background that we must view the plight of [a buyer] who staggers into a contract which could make him liable to pay the full price . . . to a finance company, with which he has not dealt directly, even though the vendor sells him a defective article" [or fails to perform the service]. "The average citizen, and particularly the financially unimportant, [is] no more likely to know the law of negotiable paper . . . than the holding in Shelley's Case.

The question here is whether this kind of paper is a "note" within the definition of the U.C.C. Code Ann. § 109A-3-104(1) states that a negotiable instrument is a writing signed by the maker containing "an unconditional promise or order to pay a sum certain in money and *no other* promise, order, obligation or power given by the maker or drawer except as authorized by this Article." [Emphasis supplied.] Ga. Code § 109A-3-112 lists certain additional terms which an instrument may contain without affecting its negotiability. The meaning of these sections read together is clear. If a writing contains any other promise, order, obligation or power, it is simply not a negotiable instrument and the concept of a holder in due course does not apply.

. . . The words "no other . . . obligation or power given by the maker" are new. The intent is that a negotiable instrument carries nothing but the simple promise to pay, with certain limited exceptions. . . .

The writing here cannot meet this new test. Among other things, it grants to the holder powers to impose a delinquency charge; to waive particular defaults or remedies without waiving others, to require its written consent for any transfer of the buyer's obligations (while keeping its own freely transferrable). It also contains an application for insurance (in effect a grant of authority to the holder to purchase it) and an agreement that the terms of the contract may apply to subsequent sales. It contains a purported waiver by the buyer of "any defense, counterclaim or cross-complaint" he could have asserted against the seller. This goes further than reiterating the rights of a holder in due course since "any defense" would also presumably include infancy, incompetence, discharge in bankruptcy, etc. This is not the type of waiver contemplated by Code Ann. § 109A-3-112. Rather, it is an attempt to impart the effect of negotiability to a writing which cannot otherwise meet the test of an Article 3 negotiable instrument. . . .

We can discover no other state which has faced this identical issue. Many states considered these writings non-negotiable under the N.I.L., so applying the U.C.C. posed no difficulty. Many other states have statutes which specifically declare conditional sale-contracts to be non-negotiable. A few states by statute provide that the holder of a note based on any consumer transaction takes it subject to all defenses. This is also an important feature of the proposed Uniform Consumer Credit Code. It is, of course, the only real solution to the problem. Even a proper note can be prolix and confusing to the layman, especially one in the grips of a fast-talking salesman. But the courts need not stand impotent while two-page, finely printed "contracts" are circulated as freely as currency. While Justice Gibson's famous "courier without luggage" may be an unobtainable ideal for most notes, allowing him to carry a bag or two does not mean that one who trucks furniture from place to place is a "courier," no matter what else he might legitimately be. The protections offered a holder in due course were evolved by merchants, bankers and lawyers to facilitate the rapid flow of *true* commercial paper. The drafters of the U.C.C. (and our legislature by its adoption) were careful to limit the type of instrument which would carry the powerful magic of negotiability under Article 3. Although theoretically possible, a retail instalment contract, or conditional-sale contract (or a writing of this nature by whatever name) is not usually a note as defined in Code §§ 109A-3-104 through 112.

Where there is any doubt, the presumption is against negotiability.

. . . The writing here is a retail instalment contract. In 1967, the General Assembly enacted Code Chapter 96-9 specifically covering retail instalment transactions. It seems clear that in so doing the legislature considered these contracts to be something other than Article 3 commercial paper. Chapter 96-9 does not give holder in due course status to an assignee or transferee of such a contract. Therefore, under simple contract law, he takes it subject to any defenses that could be asserted against the assignor.

In a well known 1953 case, the Supreme Court of Florida made this perceptive statement: "It may be that our holding here will require some changes in business methods and will impose a greater burden on the finance companies. We think the buyer . . . should have some protection somewhere along the line. We believe the finance company is better able to bear the risk of the dealer's insolvency than the buyer and in a far better position to protect his interests against unscrupulous and insolvent dealers."

Judgment affirmed.

Mourning v. Family Publications Service, Inc.
93 S.Ct. 1652 (1973)

Petitioner purchased magazines from respondent's door-to-door salesman. The contract covered four magazines for five years. Petitioner paid $3.95 down and owed $118.50, but the contract did not recite the total purchase price or the amount unpaid, and it made no reference to finance charges. Petitioner defaulted, and respondent sent her two collection letters. Petitioner filed suit alleging a violation of the Truth-in-Lending Act, asking for the statutory penalty and attorney's fees.

BURGER, C.J. . . . Section 121 of the Truth-in-Lending Act requires merchants who regularly extend credit, with attendant finance charges, to disclose certain contract informa-

tion "to each person to whom consumer credit is extended and upon whom a finance charge is or may be imposed. . . ." Among other relevant facts, the merchant must, where applicable, list the cash price of the merchandise or service sold, the amount of finance and other charges, and the rate of the charges. Failure to disclose renders the seller liable to the consumer for a penalty of twice the amount of the finance charge, but in no event less than $100 or more than $1,000. The creditor may also be assessed for the costs of the litigation, including reasonable attorney's fees, and in certain circumstances not relevant here, may be the subject of criminal charges.

Section 105 of the Act provides:

> The [Federal Reserve] Board shall prescribe regulations to carry out the purposes of [the Act]. These regulations may contain such classifications, differentiations, or other provisions, and may provide for such adjustments and exceptions for any class of transactions, as in the judgment of the Board are necessary or proper to effectuate the purposes of [the Act], to prevent circumvention or evasion thereof, or to facilitate compliance therewith.

Accordingly, the Board has promulgated Regulation Z, which defines the circumstances in which a seller who regularly extends credit must make the disclosures outlined in § 128. The regulation provides that disclosure is necessary whenever credit is offered to a consumer "for which either a finance charge is or may be imposed or which, pursuant to an agreement, is or may be payable in more than four installments."

Relying on the rule governing credit transactions of more than four installments, the District Court granted summary judgment for petitioner. The court found that respondent had extended credit to petitioner, which by agreement was payable in more than four installments, but had failed to comply with the disclosure provisions of the Act.

The Court of Appeals reversed, holding that the Board had exceeded its statutory authority in promulgating the regulation upon which the District Court relied. The regulation was found to conflict with § 121 of the Act since it required that disclosure be made in regard to some credit transactions in which a finance charge had not been imposed. . . .

Passage of the Truth-in-Lending Act in 1968 culminated several years of congressional study and debate as to the propriety and usefulness of imposing mandatory disclosure requirements on those who extend credit to consumers in the American market. By the time of passage, it had become abundantly clear that the use of consumer credit was expanding at an extremely rapid rate. From the end of World War II through 1967, the amount of such credit outstanding had increased from $5.6 billion to $95.9 billion, a rate of growth more than 4½ times as great as that of the economy. Yet, as the congressional hearings revealed, consumers remained remarkably ignorant of the nature of their credit obligations and of the costs of deferring payment. Because of the divergent, and at times fraudulent, practices by which consumers were informed of the terms of the credit extended to them, many consumers were prevented from shopping for the best terms available and, at times, were prompted to assume liabilities they could not meet. . . .

The Truth-in-Lending Act was designed to remedy the problems which had developed. The House Committee on Banking and Currency reported, in regard to the then proposed legislation:

> [B]y requiring all creditors to disclose credit information in a uniform manner, and by requiring all additional mandatory charges imposed by the creditor as an incident to credit be included in the computation of the applicable percentage rate, the American consumer will be given the information he needs to compare the cost of credit and to make the best informed decision on the use of credit.

This purpose was stated explicitly in § 102 of the legislation enacted:

> The Congress finds that economic stabilization would be enhanced and the competition among the various financial institutions and other firms engaged in the extension of consumer credit would be strengthened by the informed use of credit. The informed use of credit results from an awareness of the cost thereof by consumers. It is the purpose of this subchapter to assure a meaningful disclosure of credit terms so that the consumer will be able to compare more readily the

various credit terms available to him and avoid the uninformed use of credit.

. . . To accomplish its desired objective, Congress determined to lay the structure of the Act broadly and to entrust its construction to an agency with the necessary experience and resources to monitor its operation. Section 105 delegated to the Federal Reserve Board broad authority to promulgate regulations necessary to render the Act effective. The language employed evinces the awareness of Congress that some creditors would attempt to characterize their transactions so as to fall one step outside whatever boundary Congress attempted to establish. It indicates as well the clear desire of Congress to insure that the Board had adequate power to deal with such attempted evasion. . . .

. . . The Board was . . . empowered to define such classifications as were reasonably necessary to insure that the objectives of the Act were fulfilled, no matter what adroit or unscrupulous practices were employed by those extending credit to consumers.

One means of circumventing the objectives of the Truth-in-Lending Act, as passed by Congress, was that of "burying" the cost of credit in the price of goods sold. Thus in many credit transactions in which creditors claimed that no finance charge had been imposed, the creditor merely assumed the cost of extending credit as an expense of doing business, to be recouped as part of the price charged in the transaction. Congress was well aware, from its extensive studies, of the possibility that merchants could use such devices to evade the disclosure requirements of the Act. . . .

It was against this . . . background that the Federal Reserve Board promulgated regulations governing enforcement of the Truth-in-Lending Act.

The Four Installment Rule was included. . . .

[The court then found the delegation of authority to the Board to be valid.]

In light of our prior holdings and the legislative history of the Truth-in-Lending Act, we cannot agree with the conclusion of the Court of Appeals that the Board exceeded its statutory authority in promulgating the Four Installment Rule. Congress was clearly aware that merchants could evade the reporting requirements of the Act by concealing credit charges. In delegating rule making authority to the Board, Congress emphasized the Board's authority to prevent such evasion. To hold that Congress did not intend the Board to take action against this type of manipulation would require us to believe that, despite this emphasis, Congress intended the obligations established by the Act to be open to evasion by subterfuges of which it was fully aware. . . .

Given that some remedial measure was authorized, the question remaining is whether the measure chosen is reasonably related to its objectives. We see no reason to doubt the Board's conclusion that the rule will deter creditors from engaging in the conduct which the Board sought to eliminate. The burdens imposed on creditors are not severe, when measured against the evils which are avoided. Furthermore, were it possible or financially feasible to delve into the intricacies of every credit transaction, it is clear that many creditors to whom the rule applies would be found to have charged for deferring payment, while claiming they had not. That some other remedial provision might be preferable is irrelevant. We have consistently held that where reasonable minds may differ as to which of several remedial measures should be chosen, courts should defer to the informed experience and judgment of the agency to whom Congress delegated appropriate authority. . . .

The Truth-in-Lending Act reflects a transition in congressional policy from a philosophy of let-the-buyer-beware to one of let-the-seller-disclose. By erecting a barrier between the seller and the prospective purchaser in the form of hard facts, Congress expressly sought "to . . . avoid the uninformed use of credit." 15 U.S.C. § 1601. Some may claim that it is a relatively easy matter to calculate the total payments to which petitioner was committed by her contract with respondent; but at the time of sale, such computations are often not encouraged by the solicitor or performed by the purchaser. Congress has determined that such purchasers are in need of protection; the Four Installment Rule serves to insure that the protective disclosure mechanism chosen by Congress will not be circumvented.

That the approach taken may reflect what respondent views as an undue paternalistic concern for the consumer is beside the point. The statutory scheme is within the power granted to Congress under the Commerce Clause. It is not a function of the courts to speculate as to whether the statute is unwise or whether the evils sought to be remedied could better have been regulated in some other manner.

Reversed and remanded.

Southwestern Inv. Co. v. Mannix
540 S.W.2d 747 (Tex.) 1976

MCDONALD, J. . . . This is an appeal by defendant Southwestern Investment from summary judgment for $731.68 statutory damages, plus $1,000 attorneys' fees, in favor of plaintiff Mannix.

Plaintiff Mannix sued defendants Banner Sales Company and Southwestern Investment, alleging he purchased stereo equipment from Banner January 22, 1974, for $381.04 down payment and an unpaid balance of $800; that he signed a sales contract and finance agreement for the unpaid balance on a form provided by Southwestern, and which Southwestern acquired by assignment; that such transaction violated . . . the Federal Truth-in-Lending Act in a number of particulars; for which plaintiff sought judgment against both defendants for $731.68 statutory damages plus attorneys' fees. Plaintiff thereafter . . . moved for summary judgment against Southwestern.

The trial court . . . held plaintiff entitled to judgment for . . . 5 Federal violations; and rendered judgment for plaintiff for $731.68, plus $1,000 attorneys' fees. . . .

The parties have stipulated that if the record on summary judgment sustains the trial court on . . . any Federal violation . . . that the statutory damages awarded by the trial court are correct, and that the $1,000 attorneys' fees awarded by the trial court are reasonable. . . .

Defendant asserts, "The trial court erred in concluding the contract in incorporating the disclosure statement contract and security agreement on a single sheet of paper failed to make all necessary disclosures on the same side of the page above and adjacent to the place for the customer's signature in violation of Regulation Z, Section 226.8(a)(1)."

Regulation Z, Section 226.8(a) of the Federal Truth-in-Lending Act provides, ". . . all of the disclosures shall be made together on either (1) the note or instrument evidencing the obligation on the same side of the page and above or adjacent to the place for the customer's signature; or (2) one side of a a separate statement which identifies the transaction."

In this case the agreement is written on both sides of a single page. According to the Interpretive Ruling of the Federal Reserve Board, in instances where both the face and reverse side are used, both sides must contain the statement: "NOTICE: See other side for important information." Here the foregoing statement does not appear on either side of the agreement.

Regulation Z was violated.

. . . Under the parties' stipulation the judgment of the trial court is thus *affirmed.*

Central Finance Co., Inc. v. Stevens
558 P.2d 122 (Kan.) 1976

Plaintiff, a finance company, sued the defendant debtor to recover a deficiency judgment on a promissory note. It had previously repossessed and sold the defendant's automobile on which it held a security interest.

Kansas had enacted the Uniform Consumer Credit Code. This statute prohibits deficiency judgments in certain consumer credit transactions including repossessions in which the cash sale price was less than $1,000 (this case). The statutory restriction on deficiency judgments applies to consumer credit sales and consumer loans in which the lender is subject to defenses arising from sales. The lower court held that since the transaction was a consumer credit sale, the law applied and judgment was awarded the defendants. Plaintiff appeals.

PRAGER, J. . . . It is important to note that in order for a particular transaction to fall within the definition of a "consumer credit sale" it must be an actual sale of goods, services, or an interest in land. In this case the transaction between Central Finance and the Stevenses was not a sale. It was a loan. The sale was consummated between Cox Motors as seller and the Stevenses as buyers. Hence the trial court was in error in holding that the transaction between Central Finance and the Stevenses was a "consumer credit sale."

The transaction between Central Finance and the Stevenses does, however, fall within the definition of a "consumer loan." . . .

In this case it is undisputed that the loan made by Central Finance to the Stevenses was made by one regularly engaged in the business of making loans to a person other than an organization and was made primarily for a personal, family, household, or agricultural purpose. The debt was payable in installments and was for an amount less than $25,000. It necessarily follows that the provisions of the U.C.C.C. governing consumer loans rather than consumer credit sales are applicable in determining the rights of the parties in this case.

If a *lender* takes possession of the collateral, he is precluded from obtaining a deficiency judgment on a "consumer loan" where two conditions exist: (1) The lender is subject to defenses arising from sales . . . and (2) the amount of the loan is $1,000 or less. It is undisputed in this case that the amount of the loan from Central Finance to the Stevenses was less than $1,000. Hence the determining factor must be whether Central Finance as a lender under a consumer loan was subject to defenses arising from the sale. . . . The U.C.C.C. lists five circumstances where a lender may be subject to defenses which may be asserted by the consumer against the seller:

(1) A lender . . . who . . . makes a consumer loan for the purpose of enabling a consumer to buy . . . from a particular seller . . . goods or services, other than primarily for an agricultural purpose, is subject to all claims and defenses of the consumer against the seller . . . arising from that sale . . . of the goods and services if

(a) the lender knows that the seller . . . arranged, for a commission, brokerage, or referral fee, for the extension of credit by the lender;

(b) the lender is a person related to the seller . . . unless the relationship is remote or is not a factor in the transaction;

(c) the seller . . . guarantees the loan or otherwise assumes the risk of loss by the lender upon the loan;

(d) the lender directly supplies the seller . . . with the contract document used by the consumer to evidence the loan, and the seller . . . significantly participates in the preparation of the document; or

(e) the loan is conditioned upon the consumer's purchase . . . of the goods or services from the particular seller . . . but the lender's payment of proceeds of the loan to the seller . . . does not in itself establish that the loan was so conditioned.

As to the first four criteria, contained in section (1) (*a*), (*b*), (*c*), and (*d*), the stipulated facts clearly establish that Central Finance had no contact or relationship of any kind whatsoever with Cox Motors. Cox Motors had not referred the Stevenses to Central Finance nor had Cox prepared or helped to prepare the contract document used by the Stevenses to evidence the loan. As to the fifth criterion, contained in paragraph (1) (*e*), there is no evidence in the stipulated facts to show that the loan from Central Finance to the Stevenses was conditioned upon the consumer purchasing the goods from the particular seller, Cox Motors. The fact that Central Finance's check for the proceeds of the loan was made payable to Cox Motors as well as to the Stevenses does not in itself establish that the loan was so conditioned. In this regard the Kansas comment to section 16a-3-405 states as follows:

> 2. . . . With respect to this last element, the lender's making the proceeds check payable to a particular dealer does not in itself make the transaction an "all in the family" loan. Similarly, under subsection (5) any participation by the lender in the sales transaction solely to insure perfection of a security interest, such as notation of the lender's lien on a certificate of title, does not in itself make a "direct loan" subject to the buyer's claims and defenses against the seller.

The fact that the proceeds check in this case was made payable to both the borrower and seller and that notation of the lender's security interest was made on the borrower's certificate of title did not create an "all in the family" loan. Creditors must be permitted to perfect their security interests when they make *bona fide* direct loans under the provisions of 16a-3-405. The statute is intended only to penalize lenders and sellers who cooperate in an "all in the family" loan. If this interpretation is not given to the UCCC, a Kansas lender who does not have any contact with the seller of consumer goods will be unable to perfect and protect his security interest without becoming entangled in the provisions of 16a-3-405.

The Kansas Consumer Credit Code bestows distinct rights and duties upon sellers and lenders in consumer credit sales. By promotion and advertising, which encourages the consumer to purchase goods, the seller bears greater responsibility for the transaction as a whole and is precluded from recovering a deficiency judgment. A lender who is completely divorced from an "all in the family" type loan activity, is merely a spectator to the consumer credit sales transaction. While carefully regulated by the consumer credit loan provisions of the Kansas UCCC, a lender is not prohibited from recovering a deficiency judgment unless he falls within the provisions of K.S.A. 16a-3-405. In this case Central Finance did not make an "all in the family" loan and is not precluded from recovering a deficiency judgment on the unpaid balance of the debt arising from the loan. . . .

Reversed and remanded.

Boudreaux v. Allstate Finance Corporation
217 So.2d 439 (La.) 1968

LANDRY, J. These . . . matters involve an action in which plaintiffs, Mr. and Mrs. Adam J. Boudreaux, obtained judgment . . . against defendant, Allstate Finance Corporation (Allstate), in the sum of $1,800.00 each for alleged tortious conduct purportedly designed to harass and coerce plaintiffs into paying a debt admittedly due Allstate. . . .

We are in accord with the finding . . . that plaintiffs are entitled to damages but find the amounts awarded are excessive and reduce same to the sum of $500.00 for each plaintiff. . . .

. . . In substance plaintiffs' petition alleges that during the period April to June, 1967, Allstate, through its agents and employees, embarked upon a calculated plan of harassment designed to enforce collection of the sum of $185.00 owed by plaintiffs to defendant, together with interest, which account was admittedly in arrears. The alleged modus operandi indulged in by defendant is reputed to consist of repeated telephone calls to the homes of neighbors requested to call plaintiffs to the telephone as plaintiffs had no phone of their own. Plaintiffs further aver defendants made defamatory and insulting remarks to plaintiffs' neighbors regarding plaintiffs and used insulting language to Mrs. Boudreaux in demanding payment of the loan. Said activity, the petition urges, has caused plaintiffs mental pain and anguish, humiliation, embarrassment as well as damage to their characters and reputations.

. . . [A]n agreed narrative of fact filed in lieu of the recorded testimony indicates plaintiffs were obligated to Allstate on a promissory note in the sum of $185.00, with interest, payable in 24 monthly installments, which indebtedness was in arrears because Mr. Boudreaux was unemployed at the time. Despite his enforced idleness, Mr. Boudreaux had indicated on several occasions, in response to Allstate's collection efforts, that the obligation would be liquidated as soon as circumstances permitted. The extent of Allstate's initial tolerance is not entirely clear from the narrative. It is evident, however, that collection efforts were greatly intensified on defendant's part. It is apparent that defendant employed questionable tactics against plaintiffs consisting primarily of a concerted and calculated plan to annoy, embarrass and humiliate plaintiffs by calling plaintiffs at the homes of neighbors who allowed plaintiffs to use their telephones as plaintiffs had no phone. It is shown that defendant's employees called the neighbors frequently and at deliberately chosen inconvenient hours such as at

night and during inclement weather. It further appears that when plaintiffs responded to these measures, plaintiffs were compelled to explain their delinquency in the presence of their neighbors and acquaintances. In addition it appears that on some occasions defendant's employees explained plaintiffs' financial troubles to the neighbors to whose homes the calls were placed and although plaintiffs requested a cessation to this practice, it continued nevertheless. It also appears that on one occasion defendant's agents called at plaintiffs' home and created a most unpleasant situation by using loud and abusive language in plaintiffs' yard in such manner that the conversation could be heard for some distance. Finally, placed of record is a letter received from Allstate which communication contained disparaging remarks concerning Mr. Boudreaux's character and opined that plaintiff would lose the respect of his family because of his delinquency.

Based on the foregoing testimony, the trial court . . . rendered judgment in favor of plaintiffs . . . in the sum of $1,800.00 each.

. . . [W]e find . . . [no] merit in the argument that plaintiffs' petition does not state a cause of action. Our courts have long since declared and recognized the right to recovery of damages for the intentional infliction of emotional disturbance. The rule is based on the principle that substantial impairment of individual dignity cannot be countenanced in law. See *Nickerson* v. *Hodges*, 146 La. 735, 84 So. 37, 9 A.L.R. 361. In effect our own rule accords with the general accepted definition of conduct upon which such an action can reasonably be based as set forth as follows in Restatement, Torts Second Section 46:

> One who by extreme and outrageous conduct intentionally or recklessly causes severe emotional distress to another is subject to liability for such emotional distress and for bodily harm resulting from it.

Irrespective of whether the right to freedom from excessive unreasonable, deliberately induced emotional distress is predicated upon invasion of privacy or the closely allied tort of intentional infliction of emotional distress, efforts to coerce payment of debt is actionable under our laws when the creditor, in an attempt to collect a debt justly due, unreasonably coerces the debtor or seriously abridges the obligor's right to privacy in his personal affairs. . . .

We . . . concur in the evident finding of the trial court that defendant's representatives considerably exceeded the limits of propriety available to a creditor in circumstances of this nature. It appears defendant's repeated and persistent tactics were deliberately intended to "shame" and "harass" plaintiffs into paying the obligation. The calculated disclosure of plaintiffs' predicament to neighbors could only result in humiliation and embarrassment flowing from the realization that plaintiffs were being characterized to their neighbors and friends as "deadbeats" who did not discharge their lawful obligations. Conceding a creditor may indulge in reasonable means to collect his accounts and that repeated requests for pay-

ment do not per se constitute harassment, nevertheless defendant herein clearly exceeded the bounds of reason which are to be observed in such cases.

On the question of quantum, we find the instant case analogous to but not as aggravated as the circumstances involved in *Tuyes* v. *Chambers,* 144 La. 723, 81 So. 265 (1919), wherein the sum of $500.00 was awarded. Considering the devaluated purchasing power of the dollar and the harsher nature of the conduct involved in the Tuyes case, supra, we believe an award of $500.00 to each plaintiff will do substantial justice between the litigants at bar. . . .

Accordingly, it is ordered, adjudged and decreed that the judgment of the trial court in favor of plaintiffs is amended and judgment rendered herein in favor of petitioners, Adam J. Boudreaux and Kathryn Boudreaux, in the sum of $500.00, together with legal interest thereon from date of judicial demand until paid. . . .

Amended and affirmed.

CHAPTER 27
REVIEW QUESTIONS AND PROBLEMS

1. What is a homestead exemption? What is the purpose of allowing it?

2. What are the goals of truth-in-lending legislation?

3. What is the purpose of the Fair Credit Reporting Act? What rights are afforded the consumer by it?

4. What is the purpose of the Deceptive Trade Practices Act?

5. H requested and received credit cards from X Oil Company for himself and his wife, W. H and W separated. Thereafter, H returned his card to X Oil Company, stating that he was canceling it but that he could not return the other card because it was within the possession of his wife, from whom he was separated. When sued by X for purchases made by W, H defended on grounds that he had canceled his contract with X. Is H liable for these purchases by W? Why?

6. A salesman for X Company sold a water-softening unit to B on a "referral sale" basis. The sales agreement provided that X Company would pay to B $40 for each name of a prospect submitted if the prospect purchased a unit. X Company did not utilize the names submitted by B, with the exception of B's parents. Is this a valid sales agreement? Explain.

7. C, a lending institution, held a mortgage on D's six-unit apartment building. D fell behind on his payments and, to avoid foreclosure, agreed to execute a mortgage on his home in favor of C. This second mortgage secured a note for the amount that D was in arrears on his payments. When the second mortgage was entered, C did not inform D of the annual percentage rate. D now sues C for his actual damages plus twice the amount of the finance charge. Should D succeed? Why?

8. B purchased a wig, including monthly servicing for four years, from S Company by issuing a promissory note. S sold the note to the F Finance Company and, shortly thereafter, went out of business. B stopped making payments on the note, due to lack of consideration on S's part. F sues B, contending that the defense is not effective against him, since he took the note as a holder in due course. Is F correct? Explain.

9. In January, B purchased merchandise from the X Store's "Great 1970 Winter Sale" catalogue, which contained the following statement: "PRESEASON SPECIAL—NO MONTHLY PAYMENTS TILL JUNE." B subsequently learned that the finance charges were imposed from the date of the purchase (January), rather than from the date payment was due (June) as indicated by the catalogue. Has the store violated the Consumer Credit Protection Act? Why?

10. H, a housewife, visited the ABC Figure Salon and a signed a weight-reducing contract that provided for a program to be completed within 12 months at a cost of $300. When H returned home, she felt that she had been subjected to extreme sales pressure and, later that same day, sent a letter to ABC requesting that the contract be canceled. Should ABC be required to cancel the contract? Why?

28

Bankruptcy

1. Introduction

The law of bankruptcy is of ancient origin and is concerned with the problems that arise when a person, partnership, corporation, or municipality is unable to satisfy obligations due to creditors. Bankruptcy has its roots in the law of the Roman Empire and has been a part of English jurisprudence since 1542. The laws relating to bankruptcy have been periodically amended in the United States. The latest revision (1978) was effective October 1, 1979. The 1978 revision contained significant changes which were necessitated by certain provisions of the Uniform Commercial Code, by the rapid increase in the number of bankruptcies, and by the consumer movement. Its provisions, which are not yet "court tested" and interpreted, will be discussed in this chapter.

The bankruptcy laws provide various methods for relieving debtors of their debts or postponing the time of their payment, and for protecting some of the rights of their creditors. Bankruptcy proceedings are predicated on federal laws. The 1978 statute established a new Bankruptcy Court in each judicial district, effective April 1, 1984. The period from 1978 to 1983 is being used to determine the number of judges required in the various Bankruptcy Courts, and for the development of their rules of procedure. The same period will also be used to select the judges to serve on the courts. The judges are to be appointed by the President with Senate approval, the same as other federal judges. They will serve 14-year terms.

The law of bankruptcy is designed to accomplish several purposes. In early times, the major purpose was to provide a method of applying a debtor's assets in an equitable distribution among his creditors. It prevented the debtor from preferring one creditor over another and minimized the losses of all creditors to the extent possible. The major purpose today is to relieve honest debtors of the weight of oppressive indebtedness in order that they may start afresh, free of their former obligations.[1] This purpose reflects recognition that misfortune and poor judgment often create a situation in which a debtor will never be able to discharge his debts by his own efforts. Public policy dictates that such debtors should be able to obtain a fresh start not only in their personal lives but in businesses as well. The procedures for adjustments and corporate reorganizations are similar in purpose. Their function is the rehabilitation of debtors, whether businesses or individuals. The adjustment procedures, if utilized, prevent harassment of debtors and spare them undue hardship, while enabling most creditors eventually to obtain repayment of debts due.

2. Types of Proceedings

The United States Code on Bankruptcy provides for four types of proceedings. Each of these proceedings is the subject of a separate chapter of the law, and they are often identified by the appropriate chapter designation. The four types of proceedings are: Chapter 7, Liquidation; Chapter 9, Adjustment of Debts of a Municipality; Chapter 11, Reorganization; Chapter 13, Adjustment of Debts of an Individual with Regular Income.

Liquidation proceedings are used to eliminate most of the debts of the debtor. Adjustment and reorganization proceedings cover cases in which debtors work out a plan to pay off creditors over an extended period of time rather than have their debts discharged. The law determines which debtors are subject to the provisions of each chapter. The law also allows the conversion of a case filed under one chapter to another chapter with the debtor's consent.

Bankruptcy proceedings may be described as either voluntary or involuntary. Voluntary proceedings are at the instigation of the debtor, while involuntary proceedings are at the instigation of creditors. All debtors covered by a chapter may voluntarily seek relief under it. The statute specifies which debtors under each chapter are subject to involuntary proceedings.

Liquidation is the most common of the bankruptcy proceedings. Cases under Chapter 7 may involve individuals, partnerships, or corporations. However,

---

[1] *Kayetan v. License No. 37589, Class C-61.*

only individuals may be discharged. A discharge voids any judgment against the debtor to the extent that it creates a personal liability. It operates as an injunction against attempts to collect the debt by judicial proceedings or otherwise. Telephone calls, letters, and personal contacts to collect a debt are in effect enjoined by a discharge in bankruptcy, the same as judicial proceedings. All debt collection efforts are prohibited.

A discharge covers all debts that arose before the date of the order for relief. It is irrevelant whether or not claim was filed and whether or not it was allowed.

The debts of partnerships and corporations that go through liquidation proceedings are not discharged. These businesses are still technically liable for their debts. However, the lack of discharge is immaterial unless the partnership or corporation acquires assets later. This lack of discharge stops people from using "shell" businesses after bankruptcy for other purposes.

Certain businesses are denied the right to have liquidation proceedings. Railroads, insurance companies, banks, savings and loan associations, homestead associations, and credit unions may not be debtors under Chapter 7. This limitation includes both domestic and foreign insurance companies and financial institutions. These organizations are subject to the jurisdiction of administrative agencies which handle all aspects of such organizations, including problems related to insolvency. Under this arrangement, there are alternative legal provisions for their liquidation.

Chapter 7 has special provisions relating to liquidation proceedings that involve stockbrokers and commodities brokers. These special provisions are necessary in order to protect the customers of such brokers, because bankruptcies of this kind usually involve large indebtedness and substantial assets. Stockbrokers and commodity brokers are only subject to Chapter 7. Chapter 11 and Chapter 13 proceedings are not possible for them.

As a general rule, any debtor subject to Chapter 7 is also subject to Chapter 11. In addition, railroads are subject to Chapter 11 even though they are not subject to liquidation proceedings under Chapter 7. The public interest in railroads prevents their liquidation, but the law recognizes that financial reorganization is not only possible but often desirable and is a common occurrence for railroads.

Farmers and not-for-profit corporations are not subject to involuntary proceedings under either Chapter 7 or Chapter 11. A "farmer" is defined as a person that receives more than 80 percent of gross income for the taxable year preceding the bankruptcy case from a farming operation owned and operated by such person. The term "farming operation" includes tillage of the soil; dairy farming; ranching; production or raising of crops, poultry, or livestock; and production of poultry or livestock products in an unmanufactured state.

Chapter 9 adjustment proceedings recognize the financial plight of many governmental units such as New York City and Cleveland, Ohio. A municipal governmental entity may be debtor under Chapter 9 if state law or a public official authorized by state law authorizes the municipality to be a debtor under Chapter 9. In addition, the municipality must be unable to meet its debts as they mature, and it must desire to effect a plan to adjust its debts.

Chapter 13 adjustments apply only to individual debtors with regular income whose debts are not so large that repayment is not feasible. The statute limits its coverage to individuals that owe on the date of the filing of the petition fixed, unsecured debts of less than $100,000 and secured debts of less than $350,000. The dollar limitations are also applicable to joint cases filed by husbands and wives.

CASE ADMINISTRATION

3. Introduction

Chapter 3 of the statute is concerned with case administration. Its provisions are applicable to cases filed under any of the four types of proceedings. It covers the various aspects of the commencement of cases, the rules of law relating to the officers of the court involved in bankruptcy such as the trustee, the principles governing the administration of bankruptcy estates, and the administrative powers of the courts and officers involved in the proceedings.

The sections dealing with the administration of bankrupt estates cover such matters as the meetings of creditors, investment of the money of the estate, and the tax returns which must be filed by the trustee. This latter provision deals with such matters as loss carrybacks, investment credit carryovers, and capital gains.

The most technical portion of Chapter 3 is entitled "administrative powers." These sections grant the bankruptcy court and the trustee a wide range of powers to accomplish the statutory purposes of bankruptcy. The law recognizes that attempts by creditors to collect from the debtor must be stopped so that the bankruptcy proceeding may handle all aspects of the debtor's affairs. There is a provision for automatic stays of other litigation. In addition, the law grants the power to the trustee to use, sell, or lease the property of the debtor. The trustee is given the power to terminate executory contracts and leases. The sections which follow discuss those aspects of case administration which are applicable to all four types of proceedings.

4. Voluntary Cases — Commencement

Voluntary cases are commenced by the filing of a petition with the bankruptcy court. The petition is filed by the debtor. In recognition of the fact that husbands and wives often owe the same debts, a joint case may be filed. A joint case is a voluntary case concerning a husband and wife, and it only requires one petition. The petition must be signed by both spouses, since one spouse cannot take the other into bankruptcy without the other's consent.

A filing fee is required of all petitioners, although it may be paid in installments. Only one filing fee is required in a joint case. A petition filed by a partnership as a firm is not a petition on behalf of the partners as individuals. If they intend to obtain individual discharges, separate petitions are required.

The voluntary petition in bankruptcy constitutes an "order for relief" of the debtor as a bankrupt. The petition contains essentially four items — a list of creditors, secured and unsecured; a list of property claimed by the debtor to be exempt; and a statement of affairs of the bankrupt.

5. Involuntary Cases — Commencement

Involuntary cases are commenced by the filing of a petition by one or more creditors. If there are 12 or more creditors, the petition must be signed by at least three creditors whose unsecured claims are not contingent and aggregate at least $5,000. If there are fewer than twelve creditors, only one need sign the petition, but the $5,000 amount must still be met. Employees, insiders, and transferees of voidable transfers are not counted in determining the number of creditors. Insiders are such persons as relatives, partners of the debtor, and directors and officers of the corporation involved. The subject of voidable transfers is discussed later in this chapter.

Creditors may commence involuntary proceedings in order to harass the debtor. To protect the debtor, the court may require the petitioning creditors to file a bond to indemnify the debtor. This bond will cover the amounts for which the petitioning creditors may have liability to the debtor. Such liability may include court costs, attorney's fees, and damages caused by the taking of the debtor's property.

Until the court enters an order for relief in an involuntary case, the debtor may continue to operate his business and to use, acquire, and dispose of his property. However, the court may order an interim trustee appointed to take possession of the property and to operate the business. If the case is a liquidation proceeding, the appointment of the interim trustee is mandatory unless the debtor posts a bond guaranteeing the value of the property in his estate.

The debtor has a right to file an answer to the petition of the creditors and to deny the allegations of the petition. Some debtors against whom involuntary proceedings are commenced are not in fact bankrupt. A general partner of a partnership debtor that did not join in the partnership may file an answer to the petition. (A voluntary petition by a partnership is considered an involuntary one unless all partners sign.) If the debtor does not file an answer, the court orders relief against the debtor. If an answer is filed, the court conducts a trial on the issues raised by the petition and the answer. Courts will order relief in an involuntary proceeding against the debtor only if it finds that the debtor is generally not paying his debts as they become due. Relief may also be ordered if, within 120 days before the filing of the petition, a custodian, receiver, or agent has taken possession of property of the debtor for the purpose of enforcing a lien against the debtor.

Bankruptcy courts need not order relief against a debtor. The statute has a special rule known as "abstention." This rule allows a court to decline jurisdiction and to dismiss a petition or suspend the proceedings. Such action may be taken if the court finds that the interests of creditors and the debtor would be better served by dismissal or suspension of the proceedings. For example, assume that an arrangement is being worked out by most creditors and the debtor out of court. A few creditors seeking to extract full payment file an involuntary petition. If the court finds that the out-of-court arrangements better serve all parties, it may dismiss the petition in involuntary bankruptcy. The principle of abstention may also be followed when there are foreign bankruptcy proceedings pending and a petition is filed in the U.S. The statute contains special rules when foreign cases are pending, in order to protect U.S. assets and claims as well as to coordinate the different proceedings.

6. The Meeting of Creditors

In a voluntary case, the debtor has filed the required schedules with the petition. In an involuntary case, if the court orders relief, the debtor will be required to complete the same schedules as the debtor in a voluntary proceeding. From this point, the proceedings are identical. All parties are given notice of the order for relief. If the debtor owns real property, notice is usually filed in the public records of the county where the land is situated. The notice to creditors will include the date by which all claims are to be filed, and the date of a meeting of the creditors with the debtor. This meeting of creditors must be within a reasonable time after the order for relief. The debtor appears at the meeting with the creditors, and the creditors are allowed to question the debtor under oath. The court may also order a meeting of any equity security holders of the debtor.

At the meeting of creditors, the debtor may be examined by the creditors to ascertain if property has been omitted from the list of assets, if property has been conveyed in defraud of creditors, and other matters that may affect the right of the debtor to have his obligations discharged.

In liquidation cases, the first meeting of creditors includes the important step of electing a permanent trustee. This trustee will replace the interim trustee appointed by the court at the time the order for relief was entered. The law designates those creditors entitled to vote and the requirements for election. At least 20 percent of the creditors in amount holding allowable unsecured claims must vote, and in order to be elected the candidate must receive a majority in amount of the claims voting.

7.   The Trustee

Within five days of appointment and before beginning the official duties, the trustee is required to file a bond conditioned on the faithful performance of the trustee's duties. The trustee is the representative of the estate and has the capacity to sue and to be sued. The statute sets limits on the trustee's compensation, but it allows the court to fix the fees which may be paid to the trustee subject to the limitations.

Trustees are authorized to employ professional persons such as attorneys, accountants, appraisers, and auctioneers. Such persons must be disinterested. The court will usually fix the compensation to be paid to these professional persons.

Trustees are authorized to deposit or invest the money of the estate during the pendency of the proceedings. In making such deposits or investments, the trustee must seek the maximum reasonable net return, taking into account the safety of the deposit or investment. Unless the deposit or investment is guaranteed by the government, the trustee is required to obtain a bond from the entity with which the money is deposited or invested.

The statute has special provisions for the selection of successor trustees in the event that one dies or resigns during a case. It also has detailed provisions on the responsibilities of the trustee under the tax laws. As a general rule, the trustee has responsibility for filing tax returns for the estate. After the order for relief, income received by the estate is taxable to it and not to an individual debtor. The estate of a partnership or a corporation debtor is not a separate entity for tax purposes. While the technical requirements of the tax laws are beyond the scope of this text, it should be remembered that the bankruptcy laws contain detailed rules which are complementary to the Internal Revenue Code in bankruptcy cases and both must be followed by the trustee.

8.   Administrative Powers

Bankruptcy cases operate to stay other judicial or administrative proceedings against the debtor. The stay is not permanent but will extend for a period sufficient to allow the trustee to inventory the debtor's estate and to take possession of it. Lawsuits, collection procedures, and attempts to repossess property are all stopped by the filing of the petition. Of course, the proceedings do not stop criminal actions or the collection of such debts as alimony and child support which are not dischargeable in bankruptcy.

Such stays of proceedings may operate to the detriment of a creditor or third party. For example, a stay would prevent a utility company from shutting off service. In addition, the trustee will frequently need to use, sell, or lease property of the debtor. This is especially true when the trustee continues to operate the debtor's business. In order to prevent irreparable harm to creditors and other third parties as a result of stays and the use, sale, or lease of the debtor's property, a trustee may be required to provide "adequate protection" to third parties. In some cases, adequate protection requires that the trustee make periodic cash payments to creditors. In others, the trustee may be required to provide a lien to the creditor. For example, when the sale, lease, or rent of the debtor's property may decrease the value of an entity's interest in property held by the trustee, a creditor may be entitled to a lien on the proceeds of any sale. The court is empowered to determine if the trustee has furnished adequate protection, and when the issue is raised the burden of proof is on the trustee.

A trustee that is authorized to operate the business of the debtor is authorized to obtain unsecured credit and to incur debts in the ordinary course of business. Such debts are paid as administrative expenses. Utilities may not refuse to service the trustee or the debtor because bills due prior to the order for relief were not paid. However, a utility may discontinue service unless, within 20 days of the order, adequate assurance of payment for future service is furnished.

9.   Executory Contracts and Unexpired Leases

Bankrupt debtors are frequently parties to contracts that have not been performed. Also, they are often lessees of real property, and the leases usually cover long periods of time. The liability for future rent is generally limited to one year's rent or 15 percent of the unpaid rent, not to exceed three years' rent, whichever is greater. This is discussed further with the materials on claims later in this chapter.

As a general rule, the trustee is authorized, subject to court approval, to assume or to reject an executory contract or unexpired lease. If the contract or lease is rejected, the other party has a claim which is subject to some statutory limitations. A rejection by the trustee creates a prepetition claim for the rejected contract or lease.

If the contract or lease is assumed, the trustee will perform the contract or assign it to someone else, and the estate will presumably receive the benefits. In liquidation cases, the trustee must assume within 60 days or within an additional 60 days, if the court extends the time. Failure to act is a rejection. In cases under Chapters 9, 11, or 13, the trustee must assume or reject before confirmation of the plan. Also the court may order the trustee to act by a specified date prior to confirmation.

If the trustee assumes a contract or lease, he must cure any default by the debtor and provide adequate assurance of future performance. In shopping center leases, adequate assurance includes protection against declines in percentage rents, and preservation of the tenant mix.

A trustee may not assume an executory contract which requires the other party to make a loan or deliver equipment to or issue a security to the debtor. A party to a contract which is based on the financial strength of the debtor is not required to extend new credit to a debtor in bankruptcy.

Contracts and leases often have clauses prohibiting assignment of them. The law also prohibits the assignment of certain contract rights, such as those which are personal in nature. The trustee in bankruptcy is allowed to assume contracts notwithstanding a clause prohibiting the assumption or assignment of the contract or lease. However, the trustee is not allowed to assume a contract if applicable nonbankruptcy law excuses the other party from performance to someone other than the debtor, unless the other party consents to the assumption.

The statute invalidates contract clauses that automatically terminate contracts or leases upon filing of a petition in bankruptcy or upon the assignment of the lease or contract. The law also invalidates contract clauses that give a party other than the debtor the right to terminate the contract upon assumption by the trustee or assignment by the debtor. Such clauses hamper rehabilitation efforts and are against public policy. They are not needed, because the court can require the trustee to provide adequate protection and can insure that the other party receives the benefit of its bargain.

Debtors are sometimes lessors instead of lessees. If the trustee rejects an unexpired lease of a debtor-lessor, the tenant may treat the lease as terminated. However, the tenant may remain in possession for the balance of the lease. There is a similar provision for contract purchasers of real estate. They may treat the rejection as a termination or they may remain in possession and make the payments due under the contract. A purchaser that treats a contract as terminated has a lien on the property to the extent of the purchase price paid.

If the trustee assigns a contract to a third party and the third party later breaches the contract, the trustee has no liability. This is a change of the common law in which an assignor is not relieved of his liability by an assignment. An assignment by a trustee in bankruptcy is, in effect, a novation if the assignment is valid.

CREDITORS AND DEBTORS

10. Introduction

Chapter 5 of the new law contains three subsections. The first deals with creditors and claims. It provides for filing proof of claims and for priorities among them. The second subsection is concerned with the debtor's duties and the effect of a discharge on the obligations of the debtor. This subsection details the exemptions available to debtors and the grounds for denying a discharge. Finally, Chapter 5 has several provisions dealing with the property of the bankruptcy estate. Its sections dealing with preferences, fraudulent transfers, and set-offs are of great importance. The discussions which follow are based on Chapter 5 and are applicable to all four types of proceedings.

11. Claims

Creditors are required to file proof of their claim if they are to share in the bankrupt's estate. Filed claims are allowed unless a party in interest objects.

If an objection is filed, the court conducts a hearing to determine the validity of the claim. There are several grounds on which a claim may be disallowed. Among the grounds for disallowing a claim are that (1) it is unenforceable because of usury, unconscionability, or failure of consideration, (2) it is for unmatured interest, (3) it is of an insider or attorney and exceeds the reasonable value of the services rendered, (4) it is for unmatured alimony or child support, and (5) it is for rent or breach of an employment contract, and it exceeds the statutory limitations for such claims.

Illegality can be raised, because any defense available to the debtor is available to the trustee. Postpetition interest is not collectible, because interest stops accruing at the date of the filing of the petition. Bankruptcy operates as an acceleration of the principal due. From the date of filing, the amount of the claim is the total principal plus interest to that date.

Unreasonable attorney's fees and claims of insiders are disallowed because they encourage concealing of assets or the return of assets to the debtor. Since alimony claims are not dischargeable in bankruptcy, there is no reason to allow a claim for postpetition alimony and child support.

The amount of rent that may be included in a claim is limited. The law is designed to compensate the landlord for his loss while not allowing the claim to be so large that other creditors will not share in the estate. A landlord's damages are limited to the rent for the greater of one year or 15 percent of the remaining lease term, not to exceed three years. In liquidation cases, the time is measured from the earlier of the date of filing the petition and the date of surrender of possession. In cases filed under Chapters 9, 11, and 13, the claim is limited to three years' rent. Of course, these limitations are not applicable to rent owed by the trustee for which the estate is liable as an administrative expense.

Landlords often have a security deposit for rent. To the extent that the security deposit exceeds the rent allowed as a claim, it must be paid over to the trustee to be a part of the bankruptcy estate. If the security deposit is less than the claim, the landlord keeps the security deposit, and it will be applied in satisfaction of the claim. The limitations on claims for rent are applicable to bona fide leases and not to leases of real property, which are financing or security leases.

The limitation for damages resulting from termination of employment contracts is similar to the one for rent. Damages are limited to compensation for the year following the earlier of the date of the petition and that of the termination of employment.

Claims are sometimes contingent or otherwise unliquidated and uncertain. The law authorizes the court to estimate and to fix the amount of such claims, if necessary, to avoid undue delay in closing the estate. The same is true for equitable remedies such as specific performance. Courts will convert such remedies to dollar amounts and proceed to close the estate.

If a secured claim is undersecured — that is, if the debt exceeds the value of the collateral — the claim is divided into two parts. The claim is secured to the extent of the value of the collateral. It is an unsecured claim for the balance.

12. Priorities

The law establishes certain priorities in the payment of claims. The general order of priority is as follows:

1. Administrative expenses
2. Involuntary GAP creditors
3. Wages, salaries, and commissions
4. Contributions to employee benefit plans
5. Consumer deposits
6. Claims of governmental units for certain taxes

Administrative expenses include all costs of administering the bankrupt's estate, including taxes incurred by the estate. Typical costs include attorney's fees, appraiser's fees, and wages paid to persons employed to help preserve the estate.

The term "involuntary GAP creditor" describes a person who extends credit to the estate after the date of filing a petition under Chapter 11 and before a trustee is appointed or before the order for relief. Such claims include taxes incurred as the result of the conduct of business in this period.

The third class of priority is limited to amounts earned by an individual within 90 days of the filing of the petition or the cessation of the debtor's business, whichever occurred first. The priority is limited to $2,000 for each individual, but it includes vacation, severance and sick leave pay as well as regular earnings. The employee's share of employment taxes is included in the third priority category, provided the wages and the employee share of taxes have been paid in full.

The fourth priority recognizes that fringe benefits are an important part of many labor-management contracts. The priority is limited to claims for contributions to employee benefit plans, arising from services rendered within 120 days before commencement of the case or cessation of the debtor's business, whichever occurs first. The priority is limited to $2,000 multiplied by the number of employees less the amount paid under priority three. The net effect is to limit the total priority for wages and employee benefits to $2,000 per employee.

The fifth priority was added in 1978 as an additional method of consumer protection. It protects consumers who have deposited money in connection with the purchase, lease, or rental of property or the purchase of services for personal, family, or household use that were not delivered or provided. The priority is limited to $900.00.

The sixth priority is for certain taxes. Priority is given to income taxes for a taxable year that ended on or before the date of filing the petition. The last due date of the return must have occurred not more than three years before the filing. Employment taxes and transfer taxes such as gift, estate, sale, and excise taxes are also given sixth class priority. Again the transaction or event which gave rise to the tax must precede the petition date and the return must have been due within three years. The bankruptcy law has several very technical aspects relating to taxation and they must be carefully reviewed not only as to the tax returns filed by the trustee but also regarding claims for taxes.

After the claims which have priority are paid, all other unsecured claims are paid a proportional share out of any assets remaining. In most cases, there are no assets at this stage of the proceedings.

13. Exemptions

In order to allow a debtor to have a fresh start and to insure debtors a certain amount of property, the law grants certain exemptions. Technically, all property of the debtor becomes property of the bankruptcy estate, but the debtor is then permitted to claim certain of it as exempt from the proceedings. Such property is then returned to the debtor. Exemptions are granted by both federal laws and state and local laws.

The Bankruptcy Act exempts the following property:

1. $7,500 in real property used as a residence
2. The debtor's interest, not to exceed $1,200, in one motor vehicle
3. The debtor's interest, not to exceed $200 in any particular item, in household furnishings, wearing apparel, appliances, books, animals, crops, or musical instruments that are held primarily for the personal family or household use of the debtor and his dependents.
4. The debtor's interest in jewelry, not to exceed $500
5. The debtor's interest in other property, not to exceed $400, plus any unused real property exemption
6. The debtor's interest, not to exceed $750, in any implements, professional books, or tools of the trade of the debtor, or the trade of his dependents
7. Unmatured life insurance contracts
8. The cash value of life insurance, not to exceed $4,000
9. Professionally prescribed health aids
10. The debtor's rights to receive benefits such as Social Security, Unemployment Compensation, Public Assistance, disability benefits, alimony, child support and separate maintenance reasonably necessary, and payments of pension profit-sharing, annuity, or similar plans
11. The debtor's right to receive payment traceable to the wrongful death of an individual on whom the debtor was dependent or to life insurance on the life of such a person or to payments for personal injury not to exceed $7,500.

Every state has enacted statutes granting exemptions to persons domiciled in each state. These exemptions have varied greatly from state to state, with some states having very large exemptions. For example, California allows homestead exemptions for real property used as a residence in the amount of $20,000. Exemptions in other states are quite low. One state has a homestead exemption of $750. Individuals may claim the larger exemptions offered by states, if it is to their advantage to do so. In order to encourage states to raise their exemptions, the law provides that the federal exemptions will be available to debtors of states unless a state specifically passes a law denying its residents the larger exemptions. It is assumed that such laws will be difficult to pass because of their discriminatory effect on local citizens. Therefore, the federal exemptions previously noted are likely to be minimums which are exceeded by some states.

A debtor is permitted to convert non-exempt property into exempt property before filing a bankruptcy petition. The debtor may select the state with the most exemptions, provided he resides there 180 days prior to the petition or resides for a longer portion of the 180-day period in that state than in any other state.

As a general rule, property that is exempt is not liable during or after the case for any debts that arise before the commencement of the case. There are exceptions to the general rule for tax claims and for alimony, child support, and separate maintenance. Exempt property can be used to collect such debts after the proceeding. In addition, the discharge in bankruptcy does not prevent enforcement of valid liens against exempt property. However, judicial liens and non-possessory, non-purchase money security interests in household goods, wearing apparel, professional books, tools, and professionally prescribed health aids may be avoided. In addition, a debtor may redeem such tangible personal property from a lien securing a dischargeable consumer debt by paying the lien holder the amount of the secured claim. Exempt property is free of such liens after the proceedings. Waivers of exemptions are unenforceable. This is to prevent creditors from attempting to deny debtors the necessary property to gain the fresh start intended by the law.

14. Debts That Are Not Discharged

While the purpose of bankruptcy proceedings and especially those under Chapter 7 is to eliminate the debts of the debtor, it should be recognized that not all debts are discharged. A discharge in bankruptcy does not discharge an individual debtor from the following debts:

1. Certain taxes and customs duties[2]
2. Debts for obtaining money, property, services, or credit by false pretenses, false representations, or actual fraud

[2] *United States* v. *Sotelo,* page 549.

3. Unscheduled debts

4. Debts for fraud or defalcation while acting in a fiduciary capacity and debts created by embezzlement or larceny.

5. Alimony, child support, and separate maintenance

6. Liability for willful and malicious torts

7. Tax penalties if the tax is not dischargeable

8. Student loans less than five years old

9. Debts owed before a previous bankruptcy to which discharge was denied for grounds other than the six-year rule

The taxes which are not discharged are the same ones that receive priority under the second, third, and sixth categories discussed in Section 12. These taxes are not discharged even if the government fails to file a claim. In addition, taxes are not discharged if the debtor failed to file a return or it is filed beyond its last due date. Finally, tax claims with respect to which the debtor filed a fraudulent return are not discharged.

The second group of debts that are not discharged are those debts that were fraudulently induced. Reasonable reliance by the debtor on a false statement in writing is required.

As previously noted, it is the duty of the bankrupt to file a schedule of all creditors and the amount due each. Notice of the proceedings is then given each creditor so that a claim may be filed. The claim of any creditor who is not listed or who does not learn of the proceedings in time to file a claim is not discharged. The bankrupt, under such circumstances, remains liable for it. In the case of nonlisted creditors, the burden of proof to establish that the creditor had knowledge of the proceedings in time to file a claim rests with the bankrupt.[3] Proof of actual knowledge is required, and while such knowledge is often present, care should be taken to list all creditors so that all claims will unquestionably be discharged.

Tort liability claims based on simple negligence are discharged. Tort liability claims arising from willful and malicious acts are not discharged. For example, a judgment arising out of an assault and battery is not discharged. Many auto accident cases raise difficult questions in applying these distinctions. In many such cases the wrongful conduct of the judgment debtor was more than mere negligence but less than intentional. Such lawsuits proceed on a theory known as willful and wanton misconduct. Many cases prior to the 1978 amendment held that judgments based on willful and wanton misconduct were not dischargeable. The 1978 revision changed this, and they are now dischargeable. Only intentional torts are not dischargeable.

The provision denying discharge to student loans is new. It seeks to give creditors and the government five years to collect student loans. However, there

[3] *Brown* v. *Tucker Professional Associates,* page 550.

is an exception if the debtor is able to convince the court that undue hardship on the debtor and his dependents will result if the student loan debt is not discharged.

THE ESTATE

15. Property of the Estate

The commencement of a bankruptcy case creates an estate. The estate consists of all legal or equitable interests of the debtor in property wherever located. The property may be tangible or intangible and includes causes of action. An interest in property may be ownership or it may be only possessory. While all property is included in the estate to begin with, the debtor may exempt those portions entitled to exemption as previously discussed.

The estate includes property that the trustee recovers by using his power to avoid prior transactions. The estate also includes property inherited by the debtor, or received as a beneficiary of life insurance within 180 days of the petition. Proceeds, products, offspring, rents, and profits which are generated by or come from property in the estate are also part of the estate.

Except as previously noted, property acquired by the debtor after commencement of the case belongs to the debtor.[4] This includes earnings from employment. Property held in trust for the benefit of the debtor under a spendthrift trust does not become a part of the estate. However, other restrictions on the transfer of the property of the debtor are invalid, and property subject to such restrictions is a part of the bankruptcy estate.

16. The Trustee's Rights and Powers

A trustee in bankruptcy has several rights and powers with respect to the property of the debtor. First of all, the trustee has the rights of a creditor on a simple contract with a judicial lien on the property of the debtor as of the date of the petition. In other words, the trustee has a judicial lien on the property just as if the trustee were a creditor. Second, the trustee has the rights and powers of a judgment creditor who obtained a judgment against the bankrupt on the date of the adjudication of bankruptcy and who had an execution issued against the bankrupt that was returned unsatisfied. The trustee has these rights of a judgment creditor whether or not any judgment creditor actually exists.

Third, the trustee has the rights of a bona fide purchaser of the real property of the debtor as of the date of the petition. This gives the trustee title to the debtor's real estate free of most of the claims of others. Finally, the trustee has the rights of an actual unsecured creditor to avoid any transfer of the debtor's property and to avoid any obligation incurred by the debtor that is

[4] *Thomas* v. *Sun Realty, Inc.,* page 551.

voidable under any federal or state law. As a result of these rights, the trustee is able to set aside transfers of property and to eliminate the interests of other parties where creditors or the debtor could do so. In addition, the trustee is given a lien on the property which puts the trustee in a preferred position.

The trustee also has the power to avoid certain liens of others on the property of the debtor. Liens that first become effective on the bankruptcy or insolvency of the debtor are voidable. As a result, contract provisions and state laws which purport to give a lien to a creditor upon the commencement of bankruptcy proceedings are ineffective. In addition, as a general rule, liens that are not perfected or enforceable on the date of the petition against a bona fide purchaser of the property are also voidable. For example, assume that a seller or creditor has an unperfected lien on goods in the hands of the debtor on the date the petition is filed. Assume further that the lien is perfected later. Such a lien is voidable if it could not be asserted against a good faith purchaser of the goods. Liens for rent and for distress for rent are also voidable.

The law imposes certain limitations on the aforesaid rights and powers of the trustee. The power must be exercised within two years of the appointment of the trustee and before the case is closed or dismissed. In addition, a creditor may perfect a security interest after the petition is filed if nonbankruptcy law allows perfection against intervening interest holders. For example, a purchase money security interest under Article 9 of the code relates back to the date of the transaction if it is perfected within ten days of delivery of the property. Such a security interest cannot be avoided if properly perfected.

The rights and powers of the trustee are also subject to the rights of a seller of goods in the ordinary course of business to reclaim goods if the debtor has received the goods while insolvent. In such cases, the seller must demand the goods back within 10 days. The right to reclaim is also subject to any superior rights of secured creditors. Courts may deny reclamation and protect the seller by giving him priority as an administrative expense.

17. Preferences

One of the goals of bankrupty proceedings is to provide an equitable distribution of a debtor's property among his creditors. To achieve this goal, the trustee in bankruptcy is allowed to recover transfers that constitute a preference of one creditor over another. As one judge said, "A creditor who dips his hand in a pot which he knows will not go round must return what he receives so that all may share." To constitute a recoverable preference the transfer must (1) have been made by an insolvent debtor; (2) have been made to a creditor for, or on account of, an antecedent debt owed by the debtor before the transfer; (3) have been made within 90 days of the filing of the bankruptcy petition; and (4) enable the creditor to receive a greater percentage of his claim than he would receive under a distribution from the bankruptcy estate in a liquidation proceeding.

Insofar as the time period is concerned, there is an exception when the transfer is to an insider. In such cases, the trustee may avoid the transfer if it occurred within one year of the date of filing the petition, provided the insider had reasonable cause to believe the debtor was insolvent at the time of the transfer.

A debtor is presumed to be insolvent during the 90-day period prior to the filing of the petition. Any person contending that the debtor was solvent has the burden of coming forward with evidence to prove solvency. Once credible evidence is introduced, the party with the benefit of the presumption of insolvency has the burden of persuasion on the issue.

Recoverable preferences include not only payments of money but also the transfer of property as payment of, or as security for, a prior indebtedness. Since the law is limited to debts, payments by the debtor of tax liabilities are exempt from the preference provision and are not recoverable. A mortgage or pledge may be set aside as readily as direct payments. A pledge or mortgage can be avoided if received within the immediate 90-day period prior to the filing of the petition in bankruptcy, provided it was obtained as security for a previous debt. In the case of a mortgage, the period dates from the recording of the mortgage rather than from its signing. In the case of a security agreement covering after-acquired property, it is the date of filing that controls and not the date of the receipt of the property.

Payment of a fully secured claim does not constitute a preference and, therefore, may not be recovered. Transfers of property for a contemporaneous consideration may not be set aside, because there is a corresponding asset for the new liability. A mortgage given to secure a contemporaneous loan is valid even when the mortgagee took the security with knowledge of the debtor's insolvency. An insolvent debtor has a right to attempt to extricate himself, as far as possible, from his financial difficulty. If the new security is personal property, it must be perfected within ten days after the security interest attaches.

The law also creates an exception for transfers in the ordinary course of business or in the ordinary financial affairs of persons not in business. The payment of such debts within 45 days after they are incurred is not recoverable if the payment is made according to ordinary business terms. This exception covers ordinary debt payments such as utility bills. The law on preferences is directed at unusual transfers and payments and not to those which occur promptly in the ordinary course of the debtor's affairs.

A creditor with a floating lien under Article 9 of the code is subject to preference attack to the extent that he improves his position during the 90-day period before bankruptcy, to the detriment of other creditors. Secured creditors are not allowed to improve their position during this period to the detriment of unsecured general creditors.

18. Set-Offs

Any debtor of a bankrupt may set-off against the amount he owes the bankrupt estate any sum that the estate owes him, provided such amount would be allowable as a claim. To the extent of this set-off, he becomes a preferred creditor, but he is legally entitled to this preference. This, however, does not apply when the claim against the bankrupt has been purchased or created for the purpose of preferring the creditor. For example, assume that a bank has loaned a bankrupt $2,000 and that the bank of the bankrupt has $1,500 on deposit at the time of bankruptcy. The bank is a preferred creditor to the extent of the deposit. This set-off will be allowed unless the evidence discloses that the deposit was made for the purpose of preferring the bank. In the latter case, the deposit becomes a part of the bankrupt estate because of the collusion.

Since the filing of the petition in bankruptcy operates as a stay of all proceedings, the right of set-off operates at the time of final distribution of the estate. Since the law allows the trustee to use the funds of the debtor with court approval, parties who wish to exercise the right of set-off should seek "adequate protection."

The right of set-off will usually be exercised by a creditor against a deposit that has been made within 90 days of the filing of a petition in bankruptcy. Quite frequently, there are several such deposits, and there also may have been several payments on the debt during the 90-day period. As a result of these variables, the application of off-set principles is sometimes difficult.

The law seeks to prohibit a creditor from improving his position during the 90-day period. It does so by limiting the amount that may be set-off. This amount is calculated by determining the amount by which, on the first day of the 90-day period, the claim against the debtor exceeds the amount on deposit, in which there was an insufficiency. An insufficiency is the amount by which the debt owed exceeds the amount on deposit.

For example, assume that a petition in bankruptcy was filed on September 2. On June 1, the debtor owes $1,000 to the creditor and the debtor deposits with the creditor a total of $500. On September 1, the debtor owes the same $1,000 but the deposit totals $1,000. The set-off is limited to $500, which was the amount of insufficiency on the first day of the 90-day period.

19. Fraudulent Transfers and Obligations

A transfer of property by a bankrupt-debtor may be fraudulent under either federal or state law. The trustee may proceed under either to set aside a fraudulent conveyance. Under federal law, a fraudulent conveyance is a transfer within one year of the filing of the petition, with the intent to hinder, delay, or defraud creditors. Under state law, the period may be longer and is usually within the range of two to five years.

Actual fraudulent intent may be inferred from the fact that the consideration is unfair, inadequate, or nonexistent. Solvency or insolvency at the time of the transfer is significant, but it is not controlling. Actual fraudulent intent exists when the transfer makes it impossible for the creditors to be paid in full or for the creditors to use legal remedies that would otherwise be available.

The intent to hinder, delay, or defraud creditors may also be implied. Such is the case when the debtor is insolvent and makes a transfer for less than a full and adequate value. Fraudulent intent is present if the debtor was insolvent on the date of the transfer when the obligation was incurred, or if the debtor became insolvent as a result of the transfer or obligation.

If the debtor is engaged in business or is about to become so, the fraudulent intent will be implied when the transfer leaves the businessman with an unreasonably small amount of capital. The businessman may be solvent but he has, nevertheless, made a fraudulent transfer if the net result of the transfer is such that he is left with an unreasonably small amount of capital, provided the transfer was without fair consideration. Whether or not the remaining capital is unreasonably small is a question of fact.

The trustee may also avoid transfer or obligation when a debtor intends to incur obligations beyond the debtor's ability to repay as they mature. For example, assume that A is about to enter business and that he plans to incur debts in the business. Because of A's concern that he may be unable to meet these potential obligations, he transfers all his property to his wife without consideration. Such a transfer may be set aside as fraudulent. The requisite intent is supplied by the factual situation at the time of the transfer and the state of mind of the transferor. The actual financial condition of the debtor in such a case is not controlling but does shed some light on the intent factor and state of mind of the debtor.

The trustee of a partnership debtor may avoid transfers of a partnership property to partners if the debtor was or thereby became insolvent. This is to prevent a partnership's preferring partners who are also creditors over other partners. Such transfers may be avoided if they occurred within one year of the date of filing the petition.

If a transferee's only liability to the trustee is because the transfer was in defraud of creditors, the law limits the transferee's liability. To the extent the transferee does give value in good faith, the transferee has a lien on the property. For the purpose of defining value, in the fraudulent transfer situation, the term includes property or the satisfaction or securing of a present or existing debt. It does not include an unperformed promise to support the debtor or a relative of a debtor.

20. Liquidation Proceedings

The discussions contained in the previous sections are applicable to all four types of proceedings. The matters discussed in this and subsequent sections cover only the individual chapters indicated in the section heading.

In liquidation proceedings, the creditors may elect a committee of not less than three nor more than eleven members to consult with the trustee in connection with the administration of the estate. Such a committee may make recommendations to the trustee and submit questions to the court.

The statutory duties of the trustee in liquidation proceedings are:

1. To collect and reduce to money the property of the estate; **2.** To account for all property received; **3.** To investigate the financial affairs of the debtor; **4.** To examine proofs of claims and to object to the allowance of any claim that is improper; **5.** To oppose the discharge of the debtor if advisable; **6.** To furnish information as is requested by a party of interest; **7.** If a business is operated, to file appropriate reports with the court and the taxing authorities; and **8.** To make a final report and account and file it with the court.

In liquidation cases, the property available is first distributed among the priority claimants in the order established. (See Section 12.) Second, property is then distributed to general unsecured creditors who file their claims on time. Third, payment is made to unsecured creditors who tardily file their claims. Fourth, distribution is made to holders of penalty, forfeiture, or punitive damage claims. Punitive penalties, including tax penalties, are subordinated to the first three classes of claims as a matter of policy. Regular creditors should be paid before windfalls to persons and entities collecting penalties. Fifth, post-petition interest on prepetition claims is paid if any property is available to do so. After the interest is paid, any surplus goes to the debtor. Claims within a particular class are paid pro rata if the trustee is unable to pay them in full.

A discharge in bankruptcy is a privilege and not a right. Therefore, in addition to providing that certain debts are not discharged, the Bankruptcy Act specifies the following grounds for denying a bankrupt a discharge:

1. Fraudulent transfers

2. Inadequate records

3. Commission of a bankruptcy crime

4. Failure to explain a loss of assets or deficiency of assets

5. Refusing to testify in the proceedings or to obey a court order

6. Any of the above within one year in connection with another bankruptcy case of an insider

7. Another discharge within six years

8. Approval by the court of a waiver of discharge

The first three grounds for denying discharge are predicated on wrongful conduct by the debtor in connection with the case. Fraudulent transfers involve such acts as removing, destroying, or concealing property with the intent to hinder, delay, or defraud creditors or the trustee. The conduct must occur within one year preceding the case or it may occur after the case is commenced.

A debtor is also denied a discharge if he has concealed, destroyed, mutilated, falsified, or failed to keep or preserve any books and records relating to his financial condition. A debtor is required to keep records from which his financial condition may be ascertained, unless the act or failure is justified.

Bankruptcy crimes are generally related to the proceedings. Such crimes include the making of a false oath, the use or presentation of a false claim, or bribery in connection with the proceedings and with the withholding of records.

The six-year rule which allows a discharge only if another discharge has not been ordered within six years extends to Chapter 11 and Chapter 13 proceedings as well as to those under Chapter 7. Discharge under Chapter 11 will bar another discharge for six years, and confirmation of a plan under Chapter 13 has the same effect.

Either a creditor or the trustee may object to the discharge. The court may order the trustee to examine the facts to see if grounds exist for the denial of the discharge. Courts are also granted the authority to revoke a discharge within one year if it was obtained by fraud on the court.

21. Reorganizations — General Aspects

Chapter 11 of the Bankruptcy Act governs reorganizations, including those of railroads. It contains detailed provisions on all aspects of the plan of reorganization, its execution, and the application of the securities laws to reorganizations. There are also special tax provisions relating to the subject.

As soon as practicable after the order for relief, the court appoints a committee of creditors holding unsecured claims. The committee ordinarily will consist of those persons with the seven largest claims. The committee appointed by the court may employ attorneys, accountants, or other agents to assist it. The committee works with the trustee and the debtor concerning the administration of the case. It represents the interests of the creditors. It may investigate the financial conditions of the debtor and will assist in the formulation of the plan.

The court in reorganization cases will usually appoint a trustee before approval of the plan of reorganization. A trustee will be appointed if the court finds that there is probably fraud, dishonesty, incompetence, or gross mismanagement of the affairs of the debtor by current management, if the appointment is in the best interests of the creditors or equity security holders. If the court does not appoint a trustee, it will appoint an examiner. In such cases, the examiner conducts an investigation into the affairs of the debtor, including any mismanagement or irregularities.

After the trustee or the examiner, as the case may be, conducts the investigation of the acts, conduct, assets, liabilities, financial conditions, and other relevant aspects of the debtor, a written report of this investigation is filed with the court. The trustee may file a plan of reorganization if the debtor does not, or it may recommend conversion of the case to liquidation proceedings. The trustee will also file tax returns for the debtor and file reports with the court. the trustee may operate the debtor's business unless the court orders otherwise.

A debtor may convert a voluntary reorganization case to a liquidation case but a debtor may not convert an involuntary reorganization case to a liquidation one. The case may also be converted at the request of a creditor, if conversion is in the best interest of the creditors and if cause for conversion is established. The statute lists nine grounds for cause for conversion to a liquidation case. Of course, a case by a farmer or a not-for-profit corporation may not be converted, because this would be the same as putting the debtor into involuntary bankruptcy.

22. Reorganizations — The Plan

The debtor may file a plan of reorganization with the voluntary petition or at any time later. The plan will attempt to extricate the business from its financial difficulties so that the business may survive. For the first 120 days after the order for relief, only the debtor may file a plan. After the 120 days, the trustee, if one has been appointed, a creditors' committee, or an equity security holder may file a plan if the debtor did not do so. In addition, if a plan is filed by the debtor and it is not accepted within 180 days from the date of the order for relief, all of the aforesaid may file a plan.

The plan will classify claims. All claims within a class will be treated the same. All unsecured claims for less than a specified amount may be classified together. The plan will designate those classes of claims that are unimpaired under the plan. It will specify the treatment to be given those claims that are impaired.

The plan must provide a means for its execution. It may provide that the debtor will retain all or part of the property of the estate. It may also propose that property be sold or transferred to creditors or other entities. Mergers and consolidations may be proposed. In short, the plan will deal with all aspects of the organization of the debtor, its property, and its debts. Some debts will be paid in full, some will be partially paid over an extended period of time, and others may not be paid at all. The only limitation is that all claimants must receive as much as they would receive in liquidation proceedings.

As is the case in liquidation proceedings, the plan may provide for the assumption or rejection of executory contracts and unexpired leases. It may provide for the impairment of any secured or unsecured claim or interest in property.

Holders of claims or interests in the debtor's property are allowed to vote and to either accept or reject the proposed plan of reorganization. A class of claims has accepted a plan if at least two-thirds in amount and more than half in number of claims vote yes. Acceptance by a class of interests such as equity holders requires a two-thirds "yes" vote.

A hearing is had on the confirmation of a plan, to determine if it is fair and equitable. The statute specifies several conditions such as good faith which must be met before the plan is approved. Before the plan is approved, it must be established that each holder of a claim or interest has either accepted the plan or will receive as much under the reorganization plan as would be received in liquidation proceedings. For secured creditors, this means that they will receive the value of their security either by payment or by delivery of the property.

Confirmation of the plan makes it binding on the debtor, equity security holders, and creditors. Confirmation vests the property of the estate in the debtor and releases it from all claims. Debts which arose prior to the confirmation are discharged unless the plan provides otherwise. Of course, nondischargeable taxes remain as obligations.

23.   Adjustment of Individual Debts

Chapter 13 proceedings are used to adjust the debts of individuals with regular income whose debts are not so large and whose income is significant enough that substantial repayment is feasible. As noted earlier in this chapter, the unsecured debts of individuals utilizing Chapter 13 proceedings cannot exceed $100,000 and the secured debts cannot exceed $350,000. Persons utilizing Chapter 13 will usually be employees earning a salary, but persons engaged in business also qualify. Self-employed persons who incur trade debts are considered to be engaged in business.

The debtor files a plan which provides for the use of all or of a portion of his future earnings or income for the payment of debts. The income is under the supervision and control of the trustee. Except as provided in the plan, the debtor keeps possession of his property. If the debtor is engaged in business, the debtor continues to operate the business. The plan must provide for the full payment of all claims entitled to priority unless the creditor with priority agrees to a different treatment. The plan may divide unsecured claims into classes. If it does so, all claims within a class must be given the same treatment.

The plan may provide that unsecured claims which are not entitled to priority are to be repaid in full, or they may be reduced to a level not lower than the amount that would be paid upon liquidation. The secured creditors may be protected by allowing them to retain their lien, by payment of the secured claim in full, or by the surrender of the property to the secured claimant. The usual plan will provide for payments over three years, but the court may extend the payment period up to a total of five years.

The plan may modify the rights of holders of secured and unsecured claims, except that the rights of holders of real estate mortgages may not be modified. Claims arising after the filing of the petition may be included in the plan. This is a realistic approach, because all of the debts of the debtor must be taken into account if the plan is to accomplish its objectives.

A plan may provide for concurrent payments on secured and unsecured claims. It may reject executory leases and contracts the same as if the case were in liquidation.

The court conducts a hearing on the confirmation of the plan. If the court is satisfied that the debtor will be able to make all payments to comply with it, the plan will be approved. Of course, the plan must be proposed in good faith, be in compliance with the law, and be in the best interests of the creditors.

As soon as the debtor completes all payments under the plan, the court grants the debtor a discharge of all debts, unless the debtor waives the discharge. Debts in which the final payment is due after the plan is completed, are not discharged. Of course, debts for alimony and child support and debts incurred for willful and malicious conversion or for injury to property are not discharged.

Courts, after a hearing, may also grant a discharge even though all payments have not been made, if the debtor's failure to complete the payments is due to circumstances for which the debtor should not justly be held accountable. In such cases, the payments under the plan must be not less than those which would have been paid on liquidation, and modification must not be practicable.

It should be kept in mind that a debtor may convert a case under Chapter 13 to a liquidation proceeding under Chapter 7 at any time. Any waiver of this right is unenforceable.

BANKRUPTCY CASES

Kayetan v. License No. 37589, Class C-61
(Ariz. App.) 1977

An Arizona statute authorized the Registrar of Contractors to revoke the license of any contractor who filed a petition in voluntary bankruptcy. Hull, a licensee, was declared in voluntary bankruptcy on January 22, 1975, and his contractor's license was revoked on May 16, 1975. He appealed to the courts, contending that the Arizona statute was unconstitutional. The trial court held for Hull and the Registrar appealed.

OGG, J. . . . The sole issue raised in this appeal is whether the statutory provisions of ARS & 32-1154(8) conflict with federal law to render them constitutionally infirm under the supremacy clause of the United States Constitution. . . .

Deciding whether a state statute is in conflict with a federal statute and hence invalid under the Supremacy Clause is essentially a two-step process of first ascertaining the construction of the two statutes and then determining the constitutional question whether they are in conflict.

Once the respective purposes of the state and federal laws in question have been determined, the resolution whether there exists a statutory conflict is to be determined by "Whether a challenged state statute 'stands as an obstacle to the accomplishment and execution of the full purposes and objectives of Congress.' " The existence of a conflict with federal law is therefore to be determined by the effect of the state statute and "Cannot be determined merely by a consideration of its purpose."

Arizona case law has consistently held that the primary purpose of state regulation of construction contractors through licensing is to protect the public from unscrupulous and unquali-

fied persons acting as contractors. Similarly, the Supreme Court has stated that the purpose of the Federal Bankruptcy Act is to give debtors "a new opportunity in life and a clear field for further effort, unhampered by the pressure and discouragement of a pre-existing debt."

These purposes are not prima facie in conflict; however, for legitimate resolution of the constitutional issue . . . we must examine the effect the Arizona statute has on federal law. . . . The clear import of a statutory provision of the nature dealt with in this case is to revoke a contractor's state license to conduct business if his debts are discharged in bankruptcy for less than their full amount. Furthermore, ARS 32-1161(B) provides that once a license is revoked under 32-1154, it shall not be reissued for one year and then only after all loss caused by the act for which the license was revoked (bankruptcy) has been fully satisfied.

The effect of this statutory scheme is to frustrate the objectives of the Bankruptcy Act in three respects. First, it tends to discourage a licensed contractor from seeking bankruptcy relief. Second, once a contractor is declared bankrupt his contractor's license may be revoked, depriving him of his livelihood. Third, ARS 32-1161(B) compels the bankrupt contractor to fully repay business debts otherwise legally discharged if his contractor's license is to be reinstated.

Since the purpose of the Bankruptcy Act as interpreted by the Supreme Court is to allow a debtor to start anew unhampered by pre-existing debts, it is clear that the Arizona statute in effect frustrates this purpose by providing for the revocation of a contractor's professional license on the sole ground of personal bankruptcy and compelling complete satisfaction of discharged debts prior to reissuance of the license. . . . We therefore find ARS 32-1154(8) in conflict with federal law and declare it unconstitutional as in violation of the supremacy clause.

United States v. Sotelo
98 S. Ct. 1795 (1978)

The Internal Revenue Code provides that "any person required to collect, truthfully account for, and pay over" federal taxes who "willfully fails" to do so, shall be liable to a "penalty" equal to the amount of the taxes in question. Section 17a(1)(e) of the Bankruptcy Act makes nondischargeable in bankruptcy "taxes . . . which the bankrupt has collected or withheld from others . . . but has not paid over."

Sotelo was the principal officer and majority shareholder of a corporation. He failed to pay over taxes withheld from employees of the corporation. The corporation and Sotelo were both adjudicated bankrupt.

The bankruptcy court held that Sotelo was personally liable for the taxes and that the liability was not dischargeable in bankruptcy. The Circuit Court of Appeals reversed. The Supreme Court granted certiorari.

MARSHALL, J. . . . Section 17a of the Bankruptcy Act provides in pertinent part:

"A discharge in bankruptcy shall release a bankrupt from all of his provable debts, . . . except such as (1) are taxes which became legally due and owing by the bankrupt to the United States or to any State . . . within three years preceding bankruptcy; Provided however, that a discharge in bankruptcy shall not release a bankrupt from any taxes . . . (e) which the bankrupt has collected or withheld from others as required by the laws of the United States or any State . . . but has not paid over. . . . " 11 U.S.C. 35(a)

Relying on this statutory language, the Government presents what it views as two independent grounds for holding the 6672 liability of Onofre Sotelo (hereinafter "respondent") to be nondischargeable. The Government's primary argument is based on the specific language relating to withholding in 17a(1)(e); alternatively, it argues that respondent's liability, although called a "penalty," IRC 6672, is in fact a "tax" as that term is used in 17a(1).

Regardless of whether these two grounds are in fact independent, 17a(1)(e) leaves no doubt as to the nondischargeability of "taxes" . . . which the bankrupt has collected or withheld from others as required by the laws of the United States or any State . . . but has not paid over." The Court of Appeals viewed this provision as inapplicable here for two reasons: first, because "it was not Sotelo himself, but his employer-corporation, that was obligated by law to collect and withhold the taxes"; and second because in any event the money involved constituted a "penalty," whereas 17a(1)(e) "renders only 'taxes' nondischargeable." We believe that the first reason is inconsistent with the Court of Appeals' recognition of respondent's undisputed liability under Internal Revenue Code 6672, and that the second is inconsistent with the language of 17a(1)(e).

The fact that respondent was found liable under 6672 necessarily means that he was "required to collect, truthfully account for, and pay over" the withholding taxes, and that he willfully failed to meet one or more of these obligations. . . . It is undisputed here, moreover, that the taxes in question were "collected or withheld" from the corporation's employees and that the taxes, though collected, have not been "paid over" to the Government. It is therefore clear that the 6672 liability was not imposed for a failure on the part of respondent to collect taxes, but was rather imposed for his failure to pay over taxes that he was required both to collect and to pay over. Under these circumstances, the most natural reading of the statutory language leads to the conclusion that respondent "collected or withheld" the taxes within the meaning of Bankruptcy Act 17a(1)(e).

We also cannot agree with the Court of Appeals that the "penalty" language of Internal Revenue Code 6672 is dispositive of the status of respondent's debt under Bankruptcy Act 17a(1)(e). The funds here involved were unquestionably "taxes" at the time they were "collected or withheld from others." It is this time period that 17a(1)(e) with its modification of "taxes" by the phrase, "collected or withheld," treats as the relevant one. That the funds due are referred to as a "penalty" when the Government later seeks to recover them does not alter their essential character as taxes for purposes of the Bankruptcy Act, at least in a case in which, as here, the 6672 liability is predicated on a failure to pay over, rather than a failure initially to collect, the taxes.

The legislative history of Bankruptcy Act 17a(1)(e) provides additional support for the view that respondent's liability should be held nondischargeable. A principal purpose of the legislation, enacted in 1966 after several years of congressional consideration, was to establish a three-year limitation on the taxes that would be nondischargeable in bankruptcy; under former law, there was no such temporal limitation. The new section ensured the discharge of most taxes "which became legally due and owing" more than three years preceding bankruptcy. With regard to unpaid withholding taxes, however, the three year limitation was made inapplicable by the addition of the provision that is today 17a(1)(e).

This provision was added to the bill to respond to the Treasury Department's position that any discharge of liability for collected withholding taxes was undesirable. Because Congress specifically contemplated that those with withholding tax payment obligations would remain liable after bankruptcy for their "conversion" of the tax funds to private use, we must conclude that the liability here involved is not dischargeable in bankruptcy. . . .

Reversed.

Brown v. Tucker Professional Associates
229 S.E. 2d 541 (Ga.) 1976

CLARK, J. . . . The single issue for decision is whether plaintiff appellee had actual knowledge of appellant defendant's voluntary bankruptcy which would have discharged defendant's debt as tenant to plaintiff landlord for rent. . . .

The involved facts . . . are as follows: Just before the defendant vacated the premises he told Howell, one of plaintiff's two general partners, that he was in financial difficulty and had filed for bankruptcy. Howell, in turn, relayed this information to his partner, Green. Defendant had not in fact then filed for bankruptcy. It was not until more than five months had passed that he actually filed his voluntary petition in bankruptcy in which he did not list plaintiff as a creditor. During the intervening five-month period defendant did not further discuss his financial problems with plaintiff. There is no evidence that plaintiff learned or was informed of defendant's *actual* filing at any time.

1. [T]he Bankruptcy Act, provides that "A discharge in bankruptcy shall release a bankrupt from all of his provable debts . . . except such as . . . have not been duly scheduled in time for proof and allowance, with the name of the creditor, if known to the bankrupt, unless such creditor had notice or actual knowledge of the proceedings in bankruptcy, . . ." After a creditor has shown that he was not duly scheduled, the burden shifts to the defendant-bankrupt to prove that the creditor had notice or actual knowledge of the proceedings.

2. Notice or knowledge must come at such a time as to give the creditor an equal opportunity with other creditors to avail himself of the benefits of the law and to participate in the administration of the estate of the bankrupt.

"[A]ctual knowledge of the proceedings in bankruptcy," has been construed by one court to mean "knowledge of facts at least sufficient to apprise the creditor that a proceeding is actually commenced and where that proceeding is pending."

The undisputed facts in this case are that defendant told one of plaintiff's general partners that he *had* filed for bankruptcy. This evidence of plaintiff's "knowledge" is, however, insufficient and of no significance because the information was not in fact true at that date. Misleading information such as that given here is not calculated to afford a creditor equal opportunity with other creditors to participate in the estate, and is not "actual knowledge" of the proceedings. . . .

Judgment affirmed.

Thomas v. Sun Realty, Inc.
385 A.2d 1252 (N.J.) 1978

Anna M. Schucht filed a petition in voluntary bankruptcy on August 13, 1963. On October 10, 1963, she purchased a tract of land from the Wilmot Corporation and received a deed to it. She received a discharge in bankruptcy on November 4, 1963. In 1973, she sold the land to Browers, who sold it to the plaintiff, Thomas, in 1975. Thomas contends that Browers' title is defective because of the Schucht bankruptcy proceedings.

BOTTER, J. . . . This appeal raises the question of the effect of bankruptcy proceedings upon the marketability of title derived from a predecessor in title, Anna M. Schucht, who . . . acquired . . . the subject property between the time she filed a petition in bankruptcy and the date of discharge from bankruptcy.

It is settled law, subject to exceptions not applicable here, that the trustee in bankruptcy has no claim on property acquired by the bankrupt after the filing of the petition. The date of filing determines the rights of the trustee in bankruptcy to property possessed by the bankrupt. Bankruptcy has the force and effect of the levy of an execution for the benefit of creditors to insure an equitable distribution amongst them of the bankrupt's assets. The date of filing the petition is the point in time when the general estate passes out of the bankrupt's control and with respect to which the status and rights of the bankrupt, the creditors, and the trustees in other particulars are fixed. . . .

Thus, property not then owed but subsequently acquired by the bankrupt does not vest in the trustee, but becomes the bankrupt's, clear of all claims that are discharged by the bankruptcy proceedings.

The applicable law having been established beyond doubt, the bankruptcy proceedings created no reasonable or substantial basis for questioning the title conveyed by the Schuchts to the Browers. Accordingly, the judgment in favor of . . . Browers, is reversed and set aside.

Reversed.

CHAPTER 28
REVIEW QUESTIONS AND PROBLEMS

1. B's car, while traveling at a high rate of speed, struck P's car. B had been drinking. P obtained a judgment against B; B then filed a petition in bankruptcy. P contended that the judgment could not be discharged. Is P correct? Why?

2. B, a pauper, could not afford the $50.00 filing fee for a voluntary petition in bankruptcy. B contends that the filing fee should be waived, on the ground that bankruptcy is a "fundamental right" which the statute abridged in an unconstitutional manner by denying his Fifth Amendment right of due process. Is B correct? Why?

3. P was involved in an automobile accident with B; P then brought suit to recover for his damages. Subsequently, B filed a petition in bankruptcy but failed to list a description of the lawsuit pending against him. Consequently, P received no notice of the bankruptcy hearing. B now contends that his discharge in bankruptcy is a bar to P's lawsuit. Is B correct? Why?

4. A staged a fireworks display at which B was injured owing to A's negligence. B sued A and obtained a judgment against him. Before B could execute his judgment, A deeded all his real property to his wife, approximately three days after the judgment. Does B have a remedy? Explain.

5. C, a creditor of B Company, garnished B's checking account. B's attorney told C that the garnishment tied up B's funds so that the company could not operate, and that the company was insolvent. The garnishment was not dropped, and five days later B filed a petition in bankruptcy. The trustee subsequently sued C, contending that the garnishment amounted to an illegal preference. Should the trustee succeed? Why?

6. A divorce decree required that H deliver furniture and an automobile to his former wife, free and clear of any claim. At that time, the furniture and the automobile were mortgaged to secure a debt. H filed a decree in bankruptcy and claimed that the discharge relieved him from the liability to pay off the claims against the furniture and the automobile. Is H correct? Why?

7. B had been connected with X Company. When X Company went out of business, the new occupant of the building destroyed the books of B's business. B subsequently filed a petition in bankruptcy. At the hearing, three creditors objected to the discharge, contending that B had failed to keep books of account or records from which his financial condition might be ascertained. Is B entitled to discharge? Why?

8. When B borrowed money from C, B intentionally made false statements on the loan application. In subsequent bankruptcy proceedings, C objected to the discharge. Should B be discharged? Why?

9. On August 5, B a consumer, made purchases at a store in the amount of $1,000. Upon receiving the bill, B, while insolvent, made payment in full. Three weeks later, B filed a petition in bankruptcy. The trustee sued to recover the $1,000, contending that the payment was a preferential transfer. Should the trustee succeed? Why?

10. B filed a petition in bankruptcy on November 2. The C bank seeks to establish its right of set-off based upon the following facts: On August 1, B owed $2,000 to C; B's deposits with C totaled $2,000. One month later, on September 1, B's debt was still $2,000, but his deposits had been reduced to $1,000. On September 10, B's debt remained the same but his deposits totaled only $400. On November 1, B's debt was still $2,000, but he had increased his deposits to $2,000. What is the maximum amount of set-off to which the C bank is entitled? Why?

book five

AGENCY

Agency and the Law of Contracts

1. Introduction

The term *agency* is used to describe the fiduciary relationship that exists when one person acts on behalf of and under the control of another person.[1] The person who acts for another is called an *agent*. The person for whom he acts and who controls the agent is called a *principal*. Traditionally, issues of agency law arise when the agent has attempted to enter into a contract on behalf of his principal. However, the law of agency includes several aspects of the law of torts. Although tort litigation usually uses the terms *master* and *servant* rather than principal and agent, both relationships are encompassed within the broad legal classification of agency law. The contract aspects will be covered in this chapter and the tort aspects in the next.

The principles of agency law are essential for the conduct of business transactions. A corporation, as a legal entity, can function only through agents. The law of partnership is to a large degree a special application of agency principles to that particular form of business organization. It is not surprising, therefore, that a substantial number of agency issues are involved in litigation. Case law provides us with most of the principles applicable to the law of agency.

Agency issues are usually discussed within a framework of three parties: the principal (P), the agent (A), and the third party (T), with whom A contracts or against whom A commits a tort while in P's service. The following examples illustrate the problems and issues involved in the law of agency:

[1] *Murphy* v. *Holiday Inns, Inc.*, page 568.

1. *T* v. *P.* A third party sues the principal for breach of a contract that *T* entered into with *A,* or for damages because of a tort committed by *A.*

2. *T* v. *A.* A third party sues an agent personally for breach of the contract entered into by the agent or for committing a tort.

3. *P* v. *T.* A principal sues the third party for breach of a contract that *A* entered into with *T* for *P.*

4. *A* v. *T.* The agent sues the third party for some loss suffered by *A*—for example, the loss of a commission because of *T*'s interference with a contract.

5. *P* v. *A.* The principal sues the agent for loss caused by the latter's failure to follow his duties, such as to obey instructions.

6. *A* v. *P.* The agent sues the principal for injuries suffered in the course of employment, for wrongful discharge, or for sums due for services or advancements.

2. Agency Terminology

An agent may act on behalf of a designated principal, in which case the latter is called a *disclosed principal.* If the agent purports to act for himself and keeps his agency a secret, the principal is called an *undisclosed principal.* A third term, *partially disclosed principal,* is used to describe the situation in which the agent acknowledges that he is acting for a principal but does not disclose his identity.

Some persons who perform services for others are known as *independent contractors.* A person may contract for the services of another in such a way as to have full and complete control over the details and manner in which the work will be conducted, or he may simply contract for a certain end result. If the agreement provides merely that the second party is to accomplish a certain result and that he has full control over the manner and methods to be pursued in bringing about the result, he is deemed an independent contractor. The party contracting with an independent contractor and receiving the benefit of his service is usually called a *proprietor.* A proprietor is generally not responsible to third parties for the independent contractor's actions, either in contract or in tort. On the other hand, if the second party places his services at the disposal of the first in such a manner that the action of the second is generally controlled by the first, an agency relation is established.

Some agents are sometimes called *brokers,* and others are called *factors.* A broker is an agent with special and limited authority to procure a customer in order that the owner can effect a sale or exchange of property. For example, a real estate broker has authority to find a buyer for another's real estate. The real estate remains under the control of the owner. A factor is a person who has possession and control of another's property, usually personal property such as goods, and is authorized to sell such property. A factor has a property interest and may sell the property in his own name, whereas a broker may not.

Agents are also classified as *general* or *special* agents. A general agent has much broader authority than does a special agent. Some cases define a general agent as one authorized to conduct a series of transactions involving a continuity of service, whereas a special agent conducts a single transaction or a series of transactions without continuity of service. Third parties should always ascertain the exact nature of the agency.

3. Capacity of Parties

It is generally stated that anyone who may act for himself may act through an agent. To this rule there is one well-recognized exception. An infant may enter into a contract, and as long as he does not disaffirm, the agreement is binding. However, there is considerable authority to the effect that any appointment of an agent by an infant is void and not merely voidable. Under this view, any agreement entered into by such an agent would be ineffective, and an attempted disaffirmance by the minor would be superfluous. Many recent cases hold, however, that a contract of the agent on behalf of a minor principal is voidable only and is subject to rescission or ratification by the minor the same as if the minor had personally entered into the contract.

An infant may act as an agent for an adult, and agreements he makes for his principal while acting within his authority are binding on the principal. Although the infant agent has a right to terminate his contract of agency at his will, as long as he continues in the employment his acts within the scope of the authority conferred upon him become those of his principal.

THE CONTRACTUAL LIABILITY OF DISCLOSED PRINCIPALS

4. Introduction

A principal is liable on all contracts properly executed and entered into by an agent possessing actual or apparent authority to enter into the contract, provided that the third party knows that the agent is contracting for the principal. A principal is also liable on unauthorized contracts entered into by a purported agent, if the principal with knowledge of all the facts ratifies or affirms that he is bound by the contract. Therefore, a principal is not liable upon a contract that he has not actually or apparently authorized and has not ratified.

The burden of proving the requisite authority or ratification is on the party dealing with the agent; the principal does not have the burden of proving lack of authority or lack of ratification. The agent's authority can come only from the principal. The agent cannot by words or conduct create his own authority unless the words or conduct are consented to or ratified by the principal. In addition, one who deals with an agent, knowing that he has exceeded his authority, does so at his peril.

5. Actual Authority

Actual authority is the authority that a principal confers upon the agent or, unintentionally by want of ordinary care, allows the agent to believe himself to possess. Actual authority includes express authority and implied authority. The term *express authority* describes the authority explicitly given to the agent by the principal. *Implied authority* is used to describe authority that is necessarily incidental to the express authority or arises because of business custom and usage or prior practices of the parties. Implied authority is sometimes referred to as *incidental authority;* it is required or reasonably necessary to carry out the purpose for which the agency was created. For example, a president of a corporation is empowered without special authorization from the board of directors to do all acts of an ordinary nature incidental to his office.

Implied authority based on custom and usage varies from one locality to another and among different kinds of businesses. To illustrate: P appoints A as his agent to sell a certain used automobile for $900. As an incident to his authority to sell, A has authority to enter into a written contract with the purchaser and to sign P's name to the contract. Whether he has implied or incidental authority to sell on credit instead of cash or to warrant the condition of the car sold depends upon local custom. If it is customary for other agents in this locality to make warranties or sell on credit, this agent and the third party with whom he deals may assume he possesses such authority in the absence of knowledge to the contrary. Custom, in effect, creates a presumption of authority.

Implied authority must be distinguished from *apparent* or *ostensible authority,* which is authority predicated on the theory of estoppel. This latter type of authority is discussed in section 7 of this chapter.

Implied authority cannot be derived from the words or conduct of the agent. A third person dealing with a known agent may not act negligently in regard to the extent of the agent's authority or blindly trust his statements in such regard but must use reasonable diligence and prudence in ascertaining whether the agent is acting within the scope of his authority. Similarly, if persons who deal with a purported agent desire to hold the principal liable on the contract, they must ascertain not only the fact of the agency but the nature and extent of the agent's authority. Should either the existence of the agency or the nature and extent of the authority be disputed, the burden of proof regarding these matters is upon the third party. For this reason, it is a common practice for persons purchasing real estate from a corporation to require a certified copy of the resolution of the board of directors authorizing the sale.

6. Actual Authority from Formal Documents

As a general rule, no particular formalities are required to confer authority upon an agent. The appointment may be either written or oral. There are, however, situations in which formalities are required. First, when the purpose of the agency can be exercised only by the signing of a formal document, the agency must be created in writing. When a formal instrument is used for conferring authority upon the agent, he is said to possess a *power of attorney*. The agent is called an "attorney-in-fact" to distinguish him from an "attorney-at-law," the term used to describe lawyers. A power of attorney may be general, giving the agent authority to act in all respects as the principal could act, or it may be special, granting to the agent only restricted authority. A power of attorney is customarily acknowledged before a notary public.

Second, the statute of frauds in the majority of the states requires that any agent who is given power to sell or to convey any interest in or concerning real estate must obtain such power by a written authorization from the principal. However, the statute of frauds in most states does not require a written agreement to contract with an ordinary real estate broker. The function of the broker is merely to find a buyer with whom the seller is willing to contract. Normally, he has no authority to enter into a binding contract or to convey the property. In a few states, a "listing agreement" is required to be in writing by special statute. In these states, the real estate broker is not entitled to a commission without a written agency agreement.

A third exception exists in a few states where it is required that the act that confers authority must possess the same dignity as the act to be performed. In these states, an agent who possesses authority to sign a contract that is required to be in writing must receive his appointment by an instrument in writing.

7. Apparent or Ostensible Authority

The terms *apparent authority* and *ostensible authority* are synonymous. They describe the authority a principal, intentionally or by want of ordinary care, causes or allows a third person to believe the agent to possess. Liability of the principal for the ostensible agent's acts rests on the doctrine of estoppel. The estoppel is created by some conduct of the principal that leads the third party to believe that a person is his agent or that an actual agent possesses the requisite authority. This conduct must be known to and justifiably relied upon by the third party to his injury or damage. The injury or damage may be a change of position, and the facts relied upon must be such that a reasonably prudent person would believe that the authority of the agency existed.[2] Thus, three usual essential elements of an estoppel—conduct, reliance, and injury— are required to create apparent authority.

The theory of apparent, or ostensible, authority is that if a principal by his words or conduct has led others to believe that he has conferred authority upon an agent, he cannot be heard to assert, as against third persons who have relied thereon in good faith, that he did not intend to confer such power. The acts may include words, oral or written, or may be limited to conduct that, reasonably interpreted by a third person, causes that person to believe that the

[2] *Apex Financial Corp.* v. *Decker,* page 569.

principal consents to have the act done on his behalf by the purported agent. An agent's apparent authority to do an act for a principal must be based on the principal's words or conduct and cannot be based on anything the agent himself has said or done. Apparent authority requires more than the mere appearance of authority. The facts must be such that a person exercising ordinary prudence, acting in good faith, and conversant with business practices would be misled thereby.

Apparent authority may be the basis for liability when the purported agent is in fact not an agent. It may also be the legal basis for finding that an actual agent possesses authority beyond that actually conferred. In other words, apparent authority may exist in one not an agent or it may expand the authority of an actual agent.

An agency by estoppel or additional authority by estoppel may arise from a course of dealing on the part of an agent, which is constantly ratified by the principal, or it may result from a person's holding himself out as an agent without any dissent on the part of the purported principal under conditions where the principal owed a duty to speak. To illustrate: Upon several occasions, A indorses his principal's name to checks and has them cashed at the bank. The principal has never given the agent such authority, but no protest is lodged with the bank until the agent appropriates to his own use the proceeds from one of the checks. The principal then attempts to recover from the bank. By approval of the agent's previous unauthorized action, the principal has led the bank to reasonably assume that the agent possesses authority to indorse checks.

8. Ratification

As previously noted, a principal may become bound on an unauthorized contract by ratifying it. Ratification is the equivalent of authority at the time of the contract.

Various conditions must exist before a ratification will be effective. First, because ratification relates back to the time of the contract, ratification can be effective only where both the principal and the agent were capable of contracting at the time the contract was executed and are still capable at the time of ratification. For this reason, a corporation may not ratify contracts made by its promoters on the corporations's behalf before the corporation was formed. For the corporation to be bound by such agreements, a novation or an assumption of liability by the corporation must occur.

Second, the agent must have professed to act as an agent. A person who professes to act for himself and who makes a contract in his own name does nothing that can be ratified, even though he intends at the time to let another have the benefit of his agreement. Therefore, an undisclosed principal may not ratify an unauthorized contract.

Third, as a general rule, ratification does not bind the principal unless he acts with full knowledge of all the material facts attending negotiation and execution of the contract. Of course, when there is express ratification and the principal acts without any apparent desire to know or to learn the facts, he may not later defend himself on the ground that he was unaware of all the material facts. When, however, ratification is to be implied from the conduct of the principal, he must act with knowledge of all important details.[3]

The law is almost always concerned with mutuality of obligation. One party should not be bound to a contract if the other party is not also bound. Therefore, the law recognizes that the third party may withdraw from an unauthorized contract entered into by an agent at any time before it is ratified by the principal. If the third party were not allowed to withdraw, the unique situation in which one party is bound and the other is not would exist. However, it must be kept in mind that ratification does not require notice to the third party. As soon as conduct constituting ratification has been indulged in by the principal, the third party loses his right to withdraw.

Ratification may be either express or implied. Any conduct that definitely indicates an intention on the part of the principal to adopt the transaction will constitute ratification. It may take the form of words of approval to the agent, a promise to perform, or actual performance, such as delivery of the product called for in the agreement. Accepting the benefits of the contract or basing a suit on the validity of an agreement clearly amounts to ratification. The issue of whether or not ratification has occurred is a question to be decided by the jury.

Acceptance and retention of the fruits of the contract are probably the most certain evidence of implied ratification. As soon as a principal learns of an unauthorized act by an agent, he should promptly repudiate it, if he is to avoid liability on the theory of ratification.

An unauthorized act may not be ratified in part and rejected in part. The principal cannot accept the benefits of the contract and refuse to assume its obligations. Therefore, if an unauthorized agent commits fraud in procuring a contract, acceptance of the benefits ratifies not only the contract but the fraudulent acts as well, and the principal is liable therefor.

THE CONTRACTUAL LIABILTY OF UNDISCLOSED PRINCIPALS

9. Introduction

For various reasons, a principal may direct an agent to enter into contracts in the agent's own name, leaving the third party either unaware of the existence of the principal (undisclosed principal) or unaware of the principal's *identity* (partially disclosed principal). The law relating to partially disclosed principals is the same as that relating to undisclosed principals.

Since an agent is pledging his own credit when the principal is not disclosed,

[3] *Pillsbury Co.* v. *Ward,* page 570.

the agent is personally liable on the contract. This liability continues unless the agent is relieved of the obligation by the third party.

The undisclosed principal is also liable on all contracts entered into by the agent within the scope of his actual authority. (There is no apparent authority, because the principal is unknown.) This liability may be imposed upon discovery of the existence of the principal or upon learning his identity.

10. The Effect of an Election

When the existence of the principal or his identity becomes known to the third party, the third party may look to either the agent or the principal for performance. If the third party elects to hold the principal liable, the agent is released. Similarly, if the third party elects to hold the agent liable, the previously undisclosed but now disclosed principal is released. An election to hold one party releases the other from liability.

It is sometimes difficult to know when an election has occurred. However, it is clear that conduct by the third party that precedes the disclosure of the principal cannot constitute an election. Because of this rule, it has been held that an unsatisfied judgment obtained against the agent before disclosure of the principal will not bar a later action against the principal.

After disclosure, the third party may evidence his election by obtaining a judgment against one of the parties or by making an express declaration of his intention to hold one party and not the other. It has been held that sending a bill to one of the parties does not indicate an election. Most states also hold that the receipt of a negotiable instrument from either principal or agent does not show an election. The mere starting of a suit has been held insufficient to constitute an election, but if the case proceeds to judgment against either the agent or the principal, election has taken place even though the judgment remains unpaid.[4]

11. The Effect of a Settlement on Liability

In the preceding section, it was stated that the third party, after learning of a previously undisclosed principal's interest in a transaction, might elect to look to the principal rather than to the agent for performance. Suppose, however, that the undisclosed principal supplied the agent with money to purchase the goods, but the agent purchased on credit and appropriated the money. In such a case, the principal would be relieved of all responsibility. The same result obtains when the undisclosed principal *settles* with the agent after the contract is made and the goods are received, but before disclosure to the third party. Any bona fide settlement between principal and agent before disclosure releases the principal. A settlement cannot have this effect, however, when it is made after the third party has learned of the existence of the principal, and the principal is aware that his identity is known. The settlement rule is based on

[4] *Sherrill* v. *Bruce Advertising, Inc.,* page 572.

equitable principles. It is fair to the third party in that it gives him all the protection he originally bargained for, and it is fair to the principal in that it protects him against a second demand for payment.

THE LIABILITY OF PRINCIPALS—SPECIAL SITUATIONS

12. Introduction

Many special problems arise in the law of agency as it relates to contractual liability and authority of agents. Some of these problems are founded in the relationship of the parties. For example, a spouse is generally liable for the contracts of the other spouse when such contracts involve family necessities. In most states, this liability is statutory. Others involve special factual situations. For example, an existing emergency that necessitates immediate action adds sufficiently to the agent's powers to enable him to meet the situation. However, if time permits and the principal is available, any proposed remedy for the difficulty must be submitted to the principal for approval. It is only when the principal is not available that the powers of the agent are extended. Furthermore, the agent receives no power greater than that sufficient to solve the difficulty.

Frequently, the liability of the principal is dependent upon whether the agent is as a matter of fact a general agent or a special agent. If the agency is general, limitations imposed upon the usual and ordinary powers of the general agent do not prevent the principal from being liable to third parties where the agent acts in violation of such limitations, unless the attention of the third parties has been drawn to them. In other words, the third party, having established that a general agency exists and having determined in a general way the limits of the authority, is not bound to explore for unexpected and unusual restrictions. He is justified in assuming, in the absence of contrary information, that the agent possesses the powers that like agents customarily have. On the other hand, if the proof is only of a special or limited agency, any action in excess of the actual authority would not bind the principal.

To illustrate the foregoing, assume an instruction to a sales agent not to sell to a certain individual, or not to sell to him on credit when credit sales are customary. Such a limitation cannot affect the validity of a contract made with this individual, unless the latter was aware of the limitation at the time the contract was made. The principal, by appointing an agent normally possessed of certain authority, is estopped to set up the limitation as a defense, unless the limitation is made known to the third party prior to the making of the contract.

13. Notice to Agent

Notice to or knowledge acquired by an agent while acting within the scope of his authority binds the principal. This is based on the theory that the agent is the principal's other self, and therefore, what the agent knows, the principal knows. However, it must be recognized that while *knowledge* possessed by an agent is *notice* to the principal, the principal may not have actual knowledge of the particular fact at all.

Notice or knowledge received by an agent under circumstances where the agent would not be presumed to communicate the information to the principal does not bind the principal. This exception to the general rule will be observed in cases when the agent is acting in his own behalf and adversely to the principal, or when the agent is under a duty to some third party not to disclose the information.

As a general rule, an agent or a person ostensibly in charge of a place of business has apparent authority to accept notices in relation to the business. In addition, an employee in charge of the receipt of mail may accept written notifications.

14.   Agent's Power to Appoint Subagents

Since agents are usually selected because of their personal qualifications, as a general rule an agent may not delegate his duty to someone else and clothe the latter with authority to bind the principal. An exception exists in those cases in which the acts of the agent are purely ministerial or mechanical. An act that requires no discretion and is purely mechanical may be delegated by the agent to a third party. Acts that involve the exercise of skill, discretion, or judgment may not be delegated without permission from the principal.

An agent may, under certain circumstances, have the actual or implied authority to appoint other agents for the principal, in which case they become true employees of the principal. Such a power on the part of the agent is not often implied, but if the situation is such that the major power conferred cannot be exercised without the aid of other agents, the agent is authorized to hire such help as is required. Thus, a manager placed in charge of a branch store may be presumed to possess authority to hire the necessary personnel the size of the business demands.

15.   The Financial Powers of Agents

An agent who delivers goods sold for cash has the implied authority to collect all payments due at the time of delivery. A salesman taking orders calling for a down payment has implied authority to accept the down payment. However, salesmen by the very nature of their jobs have no implied authority to receive payments on account, and any authority to do so must be expressly given. Thus, a person in his capacity as salesclerk in a store has authority to collect any payment made at the time of sale but no authority to receive payments on account. Payment to an agent without authority to collect does not discharge the debt.

Authority to collect gives the agent no authority to accept anything other than money in payment. Unless expressly authorized, he is not empowered to accept negotiable notes or property in settlement of an indebtedness. It is customary for an agent to accept checks as conditional payment. Under such circumstances, the debt is not paid unless the check is honored.

A general agent placed in charge of a business has implied or apparent authority to purchase for cash or on credit. The implied authority is based on the nature of his position and on the fact that the public rightly concludes that a corporation or an individual acting through another person has given him the power and authority that naturally and properly belong to the character in which the agent is held out.

Authority to borrow money is not easily implied.[5] Such authority must be expressly granted or qualify as incidental authority to the express authority, or the principal will not be bound. The authority to borrow should always be confirmed with the principal.

LIABILITY OF AGENTS

16.   Based on the Contract

As a general rule, an agent is not personally liable on contracts that he has entered into on behalf of his disclosed principal, and the liability is solely that of the principal. To this rule, there are certain well-recognized exceptions. First, if the agent carelessly executes a written agreement, he may fail to bind his principal and incur personal liability. When an agent signs a simple contract or commercial paper, he should execute it in such a fashion as to clearly indicate his representative capacity. If the signatures are ambiguous in that they fail to indicate the actual relationship of the parties and to identify the party intended to be bound, the agent may be personally liable on the instrument. Many states permit the use of parol evidence to show the intention of the agent and the third party when the signature is ambiguous—the agent is allowed to offer proof that it was not intended that he assume personal responsibility.

Second, the third party may request the agent to be personally bound because of the agent's credit rating or some other personal reason. Where the agent voluntarily assumes the burden of performance in his personal capacity, he unquestionably becomes liable in the event of nonperformance by his principal. As previously noted, an agent for an undisclosed or partially disclosed principal assumes personal liability.[6] Disclosure of the principal is required in order to give the third party the opportunity to verify the authority

[5] *Bank of America, Nat. Trust & Sav. Ass'n* v. *Horowytz,* page 573.
[6] *Oxford Bldg. Services* v. *Gresham,* page 574.

of the agency and to allow the third party to decide if he wants to extend credit to the principal.

17. Based on Breach of Warranty

An agent's liability may be implied from the circumstances as well as being the direct result of the contract. Liability in such situations is usually said to be implied and to arise from the breach of an implied warranty. There are two basic warranties that are used to imply liability: the warranty of authority, and the warranty that the principal is competent.

As a general rule, an agent impliedly warrants to third parties that he possesses power to effect the contractual relations of his principal. If in any particular transaction the agent fails to possess this power, the agent violates this implied warranty, and he is liable to third parties for the damages resulting from his failure to bind the principal. The agent may or may not be aware of this lack of authority, and he may honestly believe that he possesses the requisite authority. Awareness of lack of authority and honesty is immaterial. If an agent exceeds his authority, he is liable to the third parties for the breach of the warranty of authority.

The agent may escape liability for damages arising from lack of authority by a full disclosure to the third party of all facts relating to the source of the agent's authority. Where all the facts are available, the third party is as capable of judging the limits of the agent's powers as is the agent.

The liability of the agent is qualified in one other respect. He is not liable when, unknown to him, his agency has been cut short by the death of the principal. Death of the principal terminates an agency. Such an event as death is usually accompanied by sufficient publicity to reach third parties. As indicated earlier, the facts are equally available to both parties, so that no warranty arises.

Every agent who deals with third parties warrants that his principal is capable of being bound. Consequently, an agent who acts for a minor or a corporation not yet formed may find himself liable for the nonperformance of his principal. The same rule enables the third party to recover from the agent when his principal is an unincorporated association, such as a club, lodge, or other informal group. An unincorporated association is not a legal entity separate and apart from its members. In most states, it cannot sue or be sued in the name it uses, but all members must be joined in a suit involving the unincorporated group. When an agent purports to bind such an organization, a breach of the warranty results because there is no entity capable of being bound. However, if the third party is fully informed that the principal is an unincorporated organization and he agrees to look entirely to it for performance, the agent is not liable.

LIABILITY OF THIRD PARTIES

18. Liability to Principal

A disclosed principal may enforce any contract made by an authorized agent for the former's benefit. This right applies to all contracts in which the principal is the real party in interest, including contracts that are made in the agent's name. Furthermore, if a contract is made for the benefit of a disclosed principal by an agent acting outside the scope of his authority, the principal is still entitled to performance, provided the contract is properly ratified before withdrawal by the third party.

An undisclosed principal is entitled to performance by third parties of all assignable contracts made for his benefit by an authorized agent. It is no defense for the third party to say that he had not entered into a contract with the principal. However, if the contract is one that involves the skill or confidence of the agent and would not have been entered into but for this skill or confidence, its performance may not be demanded by the undisclosed principal, since the contract would not be assignable because personal rights and duties are not transferable without consent.

In cases other than those involving commercial paper, the undisclosed principal takes over the contract subject to all defenses that the third party could have established against the agent. For example, if the third party contracts to buy from such an agent and has a right of setoff against the agent, he has this same right of setoff against the undisclosed principal. The third party may also pay the agent prior to discovery of the principal, and such payment will discharge his liability.

19. Liability to Agent

Normally, the agent possesses no right to bring suit on contracts made by him for the benefit of his principal, because he has no interest in the cause of action. Where the agent binds himself to the third party, either intentionally or ineptly by a failure to properly express himself, he may, however, maintain an action. An agent of an undisclosed principal is liable on the contract and may sue in his own name in the event of nonperformance by the third party. Thus, either the agent or the undisclosed principal might bring suit, but in case of a dispute, the right of the previously undisclosed principal is superior.

Custom has long sanctioned an action by the agent based upon a contract in which he is interested because of anticipated commissions. As a result, a factor may institute an action in his own name to recover for goods sold. He may also recover against a carrier for delay in the shipment of goods sold or to be sold.

Similarly, an agent who has been vested with title to commercial paper may sue the maker thereof. The same is true of any claim held by the principal that he definitely places with the agent for collection and suit, where such is necessary. In all cases of this character, the agent retains the proceeds as a trust fund for his principal.

AGENCY AND THE LAW OF CONTRACTS CASES

Murphy v. Holiday Inns, Inc.
219 S.E.2d 874 (Va.) 1975

Plaintiff slipped and fell on a walkway at a Holiday Inn. The Inn was operated by a licensee known as Betsy-Len Motor Corporation. Defendant, the licensor, contended that it had no liability because no principal–agent or master–servant relationship existed between the licensor and the licensee. The trial court found for the defendant and the plaintiff appealed.

POFF, J. . . . Plaintiff argues that the license agreement gives defendant "the authority and control over the Betsy-Len Corporation that establishes a true master/servant relationship. . . ."

Actual agency is a consensual relationship.

Agency is the fiduciary relation which results from the manifestation of consent by one person to another that the other shall act on his behalf and subject to his control, and consent by the other so to act.

It is the element of continuous subjection to the will of the principal which distinguishes the agent from other fiduciaries and the agency agreement from other agreements. . . .

Plaintiff and defendant . . . agree that, in determining whether a contract establishes an agency relationship, the critical test is the nature and extent of the control agreed upon.

The subject matter of the license defendant granted Betsy-Len is a "system." As defined in the agreement, the system is one "providing to the public . . . an inn service . . . of distinctive nature, of high quality, and of other distinguishing characteristics." Those characteristics include trade names using the words "Holiday Inn" and certain variations and combinations of those words, trade marks, architectural designs, insignia, patterns, color schemes, styles, furnishings, equipment, advertising services, and methods of operation.

In consideration of the license to use the "system," the licensee agreed to pay an initial sum of $5,000; to construct one or more inns in accordance with plans approved by the licensor; to make monthly payments of 15 cents per room per day (5 cents of which was to be earmarked for national advertising expenditures); and "to conduct the operation of inns . . . in accordance with the terms and provisions of this license and of the Rules of operation of said System."

Plaintiff points to several provisions and rules which he says satisfy the control test and establish the principal–agent relationship. . . .

The license agreement of which these requirements were made a part is a franchise contract. In the business world, franchising is a current phenomenon of billion-dollar proportions.

[Franchising is] a system for the selective distribution of goods and/or services under a brand name through outlets owned by independent businessmen, called "franchisees." Although the franchisor supplies the franchisee with know-how and brand identification on a continuing basis, the franchisee enjoys the right to profit and runs the risk of loss.

The franchisor controls the distribution of his goods and/or services through a contract which regulates the activities of the franchise, in order to achieve standardization.

The fact that an agreement is a franchise contract does not insulate the contracting parties from an agency relationship. If a franchise contract so "regulates the activities of the franchisee" as to vest the franchisor with control within the definition of agency, the agency relationship arises even though the parties expressly deny it. . . .

Here, the license agreement contains the principal features of the typical franchise contract, including regulatory provisions. Defendant owned the "brand name," the trade mark, and the other assets associated with the "system." Betsy-Len owned the sales "outlet." Defendant agreed to allow Besty-Len to use its assets. Betsy-Len agreed to pay a fee for that privilege. Betsy-Len retained the "right to profit" and bore the "risk of loss." With respect to the manner in which defendant's trade mark and other assets were to be used both parties agreed to certain regulatory rules of operation.

Having carefully considered all of the regulatory provisions in the agreement, we are of opinion that they gave defendant no "control or right to control the methods or details of doing the work," and, therefore, agree with the trial court that no principal–agent or master–servant relationship was created. As appears from the face of the document, the purpose of those provisions was to achieve system-wide standardization of business identity, uniformity of commercial service, and optimum public good will, all for the benefit of both contracting parties. The regulatory provisions did not give defendant control over the day-to-day operation of Betsy-Len's motel. While defendant was empowered to regulate the architectural style of the buildings and the type and style of furnishings and equipment, defendant was given no power to control daily maintenance of the premises. Defendant was given no power to control Betsy-Len's current business expenditures, fix customer rates, or demand a share of the profits. Defendant was given no power to hire or fire Betsy-Len's employees, determine employee wages or working conditions, set standards for employee skills or productivity, supervise employee work routine, or discipline employees for nonfeasance or misfeasance. All such powers and other management controls and responsibilities customarily exercised by an owner and operator of an on-going business were retained by Betsy-Len.

We hold that the regulatory provisions of the franchise contract did not constitute control within the definition of agency, and the judgment is
Affirmed.

Apex Financial Corp. v. Decker
369 A.2d 483 (Pa.Super) 1976

Apex Financial Corporation loaned money to Decker secured by a mortgage. At the time of the loan the Bethlehem Consumer Discount Company ("BAC") had a judgment lien on the property. The manager of BAC agreed to subordinate its judgment to that of the mortgage and sent Apex a letter to that effect. BAC later refused to execute a subordination agreement. Apex foreclosed its lien and the property was sold by the sheriff. The sheriff paid off BAC prior to applying any proceeds to the mortgage.

The lower court held that the sheriff's distribution was correct and Apex appealed.

WATKINS, J. . . . Apex claims that the BAC lien should have been subordinated to its lien because of the letter to Apex. To support its position Apex contends that Luhrs, BAC's manager, was clothed with the authority to make such an agreement, that Apex relied to its detriment on the . . . letter from Luhrs to Apex, and that therefore BAC should be bound by Luhrs' agreement to subordinate the BAC lien. BAC contends that Luhrs did not have the authority to subordinate BAC's liens, that the agreement was not enforceable because it was gratuitous since BAC received nothing in return for a subordination of its lien and that Apex has suffered no detriment as a result of the letter anyhow.

The liability of a principal to third parties for the act of an agent must rest on (1) express authority, or that which is directly granted; (2) implied authority, to do all that is proper, usual and necessary to the exercise of the authority actually granted; (3) apparent authority, as where the principal holds one out as agent by words or conduct; and (4) agency by estoppel. The burden of establishing an agency relationship rests with the party asserting it. The evidence adduced at the hearing below failed to establish any express or implied authority on the part of Luhrs to subordinate BAC's lien. Therefore the sole issue for determination is whether BAC had clothed Luhrs with the apparent authority or authority by estoppel by designating him as "manager" of one of its offices.

"Apparent authority" is the power to bind a principal which the principal has not actually granted but which he leads persons with whom his agent deals to believe that he has granted to the agent. The test for such is whether a man of ordinary prudence, diligence and discretion would have a right to believe that the agent possessed the authority he purported to exercise. The only evidence tending to indicate the authority of Luhrs was that he was a "manager." . . . In fact Luhrs' authority was limited to the making and collecting of loans. The subordination of a lien is a somewhat extraordinary act and is even more so when it is done without consideration. Therefore Apex should have been placed on notice as to the extent of a "manager's" authority to perform such an act. . . .

Since Luhrs, as manager, was not clothed with the apparent authority to execute a gratuitous subordination of a lien merely by his position, we hold that the court below was correct in its decision refusing to alter the sheriff's schedule of distribution. . . .

Affirmed.

Pillsbury Co. v. Ward
250 N.W.2d 35 (Iowa) 1977

Plaintiff, a grain dealer, sued the defendant for breach of a contract to sell soybeans. The lower court found for the defendant. The defendant Ward had agreed to sell 3,000 bushels to be delivered in January, 1973, but his crop only amounted to 2,000 bushels. Since other farmers had experienced similar problems, the price of soybeans was rising rapidly in January, 1973.

Dale Bullock, a friend and neighbor of the defendant, was a trucker who hauled grain to Pillsbury for local farmers. On January 25, 1973, Ward contacted Bullock in order to make delivery. For reasons personal to Bullock he called the Pillsbury facility before loading the soybeans for delivery. Weather and hauling conditions were generally unfavorable. Bullock was advised the trucks arriving with grain at the facility were lined up, causing delay before they could be unloaded.

Without consulting Ward, an agent of Pillsbury and Bullock agreed to "extend" the contract and await more favorable delivery conditions. Except for the possibility of spoilage, the extension would do little harm to Ward as to the 2,000 bushels ready for delivery. But, in view of the continuing rise in the soybean market, the delay would obviously require Ward to pay an increasing amount for the 1,000 bushels he was short.

On January 27, 1973, an agent of Pillsbury called Ward and asked what Ward intended to do. Ward referred him to Bullock's telephone conversation. The agent told Ward that an extension agreement would be forwarded. When Ward received it, he did not sign it.

On February 6, 1973, Ward advised Pillsbury in writing he considered the contract void on the ground he offered to deliver the soybeans within the specified time and delivery was refused by Pillsbury.

HARRIS, J. . . . The first question is whether the agreement between Pillsbury and Bullock to extend the delivery date of Ward's soybeans was binding on Ward. To determine this question consideration must be given the following: (1) In connection with the extension agreement was Bullock an agent of Ward? (2) even if Bullock was not such an agent of Ward did Ward ratify the extension agreement?

Was Bullock an agent of Ward for purposes of the extension agreement? The question of whether a principal–agent relationship exists is ordinarily one of fact. The trial court found Bullock was, for the purposes of the extension agreement, an agent of Pillsbury and not of Ward. . . .

The record reveals ample evidence to support the trial court's finding Bullock was not an agent of Ward, especially in view of the established elements of agency. Agency has been defined as a fiduciary relationship which results from (1) manifestation of consent by one person, the principal, that another, the agent, shall act on the former's behalf and subject to the former's control, and (2) consent by the latter to so act. There is substantial evidence Bullock was not acting in Ward's behalf in negotiating the extension, was not subject to Ward's control, and had not consented to be Ward's agent for the purpose of negotiating the extension agreement.

Did Ward nevertheless ratify the extension agreement? Pillsbury argues Ward ratified the extension agreement by failing to repudiate it in his phone conversation. . . . Pillsbury relies on the rule: ". . . [I]t is the duty of the principal to repudiate the unauthorized act of his agent within a reasonable time after knowledge of the act of the agent comes to him. If he does not repudiate, the principal is held to have ratified. . . .

Ratification is defined in the Restatement, Second, Agency, § 82 as follows:

> Ratification is the affirmance by a person of a prior act which did not bind him but which was done or professedly done on his account, whereby the act, as to some or all persons, is given effect as if originally authorized by him.

Affirmance is defined in the Restatement, Second, Agency, § 83 as follows:

> Affirmance is either
>
> (a) a manifestation of an election by one on whose account an unauthorized act has been done to treat the act as authorized, or
>
> (b) conduct by him justifiable only if there was such an election.

But it is clear ratification does not apply where, as here, the act is done by one who is not an agent or does not purport to be one. Restatement, Second, Agency, § 85 states:

> Purporting to Act as Agent as a Requisite for Ratification
>
> (1) Ratification does not result from the affirmance of a transaction with a third person unless the one acting is purported to be acting for the ratifier.
>
> (2) An act of service not involving transaction with a third person is subject to ratification if, but only if, the one doing the act intends or purports to perform it as the servant of another.

In the instant case Bullock did not act as agent for Ward in the transaction. The trial court so found and we have pointed out substantial evidence supports the finding. The record is void of any indication Bullock purported to act for Ward in connection with the extension agreement. On the contrary, the record is clear Bullock was acting in his own behalf and to the elevator's advantage in negotiating the extension agreement.

Even if we were to assume Bullock had been Ward's agent, Ward did not ratify Bullock's unauthorized act. To ratify an unauthorized act of an agent the principal must have full knowledge of the facts (actual or inferred) and must intend to ratify (expressly or impliedly). A failure to repudiate the unauthorized act of an agent within a reasonable time after learning thereof will be deemed a ratification. The receipt or retention of benefits from the unauthorized transaction may constitute ratification.

Under these principles we do not believe Ward can be said to have ratified the extension agreement. . . . Testimony in the record supports Ward's claim he believed Pillsbury was unable to accept timely delivery and such inability was the reason for the extension agreement. Hence there is substantial evidence to support a holding Ward lacked full knowledge concerning the extension agreement. Ward cannot be said to have ratified the extension. . . .

Affirmed.

Sherrill v. Bruce Advertising, Inc.
538 S.W.2d 865 (Tex.) 1976

COULSON, J. . . . This is an appeal from a suit on a contract for services rendered. Bruce Advertising, Inc. sued M. A. Sherrill, Trustee of the William W. Sherrill Trust and Crane-Maier and Associates, Inc. for services rendered in connection with the development of real property owned by the Sherrill Trust. The trial court entered judgment for Bruce Advertising. . . . The judgment against Crane-Maier has not been appealed and has become final. This appeal relates only to the judgment entered against M. A. Sherrill, Trustee of the William W. Sherrill Trust. We reverse.

In 1970, an agreement was entered between Crane-Maier and the Sherrill Trust whereby the Trust's real property located in Galveston County would be subdivided, developed and sold by Crane-Maier. Bruce Advertising dealt with Crane-Maier by supplying services to them on a contractual basis for development of the realty. Bruce Advertising was not aware that the Sherrill Trust owned the property which Crane-Maier was developing. Suit was brought against Crane-Maier for the services rendered by Bruce Advertising when payment was not forthcoming. After suit was instituted, Crane-Maier by way of its pleadings informed Bruce Advertising that the Sherrill Trust was owner of the property which Crane-Maier was developing. The trial court sitting without a jury entered judgment against both Crane-Maier and the Sherrill Trust holding them jointly and severally liable for the services rendered by Bruce Advertising. . . . The court stated that the association of and agreement between Crane-Maier and the Sherrill Trust constituted a joint venture for the development of the property. The Sherrill Trust has appealed the judgment claiming that as a matter of law there is no joint venture between it and Crane-Maier. We agree. . . .

However, we must consider whether the findings of fact will support the judgment against the Sherrill Trust on any other theory of law. The findings of fact show that Crane-Maier agreed with Bruce Advertising to handle the advertising requirements of the property belonging to the Sherrill Trust. They further show that an agreement was entered into between the Sherrill Trust and Crane-Maier for development and sale of the lots of the Sherrill Trust's property and that Crane-Maier was to be compensated for its services of promotion, development and sales of the project by a percentage of the sales price of each lot sold. These findings contain elements supporting the theory that Crane-Maier was the agent acting for the principal, the Sherrill Trust, in ordering advertising services from Bruce Advertising.

Whether Bruce Advertising may recover a judgment on a joint and several basis against both a principal and agent is the question presented. . . .

We may imply from the findings of fact that a principal and agent relationship existed between the Sherrill Trust and Crane-Maier, which theory is supported by Bruce Advertising's pleadings. Bruce Advertising did not know that Crane-Maier was acting for anyone other than itself. The Sherrill Trust is in the position of an undisclosed principal. An undisclosed principal is discharged from liability upon a contract if, with knowledge of the identity of the principal, the other party recovers judgment against the agent who made the contract, for the breach of the contract. While this rule has received some discredit, the Texas courts have consistently followed it. Here, the judgment against the agent Crane-Maier has become final. On the theory of principal and agent, the principal, Sherrill Trust, cannot now be held liable since there is a final judgment had against its agent for breach of the contract.

The judgment against Crane-Maier having been entered and now final, there is no theory which can support joint and several liability against the Sherrill Trust. . . .

Reversed.

Bank of America, Nat. Trust & Sav. Ass'n. v. Horowytz
248 A.2d 446 (N.J.) 1968

O'BRIEN, J. This is a suit on a promissory note, dated October 26, 1961, signed in the name of defendant, "Carol Horowytz d/b/a E. D. S. by J. Pearl," and endorsed on the reverse side by "Jack Pearl."

Defendant has admitted in the pretrial order that J. Pearl is her father and that he engaged in business in defendant's name from time to time.

It appears . . . that on April 8, 1957, a checking account was opened with plaintiff bank in the name of defendant doing business under the tradename E. D. S., as a men's clothing business. . . . The signature card, containing defendant's authorized signature, also contains the statement, "J. Pearl power of attorney attached." . . .

. . . The question presented is whether J. Pearl had the authority to obligate defendant on the note in question. Plaintiff relies solely upon the power of attorney as establishing such authority.

Thus the court is called upon to determine whether the power of attorney can be construed as clothing the attorney-in-fact with the authority to borrow on behalf of defendant principal.

A power of attorney is an instrument in writing by which one person, as principal, appoints another as his agent and confers upon him the authority to perform certain specified acts or kinds of acts on behalf of the principal. The primary purpose of a power of attorney is not to define the authority of the agent as between himself and his principal, but to evidence the authority of the agent to third parties with whom the agent deals.

The authority to borrow money on the credit of the principal is among the most important and also dangerous powers which a principal can confer upon an agent, since manifestly there is a great possibility of the abuse of the power. For this reason, in the absence of express authority, the authority of an agent to borrow on the principal's credit will not be inferred unless it is necessarily implied by the scope and character of the authority which is expressly granted. Unless otherwise agreed, an agent is not authorized to borrow unless such borrowing is usually incident to the performance of acts which he is authorized to perform for the principal.

These principles have been well expressed by the court in *Williams* v. *Dugan*, 217 Mass. 526 (1914):

> The power to borrow money or to execute and deliver promissory notes is

one of the most important which a principal can confer upon an agent. It is fraught with great possibilities of financial calamity. It is not lightly to be implied. It either must be granted by express terms or flow as a necessary and inevitable consequence from the nature of the agency actually created.

Courts are reluctant to find an authority to borrow where such authority is not explicitly conferred. . . .

It is apparent that the authority to borrow money is not given to the attorney-in-fact in so many words. Thus, it becomes necessary to determine whether such authority may be implied by a reasonable construction and interpretation of the instrument, or whether such power may be inferred or necessarily implied by the scope and character of the authority which is expressly granted. . . .

The instrument delegates power "to sign and endorse checks, notes and drafts and transact all business with your Day and Night Branch San Francisco Calif." The delegation is in both specific and general terms. If the power to borrow money is necessarily to be implied by the terms of the instrument, it must be expressed by the specific terms "sign . . . notes" rather than by the general term "and transact all business." For, by the law of California:

> When authority is given partly in general terms and partly in specific terms, the general authority gives no higher powers than those specifically mentioned.

Focusing, therefore, on the words "sign . . . notes," plaintiff construes that language to mean "make and deliver promissory notes as evidence of a debt," i.e., the power to borrow money. Defendant, on the other hand, construes the same language to mean "endorse notes presented for payment" or "sign notes payable at the bank," which amounts to an authorization to the bank to pay such notes from funds credited to the checking account. . . .

The power does not expressly authorize the agent to borrow money and requires construction and interpretation of the language used. Therefore, it is this court's opinion that the instrument must be construed most strongly against the party supplying it—plaintiff bank.

. . . [T]he court concludes that it cannot by any reasonable construction or interpretation construe the language used in the power of attorney supplied by plaintiff bank to authorize the attorney-in-fact to borrow money on the defendant's credit nor can the court find that such authority is to be necessarily implied by the scope and character of the authority expressly granted. . . .

Accordingly . . . the court concludes that the power of attorney does not contain an express or implied grant of power to borrow money; nor may such power be inferred as necessarily implied by the scope and character of the authority which is expressly granted; nor has any evidence been adduced of any apparent or ostensible power give to the attorney-in-fact sufficient to bind defendant principal.

Judgment will therefore be in favor of defendant.

Oxford Bldg. Services v. Gresham
221 S.E.2d 667 (Ga.) 1975

EVANS, J. . . . Oxford Building Services, Inc. operates a janitorial service, and engages in cleaning commercial buildings. Oxford contracted with William J. Gresham, d/b/a Gresham Realty, to clean certain buildings. Gresham at no time advised Oxford that Gresham was not the principal and owner of the buildings, and contracted as if he were such principal and owner. Oxford cleaned the buildings under said contract for at least two years, and rendered bills for such services and said bills were paid by Gresham.

But then Gresham got behind in his payments for such cleaning services to the extent of $7,000, and Oxford filed suit against Gresham to recover said sum.

Gresham defended and contended that he was not the owner of the buildings, but merely an agent of the owner, and that as such agent, he was not liable for his principal's default in a contractual matter. Oxford, plaintiff, won the first round, a jury verdict being returned in his favor; but Gresham, defendant, filed a motion for new trial which was granted and on the second trial the verdict was rendered in favor of defendant, Gresham. Oxford filed motion for new trial and for judgment notwithstanding the verdict, both of which were denied, and Oxford appeals. *Held:*

At the outset, we deem it advisable to set forth a certain situation in which the agent is individually liable. If the agent does not disclose to the other party his principal, then the agent is personally liable and responsible. . . . [T]here was no evidence that the agent ever disclosed the name of the principal; and the agent never did profess to act for such principal.

Enumerations of error numbers 1, 2, 3, 4, and 5 all complain because of the trial court's failure to give in charge to the jury written requests to the effect that where an agent deals with another, for a principal, but does not disclose that he is agent, or that he is acting for a principal, the agent himself is individually liable. These requests set forth the law correctly, there was evidence upon which to base same, and it was error not to give such requests in charge. . . .

Judgment reversed.

CHAPTER 29
REVIEW QUESTIONS AND PROBLEMS

1. P authorized his minor son to find a buyer for a tract of land. The son did so and signed a contract for the sale to X. P refused to honor the contract and set up the defense that his son could not legally act as an agent. Is P correct? Why?

2. A borrowed a car from B, and a place was designated for its return. While returning the car, A hit and injured X. X sued A and B, claiming an agency existed, and B could be held liable. Was X correct? Why?

3. X was in the Army for twelve years. After being stationed in Colombia, he was transferred to Germany. Before he moved, he left his automobile, which was registered in his name, with his wife, Y. While X was still in Germany, Y, without his knowledge or consent, traded the car for a newer one. Is the car dealer justified in looking to X for payment? Why?

4. X hires Y, an attorney, to sue Z for a debt. While X is out of town, Y settles the case with Z, and Y forges X's name to a release. When X returns, he accepts Z's check. May X claim Y acted without authority and avoid the release? Why?

5. A, thinking he had authority to do so, signed P's name to a contract whereby T was to drill an oil well for $7,000. Later, A and T learned P had not given A authority to do so. Is A liable if the contract was signed "P per A"? Why?

6. A brother and sister jointly owned land. T agreed to buy the property. The contract was signed by the sister individually and as agent for her brother. The brother had orally agreed to the terms of the contract. Is the brother bound on the contract? Why?

7. A, the managing agent of P, borrowed $3,500 from T upon P's behalf for use in P's business. P had not authorized A to borrow the money. P did repay $200 of the amount to T. Is T entitled to collect the balance due from P? Why?

8. P and X were competitors in business. P suspected that X would not sell to him, so he engaged A to purchase asphalt blocks from X. A purchased the blocks, but they were unmerchantable. When sued for breach of warranty by P, X defended on the ground that the contract would not have been entered if the identity of the principal had been known. Can P hold X liable on the contract? Why?

9. A was the president of P Company, which constructed new homes. A negotiated with T for plumbing work on a particular house. A identified himself as president of P Company but did not indicate that the contract was on behalf of P Company. The check in payment to T was signed by A under the printed name of P Company, with no indication of capacity of either signor. The check was not paid, because of insufficient funds. When A had negotiated with T on a previous contract, three checks signed in the same manner were cashed by T. Can T hold A personally liable on the contract? Why?

10. B purchased a new car and called the X Insurance Company's home office to transfer the insurance from his old car to his new one and obtain collision coverage. He talked to two girls before being switched to A, who replied, "O.K., you are covered." A had no authority to give additional insurance coverage. B had an accident the day after he talked to A. B sues X for damage to his car. Should he succeed? Why?

Tort Liability

1. Introduction

The fundamental principles of tort liability in the law of agency, which are discussed in this chapter, can be summarized as follows:

1. Agents, servants, and independent contractors are personally liable for their own torts.

2. Agents, servants, and independent contractors are not liable for the torts of their employers.

3. A master is liable under a doctine known as *respondeat superior* for the torts of his servant if the servant is acting within the scope of his employment.

4. A principal is liable for the torts of an agent who is also a servant in the performance of his duties if the agent is acting within the scope of his employment.

5. A principal, proprietor, employer, or contractee (each of these terms is sometimes used) is not as a general rule liable for the torts of an independent contractor.

6. Injured employees may have rights against their employers as well as against third parties who cause their injuries.

In the foregoing list, numbers 3 and 4 actually express the same basic concept. The terms *master* and *servant* are technically more accurate than the terms *principal* and *agent* in describing the parties when tort liability is discussed. Courts nevertheless frequently describe the parties as "principal" and "agent." However, a principal is liable for torts of only those agents who are subject to that kind of control that establishes the master–servant relationship.[1] For the purpose of tort liability, a servant is a person who is employed with or without pay to perform personal services for another in his affairs, and who, in respect to the physical movements in the performance of such service, is subject to the master's right or power of control. A person who renders services for another but retains control over the manner of rendering such services is not a servant but an independent contractor.

2. Liability of Agents and Servants

Every person who commits a tort is personally liable to the individual whose person or property is injured or damaged by the wrongful act. Where an agent or officer of a corporation commits or participates in the commission of a tort, whether or not he acts on behalf of corporation, he is liable to third persons injured. One is not relieved of tort liability by establishing that the tortious act was committed under the direction of someone else or in the course of employment by another. The fact that the employer or principal may be held liable does not in any way relieve the employee or agent of his liability. The agent's or servant's liability is joint and several with the liability of the principal. Of course, the converse is not true. An agent, servant, or independent contractor is not liable for the torts of the principal, master, or employer.

In the event that A commits a tort against T, T can bring action against A or against P, or T can sue A and P jointly. Assume that T sues and collects from P, as is typically the case, because P's financial standing is usually better than A's. Can P upon paying the judgment recover his loss from A? The answer is yes if the tort arose from A's negligence and there was no contributing fault on P's part. As will be discussed more fully in this chapter, a servant is liable for his own misconduct either to others or to his employer.

Suits by masters against servants for indemnity are not common, for several reasons. First, the servant's financial condition frequently does not warrant suit. Second, the employer knows of the risk of negligence by his employees and covers this risk with insurance. If indemnity were a common occurrence, the ultimate loss would almost always fall on employees or workmen. If this situation developed, it would have an adverse effect on employee morale and would make labor–management relations much more difficult. Therefore, few employers seek to enforce the right to collect losses from employees. However, in a few recent cases, some courts have allowed the insurance carrier of the employer to sue the employee under its right of subrogation. If such suits become common, it is likely that legislation will be enacted to eliminate the insurance carrier's claim against the negligent employee, on the ground that such suits are against public policy.

1 *Wilken* v. *Van Sickle*, page 587.

Just as P may have a right to reimburse or indemnify from A, under certain situations A may successfully maintain an action for reimbursement or indemnity against P. Such is the case when A commits a tort in conformity with instructions given to him by P, without knowledge that his conduct is tortious. For example, P, a retail appliance dealer, instructs A to repossess a TV set from T, who had purchased it on an installment contract. P informs A that T is in arrears in his payments. Actually, T is current in his payments, and a bookkeeping error had been made by P. In accordance with his instructions and over protest from T, A makes the repossession. A *has* committed a tort, but P must indemnify him and satisfy T's claim against A, if T elects to collect from A.

TORT LIABILITY OF PRINCIPALS AND MASTERS

3. *Respondeat Superior*

A master is liable to third persons for the torts committed by his servants *within the scope of their employment* and in prosecution of the master's business. This concept, frequently known as *respondeat superior* (let the master respond), imposes vicarious liability on employers as a matter of public policy. Although negligence of the servant is the usual basis of liability, the doctrine of *respondeat superior* is also applicable to intentional torts, such as trespass, assault,[2] libel, and fraud, that are committed by a servant acting within the scope of his employment. It is applicable even though the master did not direct the willful act or assent to it.

This vicarious liability imposed on masters, which makes them pay for wrongs they have not actually committed, is not based on logic and reason but on business and social policy. The theory is that the master is in a better position to pay for the wrong than is the servant. This concept is sometimes referred to as the "deep pocket" theory. The business policy theory is that injuries to persons and property are hazards of doing business, the cost of which the business should bear rather than have the loss borne by the innocent victim of the tort or society as a whole.

The application doctrine of *respondeat superior* usually involves the issue as to whether the servant was *acting within the scope of his employment* at the time of the commission of the tort. The agent or servant may have detoured from his employment and gone off on a frolic of his own. (The law of frolics and detours is covered in a later section.) In addition, the facts may establish that the control of the master over the servant's employment has ended. If the servant is no longer acting within the scope of his employment and on his master's business, but is acting solely on his own behalf, there can obviously be no liability.

[2] *Overton* v. *Henderson,* page 588.

As a general rule, the master cannot avoid liability by showing that he has instructed the servant not to do the particular act complained of. When a servant disobeys the instructions of his master, the fact of disobedience alone does not insulate the master from liability. In addition, the master is not released by evidence that the servant was not doing the work his master had instructed him to do, when the servant had misunderstood the instruction. As long as the servant is attempting to further his master's business, the master is liable because the servant is acting within the scope of his employment.

4. Expanding Vicarious Liability

In recent years, the law has been expanding the concept of vicarious liability, even to acts of persons who are not employees. A person engaged in some endeavor gratuitously may still be a "servant" within the scope of the master–servant doctrine. The two key elements for determination of whether a gratuitous undertaking is a part of master–servant relationship are (1) whether the actor has submitted himself to the directions and to the control of the one for whom the service is done, and (2) whether the primary purpose of the underlying act was to serve another. If so, the "master" is liable for the torts of the unpaid "servant."

Most of the expansion of the application of *respondeat superior* and vicarious liability has been by statute. Liability for automobile accidents has been a major area of expansion. Some states have adopted what is known as the "family-car doctrine." [3] Under it, if the car is generally made available for family use, any member of the family is presumed to be an agent of the parent-owner when using the family car for his or her convenience or pleasure. The presumption may be rebutted, however. Other states have gone further and provided that anyone driving a car with the permission of the owner is the owner's agent, and the owner has vicarious liability to persons injured by the driver. The family purpose doctrine may extend to nonfamily members under some circumstances.

5. Frolics and Detours

Respondeat superior requires that the agent or servant be *acting within the scope of his employment* at the time of the commission of the tort. The law imposes liability on the master only when the master's business is being carried on or where the wrongful act was authorized or ratified by the principal. The master's liability does not arise when the servant steps aside from his employment to commit the tort or does the wrongful act to accomplish some purpose of his own. If the tort is activated by a purpose to serve the master or principal, then he is liable. Otherwise, he is not. Although the scope of employment is considerably broader than explicitly authorized acts of the employee, it does

[3] *Dixon* v. *Phillips,* page 589.

not extend to cases in which the servant has stepped aside from his employment to commit a tort that the master neither directed in fact nor could be supposed, from the nature of the servant's employment, to have authorized or expected the servant to do.

However, not every deviation from the strict course of duty is a departure such as will relieve a master of liability for the acts of a servant. The fact that a servant, while performing his duty to his master, incidentally does something for himself or a third person does not automatically relieve the master from liability for negligence that causes injury to another. To sever the servant from the scope of his employment, the act complained of must be such a divergence from his regular duties that its very character severs the relationship of master and servant.

It is not possible to state a simple test to determine if the tort is committed within the scope of the employment. However, factors that are considered in determining the scope of employment include the nature of the employment; the right of control, "not only as to the result to be accomplished but also as to the means to be used"; [4] the ownership of the instrumentality, such as an automobile; whether the instrumentality was furnished by the employer; whether the use was authorized; and the time and place of the occurrence. Most courts inquire into the intent of the servant and the extent of deviation from expected conduct involved in the tort. The issue is usually one of fact and is left to the jury.

A servant is not acting within the scope of his employment if he is on a "frolic" of his own. The deviation may sometimes be described as a "detour," in which case a problem is presented as to the point at which the detour ends and the course of employment resumes. Another difficult situation is presented when the servant combines his own business with that of his master. As a general rule, this fact does not relieve the master of liability. The doctrine of *respondeat superior* has been extended to create liability for negligence of strangers while assisting a servant in carrying out the master's business, where the authority to obtain assistance is given or is required, as in the case of an emergency.

Intentional or willful torts are not as likely to occur within the scope of the servant's employment as are those predicated upon a negligence theory. If the willful misconduct of the servant has nothing to do with his master's business and is animated entirely by hatred or a feeling of ill will toward the third party, the master is not liable.

6. Procedure

As previously noted, the law of torts in most states, unlike the law of contracts, allows joinder of the master and servant as defendants in one cause of action or permits them to be sued separately. Although the plaintiff is limited to one

---

[4] *Johnson* v. *Evers,* page 590.

recovery, the master and servant are jointly and severally liable. The party may collect from either or both in any proportion until the judgment is paid in full. If the servant is sued first and a judgment is obtained that is not satisfied, such a suit is not a bar to a subsequent suit against the master, but the amount of the judgment against the servant fixes the maximum limit of potential liability against the master.

If the servant is found to be free of liability, either in a separate suit or as a codefendant with the master, then the suit against the master on the basis of *respondeat superior* will fail. The master's liability is predicated upon the fault of the servant, and if the servant is found to be free of fault, the master has no liability as a matter of law.

7.   Independent Contractors

An independent contractor is a person performing a service for one who employs him under an arrangement by which the person engaged has the power to control the details of the work being performed.[5] Because the performance is within the control of such person, he is not a servant, and his only responsibility is to accomplish the result contracted for. To illustrate: A contracts to build a boat for P at a cost of $5,000 and according to certain specifications. In such a case, it is clear that A is an independent contractor, with the completed boat as the result. However, had P engaged A by the day to assist in building the boat under P's supervision and at P's direction, the master–servant relationship would have resulted. As previously discussed, it should be kept in mind that an agent with authority to represent his principal contractually will, at the same time, be either a servant or an independent contractor for the purpose of tort liability.

The distinction between servants and independent contractors is important because, as a general rule, the doctrine of *respondeat superior* and the concept of vicarious liability in tort are not applicable to independent contractors. There is no tort liability, as a general rule, because the theories that justify liability on the master for the servant's tort are not present when the person engaged to do the work is not a servant.

The hallmark of a master–servant relationship is that the master not only controls the result of the work but has the right to direct the manner in which the work shall be accomplished; the distinguishing feature of an independent contractee–contractor relationship is that the person engaged in the work has exclusive control of the manner of performing it, being responsible for only the result and not the means. In ascertaining whether a person is a servant or an independent contractor, the basic inquiry is whether such person is subject to the alleged employer's control or right to control with respect to his physical conduct in the performance of services for which he was engaged. However, it should be kept in mind that an employer of an independent contractor may

[5] *Perryman* v. *Self,* page 591.

retain a broad general power of supervision of the work so as to ensure satisfactory performance of the contract—including the right to inspect, *to stop the work,* to make suggestions or recommendations as to details of the work, *or to prescribe alterations or deviations in the work*—without changing the relationship from that of owner and independent contractor or the duties arising from that relationship.

The application of the doctrine of *respondeat superior* and the tests for determining if the wrongdoer is an independent contractor are quite difficult to apply to professional and technically skilled personnel. For example, it can be argued that a physician's vocation requires such a high skill and learning that others, especially laymen, cannot as a matter of law be in control of the physician's activities. Such an argument if accepted would eliminate the liability of hospitals for acts of medical employees.

Notwithstanding the logic of the aforesaid argument, courts usually hold that *respondeat superior* may be applied to professional persons and that such persons may be servants. Of course, some professional and technical persons are independent contractors. Hospitals and others who render professional service through skilled employees have the same legal responsibilities as everyone else. If the person who commits a tort is an employee acting on its behalf, the employer is liable even though no one actually "controls" the employee in the performance of his art or skill. These concepts are applicable to doctors, chemists, airline pilots, lawyers, and other highly trained and specialized persons.

Since it is generally understood that one is not liable for the torts of an independent contractor, contracts frequently provide that the relationship is that of independent contractor and not master–servant. Such a provision is not binding on third parties, and the contract cannot be used to protect the contracting parties from the actual relationship as shown by the facts.

8. Exceptions

The rule of insulation from liability in the independent-contractor situation is subject to several well-recognized exceptions.[6] The most common of these is where the work involved is inherently dangerous to the public. The basis of this exception is that it would be contrary to public policy to allow one engaged in such an activity to avoid his liability by selecting an independent contractor rather than a servant to do the work.

Another exception to insulation from vicarious liability exists where the work being done is illegal. An employer cannot avoid liability by hiring an independent contractor to perform a task that is illegal. Another common exception involves employee's duties, which are considered to be nondelegable. In the law of contracts, it was noted that personal rights and personal duties could not be transferred without consent of the other party.

[6] *Boroughs* v. *Joiner,* page 592.

Many statutes impose strict duties on parties such as common carriers and innkeepers. If an attempt is made to delegate these duties to an independent contractor, it is clear that the employer upon whom the duty is imposed has liability for the torts of the independent contractor.

Finally, an employer is liable for the torts of an independent contractor if the tort is ratified. For example, if an independent contractor wrongfully repossesses an automobile and the one hiring him refuses to return it on demand, the tort has been ratified and both parties have liability.

Tort liability is also imposed where the employer is himself at fault, as when he selects the employee negligently. This is true whether the party performing the work is a servant or an independent contractor. For example, assume that X, a person with known propensities for violence, including a criminal record for assaults, is employed. X assaults a customer of his employer. There is liability even though X may be an independent contractor. There would also be liability even though X went beyond the scope of his employment. Liability exists because of the negligence of the party hiring X.

INJURIES TO EMPLOYEES

9. Claims against Third Parties

Irrespective of other legal relationships, any person injured by the commission of a tort has a cause of action against the wrongdoer. An employee who is injured by the wrongful conduct of the third person may recover from the third person. If the employee has been compensated for his injuries by his employer under the applicable workmen's compensation law, the employer is entitled to recover any workmen's compensation payments from the sum that the employee recovers from the wrongful third party.

There are three rather unusual tort situations that have a direct relation to the employment contract. First, any third party who maliciously or wrongfully influences a principal to terminate an agent's employment thereby commits a tort. The wrongful third party must compensate the agent for any damages that result from such conduct. Second, any third person who wrongfully interferes with the prospective economic advantage of an agent has liability to the agent for the loss sustained. Third, any person who influences another to breach a contract in which the agent is interested thereby renders himself liable to the agent as well as to the principal.

10. Tort Claims against the Employer

An employer owes certain nondelegable duties to his employees. These include the duty (1) to warn employees of the hazards of their employment, (2) to supervise their activities, (3) to furnish a reasonably safe place to work, and (4) to furnish reasonably safe instrumentalities with which to work. As part of the obligation to provide a safe place to work, the employer must instruct his employees in the safe use and handling of the products and equipment used in and around the employer's plant or facilities. What is reasonable for the purposes of these rules depends on all the facts and circumstances of each case. For example, what is a reasonably safe place to work can depend upon the age and ability of the worker as well as the condition of the premises. It may be negligent to furnish a minor with, or to fail to supervise a minor in the operation of, a certain instrumentality when to take the same action with a grown man or an experienced employee would not constitute negligence.

At common law, the employer who breached these duties to his employees was liable in tort for the injuries received by the employees. The employer was not an insurer of his employee's safety, but liability was based on negligence. However, the employee in his tort action was confronted with overcoming three defenses available to the employer, one or more of which frequently barred recovery. The first of these defenses was that the employee was *contributorily negligent*. If the employee was even partially at fault, this defense was successful even though the majority of the fault was the employer's. Second, if the injury was caused by some other employee, the *fellow-servant* doctrine excused the employer and limited recovery to a suit against the other employee who was at fault. Finally, in many jobs that by their very nature involved some risk of injury, the doctrine of *assumption of risk* would allow the employer to avoid liability.

The common law rules resulted for the most part in imposing on employees the burdens that resulted from accidental injuries, occupational diseases, and even death. Through the legislative process, society has rather uniformly determined that this result is undersirable as a matter of public policy. Statutes known as *workmen's compensation* have been enacted in all the states. These laws impose liability without fault (eliminate the common law defenses) on most employers for injuries, occupational diseases, and death of their employees.

11. Workmen's Compensation

Workmen's compensation laws vary a great deal from state to state as to the covered industries and employees, the nature of the injuries or diseases that are compensable, and the rates and source of compensation. In spite of the wide variances in the laws of the states in this area, certain general observations can be made.

State workmen's compensation statutes provide a system of paying for death, illness, or injury that arises out of and in the course of the employment. The three defenses the employer had at common law are eliminated. The employers are strictly liable without fault.

Most state statutes exclude certain types of employment from their coverage. Generally, domestic and agricultural employees are not covered. In the majority of states, the statutes are compulsory. In some states, employers may elect to be subject to lawsuits by their employees or their survivors. In such cases, the plaintiff must prove that the death or injury resulted proximately from the negligence of the employer. But the plaintiff is not subject to the common law defenses. In addition, there is no statutory limit to the amount of damages recoverable. Thus, few employers elect to avoid coverage.

The workmen's compensation acts give covered employees the right to certain cash payments for their loss of income. A weekly benefit is payable during periods of disability. In the event of an employee's death, benefits are provided for the spouse and minor children. The amount of such awards is usually subject to a stated maximum and is calculated by using a percentage of the wages of the employee. If the employee suffers permanent partial disability, most states provide compensation for both injuries that are scheduled in the statute and those that are nonscheduled. As an example of the former, a worker who loses a hand might be awarded 100 weeks of compensation at $90 per week. Besides scheduling specific compensation for certain specific injuries, most acts also provide compensation for nonscheduled ones, such as back injuries, based upon the earning power the employee lost owing to his injury. In addition to the payments above, all statutes provide for medical benefits.

In some states, employers have a choice of covering their workmen's compensation risk with insurance or of being self-insured (i.e., paying all claims directly) if they can demonstrate their capability to do so. In other states, employers pay into a state fund used to compensate workers entitled to benefits. In these states, the amounts of the payments are based on the size of the payroll and the experience of the employer in having claims filed.

Although the right to workmen's compensation benefits is given without regard to fault of either the employer or the employee, employers are not always liable. The tests for determining whether an employee is entitled to workmen's compensation are simply, (1) Was the injury accidental? and (2) Did the injury arise out of and in the course of the employment? Since workmen's compensation laws are remedial in nature, they have been very liberally construed. In recent years, the courts have tended to expand coverage and the scope of the employer's liability. It has been held that heart attacks as well as other common ailments where the employee had either a preexisting disease or a physical condition likely to lead to the disease were compensable as "accidental injuries." Likewise, the courts have been more and more liberal in upholding awards that have been challenged on the ground that the injury did not arise out of and in the course of the employment.[7]

---

[7] *Cavalcante* v. *Lockheed Electronics Co.*, page 593.

The system of separate and varying state workmen's compensation laws as they exist today has been subject to much criticism. The laws have been attacked as inadequate because of their restrictive coverage and limited benefits. Not all types of employment or occupational risks are covered. Many states exempt businesses that do not employ a certain minimum number of workers. Much criticism has also been leveled at the quality of administration of most workmen's compensation programs. The weaknesses in the present laws, and the fact that there are wide variations in the workmen's compensation acts (as well as case law) from state to state, have led to suggestions that workmen's compensation be modernized and reformed to better meet the social needs of today and that it be made uniform from state to state. Some have proposed a Federal Workmen's Compensation Act to replace the state ones.

TORT LIABILITY CASES

Wilken v. Van Sickle
507 P.2d 1150 (Or.) 1973

HOWELL, J. An auto driven by defendant Van Sickle collided with a vehicle in which plaintiff was riding as a passenger. Plaintiff brought this action against Van Sickle and the defendant Freightliner Corporation, contending that Van Sickle was either an agent or servant of Freightliner at the time of the accident. Plaintiff appeals from a judgment of involuntary nonsuit entered in favor of defendant Freightliner. . . .

In the instant case only one question—the vicarious liability of Freightliner—was submitted to the court sitting without a jury.

The following facts appear . . . :

On a date prior to the accident, Van Sickle applied for a job with Freightliner. On the day of the accident, he had completed his aptitude test and was given certain forms for a required medical examination to be taken that afternoon. Van Sickle was to be hired if he passed the medical examination. The appointment was made and the examination paid for by Freightliner.

After completion of the examination, he was to return the forms to Freightliner's office.

He did not return directly to Freightliner but instead drove to his girl friend's home in Milwaukee. After leaving her home and on his way to the Freightliner office, Van Sickle's car collided with the vehicle in which plaintiff was riding as a passenger.

Later, Van Sickle reported to the Freightliner office, was hired, and reported to work the next day.

Clearly Van Sickle, at the time of the accident, was not an employee of defendant Freightliner. It is true that the results of the medical examination were satisfactory to Freightliner, but Van Sickle did not actually become an employee until the day following the accident. Moreover, under the doctrine of *respondeat superior,* the plaintiff must show "the harm-producing activity was in furtherance of the employer's business and that the employer had the right to exercise some degree of control over the workman in the conduct of such activity."

There was no showing that Freightliner had the right to exercise some degree of control over Van Sickle at the time. How and when he returned the medical papers to Freightliner's office was entirely within Van Sickle's discretion.

The remaining question is whether Van Sickle was a non-servant agent of Freightliner at the time of the accident. Plaintiff contends that Van Sickle was a special agent of Freightliner for the purpose of returning the completed medical forms. Even assuming that Van Sickle was a non-servant agent of Freightliner for the purpose of obtaining an employment physical examination and returning the forms to Freightliner, it does not follow that Freightliner is vicariously liable.

A very similar case is *McLean* v. *St. Regis Paper Company,* 6 Wash.App. 727 (1972). There, the alleged agent had been directed to take a physical examination by the defendant, St. Regis, his prospective employer. The examination was paid for by St. Regis and was a prerequisite to employment. On the way to the medical clinic the prospective employee's car was involved in an accident with another vehicle. The injured plaintiff filed an action against St. Regis, claiming that the latter was vicariously liable because the prospective employee was an agent of St. Regis for the purpose of obtaining the employment physical examination and returning with the results.

The Washington court adopted and quoted the general principle set forth by Dean Prosser:

Since an agent who is not a servant is not subject to any right of control by his employer over the details of his physical conduct, the responsibility ordinarily rests upon the agent alone, and the principal is not liable for the torts which he may commit. Prosser, Law of Torts 479, § 69 (3d ed 1964).

The court noted that if the rule were otherwise, a client, for example, could be responsible for the negligent physical conduct of his attorney for an act wholly beyond the client's ability to control.

The Washington court held that in order to establish vicarious libility of St. Regis, it was necessary to show that St. Regis had control of, or the right to control, the physical acts of the prospective employee. As St. Regis did not direct how the prospective employee should get to the clinic, and, as he furnished his own transportation and was under no obligation to take the exam or to return the forms afterward, the element of right to control was lacking. . . .

In the case at bar, like the *McLean* case, the defendant had no right to control the physical movements of Van Sickle in going to or returning from the clinic. Van Sickle was under no obligation to take the physical examination or to return to the Freightliner offices afterward.

The judgment is affirmed.

Overton v. Henderson
222 S.E.2d 724 (N.C.) 1976

Plaintiff sued Cole for damages by reason of an assult by Henderson, an alleged agent of Cole. Henderson had shot plaintiff in a barbershop. Cole operated a motel and Henderson, his brother, lived at the motel and worked as a desk clerk. The lower court held that the defendant was not liable as a matter of law, and plaintiff appealed.

PARKER, J. . . . Our Supreme Court has had many occasions to examine the law ap-plicable to cases in which it is sought to hold a principal or employer liable for an assault committed by his agent or employee. . . . Insofar as pertinent to the present case, the applicable principles of law . . . may be summarized as follows: The principal is liable for the acts of his agent, whether malicious or negligent, and the employer for similar acts of his employees, which result in injury to third persons, when the agent or employee is acting within the line of his duty and exercising the functions of his employment. The test is whether the act was done within the scope of his employment and in the prosecution and furtherance of the business which was given him to do. If the servant was engaged in performing the duties of his employment at the time he did the wrongful act which caused the injury, the employer is not absolved from liability by reason of the fact that the employee was also motivated by malice or ill will toward the person injured, or even by the fact that the employer had expressly forbidden him to commit such act. . . . If the act of the employee was a means or method of doing that which he was employed to do, though the act be unlawful and unauthorized or even forbidden, the employer is liable for the resulting injury, but he is not liable if the employee departed, however briefly, from his duties in order to accomplish a purpose of his own, which purpose was not incidental to the work he was employed to do. However, it is not enough to render the employer liable that the employee did the wrongful act for the purpose of benefiting the employer.

Applying these principles to the present case, we find that the directed verdict for the employer, the defendant Cole, was properly entered. The evidence shows that she employed her brother, Henderson, to work at her motel,

and that she authorized him to deal with the guests, checking them in and out, and to supervise other employees. She also authorized him to make deposits in the bank account which she maintained in connection with the motel business and to draw checks on that account. However, when Henderson assaulted the plaintiff, he was not engaged in performing any of the work he was employed to do. He was not dealing with a guest or supervising any other employee, and he was not even on his employer's premises. Apparently his animosity toward plaintiff was aroused by a letter which plaintiff wrote to Mrs. Cole in which plaintiff claimed she was indebted to him for work plaintiff performed at the motel, but there was no evidence that it was any part of Henderson's duties to settle claims against his employer. Clearly, there was no evidence that Mrs. Cole ever expressly authorized Henderson to perform any such function on her behalf and such a function cannot be reasonably implied from the duties which she did authorize him to perform. Since there was no evidence from which the jury could find that Henderson's assault on plaintiff was committed while he was engaged in performing any duty of his employment, the directed verdict in favor of his employer was properly granted. . . .

Affirmed.

Dixon v. Phillips
217 S.E.2d 331 (Ga.) 1975

EVANS, J. . . . The owner of a family purpose automobile allowed his minor son, a member of his household, to drive the car. The son permitted another to drive, and a collision occurred. The father testified . . . that he had expressly forbidden his son to allow any other person to drive the car.

The lower court holds that notwithstanding the son was present in the automobile, retaining control and direction over it, the defendant owner's motion for summary judg-

ment should have been granted, and plaintiff appeals. *Held:*

The question here is not what instructions the father gave his son as to the way and manner in which the son operated and managed the vehicle, because the owner could not limit his liability by such private instructions, to which the injured parties were not privy. The test is as to whether the car was being operated in the scope of the owner's business. The owner had made it his business to furnish a car for the pleasure and convenience of members of his family. The law does not allow a principal to insulate and absolve himself of liability by private instructions to his agent. The "family purpose car doctrine" is an extension of the principal–agent relationship. . . .

A master is responsible for the tortious acts of his servant, done in his business and within scope of employment, although he does not authorize or know of the particular act, *or even if he disapproves or forbids.* This is so because the test of the master's responsibility for the acts of the servant is, *not whether such act was done in accordance with the instruction of the master to servant, but whether it was done in the prosecution and in the scope of the master's business.* . . .

[W]hen a family purpose car that is furnished by the owner to members of the family for their convenience and pleasure is sued for such purpose, and a member of the family is present in the automobile controlling, or who could supervise control of the operation thereof:

1. An owner of a family purpose car is liable for the acts of members of his family in driving said car.

Johnson v. Evers
238 N.W.2d 474 (Neb.) 1976

Plaintiff, while riding as a passenger in an automobile driven by her mother, was injured in a collision with a car driven by the defendant Evers. Evers was an employee (brakeman and conductor) of the Union Pacific Railroad. He worked out of North Platte, Nebraska and Torrington, Wyoming. At the time of the accident, Evers was driving to Torrington to get some of his clothes and other belongings. The trial court held that the railroad was not liable as a matter of law and the plaintiff appealed.

MCCOWN, J. . . . The plaintiff contends that there is a factual dispute and that Evers was acting in furtherance of the business of the Union Pacific Railroad Company in that the trip would incidentally or indirectly contribute to the service and benefit of the employer.

2. The owner of a family purpose car is liable for the acts of a third person, to whom his child has entrusted the driving of the car.

3. The family purpose doctrine is but an extension of the law of principal and agent.

4. So long as the car is being operated for the pleasure of some member of the owner's family, even though a third person is driving, the owner is liable.

5. An owner (master) cannot insulate himself from liability by the mere giving of private instructions to his children, such as forbidding them to allow third persons to drive the car, and as to which private instructions the injured party is not privy.

6. The test to be observed is whether or not the car was at the time being operated in the owner's business—in the business for which he furnished the car—to wit, the furnishing of pleasure to members of his family; and if so, the owner is liable.

For the foregoing reasons the lower court erred in granting the defendant father's motion for summary judgment.

Judgment reversed.

Restatement, Agency 2d, S. 228, p. 504, provides:

(1) Conduct of a servant is within the scope of employment if, but only if:

(a) it is of the kind he is employed to perform;

(b) it occurs substantially within the authorized time and space limits;

(c) it is actuated, at least in part, by a purpose to serve the master, and . . .

Comment (c) to that section makes it clear that there is no liability for the conduct of one who, although a servant in performing other services, is doing work as to which there is no control or right to control by the master.

A corporation is liable for the negligent operation of an automobile by its agent or servant only when such agent or servant is engaged in the employer's or principal's business with its knowledge and direction.

In an action against an employer for personal injuries inflicted by an employee upon a third person by the negligent use of an automobile owned and operated by the employee, the burden is on the plaintiff to prove that the employee was acting within the scope of his employment at the time of the injury. . . . It is not enough, in order to establish liability, to show that the master has an interest in what is being done. It must also be made to appear that the servant whose act is in question has authority from the master to perform the class of service to which the act belongs. . . .

The doctrine of *respondeat superior* is applicable only when the employment relation can be found to exist at the time and with respect to the conduct giving rise to the injury.

In this case the purpose for Evers' trip was personal. The trip was entirely outside the space and time limits of his employment, and driving an automobile was not in any sense within the class of work for which he was hired. It was beyond the ability of the employer to assert any control, directly or indirectly, over Evers' conduct or performance. There are many off-duty activities of employees which might be said to benefit employers to some degree, but ordinarily they constitute no part of the work employees are hired to perform. If an employer were liable under the circumstances here simply because of some remote possibility of indirect benefit to him, there would be virtually no limit to the liability which could be imposed upon an employer for the off-duty torts of any employee on his payroll. There is no justifiable reason for such an extension of doctrines of legal liability. . . .

Affirmed.

Perryman v. Self
546 S.W.2d 670 (Tex.) 1977

MCDONALD, J. . . . This is an appeal by defendant Perryman from $9,450 judgment against him in favor of plaintiffs Self.

Plaintiffs Self sued defendants Perryman and Corley Drilling Company for damages to plaintiffs' property during the drilling of an oil well on such property. Plaintiffs own the surface of 280 acres of land; Perryman owns an oil and gas lease on such property; and Corley drilled the well.

During the drilling of the well Corley's employees drove a truck into plaintiffs' barn; ruined plaintiffs' fences; used a mud pump with a defective engine; all of which the jury found was negligence and a proximate cause of $9,450 damage to plaintiffs. The jury further found (Issue 10) that Corley was "acting as an employee" of Perryman, and not as an "independent contractor. . . ."

Perryman appeals on one point: "The trial court erred in (approving) . . . the jury's finding . . . that Corley Drilling Company was acting as an employee of Perryman."

If Corley was an Independent Contractor, Perryman is not liable for Corley's negligence in damaging plaintiffs' property. If Corley is an agent or employee of Perryman, then Perryman is liable for such damages. . . .

Whether Corley is an independent contractor or an agent or employee depends on whether Perryman had the right to control the details of the work. . . .

Plaintiffs owned the surface of the land. Perryman owned an oil and gas lease authorizing him to drill for oil and gas. Perryman entered a written contract with Corley under which Corley agreed to drill a well at a site selected by Perryman "4900 feet . . ." for $15,000 furnishing all labor and material; and assuming liability for injuries to "any person or property, incident to or resulting from the operation of the contractor hereunder."

Witness Frizzell, Perryman's "accountant, trouble shooter and general manager" testified he was on the land during the drilling operation; that Perryman had a "drilling superintendent" on the ground during the drilling; that the drilling superintendent "represented us at the well to see that the work was properly done"; "he has the authority to protect our interest"; and "Q. And to correct things there at the well site in behalf of Mr. Perryman? A. That is right."

And Perryman introduced into evidence Exhibit 7, his report to the Railroad Commission of Texas of plugging the well. Such report was signed by "Corley" as "Agent."

While the foregoing does not conclusively establish that Corley was an agent or employee of Perryman . . . such constitutes some evidence which the jury had a right to believe; and we think same ample to sustain the jury's answer to Issue 10. . . .

Affirmed.

Boroughs v. Joiner
337 So.2d 340 (Ala.) 1976

Plaintiff, the owner of a fishing lake, sued the defendant for damage to the lake caused by the defendant's spraying crops on a nearby farm. Defendant had employed an independent contractor to spray a pesticide on his crops. The trial court held that the defendant was not liable as a matter of law for the tort of the independent contractor. The plaintiff appeals.

SHORES, J. . . . The general rule in this state, and in most others, is that:

> . . . one is not ordinarily responsible for the negligent acts of his independent contractor. But this rule, as most others, has important exceptions. One is that a person is responsible for the manner of the performance of his nondelegable duties, though done by an independent contractor, and therefore, that one who by his contract or by law is due certain obligations to another cannot divest himself of liability for a negligent performance by reason of the employment of such contractor.

It is also generally recognized that one who employs a contractor to carry on an inherently or intrinsically dangerous activity cannot thereby insulate himself from liability.

Although the courts have had some difficulty in stating a precise definition of activity which is inherently or intrinsically dangerous, the cases seem to agree that an intrinsic danger in an undertaking ". . . is one which inheres in the performance of the contract and results directly from the work to be done, not from the collateral negligence of the contractor, and important factors to be understood and considered are the contemplated conditions under which the work is to be done and the known circumstances attending it."

The rule is stated in Restatement of the Law, Torts 2d, Vol. 2, § 427 (1965), as follows:

> One who employs an independent contractor to do work involving a special danger to others which the employer knows or has reason to know to be inherent in or normal to the work, or which he contemplates or has reason to contemplate when making the contract, is subject to liability for physical harm caused to such others by the contractor's failure to take reasonable precautions against such danger.

Crop dusting and spraying have been the subject of much litigation in recent years. Many courts have categorized such activity as inherently or intrinsically dangerous, making inapplicable the rule that a principal is not liable for the torts of his independent contractor. . . .

The reasoning of the courts that have dealt with this problem has been summarized in 12 A.L.R.2d 438:

> There can be no doubt that farmers, orchardists, and, in fact, all horticulturists

have the right to use the many beneficial new dusts and sprays to protect their growing fruits and vegetables from the ever-increasing invasion of insects, worms, borers, weevils, etc., and to assure the best possible product by dusts and sprays which eliminate weeds that would otherwise choke out or stunt growth.

But such preventive measures cannot be used with absolute impunity. Due care must be exercised in seeing to it that the weather conditions are right, that the operator spreading the material does not place it so close to fence lines that cattle can reach through and eat poisoned grass; that airplane spreaders cut off the dust or spray distributor when making turns over the crops of others which the material would injure or over pasture land of others which would be poisoned for animals thereon, and that they do not spread dust when the wind is so blowing as to float it to the crops of others or the hives of bees and kill them. Care must likewise be taken that poisonous spray is not blown on pasture land.

In other words, an owner of premises may be liable to damages for spreading poisonous dusts and sprays negligently.

The Legislature of Alabama has recognized that insecticides and pesticides are intrinsically dangerous and has adopted statutes regulating the sale, distribution and application of those products in this state. . . .

We hold that aerial application of insecticides and pesticides falls into the intrinsically or inherently dangerous category and, therefore, the landowner cannot insulate himself from liability simply because he has caused the application of the product to be made on his land by an independent contractor. . . .

Reversed and remanded.

Cavalcante v. Lockheed Electronics Co.
204 A.2d 621 (N.J.) 1964

This was an appeal by Lockheed Electronics Company from an award of statutory compensation benefits to the petitioner, who was the widow of a former Lockheed employee. The deceased employee had been working long and odd hours on a special "cleanup" job for Lockheed in New London, Connecticut, about 150 miles from his regular place of employment. After dinner, at about 10 P.M. of the third day of this job, he and four co-workers decided to leave their motel and to "go out and see what New London was like." They drove to "a bar and a restaurant and dance hall" where they were "drinking beer, listening to the music and talking over our work and what had to be done and what we had accomplished so far." They were also dancing and drinking scotch and soda, decedent included. Driving back at 12:30 A.M. the next morning, decedent failed to negotiate a hidden curve in the road and died as a result of the accident.

HOPKINS, J. . . . In its appeal Lockheed argues strenuously that decedent's accident and death did not arise out of and in the course of his employment, that there was no causal connection between the conditions of the work and the resulting injury, and that the injury did not have its origin in a risk connected with the employment, nor did it flow from that source as a natural consequence. . . .

Lockheed argues that the acts of the decedent and his associates in the present case were not reasonably necessary to serve their basic subsistence needs, and that in fact the decedent had finished his work for the day, had had his evening meal, and from that time on his time was his own, just as if he had finished a long overtime session at the Plainfield plant at home. It contends that the evening trip from its start to its unfortunate finish was clearly an abandonment of and departure from the employment on a purely personal matter, having no connection whatever with the duties of his employment, his meals, his travel or his living conditions.

It is basic that an accident arises "in the course of" employment when it occurs (a) within the period of employment, (b) at a place where the employee may reasonably be, and (c) while he is fulfilling the duties of the employment, or doing something incidental to it. It arises "out of" the employment when the risk of such an occurrence is reasonably incident to the employment. Such a risk is one that grows out of or is connected with what a workman has to do in fulfilling his contract of service. It immediately becomes evident that the standard always is reasonableness. . . .

Where an employee is traveling on a business trip away from his home, "reasonableness" . . . is given a very liberal construction. In *Robinson* v. *Federal Telephone & Radio,* the court quoted with approval from *Thornton* v. *Hartford Accident & Indemnity Co.,* when it said:

> The eating of meals, while a pleasure indulged in by a traveling salesman and all mankind, is as necessary to the continuance of his duties as the breath of life; and where his duties take him away from his home his acts of ministration to himself should not—and we believe do not—take him outside the scope of his employment so long as he performs these acts in a normal and prudent manner. Such activities, the performance of which are necessary to his health and comfort, while in a sense personal to himself are nevertheless incidents of his employment.

It therefore becomes necessary to examine what acts, which "are reasonably necessary to serve the basic subsistence needs of the employee," and are to be "reasonably included within the scope of the employment," come within the meaning of the *Robinson* case. . . .

It must be kept in mind that "work-connected activity goes beyond the direct services performed for the employer and includes at least some ministration to the personal comfort and human wants of the employee." . . .

In *Schneider* v. *United Whelan Drug Stores,* decedent and his superior were in Miami, Florida on business. Because they had about 24 hours to await the return flight for which they had reservations, they accepted the invitation of a local employee to go boating. Decedent drowned when the boat capsized. The court reversed the denial of the award and held this act of boating was reasonable to engage in.

The facts of *Hancock* v. *Ingersoll-Rand Co.* are clearly distinguishable [from those of the case at bar]. . . . In *Hancock* recovery was denied because the court was of the opinion that the frequenting of cocktail lounges with unknown female companions was completely unreasonable. There is no difference in the principle or rule to be applied, as it is only a question of degree. In the instant case the visit to the tavern was with fellow employees simply seeking some reasonable relaxation. Reasonableness is the key to recovery. . . .

In *Lewis* v. *Knappen Tippetts Abbett Engineering Co.,* decedent had been sent to Israel as a consultant to the Israeli Government. Before his work was fully completed, he went from Tel Aviv to Jerusalem with a United Nations convoy for the sole purpose of sight-seeing. The convoy was attacked by unknown Arabs, who broke a period of truce then in effect and decedent was fatally shot. The Court of Appeals of New York found that this employee was acting within the scope of his employment and that the accident occurred during the course of his employment because he was acting in a reasonable manner and the accident happened at a place where he might reasonably have been expected to have been. . . .

Because it is reasonable for a traveling employee to seek some physical relaxation, and because this was done in a reasonable manner, this accident and the consequent death did arise out of and in the course of decedent's employment.

The judgment below is affirmed.
Affirmed.

CHAPTER 30
REVIEW QUESTIONS AND PROBLEMS

1. S was employed by M as a trainee photographer. Late one night, after photographing a wedding, S was returning the camera equipment to the studio (he was not required to return the equipment that night) when his auto collided with T's auto. T was killed, and T's estate wants to join M in the suit against S. Should this be allowed? Why?

2. S used the family car to pick up groceries ordered by his mother. S's father, F, did not give, and would not have given had he been asked, permission for S to use the car. While on route to the store, S struck and injured T. Can T recover from F? Why?

3. T, an employee of X Company, was discharged from his job by M, manager of X Company. M told S, another employee of X Company, "If T comes back, throw him out." When T returned to the premises, he was attacked by S. Is X Company liable? Why?

4. A construction company engaged a subcontractor to procure fill dirt. The subcontractor's employee, operating a bulldozer, scraped a high-pressure gas line under the surface of the ground. The gas line exploded, damaging the plaintiff's property. May the plaintiff recover from the construction company? Why?

5. A, a doctor, was employed at a regular salary by the QRS Shipping Line to serve aboard ship and treat passengers. A treated B, a passenger, and B died as a result of A's negligence. May A's heirs recover from the QRS Lines? Why?

6. T was shopping in P's store when E, an employee, brushed at P's ankle with a shopping cart. A short time later, while still shopping, T told E that he should say "Excuse me," and then people would get out of his way. E then punched T in the face, knocking her to the floor. T now sues P. Should she collect? Why?

7. E was employed by P Company as a timekeeper. E's superior told him to "jump in the car and get the payroll." Since he was not instructed as to which car to take or which route to follow, E decided to use his own car, and he took the most direct route. There was an accident on the way, owing to E's negligence. The injured party now sues P. Is P liable? Why?

8. E, an employee of P Company, was involved in an automobile accident owing to her negligence. She was driving her own car but did receive a car allowance and mileage for use of the car for business purposes. She had left her office with a customer, and they had gone to a bar and had a drink.

She then left for home, and on the way, the accident occurred. E frequently did paperwork at home. Is P liable to the driver of the other car? Why?

9. E worked for P Life Insurance Company under an employment contract to solicit applications for insurance. Under the contract, E was to cover "New Mexico as directed." He was to choose his own transportation, hours, and places of work. The contract provided that E was "an independent contractor" working on a commission basis, and that he would pay for his own expenses. E negligently struck and killed T while returning to his home, after calling on prospective customers. Is P liable? Why?

10. P Company employed E as a distributor to solicit customers and sell its products. At the time of employment, E had committed numerous traffic violations and had been involved in several motor vehicle accidents. While on the way to call on a customer, E's car negligently struck another car. Assuming that E is an independent contractor, can the passengers of the other car recover from P? Why?

11. E was formerly employed at R Company's store. Following her discharge, she sought other employment. A prospective employer telephoned O's office and inquired as to the reason for E's discharge. A secretary said that all the supervisors were out and that all she could do was to pull E's personnel file, which, she did, and advised E's prospective employer that E was discharged for shortages. The notation was false and E sued R Company for defamation of character. Should E succeed? Why?

12. S was an employee of M. S's job was to drive an ice cream truck and sell ice cream to persons from the truck. When the truck became stalled, he asked T and T's friend to push the truck. They agreed and were compensated for their services with a can of whipped cream each, given to them by S. T's whipped cream exploded and injured him. When sued by T, M defended on the grounds that S was acting outside the scope of his employment at the time he gave T the whipped cream. Is this correct? Explain.

Duties of Principal and Agent to Each Other

DUTIES OF AGENT TO PRINCIPAL

1. Introduction

The nature and extent of the duties imposed upon agents and servants are governed largely by the contract of employment. In addition to the duties expressly designated, certain others are implied by the fiduciary nature of the relationship and by the legal effects on the principal of actions or omissions by the agent. The usual implied duties are (1) to be loyal to his principal; (2) to obey all reasonable instructions; (3) not to be negligent; (4) to account for all money or property received for the benefit of the principal; and (5) to inform the principal of all facts that materially affect the subject matter of the agency. These implied duties are essential to the employer–employee relationship.

2. Duty of Loyalty

The duty of loyalty is the hallmark of a fiduciary relationship. This duty prevents an agent from directly or indirectly undertaking a business venture that competes or interferes in any manner with the business of his employer or making any contract for himself when he should have made it for his principal. An agent is not allowed to sell or to lease his principal's property to himself unless the principal assents to the sale or lease. Purchasing agents are prohibited from buying from themselves. Real estate brokers and other agents are not allowed to represent both parties to a transaction.[1] Transactions that

[1] *Meerdink* v. *Krieger,* page 604.

violate these rules are voidable by the principal. The remedy of rescission is available even though the contracts are fair and on as favorable terms as could be obtained elsewhere.

In addition to the remedy of rescission, a principal is entitled to receive any profit or gain realized by the agent in violation of this duty. The principal may also collect from the agent any damages sustained as a result of the breach of the duty of loyalty.

An agent may deal with himself if he obtains the permission of the principal. In such cases, the agent must disclose fully all facts that materially influence the situation.

The duty of loyalty demands that information of a confidential character acquired while in the service of the principal shall not be used by the agent to advance his interests in opposition to those of the principal. This confidential information is usually called *trade secrets*. Trade secrets include plans, processes, tools, mechanisms, compounds, and informational data used in business operations. They are known only to the owner of the business and to such limited other persons in whom it may be necessary to confide. An employer seeking to prevent the disclosure or use of trade secrets or information must demonstrate that he pursued an active course of conduct designed to inform his employees that such secrets and information were to remain confidential. An issue to be determined in all cases involving trade secrets is whether the information sought to be protected is, in fact and in law, confidential. The result in each case depends on the conduct of the parties and the nature of the information.

An employee who learns of secret processes or formulas or comes into possession of lists of customers may not use this information to the detriment of his employer. Former employees may not use such information in a competing business regardless of whether the trade secrets were copied or memorized. The fact that a trade secret is spied out does not make it any less a secret, nor does the fact that a product is on the market amount to a divulgence or abandonment of the secrets connected with the product. The employer may obtain an injunction to prevent their use. Such use is a form of unfair competition. The rule relating to trade secrets is applied with equal severity whether the agent acts before or after he severs his connection with the principal.

Knowledge that is important but that does not amount to a trade secret may be used, even if it affects the agent's former employer injuriously. That which by experience has become a part of a former employee's general knowledge cannot and ought not be enjoined from further and different uses. For this reason, there is nothing to hinder a person who has made the acquaintance of his employer's customers from later circularizing those whom he can remember. His acquaintanceship is part of his acquired skill. The employer may protect himself in the later case by a clause in the employment agreement to the effect that the employee will not compete with the employer or work for a competitor for a limited period of time after his employment is terminated.

3. Duty to Obey Instructions

It is the duty of an agent to obey all legal instructions issued by his principal as long as they refer to duties contemplated by the contract of employment. Burdens not required by the agreement cannot be indiscriminately imposed by the employer. An instruction may not be regarded lightly merely because it departs from the usual procedure and seems fanciful and impractical to the employee. It is not his business to question the procedure outlined by his superior. Any loss that results while he is pursuing any other course makes him liable to the principal for any resulting loss.

Furthermore, an instruction of the principal does not become improper merely because the motive of the principal is bad, unless it is illegal or immoral. He may well be aware of the agent's distaste for certain tasks, yet if those tasks are such as may be called for under the employment agreement, it becomes the agent's duty to perform them. Failure to perform often results in proper grounds for his discharge.

Closely allied to the duty to follow instructions is the duty to remain within the scope of the authority conferred. Because of the doctrine of estoppel, it often becomes possible for an agent to exceed his authority and still bind his principal. In case of such a violation of his contract, the employee becomes responsible for any resulting loss.[2]

Occasionally, circumstances arise that nullify instructions previously given, or at least allow a deviation from them. Because of the new conditions, the old instructions would, if followed, practically destroy the purpose of the agency. Whenever such an emergency arises, it becomes the duty of the agent, provided the principal is not available, to exercise his best judgment in meeting the situation.

4. Duty Not to Be Negligent

As was discussed in Chapter 30, the doctrine of *respondeat superior* imposes liability upon a principal or master for the torts of an agent or servant acting within the scope of his employment. The agent or servant is primarily liable, and the principal or master is secondarily liable.

It is an implied condition of employment contracts, if not otherwise expressed, that the employee has a duty to act in good faith and to exercise reasonable care and diligence in performing his tasks. Failure to do so is a breach of the employment contract. However, it should be kept in mind that an agent must only exercise ordinary and reasonable care, skill, and diligence. He is not an insurer for his principal.

[2] *Crawford* v. *DeMicco,* page 606.

If the employer has liability to third persons owing to the employee's acts or omissions of negligence and the application of the doctrine of *respondeat superior,* the employer may recover his loss from the employee. This right may be transferred by the doctrine of subrogation to the liability insurance carrier of the employer.

5. Duty to Account

Money or property entrusted to the agent must be accounted for to the principal even if received in an illegal transaction. An agent is required to keep proper records. Any money collected by an agent for his principal should not be mingled with funds of the former. If they are deposited in a bank, they should be kept in a separate account. Failure to do so makes the agent liable for interest and any loss that may result.

An agent who receives money from third parties for the benefit of the principal owes no duty to account to the third parties. The only duty to account is owed to the principal. On the other hand, money paid to an agent who has no authority to collect it, and who does not turn it over to the principal, may be recovered from the agent in an action by the third party.

A different problem is presented when money is paid to an agent in error, such as occurs by overpayment of an account. If the agent has passed the money on to his principal before the mistake is discovered, it is clear that only the principal is liable. Nevertheless, money that is still in the possession of the agent when he is notified of the error should be returned to the third party. The agent does not relieve himself of this burden by subsequently making payment to his principal.

Any payment made in error to an agent and caused by the agent's mistake or misconduct may always be recovered from him, even if he has surrendered it to his principal. Also, any overpayment may be recovered from the agent of an undisclosed principal, because the party dealing with the agent was unaware of the existence of the principal.

6. Duty to Give Notice

It was previously noted that knowledge acquired by an agent within the scope of his authority binds the principal, or more succinctly, knowledge of an agent is notice to the principal. Therefore, the law imposes on the agent the duty to inform his principal of all facts that affect the subject matter of the agency and are obtained within the scope of the employment. Information learned while outside the scope of employment and beyond the agent's authority need not be communicated to the principal. In addition, there are certain exceptions to the rule of imputed knowledge. These exceptions arise in situations where it is not expected that the agent will inform the principal.[3]

---

[3] *Imperial Finance Corp.* v. *Finance Factors, Ltd.,* page 606.

This rule extends beyond the duty to inform the principal of conflicting interests of third parties or possible violations of the duty of loyalty in a particular transaction. It imposes upon the agent a duty to give his principal all information that materially affects the interest of the principal. For example, knowledge of facts that may have greatly advanced the value of property placed with an agent for sale must be communicated before the property is sold at a price previously established by the principal.

DUTIES OF PRINCIPAL TO AGENT

7. Duty to Compensate in General

The agent is entitled to be compensated for his services in accordance with the terms of his contract of employment. If no definite compensation has been agreed upon, there arises a duty to pay the reasonable value of such services. Whenever the party performing the services is a stranger to the employer, the obligation to compensate exists. However, where relatives are working for one another and no express agreement has been formulated, the courts are likely to infer that the services so rendered should be considered gratuitous. This question frequently arises in claims against an estate for the value of care given the deceased prior to his death by a relative. Following this rule, the claims are usually denied in the absence of an express contract to pay for the care.

If the contract is silent on the amount of compensation, the reasonable value will be the customary rate in the community, if any. If no customary rate is available, opinion evidence is received in determining the value of the services. Difficult issues often arise as to the obligation to pay for "fringe benefits," such as vacation pay and pension plans. Since the right to compensation is essentially contractual, courts are hesitant to expand the duty beyond the obligation actually established by proof.

Many employment contracts include provisions for paying a percentage of profits to a key employee. In the absence of a detailed enumeration in the employment contract of the items to be considered in determining net income, it will be computed in accordance with generally accepted accounting principles, taking into consideration past custom and practice in the operation of the employer's business. It is assumed that the methods of determining net income will be consistent and that no substantial changes will be made in the methods of accounting without the mutual agreement of the parties. The employer cannot unilaterally change the accounting methods, nor can the employee require a change in order to effect an increase in his earnings.

8. Duty to Compensate Real Estate Brokers

The right of a real estate broker or agent to a commission is frequently the subject of litigation. In the absence of an express agreement, the real estate broker earns a commission in either of two situations. First, he will be entitled to it if he finds a buyer who is ready, willing, and able to meet the terms outlined by the seller in the listing agreement. The owner cannot deprive the agent of a commission by refusing to deal with the prospective purchaser or by withdrawing the property from sale. The owner cannot relieve himself of the duty to pay the commission by terminating the agency and later contracting directly with the broker's prospect. The fee is earned if it is shown that the broker was the inducing cause of the sale.

The commission is also earned if the owner contracts with the purchaser (whether or not the price is less than the listed price), even though it later develops that the buyer is unable to meet the terms of the contract. The contract is conclusive evidence that the broker found a ready, willing, and able buyer. The seller assumes the risk of performance upon executing the contract with the buyer presented by the broker. This is true even if the law allows the buyer to avoid liability, as for example where the property is destroyed. However, if a prospective purchaser conditions his obligation to purchase on an approval of credit or approval of a loan, he is not a ready, willing, and able buyer until such approval. If it is not forthcoming, the broker is not entitled to a commission.

The broker's commission is contingent on payment by the purchaser when his contract of employment so states. An owner who lists property with several brokers is obligated to pay the first one to find a satisfactory purchaser, at which time the agency of other brokers is automatically terminated, assuming a simple listing.

There are three distinct types of real estate listings—placing of property with real estate brokers for sale. First is the simple listing of the property for sale on the terms set forth by the seller, in which case the listing may be with several brokers and the right to withdraw or terminate the relationship at any time is reserved by the seller. Under such circumstances, the seller pays the commission to the first broker who finds a buyer. The owner is free to sell on his own behalf without a commission. The second type consists of an exclusive listing, which usually gives to the broker the exclusive right to find a buyer for an agreed period of time. In this case, the seller is not free to list the property with other brokers, and a sale through other brokers would be a violation of the contract of listing, although the seller himself is free to find a buyer of his own. Third is a listing in which the broker is given an exclusive right to sell. In this case even the seller is not free to find a buyer of his own choosing.[4] If the seller does sell on his own behalf, he is obliged to pay a commission to the broker holding an exclusive right to sell listing.

In recent years, there has developed what is known as a "Multiple Listing Agreement." This is a method of listing property with several brokers simultaneously. These brokers belong to an organization whose members share listings and divide the commissions. For example, a typical commission would

4 *Wade* v. *Austin*, page 608.

be split 60 percent to the selling broker, 30 percent to the listing broker, and 10 percent to the organization for operating expenses. These multiple listing groups give homeowners the advantage of increased exposure to potential buyers. In return for this advantage, most multiple listing agreements are of the exclusive right to sell type.

The right to a real estate commission is subject to statutory limitations in most states. Some of these require a written contract or written authority to place signs on property. Almost every state requires a license before a person may engage in this activity. Some courts have gone so far as to hold that a broker selling property in a state in which he is licensed is not entitled to a fee if the buyer is found or the sale completed in another state. Strict adherence to the licensing statutes is usually required. A broker may forfeit his right to compensation by improper conduct, breach of the duty of loyalty, or lack of good faith. A real estate broker is a fiduciary, and his actions must be for the sole benefit of his principal.

9. Duty to Compensate Sales Representatives

Salesmen who sell merchandise on a commission basis are confronted by problems similar to those of the broker, unless their employment contract is specific in its details. Let us assume that X Company appoints A as its exclusive sales representative in a certain territory on a commission basis, and that the employer is engaged in producing and selling electrical equipment. T, a businessman in the area involved, sends a large order for merchandise directly to the home office of X Company. Is A entitled to a commission on the sale? It is generally held that such a salesman is entitled to a commission only on sales solicited and induced by him, unless his contract of employment gives him greater rights.

The salesman usually earns his commission as soon as an order from a responsible buyer is obtained, unless his contract of employment makes payment contingent upon delivery of the good or collection of the sale price. If payment is made dependent upon performance by the purchaser, the employer cannot deny the salesman his commission by terminating the agency prior to collection of the account. When the buyer ultimately pays for the goods, the seller is obligated to pay the commission.

An agent who receives a weekly or monthly advance against future commissions is not obligated to return the advance if commissions equal thereto are not earned. The advance, in the absence of a specific agreement, is considered by the courts as a minimum salary.

10. Duty to Reimburse and Indemnify

A servant is entitled to indemnity for certain tort losses. They are limited to factual situations in which the servant is not at fault and his liability results from following the instructions of the master. An agent or a servant is justified in presuming that instructions given by the principal are such as he lawfully has a right to give, and that performance resulting from such instructions will not injuriously affect third parties. Where this is not the case, and the agent incurs a liability to some third party because of trespass or conversion, the principal must indemnify the agent against loss. There will ordinarily be no indemnification for losses incurred in negligence actions, because the servant's own conduct is involved. The indemnification is usually of the master by the servant in tort situations. However, if the agent or servant is sued for actions within the course of employment, the agent or servant is entitled to be reimbursed for attorney's fees and court costs incurred if the principal does not furnish them in the first instance when obligated to do so.[5]

An agent has a general right to reimbursement for money expended on behalf of his principal. It must appear that the money was reasonably spent and that its expenditure was not necessitated by the misconduct or negligence of the agent. It is the duty of the principal to make performance by the agent possible whenever the latter has entered into a contract in his own name for the former's benefit. The undisclosed principal must fully protect his agent by making the funds available to perform the contract as agreed.

DUTIES OF PARTIES CASES

Meerdink v. Krieger
550 P.2d 42 (Wash. App.) 1976

GREEN, J. . . . Plaintiffs, purchasers, brought an action against defendant realtors, alleging nondiscosure of a dual agency relationship. Defendants appeal from a verdict in favor of plantiffs. . . .

Plaintiffs, widowed sisters contemplating retirement, desired to exchange their homes for an apartment house in which they could live and receive rental income. They contacted defendant Glen Bunger, a real estate agent, seeking his advice and expertise to help them find an apartment house in the $80,000 to $90,000 range. Plaintiffs, unknowledgeable in real estate and business transactions, told Mr. Bunger they were depending solely upon him for advice. Unable to find a suitable apartment house, Mr. Bunger suggested that plaintiffs build one. He stated they could expect

to receive a total net credit of $46,000 for their homes on a trade with a builder. Mr. Bunger and his employer, Mr. Krieger, d/b/a Krieger & Associates, introduced Mr. Johnson, a builder, to plaintiffs who stated their desired $80,000 to $90,000 price range. Mr. Johnson obtained plans which were viewed by plaintiffs who were then presented with an offer to purchase, prepared in Mr. Krieger's office and citing a purchase price of $120,000. Upon inquiry, plaintiffs were told that this figure had to be high to cover unforeseeable problems and, if possible, it would be adjusted downward to allow a small profit over costs. Plaintiffs were reluctant, but a few days later, signed the offer to purchase, relying on Mr. Bunger's statements that the transaction was a "good deal" and that they should pay more so that they

---

[5] *Douglas* v. *Los Angeles Herald-Examiner,* page 609.

could "get more money out of it." This offer was later accepted by Mr. Johnson with the following additional term:

> I agree with the above sale and the foregoing terms and conditions and agree to pay Krieger & Associates, as agent, a fee of $10,000 for services.

Upon receipt of a copy of the accepted offer, plaintiffs did not notice the additional recitation. Thereafter, they attached no legal significance to it but thought, throughout the transaction, that they were obligated to pay a commission.

During construction, plaintiffs continued to express to Mr. Bunger their dissatisfaction with the price and their reservations about going through with the transaction, but he advised them that they could not lose and urged them not to back out. At the suggestion of Mr. Bunger, plaintiffs put their residences on the market through a listing agreement with him, reciting selling prices of $35,000 for Mrs. Meerdink's home and $15,000 from Mrs. Cranfill's home. No results were obtained and plaintiffs ultimately conveyed their properties to Mr. Johnson, receiving a total net credit of $33,000 for both homes. Upon completion of construction, plaintiffs executed a real estate contract for a purchase price of $115,000. Thereafter, Mr. Bunger and Krieger & Associates held an open house to obtain tenants for the apartment units.

Plaintiffs testified that they thought Krieger & Associates and Mr. Bunger were working for them; that it was never discussed how they were to pay defendants for services; that they did not know the builder was paying a commission; and that they would not have gone through with the deal had they known the defendants were not working for them. Mr. Johnson, the builder, testified that he knew plaintiffs were relying on Mr. Bunger and depending upon him for advice. It was further apparent to Mr. Johnson that the plaintiffs had very little knowledge of realty transactions

and he questioned Mr. Bunger as to whether plaintiffs should be getting into the deal. Mr. Johnson stated that the price was reduced by $5,000 out of kindness and a desire to be fair to the plaintiff "neophytes." He testified the actual cost of the apartment house was around $80,000 and his usual profit was 15 percent. Both parties produced expert testimony regarding the value of the apartment house, ranging from $87,500 to $115,000. . . .

We begin with the fundamental rule that a real estate agent has the duty to exercise the utmost good faith and fidelity toward his principal in all matters falling within the scope of his employment. Such agent must exercise reasonable care, skill and judgment in securing the best bargain possible, and must scrupulously avoid representing interests antagonistic to that of the principal without the explicit and fully informed consent of the principal. Further, the agent must make a full, fair and timely disclosure to the principal of all facts within the agent's knowledge which are, or may be, material to the transaction and which might affect the principal's rights and interests or influence his actions. Consequently, a dual agency relationship is permissible "when both parties have full knowledge of the facts and consent thereto."

Before such consent can be held to exist, clear and express disclosure of the dual agency relation and the material circumstances that may influence the consent to the dual agency must be made.

Whether defendants violated these obligations raises questions of fact for the jury under proper instructions.

Defendants . . . contending that the only proper measure of damages is refund or forfeiture of the commission paid. We disagree.

An agent is subject to liability for any loss to the principal arising from breach of duty. Breach of duty by an agent may result in forfeiture of the agent's commission as well as liability for damages. . . .

Affirmed.

Crawford v. DeMicco
216 So.2d 769 (Fla.) 1968

Plaintiff sued an insurance company to recover the value of a boat lost in a storm. The agent that issued the binder on the boat had been instructed not to issue coverage on boats more than three years old or worth more than $5,000, without a condition survey. The boat in question was thirteen years old and insured for $5,000. The defendant insurance company filed a cross claim against its agent. The lower court found for the agent on the indemnity claim, and the defendant insurance company appealed.

CROSS, J. [After discussing other issues] . . . Turning now to the action by the cross-plaintiff-insurer against the cross-defendant-agency, we are to determine if an insurance agent binds a contract of insurance which he is not authorized to do, is such agent liable to indemnify the company for its losses arising from the enforcement of the insurance contract so bound.

The facts as alluded to above are simple, and the law is equally so. It has long been well settled that an agent owes to his principal the obligation of high fidelity, and that he may not proceed without or beyond his authority, particularly where he has been forbidden to act and that so proceeding, his actions caused loss to his principal, the agent is fully accountable to the principal therefor. 2d Restatement of Agency, § 401. An elementary factor in the principal–agent relationship is control. As stated in 2d Restatement of Agency, § 14B(f), "An agent acts for and on behalf of his principal and subject to his control. . . . The agent

owes a duty of obedience to his principal."

The record in this case reveals that the agency through its employee proceeded without and went beyond its authority. . . .

The record further indicates that the agent's employee was informed on a prior occasion when dealing with insurance being placed on another vessel, that as a matter of course the insurer specifically instructed the agent's employee that a survey is required on vessels that are valued at $5,000 or over or are more than three years old, if the vessel was to be submitted to the insurer for insurance.

Under the facts of the instant case and the settled law applicable thereto, unless and until the principal with full knowledge of all the applicable facts waived the breach of its instructions, ratified or adopted the agent's act as its own, or facts otherwise raising an estoppel against the principal, the agent became and remained liable to the principal for the damages incurred in acting without authority to the disadvantage of its principal. The facts herein reveal no adoption, ratification or estoppel on the part of the principal-insurer.

The cross-defendant-agency, through its employee, acted precipitatively, unreasonably and without authority. The testimony reveals vividly that the agency's employee admittedly and grievously breached his duty to the insurer by his initial unauthorized act in binding the vessel, and therefore the cross-defendant-agent cannot escape the loss or any part thereof and throw such loss upon the principal-insurer. . . .

Reversed.

Imperial Finance Corp. v. Finance Factors, Ltd.
490 P.2d 662 (Hawaii) 1971

KOBAYASHI, J. This appeal comes from the decision of the trial court that appellee, Finance Factors, Ltd., did not breach a fiduciary duty owed appellant, Imperial Finance Corporation, in securing an attachment bond

on certain property for appellant. . . .

In January, 1967, an officer of appellant, Arthur Muraoka, acting on behalf of appellant, reached an agreement with Richard Kuga, a special representative in the insurance division of appellee, with regard to obtaining an attachment bond. The bond was to issue against real property owned by Alice Chong, who was indebted to appellant. Muraoka requested and Kuga agreed that information as to the attachment be kept confidential because an employee of one of appellee's subsidiaries was the son-in-law of Mrs. Chong.

Simultaneously with' or immediately subsequent to the acts above, Mrs. Chong went to appellee's loan offices to obtain a loan. Appellee's loan division, unaware of appellant's application for an attachment bond, approved the loan, took as security a mortgage on the same Chong property and duly recorded the mortgage.

Within a matter of a few days thereafter appellant, unaware of appellee's loan to Mrs. Chong and of appellee's taking as security a mortgage on the Chong property, perfected its attachment on the same property. Subsequently appellee foreclosed on its mortgage and the property was sold at a judicial sale. Because appellant's attachment was subordinate to appellee's mortgage, the proceeds from the sale went first to satisfy the amount owed appellee with the balance going to appellant. Consequently appellant suffered a loss amounting to the difference between the balance remaining of the judicial sale and the amount of its attachment.

ISSUE

. . . [I]t is sufficient for purposes of this appeal to assume that when appellant requested appellee's employee, Kuga, to obtain an attachment bond and such request was accepted, a duty was created in appellee to perform effectively in accordance with their agreement. The question is whether that duty was breached when appellee itself obtained a superior mortgage on the same property. Incident to considering said question we must first resolve the issue of whether the knowledge Kuga had of the attachment bond should be imputed to appellee, regardless of how the duty owed appellant by appellee is characterized. In deciding this issue the effect given to appellant's request of confidentiality becomes determinative.

IMPUTING KNOWLEDGE OF AGENT TO PRINCIPAL

The duty of an agent to give information to his principal is set forth in Restatement (Second) of Agency § 381 (1958): "Unless otherwise agreed, an agent is subject to a duty to use reasonable efforts to give his principal information which is relevant to affairs entrusted to him and which, as the agent has notice, the principal would desire to have and which can be communicated without violating a superior duty to a third person." An exception to this rule concerns the disclosure of confidential information and provides that an agent is not to communicate to the principal any information, the disclosure of which would be a breach of duty to a third person. Restatement (Second) of Agency § 381, comment *e* at 184 (1958). This provision is in accord with § 281 which provides essentially that "where an agent's duties to others prevent him from disclosing facts to the principal, the latter is not bound because of the agent's knowledge." . . .

The rationale for the rule that imputes an agent's knowledge to his principal and exceptions to that rule have been aptly stated in *Sands* v. *Eagle Oil and Refining Co.,* 83 Cal. App.2d 312 (1948):

It is true that in general the knowledge of an agent which he is under a duty to disclose to his principal or to another agent of the principal, is to be imputed to the principal. Rest. Agency, sec. 275; . . . However this rule is not without exceptions pertinent to this case. One is that if the agent and the third party act in collusion against the principal the principal will not be held bound by the knowledge of the agent. *Another excludes application of the general rule when the third party knows that the agent will not advise the principal. . . .*

THE REQUEST OF CONFIDENTIALITY

An exception to the general rule imputing knowledge from the agent to the principal is most frequently applied when either the agent is acting to defraud the principal, the agent and a third party have acted together in collusion against the principle, or the agent acquires confidential information, creating a duty not to disclose such information to his principal. In applying the facts of this case to the principles of law in this area as cited above, an exception is applicable to the general rule.

Muraoka, acting on behalf of appellant, had definite reason to know that Kuga would not be relaying the information about the attachment bond on to the other divisions of his corporate principal. Muraoka had specifically requested that Kuga not disclose the information because he knew that a relative of Chong's was an officer of appellee corporation and Muraoka did not want Chong to learn about the pending attachment bond prior to its being perfected. . . . Mr. Kuga agreed to keep the information confidential and volunteered that he would not even keep a file on the matter in his office.

Muraoka could have gone to another concern to obtain the attachment bond but instead he went to Kuga, appellee's agent, who agreed to keep it confidential, thus creating a duty for him to do so. As such, appellant is estopped from presently asserting that knowledge of the attachment bond should be imputed to appellee. Muraoka's request of confidentiality nullifies any knowledge about the attachment bond that would otherwise be imputed to appellee.

Therefore, even if there did exist an agency relationship, appellee violated no duty, fiduciary or otherwise, when it secured the mortgage lien that turned out to have priority over appellant's attachment bond on the Chong property.

Judgment affirmed.

Wade v. Austin
524 S.W.2d 79 (Tex.) 1975

Plaintiff, a real estate broker, sued the defendants for a real estate commission. Defendants had listed their property with plaintiff under an "exclusive right to sell listing." Plaintiff had conducted an open house and had advertised the property in the newspaper. The defendants learned of a prospective purchaser and sold the property directly to the purchaser. When the defendants refused to pay the real estate commission, plaintiff brought this action. The lower court found for the plaintiff.

RAY, J. . . . Under the contract, appellee had the sole right to sell the property during the listing period, and the contract expressly provided that appellee would be compensated for services rendered in the event of sale, regardless of who sold the property. . . .

Appellant's first point of error contends that appellee Austin was not entitled to recover . . . because appellee Jac A. Austin was not the procuring cause of the sale of the real property nor did he produce a purchaser ready and willing to purchase the property on the terms of the contract. . . . [W]e are convinced that the "procuring cause" contention is without merit under an "exclusive right to sell" contract. The test is whether the broker rendered services as required by the contract and whether the property is sold during the listing period, regardless of by whom. The purpose of the "exclusive right to sell" contract is to avoid a broker rendering all reasonable efforts to sell a piece of listed property and then encounter the claim of the owner that the broker is not entitled to be compensated because the owners sold the property directly without the broker being the procuring cause. The "procuring cause" contention is tenable under an "exclusive agency to sell" contract but not "exclusive agency with sole right to sell" contract.

It is undisputed that the Wade property was sold to Florence during the listing period. . . .

Affirmed.

Douglas v. Los Angeles Herald-Examiner
123 Cal. Rptr. 683 (1975)

Plaintiff, an investigative reporter for the defendant newspaper, wrote a series of articles about the connection between certain union officials and a local business. As a result of these articles, the plaintiff was sued for libel. Plaintiff requested the defendant to provide an attorney to defend the libel action. When the defendant refused to do so, plaintiff hired an attorney and was successful in defending the suit. Plaintiff then sued the defendant on the theory of indemnity for the fees and costs incurred in defending the libel action. The lower court held for defendant and the plaintiff appeals.

LORING, J. . . . Labor Code section 2802 reads:

> An employer shall indemnify his employee for all that the employee necessarily expends or loses in direct consequence of the discharge of his duties as such, or of his obedience to the directions of the employer, even though unlawful, unless the employee, at the time of obeying such directions, believed them to be unlawful. . . .

The Restatement of the Law of Agency, section 439 . . . provides:

> § 439. When Duty of Indemnity Exists

> Unless otherwise agreed, a principal is subject to a duty to exonerate an agent who is not barred by the illegality of his conduct to indemnify him for: . . .

> (d) expenses of defending actions by third persons brought because of the agent's authorized conduct, such actions being unfounded but not brought in bad faith; . . .

In the "Comment on Clause (d)" at 333 the Restatement states:

> h. An agent who has done an authorized act which brings him into contact with others, such as the making of a contract or the taking possession of a chattel, is ordinarily entitled to indemnity for the expenses of a successful defense to actions brought by third persons acting under the mistaken belief that the agent's conduct was a breach of contract, a tort, or otherwise created liability to them. If the action is the result of a reasonable mistake of law or fact by the third person, it is within the risks attendant upon authorizing the conduct and one which the principal customarily assumes. . . .

In the Appendix at 685, the following comment on clause (d) is made:

Comment d. Indemnity for the expense of defending actions **brought** against an agent because of a transaction entered into on account of the principal is granted as a matter of course where a judgment is obtained against the agent, if the principal has been notified. The same rule should apply where suit is brought and successfully defended. . . . No statement is made as to the corporate directors who have successfully defended actions by minority stockholders, since directors are in a special category. There is, however, no reason why they should not be indemnified and it is suggested that the adverse decisions were made at a time when the principles of indemnity were not well understood. . . .

We have no doubt that Labor Code section 2802 requires an employer to defend or indemnify an employee who is sued by third persons for conduct in the course and scope of his employment. . . .

However, we cannot endorse the requirement of the Restatement that the action by the third person (for which the employee is entitled to indemnity) must be one which was "not brought in bad faith" since no such distinction appears in Labor Code section 2802. The employee who is sued for authorized acts in the scope of his employment is as much in need of and deserving of indemnity if the third person acts in bad faith as the employee is if the third person acts in good faith. The needs and rights of the employee should not be measured by the state of mind of the third person plaintiff. If the term "bad faith" is intended to only exclude actions brought as a result of

collusion between the third person and the employee, then we have no quarrel with the term.

Consequently, we conclude that if Bursten sued Douglas "solely and exclusively because of acts performed for, at the direction of, and with the authorization and approval of (Herald) which acts of (Douglas) were specifically ratified and approved by (Herald)" as alleged in paragraph XIII of the complaint, then Douglas would be entitled to indemnity from Herald for the costs and expenses incurred in defending the case of *Bursten* v. *Douglas*.

. . . The test of whether or not Douglas is entitled to recover under Labor Code section 2802 is . . . whether Douglas was required to defend the federal action solely because of acts which he performed within the course and scope of his employment. . . . An employer does not have a duty to defend an employee who is sued solely because he was off on a frolic of his own not within the scope of his employment and not in obedience to the directions of his employer. . . .

In our view when an employer refuses to defend an employee in an action which may or may not be unfounded for conduct which may or may not have been within the course and scope of his employment and it is ultimately established that the action was unfounded and the employee acted within the course and scope of his employment, then the employer has an obligation under Labor Code section 2802 to indemnify the employee for his attorney's fees and costs in defending the action. . . .

Reversed.

CHAPTER 31
REVIEW QUESTIONS AND PROBLEMS

1. The X Insurance Company instructed its agent, Y, to cancel an insurance policy that had been issued on property owned by Z. Y failed to cancel the policy, and five weeks later, the property was destroyed by fire. X was forced to pay the claim. Can X recover from Y? Why?

2. P borrowed money from a bank for the construction of a house. A orally promised to act as agent in the payment of bills incurred in the construction. A paid out money without requiring the construction company to submit releases as required by the mechanic's lien law of Ohio. Filed against the house was $5,500 of liens, and P sued A for failure to exercise due care. Can P recover? Why?

3. P employed A, as agent, to operate and manage a business. A kept all the records and books of the business for 20 years. In the last four years of service, A prepared an annual income report. The reports were not checked, and no audit was made. When A resigned, he claimed that P was not entitled to an accounting, since the annual reports had been issued. Was A correct? Why?

4. A, a real estate agent, while attempting to sell P's property, lent T funds from his commission, which T used as a down payment on P's property. Is A entitled to his commission? Assuming a contract was signed, may T specifically enforce the contract? Why?

5. X, while delivering goods for Y, negligently ran into a train, damaging Y's automobile. May Y recover from X? Why?

6. A was sales manager of P, a turkey-packing company. As a member of the "management group," A was consulted on all phases of P's business. He persuaded the company to enter into a contract to purchase 20,000 turkeys from him, but concealed for some time the fact that the turkeys were being purchased from him. P Company did not carry out the contract, and A brings suit. Is the contract enforceable? Why?

7. S listed his real property for sale with A, a real estate agent. B was interested in purchasing land and engaged A to represent him. A arranged for S to sell his property to B and collected a commission from both parties. Neither S nor B was aware that A was acting as an agent for both of them. B now sues to rescind the contract of sale. Should B succeed? Why?

8. When E was working for P Company, he accrued vacation time but did not take a vacation. After the employment relationship was terminated, E brought suit to recover wages for the period of time that vacation had accrued. The contract of employment was silent on this point. Should E succeed? Why?

9. S listed his residence for sale with A, a real estate broker. Through A's efforts, a contract of sale was entered with B. However, before the closing date (the date that the title would pass), S's house was destroyed by fire. B elected to rescind the contract, as state law provided him with this right. S refused to pay a commission to A. Is A entitled to a commission? Why?

10. E, an employee of P Company, had as one of his duties the initiation and negotiation of contracts on behalf of P. E was instrumental in securing the awarding of a contract to X Construction Company. Shortly thereafter, E received $50,000 from X. P sues E for damages in the amount of $50,000. Should P succeed? Why?

32

Termination of the Agency Relationship

1. Introduction

Two basic issues are involved with the subject of termination of an agency relationship. First, what acts or facts are sufficient to terminate the authority of the agent insofar as the immediate parties are concerned? Second, what is required to terminate the agent's authority insofar as third parties are concerned? The latter question recognizes that an agent may continue to have the *power* to bind the principal but not the *right* to do so.

The methods of termination are usually divided into termination by act of the parties and termination by operation of law. The discussion that follows is limited to termination of the agency relationship and is not applicable to employment generally.

It should be recognized that termination of the employer-employee relationship will frequently be subject to the terms of an applicable collective-bargaining agreement. In addition, public policy considerations may deny the employers the right to terminate the employment relationship with impunity. Public policy preventing termination of employment is found in the provisions of the civil-rights laws relating to hiring, firing, promotion, and tenure of the employment. Courts in recent years have added other grounds for imposing liability on employers for wrongful discharge even if the employment relationship is one described as at will. Liability has been imposed for discharges that resulted from (1) refusing to give perjured testimony, (2) resisting sexual advances, and (3) serving on a jury.[1]

[1] *Nees* v. *Hocks,* page 616.

2. By Act of the Parties

Termination by act of the parties includes termination by force of their agreement or by the act of one or both of the parties. An example of the former is an agency that is created to continue for a definite period of time. It ceases, by virtue of the terms of the agreement, at the expiration of the stipulated period. If the parties consent to the continuation of the relationship beyond such period, the courts imply the formation of a new contract of employment. The new agreement contains the same terms as the old one and continues for a like period of time, except that no implied contract can run longer than one year because of the statute of frauds.

Another example of termination by force of the agreement is an agency created to accomplish a certain purpose, which automatically ends with the completion of the task assigned. In such a case, third parties are not entitled to notice of the termination. Furthermore, when it is possible for one of several agents to perform the task, such as selling certain real estate, it is held that performance by the first party terminates the authority of the other agents without notice of termination being required.

Many, if not most, agency contracts do not provide for the duration of the agreement. A contract for permanent employment, not supported by any consideration other than the performance of duties and payment of wages, is a contract for an indefinite period and terminable at the will of either party at any time.[2] Some agency agreements purport to be for a definite period but, on close examination, are found to be actually terminable at will.

Any contract may be terminated by mutual agreement; therefore, the agency relationship may be canceled in this manner. Furthermore, as a general rule, either party to the agreement has full *power* to terminate it whenever he desires, although he possesses no *right* to do so. Wrongful termination of the agency by either party subjects him to a suit for damages by the other party.

3. Wrongful Termination and Its Effect

As a general rule and subject to the exceptions previously noted, an employment that continues at the will of the parties may be rightfully terminated by either party at any time. Termination is not a breach of contract, but tort liability may be injured if public policy demands it. On the other hand, if the employer wrongfully terminates a contract that was to continue for an agreed period, there is liability for damages for breach of contract. Of course, if the agent is discharged for cause, such as for the failure to follow instructions, he may not recover damages from the employer.

The employee whose employment has been wrongfully cut short is entitled to recover compensation for work done before his dismissal and an additional sum for damages. Most of the states permit him to bring an action either immediately following the breach, in which case he recovers prospective damages,

---

[2] *Singh* v. *Cities Service Oil Company*, page 618.

or after the period has expired, in which event he recovers the damages actually sustained. In the latter case, he is compelled to deduct from the compensation called for in the agreement the amount that he has been able to earn during the interim.[3] Under such circumstances, the employee is under a duty to exercise reasonable diligence in finding other work of like character. Apparently this rule does not require him to seek employment in a new locality or to accept work of a different kind or more menial character. His duty is to find work of like kind, provided it is available in the particular locality.

4. Termination by Law

Certain acts are held by law to terminate the agency. Among these are death, insanity, bankruptcy of either of the parties, or any event creating true impossibility of performance, such as destruction of the subject matter of the agency. Bankruptcy has such an effect only if it affects the subject matter of the agency.

It is said of such cases that the agency is immediately terminated and that no notice need be given to either the agent or the third parties. However, with reference to insanity, unless the principal has been publicly adjudged insane, it is believed that an agent's contracts are binding on the principal unless the third party is aware of the mental illness, especially where the contract is beneficial to the insane principal's estate.

5. Agency Coupled with an Interest

As a general rule, an agency contract can be terminated at any time by either party. As previously noted, the power to terminate exists without the right to do so, and if the power is exercised wrongfully, a suit at law for damages may be brought. Agency contracts are not specifically enforceable against the principal because of the lack of mutuality in the remedy, even though equity courts will restrain violation of an express or implied covenant not to compete. Since the principal could not require the agent to work (involuntary servitude), the agent cannot, as a general rule, compel the principal to continue the agency.[4]

To the general rule, however, there is one well-recognized exception, known as *an agency coupled with an interest*. This term describes the relationship that exists when the agent has an actual beneficial interest in the property that is the subject matter of the agency. For example, a security agreement that contains a provision naming the secured party as agent to sell the property in the event of default creates an agency coupled with an interest in property. An agency coupled with an interest in property cannot be terminated unilaterally by the principal and is not terminated by events (such as death or bankruptcy

---

[3] *Cornell* v. *T.V. Development Corp.*, page 618.
[4] *Sarokhan* v. *Fair Lawn Memorial Hospital, Inc.*, page 620.

of the principal) that otherwise terminate agencies by operation of law. The net effect is that an agency coupled with an interest in property cannot be terminated without the consent of the agent.

An agency coupled with an interest in property must be distinguished from *an agency coupled with an obligation*. This latter term describes the situation in which the agency is created as a source of reimbursement to the agent. Such an agency is a hybrid between the usual agency and the agency coupled with an interest in property. The agency coupled with an obligation cannot unilaterally be terminated by the principal, but death or bankruptcy of the principal will terminate the agency by operation of law.

Under either type of agency, it should be clear that the interest in the subject matter must be greater than the mere expectation of profits to be realized or the proceeds to be derived from the sale of the property. The interest must be in the property itself. For example, a real estate broker is not an agent coupled with an interest, even though he expects a commission from the proceeds of the sale. Likewise, a principal who has appointed an agent to sell certain goods on commission has the power to terminate the agency at any time, although such conduct might constitute a breach of the agreement.

6. Notice in Event of Termination

Termination of the agency, as explained above, may take place by act of the parties or by operation of law. If the parties or either of them by their own action have terminated the agency, it is the duty of the principal to notify of its termination all third parties who have learned of the existence of the agency. Without such notice, the agent would still possess apparent authority to act for his principal. Those persons entitled to such notice may be divided into two groups: (1) those who have previously relied upon the agency by dealing with the agent, and (2) those who have never previously dealt with the agent, but who, nevertheless, have learned of the agency. The principal's duty to the first class can be satisfied only by the actual receipt of notice of the termination by the third party.[5] The principal satisfies his duty to the second group by giving public notice, such as newspaper publicity, in the location involved. If any one of the second group, not having seen the newspaper account of the termination, relies upon the continuation of the agency to his detriment, he has no cause of action against the principal. If a member of the first group has not received direct notice from the principal, but has learned indirectly of the severance of relation or of facts sufficient to place him on inquiry, he is no longer justified in extending credit to the agent or otherwise dealing with him as a representative of the principal.

Where the agency is terminated by action of law, such as death, insanity, or bankruptcy, no duty to notify third parties is placed upon the principal. Such matters receive publicity through newspapers, official records, and otherwise,

[5] *Zukaitis* v. *Aetna Cas. & Sur. Co.*, page 621.

and third parties normally become aware of the termination without the necessity for additional notification. If the death of the principal occurs before an agent contracts with a third party, the third party has no cause of action against either the agent or the estate of the principal unless the agent is acting for an undisclosed principal. In the latter case, since the agent makes the contract in his own name, he is liable to the third party. Otherwise, the third party is in as good a position to know of the death of the principal as is the agent.

A special problem exists in regard to notice in cases of special agents as distinguished from general agents. Ordinarily, notice is not required to revoke the authority of a special agent, since the agent possesses no continuing authority and no one will be in a habit of dealing with him. However, if the principal has directly indicated that the agent has authority in a certain matter or at a certain time, notice will be required to prevent reliance on the principal's conduct by a party dealing with the agent. This is especially true if the agent is acting under a special power of attorney. Actual notice of termination is required in these cases.

TERMINATION OF THE AGENCY RELATIONSHIP CASES

Nees v. Hocks
536 P.2d 512 (Or.) 1975

DENECKE, J. . . . . The principal question is whether the plaintiff alleged and proved conduct of the defendants which amounts to a tort of some nature. . . .

The plaintiff performed clerical duties for defendants. She started work in 1971. In 1972 she was called for jury duty; however, as she informed defendants, she requested and was granted a 12-month postponement because of her honeymoon. On February 2, 1973, plaintiff was again subpoenaed to serve on the jury. She told defendants and they stated that a month was too long for her "to be gone." Defendants gave her a letter which stated defendants could spare plaintiff "for awhile" but not for a month and asked that she be excused. Plaintiff presented this letter to the court clerk and told the clerk that she had been called before and had to be excused, but she would like to serve on jury duty. The clerk told plaintiff she would not be excused. The plaintiff

immediately came back to the office and told defendants that she would have to serve a minimum of two weeks' jury duty. She did not tell defendants she had told the court clerk she really wanted to serve.

Plaintiff started her jury duty on February 26, 1973. On March 1, 1973, she received a termination letter from defendants. The letter stated, in part: "Although we asked you to request an excusal from Jury Duty and wrote a letter confirming the Labls [defendants'] position, it has been brought to our attention you, in fact, requested to be placed on Jury Duty. . . ."

A representative of the firm that employed plaintiff after she was terminated by defendants testified one of the defendants told him plaintiff was terminated because she went on jury duty.

Plaintiff testified she suffered emotional distress because of her termination. She secured employment commencing one week after she finished jury duty for a higher salary than she had received from defendants. The jury awarded plaintiff compensatory . . . damages. . . .

We recognize, as defendants assert, that, generally, in the absence of a contract or legislation to the contrary, an employer can discharge an employee at any time and for any cause. Conversely, an employee can quit at any time for any cause. Such termination by the employer or employee is not a breach of contract and ordinarily does not create a tortious cause of action. The question to us is, however, are there instances in which the employer's reason or motive for discharging harms or interferes with an important interest of the community and, therefore, justifies compensation to the employee?

Other courts have held that there are such instances. In *Petermann* v. *International Brotherhood of Teamsters,* 174 Cal. App.2d 184, 344 P.2d 25 (1959), the plaintiff was discharged by his employer for refusing to give perjured testimony before a committee of the legislature. A judgment on the pleadings for the defendant employer was reversed.

In *Monge* v. *Beeve Rubber Company,* 114 N.H. 130, 316 A.2d 549 (1974), the plaintiff employee claimed "she was harassed by her foreman because she refused to go out with him and that his hostility, condoned if not shared by defendant's personnel manager, ultimately resulted in her being fired." 316 A.2d at 550. The court reversed an order of a trial court setting aside the verdict of the jury in favor of plaintiff.

In *Frampton* v. *Central Indiana Gas Company,* 297 N.E.2d 425 (Ind. 1973), the plaintiff employee alleged he was discharged for filing a workmen's compensation claim. The court reversed the order of the trial court dismissing the complaint for failing to state a cause of action. . . .

We conclude that there can be circumstances in which an employer discharges an employee for such a socially undesirable motive

that the employer must respond in damages for any injury done. The next question is, does the evidence in this case permit a finding that such circumstances are present?

. . . [T]he immediate question can be stated specifically, is the community's interest in having its citizens serve on jury duty so important that an employer, who interferes with that interest by discharging an employee who served on a jury, should be required to compensate his employee for any damages she suffered?

Art. VII, § 3, of the Oregon Constitution provides that jury trial shall be preserved in civil cases. Art. I, § 11, provides a defendant in a criminal case has a right of trial by jury. Art. VII, § 5, provides: "The Legislative Assembly shall so provide that the most competent of the permanent citizens of the county shall be chosen for jurors."

ORS 10.040 provides for certain exemptions from jury duty. ORS 10.050 provides for certain excuses from jury duty including health, age and "(c) When serving as a juror would result in extreme hardship to the person including but not limited to unusual and extraordinary financial hardship." ORS 10.055 provides for deferment of jury duty "for good cause shown" for not more than one year. ORS 10.990 provides that if a juror, "without reasonable cause," neglects to attend for jury service the sheriff may impose a fine, not exceeding $20 for each day the juror does not attend.

People v. *Vitucci,* 49 Ill.App.2d 171 (1964), stated that an employer who discharged an employee who was absent because of jury duty was guilty of contempt of court. Massachusetts has a statute making such conduct contemptuous.

These actions by the people, the legislature and courts clearly indicate that the jury system and jury duty are regarded as high on the scale of American institutions and citizen obligations. If an employer were permitted with impunity to discharge an employee for fulfilling her obligation of jury duty, the jury system would be adversely affected. The will of the community would be thwarted. For these reasons we hold that the defendants are liable for discharging plaintiff because she served on the jury. . . .

Affirmed.

Singh v. Cities Service Oil Company
554 P.2d 1367 (Okl.) 1976

The defendant oil company offered the plaintiff a position as a research geophysicist at a salary of $26,400. The defendant accepted the offer but before he commenced work, the defendant withdrew its offer of employment. Plaintiff brought suit for breach of contract in the Federal Court. That court certified the following question to the Oklahoma Supreme Court: Under Oklahoma law, does a hiring at a specified sum "per year" dictate the duration of the employment, or does such language merely connote the rate of compensation for an employment agreement which is otherwise terminable at will?

HODGES, J. . . . The determination of whether an employment contract is for a definite period of time or for an indefinite period terminable at the will of either party presents a question which is not free from doubt. Although the authorities are numerous, they are sharply conflicting. The minority of jurisdictions adhere to the English doctrine which holds where the duration of the contract is not specified, but where compensation is designated at a rate per day, week, month or year, it imports an employment for the stipulated period. The other presumption, the more modern American doctrine, repudiates the English doctrine and is the majority rule. It provides unless the circumstances indicate otherwise or in the absence of special consideration a contract of employment which provides that the employee shall receive a fixed sum for each day, week, month, or year of service, but makes no provision as to the duration of such service is an indefinite hiring terminable at the will of either party without incurring liability for breach of contract. The fact that an employee enters into a contract which merely specifies a salary proportionate to units of time which are utilized for the purposes of accounting or payment, such as a month or a year, does not, of itself, indicate the parties have agreed the employment is to continue for the stated unit of time. The specification is merely the indicia of the rate at which the salary is earned or is to be paid.

We therefore find, in the absence of facts and circumstances which indicate that an agreement is for a specific term, an employment contract which provides for an annual rate of compensation, but makes no provision as to the duration of the employment, is not a contract for one year, but is terminable at will by either party.

Cornell v. T.V. Development Corp.
215 N.E.2d 349 (N.Y) 1966

Plaintiff was wrongfully discharged as general manager of defendant corporation. Plaintiff sued for the unpaid salary to the end of his five-year employment contract. Plaintiff had formed a new company after his discharge but had not received a salary from it. The lower courts denied plaintiff any recovery for salary after he went to work for the new corporation, and plaintiff appealed.

SCILEPPI, J. . . . "There is a finding by both lower courts that the defendant wrongfully discharged the plaintiff. The only question presented is whether the plaintiff is then entitled to a judgment for the salary called for in the contract to its termination date. The breach of contract action is an action at law and the principles applicable thereto must be applied.

"The plaintiff is entitled to damages which will compensate him for the defendant's breach of contract. *Prima facie* the measure of such damage is 'the wage that would be payable during the remainder of the term'; but this is only the *prima facie* measure. The actual damage is measured by the wage that would be payable during the remainder of the term reduced by the income which the discharged employee has earned, will earn, or could with reasonable diligence earn during the unexpired term. The discharged employee's damages may be measured *prima facie* by the unpaid wage, but it is the present worth of the obligation to pay the wages at a time in the future that fixes the damages. Indeed, in the case of breach of contract of employment, not only time but the uncertainty of human life may be taken into consideration in fixing the present worth of an obligation to pay money due at some time in the future, after the trial." . . .

Here the proof shows that the plaintiff was borrowing funds to form a corporation for the purpose of going into the electronic business. At the time of trial, the corporation had no bank account; it owned no assets; and the plaintiff received no employment income after his discharge, but did receive $600 in unemployment insurance payments.

Defendant appears to have offered no proof of what, if anything, plaintiff earned or could have earned after his wrongful discharge. Instead, defendant makes the bare and . . . incorrect assertion that plaintiff had the burden of showing his prospective income from his newly formed corporation. From this incorrect premise, defendant concludes that, because plaintiff chose to form his own business venture, he is barred from further recovery.

The record shows that the plaintiff attempted to obtain employment after his wrongful discharge, and, failing to do so, started his own business with intention of promoting his invention, if upon trial he was awarded the right to use the invention. Under these circumstances, we fail to see how it could be held that the plaintiff's entry into corporate business barred his right to damages accruing after that date. . . .

After the plaintiff's failure to obtain employment, his decision to form a corporation from which he might reasonably expect to derive some financial benefit was consonant with his obligation to mitigate damages. . . . Therefore, the mere fact that plaintiff organized a corporation should not bar recovery on the ground that he took himself out of the employment field. By so holding, we avoid the absurdity of one rule of law calling upon the plaintiff to make reasonable efforts to mitigate his damages "while another rule required him to remain idle in order that he may recover full wages." . . .

In sum, the lower courts improperly concluded that plaintiff was barred from recovering anything for the period following formation of his corporation. Although defendant offered no proof of mitigation of damages, on this record, it would be needlessly harsh for us to require the defendant to pay over the balance due on the employment contract. Rather, we remit this case for a new trial on the question of damages only, at which trial the defendant will now be in a better position to show, if it can, the actual and prospective earnings of plaintiff from his corporate business. Plaintiff's corporation was just created about the time of trial. Enough time has now elapsed to permit an evaluation of his potential income from the corporation and the ascertainment of the income so far actually received by plaintiff therefrom.

We conclude that, in addition to the amount already paid, plaintiff is entitled to receive the present value of the money that would have been due him under the original contract, less what he has earned and can reasonably be expected to earn in his new corporate venture during the unexpired term of the contract. . . .

Order reversed, etc.

Sarokhan v. Fair Lawn Memorial Hospital, Inc.
199 A.2d 52 (N.J.) 1964

A doctor brought suit to enjoin a hospital from terminating his services as medical and surgery director and for other relief. Plaintiff had no financial investment in the hospital but had a written contract for ten years. The agreement provided that it could not be revoked or altered during the period. Plaintiff had organized the hospital and was given rather complete control over it. A controversy developed, and the board of directors of the hospital sought to discharge the plaintiff.

KILKENNY, J. The contract herein was one for the rendition of personal services. This is so even though the duties of the job required a person "knowledgeable in the medical arts and in the process of medical administration," as the contract noted. Personal service contracts are generally not specifically enforceable affirmatively. Equity will not compel performance of the personal services, even where the contract involves a "star" of unique talent, because equity will not make a vain decree. At most, equity will restrain violation of an express or implied negative covenant, thus precluding the performer from performing for somebody else.

So, too, it is a general rule that agency contracts are not specifically enforceable in a suit brought by the agent against his principal. Courts are not wont to force a principal to keep an agent against his will, "because the law has allowed every principal a power to revoke his deputation at any time." To do so would violate the basic concept in the law of agency, *viz.,* the right of the principal to select his own *alter ego,* to exercise his *delectus personarum.*

The mere fact that the appointment recites that it will be irrevocable during the term of the appointment does not preclude the principal from exercising the power to revoke it. So, too, "it is not necessary for the principal to have any good reasons for his action in revoking the agency, and he may cancel the

agent's authority at his caprice, even though the instrument creating the agency contains an express declaration of irrevocability." This does not mean that the principal may breach such a contract with impunity. For a wrongful breach, the agent may sue at law and recover money damages. Normally, that is the only remedy available to him. The same rule is applicable to a partnership agreement, a mutual agency relationship in which co-owners carry on a business for profit. . . .

Specific performance of personal services contracts is refused for the further reason that they lack mutuality of enforcement. The employee or agent, reinstated by judicial decree, might abandon his duties on the next day, and a court of equity could not compel him to perform. The wronged principal's only remedy would be an action at law for money damages. . . . [A] want of mutuality in the remedy warrants denial of specific performance. "If the enforcement of the obligation may not be granted to both contracting parties, it should not be enforced against one party."

The law has recognized, as an exception to the general rule, that "an agency coupled with an interest" cannot be revoked by the principal during the term fixed for its existence. Even the death of the principal does not terminate it. The best known case setting forth this exception is *Hunt* v. *Rousmanier* (8 Wheat. (U.S.) 174, 5. L.Ed. 589 (1823)). In that case, Hunt loaned money to Rousmanier and to secure repayment of the debt the borrower gave the lender a power of attorney to sell a vessel, with authority to deduct from the proceeds the balance due on the loan and turn over the residue to the borrower. The issue was whether the power survived the death of Rousmanier, the giver of the power. The rule was laid down that the death of the principal does not revoke an agency coupled with an interest.

Defendants concede that, if the contract herein created an agency coupled with an in-

terest, they would not have the power to revoke it. They maintain that such an agency was
not created. We agree. The test of an agency
coupled with an interest is stated in 2 Williston,
Contracts (3rd Ed.), § 280, pp. 301–302, as
follows:

> Does the agent have an interest or
> estate in the subject matter of the agency
> independent of the power conferred, or
> does the estate or interest accrue by or
> after the exercise of the power con-
> ferred?
>
> If the former, it is an agency coupled
> with an interest, or as has been suggested,
> a proprietary power; if the latter, it is
> not.

If the agency is given as security for a debt
or obligation, it is regarded as an agency
coupled with an interest. "In order that a power
may be irrevocable because coupled with an
interest, it is necessary that the interest shall
be in the subject matter of the power, and not
in the proceeds which will arise from the exercise of the power." (3 Am.Jur.2d, *Agency,*
§ 62.) The agency herein was not given as
security for some obligation due plaintiff. He
had no interest in the subject matter of the
power independent of the power conferred.
The power conferred by defendant hospital was
not one "coupled with an interest." Accordingly, it is not irrevocable, despite the terminology used by the parties.

We conclude that the contract in issue did
not create an agency coupled with an interest
and that defendants had and have the *power* to
terminate it. . . .

Reversed and remanded.

Zukaitis v. Aetna Cas. & Sur. Co.
236 N.W.2d 819 (Neb.) 1975

BLUE, J. . . . This is an action for a
declaratory judgment brought to determine
whether defendant-appellee, the Aetna Casualty
and Surety Company, was obligated under its
professional liability insurance policy to defend plaintiff-appellant, Raymond R. Zukaitis,
in a medical malpractice suit.

. . . Raymond R. Zukaitis was a physician practicing medicine in Douglas County,
Nebraska. Aetna issued Dr. Zukaitis a policy
of professional liability insurance through its
agent, the Ed Larsen Insurance Agency, Inc.
This policy was for a period from August 31,
1969, to August 31, 1970.

On August 7, 1971, Dr. Zukaitis received
a written notification of a claim for malpractice
which allegedly occurred on September 27,
1969. On August 10, 1971, Dr. Zukaitis telephoned the Ed Larsen Insurance Agency. At
the request of the agency the written claim
was forwarded to it by Dr. Zukaitis. This was
received on August 11, 1971, and was erroneously referred to the St. Paul Fire and
Marine Insurance Company on that date by the
agency.

Dr. Zukaitis was insured with St. Paul Fire
and Marine Insurance Company from August
31, 1970, to August 31, 1971. But on the date
of the alleged malpractice, he was insured with
Aetna. . . .

On November 22, 1971, a malpractice
action was brought against Dr. Zukaitis based
on the alleged malpractice of September 27,
1969. Attorneys for St. Paul undertook the
defense of the lawsuit. On January 25, 1974,
St. Paul discovered that it was not the insurance carrier for Dr. Zukaitis on September 27,
1969, the date of the alleged malpractice, and
advised Aetna of this at that time. Dr. Zukaitis
was also advised of this, and the attorney retained for St. Paul to represent Dr. Zukaitis
withdrew. Dr. Zukaitis made demand upon
Aetna on May 28, 1974, for it to undertake the
defense of Dr. Zukaitis, but this demand was
refused.

Dr. Zukaitis retained his own attorney to
represent him in the malpractice case. A motion for summary judgment was filed by Dr.
Zukaitis in that case, which motion was sustained. This action for a declaratory judgment

against Aetna therefore resolved itself into an effort to recover attorney's fees and costs. The District Court found for Aetna. . . .

Aetna contends that it is relieved from its obligation to Dr. Zukaitis since notice was given as required by paragraph 4(b) of the policy which provides: "If claim is made or suit is brought against the insured, the insured shall immediately forward to the company every demand, notice, summons or other process received by him or his representative."

Dr. Zukaitis contends that under the circumstances, notice to Aetna was given within a reasonable period in that the agent who wrote the policy was given notice. . . .

Ordinarily notice to a soliciting agent who countersigns and issues policies of insurance is notice to the insurance company. This is also true even if the agent forwards the notice to the wrong company. . . .

The question then is whether this is true after the agency contract between the insurance company and the agent has been terminated as it was in this case. To answer this, it is necessary to refer to the general law of agency.

The rule is that a revocation of the agent's authority does not become effective as between the principal and third persons until they receive notice of the termination.

Here, Dr. Zukaitis did what most reasonable persons would do in this situation; he notified the agent who sold him the policy. There is no evidence that notice of the termination was sent to him or that he knew the agency contract had been canceled.

It is stated in 3 Couch on Insurance 2d, § 26:50, p. 513: "When the insurer terminates the agency contract, it is its duty to notify third persons, such as the insureds with whom the agent dealt, and inform them of such termination. If it does not so notify and such third persons or insureds deal with the agent without notice or knowledge of the termination, and in reliance on the apparently continuing authority of the agent, the insurer is bound by the acts of the former agent."

The following appears in 3 Couch on Insurance 2d, § 26:50, p. 515: "The principle of the carrying over of the authority of an agent after termination with respect to third persons having no notice or knowledge thereof has been applied so as to bind the insurer when the third person dealt with the apparent agent by contracting with him, or by forwarding or delivering to him suit papers and proofs of loss. . . ."

The general rule . . . is that an insured is entitled to assume that an insurance agent is continuing to act within the scope of his agency, unless and until he has either actual or constructive notice to the contrary; and "a revocation by the principal, of the general authority of his agent, is ineffective as between the principal and such third persons as deal with the agent, as such, on the faith of the continued existence of his authority, without notice of the revocation."

We conclude that under the facts and circumstances of this case, the notice given by the plaintiff to the agent of the defendant constitutes notice to the defendant and would obligate defendant to carry out the terms of its insurance contract with plaintiff. . . .

Reversed.

CHAPTER 32
REVIEW QUESTIONS AND PROBLEMS

1. In December, P authorized A to act as his agent to sell stock. The power of attorney was to be "irrevocable" for one year. In April, P notified A that the power of attorney was terminated. Was the termination valid? Why?

2. X hired B to sell real estate. C was interested in purchasing the land and contacted B. A few days later, X died, and C learned about the death when he tried to contact X to get some information about the property. Y, the administratrix of the estate, sold the land to C, and B sued for a commission. Can B win? Explain.

3. X Mortgage Company lent money for the construction of a hotel and was to lease the entire second floor for the sum of $10 for a period of 20 years. The lease and agreement also appointed X as sole and exclusive agent for the management of the building. One year later, the hotel company assigned the lease and building to A. A then took over management of the building and claimed the agency was revocable by them at any time. Can A continue to manage the building? Why?

4. P owned a farm operated by his agent, A. A hired X to bale hay and bill P for the work. The next year, the agency was terminated. A again hired X to bale hay and send the bill to P. This time, P refused to pay because A was not his agent. Can X recover? Why?

5. A, a buyer for the X department store, was discharged. Y had never sold to A but knew that A was X's buyer. After A was discharged, an article about his changing jobs was in the newspaper, but Y did not read it. If A purchases goods on credit from Y, charging them to X, is X liable? Why?

6. P was employed by D under a contract stating that the employment "shall remain in effect for a period of twelve months and will be automatically renewed for twelve-month terms unless sooner terminated." P was discharged before the completion of the first twelve-month period. Was P wrongfully discharged? Why?

7. P had a ten-month teaching contract with the D School beginning August 31. In November, P was hospitalized for surgery and was unable to resume her teaching duties until April. In the interim, the school hired a replacement teacher. P sues, claiming that she is entitled to damages equal to her full salary for April, May, and June. Is P correct? Why?

8. P worked for D on an employment-at-will basis. While at work, P sustained an injury to his lower back. When P filed a claim for workmen's compensation, he was discharged by D. P brought suit, but D claimed that an "employee at will" can be discharged for any reason. Is D correct? Why?

9. A agreed in writing to employ B as a research assistant at an annual salary of $10,800. Four months later, A discharged B. B brought suit, claiming that the contract of employment was for one year and, therefore, she is entitled to compensation for eight months' salary. Is B correct? Why?

10. X was one-third owner of property upon which an apartment complex was constructed by the three owners. An agreement was then entered whereby X would receive an additional 12 percent of the profits for supervising the operation of the apartment building. Is X an agent coupled with an interest? Why?

book six

BUSINESS ORGANIZATIONS

Choosing the Form
of Organization

1. Introduction

Business organizations may operate under a variety of legal forms. The most common ones are sole proprietorships, partnerships, limited partnerships, and corporations. There are also some specialized organizations, such as professional service corporations, that are authorized by statute so that doctors, lawyers, dentists, and other professional persons are able to obtain the tax advantages of corporations.

This chapter will examine the various forms of organization and the factors that influence the actual selection of a particular form. The factors involved in in this selection are applicable to all businesses, from the smallest to the largest, but the relative influence of the various factors varies greatly depending on the size of the business. As a practical matter, the very large business must be incorporated, because this is the only method that can bring a large number of owners and investors together for an extended period of time. The difficulty of deciding which is the best form of organization to select is most often encountered in the closely held business. It should also be kept in mind that taxation is usually the most significant contributing factor. Although a detailed discussion of the tax laws is beyond the scope of this text, some of the general principles of taxation will be presented in order to illustrate the influence taxation brings to bear in choosing diverse organizational forms.

2. General Partnerships

Partnerships developed logically in the law merchant, and the common law of partnerships has been codified in most states in the Uniform Partnership Act. A *partnership* is an association of two or more persons to carry on as co-owners, a business for profit. It is the result of an agreement.

This form of organization has many advantages: (1) Since it is a matter of contract between individuals to which the state is not a party, it is easily formed; (2) the costs of formation are minimal; (3) it is not a taxable entity; (4) each owner as a general rule has an equal voice in management; (5) it may operate in more than one state without being required to comply with many legal formalities; and (6) partnerships are generally subject to less regulation and less government supervision than corporations are. The fact that a partnership is not a taxable entity does not mean that partnership income is tax free. A partnership files an information return allocating its income or losses among the partners, and each partner pays income tax on the portion of income or deducts the loss allocated to him.

Several aspects of partnerships may be considered disadvantageous in many cases. First, as a practical matter, only a limited number of people may own such a business. Second, a partnership is dissolved any time a member ceases to be a partner either by withdrawal or death. Although dissolution is the subject matter of Chapter 36, it should be observed here that the perpetual existence of a corporation is often a distinct advantage as compared to easily dissolved partnerships.

Third, the liability of a partner is unlimited as contrasted with the limited liability of a shareholder. The unlimited liability of a partner is applicable to both contract and tort claims. Fourth, since a partner is taxed on his share of the profits of a partnership whether distributed to him or not, a partner may be required to pay income tax on money that is not received. This burden is an important consideration in a new business that is reinvesting its profits for expansion. A partner in such a business would have to have an independent means of paying the taxes on such income.

3. Limited Partnerships

A *limited partnership,* just like other partnerships, comes into existence by virtue of an agreement. However, a limited partnership is like a corporation in that it is authorized by statute, and the liability of one or more of the partners, but not of all, is limited to the amount of capital contributed at the time of the creation of the partnership. A limited partnership is composed of one or more general partners who manage the business and who are personally liable for its debts. It also includes one or more limited partners who contribute capital and share in profits and losses but who take no part in running the business, and who incur no liability with respect to partnership obligations beyond their contribution to capital. Because of the limited liability of the limited partners, the organization is called a limited partnership.

Such organizations are governed in most states by the Uniform Limited Partnership Act provisions. The purpose of this statute is to encourage trade by permitting persons possessing capital to invest in the business and reap their share of the profits without becoming liable for debts, or risking in the venture more than the capital contributed. This reduced risk is conditioned on the investor's not holding himself out as general partner or participating actively in the conduct of the business.

To create a limited partnership under the Uniform Limited Partnership Act, the parties must sign and swear to a certificate containing the following information: the name of the partnership; the character of the business; its location; the name and place of residence of each member; those who are to be the general and those who are to be the limited partners; the term for which the partnership is to exist; the amount of cash or the agreed value of property to be contributed by each partner; the additional contributions, if any, to be made from time to time by each partner; the time that any such contributions are to be returned to the limited partner; the share of profit or compensation each limited partner shall receive and the rights of the limited partners, if any; and the right of the remaining general partners to continue the business on the death, retirement, or incapacity of other partners.

The certificate must be recorded in the county where the partnership has its principal place of business or with the secretary of state, depending on state law. In addition, most states require notice by newspaper publication. In the event of any change in the facts contained in the certificate as filed, such as a change in the name of the partnership, the capital, or other matters, a new certificate must be filed. If such a certificate is not filed and the partnership continues, the limited partners immediately become liable as general partners.

The statutes of most states require the partnership to conduct its business in a firm name that does not include the name of any of the limited partners or the word *company*. Some states specify that the word *limited* shall be added to the name.

A limited partner is not liable beyond his contribution to creditors of the partnership in the pursuit of the partnership business, unless the limited partner participates in the management and control of the business. Participation in management makes the limited partner a general partner with unlimited liability, notwithstanding the certificate. This unlimited liability cannot be avoided by use of a corporation as the general partner if the limited partners are in control of the corporate general partner.[1]

A limited partnership cannot be dissolved voluntarily before the time for its termination as stated in the certificate without the filing and publication of

---

[1] *DeLaney* v. *Fidelity Lease Limited,* page 636.

the notice of dissolution. Upon dissolution, the distribution of the assets of the firm is prescribed in the statute that gives priority to limited partners over general partners after all creditors are paid.

The limited partnership as a tax shelter is of special value in many new businesses, and especially in real estate ventures such as shopping centers and apartment complexes. It gives the investor limited liability and the operators control of the venture. It allows the maximum use of the tax advantages of accelerated depreciation and the investment credit. Accelerated depreciation usually results in a tax loss in early years, which can be immediately deducted by the limited partner. (If the investor were a corporate shareholder, the loss would be carried forward until an offsetting profit existed.) However, there is usually a positive cash flow to the organization, notwithstanding the tax loss. Thus, a limited partner may be able to receive income and at the same time a loss for tax purposes. When such ventures start to show a taxable gain, the limited partnership is often dissolved and a corporation formed, or the venture is sold.

The obvious disadvantage in a limited partnership is the fact that the limited partner cannot participate in management without a change of status to that of a general partner. However, a limited partner does have a right to inspect the books of the business, to receive an accounting, and to engage in activities that are of an advisory nature and do not amount to participation in the control of the business.[2]

4. Revised Uniform Limited Partnership Act

In 1976, the Commissioners on Uniform State Laws issued a revised Uniform Limited Partnership Act. Although this act has not yet been adopted by very many states, it will in all probability become the law in most states in the future. The revised act tends to make a limited partnership more like a corporation.

Under the revised act, the name of the limited partnership must contain the words "limited partnership." The name may not contain the name of a limited partner unless his name is also the name of a general partner or the name had been used prior to the admission of that limited partner.

A limited partnership under the new law is required to maintain a registered office within the state and an agent to receive notices for it. The law requires that certain records, such as a list of all partners and a copy of the certificate of the limited partnership, be maintained at this office. There must also be kept copies of the partnership tax returns for three years and copies of all financial statements for the same period.

Under the revised act, the certificate creating the partnership is filed with the secretary of state. If it is later amended or canceled, the certificates of amendment and cancellation are also filed in that office.

[2] *Trans-Am Builders, Inc.* v. *Woods Mill Ltd.*, page 637.

The revised act makes a substantial change in the liability of a limited partner who participates in the control of the business. The liability of a general partner is imposed on a limited partner who participates in the control of the business only if the third party had knowledge of the participation. In addition, the act provides that a limited partner does not participate in the control of the business by (1) being an agent or employee of the business, (2) consulting with or advising a partner with respect to the partnership, (3) acting as surety of the limited partnership, (4) approving or disapproving of an amendment to the certificate, and (5) voting on such matters as dissolution, sale of assets, or a change of name.

5. Joint Venture

A joint venture, or joint adventure, occurs when two or more persons combine their efforts in a particular busines enterprise and agree to share the profits or losses jointly or in proportion to their contributions. It is to be distinguished from a partnership in that the joint venture is a less formal association and contemplates a single transaction or a limited activity, whereas a partnership contemplates the operation of a general business. It is a specific venture without the formation of a partnership or corporation.

While a partnership in most states is a legal entity, apart from the partners, a joint venture is not. A joint venture cannot sue or be sued except by or on behalf of the joint venturers individually.

Joint ventures file a partnership tax return and have many of the other legal aspects of partnerships. For example, the parties stand in a fiduciary relationship with each other and are agents for purposes of tort liability.

6. The Business Corporation

A *corporation* comes into existence by an act of the state. It is a legal entity that usually has perpetual existence. The liability of the owners is limited to their investment unless there is a successful "piercing of the corporate veil." This is discussed in Chapter 37. A corporation is a taxable entity paying a tax on its net profits. In addition, dividends paid to stockholders are also taxable, giving rise to the frequently made observation that corporate income is subject to double taxation. The accuracy of this observation will be discussed later.

The advantages of the corporate form of organization may be briefly summarized as follows: (1) It is the only method that will raise substantial capital from a large number of investors; (2) the investors have limited liability; (3) the organization can have perpetual existence; (4) it is possible for control to be vested in those with a minority of the investment by using such techniques as nonvoting or preferred stock; (5) ownership may be divided into many separate and unequal shares; (6) the investors, notwithstanding their status as owners, may also be employees entitled to such benefits as workmen's compensation; (7) certain laws, such as those relating to usury, are not applicable to corporations; and (8) the tax laws have several provisions that are favorable to corporations.

Among the frequently cited disadvantages of the corporate form of organization are (1) the cost of forming and maintaining the corporate form, with its rather formal procedures; (2) expenditures such as license fees and franchise taxes that are assessed against corporations but not against partnerships; (3) the double taxation of corporate income and the frequently higher tax rates; (4) the requirement that it must be qualified to do business in a state; [3] (5) the fact that corporations are subject to more regulation by government at all levels than are other forms; and (6) that a corporation must use an attorney in litigation, whereas a layman can proceed on his own behalf. [4]

7. Taxation of Corporate Income

The fact that taxation was listed as both an advantage and a disadvantage of the corporate form illustrates the overwhelming importance of the tax factor in choosing this particular form of organization. One of the forces that has given great impetus to the incorporation of thousands of businesses and professional practices is the Internal Revenue Code provisions on qualified pension and profit-sharing plans.

These provisions allow a corporation to deduct from taxable income its payments under qualified plans. These payments are invested, and the earnings are not subject to taxation when earned. Income tax is paid by the recipients on retirement at a time when the taxpayer has additional exemptions and probably a lower tax rate. To illustrate the advantages of such plans, assume that A, B, and C are shareholders and employees of the ABC Company. Assume also that the company has five additional employees and that the net income of the company is $100,000. If ABC Company pays $20,000 to a qualified plan, the income tax deduction is $9,600 (assuming a 48 percent rate). The net cost of the payment to the company is $10,400. The $20,000 is credited to the accounts of the employees by a formula based on wages and years of service. Assume that the amount credited to A, B, and C is $12,000. This gives them an initial gain of $1,600 and a tax-free investment. In addition, the employees have received benefits and security. A, B, and C, as well as the other employees, would receive their benefits upon retirement at a time when their tax rates would be lower and exemptions increased.

Other advantages of the tax laws to corporations are that (1) health-insurance payments are fully deductible and are not subject to the limitations applicable to individuals; (2) deferred compensation plans may be adopted; (3) earnings up to $25,000 are currently taxed at a rate of 20 percent, and the next $25,000 of earnings are currently taxed at the rate of 22 percent, both of which are often lower than the individual investor's tax rate; (4) in-

3 *Eli Lilly and Company* v. *Sav-On-Drugs, Inc.,* page 640.
4 *Land Management* v. *Department of Envir. Protec.,* page 641.

come that is needed in the business is not taxed to a person who does not receive it; (5) accumulated income can be taken out as a capital gain on dissolution; (6) the corporation may provide life insurance for its employees as a deductible expense; and (7) medical expenses in excess of health-insurance coverage may be paid on behalf of employees as a deductible expense.

The corporate form is frequently at a disadvantage from a tax standpoint because of the double-taxation aspect and because the 48 percent rate often exceeds the individual rate of the owners of the business. In addition, some states impose a higher tax on corporate income than on individual income. There are also many taxes that are imposed on corporations but not on individuals or partnerships.

In connection with the double taxation of corporate income, it should be noted that certain techniques may be used to avoid, in part, this double taxation. First of all, reasonable salaries paid to corporate employees may be deducted in computing the taxable income of the business. Thus, in a closely held corporation, in which all or most shareholders are officers or employees, this technique can be used to avoid double taxation of much of the corporate income. However, the Internal Revenue Code disallows a deduction for excessive or unreasonable compensation, and such payments are taxable as dividends. Therefore, the determination of the reasonableness of corporate salaries is an ever-present tax problem in the closely held corporation.

Second, the capital structure of a corporation may include both common stock and interest-bearing loans from shareholders. For example, assume that a company needs $200,000 to commence business. If $200,000 of stock is purchased, there will be no expense to be deducted. However, assume that $100,000 worth of stock is purchased and $100,000 is lent to the company at 8 percent interest. In this case, $8,000 of interest each year is deductible as an expense of the company, and thus subject to only one tax as interest income to the owners. Just as in the case of salaries, the Internal Revenue Code contains a counteracting rule relating to corporations that are undercapitalized. If the corporation is undercapitalized, interest payments will be treated as dividends and disallowed as deductible expenses.

The third technique for avoiding double taxation, at least in part, is simply not to pay dividends and to accumulate the earnings. After the earnings have been accumulated, the shareholders can sell their stock or dissolve the corporation. In both situations, the difference between the original investment and the amount received is given capital gains treatment, and thus double taxation is partially avoided. Here again, we have tax laws designed to counteract the technique above. There is a special income tax imposed on "excessive accumulated earnings" in addition to the normal tax, and rules relating to collapsible corporations.

Finally, there is a special provision in the Internal Revenue Code that allows small, closely held business corporations to be treated similarly to partnerships for income tax purposes. These corporations, known as Subchapter S corporations, are discussed more fully in the next section.

8.   The Subchapter S Corporation

The limited partnership is a hybrid between a corporation and a partnership in the area of liability. A similar hybrid, known as a *tax-option* or *Subchapter S corporation,* exists in the tax area of the law. Such corporations have the advantages of the corporate form of organization without the problem of double taxation of income.

The tax-option corporation is one that elects to be taxed in a manner similar to that of partnerships—i.e., to file an information return allocating income among the shareholders for immediate reporting regardless of dividend distributions, thus avoiding any tax on the part of the corporation.

A Subchapter S corporation cannot have more than ten shareholders to begin with. After it is in existence for five years, it may have up to fifteen shareholders, each of whom must sign the election to be taxed in the manner similar to a partnership. Corporations with more than 20 percent of their income from rents, interest, dividends, or royalties do not qualify. There are many technical rules of tax law involved in Subchapter S corporations, but as a rule of thumb, this method of taxation has distinct advantages for a business operating at a loss, because the loss is shared and immediately deductible on the returns of the shareholders. It is also advantageous for businesses capable of paying out net profits as earned. In the latter case, the corporate tax is avoided. If net profits must be retained in the business, Subchapter S tax treatment may be disadvantageous because income tax is paid on earnings not received. There is also a danger of double taxation to the individual, because undistributed earnings that have been taxed once are taxed again in the event of the death of a shareholder. However, the tax laws relating to pension plans reduce the advantages of such corporations. They have equal status with partnerships and sole proprietorships for pension plan purposes. This status is discussed more fully in the next section.

9.   The Professional Service Association

Traditionally, professional services, such as those of a doctor, lawyer, or dentist, could be performed only by an individual and could not be performed by a corporation because the relationship of doctor and patient or attorney and client was considered a highly personal one. The impersonal corporate entity could not render the personal services involved.

The tax advantages of profit-sharing and pension plans previously discussed in connection with corporations are not available to sole proprietors and to partners in partnerships to the same extent that they are available in corporations. An individual proprietor or partner is limited to a deduction of 15 percent of income or $7,500, whichever is less, under what is usually referred to as the *H.R. 10,* or *Keogh, pension-plan provision.* Therefore, professional persons often desire to incorporate or to form a professional association in order to obtain these tax advantages. To make this possible, every state has enacted statutes authorizing professional associations. These associations are legal entities similar to corporations, and they are allowed deductions for payments to qualified pension and profit-sharing plans.

To illustrate the advantages of a professional corporation or association, assume that a doctor has a net income of $100,000. If he is unincorporated, he may pay $7,500 into a retirement plan. However, if he incorporates his practice, he may pay $25,000 into a qualified pension (10 percent, or $10,-000) and profit-sharing (15 percent, or $15,000) plan. Of this $25,000, one-half, or $12,500, is in tax savings, since his income would be taxed at the 50 percent rate. The earnings of the $25,000 invested are tax free until retirement. In addition, he can deduct health-insurance premiums, pay additional personal medical expenses as a deductible expense, and provide up to $50,000 of life insurance with tax-free dollars. The cost of these savings is whatever is paid into the plan to cover his employees.

Although the foregoing illustration may not be typical of all professional persons, there is obviously great impetus in the law for the formation of professional associations. Today, there are thousands of professional corporations. They can be identified by the letters *S.C.* (Service Corporation), *P.C.* (Professional Corporation), or *Inc.* (Incorporated), or by the word *company* in the name of the firm.

10. Making the Decision

The business with substantial capitalization will be a corporation for the reasons previously noted. If the business is to be owned and operated by relatively few persons, the decision as to the form of organization involves a consideration of the factors previously discussed, the most significant of which are (1) taxation, (2) liability, (3) control, (4) continuity, and (5) legal capacity. *Legal capacity* is the power of the business to sue and be sued in its own name and the power to own and dispose of property as well as to enter into contracts in its own name.

In evaluating the impact of taxation, an accountant or attorney will look at the projected profits or losses of the business, the ability to distribute earnings, and the tax brackets of the individuals involved as owners. A computation of the estimated total tax burden under the various forms of organization will be made. The results will be considered, along with the other factors, in making the decision as to the form of business organization to be used.

The generalization that partners have unlimited liability and stockholders limited liability must be qualified in the case of a closely held business. A small, closely held corporation with limited assets and capital will find it difficult to obtain credit on the strength of its own credit standing alone, and as a practical matter, the shareholders will usually be required to add their own individual liability as security for the debts. For example, if the XYZ Company seeks a loan at a local bank, the bank will require the owners X, Y, and Z to personally guarantee repayment of the loan. This is not to say that closely held corporations do not have some degree of limited liability. The investors in those types of businesses are protected with limited liability for contractlike obligations that are imposed as a matter of law (such as taxes) and for debts resulting from torts that are committed by company employees while engaged in company business.

If the tax aspects dictate a partnership, and limited liability is desired by some investors, the limited partnership will be considered.

The significance of the law relating to control will be apparent in the discussions on formation and operation of partnerships and corporations in the chapters that follow. The desire of one or more individuals to control the business is a major factor in selecting the form, and the control issues are second only to taxation in importance.

The table on pages 638 and 639 summarizes the factors that are considered in choosing a form of organization.

CHOOSING THE FORM OF ORGANIZATION CASES

DeLaney v. Fidelity Lease Limited
526 S.W.2d 543 (Tex.) 1975

Fidelity Lease Limited is a limited partnership consisting of 22 limited partners and a corporate general partner. Three of the limited partners were the officers and directors of the corporate general partner. When the limited partnership breached a contract with the plaintiff, suit was brought against three of the limited partners individually. It was contended that they had become general partners by participating in the management of the limited partnership. The lower courts held that the individuals were not liable and the plaintiff appealed.

DANIEL, J. . . . The question here is whether limited partners in a limited partnership become liable as general partners if they "take part in the control of the business" while acting as officers of a corporation which is the sole general partner of the limited partnership. . . .

Pertinent portions of the Texas Uniform Limited Partnership Act, Article 6132a, provide:

> Sec. 8. A limited partner shall not become liable as a general partner unless, in addition to the exercise of his rights and powers as a limited partner, he takes part in the control of the business. . . .

It was alleged by plaintiffs, and there is summary judgment evidence, that the three limited partners controlled the business of the limited partnership, albeit through the corporate entity. The defendant limited partners argue that they acted only through the corporation and that the corporation actually controlled the business of the limited partnership. In response to this contention, we adopt the following statements in the dissenting opinion of Chief Justice Preslar in the court of civil appeals:

> I find it difficult to separate their acts for they were at all times in the dual capacity of limited partners and officers of the corporation. Apparently the corporation had no function except to operate the limited partnership and Appellees were obligated to their other partners to so operate the corporation as to benefit the partnership. Each act was done then, not for the corporation, but for the partnership. Indirectly, if not directly, they were exercising control over the partnership. Truly "the corporation fiction" was in this instance a fiction.

Thus, we hold that the personal liability, which attaches to a limited partner when "he takes part in the control and management of the business," cannot be evaded merely by acting through a corporation.

Crombie, Kahn, and Sanders argue that, since their only control of Fidelity's business was as officers of the alleged corporate general partner, they are insulated from personal liability arising from their activities or those of the corporation. This is a general rule of corporate law, but one of several exceptions in which the courts will disregard the corporate fiction is where it is used to circumvent a statute. That is precisely the result here, for it is undisputed that the corporation was organized to manage and control the limited partnership. Strict compliance with the statute is required if a limited partner is to avoid liability as a general partner. It is quite clear that there can be more than one general partner. Assuming that Interlease Corporation was a legal general partner . . . this would not prevent Crombie, Kahn, and Sanders from taking part in the control of the business in their individual capacities as well as their corporate capacities. In no event should they be permitted to escape the statutory liability which would have devolved upon them if there had been no attempted interposition of the corporate shield against personal liability. Otherwise, the statutory requirement of at least one general partner with general liability in a limited partnership can be circumvented or vitiated by limited partners operating the partnership through a corporation with minimum capitalization and therefore minimum liability. We hold that . . . if . . . either of these three limited partners took part in the control of the business, whether or not in his capacity as an officer of Interlease Corporation, he should be adjudged personally liable as a general partner.

Reversed.

Trans-Am Builders, Inc. v. Woods Mill, Ltd.
210 S.E.2d 866 (Ga.) 1974

STOLZ, J. . . . The litigation before us arose out of the construction of an apartment complex involving Trans-Am Builders, Inc., as general contractor (appellant) and Woods Mill, Ltd., a limited partnership (appellee) with a number of individuals as limited partners and The Baier Corporation as the general partner. . . .

During the construction of the project, financial difficulties arose, resulting in appellant's either abandoning or being removed from the project. Suits and countersuits were filed. However, there is but one issue before us, that is, have the limited partners conducted themselves in such a manner as to "take part in the control of the business" and thus become liable as a general partner? . . .

Code Ann. § 75-411 provides as follows: (1) A limited partner shall have the same rights as a general partner to (a) Have the partnership books kept at the principal place of business of the partnership, and at all times to inspect and copy any of them. (b) Have on demand true and full information of all things affecting the partnership, and a formal account of partnership affairs whenever circumstances

COMPARISON OF CHARACTERISTICS OF BUSINESS ORGANIZATIONS

| Characteristic | Corporations | | Partnerships | |
	General	Subchapter S	General	Limited
1. Method of creation	Charter issued by state	Same + file agreement with IRS	Created by agreement of the parties	Same + file statutory form in public office
2. Liability of members	Shareholders have limited liability	Same	Partners have unlimited liability	General partners—unlimited liability; limited partners—limited liability
3. Duration	May be perpetual	Same	Termination by death, agreement, bankruptcy, or withdrawal of a partner	The term provided in the certificate
4. Transferability of interest	Generally freely transferable subject to limits of contacts between shareholders	Same	Not transferable	General partner—not transferable; limited partner—transferable
5. Management	Shareholders elect directors who set policy	Same	All partners in absence of agreement have equal voice	General partners have equal voice; limited partners have no voice
6. Taxation	Income taxed to corporation; dividends taxed to shareholders	Net income taxed to shareholders whether distributed or not	Not a taxable entity—net income taxed to partners whether distributed or not	Same

COMPARISON OF CHARACTERISTICS OF BUSINESS ORGANIZATIONS—Continued

Characteristic	Corporations		Partnerships	
	General	Subchapter S	General	Limited
7. Legal entity for progress of: a. Suit in firm name b. Owning property in firm name c. Bankruptcy d. Limiting liability	Is a legal entity in all states; for all purposes	Same	By modern law is an entity for a. Yes b. Yes c. Yes d. No	Same
8. Transact business in other states	Must qualify to do business and obtain certificate of authority	Same	No limitation	Copy of certificate must be filed in all counties where doing business
9. Organization fee, annual license fee, and annual reports	All required	Same	None	None
10. Modification of or amendment of articles	Must obtain state approval	Same	No requirement	Must file changes
11. Agency	A shareholder is not an agent of the corporation	Same	Each partner is both a principal and an agent of his copartners	Limited partners are not principals or agents; general partners are the same as in general partnership

render it just and reasonable. (c) Have dissolution and winding up by decree of court. (2) A limited partner shall have the right to receive a share of the profits or other compensation by way of income, and to the return of his contribution. . . .

The evidence before us reveals that the limited partners (with one exception) held at least two meetings after it became apparent that the project was in financial difficulty. At these meetings the situation was presented by a representative of the general partner, discussions were participated in, and additional money was raised to meet financial obligations. At least one of the limited partners went to the project and went over it with the appellant's superintendent, and "obnoxiously" complained and objected to the way the work was being conducted, but there is nothing to indicate that he gave any directions which may have been followed by the plaintiff's superintendent. . . . The appellant contends that these actions violated Code Ann. § 75-411, *supra,* and that the limited partners thus became general partners. The trial judge held otherwise and sustained the limited partners' motion for summary judgment, from which judgment the plaintiff appeals. . . .

It is well established that just because a man is a limited partner in an enterprise he is not by reason of that status precluded from continuing to have an interest in the affairs of the partnership, from giving advice and suggestions to the general partner or his nominees, and from interesting himself in specific aspects of the business. Such casual advice as limited partners may have given to [the employees] can hardly be said to be interference in day-to-day management. Certainly common sense dictates that in times of severe financial crisis all partners in such an enterprise, limited or general, will become actively interested in any effort to keep the enterprise afloat and many abnormal problems will arise that are not under any stretch of the imagination mere day-to-day matters of managing the partnership business. This is all that occurred in this instance. . . .

It would be unreasonable to hold that a limited partner may not advise with the general partner and visit the partnership business, particularly when the project is confronted with a severe financial crisis.

Judgment affirmed.

Eli Lilly and Company v. Sav-On-Drugs, Inc.
366 U.S. 276 1961

BLACK, J. The appellant Eli Lilly and Company, an Indiana corporation dealing in pharmaceutical products, brought this action in a New Jersey state court to enjoin the appellee Sav-On-Drugs, Inc., a New Jersey corporation, from selling Lilly's products in New Jersey at prices lower than those fixed in minimum retail price contracts into which Lilly had entered with a number of New Jersey drug retailers. . . . Sav-On moved to dismiss this complaint under a New Jersey statute that denies a foreign corporation transacting business in the State the right to bring any action in New Jersey upon any contract made there unless and until it files with the New Jersey Secretary of

State a copy of its charter together with a limited amount of information about its operations and obtains from him a certificate authorizing it to do business in the State.

Lilly opposed the motion to dismiss, urging that its business in New Jersey was entirely in interstate commerce and arguing, upon that ground, that the attempt to require it to file the necessary information and obtain a certificate for its New Jersey business was forbidden by the Commerce Clause of the Federal Constitution. Both parties offered evidence to the Court in the nature of affidavits as to the extent and kind of business done by Lilly with New Jersey companies and people. On this evidence, the trial court made findings of fact and granted Sav-On's motion to dismiss, stating as its ground that "the conclusion is inescapable that the plaintiff [Lilly] was in fact doing business in this State at the time of the acts complained of and was required to, but did not, comply with the provisions of the Corporation Act." . . . The State Supreme Court . . . affirmed the judgment upholding the statute. . . . We noted probable jurisdiction to consider Lilly's contention that the constitutional question was improperly decided by the state courts.

The record shows that the New Jersey trade in Lilly's pharmaceutical products is carried on through both interstate and intrastate channels. Lilly manufactures these products and sells them in interstate commerce to certain selected New Jersey wholesalers. These wholesalers then sell the products in intrastate commerce to New Jersey hospitals, physicians and retail drugstores, and these retail stores in turn sell them, again in intrastate commerce, to the general public. It is well established that New Jersey cannot require Lilly to get a certificate of authority to do business in the State if its participation in this trade is limited to its wholly interstate sales to New Jersey wholesalers. Under the authority of the so-called "drummer" cases . . . Lilly is free to send salesmen into New Jersey to promote this interstate trade without interference from regulations imposed by the State. On the other hand, it is equally well settled that if Lilly is engaged in intrastate as well as interstate aspects of the New Jersey drug business, the State can require it to get a certificate of authority to do business. In such a situation, Lilly could not escape state regulation merely because it is also engaged in interstate commerce. We must then look to the record to determine whether Lilly is engaged in intrastate commerce in New Jersey.

The findings of the trial court, based as they are upon uncontroverted evidence presented to it, show clearly that Lilly is conducting an intrastate as well as an interstate business in New Jersey. . . .

We agree with the trial court that "[t]o hold under the facts above recited that plaintiff [Lilly] is not doing business in New Jersey is to completely ignore reality." Eighteen "detailmen," working out of a big office in Newark, New Jersey, with Lilly's name on the door and in the lobby of the building, and with Lilly's district manager and secretary in charge, have been regularly engaged in work for Lilly which relates directly to the intrastate aspects of the sale of Lilly's products. These eighteen "detailmen" have been traveling throughout the State of New Jersey promoting the sales of Lilly's products, not to the wholesalers, Lilly's interstate customers, but to the physicians, hospitals and retailers who buy those products in intrastate commerce from the wholesalers. To this end, they have provided these hospitals, physicians and retailers with up-to-date knowledge of Lilly's products and with free advertising and promotional material designed to encourage the general public to make more intrastate purchases of Lilly's products. And they sometimes even directly participate in the intrastate sales themselves by transmitting orders from the hospitals, physicians and drugstores they service to the New Jersey wholesalers. . . .

Affirmed.

Land Management v. Department of Envir. Protec.
368 A.2d 602 (ME) 1977

ARCHIBALD, J. . . . The sole issue raised by this appeal is whether the presiding Justice acted properly in dismissing the plaintiff's complaint on the ground that the plaintiff was a corporation not represented by a duly admitted attorney. We conclude that the Justice below correctly dismissed the complaint, and we therefore deny the plaintiff's appeal.

The plaintiff, Land Management, Inc., is a corporation doing business in the State of

Maine. On April 9, 1976, it commenced an action in the Superior Court seeking declaratory and injunctive relief against the defendants. Throughout the proceedings in the Superior Court the plaintiff was represented by its president who, admittedly, is not an attorney admitted to practice law in Maine.

All of the defendants filed motions to dismiss the plaintiff's complaint. . . . [These were granted] solely on the basis

> that the Plaintiff Land Management, Inc. is not entitled to proceed in this action acting *pro se* by and through a person who is not an attorney licensed to practice law.

In support of its position that a corporation may represent itself in Maine courts through a corporate officer who is not a duly admitted attorney, the plaintiff relies upon language found in 4 M.R.S.A. §§ 807 and 811.

4 M.R.S.A. § 807 provides:

> Unless duly admitted to the bar of this State, no person shall practice law or any branch thereof, or hold himself out to practice law or any branch thereof, within the State or before any court therein, or demand or receive any remuneration for such services rendered in this State. Whoever, not being duly admitted to the bar of this State, shall practice law or any branch thereof, or hold himself out to practice law or any branch thereof, within the State or before any court therein, or demand or receive any remuneration for such services rendered in this State, shall be punished by a fine of not more than $500 or by imprisonment for not more than three months, or by both. This section shall not be construed to apply to practice before any Federal Court by any person duly admitted to practice therein nor to a person pleading or managing his own cause in court. . . .

4 M.R.S.A. § 811 defines a "person" as "any individual, corporation, partnership or association."

On the basis of these statutory provisions, the plaintiff contends that since a corporation can only act through its agents, it may authorize a non-attorney to represent it in court. We do not agree with the plaintiff's assertion that the Legislature, in enacting §§ 807 and 811, intended to permit a corporation to be represented before the courts of this State by a person who is not authorized to practice law. To accept plaintiff's argument would require us to hold that a corporation may authorize a non-attorney to represent it in court, while an individual may not. We do not believe that the Legislature intended such an illogical result. The purpose of § 811 for including a corporation within the definition of the word "person" was to make it clear that a corporation, as well as anyone else, is prohibited from engaging in the unauthorized practice of law. This section modified the § 807 prohibition against unauthorized practice rather than expanding the right of individuals to represent themselves in either the Federal or State courts.

The rule that a corporation may appear in court only through a licensed attorney was stated succinctly in *Paradise* v. *Nowlin,* 86 Cal. App.2d 897, 195 P.2d 867 (1948):

> A natural person may represent himself and present his own case to the court although he is not a licensed attorney. A corporation is not a natural person. It is an artificial entity created by law and as such it can neither practice law nor appear or act in person. Out of court it must act in its affairs through its agents and representatives and in matters in court it can act only through licensed attorneys. A corporation cannot appear in court by an officer who is not an attorney and it cannot appear in *propria persona.*

Sound public policy reasons also require such a rule. As stated by the Ohio Supreme Court:

> To allow a corporation to maintain litigation and appear in court represented by corporate officers or agents only would

lay open the gates to the practice of law for entry to those corporate officers or agents who have not been qualified to practice law and who are not amenable to the general discipline of the court.

There is abundant authority, both state and federal, rejecting the argument, as ad-vanced by the plaintiff, that a corporation has the right to appear in court without the aid of a licensed attorney.

Since the plaintiff was not represented by counsel licensed to practice law, its complaint was a nullity and was properly dismissed by the presiding Justice.

Appeal denied.

CHAPTER 33
REVIEW QUESTIONS AND PROBLEMS

1. A and B each had a license to sell cars. They agreed to share the same lot, building, furnishings, telephone, etc., but the businesses would be run independently. C sued A and B for fraud, committed by B, claiming they were joint venturers. Is A liable for the fraudulent conduct of B? Why?

2. A, B, and C, three physicians, operated the Sunnyhill Sanitarium as partners. As a result of C's medical negligence, X, a patient, died. May X's wife recover for wrongful death from A and B? Why?

3. A and B orally agreed to purchase and to operate a motel-restaurant, although no formal partnership agreement was ever executed. B purchased the motel-restaurant personally, without informing A of the transaction. Does A have a remedy against B? Why?

4. A, B, and C filed articles of incorporation with the state of Ohio, but failed to perfect the corporation by fulfilling all the statutory requirements. They proceeded to operate a warehouse together. X entered the warehouse and because of A's negligence fell down an abandoned elevator shaft. May X recover from the personal assets of B and C? Why?

5. John Doe and Richard Roe wish to enter the camping-equipment manufacturing business. Assume each of the following facts. In each case, which type of business association would be most advantageous? Explain.

    a. Doe is an expert in the field of camping-gear production and sale, but has no funds. Roe knows nothing about such production, but is willing to contribute all necessary capital.

    b. Camping-gear production requires large amounts of capital, much more than Doe and Roe can raise personally or together, yet they wish to control the business.

    c. Some phases of production and sale are rather dangerous, and a relatively large number of tort judgments may be anticipated.

d.   Sales will take place on a nationwide basis.

e.   Doe and Roe are both 65 years old. No profits are expected for at least five years, and interruption of the business before that time will make it a total loss.

f.   Several other people wish to put funds into the business, but are unwilling to assume personal liability.

g.   The anticipated earnings over cost, at least for the first few years, will be approximately $70,000. Doe and Roe wish to draw salaries of $25,000 each; they also want a hospitalization and retirement plan, all to be paid from these earnings.

h.   A loss is expected for the first three years, owing to the initial capital outlay and the difficulty in entering the market.

6.   A and B purchased a tavern. They orally agreed that A would manage the business at a stipulated salary and receive 50 percent of all profits but would not be liable for any losses. Subsequently, the Internal Revenue Service assessed a deficiency in cabaret taxes in the amount of $46,000. A contended that the taxes constituted a loss for the business, and since he was a limited partner, he was not liable for such loss. Is A correct? Why?

7.   The credit manager of X Company brought suit against D in the small-claims court without the assistance of an attorney. The state statute provided that actions may be maintained in the small-claims court by any person who executes an affidavit setting forth the nature of the claim. A judgment was entered on behalf of X Company. Should the judgment be enforced? Why?

8.   On November 23, 1973, X and Y formed a limited partnership. Prior to this, X had entered into a land-purchase contract with S. The sale was not closed, however, until December 12, 1973, when the contract was signed, "X Limited, a limited partnership, by X." The certificate of limited partnership was recorded on April 19, 1974. The partnership defaulted on the contract. S recovered a judgment against the partnership and X but was unable to fully enforce it. In February 1976, S brought suit against Y. Should Y be held liable as a general partner? Why?

9.   X was injured when his car was struck by a car driven by A. At the time of the accident, A and B, brothers, were returning home from a deer-hunting trip. The brothers hunted on a regular basis and would take turns driving their own car. Each brother would hunt on his own but assisted the other in bringing home any deer killed. Later, their father would butcher the meat, and it would be divided equally between the two brothers. X brought suit against A and B, claiming that B was liable as a joint venturer. Is B liable to X? Why?

10. A and B formed a limited partnership. Articles of partnership were drawn up establishing that A was a limited partner. Both A and B signed the agreement, but a certificate of limited partnership was not recorded. Eleven years later, the business went into bankruptcy. Should A be held liable as a general partner? Why?

11. L & G formed a limited partnership with G as general partner. The partnership purchased land from S, giving a promissory note on behalf of the partnership to S. The partnership subsequently defaulted on its payments and S brought suit. If there are insufficient assets in the partnership to cover the balance due on the note, can S hold G personally liable? Why?

12. The Green River Club, a voluntary unincorporated recreational club, brought an action to enjoin the enforcement of a state civil rights statute against the club, maintaining the statute was inapplicable. May the club bring the action? Explain.

13. A, B, and C formed a limited partnership. C, the limited partner, contributed the goods instead of cash as required by statute. In an action by a creditor, it was claimed C was a general partner. Was the creditor correct? Why?

Formation of Partnerships

1. Introduction

A *partnership* is an association of two or more persons to carry on as co-owners a business for profit. It is the result of an agreement between competent parties, either expressed or implied, to place their money, effects, labor, or skill, or a combination of them in a business and to divide the profits and losses. Express partnership agreements may be either oral or written, but such agreements should be reduced to writing and be carefully prepared. The provisions usually contained in articles of partnership will be discussed later in this chapter.

Issues concerning the existence of a partnership may arise between the parties or between the alleged partnership and third parties. The legal issues in these two situations are substantially different. When the issue is between the alleged partners, it is essentially a question of intention.[1] When the issue concerns liability to a third person, the question involves not only intention as to the actual existence of the partnership but issues of estoppel as well.

2. Implied Partnerships

As between the parties, the intention to create a partnership may be expressed or it may be implied from the conduct of the parties. The basic question is whether the parties intend a relationship that includes the essential elements of a partnership, not whether they intend to be partners.

[1] *Cyrus* v. *Cyrus,* page 651.

If the essential elements of a partnership are present, the mere fact that the parties do not think they are becoming partners is immaterial. If the parties agree upon an arrangement that is a partnership in fact, it is immaterial whether they call it something else or that they declare that they are not partners. On the other hand, the mere fact that the parties themselves call the relation a partnership will not make it so, if they have not, by their contract, agreed upon an arrangement that by the law is a partnership in fact.

The essential attributes of a partnership are a common interest in the business and management and a share in the profits and losses. However, if there is a sharing of profits, a partnership may be found to exist even though there is no sharing of losses.

The presence of a common interest in property and management is not enough to establish a partnership by implication. Also, an agreement to share the gross returns of a business, sometimes called gross profits, does not of itself prove an intention to form a partnership. However, the receipt by a person of a share of the real or net profits in a business is *prima facie* evidence that he is a partner in the business. The presumption that a partnership exists by reason of sharing net profits is not conclusive and may be overcome by evidence that the share in the profits is received for some other purpose, such as payment of a debt by installments, wages, rent, annuity to a widow of a deceased partner, interest on a loan, or payment for goodwill by installments.[2] For example, bonuses are frequently paid as a percent of profit, and such a payment does not make the employee a partner.

3. Partner by Estoppel

Insofar as third persons are concerned, partnership liability, like the apparent authority of an agent, may be predicated upon the legal theory of *estoppel*. Where a person by words, spoken or written, or by conduct represents himself or consents to another's representing him to another to be a partner in an existing partnership, or a partner with other persons not in a partnership, he is not a partner but is liable to any party to whom such representation has been made.[3] If the representation is made in a public manner either personally or with consent of the apparent partner, the apparent partner is liable if credit is extended to the partnership, even if the creditor did not actually know of the representation. This is an exception to the usual estoppel requirement of actual reliance.

The courts are not in accord as to whether a person is under a duty to affirmatively disclaim a reputed partnership where the representation of partnership was not made by or with the consent of the person sought to be charged as a partner. Some court cases hold that if a person is held out as a partner and he knows it, he should be chargeable as a partner unless he takes

[2] *P & M Cattle Co.* v. *Holler,* page 653.
[3] *Phillip Van Heusen, Inc.* v. *Korn,* page 655.

reasonable steps to give notice that he is not, in fact, a partner. Other cases indicate that there is no duty to deny false representations of partnership where the ostensible partner did not participate in making the misrepresentation.

THE ARTICLES OF PARTNERSHIP

4. Introduction

The partnership agreement, usually called the *articles of partnership,* will vary from business to business. Among the subjects usually contained in such agreements are the following: the names of the partners and of the partnership; its purpose and duration; the capital contributions of each partner; the method of sharing profits and losses; the effect of advances; the salaries, if any, to be paid the partners; the method of accounting and the fiscal year; the rights and liabilities of the parties upon the death or withdrawal of a partner; and the procedures to be followed upon dissolution.

The Uniform Partnership Act is a part of the agreement as if it had actually been written into the contract or made part of its stipulations. The sections that follow discuss some of the more important provisions of partnership agreements and indicate the effect of the Uniform Act on the agreement.

5. The Profit-and-Loss Provision

Unless the agreement is to the contrary, each partner has a right to share equally in the profits of the enterprise, and each partner is under a duty to contribute equally to the losses. Capital contributed to the firm is a liability owing by the firm to the contributing partners. If, on dissolution, there are not sufficient assets to repay each partner his capital, such amount is considered as a loss and must be met like any other loss of the partnership. For example, a partnership is composed of A, B, and C. A contributed $20,000, B contributed $10,000, and C contributed $4,000. The firm is dissolved, and upon the payment of firm debts there remains only $10,000 of firm assets. Since the total contribution to capital was $34,000, the operating loss is $24,000. This loss must be borne equally by A, B, and C, so that the loss for each is $8,000. This means that A is entitled to be reimbursed to the extent of his $20,000 contribution less $8,000, his share of the loss, or net of $12,000. B is entitled to $10,000, less $8,000, or $2,000. Since C has contributed only $4,000, he must now contribute to the firm an additional $4,000 in order that his loss will equal $8,000. The additional $4,000 contributed by C, plus the $10,000 remaining will now be distributed so that A will receive $12,000 and B $2,000.

Occasionally, articles of copartnership specify the manner in which profits are to be divided but neglect to mention possible losses. In such cases, the losses are borne in the same proportion that profits are to be shared. In the event that losses occur when one of the partners is insolvent and his share of the loss exceeds the amount owed him for advances and capital, the excess must be shared by the other partners. They share this unusual loss, with respect to each other, in the same ratio that they share profits.

Thus in the example above, if C is insolvent, A and B would each bear an additional $2,000 loss.

In addition to each partner's having the right to be repaid his contributions, whether by way of capital or advances to the partnership property, the partnership must indemnify every partner in respect of payments made and personal liabilities reasonably incurred by him in the ordinary and proper conduct of its business, or for the preservation of its business or property.

6. The Partnership Capital Provision

Partnership capital consists of the total credits to the capital accounts of the various partners, provided the credits are for permanent investments in the business. Such capital represents that amount that the partnership is obligated to return to the partners at the time of dissolution, and it can be varied only with the consent of all the partners. Undivided profits that are permitted by some of the partners to accumulate in the business do not become part of the capital. They, like temporary advances by firm members, are subject to withdrawal at any time unless the agreement provides to the contrary.

The amount that each partner is to contribute to the firm, as well as the credit he is to receive for assets contributed, is entirely dependent upon the partnership agreement. A person may become a partner without a capital contribution. For example, he may contribute services to balance the capital investment of the other partners. Such a partner, however, has no capital to be returned at the time of liquidation. Only those who receive credit for capital investments—which may include goodwill, patent rights, and so forth, if agreed upon—are entitled to the return of capital when dissolution occurs.

If the investment is in a form other than money, the property no longer belongs to the contributing partner. He has vested the firm with title and he has no greater equity in the property than any other partner. At dissolution he recovers only the amount allowed to him for the property invested.

7. Provisions Relating to Partnership Property

A partnership may use its own property, the property of the individual partners, or the property of some third person. It frequently becomes important, especially on dissolution and where claims of firm creditors are involved, to ascertain exactly what property constitutes *partnership property* in order to ascertain the rights of partners and firm creditors to specific property.[4]

As a general rule, the agreement of the parties will determine what property is properly classified as partnership property. In absence of an express agree-

[4] *Cyrus* v. *Cyrus,* page 651.

ment, what constitutes partnership property is ascertained from the conduct of the parties, and from the purpose for and the way in which property is used in the pursuit of the business. In general, all property originally brought into the partnership, or subsequently acquired on account of the partnership, is partnership property. Unless a contrary intention appears, property acquired with partnership funds is partnership property regardless of the manner in which title is formally held.

Because a partnership has the right to acquire, own, and dispose of personal property in the firm name, legal documents affecting the title to partnership personal property may be executed in the firm name by any partner. A partnership is a legal entity for the purposes of title to real estate that may be held in the firm name. Title so acquired can be conveyed in the partnership name. Where title to real property is in the partnership name, any partner may convey title to such property by a conveyance executed in the partnership name. To be effective, such a conveyance must be within the terms of the partnership agreement or within the pursuit of the partnership business.

8. The Firm Name

Since a partnership is created by the agreement of the parties, they select the name to be used. If the name is other than that of the partners, most states have assumed name statutes that require the giving of public notice as to the actual identity of the partners. Failure to comply with these assumed name statutes may result in the partnership's being denied access to the courts to sue its debtors, or it may result in criminal actions being brought against those operating under the assumed name.

The firm name is an asset of the firm, and as such it may also be sold, assigned, or disposed of in any manner the parties agree upon.[5]

At common law, a partnership was not a legal entity that could sue and be sued in the firm name. All actions had to be brought on behalf of or against all the partners as individuals. Today, most states by statutes have changed the common law, and partnerships in such states may sue or be sued in the firm name. They may also declare bankruptcy as a firm. To this extent, and to the extent that it can own and dispose of property in the firm name, a partnership is a legal entity. It is not a legal entity to the same extent as a corporation, however.

9. Provisions Relating to Goodwill

Goodwill, which is usually transferred with the name, is based upon the justifiable expectation of the continued patronage of old customers and the probable patronage of new customers resulting from good reputation, satisfied customers, established location, and past advertising. Goodwill is usually considered in an evaluation of the assets of the business, and it is capable of being

---

[5] *O'Hara* v. *Lance et ux.*, page 656.

sold and transferred. Upon dissolution caused by the death of one of the partners, it must be accounted for by the surviving partner to the legal representative of the deceased partner, unless otherwise agreed upon in the *buy and sell agreement*.

When goodwill and the firm name are sold, an agreement not to compete is usually part of the sales agreement. Such an agreement may be implied but should be a part of the buy and sell provisions.

10. The "Buy and Sell" Provisions

Either as part of the partnership agreement or by separate contract, the partners should provide for the contingency of death or withdrawal of a partner. This contingency is covered by a *buy and sell agreement,* and it is imperative that the terms of the buy and sell provisions be agreed upon before either party knows whether he is a buyer or a seller. Agreement after the status of the parties becomes known is extremely difficult, if not impossible. If such agreement is lacking, many additional problems will arise upon the death or withdrawal of a partner, and there are many possibilities of litigation and economic loss to all concerned.

A buy and sell agreement avoids these types of problems by providing a method whereby the surviving partner or partners can purchase the interest of the deceased partner, or the remaining partner or partners can purchase the interest of the withdrawing partner. A method of determining the price to be paid for such interest is provided. The time and method of payment are usually stipulated. The buy and sell agreement should specify whether a partner has an option to purchase the interest of a dying or withdrawing partner or whether he has a duty to do so.

It is common for partners to provide for life insurance on each other's lives as a means of funding the buy and sell provisions. In the event of a partner's death, proceeds of the insurance are utilized to purchase the deceased partner's interest. Premiums on such life insurance are not deductible for tax purposes but are usually treated as an expense for accounting purposes. There are a variety of methods for holding title to the insurance. It may be individually owned or business owned. The provisions of the policy should be carefully integrated into the partnership agreement; each partner's estate plan should also properly consider the ramifications of this insurance and of the buy and sell agreement.

FORMATION OF PARTNERSHIPS CASES

Cyrus v. Cyrus
64 N.W.2d 538 (Minn.) 1954

MATSON, J. Plaintiff, as administratrix of the estate of her deceased husband, Cecil Cyrus, brought this action to establish the existence of a partnership from November 1, 1936 to December 17, 1944 (date of decedent's death) between her husband and his brother, Curtis, the defendant herein, and to provide for a liquidation of said partnership and a division of its assets.

In 1934, Cecil Cyrus, Edna Cyrus (the plaintiff), and their children were living on a farm in North Dakota. In 1935 Cecil Cyrus served time in the penitentiary at Burleigh, North Dakota, and the plaintiff and children lived in Minot. During the years 1934 and 1935, both Cecil and the plaintiff received letters from Curtis, Cecil's brother, in which Curtis urged them to move to Minnesota and enter into a "partnership" for the building and operating of a tourist camp or resort on Lake of the Woods. In response to the requests of Curtis, the family moved to Minnesota in December of 1936 and entered into an agreement with a third person to live in a house situated on property close to the 60-acre tract which Curtis had purchased in his own name in 1935. Curtis's property was vacant except for one old "shack," and in accordance with the agreement to start a resort, Cecil and his father built a cabin on Curtis's land. . . . [T]his cabin, and all subsequent improvements, were thereafter paid for out of earnings derived from the operation of the resort. . . . Sometime after 1936 an additional 40-acre tract was acquired in Curtis's name, but . . . it . . . was paid for out of resort earnings. Although out of the resort earnings Cecil was allowed the living expenses for his family, he contributed his labor, and his wife did all the washing and ironing and cleaned and took care of the cabins. In addition Cecil's three children, especially the older one who was 18 years old when Cecil died, helped with the resort work.

During the entire period involved herein Curtis was regularly employed in Minneapolis and did not contribute any personal work to the operation of the resort other than to build an occasional cabin shelf while on his vacation. Every fall when Curtis visited the resort, the earnings were accounted for and Curtis was given his one-half share. This continued until Cecil died in December of 1944. At that time

the value of the resort was estimated to be $10,000. . . .

Plaintiff, as special administratrix of Cecil's estate, brought her action . . . for an adjudication that a partnership existed and for the liquidation of such partnership and a division of its assets. Judgment was entered in favor of the plaintiff declaring that a partnership had been formed and that the same was dissolved when Cecil died on December 17, 1944, and that Cecil's interest therein was then of the value of $5,000. . . . Defendant's appeal is from said judgment.

We are concerned with the specific issue of whether Cecil and Curtis were partners as between themselves and not whether they were partners as to third persons. Except in those rare cases where the evidence is conclusive, partnership or no partnership is a question of fact. Since there is no arbitrary test for determining the existence of a partnership, each case must be decided according to its own peculiar facts. . . .

The evidence as a whole . . . reasonably tends to indicate an intent of the parties to combine their property, labor, and skill as co-owners of a business for joint profit. There is credible evidence that the resort equipment and improvements were paid for out of the resort earnings. Significantly there was a splitting of the profits each fall. In addition Cecil was never paid a fixed wage or salary. Although he had no fixed salary, he did receive out of the resort's income the living expenses for himself and his family. . . . Although Cecil may have contributed nothing but his services to the resort business, this does not preclude the existence of a partnership. It is not unusual for two or more persons to unite in business, one contributing money and the other labor, the profits being divided between them; and in such cases it is often held that a partnership is formed. Although not of controlling significance, the fact that Cecil handled the money taken in and managed the resort is indicative of something more than an employer-employee relationship; and it is generally recognized that such fact tends to show a partnership. Furthermore, it is evident that there was a community of interest between Cecil and Curtis in the development of the resort, and this circumstance is an additional indicium of a partnership. . . . Separately, the evidentiary items are of no controlling significance; nevertheless, when combined together they present an evidentiary pattern which, in light of the evidence as a whole, presented an issue of fact for the trial court. The trial court's finding that a partnership existed must be affirmed.

It is particularly urged, however, that the real estate in defendant's name which was used in the operation of the resort never became a part of the partnership assets. A 60-acre tract was purchased by the defendant in 1935 before the partnership existed. After the partnership was formed an additional tract of 40 acres was bought. Both tracts were used solely for partnership purposes.

The trial court was justified in finding that the 40-acre tract was partnership property. The evidence supports a finding that it was purchased with earnings from the resort, a fact which in the absence of other circumstances denotes that the property belonged to the partnership. M.S.A. defines partnership property as follows:

> Unless the contrary intention appears, property acquired with partnership funds is partnership property.

Section 323.08 provides that every partner is an agent of the partnership for the purpose of its business. The mere fact that the title was taken in defendant's name does not prevent it from being partnership property. It is elementary that, where one partner purchases real estate with partnership funds and takes the title in his own name, he will be deemed a trustee holding such title for the benefit of the partnership. We have the further factor that Curtis was reimbursed out of resort earnings for taxes paid on the realty. The trial court could reasonably find not only that there was an absence of any intent that the tract should belong to Curtis but that there was an actual intent that it should belong to the partnership.

It is uncontradicted that the original 60-acre tract was purchased by the defendant with his own money and that the title was taken in his own name. As already noted it was acquired prior to the creation of the partnership. If the 60-acre tract constitutes partnership property, it must be on the theory that it was contributed to the partnership by the defendant. Whether real property acquired by a partner individually prior to the formation of a partnership belongs to or has been appropriated to the partnership is a question of intent. The fact that such realty is used for partnership purposes is not of itself, when standing alone, sufficient to establish an intent to contribute it to the partnership assets. In addition to the element of partnership use, we have, however, certain other evidentiary factors. Cabins, docks, and other improvements were built upon this land for the use of the partnership and were paid for out of partnership earnings. Improvements so made at partnership expense, although not of controlling significance, tend to show an intent that the land should be partnership property. As with the 40-acre tract, we have the salient fact that the evidence sustains a finding that the taxes were ultimately paid for out of partnership earnings. . . . Under the circumstances we can only conclude that the evidence sustains the trial court's conclusion that the entire realty was partnership property. . . .

Affirmed.

P & M Cattle Co. v. Holler
559 P.2d 1019 (Wyo.) 1977

RAPER, J. . . . In the district court, the plaintiff-appellant, a partnership, sought and was denied recovery for losses incurred in 1974 under an alleged "oral joint venture agreement" to purchase, lease and sell livestock. . . .

The only real issue is whether the parties to this appeal were parties to a joint venture or partnership agreement to share losses as well as profits from a cattle purchase, feed and sell operation.

In 1971, the defendant was looking for someone to pasture cattle on the defendant's land at $3.00 per head per month. One of two partners in the plaintiff partnership expressed an interest and invited defendant to talk. As a result, the following written agreement was entered into:

2-23-1971

Contract—Rusty Holler (60 Bar Ranch) —L. W. Maxfield and Bill Poage

Rusty to furnish grass for est 1000 yr st and 21 heifers

Maxfield & Poage to furnish money for cattle plus trucking & salt—and max of $300 per month for labor

Rusty to take cattle around May 1st and cattle to be sold at a time this fall agreed upon by all parties involved

Cost of cattle plus freight—salt and labor to be first cost

Net money from sale of cattle less first cost to be split 50–50 between Rusty (½) and Maxfield and Poage (½) (death loss to be part of first cost)

/s/ L. W. Maxfield
/s/ Bill Poage
LM
/s/ Rusty Holler

The 1971 agreement was orally renewed for the years 1972, 1973 and 1974. Plaintiff and defendant each realized substantial returns in the first three years but in 1974 there was not enough realized from the sale of cattle to pay first costs and a loss resulted. Plaintiff insists that the defendant is bound to pay it $44,500 representing one-half of the total cash loss in the sum of $89,000. . . .

The parties never discussed nor is there any mention in the contract of what would happen if the cattle sold at a loss. Nor was any mention made of reimbursement or credit to the defendant for the value of his services and pasture or grass he contributed, in the event cattle sold at a loss.

A broad overview of the entire record suggests that this case involves only a contract in which plaintiff agreed to put up the money and defendant agreed to put up grazing land and grass, along with services, with a view to profit to both, each to bear their own losses. . . .

Since joint adventures . . . are a species of and governed by the law of partnerships, we must go to the Uniform Partnership Act which defines a partnership as follows: "A partnership is an association of two or more persons to carry on as co-owners a business for profit." "In determining whether a partnership exists, these rules shall apply: . . .

'(4) The receipt by a person of a share of the profits of a business is prima facie evidence that he is a partner in the business, but no such inference shall be drawn if such profits were received in payment:

(a) As a debt of installments or otherwise.

(b) As wages of an employee or rent to a landlord,

(c) As an annuity to a widow or representative of a deceased partner,

(d) As an interest on a loan, though the amount of payment vary with the profits of the business,

(e) As the consideration for the sale of the good-will of a business or other property by installments or otherwise.' "

As can be seen from above . . . an agreement to share profits is far from decisive that a partnership is intended.

As in any contractual relationship, the intent of the parties is controlling. The parties must intend to create the relationship of . . . partnership. . . . There is no automatic solution to the question of the existence of a partnership but it turns upon the facts and circumstances of association between the parties.

. . . No single fact may be stated as the complete and final test of a partnership. Even a written agreement, designating the parties as partners and providing for a sharing of the profits, is only evidential and not conclusive of the existence of a partnership.

In the case before us there was no express agreement to form a partnership. True, there was an agreement but nowhere in that document is there anywhere mentioned the term partnership. Nor is there anywhere mentioned any sharing of losses, which is normally concomitant with a sharing of profits in a partnership.

Since we cannot look at the face of the instrument here and determine whether there is a partnership, it is necessary that we examine into the complete relationship between plaintiff and defendant.

In the first place, the agreement is not labeled a "partnership agreement" nor is the term "partnership" anywhere mentioned within its terms. The plaintiff was itself a partnership made up of two ranchers well acquainted with that arrangement, one of whom drew the contract. From its inception, then, none of the parties ever identified it as such. The pact was conceived in an atmosphere created by defendant's desire to sell grass. The division of losses was never discussed between the parties until the plaintiff delivered the bad news to the defendant following fall cattle sales in 1974. No partnership federal income tax return in any of the years 1971–74 was prepared and submitted to the Internal Revenue Service of the United States. On the income tax returns made by the plaintiff during the period in question, the part of profits paid to the defendant was carried as a business expense listed as "contract feeding." The defendant included such payments on his individual income tax return as a sale of "crops," nor were the cattle grazed on his place by the defendant carried on defendant's income tax return livestock inventory. The livestock were carried on plaintiff's partnership income tax returns. On the check given by plaintiff to defendant in 1973, for defendant's share of profits at the end of season, it was shown as being for "pasture."

Within the framework of the Uniform Partnership Act, we find rules available to the trial judge to determine that there was no partnership. The division of profits was only a measure—a standard of payment by plaintiff to defendant in discharge of a debt for services and grass . . . or in payment to defendant for wages of an employee in caring for the cattle while on his ranch and rent to him as landlord for his pasture or sale of grass as personal property or through a combination . . . for wages and rent or sale of property. We are satisfied that no partnership was intended. The agreement was only an apparatus to pay defendant for his grass and services and we return to its terms after reconnoitering the outer regions. . . .

Affirmed.

Phillip Van Heusen, Inc. v. Korn
460 P.2d 549 (Kan.) 1969

Plaintiff sued a father and son on an open account, contending that they were partners. The father was in the power lawn mower business, and he had assisted in setting his son up in a clothing business in some extra space in the father's building. The son was to pay rent when the business became self-supporting. The son by letter solicited supplies for his clothing business on his father's letterhead. The father joined the son in signing the letters. The father signed a note at the bank with the son, and the proceeds of the loan were deposited in a "Varsity Shop" account. Both the father and the son were on the signature card for the account.

After the Varsity Shop was opened, the son ordered goods from the plaintiff. Earlier, Dun & Bradstreet had called the father's power lawn mower business and inquired about the new clothing store. A report was then prepared showing that the two businesses had common ownership. A Dun & Bradstreet report had been furnished the plaintiff.

FATZER, J. . . . It is . . . contended the district court erred in finding the appellant was estopped to deny his liability to the appellee. The district court found there was no actual partnership between the father and son, but further found from the evidence that credit was extended by the appellee on the basis of representations made by the appellant, or on representations made with his knowledge and assent and that he was liable for the goods furnished. Based on that finding, the district court concluded the appellant was estopped to deny his liability. We find no error.

. . . When the appellee's allegation of partnership was denied, it had to fall back on the rule of law which holds that a person whose course of conduct leads another to believe he is a partner, and the party misled extends credit in reliance thereon, such person is liable as if he were a partner in fact. This court has consistently applied the rule that one may estop himself from denying his liability as a partner, where such relationship does not exist in fact, by holding himself out as such, or by negligently permitting one with whom he is engaged in business to do so. The rule is stated in 68 C.J.S. Partnership § 32, p. 457, as follows:

> Any act, representation, or conduct on the part of a person, reasonably calculated to induce the belief that he is a partner, constitutes a holding out, with respect to whether a partnership will be held to exist as to third persons.

. . . We have fully reviewed the record and conclude the judgment entered by the district court was correct. The appellant should not be allowed to escape the consequences of holding out his credit in the manner disclosed by the record, and then withdraw it when it appears that the business would fail and he might become liable.

Affirmed.

O'Hara v. Lance et ux.
77 Ariz. 84, 1954

Defendant, General W. Lance, established a business known as the Ace-Lance Refrigeration Company in Phoenix in 1942. In 1946 defendant and plaintiff entered into a partnership agreement and continued in the same business as "Ace-Lance & O'Hara Refrigeration Company." In 1949 the partnership was dissolved, Lance selling all partnership assets, including goodwill, to O'Hara. Lance agreed not to compete for a period of two years and granted to O'Hara the exclusive right to the firm name except for the condition that after December 21, 1950. O'Hara might not further use Lance's name without his consent. In 1951 plaintiff sued to enjoin defendant from competing and to restrain him from using the word "Ace" in the firm name of any refrigeration business in Arizona. The lower court denied the relief requested by plaintiff and held that defendant had the right to use the word "Ace" as well as the word "Lance" in a new business. Plaintiff appealed.

TULLAR, J. . . . The first and primary step is to determine what was bought and sold at the time of the dissolution of the partnership. Happily, the agreement of the parties is explicit. Lance, "the retiring partner," is being paid, "for his share in the business and the capital, stock, equipment, effects and good will thereof." The agreement recites that valuations and estimates have been placed upon these items, and agreed to, specially including the good will, and a balance has been struck.

In the law of partnership, it is the rule that, in the absence of agreement to the contrary, a sale of assets and good will of a commercial partnership carries with it the right to use the partnership name. We are not here dealing with a "professional" partnership, wherein the law is quite different.

A conveyance of the good will of a business carries with it an implied covenant to do nothing which would derogate from the grant. If the vendor of the good will re-engage in business, it is his duty to conduct his new business in such a way that it will not appear to be a continuation of the business that he has sold. The vendor has a duty not only to his vendee, but to the public, not to confuse or deceive the customer into thinking he is in one place of business when he is in another. This type of confusion and deceit is the keystone of unfair competition. And, we have previously pointed out, this is the universal test for the presence of unfair competition: Is the public likely to be deceived?

So in this case, when Lance included in his sale the good will of the business, he sold to O'Hara the right to the use of the firm name, Ace-Lance & O'Hara Refrigeration Company. And, as the agreement recites, this was "to hold the same unto O'Hara absolutely."

This does not necessarily mean, in law, that Lance has parted with the right henceforth to use his own personal name. Indeed, there is a presumption that no one intends to part with this right, and that an assignment of good will does not, *ipso facto,* confer upon the assignee the exclusive right to the use of assignor's personal name. While one may sell his own name as a trade name servient to the business to which it is attached, the intent so to divest oneself must clearly be shown.

Lance . . . sold to O'Hara the exclusive use of his personal name as a trade name in the refrigeration business, but only for a limited time. The time limit having expired, there is now no restraint upon Lance's use of his personal name for any lawful purpose he may desire, so long as he does not transgress his obligation not to interfere with O'Hara's right to receive the benefits of his purchase.

. . . Fact and law conclusively show O'Hara's right in and to the use of the word "Ace," in the refrigeration business in his trade area. Lance does not have the same right.

O'Hara has prayed for state-wide restraint. He is, however, entitled to protection only in the territory from which he received business or might reasonably be expected to receive business in the future. His protection should extend as far as his business reputation and his goods have become known.

The judgment of the trial court is reversed. Plaintiff . . . [is granted] an injunction restraining the defendant from using the name, "Ace," in any refrigeration business within the area or served by the Phoenix metropolitan area telephone directory.

Reversed.

CHAPTER 34
REVIEW QUESTIONS AND PROBLEMS

1. A and B formed a partnership. In a lawsuit, A claimed the attempted partnership was a nullity because B was a minor. Was A correct? Explain.

2. Company A entered into a contract with Company C, and Company B assured the contract would be performed. Company B paid damages for breach of contract and then brought suit against Company A and Company C. Company C was an investment company that financed and often furnished machinery to Company A. Under the agreements, Company C would share in the profits of Company A's contracts. B claimed A and C were partners and its suit against C was justified. Did a partnership exist? Explain.

3. A and H formed a partnership. Sometimes thereafter, H and his wife, W, divorced. The divorce decree granted W the interest in the partnership owned by H. Did this make W a partner? Why?

4. X allowed Y and Z to construct a greenhouse on his property with the understanding that the physical structure would be the property of X. Later, a partnership was formed, with all partners sharing profits and losses equally. Four more greenhouses were built. When Y died, a dispute arose over who owned the four greenhouses. Did X own all the greenhouses? Why?

5. A was the principal stockholder in the XYZ Stockyards Corporation, and B was his secretary-bookkeeper. They married, and in the same year, the XYZ Corporation was dissolved. A continued to operate the business as sole owner. B continued to work in the same capacity as before, but without salary, and she testified that A orally made her a partner. Twenty years later, B divorced A and asked for a one-half interest in all partnership property. Should she recover? Why?

6. A, B, and C signed a "partnership agreement." The contract stipulated the following: A would provide the barbershop and equipment, while B and C would furnish their tools of the trade; upon dissolution of the partnership, ownership of the property would revert to each party; each partner would share in the income of the business; and all partnership policy would be decided by A. Have A, B, and C formed a partnership? Why?

7. F had been in business with his son, S, under the name of "F and Son." F withdrew from the business. The telephone number was then carried in the name of S. One year later, S, without the knowledge of F, requested the telephone company to list the number under the name of F and S. Two years later, S did not pay a monthly bill for $1,200 and the telephone company claimed that F is liable. Is F liable? Why?

8. F signed a contract to plant and harvest popcorn for X Company. X Company sent F a letter signed by A, manager of X Company, advising F that he should store the popcorn in his own bins and that company trucks would pick it up. F stored the popcorn in the bins and demanded payment. When F demanded payment, A informed him that X Company was now doing business as A and Company, but that the popcorn would still be picked up and the contract price paid. The popcorn was picked up at A's direction, but F never received his money. F contends that A is liable as a partner, but A claims that he was only an employee. Is A liable? Why?

9. O and T entered into a written agreement whereby T was to farm part of O's land; in exchange, O was to receive one-third of the crop as rental

The contract provided that O was to advance financing and T was to furnish the equipment. It was also agreed that after payment of O's share, all of the net proceeds were to be divided equally, and losses were also to be shared equally. The contract specifically stated that O and T were not engaged in the transaction as partners but as landlord and tenant. Are O and T partners? Why?

10. A and B formed a partnership dealing in real estate. When A died, his widow claimed that the property A and B had purchased with the deed listing A and B as "tenants in common" should not be inventoried in the estate as partnership property. At the trial it was determined that this property had been purchased with partnership funds. Did this property belong to the partnership, or to A and B individually as joint owners? Why?

11. A and B commenced a retail propane gas business. A put up all the money, bought all the supplies and equipment, and B began selling and delivering gas for which he was paid $65 a week. At the end of the year partnership income tax returns were filed which showed a percentage of partnership of two-thirds in A and one-third in B. Were A and B partners? Explain.

12. S purchased a farm and shortly thereafter, entered into negotiations to sell the farm to B. S hired A, an attorney, to represent him in the negotiations. A contract to sell was executed but S subsequently refused to sell the farm to B. B sued S and A, contending that A is liable as a partner since he was to receive a share of the profits had the sale been consummated. Should A be held liable as a partner? Why?

13. A and B formed a partnership under the name "Richter Brothers." The business was operated for years and the firm name constituted an asset of the partnership. Upon A's death a corporation was formed using the name "Richter Brothers Company, Inc." The company advertised that it had been in business for seventy years. A suit was brought to restrain the corporation from using the name "Richter Brothers" as part of the corporate name. What result? Why?

35

Operating the Partnership

1. Introduction

The operation of a partnership is governed by the provisions of the partnership agreement and by the applicable statutory law, which in most states is the Uniform Partnership Act. Thus, the rights, duties, and powers of partners are both expressed (those in the agreement) and implied (those created by law). Many of the expressed rights, duties, and powers were discussed in the preceding chapter, which covered the typical subjects found in articles of partnership. Those that are implied will be discussed in this chapter, along with some additional observations about the partnership agreement as it affects operations. Throughout the discussion, it should be kept in mind that a partner is essentially an agent for the other partners and that the general principles of the law of agency are applicable.

Before examining the rights, duties, and powers of partners, certain additional terminology should be understood. A *silent partner* is one that does not participate in management. However, if the silent partner is to have limited liability, the provisions of the Uniform Limited Partnership Act would have to be complied with. A *secret partner* is unknown to third parties. He may advise management and actually participate in decisions, but his interest is not known to third parties. A *dormant partner* is both secret and silent.

RIGHTS OF PARTNERS

2. Right to Participate in Management

All partners have equal rights in the management and conduct of the firm business. The partners may, however, by agreement, place the management within the control of one or more partners. The right to an equal voice in the management and conduct of the business is not determined by the share that each partner has invested in the business.

In regard to ordinary matters arising in the conduct of the partnership business, the opinion of the majority of the partners is controlling. If the firm consists or only two persons, and they are unable to agree, and the articles of partnership make no provision for the settlement of disputes, dissolution is the only remedy. The partnership agreement usually provides for some form of arbitration of deadlocks between partners in order to avoid dissolution.

The majority cannot, however, without the consent of the minority, change the essential nature of the business by altering the partnership agreement or by reducing or increasing the capital of the partners; or embark upon a new business; or admit new members to the firm.

Certain acts other than those enumerated above require the unanimous consent of the partners in order to bind the firm, namely: (1) assigning the firm property to a trustee for the benefit of creditors; (2) confessing a judgment; (3) disposing of the goodwill of the business; (4) submitting a partnership agreement to arbitration; and (5) doing any act that would make impossible the conduct of the partnership business.

3. Right to Be Compensated for Services

It is the duty of each partner, in the absence of an agreement to the contrary, to give his entire time, skill, and energy to the pursuit of the partnership affairs. No partner is entitled to payment for services rendered in the conduct of the partnership business, unless an agreement to that effect has been expressed or may be implied from the conduct of the partners.[1] Often, one of the partners does not desire to participate in the management of the business. The partnership agreement in such case usually provides that the active partners receive a salary for their services in addition to their share in the profits. A surviving partner is entitled to reasonable compensation for his services in winding up the partnership affairs, unless he is guilty of misconduct in winding up the affairs.

4. Right to Interest

Contributions to capital are not entitled to draw interest unless they are not repaid when the repayment should be made. The partner's share in the profits

---

[1] *Waagen* v. *Gerde,* page 667.

constitutes the earnings upon his capital investment. In the absence of an expressed provision for the payment of interest, it is presumed that interest will be paid only on advances above the amount originally contributed as capital. Advances in excess of the prescribed capital, even though credited to the capital account of the contributing partners, are entitled to draw interest from the date of the advance.

Unwithdrawn profits remaining in the firm are not entitled to draw interest. Such unwithdrawn profits are not considered advances or loans by the mere fact that they are left with the firm. However, custom, usage, and circumstances may show an intention to treat such unwithdrawn profits as loans to the firm.

5. Right to Information and to Inspection of Books

Each partner, whether active or inactive, is entitled to full and complete information concerning the conduct of the business. A partner has the right to inspect the books to secure such information. The partnership agreement usually provides for a bookkeeper, and each partner is under a duty to give the bookkeeper whatever information is necessary to carry on the business efficiently and effectively. It is the duty of the person keeping the records at the firm's place of business to allow each partner access to them. No partner has a right to remove the records without the consent of the other partners. Each partner is entitled to inspect the books and make copies therefrom, provided he does not make such inspection or copies to secure an advantageous position or for fraudulent purposes.

6. Right to an Accounting

The partners' proportionate share of the partnership assets or profits, when not determined by a voluntary settlement of the parties, may be ascertained in a suit in equity for an accounting. As a general rule, a partner cannot maintain an *action at law* against other members of the firm on the partnership agreement, because until there is an accounting and all partnership affairs are settled, the indebtedness between the firm members is undetermined. This general rule is subject to a few commonsense exceptions.

Because partners ordinarily have equal access to the partnership records, there is usually no need for formal accountings to determine partnership interests. A suit for an accounting is not permitted for settling incidental matters or disputes between the partners. However, if a dispute is of such grievous nature as to make impossible the continued existence of the partnership, a suit for an accounting in equity is allowed.

In all cases, a partner is entitled to an accounting upon the dissolution of the firm. In addition, he has a right to a formal accounting without a dissolution of the firm in the following situations:

1. Where there is an agreement for an accounting at a definite date

2. Where one partner has withheld profits arising from secret transactions

3. Where there has been an execution levied against the interest of one of the partners

4. Where one is in such a position that he does not have access to the books

5. Where the partnership is approaching insolvency and all parties are not available.

Upon an agreement between themselves, the partners may make a complete accounting and settle their claims without resort to a court of equity.

7. Property Rights

A partner is a co-owner with his partners of partnership property. Subject to any agreement between the partners, a partner has an equal right among his partners to possess partnership property for partnership purposes. He has no right to possess specific partnership property for other purposes without the consent of the other partners.

A partner has a right that the property shall be used in the pursuit of the partnership business and to pay firm creditors. A partner does not own any specific item of the partnership property. He therefore has no right in specific partnership property that is transferable by him. A partner has no right to use the firm property in satisfaction of his personal debts, and he has no interest in specific partnership property that can be levied upon by his personal creditors.

When a partner dies, his interest in specific partnership property passes to the surviving partner or partners, who have the duty of winding up the affairs of the partnership in accordance with the partnership agreement and the applicable laws. When the winding-up process is complete, the estate of the deceased partner will be paid whatever sum the estate is entitled to according to law and the partnership agreement. The surviving partner may sell the property, real and personal, of the partnership in connection with winding up the business in order to obtain the cash to pay the estate of the deceased partner.

A partner's interest *in the firm* consists of his rights to share in the profits that are earned and, after dissolution and liquidation, to the return of his capital and such profits as have not been distributed previously. This assumes, of course, that his capital has not been absorbed or impaired by losses.

A partner may assign his interest in or his right to share in the profits of the partnership. Such an assignment will not of itself work a dissolution of the firm. The assignee is not entitled to interfere in the management of the business. The only right of the assignee is to receive the profits to which the assignor would otherwise have been entitled and, in the event of dissolution, to receive his assignor's interest.

A partner's interest in the partnership cannot be levied upon by his separate creditors and sold at public sale. A judgment creditor of a partner must proceed by obtaining a "charging order" from the court. This order charges the interest of the debtor partner with the unsatisfied amount of the judgment debt. The court will ordinarily appoint a receiver who will receive the partner's share of the profits and any other money due or to fall due to him in respect of the partnership and apply the same upon the judgment. Likewise, the court may order that the interest charged be sold. Neither the charging order nor the sale of the interest will cause a dissolution of the firm, unless the partnership is one that is terminable at will.

DUTIES AND POWERS OF PARTNERS

8. Duties in General

A partnership is a fiduciary relationship, and each partner owes the duty of undivided loyalty to the other.[2] Therefore, every partner must account to the partnership for any benefit, and hold as a trustee for it any profits, gained by him without consent of the other partners, and account for any use by him of the partnership property. This duty also rests upon representatives of deceased partners engaged in the liquidation of the affairs of the partnership.

The partnership relation is a personal one, and each partner is under duty to exercise good faith and to consider the mutual welfare of all the partners in his conduct of the business. If one partner attempts to secure an advantage over the others, he thereby breaches the partnership relation, and he must account for all benefits that he obtains. This includes transactions with partners and with others.

9. Powers in General

A partner is an agent of the partnership for the purpose of its business, and the general laws of agency are applicable to his conduct. He has the power to bind the partnership both in tort and in contract. Each partner has authority to bind the partnership whenever the partner is apparently carrying on, in the usual way, the business of the partnership. Of course, if the partner so acting has in fact no authority to act for the partnership in the particular matter, and the person with whom he is dealing has knowledge of the fact that he has no such authority, there is no liability. An act of a partner that is not apparently for the carrying on of the business of the partnership in the usual way does not bind the partnership unless authorized by the other partners.[3]

[2] *Huffington* v. *Upchurch,* page 668.
[3] *Bole* v. *Lyle,* page 669.

The Uniform Partnership Act imposes tort liability upon the partnership for all wrongful acts or omissions of any partner acting in the ordinary course of the partnership and for its benefit.[4]

The rules of agency relating to authority, ratification, and secret limitations on the authority of a partner are applicable to partnerships, but the extent of implied authority is generally greater for partners than for ordinary agents. Each partner has implied power to do all acts necessary for carrying on the business of the partnership. The nature and scope of the business and what is usual in the particular business determine the extent of the implied powers. Among the common implied powers are the following: to compromise, adjust, and settle claims or debts owed by or to the partnership; to sell goods in the regular course of business and to make warranties; to buy property within the scope of the business for cash or upon credit; to buy insurance; to hire employees; to make admissions against interest; to enter into contracts within the scope of the firm; and to receive notice. In a trading partnership, a partner has the implied authority to borrow funds and to pledge the assets of the firm. Some of these implied duties are discussed more fully in the sections that follow.

A partner has the power to impose tort liability through the doctrine of *respondeat superior*. The law imposes tort liability upon a partnership for all wrongful acts or omissions of any partner acting in the ordinary course of the partnership and for its benefit.

If a partnership has liability because of a tort of a partner, the firm has the right to collect its losses from the partner at fault. In effect, a partnership that is liable in tort to a third person has a right of indemnity against the partner at fault. Likewise, if the injured third party collects directly from the partner at fault, the partner cannot seek contribution from his copartners.

10. Powers over Property

Each partner has implied authority to sell to good-faith purchasers personal property that is held for the purpose of resale and to execute such documents as are necessary to effect a transfer of title thereof. Of course, if his authority in this connection has been limited and such fact is known to the purchaser, the transfer of title will be ineffective or voidable. A partner has no power to sell the fixtures and equipment used in the business unless he has been duly authorized. Such acts are not a regular feature of the business, and a prospective purchaser of such property should make certain that the particular partner has been given authority to sell. The power to sell, where it is present, gives also the power to make such warranties as normally accompany similar sales.

The right to sell firm real property is to be inferred only if the firm is engaged in the real estate business. In other cases, there is no right to sell and convey realty, except where such sale has been authorized by a partnership agreement.

[4] *Flynn v. Reaves,* page 669.

Title to real property may be taken in the firm name as a "tenancy in partnership," and any member of the firm has power to execute a deed thereto by signing the firm name. In such a case, what is the effect of a wrongful transfer of real estate that has been acquired for use in the business and not for resale? The conveyance may be set aside by the other partners, since the purchaser should have known that one partner has no power to sell without the approval of the others. However, if the first purchaser has resold and conveyed the property to an innocent third party, the latter takes good title.

If the title to firm property is not held in the firm name but is held in the names of one or more of the partners, a conveyance by those in whose names the title is held passes good title, unless purchaser knows or should know that title was held for the firm. There is nothing in the record title in such a situation to call the buyer's attention to the fact that the firm has an interest in the property.

The power to mortgage or pledge firm property is primarily dependent upon the power, later discussed, to borrow money and bind the firm. A partner with authority to borrow may, as an incident to that power, give the security normally demanded for similar loans. Since no one partner, without the consent of the others, has the power to commit an act that will destroy or terminate the business, the power to give a mortgage on the entire stock of merchandise and fixtures of a business is usually denied. Such a mortgage would make it possible, upon default, to liquidate the firm's assets and thus destroy its business. Subject to this limitation, the power to borrow carries the power to pledge or mortgage.

11. Financial Powers

For the purpose of determining the limit of a partner's financial powers, partnerships may be divided into two general classes—trading and nontrading partnerships. A *trading partnership* is one that has for its primary purpose the buying and selling of commodities. In such a trading firm, each partner has an implied power to borrow money and to extend the credit of the firm, in the usual course of business, by signing negotiable paper.[5]

A *nontrading partnership* is one that does not buy and sell commodities, but that has for its primary purpose the production of commodities or is organized for the purpose of selling services—for example, professional partnerships. In such partnerships, a partner's powers are more limited, and a partner does not have implied power to borrow money or to bind the firm on negotiable paper. However, where the act is within the scope of the partnership business, a member of a nontrading partnership may bind the firm by the exercise of implied authority just as a partner in a trading partnership may.

[5] *Holloway* v. *Smith et al.,* page 670.

12. Notice and Admissions

Each partner has implied authority to receive notice for all the other partners concerning matters within the pursuit of the partnership business; and knowledge held by any partner in his mind, but not revealed to the other partners, is notice to the partnership. Knowledge of one partner is knowledge of all. This knowledge, however, must be knowledge obtained within the scope of the partnership business. If the partner could have and should have communicated knowledge to the other partners and fails to do so, his failure would be chargeable to the firm. This rule does not apply, however, if fraud is perpetrated on the partnership by the partner having such knowledge.

Admissions or representations pertaining to the conduct of the partnership business and made by a partner may be used as evidence against the partnership.

OPERATING THE PARTNERSHIP CASES

Waagen v. Gerde et ux.
219 P.2d 595 (Wash.) 1950

Plaintiff and defendants were partners in the ownership and operation of a fishing vessel. Plaintiff brought this action for an accounting and alleged that defendants had wrongfully withheld partnership earnings from plaintiff. Defendant Karl Gerde perfected a new type of net for catching sharks and contended that he was entitled to compensation for the time and effort expended in constructing the shark nets. The lower court held in favor of plaintiff, and defendants appealed.

DONWORTH, J. . . . Appellant's final assignment of error is that the trial court erred in refusing to allow appellant any credit for work done by him in constructing the shark nets.

The evidence shows that appellant with some help from his two sons designed and built the shark nets. Respondent did not in any way assist him in this job. According to appellant, the value of this work was $2,500 and he claims that he should be compensated for this work.

The general rule is clear that one partner is not entitled to extra compensation from the partnership, in the absence of an express or an implied agreement therefor. Each case must depend largely upon its own facts, and thus other cases are generally of little or no assistance in deciding the case at hand.

The exception to the general rule is well stated in 1 Rowley, *Modern Law of Partnership* 412, § 354, as follows: "Where it can be fairly and justly implied from the course of dealing between the partners, [or] from circumstances of equivalent force, that one partner is to be compensated for his services, his claim will be sustained." The partnership may be of such a peculiar kind, and the arrangements and the course of dealing of the partners in regard to it may be such as pretty plainly to show an expectation and understanding, without an express agreement upon the subject, that certain services of a copartner should be paid for. Such cases, presenting unusual conditions, are exceptions to the general rule.

While appellant's ingenuity and industry were largely responsible for the success of the *Princess* in shark fishing, we cannot find anything in the record from which an agreement to pay him special compensation could be implied. Appellant did inform respondent that he was busy getting the nets ready and that it would "be lots of work to fix" them, but never at any time did he inform respondent what the work actually entailed or that he expected any compensation for it. Since respondent had so little knowledge of the conduct of the net operations, there could not be any implied agreement for compensation. The trial court found no factual basis for such an allowance, and we can find none in the record.

Affirmed.

Huffington v. Upchurch
532 S.W.2d 576 (Tex.) 1976

The parties to this lawsuit are partners in an oil and gas investment firm. The purposes of the partnership are to acquire, own, develop and operate oil, gas and mineral leases. The partnership agreement provided that the partners were "free to conduct, in their individual capacities, or in association with others, any other business transaction not directly related to the business of acquiring mineral leases and other mineral or royalty interests and the exploration for and production of oil, gas and other minerals."

The defendant was the managing partner. He learned of an "Indonesian" oil deal and acquired 10 per cent of it for himself. When the plaintiff learned that the defendant had acquired the 10 per cent interest, he demanded the right to contribute his share and to participate in the venture. When the defendant refused to allow plaintiff to participate, plaintiff filed suit contending that the investment was partnership property. The lower court found for the plaintiff and the defendant appealed.

POPE, J. . . . It is undisputed that the Indonesian venture fell within the nature of the partnership business as defined by the written contract. However, it was defendant's contention that Upchurch failed to plead and prove the partnership's financial capability to take advantage of this particular venture. . . .

The partnership contract obligated Roy Huffington to "give his attendance to, and to the utmost of his skill and power shall exert himself for, the joint interest, benefit and advantage of said partnership business." In a case of this kind, where the partner who has misappropriated a particular opportunity is also the partner who is primarily responsible for finding financial backing, the burden of proving financial incapability should be on him so as to encourage the exertion of his best efforts. . . .

As managing partner of Huffington Associates, Roy Huffington owed to his copartners one of the highest fiduciary duties recognized in the law. In *Smith* v. *Bolin,* 153 Tex. 486, 271 S.W.2d 93, 96 (1954), this court quoted at length from Justice Cardozo's opinion in *Meinhard* v. *Salmon,* 249 N.Y. 458, 164 N.E. 545 (1928) concerning the fiduciary duties of managing partners.

> As managing partner of their partnership enterprise, respondent owed his partners even a greater duty of loyalty than is normally required. In the *Meinhard* v. *Salmon* case, *supra,* the court said: "Salmon had put himself in a position in which thought of self was to be renounced, however hard the abnegation. He was much more than a coadventurer. He was a managing coadventurer. . . . For him and for those like him the rule of undivided loyalty is relentless and supreme." . . .

We affirm . . . the judgment of the court of civil appeals which awarded Upchurch a judgment against Huffington and Huffington, Inc. for 14.285 per cent of the interest created by the joint venture agreement standing in the name of Roy M. Huffington, Inc.

So ordered.

Bole v. Lyle
287 S.W.2d 931 (Tenn.) 1956

Lyle, Peters, and Barton were partners operating a business which manufactured packing crates and other wood products. The partnership had purchased a tract of timber and were cutting it into lumber to supply their needs. Barton, the managing partner, entered into a contract to sell lumber to plaintiff and received payment therefor. The lumber was never delivered to plaintiff, and Barton never accounted to the partnership for the money received. Plaintiff sought to hold the partnership accountable. The lower court held that Lyle and Peters were not liable. Plaintiff appealed.

McAMIS, J. . . . The general rule is that each partner is a general agent of the firm but only for the purpose of carrying on the business of the partnership. Any sale by a partner to be valid must be in furtherance of the partnership business, within the real scope of the business or such as third persons may reasonably conclude, from all the circumstances, to be embraced within it. If the act is embraced within the partnership business or incident to such business according to the ordinary and usual course of conducting it, the partnership is bound regardless of whether the partner, in performing the act, proceeds in good faith or bad faith toward his copartners.

Sales made by a partner in a trading firm are, of course, not viewed with the same strictness as in nontrading firms such as here involved, because in trading firms sales are usually within the scope of the business while in nontrading firms they are exceptional and only incidental to the main business. *A priori,* in determining whether an act is within the scope of the business it is of importance, first, to determine the character of the partnership operations.

We think the case here presented is simply that of a nonresident, unfamiliar with the partnership operations, being defrauded by one of the partners acting in a matter beyond both the real and apparent scope of the business and beyond the real or apparent scope of the agency. There was nothing in the firm name to suggest that it was in the business of selling lumber. Complainant chose to deal with one of the partners without knowing anything of the nature of the partnership operations and we agree with the Chancellor that the nonparticipating partners were in no way responsible for his loss and that recovery should be against Barton alone.

Affirmed.

Flynn v. Reaves
218 S.E.2d 661 (Ga.) 1975

CLARK, J. . . . The circumstances giving rise to this appeal may be summarized as follows: Seeking damages for medical malpractice, plaintiffs, husband and wife, brought suit only against defendant, Dr. Charles R. Moore, alleging him to have been negligent in his diagnosis and treatment of the eyes of plaintiff wife. Defendant answered, denying the allegations of negligence. Thereafter, defendant initiated a third-party action against his former co-partners, Dr. James T. Flynn, Jr., Dr. Robert E. Fokes, Jr. and Dr. James R. Paulk.

In this third-party complaint, "while in no way admitting that either he or the named third-party defendants are liable to the plaintiffs, defendant does show that the third-party defendants are equally responsible with him should there be found any violation of a duty to plaintiffs." This pleading alleges that he had been an equal partner with the three third-party defendants, hereafter referred to as "co-partners," in a medical practice partnership operated under the name of "The Eye, Ear, Nose and Throat Clinic" at the time when he had diagnosed and treated plaintiff wife; that his diagnosis and treatment of plaintiff wife was performed within the course of the partnership business; that he and his copartners shared equally in the profits and losses of the partnership; and that the three copartners were liable to him for three-fourths of any sum which plaintiffs might recover against him in the principal suit. . . .

The copartners . . . challenged the sufficiency of the third-party complaint via motion for a judgment decreeing that it failed to state a claim entitling defendant to the relief sought against the third-party defendants. This motion was denied and the copartners have appealed. . . .

1. The law of partnership is the law of agency: "Each partner being the agent of the firm, the firm is liable for his torts committed within the scope of his agency, on the principle of *respondeat superior,* in the same way that a master is responsible for his servant's torts, and for the same reason [that] the firm is liable for the torts of its agents or servants." . . . Thus, "where several physicians are in partnership, they may be held liable in damages for the professional negligence of one of the firm."

In the case at bar, therefore, the copartners and defendant would be jointly and severally liable to plaintiffs if it were established that defendant in fact negligently diagnosed and treated plaintiff wife in the course of the partnership business. Therefore, plaintiffs had the choice of suing the defendant individually, or all of the partners including defendant jointly. But defendant cannot seek contribution from his copartners simply because they are jointly liable to plaintiffs. "[T]here may be cases in which a person who has suffered loss or damage may have the right to sue two persons as if they were joint wrong-doers, without their being, as among themselves, joint wrongdoers. A.'s servant, B., negligently injures C. in the performance of A.'s work. From C.'s standpoint, A. and B. are joint wrongdoers, but as among themselves B. is the wrongdoer and A. is subjected to liability merely by the doctrine of *respondeat superior;* so that, if C. sues A. alone and compels him to pay the damage, A., in turn, may compel B. to indemnify him for the loss. So in this class of cases it is always relevant to inquire, 'Whose wrong really caused the damage?' . . . Generally speaking, a right of action over in such cases exists only where the negligence of him who has been compelled to satisfy the damages is imputed or constructive only, and the negligence of him against whom the remedy over is asserted was actual or more immediately causal."

Here, the copartners and defendant are not joint tortfeasors as among themselves. For the copartners are subjected to liability only by the doctrine of *respondeat superior*. Thus, defendant whose negligence, if any, was actual, cannot seek contribution from his copartners, who are merely constructively negligent. Of course, had defendant alleged that his copartners were actual tortfeasors, a third-party action for contribution would lie. But such is not the case.

Therefore, we hold, as other courts have held, that where a partner is sued individually by a plaintiff injured by the partner's sole negligence, the partner cannot seek contribution from his copartners even though the negligent act occurred in the course of the partnership business.

2. Since defendant's third-party complaint failed to state a claim upon which relief can be granted, the denial of the copartners' motion was error.

Judgment reversed.

Holloway v. Smith et al.
88 S.E.2d 909 (Va.) 1955

Defendants Smith and Ten Brook were partners in the automobile business under the name of Greenwood Sales and Service. Defendant Ten Brook borrowed $6,000 from plaintiff and gave a partnership note in return. It is contended by the Smiths that Ten Brook borrowed the money to make his initial capital contribution to the partnership and that the obligation to repay was solely that of Ten Brook. They also contended that Ten Brook lacked the authority to bind the partnership on the note. The lower court held that the Smiths were not liable on the note.

SPRATLEY, J. Greenwood Sales & Service was a trading or commercial partnership, and in the course of its business, it borrowed money for carrying on its business in the usual way.

. . . It is settled law in Virginia, both by statute and in numerous decisions, that a partner is an agent of the firm for the purpose of the partnership business, and may bind all partners by his acts within the scope of such business. It is of no consequence whether the partner is acting in good faith with his copartners or not, provided the act is within the scope of the partnership's business and professedly for the firm, and third persons are acting in good faith.

. . . Pertinent here is this statement from 40 Am. Jur., *Partnership,* § 11 at p. 134:

The character and nature of partnerships ordinarily determine the powers and liabilities of different classes of partners. In this connection, the most important distinction exists between trading or commercial partnerships and those which are not organized for the purpose of trade or commerce. Greater powers are impliedly given to members of the former as compared with the second type of partnerships, such as in the matter of drawing or endorsing negotiable instruments.

The Smiths selected Ten Brook as their partner. The partnership was a going concern when the $6,000 note was executed. In the absence of a restriction on his authority, known to Mrs. Holloway, Ten Brook had the same power to bind the partnership as his copartners had. Ten Brook, as the agent of the partnership, solicited the loan professedly for the firm, and executed the note evidencing it, for "apparently carrying on in the usual way the business of the partnership" of which he was a member.

[*The court held that the Smiths as well as Ten Brook were liable on the note.*]

CHAPTER 35
REVIEW QUESTIONS AND PROBLEMS

1. X is a partner in the XYZ Company. X used profits from the partnership to buy stock in his own name. In a suit for an accounting, the question arises as to whether the firm is entitled to the profit from the sale of the stock. Who is entitled to the profit?

2. A, B, and C were members of X Company, a partnership. A and C paid themselves large salaries, rented partnership property at low rates, and excluded B from participating in management of the business. Did B have any legal basis for a suit against A and C?

3. X, Y, and Z, in partnership, operated a construction business. Y contracted to build a ferryboat and ordered materials from A. When Y did not make payment, A brought suit against the partnership to enforce a lien against the ferryboat. A claimed that all the members of the partnership were bound by the contract made by Y. Was A correct?

4. A and B were partners in a buying and selling business. B borrowed money from a bank in the partnership name. The bank brought an action against A and B to recover the loan. A claimed B had no authority to bind the partnership; thus, he could not be held liable for the debt. Was A correct?

5. A and B were partners in a jewelry business. B learned that A had a malignant cancer and was not expected to live very long. A was unaware she had cancer when the following agreement was made: Upon the death of either partner, all the partnership assets would become the sole and exclusive property of the surviving partner. A died a few months later, and the executor of the estate sued B for A's interest in the partnership. Can the executor recover A's interest in the business?

6. P was a partner in a firm operating a coal mine. P's personal truck was being used by the firm to haul coal when it was destroyed, owing to the negligence of an employee of the partnership. P claimed negligence on the part of the firm and sued the partnership, including himself as a partner. Should P be allowed to sue the partnership? Why?

7. A and B were partners in the used-car business. B was driving home from the business in a car that was part of the partnership inventory when he negligently injured P, who sued the partners individually and the partnership. B worked irregular hours, usually returning to the used-car lot after going home. Should A and the partnership be held liable? Why?

8. A and B formed a partnership and built a shopping center. Three years later, A, the managing partner, informed B that the business was in deep financial trouble, and that he had tried to sell the complex but had failed. A said that the best thing to do would be for one to buy the other out, and that their equity in the business was not worth more than $3 million. B sold his one-half interest in the partnership to A for $1,500,000. B later discovered that their equity in the business amounted to over $10 million, and that A had received several offers to purchase the business. B brought suit to rescind the sale, to have the partnership dissolved, and for accounting. Should B succeed? Why?

9. X and Y owned and operated a cafe as partners. While P was in the cafe, drinking at the bar, X assaulted him without provocation, causing serious injuries. X was sent to prison. P sues Y to recover damages for his injuries. Should P succeed? Why?

10. X and Y entered into a partnership agreement by which the partnership would construct and manage small drive-in shopping centers. It was agreed that Y would be the general contractor. Y performed his part of the partnership agreement through the Y Construction Company, of which he was president and owner. When the Y Construction Company submitted a bill to the partnership, X objected, claiming that the charges were excessive. Y Company then purchased a partnership note from the bank, which was secured by partnership property, and began foreclosure proceedings on the property. Has Y breached a duty owed to X? Why?

11. A and B operated a sawmill. A agreed to sell timber to the partnership at market prices. B brought suit against A for refusing to sell timber to the partnership on credit. Did A breach his partnership duties? Why?

12. A advances to a partnership, for a period of sixty days, the sum of $19,000 in addition to his agreed capital. Is he entitled to interest on the advance? Why?

13. A and B have been partners for a number of years. Upon A's death, B spent considerable time in winding up the partnership affairs. Is he legally entitled to compensation for his services? Explain.

Dissolution of Partnerships

1. Introduction

The term *dissolution* is used to describe the legal destruction of the partnership relationship. Dissolution occurs whenever a partner ceases to be a member of the firm or whenever a new partner is admitted to the firm.

There are three separate steps necessary for the complete extinguishment of an existing partnership. They are (1) dissolution, (2) winding up, and (3) termination. *Dissolution* is the change in the relation of the partners caused by any partner's ceasing to be associated in the carrying on as distinguished from the winding up of the business. Dissolution alone does not act to terminate the partnership but rather designates the point in time when the partners cease to carry on the business together. *Winding up* involves the process of reducing the assets to cash, paying off the creditors, and distributing the balance to the partners. *Termination* occurs only when the winding-up process is completed.

Dissolution will occur without violation of the partnership agreement (1) by the termination of the stipulated term or particular undertaking specified in the agreement; (2) by the express will of any partner when no definite term or particular undertaking is specified; [1] (3) by the agreement of all the partners; or (4) by the expulsion, in good faith, of any partner from the business, in accordance with such a power conferred by the partnership agreement.

[1] *Johnson* v. *Kennedy,* page 682.

674

2. Dissolution by Act of the Partners

A partnership at will may be legally dissolved without liability by the express will of any partner when no definite term or particular undertaking is specified. The dissolution may be accomplished by giving notice to the other parties, and no particular form of notice is required. The notice of dissolution may be express or it may be implied from circumstances that are inconsistent with the continuation of the partnership. For example, a partner whose services are essential leaves the community. This is an act of and notice of dissolution.

Expulsion of a partner is a breach of the partnership agreement unless the agreement confers the power of expulsion upon a majority of the partners. For example, assume that A, B, and C are partners. A and B cannot expel C unless that power is specifically granted in the agreement. However, if there is no power to expel, partners may seek judicial dissolution if one partner is guilty of violating the partnership agreement (see the next section). To illustrate, assume that C in the case above was not devoting his time to the business as required by the partnership agreement. A and B could seek a judicial dissolution on these grounds, although they could not expel C.

Dissolution may also occur in violation of the partnership agreement. Although the agreement stipulates the length of time the partnership is to last, dissolution is always possible, because the relationship is essentially a mutual agency not capable of specific performance and, therefore, each partner has the power, though not necessarily the *right,* to revoke the relationship. In the event of wrongful dissolution, the wrongdoer is liable for damages.

3. By Operation of Law

If, during the period of the partnership, events occur that make it impossible or illegal for the partnership to continue, it will be dissolved by operation of law. Such events or conditions are death or bankruptcy of one of the partners, or a change in the law that makes the continuance of the business illegal.

A partnership is a personal relationship existing by reason of contract. Therefore, when one of the partners dies, the partnership is dissolved. However, it is not terminated on dissolution but continues for the purpose of winding up the partnership's affairs. The process of winding up is, in most states, the exclusive obligation and right of the surviving partner or partners. The executor or administrator of the deceased partner has no right to participate unless the deceased was the last surviving partner or unless specifically authorized by a court to do so. As a general rule, the estate of the deceased partner is not bound on new contracts unconnected with winding up that are entered into after dissolution, even though the partnership agreement provided that the partnership be continued.

The bankruptcy of a partner will dissolve the partnership, because the control of his property passes to his assignee or trustee for the benefit of the creditors in somewhat the same way that the control of the property passes to the legal representatives upon the death of a partner. The mere insolvency of a partner will not be sufficient to justify a dissolution, unless there has been an assignment of his assets. The bankruptcy of the firm itself is a cause for dissolution, as is also a valid assignment of all the firm assets for the benefit of creditors.

4. Dissolution by Court Decree

When a partnership, by its agreement, is to be continued for a term of years, circumstances may arise that might make the continued existence of the firm impossible and unprofitable. Therefore, upon the application of one of the partners to a court of equity, the partnership may be dissolved. The following are the circumstances and situations in which a court of equity may order dissolution:

1. Total incapacity of a partner to conduct business and to perform the duties required under the contract for partnership.

2. A declaration by judicial process that a partner is insane.

3. Gross misconduct and neglect or breach of duty by a partner to such an extent that it is impossible to carry out the purposes of the partnership agreement. The court will not interfere and grant a decree of dissolution for mere discourtesy, temporary inconvenience, differences of opinion, or errors in judgment. The misconduct must be of such gross nature that the continued operation of the business would be unprofitable.

4. Willful and persistent commitment of breach of the partnership agreement, misappropriation of funds, or commitment of fraudulent acts.

5. A partnership that was entered into by reason of fraud may be dissolved on the application of an innocent party.

5. Effect of Dissolution on Powers and Duties of Partners

The process of winding up, except when the agreement provides for continuation by purchase of a former partner's share, involves the liquidation of the partnership assets so that cash may be available to pay creditors and to make a distribution to the partners. When the agreement provides for continuation and purchase of a deceased partner's interest, the technical dissolution is followed by valuation and payment, and the new firm immediately commences business.

As a general rule, dissolution terminates the actual authority of any partner to act for the partnership, except so far as may be necessary to wind up partnership affairs, to liquidate the assets of the firm in an orderly manner, or to complete transactions begun but not then finished.[2] This termination of authority eliminates actual authority as it relates to the partners; but when it

---

[2] *North Star Coal Company* v. *Eddy,* page 683.

concerns third persons who had dealings with the firm, apparent authority still exists until notice of termination is given.

This apparent authority means that one partner of a dissolved partnership may bind the firm on contracts unconnected with winding up the firm's affairs. When he does so, issues arise as to whether or not the new obligations may be met with partnership funds or whether the contracting partner is entitled to contribution toward payment of the debt or obligation from the other partners.

The resolution of these issues depends upon the cause of the dissolution. If the dissolution is caused by (1) the act of a partner, (2) bankruptcy of the partnership, or (3) the death of a partner, each partner is liable to the other partner for his share of any liability incurred on behalf of the firm after dissolution, just as if there had been no dissolution, unless the partner incurring the liability had knowledge of the dissolution. In these situations, where knowledge of the dissolution is present, the partner incurring the liability is solely responsible, and he cannot require his fellow partners to share the burden of his unauthorized act. If the dissolution is not caused by the act, bankruptcy, or death of a partner but by some event such as a court decree, no partner has authority to act and therefore no right to contribution from other partners exists for liabilities incurred after dissolution.

When dissolution results from the death of a partner, title to partnership property remains in the surviving partner or partners for puposes of winding up and liquidation. Both real and personal property is, through the survivors thus made available to a firm's creditors. All realty is treated as though it were personal property; it is sold and the surviving partners finally account, usually in cash, to the personal representative of the deceased partner for the latter's share in the proceeds of liquidation.

Upon dissolution, it is the duty of the remaining partner or partners to wind up the affairs. If they fail to do so and instead continue the business, they have liability to the withdrawing partner, his assignee, or personal representative for use of partnership assets. The liability may include interest if the value of the former partner's portion of the partnership can be ascertained. It may also include liability for a share of postdissolution profits. This liability arises because the business is continuing to use the assets of all the former partners.

6. Rights of Partners after Dissolution

Upon dissolution, a withdrawing partner who has not breached the partnership agreement has certain options with regard to his interest in the dissolved partnership. First, he may require the partnership to be wound up and terminated. Upon the exercise of this option, the partnership is liquidated and the assets are distributed among the partners. In the alternative, the withdrawing partner may allow the business to continue or accept the fact that it has continued.

If the withdrawing partner allows the business to continue, the value of his interest in the partnership as of the date of dissolution is ascertained. He then has the right to receive, at his option after an accounting, either the value of his interest in the partnership with interest or, in lieu of interest, the profits attributable to the use of his right in the property of the dissolved partnership. The portion of profits to which a withdrawing partner is entitled because of the use of property will almost always be less than his portion prior to dissolution. This is true because a portion of the profit is usually attributable to services of the continuing partners.[3]

Where the dissolution is caused in any way other than the breach of the partnership agreement, each partner has a right to insist that all the partnership assets be used first to pay firm debts. After firm obligations are paid, remaining assets are used to return capital contributions and to distribute profits. All the partners, except those who have caused a wrongful dissolution of the firm, have the right to participate in the winding up of the business. The majority may select the method or procedure to be followed in the liquidation, but the assets, other than real estate, must be turned into cash unless all the partners agree to distribution in kind.

If a partnership that is to continue for a fixed period is dissolved by the wrongful withdrawal of one partner, the remaining members may continue as partners under the same firm name for the balance of the agreed term of the partnership. They are required to settle with the withdrawing partner for his interest in the partnership, however. The remaining partners are required to compensate the withdrawing partner, but they are allowed to subtract from the amount due in cash the damages caused by his wrongful withdrawal. In the calculation of his share, the goodwill of the business is not taken into consideration.

Just as a partner whose property is used to earn postdissolution profits is entitled to share in such profits, one who continues the partnership business after dissolution and contributes substantial labor and management services thereto is entitled to compensation for that share of the profits attributable to such services. A partner who withdraws from a partnership has no interest in profits that are attributable to labor and management services of continuing partners and that are earned after dissolution and before final accounting.

It is often difficult to accurately value the interest of a withdrawing or deceased partner when the business continues. The buy and sell provisions will control the method for establishing the value of the interest as of the date of dissolution. However, it should be recognized that mathematical certainty is impossible when valuing a withdrawing partner's interest in a dissolved partnership.

7.   Effect of Dissolution on Third Parties

Dissolution of a partnership terminates the authority of the partners to create future liability, but it does not discharge the existing liability of any partner. An agreement between the partners themselves that one or more of the

---

[3] *Hilgendorf* v. *Denson,* page 684.

partners will assume the partnership liabilities and that a withdrawing partner will be discharged does not bind the firm creditors. However, upon dissolution, a partner who withdraws may be discharged from any existing liability by an agreement to that effect with the creditors.

When firm assets are insufficient to pay firm debts, the individual property of partners, including the estate of a deceased partner, is subject to the claims of third parties for all debts created while the partnership existed. This liability is subject to the payment of individual debts, however.

8. Notice on Dissolution

After dissolution, two categories of parties are entitled to notice of the dissolution. First of all, firm creditors, including all former creditors, are entitled to actual notice of the dissolution. Transactions entered into after dissolution without such notice continue to bind withdrawing partners and the estate of deceased partners.[4] However, if proper notice is given, former partners are not liable for contracts unconnected with winding up the partnership's affairs. The giving of actual notice eliminates the apparent authority to bind the former firm and its partners.

Notice of dissolution is required whether the dissolution is caused by an act of the parties or by operation of law, except where a partner becomes bankrupt or the continuation of the business becomes illegal. Therefore, upon death of a partner, the personal representative should give immediate notice of the death and dissolution in order to avoid further liability.

The second category of parties entitled to notice of dissolution consists of persons who knew about the partnership but who were not creditors. Where the dissolution is caused by an act of the parties, the partners will continue to be liable to all such parties unless public notice of such dissolution is given. Notice by publication in a newspaper in the community where the business has been transacted is sufficient public notice.

Where a partner has not actively engaged in the conduct of the partnership business, and creditors have not learned that he was a partner and have not extended credit to the firm on the faith of such partner, there is no duty to give notice to either of the groups mentioned above.

9. New Partners and New Firms

A person admitted as a partner into an existing partnership is, as a member of the firm, liable to the extent of his investment for all obligations created before his admission, as though he had previously been a partner. His separate estate is not liable for such obligations, and the creditors of the old firm can look only to the firm assets and to the members of the old firm.

If a business is continued without liquidation of the partnership affairs,

[4] *Letellier-Phillips Paper Co.* v. *Fiedler et al.,* page 685.

creditors of the first, or dissolved, partnership are also creditors of the partnership continuing the business. Likewise, if the partners assign all their interest to a single partner, who continues the business without liquidation of the partnership affairs, creditors of the dissolved partnership are also creditors of the single person so continuing the business.

DISTRIBUTIONS ON DISSOLUTION

10. Solvent Partnerships

Upon the dissolution of a solvent partnership and a winding up of its business, an accounting is had to determine its assets and liabilities. Before the partners are entitled to participate in any of the assets, whether such partners are owed money by the firm or not, all firm creditors other than partners are entitled to be paid. After firm creditors are paid, the assets of the partnership are distributed among the partners, as follows:

1. Each partner who has made advances to the firm, or has incurred liability for or on behalf of the firm, is entitled to be reimbursed.[5]

2. Each partner is then entitled to the return of the capital that he has contributed to the firm.

3. Any balance is distributed as profits, in accordance with the partnership agreement.

In many partnerships, one partner contributes capital and the other partner contributes labor. In such cases, the partner contributing labor has nothing to be returned in step number 2 above. Of course, the original agreement could place a value on such labor, but unless it does so, only the partner who actually contributes cash or other property will be repaid in step number 2.

11. Insolvent Partnerships

When the firm is *insolvent* and a court of equity is responsible for making the distribution of assets, the assets are distributed in accordance with a rule known as "marshalling of assets."

Persons entering into a partnership agreement impliedly agree that the partnership assets shall be used for the payment of the firm debts before the payment of any individual debts of the partners. Consequently, a court of equity, in distributing firm assets, will give priority to firm creditors in firm assets as against the separate creditors of the individual partners and will give priority to private creditors of individual partners in the separate assets of the partners as against firm creditors. Each class of creditors is not permitted to

[5] *Park Cities Corporation* v. *Byrd,* page 686.

use the fund belonging to the other until the claims of the other have been satisfied. Because the firm creditors have available two funds out of which to seek payment—firm assets and the individual assets of the partners—and individual creditors of the partners have only one fund—the personal assets of the partners—equity compels the firm creditors to exhaust firm assets before having recourse to the partners' individual assets.[6]

The doctrine of marshalling of assets does not apply, however, if a partner conceals his existence and permits the other member of the firm to deal with the public as sole owner of the business. Under these circumstances, the dormant partner by his conduct has led the creditors of the active partner to rely upon firm assets as the separate property of the active partner, and by reason of his conduct, the dormant partner is estopped from demanding an application of the equity rule that firm assets shall be used to pay firm creditors in priority, and individual assets to pay individual creditors. Thus, the firm assets must be shared equally with firm creditors and the individual creditors of the active partner. In such a case, since the firm assets may not be sufficient to pay all the firm debts when depleted by payments to individual creditors, there may be unpaid firm creditors, and dormant partners will be personally liable. Since the firm creditors' right to firm property rests upon the partners' right that firm assets be used to pay firm debts, the conduct that estops a dormant partner also denies the creditors such a preference. Furthermore, the creditors who relied upon the assets in the hands of the sole active partner cannot claim a preference when later they learn such assets were partnership assets.

Just as the individual creditors are limited to individual assets, firm creditors are limited to firm assets. Therefore, firm creditors are not entitled to payment out of the individual assets of the partners until the individual creditors have been paid. This rule applies even though the firm creditors may, at the same time, be individual creditors of a member of the firm. There are two main exceptions to this general rule: (1) Where there are no firm assets and no living solvent partners. The rule for the limit of firm creditors to firm assets applies only where there are firm assets. If no firm assets and no living solvent partner exist, the firm creditors may share equally with the individual creditors in the distribution of the individual estates of the partners. (2) If a partner has fraudulently converted the firm assets to his own use, it follows that the firm creditors will be entitled to share equally with individual creditors in such partner's individual assets.

The doctrine of marshalling of assets was not applicable to tort claims at common law and is not applicable to tort claims under the Uniform Partnership Act. Partners are individually liable in tort for the acts of the firm, its agents, and servants. The liability is joint and several. Thus, the injured party may sue the partners individually or as a partnership. The firm assets need

---

[6] *Casey et al.* v. *Grantham et al.,* page 687.

not be first used to collect a judgment, and direct action may be taken against individual assets.

DISSOLUTION OF PARTNERSHIPS CASES

Johnson v. Kennedy
214 N.E.2d 276 (Mass.) 1966

Plaintiff brought suit in equity for an accounting and for damages based on an alleged wrongful dissolution of an oral partnership. The issue was whether the dissolution was wrongful. The lower court found that it was not and entered a decree for the defendants.

KIRK, J. . . . In April, 1961, the plaintiffs Johnson and Walker joined with the defendant Donald C. Kennedy (Kennedy) in forming an insurance agency partnership to be known as the Triangle Insurance Agency (Triangle). The arrangement was oral. There was no agreement as to how long the partnership would continue. It was agreed that each would have a one-third interest in the partnership. . . .

In August, 1963, the partners retained counsel to prepare a written partnership agreement. By December 7, 1963, the agreement was drawn. It provided that the partnership was to last for twenty-five years from January 1, 1964. The three partners were to meet, discuss, and sign the agreement on December 16, 1963.

Meanwhile, early in December, 1963, Kennedy secretly consulted an attorney about owning the business himself, and, without consulting Johnson and Walker, arranged that the Triangle bank accounts be held jointly with his wife. In November, Kennedy drew more than twice his salary from the agency. This caused some dispute among the partners, and Johnson took the agency's books to his home for review. On December 13, Kennedy transferred the agency funds to two Boston banks, concealing their location from the other partners, opening one account in his wife's name alone, and the other in the name of Triangle with his wife having the right to withdraw. On the night of December 14, 1963, Kennedy secretly removed all books, records, and furniture from the office to another office a block away where he opened for business under the Triangle name. On December 17, Johnson and Walker brought this bill, claiming wrongful dissolution and a right to damages. Kennedy denied . . . that the dissolution was wrongful or that damages were due. . . .

The . . . lower court adjudged that the dissolution was not wrongful and that the plaintiffs were not entitled to damages for breach of the agreement. Kennedy was ordered to pay Johnson $1,330.15 and to pay Walker $980.15. Johnson and Walker were ordered to convey all of their interest in the physical property of the partnership to Kennedy. . . .

We consider the final decree. There was no error in the rulings that the dissolution of the partnership was not wrongful and that the plaintiffs were not entitled to damages for breach of the agreement. Inasmuch as the oral agreement did not specify the life of the agency, the partnership was at the will of the partners. As G.L. c. 108A, § 31, provides, "Dissolution is caused: (1) Without violation of the agreement between the partners . . . (b) By the express will of any partner when no definite term or particular undertaking is specified." Thus, in a partnership of indefinite duration, any partner may lawfully dissolve the firm at any time. The unexecuted agreement specifying a duration of twenty-five years did not affect the nature of the existing partnership. Because the firm was a partnership at will, Kennedy's termination of it, however unseemly in manner and method, was not a legal wrong. . . .

Affirmed.

North Star Coal Company v. Eddy
277 A.2d 154 (Pa.) 1971

ROBERTS, J. This appeal . . . presents an issue . . . concerning the proper method of serving process upon a dissolved but unterminated partnership. The pertinent facts are as follows.

In the summer of 1961, appellant Carlo Teodori and one Thomas Eddy formed a partnership. . . .

On February 13, 1964, appellant and Eddy, as partners trading and doing business as the Mac Coal Company, purchased certain unmined coal from appellee North Star Coal Company and executed a purchase money mortgage and bond in appellee's favor to secure payment of an $80,000 purchase price. The terms of the bond provided that quarterly payments be made to the mortgagee, and for some time thereafter the required installments were remitted in timely fashion from the partnership office. . . .

On April 30, 1965, appellant withdrew from the partnership. He did not at that time inform any of the partnership creditors of his withdrawal but instead assumed that his attorney would perform any necessary notifications. Appellant took no further steps to publicize his withdrawal until July 10, 1969, when notice of the partnership's dissolution was filed with the Allegheny County Prothonotary.

Notwithstanding the partnership's dissolution in 1965 and for several years thereafter, quarterly mortgage payments were made to appellee, at first from the partnership office . . . and later from Thomas Eddy's private law office. . . .

The mortgage payment due May 1, 1969 was not made and appellee instituted an action of mortgage foreclosure . . . against appellant and Eddy as partners in the Mac Coal Company. Appellee's complaint was filed on July 11, 1969, one day after the filing in Allegheny County of the notice of partnership dissolution. Service was made on Thomas Eddy's private secretary at Eddy's law office. . . .

When neither appellant nor Eddy answered or appeared within the prescribed time, default judgment in the sum of $70,000 with interest was entered in favor of appellee, and on November 7, 1969, the mortgaged partnership property was sold at a sheriff's sale. On December 26, 1969, appellant petitioned the Court . . . to set aside the sheriff's sale on the ground that he had not been properly served with process in the underlying mortgage foreclosure action. Following a hearing the petition was denied . . . and the present appeal followed.

The legal norm governing service of process upon a partnership is contained in Rule 2131(a) of the Pennsylvania Rules of Civil Procedure, 12 P.S. Appendix, which provides:

> (a) Service of process upon a partner or a registered agent of a partnership, or upon the manager, clerk or other person for the time being in charge of any regular place of business of a partnership shall be deemed service upon the partnership and upon each partner individually named in the action, provided the person served is not a plaintiff in the action.

Appellant contends that Rule 2131(a) does not apply in the case of a dissolved partnership where the serving party has at least constructive notice of the dissolution and that Thomas Eddy's private secretary was not a "person for the time being in charge of any regular place of business . . . [of the] partnership."

In so arguing appellant overlooks the fundamental distinction between the dissolution of a partnership and its termination. "The dissolution of a partnership is the change in the relation of the partners caused by any partner ceasing to be associated in the carrying on, as distinguished from the winding up, of the business." Even after dissolution, a partnership is not terminated but continues to exist until the winding up of partnership affairs is completed, and the authority remains to act for the partnership in winding up partnership affairs and completing transactions begun but not yet finished at the time of dissolution.

In light of a partnership's continuing and substantial post-dissolution existence, there is no reason to conclude that the mere act of dissolution in and of itself renders inoperative the service of process provisions of Rule 2131(a). To the contrary, we are persuaded by the view adopted by the California Supreme Court in the similar case of *Cotten* v. *Perishable Air Conditioners,* 18 Cal.2d 575, 116 P.2d 603 (1941).

> In general a dissolution operates only with respect to future transactions; as to everything past the partnership continues until all preexisting matters are terminated. . . . The dissolution does not destroy the authority of a partner to act for his former associates in matters in which they still have a common interest and are under a common liability.

. . . There is no reason, therefore, why the statute authorizing a judgment against a partnership by service upon one partner . . . should not be just as effective and applicable during the period subsequent to dissolution but prior to termination of the partnership as it is during the period before dissolution. . . .

The partnership in the instant case continued to exist after its dissolution for purposes of satisfying its obligation to appellee, and for several years subsequent to its dissolution that obligation was in fact satisfied by the remitting of quarterly mortgage payments from Eddy's private law office. . . . That being so, Eddy's private office was unquestionably a "regular place of business of . . . [the] partnership" within the meaning of Rule 2131, and Eddy's private secretary was a "person for the time being in charge of" that office. We therefore hold that appellee's service of process upon Eddy's secretary fully complied with Rule 2131.

Affirmed.

Hilgendorf v. Denson
341 So.2d 549 (Fla. App.) 1977

PER CURIAM. Once again, Hilgendorf appeals from a Final Judgment entered upon Denson's claim for an accounting of the profits earned by Hilgendorf after Hilgendorf dissolved a partnership previously known as "Gateway Realty." . . . In effect . . . The Judgment required Hilgendorf to pay Denson one-half of all earnings made by her for a period of eleven months following the dissolution of the partnership.

In January, 1972, Hilgendorf and Denson formed a partnership known as "Gateway Realty." The nature of that business was to sell real estate. The partnership was compensated by earning real estate commissions. The partnership was a verbal one, with the understanding that the parties would share expenses and profits. It was not for a fixed period of time and, therefore, was subject to being dissolved at anytime by the expressed

decision of either party. . . . In January, 1973, Hilgendorf told Denson that the partnership was over and Denson left February 2, 1973.

Hilgendorf and her husband owned the premises where the partnership had previously existed. Hilgendorf remained there and continued to operate a real estate business. For six or seven weeks she operated under the name of Gateway Realty of Gainesville, Inc., and thereafter as Betty Hilgendorf, Realtor. There had recently been a classified ad placed in the telephone directory which would continue until January of 1974. Hilgendorf continued to use the same telephone number. Hence, Hilgendorf had the benefit of the telephone number and the classified advertising. Denson set up her own business at a different location. Hilgendorf accounted for and paid to Denson one-half of all the sales which resulted from listings that were in the office at the time of the dissolution of the partnership. The Judgment entered against Hilgendorf was in addition to those figures.

. . . Denson's rights are governed by the provisions of Section 620.765, Florida Statutes. Under that Statute Denson had the right to have the value of her interest on the date of dissolution ascertained and to receive the value of that interest or, at her option, to receive the profits attributable to the use of her right in the property of the dissolved partnership. As stated in *Sechrest* v. *Sechrest,* 248 Wis. 516, 22 N.W.2d 594 (1946):

> The reason for the provision in the partnership law for payment of either interest on the retiring partner's share of the assets or profits, at his option, is not because the retiring partner still retains an interest in the business but rather is intended to give him a return on assets belonging to him which still are being employed in the business by the remaining partner. . . .

By accepting the proceeds of the sales from listings which were in the office at the time of the dissolution of the partnership, Denson elected to receive a part of the profits. Any additional profits which have not been distributed to her would of necessity be limited to that part which her share of the assets of the partnership produced.

As this Court previously stated, Denson seeks to sustain her participation in Hilgendorf's profits for the eleven months period ending January 3, 1974, on the ground that under all the circumstances that is an ap-propriate period for an accounting by Hilgendorf of post-dissolution profits earned with partnership assets. . . . The difficulty from that proposition is that other than the sales already accounted for, as mentioned above, there is no evidence that any of the sales or profits made by Hilgendorf were related in any way to the assets of the partnership. The best considered authorities hold that the former partner or his estate is entitled to the profits which are earned by his share of the assets, or according to his share of the capital, after deducting such share as is attributable to the skill and services of those who have continued to carry on the business. . . .

It must be borne in mind that the profits of the partnership were the result primarily of the performance of personal services. In the absence of particular circumstances affecting the situation, a partner whose only contribution to the firm is personal services or skill is not entitled to share the profits earned after dissolution of the partnership when his services ended upon the dissolution. . . .

We agree with the proposition that if a surviving or remaining partner continues the partnership business with the partnership assets, the remaining partner is required to account to the withdrawing partner. . . .

The assets remaining at the time of the dissolution were so minimal that except for the listings already accounted for there was no basis upon which one could claim that subsequent earnings by Hilgendorf were derived therefrom. . . .

Reversed.

Letellier-Phillips Paper Co. v. Fiedler et al.
222 S.W.2d 42 (Tenn.) 1949

Plaintiffs brought this action to recover from defendants as individuals and members of a partnership for merchandise sold and delivered to them. A corporation had been formed by defendants which took over their individual and partnership assets. Plaintiffs alleged that they were not aware that the part-nership had been converted into a corporation. From a judgment in favor of plaintiffs, defendants appealed.

SWEPSTON, J. . . . The suit is on account for merchandise sold and delivered and the essential question in the trial below was whether there was partnership liability or corporate liability, the partners having operated as such for about a year and having later formed a corporation.

. . . The bill alleges that about December 24, 1945, complainant agreed to extend credit to defendants, Fiedler & Sullivan, individually and as partners trading as Fied-Sul Paper Mills. That upon the pledge of the individual credit of the defendants complainant began shipping them merchandise.

That the account about January 1, 1947, was current and amounted to $6,855.26. That subsequently the balance began to grow larger until on August 1, 1947, it amounted to $26,890.70, which later upon demand was reduced to $24,060.74 at which figure it has remained, because all purchases lately have been for cash.

That about August 1, 1947, complainant learned for the first time that a corporation had been formed by defendants and that it had taken over certain assets of the individuals and of the partnership all without notice to complainant.

That it had never dealt with the corporation and had relied upon the credit of the partnership and the individuals composing it and that said transfer of assets was fraudulent, etc.

. . . The cases show that the notice may be an express notice or may be implied from sufficient circumstances. However obtained, it must be sufficient to amount to actual knowledge where one who has been dealing with the firm before dissolution is involved. The knowledge may be constructive as to those who have not dealt with the firm before dissolution.

Affirmed.

Park Cities Corporation v. Byrd
522 S.W.2d 572 (Tex.) 1975

Mr. Byrd was the general partner in a limited partnership. She made numerous loans to the partnership during her lifetime. These loans were evidenced by promissory notes bearing interest. When Mrs. Byrd died, the executors of her estate filed this suit for instruction as to the proper method for winding up the partnership. The limited partners contended that the loans were capital contributions and should be repaid as such.

KEITH, J. . . . The partnership agreement provided that the general partner "shall have the sole and exclusive control of the management of the business of the partnership and shall devote such part of her time, attention, talent, capital, credit and business capacity to the business of the partnership as is necessary for its successful operation." The agreement did *not* require Mrs. Byrd to contribute a fixed or stated dollar amount of capital contribution; and, although granting her sole and exclusive control of the management, did not contain any provision prohibiting the borrowing of funds.

Upon a complete record, the trial court found as a fact that the loans so made by Mrs. Byrd were actual "bona fide loans made to the Limited Partnership by the General Partner, and are not capital contributions." Whether an advance by a partner is a loan or an added contribution to the capital of the firm is a question of fact. . . .

It is neither illegal nor improper for a partner to make a loan to a partnership of which he is a member. As stated in 60 Am. Jur. 2d, *Partnership* § 309 at 204 (1972):

> Under the Uniform Partnership Act, the second rank in order of payment is for those liabilities owing to partners other than for capital and profits. This provision is in accord with the general rule that in the absence of an agreement which will determine rights as to advances, each partner is a creditor of the firm as to money loaned it and has a right to repayment after the debts to other creditors have been met. The payment of interest on advances apparently also falls within the second rank in order

of payment if there is an express or implied agreement to pay interest. . . .

In *Moore* v. *Steele,* 67 Tex. 435, 3 S.W. 448, 450 (1887), Judge Gaines held that a partner "who has advanced money to the firm beyond his share of the capital is entitled to retain the amount due him before the other partners are entitled to recover any of the assets."

In Crane & Bromberg, *supra* (§ 65 at 369), the authors state:

Before profits are shared on dissolution, payments must be made to creditors, and partners must be *repaid their advances* and their capital contributions. Presumably the partner making advances is entitled to interest thereon until paid.

. . . We hold that . . . the partner is entitled to be repaid the advances, with interest, before payments are made for those owing to partners in respect of capital or in respect of profits. . . .

Affirmed.

Casey et al. v. Grantham et al.
79 S.E. and 735 (N.C.) 1954

Plaintiff, Casey, brought this action against defendant Harold J. Grantham, his partner in the sawmill and cotton gin business, for a partnership accounting and against defendant Clarence Grantham to enjoin the foreclosure of a deed of trust on partnership property and on the home and farm of plaintiffs until a partnership accounting had been obtained. The deeds of trust had been given to secure a loan made to the partnership by defendant Clarence Grantham. Plaintiffs contended that the partnership property was well worth the amount of the debt owed by the partnership to Clarence Grantham. The lower court sustained a demurrer to the complaint, and plaintiffs appealed.

PARKER, J. . . . G.S. § 59-68(1) reads:

When dissolution is caused in any way except in contravention of the partnership agreement, each partner, as against his copartners and all persons claiming through them in respect of their interest in the partnership, unless otherwise agreed, may have the partnership property applied to discharge its liabilities, and the surplus applied to pay in cash the net amount owing to the respective partners.

. . . It is said in 68 C.J.S., *Partnership,* § 185, p. 639, "The right, in equity, to have

the partnership and individual assets marshaled is for the benefit and protection of the partners themselves, and, therefore, the equity of a creditor, to the application of this doctrine, is of a dependent and subordinate character, and must be worked out through the medium of the partners or their representatives." . . .

Each partner has the right to have the partnership property applied to the payment or security of partnership debts in order to relieve him from personal liability.

It appears that under the general rule as to marshaling partnership and individual assets, or under the application of a principle of equity similar to that rule, the rule that partnership debts may be paid out of individual assets is subject to the modification that the individual assets may be so applied where, and only where, there are no firm assets, or where the firm assets have become exhausted. It would seem that the rationale for this modification to the rule rests upon the fact that the partners occupy the position of sureties in respect to their individual property being liable for the payment of partnership debts.

. . . It may be that the property of the partnership conveyed in the deed of trust may not sell for enough at a forced sale to pay Clarence Grantham's debt in full—though the demurrer admits that it will—but that Harold J. Grantham may be indebted to the partnership in an amount to make up such deficiency, if such a deficiency should exist. How can that be determined, until there is an accounting between the parties of the partnership affairs?

Under the rules laid down above it would seem to be plain that the plaintiffs have alleged sufficient facts to enjoin a foreclosure sale under the deed of trust until there has been an accounting and settlement of the partnership affairs between the partners, Casey and Harold J. Grantham. Under such circumstances it is the rule with us that an injunction should be granted where the injury, if any, which the defendant Clarence Grantham, would suffer from its issuance would be slight as compared with the irreparable damage which the plaintiffs would suffer from the forced sale of their home and farm from its refusal, if the plaintiffs should finally prevail.

Reversed.

CHAPTER 36
REVIEW QUESTIONS AND PROBLEMS

1. X Company was a partnership owned by A and B. On the death of A, B had a suit brought against him, by the receiver of the firm, to liquidate the business and make an accounting. B claimed he was entitled to compensation for his services "in winding up the partnership affairs." It was shown that B had used a partnership truck and funds and never accounted for them. Is B entitled to compensation? Explain.

2. The X Company was owned by A, B, and C. Upon the deaths of A and C, B made an agreement with their estates to continue the partnership. B brought an action for a decree to declare himself the sole remaining partner and owner of the business. Was B the sole owner? Explain.

3. A and B ran a partnership. A was permitted to be absent from the business for a period of two years because of a nervous condition. At the end of the two years, A did not return to work but did continue to draw money from the firm's bank account. B was unable to determine the firm's bank balance at any point in time and could not run the business efficiently. A suit was brought by B for the appointment of a receiver and the dissolution of the partnership. What result? Why?

4. A Company sold machinery to X, Y, and Z, a limited partnership. The partnership was dissolved, and the capital contributions of X and Y, the limited partners, were returned to them. The partnership then could not pay its debts, and A sued for payment. Can A collect from the limited partners X and Y? Why?

5. A, B, and C take a new partner, D, into their business. He invests $3,000. What is the extent of his liability, if any, to creditors of the old firm? What are the rights of creditors of the old firm, in comparison with creditors of the new firm, in the firm assets? Explain.

6. A, B, and C operated an insurance and real estate partnership. B and C discovered that A had failed to account for various sums to the partnership, and they "permanently suspended" A from the partnership and divided his interest between themselves. The partnership agreement did not contain any provisions for expulsion of a partner from the business. A brought suit for dissolution and an accounting for his share of the partnership. Should A succeed? Why?

7. X and Y formed a partnership, but one year later mutually agreed to dissolution. The only notice of dissolution was by publication in a newspaper in the community where their business had been transacted. By agreement, X continued to operate the business. Z Company, which had been a previous creditor of the partnership, continued to extend credit to the business. When Z Company was not paid, it brought suit against both X and Y. Should Y be held liable for the credit extended after dissolution? Why?

8. A and B owned a newspaper as a partnership. A died, and B continued to operate the business even though the representative of A's estate attempted, unsuccessfully, to sell the newspaper. Three years after the death of A, B began to wind up the business. X, an accountant, performed services of the same type for the newspaper both before and after A's death. Should the estate of A be partially liable for these services? Why?

9. A and B operated a cosmetics concern as a partnership. X performed printing services for the business and was paid in full. The partnership incorporated, becoming A and B, Inc., but X was not informed of this change of status. Shortly thereafter, X performed additional services but was not paid. Can X hold A and B liable in their individual capacities? Why?

10. A and B operated a farm as partners under an agreement that expired by its own terms in 1956. Even though the business had been financially successful, A and B became involved in a series of arguments over matters of a trivial nature. B brought suit to dissolve the partnership in 1955. Should dissolution be granted? Why?

The Formation of Corporations

1. Introduction

Corporations may be classified in a variety of ways. Public corporations may be contrasted with private corporations. Corporations for profit, or business corporations, are distinguished from not-for-profit corporations. Each state classifies corporations doing business within that state as foreign or domestic, to denote the state where incorporation took place. Moreover, each state has a variety of statutes relating to such specialized corporations as cooperatives, church and religious corporations, and fraternal organizations. In this chapter and those that follow, we are primarily concerned with the private business corporation.

The statutes relating to business corporations vary from state to state, yet they are quite similar. For our discussion, the basic principles of the Model Business Corporation Act will be used. This model act, prepared by the Commissioners on Uniform State Laws, has been adopted in substance by a majority of the states, and other states have enacted many of its provisions. Thus, it is a major influence on the law of corporations throughout the country. However, it is necessary to check one's own state statute relating to corporations in order to be adequately advised on any particular issue.

A *corporation* is an artificial, intangible being, created by law. It is a method by which individuals unite under a common name, for common purposes, as long as the entity continues to exist. As a legal entity, the corporation is not affected by the death, incapacity, or bankruptcy of a member. Its owners do not have personal liability on its contracts [1] and it has no liability for the obligations of its shareholders. It owns property and can sue or be sued the same as a natural person.

A corporation is also a person for purposes of both tort and criminal law. As an impersonal entity, it can act only through agents and servants, but the corporation is subject to the doctrine of *respondeat superior* and may be punished for certain criminal acts of its agents or servants.

Although a corporation is considered a person under most statutes, there are a few, such as those allowing the appointment of "suitable persons" as parole officers, in which it is not a "person." A corporation is a person for purpose of the due process clause of the Fifth and Fourteenth Amendments to the United States Constitution. However, for purposes of the privilege against compulsory self-incrimination, it is not a person.

2. Procedure for Incorporation

The law defines the purposes for which corporations may be formed and prescribes the steps to be taken for the creation of the corporation. Most statutes provide that a specified number of adult citizens, usually not less than three, may file an application for a charter. The application contains the names and addresses of the incorporators; the name of the proposed corporation; the purposes for which it is to be formed; its proposed duration; the location of its registered office; the name of its registered agent; and information about its capital stock. For example, it will indicate if there are to be both common stock and preferred stock and the par value, if any, of each.

Some states also require the names and addresses of the subscribers to the capital stock and the amount subscribed and paid in by each. It is usually indicated whether the stock is to be paid for in cash or in property.

The application, signed by all the incorporators and acknowledged by a notary public, is forwarded to a state official, usually the secretary of state. The official then issues a charter. Upon receipt of the charter, it is filed by the incorporators in the proper recording office. The receipt of the charter and its filing are the operative facts that bring the corporation into existence and give it authority and power to do business.

After the charter has been received and filed, the incorporators and all pre-incorporation subscribers to stock meet and elect a board of directors. They may also adopt the bylaws of the corporation if the applicable law so provides. In most instances, the bylaws are adopted by the board of directors and not by the shareholders. The board of directors that has been elected then meets, adopts the bylaws, elects the officers, calls for the payment of the subscription price for the stock, and makes whatever decisions are necessary to commence business.

[1] *Lamas* v. *Baldwin*, page 703.

3.   The Bylaws

The power to alter, amend, or revoke the bylaws is vested in the board of directors unless reserved to the shareholders by statute or by the articles of incorporation. The board cannot, however, repeal, amend, or add to the bylaws where such change will affect the vested rights of a shareholder.

A bylaw is a rule for governing and managing the affairs of the corporation that is binding upon all shareholders. The provisions of the bylaws are not binding on third parties unless the third parties have knowledge of them. The bylaws contain provisions establishing the corporate seal and the form of stock certificate to be used. They also contain provisions covering the number of officers and directors, the method of electing them and removing them from office, and the enumeration of their duties. They also specify the time and place of the meetings of the directors and the shareholders. Together with the articles of incorporation and the applicable statute, the bylaws provide the rules for operating the corporation. The bylaws are subservient to the articles of incorporation and the statute but are of greater authority than, for instance, a single resolution of the board. Failure to follow the bylaws constitutes a breach of the fiduciary duties of a director or officer.

4.   Entity Disregarded

One of the basic advantages of the corporate form of business organization is the limitation of shareholder liability. Corporations are formed for the express purpose of limiting one's risk to the amount of his investment in the stock. Sometimes suits are brought to hold the shareholders personally liable for an obligation of a corporation. Such suits attempt to "pierce the corporate veil" and ask the court to look behind the corporate entity and take action as though no entity separate from the members existed. However, the corporate entity may not be disregarded simply because all the stock is owned by the members of a family or by one person, or by another corporation.[2]

In certain situations, the corporate entity may be disregarded. For example, if the use of the corporation is to defraud or to avoid an otherwise valid obligation, the court may handle the problem as though no corporation existed. To illustrate, let us assume that A and B sold a certain business and agreed not to compete with the buyer for a given number of years. Desirous of re-entering business, in violation of the contract term, they organize a corporation, becoming the principal stockholders and managers. The buyer may have the corporation enjoined from competing with him as effectively as he could have enjoined A and B from establishing a competing business. Likewise, if the corporate device is used to evade a statute, the corporate entity may be disregarded. For example, if a state law provides that a person may not hold more than one liquor license at a time, this law cannot be circumvented by

---

[2] *Divco-Wayne Sales Fin. Corp.* v. *Martin Vehicle Sales*, page 704.

forming multiple corporations. The attempt to evade the statute would justify "piercing the corporate veil."

Finally, the corporate entity is sometimes disregarded when a court determines that the ends of justice require "piercing the corporate veil." Today, courts may treat an individual and a corporation as identical where unusual facts and the conduct of the parties are such that the distinct corporate entity ought to be disregarded.

5. Foreign Corporations

A corporation organized under the laws of a particular state or country is called, within that particular state or country, a "domestic corporation." When such a corporation does business within another state or country, it is called a "foreign corporation" in such state or country. Domestic corporations become qualified to do business upon receipt and recording of their charter. Foreign corporations with significant intrastate activities must also "qualify" to do business by obtaining a certificate of authority and by paying the license fees and taxes levied on local businesses. A foreign corporation engaged wholly in *interstate* commerce through a state need not qualify in such state.

Most state statutes require foreign corporations to qualify to do business by filing a copy of their articles of incorporation with the secretary of state. They are also required to appoint an agent upon whom service of process may be served, and to maintain an office in the state. Failure to comply results in a denial of the right of access to the courts.[3] In a real sense this prevents them from conducting business, because the corporation's contracts are not enforceable by suit and debtors would thus be able to avoid payment to the corporation. However, a corporation that has not qualified may still be sued, and noncompliance cannot be used as a defense by the corporation when sued by a third party. Transacting business within the state without complying with the statute also subjects the corporation and its officers to statutory penalties, such as a fine.

The term *doing business* is not reducible to an exact and certain definition. The Model Business Corporation Act defines the term by saying that a foreign corporation is *doing business* when "some part of its business substantial and continuous in character and not merely casual or occasional" is transacted within a state. A corporation is not *doing business* in a state merely because it is involved in litigation or maintains a bank account or an office within a state for the transfer of its stock. It also states that a foreign corporation is not required to obtain a license to do business by reason of the fact that (1) it is in the mail-order business and receives orders from a state that are accepted and filled by shipment from without the state, and (2) it uses salesmen within a state to obtain orders that are only accepted and approved from without the state. However, a foreign corporation is required

[3] *Farmers Bank* v. *Sinwellan Corporation,* page 705.

to obtain a license if the orders are accepted or filled from within the state or if any sale, repair, or replacement is made from stock physically present within the state in which the order is obtained.

6. Powers of Corporations

The application for a charter includes a statement of the powers desired by the corporation. These are usually stated in quite broad language. A corporation has only such powers as are conferred upon it by the state that creates it. The charter, together with the statute under which it is issued, sets forth the express powers of the corporation. In addition, all powers reasonably necessary to carry out the expressed powers are implied.

The following general powers are ordinarily granted to the corporation by statute: (1) to have perpetual existence; (2) to sue and be sued; (3) to have a corporate name and corporate seal; (4) to own, use, convey, and deal in both real and personal property; (5) to borrow and lend money other than to officers and directors; (6) to purchase, own, and dispose of securities; (7) to enter into contracts of every kind; (8) to make charitable contributions; (9) to pay pensions and establish pension plans; and (10) all powers necessary or convenient to effect any of the other purposes.

The power to acquire securities includes the power to own a corporation's own stock. Such stock, called treasury stock, has been legally issued, fully paid for, and reacquired by gift or purchase but has not been formally canceled. A corporation is restricted in its power to purchase treasury stock, because the purchase might effect a reduction of its capital to the detriment of creditors. In most states, a corporation is permitted to purchase shares of its own stock only out of accumulated profits or surplus. This retains an investment in the corporation by stockholders equivalent to the original capital as a protective cushion for creditors in case subsequent losses develop.

A corporation that has issued preferred stock has the power to redeem such stock, where there is no injury to, or objection by, creditors. Here again, many of the states require the preferred stock to be redeemed out of surplus or demand that authority to reduce capital stock be obtained from the state.

7. Ultra Vires

Any acts of a corporation that are beyond the authority, express or implied, given to it by the state are said to be *ultra vires* acts—"beyond the authority." If a corporation performs acts or enters into contracts to perform acts that are *ultra vires,* the state creating such a corporation may forfeit its charter for misuse of its corporate authority. The extent of the misuse is controlling in determining whether the state will take away its franchise or merely enjoin the corporation from further *ultra vires* conduct.

At common law, a corporation had no liability on contracts beyond its corporate powers, because the corporation has capacity only to do those things expressly authorized within its charter or incidental thereto. However, most modern statutes, including the Model Business Corporation Act, provide that all *ultra vires* contracts are enforceable. Neither party to such a contract may use *ultra vires* as a defense. *Ultra vires* conduct on the part of the corporation may be enjoined by the state or any shareholder, but otherwise, contracts previously made are binding whether they be wholly executory, partially executed, or fully performed. In such cases, the directors are liable to the shareholder for losses suffered as a result of engaging in *ultra vires* activities.

OTHER ASPECTS OF CORPORATE FORMATION

8. Promoters

A *promoter,* as the name implies, is one who promotes the corporation and assists in bringing it into existence. One or more promoters will be involved in making application for the charter, holding the first meeting of shareholders, entering into preincorporation subscription agreements, and engaging in other activities necessary to bring the corporation into existence. Promoters are responsible for compliance with the applicable blue-sky laws (statutes relating to the sale of securities), including the preparation of a prospectus if required.

Many of these activities involve the incurring of contractual obligations or debts. For example, the preparation of the application for a charter requires the assistance of a lawyer, and it must be accompanied by the required filing fee. Legal questions frequently arise as to who has liability for these obligations and debts. Is the promoter liable? Is the corporation after formation liable? Are both liable?

Certain general principles of contract and agency law prevent simple answers to these questions. First of all, a promoter is not an agent prior to incorporation, because there is no principal. A party who purports to act as an agent for a nonexistent principal is generally liable as a principal. Second, the corporation technically cannot ratify the contracts of promoters, because ratification requires capacity to contract both at the time of the contract and at the time of the ratification.

To avoid the difficulties caused by these legal theories, the law has used certain fictions to create an obligation on the part of the corporation and to provide a means to eliminate liability on the part of the promoters. One fiction is that a novation occurs. This theory proceeds on the premise that when the corporation assents to the contract, the third party agrees to discharge the promoter and to look only to the corporation. The discharge of the promoter by the third party is consideration to make binding the corporation's promise to be bound upon the contract. In the absence of a novation, the promoter will continue to be personally liable. Establishing a novation often fails because of a lack of proof of any agreement to release the promoter.

Another theory that is used to determine liability on preincorporation obligations may be described as the *offer and acceptance theory*. Under this theory, a contract made by a promoter for the benefit of the corporation is an offer that may be accepted by the corporation after it comes into existence. Acceptance of the benefits of the contract constitutes a formal ratification of it.[4]

In cases where the corporation does not accept the offer, the corporation is not liable. The promoter may or may not be liable, depending on the degree of disclosure as discussed below.

Corporations have also been held liable on promoters' contracts on theories that may be called the *consideration theory* and the *quasi-contract theory*. Under the consideration theory, a promise made after incorporation by the directors to pay for the expenses and services of promoters will be binding and supported by sufficient consideration, on the theory of services previously rendered. The quasi-contract theory holds that corporations are liable by implication for the necessary expenses and services incurred by the promoters in bringing them into existence, because such expenses and services accrue, or inure, to the benefit of the corporation. Finally, it should be noted that some states have abandoned trying to justify corporate liability with a legal theory and have simply provided by statute that corporations are liable for the reasonable expenses incurred by promoters.

The parties frequently do not intend the promoter to be liable on a preincorporation contract. A promoter may avoid personal liability by informing the other party that he does not intend to be liable and that he is acting in the name of and solely on the credit of a corporation to be formed. But if the promoter represents that there is an existing corporation when there is none, the promoter is liable. A promoter should make sure that contracts entered into on behalf of the proposed corporation are so worded as to relieve him of personal liability.

Promoters occupy a fiduciary relationship toward the prospective corporation and have no right, therefore, to secure any benefit or advantage over the corporation itself or over other shareholders, because of their position as promoters. A promoter cannot purchase property and then sell it to the corporation at an advance, nor has he a right to receive a commission from a third party for the sale of property to the corporation. In general, however, he may sell property acquired by him prior to the time he started promoting the corporation, provided he sells it to an unbiased board of directors after full disclosure of all pertinent facts.

9. Stock Subscriptions

A *preincorporation stock subscription* is an agreement to purchase stock in a corporation. It is a binding agreement (a subscriber cannot revoke his subscription) created among the subscribers for stock in a corporation to be

---

[4] *Fortune Furn. Mfg. Co., Inc.* v. *Mid-South Plastic Fab. Co.,* page 707.

formed. The subscription is usually drafted in such a manner as to create a contract. Some states have provided by statute that a preincorporation subscription constitutes a binding, irrevocable offer to the corporation, by reason of the mutual promises of the parties. The offer is usually limited to a stated period of time, such as six months.

Certain conditions are inherent in the preincorporation subscription contract. The subscriber will not be liable unless the corporation is completely organized, the full amount of the capital stock has been subscribed in the absence of an express agreement to the contrary, and the purpose, articles, and bylaws of the corporation are as originally stated and relied upon by the subscriber. Conditions, express or implied, in the stock subscription agreement are often waived by the subscriber if, with knowledge of the nonperformance, he participates in shareholders' meetings, pays part or all of his subscription, or acts as an officer or a director of the corporation.

A subscription to stock of a corporation already in existence is a contract between the subscriber and the corporation. Such a contract may come into existence by reason of an offer either made by the corporation and accepted by the subscriber or made by the subscriber and accepted by the corporation. If the corporation opens subscription books and advertises its stock, it is seeking an offer to be made by the subscriber. The corporation may, however, make a general offer to the public, which may be accepted by the subscriber in accordance with the terms of the general offer.

10. The Corporate Names

One of the provisions in the application for a corporate charter is the proposed name of the corporation. In order that persons dealing with a business will know that it is a corporation and that the investors therefore have limited liability, the law requires that the corporate name include one of the following words or end with an abbreviation of them: *corporation, company, incorporated,* or *limited.* In addition, a corporate name must not be the same as or deceptively similar to the name of any domestic corporation or that of a foreign corporation authorized to do business in the state to which the application is made.[5]

Most states have procedures for reserving a corporate name for a limited period. Inquiry is usually made as to the availability of a name, and if it is available, it is reserved while the articles are being prepared. The name may be changed by charter amendment at any time without affecting corporate contracts or title to corporate property in any way.

11. The Corporate Buy and Sell Agreement

The importance of a buy and sell agreement between partners was previously mentioned. A buy and sell agreement between shareholders in a closely held

[5] *American Legal Aid, Inc.* v. *Legal Aid Services, Inc.,* page 708.

corporation is equally desirable. It is just as important to have a means of getting a shareholder out of a closely held corporation as it is to have a means of getting a partner out of a partnership.

Shareholder buy and sell provisions should be worked out before any shareholder knows whether he is a buyer or a seller. Although withdrawal from active participation will not effect a dissolution, it can have the serious effect of precipitating a lawsuit, or a shareholder may continue to participate in management when he does not desire to do so. Frequently, a withdrawing shareholder will be forced to sell his stock for less than it is worth because a buy and sell agreement was not worked out in advance.

Corporate buy and sell provisions are similar to those in a partnership, except that the corporation as an entity is frequently a party to them. Many contracts provide that before a shareholder can sell his stock to an outsider, it must first be offered to the corporation. Some contracts also require that it be offered to other shareholders. Such rights of first refusal are legal.

Corporations may buy life insurance on the life of an officer-shareholder and use the proceeds to repurchase his stock. Stock redemptions on the death of a shareholder are an integral part of estate planning, and the various alternatives and plans to redeem such stock should be carefully studied at the time the corporation is formed.

THE BLUE-SKY LAWS

12.   Introduction

Government at both the federal and state levels is actively involved in the regulation of the sale of securities. Numerous statutes have been enacted not only to protect the investing public but to impose liability on anyone assisting in the sale of securities in violation of the law. These laws are commonly known as blue-sky laws because of their avowed purpose of preventing one person from selling another a patch of blue sky.

The responsibility for administering the federal securities law is vested in an independent regulatory agency, the Securities and Exchange Commission. The SEC exercises vast quasi-legislative and quasi-judicial powers. It employs many technical experts, including lawyers, accountants, and securities analysts. To prevent fraudulent sales of securities, the agency has adopted rules and regulations relating to financial and other information, which must be included in the documents filed with the commission as well as those given to potential investors. It also regulates the various stock exchanges, utility holding companies, investment trusts, and investment advisors.

Because the objective of the securities laws is to protect innocent persons from investing their money in speculative enterprises over which they have little or no control, the laws are paternalistic in character and are liberally construed to protect the investing public. The securities laws therefore cover not only stocks and bonds but every kind of investment in which one person invests money and looks to others for the success of the venture. Thus, the term *security* is broadly defined to include any investment in which a person turns his money or property over to another to manage for profit.

13. The Securities Act of 1933

The Securities Act of 1933 is a disclosure law. It requires that securities subject to its provisions be registered and that a prospectus be furnished each investor. The function of the prospectus is to provide the investor with sufficient facts, including financial information about the issuer, to enable the prospective buyer to make an intelligent investment decision.

This law is applicable to transactions in which a security is sold to the general public by the issuer, an underwriter, or a controlling person. A *controlling person* is one who controls or is controlled by the issuer, such as the major stockholder of a corporation. An *underwriter* is anyone who participates in the distribution by selling it for the issuer or by guaranteeing its sale.

The 1933 act is not applicable to transactions by securities dealers after 40 days have elapsed from the effective date of the public offer. If the security is offered by a company with no prior registration statements, this period is 90 days. This exemption allows a dealer to enter into transactions in securities after a minimum period has elapsed. In addition, brokers' transactions executed on any exchange or in the over-the-counter market are exempt if they are unsolicited.

The law covers public sales; private sales are exempt. This exemption for private sales is often difficult to apply. In determining whether or not a sale is being made to the general public, the SEC will examine (1) the number of offerees, (2) their knowledge about the company in which they are investing, (3) the relationship between the offeror and offeree, (4) whether the security comes to rest in the hands of the offeree or is resold, and (5) the amount of advertising involved. At one time, a sale to fewer than 25 persons was not a public sale. Although the SEC does not always follow it, the 25-persons figure is still a good rule of thumb for defining the private exemption.

The law also exempts certain securities from the registration and prospectus requirement. Securities such as those of banks, which are regulated by other government agencies, fall into this category. In addition, sales wholly in intrastate commerce as contrasted with interstate commerce are exempt. The intrastate exemption covers securities that are offered and sold only to persons who reside within the state of incorporation; or if the issuer is unincorporated, the purchasers must reside within the state of its residence and place of business. If the sale is to a resident with the intention that it will be resold to a nonresident, the intrastate exemption is lost.

The law also authorizes the SEC to create additional exemptions if it finds that the registration requirement is not necessary in the public interest and is not necessary for the protection of investors by reason of the small amount involved or the limited character of the public offering. The SEC may not exempt an issue where the total dollar value exceeds $500,000. Offerings involving under $500,000 are covered by special regulations. The SEC may also exempt securities issued under the Small Business Investment Act.

This law does not prevent the sale of low-grade or highly speculative securities. As a disclosure law, all that is required is that the negative aspects of the.offering be disclosed. A prospectus always contains a warning that the securities have not been approved by the commission and that the commission has not passed upon the accuracy of the information contained in the prospectus.

14. Liability under the 1933 Act

The 1933 Securities Act imposes both civil and criminal liability for violation of its provisions. The criminal liability is for fraud in *any* offer or sale of securities. Fraud in the sale of an exempt security is still a criminal violation if the mail is used or if an instrumentality of interstate commerce has been used.

The civil liability provisions relating to registration statements impose liability on the following persons in favor of purchasers of securities:

1. Every person who signed the registration statement

2. Every director of the corporation or partner in the partnership issuing the security

3. Every person who with his consent is named in the registration statement as about to become a director or partner

4. Every accountant, engineer, or appraiser who assists in the preparation of the registration statement or its certification

5. Every underwriter

For purposes of civil liability in connection with a registration statement, it is imposed if the registration statement (1) contains untrue statements of material facts, (2) omits material facts required by statute or regulation, and (3) omits information that if not given makes the facts stated misleading. This last stipulation describes the factual situation of a statement containing a half-truth that has the net effect of misleading the reader. The test of accuracy and materiality is as of the date the registration statement becomes effective.

A plaintiff-purchaser need not prove reliance on the registration statement, but actual knowledge of falsity is a defense. Scienter is not an element of proof, but, except for the issuer, reliance on an expert such as an accountant is a defense. The liability here is usually for the difference between the price paid by the investor, not to exceed the original offering price, and the value of the security at the time of the suit.

The law contains a separate provision relating to liability arising in connection with prospectuses and communications. It imposes liability on any person who sells or offers to sell a security without complying with the legal requirements relating to the furnishing of a proper prospectus. It also imposes liability on anyone who sells a security by use of a prospectus or an oral statement that includes untrue information or omits a material fact necessary so that the statements made will not be misleading.

The statute of limitations for both civil and criminal liability is one year. The statute does not start to run until the discovery of the untrue statement or omission, or from the time such discovery would have been made with reasonable diligence. In no event may a suit be brought more than three years after the sale.

15. The Securities Exchange Act of 1934

The 1934 act, as the title implies, is concerned with securities exchanges and with the trading of securities after the primary offering stage. In addition to creating the SEC, the 1934 act contains provisions regulating the various stock exchanges. It regulates brokers and dealers in securities and contains numerous provisions relating to such matters as proxy solicitation and insider transactions.

The Securities Exchange Act prohibits the sale of a security on a national exchange unless a registration is effective for the security. Registration under the 1934 act is somewhat different from registration under the 1933 act. Registration under the Securities Exchange Act requires the filing of prescribed forms with the applicable stock exchange and with the SEC. As a general rule, all equity securities that are held by 500 or more owners must be registered if the issuer has more than $1 million in gross assets. This rule picks up issues that are traded over the counter, and it applies to securities that might have qualified under one of the exemptions in the 1933 act.

Issuers of registered securities are required by the 1934 act to file periodic reports with the SEC, as well as to report significant developments to it. The SEC rules on proxies apply to all securities registered under the act. These rules regulate all aspects of proxy solicitation in great detail. The law also prohibits market manipulations and regulates such activities as short sales.

The provisions relating to stockbrokers and dealers prohibit the use of the mails or any instrumentality of interstate commerce to sell securities unless the broker or the dealer is registered. The language is sufficiently broad to cover advertising as well as actual sales. Brokers and dealers are required to keep detailed records and to file annual reports with the SEC.

In order to prevent "insiders" from profiting from the use of information not available to the general public, the law contains provisions on insider transactions. The law prevents short-swing profits by such insiders. Thus, if a director, officer, or principal owner realizes profits on the purchase and sale of a security within a six-month period, the profits inure to and belong to the company. The profit is calculated on the lowest price in, highest price out, in any six-month period.

The "insider" provisions also give reporting requirements for directors, officers, and any principal owner. (The last is anyone who owns more than 10 percent of any class of nonexempt securities.) The law requires that these persons file, at the time of the registration of such security or within ten days after they become such owners, directors, or officers, a statement with the commission and with the exchange of the amount of all equity securities of such issuer of which they are owners. Filing is also required within ten days after the close of each calendar month, if there has been any change in ownership. There are certain exemptions to the insider rules. For example, executors or administrators of estates are exempt for twelve months. Odd-lot dealers are also generally exempt.

16. Liability under the 1934 Act

Liability is imposed under the 1934 Securities Exchange Act for violations in addition to those relating to insider transactions and short-swing profits. Section 18, for example, imposes liability on any person who shall make or cause to be made any false and misleading statements of material fact in any application, report, or document filed under the act. This liability based on fraud is in favor of both purchasers and sellers. Plaintiffs under this section must prove scienter, reliance on the false or misleading statement, and damage. It is a defense that the person sued acted in good faith and without knowledge that the statement was false and misleading. In other words, freedom from fraud is a defense under an action predicated on Section 18. There is no liability under this section for simple negligence.

Most of the litigation under the 1934 act is brought under Section 10b and Rule 10b-5 of the SEC. These provisions are concerned with manipulative and deceptive devices and contrivances. Rule 10b-5 declares that it is unlawful to use the mails or any instrumentality of interstate commerce or any national securities exchange to defraud *any person* in connection with the *purchase or sale* of any security. As a result of judicial interpretation, this section and the rules promulgated under it provide a private remedy for defrauded investors. This remedy may be invoked against "any person" who indulges in fraudulent practices in connection with the purchase or sale of securities. In actual practice, defendants in Section 10b and Rule 10b-5 cases have tended to fall into four general categories: (1) insiders, (2) broker-dealers, (3) corporations whose stock is purchased or sold by plaintiffs, and (4) those who "aid and abet" or conspire with a party in one of the first three categories. Accountants are an example of those who may fall into the fourth category.[6] Silence may constitute aiding and abetting. Although there is no general duty on all persons who have knowledge of improper activities to report them, a duty to disclose

[6] *Ernst & Ernst* v. *Hochfelder et al.,* page 709.

may arise in the face of a special relationship or set of circumstances, such as an accountant's certifying financial statements.

The concept of fraud under Section 10b encompasses not only untrue statements of material facts but the omission to state material facts necessary to prevent the statements actually made from being misleading. In other words, a half-truth that misleads is fraudulent. Finally, a failure to correct a misleading impression left by statements already made or silence where there is a duty to speak gives rise to a violation of Rule 10b-5.

The application of Rule 10b-5 is not limited to securities subject to the act. It applies to all sales of any security. The rule requires that those standing in a fiduciary relationship disclose all material facts before entering into transactions. This means that an officer, a director, or a controlling shareholder has a duty to disclose all material facts. Failure to do so is a violation and in effect fraudulent.

The 1934 act provides for criminal penalties for willful violations. The punishment for individuals is a $10,000 fine, or imprisonment for two years, or both. Failure to file the required reports and documents makes the issuer subject to a $100 forfeiture per day.

FORMATION OF CORPORATIONS CASES

Lamas v. Baldwin
230 S.E.2d 13 (Ga.) 1976

Plaintiff, an electric contractor, sued the defendant Arthur Lamas for electrical work upon premises occupied by "Happy Herman's." In suing Lamas as an individual, plaintiff alleged that the defendant was a general contractor operating under the name of "Lamas Construction Company." Defendant contended that he had no personal liability because the contract was that of the corporation. The trial court found for the plaintiff and the defendant appealed.

CLARK, J. . . . The Lamas Company, Inc., had been doing business as a corporation since its charter had been obtained in 1958. All statutory requirements applicable to corporations had been regularly complied with. The business licenses were obtained in the corporate name. Lamas had at no time been engaged individually in the construction business. The corporation had entered into an agreement with Happy Herman's, Inc., to renovate the latter's business establishment. . . .

Plaintiff met with Lamas at the job site. The building permit at the site showed The Lamas Company, Inc., as the general contractor. Moreover, a large sign reading "Construction by The Lamas Company, Inc." adorned the construction site. Plaintiff testified he looked at the building permit but that he could not remember the name of the general contractor thereon. Plaintiff further testified that he did not know Lamas was representing the corporation when the meeting took place; that Lamas did not inform him that he was acting on behalf of the corporation; . . . and that he understood that he contracted with Lamas individually. Lamas testified that he himself was not the general contractor and that he did not engage in the construction business as an individual.

Plaintiff's wife worked in plaintiff's business office as a bookkeeper. Shortly after the work had progressed, she called the general contractor to learn how it should be billed by plaintiff. She was told that the bills should be sent to The Lamas Company, Inc. Plaintiff's statements therefore were addressed to the corporation. Lamas was never billed personally for plaintiff's work. Partial payments made to plaintiff were made on checks bearing the name "The Lamas Company, Inc." as payor. . . .

In the main appeal, defendant Lamas contends the court erred in entering judgment against him. We agree. . . . The trial court's finding that plaintiff contracted with defendant individually is clearly erroneous.

It is settled law that an agent of a corporation may be held liable individually where he does not disclose his agency. But no express words disclosing the agency are necessary, especially where the agent could reasonably believe that the other contracting party knew the real facts. The attendant circumstances in this case are such that plaintiff cannot claim defendant's agency was not disclosed. Defendant could reasonably have believed that plaintiff knew the real facts by virtue of the building permit and construction sign. Moreover, the evidence shows that *during* the course of dealing plaintiff had actual knowledge that he contracted with The Lamas Company, Inc.

Shortly after plaintiff undertook to do the work, the corporate entity and the agency relationship of Lamas were disclosed upon plaintiff's express inquiry made through his wife as his bookkeeper. Plaintiff's statements were sent to the corporation; none of the billing was in the name of defendant Lamas, personally. . . . In sum, one cannot conclude that plaintiff did not have knowledge that he was dealing with a corporation, notwithstanding the fact that at the time of the contract he did not get that specific information from Lamas.

"[A] corporation . . . is an artificial person. This legal entity retains its separate and independent character, regardless of the ownership of its capital stock; and as such it cannot be held liable for the obligations of a stockholder. Nor are the stockholders liable for the obligations of the corporation." "One person may own all the stock of a corporation, and still such individual shareholder and the corporation would, in law, be two separate and distinct persons." And one who deals with a corporation as such an entity cannot, in the absence of fraud, deny the legality of the corporate existence for the purpose of holding the owner liable. Having dealt with the corporation as his debtor, plaintiff cannot claim defendant is personally liable for its debts. . . .

Reversed.

Divco-Wayne Sales Fin. Corp. v. Martin Vehicle Sales
195 N.E.2d 287 (Ill.) 1963

Plaintiff, Divco-Wayne Sales Financial Corp., sued defendant in replevin for repossession of seven hearses. Defendant attempted to assert a counterclaim based on a contract with plaintiff's parent corporation, Divco-Wayne. The lower court allowed defendant's counterclaim to stand, and plaintiff appealed.

BURKE, J. . . . Plaintiff maintains that the counterclaim does not state a cause of action against it and that its motion to dismiss should have been allowed. The exhibit attached

to Martin's counterclaim is not an agreement between plaintiff and Martin. It is a contract between Martin and Divco-Wayne Corporation. . . .

The evidence is uncontroverted that Sales Financial, although a wholly owned subsidiary, is a separate corporation independent of the parent. The principle that a corporation is an entity separate from its shareholders and from other corporations with which it may be associated has long been recognized in Illinois, as it has universally in the United States. In the *Donnell* case Mr. Justice Holmes said, 208 U.S. p. 273, 28 S.Ct. p. 289, 52 L.Ed. 481: "A leading purpose of such statutes and of those who act under them is to interpose a nonconductor, through which, in matters of contract, it is impossible to see the men behind." In *Superior Coal Co.* v. *Department of Finance,* 377 Ill. 282, p. 289, the court said: "Ownership of capital stock in one corporation by another does not, itself, create an identity of corporate interest between the two companies, nor render the stockholding company the owner of the property of the other, or create the relation of principal and agent, representative, or *alter ego* between the two. Nor does the identity of officers of two corporations establish identity of the corporations." Divco-Wayne Corporation is engaged in the business of manufacturing vehicles. Sales Financial is in the business of financing vehicles.

The relationship of parent and subsidiary corporation will not, standing alone, render the subsidiary liable on the parent's contract. The decisions on this point are colleced in an annotation in 102 A.L.R. 1054, entitled "Liability of holding corporation on contracts of subsidiary," where the annotator says: ". . . a holding company is not, as a general rule, liable on the contracts of its subsidiary corporation."

One who seeks to have the Court apply an exception to the rule of separate corporate existence must seek that relief in his pleading and carry the burden of proving actual identity or a misuse of corporate form which, unless disregarded, will result in a fraud on him. Martin did not assert in any of its pleadings that Sales Financial and Divco-Wayne Corporation were one and the same or that it had been misled, nor did it ask the court to disregard corporate form in order to prevent a fraud from being perpetrated. . . .

The Martins had been dealers in Divco-Wayne professional cars for several years prior to the signing of the contract exhibited in this case. The three Martins testified and not one of them asserted that he was confused or misled by these two corporations or that they or the Martin Company were in any manner defrauded because of the two corporations. There is no basis in the evidence justifying the court in refusing to treat the two corporations as separate entities. The burden was upon Martin to prove either (1) identity in fact, or (2) the fraudulent misuse of corporate form. This it failed to do. The judgment against Sales Financial for commissions allegedly owed not by it but by Divco-Wayne Corporation has no basis in law. . . .

Reversed.

Farmers Bank v. Sinwellan Corporation
367 A.2d 180 (Del. Super.) 1976

DUFFY, J. . . . Plaintiff, Sinwellan Corporation, has a checking account in the Farmers Bank of the State of Delaware, defendant. The gravamen of the complaint is that Farmers wrongfully dishonored certain checks drawn on Sinwellan's account. . . . The Superior Court denied Farmers' motion to dismiss the complaint and this appeal followed.

Sinwellan is a Maryland corporation which has not registered or otherwise qualified to do business in Delaware. The State Constitution, Art. IX § 5 provides:

No foreign corporation shall do any business in this State through or by branch offices, agents or representatives located in this State, without having an authorized agent or agents in the State upon whom legal process may be served.

That provision, which is not self-executing . . . has been implemented by two statutes, the first of which is 8 Del.C. § 371; it reads:

a. As used in this chapter, the words "foreign corporation" mean a corporation organized under the laws of any jurisdiction other than this State.

b. No foreign corporation shall do any business in this State, through or by branch offices, agents or representatives located in this State, until it shall have paid to the Secretary of State of this State for the use of this State, $50, and shall have filed in the office of the Secretary of State:

1. A certificate issued by an authorized officer of the jurisdiction of its incorporation evidencing its corporate existence. . . ;

2. A sworn statement executed by an authorized officer of each corporation setting forth (i) the name and address of its registered agent in this State, which agent shall be either an individual resident in this State when appointed or another corporation authorized to transact business in this State, (ii) a statement, as of a date not earlier than 6 months prior to the filing date, of the assets and liabilities of the corporation, and (iii) the business it proposes to do in this State, and a statement that it is authorized to do that business in the jurisdiction of its incorporation.

The penalty for failure to comply with § 371 is found in 8 Del.C. § 383, which provides:

(a) A foreign corporation which is required to comply with §§ 371 and 372 of this title and which has done business in this State without authority shall not maintain any action or special proceeding in this State unless and until such corporation has been authorized to do business in this State and has paid to the State all fees, penalties and franchise taxes for the years or parts thereof during which it did business in this State without authority. This prohibition shall not apply to any successor in interest to such foreign corporation.

This case does not call for an exhaustive analysis of these statutes or their rationale. . . .

It is sufficient, we think, to make two observations about them. First, the test for applicability of § 371 is whether the foreign corporation does *any* business in this State, not whether it is "doing business" here. . . . The latter test is applicable for purposes of the long arm statute . . . but not for maintenance of an action within the meaning of § 383. The "any" business test is more comprehensive in meaning than the "doing business" test. . . . Second, non-compliance with § 371 bars a foreign corporation from maintaining "any action" in the Courts of this State. That is the penalty.

We turn now to what the record reveals about Sinwellan's activities in Delaware. It is undisputed that Sinwellan maintained a Delaware bank account in its corporate name, advertised in two Delaware newspapers of general circulation, stored its financial records in this State, executed contracts in Delaware with Delaware residents, sold or attempted to sell securities here, engaged in credit transactions with Delaware residents, and provided taxi service in Delaware to transport persons to and from places in this State.

The Superior Court was aware of these activities but found them to be "incidental" to Sinwellan's "major purpose of operating and maintaining Great Oaks Lodge in Maryland." Apparently, the Court applied the "doing business" test and found the activities inadequate to require compliance by that standard. But, as we have said, that is not the test under § 371.

We conclude that in the aggregate, at least, Sinwellan's activities in this State clearly go beyond the minimum requirements of the "any" business criterion in § 371. As this Court observed long ago . . . the primary object of the Statute is to secure to the State and its people a way to serve process on a corporation which is organized elsewhere and which comes here to act through officers or agents. Given the scope of intra-State activities in which Sinwellan is engaged, the Statute wisely requires that it formalize its presence here through the nomination of an agent, the identification of an office and by otherwise complying with § 371. Accordingly, Sinwellan must comply with § 371 before it may maintain this action. . . .

Reversed.

Fortune Furn. Mfg. Co., Inc. v. Mid-South Plastic Fab. Co.
310 So.2d 725 (Miss.) 1975

Plaintiff, a corporation, sued to collect on open account. The defendant filed a counter-claim based on an agreement with two executives of the plaintiff corporation. The agreement, which was in the form of a letter signed by W.E. Walker as President, provided that the plaintiff was to rebate 2% of all purchases with the rebate to be used by the defendant for advertising.

The agreement was entered into on July 8, 1968 but the plaintiff was not incorporated until July 22, 1968. Plaintiff's contention ·that it was not bound by the agreement entered into prior to its incorporation was accepted by the trial court.

GILLESPIE, J. . . . Is Mid-South bound by the letter?

The principal argument of Mid-South is that the letter dated July 8, 1968, written by Walker, purportedly on behalf of Mid-South and as president thereof, is not binding because Mid-South did not come into existence until July 22, 1968, the date of the charter. It is contended by Mid-South that the letter could not have been the act or the creation of Mid-South which was not then a corporate entity and that there was no ratification or adoption of the contract by affirmative action of the company after its incorporation.

The general rule is that a contract made by promoters with a view towards incorporation will be binding upon the corporation if it accepts benefits of the contract with the full knowledge of the terms of the contract.

There are several theories upon which corporations have been held liable, including the theory of adoption and the theory of ratification. In *Pearl Realty Co. v. Wells,* 164 Miss. 300, 145 So. 102 (1933), the Court spoke in terms of "ratification" and upheld a contract for services rendered in obtaining a cancellation of a lease to a lot upon which Pearl Realty Company subsequently erected a building. Pearl Realty Company was incorporated after the negotiations between the promoter of the corporation and Wells. In concluding that the corporation had ratified the contract made by the promoters, the Court said:

> It is permissible for promoters to make contracts which, if ratified by corporations after they are organized, will bind the corporations.

An analysis of *Pearl Realty Company* indicates that the term "ratification" in that opinion does not refer to any formal act of the corporation, but rather that the corporation adopted the contract and received the benefits of it with full knowledge on the part of all parties concerned in the corporation's organization of the manner and conditions under which it had been obtained. The Court held that under such circumstances the contract was binding on the corporation.

The general rule is that adoption may be implied from the acts or acquiescence of a corporation without express acceptance or ratification, and the adopting corporation will be liable if its responsible officers have or are chargeable with knowledge of the facts upon which it acts.

Stillpass and Walker, the only executive officers of Mid-South, initiated and concluded the agreement that was reduced to writing in the letter to Fortune. Stillpass admitted that Mid-South would not have been organized without Fortune's account. The jury was fully justified in finding that these two officers had full knowledge of the terms of the contract and took advantage of it to sell more than $1,000,-

000 in goods to Fortune as a result of the contract. We are of the opinion that the jury was justified under the evidence in finding that Mid-South was bound by the terms of the letter of July 8, 1968. . . .

Reversed.

American Legal Aid, Inc. v. Legal Aid Services, Inc.
503 P.2d 1201 (Wyo.) 1972

McEWAN, J. . . . This was an action by Legal Aid Services, Inc. (plaintiff below and appellee here) to enjoin the defendant, American Legal Aid, Inc. from using the term "Legal Aid" in defendant's corporate title, sales presentations, or contracts on the grounds that it was deceptively similar and therefore violated plaintiff's right as a prior incorporator to the exclusive use of the name "Legal Aid." . . . The trial court . . . entered judgment in favor of the plaintiff and against the defendant enjoining the defendant from using the term "Legal Aid" in its corporate name, contracts, sales promotions, or in any other manner, from which judgment the defendant has appealed.

Plaintiff was organized as a Wyoming non-profit corporation on December 19, 1966 . . . for the purpose of rendering free legal services to persons of low income. It was funded by a Federal grant through the Office of Economic Opportunity, and is sponsored by the Natrona County Bar Association which contributes through its members approximately 700 hours in free legal service to the poor each year. . . . It has made itself and its services known through various governmental sponsored agencies and via news media, and has rendered legal services to over 3,700 qualified individuals during its existence.

American Legal Aid commenced business as a proprietorship in 1970 and was financially backed by the DeBuse family. It sold memberships to the general public for reimbursement of attorney's fees incurred in specified areas according to a schedule. William A. DeBuse, Jr. prepared Articles of Incorporation for American Legal Aid and filed them in the office of the Wyoming Secretary of State on June 16, 1970. In the spring of 1971 the defendant corporation conducted a rather extensive selling campaign and contacted as many as 20,000 people in Natrona County, Wyoming. Through July of 1971 it had sold about 2,300 memberships. . . .

The trial court found that the evidence disclosed there was confusion as to the identities of the two corporations. It also found that the predominant words were "Legal Aid," and that those words had acquired a secondary meaning in the Natrona County community where, through extensive public relations and operational activity since 1966, the plaintiff had become known for its free services to the indigent. The trial court further found that the evidence disclosed the defendant exploited this; that the public was deceived and misled into believing the two corporations were in some way connected; and that the standing and goodwill of the plaintiff corporation was entitled to protection. . . .

There was considerable evidence that many people were confused about the two corporations, especially following the extensive telephone campaign of the defendant in the spring. Curtis L. Harden, attorney at law and executive director of plaintiff, Legal Aid Services, Inc., testified without objection that in the winter and spring of 1971 members of the Natrona County Bar Association were besieged by telephone calls from clients asking about the telephone solicitations which were thought to have been made by the plaintiff, Legal Aid Services, Inc. A committee was appointed to look into the matter and it was determined that the solicitations were not being made by plaintiff but were made by the defendant. There was evidence that some people contacted the defendant corporation when in fact they sought plaintiff corporation, and some people sought the plaintiff but contacted the defendant. Many people thought the two corporations were one and the same. As stated in 6 Fletcher Cyclopedia Corporations, § 2429, pp. 93–95 (Permanent Edition):

> What degree of resemblance or similarity between the names of the two companies will warrant the interference of the court is not capable of exact definition. It is and must be a matter to be determined from the facts and circumstances accompanying each particular case, and no inflexible rule can be laid down as to what use of names will constitute unfair competition; this is a question of fact. It has been remarked by the courts that authorities upon the question are of little help, so varied are the facts and circumstances surrounding each case.

We think that here there was sufficient credible evidence to support the findings of the trial court. . . .

There was evidence that the defendant, William A. DeBuse, Jr., deliberately or thoughtlessly selected a name to which plaintiff had acquired a prior right. A court of equity may grant injunctive relief against a defendant corporation wrongfully using a name similar to a plaintiff corporation's name, particularly where hardship or damage to defendant is not great. The defendant may under the Wyoming Business Corporation Act by a comparatively simple process change its name. It would thus appear that the defendant need not interrupt its business but could in a few days' time change its name and continue to conduct its activities with any of the rights and privileges that it had before the name change. . . .

Affirmed.

Ernst & Ernst v. Hochfelder et al.
96 S.Ct. 1375 (1976)

POWELL, JUSTICE: The issue in this case is whether an action for civil damages may lie under § 10(b) of the Securities Exchange Act of 1934 (1934 Act) and Securities and Exchange Commission Rule 10b-5 in the absence of an allegation of intent to deceive, manipulate, or defraud on the part of the defendant.

I

Petitioner, Ernst & Ernst, is an accounting firm. From 1946 through 1967 it was retained by First Securities Company of Chicago (First Securities), a small brokerage firm and member of the Midwest Stock Exchange and of the National Association of Securities Dealers, to perform periodic audits of the firm's books and records. In connection with these audits Ernst & Ernst prepared for filing with the Securities and Exchange Commission (the Commission) the annual reports required of First Securities under § 17(a) of the 1934 Act. It also pre-

pared for First Securities responses to the financial questionnaires of the Midwest Stock Exchange (the Exchange).

Respondents were customers of First Securities who invested in a fraudulent securities scheme perpetrated by Leston B. Nay, president of the firm and owner of 92% of its stock. Nay induced the respondents to invest funds in "escrow" accounts that he represented would yield a high rate of return. Respondents did so from 1942 through 1966, with the majority of the transactions occurring in the 1950's. In fact, there were no escrow accounts as Nay converted respondents' funds to his own use immediately upon receipt. These transactions were not in the customary form of dealings between First Securities and its customers. The respondents drew their personal checks payable to Nay or a designated bank for his account. No such escrow accounts were reflected on the books and records of First Securities, and none was shown on its periodic accounting to respondents in connection with their other investments. Nor were they included in First Securities' filings with the Commission or the Exchange.

This fraud came to light in 1968 when Nay committed suicide, leaving a note that described First Securities as bankrupt and the escrow accounts as "spurious." Respondents subsequently filed this action for damages against Ernst & Ernst . . . under § 10(b) of the 1934 Act. The complaint charged that Nay's escrow scheme violated § 10(b) and Commission Rule 10b-5, and that Ernst & Ernst had "aided and abetted" Nay's violations by its "failure" to conduct proper audits of First Securities. As revealed through discovery, respondents' cause of action rested on a theory of negligent nonfeasance. The premise was that Ernst & Ernst had failed to utilize "appropriate auditing procedures" in its audits of First Securities, thereby failing to discover internal practices of the firm said to prevent an effective audit. The practice principally relied on was Nay's rule that only he could open mail addressed to him at First Securities or addressed to First Securities to his attention, even if it arrived in his absence. Respondents contended that if Ernst & Ernst had conducted a proper audit, it would have discovered this "mail rule." The existence of the rule then would have been disclosed in reports to the Exchange and to the Commission by Ernst & Ernst as an irregular procedure that prevented an effective audit. This would have led to an investigation of Nay that would have revealed the fraudulent scheme. Respondents specifically disclaimed the existence of fraud or intentional misconduct on the part of Ernst & Ernst.

After extensive discovery the District Court granted Ernst & Ernst's motion for summary judgment and dismissed the action. . . .

The Court of Appeals for the Seventh Circuit reversed and remanded, holding that one who breaches a duty of inquiry and disclosure owed another is liable in damages for aiding and abetting a third party's violation of Rule

10b-5 if the fraud would have been discovered or prevented but for the breach. . . .

We granted certiorari to resolve the question whether a private cause of action for damages will lie under § 10(b) and Rule 10b-5 in the absence of any allegation of "scienter" —intent to deceive, manipulate, or defraud. We conclude that it will not and therefore we reverse.

II

Federal regulation of transactions in securities emerged as part of the aftermath of the market crash in 1929. The Securities Act of 1933 (1933 Act) was designed to provide investors with full disclosure of material information concerning public offerings of securities in commerce, to protect investors against fraud and, through the imposition of specified civil liabilities, to promote ethical standards of honesty and fair dealing. The 1934 Act was intended principally to protect investors against manipulation of stock prices through regulation of transactions upon securities exchanges and in over-the-counter markets, and to impose regular reporting requirements on companies whose stock is listed on national securities exchanges. Although the Acts contain numerous carefully drawn express civil remedies and criminal penalties, Congress recognized that efficient regulation of securities trading could not be accomplished under a rigid statutory program. As part of the 1934 Act Congress created the Commission, which is provided with an arsenal of flexible enforcement powers.

Section 10 of the 1934 Act makes it "unlawful for any person . . . (b) [t]o use or employ, in connection with the purchase or sale of any security . . . any manipulative or deceptive device or contrivance in contravention of such rules and regulations as the Commission may prescribe as necessary or appropriate in the public interest or for the protection of investors." In 1942, acting pursuant to the power conferred by § 10(b), the Commission promulgated Rule 10b-5, which now provides:

> Employment of manipulative and deceptive devices.
>
> It shall be unlawful for any person, directly or indirectly, by the use of any means or instrumentality of interstate commerce, or of the mails, or of any facility of any national securities exchange,
>
> 1. To employ any device, scheme, or artifice to defraud,
>
> 2. To make any untrue statement of a material fact or to omit to state a material fact necessary in order to make the statements made, in the light of the circumstances under which they were made, not misleading, or
>
> 3. To engage in any act, practice, or course of business which operates or would operate as a fraud or deceit upon any person, in connection with the purchase or sale of any security.

Although § 10(b) does not by its terms create an express civil remedy for its violation . . . the existence of a private cause of action for violations of the statute and the rule is now well established. During the 30-year period since a private cause of action was first implied under § 10(b) and Rule 10b-5, a substantial body of case law and commentary has developed as to its elements. Courts and commentators long have differed with regard to whether scienter is a necessary element of such a cause of action, or whether negligent conduct alone is sufficient. In addressing this question, we turn first to the language of § 10(b), for "[t]he starting point in every case involving construction of a statute is the language itself."

Section 10(b) makes unlawful the use of employment of "any manipulative or deceptive device or contrivance" in contravention of Commission rules. The words "manipulative or deceptive" used in conjunction with "device or contrivance" strongly suggest that § 10(b) was intended to proscribe knowing or intentional misconduct.

In its *amicus curiae* brief, however, the Commission contends that nothing in the language "manipulative or deceptive device or contrivance" limits its operation to knowing or intentional practices. In support of its view, the Commission cites the overall congressional purpose in the 1933 and 1934 Acts to protect investors against false and deceptive practices that might injure them.

The Commission then reasons that since the "effect" upon investors of given conduct is the same regardless of whether the conduct is negligent or intentional, Congress must have intended to bar all such practices and not just those done knowingly or intentionally. . . . The argument simply ignores the use of the words "manipulative," "device," and "contrivance," terms that make unmistakable a congressional intent to proscribe a type of conduct quite different from negligence. Use of the word "manipulative" is especially significant. It is and was virtually a term of art when used in connection with securities markets. It connotes intentional or willful conduct designed to deceive or defraud investors by controlling or artificially affecting the price of securities. . . .

. . . When a statute speaks so specifically in terms of manipulation and deception, and of implementing devices and contrivances—the commonly understood terminology of intentional wrongdoing—and when its history reflects no more expansive intent, we are quite unwilling to extend the scope of the statute to negligent conduct.

[*The judgment of the Court of Appeals is reversed.*]

CHAPTER 37
REVIEW QUESTIONS AND PROBLEMS

1. A, sole owner of the stock of XYZ Company, Inc., sold all his stock to B for $10,000. However, B, at the time of transfer of the stock, paid A only part of the agreed price and gave his promissory note for the remainder. When the note came due, B did not pay, and A sued him on the note. B's defense was that A owed XYZ Company more than the amount due on the note. Is this a valid defense? Explain.

2. Shareholders of the XYZ Corp. borrowed money from B Bank. XYZ Corp. had an account at B Bank. The shareholders did not repay the borrowed money when it came due. B Bank deducted the amounts from the account of XYZ Corp., claiming that the shareholders used the money for the benefit of the corporation. Must the bank return the money to the account of the XYZ Corp.? Why?

3. The XYZ Theater Co. leased a theater from XYZ, Inc. In the lease there was a clause prohibiting the transferring of the lease by the lessee to another. If the shareholders of the XYZ Theater Co. sell all their stock to B, is there a violation of the antiassignment clause of the lease? Explain.

4. A Company was the parent company and B Company was a subsidiary. A Company extended credit to B Company. The latter became insolvent, and the other creditors objected to A Company's sharing equally in the assets. Is A Company entitled to its pro rata share of B's assets? Why?

5. The P Company, a corporation, owns real and personal property in state X. X has a statute requiring qualification by foreign corporations, but the P Company has not qualified. P Company leases its property to D, the lease being executed in state Y. If D fails to pay the rent, may the P Company sue him in state X? Why?

6. A, B, and C were the directors of X Company. At the annual stockholders' meeting, A and B, the sole shareholders, voted to amend the bylaws to reduce the number of directors from three to two. A and B then elected themselves as the two directors. C claimed that this action should be nullified, since neither the state statute nor the articles of incorporation gave the stockholders the power to amend the bylaws. Is C correct? Why?

7. X Corporation gave one of its employees the option to purchase 40,000 shares at $3 per share, the market price at that time. The employee exercised the option when the market price had risen to $8 per share. S, a shareholder, contends that the action is invalid, because the state statute does not empower a corporation to issue a stock option, and that such action is in violation of his preemptive rights. Is S correct? Why?

8. A owned all the stock in A Company. A contract was entered whereby the company purchased A's stock for $4,000 cash and a $20,000 unsecured promissory note. The liabilities of the company exceeded its assets. Was the contract between A and A Company valid? Why?

9. P, a promoter, executed a contract to purchase land from S. The contract was signed, "X Company, Inc., by P, Pres." S was aware at the time of contracting that the corporation did not exist, either *de jure* or *de facto,* and that P expressly declined to be named as a party individually. The buyer named in the contract, "X Company, Inc.," was never organized in accordance with the representations of P. S brought suit, claiming that P is personally liable on the contract. Is S correct? Why?

10. A proposition was scheduled to be submitted to the voters of San Francisco. The board of directors of X Utility Company, which serviced the San Francisco area, concluded that the adoption of the proposition would have a direct, adverse bearing upon its business affairs. The board therefore authorized a $10,000 contribution to an association that advocated the defeat of the proposition. Was the contribution *ultra vires?* Why?

Operating the Corporation

1. Introduction

The preceding chapter was concerned with the legal aspects of forming a corporation. Many of the legal principles that were discussed there are also applicable to the operation of a corporate entity. For example, many bylaw provisions are directly concerned with operations. Some of the subjects dealt with in this chapter, such as stock and the rights of shareholders, have a bearing on formation problems. Therefore, the discussion in the preceding chapter and the materials in this chapter should be considered complementary.

Three distinct groups participate in the management of a corporation. The *shareholders* or *stockholders* (the words are synonymous) make up the basic governing body. Shareholders exercise their control by electing the *board of directors* and by voting on such matters as merger, consolidation, or dissolution. The board of directors adopts the bylaws, makes corporate policy, and, in addition, has the responsibility for electing *officers* who carry out the policies. The duties and powers of the shareholders, the board of directors, and the various officers are regulated by statute and by the bylaws of the corporation. These duties and powers will be discussed in this chapter.

SHAREHOLDERS

2. Meetings

Action by the shareholders normally binds the corporation only when taken in a regular, or properly called, special meeting after such notice as is required by the bylaws or statute has been given. However, it is generally conceded, and many states so provide by statute, that action approved informally by *all shareholders* will bind the corporation. Informal action is not possible with less than unanimous approval.

Notice of a special meeting must include a statement concerning the matters to be acted upon at the meeting, and any action taken on other matters will be ineffective. If unusual action, such as a sale of corporate assets, is to be taken at a regular annual meeting, notice of the meeting must call specific attention to that fact; but otherwise, any business may be transacted at the annual meeting.

Failure to give proper notice of a meeting generally invalidates the action taken at the meeting. A shareholder who, having failed to receive notice, attends and participates in a meeting is said to waive the notice by his presence.

A quorum of shareholders must be present in order to transact business, such quorum being a majority of the voting shares outstanding, unless some statute or the bylaws provide for a larger or smaller percentage. Affirmative action is approved by majority vote of the shares represented at a meeting, provided a quorum exists. Certain unusual matters, such as mergers or sale of all corporate assets, require approval by a vote of two-thirds or three-fourths of the shareholders.

The annual meeting of shareholders of the large, publicly held corporation is a curious phenomenon. Management has usually solicited enough proxies in advance to control any vote that is taken. Nevertheless, many shareholders attend such meetings in order to question management on a variety of social and political issues and to "lobby" for certain policies. The meeting is also used by management as a public-relations opportunity, to educate the shareholders on company accomplishments as well as its problems.

3. Voting

The statutes of the various states and the charters issued under their authority prescribe the matters on which shareholders are entitled to vote. Shareholders are usually entitled to vote on the election of directors; on such major policy issues as mergers and consolidations, and on dissolution; and, in some instances, on a change in the bylaws.

Some state laws allow a corporation to deny the vote to some shareholders on certain issues. For example, state law may allow for stock to be nonvoting on the election of directors. This provides a method by which a minority of the shareholders can obtain control. Since public policy supports the right of an investor to vote, the status of stock as nonvoting must be communicated to the investor or the stock purchase may be rescinded.

As a general rule, every shareholder is entitled to as many votes as he owns shares of stock. The shareholder whose name appears upon the corporate record is usually designated by the bylaws as the person entitled to vote. Preferred shareholders, by their contract with the corporation, may or may not be entitled to vote.

The statutes of some states provide for cumulative voting in the election of directors. In cumulative voting, a shareholder may cast as many votes for one candidate for director as there are directors to be elected, multiplied by the number of his shares of stock, or he may distribute this same number of votes among the candidates as he sees fit. For example, a shareholder owning 100 shares of stock has 300 votes if three directors are to be elected. He may cast all 300 votes for one candidate, or spread them among the candidates.

A shareholder is entitled to vote only by virtue of his ownership of the stock. A shareholder may specifically authorize another to vote his stock. This authorization is made by power of attorney and must specifically state that the agent of the shareholder has power to vote his principal's stock. This method of voting is called *voting by proxy*. It is a personal relationship and may be revoked at any time by the shareholder before the authority is exercised. The laws relative to principal and agent control this relationship.

A shareholder, unlike a director, is permitted to vote on a matter in which he has a personal interest. The majority of shareholders may not take action, however, that is clearly detrimental to the corporation and minority interests.

4. The Rights and Duties of Shareholders

A shareholder has the following rights, usually created by statute and reiterated in the bylaws: (1) the right to inspect the books and papers of the corporation,[1] (2) the right to attend stockholders' meetings and to vote for directors and on certain other matters such as dissolution or merger, (3) a right to share in the profits when a dividend is declared, (4) the preemptive right, and (5) the right to bring a shareholder's derivative suit.

The right to inspect the books and papers is limited to good-faith inspections for proper and honest purposes at the proper time and the proper place. A *proper purpose* is one that seeks to protect the interest of the corporation as well as the interest of the shareholder seeking the information. The inspection must be made with a justifiable motive and not through idle curiosity or for vexatious purposes. The business hours of the corporation are the reasonable and proper hours in which a stockholder is entitled to inspect the books.

In some states, a shareholder who is refused access to the books and records is entitled to damages as provided by statute. For example, a typical statute provides that a shareholder who is denied the right to inspect books and records is entitled to damages equal to 10 percent of the value of the stock owned.

The right to inspect includes contracts and correspondence as well as books and records. These statutes are given a broad and liberal interpretation. The

---

[1] *G. S. & M. Company* v. *Dixon*, page 727.

right extends even to confidential records, such as those relating to bank loans.

The shareholders in a close corporation owe one another substantially the same fiduciary duty in the operation of the enterprise that partners owe to one another. They must discharge their management and shareholder responsibilities in conformity with the strict good-faith standard, and they may not act out of avarice, expediency, or self-interest in derogation of their loyalty to other shareholders and to the corporation. This good-faith standard that shareholders in a close corporation must observe is in contrast to the relationship of the shareholders in a publicly held corporation. As a general rule, there is no fiduciary relationship between shareholders in publicly held corporations. One owner of stock listed on the New York Stock Exchange owes no duty to other owners of the same stock unless, of course, the shareholder is also an insider subject to SEC regulation.

5.   Preemptive Right

The original application for a charter specifies the amount of stock the corporation will be authorized to issue. It also specifies the amount that will be ·issued without further notice to the state. The amount of authorized stock and the amount of issued stock are used to compute the license fees and franchise taxes due to the state of incorporation. These amounts cannot be increased or exceeded without the authority of the state.

The shareholders may authorize an increase in the authorized capital stock. Such action may not be taken by the directors. An increase in the authorized capital stock is an amendment to the corporate charter that requires state approval.

The board of directors may authorize the sale of unissued capital stock when the amount previously issued is less than the amount authorized. This does not require an amendment to the charter. All that is required in such a case is that the state be informed of the additional issue of the stock so that the correct taxes may be collected.

When an increase in the capital stock has been properly authorized, the existing shareholders have a prior right against third parties to subscribe to the increased capital stock. This right is called the shareholder's *preemptive right*. It is based upon the shareholder's right to protect and maintain his proportionate control and interest in the corporation.[2]

The preemptive right may be limited or waived by contract and by provisions in the charter or bylaws of the corporation in most states. In many states, it is not applicable to treasury stock.

The preemptive right is applicable to new authorizations of stock. It is generally not applicable to new issues of stock previously authorized. How-

---

[2] *Ross Transport, Inc. et al.* v. *Crothers et al.,* page 729.

ever, if the new issue of an original authorization takes place a long time after the original issue, many states provide that the preemptive right exists. Most states approve the issuance of stock to employees under stock option plans without regard to the preemptive right.

6. Derivative Suits

A shareholder cannot maintain an *action at law* for injuries to the corporation, because the corporation is a legal entity and by law has a right to bring a suit in its own name. Nor can a shareholder bring a suit in law against the directors or other officers of the corporation for negligence, waste, and mismanagement in the conduct of the corporate business. The right to sue for injuries to the corporation rests strictly with the corporation itself, unless modified by statute.

A shareholder may, however, bring a *suit in equity,* known as a shareholder's derivative suit, to enjoin the officers of a corporation from entering into *ultra vires* contracts or from doing anything that would impair the corporate assets. Likewise, the shareholder has a right to bring suit in equity for, or on behalf of, the corporation itself if the officers are acting outside the scope of their authority, are guilty of negligent conduct, or are engaging, or about to engage, in illegal, oppressive, or fraudulent transactions in such a way as to be injurious to the corporation itself.

Before a shareholder may enter into a suit in equity for and on behalf of the corporation, he must show that he has done everything possible to secure action by the managing officers and directors and that they have refused to act. For example, if the action involves a lawsuit, there must be a demand to sue or it must be apparent that a demand would be futile under the circumstances. Any judgment received in such an action benefits the corporation and only indirectly the shareholder who initiates the action. He is permitted, however, to recover the expenses involved in the suit.

Mere dissatisfaction with the management of the corporation will not justify a derivative suit. In the law of corporations, it is fundamental that the majority of the shareholders control the corporation. Every shareholder impliedly agrees that he will be bound by the acts and decisions of a majority of the shareholders or by the agents of the corporation duly chosen by such majority. Courts will not undertake to control the business of a corporation even though it may be seen that better decisions might be made and the business more successful if other methods were pursued. The majority of shares of stock are permitted to control the business of a corporation in their discretion, when not in violation of its charter or some public law, or corruptly, oppressively, and fraudulently subversive of the rights and interests of the corporation or of a shareholder. If a majority of disinterested directors acting in good faith and with reasonable business judgment adopt a course of action, it will not be overturned by a derivative suit.

DIRECTORS

7. Qualifications and Powers

The directors of a corporation are elected by the shareholders. The duties of directors ordinarily consist of attending meetings, exercising judgment on propositions brought before the board, and voting. A corporation is managed under the direction of the board of directors. A director need not be involved actively in the day-to-day operation of the business. A director has no power to issue orders to any officer or employee, nor can he institute policies by himself, or command or veto any other action by the board.

It is not essential that directors hold stock in the corporation. Because they are to supervise the business activities, select key employees, and plan for the future development of the enterprise, they are presumably elected because of their business ability.

The directors have power to take such actions as are necessary or proper to conduct the ordinary business activities of the company. They may not amend the charter, approve a merger, or bring about a consolidation with another corporation without the approval of the shareholders.

8. Meetings

The bylaws usually provide for the number of directors. Historically, not less than three directors were required, but in recent years, many corporate statutes have authorized two directors—and in some cases, one director. This development is especially prevalent in professional associations or corporations, which frequently have only one shareholder and thus only one director.

Since the board of directors must act as a unit, it is traditional that it assemble at board meetings. The bylaws provide for the method of calling directors' meetings and for the time and the place of meeting. A record is usually kept of the activities of the board of directors, and the evidence of the exercise of its powers is stated in resolutions kept in the corporate minute book. A majority of the members of the board of directors is necessary to constitute a quorum unless a bylaw provides to the contrary. Special meetings are proper only when all directors are notified or are present at the meetings. Directors may not vote by proxy, having been selected as agents because of their personal qualifications.

Modern statutes make informal action possible by a board of directors (usually by telephone), provided the action taken is subsequently reduced to writing and signed by the directors. This gives a board the flexibility and capability to make decisions when needed without delay.

Traditionally, a director was forbidden to vote on any matter in which he had a personal interest. Even though his vote was not necessary to carry the proposition considered, many courts would regard any action taken as a result of that vote to be voidable. Some courts went so far as to hold that if he was present at the meeting, favorable action was not binding. Most courts held that if his presence was required to make a quorum, no transaction in which he was interested could be acted upon. These rather severe rules were developed so that directors would not be tempted to use their position to profit at the expense of the corporation.

Today, many of the traditional rules on director voting and participation have been relaxed somewhat. The trend of the law is to allow interested directors to be present and to be counted as a part of the quorum. Actions taken with such directors are valid if the participating director's interest is fully and completely disclosed, provided the action is approved by a majority of disinterested directors.[3] This problem of acting in good faith is discussed in more detail in Section 11 of this chapter.

9. Compensation

In the absence of a stipulation in the charter or bylaws or resolution of the shareholders, directors receive no compensation for their services as such. Such compensation is usually provided for, however. Directors who are appointed as officers of the corporation should have their salaries fixed at a meeting of the shareholders or in the bylaws. Because directors are not supposed to vote on any matter in which they have a personal interest, director-officers of small corporations usually vote on salaries for each other but not their own, and the action on salaries is ratified by the shareholders in order to ensure the validity of the employment contracts.

10. Liability—Generally

The directors of a corporation may have personal liability both in tort and in the contract. The principles of the law of agency are applicable. The liability is usually to the corporation. It may extend to shareholders and third parties as well. It should be noted that officers of corporations may also have personal liability, and the principles herein discussed are applicable to officers as well as to directors.

The liability of corporate officers and directors for tortious conduct is predicated upon basic common law principles. For example, a director who participates in fraudulent conduct by the corporation has personal liability to the third party on the usual common law tort theories just as does any other agent or servant. Moreover, the director need not personally commit fraud. He is liable if he sanctions or approves it.

The liability of corporate directors is most frequently based on a violation of the fiduciary duties owed to the corporation. A director occupies a position of trust and confidence with respect to the corporation and cannot, by reason of

---

[3] *Rapoport v. Schneider*, page 730.

his position, directly or indirectly derive any personal benefits that are not enjoyed by the corporation or the shareholders.

There are several statutes that impose liability on directors and officers.[4] They may be liable to the U.S. government for failure to pay federal withholding and Social Security taxes for the employees of the corporation if they have responsibility in that area. Likewise, a director or officer is subject to third-party liability for aiding a corporation in such acts as patent, copyright, or trademark infringements, unfair competition, antitrust violations, violation of the laws relating to discrimination, or violations of the securities laws.

The law requires that a director perform his duties in good faith and in a manner that he reasonably believes to be in the best interests of the corporation. A director is also required to exercise such care as an ordinarily prudent person in a like position would use under similar circumstances. These standards of "good faith" and "due care" arise out of the fiduciary relationship existing between the corporation and its directors and the duty of loyalty that exists in such relationships.[5] They are discussed further in the sections that follow.

11. Good Faith

The duty of loyalty, or the duty to act in good faith, prohibits directors from acting with a conflict of interest. The most common violation of this duty occurs when a director enters into a contract with or personally deals with the corporation. A conflict of interest also arises in transactions between the director's corporation and another entity of which he may be a director, employee, investor, or in which he is otherwise interested. In all circumstances, the director or officer must fully disclose his conflict of interest to the corporation. If he fails to do so, the contract may be rescinded.

At common law, such a contract was voidable unless it was shown to be (1) approved by a disinterested board, and (2) "fair" to the corporation, in that its terms were as favorable as those available from any other person. Under some modern statutes, the transaction is valid if (1) it is approved, with knowledge of the material facts, by a vote of (a) disinterested directors *or* (b) shareholders; *or* (2) the director can show it to be "fair."

The good-faith requirement is also lacking when a director or officer takes an opportunity for himself that the corporation should have had. A director is required to first present all possible corporate opportunities to the corporation. Only after an informed determination by the disinterested directors that the corporation should not pursue such opportunities can a director pursue them for his own benefit.

There are three other common conflict-of-interest situations that are re-

---

[4] *Wyrybkowski* v. *Cobra Pre-Hung Doors, Inc.,* page 731.
[5] *Wilkes* v. *Springside Nursing Home, Inc.,* page 731.

solved by the same fiduciary standards as set out above. The first involves the setting of executive compensation for officer-directors. This was discussed in Section 9. Another conflict arises when the incumbent directors become engaged in a proxy contest in order to preserve their positions. It is generally recognized that the expense of such a proxy fight cannot be paid by the corporation. Only if a shareholder vote is concerned with a matter of corporate policy can corporate funds be used for proxy fights. Finally, a fiduciary duty arises when a director who is also a majority shareholder sells control of the corporation to another. Although the director can and should resign his position upon the sale, he may be liable for placing the corporation in the hands of unscrupulous buyers if he had warning of the intentions of the buyer to, for example, loot the corporation.

12.   Due Care

In its simplest terms, the duty of care is synonymous with a duty not to be negligent. The standard may be stated in a variety of ways, but the most common is that a director must exercise that degree of care that an ordinarily prudent man would exercise in managing his own affairs.

Since many directors are not actively engaged in the day-to-day operation of the business, the law recognizes that they need to rely on others for much of the information used in decision making. In performing his duties, a director is entitled to rely on information, opinions, reports, and statements of others. These include officers and employees whom the director reasonably believes to be reliable and competent in the matters presented. A director may also rely on legal counsel, public accountants, and other expert professionals. Finally, a director may also rely on committees of the board if they act within the designated authority and he reasonably believes that they merit confidence. A director does not fulfill his duties and does not act in good faith if he has knowledge that would cause the reliance to be unwarranted.

The purpose of the foregoing is to allow directors to use their best business judgment without incurring liability for honest mistakes. Directors must make difficult policy decisions, and they should not have liability if their decisions are based on information that later turns out to be false.

The liability of directors for negligence in the management of the corporation is to the corporation. Since no duty runs to third-party creditors, there is no liability to them or to the shareholders. Of course, a shareholder may enforce this liability through a derivative suit.

13.   Indemnification and Insurance

In recent years, there has been a dramatic increase in the number of lawsuits filed against directors and officers of publicly held corporations. These lawsuits have been filed by dissenting shareholders, public-interest groups, and government regulators. Many of the lawsuits result from the failure of directors to prevent activities such as bribery of foreign officials and illegal political contributions.

It has been a corporate practice in most large corporations to purchase liability insurance coverage for directors. Because of the increased number of suits, the cost of this insurance is soaring.

In order to reimburse directors and officers for the expenses of defending lawsuits if the insurance is nonexistent or inadequate, most states provide by statute for indemnification by the corporation. The Model Business Corporation Act provides that the standard for indemnification is that the director must have "acted in good faith and in a manner he reasonably believed to be in or not opposed to the best interests of the corporation" and, if a criminal action, "had no reasonable cause to believe his conduct was unlawful." The indemnification is automatic if the director has been successful in the defense of any action.

CORPORATE STOCK

14. Introduction

A certificate of stock is written evidence of the ownership of a certain number of shares of stock of a corporation. The certificate is the physical evidence that the corporation recognizes a certain person as a shareholder. The rights of a shareholder are primarily three in number: the right to share in profits, the right to participate indirectly in the control of the corporation, and the right to receive a portion of the assets at time of dissolution. A share of stock gives the holder no right to share in the active management of the business.

The term *stock* must be distinguished from the term *bond*. A bond is an obligation of the corporation to pay a certain sum of money in the future at a specified rate of interest. Corporate bonds are often secured by a mortgage on the assets of the corporation, but many corporate bonds, called *debentures,* do not have such security. A bondholder is a creditor of the corporation. A bondholder has no right to vote or to participate in the management and control of a corporation, unless, upon insolvency, such rights are given by contract.

15. Kinds of Stock

Common stock is the simplest type of corporate stock. It entitles the owner to share in the control, profits, and assets of the corporation in proportion to the amount of common stock he holds. Such a shareholder has no advantage, priority, or preference over any other class of shareholders.

Preferred stock is stock that has a prior claim to dividends, or to assets on dissolution, over other classes of stock. The most important right given to a preferred stockholder is the right to receive a certain specified dividend, even though the earnings are not sufficient to pay a like dividend to common sharholders.

Preferred stock may be *cumulative* or *noncumulative*. If cumulative, any dividends that are not paid because of lack of earnings accrue and are paid when earnings are available. If noncumulative, only the current year's preferred dividend is paid out of current earnings. If nothing is stated about the payment of the dividends, the preferred stock is cumulative, and preferred dividends and all arrears thereon must be paid before a dividend is declared on common stock.

The statutes of most states provide that a corporation may issue stock with *no par* value. The value of no-par stock is determined by its sale value in the open market or by the price set by the directors as a "stated value." Shareholders, creditors of the corporation, and the public will not be misled or prejudiced by this type of stock, because there is no holding out that the stock has any particular face value. All persons dealing in such stock are put on notice that they should investigate the corporation's assets and its financial condition. Stock with no par value represents the proportionate part of the total assets of the corporation it stipulates but does not indicate the monetary value or par value of the share. The state law usually permits the directors to determine what portion of the amount received from the sale of no-par stock shall be credited to the capital stock account and how much, if any, shall be credited to paid-in surplus.

A *stock warrant* is a certificate that gives to the holder thereof the right to subscribe for and purchase a given number of shares of stock in a corporation at a stated price. It is usually issued in connection with the sale of other shares of stock or of bonds, although the law of some states permits the issuance of stock warrants entirely separate and apart from the sale of other securities. Warrants are transferable. The option to purchase contained in the warrants may or may not be limited as to time or otherwise conditioned. Warrants have value and can readily be sold on the market in the same fashion as other securities.

Watered stock is stock that has been issued as fully paid, when in fact its full par value has not been paid in money, property, or services.[6] The capital stock of a corporation represents the total par value of all the shares of the corporation (plus the stated value of no-par stock), and the public, including corporate creditors, has a right to assume that the capital stock issued has been paid for in full. The corporation represents that assets have been received in payment equal in amount to its issued capital stock. If watered stock is issued, the original holders of such stock are liable to corporate creditors for the difference between its par value and the amount they actually paid for the stock.

Treasury stock is that which has been issued by the corporation for value and returned by gift or purchase to the corporation. It may be sold below par

[6] *Bing Crosby Minute Maid Corp.* v. *Eaton*, page 733.

and the proceeds returned to the treasury of the corporation for working capital. It differs from stock originally issued below par, in that the purchaser is not liable for the difference between par and the sale price. It may be sold at any price the company sees fit to charge.

16. Dividends

Although a shareholder has a right to his share of dividends when declared, whether or not a dividend is declared is within the discretion of the board of directors. The shareholders of a corporation are not entitled to the payment of a dividend simply because earned surplus exists. The board of directors, at its discretion, may see fit to continue the profits in the business for the purpose of expansion. A board of directors, however, must act reasonably and in good faith. Where fraud or a gross abuse of discretion is shown and there are profits out of which dividends may be declared, the shareholders may compel the board of directors to declare dividends. It must be clear, however, that the board of directors has refused to declare dividends illegally, wantonly, and without justification before there is a right to interfere by asking a court to order the payment of dividends.

When a cash dividend is declared, it becomes a debt of the corporation. It will be paid to the person whose name appears on the corporate stock records as the owner of the share on the record date as of which the dividend is payable. A cash dividend, once its declaration has been made public, may not be rescinded.

A declaration of dividends is proper as long as it does not impair the capital stock. Any declaration, however, that reduces the net assets of the corporation below the outstanding capital stock is illegal.

Dividends are permissible only after provision has been made for all expenses, including depreciation. In those industries with wasting or depleting assets, such as mines and oil wells, it is not necessary to allow for the depletion before declaring dividends.

Directors are personally liable to creditors for dividends improperly declared. In most states, shareholders who receive such dividends may be compelled to return them.

A *stock dividend* is a transfer of retained earnings to capital and is used where the earnings are required for growth of the business. Stock dividends of the issuing company are not taxable income to shareholders. A *stock split* differs from a *stock dividend* in that in the former, there is no transfer of surplus to capital but only a reduction in par value and an increase in the number of shares.

17. Shareholder Agreements

The right to transfer freely one's share in the ownership of the business is inherent in corporations. It is one of the features of corporate life that distinguishes it from a partnership. However, shareholders of "close" corporations often attempt by agreement or bylaw to limit the group of potential purchasers. A corporate bylaw that provides that the shares of stock can be transferred only to the corporation or to those approved by the board of directors is un-enforceable. It places too severe a restraint upon the alienation of property. Society is best protected when property may be transferred freely. However, an agreement or a bylaw approved by all shareholders to the effect that no transfer of stock shall be made until it has first been offered to the other share-holders or to the corporation is generally enforced. Notice of the bylaw or agreement should be set forth in the stock certificate, because an innocent purchaser without notice of the restriction on alienation receives ownership free from the restriction.

Sometimes the buy and sell agreements between shareholders go even further and provide for such matters as salary continuation in the event of death or disability, and the amount of dividends to be paid in the future. Some agreements even commit the shareholders to vote for certain persons in the election of directors. Such agreements are valid in closely held corporations, provided the duration of the agreement is not so long as to be contrary to public policy and provided the agreement does not adversely affect minority interests in the corporation. These agreements are used by the majority owners to ensure the election of the desired board of directors. Corporations are governed by the republican principle that the whole are bound by lawful acts of the majority. It is not against public policy or dishonest for shareholders to contract for the purpose of control.

18.   Transfer of Stock and Other Investment Securities

A share of stock is personal property, and the owner has the right to transfer it just as he may transfer any other personal property. A share of stock is generally transferred by an endorsement and the delivery of the certificate of stock. A share may be transferred or assigned by a bill of sale or by any other method that will pass title to a chose in action or other intangible property. Whenever a share of stock is sold and a new stock certificate issued, the name of the new owner is entered on the stock records of the corporation. In a small corporation, the secretary of the corporation usually handles all transfers of stock and also the canceling of old certificates and issuing of new. Large corporations, in which there are hundreds and even thousands of transactions, employ transfer agents. The transfer agents transfer stock, cancel old certifi-cates, issue new ones, prepare and keep up-to-date the names of the share-holders of the corporation, distribute dividends, mail out shareholders' notices, and perform many functions to assist the corporation secretary. Stock ex-change rules provide that corporations listing stock for sale must maintain a transfer agency and registry, operated and maintained under exchange regula-tions. The registrar of stock is an agent of the corporation whose duty is to see that no stock certificates are issued in excess of the authorized capitalization of the corporation.

The volume of transactions in stock sold publicly is so large that many techniques have been developed to reduce the cost and confusion of transfers. One such technique is for the title to the stock to be held in the "house name" of a brokerage firm. If the firm has transactions with both buyers and sellers in the same stock, a transfer can be effected by a bookkeeping entry, and new certificates need not be issued. The firm will, however, solicit proxies and vote the stock in accordance with the instructions of the actual owner. As another means of reducing transfers, many companies are discouraging small shareholders from investing. For example, a company may try to purchase back the stock of every holder of ten shares or less. Such a policy will greatly reduce corporate administrative expenses.

Many people are advocating replacing stock certificates with punch cards that can be easily transferred by computer. It is anticipated that in the near future, formal stock certificates may disappear from use by large corporations.

Article 8 of the Uniform Commercial Code deals with investment securities. It must be considered along with the blue-sky laws on issues concerning the transfer of stock.

The general approach of Article 8 is that securities are negotiable instruments and that bona fide purchasers thereof have greater rights than they would have "if things bought were chattels or simple contracts." The particular rules of Article 3 that relate to the establishment of preferred status for commercial paper are applied to securities. Defenses of the issuer are generally not effective against a purchaser for value who has received the securities without being given notice of the particular defense raised.

A bona fide purchaser is one who purchases in good faith and without notice of any adverse claim. He is the equivalent of a holder in due course. A bona fide purchaser takes free "adverse claims," which include a claim that a transfer was wrongful or that some other person is the owner of, or has an interest in, the security.

OPERATING THE CORPORATION CASES

G. S. & M. Company v. Dixon
138 S.E.2d 662 (Ga.) 1964

The petitioner, Dixon, was the administrator of the estate of a decedent who at the time of his death owned three-fourths of a share of stock in the defendant corporation. Petitioner sought a court order allowing him to inspect the corporate records. The trial court entered a summary judgment for petitioner, and the corporation appealed.

GRICE, J. . . . Petitioner, a bona fide stockholder, has requested the right to inspect the books of the corporation, including its bylaws, its minute books, and its financial records.

Although his counsel has been allowed a limited examination of its financial records, the corporation has persistently refused to allow him to examine such minute books or bylaws.

The examination was asked in good faith for a specific and honest purpose, and not to gratify curiosity or for speculative or vexatious purposes. The purpose is germane to petitioner's interest as a stockholder, is proper and lawful in character, and is not inimical to the interest of the corporation. He has asked that such inspection be allowed during reasonable business hours at the corporation's principal office in a named Georgia county.

A stockholders' meeting has been called for a specified date and place in the State of New York. The corporate charter does not provide that stockholders' meetings may be held outside the State of Georgia.

Petitioner has made persistent and repeated efforts to examine the corporation's books, records, and bylaws in order to ascertain the legality of such meeting, to determine the worth of the decedent's share for inventory and estate tax purposes, to ascertain whether the corporation's assets have been properly administered, and for other proper and legitimate purposes. But the corporation has refused to allow such examination. . . .

The instant petition . . . rests upon the right of a stockholder to inspect the corporate records, which right is not dependent upon fraud or such other acts.

That right is recognized in this State. A leading case declares: "A bona fide stockholder has the legal right to inspect the books and records of the company, where the examination is asked for in good faith for a specific and honest purpose, and not to gratify curiosity, or for speculating or for vexatious purposes, and provide, further, that the purpose of the stockholder desiring to make the examination is germane to his interest as a stockholder, proper and lawful in character, and not inimical to the interests of the corporation itself, and

the inspection is made during reasonable business hours." In this State, the right of inspection stems from the common law. Furthermore, the rule is that "A stockholder may inspect the books of the corporation for the purpose of informing himself as to the manner and fidelity with which the corporate affairs are being conducted. . . . Inspection may also be required for the purpose of ascertaining the financial condition of the company, the value of its stock. . . ."

The basis of this right is simple and logical: "The basis of the right of stockholders to inspect the books and records is the ownership of the corporate property and assets through ownership of shares; as owners, they have the right to inform themselves as to the management of their property by the directors and officers who are their trustees in direct charge of the property." . . .

This right is not dependent upon the amount of stock held. It is ". . . immaterial whether a stockholder asserting a right of inspection holds a few shares or many."

The stockholder's allegations here fit the requirements for inspection. The purposes of the desired inspection are proper. The petitioner alleged that he desires the right to inspect the books and records of the company in order that he may ascertain the legality of the stockholders' meeting, determine the worth of the shares of the decedent for inventory and estate tax purposes, ascertain whether the assets of the corporation have been properly administered, and for other proper and ligitimate purposes. It alleged that the examination was asked in good faith and not to gratify curiosity, speculate or vex; that his purposes are germane to his interest as a stockholder and not inimical to the interest of the corporation; and that his request was reasonable as to time and place. Thus, the petition sufficiently shows that the stockholder has the right to inspect and has been denied it. . . .

Affirmed.

Ross Transport, Inc. et al. v. Crothers et al.
45 A.2d 267 (MD) 1946

The plaintiffs, Crothers and other stockholders, brought this action against the corporation, its directors, and certain stockholders to set aside the issuance of certain shares of stock. The stock was sold to a director and to the family of the president, who was also a director. The lower court decreed that the stockholders who had received the additional stock must repay to the corporation the dividends received by them. The stock was declared to be illegally issued and ordered canceled. The defendants appealed.

MARBURY, C. J. . . . The sale of this additional stock to a director and to the family of the president . . . without opportunity to buy given to other stockholders, is sought to be justified on the ground that it was originally planned, and that the money was needed to purchase additional buses at a cost of about $16,000. The facts, however, show no such need. The company was an immediate financial success.

. . . The appellees give two reasons for their contention that the stock sales of August 26th were void: First, because they deprive them and the other original stockholders of their pre-emptive rights to purchase a proportionate amount of the remaining shares, and, second, because, in selling to themselves and their nominees, Williams and Ross have abused their trust as officers and directors. They claim to be injured in two ways. Their voting powers have been proportionately lessened, and the control of the company has passed to Williams and Ross. And the amount paid in dividends has to be divided among 365 more shares of stock to the consequent financial loss of the holders of the original shares.

. . . The doctine known as the pre-emptive right of shareholders is a judicial interpretation of general principles of corporation law. Existing stockholders are the owners of the business, and are entitled to have that ownership continued in the same proportion. Therefore, when additional stock is issued, those already having shares are held to have the first right to buy the new stock in proportion to their holdings. This doctrine was first promulgated in 1807 in the case of *Gray* v. *Portland Bank,* 3 Mass. 364, 3 Am. Dec. 156. At that time, corporations were small and closely held, much like the one before us in this case. But in the succeeding years, corporations grew and expanded. New capital was frequently required. New properties had to be acquired for which it was desirable to issue stock. Companies merged, and new stock in the consolidation was issued. Stock was issued for services. Different kinds of stock were authorized—preferred without voting power but with prior dividend rights—preferred with the right to convert into common—several classes of both common and preferred with different rights. Some stock had voting rights. Other stock did not. Bonds were issued, convertible into stock. All of these changes in the corporate structure made it impossible always to follow the simple doctrines earlier decided. Exceptions grew, and were noted in the decisions.

Only one of these exceptions is involved in the present case. It has been held that pre-emptive rights do not exist where the stock about to be issued is part of the original issue. This exception is based upon the fact that the original subscribers took their stock on the implied understanding that the incorporators could complete the sale of the remaining stock to obtain the capital thought necessary to start the business. But this gives rise to an exception to the exception, where conditions have changed since the original issue. The stock sold the Williams family and Ross was part of the original issue and it is claimed by the appellants that it comes within the exception, and the appellees and the other stockholders have no pre-emptive rights.

The appellees, on the other hand, contend, and the chancellors found that changed conditions made it unnecessary to use the remaining unsold stock to obtain capital, and pre-emptive rights exist in it just as they would exist in newly authorized stock.

It is unnecessary for us to decide which of these two conflicting points of view applies to this cause, because another controlling consideration enters. The doctrine of pre-emptive right is not affected by the identity of the purchasers of the issued stock. What it is concerned with is who did not get it. But when officers and directors sell to themselves, and thereby gain an advantage, both in value and in voting power, another situation arises, which it does not require the assertion of a pre-emptive right to deal with.

It has long been the law in this State that trustees cannot purchase at their own sale, and trustees, in this sense, include directors of corporations.

. . . *The decree will be affirmed.*

Rapoport v. Schneider
278 N.E.2d 642 (N.Y.) 1972

Plaintiffs, as directors and as stockholders of a corporation, brought a derivative action on behalf of the corporation against other directors to prevent the payment of a real estate commission. The corporation, New York Equities, had seven directors. Its real property was first managed by Strand Management, Inc., and later by Helmsley-Spear, Inc. One plaintiff, Rapoport, was the sole owner of Strand. Three of the defendants were officers of Helmsley.

At a special meeting, the board of directors by a vote of four to two agreed to pay a commission to Helmsley. Two of the three directors who were officers of Helmsley voted for the resolution, as did two directors who had no interest in Helmsley or Strand. Rapoport voted against it, as did one other director who had no interest in Helmsley or Strand. One director was absent. The lower court held that the complaint did not state a cause of action, and plaintiffs appealed.

BREITEL, J. . . . Plaintiffs allege . . . that the resolution is invalid because of participation by interested directors. Defendant directors Schneider and Winter, who voted for the resolution, were . . . officers of Helmsley. Plaintiff Rapoport, who voted against the resolution, was the sole owner of Strand, the competing claimant for the commissions. . . .

The Business Corporation Law provides that where "interested" directors, who have disclosed their interest, vote on a resolution, the resolution is nonetheless valid if a majority of the disinterested directors vote in its favor. A director is "interested" if he is an officer or director of another corporation apparently involved in the questioned transaction. Thus, all three of the directors mentioned are "interested." Not counting the votes of these directors, there remain the votes of two disinterested directors in favor of the resolution, H. Klein and I. Klein, and the vote of one disinterested director, Giber, opposed to the resolution. A quorum of votes cast by disinterested directors is not required . . . therefore, the resolution is not invalid because of the participation of interested directors.

Despite the validity of the resolution . . . the interested directors may in any event be liable for having participated in a transaction from which they may derive an indirect personal benefit. It is not necessary, however, to reach this question. To assert liability for waste, it is sufficient to allege that the directors have knowingly authorized payment of a duplicate claim out of corporate funds. It is and has always been general law that a director may be held accountable for the waste of corporate assets whether intentional or negligent without limitation to transactions from which he benefits. The cause of action alleges that Equities had been sued by Strand to recover commissions, that the lawsuit had already been partly settled, and that the Helmsley claim was for substantially the same services as the Strand claim. Although this is a rather skimpy allegation of a duplicated claim, its thrust is plain and unmistakable in establishing, if true, that the claim was a false one.

Accordingly, the order of the Appellate Division should be reversed and the motion to dismiss the complaint denied, with costs in all courts.

Order reversed, etc.

Wyrybkowski v. Cobra Pre-Hung Doors, Inc.
239 N.W.2d 660 (Mich.) 1976

The plaintiff was injured while working for the corporate defendant. The state workmen's compensation bureau awarded plaintiff 215 weeks of compensation at $95 per week plus $81 in medical expenses. The corporation paid $5,000 and then filed a petition in voluntary bankruptcy. The trustee in bankruptcy paid plaintiff an additional $1,700. Plaintiff then sued the officers and directors of the corporation for the unpaid balance of his workmen's compensation claim.

BRENNAN, J. . . . M.S.A. § 17.237 (61) lists methods by which an employer shall provide for the payment of compensation under the act. One approved means is by insuring against such liability with an insurer authorized to transact the business of workmen's compensation insurance within the State of Michigan. M.S.A. § 17.237(647) provides that if the officers and directors of a corporation have not complied wtih M.S.A. § 17.237(611), "[i]f the employer is a corporation, the officers and directors thereof shall be individually and jointly and severally liable for any portion of any such judgment as is returned unsatisfied after execution against the corporation."

By these statutes the Michigan Legislature has sought to protect the interests of persons with the workmen's compensation awards by providing . . . that officers and directors of corporations who fail to see to it that the corporations are able to meet these obligations shall be individually and jointly and severally liable for unpaid awards. The statutory design, therefore, is clear. Corporations are required to provide insurance so that workmen's compensation awards can be paid. If the officers and directors of a corporation fail to arrange for such insurance, the claimant may proceed against the assets of the corporation. If the assets of a corporation prove to be inadequate to pay the award, the officers and directors can be held jointly and severally liable for any balance remaining unpaid. . . .

We hold, therefore, that where the officers and directors of a bankrupt corporation are individually and jointly and severally liable for a workmen's compensation award, due to non-compliance with M.S.A. § 17.237(611), a judgment may be entered against them in circuit court pursuant to M.S.A. § 17.237(647) for any portion of the award remaining unpaid after the distribution of assets by the trustee in bankruptcy and the closing of the bankrupt estate. . . . Plaintiff may, therefore, petition the circuit court for entry of a judgment against the officers and directors for the unpaid portion of his award.

Remanded.

Wilkes v. Springside Nursing Home, Inc.
353 N.E.2d 657 (Mass.) 1976

Plaintiff and the three individual defendants formed a corporation to operate a nursing home. Each shareholder owned one-fourth of the stock and each of them served as a director of the corporation. In addition, each of the parties received a salary of $100 per week for services rendered to the corporation.

After several years of successful operation, the plaintiff and one of the other shareholders by the name of Quinn had a falling out. As the result of this strained relationship, plaintiff in January 1967 gave notice of his intention to sell his shares for their appraised value. In February 1967 the Board of Directors raised Quinn's salary and canceled plaintiff's salary. At the annual meeting in March, plaintiff was not reelected as a director nor was he reelected as an officer. He was told to stay away from the nursing home.

Plaintiff sued the corporation and the individual defendants for damages for lost salary and for breach of the fiduciary duties owed to minority stockholders. The lower court dismissed plaintiff's suit and he appealed.

HENNESSEY, J. . . . We turn to Wilkes's claim for damages based on a breach of the fiduciary duty owed to him by the other participants in this venture.

. . . [S]tockholders in the close corporation owe one another substantially the same fiduciary duty in the operation of the enterprise that partners owe to one another. . . . The standard of duty owed by partners to one another is one of "utmost good faith and loyalty." . . . Thus . . . [s]tockholders in close corporations must discharge their management and stockholder responsibilities in conformity with this strict good faith standard. They may not act out of avarice, expendiency or self-interest in derogation of their duty of loyalty to the other stockholders and to the corporation.

. . . [O]ne peculiar aspect of close corporations [is] the opportunity afforded to majority stockholders to oppress, disadvantage or "freeze out" minority stockholders. . . .

"Freeze outs" . . . may be accomplished by the use of [many] devices. One such device which has proved to be particularly effective in accomplishing the purpose of the majority is to deprive minority stockholders of corporate offices and of employment with the corporation. This "freeze-out" technique has been successful because courts fairly consistently have been disinclined to interfere in those facets of internal corporate operations, such as the selection and retention or dismissal of officers, directors and employees, which essentially involve management decisions subject to the principle of majority control. . . .

The denial of employment to the minority at the hands of the majority is especially pernicious in some instances. A guaranty of employment with the corporation may have been one of the basic reason[s] why a minority owner has invested capital in the firm. The minority stockholder typically depends on his salary as the principal return on his investment, since the earnings of a close corporation . . . are distributed in major part in salaries, bonuses and retirement benefits. Other noneconomic interests of the minority stockholder are likewise injuriously affected by barring him from corporate office. Such action severely restricts his participation in the management of the enterprise, and he is relegated to enjoying those benefits incident to his status as a stockholder. In sum, by terminating a minority stockholder's employment or by severing him from a position as an officer or director, the majority effectively frustrate the minority stockholder's purposes in entering on the corporate venture and also deny him an equal return on his investment. . . .

Nevertheless, we are concerned that untempered application of the strict good faith standard enunciated . . . will result in the imposition of limitations on legitimate action by the controlling group in a close corporation which will unduly hamper its effectiveness in managing the corporation in the best interests of all concerned. The majority, concededly, have certain rights to what has been termed "selfish ownership" in the corporation which should be balanced against the concept of their fiduciary obligation to the minority.

Therefore, when minority stockholders in a close corporation bring suit against the majority alleging a breach of the strict good faith duty owed to them by the majority, we must carefully analyze the action taken by the controlling stockholders in the individual case. It must be asked whether the controlling group can demonstrate a legitimate business purpose for its action. In asking this question, we acknowledge the fact that the controlling group in a close corporation must have some room to maneuver in establishing the business policy of the corporation. . . .

When an asserted business purpose for their action is advanced by the majority, however, we think it is open to minority stockholders to demonstrate that the same legitimate objective could have been achieved through an alternative course of action less harmful to the minority's interest. If called on to settle a dispute, our courts must weigh the legitimate business purpose, if any, against the practicability of a less harmful alternative.

Applying this approach to the instant case it is apparent that the majority stockholders in Springside have not shown a legitimate business purpose for severing Wilkes from the payroll of the corporation or for refusing to reelect him as a salaried officer and director. . . .

It is an inescapable conclusion from all the evidence that the action of the majority stockholders here was a designed "freeze out" for which no legitimate business purpose has been suggested. Furthermore, we may infer that a design to pressure Wilkes into selling his shares to the corporation at a price below their value well may have been at the heart of the majority's plan.

In the context of this case, several factors bear directly on the duty owed to Wilkes by his associates. At a minimum, the duty of utmost good faith and loyalty would demand that the majority consider that their action was in disregard of a long-standing policy of the stockholders that each would be a director of the corporation and that employment with the corporation would go hand in hand with stock ownership; that Wilkes was one of the four originators of the nursing home venture; and that Wilkes, like the others, had invested his capital and time for more than fifteen years with the expectation that he would continue to participate in corporate decisions. Most important is the plain fact that the cutting off of Wilkes's salary, together with the fact that the corporation never declared a dividend, assured that Wilkes would receive no return at all from the corporation. . . .

Reversed and remanded.

Bing Crosby Minute Maid Corp. v. Eaton
297 P.2d 5 (Cal.) 1956

Plaintiff corporation was a judgment creditor of a corporation in which defendant, Eaton, was the principal stockholder. The judgment was not paid, and plaintiff brought this action to recover from defendant. Defendant had received 4,500 shares of stock having a par value of $10 in return for consideration from defendant of $34,780.83. The lower court rendered a judgment against defendant in the amount of $10,219.17. The lower court granted a new trial, and plaintiff appealed.

SHENK, J. . . . In this state a shareholder is ordinarily not personally liable for the debts of the corporation; he undertakes only the risk that his shares may become worthless. There are, however, certain exceptions to this rule of limited liability. For example, a subscriber to shares who pays in only part of what he agreed to pay is liable to creditors for the balance.

. . . The plaintiff seeks to base its recovery on the only other exception to the limited liability rule that the record could support, namely, liability for holding watered stock, which is stock issued in return for properties or services worth less than its par value. Accordingly, this case calls for an analysis of the rights of a creditor of an insolvent corporation against a holder of watered stock. Holders of watered stock are generally held liable to the corporation's creditors for the difference between the par value of the stock and the amount paid in.

. . . The liability of a holder of watered stock has been based on one of two theories: the misrepresentation theory or the statutory obligation theory. The misrepresentation theory is the one accepted in most jurisdictions. The courts view the issue of watered stock as a misrepresentation of the corporation's capital. Creditors who rely on this misrepresentation are entitled to recover the "water" from the holders of the watered shares.

Statutes expressly prohibiting watered stock are commonplace today. In some jurisdictions where they have been enacted, the statutory obligation theory has been applied. Under that theory the holder of watered stock is held responsible to creditors whether or not they have relied on overvaluation of corporate capital.

. . . In his answer the defendant alleged that in extending credit to the corporation the plaintiff did not rely on the par value of the shares issued, but only on independent investigation and reports as to the corporation's current cash position, its physical assets and its business experience. At the trial the plaintiff's district manager admitted that during the period when the plaintiff extended credit to the corporation, (1) the district manager believed that the original capital of the corporation amounted to only $25,000, and (2) the only financial statement of the corporation that the plaintiff ever saw showed a capital stock account of less than $33,000. These admissions would be sufficient to support a finding that the plaintiff did not rely on any misrepresentation arising out of the issuance of watered stock. The court made no finding on the issue of reliance. If the misrepresentation theory prevails in California, that issue was material and the defendant was entitled to a finding thereon. If the statutory obligation theory prevails, the fact that the plaintiff did not rely on any misrepresentation arising out of the issuance of watered stock is irrelevant and accordingly a finding on the issue of reliance would be surplusage.

It is therefore necessary to determine which theory prevails in this state. The plaintiff concedes that before the enactment of § 1110 of the Corporations Code in 1931, the misrepresentation theory was the only one available to creditors seeking to recover from holders of watered stock.

. . . In view of the cases in this state adopting the misrepresentation theory, it is reasonable to assume that the Legislature would have used clear language expressing an intent to broaden the basis of liability of holders of watered stock had it entertained such an intention. In this state the liability of a holder of watered stock may only be based on the misrepresentation theory.

The plaintiff contends that even under the misrepresentation theory a creditor's reliance on the misrepresentation arising out of the issuance of watered stock should be conclusively presumed. This contention is without substantial merit. If it should prevail, the misrepresentation theory and the statutory obligation theory would be essentially identical. This court has held that under the misrepresentation theory a person who extended credit to a corporation (1) before the watered stock was issued, or (2) with full knowledge that watered stock was outstanding, cannot recover from the holders of the watered stock. These decisions indicate that under the misrepresentation theory reliance by the creditor is a prerequisite to the liability of a holder of watered stock. The trial court was therefore justified in ordering a new trial because of the absence of a finding on that issue.

. . . *The order granting the new trial is affirmed.*

CHAPTER 38
REVIEW QUESTIONS AND PROBLEMS

1. If a shareholder owns stock in separate corporations that are competitors, is he allowed to inspect the shareholders list of the particular corporations? Explain.

2. Assume that a person purchases stock in a company and presents the company with a properly indorsed certificate. If the company refuses to reissue a new certificate in his name and recognize his rights as a shareholder, can he require the company to pay him the face value of the certificate? Why?

3. A sold B some stock of the XYZ Company. A gave the stock to B and received the funds, but he did not indorse the stock. A died, and A's executor now claims that the stock, which has greatly increased in value, should be returned, since it was not indorsed. Should it be? Explain.

4. The ABC Company authorized a director, Z, to negotiate the purchase of some land. Instead, Z secretly bought the land himself and sold it to the corporation at a profit. After learning of the deceit, the corporation failed to act. Does B, a minority shareholder, have any remedy? Explain.

5. On March 1, Y Company declared a cash dividend of 5 percent, payable on June 1 to all stockholders of record on May 1. On April 10, A sold ten shares of Y Stock to B, but the transfer was not recorded on the corporation's books until May 15. To whom will the company pay the dividend? Who is entitled to the dividend? Explain.

6. Class B stock in X Company had no voting power, as provided in the certificate of incorporation. S purchased the stock, but the stock certificate did not state that the stock was nonvoting. S was denied the right to vote in the election of directors and brought suit to rescind the contract of purchase. Should S succeed? Why?

7. A creditor of X Company sued the directors of the corporation because of alleged negligent mismanagement of corporate business. In defense, the directors contend that the creditor does not have standing to sue. Are the directors correct? Why?

8. A, the director, general manager, and treasurer of X Company, sold to himself certain boats and engines from the corporation's inventory. At the time of the sale, A was aware that he was going to be discharged shortly. When X Company brought suit to have the sale set aside, A claimed that the property sold was surplus to X Company's needs and that the selling price was fair. Should the sale be set aside? Why?

9. A owned a majority of the stock of X Company, and he ran the corporation by himself. The balance of the stock was owned by A's brother and sister, who agreed to sell all their stock to A. At the time of the purchase, A was negotiating a sale of X Company to another company, but A did not reveal this fact to his brother and sister. The sale of the company resulted in A's selling the stock for a greater amount than he had paid for it. The brother and sister brought suit to recover the difference. Should the brother and sister succeed? Why?

10. All stockholders were present at the annual stockholders' meeting of X Company, whose bylaws required only a majority of shareholders to constitute a quorum. During the meeting, two shareholders, who owned a majority of the stock, withdrew from the meeting while it was in progress. Following the withdrawal, the remaining stockholders elected five new members to the board of directors. Should the election of the directors be invalidated? Why?

11. The directors of a non-profit automobile club, which provided automobile service and other benefits to its membership under a franchise from the Automobile Association of America (AAA), purchased the Y Insurance Agency for themselves. The club already owned the X Insurance Agency, located in a different county, and the Y Agency operated in a manner indistinguishable from X. Both agencies referred "leads" to one another. Y advertised as if it were affiliated with the club and received free advertising space in the club's newsletter. When the membership learned of the acquisition several years later, a shareholder brought suit contending the directors had breached their fiduciary obligation. Should the directors be held liable? Why?

12. P sued D Company for breach of contract. P was a director of D Company, and his presence and vote were necessary to the approval of the contract with him. D Company contends that the contract is not binding. Is the company correct? Explain.

39

Corporate Dissolutions, Mergers, and Consolidations

1. Introduction

Corporate existence terminates upon the expiration of the period set forth in the charter or upon the voluntary or involuntary dissolution of the corporation. In a consolidation, corporate existence technically ceases for both corporations when the new corporation is formed. In a merger, it does so for the corporation that is merged into the continuing one. This chapter will discuss these various methods of terminating the corporate existence.

Most corporate charters provide for perpetual existence. However, where the charter stipulates that the corporation shall exist for a definite period, it automatically terminates at the expiration of the period, unless application to continue the corporation is made and approved by the authority granting the charter.

2. Voluntary Dissolutions

A corporation that has obtained its charter but that has not commenced business may be dissolved by its incorporators. The incorporators file articles of dissolution with the state, and a certificate of dissolution is issued if all fees are paid and the articles are in order.

A corporation that has commenced business may be voluntarily dissolved either by the written consent of *all* its shareholders or by corporate action instituted by its board of directors and approved by a majority of the shareholders. The board action is usually in the form of a recommendation, and it directs that the issue be submitted to the shareholders. A meeting of the shareholders is called to consider the dissolution issue, and if the vote is in favor of it, the officers follow the statutory procedures for dissolution.

These procedures require that the corporate officers file a statement of intent to dissolve with the state of incorporation. This statement of intent includes the consent of all shareholders, if that method is used, or the resolution if the dissolution was instituted by board action. Upon filing the statement of intent, the corporation must cease to carry on its business, except for winding up its affairs, but its corporate existence continues until a certificate of dissolution is issued by the state.

In winding up its affairs, the corporation must give notice to all creditors of the corporation. Directors become personally liable for any debt about which notice is not given.[1]

In dissolution proceedings, corporate assets are first used to pay debts. After all debts are paid, the remainder is distributed proportionately among the shareholders. If there are insufficient assets to pay all debts, a receiver will be appointed by a court and the proceedings will be similar to those of involuntary dissolutions, discussed later.

When all funds are distributed, the corporation will prepare "articles of dissolution" and forward them to the state for approval. When these have been signed by the appropriate state official, usually the secretary of state, one copy is filed with state records and one copy is returned to the corporation to be kept with the corporate records.

The filing of a statement of intent to dissolve is not irrevocable. If the shareholders change their minds before the articles of dissolution are issued, the decision may be revoked by filing a statement of revocation of voluntary dissolution proceedings. When such a statement is filed, the corporation may resume its business.

INVOLUNTARY DISSOLUTIONS

3. Proceedings Commenced by the State

The state, having created the corporation, has the right to institute proceedings to cancel the charter. Suits by a state to cancel or forfeit a charter are known as *quo warranto* proceedings. They are filed by the attorney general and usually at the request of the secretary of state, although they are sometimes filed at the request of a private party.

Quo warranto proceedings may be brought by the attorney general if a corporation (1) fails to file its annual report; (2) fails to pay its franchise tax and license fees; (3) procured its charter by fraud; (4) abuses and misuses its authority; (5) fails to appoint and maintain a registered agent for the service of notices and process, or fails to inform the state of the name and address of

1 *People* v. *Parker,* page 742.

its registered agent; or (6) ceases to perform its corporate functions for a long period of time. The attorney general may also, without charter forfeiture, by proper proceedings enjoin a corporation from engaging in a business not authorized by its charter.

4. Proceedings Commenced by Shareholders

Involuntary dissolution may be ordered by a court of equity at the request of a shareholder when it is established that the directors are deadlocked in the management of the corporate affairs or that the shareholders are deadlocked in voting power and unable to elect a board of directors. Deadlocks require proof that the corporation cannot perform its corporate powers and that the deadlock cannot be broken.

The general rule throughout the country is that a minority shareholder or group of shareholders of a going and solvent corporation cannot maintain a suit to have it dissolved, absent statutory authority. Most states have statutes that authorize courts of equity to liquidate a corporation at the request of a shareholder when it is proved that those in control of the corporation are acting illegally, fraudulently, or oppressively. It is difficult to define oppressive conduct, and each case must be decided on its own facts. In the early law, courts followed what had been described as the "robber-baron" theory. This theory allowed the majority to do anything, including a "squeeze out" of minority stockholders, as long as no specific laws were violated and no actual fraud was committed. The robber baron theory was based on the concept that the majority owed no fiduciary duty to minority shareholders.

Modern decisions tend to reject the robber baron theory. Actions that tend to "squeeze out" or "freeze out" minority shareholders may provide grounds for dissolution or other equitable relief. For example, relief has been granted minority shareholders where the majority have refused to declare dividends but have paid out all profits to themselves in the form of salaries and bonuses. Relief was also granted in a case where the majority shareholders of a corporation that was not in need of funds sold additional stock in order to dilute the percentage of control of the minority, who the majority knew were unable financially to exercise their preemptive right.

Today, conduct that is not illegal or fraudulent may be held to be oppressive. Although controlling shareholders in a closely held corporation are not fiduciaries in the strict sense of the word, the general concepts of fiduciary duties are useful in deciding if conduct is oppressive. The law imposes equitable limitations on dominant shareholders. They are under a duty to refrain from using their control to profit for themselves at the expense of the minority. Repeated violations of these duties will serve as a ground for dissolution. Even though it takes substantially less evidence to justify dissolution of a partnership than of a close corporation, the trend is to treat the issues as quite similar. Oppressive conduct may be summarized as conduct that is burdensome, harsh, and wrongful. It is a substantial deviation from fair dealing and a violation of fair play. It is a violation of the fiduciary duty of good faith in those states that recognize such a duty.

All states allow minority shareholders to obtain dissolution when it is established that corporate assets are being wasted or looted, or that the corporation is unable to carry out its purposes. In addition, some states have by statute broadened the grounds for court-ordered dissolution. These states allow courts to order dissolution when it is reasonably necessary for the protection of the rights or interests of minority shareholders.[2] A corporation will not be dissolved by a court for errors of judgment or because the court, confronted with a question of policy, would decide it differently from the way the directors would. Dissolutions by decree at the request of a shareholder are rare, but as previously noted, the trend is to give greater protection to the minority shareholders and to reject the robber baron theory.

5. Proceedings Commenced by Creditors

A corporation is in the same position as a natural person insofar as its creditors are concerned. A suit may be brought against it, and if judgment is obtained, an execution may be levied against its property, which may then be sold. Also, corporate assets may be attached, and if the corporation has no property subject to execution, its assets may be traced by a bill in a court of equity.

The creditors have no right, just because they are creditors, to interfere with the management of the business. A creditor who has an unsatisfied judgment against a corporation, because there is no corporate property upon which a levy can be made, may bring a bill in equity to set aside conveyances and transfers of corporate property that have been fraudulently transferred for the purpose of delaying and hindering creditors. Creditors may also, under the circumstances above, ask for a receiver to take over the assets of the corporation and to apply them to the payment of debts.

When there is an unsatisfied execution and it is established that the corporation is insolvent, a court may order a dissolution. The same is true if the corporation admits its insolvency. Dissolution in such cases proceeds in the same manner as if instituted by the state or by voluntary proceedings when insolvent. These procedures are discussed in the next section.

6. Procedure on Involuntary Dissolution

In liquidating a corporation, courts have the full range of judicial powers at their disposal. They may issue injunctions, appoint receivers, and take whatever steps are necessary to preserve the corporate assets for the protection of creditors and shareholders. The receiver will usually collect the assets, includ-

2 *Stumpf* v. *C. S. Stumpf & Sons, Inc.,* page 743.

ing any amount owed to the corporation for shares. The receiver will then sell the assets, pay the debts and expenses of liquidation, and, if any funds are left, divide them proportionately among the shareholders. Courts usually require creditors to prove their claims in court in a manner similar to that in bankruptcy proceedings. When all funds in the hands of a receiver are paid out, the court issues a decree of dissolution that is filed with the secretary of state. Funds due persons who cannot be located are deposited with the state treasurer and held for a stated number of years. If not claimed within the stated period by the creditor or shareholder, the funds belong to the state.

7. Liability of Shareholders on Dissolution

As a general rule, shareholders are not liable for the debts of the firm. However, a shareholder who has not paid for his stock in full is liable to the receiver or to a creditor for the unpaid balance. In addition, statutes in most states allow creditors to reach assets of the former corporation in the hands of shareholders.[3] The assets of a corporation are a fund for the payment of creditors, and the directors must manage this fund for their benefit. The liability of shareholders is often predicated upon the theory that the transfer of corporate assets on dissolution is in fraud of creditors and a shareholder knowingly receiving such assets ought to have liability.

Most states have statutory provisions for survival, for a stated period after dissolution, of remedies against a corporation, its directors, officers, and shareholders for claims existing prior to dissolution. Suits against the corporation may be prosecuted or defended in the corporate name. The statutory period is not a statute of limitation; it is simply the period during which claims survive. A judgment on such a claim may be collected from property distributed to shareholders on dissolution, or the creditor may proceed directly against the shareholder receiving the property.

CONSOLIDATIONS AND MERGERS

8. Definitions

Consolidation is the uniting of two or more corporations, whereby a new corporation is created and the old entities are dissolved. The new corporation takes title to all the property, rights, powers, and privileges of the old corporations, subject to the liabilities and obligations of the old corporations.

In a *merger,* however, one of the corporations continues its existence but absorbs the other corporation, which ceases to have an independent existence. The continuing corporation may expressly or impliedly assume and agree to pay the debts and liabilities of the absorbed corporation. If so, the creditors

---

[3] *United States Fire Ins. Co.* v. *Morejon,* page 744.

become third-party creditor beneficiaries. By statute in most states, the surviving corporation is deemed to have assumed all the liabilities and obligations of the absorbed corporation. In recent years, this has even been extended to product liability claims arising out of sales by the former corporation.

Mergers and acquisitions occupy a major segment of the antitrust laws. This aspect will be discussed more fully in the next chapter.

9. Procedures

The procedures for consolidations and mergers are statutory. The usual procedure is for the board of directors of each corporation to approve the plan by resolution. The resolution will set forth in detail all the facts of the planned merger or consolidation. The plan is then submitted to the shareholders of each corporation for approval. Notice is given of the meeting, and the resolution passed by the directors is usually a part of the notice. The shareholders are entitled to be informed of all facts that may affect their vote. If proxies are solicited for such a vote, the proxy material must disclose these facts. The shareholders must approve the plan by a two-thirds vote of all shares, and two-thirds of each class if more than one class of stock is voting. If the consolidation or merger is approved by the shareholders of both corporations, articles of consolidation or articles of merger will be prepared and filed with the state. If the papers are in order and all fees are paid, a certificate of consolidation or a certificate of merger will be issued.

A shareholder who dissents to a consolidation or merger and who makes his dissent a matter of record by serving a written demand that the corporation purchase his stock is entitled to be paid the fair market value of his stock on the day preceding the vote on the corporate action. Procedures are established for ascertaining the fair market value and for a judicial decision of that issue if necessary.[4] When the statutory procedures are followed, the dissenting shareholder ceases to be a shareholder when notice is given, and he becomes a creditor at that time. A shareholder who dissents from a sale or exchange of all or substantially all the assets or property of the corporation, other than in the usual course of business, has the same right to be paid for his stock.

CORPORATE DISSOLUTIONS, MERGERS, AND CONSOLIDATIONS CASES

People v. Parker
197 N.E.2d 30 (Ill.) 1964

HERSHEY, J. The People of the State of Illinois recovered a judgment of $1,024.40 against Paul A. Parker, a former director of the dissolved corporation, Parker Laundry

---

[4] *Brown v. Hedahl's–Q B & R, Inc.,* page 745.

Company, for unpaid personal property taxes levied against the corporation for the years 1953 and 1954. Parker appeals . . . urging that the action was barred by the two-year limitation contained in section 94 of the Business Corporation Act.

Parker Laundry Company, an Illinois corporation, with offices in the city of Rock Island, on December 31, 1954, filed with the Secretary of State a statement of intent to dissolve. The defendant, Parker, was a director at the time, as well as the sole stockholder. The corporation was then liable for personal property taxes for the year 1953 in the amount of $295.46, and for the year 1954, $286.27. Although section 79 of the Business Corporation Act requires that notice of intent to dissolve be given each known creditor, no such notice was given the county treasurer for Rock Island County. The corporation was dissolved February 15, 1955.

The State's Attorney for Rock Island County on October 16, 1961, filed the complaint which initiated this civil action. The basis for recovery was section 42(f) of the Business Corporation Act, which imposes liability on directors of a corporation which has filed a statement of intent to dissolve and fails to mail notice of such action to known creditors of the corporation to the extent of "all loss and damage occasioned thereby." A motion to dismiss the complaint on the basis that the action was outlawed by section 94 of the Business Corporation Act was denied. . . .

Section 94 reads as follows: "The dissolu-tion of a corporation either (1) by the issuance of a certificate of dissolution by the Secretary of State, or (2) by the decree of a court of equity when the court has not liquidated the assets and business of the corporation, or (3) by expiration of its period of duration, shall not take away or impair any remedy available to or against such corporation its directors, or shareholders, for any right or claim existing, or any liability incurred, prior to such dissolution if action or other proceeding thereon is commenced within two years after the date of such dissolution. . . ."

The foregoing provision appears to be a survival statute rather than a statute of limitation. . . .

Unless the liability imposed on corporate directors by section 42(f) abates upon dissolution of the corporation involved, section 94 has no application. Defendant offers no authority for the necessary premise that dissolution of a corporation abates liability incurred by its directors, and we do not know of any principle that requires that result. . . .

Logic . . . suggests that the liability created by section 42(f) does not abate upon dissolution of the corporation involved. It would be anomalous that the occasion giving rise to the liability, dissolution of the corporation, would also cause it to abate.

. . . Section 94 has no application to the directors' liability imposed by section 42(f), and it is conceded that the general statute of limitations has no application to plaintiff. . . .

Judgment affirmed.

Stumpf v. C.S. Stumpf & Sons, Inc.
120 Cal.Rptr. 671 (1975)

A father and his two sons formed a corporation to conduct a general contracting business. The business had previously been conducted as a partnership, and each shareholder had an equal number of shares in the new corporation. Three years later, plaintiff, one of the sons, ceased to be employed by the corporation. There had been a dispute, and the plaintiff had been removed as an officer and director of the corporation. The corporation pays no dividends but invests its profits in real estate. There was no evidence of abuse of authority or persistent unfairness by the defendants. Plaintiff filed suit to dissolve the corporation. California law allows courts to order dissolution where "liquidation is reasonably necessary" for the protection of the rights or interests of the complaining shareholders. The lower court ordered dissolution and the defendants appealed.

CHRISTIAN, J. . . . Appellant contends that respondent's rights and interests are not jeopardized and that dissolution was not justified. Implied in this contention is the argument that [the statute] is not applicable in the absence of some finding of deadlock, mismanagement of the corporation, or display of unfairness toward respondent. The court specifically found that there had been no mismanagement or unfairness; there was no evidence of corporate deadlock. . . .

It is true that courts of some states have narrowly construed provisions similar to subdivision (f), requiring a showing of some kind of management misconduct or deadlock before relief will be granted. In California, a narrow construction of the involuntary dissolution statute has been urged by Ballantine, who suggested that a broad construction of the statute "make[s] it too easy for an obstreperous minority to interfere with the legitimate control and management of the majority by creating a cash nuisance value."

But the danger of minority abuse was evidently recognized and dealt with by the Legislature. The procedure created by the statute does not authorize dissolution at will. The minority must persuade the court that fairness requires drastic relief under section 4651, subdivision (f); involuntary dissolution is not an automatic remedy but, rather, a matter for the court's discretion. "[A] minority stockholder suing under a statute, just as if he were suing in the absence of statute, must still convince the court that his application is meritorious. If the objection were that, because of the possibility of abuse, minority stockholders should not be permitted to ask a court to wind up a corporation, however meritorious the case, the solution would seem to lie in total abolition of the remedy. The reluctance to authorize winding-up a corporation even where such action would be just and equitable contrasts strangely with the arbitrary manner in which a ministerial state official terminates, at a stroke, the existence of great numbers of corporations for failure to comply with comparatively unimportant formalities, such as filing reports or paying a nominal annual tax.". . .

The court's exercise of discretion to order dissolution under section 4651, subdivision (f), was consistent with the intent of the Legislature in adopting that provision.

Appellant next contends that the court's conclusion that the case called for relief under section 4651, subdivision (f), was not supported by the evidence. . . . There was, however, substantial evidence supporting the findings and judgment. The hostility between the two brothers had grown so extreme that respondent severed contact with his family and was allowed no say in the operation of the business. After respondent's withdrawal from the business, he received no salary, dividends, or other revenue from his investment in the corporation. . . .

The decree is affirmed.

United States Fire Ins. Co. v. Morejon
338 So.2d 223 (Fla. App.) 1976

PER CURIAM. . . . On April 17, 1971, plaintiff Morejon was injured in a laundromat owned and operated by Washwell, Inc., which has since been dissolved. At the time of the injury, Rebozo was an officer, director and sole stockholder of Washwell and both Rebozo and Washwell were insured under a liability policy issued by Royal Indemnity with limits of $100,000. Morejon filed suit against Washwell prior to its dissolution, and recovered a judgment in the amount of $385,000. On appeal, this court ordered a remittitur to $150,000. Royal Indemnity paid the $100,000 limit of its liability, leaving $50,000 outstanding.

Morejon then brought the instant action, alleging that she had obtained a prior judgment against Washwell, and that Rebozo, as director, sole stockholder and holder of the proceeds from the dissolution of Washwell, was indebted to her.

Following extensive discovery . . . the trial court granted summary final judgments in favor of Morejon against Rebozo.

We find no error in the trial court's entry of the judgment against Rebozo individually because after plaintiff's accident, but prior to the judgment against Rebozo, Rebozo liquidated Washwell and as sole stockholder received all of the assets. Pursuant to Section 608.30, Florida Statutes (1975), Rebozo must maintain a sufficient amount of the dissolved corporation's assets in order to pay the claims of creditors. The properties of the corporation constitute a fund for the payment of the corporation's debts, and the surviving directors are charged with managing such fund for the interest of the creditors. The judgment against Rebozo is affirmed. . . .

Affirmed.

Brown v. Hedahl's–Q B & R, Inc.
185 N.W.2d 249 (N.Dak.) 1971

The owner of shares of stock in a closely held corporation dissented to a proposed merger that was approved by the remaining shareholders. By state statute, the dissenting shareholder who filed written objections to the merger was entitled to be paid the "fair value" of his shares as of the day preceding the approval of the merger by the other shareholders. The shareholder contended that the stock was worth $322 per share, and the corporation contended that it was worth $100 per share. The lower court found the "fair value" to be $230 per share, and the corporation which had to purchase the stock appealed.

TEIGEN, J. . . . It appears, as a matter of general law, that there are three primary methods used by courts in determining the fair value of shares of dissenting shareholders. These three methods are the market value method, the asset value method, and the investment or earnings value method. The market value method establishes the value of the share on the basis of the price for which a share is selling or could be sold to a willing buyer. This method is most reliable where there is an established market for the stock. The asset value method looks to the net assets of the corporation valued as a "going concern," each share having a pro rata value of the net assets. The net assets value depends on the real worth of the assets as determined by physical appraisals, accurate inventories, and realistic allowances for depreciation and obsolescence. The investment value method relates to the earning capacity of the corporation and involves an attempt to predict its future income based primarily on its previous earnings record. Dividends paid by the corporation are considered in its investment value. Generally, all the elements involved in these methods are considered in determining the value of the dissenter's stock. . . .

In redetermining the "fair value" of a share of Q B & R stock as of March 8, 1968, we have used all three methods of valuation and have established a value under each method which we have assigned a certain percentage weight in determining the fair value of the Q B & R stock. In determining the asset value as of March 8, 1968, we have used the consolidated statement of February 29, 1968, as that is the closest statement to the date in question. We have made certain adjustments to this statement to more properly reflect the true value of the assets of Q B & R as a "going concern." . . . [After explaining the adjustments.] The book value and the adjusted value of the Q B & R assets as of February 29, 1968, are shown on the following page.

The asset value per share, then, based on

Q B & R CONSOLIDATED STATEMENT
February 29, 1968

	Book Value	Adjusted Value
Current Assets:		
Cash on hand and in banks	10,583.75	10,583.75
Notes Receivable	6,641.27	3,000.00
Accounts Receivable	184,800.00	166,320.00
Inventories	469,932.77	469,932.77
Stocks and Bonds	5,423.98	4,000.00
Cash Value Life Insurance	10,860.00	10,860.00
Fixed Assets:		
Real Estate—Lots	34,916.73	207,300.00
Real Estate—Buildings	56,150.59	(Bldgs. included above)
Furniture & Fixtures	4,792.50	9,000.00
Shop Equipment	13,450.98	20,250.00
Autos & Trucks	14,223.92	11,385.00
Total Assets:	811,776.89	912,631.52
Total Liabilities:	203,228.93	203,228.93
Net Asset Value:	608,547.96	709,402.59

Total Shares Outstanding: 2,922
Asset Value Per Share based on the adjusted
statement value of Q B & R:

$$\begin{array}{r} 242.81 \\ \hline 2,922 \overline{\smash{\big)}\ 709,402,59} \end{array}$$

the adjusted value of the Q B & R assets as of February 29, 1968, is $242.81 per share.

Under the investment value (or earnings value) method of valuation, the value per share of Q B & R stock as of March 8, 1968, is zero. Q B & R had sustained a series of losses for several years prior to its merger with Hedahl's, Inc. Plaintiffs' exhibit showing the comparative net profits between Q B & R and Hedahl's, Inc., from 1962 through 1967 shows that Q B & R's five-year average net earnings per share, disregarding 1967, the year prior to the merger, was a loss of 14¢ per share. Based on a six-year average, which includes 1967, the earnings per share was a loss of $4.62 per share. Based on its earnings record, Q B & R was not a good investment and its earnings value is properly fixed at zero. . . . It appears that there is no established market for the Q B & R shares and thus there is no apparent market value that can be assigned to a share of Q B & R stock. However, a reconstructed market value can be established based on the limited transactions that have occurred. . . .

Averaging all Q B & R stock transactions from June of 1963 up to December 6, 1967, the result is a reconstructed market price of $69 per share. This figure appears to be a reasonable reconstructed market price and, accordingly, will be established as the market value for a share of Q B & R stock. . . .

We hold that all three methods of valuation must be used in determining the "fair value" of a share of Q B & R stock as of March 8, 1968. We have determined the value of a share of Q B & R stock by each method. The asset value of a share of Q B & R stock is $242.81 per share; the investment or earnings value of a share of Q B & R stock is zero; and the market value of a share of Q B & R stock is $69 per share. Having determined the value of a share of Q B & R stock by each method, the problem becomes one of weighing the various factors to reach a final result that properly takes into consideration all of the elements and factors involved in determining the "fair value" of a share of Q B & R stock as of March 8, 1968. . . .

In weighing the various values involved we have considered all aspects of Q B & R as a "going concern" prior to its merger with Hedahl's, Inc. Although we have assigned weights to the several values involved, we have not used any set formula; rather, we have relied on an analysis of the particular facts of this case as being determinative of the weight given each value. We have assigned a weight of 25% to the market value of Q B & R. Normally, where there is an established market for the stock of a corporation the market price is given great weight. In other cases where there is no reliable market and none can be reconstructed, market price is not considered at all. However, as to the Q B & R stock, there has been a limited market such that we can properly reconstruct a realistic market price for a share of Q B & R stock. We have assigned a weight of 50% to the asset value of Q B & R. Normally, a higher value is assigned only in cases where the primary purpose of the corporation is to hold assets, such as real estate, for the purpose of allowing them to appreciate in value. In other words, assets are weighed more heavily when they are held for appreciation purposes rather than for commercial retail or wholesale purposes designed to generate earnings. Here the assets of Q B & R primarily consisted of inventories for sale and the necessary buildings and equipment to carry out this business purpose. The inventories held by Q B & R would depreciate in value rather than appreciate but the value of the lots and buildings is substantial in relation to the inventories and will likely appreciate in value. We have assigned a weight of 25% to the investment or earnings value of Q B & R. Normally, in a commercial business, earnings are given great weight as the primary purpose of the business is to generate earnings and not to hold assets that will appreciate in value. Q B & R was such a business, whose primary purpose was to generate earnings for its shareholders. The fact that Q B & R has failed in the past several years to generate such earnings does not mean that earnings are not an important part of the value of Q B & R stock. . . . Although earnings should ordinarily weigh heavily in determining the true value of the stock in a commercial corporation, we believe, under the circumstances, it is proper to give less weight in this case. Accordingly, we have determined that the "fair value" of a share of Q B & R stock as of March 8, 1968, is $138.65 per share.

	Value		Weight		Result
Asset	$242.81	×	50%	=	$121.40
Market	69.00	×	25%	=	17.25
Earnings	0.00	×	25%	=	0.00
Total Value Per Share					$138.65

We therefore direct that the judgment be modified to conform to this opinion and as modified, it is affirmed.

Affirmed.

CHAPTER 39
REVIEW QUESTIONS AND PROBLEMS

1. The X Company was dissolved and all its business wound up. A sale of some assets was made to prepare for distribution to the shareholders. The Y Corporation, a creditor of X, had not been paid and therefore brought suit against X to collect its account. Can Y receive payment? Explain.

2. The Paper Corporation breached a contract with Y. A short while later, Paper merged with the Towel Corporation to form the Paper Towel Corporation. Can Y collect damages from Paper Towel? Explain.

3. The minority stockholders of X Corporation seek to enjoin a sale of its assets and dissolution of the firm. Do the majority of the shareholders have the right to sell the corporate assets and dissolve the company? Explain.

4. A, the owner of all the capital stock of the XYZ Corporation, a newspaper business, sold all his shares to B and promised to serve as adviser to the newspaper for a period of five years, in return for $11,000. After three years, B dissolved the corporation. Only $4,000 had been paid to A. Is A entitled to collect the $7,000 balance? Why?

5. A, B, and C were owners of some orange groves in Florida. X wished to enter the orange-growing business and approached A, B, and C with an offer to form a corporation. The corporation was formed, and the land owned by A, B, and C was transferred to the corporation. X was to manage the corporation, and A, B, and C were to retire, leaving the operation of the groves to X. X failed to manage the groves; in fact, he did nothing. May A, B, and C obtain dissolution of the corporation? Explain.

6. X Company was operated by D, who owned 53 percent of the common stock. D received a salary of $10,000 per year and bonuses of $7,000 per year. The corporation had a net worth of $100,000 and sales of $245,000. The net profit of X Company had been under $2,000, and dividends were either small or nonexistent. Minority shareholders brought suit to compel dissolution of the corporation on the ground of waste, alleging that the waste occurred in the payment of bonuses to D. Should X Company be dissolved? Why?

7. P, the past president of a dissolved corporation, brought suit against two shareholders of the corporation to recover the amount of his unpaid salary. The state statute provided that the shareholders are personally liable for the unpaid salaries and wages of employees and laborers of the corporation in an amount equal to the value of the stock owned by them. The stockholders contend that the statute is not applicable to the chief executive officer who had complete control of the corporation. Should P succeed? Why?

8. A, B, and C formed a corporation for the purpose of operating a Chevrolet franchise. C was the franchise dealer; when he died, it became necessary to pick a new dealer. A and B, however, could not agree on a dealer, and the Chevrolet franchise was lost. B opened his own repair shop on part of the company's property. F, a friend of A's wanted to lease the remainder of the property to operate a new Chevrolet franchise, but B objected to the lease. B and the administrator of C's estate brought suit to dissolve the corporation. Should the corporation be dissolved? Why?

9. The assets of A Company were transferred to B Company. Two years later, C Company purchased for $1 million the assets of B Company. Three years later, X, a machinist, was injured as a result of a defect in a punch press that had been manufactured by A Company. X sues C Company in tort for his injuries. Is C Company liable to X? Why?

10. A Company owed $35,000 in personal property taxes to the city. The city agreed not to levy on the personal property of the corporation, and in turn, A Company agreed to pay the delinquent taxes in installments. The directors then caused the corporation to move personal property outside the jurisdiction of the city and dissolved the corporation, while disposing of the assets. The city brought suit to hold the directors personally liable for the delinquent taxes. Are the directors liable? Why?

11. A Company purchased the assets of B Company. P was injured while using a power press, which was defective and had been manufactured by B Company. P brought a product liability suit against A Company. A Company contended that it was a corporate stranger to the manufacturer of the press and hence not liable. Should A Company be held liable? Why?

12. The X Company and the Y Company form an "agreement of consolidation." The Y Company has cumulative preferred stock which has dividends in arrears. Suit is brought by a stockholder of Y against the consolidated firm, the X-Y Company. The stockholder claims he is entitled to the liquidating value and dividends in arrears on the preferred stock. The preferred stock contract states, "Upon dissolution, liquidation or winding up of the corporation, preferred shareholders shall receive $102.50 per share plus all dividends in arrears." Is the stockholder entitled to his claim? Explain.

Government Regulation

of Business

1. Introduction

The business environment is the product of political, social, economic, and legal forces. Each of these forces has its own substantial impact on our society; it is the law that possesses the cohesive quality to unite them and make our private property system and competitive economic system workable. The law not only creates and protects property rights, it also regulates business activity in an infinite variety of ways. Government regulations affect every aspect of business and are a major part of "business law" today.

Regulation of business is the result of statutes enacted by the legislative branch of government and the execution of the policies set forth in such statutes by the executive branch and the independent regulatory agencies. The policies set forth in statutes are usually carried out by administrative agencies exercising their rule-making, enforcing, and quasi-judicial powers. The determination of the constitutionality and legality of all regulatory activities, as well as the application of the rules issued, ultimately rests with the courts. Therefore, as a practical matter, all branches of government are actively engaged in placing limitations on business activity.

This chapter will discuss the legal basis of the power of federal, state, and local governments to regulate business, the regulation of competition and the regulation of employment.

2. The Federal Power to Regulate Business

The power of the federal government to regulate business activity is found in the commerce clause of the Constitution, which provides, "Congress shall have the power to regulate commerce with foreign nations, among the several States and with the Indian tribes." The power to regulate foreign commerce is vested exclusively in the federal government. State and local governments cannot regulate foreign commerce. Any attempt to do so is unconstitutional. The power to regulate foreign commerce extends to all aspects of foreign trade. No sort of trade to which this power does not extend can be carried on between this country and any other.

The language "among the several states" has been interpreted to mean that Congress has the power not only to regulate interstate commerce but also to regulate any intrastate business activity that has a substantial effect on interstate commerce.[1] The effect on interstate commerce may be positive or negative. For example, Congress may pass a law prohibiting a specific activity and thereby prevent interstate commerce. The effect of any individual business on interstate commerce need not be substantial, if the cumulative effect of all similar businesses is substantial.

Although the power of Congress to regulate an infinite variety of business activities by use of the commerce clause is quite broad, it is subject to some limitations. These limitations are found in other provisions of the Constitution, such as the Sixth Amendment's guarantee of a right to a trial by jury and the Fifth Amendment's due process clause. In addition, a recent decision has made it clear that the power to regulate commerce cannot be used to destroy state and local governments. In that case, Congress attempted to regulate the wages of the employees of state and local governments. The Supreme Court held that Congress may not exercise its power to regulate commerce so as to force directly upon the states its choices as to how essential decisions regarding the conduct of integral government functions are to be made.

3. State Regulation of Business

State and local governments use their "police power" to enact laws to promote the public health, safety, morals, and general welfare. Of necessity, such laws frequently result in the regulation of business activity. The commerce clause does not expressly prohibit the use of a state's police power merely because a law results in the regulation of business activity. However, the

---

[1] *Perez* v. *United States,* page 764.

commerce clause and the supremacy clause of the Constitution do impose several restrictions on the use of police power as it affects business.

The first restriction is that state and local governments cannot enact laws on subjects that are considered to be exclusively federal. For example, a state could not pass a law establishing the width of a railroad track or a law concerning air traffic, because such subjects require national uniformity. For this reason, any state law concerning a subject that is exclusively under the federal government's jurisdiction is unconstitutional under the commerce and supremacy clauses. This is true even if there is no federal law on the subject.

The second limitation concerns subject matters over which the federal government has taken exclusive jurisdiction by enacting legislation. Federal laws that assert exclusive jurisdiction over a subject are said to preempt the field. Preemption may result from express language or by comprehensive regulation showing an intent by Congress to exercise exclusive dominion over the subject matter. When a federal statute has preempted the field, *any* state or local law pertaining to the same subject matter is unconstitutional and the state regulation is void.

Not every federal regulatory statute preempts the field. When a federal law does not preempt the field and the subject matter is not exclusively federal, state regulation under the police power is permitted. However, if a state law is inconsistent or irreconcilably in conflict with the federal statute, the state law is unconstitutional and void. Moreover, state laws are invalid if they discriminate against interstate commerce or impose an undue burden on it.

In addition to the commerce clause limitations, a state's exercise of police power may be challenged under the constitutional provisions relating to "due process" and "equal protection of the laws," and under all provisions of the Bill of Rights. Challenges to the constitutionality of a law based on "due process" and "equal protection" are frequently used to challenge a tax imposed on interstate commerce. Taxation is a very significant form of regulation. The Bill of Rights provisions are employed to challenge such laws as Sunday-closing statutes or censorship of obscenity ordinances.

The commerce clause also imposes limitations on the taxing power of state and local governments. Although the issues involved are varied and complex, it may be said as a general rule that a state may impose a tax such as an income tax or a property tax on a business engaged in interstate commerce provided that the tax is *apportioned* by some reasonable formula to local activities within the state and does not discriminate against interstate commerce in favor of intrastate commerce. There must be a connection between the tax and the local enterprise being taxed (*nexus*), or the tax will violate the commerce clause. The concepts of nexus and apportionment are used to ensure that interstate commerce pays its fair share for benefits received from the state.

THE REGULATION OF COMPETITION—THE ANTITRUST LAWS

4. The Sherman Act

In 1890, under its power to regulate interstate commerce, Congress passed the Sherman Antitrust Act. The Sherman Act was directed essentially at two areas: (1) contracts, combinations, or conspiracies in restraint of trade; and (2) monopoly and attempts to monopolize. The law sought to preserve workable competition.

The Sherman Act contains four separate legal sanctions. First, it is a federal crime punishable by fine or imprisonment or both for any person or corporation to violate its provisions. Although originally they were only misdemeanors, today crimes under the Sherman Act are felonies. An individual found guilty may be fined up to $100,000 and imprisoned up to three years. A corporation found guilty may be fined up to $1 million for each offense.

Second, the Sherman Act authorizes injunctions to prevent and restrain violations or continued violations of the act. Failure to obey may be punished by contempt proceedings resulting in a fine or jail sentence.

Third, a remedy is given to those persons who have been injured by violation of the act. Such persons are given the right, in a civil action, to collect treble damages plus court costs and reasonable attorney's fees. This remedy may be enforced on behalf of the citizens of a state by the attorney general of the state. Such suits are instituted when the injured parties are consumers who have been the victim of violations such as price-fixing. Normally, the objective of money damages is to place the injured party in the position he would have enjoyed, as nearly as this can be done with money, had his rights not been invaded. The treble-damage provision serves not only as a means of punishing the defendant for his wrongful act but also of compensating the plaintiff for his actual injury.

Finally, if any property owned in violation of the restraint of trade provisions of the act is being transported from one state to another, it is made subject to seizure by and forfeiture to the United States. This last sanction has rarely been used.

The most common type of Sherman Act violation is price-fixing. Price-fixing is as a matter of law in restraint of trade. It is no defense that the prices fixed are fair or reasonable. It also is no defense that price-fixing is engaged in by small competitors to allow them to compete with larger competitors. It is just as illegal to fix a low price as it is to fix a high price. Today, it is as illegal to fix the price of services as it is to fix the price of goods.[2] Price-fixing in the service sector has been engaged in by professional persons as well as by service occupations such as automobile- and TV-repair workers, barbers, and refuse collectors. For many years, it was contended that persons performing services were not engaged in trade or commerce. That contention has been

---

[2] *Goldfarb et ux.* v. *Virginia State Bar et al.,* page 766.

rejected, and suits to prevent price-fixing in the service sector are common today.

There are many other examples of Sherman Act violations. Many of these involve concerted activities among competitors. For example, an exchange of price information has been held to be a Sherman Act violation. Agreements to divide up territories among competitors, or to limit the supply of a commodity, are outlawed.

From its adoption, the Sherman Act proved unable to achieve all its goals. This was because of its very broad language and the favorable treatment given "big business" by the courts early in this century. Various amendments designed to make the act more specific have been enacted through the years. These amendments and some other statutes are discussed more fully in the sections that follow.

5. The Clayton Act

In 1914, Congress enacted the Clayton Act, which was designed to make the Sherman Act more specific. The act declared illegal certain practices that might have an adverse effect on competition but were something less than contracts, combinations, or conspiracies in restraint of trade, and did not constitute actual monopolization or attempts to monopolize. The practices it enumerated were outlawed if their effect *might* be to substantially lessen competition, or *tend* to create a monopoly. This is sometimes referred to as the "prohibited effect" in the Clayton Act.

The Clayton Act contains four major provisions. Section 2 makes it unlawful for a seller to discriminate in price between purchasers of commodities when the prohibited effect or tendency might result. This provision on price discrimination was amended in 1936, by the Robinson-Patman Amendment, discussed in Section 7 of this chapter.

Section 3 is directed at tying and exclusive contracts. Such contracts may be contracts of sale or lease. They usually contain a provision or condition that the lessee or purchaser shall not use or deal in the commodities of a competitor of the lessor or seller. This section of the act prevents a seller of a product that is in high demand from forcing a purchaser to purchase a less desirable product in order to obtain the former. It results in every product's standing on its merits. For example, a seller or lessor of a computer cannot require that the buyer or lessee purchase all punch cards from it. Such a requirement is an unreasonable restraint that might substantially lessen competition, by foreclosing competitors from a substantial market. Full-line forcing is another example of a Section 3 violation.

Section 7 prohibits the acquisition of all or part of the stock of other corporations, where the effect *might* be to lessen competition substantially or to *tend* to create a monopoly. This section was substantially amended, and its provisions as amended will be discussed in Section 8 later.

Section 8 of the Clayton Act is aimed at interlocking directorates. It prohibits a person from being a member of the board of directors of two or more corporations at the same time when one of them has capital, surplus, and undivided profits totaling more than $1,000,000, where elimination of competition by agreement between such corporations would amount to a violation of any of the antitrust laws.

6. The Federal Trade Commission Act

Congress enacted a second antitrust law in 1914. This law created the Federal Trade Commission as one of the expert independent regulatory agencies. The Federal Trade Commission was given jurisdiction over cases arising under Sections 2, 3, 7, and 8 of the Clayton Act. In addition, the commission has been directed to prevent unfair methods of competition and unfair or deceptive acts or practices. Its jurisdiction over unfair methods of competition gives it the responsibility to ensure that overcompetitive economic systems work. Its jurisdiction over unfair and deceptive acts or practices makes the commission the primary consumer protection agency at the federal level.

Today, the FTC is a very active federal agency. It is involved in attempts to break oligopolies and shared monopolies. For example, it is seeking to create competition in the breakfast-food market in a complicated case involving the "Big Four" cereal companies.

Advertising is of great concern to the commission. It is attempting to limit ads directed at children contending that they constitute an unfair method of competition. It has required advertisers to run corrective ads when it has been established that an advertisement was deceptive. It requires manufacturers to prove the truthfulness or to substantiate the claims made in advertising. The government is not required to prove that an ad is false for the FTC act to be violated. Great deference is given to the decisions of the commission as they affect the marketing of goods. An activity may be an unfair method of competition without being a violation of the Sherman or Clayton acts.

7. The Robinson-Patman Act

In 1936, Congress enacted the Robinson-Patman Amendment of Section 2 of the original Clayton Act, dealing with price discrimination. This amendment, sometimes referred to as "the chain-store act," was designed to ensure equality of treatment to all buyers of a seller, in those cases when the result of unequal treatment might substantially lessen competition or tend to create a monopoly in any line of commerce. Section 2 of the Clayton Act had not achieved this end, partly owing to the legality of quantity discounts under it, and partly because some buyers were able to obtain indirect benefits such as promotional or brokerage allowances. Such allowances were actually discounts that gave competitive advantage to one buyer over other buyers dealing with the same seller.

The Robinson-Patman Act made it a crime for a seller to sell at lower prices in one geographical area than in another in the United States in order to eliminate competition or a competitor, or to sell at unreasonably low prices to drive out a competitor. In addition, the Federal Trade Commission was given jurisdiction and authority to eliminate quantity discounts and to forbid brokerage allowances, except to independent brokers. The statute also prohibited promotional allowances, except on an equal basis.

The law applies to both buyers and sellers. It is just as illegal to receive the benefit of price discrimination as it is to give a lower price to one of two buyers. As a result of Robinson-Patman, the small businessman is able to purchase merchandise at essentially the same price as the large business. He is entitled to the same price for identical goods and to proportionately equal promotional allowances. A large competitor cannot legally reduce his price to drive out the small competitor.

The original Clayton Act required a showing of general injury to competitive conditions. The 1936 amendment provided that there could be a finding of injury to competition by a showing of "injury to the competitor" victimized by the discrimination. This proviso gave additional protection to small businessmen.

8. Mergers and Acquisitions

Section 7 of the Clayton Act as originally written was extremely limited in its application. In 1950, this act was amended to prohibit the acquisition of the stock *or assets* of other corporations when the effect might be or tend to create a monopoly *in any line of commerce* in any section of the country. Section 7 as originally written covered horizontal mergers—those between competitors. It did not cover vertical (those between a buyer and seller) or conglomerate mergers. Moreover, a major gap existed in the language concerning stock of another company but not its assets. Acquisition could occur simply by the purchase of a plant instead of the corporate stock. The 1950 amendment plugged this loophole by adding "assets" to "stock." It was also broadened to cover vertical and conglomerate mergers with the deletion of the language "of a competitor" and the insertion of "any line of commerce."

Section 7 requires only a finding and conclusion that a given acquisition or merger has a reasonable probability of lessening competition or tending toward monopoly. It does not deal with certainties, only with probabilities. The goal of the law is to arrest anticompetitive effects and trends toward undue concentration of economic power at their incipiency. In determining whether or not a given merger or acquisition is illegal, courts examine both the product market and the geographic market affected.

A significant concept in the merger field today is the "potential-entrant" doctrine. This doctrine finds that the prohibited effect may exist where an acquisition or a merger involves a potential entrant into a market. An acquisition of a company by a potential competitor is thus illegal where the effect may be to substantially lessen competition.[3] The potential-entrant doctrine applies to product extension and to geographic expansion by mergers and acquistions. The potential-entrant doctrine is applied not only because if entry does occur there is an additional competitor, but also because the mere presence of a potential competitor at the edge of the market has positive effects on those companies actually competing.

The law recognizes that stimulation of competition might flow from a particular merger. It does not impede, for example, a merger between two small companies to enable the combination to compete more effectively with larger corporations dominating the relevant market, nor a merger between a corporation that is financially healthy and a failing one that can no longer be a vital competitive factor in the market.

Congress neither adopted nor rejected any particular tests for measuring the relevant markets. Nor did it adopt a definition of the word *substantially,* whether in quantitative terms of sales or assets or market shares, or in designated qualitative terms, by which a merger's effects on competition were to be measured. Congress merely indicated plainly that a merger had to be functionally viewed, in the context of its particular industry. If the merger or acquisition involved a concentrated industry or one tending toward concentration, a challenge would be more likely. If the industry was fragmented and without significant barriers to entry, there would be less likelihood of challenge.

By a 1976 amendment, a company with annual net sales amounting to $10 million or more that is being acquired by a firm with total annual sales of $100 million or more must give the Justice Department 30 days' notice before any proposed merger is consummated. This enables the government to take action to stop any merger in advance. Mergers meeting these tests are likely to have anticompetitive effects.

A significant portion of antitrust litigation falls under Section 7. Recent years have seen a rash of corporate mergers, since growth by acquisition or merger is usually deemed more desirable than internal growth. In addition to creating antitrust problems, these mergers have also caused problems for accountants and financial experts. Financial reporting for conglomerates is obviously difficult when one considers that such statements may combine the sales of a distillery and an airline, for example. Solving the numerous problems raised by mergers will be a matter of concern for many years to come.

THE REGULATION OF EMPLOYMENT

9. Introduction

Many legislative enactments affect the employment relationship. First, there are the federal statutes that regulate labor–management relations and collec-

---

[3] *FTC* v. *Procter & Gamble Co.,* page 768.

tive bargaining. These statutes, the judicial decisions interpreting them, and the actions of the administrative agency (NLRB) that enforces and administers them compose a major segment of the law relating to employment.

Second, there are the federal statutes that regulate wages, hours, and working conditions. The Fair Labor Standards Act, which controls such matters as minimum wages, hours, and the records to be kept by employers, is an example of such a statute. The Occupational Safety and Health Act, commonly referred to as OSHA, is an attempt by the federal government to ensure, as far as possible, safe and healthful working conditions for every working man and woman.

Third, there are the state laws that deal with such matters as child labor, safety devices, unemployment compensation, and fair employment practices. It must be recognized that many of the rights and duties of both employers and employees are determined by these statutes and the administrative agencies operating pursuant to them. The businessman must be familiar with these statutes and the regulations related to them and must comply with those applicable to his business. This chapter will discuss the Fair Labor Standards Act, OSHA, and laws relating to discrimination in employment.

10.   The Fair Labor Standards Act

The Fair Labor Standards Act originally required covered employers to pay their employees at least 25 cents an hour for a regular workweek of 44 hours, to pay such employees at least time and one-half for all work performed over the 44-hour week, and to keep certain records for each worker that would demonstrate compliance or noncompliance with the act. This minimum hourly wage has been increasing each year recently, and by laws already enacted, it will go to $3.20 per hour. The standard workweek is now 40 hours, with overtime pay at a rate of not less than one and one-half times the employee's regular rate of pay. The wage and overtime provisions apply whether an employee is paid on a time, piecework, job, incentive, or other basis. Of course, record-keeping requirements remain.

Not all types of employment were covered by the original FLSA, nor are they today. However, the amendments have expanded coverage greatly along with the minimum wage, so that now most workers are protected by it. Categories of persons who are not currently covered include many who do not need the protection, such as those engaged in the practice of a profession and managerial personnel.

The FLSA contains sections that regulate the employment of child labor. Under these, 18 is the minimum age for employment in hazardous occupations. These include work involving exposure to radioactivity, the operation of various kinds of dangerous machinery, mining, and roofing. Otherwise the basic minimum age for employment is 16, at which children may be employed in any nonhazardous work. The employment of 14- and 15-year-olds is limited to such occupations as sales and clerical work, under specific conditions of work, for limited hours, and outside school time only. Children under 14 may not be employed, except for a few jobs that are specifically exempt. For example, children employed in agriculture outside of school hours, children employed by their parents in nonhazardous occupations, child actors, and newspaper deliverers are exempt.

The FLSA authorizes the three usual sanctions for violations of its provisions. The criminal sanctions carry $10,000 fines and imprisonment for up to six months as penalties. Federal courts may issue injunctions to prevent violations. Finally, an employee who is injured by a violation may bring a civil suit against his employer and recover unpaid wages or overtime compensation and punitive damages, plus reasonable attorney's fees and cost of the action. The administrator of the Wage and Hour Division of the Department of Labor may bring suit on behalf of the employee.

11. OSHA

The enactment of workmen's compensation and the imposition of employer liability without fault did not eliminate occupational diseases and industrial accidents or reduce them to a satisfactory level. To further the goal of ensuring safe and healthful working conditions, Congress in 1970 enacted an Occupational Safety and Health Act under its powers in the commerce clause. This act, commonly referred to as OSHA, created a three-member Occupational Safety and Health Review Commission to handle the quasi-judicial functions under the act and delegated to the secretary of labor certain quasi-legislative powers.

The quasi-legislative powers delegated to the secretary of labor include the authority to set mandatory occupational safety and health standards applicable to businesses affecting interstate commerce. Pursuant to this authority, the Department of Labor has issued detailed rules and regulations setting forth safety standards for almost every industry. Some of these standards apply to all industries, and others apply only to certain types of activities, such as construction. For example, the standards relating to fire extinguishers, exits from buildings, electrical groundings, and machine guards are of general applicability, whereas rules relating to the wearing of hard hats would be directed to a particular work task or activity.

These rules and regulations came from a variety of sources, but they were generally the standards for health and safety recognized by such organizations as the National Fire Protection Association and the American Standards Institute. When these standards were adopted, they became legislative means to which all employers must conform. Although conformance has not usually been difficult for the very large corporation with a substantial staff that was devoted to safety matters prior to the enactment of OSHA, there have been many problems for the small business in the early years of OSHA, and heavy costs involved in compliance.

To determine if the health and safety standards adopted by the secretary of labor are being complied with, there are inspectors whose job it is to visit places of work and make on-site inspections. These inspectors may appear at a place of business on their own initiative, or they may appear as the result of an employee complaint. An employee who believes that a violation of job safety or health standards exists or that he is in danger may request an inspection in writing by sending a letter to the Department of Labor. The inspectors have authority to issue citations if they find a violation of the applicable rules and regulations. It should be noted that the great majority of all inspections do result in citations. The employer may be fined up to $1,000 for every citation, but if the employer does not agree that the alleged violation exists, he may appeal to the Review Commission, which will hold a quasi-judicial hearing to determine if a violation, in fact, exists. Decisions of the commission, as well as appeals from rules enacted pursuant to the delegated authority, may be appealed to the courts.

An employer who willfully or repeatedly violates the safety and health rules and standards may be penalized up to $10,000 for each violation. As previously noted, the penalty for a simple citation is any amount up to $1,000, and an employer who fails to correct a violation within the period permitted for its correction may be penalized $1,000 for each day the violation continues.

OSHA has been a very controversial law. Although its goals have been accepted, its approach has not. In the early years, the administration of the law was primarily directed at job safety. This resulted in billions of dollars in costs to industry to comply with the OSHA standards. Many people felt that the benefits derived from these costs were relatively insignificant. Moreover, the unannounced inspection procedure was held to violate the Fourth Amendment and search warrants may be required if the employer objects to the inspection without one. Today OSHA is directing its efforts more at health and less at safety. For example, those charged with administering the law are attacking working conditions likely to cause cancer or heart attacks.

In addition, inspectors are working with businesses seeking to correct unsafe conditions without imposing fines. The Department of Labor is attempting to make sure that OSHA enforcement does not affect labor–management relations. Record-keeping requirements are being reduced, and an attempt is being made to grant reasonable variances to OSHA standards where no significant danger to employees would exist. It is yet too early to know whether or not OSHA will accomplish its purposes and whether the administration of the law by the Department of Labor will be such that it will merit the support of the business community and the rest of society.

DISCRIMINATION IN EMPLOYMENT

12. Introduction

Many cities, most states, and the federal government have enacted statutes designed to prevent discrimination in hiring, promotion, pay, or layoffs, because of race, color, creed, sex, national origin, or age—the last category covering workers between 40 and 65 years of age. A federal law also prohibits discrimination against the handicapped. These statutes have modified the basic common law concept that an employer had a free choice in selecting his employees and, in the absence of a contract, a free choice in discharging them. They have been enacted as a part of the general philosophy of government that all persons should have equality of opportunity. These statutes frequently contain criminal sanctions and authorize civil suits for damages.

The basic federal law on equal employment opportunity was enacted in 1964. The Civil Rights Act of 1964, as now amended, covers all employers with fifteen or more employees, labor unions with fifteen or more members, labor unions that operate a hiring hall, and employment agencies. The 1972 amendment extended coverage to state and local governments and to educational institutions with respect to persons whose work involves educational activities.

The types of employer action in which discrimination is prohibited include discharge; refusal to hire; compensation; and terms, conditions, or privileges of employment. The act proscribes not only overt discrimination but also practices that are fair in form but discriminatory in operation.

13. EEOC

A federal administrative agency known as the Equal Employment Opportunity Commission has the primary responsibility for enforcing the act. The EEOC is composed of five members, not more than three of whom may be members of the same political party. In the course of its investigations, the commission has broad authority to examine and copy evidence, require the production of documentary evidence, hold hearings, and subpoena and examine witnesses under oath.

By a 1972 amendment, the EEOC has the power to file a civil suit in court and to represent a person charging a violation of the act. However, it must first exhaust efforts to conciliate the claim. The remedies available in such an action include reinstatement with back pay for the victim of an illegal discrimination and injunctions against future violations of the law.

The federal law seeks to preserve state and local employment-practice laws. Where an alleged violation of federal law, if true, is violative of a state or local law, the commission may not act until 60 days after the proceedings, if any, have been commenced under that law. Similarly, the commission must notify the appropriate officials and defer all action until the local authority has had, in general, at least 60 days to resolve the matter. In either case, the 60-day waiting requirement is dispensed with if the local proceeding is terminated before that time.

14. Tests

Practices involving recruiting, hiring, and promotion of employees are often charged with being discriminatory and in violation of the law. For example, the courts have held that the use of a standardized general intelligence test in selecting and placing personnel is prohibited as being discriminatory on the basis of race. Tests neutral on their face, and even neutral in terms of intent, cannot be maintained if they operate to "freeze" the *status quo* of prior discriminatory employment practices. If an employment practice cannot be shown to be related to job performance, the practice is prohibited. The Civil Rights Act proscribes not only overt discrimination but also practices that are fair in form but discriminatory in operation. As a result, job tests have been dropped by many companies because of the difficulty of proving that all questions are validly related to job performance.[4]

Discrimination on the basis of religion, sex, or national origin is permissible in hiring, referrals, advertising, and admission to apprenticeship programs if these considerations are bona fide occupational qualifications. The omission of race and color from this exception means the Congress does not feel that these two factors are *ever* bona fide occupational qualifications. In addition, religion, sex, and national origin are not usually considered bona fide occupational qualifications.

15. Seniority

Bona fide seniority systems are often used to select persons to be laid off in the event an employer is reducing its labor force. They are also used to provide the basis for many promotions. As a result of seniority, the last hired are usually the first fired. Decisions based on seniority have been challenged as violating the laws relating to equal employment opportunity. The challenges arose when recently hired members of minority groups were laid off during periods of economic downturn.

Although the law that is to be applied when seniority systems conflict with equal employment opportunity is still developing, certain principles are emerging. If a company has not discriminated in its employment practices since the adoption of the Civil Rights Act, its seniority system for purpose of layoff is probably valid. However, promotions cannot be awarded on the basis of seniority if the effect is to lock minorities into less desirable jobs and to legally carry forward the effects of past discrimination. In addition, the law

---

[4] *Griggs* v. *Duke Power Company,* page 771.

requires that employees be given retroactive seniority if they have been discriminated against and denied equal employment opportunity since 1964. In addition to retroactive seniority to the date of the original employment application, minority employees are entitled to back pay and to priority consideration for vacancies when discrimination in violation of statute is proven.

16. Sex Discrimination

Discrimination based on sex is a major area of equal employment opportunity litigation. Historically, states have enacted many laws designed to protect women. For example, many states prohibited by statute the employment of women in certain occupations, such as those that require lifting heavy objects. Others barred women from working during the night or working more than a given number of hours per week or day. Under EEOC guidelines and court decisions, such statutes are not a defense to a charge of illegal sex discrimination. Other EEOC guidelines forbid (1) classifying jobs as male or female by employers, and (2) advertising in help-wanted columns that are designated male or female, unless sex is a bona fide job qualification. Courts construe this exception narrowly. No bona fide occupational qualification was found to exist where there was (1) a rule requiring airline stewardesses to be single, (2) a policy of hiring only females as flight-cabin attendants, (3) a rule against hiring females with preschool-age children, and (4) a telephone company policy against hiring females as switchmen because of the alleged heavy lifting involved in the job. For sex to be a valid job qualification, it must be demonstrably relevant to job performance. Very few jobs meet this test. Moreover, employers may establish job criteria that tend to result in job discrimination unless the criteria meet the test of business necessity.[5]

There is also a federal law that requires that women be paid wages equivalent to those paid men for equivalent work (or vice versa). Executive personnel are exempt from the Equal Pay Act.

The desire to eliminate the adverse effects of past discrimination has prompted most government bodies and many private employers to adopt policies and practices described as affirmative-action programs. These affirmative-action programs usually establish goals for hiring and promoting members of minority groups. These goals are to be achieved by active recruitment programs and by giving priority to minorities. Members of such groups are to be given priority when there are fewer of them working in a given job category than one would reasonably expect there should be, considering their availability.

Affirmative-action programs and similar efforts have resulted in charges of reverse discrimination by white males. Courts have recently held that the law prohibits discrimination of any kind and that overt attempts to favor minori-

[5] *Boyd v. Ozark Air Lines, Inc.*, page 773.

ties are also illegal. Double standards in selection and promotion policies are illegal today. The law is trying to achieve equality of opportunity without discrimination against either the majority of persons or the members of minority groups.

GOVERNMENT REGULATION OF BUSINESS CASES

Perez v. United States
91 S.Ct. 1357 (1971)

The defendant was convicted of violating the Federal Consumer Credit Protection Act by engaging in "loan sharking." The defendant challenged the constitutionality of the federal law on the ground that the activity was local and thus beyond the power of the federal government.

DOUGLAS, J. . . . The constitutional question is a substantial one. . . .

The Commerce Clause reaches in the main three categories of problems. First, the use of channels of interstate or foreign commerce which Congress deems are being misused, as for example, the shipment of stolen goods or of persons who have been kidnapped. Second, protection of the instrumentalities of interstate commerce, as for example, the destruction of an aircraft, or persons or things in commerce, as for example, thefts from interstate shipments. Third, those activities affecting commerce. It is with this last category that we are here concerned. . . .

Chief Justice Stone wrote for a unanimous Court in 1942 that Congress could provide for the regulation of the price of intrastate milk, the sale of which, in competition with interstate milk, affects the price structure and federal regulation of the latter. The commerce power, he said, "extends to those activities intrastate which so affect interstate commerce, or the exertion of the power of Congress over it, as to make regulation of them appropriate means to the attainment of a legitimate end, the effective execution of the granted power to regulate interstate commerce."

Wickard v. *Filburn,* 317 U.S. 111, soon followed in which a unanimous Court held that wheat grown wholly for home consumption was constitutionally within the scope of federal regulation of wheat production because, though never marketed interstate, it supplied the need of the grower which otherwise would be satisfied by his purchases in the open market. We said:

> . . . even if appellee's activity be local and though it may not be regarded as commerce, it may still, whatever its nature, be reached by Congress if it exerts a substantial economic effect on interstate commerce, and this irrespective of whether such effect is what might at some earlier time have been defined as "direct" or "indirect." 317 U.S., at 125.

As pointed out in *United States* v. *Darby,* 312 U.S. 100, the decision sustaining an Act of Congress which prohibited the employment of workers in the production of goods "for interstate commerce" at other than prescribed wages and hours—*a class of activities*—was held properly regulated by Congress without proof that the particular intrastate activity against which a sanction was laid had an effect on commerce. A unanimous Court said:

> . . . Congress has sometimes left it to the courts to determine whether the intrastate activities have the prohibited effect on the commerce, as in the Sherman Act. It has sometimes left it to an administrative board or agency to deter-

mine whether the activities sought to be regulated or prohibited have such effect, as in the case of the Interstate Commerce Act, and the National Labor Relations Act, or whether they come within the statutory definition of the prohibited Act, as in the Federal Trade Commission Act. And sometimes Congress itself has said that a particular activity affects the commerce, as it did in the present Act, the Safety Appliance Act and the Railway Labor Act. In passing on the validity of legislation of the class last mentioned the only function of courts is to determine whether the particular activity regulated or prohibited is within the reach of the federal power.

That case is particularly relevant here because it involved a criminal prosecution, a unanimous Court holding that the Act was "sufficiently definite to meet constitutional demands." Petitioner is clearly *a member of the class* which engages in "extortionate credit transactions" as defined by Congress and the description of that class has the required definiteness.

It was the "class of activities" test which we employed in *Heart of Atlanta Motel, Inc. v. United States,* 379 U.S. 241, to sustain an Act of Congress requiring hotel or motel accommodations for Negro guests. The Act declared that " 'any inn, hotel, motel, or other establishment which provides lodging to transient guests' affects commerce *per se.*" That exercise of power under the Commerce Clause was sustained.

> . . . our people have become increasingly mobile with millions of people of all races traveling from State to State; that Negroes in particular have been the subject of discrimination in transient accommodations, having to travel great distances to secure the same; that often they have been unable to obtain accommodations and have had to call upon friends to put them up overnight . . . and that these conditions had become so acute as to require the listing of available lodging for Negroes in a special guidebook. . . .

In a companion case, *Katzenbach v. McClung,* 379 U.S. 294, we ruled on the constitutionality of the restaurant provision of the same Civil Rights Act which regulated the restaurant "if . . . it serves or offers to serve interstate travelers or a substantial portion of the food which it serves . . . has moved in commerce." Apart from the effect on the flow of food in commerce to restaurants, we spoke of the restrictive effect of the exclusion of Negroes from restaurants on interstate travel by Negroes.

> . . . there was an impressive array of testimony that discrimination in restaurants had a direct and highly restrictive effect upon interstate travel by Negroes. This resulted, it was said, because discriminatory practices prevent Negroes from buying prepared food served on the premises while on a trip, except in isolated and unkempt restaurants and under most unsatisfactory and often unpleasant conditions. This obviously discourages travel and obstructs interstate commerce for one can hardly travel without eating. Likewise, it was said, that discrimination deterred professional, as well as skilled, people from moving into areas where such practices occurred and thereby caused industry to be reluctant to establish there.

In emphasis of our position that it was the *class of activities* regulated that was the measure, we acknowledge that Congress appropriately considered the "total incidence" of the practice on commerce.

Where the *class of activities* is regulated and that *class* is within the reach of federal power, the courts have no power, "to excise, as trivial, individual instances" of the class.

Extortionate credit transactions, though purely intrastate, may in the judgment of Congress affect interstate commerce. In an analogous situation, Mr. Justice Holmes, speaking for a unanimous Court, said ". . . when it is necessary in order to prevent an evil to make the law embrace more than the precise thing to be prevented it may do so." . . .

In the setting of the present case there is a tie-in between local loan sharks and interstate crime.

The findings by Congress are quite adequate on that ground. . . .

"Even where extortionate credit transactions are purely intrastate in character, they nevertheless directly affect interstate and foreign commerce." . . .

It appears . . . that loan sharking in its national setting is one way organized interstate crime holds its guns to the heads of the poor and the rich alike and syphons funds from numerous localities to finance its national operations.

Affirmed.

Goldfarb et ux. v. Virginia State Bar et al.
95 S.Ct. 2004 (1975)

BURGER, CHIEF JUSTICE: We granted certiorari to decide whether a minimum fee schedule for lawyers published by the Fairfax County Bar Association and enforced by the Virginia State Bar violates § 1 of the Sherman Act, 15 U. S. C. § 1. The Court of Appeals held that, although the fee schedule and enforcement mechanism substantially restrained competition among lawyers, publication of the schedule by the County Bar was outside the scope of the Act because the practice of law is not "trade or commerce. . . . "

In 1971 petitioners, husband and wife, contracted to buy a home in Fairfax County, Virginia. The financing agency required them to secure title insurance; this required a title examination, and only a member of the Virginia State Bar could legally perform that service. Petitioners therefore contacted a lawyer who quoted them the precise fee suggested in a minimum fee schedule published by respondent Fairfax County Bar Association; the lawyer told them that it was his policy to keep his charges in line with the minimum fee schedule which provided for a fee of 1% of the value of the property involved. Petitioners then tried to find a lawyer who would examine the title for less than the fee fixed by the schedule. They sent letters to 36 other Fairfax County lawyers requesting their fees. Nineteen replied, and none indicated that he would charge less than the rate fixed by the schedule; several stated that they knew of no attorney who would do so.

The fee schedule the lawyers referred to is a list of recommended minimum prices for common legal services. Respondent Fairfax County Bar Association published the fee schedule although, as a purely voluntary association of attorneys, the County Bar has no formal power to enforce it. Enforcement has been provided by respondent Virginia State Bar which is the administrative agency through which the Virginia Supreme Court regulates the practice of law in that State; membership in the State Bar is required in order to practice in Virginia. Although the State Bar has never taken formal disciplinary action to compel adherence to any fee schedule, it has published reports condoning fee schedules, and has issued two ethical opinions indicating fee schedules cannot be ignored. The most recent opinion states that "evidence that an attorney *habitually* charges less than the suggested minimum fee schedule adopted by his local bar association raises a presumption that such lawyer is guilty of misconduct. . . ."

Because petitioners could not find a lawyer willing to charge a fee lower than the schedule dictated they had their title examined by the lawyer they had first contacted. They then brought this class action against the State Bar and the County Bar alleging that the operation of the minimum fee schedule, as applied to fees for legal services relating to residential real estate transactions, constitutes price fixing in violation of § 1 of the Sherman Act. Practitioners sought both injunctive relief and damages. . . .

[The Court then reviewed the decisions of the lower courts which had resulted in a denial of relief to petitioners.]

We granted certiorari, and are thus confronted for the first time with the question of whether the Sherman Act applies to services performed by attorneys in examining titles in connection with financing the purchase of real estate. . . .

The County Bar argues that because the fee schedule is merely advisory, the schedule and its enforcement mechanism do not constitute price fixing. Its purpose, the argument continues, is only to provide legitimate information to aid member lawyers in complying with Virginia professional regulations. Moreover, the County Bar contends that in practice the schedule has not had the effect of producing fixed fees. The facts found by the trier belie these contentions, and nothing in the record suggests these findings lack support. . . .

The record here . . . reveals that . . . a fixed, rigid price floor arose from respondents' activities: every lawyer who responded to petitioners' inquiries adhered to the fee schedule, and no lawyer asked for additional information in order to set an individualized fee. The price information disseminated did not concern past standards, but rather minimum fees to be charged in future transactions, and those minimum rates were increased over time. The fee schedule was enforced through the prospect of professional discipline from the State Bar, and the desire of attorneys to comply with announced professional norms; the motivation to conform was reinforced by the assurance that other lawyers would not compete by underbidding. This is not merely a case of an agreement that may be inferred from an exchange of price information, for here a naked agreement was clearly shown, and the effect on prices is plain.

Moreover, in terms of restraining competition and harming consumers like petitioners the price-fixing activities found here are unusually damaging. A title examination is in-dispensable in the process of financing a real estate purchase, and since only an attorney licensed to practice in Virginia may legally examine a title, consumers could not turn to alternative sources for the necessary service. All attorneys, of course, were practicing under the constraint of the fee schedule. . . . These factors coalesced to create a pricing system that consumers could not realistically escape. On this record respondent's activities constitute a classic illustration of price fixing. . . . The County Bar argues that Congress never intended to include the learned professions within the terms "trade or commerce" in § 1 of the Sherman Act, and therefore the sale of professional services is exempt from the Act. No explicit exemption or legislative history is provided to support this contention, rather the existence of state regulation seems to be its primary basis. Also, the County Bar maintains that competition is inconsistent with the practice of a profession because enhancing profit is not the goal of professional activities; the goal is to provide services necessary to the community. That, indeed, is the classic basis traditionally advanced to distinguish professions from trades, businesses, and other occupations, but it loses some of its force when used to support the fee control activities involved here.

In arguing that learned professions are not "trade or commerce" the County Bar seeks a total exclusion from antitrust regulation. Whether state regulation is active or dormant, real or theoretical, lawyers would be able to adopt anticompetitive practices with impunity. We cannot find support for the proposition that Congress intended any such sweeping exclusion. The nature of an occupation, standing alone, does not provide sanctuary from the Sherman Act, nor is the public service aspect of professional practice controlling in determining whether § 1 includes professions. Congress intended to strike as broadly as it could in § 1 of the Sherman Act, and to read into it so wide an exemption as that urged on us would be at odds with that purpose.

The language of § 1 of the Sherman Act, of course, contains no exception. "Language more comprehensive is difficult to conceive." And our cases have repeatedly established that there is a heavy presumption against implicit exemptions. Indeed, our cases have specifically included the sale of services within § 1. Whatever else it may be, the examination of a land title is a service; the exchange of such a service for money is "commerce" in the most common usage of that word. It is no disparagement of the practice of law as a profession to acknowledge that it has this business aspect, and § 1 of the Sherman Act

> [o]n its face shows a carefully studied attempt to bring within the Act every person engaged in business whose activities might restrain or monopolize commercial intercourse among the states.

In the modern world it cannot be denied that the activities of lawyers play an important part in commercial intercourse and that anticompetitive activities by lawyers may exert a restraint on commerce. . . .

We recognize that the States have a compelling interest in the practice of professions within their boundaries, and that as part of their power to protect the public health, safety, and other valid interests they have broad power to establish standards for licensing practitioners and regulating the practice of professions. We also recognize that in some instances the State may decide that "forms of competition usual in the business world may be demoralizing to the ethical standards of a profession." The interest of the State in regulating lawyers is especially great since lawyers are essential to the primary governmental function of administering justice, and have historically been "officers of the courts." In holding that certain anticompetitive conduct by lawyers is within the reach of the Sherman Act we intend no diminution of the authority of the State to regulate its professions. . . .

Reversed and remanded.

FTC v. Procter & Gamble Co.
87 S.Ct. 1224 (1967)

DOUGLAS, J. . . . This is a proceeding initiated by the Federal Trade Commission charging that respondent, Procter & Gamble Co., had acquired the assets of Clorox Chemical Co. in violation of § 7 of the Clayton Act, as amended. The charge was that Procter's acquisition of Clorox may substantially lessen competition or tend to create a monopoly in the production and sale of household liquid bleaches. . . .

It does not particularly aid analysis to talk of this merger in conventional terms, namely, horizontal or vertical or conglomerate. This merger may most appropriately be described as a "product-extension merger. . . ." The facts are not disputed. . . .

At the time of the merger, Clorox was the leading manufacturer in the heavily concentrated household liquid bleach industry. It is agreed that household liquid bleach is the relevant line of commerce. . . .

The relevant geographical market is the Nation and a series of regional markets. Because of high shipping costs and low sales price, it is not feasible to ship the product more than 300 miles from its point of manufacture. Most manufacturers are limited to competition within a single region since they have but one plant. Clorox is the only firm selling nationally; it has 13 plants distributed throughout the Nation. Purex, Clorox's closest competitor in size, does not distribute its bleach in the northeast or middle-Atlantic States; in 1957 Purex's bleach was available in less than 50% of the national market.

At the time of the acquisition, Clorox was the leading manufacturer of household liquid bleach, with 48.8% of the national sales. . . . Its market share had been steadily increasing for the five years prior to the merger. Its nearest rival was Purex. . . . Purex accounted for 15.7% of the household liquid bleach market.

The industry is highly concentrated; in 1957 Clorox and Purex accounted for almost 65% of the Nation's household liquid bleach sales, and, together with four other firms, for almost 80%. The remaining 20% was divided among over 200 small producers. . . .

Since all liquid bleach is chemically identical, advertising and sales promotion is vital. In 1957 Clorox spent almost $3,700,000 on advertising, imprinting the value of its bleach in the mind of the consumer. In addition, it spent $1,700,000 for other promotional activities. The Commission found that these heavy expenditures went far to explain why Clorox maintained so high a market share despite the fact that its brand, though chemically indistinguishable from rival brands, retailed for a price equal to or, in many instances, higher than its competitors.

Procter is a large, diversified manufacturer of low-price, high-turnover household products sold through grocery, drug, and department stores. Prior to its acquisition of Clorox, it did not produce household liquid bleach. Its 1957 sales were in excess of $1,100,000,000, from which it realized profits of more than $67,000,-000; its assets were over $500,000,000. Procter has been marked by rapid growth and diversification. It has successfully developed and introduced a number of new products. Its primary activity is in the general area of soaps, detergents, and cleaners; in 1957, of total domestic sales, more than one-half (over $500,-000,000) were in this field. Procter was the dominant factor in this area. It accounted for 54.4% of all packaged detergent sales. The industry is heavily concentrated—Procter and its nearest competitors, Colgate-Palmolive and Lever Brothers, account for 80% of the market.

In the marketing of soaps, detergents, and cleansers, as in the marketing of household liquid bleach, advertising and sales promotion are vital. In 1957, Procter was the Nation's largest advertiser, spending more than $80,-000,000 on advertising and an additional $47,-000,000 on sales promotion. Due to its tremendous volume, Procter receives substantial discounts from the media. As a multi-product producer Procter enjoys substantial advantages in advertising and sales promotion. Thus, it can and does feature several products in its promotions, reducing the printing, mailing, and other costs for each product. It also purchases network programs on behalf of several products, enabling it to give each product network exposure at a fraction of the cost per product that a firm with only one product to advertise would incur.

Prior to the acquisition, Procter was in the course of diversifying into product lines related to its basic detergent-soap-cleanser business. Liquid bleach was a distinct possibility since packaged detergents—Procter's primary product line—and liquid bleach are used complementarily in washing clothes and fabrics, and in general household cleaning. . . .

The decision to acquire Clorox was the result of a study conducted by Procter's promotion department designed to determine the advisability of entering the liquid bleach industry. The initial report noted the ascendancy of liquid bleach in the large and expanding household bleach market, and recommended that Procter purchase Clorox rather than enter independently. Since a large investment would be needed to obtain a satisfactory market share, acquisition of the industry's leading firm was attractive. "Taking over the Clorox business . . . could be a way of achieving a dominant position in the liquid bleach market quickly, which would pay out reasonably well." The initial report predicted that Procter's "sales distribution and manufacturing setup" could increase Clorox's share of the markets in areas where it was low. The final report confirmed the conclusions of the initial report and emphasized that Procter would make more effective use of Clorox's advertising budget and that the merger would facilitate advertising economies. A few months later, Procter acquired the assets of Clorox in the name of a wholly owned subsidiary, the Clorox Company, in exchange for Procter stock.

The Commission found that the acquisition might substantially lessen competition. The findings and reasoning of the Commission need be only briefly summarized. The Commission found that the substitution of Procter with its huge assets and advertising advantages for the already dominant Clorox would dissuade new entrants and discourage active competition from the firms already in the industry due to fear of retaliation by Procter. The Commission thought it relevant that retailers might be induced to give Clorox preferred shelf space since it would be manufactured by Procter, which also produced a number of other products marketed by the retailers. There was also the danger that Procter might underprice Clorox in order to drive out competition, and subsidize the underpricing with revenue from other products. The Commission carefully reviewed the effect of the acquisition on the structure of the industry, noting that "the practical tendency of the . . . merger . . . is to transform the liquid bleach industry into an arena of big business competition only, with the few small firms falling by the wayside, unable to compete with their giant rivals." Further, the merger would seriously diminish potential competition by eliminating Procter as a potential entrant into the industry. Prior to the merger, the Commission found that Procter was the most likely prospective entrant, and absent the merger would have remained on the periphery, restraining Clorox from exercising its market power. If Procter had actually entered, Clorox's dominant position would have been eroded and the concentration of the industry reduced. The Commission stated that it had not placed reliance on postacquisition evidence in holding the merger unlawful. . . .

Section 7 of the Clayton Act was intended to arrest the anticompetitive effects of market power in their incipiency. The core question is whether a merger may substantially lessen competition, and necessarily requires a prediction of the merger's impact on competition, present and future. The section can deal only with probabilities, not with certainties. And there is certainly no requirement that the anticompetitive power manifest itself in anticompetitive action before § 7 can be called into play. If the enforcement of § 7 turned on the existence of actual anticompetitive practices, the congressional policy of thwarting such practices in their incipiency would be frustrated.

All mergers are within the reach of § 7, and all must be tested by the same standard, whether they are classified as horizontal, vertical, conglomerate or other. As noted by the Commission this merger is neither horizontal, vertical, nor conglomerate. Since the products of the acquired company are complementary to those of the acquiring company and may be produced with similar facilities, marketed through the same channels and in the same manner, and advertised by the same media, the Commission aptly called this acquisition a "product-extension merger"; . . .

The anticompetitive effects with which this product-extension merger is fraught can easily be seen: (1) the substitution of the powerful acquiring firm for the smaller, but already dominant, firm may substantially reduce the competitive structure of the industry by raising entry barriers and by dissuading the smaller firms from aggressively competing; (2) the acquisition eliminates the potential competition of the acquiring firm.

. . . The acquisition may also have the tendency of raising the barriers to new entry. The major competitive weapon in the successful marketing of bleach is advertising. Clorox was limited in this area by its relatively small budget and its inability to obtain substantial discounts. By contrast, Procter's budget was much larger; and, although it would not devote its entire budget to advertising Clorox, it could divert a large portion to meet the short-term threat of a new entrant. Procter would be able to use its volume discounts to advantage in advertising Clorox. Thus, a new entrant would be much more reluctant to face the giant Procter than it would have been to face the smaller Clorox.

Possible economies cannot be used as a defense to illegality. Congress was aware that some mergers which lessen competition may also result in economies, but it struck the balance in favor of protecting competition.

. . . It is clear that the existence of Procter at the edge of the industry exerted considerable influence on the market. First, the market behavior of the liquid bleach industry was influenced by each firm's predictions of the market behavior of its competitors, actual and potential. Second, the barriers to entry by a firm of Procter's size and with its advantages were not significant. There is no indication that the barriers were so high that the price Procter would have to charge would be above the price that would maximize the profits of the existing firms. Third, the number of potential entrants was not so large that the elimination of one would be insignificant. Few firms would have the temerity to challenge a firm as solidly entrenched as Clorox. Fourth, Procter was found by the Commission to be the most likely entrant. These findings of the Commission were amply supported by the evidence.

The judgment of the Court of Appeals is reversed and remanded with instructions to affirm and enforce the Commission's order. . . .

Reversed and remanded.

Griggs v. Duke Power Company
91 S.Ct. 849 (1971)

BURGER, C. J. We granted the writ in this case to resolve the question whether an employer is prohibited by the Civil Rights Act of 1964, Title VII, from requiring a high school education or passing of a standardized general intelligence test as a condition of employment in or transfer to jobs when (a) neither standard is shown to be significantly related to successful job performance, (b) both requirements operate to disqualify Negroes at a substantially higher rate than white applicants, and (c) the jobs in question formerly had been filled only by white employees as part of a long-standing practice of giving preference to whites.

. . . All the petitioners are employed at the Company's Dan River Steam Station, a power generating facility located at Draper, North Carolina. At the time this action was instituted, the Company had 95 employees at the Dan River Station, 14 of whom were Negroes; 13 of these are petitioners here.

The District Court found that prior to July 2, 1965, the effective date of the Civil Rights Act of 1964, the Company openly discriminated on the basis of race in the hiring and assigning of employees at its Dan River plant. The plant was organized into five operating departments: (1) Labor, (2) Coal Handling, (3) Operations, (4) Maintenance, and (5) Laboratory and Test. Negroes were employed only in the Labor Department where the highest paying jobs paid less than the lowest paying jobs in the other four "operating" departments in which only whites were employed. Promotions were normally made within each department on the basis of job seniority. Transferees into a department usually began in the lowest position.

In 1955 the Company instituted a policy of requiring a high school education for initial assignment to any department except Labor, and for transfer from the Coal Handling to any "inside" department (Operations, Maintenance, or Laboratory). When the Company abandoned its policy of restricting Negroes to the Labor Department in 1965, completion of high school also was made a prerequisite to transfer from Labor to any other department. From the time the high school requirement was instituted to the time of trial, however, white employees hired before the time of the high school education requirement continued to perform satisfactorily and achieve promotions in the "operating" departments. Findings on this score are not challenged.

The Company added a further requirement for new employees on July 2, 1965, the date on which Title VII became effective. To qualify for placement in any but the Labor Department it became necessary to register satisfactory scores on two professionally prepared aptitude tests, as well as to have a high school education. Completion of high school alone continued to render employees eligible for transfer to the four desirable departments from which Negroes had been excluded if the incumbent had been employed prior to the time of the new requirement. In September 1965 the Company began to permit incumbent employees who lacked a high school education to qualify for transfer from Labor or Coal Handling to an "inside" job by passing two tests—the Wonderlic Personnel Test, which purports to measure general intelligence, and the Bennett Mechanical Aptitude Test. Neither was directed or intended to measure the ability to learn to perform a particular job or category of jobs. The requisite scores used for both initial hiring and transfer approximated the national median for high school graduates.

The District Court had found that while the Company previously followed a policy of overt racial discrimination in a period prior to the Act, such conduct had ceased. . . .

The Court of Appeals . . . concluded that a subjective test of the employer's intent should govern, particularly in a close case, and that in this case there was no showing of a discriminatory purpose in the adoption of the diploma and test requirements. On this basis, the Court of Appeals concluded there was no violation of the Act. . . .

The objective of Congress in the enactment of Title VII is plain from the language of the statute. It was to achieve equality of employment opportunities and remove barriers that have operated in the past to favor an identifiable group of white employees over other employees. Under the Act, practices, procedures, or tests neutral on their face, and even neutral in terms of intent, cannot be maintained if they operate to "freeze" the status quo of prior discriminatory employment practices.

The Court of Appeals' opinion, and the partial dissent, agreed that, on the record in the present case, "whites fare far better on the Company's alternative requirements" than Negroes. This consequence would appear to be directly traceable to race. Basic intelligence must have the means of articulation to manifest itself fairly in a testing process. Because they

are Negroes, petitioners have long received inferior education in segregated schools and this Court expressly recognized these differences in *Gaston County* v. *United States.* There, because of the inferior education received by Negroes in North Carolina, this Court barred the institution of a literacy test for voter registration on the ground that the test would abridge the right to vote indirectly on account of race. Congress did not intend by Title VII, however, to guarantee a job to every person regardless of qualifications. In short, the Act does not command that any person be hired simply because he was formerly the subject of discrimination, or because he is a member of a minority group. Discriminatory preference for any group, minority or majority, is precisely and only what Congess has proscribed. What is required by Congress is the removal of artificial, arbitrary, and unnecessary barriers to employment when the barriers operate invidiously to discriminate on the basis of racial or other impermissible classification.

. . . The Act proscribes not only overt discrimination but also practices that are fair in form, but discriminatory in operation. The touchstone is business necessity. If an employment practice which operates to exclude Negroes cannot be shown to be related to job performance, the practice is prohibited.

On the record before us, neither the high school completion requirement nor the general intelligence test is shown to bear a demonstrable relationship to successful performance of the jobs for which it was used. Both were adopted . . . without meaningful study of their relationship to job-performance ability. Rather, a vice president of the Company testified, the requirements were instituted on the Company's judgment that they generally would improve the overall quality of the work force.

The evidence, however, shows that employees who have not completed high school or taken the tests have continued to perform satisfactorily and make progress in departments for which the high school and test criteria are now used. The promotion record of present employees who would not be able to meet the new criteria thus suggests the possibility that the requirements may not be needed even for the limited purpose of preserving the avowed policy of advancement within the Company. . . .

The Court of Appeals held that the Company had adopted the diploma and test requirements without any "intention to discriminate against Negro employees." We do not suggest that either the District Court or the Court of Appeals erred in examining the employer's intent; but good intent or absence of discriminatory intent does not redeem employment procedures or testing mechanisms that operate as "built-in headwinds" for minority groups and are unrelated to measuring job capability. . . .

The facts of this case demonstrate the inadequacy of broad and general testing devices as well as the infirmity of using diplomas or degrees as fixed measures of capability. History is filled with examples of men and women who rendered highly effective performance without the conventional badges of accomplishment in terms of certificates, diplomas, or degrees. Diplomas and tests are useful servants, but Congress has mandated the common-sense proposition that they are not to become masters of reality.

The Company contends that its general intelligence tests are specifically permitted by § 703(h) of the Act. That section authorizes the use of "any professionally developed ability test" that is not "designed, intended, *or used* to discriminate because of race. . . ." (Emphasis added.)

The Equal Employment Opportunity Commission, having enforcement responsibility, has issued guidelines interpreting § 703(h) to permit only the use of job-related tests. The administrative interpretation of the Act by the enforcing agency is entitled to great deference. Since the Act and its legislative history support the Commission's construction, this affords good reason to treat the Guidelines as expressing the will of Congress. . . .

Nothing in the Act precludes the use of testing or measuring procedures; obviously they are useful. What Congress has forbidden is giving these devices and mechanisms controlling force unless they are demonstrably a reasonable measure of job performance. Congress has not commanded that the less qualified be preferred over the better qualified simply because of minority origins. Far from disparaging job qualifications as such, Congress has made such qualifications the controlling factor, so that race, religion, nationality, and sex become irrelevant. What Congress has commanded is that any tests used must measure the person for the job and not the person in the abstract. . . .

Reversed.

Boyd v. Ozark Air Lines, Inc.
419 F.Supp. 1061 (1976)

Plaintiff, representing a class composed of all future female applicants meeting reasonable qualifications for serving as airline pilots, brought this action challenging a commercial airline's minimum height requirement for pilots as sexually discriminatory. The defendant airline employs 380 male pilots and no female pilots. Its criteria for pilots consists of:

(a)   Age: 20–30 years old;
(b)   Minimum flight experience (correlated to age);

(c)   Professional permits and certificates;
(d)   Education: high school graduate with college preferred;
(e)   Satisfactory completion of defendant's examination;
(f)   Height: 5′ 7″ to 6′ 2″.

Plaintiff meets all of the employment criteria except the height requirement. Statistics presented by plaintiff establish that for the age group encompassing 18 to 34 years, a 5′ 7″

height requirement excludes approximately 25.8% of the males and approximately 93% of the females. Among active fliers, without a distinction made for age, the height requirement eliminates 11.24% of the males and 74.19% of the females. Thus, the evidence established that defendant's height requirement had a disparate impact upon women.

NANGLE, J. . . . Plaintiff has asserted that she was denied a position as a pilot because of her sex. The Court has concluded that plaintiff's sex was not a factor in defendant's decision but instead, that the decision was based on the fact that plaintiff did not meet the minimum height requirements. The statistical evidence adduced, however, establishes that defendant's minimum height requirement has a disparate impact upon women. This, combined with the fact that defendant does not employ any women among its 380 pilots, establishes a *prima facie* case of discrimination.

Accordingly, the burden shifts to defendant to establish that this height requirement is both job-related and a business necessity.

To establish that a practice is a business necessity, which operates as a defense to a charge of sex discrimination, defendant must show that the requirement fosters safety and efficiency and is *"essential* to that goal."

. . . [T]he business purpose must be sufficiently compelling to override any . . . [sexual] impact; the challenged practice must effectively carry out the business purpose it is alleged to serve; and there must be available no acceptable alternative policies or practices which would better accomplish the business purpose advanced, or accomplish it equally well with a lesser differential . . . [sexual] impact.

Defendant has amply met its burden of establishing that a height requirement is a business necessity. The evidence showed that pilots must have free and unfettered use of all instruments within the cockpit and still have the ability to meet the design eye reference point. In view of the cockpit design, over which defendant has little control, a height requirement must be established. The cockpit can only accommodate a range of heights. Defendant has chosen to draw the line at 5′ 7″. The evidence established, however, that a requirement of 5′ 5″, which would lessen the disparate impact upon women, would be sufficient to insure the requisite mobility and vision. Accordingly, the Court will order defendant to lower its height requirement to 5′ 5″.

Plaintiff argues that the necessity of imposing a height requirement must be validated empirically. . . . In *Spurlock* v. *United Airlines, Inc.,* 457 F.2d 216, 219 (10th Cir. 1972), the court stated:

> When a job requires a small amount of skill and training and the consequences of hiring an unqualified applicant are insignificant, the courts should examine closely any pre-employment standard or criteria which discriminate against minorities. In such a case, the employer should have a heavy burden to demonstrate to the court's satisfaction that his employment criteria are job-related. On the other hand, when the job clearly requires a high degree of skill and the economic and human risks involved in hiring an unqualified applicant are great, the employer bears a correspondingly lighter burden to show that his employment criteria are job-related. . . . The job of airline flight officer is clearly such a job. United's flight officers pilot aircraft worth as much as $20 million and transport as many as 300 passengers per flight. The risks involved in hiring an unqualified applicant are staggering. The public interest clearly lies in having the most highly qualified persons available to pilot airliners. The courts, therefore, should proceed with great caution before requiring an employer to lower his pre-employment standards for such a job.

The Court agrees with this reasoning. A height requirement is unquestionably job-related. The evidence on this point . . . is overwhelming. Empirical data are not required. . . .

The Court has concluded that the imposition of a height requirement is both job-related and a business necessity. The Court has further concluded, however, that defendant's height requirement is unnecessarily high and, to that extent, is violative of Title VII, 42 U.S.C. § 200e *et seq.* The Court will order that defendant lower its minimum height requirement to 5′ 5″. . . .

So ordered.

CHAPTER 40
REVIEW QUESTIONS AND PROBLEMS

1. South Carolina, concerned with the condition of its highways, passed legislation banning from the highways all trucks over ninety inches in width and over 20,000 lbs. gross weight. Evidence shows 85 percent of all semi-trailer trucks exceed that limit. Is the statute constitutional? Why?

2. Federal law regulates the construction of the last car on all interstate trains. A Pennsylvania railroad complied with a state law that made different regulations but did not comply with the federal law. The railroad contended the state law applied because it was a Pennsylvania company. Was the railroad correct? Explain.

3. Company A brought suit against Company B, claiming it improperly cut prices. B argued A could not bring suit because A was a foreign corporation not licensed in that state. A state statute supported B's argument. A claimed the law was an unconstitutional burden on interstate commerce. What result? Why?

4. State A imposed an income tax on all residents of the state. X claimed his salary was not taxable because his work with the Federal Home Owners Loan Corporation advanced the interest of the national government. Is X correct? Explain.

5. X, Y, and Z, sugar refineries, together agreed to pay sugar-beet farmers a set price for their crops. The farmers sued X under the Sherman Act, charging that the agreement among the refineries was an illegal trust. The refined sugar was to be sold in interstate markets. Can the farmers collect treble damages? Why?

6. X Company produced and sold bread only in Virginia. Y Company, a competitor, operated an interstate business, including the area covered by X. Y cut the price of bread in half in Virginia, forcing X Company out of business. No price cuts were made in any other state. Can X collect damages for violation of the Clayton and Robinson-Patman Acts?

7. Major oil companies agreed to purchase all the gas produced by independent refineries in a certain area of the United States. This allowed them to maintain the retail price by reducing competition; thus a stable market could be sustained. Has the Sherman Act been violated? Explain.

8. P had a home delivery route for the newspaper of D Company. The contract provided that carriers with exclusive territories were subject to termination if their prices exceeded the suggested maximum. P raised the price to his customers, and D objected. D hired a company to solicit readers away from this route and hired another carrier to take over part of the route. P brought suit, claiming that D was in violation of the Sherman Act. Is P correct? Why?

9. Manufacturers of containers entered into an agreement whereby they would exchange price information concerning specific sales to identified customers, but there was no agreement to adhere to a price schedule. The Justice Department brought suit, charging a price-fixing agreement in violation of § 1 of the Sherman Act. Was this agreement in violation of the Sherman Act? Why?

10. X Company and Y Company, two highly successful grocery chains in the Los Angeles area, agreed to a merger. During the preceding ten years, both companies had doubled their number of stores, and X's share of the market doubled while Y's share of the market tripled. The merger created the second largest chain in Los Angeles. During this same time period, the number of owners operating a single store dropped 40 percent. The Justice Department claimed that the merger violated § 7 of the Clayton Act; in defense, the companies argued that the Los Angeles market was competitive before the merger and would continue to be so in the future. Did the merger violate § 7 of the Clayton Act? Why?

11. The National Collegiate Athletic Association, a voluntary association of 800 colleges and universities located throughout the United States, adopted a bylaw limiting the number of football coaches that a member of Division I may employ to one head coach, eight assistant coaches, and two part-time assistant coaches. A university brought suit, contending that this action was an unreasonable restraint of trade and in violation of the Sherman Act. Is the bylaw an unreasonable restraint of trade? Why?

12. A, owner of a lounge, hired women bartenders, contrary to a state statute that prohibited women from tending bar except when the woman was the holder of a liquor license. The state revoked A's liquor license and A brought suit, claiming that the state statute violated the 1964 Civil Rights Act. In defense, the state contends that a bartender must be physically strong enough to protect himself against inebriated customers and to maintain order in the bar, and that women as a class are unable to do so. Is the state law invalid? Why?

13. A Company was the principal supplier of certain raw materials to B Company and was also the holder of 23 percent of B Company's stock. The Justice Department brought suit, claiming that the acquisition of this stock by A Company violated § 7 of the Clayton Act. In defense, A Company contended that the Clayton Act was not applicable, since A Company and B Company were not in competition with each other. Is A correct? Why?

14. A Shoe Company entered into franchise agreements with 650 retail stores. The agreements prohibited the stores from handling any shoes other than A Company's. Those stores that so agreed received valuable benefits not available to other customers of A, including architectural plans, merchandising records, and group insurance. It was determined that A's activities were not in violation of either the Sherman or Clayton Acts. The FTC brought suit, contending that the franchise agreement constituted an unfair method of competition. Was this action by the FTC proper? Why?

15. The National Society of Professional Engineers adopted an ethical standard that prohibited price bidding for professional engineering work. The rule was adopted to prevent unsafe designs by engineers and unsafe construction as well as to prevent deceptively low bids. The Department of Justice claimed that the ethical standard violated § 1 of the Sherman Act. Did the National Society of Professional Engineers violate the Sherman Act? Why?

16. X Railroad Company sold and leased several million acres of land using deeds that contained "preferential routing clauses." Under these deeds, purchasers and lessees agreed to ship their products on the X Railroad as long as it offered rates and services equal to those of other available carriers. The U.S. government brought suit against X charging that the "preferential routing clauses" were violations of the Sherman Act. Should the clauses be declared void? Explain.

book seven

PROPERTY

Personal Property

1. Introduction

The term *property* is meaningless unless it is associated with people or individuals. Some of the terms frequently used in expressing this association are *ownership, title,* and *possession.* The word *owner* usually describes someone who possesses all the rights or interests associated with the subject matter or thing involved. The word *title* is often used synonymously with *ownership.* *Title* is also used to signify the method by which ownership is acquired, as by a transfer of title. It may also be used to indicate the evidence by which ownership is established—a written instrument called a title, as, for example, a car title. Thus, the word *title* has a variety of meanings, depending upon the context in which it is used.

The word *possession* is equally difficult to define accurately, and its meaning is also dependent somewhat on the context in which it is used. Possession implies the concept of physical control or dominium by a person over property and the personal and mental relationship to it. One can physically possess a watch or a ring, but it is obviously impossible to physically possess a thousand acres of land in the same manner; and yet the word *possession* as a legal term is used in both instances. Possession describes not only physical control but the power to obtain physical control by legal sanctions, if necessary.

In the early law, property was thought of as a thing that could be touched, possessed, and delivered. As the law of property developed, courts began to recognize that property was more accurately described as the "bundle of rights" a person had in respect to a thing. Today, property is thought of as an object or a thing over which someone exercises legal rights.

Defining property as a "bundle of rights" enables courts and the law to develop a variety of interests in property. A person may possess the entire bundle of rights in relation to a thing, in which case he is the only owner. On the other hand, the bundle of rights may be divided among several people, in which case there is incomplete ownership by any one person, and property rights exist for several people. For example, assume that the owner of a tract of land authorizes the local public utility companies to install power and telephone lines underground through his land. The utility companies are granted what is called an *easement,* which is a property right, and as a result, the owner has less than the full bundle of rights and his title is subject to an *encumbrance.*

One other fact of life must be recognized when studying the law of property. There can be no property rights without a government and a legal system to create and enforce them. Private property rights cannot exist without some method of keeping the bundle of rights for the true owner and for restoring these rights to him when he is deprived of them. It should also be recognized that no one person has a complete bundle of rights, since the law limits private property rights and the use of private property to some extent in the public interest. The owner of land may not use it in violation of the local zoning ordinance. The owner of an automobile may not use it contrary to the law without penalty. Much of our legal system is designed to provide a means of creating, transferring, and limiting the bundle of rights that individuals possess in relation to land, movable objects or things, or intangibles—which we collectively call property.

2.   Classifications

From the standpoint of its physical characteristics, property is classified as either personal property or real property. Land and things affixed to or growing upon the land come under the heading of *real property*. All other property is said to be *personal property*. In general, personal property is subject to different treatment under the law from real property.

Personal property may be classified as either tangible or intangible. The term *tangible personal property* includes objects such as goods. The term *intangible personal property* refers to such things as accounts receivable, goodwill, patents, and trademarks. Intangible personal property has value just as has tangible property, and each can be transferred.

The term *chattel* is used to describe personal property generally. Chattels may also be classified as *chattels real* and *chattels personal. Chattels real* describes an interest in land, such as a leasehold. *Chattels personal* is applied to movable personal property.

When the term *chattel* is used in connection with tangible personal property, such property is referred to as *chattels personal in action.* A chattel personal in action, or *chose in action,* as it is frequently called, is something to which one has a right to possession, but concerning which he may be required to bring some legal action in order to ultimately enjoy possession. For example, a contract right may be said to be a chose in action because a lawsuit may be necessary to obtain the rights under the contract. A negotiable instrument is a common form of chose in action. Although the instrument itself may be said to be property, in reality it is simply evidence of a right to money, and it may be necessary to maintain an action to reduce the money to possession.

3. The Distinction between Real and Personal Property

The distinction between *real* and *personal* property is significant in three situations: (1) in determining the law applicable to a transaction; (2) in matters of inheritance; and (3) in the methods that may be used to transfer the property. The first situation refers to the principles and problems of conflicts of laws that arise in connection with various types of property. Conflict-of-laws problems arise when a legal issue has contact with more than one state.

As a general rule, conflict-of-laws principles provide that the law of the situs—the law of the state where real property is located—determines all legal questions concerning such property. Legal issues concerning conflict of laws relating to personal property are not so easily resolved. Conflict-of-laws rules may refer to the law of the owner's domicile to resolve some questions and to the law of the state with the most significant contacts with the property to resolve others. The law of the situs of the property is also used to resolve some legal issues, especially when the property involved is movable. Therefore, the designation of property as real or personal has a significant impact on the determination of the body of law that is used to decide legal issues concerning the property.

The second situation in which the distinction may be important is in matters of inheritance. If a person dies leaving a will, he is said to die testate. His personal property passes to the executor named in the will, to be distributed in accordance with the terms of the will, and his real property passes to the devisees named in the will.

When a person dies without leaving a will, he is said to die intestate, and his property passes in conformity with the laws of "intestate succession." The laws of intestate succession frequently have different provisions for real estate and for personal property. For example, assume that D died leaving W, his widow, and C, a child, as his only heirs at law. A typical intestate statute might provide that the widow is entitled to all personal property but to only one-half the real property of the deceased. In such cases, the importance of the distinction between real and personal property is obvious.

The distinction between real and personal property is also significant during the lifetime of the owner in determining the methods by which the property can be transferred. The methods of transferring personal property and real property are substantially different. Formal instruments such as deeds are required to transfer an interest in land, whereas few formalities are required in the case of personal property. A bill of sale may be used in selling personal property, but it is not generally required and does not in any event involve the technicalities of a deed. For example, a motor vehicle transfer may require the delivery of a certificate of title, but, as mentioned above, the transfer of personal property is as a rule quite simply accomplished, whereas formality is required to transfer real property.

METHODS OF ACQUIRING TITLE TO PERSONAL PROPERTY

4. Introduction

Title to personal property may be acquired through any of the following methods: original possession, transfer, accession, or confusion. Original possession is a method of extremely limited applicability. It may be used to obtain title over things such as wild animals and fish that are available for appropriation by individuals. Property that is in its native state and over which no one has as yet taken full and complete control belongs to the first person who reduces such property to his exclusive possession. Property once reduced to ownership, but later discarded, belongs to the first party next taking possession.

In addition, it might be said that property created through mental or physical labor belongs to the creator unless he has agreed to create it for someone else, being induced to do so because of some compensation that has been agreed to by the interested parties. Such items as books, inventions, and trademarks might be included under this heading. This kind of property is usually protected by the government through means of copyrights, patents, and trademarks.

5. Title by Transfer

Personal property may be transferred by sale, gift, will, or operation of law. The law relating to transfer by sale has previously been discussed in connection with Article 2 of the Uniform Commercial Code. Transfers by operation of law include such transfers as judicial sales, mortgage foreclosures, and intestate succession.

As a general rule, a transferee receives the rights of the transferor, and a transferee takes no better title than the transferor had. If the transferor of the personal property did not have title to the property, the transferee would not have title either. This is true even though the transferee believes that his transferor has a good title. For example, an innocent purchaser from a thief obtains no title to the property purchased, and no subsequent purchaser stands in any better position. Because the thief had no title or ownership, persons who acquired the property from or through the thief have no title or ownership. However, if the transferor of the property has a voidable title and he sells property to an innocent purchaser, the transferee may obtain good title to the property. For example, assume that X acquires the title to property from Y through fraudulent representations. Y could avoid the transaction with X and obtain a return of his property. However, if X sells the property to Z and Z does not know about X's fraudulent representations, Y cannot disaffirm against Z, and Z has good title to the property, since he is a good-faith purchaser for value.

6. Title by Gift

There are three elements of a valid gift—intention to make the gift, delivery, and acceptance of the gift. From a legal standpoint, the element of delivery is the most significant, because the law requires an actual physical change in possession of the property, with the owner's consent.

In the case of choses in action, the transfer of possession usually takes place by means of an assignment, the exception being negotiable instruments, which may be transferred either by assignment or by negotiation.

An executed gift—one accomplished by delivery of the property to the donor—cannot be rescinded except in the case of a gift *causa mortis,* discussed later. The delivery can be actual or constructive or symbolic, if the situation demands. Thus, if the property is in storage, the donor could make a delivery by giving the donee the warehouse receipt. A donor may also accomplish delivery by giving the donee something that is a token representing the latter's dominion and control. For example, a delivery of the keys to an automobile may be a valid symbolic delivery. However, a symbolic or constructive delivery will not suffice if actual delivery is reasonably possible.[1]

It was previously noted that gifts *causa mortis* constitute an exception to the general rule on the finality of completed gifts. A gift *causa mortis* is in contemplation of death and refers to the situation in which a person who is, or who believes that he is, facing death makes a gift on the assumption that death is imminent. A person about to embark on a perilous trip or to undergo a serious operation, or one who has an apparently incurable and fatal illness, might make a gift and deliver the item to the donee on the assumption that he is not long for this world. If he returns safely or does not die, the donor is allowed to revoke the gift and recover the property from the donee.[2]

7. Accession

Accession literally means "adding to." In the law of personal property accession has two basic meanings. First of all, it refers to the right of an owner to

---

[1] *In re Estate of Evans,* page 789.
[2] *Fendley* v. *Laster,* page 791.

all that his property produces. For example, the owner of a cow is also the owner of each calf born, and the owner of lumber is the owner of a table made from the lumber by another. Accession is also the legal term used to signify the acquisition of title to personal property when it is incorporated into other property or joined with other property.

When accession occurs, the issue of who has title is frequently litigated. The general rule is that when the goods of two different owners are united together without the willful misconduct of either party, the title to the resulting product goes to the owner of the major portion of the goods. The same is true if one person adds labor to the raw materials of another. Title is in the owner of the materials. These rules are based on the principle that personal property permanently added to other property and forming a minor portion of the finished product becomes part and parcel of the larger unit; and since the title can be in only one party, it is in the owner of the major portion. The owner of the minor portion may recover damages, if his portion was wrongfully taken from him. The law of accession simply prevents the owner of the minor portion from recovering the property.

To illustrate the foregoing, assume that X owns some raw materials and that Y inadvertently uses these materials to manufacture a product. The product belongs to X. If Y also adds some raw materials of his own, the manufactured product belongs to the party who contributed the major portion of the materials. If Y becomes the owner, X is entitled to recover his damages. If X is the owner, Y is not entitled to anything, since he used X's materials.

A similar issue arises when one party repairs goods of another without authority. In such a case, the owner is entitled to the goods as repaired irrespective of the value of the repair, unless the repairs can be severed without damaging the original goods.

The law of accession distinguishes between the rights of "innocent" and of "willful" trespassers, although both are wrongful. An innocent trespasser of personal property is one who acts through mistake or conduct less than intentionally wrongful. A willful trespasser cannot obtain title, as against the original owner, under any circumstances.

If the property involved in an issue of accession is sold to a good-faith purchaser, the rights and liabilities of the owner and the third party are the same as those of the original trespasser. A willful trespasser has no title and can convey none. The owner can get the property back without any liability to the third party. If the third party makes improvements or repairs, he has the right to remove his additions if they can be removed without damaging the original goods.[3] An innocent trespasser can convey this right to remove to a good-faith purchaser.

[3] *Farm Bureau Mut. Automobile Ins. Co.* v. *Moseley,* page 792.

8. Confusion

Property of such a character that one unit may not be distinguished from another unit and that is usually sold by weight or measure is known as fungible property. Grain, hay, logs, wine, oil, and other similar articles afford illustrations of property of this nature. Such property, belonging to various parties, is often mixed by intention of the parties, and occasionally by accident, unintentional mistake, or the wrongful misconduct of an owner of some of the goods. Confusion of fungible property belonging to various owners, assuming that no misconduct (confusion by consent, accident, or unintentional mistake) is involved, results in an undivided ownership of the total mass. To illustrate: Grain is stored in a public warehouse by many parties. Each owner holds an undivided interest in the total mass, his particular interest being dependent upon the amount stored by him. Should there be a partial destruction of the total mass, the loss would be divided proportionately.

Confusion of goods that results from the wrongful conduct of one of the parties causes the title to the total mass to pass to the innocent party. If the mixture is divisible, an exception exists, and the wrongdoer, if he is able to show that the resultant mass is equal in value per unit to that of the innocent party, is able to recover his share. Where the new mixture is worth no less per unit than that formerly belonging to the innocent party, the wrongdoer may claim his portion of the new mass by presenting convincing evidence of the amount added by him. If two masses are added together and the wrongdoer can establish only his proportion of one mass, he is entitled to that portion of the combined mass.[4]

9. Abandoned, Lost, and Mislaid Property

Property is said to be abandoned whenever it is discarded by the true owner, who, at that time, has no intention of reclaiming it.[5] Such property belongs to the first individual again reducing it to possession.

Property is lost whenever, as a result of negligence, accident, or some other cause, it is found at some place other than that chosen by the owner. Title to lost property continues to rest with the true owner. Until the true owner has been ascertained, the finder may keep it, and his title is good as against everyone except the true owner. The rights of the finder are superior to those of the person in charge of the property upon which the lost article is found unless the finder is a trespasser. Occasionally, state statutes provide for newspaper publicity concerning articles that have been found. Under these statutes, if the owner cannot be located, the found property reverts to the state or county if its value exceeds an established minimum.

[4] *Troop* v. *St. Louis Union Trust Co.,* page 792.
[5] *Stankiewicz* v. *Hawkes,* page 793.

Mislaid or misplaced property is such as is intentionally placed by the owner at a certain spot in such a manner as to indicate that he merely forgot to pick it up. In such a case, the presumption is that he will later remember where he left it and return for it. The owner of the premises upon which it is found is entitled to hold such property as bailee until the true owner is located.

10. Multiple Ownership

There are three distinct methods by which two or more people may own personal property at the same time: (1) tenancy in common, (2) joint tenancy or tenancy by the entireties, and (3) community property. A tenancy by the entireties is a joint tenancy between spouses. It is recognized in some states. Community property as a method of common ownership is limited to only a few states. Several states have modified the common law characteristics of these forms of ownership, so it is essential that each state's law be consulted for the technicalities of these tenancies.

The main distinction between a tenancy in common and a joint tenancy or tenancy by the entireties is the effect of death on the tenancy. In the event of the death of a tenant in common, his share in the property passes to the executor named in the will or to the administrator of his estate. If property is held in joint tenancy or tenancy by the entireties, the interest of a deceased owner automatically passes to the surviving joint owner. These tenancies are ownership with the right of survivorship. Such property is not subject to probate or to the debts of the deceased joint tenant. Thus, a tenancy with the right of survivorship passes the title of the deceased by operation of law to the survivor or survivors free of the claims of anyone else.

Both joint tenancy and tenancy in common ownership may include two or more persons who may or may not be related. In tenancy in common, the share of the tenants may differ; for example, A may own an undivided two-thirds and B an undivided one-third. In joint tenancy, the interests not only must be equal but must be created at the same time.

In some states, property acquired by either spouse after the marriage is community property. Although there are slight deviations in the approach to community property, such laws usually provide that the husband shall have the management and control of community personal property just as if he were the sole owner. However, he may not transfer more than one-half of it by will, and the other half automatically passes to the surviving spouse on death. The community property laws often provide additional limitations on the disposition of community property real estate. The usual requirement is that the wife must join in any conveyance of real estate, but not of personal property.

11. Special Aspects of Joint Tenancy

When there is a question as to which form of ownership actually exists in any specific case, the law usually favors property's passing by will or intestacy to its passing by right of survivorship. Courts do not find that property is held in joint tenancy with the right of survivorship unless there is a contract between the two co-owners clearly stating that such is the case and that the right of survivorship is to apply. Bank signature cards and stock certificates that use the term *joint tenancy* or "with the right of survivorship" create such a contract, as does the language "as joint tenants and not as tenants in common." In most states, the contract must be signed by both parties to be effective. Failure to use the proper language or have a properly executed contract results in a tenancy in common.

Several additional aspects of holding property in joint tenancy frequently result in litigation. First of all, joint tenancy is often used as a substitute for a will. A party wanting to leave property to another on death sometimes puts the property in joint tenancy. Is a present gift intended? Does the new joint tenant have the right to share in the income of the property prior to the death of the original owner? [6] Such issues are frequently litigated.

A similar issue arises when one person, who may be in ill health or incapacitated, adds another person's name to a savings or a checking account in order to allow the latter to pay bills and handle the former's business transactions. The signature card often provides for a joint tenancy. Was a joint tenancy or mere agency intended? Joint-tenancy arrangements are frequently challenged successfully on the ground that the right of survivorship was not intended.

A disadvantage of the joint tenancy arrangement is the ease with which it may be severed. Each joint tenant has the power to terminate the right of survivorship by a simple transfer or conveyance of his interest to a third party. The severance converts the joint tenancy to a tenancy in common.

PERSONAL PROPERTY CASES

In re Estate of Evans
356 A.2d 778 (Pa.) 1976

Appellant contended that she was the donee of a gift of the contents of a safe deposit box. The deceased had given the appellant the keys to the box which contained $800,000 in stocks and bonds. There was no question that a gift of the contents was intended. However, the lower court held that there was no gift because there had been no actual or constructive delivery of the contents of the box. The trial court found that the deceased had not divested himself of complete dominion and control over the contents of the box.

NIX, J. . . . In order to effectuate an inter vivos gift there must be evidence of an intention to make a gift and a *delivery*, actual or constructive, of a nature sufficient not only to *divest the donor* of all dominion over the property but also *invest the donee* with complete control over the subject-matter of the gift. . . .

In the instant case, the controversy focuses on whether there was an adequate delivery. . . . Without a complete delivery during the lifetime of the donor there can be no valid gift inter vivos. Though every other step be

[6] *Kinney* v. *Ewing*, page 794.

taken that is essential to the validity of the gift, if there is no delivery, the gift must fail. Intention cannot supply it; words cannot supply it; actions cannot supply it. It is an indispensable requisite, without which the gift fails, regardless of consequence. The consequence is that no matter how often or how emphatically the desire or intention of the donor to make the gift has been expressed, upon his death before delivery has been completed, the promise or purpose to give is revoked.

We have recognized that in some cases, due to the form of the subject matter of the gift or due to the immobility of the donor actual, manual delivery may be dispensed with and constructive or symbolic delivery will suffice. In *Ream Estate,* 413 Pa. 489, 198 A.2d 556 (1964), for example, the Court found there had been a valid constructive delivery of an automobile where the donor gave the keys to the alleged donee and also gave him the title to the car after executing an assignment of it leaving the designation of the assignee blank. The assignment was executed in the presence of a justice of the peace and the evidence was overwhelming that the name of the donee was to be inserted upon the death of the decedent.

In *Elliott's Estate,* 312 Pa. 493, 167 A. 289 (1933), we held there was a valid constructive delivery of the contents of a safe deposit box where the donor turned over to the alleged donee the keys. There, however, just prior to the delivery of the keys a doctor had informed the non-ambulatory donor that death was imminent. Under those circumstances manual delivery was impossible.

Appellant relies heavily on *Leadenham's Estate,* 289 Pa. 216, 137 A. 247 (1927). . . . This decision, however, supports the Court's finding that there was no delivery in the instant case. In *Leadenham's Estate,* the donor had rented a separate safe deposit box in the name of the intended donee, put the contents of his box into the newly rented one and delivered the keys to it to the donee. On those facts we held that the constructive delivery of the keys

was sufficient to sustain the inter vivos gift because the donor had divested himself of dominion and control and invested the donee with complete dominion and control. . . .

In the instant case, appellant did not have dominion and control over the box even though she was given the keys to it. The box remained registered in Mr. Evans' name and she could not have gained access to it even with the keys. Mr. Evans never terminated his control over the box, consequently he never made a delivery, constructive or otherwise.

Although appellant suggests that it was impractical and inconvenient for Mr. Evans to manually deliver the contents of his box to her because of his physical condition and the hazards of taking such a large sum of money out of the bank to her home, we need only note that the deceased was obviously a shrewd investor, familiar with banking practices, and could have made delivery in a number of simple, convenient ways. First, he was not on his deathbed. He was ambulatory and not only went to the bank on October 22, 1971, but took walks thereafter and did not enter the hospital until November 5, 1971. On the day he went to the bank he could have rented a second safe deposit box in appellant's name, delivered the contents of his box to it and then given the keys to appellant. He could have assigned the contents of his box to appellant. For that matter, he could have written a codicil to his will.

The lower court noted that the deceased was an enigmatic figure. It is not for us to guess why people perform as they do. On the record before us it is clear that regardless of Mr. Evans' intention to make a gift to appellant, he never executed that intention and we will not do it for him. On these facts, we are constrained to hold that there was not an inter vivos gift to appellant and that the contents of the safe deposit box were properly included in the inventory of Mr. Evans' estate. . . .

Affirmed.

Fendley v. Laster
538 S.W.2d 555 (Ark.) 1976

WILLIAMS, J. . . . This Appeal involves the validity of a gift causa mortis.

Briefly, Stanley Claude Fendley owned the Economy Drug Stores in Little Rock and the Appellee, Johnnie Faye Laster, was his trusted employee for many years. On December 23, 1967, Fendley suffered a severe and disabling heart attack from which he remained hospitalized for approximately two months.

On March 1, 1968, after returning home, he wrote and delivered a check to Johnnie Faye Laster for $10,000.00, which is the subject of the purported gift. In the left-hand corner he penned the following words, "Only Good In Case of Death SCF."

After the heart attack he only returned to the active management of his business affairs on a part time basis for the period of about a year. He died on June 21, 1973 at the age of 71. Prior to his death, on the 16th day of October, 1972, E.B. Fendley and C.B. Fendley were appointed Co-Guardians of the Person and Estate of Stanley Claude Fendley, because of his mental and physical incompetency.

Fendley died testate and Appellants, who were appointed Co-Executors of his Estate, disallowed the claim of Johnnie Faye Laster for $10,000.00. Subsequently, the Probate Court of Pulaski County allowed it as a gift causa mortis.

Under these facts, about which there is no dispute, most of them having been stipulated, there is no question but that Stanley Claude Fendley attempted to make a gift to Johnnie Faye Laster of $10,000.00 and effectively delivered the check representing the money to her. Also, in the opinion of the Court, there is no doubt but that he was apprehensive of death at the time he wrote and delivered the check to her. It is not difficult to conceive his state of mind at that time, having just undergone such a serious brush with death.

We reaffirm the rule . . . that a check may be the subject of a gift causa mortis.

There is no difficulty, therefore, in finding that the subject matter of a gift has been delivered by the donor to the donee at a time when the donor was under the apprehension of death from some existing disease, two of the requirements of a valid gift causa mortis.

The difficulty in this case, however, comes with the third requirement, that is, that the donor must die without recovering from the disease (or surviving the peril).

Did Fendley die without recovering from the disease which placed him in a state of apprehension during the last few days of 1967 and the first two months of 1968?

Under the stipulation of facts, Fendley did not return to full time management of his business interests but during the period between the heart attack and his death he did actively conduct some of his business affairs on a part time basis for about one year; and ultimately died from the existing heart condition on June 21, 1973. . . .

The cause of death as reflected on the Death Certificate signed by the attending physician was "acute pulmonary edema, arteriosclerotic heart disease, congestive heart failure chronic."

In view of the time that Fendley lived after the apprehensive incident, in excess of five years, and of his activities during that period of time, though limited to some extent, we are of the opinion that it is not reasonable to say that he had not recovered from the disease which caused his apprehension and that the effort to establish a gift causa mortis must fail. . . .

When a gift causa mortis is made during sickness, it is essential, in order to perfect it and prevent a revocation, that the donor should die of the very same sickness from which he was then suffering, and there should be no intervening recovery between the illness and his final death; and it seems that the donee must affirmatively show the existence of all these facts. . . .

That Fendley did leave his hospital bed and the hospital and did show some interest and activity in his business is at least convincing evidence that he "recovered" from the depth of the disease that caused him to be overly concerned about his chances of pro-longed life. This, in addition to five years of prolonged life, convinces the Court that there was an intervening recovery between the illness and his final death. . . .

Reversed.

Farm Bureau Mut. Automobile Ins. Co. v. Moseley
90 A.2d 485 (Ill.) 1950

Plaintiff sued to recover a stolen automobile. The defendant had purchased the automobile from a used car dealer. The motor in the car had been removed, and a new one had been put in its place by the thief. Defendant had added a sun visor, seat covers, and gasoline tank.

RICHARDS, J. . . . The owner of goods or chattels which have been stolen is not divested of his ownership of the property by the larcenous taking. He may follow and reclaim the stolen property wherever he finds it.

A sale by the thief, or by any person claiming under the thief, does not divest title to the property in the purchaser as against the legal owner. The fact that the sale was made in the ordinary course of business and the purchaser acted in good faith makes no difference.

The subsequent possession by the thief is a continuing wrong, and if the wrongdoer increases the value of the property by his labor upon it, or by substituting parts for those which were on it when he acquired it, or by adding new parts to it, the property in its enhanced value or changed condition still be-longs to the original owner and he may retake it with the accessions thereto.

The automobile in question having been identified as stolen property, the defendant Moseley has no title to it as against the claim of the plaintiff. . . .

The property right to the automobile being in the plaintiff, I render judgment in its favor for the automobile.

The engine which was in the automobile at the time it was stolen from Mr. Grunwell, having been removed by the thief, or someone who claimed under the thief, and another engine put in its place, the new engine became a part of the automobile and the plaintiff is entitled to retain it as his property.

It does not appear that the defendant Moseley knew that the automobile had been stolen when he purchased it, consequently there was no wilful wrongdoing by him. This being true, he is entitled to the sun visor, seat covers, and gasoline tank which he attached to the automobile while it was in his possession. The distinction between a wilful and involuntary wrongdoer is recognized by the authorities.

So ordered.

Troop v. St. Louis Union Trust Co.
166 N.E.2d 116 (Ill.) 1960

Plaintiff, Troop, the owner of a three-fourths working interest in an oil and gas lease and the manager of it, sued the defendant, the owner of the other one-fourth, to foreclose a partnership lien because the defendant had not paid his share of the operating expenses for eight years. Plaintiff also owned another lease and had commingled the oil of the two leases. Defendant counterclaimed and asserted that he was entitled to one-fourth of the total oil as commingled. The trial court held that defendant was entitled to one-fourth of the total oil from both leases, and plaintiff appealed.

SCHEINEMAN, J. . . . The doctrine of confusion of goods has been a part of English and American law for continuous centuries. It applies to any type of goods of such uniformity that, after mixing, there is no possibility of identification of the component parts. If the proportionate parts are not ascertainable, equity will declare the innocent party owner of the whole.

. . . [W]hen the commingling is proved, the burden of going forward with evidence to show the correct proportions is on the party who commingled. In the absence of such proof he bears the whole loss.

This appears to be the first case in a court of review in this state involving the doctrine as applied to oil. We hold that oil is a type of uniform substance to which the doctrine applies. It has been so applied in other states. We cite only one of these cases, which bears some resemblance to this case. *Stone* v. *Marshall Oil Co.,* 208 Pa. 85. In that case the plaintiff owned one-fourth of the gas on one lease, which the defendant had commingled with the gas from eighteen other wells. The master applied the doctrine in question and, of the net proceeds, awarded one-fourth of the total to plaintiff. The trial court sustained exceptions, and required a computation, with the limitation that all doubts be resolved in favor of plaintiff. This rule was reversed by the court of review, which held the master was correct, that plaintiff should have his fraction of the entire amount.

We conclude that the decree properly awarded one-fourth of the commingled oil to Rust, less the expenses properly charged. . . . The decree is affirmed in all respects.

Decree affirmed.

Stankiewicz v. Hawkes
369 A.2d 253 (Conn.) 1976

PARSKEY, J. . . . The limited issue which is dispositive of this appeal is whether the trial court was justified in finding that the plaintiff had abandoned her personal property.

The facts as found by the trial court may be summarized as follows: The plaintiff was a tenant of an apartment rented to her by the defendant. In August, 1973, the plaintiff and her children were required to vacate the apartment which was in urgent need of redecorating because its physical condition was a health hazard to the plaintiff's children. When the plaintiff moved from the apartment she took some of her possessions and some of her children's possessions, but she left behind many items and belongings. Among the items left behind were dishes, silverware, children's clothing, four winter coats, three bureaus, a table and chairs, a radio, and a tool set. The defendant inspected the apartment, found the place "in a mess" and concluded that the items remaining were abandoned junk. The defendant's workers removed the items from the apartment and placed them in a pile in the yard where they were left unprotected and exposed to rain. Subsequently, the property was removed to the junkyard by order of the police. The court found that the plaintiff had abandoned the personal property she left in the apartment.

Abandonment implies a voluntary and intentional relinquishment of a known right. If that test is applied to the facts of this case, the record does not support the court's finding of abandonment. The plaintiff was a tenant of the defendant's. As such she had the exclusive right to the possession of her apartment. Nothing in the finding suggests that her right to possession had terminated for any reason. In the absence of an agreement to the contrary, the landlord had no right to enter it without her consent. The plaintiff did not move out voluntarily. She was required to leave because the physical condition of the apartment exposed her children to a health hazard. There is no finding that the plaintiff permitted the defendant to enter the apartment for any purpose other than to make necessary repairs. The numerous personal belongings which she left behind, items such as winter clothing, sheets, blankets and pillow cases, bureaus, a table and chairs, bespeak an expectation of early return and not of permanent removal. The plaintiff's property rights are not measured by the state of her finances. However humble her possessions, they were hers to use. The fact that the defendant considered those possessions rags and junk gave him no right to exercise dominion over them. The removal of the plaintiff's property from the apartment and its exposure to the elements, under the circumstances of this case, constituted a conversion. Since the plaintiff's removal from the apartment was involuntary and since there is no evidence of any other act by the plaintiff prior to the conversion from which one could reasonably infer a voluntary relinquishment by the plaintiff of her right to her possessions, the court's finding of abandonment cannot stand.

The plaintiff is entitled to a judgment because of the conversion of her property. A new trial will be necessary to assess damages. . . . The case is remanded with direction to render judgment for the plaintiff to recover such damages as she may prove on a new trial limited to the issue of damages.

Reversed.

Kinney v. Ewing
492 P.2d 636 (N.M.) 1972

A mother brought suit against her daughter for a declaratory judgment that the daughter had no interest in certain securities. The mother had purchased the securities with her own funds, but they were registered in the names of the mother and her daughter as joint tenants with the right of survivorship so that the property would go to the daughter upon the mother's death without probate proceedings. The mother had custody of the certificates. The daughter had been seeking and claiming half the dividends on the securities. The lower court found for the mother, and the daughter appealed.

STEPHENSON, J. . . . The basic question presented is whether a valid gift was made and completed. . . .

The decisive question concerning the Securities is whether there existed the requisite donative intent. The trial court found that:

6. In registering said securities in the names of herself and defendant as joint tenants, plaintiff did not thereby intend to give defendant any interest in said securities during plaintiff's lifetime, but only to provide for the passing of the ownership of said securities to defendant upon the death of plaintiff; plaintiff's intention was to make a gift of said securities to defendant to take effect upon the death of plaintiff, and not before.

Defendant relies upon § 70-1-14.1, N.M. S.A., 1953, which effected profound changes in our law in the field of joint tenancies, and which provides:

An instrument conveying or transferring title to real or personal property to two [2] or more persons as joint tenants, to two [2] or more persons and to the survivors of them and the heirs and assigns of the survivor, or to two [2] or more persons with right of survivorship, shall be prima-facie evidence that such property is held in a joint tenancy and shall be conclusive as to purchasers or encumbrancers for value. In any litigation involving the issue of such tenancy a preponderance of the evidence shall be sufficient to establish the same.

She argues that by virtue of this statute, the certificates for the Securities constituted prima facie evidence that the stocks were held in joint tenancy; that since the certificates were so registered at plaintiff's direction without consideration passing from defendant to plaintiff, they are also prima facie evidence of plaintiff's intent to give defendant a gift of a present interest in the securities; that it was therefore incumbent upon plaintiff to meet this prima facie evidence or rebut these presumptions; and that the registration of stock certificates in joint tenancy at the direction of the donor creates a presumption of donative intent. We have no quarrel with defendant's reasoning to this point, but she then argues that it was incumbent upon plaintiff to rebut this presumption by clear and convincing evidence which, as a matter of law, she failed to do, and it is here that we take our departure from her position. . . .

We have no hesitation in holding that the trial court's finding as to lack of donative intent as to the Securities is sustained by substantial evidence. Plaintiff relied on the advice of a banker friend in selecting the joint tenancy vehicle. Legal advice from bankers, although historically a boon to the legal profession, is attended with hazards to its recipient, albeit likely to no greater degree than financial advice from lawyers. The question posed is not whether the advice was good or bad—accurate or inaccurate. Rather, the issue is what intention the advice engendered as evidenced by plaintiff's subsequent actions and her testimony.

The true situation is that plaintiff wished to make provision for defendant following the former's death. The means she chose, based upon the advice she received, was inappropriate. She desired to avoid probate proceedings. She is not to be criticized for this. Probate proceedings have not achieved popularity with the laity and are unlikely to do so.

Testamentary intentions are transitory. The lady changed her mind. . . .

Affirmed.

CHAPTER 41
REVIEW QUESTIONS AND PROBLEMS

1. X had a safe deposit box at Y Bank. The only people with access to the safe deposit box area were bank personnel and box renters. X, while in the area, found a $100 bill which he turned over to the bank. After one year, no one had claimed the money, and X sued the bank for the $100. Should he receive it? Why?

2. X gave Y an engagement ring in contemplation of marriage. X was killed in an accident before the marriage, and his estate sued to recover the ring. Should it succeed? Explain.

3. X bought ten lottery tickets on an automobile. She wrote her niece's name on the back of one of the tickets, then called her niece's mother and informed her that she had bought a chance for her niece. The niece's ticket won the car, but X claimed the car belonged to her. Is she correct? Why?

4. X, by will, left his brother Y "all my tangible personal property." Would this include jewelry? stocks and bonds? an automobile? a leasehold interest in some land? Explain.

5. X purchased a car from Y on the installment plan. He then purchased tires from Z to put on the car, also via installments. X defaulted, and the car was repossessed by Y. Z then sued Y for the tires. Y claims ownership through accession. Should Z recover? Why?

6. B purchased feed-mill equipment from S but left the equipment in S's warehouse with the understanding that he would remove it later. B removed certain major items of the equipment within six months; however, when B went to the warehouse four years later, S prevented him from removing further equipment. B brought suit for the return of the equipment. Should B succeed? Why?

7. S sold several tracts of land on contract, retaining legal title to the land, with the buyers owing the unpaid principal on the contracts. S was indebted to C. In consideration of C's cancellation of the indebtedness, S agreed to transfer by deed and assignment the real estate contracts to C. Subsequently C, without the knowledge of his wife, changed the agreement and executed a quitclaim deed to S covering all the land covered by the contract. C and his wife later brought suit to rescind the deed, on the ground that it was contrary to the community property laws of the state. Is C correct? Why?

8. A certificate of deposit of a bank noted the following: "U or N as joint tenants with the right of survivorship." The accompanying signature card bore the signatures of U and N. After U died, N admitted that he had no previous knowledge of the certificate and that he did not sign the signature card. Did the certificate of deposit create a joint tenancy? Why?

9. A mother deposited $10,000 of her money in a joint account in a savings and loan association. Both signatures were required for withdrawal, and the signature card contained the following: "Any funds placed in or added to the account by any one of the parties is and shall be conclusively intended to be a gift to the other party to the extent of his pro rata share." The mother retained possession of the certificate of deposit and subsequently brought suit, claiming that she is the sole owner of the funds. Is the mother correct? Why?

10. A and B owned property as joint tenants. B leased the property to L for a period of ten years without the knowledge or consent of A. B died three months after the execution of the lease. Did the granting of the lease by B sever the joint tenancy? Did the lease become invalid when B died? Why?

42

Bailments

1. Introduction

Possession of personal property is often temporarily surrendered by the owner to another person. In such cases, the person to whom the goods are delivered may perform some service pertaining to the goods, such as a repair, after which he returns them to the owner. Upon many occasions, one person borrows or rents an article that belongs to another, or a person may store his goods in a warehouse.

A contract whereby possession of personal property is surrendered by the owner with provision for its return at a later time forms a *bailment*. The owner of the goods is known as the *bailor,* whereas the one receiving possession is called the *bailee.*

There are three distinct requirements for a bailment: (1) retention of title by bailor; (2) possession and temporary control of the property by the bailee; [1] and (3) ultimate possession to revert to the bailor unless he orders it transferred to some designated third person.

A bailment occurs when personal property is leased. A lease by a merchant dealing in goods of the type involved is similar to a sale of the goods. As a result, the bailor (lessor) makes the same warranties as a seller of goods, and the provisions of the Code are applicable to such bailments.

[1] *Simons* v. *First National Bank of Denver,* page 807.

797

2. Types of Bailment

Bailments group naturally into three classes: bailments for the benefit of the bailor; bailments for the benefit of the bailee; and bailments for the mutual benefit of the bailor and the bailee. Typical of the first group are those cases in which the bailor leaves goods in the safekeeping of the bailee under circumstances that negate the idea of compensation. Because the bailee is not to be paid in any manner, the bailment is for the exclusive benefit of the bailor. A bailment for the benefit of the bailee is best exemplified by a loan of some article. Thus, A borrows B's automobile for a day. The bailment is one for the sole benefit of A.

The most common type of bailment is the one in which both parties are to benefit. Contracts for repair, carriage, storage, or pledge of property fall within this class. The bailor receives the benefit of some service; the bailee benefits by the receipt of certain agreed compensation; thus, both parties profit as a result of the bailment. To constitute a bailment for mutual benefit, it is not essential that the bailee actually receive compensation in money or tangible property. If the bailment is an incident of the business in which the bailee makes a profit, or was accepted because of benefits expected to accrue, it is a mutual benefit bailment.

3. Degree of Care Required by Bailee

Provided that proper care has been exercised by the bailee, any loss or damage to the property bailed follows title and consequently falls upon the bailor. Each type of bailment requires a different degree of care. In a bailment for the benefit of the bailor, the bailee is required to exercise only slight care, whereas in one for the benefit of the bailee, extraordinary care is required. A bailment for the mutual benefit of the parties demands only ordinary care on the part of the bailee. *Ordinary care* is defined as care that the average individual usually exercises over his own property.[2]

In addition to the duty to exercise care, the bailee promises to return the property undamaged upon termination of the bailment. In an action by a bailor against a bailee based upon a breach of the contract of bailment, when the bailor proves delivery of the bailed property and the failure of the bailee to redeliver upon legal demand therefor, a *prima facie* case of want of due care is thereby established, and the burden of going forward with the evidence shifts to the bailee to explain his failure to redeliver.

The Uniform Commercial Code, Article 7—Documents of Title—provides, "A warehouseman is liable for loss of or injury to the goods caused by his failure to exercise such care in regard to them as a reasonably careful man would exercise under like circumstances but unless otherwise agreed he is not liable for damages which could not have been avoided by the exercise of such

---

[2] *Stovall Tire & Marine, Inc.* v. *Fowler*, page 808.

care." However, provision is made for the continued effective operation of any statute, state or federal, that imposes more rigid standards of responsibility for some or all failures.

Furthermore, the amount of care demanded varies with the nature and value of the article bailed. The care found to be sufficient in the case of a carpenter's tool chest would probably not be ample for a diamond ring worth $10,000. A higher standard of protection is required for valuable articles than for those less valuable.

4. Degree of Care Required by Bailor

Property leased by the bailor to the bailee (a mutual benefit bailment) must be reasonably fit for the intended purpose. For this reason, it is the duty of the bailor to notify the bailee of all defects in the property leased, of which he might reasonably have been aware. The bailor is responsible for any damage suffered by the bailee as the result of such defects unless he notifies the bailee of them. This rule holds true even though the bailor is not aware of the defect if, by the exercise of reasonable diligence, he could have discovered it.

If, on the other hand, the article is merely loaned to the bailee—a bailment for the benefit of the bailee—the bailor's duty is to notify the bailee only of known defects. A bailor who fails to give the required notice of a defect is liable to any person who might be expected to use the defective article as a result of the bailment. For example, employees of the bailee and members of the bailee's family may usually recover of the bailor for injuries received as a consequence of the defect.

5. Exculpatory Clauses

Bailees frequently desire to disclaim liability for damage to the property that may occur while it is in their possession. An exculpatory clause disclaiming liability for negligence is illegal if the bailee is a quasi-public institution, because such contracts are against public policy. This subject was discussed in detail in the Book on Contracts.

More and more bailees are being classified as quasi-public because of the inequality of bargaining power between the bailor and bailee that prevails in many situations. Not all exculpatory clauses seek to eliminate liability completely; some seek to limit the amount of damages. Contracts limiting the amount of damages are looked upon more favorably than absolute disclaimers because it is fair for both parties to know the value of the property and the risk it presents. In accordance with this theory, the Uniform Commercial Code provides that damages may be limited by a term in the warehouse receipt or storage agreement limiting the amount of liability in case of loss or damage. However, a warehouseman cannot disclaim the obligation of reasonable care by such agreement. Limitations on the liability of carriers is discussed later in this chapter.

6.   Rights and Duties of Bailee

The bailment agreement governs the duties and rights of the bailee. Should he treat the property in a different manner, or use it for some purpose other than that contemplated by the contract, he becomes liable for any loss or damage to the property in the interim. This is true even though the damage can in no sense be attributed to the conduct of the bailee. To illustrate: Let us assume that A stores his car in B's public garage for the winter. B, because of a crowded condition, has the car temporarily moved to another garage without the consent of A. As the result of a tornado, the car is destroyed while at the second location. The loss falls upon B, as he exceeded the terms of the bailment contract. In a restricted sense, the bailee is guilty of conversion of the bailor's property during the period in which the contract terms are being violated.

The bailee has no right to deny the title of the bailor unless the bailee has yielded possession to one having paramount title. In other words, the bailee has no right to retain possession of the property merely because he is able to prove that the bailor does not have title. In order to defeat the bailor's right to possession, the bailee must show that he has turned the property over to someone having better title, or that he is holding the property under an agreement with the true owner.

COMMON CARRIERS

7.   Definition

A *common* or *public carrier* is distinguished from a *private carrier* in that the former performs a public service for all, so that it will be liable for refusal, without excuse, to carry for all who might apply. A private carrier is one who undertakes by special arrangement to transport property without being bound to serve everyone who may request service. A private carrier may advertise and secure as much business as possible without losing the status of a private carrier.

Common carriers are licensed by public bodies such as the Interstate Commerce Commission or the commerce commissions of the various states. They are licensed to serve a designated territory with specified points of departure and destination. Their rates are uniform and a matter of public record in their tariffs.

A common carrier may specialize; that is, it may restrict itself to carrying a particular type of goods, it may specialize in the means of transportation it employs, or it may limit its services to a specific area. Common carriers do not undertake to carry, by any means, any and all property to any place. The area served by the carrier, the types of goods carried, and the methods employed are all set forth in the certificate of public convenience and necessity issued by the appropriate regulatory agency. The terms of the certificate must be complied with. Carriers do not have the right to transport wherever they please.[3] They do not have freedom of contract as to rates or territory.

8. Care Required of the Common Carrier

The contract for carriage of goods constitutes a mutual benefit bailment, but the care required of the carrier greatly exceeds that of the ordinary bailee. A common carrier is an absolute insurer of the safe delivery of the goods to their destination. This rule is subject to only five exceptions: any loss or damage that results from (1) an act of God,[4] (2) action of an alien enemy, (3) order of public authority, (4) inherent nature of the goods, or (5) misconduct of the shipper. Thus, any loss that results from an accident or the willful misconduct of some third party must be borne by the carrier. For example, A, in order to injure a certain railway company, sets fire to several boxcars loaded with freight. Any damage to the goods falls upon the carrier. On the other hand, if lightning, an act of God, has set fire to the cars, the loss would have fallen upon the shipper.

Any damage to goods in shipment that results from the very nature of the goods, from improper crating, or from failure to protect the property must be suffered by the shipper. Thus, if a dog dies because his crate was poorly ventilated, the shipper is unable to recover from the carrier. However, it must be kept in mind that the carrier has the burden of proving that it was free from negligence and that the damage falls within one of the exceptions to the rule establishing the carrier's liability as an insurer of the shipment.

Goods may be damaged while in the possession of either the receiving, a connecting, or the delivering carrier. Damages arising while goods were being transported may be recovered by the shipper or the consignee from the delivering carrier. This result is based on a federal statute that relieves shippers and consignees of the impossible burden of proving which specific carrier along the chain of transportation caused the actual damage of the goods. If the shipper files a claim against the original carrier, it in turn may demand restitution from the connecting carriers.

The burden is on the shipper to prove that the goods were in good condition at the time and place of shipment. As previously noted, proof that the goods were in good condition when delivered to the carrier and that they were damaged when delivered by the carrier creates a *prima facie* case of liability. However, there is no presumption that the goods were in good condition when delivered to the carrier. Actual proof is required.

A common carrier, while not an insurer of passengers, owes the highest degree of care to them. In other words, a common carrier will be liable to passengers for injuries for even slight negligence. This high duty is not required to persons who are on the premises of the carrier but not on board the

---

[3] *Mars Express, Inc.* v. *David Masnik, Inc.,* page 809.
[4] *Southern Pacific Company* v. *Loden,* page 811.

carrier. Persons in the act of boarding are considered to be on board, as are persons alighting. The highest degree of care is owed to passengers, whereas ordinary care is owed to visitors on the premises who are not in the status of passengers.[5]

9.   Contract against Liability of Carrier

The discussion in Section 5 on exculpatory clauses is applicable to carriers. Although a common carrier may not contract away its liability for goods damaged in shipment, it may limit the liability to a stated amount. A carrier may also, where lower rates are granted, relieve itself from the consequences of causes or of conduct over which it has no control. Such a provision in effect incorporates the five exceptions to the insurer rule stated above.

The Uniform Commercial Code provides, "A carrier who issues a bill of lading whether negotiable or nonnegotiable must exercise the degree of care in relation to the goods which a reasonably careful man would exercise under like circumstances." However, it must be noted that federal legislation controls interstate shipments, and the Code stipulates that the section quoted "does not repeal or change any law or rule of law which imposes liability upon a common carrier for damages not caused by its negligence."

Since a carrier may limit liability to an agreed valuation, the shipper is limited in his recovery to the value asserted in the bill of lading or other contract. The rate charged for transportation will vary with the value of the property shipped. It is for this reason that the agreed valuation is binding, provided the tariff on file authorizes the limitation.[6]

10.   Duration of the Relation

The liability of the carrier attaches as soon as the goods are delivered to him. The receipt of the goods is usually acknowledged by a *bill of lading,* which sets forth the terms and conditions of shipment. The carrier becomes responsible for a carload shipment as soon as the car has been delivered to him. If the car is loaded while located upon railroad property, the carrier becomes liable at the moment the car is fully loaded.

The extreme degree of care required of the carrier may be terminated before the goods are actually delivered to the consignee. Three views prevail in this country as to when the relationship of the carrier ceases. Some states hold that the duties of the carrier end and those of a warehouseman begin as soon as the local shipment is unloaded from the car into the freight house. Others hold the carrier to strict liability until the consignee has had a reasonable time in which to inspect and remove the shipment. Still other states hold that the consignee is

[5] *Katamay* v. *Chicago Transit Authority,* page 813.
[6] *Greyhound Lines, Inc.* v. *Mah,* page 814.

entitled to notice and that he has a reasonable time after notice in which to remove the goods before the liability of the carrier as a carrier is terminated. To illustrate: Let us assume that goods arrive at their destination and are unloaded in the freight house. Before the consignee has had time to take them away, the goods are destroyed by fire, although the carrier has exercised ordinary care. Under the first of these views, the loss would fall upon the shipper, as at the time of the fire, the railway was no longer a carrier but a warehouseman. Under the other two views, the loss would fall on the carrier, as the extreme liability had not yet terminated, inasmuch as no time had been given for delivery.

The carload shipment is delivered as soon as it is placed on the private switch of the consignee or "spotted" at the unloading platform. Any subsequent loss, unless it results from the negligence of the carrier, must fall upon the owner of the goods.

11. Rates

Rates charged by common carriers must be reasonable. Carriers engaged in interstate business are subject to the regulation of the Interstate Commerce Commission, and all tariffs or rate schedules must be filed with the ICC and approved. Almost all the states have commissions for the purpose of establishing rates for intrastate business. These commissions also require tariffs to be filed with them. Any rate either higher or lower than that shown in the approved tariff is illegal. Discriminatory rates by the use of rebates are also forbidden, and the giving or receiving of rebates constitutes a crime.

A carrier may insist upon the payment of the charges at the time it accepts the delivery. Since it has a lien upon the goods as security for the charges, however, it customarily waits until the goods are delivered before collecting. The carrier usually refuses to surrender the goods unless the freight is paid, and if the freight remains unpaid for a certain period of time, it may advertise the property for sale. Any surplus, above the charges, realized from the sale reverts to the owner of the goods.

Any undue delay on the part of the consignee in removing the goods from the warehouse or the tracks of the railway permits the carrier to add a small additional charge known as *demurrage*.

12. Innkeepers' Liability

Issues similar to those involved with common carriers frequently arise in suits against hotel and motel operators. At common law, an innkeeper was an insurer of the safety of the goods of its guests. This rule came from the amount of control the innkeepers had over such goods as the result of the retention of keys to each room. Because of the ease of access of its employees to each guest room, the law imposed liability as a matter of public policy. There were exceptions to this general rule, however. As exceptions, the innkeeper was not liable for loss caused by an act of God, a public enemy, an act of public authority, the inherent nature of the property, or the fault of the guest.

Most states have enacted statutes pertaining to hotel or motel operators' liability. These statutes usually provide that if the operator maintains a safe or lockbox for guests to deposit valuable property in, then there is no liability if such property is stolen from the room. Such laws usually cover property of "small compass," which includes money, negotiable instruments, jewelry, and precious stones.[7] These laws further require that notice of the availability of the safe be given with notice of the liability limitation.

Some states also have laws that limit the maximum liability of hotel and motel operators to a stated amount, such as $500. Others have changed the liability from that of an insurer to that of a bailee of a mutual benefit bailment (ordinary care as the duty). In all states, the liability of the innkeeper is limited to the value of the property. There is no liability for consequential damages that may flow from the loss of the property.

DOCUMENTS OF TITLE

13.   General Concepts: Definitions

A *document of title* is broadly defined as any "document which in the regular course of business or financing is treated as adequately evidencing that the person in possession of it is entitled to receive, hold and dispose of the document *and the goods it covers*" (1-201[15]). Such a document must indicate that it was issued by a bailee or directed to a bailee and that it covers goods in the bailee's possession. The term primarily covers bills of lading and warehouse receipts.

Documents of title are covered by Article 7 of the Code. Numerous other statutes, both state and federal, also regulate the business of carriers and warehousemen. The federal Bills of Lading Act, for example, controls bills of lading covering foreign exports and interstate shipments of goods. The Code does not displace such statutes. Article 7 deals only with rights related to documents of title and not to the regulation of the services rendered by carriers or warehousemen.

Documents of title can serve a dual function. They may serve as receipts for goods stored or shipped, and they may also be representative of the goods. In the latter capacity, they are most useful in financing commercial transactions.

A *warehouse receipt* is a receipt issued by a person engaged in the business of storing goods for hire (1-201[45]). A *bill of lading* is a document evi-

---

[7] *Walls* v. *Cosmopolitan Hotels, Inc.,* page 814.

dencing the receipt of goods for shipment. An *issuer* is a bailee who prepares the document of title. A *consignor* is the person named in a bill of lading as the person from whom the goods have been received for shipment. A *consignee* is the person named in a bill of lading as the one to whom delivery is to be made.

Documents of title may be negotiable or nonnegotiable. The concept of negotiability was discussed in connection with commercial paper. The concept of negotiability for a document of title is similar to that of negotiability of commercial paper. The holder of a negotiable document is in a much more favorable position than one who holds a nonnegotiable one. The holder of a negotiable document obtains the direct obligation of the issuer to hold or deliver the goods free from most defenses and claims. In essence, the holder is so well protected that he can almost regard the document as the equivalent of the goods it represents.

14. Negotiation and Transfer

A warehouse receipt, bill of lading, or other document is negotiable if by its terms the goods are to be delivered to the bearer or to the "order of" a named person. A document not containing these "words of negotiability" is not negotiable. Thus, a bill of lading that states that goods are consigned to John Doe would not be negotiable.

Both negotiable and nonnegotiable documents can be transferred, but the method of transfer is different. A nonnegotiable document can be "assigned"; then the assignee acquires only the rights of the assignor and is subject to all defenses that are available against the assignor. The assignee is burdened with all defects in the assignor's title. *Negotiation* of a negotiable document places the transferee in a much more favorable position. If there is "due negotiation," the transferee is free from the defects of the transferor's title and the claims of third persons.

The method of negotiating a document of title depends upon whether it is an "order" document or a "bearer" document. The former is negotiated by indorsement and delivery; the latter, by delivery alone. The effects of blank and special indorsements are the same as those for commercial paper, and the last indorsement controls.

In order for the holder of a negotiable document of title to have the preferred status, there must have been a due negotiation. This means not only any necessary indorsement and/or delivery but also that the holder must satisfy certain requirements similar to those of a holder in due course of commercial paper. He must have purchased the document in good faith, without notice of a defense against or claim to it on the part of any person. He must have paid value for it, and the negotiation must have been in the regular course of business or financing. One to whom a document is negotiated in satisfaction or payment of a prior debt has not paid value.

If there has been due negotiation, the holder acquires title to the document, title to the goods, and the direct obligation of the issuer to hold or deliver the goods according to the terms of the document. The holder's rights cannot be defeated by any stoppage of the goods or surrender of them by the bailee. His rights are not impaired even if the negotiation or any prior negotiation constituted a breach of duty; even if any person has been deprived of possession of the document by misrepresentation, fraud, accident, mistake, duress, loss, theft, or conversion; and even if a previous sale or other transfer of the goods or document has been made to a third person (7-502[2]).

15. Liability of Indorser or Transferor

The indorser or transferor of a document of title makes three warranties to his immediate purchaser:

1. He warrants that the document is genuine. One who purchases a forged document of title may, upon discovery of the forgery, recover from the person who sold it to him.

2. He warrants that he has no knowledge of any facts that would impair its validity or worth.

3. He warrants that his sale of the document is rightful and fully effective with respect to the title to the document and the goods it represents. However, unless he has also sold the goods, he does not make any additional warranties as to the goods. If he is also the seller of the goods, he makes the usual seller's warranties. The indorser of a document of title does not warrant performance by the bailee.

His warranties are satisfied when the purchaser obtains a good right against the warehouseman or carrier. If the bailee has misappropriated the goods or refuses to surrender them, the holder of the document has as his only recourse an action against the bailee who issued the document.

If a bank or other person has been authorized to deliver a document of title, acting as an agent for this purpose, the delivery of the document creates no warranty by the agent as to the document itself. Thus, no liability would be assumed by any such agent if the document were not genuine.

16. Obligations of Bailees under Documents of Title

A public warehouse that issues a negotiable receipt is not at liberty to surrender the goods to the original bailor unless he surrenders the receipt for cancellation. The receipt represents the goods and must be surrendered before the goods may be obtained. A warehouse that surrenders goods without the return of the receipt may be called upon for the goods by someone who has purchased the document. The goods should be delivered only to the person who possesses the receipt, and then only if the receipt has been properly indorsed when such indorsement is required.

A bailee can refuse to deliver the goods called for by the document until payment of his just charges has been made. Applicable law may actually prohibit delivery without payment.

If a receipt was complete when issued but was later altered without authority, the warehouse's liability is determined by the original terms of the document. If a receipt was issued with blanks, a good-faith purchaser of the completed receipt may recover from the warehouse that issued the incomplete receipt.

A warehouse receipt, even though it has been properly negotiated, will in one situation be inferior to the rights of a buyer of the goods represented by the receipt. When a buyer in ordinary course of business buys fungible goods from a warehouseman who is also engaged in the business of buying and selling such fungible goods, he takes the goods free of any claim under the receipt. A typical case might involve the purchase of grain from an elevator. The holder of a receipt for grain stored would have no claim to grain purchased by a person from the owner of the elevator if the latter became insolvent and unable to deliver to the receipt holder.

BAILMENTS CASES

Simons v. First National Bank of Denver
491 P.2d 602 (Colo.) 1972

DUFFORD, J. . . . Plaintiff is the owner of an aircraft which he parked and tied to a ramp owned by defendant . . . Bank . . . at Jefferson County Airport . . . under an arrangement whereby plaintiff paid $15 per month. The aircraft was overturned and demolished by high winds. Plaintiff brought this action to recover the amount of $4,700 for the damage done to his aircraft. . . . Plaintiff alleged that defendants were bailees of his airplane and as such were responsible for its safety and had the duty of returning it to him undamaged. Defendants' answer denied that bailment was created and asserted affirmatively that the relationship which arose from the tie-down arrangement under which the plaintiff's airplane was parked on their facilities was merely a lease or a license.

The evidence at trial was uncontroverted in showing that plaintiff at all times had full control over his aircraft, tied the airplane to the ramp himself, and discouraged all parties from disturbing the aircraft. No evidence was introduced which suggested that defendants had agreed to a bailment either orally or in writing, or that they had exercised control over the aircraft at any time. . . . [T]he trial court ruled that a bailment had been created, as a matter of law. . . . Defendants appeal. . . .

It is the position of the defendants . . . that it was error on the part of the trial court to determine that they were bailees as a matter of law. . . . The defendants further assert that the trial court should have held, as a matter of law, that a lease or license relationship existed between the defendants and the plaintiff, under which the defendants owed only limited duties, and as to which there was no proof given of any breach on their part. Accordingly, they claim the trial court should have directed a verdict against the plaintiff and dismissed his complaint. We find the defendants are correct in these assertions.

Bailment is the delivery of personal property by one person to another in trust for a specific purpose with a contract, express or implied, that the trust shall be faithfully executed and the property returned or duly accounted for when the special purpose is accomplished or kept until the bailor reclaims the property. However, a bailment does not arise in those situations where the owner of the property retains control over his property. Consistent with these general principles of bailment law, it has been ruled that, where an aircraft is placed in an airport parking or tie-down space and the owner of the airport facility is not given and does not assert any control over the aircraft, only a lease relating to the space or facilities occupied by the aircraft is created as opposed to a bailment of the aircraft into the hands of the owner of that space.

In the case before us, there is a void of any evidence which would establish that control over the plaintiff's airplane was voluntarily passed to the defendants or that they attempted to exercise any such control. . . . Such being the case, the trial court erred in ruling, as a matter of law, that a bailment existed. . . .

Reversed.

Stovall Tire & Marine, Inc. v. Fowler
217 S.E.2d 367 (Ga.) 1975

QUILLIAN, J. In the fall of 1971 plaintiff requested defendant to install a reconditioned engine in his 18 foot Chris-Craft boat. Defendant performed the work and returned the boat to plaintiff in April 1972. Plaintiff hired a trailer to haul the boat to Lake Lanier. The engine would not run satisfactorily and the boat was returned to defendant's place of business in DeKalb County. Approximately three weeks later, "the latter part of May," the boat was returned to plaintiff and he again transferred it to Lake Lanier. The engine ran approximately 400 yards and plaintiff had to be towed ashore. The next week plaintiff contacted Mr. Ben Beard, chief mechanic for defendant, the person who had performed the earlier work on the boat. Beard told plaintiff to take the boat to Aqualand at Lake Lanier where Stovall had leased a slip, "until he could get up there and work on it. He said he would go up there and do the repairs at Lanier, rather than bring it back to Atlanta." Plaintiff placed his boat in defendant's slip at the Aqualand pier and secured it with four lines, one each to the bow and stern—on both sides. Plaintiff testified that after leaving the boat where he had been directed, he told "Mr. Stovall that the boat was there and it was ready for them to get up there and work on it. . . . I contacted Mr. Stovall at least twice to ask him if the boat had been repaired. . . . I went back to Stovall about the middle of July and asked him if the boat had been repaired and . . . he told me that the boat had been sunk." A severe storm occurred at Lake Lanier on July 4, 1972. A "Day Cruiser" had been placed in the defendant's slip with plaintiff's "runabout." During the storm the lines securing the cruiser "parted" and the "stern of the cruiser rode up on and hit the stern of the mahogany [plaintiff's boat]. . . ." The plaintiff's boat was afloat the next day but sank later in the week. The cruiser departed during the latter part of the week and was never identified. Defendant denied that his chief mechanic had any authority to direct plaintiff to leave his boat in the defendant's slip at Lake Lanier. Defendant further denied that he knew plaintiff's boat was in his slip until after it sank.

At trial, and here on appeal, defendant has asserted that there was no bailment and the cause of the damage to plaintiff's boat was an "Act of God." The case was tried before a judge without a jury and he gave judgment for plaintiff. Defendant appeals.

Held:

1. The issue of whether the evidence proved . . . a bailment was created . . . was for determination by the trier of fact, in this instance, the judge. There is sufficient evidence

of record to support . . . this determination.

2. Appellant contends the trial court failed to recognize and apply the "Act of God" defense. For a bailee to avail himself of an "Act of God" defense he must establish that his own negligence did not contribute to the damage or loss. . . . The trial court advised the defendant "[t]he boat was bailed to Stovall and Stovall was to make repairs and the plaintiff has testified that the repairs were not made. . . . Nothing was done from the last of May until some time in July when he called up and asked about his boat. . . . And as far as the Court is concerned, in order to show due diligence, there's going to have to be some testimony to show that Mr. Beard within a very brief time went up there to see that the boat was properly stored or tied up or whatever you do with boats, and that periodic checks were made to see that the bailed property was there and in good condition . . . to see if it was being looked after or cared for properly . . . where they told me to take it, then they're not using due diligence."

The court correctly applied the rule that in cases of bailment, after proof of loss the burden of proof is on the bailee to show proper diligence. . . . The court clearly advised defendant that bailment and loss had been shown by plaintiff and—in his opinion, due diligence had not been shown by defendant in permitting plaintiff's boat to remain in the defendant's slip for approximately six weeks—without action.

Where property is delivered for repair under a bailment and there is no agreement as to time the work is to be completed, a reasonable time will be allowed, and what is a reasonable time is a question for the trier of fact. . . . The court strongly advised defendant his actions did not constitute due diligence—thus he could not avail himself of the "Act of God" defense. . . . We find that where plaintiff first delivered his boat to defendant for repair "in the fall" of one year and in July of the succeeding year those repairs have not been completed—we cannot say there is insufficient evidence in the record to support the finding of the court that due diligence of defendant was not established. . . .

Judgment affirmed.

Mars Express, Inc. v. David Masnik, Inc.
401 F.2d 891 (1968)

SMITH, J. . . . This is an action brought by a trucking company to recover undercharges for the transportation of 290 truckloads of liquor from Peekskill, New York, to Bridgeport, Connecticut, where the defendant operated a wholesale liquor business. Plaintiff's claim is based on section 217(b) of the Interstate Commerce Act, which provides in pertinent part:

> No common carrier by motor vehicle shall charge or demand or collect or receive a greater or less or different compensation for transportation . . . between the points enumerated in such tariff than the rates, fares, and charges specified in the tariffs in effect at the time; and no such carrier shall refund

or remit in any manner or by any device, directly or indirectly . . . any portion of the rates, fares, or charges so specified.
. . . 49 U.S.C. § 217(b).

The amount involved is stipulated to be $19,023.50, plus interest. This represents the difference between the freight charges actually paid by defendant and a higher figure calculated by reference to the published tariff.

The United States District Court for the District of Connecticut gave judgment for the defendant shipper, and the plaintiff carrier appeals. We find no error and affirm the judgment.

The plaintiff, Mars Express, Inc. ("Mars"), was a common carrier operating under the jurisdiction of the Interstate Commerce Commission. By the terms of its certificate of public convenience and necessity, Mars was authorized to operate (1) between certain New Jersey counties and parts of New York, including Peekskill, and (2) between those same New Jersey counties and parts of Connecticut, including Bridgeport. Mars was not authorized, however, to operate directly between Peekskill and Bridgeport.

From 1956 through December 1963, Mars billed defendant for shipping charges at a rate of 40 cents per hundredweight on loads of 36,000 pounds or over. This was pursuant to a rate application approved by the ICC in 1956. In that application, Mars represented that it would transport the liquor from Peekskill to Bridgeport by way of New Jersey. It also represented that it would transport the liquor in conjunction with another common carrier, Apex Express, Inc. ("Apex"). More specifically, Apex was to transport the liquor from Peekskill to New Jersey, and Mars would then transport it from New Jersey to Bridgeport.

In 1962, the New England Motor Rate Bureau, Inc., an association authorized by power of attorney to make rate applications for Mars, filed a new liquor rate with the ICC. The application was made without Mars' knowledge, and raised the applicable rate to 56 cents per hundredweight for loads of 36,000 pounds or more. The new rate was deemed "accepted" by the ICC effective March 1, 1962, and was subsequently published. For some inexplicable reason, however, neither plaintiff nor defendant learned of the new rate until December 1963, when Mars demanded that defendant pay additional charges on shipments delivered after March 1, 1962.

If this was all that had happened, then plainly Mars would be entitled to recover undercharges under section 217(b) of the Act. As Mr. Justice Hughes said in *Louisville & Nashville Railroad Company* v. *Maxwell*, 237 U.S. 94, 97, 35 S.Ct. 494, 59 L.Ed. 853 (1915):

> Ignorance or misquotation of rates is not an excuse for paying or charging either less or more than the rate filed. This rule

is undeniably strict and it obviously may work hardship in some cases, but it embodies the policy which has been adopted by Congress. . . .

In a recent decision the Third Circuit remarked: "The rate filed is a matter of public record of which the shipper must take notice at his peril."

The district court found, however, that Mars exceeded the scope of its authority as a common carrier by transporting the liquor directly from Peekskill to Bridgeport without going by way of New Jersey as its certificate stipulated. The finding of the court below was that Apex did not participate "to any appreciable extent, if at all" in this arrangement. "The trucks carrying the liquor went directly from Peekskill to Bridgeport. They were trucks operated by Mars." Since Mars was operating beyond its authority as a common carrier, the lower court ruled that Mars could not bring a section 217(b) action for undercharges, and gave judgment for the defendant.

While Mars was a common carrier within the Act . . . it cannot recover undercharges for illegal carriage off route. . . . [M]ere possession of a certificate of public convenience and necessity [does not] automatically entitle a common carrier to the rate of file with the ICC.

A common carrier may not operate "unless there is in force with respect to such carrier a certificate of public convenience and necessity issued by the Commission *authorizing* such operations." Certificates prescribe the points of origin and destination which the trucker may serve, and also restrict him to specified routes. Plainly Mars' certificate does not authorize it to transport liquor *directly* from Peekskill to Bridgeport. Lacking the necessary authorization, Mars was not operating legally as a common carrier when it transported defendant's liquor, and thus cannot assert a claim for undercharges based on the published tariff.

A certificate of public convenience and necessity is not a certificate authorizing common carriers to roam wherever they choose.

Indeed, when the Interstate Commerce Act was amended in 1935 to give the ICC jurisdiction over trucking activities, it was thought that destructive competition could be prevented, as well as the "public interest" promoted, by restricting routes and stabilizing rates. It seems basic to the policy underlying the Act that

before a common carrier can take advantage of its published tariff rates, it must follow its authorized route. To allow common carriers to transport goods by whatever route they choose would be to invite the kind of chaos that the Act was intended to forestall.

The judgment for defendant is affirmed.

Southern Pacific Company v. Loden
508 P.2d 347 (Ariz.) 1972

HOWARD, J. Plaintiff-appellee brought a breach of contract action to recover damages in the sum of $10,047.68 resulting from the defendant carrier's failure to deliver certain perishable produce shipped from Nogales, Arizona to Los Angeles, California within the ordinary and usual time.

Southern Pacific Company admitted that appellee's shipment was delayed and not delivered to its destination within the usual time, but alleged that the delay was caused by an act of God and was unavoidable due to unusually heavy rains and flood conditions causing damage to its track and rail facilities. . . .

On June 12, 1972, the court entered judgment in favor of the plaintiff in the sum of $10,047.68, and Southern Pacific appeals from this judgment. . . .

The delay [in the delivery of the produce] . . . was caused under the following circumstances:

It had been raining in the Los Angeles area for about a week prior to January 25, 1969. On the morning of Saturday, January 25th, Milford Smith, Assistant Bridge and Building Supervisor for Southern Pacific, was dispatched from Los Angeles to inspect track structures on the railroad line from Los Angeles to Yuma, Arizona. At Ontario, California, east of Los Angeles, he encountered water flowing under one track structure causing a scour (the washing away of dirt from behind the wing-walls or abutment of the structure). He fortified the structure with burlap sacks and reported the condition by telephone for repair.

Mr. Smith continued his inspection eastward, and at Whitewater, California he en-

countered water which had overflowed its channel and was running over the tracks. This was reported on the evening of January 25, 1969. Smith received orders to proceed to Thermal, California where on arrival he discovered that both railroad bridges had fallen into the channel and were in the water. He returned to Indio to report the condition and made arrangements for a repair crew and materials to be brought in. On Sunday, January 26th, pile-driving operations commenced. The tracks were joined on Tuesday, January 28th and at 5:30 P.M. the train on which Loden's cucumbers were loaded departed from Yuma, arriving at Los Angeles a 6:40 A.M. January 29, 1969.

Common carriers impliedly agree to carry safely, and at common law they are held to a very strict accountability for the loss or damage of goods received by them. In this state a common carrier's liability for damage to goods in transit is based on the substantive rule of law that the carrier is an insurer for the safe transportation of goods entrusted to its care, unless the loss is caused by an act of God, the public enemy, negligence of the shipper, or the inherent nature of the goods themselves.

Furthermore, common carriers undertaking to carry perishable goods are held to a higher degree of care than when engaged in the shipment of other articles not inherently perishable and a failure to comply with this duty which results in a loss or injury to the shipper renders the carrier liable for the loss sustained, unless a proper defense is alleged and proved.

In addition, common carriers undertaking to transport property must, in the absence of an express contract providing for the time of delivery, carry and deliver within a reasonable time. The carrier is required to exercise due diligence to transport and deliver the property and guard against delay. Mere delay in transportation does not create a liability to respond in damages, and the rule is that the carrier is bound to use reasonable diligence and care, and only negligence will render it liable.

The law recognizes various fact situations as an excuse for delay which constitutes a good defense. Examples of such facts are accidents or misfortunes without fault or negligence on the carrier's part, or an act of God; an act or fault of the shipper or consignee; the press of business; strikes; extreme weather conditions; and accidents not amounting to acts of God. The delay, however, must have been due to an occurrence as could not have been anticipated in the exercise by the carrier of reasonable prudence, diligence and care.

In the case at bar, appellant at all times prior to judgment and appeal alleged an act of God as justification for the delay in transportation and consequent spoilage of appellee's perishable produce. . . .

The question on appeal therefore resolves itself to whether or not appellant sufficiently met its burden of proving that an act of God occurred excusing its delay in transporation and delivery of appellee's goods.

The various definitions of an act of God practically all require the entire exclusion of human agency from the cause of the loss or injury. A casualty cannot be considered an act of God if it results from or is contributed to by human agency, and that which may be prevented by the exercise of reasonable diligence is not an act of God.

The only acts of God that excuse common carriers from liability for loss or injury to goods in transit are those operations of the forces of nature that could not have been anticipated and provided against and that by their superhuman force unexpectedly injure or destroy goods in the custody or control of the carrier.

Extreme weather conditions which operate to foil human obligations of duty are regarded as acts of God. However, every strong wind, snowstorm, or rainstorm cannot be termed an act of God merely because it is of unusual or more than average intensity. Ordinary, expectable, and gradual weather conditions are not regarded as acts of God even though they may have produced a disaster, because man had the opportunity to control their effects. . . .

Application of the above principles to the evidence presented at trial leads to the conclusion that Southern Pacific failed to prove its defense of an act of God. Two of appellant's employees testified that it had rained in the Los Angeles area for a week prior to January 25, 1969, and it was not until a week after the rain began that Southern Pacific dispatched its employee Smith to patrol the track between Los Angeles and Yuma. Appellant offered knowledge and evidence of a week-long rain but offered no evidence of precautions to avoid possible consequences of this rainfall. Southern Pacific, through the testimony of its own witnesses, demonstrated notice of a gradual weather condition which could foreseeably cause damage to its facilities and consequent delay in transportation.

One of appellant's employees testified that he had not experienced the "conditions" on the line between Yuma and Los Angeles in his 29 years with the railroad. The appellant, however, offered no weather records in evidence to indicate how much rain fell during the period in question or the amount of water runoff at the bridge at Thermal or elsewhere, nor any comparison of the purported rainfall with that which had occurred previously. Appellant did not meet its burden to establish that the rainfall in the instant case was of unusual or more than average intensity.

A rainstorm of unusual duration or intensity is not necessarily a superhuman cause or an act of God. The rainfall in the instant case was not shown to be totally unforeseeable or of greater intensity than other rainfalls in the region so as to justify being called an "act of God" and, therefore, the judgment of the trial court is. . . .

Affirmed.

Katamay v. Chicago Transit Authority
289 N.E.2d 623 (Ill.) 1972

Plaintiff was standing on defendant's elevated platform waiting to board defendant's train. Defendant's train stopped at the platform, its doors opened, several people boarded, and as plaintiff started toward the train she fell —her shoes were off her feet and the heels were wedged in the spaces between the wooden planks of the platform. The jury found for plaintiff and awarded $27,500 as damages. The appellate court reversed, holding as a matter of law that plaintiff was not a passenger at the time of her injury, and defendant, therefore, did not owe her the highest degree of care; that it owed her the duty of ordinary care but that no breach of that duty was shown for the reason that plaintiff's evidence failed to show that defendant had either actual or constructive notice of the condition which caused her to fall. Plaintiff was granted leave to appeal.

GOLDENHERSH, J. . . . Defendant contends that "The law is well established in this state that a party does not have the status of a passenger unless he is injured while in the actual process of boarding a train."

The passenger to whom the carrier owes the duty to exercise the highest degree of care is one who is in the act of boarding, is upon, or is in the act of alighting from, the carrier's vehicle. We are not persuaded that, to come within this definition a passenger, of necessity, must have come into actual contact with the vehicle. This court has said that the rationale for the imposition of the duty upon a carrier to exercise the highest degree of care for the safety of an individual while he is a passenger as distinguished from the lesser duty owed at all other times is that the degree of care should be commensurate with the danger to which the passenger is subjected, and the degree of care required to be exercised increases as the danger increases.

In *Chicago Terminal Transfer R.R. Co.* v. *Schmelling,* 197 Ill. 619, at page 629, 64 N.E. 714, at page 717, the court said, "The duty

of a carrier to its passengers is, not only to exercise the highest degree of care and prudence in carrying them to their destinations, but also to afford them reasonable opportunities to leave the trains of the company with safety. The relation of carrier and passenger does not terminate until the passenger has alighted from the train and left the place where passengers are discharged, and the duty of the carrier to its passenger continues until the passenger has had a reasonable time in which to leave the depot or alighting place. What is such reasonable time must often depend upon the circumstances of the particular case. . . ."

In *Zorotovich* v. *Washington Toll Bridge Authority,* 80 Wash.2d 106, 491 P.2d 1295, while plaintiff was waiting to buy a ticket to ride defendant's ferry, he was struck by a vehicle being driven across the platform. In holding that the plaintiff was a passenger, the Supreme Court of Washington said: "The matters to be considered in determining the status as a passenger are: (1) place (a place under the control of the carrier and provided for the use of persons who are about to enter carrier's conveyance); (2) time (a reasonable time before the time to enter the conveyance); (3) intention (a genuine intention to take passage upon carrier's conveyance); (4) control (a submission to the directions, express or implied, of the carrier); and (5) knowledge (a notice to carrier either that the person is actually prepared to take passage or that persons awaiting passage may reasonably be expected at the time and place)." At page 1298 the court said: "We are not overlooking the contention of the defendant, Washington Toll Bridge Authority, that plaintiff was not in the act of boarding the ferry and that the dock was several hundred feet in length. The statement as to the length of the dock is factually correct but does not change the situation. The use of the dock was a necessary part of the act of boarding the ferry."

We hold that plaintiff was not required to be in physical contact with defendant's train in order to occupy the status of passenger. She was standing on the platform provided for boarding and alighting from defendant's trains and was engaged in the "act of boarding" if, with intent to board the standing train and pay the required fare, she moved toward it for that purpose.

If, at the time she fell, she was in the act of boarding, defendant owed her the duty to exercise a degree of care for her safety equal to the duty owed to provide her a safe place to alight. These issues were submitted to the jury under proper instructions, and were decided favorably to plaintiff. . . .

Appellate court reversed; circuit court affirmed.

Greyhound Lines, Inc. v. Mah
219 S.E.2d 842 (Va.) 1975

Plaintiff, Mah, sued the defendant to recover damages for the value of lost luggage. Its value was $1,000.55. Defendant's tariff on file with the Interstate Commerce Commission limited its liability to $50. The claim check contained the following notation on the front: "BAGGAGE LIABILITY LIMITED TO $50 (SEE OVER)." The reverse side of each claim check contained language stating that Greyhound's liability was limited to $50 for all baggage checked on one full fare ticket unless a greater value of the baggage was declared in writing at the time of the checking, in which case charges for excess value would be collected and a receipt issued therefor; and that "This check is accepted subject to all conditions of published tariffs."

Plaintiff did not read the claim check and did not notice the posters on the wall in the bus terminal advising passengers of the limitations.

I'ANSON, J. . . . Since the loss sustained by the plaintiff resulted from the movement of baggage in interstate commerce, the rights of the parties must be determined by the application of appropriate federal statutes.

The Interstate Commerce Act permits motor carriers to limit their liability for loss of a passenger's baggage if the carrier complies with the applicable terms of the Act and the rules and regulations of the Interstate Commerce Commission. . . . Many cases have recognized the right of motor carriers to limit their liability through tariffs duly filed with the Interstate Commerce Commission, pursuant to these federal statutes.

Before a motor carrier engaged in interstate commerce can limit its liability for negligent loss of baggage entrusted to it, it must show each of the following: (1) that it received the baggage as a common carrier; (2) that it issued a written receipt which contained the asserted limitation; and (3) that the Interstate Commerce Commission had on file at the time of the loss a tariff setting forth an authorized limitation, which is based on a rate differential.

Here the evidence established that Greyhound met each of the above conditions. . . . Hence, the judgment of the court below is modified by reducing the judgment for the plaintiff to the amount of the limitation of liability under the tariff and contract, and judgment is here entered for the plaintiff in the amount of $50.00.

Affirmed as modified, and final judgment.

Walls v. Cosmopolitan Hotels, Inc.
534 P.2d 1373 (Wash.App.) 1975

MUNSON, J. . . . Plaintiff, Paul Walls, instituted this action against defendant Cosmopolitan Hotels, Inc., to recover the value of a wristwatch he claimed had been stolen from his room while he was a guest in the defendant's hotel. The trial court granted summary judgment to the defendant, based upon the failure of Mr. Walls to deposit his watch with the hotel as required by RCW 19.48.030. Plaintiff appeals. We affirm.

Plaintiff was a registered guest in the defendant's hotel. Plaintiff contends that when he left his hotel room for dinner he had locked the door and left the watch on a nightstand. However, upon his return the watch was gone. He noticed that the door was damaged, and upon closer inspection, had been severely damaged on some prior occasion. Apparently the screws holding the repaired portions to the lock were loose and one could easily obtain entry by merely pushing gently upon the door, even though it was locked.

Plaintiff contends that the maintenance of the door in this condition constituted willful and wanton misconduct and such a disregard for the protection of plaintiff's property that the defendant should be liable for the loss of his watch, which he values at $3,685. On the other hand, defendant contends that the failure of the plaintiff to deposit his watch pursuant to RCW 19.48.030 is dispositive of all issues, namely: (1) whether a wristwatch is an includable item, subject to the terms of RCW 19.48.030; and (2) whether the alleged willful and wanton misconduct of the defendant in allowing the disrepair of the door to exist entitles plaintiff to recover within the terms of RCW 19.48.030. . . .

As to the first issue, we hold that a wristwatch valued at $3,685 is "valuable property of small compass" and therefore subject to the provisions of RCW 19.48.030.

As to the second issue, we hold that when the plaintiff failed to deposit his "valuable property of small compass" with the hotel pursuant to RCW 19.48.030, the defendant was relieved of all liability regardless of the cause of the loss. The statute specifically states that

> if such guests . . . shall neglect to deliver such property to the person in charge of such . . . safe . . . the proprietor . . . shall not be liable for any loss . . . of . . . such property . . . sustained by such guests . . . by negligence of such proprietor . . . or by fire, theft, burglary, or *any other cause whatsoever;* . . .

(Italics ours.) Therefore, plaintiff's contention that the cause of his loss was the willful and wanton misconduct of the defendant is not well taken in that the claimed cause of plaintiff's loss is contained within the terms "any other cause whatsoever." . . .

Judgment is affirmed.

CHAPTER 42
REVIEW QUESTIONS AND PROBLEMS

1. X had his car serviced regularly at Y's service station. Sometimes the car was left overnight in Y's possession. On one occasion when the car was left overnight to be serviced, an employee of Y used the car without authorization and demolished it. X then sued Y for breach of an implied contract of bailment. Should X recover his loss? Explain.

2. X left her mink jacket in the unattended cloakroom at Y's hotel while having lunch. When she returned to the cloakroom, the jacket had been stolen. X sued Y for the value of the jacket, contending that a bailment existed. May she recover? Explain.

3. X entered into a logging contract with Y Lumber Company. Y furnished an engine to be used by X. X signed an agreement to redeliver the engine at a set date in good condition. Through no negligence of X, a fire started and burned the engine. Y sued X for the value of the engine. Should he recover? Why?

4. X entered into a bailment agreement to store certain household goods in Y's warehouse. The warehouse burned and the goods were destroyed. X sued Y to recover his loss. Y cannot establish that the fire was not caused by negligence on his part. Should X recover? Why?

5. A rented a safe-deposit box from B Company. A placed a considerable amount of money in the box and informed B of this. B exercised great care in selecting employees, supervising access to the vault, and accounting for the keys. When A returned for the money, it was gone. He sued B for the money. Should he recover? Why?

6. O left his car in B's parking garage overnight, receiving a claim check stating that the garage is liable for damages up to $250 only. During the night, an intoxicated sailor stole the car and wrecked it. B's employee saw an intoxicated man in the garage that night. O brought suit against B, claiming damages in the amount of the value of his car. Is B liable? Why?

7. O brought his show horse to B's horse farm for breeding purposes and paid for this service. While there, the horse broke her leg and had to be destroyed. The horse had been skittish as a result of a prior surgical operation, but no one knows how the injury occurred. Is B liable to O for damages? Why?

8. B was planning to purchase a car from O, a dealer. Pending alterations in the car, O lent B an 11-year-old car. B had driven the car a distance of six miles when the enigne exploded, causing injuries to B. As the fire was being extinguished, B noticed that the clamp used to fasten the hose connecting the radiator and the engine block was off, and that alcohol was seeping onto the engine block. Is O liable for B's injuries? Why?

9. X Company shipped by railroad four carloads of apples from Seattle, Washington, to Washington, D.C. The apples arrived spoiled, and X brought suit, alleging that the negligence of the railroad caused the apples to arrive in improper condition. The owner of X Company, who was not present when the apples were inspected or shipped, testified that the apples were in good condition when delivered to the carrier. His testimony was based upon inspection reports of the Department of Agriculture, which were prepared six weeks prior to shpiment. Should the railroad be held liable? Why?

10. X took C Company's airline flight from New Orleans to Chicago. The plane passed through turbulence while making an intermediate stop in St. Louis, causing X to strike his head against the window trim and break his glasses. The predicted weather conditions included heavy thunderstorms, surface-wind gusts of 50 to 70 miles per hour, isolated tornadoes, and moderate to severe turbulence. C did not inform the passengers of the possibility of serious weather conditions before departing New Orleans. Is C liable for X's injuries? Why?

11. A left his TV set at B's shop for repairs. The shop had been broken into several times over the past few months, but B did not bother to install any additional burglary protection. During the night, A's set was stolen from B's shop. Can A collect from B for the loss of the set? Why?

12. A purchased construction equipment from the XYZ company. However, because delivery would take over a month, the company loaned A some used equipment. On demand A returned all but one truck, which had been destroyed. May the XYZ company recover the value of the truck from A? Why?

13. The XYZ company, duly licensed by the ICC as a motor carrier, delivered some wood shipped by B to A. The wood was watersoaked, although there was no evidence that this resulted from the XYZ company's negligence or fault. May A recover from XYZ? Why?

Real Property

1. The Nature of Real Property

The preceding chapters dealt with personal property; the following discussion concerns land and the rules of law concerning it. Real property includes not only land but also things permanently affixed thereto, such as buildings, fences, trees, and the like. The Uniform Commercial Code has special provisions relating to the sale of goods to be severed from the land. Its provisions apply to contracts for the sale of timber, minerals, or other items that are to be severed by the seller. However, transactions involving items to be severed from real estate are subject to any third-party rights as disclosed by real estate records.

Sometimes property has characteristics of both personal and real property. Such property is commonly referred to as *fixtures*. A fixture is an article of personal property that has become attached, annexed, or affixed to real property. It is personal property such as a furnace or air conditioner that has become part of the real property. The question as to whether or not a given item is a fixture and thus part of the real estate arises in several situations: (1) in determining the value of real estate for tax purposes; (2) in determining whether or not a sale of the real estate included the item of property in question; (3) in determining whether or not the item of property is a part of the security given by a mortgagor of the real estate to a mortgagee; and (4) in determining whether the item belongs to the owner of the building or the tenant on termination of a lease. Fixtures issues also arise under Article 9 of the

Uniform Commercial Code in disputes between secured creditors and persons with interest in the land.

If property is a fixture, (1) it is included in the value of real estate for tax purposes; (2) it is sold and title to it passes with the real estate; (3) it is a part of the security covered by a mortgage; and (4) it belongs to the landlord owner and not to the tenant on termination of a lease. The Uniform Commercial Code provides that no security interest exists in "goods incorporated into a structure in the manner of lumber, bricks, tile, cement, glass, metal work and the like." A party with a security interest in such goods loses it when the goods are incorporated into the real estate.

There are several tests used by courts in making the decision as to whether or not an item of personal property has become a part of the real estate so that it is a fixture: [1]

1. *Annexation test.*   The common law required the chattel to be "let into" or "united" to the land. The test of annexation alone is inadequate, for many things attached to the soil or buildings are not fixtures, and many things not physically attached to the soil or buildings are considered fixtures. For example, articles of furniture substantially fastened but capable of easy removal are not necessarily fixtures. Physical annexation may be only for the purpose of more convenient use. On the other hand, machinery that has been annexed, but detached for repairs or other temporary reason, may still be considered a fixture although severed.

Doors, windows, screens, storm windows, and the like, although readily detachable, are generally considered fixtures because they are an intergal part of the building and pertain to its function. The mode and degree of attachment and whether the article can be removed without material injury to the article, the building, or the land are often important considerations in determining whether the article is a fixture. Electric ranges connected to a building by a plug or vent pipe under the material-injury test are not fixtures, but the removal of wainscoting, wood siding, fireplace mantels, and water systems, including connecting pipes, would cause a material injury to the building and land, and these items are fixtures.

2. *Adaptation test.*   Because the annexation test alone is inadequate to determine what is a fixture, the adaptation test has been developed. *Adaptation* means that the article is used in promoting the purpose for which the land is used. Thus, if an article is placed upon or annexed to land to improve it, make it more valuable, and extend its use, it is a fixture. For example, pipes, pumps, and electric motors for an irrigation system are chattels that may be so adapted as to become fixtures. This test alone is not adequate, because rarely is an article attached or placed upon land except to advance the purpose for which the land is to be used.

[1] *Dean Vincent, Inc.* v. *Redisco, Inc.,* page 829.

3. *Intention test.* Annexation and adaptation as tests to determine whether a chattel has become realty are only part of the more inclusive test of intention. Annexation and adaptation are evidence of an intention to make a chattel a fixture. In addition to annexation and adaptation as evidence of an intention, the following situations and circumstances are also used from which intention is deduced: (a) the kind and character of the article affixed; (b) the purpose and use for which the annexation has been made; and (c) the relation and situation of the parties making the annexation. For example, the relation of landlord and tenant suggests that such items as showcases, acquired and used by the tenant, are not intended to become permanently part of the real property. Such property, called trade fixtures, is an exception to the general rule of fixtures because such items are generally intended to be removed by the tenant at the end of the lease. Trade fixtures retain their character as personal property.

2. Describing Real Property

Real property may be described by using (1) the metes and bounds system, (2) the congressional survey system, and (3) the plat system. The *metes and bounds* system establishes boundary lines by reference to natural or artificial monuments—that is, to fixed points, such as roads, streams, fences, trees. A metes and bounds description starts with a monument, determines the angle of the line and the distance to the next monument, and so forth until the tract is fully enclosed and described. Because surveyors may not always agree, the law of metes and bounds creates an order of precedence. Courses (angles) control over distances, and it is presumed that lines connect the monuments if the angle is wrong. Some metes and bounds descriptions use only courses and distances starting from a known point.

The term *congressional survey* refers to a system of describing land by using a known base line and principal meridians. The base line runs from east to west, and principal meridians run from north to south. Townships are thus located in relation to these lines. For example, a township may be described as 7 North, Range 3 East of the 3rd Principal Meridian. This township is seven townships north of the base line and three east of the 3rd principal meridian. The townships, then, would be divided into 36 sections, each section being one square mile. (There will be fractional sections, owing to the convergence of the meridians.) With the exception of the fractional sections, each section consists of 640 acres. Parts of the section are described by their location within it, as the drawing on page 821 illustrates.

A *plat* is a recorded document dividing a tract described by metes and bounds or congressional survey into streets, blocks, and lots. The land may thereafter be described in relation to the recorded plat by simply giving the lot number, block, and subdivision name. For example, Lot 8 in Block 7 of Ben Johnson's Subdivision in the City of Emporia, Kansas, might describe real property located in that municipality.

W 1/2 NW 1/4 80 acres	E 1/2 NW 1/4 80 acres	NE 1/4 160 acres
NW 1/4 SW 1/4 40 acres		N 1/2 SE 1/4 80 acres
	SE 1/4 SW 1/4 40 acres	5 A — NE 1/4 of SE 1/4 of SE 1/4 10 acres / 20 acres

3. Methods of Acquisition

Title to real property may be acquired in several different ways: (1) by original entry, called title by occupancy; (2) by transfer through, and with the consent of, the owner; (3) by judicial sale; (4) by possession of a party under claim of title for the period of the statute of limitations, usually 20 years, called adverse possession; (5) by will; (6) by descent, under intestacy statutes; and (7) by accretion, as when a river or a lake creates new land. Transfers by will and by descent are discussed in Chapter 45.

Original entry refers to a title obtained from the sovereign. Except in those portions of the United States where the original title to the land was derived from grants that were issued by the king of England and other sovereigns who took possession of the land by conquest, title to all the land in the United States was derived from the U.S. government. Private individuals who occupied land for the period of time prescribed by federal statute and met such other conditions as were established by law acquired title by patent from the federal government.

4. Transfer with the Consent of the Owner

The title to real property is most commonly transferred by the owner's executing a document known as a deed and delivering it to his transferee. A deed is generally a formal instrument under seal that is executed and acknowledged in the presence of a notary public. The deeds most generally used are *warranty* and *quitclaim* deeds. Many states have by statute prescribed the form for a deed.

A warranty deed and the statutory deeds convey the fee simple title to the grantee. Such deeds are called warranty deeds, because of the covenants on the part of the grantor by which he warrants (1) that, at the time of the making of the deed, he has fee simple title therein and right and power to convey the same; (2) that the property is free from all encumbrances, except those encumbrances enumerated therein; [2] (3) that the grantee, his heirs, or assigns will have the quiet and peaceful enjoyment thereof and that the grantor will defend the title to the property against all persons who may lawfully claim it. In most states, the warranties above are implied from the words written in the deed.

There may be circumstances under which the grantor would not wish to make warranties with respect to the title, and under such conditions, he may execute a quitclaim deed. Such a deed merely transfers all of the "right, title, and interest" of the grantor to the grantee. Whatever title the grantor has, the grantee receives, but the grantor makes no warranties. A quitclaim deed is used where the interest of the grantor is not clear, as for example where a deed will clear defective title.

The statutes of the various states provide the necessary requirements as to the form of the deed and the formalities necessary for proper execution of deeds. A deed is ordinarily required to be signed, sealed, acknowledged, and delivered. A deed is not effective until it is delivered to the grantee—that is, placed entirely out of the control of the grantor. This delivery usually occurs by the handing of the instrument to the grantee or his agents. Where property is purchased on installment contract, and occasionally in other cases, the deed is placed in the hands of a third party to be delivered by him to the grantee upon the happening of some event, usually the final payment by the grantee. Such delivery to a third party is called *delivery in escrow* and takes control over the deed entirely out of the hands of the grantor. Only if the conditions are not satisfied is the escrow agent at liberty to return the deed to the grantor.

In order that the owner of real estate may notify all persons that he has title to the property, the statutes of the various states provide that deeds shall be recorded in the recording office of the county in which the land is located. Failure to record a deed by a new owner who has not entered into possession makes it possible for the former owner to convey and pass good title to the property to an innocent third party, although the former owner has no right to do so and would be liable to his first grantee in such a case.

5.   Transfer by Judicial Sale

Title to land may be acquired by a vendee at a sale conducted by a sheriff or other proper official. Such sale is one made under the jurisdiction of a court having competent authority to order the sale. In order to secure the money to

---

[2] *Jones* v. *Grow Investment and Mortgage Company,* page 830.

pay a judgment secured by a successful plaintiff, it may be necessary to sell the property of the defendant. Such a sale is called a *judicial sale*. A *tax sale* is a public sale of land, owned by a delinquent taxpayer, for the collection of unpaid taxes. The purchaser at such sale acquires a *tax title*. A *mortgage foreclosure sale* is a proceeding in equity by which a mortgage secures, by judicial sale, money to pay the obligation secured by the mortgage. The word *foreclosure* is also applied to the proceedings for enforcing other types of liens, such as mechanic's liens, assessments against realty to pay public improvements, and other statutory liens. The character of title acquired by a purchaser at such judicial sale is determined by state statute.

6. Title by Adverse Possession

Title to land may be acquired under a principle known as *adverse possession*. Thus, a person who enters into actual possession of land and remains thereon openly and notoriously for the period of time prescribed in the statute of limitations, claiming title thereto in denial of, and adversely to, the superior title of another, will at the end of the statutory period acquire legal title. Actual knowledge by the true owner that his land is occupied adversely is not essential.[3] However, the possession must be of such a nature as to charge a reasonably diligent legal owner with knowledge of the adverse claim. It has also been held that adverse possession will not run against a municipal corporation.

In many states, adverse possession by one with color of title who pays the real estate taxes will ripen into title in a much shorter period than is required for adverse possession without color of title. For example, the usual period of the statute of limitations may be 15 or 20 years. The period for one holding with color of title may be five to seven years, depending on the state law involved. *Color of title* refers to a defective title but one that except for the defect would be a good title. For example, a mistake in a deed does not convey clear title, but does convey color of title. This use of adverse possession is very important in clearing defective titles. Errors can be ignored after the statutory period if there is adverse possession, color of title, and payment of taxes.

7. Title by Accretion

An *accretion* is the accumulation of land to the land of an owner by action of water. If land is added to that of an owner by the gradual addition of matter deposited by water, thereby extending the shore or bank, such increase is called *alluvion*. If a gradual increase in the land of an owner is caused by the receding of water, such increase is called *reliction*. A sudden deposit of land such as that caused by a flood does not make a change in ownership or boundary lines. However, if such change is slow and gradual by alluvion or

3 *Vetick* v. *Kula,* page 831.

reliction, the newly formed land belongs to the owner of the bed of the stream in which the new land is formed. If the opposite bank of a private stream belongs to different persons, it is a general rule that each owns the bed to the middle line of the stream. However, title to lands created by accretion may be acquired by adverse possession.[4] In public waters, such as navigable streams, lakes, and the sea, the title of bed of the water, in the absence of special circumstances, is in the United States. Accretion to the land belongs to the riparian owner; islands created belong to the government.

8. Covenants and Conditions

Quite often, the grantor places restrictions upon the use that may be made of the land conveyed. These restrictions may be contained in the deed, or they may be made applicable to several tracts of land by including them with the plat of a subdivision. Where such restrictions are contained in a plat, they are binding on all subsequent purchasers and they supplement the applicable zoning laws. The plat may, for instance, provide that the land shall be used exclusively for residential purposes and that the style and cost of the residence must meet certain specifications. Restrictions inserted in a deed are covenants or promises on the part of the grantee. If they purport to cover the land instead of the grantee, they are said to run with the land. Even though the grantee fails to include them in a subsequent deed made by him, a new owner is nevertheless subject to them. They remain indefinitely as restrictions against the use of the land. Such restrictions will not be enforced, however, if conditions have changed substantially since the inception of the covenants.

Most of these covenants are inserted in part for the benefit of surrounding property, and they may be enforced by the owners of such property. This is particularly true when the owner of land that is being divided into a subdivision inserts similar restrictions in each deed or in the plat. The owner of any lot that is subject to the restrictions is permitted to enforce the restrictions against the other lot owners located in the same subdivision. However, restrictions in a deed are strictly construed against the party seeking to enforce them. Doubts about restrictions are resolved in favor of freedom of the land from servitude as a matter of public policy.[5]

Occasionally, a covenant is inserted for the personal benefit of the grantor and will not run with the land. For example, if grantee A as part of the consideration covenants to repair a dam on land owned by grantor B, such covenant will not run with the land and place a duty upon a grantee of A. The promise does not touch and concern the land granted from A to B but is only a personal covenant for the benefit of B.

It should be noted that covenants and conditions that are designed to discriminate on the grounds of race, creed, color, or national origin are unconsti-

[4] *Rieke* v. *Olander,* page 832.
[5] *Walker* v. *Gross,* page 833.

tutional as a denial of equal protection of the laws. Such covenants were common at one time, and many are still incorporated in restrictions that accompany plats. When challenged, such restrictions have been held to be unconstitutional; they should today be considered a nullity without a court test case.

9. Proving Ownership

Ownership of real estate is a matter of public record. Every deed, mortgage, judgment, lien, or other transaction that affects the title to real estate must be made a matter of public record in the county in which the real estate is located. Deeds and other documents are usually recorded in the county's recorder's office. The records of the probate court furnish the public documents necessary to prove title by will or descent. Divorce proceedings and other judicial proceedings that affect the title to real estate are also part of the public record.

To establish title to real estate, it is necessary to examine all the public records that may affect the title. In a few states, lawyers actually examine all the public records to establish the title to real estate. Because it is extremely difficult for an individual or his attorney to examine all the records in most states, businesses have been formed for the express purpose of furnishing the appropriate records for any given parcel of real estate. These companies, known as *abstract companies,* are usually well-established firms that have maintained tract indexes for many years that they keep current on a daily basis. Upon request, these companies prepare an abstract of record that sets forth the history of the parcel in question and all matters that may affect the title. The abstract of title is examined by an attorney, who furnishes his written opinion concerning the title. The opinion will set forth any defects in the title as well as encumbrances against it. The abstract of title must be brought down to date each time the property is transferred or proof of title is required, in order that the chain of title might be complete. The opinion on title will be useless unless all court proceedings, such as foreclosures, partitions, transfers by deed, and probate proceedings, are shown. It should be noted that an attorney's opinion on title is just that—an opinion. If the attorney makes a mistake—for example—his opinion states that X has title to Blackacre, when in fact X does not have title to Blackacre—X does not have title. X's only recourse would be a malpractice suit against the attorney.

Because of limited resources, many lawyers are unable to respond in damages to pay losses caused by their mistakes. Therefore, the abstract of title and attorney's opinion as a means of protecting owners is in many cases not satisfactory. In addition, there may be title defects that do not appear of record and that the attorney does not cover in his title opinion. For example, an illegitimate child may be an unknown heir with an interest in property, as may be a spouse in a secret marriage. To protect owners against such hidden claims and to offset the limited resources of most lawyers, *title insurance* has been developed.

Title insurance is in effect an opinion of the title company instead of the lawyer. The opinion of the title company is backed up to the extent of the face value of the title insurance policy. If the purported owner loses his property, he collects the insurance just as if it were life insurance and the insured had died. Title insurance can cover matters beyond those in a title opinion. It has the financial backing of the issuing company, which is financially more secure than any law firm. Modern real estate practice uses abstracts and title policies rather than abstracts and title opinions. Title insurance companies usually maintain their own tract records, thus eliminating the cost of bringing the abstract down to date.

Another method of proving ownership that is used in some localities is known as the *Torrens System*. This system is based on a registered title that can be transferred only upon the official registration records. The original registration of any title usually requires a judicial determination as to the current owner, and then all subsequent transfers merely involve the surrender of the registered title, in much the same way that an automobile title is transferred. The Torrens System is a much simpler system to use after a title has once been registered. However, the high cost of obtaining the original registration has prevented the Torrens System from replacing abstracts and title policies as proof of title in most areas.

INTERESTS IN REAL PROPERTY

10.   Estates in Fee Simple

A person who owns the entire estate in real property is said to be an *owner in fee simple*. A fee simple title is that which is usually received by the grantee of a warranty deed.

11.   Life Estates

An owner of land may create, either by will or by deed, a *life estate* therein. Such a life estate may be for the life of the grantee, or it may be created for the duration of the life of some other designated person. Unless the instrument that creates the life estate places limitations upon it, the interest can be sold or mortgaged like any other interest in real estate. The buyer or mortgagee takes into consideration the fact that he receives only a life estate and that it may be terminated at any time by the death of the person for whose life it was created.

The life tenant is obligated to use reasonable care to maintain the property in the condition in which it was received, ordinary wear and tear excepted. It is his duty to repair, to pay taxes, and out of the income received to pay interest on any mortgage that may have been outstanding at the time the life estate was created. The life tenant has no right to make an unusual use of the property if such a use tends to deplete the value of the property, unless the property was so used at the time the estate was created. For instance, a life tenant would have no right to mine coal or to cut and mill timber from land in which he held only a life estate, unless such operations were being conducted or contemplated at the time the life estate was created.

12. Remainders and Reversions

After the termination of a life estate, the remaining estate may be given to someone else, or it may revert to the original owner or his heirs. If the estate is to be given to someone else upon the termination of a life estate, it is called an estate in *remainder*. If it is to revert back to the original owner, it is called a *reversion*. If the original owner of the estate is dead, the reversion comes back to his heirs. A remainder or a reversionary interest may be sold, mortgaged, or otherwise disposed of in the same manner as any other interest in real property.

13. Easements

An *easement* is a right, granted by the grantor to the grantee, to use real property. For example, the grantor may convey to the grantee a right of way over land, the right to lay drain tile under the land, or the right to extend utility lines in or over the land. If these rights of easement are reserved in the deed conveying the property, or granted by a separate deed, they pass along with the property to the next grantee and are burdens upon the land. Such easements may be made separate and distinct by contract and are binding only on the immediate parties to the agreement. If such right to use another's land is given orally, it is not an easement but a license, and the owner of the land may revoke it at any time unless it has become irrevocable by estoppel; whereas an easement given by grant cannot be revoked or taken away except by deed, as such a right of way is considered a right in real property. An easement, like title to property, may be acquired by prescription, which is similar to adverse possession.

Easements may also be obtained through judicial proceedings in certain cases. Since the law takes the position that an owner of land should be entitled to access to that land, owners of land that would otherwise be landlocked may be entitled to an easement by necessity. Such an easement is in effect one that is granted by the owner of the servient land (access that the easement passes) to the owner of the other land by implication.[6]

14. Multiple Ownership

Multiple ownership of personal property was discussed in Chapter 41. The principles discussed there are generally applicable to real estate also. Real

[6] *Burrow* v. *Miller,* page 834.

property may be owned by two or more unrelated persons, either as tenants in common or as joint tenants. The nature of the granting clause in the deed or will by which the title is transferred will determine which form of multiple ownership exists. A joint tenancy can be created only by a specific statement that the grantees shall hold title as joint tenants with the right of survivorship, and not as tenants in common. Without such a clause, the grantees are tenants in common. It should be kept in mind that on death, joint-tenancy property passes to the surviving joint tenant. Tenancy-in-common property passes to one's heirs or pursuant to the will of the deceased tenant in common.

If the grantees are related by marriage and the state law so provides, a conveyance to a husband and wife creates a *tenancy by the entireties*. A tenancy by the entirety in states that authorize such common ownership of real estate can exist only between husband and wife. A conveyance of real estate to a husband and wife in these states is automatically a tenancy by the entireties. Neither tenant can unilaterally sever or end the tenancy. It may only be terminated by divorce, a joint transfer to a third party, or a conveyance by one spouse to the other. The inability of either spouse to terminate the tenancy unilaterally is the primary difference between a joint tenancy and a tenancy by the entireties, as the basic characteristic of each is the right of survivorship. In most states that authorize tenancy by the entireties, not only is there a prohibition on one tenant's making a voluntary transfer of his or her share but there are also severe restrictions on the rights of creditors to collect an individual debt of one tenant of the property. For example, assume that H and W own their home as tenants by the entireties. X has a judgment for $10,000 against H alone. In most states, X could not cause a sale of the house to collect the debt. Of course, if X had a judgment against both H and W, he could collect from a judicial sale of the property.

Some states have abolished joint tenancies and tenancies by the entireties. The law has always favored tenancy in common. This favoritism has been seen in cases that resolve doubts about which tenancy was created in favor of tenancy in common. The right of survivorship has often been used to defeat the justifiable expectations of creditors and sometimes results in property's passing to other than those intended. Hence, there is pressure to abolish this form of ownership in many states.

Several of the southwestern and western states have what is known as *community property,* having inherited it in part from their French and Spanish ancestors. In these states, most property acquired after marriage other than by devise, bequest, or from the proceeds of noncommunity property becomes the joint property of husband and wife. Control of the property is vested primarily in the husband, and he is authorized, in most states, to sell or to mortgage it. The proceeds of the sale or mortgage in turn become community property. Upon the death of one of the parties, title to at least half the community property passes to the survivor. In most of the states, the disposition of the remainder may be by will or under the rules of descent.

REAL PROPERTY CASES

Dean Vincent, Inc. v. Redisco, Inc.
373 P.2d 995 (Or.) 1962

GOODWIN, J. This is a contest for priority between secured creditors. It arises out of the building of an apartment house. The plaintiff holds a first mortgage on the real property. The defendant, Redisco, Inc., holds a conditional sales contract and a second mortgage for the price of the floor coverings and the installation charges therefor. From a decree according priority to the plaintiff's mortgage, Redisco appeals. . . .

Carpeting, like electrical ornaments, plumbing bowls, hardware, and an infinite variety of other personal property, may or may not be so annexed to the real property as to lose its identity as personal property. . . . Whether such property retains its character as personal property or loses its separate identity in the real property depends upon a combination of factors. These factors are usually spoken of as annexation, adaptation, and intention. Intention is the most important and the most difficult factor to apply. It must be objective, and not some secret plan or mental reservation. . . .

Except for the semantical influence of cases concerning "rugs," there is no reason to say that installed floor covering is any more or less movable than installed plumbing fixtures, as either may be removed by experts, properly outfitted with tools, without doing appreciable harm to the freehold. See *Roseburg Nat. Bank v. Camp*, 89 Or. 67, where we said:

> The old rule that all things annexed to the realty become a part of it has been much relaxed. Annexation is not the sole test for determining whether a fixture is removable or irremovable. The line between removable and irremovable fixtures is sometimes so close and difficult to ascertain that it is impossible to frame a precise, unbending and infallible rule which can be applied to all cases. Each case must depend largely upon its own

special facts and peculiar circumstances.
. . .

The record shows that the trial judge had our former cases in mind when he ruled upon the question below. His ruling was based upon a careful consideration of the intention of the parties as disclosed by their behavior. He also considered the manner of installation (annexation), and the actual as well as the intended adaptation and adaptability of the material installed. Insofar as his evaluation of the facts is concerned, we can find no basis for reaching a different conclusion.

It may well be true that Redisco did not intend to give up the security title it retained under its conditional sales contract. However, no vendor is likely to intend to forfeit any security. The important question is not what the vendor intended, but what an objective bystander would make of the total factual situations. . . .

The controlling intent would seem to be that of the buyer and seller concerning the function of the floor covering. Did the parties intend that the floor covering be installed in the building, there to remain during its useful life, or did they intend to put down the floor covering to be used as such only until someone might see fit to take it out and use it elsewhere?

Since it is reasonable to assume that all parties expected the financial aspects of the transaction to proceed according to plan, the principal intention of the parties, from a functional point of view, was to put the carpet down and leave it there until it wore out. If such was their intention, then the nature of the order to the factory for custom-made carpet and the cutting and fitting within the seventy units is completely consistent with the view taken by the trial court that the floor covering was intended to become a permanent part of the building.

There is no particular policy or equitable reason to favor either party in a transaction of this character. To permit the conditional seller of merchandise to go into the building and remove part of the building is no better or no worse than to wash out the security of the seller by forbidding such relief. The parties were dealing at arms' length at all times.

The first mortgage is a prior lien on the building and its fixtures. The carpet is a fixture under all the tests of annexation, adaptation, and function intention. We concur in the trial court's analysis of the factual situation, and in its application of the law of fixtures.

Affirmed.

Jones v. Grow Investment and Mortgage Company
358 P.2d 909 (Utah) 1961

CALLISTER, J. Action to recover damages for breach of covenant against encumbrances. The trial court, sitting without a jury, awarded judgment to the plaintiffs and defendant appeals.

Defendant conveyed to plaintiffs by a statutory form of warranty deed a residential lot located in Orem, Utah County. The deed provided, in addition to the form language, that the described tract of land was "subject to deed restrictions and easements of record."

At the time of the conveyance there existed an open irrigation ditch which ran the length of the east side or rear of the lot. The ditch terminates at the southeast corner of the lot and an underground cement pipe commences at that point and runs westerly along the south of the lot. It is conceded that the ditch is a prescriptive easement and not of record. Plaintiffs attempted to fill the ditch but were prevented by the owners of the dominant estate.

Defendant makes numerous assignments of error, but, in the main, they boil down to the question as to whether the lower court erred in refusing to find that the ditch was an easement excepted from the covenant against encumbrances. It is the contention of defendant that the ditch was an open and visible easement of which the plaintiffs had notice or knowledge.

The trial judge made findings to the effect that the plaintiff, Larry L. Jones, made a personal inspection of the lot in the company of defendant's agent prior to the conveyance and saw the visible and open irrigation ditch which appeared to dead-end at the south line; that at

that time the ditch appeared to be abandoned and contained tree limbs, building refuse, weeds, and trash; that the cement pipe was completely covered and not visible on a casual inspection; that Larry L. Jones made inquiry of defendant's agent and was advised that the ditch could be filled in and the yard leveled; and that the ditch was an easement by prescription and not of record. The trial judge concluded that the existence of the ditch was a breach of warranty and entered judgment in favor of the plaintiffs in the amount of $750.

There is considerable conflict among the authorities as to whether or not a visible or known easement is excepted from a covenant against encumbrances. A distinction is made in some cases between encumbrances which affect the title and those which simply affect the physical condition of the land. In the first class, it is universally held that the encumbrances are included with the covenant, regardless of the knowledge of the grantee. Those encumbrances relating to physical conditions of the property have, in many instances, been treated as excluded from the covenant. Some of these cases are decided upon the theory that, whenever the actual physical conditions of the realty are apparent, and are in their nature permanent and irremediable, such conditions are within the contemplation of the parties when contracting, and are therefore not included in a general covenant against encumbrances.

There seems to be a tendency toward the proposition that certain visible public easements, such as highways and railroad rights of way, in open and notorious use at the time of the conveyance, do not breach a covenant against encumbrances. However, it still seems to be the general rule, particularly in those cases involving private rights of way, that an easement which is a burden upon the estate granted and which diminishes its value constitutes a breach of the covenant against encumbrances in the deed, regardless of whether the grantee had knowledge of its existence or that it was visible and notorious.

Ordinarily, parol evidence is inadmissible to show exceptions to express covenants in a deed or to show that a purchaser knew of the existence of an easement not referred to in the deed and took the conveyance subject to it. This rule should not be lightly disregarded for titles to real estate would be uncertain and recordation of deeds useless if their contents were to be determined by the testimony of witnesses.

Certainly, if the deed contains anything which would indicate that a known encumbrance was not intended to be within the covenant, the purchaser cannot complain that such an encumbrance was a breach of the covenant. However, with the possible exception of public easements that are apparent and in their nature permanent and irremediable, mere knowledge of the encumbrance is not sufficient to exclude it from the operation of the covenant. The intention to exclude an encumbrance should be manifested in the deed itself, for a resort to oral or other extraneous evidence would violate settled principles of law in regard to deeds.

In the instant case, the defendant's deed to plaintiffs was in the statutory form which carries with it a covenant that the premises conveyed are free from all encumbrances. The defendant saw fit to except from this covenant "deed restrictions and easements of record." Nothing is manifested in the deed that any other encumbrances were to be excluded. It would have been a simple matter for the defendant, as grantor, to exclude from the covenant the existing ditch. Under the deed, as written and delivered, a grantee could reasonably assume that the ditch was included within the encumbrance. The very purpose of the covenant is to protect a grantee against defects and to hold that one can be protected only against unknown defects would be to rob the covenant of most of its value. If from the force of the covenant it is desired to eliminate known defects, or to limit the covenant in any way, it is easy to do so. It must be concluded that the ditch was a breach of the covenant against encumbrances. . . .

Affirmed.

Vetick v. Kula
247 N.W.2d 637 (Neb.) 1976

CLINTON, J. This is a boundary line dispute between plaintiff-appellant Vetick, the owner of the northwest quarter of Section 6, Township 15 North, Range 4, West of the 6th P.M. Merrick County, and defendant-appellee Kula, the owner of the adjoining northeast quarter.

The evidence undisputedly establishes that a fence line had been the acknowledged boundary line between the adjoining properties for at least 56 years. Kula farmed the disputed tract for over 20 years, during which time he had grown crops, leveled the land, and put in an irrigation pump.

A Survey taken in the fall of 1975 established that the fence was not the actual boundary, the actual boundary lying east of the fence. It established that a tract of land of approximately 5.09 acres, which both parties thought belonged to Kula, was within the tract to which Vetick held record title. Vetick brought an action of ejectment to recover this tract and for a mandatory injunction requiring removal of the fence. Kula denied generally and pled a claim of title by adverse possession. The trial court entered judgment for Kula. We affirm.

The case of *McCain* v. *Cook,* 184 Neb.

147, 165 N.W.2d 734, is controlling. "It is the established law of this state that, when a fence is constructed as a boundary line between two properties, and parties claim ownership of land up to the fence for the full statutory period and are not interrupted in their possession or control during that time, they will, by adverse possession, gain title to such land as may have been improperly enclosed with their own." The above evidence fully establishes Kula's title under McCain rationale.

Affirmed.

Rieke v. Olander
485 P.2d 1335 (Kan.) 1971

PRICE, J. This law suit between two neighboring landowners was an action to quiet title to certain land immediately north of the Kansas (Kaw) River in Leavenworth county.

Judgment was for defendant Olander, and plaintiffs Rieke have appealed. . . .

The land in dispute was the *northeast* quarter of section 27-12-22 lying north of the river. Much of it was the result of accretion from periodic flooding—particularly the great flood of 1951. Section 22-12-22 is directly north of section 27, and defendant was the owner of the southeast quarter of that section. Plaintiffs were the owners of the northwest quarter of section 27. It will be seen, therefore, that the quarter in dispute is adjacent to and directly south of the quarter owned by defendant in section 22.

Considerable evidence—including maps and aerial photographs—was introduced. It would add nothing to this opinion to discuss the evidence at length. It established that as far back as the 1930s defendant's father and other predecessors in title had from time to time farmed portions of the property in dispute—depending upon the whims of the river—and that they had cut and removed timber from it and had pastured livestock on it. The "understanding" in the neighborhood was that defendant was the owner. A north-south fence running through the middle of the section had been erected and maintained, but plaintiffs had cut a portion of it.

At the conclusion of the trial the court found that defendant Olander and his wife were the owners of the disputed land—being the northeast fractional quarter of section 27— and all accretions lying directly south of such fractional quarter extending to the north bank of the river, and that they and their predecessors in interest had been in the open, adverse, continuous and exclusive possession of such land for more than fifteen years under claim of title—and entered judgment quieting their title to the same. In addition, defendant was granted a money judgment for $35.00 for cost of repairing the fence in question.

In this appeal plaintiffs contend the trial court erred in finding that defendant was the owner of the accretion land in dispute by virtue of adverse possession because he was not in continuous, actual, open and notorious possession of it, and that adverse possession could not extend constructively to the newly created accretion lands.

Our law of adverse possession is based on K.S.A. 60-503 which provides that no action shall be maintained against any person for the recovery of real property who has been in open, exclusive and continuous possession of such real property, either under a claim knowingly adverse or under a belief of ownership— for a period of fifteen years. The underlying principle of that statute has long been the law. It has been held many times that adverse possession is largely a matter of intent—coupled, of course, with overt acts on the part of claimant; that acts, in order to constitute adverse possession, are relative to the type and nature of the property and surrounding circumstances, taking into consideration the particular land, its condition, character, locality and appropriate use; and that whether one has acquired title by adverse possession is a question of fact to be determined by the trier of the facts, and the determination so made, if based on substantial evidence, is binding on appeal.

There was much substantial evidence before the trial court to support its finding of adverse possession, and such finding is not to be disturbed on appeal.

On this point—as stated above, plaintiffs also contend that any adverse possession could not extend constructively to the newly created accretion land. The rule is to the contrary. In 2 C.J.S. Adverse Possession § 205, p. 806, it is stated—

> *Accretion.* The title to an accretion follows the title of the riparian land to which it is attached regardless of whether the latter title was acquired by deed or adverse possession. Where accretions are formed to riparian lands held adversely, the title of claimant after the bar of the statute has attached carries

with it title to the accretions formed during the statutory period. This is true, however recent the formation.

To the same effect is 3 Am.Jur.2d Adverse Possession § 203, p. 293, where it is said that the ownership of accretions may be acquired by adverse possession and that one who has acquired title to land by adverse possession is entitled to any accretions thereto, regardless of the time of their formation.

Here it is clear that for many years more than the fifteen required, defendant and/or his predecessors in interest occupied, used and possessed the farm all the way to the north bank of the river, including accretions as they periodically occurred. . . .

We think that the conclusions reached by the trial court were correct, and the judgment is

Affirmed.

Walker v. Gross
290 N.E.2d 543 (Mass.) 1972

Plaintiffs sought a determination that a deed restriction providing that no part of their premises in Waltham shall be "used for any business purpose" (except for the sale of bait, fishing tackle, and sporting goods) does not prevent the use of the premises for an apartment house. The defendants are the other landowners in the neighborhood. The lower court held for plaintiffs, and defendants appealed.

WILKINS, J. . . . The defendants contend that the ownership and operation of an apartment building is a business and that, therefore, the plaintiffs' premises are to be used for a business purpose. In many respects and for certain purposes, ownership and operation of an apartment house is a business. . . .

The plaintiffs . . . point out that the restriction relates to the *use* of the premises for a business purpose and that clearly the tenants will use the premises for residential purposes. The issue thus is clearly drawn, namely, whether land used for an apartment house is "used for

any business purpose" within the meaning of those words in the restrictive covenant applicable to the plaintiffs' land.

The restriction itself gives no significant guidance on the question whether an apartment house use is a use for a business purpose. No extrinsic evidence has been presented to assist us in interpreting the intent of the parties in light of the material circumstances and pertinent facts known to the parties to the deed at the time it was executed.

We know only that the retail sale of fishing tackle and sporting goods was regarded as a business purpose because those activities were expressly excluded from the prohibition of the restriction. In these circumstances we are guided in reaching our conclusion by the general rule that restrictions in a deed are to be strictly construed against the party seeking to enforce those restrictions. Thus any doubt should be "resolved in favor of the freedom of land from servitude."

We hold that the use of the plantiffs' premises for apartment house purposes does not violate the deed restriction against the use of those premises for any business purpose. The plaintiffs' apartment building will be used by its occupants for residential purposes. The fact that the apartment house may be owned for income producing purposes does not make the *use* of the premises a use for a business purpose. If we were to accept the view asserted by the defendants, the renting of a single family house and the construction of such a house for sale would seemingly be in violation of this restriction as well. We think that the language of the restriction is concerned with the physical activity carried on upon the premises and not with the presence or absence of a profit making motive on the part of the landowner. . . .

The defendants basically object to the construction of an apartment house instead of single family houses. The restriction, however, does not speak in terms of allowing only single family houses, but rather it speaks in words of exclusion to prevent any use for business purposes. If use of an apartment house is, as we hold under the language of the deed restriction, not a use for a business purpose, the scope of the limitation contained in the deed obviously fails to reach the proposed apartment house use. What the grantor might have done if he had anticipated present circumstances need not concern us. Construed, as it must be, strictly against the parties asserting the applicability of the restriction, the restriction simply fails to do what the defendants assert.

Decree affirmed.

Burrow v. Miller
340 So.2d 779 (Ala.) 1976

JONES, J. This case involves the right of ingress and egress by the appellees Bruce and Wendell Miller and Lura Howell, over the appellants', Swansie and Maggie Burrow's, property. The trial Court, hearing the evidence . . . granted to the appellees the right of ingress and egress over the Burrow's property and enjoined the Burrows from interfering with the appellees' rights. We affirm.

The opposing parties are coterminous landowners. Their common source of title is J.C. Clark. The Howells' land is located south of the Burrows.

The Howells' right of ingress and egress has a road separating the lands of the Burrows and Flurrie Shotts. There was testimony to the effect that this road was the only one to the Howells' land and that it had been continuously used since 1948.

The trial Judge, hearing the evidence . . . determined that an implied easement or an easement of necessity existed. . . .

We find ample evidence in the record to support the trial Judge's findings of fact and that these facts satisfy the requirements necessary for the creation of an implied easement as set out in *Hamby* v. *Stepleton,* 221 Ala. 536, 130 So. 76 (1930). There the Court stated that two elements are necessary for the finding of an easement of necessity. First, the properties in controversy must come from a common source, which in this case is J.C. Clark. Secondly, there must be a reasonable necessity for the creation of this easement; that is, it must be the only practical avenue of ingress and egress. As Chief Justice Anderson, quoting from 9 R.C.L. § 31, Page 768, stated in *Hamby,* " 'Necessity does not of itself create a right of way, but it is evidence of the grantor's intention to convey one, and raises an implication of a grant. The presumption, however, is one of fact, and whether or not the grant is to be implied in a given case depends upon the terms of the deed and the facts in that case.' "

The deed referred to in the above quoted portion of *Hamby,* like the deed here, was not an express conveyance of the easement in question but the deed to the property to be served by the claimed easement. Chief Justice Anderson, in *Hamby*, continues:

> "Following [this] general rule . . . a similar right may be created by implied reservation, notwithstanding general covenants in a warranty deed. The underlying principle is that whenever one conveys property, he also conveys whatever is necessary to its beneficial use, coupled with the further consideration that it is for the public good that land should not be unoccupied."

It should be noted that this rule of "granting by implication an easement of necessity" is an exception to the general rule that an easement can only be created by deed, by prescription, or by adverse use for the statutory period.

The trial Judge, sitting as trier of the facts, determined, with ample supportive evidence, that an implied easement of necessity did indeed exist. Therefore, we affirm the decision of the trial Court.

Affirmed.

CHAPTER 43
REVIEW QUESTIONS AND PROBLEMS

1. X operated a ski lift on land leased from the state. The lease stipulated that the lift might not be removed under any circumstances. The state taxed the lift as personal property, and X sought to have it classified as real property. Who was correct? Explain.

2. X and Y had adjoining property. There was a plot on the boundary of their land that was in dispute as to ownership. X had been using the land for ten years as a garden. Y had a survey made that indicated the plot was his. During the ten years X had worked the land, Y had made no claim to ownership. X claims ownership by adverse possession. May X keep the land? (Assume a seven year statute.) Explain.

3. H married W and then conveyed a house previously owned by him to H and W as joint tenants. H later filed a declaration to sever the survivorship of joint tenancy and executed a will to preserve an interest in the house for a daughter by a prior marriage. Upon H's death, W claimed ownership of the property. Did W receive the property as surviving joint tenant? Explain.

4. X and Y owned adjoining property. There was a passway that crossed both these sections of land to connect two major highways. The passway had been used by X and Y for many years. Y put a gate across the passway on his land and refused to let X pass through. X sues to enjoin Y from blocking the road. Should he succeed? Explain.

5. A sold Whiteacre to B, inserting the provision in the deed, "Whiteacre shall not be transferred to any Negro or colored person." B sells Whiteacre to C, a black. May A obtain an injunction forbidding the sale or, in the alternative, damages from B? Why?

6. O owned land in a subdivision and planned to construct two apartment buildings on the land. Some residents of the subdivision brought suit for an injunction, contending that the construction would violate the covenants contained in the plat of the subdivision, which restricts buildings to single-family residences. O claimed that the covenant is no longer effective, because the land had been rezoned for apartment buildings. Should the restrictive covenant be enforced? Why?

7. For more than 20 years, X used a lane across land belonging to O for taking his cattle to pasture. During this time, O had always paid the taxes on the property. Is X entitled to an easement by prescription? Why?

8. C Company owned and operated a comprehensive television cable system that contained about 630 miles of feeder cable. The cable was annexed to telephone poles owned by the telephone company, under a lease that required removal if the telephone company should need the space for their own service needs. The county assessed the television cable system as real property, contending that the cable is a fixture under common law principles. Should the television cable be classified as a fixture? Why?

9. H and W, husband and wife, owned property as tenants by the entirety. H, who did not carry liability insurance, was involved in an automobile accident when his car negligently struck P's car. P brought suit, claiming damages from H. One month later, H and W conveyed the property to their sons, but no consideration was paid by the sons. P was unable to enforce her judgment against H's personal property and brought suit, contending that the conveyance should be set aside because it was fraudulent. Is P correct? Why?

10. A sold land to B, reserving to A the right of free egress and ingress over the private road. B sold the land to C, but the deed did not mention that C was taking the land subject to the easement contained in the conveyance by A to B. Is the easement effective against C? Why?

Real Estate Transactions

1. Introduction

Real property is involved in a variety of transactions, such as contracts of sale, contracts for a deed, and leases. There are three distinct interests in land—surface rights, mineral rights, and air rights. Some real estate transactions may involve only some of these rights. For example, a sale or lease of surface rights only may be executed. Such a contract would not affect either the air rights or the mineral rights. Similarly, a party may sell or lease part of or all mineral rights, such as the rights to oil and gas, without affecting the surface or the air rights. However, unless the instrument transferring the property clearly separates the interests in real property, all three interests are included in a sale or lease.

Contracts involving real estate are subject to the same general principles of contract law as are other contracts. The sections on offer and acceptance, consideration, and competent parties in Book Two on contracts noted several aspects of the law as it relates to contracts involving real estate. Your attention is also called to these sections and to the provisions of the statute of frauds relating to real estate contracts. It will be extremely helpful to review these subjects at this time.

THE CONTRACT FOR SALE

2. The Offer to Purchase

The typical contract for sale of real estate originates with an *offer to purchase* from the buyer to the seller. This offer to purchase is frequently obtained by a real estate broker or an agent. In most states, an offer to purchase may be prepared by a real estate broker without his being guilty of unauthorized practice of law. The offer is submitted to the seller for acceptance or rejection. In many cases, this offer upon acceptance is the only contract between the parties. In other cases, if it is accepted, the informal offer and acceptance are then taken to the buyer's or the seller's attorney for preparation of the actual contract. After acceptance of the offer to purchase by the seller, an enforceable contract does exist in most states. However, it is desirable to have an attorney prepare a formal contract that will set forth all aspects of the transaction. Unfortunately, this often does not occur. Real estate brokers cannot legally prepare such contracts in most states, since the preparation would constitute unauthorized practice of law.

Not only is it important that an attorney prepare an actual contract of sale after the offer and acceptance are complete; it is equally important that the other party's attorney review the contract so prepared. Each party to a real estate contract needs the advice of legal counsel for several reasons. First of all, historically, the doctrine of *caveat emptor* applied to real estate transactions. Although there is a trend developing toward holding that a contractor impliedly warrants new construction to be of workmanlike quality for a short period of time, it is clear that buyers should require that the contract include those express warranties relating to the quality of construction or the condition of the premises actually relied upon. For example, if there is to be a warranty that the premises are free of termites, the contract should so provide.

Second, it should always be recognized that the interests of the seller and the interests of the buyer are in conflict and adversary. For example, a seller is best served by a contract requiring delivery of a quitclaim deed, whereas a buyer's interests are best served by a contract calling for a warranty deed. It is neither wise nor ethical for one attorney to represent both parties to a real estate transaction, because of these conflicts of interest.

Third, several essential provisions are usually omitted from offers to purchase. Among the provisions that may not be found in offers to purchase are those relating to grace periods upon default, the terms of escrow, and forfeiture clauses. These and other provisions are discussed in the next section.

3.   Terms of the Contract

The typical real estate contract of sale, in addition to such obvious matters as describing the property and setting forth the price, the method of payment, and the date of possession, will contain provisions concerning the prorating of the real estate taxes, the assignment of hazard insurance, the selection of an escrow agent, and whether the proof of title will be made by furnishing an abstract or a title-insurance policy. The contract will also contain provisions concerning such contingencies as default by the buyer or destruction of the premises.

An escrow provision is desirable because a deed must be delivered during the lifetime of the grantor to be effective.[1] Because it is always possible for the grantor to die between the time of executing the contract and the delivery of possession and final payment, the deed is executed concurrently with the contract and is delivered to a third person, known as the escrowee or escrow agent, to be delivered to the grantee upon final payment. If the seller-grantor dies, the transaction can still be consummated, his death notwithstanding. Delivery of a deed in escrow will also cut off attaching creditors of the seller and pass title clear of any claims perfected after the escrow.

4. Closing the Transaction

After the execution of the contract and deed, these documents are placed in escrow until the date for delivery of possession and final payment. During the interim period, the buyer's attorney will seek to verify that the seller has marketable title to the property. This may be done by checking the original records, but it will usually be accomplished by use of either an abstract of title or a title report from a title-insurance company.

The *title report* is a letter committing the title company to issue a title policy upon payment of the premium. The preliminary commitment serves as a check of the records to date to make sure that the title is clear. If the buyer obtains a loan on the premises, the lender will also want its lawyer to examine the title and to prepare the mortgage documents. In addition, many contracts require the seller to furnish to the buyer a survey of the premises. Some contracts require the seller to prepare an affidavit concerning repairs and improvements to the premises within the applicable time period for merchant's liens. When the premises that are being sold have been constructed recently, an affidavit of the building contractor will be obtained showing what mechanic's liens exist, if any.

At the time of closing the transaction, a closing statement will be prepared showing all sums due the seller and all credits due the buyer. In the event that a mortgage is being assumed, it would serve as a credit to the buyer. Other credits would include abstract costs, documentary revenue stamps if required by state law, and taxes and special assessments that are liens. The buyer will pay the net amount due to the seller or to the escrow agent for delivery to the seller, and the escrow agent will deliver the deed to the buyer for recording. At the same time, the seller will deliver possession of the premises to the buyer, and the transaction will be completed.

5. A Contract for a Deed

There is a special type of real estate contract that is generally referred to as a *contract for a deed*. Such a contract is actually a conditional sale of real estate

[1] *Donnelly* v. *Robinson*, page 849.

in which the seller retains title to the property, and the buyer makes payments for an extended period of time. The buyer's right to a deed to the property is conditioned on his making all the payments. Such contracts are sometimes called *installment land contracts,* and they contain the usual provisions found in other real estate contracts. The purchaser has the risk of loss during the period of the contract unless there is a state statute to the contrary.[2] The escrow provision is absolutely essential in contracts for a deed because there is usually a period of several years between execution of the contract and delivery of the deed. In such cases, payments by the buyer are usually made to the escrow agent, so that at all times the escrow agent is aware of the status of the contract.

Two additional clauses in most installment land contracts are of particular significance. One of them is known as the *acceleration clause;* the other is known as the *forfeiture clause.* The acceleration clause allows the seller to declare the full amount of the contract due and payable in the event the buyer fails to make any of the payments or fails to perform any other of the contract's provisions as agreed. The default or forfeiture clause allows the seller, when the buyer is in default, to terminate the contract and to get the deed back from the escrow agent. The net effect of this clause is to allow the seller to keep all payments and improvements made as liquidated damages for breach of contract.

In contracts for a deed where the buyer has made substantial payments or in which he has a substantial equity, it is apparent that forfeiture of the contract might be inequitable. The principles discussed in Chapter 7 that apply to liquidated damages and forfeitures are also applicable to these contracts, because courts of equity abhor forfeitures. When the buyer's equity is substantial and forfeiture would be inequitable, a court upon proper application may prohibit the forfeiture and order the sale of the property with the proceeds being distributed to the seller to the extent necessary to pay off the contract and the balance being paid to the buyer.

No general rule can be stated to describe those cases in which a forfeiture will be allowed and those in which it will not. As a part of its equitable jurisdiction, the court will examine all the facts. If the buyer has made only a small payment, and it is not inequitable to do so, forfeiture will be permitted. However, if the buyer has made only a slight default with regard to the amount and time of payment, or has largely completed his payments, and the amount of the unpaid purchase price is much less than the value of the property involved, forfeiture will be denied. Forfeiture clauses are easily waived, and notice is usually required to reinstate the forefeiture provisions when default occurs without the forfeiture clause being enforced.

[2] *Briz-Ler Corporation* v. *Weiner,* page 850.

6. The Doctrine of Equitable Conversion

In contracts for the sale of real estate and in contracts for a deed, there is frequently a substantial time lag between the execution of the contract and its performance. During this period, one or more of the parties may die, the property may be destroyed, or the original parties may enter into other transactions, such as an assignment of the contract. The legal effect of these events and transactions is frequently affected by whether or not the interest of a party is real estate or personal property. For example, in community property states, a husband may transfer personal property without his wife's joining in the transfer, whereas if the interest is real estate, the wife must join in conveyance.

The interest of a party to a contract involving real estate is not determined by legal title to the property involved. Rather, the interest is determined by equitable principles and a doctrine known as the *doctrine of equitable conversion*. The doctrine of equitable conversion operates on the execution of a contract involving real estate and converts the interest of the seller who has legal title to real property to an interest in personal property, and it converts the interest of the buyer who owes money to an interest in real estate. In other words, after the execution of a contract, the law considers that the seller's interest in the transaction is personal property and that the buyer's interest is real estate. This result comes from the concept that equity regards the transaction as being completed.

To illustrate the foregoing, assume that X by will leaves all his real estate to Y and all his personal property to Z. X thereafter enters into a contract to sell his house for $10,000 and dies before receiving the money. Although X has legal title to the real estate at the time of his death, the doctrine of equitable conversion converts that to personal property, and the $10,000 would be paid to Z and not Y under X's will.

7. Housing Warranties

Historically, the doctrine of *caveat emptor* has been applied to real estate transactions, including the sale of new homes. Buyers have been allowed to rescind purchases on the ground of fraud or misrepresentation, but warranties have been found to exist only when specifically included in the contract of purchase. In other words, historically, the seller of housing did not by the simple act of sale make any warranties as to either the habitability of the structure or the quality of workmanship and materials.

In recent years, several states have changed the law as it relates to the sale of housing. The courts in these states have imposed liability on sellers and builders of housing by use of a variety of theories. Some courts have held that there is an implied warranty against structural defects similar to the implied warranty of fitness in the sale of personal property. These courts have held that there is no rational basis for differentiating between the sale of a newly constructed house by the builder-vendor and the sale of any other manu-factured product.[3] These courts usually have not extended the warranty against structural defects to the case where an individual builds a house him-self and later decides to sell it. Casual sales are not included because the warranty arises when the seller is in the business of selling housing.

Other courts have created an implied warranty that a home is built and constructed in a reasonably workmanlike manner and that it is fit for its intended purpose—habitation. In one case, there was no water supply, and the subdivider-seller was held liable for breach of this warranty. In another case, the air-conditioning system did not work properly, and the seller was held to have breached an implied warranty. In some cases, the buyer is entitled to damages. If the breach is so great that the home is unfit for habitation, of course rescission is the remedy. In this regard, it should be kept in mind that the theory of implied warranty does not impose on the builder an obligation to build a perfect house.

Congress is currently considering legislation that would require builders to furnish buyers of new homes with a warranty for a stated period. Such a warranty would require the builders to repair defects discovered within the period and to replace defective portions of the structure if necessary. Con-sumer protection is gradually being extended to housing.

8.   Buyer Protection

In 1968, Congress enacted the Interstate Sales Full Disclosure Act. The Commission on Uniform State Laws has prepared a Uniform Land Sales Practices Act, which as of this writing has been adopted by seven states. At least half of the other states have statutes dealing with promotional sales of real estate. The Office of Interstate Land Sales Registration of the Department of Housing and Urban Development (HUD) has promulgated tough dis-closure regulations relating to the sale of land by developers. These statutes and the regulations issued pursuant to them have resulted from the sale of "swampland to the unwitting public" and other abuses, especially in adver-tising. Land in tourist and vacation states has been the subject of extensive worldwide sales campaigns, many of which have been fraudulent. The promo-tional sale of such land in Arizona, California, Florida, and a few other states, as well as the Virgin Islands, usually involves a long-term contract with a low down payment.

There are three major problems that all the laws and regulations are de-signed to eliminate. First of all, most promotions represent that there will be many offsite improvements, such as swimming pools, golf courses, clubhouses, and lakes. These improvements are seldom in existence at the time of the sale, and safeguards are needed to ensure that they will be completed as represented.

Second, the seller must be able to convey clear title to the tract sold, in-cluding the presence of a means of ingress and egress and the usual required

---

[3] *Tavares* v. *Horstman,* page 851.

utilities such as electricity and water. Many new developments are "platted" out of desert land or swampland. Although the plats show streets and sewers, frequently these do not exist at the time of the sale. Moreover, the land is sometimes under "option" to the seller and is not actually owned. The law needs to ensure that the seller has title and that the land is or will be as platted, including streets and utilities.

Third, the buyer is often not in a position to inspect the property, and he must rely on the promotional material furnished by the seller. This puts the parties in an unequal bargaining position, and therefore the law seeks to require a full and fair disclosure to buyers by regulating the promotional material. Of course, these statutes are designed to prevent fraudulent practices.

The federal law covers interstate sellers of over 50 lots. The following rules illustrate the breadth and depth of the law and HUD's regulations:

1. Developers must give buyers an audited financial statement of the seller if its sales exceed 300 lots or $500,000 in value.

2. Developers must disclose, in a property report, past or pending disciplinary proceedings, bankruptcies, or litigation connected with land sales.

3. In the property report, buyers must be given information on environmental factors, such as "unusual noises," flooding conditions, odors, stagnant ponds, and sewage-treatment facilities.

4. The developer must state whether it is legally obligated and financially able to make the represented improvements.

5. The front page of the property report must be overprinted in red capital letters with: PURCHASERS SHOULD READ THIS DOCUMENT BEFORE SIGNING ANYTHING.

6. Ads must advise buyers to read the property report and must state whether the pictured improvements exist or are merely proposed. Ads must give the mileage to reference points, and it must be measured on roads accessible by car.

As can be seen from the foregoing, these laws are intended to furnish the facts to potential buyers so that the consuming public can make intelligent decisions. It is still legal to sell land that is under water—you just have to tell the buyer that it is under water. Although these laws may hurt sales to some extent, they do not greatly damage the legitimate businesses, of which there are many. Land sales abuses have not been eliminated by these laws, but substantial progress has been made.

LEASES

9. General Principles

A *lease* is a transfer of possession of real estate from a landlord (lessor) to a tenant (lessee) for a consideration called rent. A lease may be oral or written.

It may be expressed or simply implied from the facts and circumstances. A lease differs from a mere license, which is a privilege granted by one person to another to use land for some particular purpose. A license is not an interest in the land. A license to the licensee is personal and is not assignable.

A lease may be (1) a tenancy for a stated period; (2) a tenancy from period to period; (3) a tenancy at will; or (4) a tenancy at sufferance. As its name implies, a tenancy for a stated period lasts for the specific time stated in the lease. A lease is required to be in writing by the statute of frauds if the period exceeds one year. The lease for a stated period terminates without notice at the end of the period. It is not affected by the death of either party during the period. A lease of land for a stated period is not terminated by destruction of the improvements during the period unless the lease so provides. However, if a lease covers only the improvements on the land, destruction of them creates impossibility of performance.

A tenancy from period to period may be created by the terms of the lease. For example, a lease may run from January 1, 1979, to December 31, 1979, and from year to year thereafter unless terminated by the parties. Many leases from period to period arise when the tenant holds over after the end of a lease for a stated period. When such a holdover occurs, the landlord may evict the former tenant as a trespasser. However, the landlord may also elect to treat the tenant as a tenant, in which case the lease continues from period to period, with the period being identical to that of the original lease, not to exceed one year. The one-year limitation results from the language of the statute of frauds. The amount of rent is identical to that of the original lease.

Leases from year to year or from month to month can be terminated only upon the giving of proper notice. The length of the notice is prescribed by state statute. For example, most state statutes require 30 days' notice to terminate a month-to-month lease. They also usually require that the notice be given on rent day—the day the rent is due.

A tenancy at will by definition has no period and can be terminated by either party at any time upon giving the prescribed statutory notice. A few states do not require notice, but if legal action is necessary to obtain possession for the lessor, a time lag will be automatically imposed. A tenancy at sufferance occurs when a tenant holds over without the consent of the landlord. Until the landlord decides to evict him or to allow him to stay, he is a tenant at sufferance.

10. Rights of Lessees

The rights and duties of the parties to the lease are determined by the lease itself and by the statutes of the state in which the property is located. Several rights of lessees are frequently misunderstood. For example, the lessee is entitled to exclusive possession and control of the premises unless the lease provides to the contrary. The landlord has no right to go upon the premises except to collect rent. This means that the owner of an apartment building cannot go into the leased apartments and inspect them unless the lease specifically reserves the right to do so. Of course, at the end of the lease, the landlord may retake possession of the premises, and at this time he may inspect for damage. A landlord may also retake possession for purposes of protecting the property, if the tenant abandons the premises.

An important right in many leases of commercial property is the right that the tenant has to remove movable trade fixtures that he has installed during the lease period. However, the right of removal terminates with the lease, and unremoved fixtures become the property of the lessor.

Another important right of the tenant relates to his corresponding duty to payment. The duty to pay rent is subject to setoffs for violations of the provisions of the lease by the landlord. The duty to pay rent is released in the event of an eviction, actual or constructive. Constructive eviction occurs when the premises become untenantable due to no fault of the tenant or because some act of the landlord deprives the tenant of quiet enjoyment of the premises. For example, assume that X rents a basement apartment. A spring rain floods the apartment and makes it uninhabitable. The tenant has been constructively evicted. He may move out, and his duty to pay rent is released. Failure to vacate the premises is a waiver of constructive eviction grounds, however. A tenant who continues in possession despite grounds for constructive eviction must continue to pay rent, unless this duty is relieved by statute. Some states and cities in recent years have enacted such laws in an attempt to force landlords to maintain their property in a tenantable condition. Such laws protect low-income tenants from slum landlords.

As a general rule, a tenant has a right to sublease the premises or to assign the lease to a third party without the consent of the lessor. However, many leases contain provisions prohibiting subleases and assignments. Such provisions are strictly construed against the lessor in cases of ambiguity or doubt about the tenant's rights.

11. Warranty of Habitability

In recent years, courts have been called upon to decide if there is an implied warranty of habitability in a lease. (This is similar to the issue of warranties on the sale of new housing and is part of the broadened protection given the consuming public.) Some courts have held that in all housing leases, there is an implied warranty of habitability. One court held that the fact that a tenant knew of a substantial number of defects when he rented the premises and that rent was accordingly reduced did not remove the tenant from protection of the warranty. The court reasoned that permitting that type of bargaining would be contrary to public policy and the purpose of the doctrine of implied warranty of habitability. In determining the kinds of defects that will be deemed to constitute a breach of warranty and habitability, several factors are considered. Among the common factors are (1) the violation of any applicable housing code or building or sanitary regulations, (2) whether the nature of the deficiency affects a vital facility, (3) the potential or actual effect upon safety and sanitation, and (4) whether the tenant was in any way responsible for the defect. A breach of this warranty may allow a tenant to terminate the lease. In addition, it may serve as a defense to a suit for rent and as a means to obtain a rent reduction.[4]

Defects in vital portions of the premises that may affect health are more important than defects in extras such as swimming pools or recreational facilities. Defects in the latter are not likely to render the premises uninhabitable. It should also be kept in mind that not all states recognize that there is an implied warranty of habitability in leases. Even though holding that such a warranty exists is a definite trend in the law, it is not universal.

12. Rights of Lessors

A landlord is entitled to possesion of the premises upon termination of the tenancy. If the tenancy is lawfully terminated, the right to possession is absolute. The motive of the landlord in termination is usually immaterial.[5] Of course, a landlord may not discriminate in leasing or termination on the basis of race, color, creed, sex, or national origin.

A landlord is entitled to recover from either the tenant or a third party for injuries to the property. In addition, in many states and by the express terms of many leases, the landlord has a lien for unpaid rent on the personal property of the tenant physically located on the premises. This lien right is exercised in a statutory proceeding known as *distress for rent*. By following the prescribed procedures, the landlord is able to distrain or physically hold personalty on the premises until the rent is paid. If not paid, the tenant's personal property may be sold pursuant to court order. The proceeds of the sale, after deducting court costs, are applied to the rent.

It is common practice for a landlord to require that the tenant deposit a stated sum of money, such as one month's rent, as security for the lease. This security deposit covers nonpayment of rent and possible damage to the premises. Many landlords have been reluctant to return these security deposits, contending in most cases that damages were present requiring repairs. As a result, many tenants have refused to pay the last month's rent, demanding that the security deposit be applied. Such practices by landlords and tenants have created a great deal of animosity and litigation. To alleviate this problem, the legislatures of many states have passed laws governing lease security deposits. Such laws usually require that the landlord pay interest on the

[4] *Timber Ridge Town House* v. *Dietz,* page 854.
[5] *Aluli* v. *Trusdell,* page 855.

deposits, and itemize the cost of any repairs that were made from the deposit. They further require the landlord to return the deposit promptly and prohibit the landlord from using it to repair conditions caused by normal wear and tear. In the event a tenant is required to sue the landlord to recover the deposit, the tenant is entitled to collect attorney's fees. Finally, under these statutes, the tenant usually is not allowed to set off the deposit against the last month's rent.

A tenant is estopped from denying his landlord's title and has a duty to redeliver the premises upon expiration of the lease in the same condition as received, ordinary wear and tear excepted. Unless the lease or a statute provides to the contrary, the lessee has the duty to make ordinary repairs but not to make improvements. Conversely, the landlord is not bound to make repairs unless the lease expressly so provides. Moreover, even if an express covenant to repair has been given the tenant by the landlord, the usual construction is that the covenants of a landlord and a tenant are independent, and therefore a tenant may not treat a landlord's failure to repair as a basis for stopping rent payments.

13. Liability to Third Persons

Difficult legal questions arise in cases involving the landlord's and tenant's liability for injuries to persons on the premises. As a general rule, a landlord makes no warranty that the premises are safe or suitable for the intended use by the tenant, and third persons are on the premises at their own peril. A landlord owes no greater duty to a tenant's guests than is owed to the tenant.[6] A landlord does have a duty to give notice of latent defects of which he has knowledge. Some states add, for the purposes of this notice rule, unknown defects of which he should have knowledge in the exercise of ordinary care.

The owner of business property, knowing that business invitees of the lessee will be constantly entering it to transact business, has an increased responsibility. This increased responsibility is known as the "public use" exception to the general rule. The basis of the exception is that the landlord leases premises on which he knows or should know that there are conditions likely to cause injury to persons entering on them, that the purpose for which the premises are leased involves the fact that people will be invited upon the premises as patrons of the tenant, and that the landlord knows or should know that the tenant cannot reasonably be expected to remedy or guard against injury from the defect. Thus, a landlord of a business owes a higher duty than does the landlord of essentially private premises. Moreover, landlords of business premises have a duty to care for the common areas. In such cases, they have a duty to inspect, repair, and maintain common areas in a reasonably safe condition.

[6] *Amburgy* v. *Golden,* page 857.

Many suits against lessors by third persons result from falls on the premises. These falls are often associated with ice and snow or waxed floors. As a general rule in most states, a landlord has no duty to remove ice and snow. The landlord has a duty to use reasonable care, and, in the absence of an agreement, most courts hold that this does not require removal of ice and snow. However, if the landlord undertakes to remove snow and ice, he must do so with ordinary care. This includes the duty to take into account dangerous conditions caused by the subsequent thawing and freezing of snow placed near the walkway. This duty to use reasonable care in removing ice and snow has been found to exist by many courts when the lease is a business one. This is part of the "public use" exception previously noted.

14. Condominiums

A condominium is an individually owned apartment or town house in a multi-unit structure, such as an apartment building, or in a complex. It is a method of owning and transferring property that possesses some of the characteristics of a lease and some of a contract of sale. In addition to the individual apartment or townhouse, the owner has an undivided interest in the common areas of the building and land, such as hallways, entrances, yard, and recreation areas. Thus, the deed to a condominium covers the housing unit involved and an undivided fractional interest in the common areas. There is usually an organization to operate the common areas, to make repairs, and to make improvements. Each owner of a unit has one vote in the management of this organization. Taxes are usually prorated on the common areas by using the fractional proportion of the undivided interests. Condominiums are of growing importance in metropolitan areas, and a determination of an owner's rights requires a study of not only the law of real property but also the law of business organizations.

There is a distinction between a *condominium* and a *cooperative* insofar as the ownership of real estate is concerned. A cooperative venture may involve an activity such as a retail store or it may involve the ownership and operation of a residential development. If a person buys an interest in a cooperative, he is purchasing a share of a not-for-profit corporation. Strictly speaking, the owner of an interest in a cooperative does not own real estate. He owns personal property—his share of the cooperative. The cooperative would pay taxes and upkeep out of the assessments to its members. A condominium contains multiple units for taxing purposes; the cooperative is a single unit. The same may be said for the financing. Each owner of a condominium may mortgage his or her own portion. In a cooperative, if there is financing, there will be only one mortgage. In both the condominium and the cooperative, there is a special form of business organization to coordinate the operation of the property.

REAL ESTATE TRANSACTIONS CASES

Donnelly v. Robinson
406 S.W.2d 595 (1966)

James Egan and Bessie Egan had a life estate in a tract of land and Melford Egan owned the remainder. An agreement between the life tenants and the remainderman provided for a fifty-fifty division of the proceeds of any sale of the property, including a sale in condemnation proceedings. On October 5, 1960, the parties executed a contract of sale and deed to the state of Missouri which provided for a sale price of $30,500. The contract and deed were placed in escrow to be held until a check in the amount of the purchase price was received from the state. The check was received November 9, 1960. James and Bessie Egan were killed October 25, 1960, and their estates claim one-half of the proceeds. Melford Egan contends that he is entitled to all of the proceeds as the remainderman. The lower court found for the estates, and the remainderman appealed.

WOLFE, J. . . . In pressing their claim for the one-half of the purchase price paid to the administrators of the life tenants' estates the appellants intervenors first assert that title had not passed to the State of Missouri at the time of James and Bessie Egan's deaths because there was no delivery of the deed to the State of Missouri. Among other cases relating to delivery, the appellants cite *Klatt* v. *Wolff,* Mo., 173 S.W.2d 933, in which this court restated the established rule that a deed, to be operative as a transfer of ownership of land, must be delivered to the grantee or someone for him. In *Harrison* v. *Edmonston,* Mo., 248 S.W. 586, also cited, this court restated the necessity of delivery of a deed with the intention to part with control over it, in order to pass title.

The respondents do not question these rules but they rely, as the trial court did, upon the effect of the delivery of the fully executed deed dated October 5, 1966, to the Wayne County Bank. The bank was to deliver this deed to the Missouri Highway Department upon payment of the purchase price. The purchase money was paid; the deed was delivered and the respondents contend that the trial court properly held that the date of the concluded transaction related back to the date of the deed and its delivery to the bank. After so holding the court logically divided the sum paid for the property in accordance with the interests of the grantors existing at the time of the execution and delivery to the bank.

The court invoked the rule that upon final delivery by a depository of a deed deposited in escrow the instrument will be treated as relating back to, and taking effect at the time of, the original deposit in escrow. This shall apply even though one of the parties to the deed dies before the second delivery. This relation back doctrine has wide and general acceptance. Its roots are ancient, for as far back as the Sixteenth Century we find the Perryman's Case, 77 Eng.Rep. 181, 1. c. 183, in which it was said:

> . . . if a man delivers a writing (d) as an escrow to be his deed on certain conditions to be performed, and afterwards the obligor or obligee dies, and afterwards the condition is performed, the deed is good, for there was *traditio inchoata* in the life of the parties, *sed postea consummata existens* by the performance of the condition takes its effect by force of the first delivery, without any new delivery. . . .

The same doctrine was pronounced by this court in *Savings Trust Co. of St. Louis* v. *Skain,* 345 Mo. 46, 131 S.W.2d 566, 1. c. 570, wherein it was said:

> . . . The relation of vendor and purchaser exists as soon as a contract for the sale and purchase of land is entered into.

Equity regards the purchaser as the owner and the vendor as holding the legal title in trust for him: . . . This equitable principle may be invoked in actions at law: . . . and that even though the purchaser has not been put in possession. . . .

There are also numerous cases in which the rule is applied to deeds given to one other than the grantee to be unconditionally delivered to the grantee upon the grantor's death.

Appellants concede that the "relation back doctrine" is a recognized rule in Missouri but contend that it should only be used for the protection of the buyer. They assert that upon

the death of the life tenants they as remaindermen held title and the life tenants had nothing to convey. . . .

When James and Bessie Egan signed the deed with Melford and Alberta Egan all parties disposed of their interest in one deed with full agreement and knowledge of what each would receive. For them it was a completed transaction. It therefore appears that the application of the doctrine of relation back to these facts is within the intended use of the doctrine as an equitable means to effectuate the intent of the parties.

Affirmed.

Briz-Ler Corporation v. Weiner
171 A.2d 65 (Del.) 1961

In October 1954, plaintiff entered into a contract to purchase a four-story hotel containing a bar and liquor store together with equipment and fixtures from the defendants. Plaintiff paid $11,500 down and agreed to pay the balance of $102,500 plus interest at 6 percent in monthly installments of $865. Plaintiff also deposited sums for taxes and insurance with the escrow agent.

In December 1957, a fire occurred on the premises causing considerable damage. At this time a substantial balance was still owing on the total purchase price. After the fire plaintiff remained in possession of the premises and operated its first floor bar and liquor store.

Plaintiff subsequently commenced negotiations with the insurance company to settle for the loss caused by the fire. Ultimately, plaintiff settled with the insurance company for a payment of $31,454.78, which sum was insufficient to meet the cost of $107,000 required to restore the entire structure in accordance with the City Building Code.

In August 1958, a dipute arose between the parties, the defendants claiming that the plaintiff was in default. Shortly thereafter plaintiff abandoned the premises, leaving all the equipment there, and defendants applied the

entire amount of the settlement to repair the building by reducing it to one level for use as a restaurant, bar and grill, and package liquor store.

Plaintiff claims that it should be repaid all the money paid by it pursuant to the installment contract because defendants cannot now deliver what they contracted to deliver, viz., a four-story hotel structure. In the alternative, plaintiff claims that it is entitled to an equitable lien on the premises, or on the proceeds of insurance, in the full amount paid by it under the contract.

The lower court dismissed plaintiff's complaint, and plaintiff appeals.

WOLCOTT, J. . . . The basic question involved in this appeal is whether or not a loss occasioned by fire to premises under an installment contract of sale shall fall upon the seller or the purchaser. Presumably, if the loss as a matter of law falls upon the seller, then plaintiff should be entitled to relief of some nature. If, on the contrary, the loss falls upon the purchaser, the complaint was properly dismissed.

The rule followed in a majority of American jurisdictions is that an executory contract for the sale of lands requiring the seller to execute a deed conveying the legal title upon payment of the full purchase price works an equitable conversion so as to make the purchaser the equitable owner of the land and the seller the equitable owner of the purchase money. The result is that the purchaser, the equitable owner, takes the benefit of all subsequent increase in value and, at the same time, becomes subject to all losses not occasioned by the fault of the seller. . . .

The basic reason for the rule is that if a party by a contract has become in equity the owner of land and premises, they are his to all intents and purposes and, as such, any loss caused to them must be borne by him. . . .

In the case at bar the plaintiff entered into possession of the premises sold upon execution of the contract. Thereafter, it exercised all the rights ordinarily incident to ownership. We think that under any view of the rule of equitable conversion of title to real estate the fact that the purchaser has possession of the land sold and exercises sole control over it requires that any loss occasioned accidentally to the premises must fall upon him. . . .

Plaintiff argues that the destruction of the building made it impossible for the defendants to convey what they had contracted to convey, viz., the premises as they existed before the fire. There is, however, no provision in the contract providing for such event. It follows, therefore, that plaintiff wants us to hold, with a small minority of the States, that destruction of the subject matter makes inoperative the doctrine of equitable conversion. Such a view, however, is a rejection of the doctrine which we have found to be the law of this State, at least under the circumstance of admitting the purchaser into possession. It follows, therefore, that plaintiff upon the execution of the contract for the purchase of the Hotel Grande became the equitable owner of it and, as such, subject to losses occasioned other than by the fault of the defendants.

When this loss by fire occurred, the plaintiff as equitable owner became entitled under the law to two options. It could require either that the proceeds of the insurance be credited on the purchase price thus reducing its obligation, or it could require that the proceeds of the insurance be used to repair and restore the damaged premises. While it does not clearly appear that plaintiff made any election, it is clear beyond question that the entire proceeds of the insurance and more were applied by the defendants to the repair of the premises. Plaintiff therefore obtained that to which it was entitled. . . .

The judgment below is affirmed.

Tavares v. Horstman
542 P.2d 1275 (Wyo.) 1975

RAPER, J. . . . We are going to affirm the trial court and discuss three primary issues in the following light: (1) The rule of *caveat emptor* (let the buyer beware) does not apply to the sale of new housing by a builder-vendor to the vendee; (2) There is an implied warranty of liability that goes with the sale of new housing by a builder-vendor to the vendee; (3) Damages are recoverable by a vendee for negligent design and construction of new housing by the builder-vendor. . . .

The defendant, a land developer and builder, sold the plaintiffs a tract of land; the defendant built a home for plaintiffs on the property under an oral agreement with no express warranty. A warranty deed with only the usual covenants of title was delivered. Within a little over a year, the septic tank system backed sewage to a depth of about three inches into the plaintiffs' basement before it was discovered. A plumber was called; after pumping out the tanks a couple of times, he advised that something would have to be done about the system. Defendant was called and informed of this nasty predicament. He dug down to the discharge pipe, perforated the line and let the raw sewage flow into an open trench. Nothing further was done. Plaintiffs called him to do something further but he said he could not work on it because he had to go on a vacation. The stinking situation was so deplorable that plaintiffs called in an experienced septic tank contractor. The system had to be rebuilt because of its inadequacy. The soil in the area of the drainage field was of tight gumbo so a particular design and manner of installation was necessary. The contractor who rebuilt the system testified that the problems with the one he replaced were several. The defendant had installed foundation drainage pipe all around the house and constructed it to discharge into the septic tank system, causing an overload of the sewage disposal scheme. There was not enough capacity for the size home it was to serve. The excess water caused the drainage field to waterlog, backed effluent into the tanks, killed the bacterial actions supposed to be taking place there and, in turn, blocked the flow of sewage from the house. Having no place else to go, the noxious wastes covered the basement floor. Plaintiffs expended $2,083 to correct the condition. . . .

Judgment for plaintiffs in the sum of $2,083 was entered (by the trial court). . . .

It appears that the rule of the past and still existing in a few jurisdictions is that no implied warranties of quality in the sale of realty existed in the common law. The doctrine of *caveat emptor* reigned supreme. Cracks, however, began to appear in that tenet with respect to the sale of new housing. Favorite references used in the cases and work of scholars come from the thoughts of Cardozo, *The Nature of the Judicial Process* (1921), p. 152:

> . . . If judges have woefully misinterpreted the *mores* of their day, or if the *mores* of their day are no longer those of ours, they ought not to tie, in helpless submission, the hands of their successors.

Later, Cardozo in his treatise, *The Growth of the Law* (1924), pp. 136–7, refined the idea to:

> . . . A rule which in its origin was the creation of the courts themselves, and was supposed in the making to express the *mores* of the day, may be abrogated by courts when the *mores* have so changed that perpetuation of the rule would be violence to the social conscience. . . .

Since World War II homes have been built in tremendous numbers. There have come into being developer-builders operating on a large scale. Many firms and persons, large and small operators, hold themselves out as skilled in home construction and are in the business of building and selling to individual owners. Developers contract with builders to construct for resale. Building construction by modern methods is complex and intertwined with governmental codes and regulations. The ordinary home buyer is not in a position, by skill or training, to discover defects lurking in the plumbing, the electrical wiring, the structure itself, all of which is usually covered up and not open for inspection.

A home buyer should be able to place reliance on the builder or developer who sells him a new house. The improved real estate the average family buys gives it thoughtful pause not only because of the base price but the interest involved over a long period of time. This is usually the largest single purchase a family makes for a lifetime. Some may be able to pay cash but we cannot single out that buyer in the formulation of a rule.

It ought to be an implicit understanding of the parties that when an agreed price is paid that the home is reasonably fit for the purpose for which it is to be used—that it is reasonably fit for habitation. Illusory value is a poor substitute for quality. There is no need for the buyer to be subjected to the harassment caused by defects and he deserves the focus of the law and its concern. The significant purchase of a new home leads logically to the buyer's expectation that he be judicially protected. Any other result would be intolerable and unjust, as the cases which follow demonstrate.

One of the first courts in the United States recognizing the worthiness of concern by the courts in this area was the Supreme Court of Colorado. In *Carpenter* v. *Donohoe,* 1964, 154 Colo. 78, 83–84 . . . it was held that where a home is the subject of sale, there are implied warranties that it was built in a workmanlike manner, that applicable building codes were complied with and it is suitable for habitation. The rule of *caveat emptor* was shoved aside. In that case, within a short time after the plaintiffs moved in, the walls began to crack and a wall of the basement began to cave in. It is startling that in such a situation a seller would have the courage to plead *caveat emptor* but he did; the trial court bought it but the supreme court reversed.

In [another case] . . . the Texas court held that *caveat emptor,* as applied to new housing, was outdated and out of harmony with modern home buying practices, so, therefore, the builder-vendor impliedly warrants that such a house was constructed in a good, workmanlike manner and was suitable for human habitation. The court said:

> The *caveat emptor* rule as applied to new houses is an anachronism patently out of harmony with modern home buying practices. It does a disservice not only to the ordinary prudent purchaser but to the industry itself by lending encouragement to the unscrupulous, fly-by-night operator and purveyor of shoddy work.
> . . .

In [an Idaho case, the court] . . . said:

> The implied warranty of fitness does not impose upon the builder an obligation to deliver a perfect house. No house is built without defects, and defects susceptible of remedy ordinarily would not warrant rescission. But major defects which render the house unfit for habitation, and which are not readily remediable, entitle the

buyer to rescission and restitution. The builder-vendor's legitimate interests are protected by the rule which casts the burden upon the purchaser to establish the facts which give rise to the implied warranty of fitness, and its breach. . . .

The cases assessing liability to the vendor under an implied warranty or negligence, or both, continue to pile up. The rule even extends to personal injuries suffered as a result of defective construction. It would appear that the desires expressed in 7 Williston on Contracts (3d Ed.) § 926A, p. 818, have come to pass, when it was said early in the development of the law we now approve:

> It would be much better if this enlightened approach were generally adopted with respect to the sale of new houses for it would tend to discourage much of the sloppy work and jerry-building that has become perceptible over the years.

The wildfire spread of cases we cite demonstrates the need for the approach to which Williston refers. . . .

In summary, then, we hold that under the circumstances of this case, the rule of *caveat emptor* no longer protects the builder-vendor because it is unrealistic in the light of the change that has emerged in the morals of the marketplace. That doctrine was based upon an arms-length transaction between seller and buyer and contemplated comparable skill and experience, which does not now exist; they are not in an equal bargaining position and the buyer is forced to rely on the skill and knowledge of the builder.

We further hold along with a vast majority of courts that where a vendor builds new houses for the purpose of sale, the sale carries with it an implied warranty that it is constructed in a reasonably workmanlike manner and is fit for habitation. For the moment, we confine this holding to the sale of new housing.

We finally hold that a buyer may proceed not only upon the basis of implied warranty but upon the basis of negligent design and construction. There obviously can be and probably is in some cases an indistinguishable overlap but an implied warranty would embrace a wider range of causes and be less restrictive in proof.

Affirmed.

Timber Ridge Town House v. Dietz
338 A.2d 21 (N.J.) 1975

KING, J. . . . . This is an action for summary dispossession alleging a default in rental payments for the month of October 1974. The monthly rental is $285 for this 3-bedroom, 2½-bath, 2-story garden apartment or townhouse in Lindenwold. Defendants withheld rent due for one month, depositing the funds in their attorney's escrow account. Thereafter the monthly rentals were deposited in escrow pending this court's decision. . . .

Defendants raise so-called habitability defenses and request an abatement of a portion of the rent. The questions are novel because the allegedly affected area is external to the actual leased premises. . . .

Timber Ridge was designed as a family community. . . . A brochure used in the rental of the properties was placed in evidence. Defendants leased the property in December 1973 in partial reliance upon the representations in the brochure. The brochure described the project as: "Quietly nestled in a gently rolling wooded glen . . . [offering] serene living in a beautiful country setting with on-site recreational facilities including a swimming pool and childrens' play area . . . and individual patio facing a spacious landscaped court yard." The written lease agreement executed on December 1, 1973 for a term of one year refers to the premises as "the apartment consisting of 5 rooms and baths."

Tenants here seek to extend the doctrine of implied warranty of habitability beyond the actual physical structure. . . . There is no doubt that the external conditions detract substantially from the tenants' living pleasure. Defendants' townhouse is immediately adjacent to the area where a large retaining wall is being constructed. Construction has been in progress for four months, and from the court's observation may continue for at least several more months. These defendant tenants are almost uniquely affected by the construction because of their proximity to the conditions. No other occupied unit is affected in such a severe manner. Their "individual patio facing a spacious landscape court yard" is unusable, as it is surrounded and overflowed by mud and water. The mud flows over the walkway connecting defendants' main entranceway and the common parking area. The parking area itself, especially where defendants or their visitors would park their vehicles, is covered with mud. The "court yard" which these tenants could legitimately anticipate appreciating is nonexistent throughout the course of construction. The construction prevents use of the patio and affects ingress and egress, use of the parking area and any outdoor recreational use of the area adjacent to the premises for either the two adult tenants or their three children. The subject premises is the highest price townhouse or apartment available in this municipality (oriented to multi-family dwellings). Tenants had a reasonable expectancy of a decent exterior environment from the sales promotion, the initial condition of the premises, and the higher price of the apartment compared to others in the community, whether the expectancy be characterized as one of amenity or necessity. They are deprived of a substantial attribute of the premises through no fault of their own and they have no control over any possible remedy to the situation. Plantiff landlord and developer was required to install the new concrete retaining wall by the municipality after defendants took possession. The initial wooden railroad tie wall had become unsafe.

The landlord argues that the implied warranty of habitability should not be extended beyond the scope of the presently controlling cases so as to encompass conditions exterior to the premises. The evolution of the doctrine to date has not explicitly included exterior conditions within its scope. . . .

. . . [T]he covenant on the part of a tenant to pay rent, and the convenant—whether express or implied—on the part of the landlord to maintain the demised premises in a habitable condition are for all purposes mutually dependent. Accordingly in an action by a landlord for unpaid rent a tenant may plead, by way of defense and setoff, a breach by the landlord of his continuing obligation to maintain an adequate standard of habitability.

In deciding what kind of defect will be deemed to constitute a breach of the warranty of habitability, the court is guided by the factors . . . as follows:

1. Has there been a violation of any applicable housing code or building or sanitary regulations?

2. Is the nature of the deficiency or defect such as to affect a vital facility?

3. What is its potential or actual effect upon safety and sanitation?

4. For what length of time has it persisted?

5. What is the age of the structure?

6. What is the amount of the rent?

7. Can the tenant be said to have waived the defect or be estopped to complain?

8. Was the tenant in any way responsible for the defective condition?

Here, no housing code violation is present, but the work on the retaining wall, causing the unsavory condition, was required by the borough engineer as a public safety measure. The defect affects all outside use of the premises. In the context of the promotional effort and type of townhouse development promised, the court feels a vital facility is affected. There is a possible effect on sanitation and safety. The defect has persisted now for a period of four to five months and is not transitory. The structure and the project are virtually new. Defendants were original occupants and had a reasonable right to expect first quality facilities. The rental was the highest in the municipality. Defendant tenants cannot in any sense be charged with waiver or estoppel and are in no way responsible for the defective condition. All of these factors support their position.

The court has considered the intention of the parties to this agreement as indicated by the representations of Timber Ridge to defendants, and defendants' reasonable expectations with respect to those representations, the location and type of residential environment of Timber Ridge, and the high rental fee for the premises. It is the finding of the court that an implied covenant arose between the parties, whether it is characterized as an implied warranty of habitability or an implied covenant to provide certain amenities. Further, the court finds that the implied covenant or warranty has been breached. An abatement of rent in the amount of 15% a month will be allowed from the date the rent was initially withheld and the summary dispossession action commenced.

So ordered.

Aluli v. Trusdell
508 P.2d 1217 (Hawaii) 1973

Plaintiff-landlord leased an apartment to defendant-tenant on a month-to-month tenancy. The landlord served a notice of termination of tenancy on the tenant, and the tenant refused to vacate the premises. When the plaintiff sued for possession, the defendant contended that the primary purpose of the eviction was to obstruct a tenant's union in which the defendant was an organizer and active member. The defendant contended that to allow the landlord to evict him would deprive him of freedom of speech, freedom of association, and freedom to petition in denial of his First Amendment rights. The lower court found against the defendant, and he appealed.

The primary issue in this appeal is whether the tenant had any valid constitutional defense to the action.

ABE, J. . . . Before stating our reasons for concluding that the tenant's allegations do not raise a constitutional defense, we wish to point out what we consider inadequacies and one sidedness of the tenant's argument on the issue.

First, we believe that the rights of the landlord and tenant should be balanced. The landlord seeks to vindicate his right of possession as an incident of the ownership of the subject premises. On the other hand, the tenant's right is a permissive right of possession pursuant to a month-to-month tenancy terminable at the end of any month at the option of either party. Thus, these two "rights" may be the opposite sides of the same coin.

Second, the tenant appears to have assumed that the landlord does not have any First Amendment rights. If it is true that he is seeking possession of the rented premises for the sole reason that he disagrees or dislikes the tenant's communicative or associative activities, is not the landlord also protected by the First Amendment in expressing these disagreements or dislikes? Is not the requesting of judicial relief "petitioning government for redress of grievances"?

. . . [T]he landlord-tenant relationship is a contractual one in our jurisdiction. If we accept the tenant's contention, it would mean that we would be substantially altering this relationship and impairing the traditional right of a landlord to recover possession of the demised premises under the terms of a lease. Or otherwise stated, the tenant's obligation under a month-to-month tenancy to return the possession of the demised premises to the landlord upon the termination of such tenancy is abrogated. If this court were to rule as contended by the tenant, its ruling might contravene the provisions of the United States Constitution, Article I, Section 10, which states in part: "No State shall . . . pass any . . .

law impairing the Obligation of Contracts."

We are upholding the district court's ruling that the First Amendment rights claimed by the tenant did not constitute a defense to the summary possession action brought by the landlord for the following two reasons:

We do not believe that the tenant's First Amendment rights have been infringed upon or abrogated by the actions of the landlord. Even after the landlord regains possession of the premises under the summary possession action, the tenant may retain membership in the tenant's union, petition the government for the redress of grievances and speak as freely about the condition of the premises, as when he is in possession of the premises. Furthermore, we do not see how the tenant is punished in any way for his activities. Being a month-to-month tenant, he had no right to demand that his tenancy be extended once the current term expired. When the landlord repossesses the premises at the end of the current term, the tenant is not being deprived of anything except his nonproprietary expectancy that his tenancy will be extended another term.

At most, the tenant's only complaint is that allowing the landlord to regain possession of the premises will lessen his interest in the subject matter about which he wishes to exercise his First Amendment rights. We do not believe the First Amendment rights claimed by the tenant operate to prefer the tenant's expectancy of continued possession of the premises over the right of the landlord to regain possession at the end of the tenant's term, so as to encourage the tenant to continue exercising his First Amendment rights in the hopes that the conditions of his tenancy would be improved.

As we have already stated, whether he is dispossessed or not, he can continue to exercise the constitutional rights he claims that the summary possession action deprives him of. Nothing is being taken away from him by the summary possession action because the landlord, under the terms of the month-to-month tenancy as incidental to the ownership of the premises, has the right to regain possession of the premises upon the termination thereof.

The summary possession statute, HRS § 666-1 of this state, does not, on its face, limit the exercise of First Amendment rights of the tenant. Our construction of this statute in no way abridges a tenant's exercise of First Amendment rights. The exercise of state power here is aimed at restoring possession of the premises to the person entitled thereto. There is no attempt here by the exercise of judicial or legislative law making power to regulate or limit the content or mode of communication or association in which a tenant may desire to engage in.

We hold that when a court of this state awards possession to a landlord, even if the landlord is motivated by his disagreement with the actions and speech of the tenant he is evicting, no state action is involved which denies or infringes the tenant's right to exercise his First Amendment Constitutional rights.

Affirmed.

Amburgy v. Golden
557 P.2d 9 (Wash.App.) 1976

FARRIS, J. . . . This action was initiated by Samuel and Sharon Amburgy to recover for injuries to her resulting from a fall over a 2-foot retaining wall in an apartment complex owned by Dan Golden and Max Kessler. The trial court granted Golden and Kessler's motion for a directed verdict at the close of the Amburgys' case. The Amburgys appeal.

Sharon Amburgy was injured when she stepped off the edge of a retaining wall while walking after dark between her brother-in-law's apartment and a neighboring apartment; she was not following a prepared pathway. The record fails to establish that anyone else ever took the route that she chose or that the owner knew or had reason to know that anyone would choose it. The trial court granted the defendants' motion for a directed verdict at the close of the Amburgys' case on two grounds: (1) knowledge of a tenant is imputed to a social guest who stands in the same legal relation to the landlord as the tenant and (2) the landlord has no affirmative duty to illuminate areas that are not "common areas."

Landlords owe their tenants' guests no greater standard of care than is owed to the tenants. They do not guarantee safety, but they have an affirmative duty to exercise reasonable care to inspect, repair and maintain common areas "in a reasonably safe condition for the tenant's use." Before this duty is found to exist, however, it must be shown that the alleged common area (1) is an area upon which the tenant or guest may be reasonably expected to go and is being put to its intended use. . . .

We find as a matter of law that the case presented by the Amburgys, given all reasonable inferences, would not sustain a jury verdict in their favor. They have failed to present evidence which would support a finding that the defendants breached a duty to them.

Further, the retaining wall here is not a "latent defect," a circumstance which, if it existed, would, together with other circumstances, create an issue of liability. Nor does maintenance of the wall constitute an act of wanton misconduct, an occurrence which would establish liability.

Affirmed.

CHAPTER 44
REVIEW QUESTIONS AND PROBLEMS

1. A, owner of Blackacre, allowed B to occupy a cabin on the land. There was no provision for rent, nor was there any agreement as to the duration of the agreement, and either could terminate the relationship at any time. When B died, A locked the cabin and put B's belongings outside the door. C, the executor of B's estate, claimed he had the right to occupy the cabin. Is this correct? Explain.

2. A leased land to B. A was aware of the fact that B was strip-mining coal from the land. This method of mining displaced portions of the topsoil, rock, and shale. Neither B nor A restored the soil, and following a heavy rainfall, rock, dirt, and coal washed down the mountainside and obstructed natural waterways. Consequently, C's property was damaged. Is A liable for such damages? Why?

3. B, the buyer, issued a check payable to the order of S, the seller, and delivered it to S. On the face of the check, B wrote, "Deposit for land on Galvin Road, Watertown, price thirty-two cents a foot." The land on Galvin Road was all that S owned. Is this sufficient for a contract of sale? Why?

4. A rented an apartment from B. A was made aware of the condition that the apartment was for adults only. When B sought to reclaim the premises because A had a child, A defended on the grounds that the clause in the lease restricting the occupancy to adults was against public policy and, therefore, void. Is the defense good? Explain.

5. S, seller, and B, buyer, executed a contract for the sale of Blackacre for $12,000. B paid $4,000 down, and the deed was placed in escrow pending payment of the $8,000 balance by B on March 12, 1963. On March 5, 1963, S died. B paid the $8,000 to the escrowee and received the deed on March 12. S's heirs challenge the transaction. What result? Why?

6. The H Hotel leased store space to T for a one-year term ending February 28, 1971. In September and November, H sent letters to T informing him that the lease would not be renewed. However, when the lease expired, T did not vacate the premises but mailed a check to H with the notation "March rent" on the reverse side. The check was deposited by H, and T claimed that the lease had been renewed for another year? Is T correct? Why?

7. T slipped on ice in the parking lot in which he rented a parking space from L. T also leased from L office space across the street from the parking lot. Did L have a duty to remove the ice from the parking lot? Why?

8. In 1968, C Construction Company built and sold a house to X. X sold the house to Y in 1971. After moving into the house, Y discovered that the basement leaked and that there was a large crack around three of the basement walls. Should C be liable to Y for the cost of repairs, which amounted to $3,500? Why?

9.   O and C entered into a contract whereby C, a general contractor, agreed to erect a building on O's land. Upon completion, the roof leaked whenever it rained. O brought suit, claiming that C had breached the implied warranty of habitability. Is O correct? Why?

10.   L agreed to lease a 105-acre tract of land to T for a term of five years. The lease provided, "Lessee will not sublet the premises to any person without the consent of Lessor in writing, thereto first obtained." Subsequently, T subleased the land to S without obtaining the consent of L. Should L be entitled to terminate the lease and collect the amount of the unpaid rent from T? Why?

11.   X, the owner of an apartment building, leased an apartment to Y. During Y's absence X inspected the property to ascertain if Y had alcoholic beverages on the premises. When X confronted Y with some empty beer bottles he had taken from the apartment, Y sued X for trespass. Is X guilty? Explain.

12.   X executed a contract for the purchase of a commercial building from Y. The contract contained a provision stating that if the payments by X were more than thirty days overdue, Y could declare a default and obtain the deed back from the escrowee. After twelve years of the twenty-year contract, X fell on hard times and made no payments for almost a year. Would a court allow Y to default the contract, cancel the deed, and reacquire possession of the property? Explain.

Wills, Estates, and Trusts

1. Introduction

Perhaps no problem associated with the ownership of property is of greater significance than the various methods available for disposing of that property on death. While the methods and techniques for distributing property on death have always been of considerable importance, their significance is greatly increased today because of the very substantial death taxes imposed by both federal and state governments. As a result of these death taxes, associated income tax problems, and other related concerns, there has developed an activity commonly referred to as *estate planning,* in which many business specialists are actively engaged.

Lawyers play a key role in estate planning, in drafting the various legal documents and analyzing the legal effect of various ideas that people have as to the disposition of their estates. Life insurance salesmen and banking personnel are also actively engaged in the field of estate planning. Life insurance not only creates estates for many people but is a method used to provide the liquid assets to pay the death taxes and other substantial costs of dying in our society. Numerous techniques for reducing income and death taxes utilize life insurance. The trust departments of a bank frequently serve as personal representative of the estate of a deceased person, as well as trustee of living and testamentary trusts used to accomplish the desired goals of an estate plan. Besides providing management of capital, the professional personal representative possesses special skills and techniques that help the property owner accomplish his goals both during his lifetime and upon his death. In addition to the attorney, the insurance broker, and the trust officer, other professional persons are actively a part of the estate-planning endeavor. The investment broker is frequently asked for advice on his area of specialty, and of course, the accountant provides much of the data, income tax information, and tax planning that goes into the development of an estate plan.

Since all these business specialists are involved in the estate-planning activity, this chapter discusses some of the general principles of the law of wills, estates, and trusts so that the legal aspects of estate planning will be understood.

2. Terminology

The law of wills and estates has certain terminology that is commonly used by those engaged in estate planning. If a person dies without a will, he or she is said to die *intestate.* When a person dies intestate, his property passes according to the applicable statute on descent and distribution to his heirs or next of kin. These statutes provide that property will in effect pass to the deceased's closest relatives, since the law presumes that this would be the intent of the deceased. For example, a typical statute provides that property of a person dying leaving a spouse and children will pass one-third to the spouse and two-thirds to the children.

A person making a will is generally referred to as the *testator.* The personal representative of a deceased who dies without a will is an *administrator,* whereas the personal representative of a testator is an *executor.* A *guardian* is the personal representative of a living person known as a *ward,* who is usually a child, and a *conservator* is the personal representative of a living person who is mentally incompetent for reasons other than age.

A gift by will of real estate is usually called a *devise;* a gift of personal property is called a *bequest.* Devises and bequests are further classified as *specific, general,* and *residuary.* A *specific legacy,* or *specific devise,* is a gift of particular property so described as to identify it and to distinguish it from all other parts of the deceased's property. If property described in a specific devise or legacy is not owned by the testator on death, the gift fails or is adeemed. A *general legacy* is one that does not describe any particular property, and it may be satisfied by delivery of any property of the general kind described. For example, a gift of a specified sum of money is a general legacy. A *residuary gift* is one that includes all the rest of that type of property. For example, a residuary gift of personal property would include all the personal property not included in the specific or general legacies. The aforesaid terms are important in the payment and distribution of the shares of an estate and in determining which party actually receives a specific item of property.

WILLS

3.   General Characteristics

A *will* is a document that expresses a person's intention as to the disposition of his or her property on death. However, a will has several additional functions. It designates the personal representative who is to be responsible for settling the affairs of the deceased. A will may make provisions for the appointment of a guardian of the person and a guardian of the estate of a minor child. Many wills contain provisions relating to the payment of taxes that may be due on the death of the deceased and such matters as whether or not the personal representative should be required to have sureties on the official bond.

Legal provisions vary from state to state, but the law generally stipulates that to be valid, a will must be executed by a person possessing testamentary capacity and must be signed either by the testator or by someone in his presence and at his direction. In most states, a will must be attested in the presence of the testator by two or more credible witnesses.

Testamentary capacity does not require a perfect mind or average intelligence. Testamentary capacity first of all requires that the minimum age be met, which in most states is 18. The person executing the will must have sufficient mental capacity to comprehend and remember who are the natural objects of his affection, to comprehend the kind and character of his property, and to understand that he or she is engaged in making a will. Less mental capacity is required to execute a will than is required to execute ordinary business transactions and contracts. Since many people at the time of making a will are in poor health, the law recognizes that many testators will not be of perfect mind, and all that is required is a minimum capacity to understand the nature and the plan involved in making a will.[1]

It should be noted that the testator need not actually sign the will, since many people who are physically incapacitated cannot do so. Thus, a will may be signed by someone else in the testator's presence and at his direction. It will not be set aside simply by proving that the signature on it is not that of the deceased.

In most states, the testator need not sign in the presence of witnesses if he acknowledges that the instrument is his own and that it bears his signature. The witnesses need not be informed that the document is a will, but only that it is the testator's instrument. The signature aspect of attestation is that the testator watch the winesses sign, and in most states it is essential that the witnesses testify that the testator watched them sign as attesting witnesses.

A credible witness is one who is competent to testify to support the will. If the witness is an interested party—takes something under the will—then in most states, the witness will not be allowed to receive any more property as a result of the will than he would have received had there been no will. In other

[1] *Hellams* v. *Ross,* page 870.

words, a witness to the will cannot profit or gain any property as a result of the will. He will be required to testify and will lose whatever the will gives him in excess of his intestate share of the deceased's estate.

A will that on its face is properly executed may be challenged on several grounds. With the exception of lack of testamentary capacity, the most frequently cited ground for a will contest is undue influence. This ground for challenging a will is defined as influence that overpowers the mind of the testator and deprives him of his free agency in the execution of the will. It is the equivalent of saying, "This is not my wish, but I must do it." It is more than mere persuasion, for here there is an exercise of independent judgment and deliberation. A presumption of undue influence is often found to exist where there is a fiduciary relationship between a testator and a beneficiary who takes substantial benefits from the will. This is especially true where the beneficiary is a nonrelated dominant party and the testator a dependent party and the will is written or its preparation procured by the beneficiary.[2]

4. Revocation of Wills

A will is said to be *ambulatory,* or not effective, until the death of the testator. It may be revoked at any time. Among the common methods of revoking a will are physical destruction, the making of a will declaring the revocation, a later will that is inconsistent with the prior will, marriage, and divorce. In many states, divorce revokes the will only to the extent of bequests or devises to the former spouse. Marriage revokes a will because it is presumed that the testator would want a different plan of distribution as the result of the marriage. It is therefore important that whenever there is a marriage or a divorce, the law of the state of the domicile be consulted to determine its effect on a prior will.

Most state laws prohibit partial revocation of a will except by a duly signed and attested instrument. Additions, alterations, substitutions, interlineations, and deletions on the face of a will are therefore ineffective, and the will stands as originally executed. The law prohibits partial revocation because of the ease with which such minor changes could be made by third parties even after the death of the person whose will is involved.

In most states, unless a provision is made for a child born after the execution of the will, or unless the will by clear and convincing language indicates that after-born children are to be disinherited, the after-born child takes from the estate whatever he or she would have received had there been no will. A legal adoption has the same effect. This stipulation is based on the assumption that the testator at the time of the execution of the original will would not have considered the after-born child and that a provision would have been intended had the child been considered.

In most states, a will that is in any manner totally revoked can be revived

[2] *Barton v. Beck Estate,* page 872.

only by the reexecution of the will or by an instrument in writing declaring the revival and executed in the same manner as a new will. To illustrate, assume that a person during his lifetime has executed four wills, each will specifically revoking the former. Assume also that none of these wills has been destroyed and that the testator shortly before his death physically destroyed will No. 4. The question arises as to whether or not will No. 3 is then valid. In most states, the answer is no. Wills are not stacked one on the other so that the revocation of the latest will revives the earlier will. In such a situation, the person would die without a will. A similar problem arises when a person executes a codicil or a minor change to a will. When a codicil is executed and it specifically refers to a former will, it has the effect of bringing the former will down to the date of the codicil, and the will is then construed as of the date of the codicil. A codicil can validate a previously invalid will. It can also validate a will that has been revoked by marriage or divorce.

5. The Administration of Estates

The statutes of each state specify the steps to be taken by the executor or the administrator in the settlement of an estate. These usually require that a petition be filed informing the court of the death of the deceased, together with a copy of the will, if any, requesting the court to hold a hearing at which time the will will be presented for probate. If the person dies without a will, the petition would be signed by someone entitled under the law to be administrator of the estate. This is usually the closest relative. In either case, every person interested in the estate as a beneficiary under the will, or as an heir or next of kin of the deceased, is entitled to notice of the time and place of the hearing. This notice may be waived by a written document filed with the court.

At the time of the hearing, there will be testimony about the death of the deceased, and the attesting witnesses will be called upon to testify about the execution of the will. The evidence offered will be for the purpose of establishing that at the time of the execution, the deceased possessed the requisite mental capacity; that the instrument was signed either by the deceased or by someone in his presence and at his direction; and that it was properly attested to by the required number of witnesses. There will also be a report to the court as to the approximate value of the estate so that the personal representative may be properly bonded. If it appears to the court that the will was properly executed, it will be admitted to probate and an executor named by the testator will be appointed. If there was no will and the person entitled to administer has so requested, then an administrator will be appointed. The executor or the administrator will then file an oath of office and an appropriate bond to guarantee the faithful discharge of the duties of personal representative. In the case of an administrator, sureties on the bond will be required. In the case of an executor, sureties will be required unless these are waived by the will.

After the executor or the administrator is appointed, there will usually be a notice of publication in an appropriate newspaper informing all creditors that they may file their claims against the estate. In addition, the executor or the administrator will gather up the personal property of the deceased, inventory it, and file an inventory with the court. The inventory will include all real estate and all personal property owned by the deceased. It will not include joint-tenancy property. Should there be any disputed claims, the court will hold an appropriate hearing and determine which claims, if any, will be paid.

During the period of administration, the personal representative will file the deceased's final income tax returns, the necessary income tax returns for the estate, the federal estate tax return if one is required, and the appropriate state death-tax returns. The personal representative will also attempt to collect any sums due the deceased and compromise any claims owing to, or debts owed by, the deceased. At the end of the period of administration, the property remaining after the payment of all debts and taxes will be distributed by the personal representative to the persons entitled to it. If the deceased died intestate, these will be the persons who are determined by the court to be the legal heirs of the deceased as of the date of death. In most states, if the deceased leaves a spouse and children, they will constitute the heirs. If there are no spouse and children, then the court will determine which blood relatives are next in line to receive the property.

It should be noted that the law in most states gives a spouse certain rights that cannot be denied by will. These rights include the right to support during the period of administration, with a statutory minimum usually provided. The exact amount will be determined by the court, based on the size of the estate and the standard of living of the surviving spouse. The laws of most states also give a spouse the right to *renounce* a will and to take a statutory share in lieu of provisions made by the will. In other words, in most states, one spouse cannot completely prevent his or her property from passing to a surviving spouse by making different provisions in the will. In many states, a spouse receives one-half the estate upon renunciation, irrespective of the provisions of the will. It should be recognized that the right to renounce usually exists for spouses only—children can be completely disinherited.

6. Substitutes for Wills

Many methods, legal devices, and techniques can serve as a valid substitute for a will. In one sense, the law of intestacy is a substitute for a will, because it is in effect a state-made will for people who have not taken the trouble to execute one for themselves. Among the more common substitutes for wills are contracts, including life insurance contracts, trusts, and joint-tenancy property.

Life insurance policies name a beneficiary to receive the proceeds on the death of the insured. This beneficiary may be the estate of the insured, in which case the proceeds will pass under the will of the deceased, or if the insured dies without a will, the proceeds will go according to the laws of intestacy. However, the usual arrangement is to name an individual beneficiary and successive beneficiaries, in the event the primary beneficiary predeceases the insured. In such a case, the provisions of the will are immaterial, and the life insurance will be paid in accordance with the terms of the policy. This is true even if the will purports to cover life insurance.

Individuals enter into numerous contracts that have the effect of disposing of property on death. Some contracts stipulate the terms of a will or surrender rights to renounce a will or to take an intestate share. Such contracts are known as antenuptial agreements.[3] In the material on business organizations, reference was made to buy and sell agreements between partners and between the shareholders of closely held corporations. These contracts in effect dispose of the interest of partners and shareholders on death. The contractual agreement will dispose of the property irrespective of any provision in a will in much the same manner as life insurance. Other contracts, including employment contracts and leases, may have a similar effect.

A *living trust* is another substitute for a will when it contains provisions as to the disposition of property on the death of a life tenant. Since this device is so important and so commonly used, it is discussed more fully in the sections that follow.

The use of joint tenancies as a means of common ownership was previously discussed. Joint tenancy is a substitute for a will because ownership passes to the surviving joint tenant on the death of one joint tenant. It will be recalled that joint-tenancy property is unaffected by the will of the deceased and that joint-tenancy property is not subject to probate or to the debts of a deceased joint tenant.

TRUSTS

7. Introduction

Although the law recognizes four distinct types of trusts, the term *trust* is generally used to describe an express private trust. The other types of trusts are known as charitable, resulting, and constructive trusts. These will be discussed later.

An *express private trust* is a fiduciary relationship with respect to property, which subjects the person with legal title to property (the trustee) to equitable duties with the property for the benefit of another (the beneficiary). In other words, a *trust* is a fiduciary relationship under which one person, the trustee, holds title to property and deals with it for the benefit of another person, known as the *beneficiary*. The most important single aspect of the relationship is its fiduciary character. The trustee is under an absolute obligation to act solely for the benefit of the beneficiary in every aspect of the relationship.

3 *Watson* v. *Watson,* page 873.

A trust may be created by a transfer of property during one's lifetime, or it may be created by a transfer on death. The former is generally called a *living* or *inter vivos trust,* the latter a *testamentary trust.* The person creating the trust is usually called the *settlor,* although he is sometimes referred to as the *creator* or the *trustor* in estate-planning literature. The settlor may create the trust by a transfer of property to the trustee, or the settlor may declare himself to be trustee of described property for the benefit of designated beneficiaries.

The intention to create a trust must be clear. Precatory words, which merely indicate a desire or hope, will not create a trust. For example, if A leaves his property to B with the hope that B will take adequate care of C, there is no trust and B is free to do with the property as he may see fit. Consideration is not required to create a trust, and of course, consideration is rarely present in a testamentary trust. The statute of frauds is applicable to the creation of a trust, and therefore, to be valid, a trust involving real estate requires written evidence of the intention to create the trust and of the exact property held in trust.

A trust may have several beneficiaries, and their rights may be dependent upon several variable factors. For example, the trustee may be authorized to determine which of the beneficiaries shall receive the income of the trust and how much each shall receive. The right of a trustee to allocate the income of the trust among the beneficiaries is sometimes referred to as a "sprinkling trust" provision. It has the advantage of allowing the trustee with actual knowledge of the needs of the beneficiaries to take those needs into account in the distribution of income. A trust may also have successive beneficiaries. For example, a trust could provide that the income should go to the deceased's spouse for life, on the death of the spouse to their children for life, and on the death of the children to the grandchildren. This would provide the equivalent of a life estate in real estate in personal property.

A settlor may be a trustee as well as one of the beneficiaries of a trust. A trustee may be one of the beneficiaries of a trust, but the sole trustee cannot be the sole beneficiary. If the sole trustee is the sole beneficiary of a trust, there is a merger of the legal and equitable interests, causing a termination of the trust by operation of law.

When the settlor is also the trustee and life beneficiary, the trust operates in effect as a will. It is nevertheless valid in most states, even though it is not executed with the formality required of a will. In such a case, it is used to avoid probate proceedings and to save the costs involved in such proceedings.

8.   The Administration of a Trust

Since a trust is a fiduciary relationship, the trustee owes a high duty of loyalty to the beneficiary. The trustee is not allowed to individually enter into transactions with the trust. Such contracts or transactions are voidable without regard to fairness, and good faith is no defense. A trustee also has a duty not to delegate his responsibility to another.

Perhaps the most important duty of the trustee is in regard to investments. The trustee has a duty not to commingle trust funds with his individual funds and a duty to earmark and segregate trust property. The trustee has a duty to diversify investments. The trustee's duty to diversify investments is sometimes described as horizontal and vertical. *Horizontal diversity* means that the trustee should diversify his investments geographically and in various industries throughout the country. *Vertical diversity* means that he should diversify by investing in different companies within the same industry.

In the selection of trust investments, it is frequently stated that a trustee must exercise that degree of care that men of prudence and intelligence exercise in the management of their own affairs not in regard to speculation but in regard to the permanent disposition of their funds, considering probable income as well as probable safety of the investment. This is generally known as the *prudent-man rule*.

To have the requisite diversification, especially in trusts with relatively small amounts of assets, there have developed in recent years what are known as *common trust funds*. These common trust funds allow a trustee, such as a bank or a trust company that holds several trusts, to invest the trust funds together to obtain the requisite diversity. The duty not to commingle is not violated, because each trust fund has its stated proportion of the total investment.

The trustee has all necessary powers to carry out the duties of trustee. These generally include the power to sell if necessary, to lease, to incur necessary expenses, to settle claims, and to retain investments. A trustee generally has no power to borrow money or to mortgage the trust assets. A trustee is liable to the beneficiary for any loss caused by a breach of trust and for any personal profit made in breach of his duty of loyalty. A trustee who makes improper investments cannot set off the gains on one against the losses on the other. Any gain in an improper investment remains in the trust, and the trustee is required to make up the losses on improper investments.

9. Termination of Trusts

In the absence of fraud or mistake, a settlor cannot revoke a trust unless he has specifically reserved the power to do so. The same principle applies to modifications of the trust. A trust may be terminated when its purposes have been accomplished or if the trust purpose becomes illegal. A trust may be terminated by the consent of all beneficiaries, provided they are all of legal age and all consent, and provided also that termination will not defeat the purpose for which the trust was created. This latter provision is especially important in the so-called spendthrift trust. If the purpose of the settlor was to conserve the estate of a spendthrift, it cannot be terminated even with the consent of the beneficiaries.

In regard to spendthrift trusts, it should be noted that all trusts are spendthrift trusts to a certain extent. That is, as a general rule, a creditor cannot collect a debt of the beneficiary directly from the trust estate if the trust was created by someone other than the beneficiary. One of the purposes of a trust is to protect the beneficiary from the claims of his creditors, and allowing a creditor to collect directly from the trust estate would defeat this purpose. Therefore, with the exception of a few claims, such as alimony, child support, and taxes, the trustee is not obligated to pay over the income or principal of the trust estate to anyone other than the beneficiary.[4] Of course, after the beneficiary has received the income, a creditor may use legal process to collect a claim. The fact that all trusts are spendthrift as to involuntary transfers is a major reason for use of the trust device.

10. Other Types of Trusts

As previously noted, in addition to the express private trust, the law recognizes charitable trusts, resulting trusts, and constructive trusts. The latter terms are used to describe trusts created by operation of law. For example, a court of equity will create a *constructive trust* in order to prevent unjust enrichment, as in the situation where a transfer of property is procured by fraud or violation of some fiduciary duty. Courts of equity also create *resulting trusts,* which result where the person with legal title is not intended to have it. For example, if a child purchases property in the name of a parent, there is no presumption of a gift and the child may establish that the parent holds title in trust for the child.

The *charitable trust* is a valuable estate-planning tool. It differs from a private trust in that it can benefit an indefinite group and can have perpetual existence. Among typical charitable purposes for which a trust can be created are the promotion of religion, the promotion of education, the promotion of health, public comfort, and the relief of poverty.

Perhaps the single most important principle in the law of charitable trusts is a doctrine known as *cy pres*. The doctrine of *cy pres* provides that if a particular charitable purpose cannot be carried out in the manner directed by the settlor, the court can carry out the general charitable intention by directing the application of the trust property to another charitable purpose consistent with the general charitable intention.[5] The words *cy pres* mean "as nearly as," and the courts simply choose another charitable purpose that is as nearly like the one selected by the settlor as possible. For example, a trust was created to provide money for a volunteer fire department. When the area in question was incorporated and the taxpayers supplied the volunteer fire department, the money was used to support a local library under the doctrine of *cy pres*.

[4] *United Mine Workers of America* v. *Boyle,* page 874.
[5] *Estate of Tomlinson,* page 876.

Charitable trusts provide a valuable estate-planning tool, as such gifts are not subject to death taxes. In addition, living gifts to a charitable trust qualify for income tax deduction.

11.   The Role of Trusts in Estate Planning

The trust device performs several useful functions as an estate-planning tool. As was previously mentioned, it can be used to protect the property of a spendthrift and to ensure that property continues to produce income in spite of the claims of creditors of a beneficiary. It can also be used to secure professional management advice for the beneficiary and to eliminate the worry, decision making, and so forth, that are involved in handling a person's investments.

The trust device allows decisions to be postponed until all the facts are known. The sprinkling device previously noted, and a trustee's authority to make investments and to sell property under changing conditions, illustrate this principle.

Perhaps the best use of the trust device is in tax planning. The trust device allows property to pass through more than one generation with only one tax, thus reducing death taxes or, in some cases, eliminating them altogether. The trust device allows for the maximum use of such estate-tax-planning devices as the marital deduction. The trust device is also used where the beneficiaries are minors or are suffering from disabilities and it is desired that someone with legal capacity to contract have title to trust property.

WILLS, ESTATES, AND TRUSTS CASES

Hellams v. Ross
233 S.E.2d 98 (S.C.) 1977

LEWIS, J. The issues involve the validity of the will of the late Marvin Robert Bass and, particularly, his testamentary capacity at the time he executed the instrument.

The testator died in Laurens County on March 9, 1975, leaving a will dated May 2, 1974, under which he devised all of his property to the Rabon Creek Baptist Church to the exclusion of his wife, the respondent herein. He had no children.

The respondent-widow objected to the probate of the will upon the ground that the testator lacked testamentary capacity to make it. . . . The Probate Court subsequently overruled the attack upon the validity of the will

and admitted it to probate. However, upon appeal to the Circuit Court, a jury found that . . . the deceased . . . did not have sufficient mental capacity to make a will on May 2, 1974, the date upon which he signed the instrument offered for probate.

The executor (appellant) took the position at the trial that there was no evidence to sustain the conclusion that the deceased was mentally incompetent . . . at the time of the execution of the will and, accordingly, moved for a directed verdict in favor of the will upon that ground. This motion was refused. . . . This appeal by the executor . . . presents the sole issue of whether there was any evidence to support the finding of the jury that the testator lacked mental capacity to make a will. . . .

It is conceded that the will was properly executed. The charge of testamentary incapacity was based upon allegations that the excessive use of alcohol and drugs had affected the testator's mental faculties. The testimony showed that the testator had been a heavy consumer of alcoholic beverages for a number of years. In fact, it is inferable that his consumption of intoxicating beverages had reached a point that he was an habitual drunkard; but the testimony shows conclusively that the testator was not under the influence of intoxicants on the date of execution of the will. The issue then is whether there was any evidence from which a reasonable inference could be drawn that the testator's intemperance had so affected his mental faculties as to render him incompetent to make a will even though he was not actually intoxicated at the time he executed it.

The burden of proof was upon respondent, as the contestant, to show a lack of mental capacity. . . .

The general principles governing the determination of testamentary capacity apply in cases where it is charged that the testator was affected by the use of alcohol or drugs. Therefore, the capacity of the testator to make a will is tested by whether he knew (1) his estate, (2) the objects of his affections, and (3) to whom he wished to give his property.

Since intoxication is a temporary condition, even an habitual drunkard is presumed to be competent, when sober, to make a will; and the person, who asserts that the excessive use of intoxicants rendered a testator incompetent to make a valid will, must affirmatively show either (1) that at the time the will was made the testator's use of intoxicants had so impaired or deranged his mind that he lacked testamentary capacity even when he was not under the immediate influence of intoxicants or (2) that he was in fact incompetent due to intoxication existing at the time of the making and execution of the will.

A careful review of the record convinces us that the evidence failed to show mental incapacity of the testator at the time the will was made. Although the testimony is undisputed that the testator was a heavy drinker and would sometimes, when on one of his frequent drinking sprees, fire his gun into the ceiling of the house and through the windows, there was no evidence of probative value that his drinking had produced a derangement of his mental faculties when he was not under the influence of intoxicants.

One of the witnesses to the will was dead, but the other two testified. One was the attorney who prepared and supervised the execution of the will and the other was the attorney's secretary. Both certified that the testator came to the attorney's office and requested that the will be prepared, giving directions as to the disposition to be made of his estate. These witnesses were positive in their testimony that the testator was sober, normal in his actions, and possessed of testamentary capacity when he signed the will.

We find no evidence of probative value to counter the positive testimony of the attesting witnesses that the testator was possessed of testamentary capacity when he signed the instrument. The lower court was therefore in error refusing to grant appellant's motion for a directed verdict. . . .

The fact alone that the testator disposed of property contrary to what others usually consider fair is not sufficient to declare his will void. . . . The right to make a will carries with it the right to disregard what the world considers a fair disposition of property. . . . That a will is unjust to one's relations is no legal reason that it should be considered an irrational act. The law puts no restrictions upon a man's right to dispose of his property in any way his partialities, or pride, or caprice may prompt him.

There was also testimony that the testator brought two trailers for considerably more than they were worth; took the sink and some furniture from his home and put it in a rental house; and that about five (5) years before his death he expressed a belief that, if he gave his money to the church, he would go to Heaven. Respondent argues that the bad business deal, using articles from his home to fix rental property, and the belief that by giving his property to the church he would go to Heaven constituted some evidence that the testator was of unsound mind. The belief that the giving of his property to the church would, within itself,

get him into Heaven might have been inaccurate but we are not prepared to say that it was evidence of an unsound mind. Neither does the bad business deal nor using his household articles to furnish his rental property reach, under this record, probative value on the question of testamentary capacity. . . .

Reversed in favor of the validity of the will.

Barton v. Beck Estate
195 A.2d 63 (Me.) 1963

WILLIAMSON, J. This case is before us on appeal from the disallowance of the will of Winifred M. Beck in the Supreme Court of Probate (on the ground of undue influence). . . . [T]he decisive issue is whether there was evidence warranting the finding of undue influence and the disallowance of the will in its entirety. . . .

"Undue influence" has been defined in language repeatedly approved by our Court, as follows:

> By undue influence in this class of cases is meant influence, in connection with the execution of the will and operating at the time the will is made, amounting to moral coercion, destroying free agency, or importunity which could not be resisted, so that the testator, unable to withstand the influence, or too weak to resist it, was constrained to do that which was not his actual will but against it. . . .

When there exists a confidential or trust relationship on the part of a beneficiary with the alleged testator, the law requires "the closest scrutiny and most careful examination of all of the surrounding circumstances. . . . Such a condition might, as a matter of fact, cast upon the proponent the burden of explanation, and the absence of satisfactory explanation would be an additional fact of more or less weight."

(Turning to the facts)

Miss Winifred M. Beck, eighty years of age, executed the purported will at Freeport on March 24, 1960. For many years prior to 1959 she lived in Boston where she had been employed as a secretary until retirement. Occasionally she had made visits to Freeport where she was born.

In 1959 on the death of two cousins she returned to Freeport. Russell G. Jeannotte (the proponent), an undertaker in Freeport, and Miss Bertha E. Rideout, his attorney, brought her from Boston. She occupied a house formerly belonging to a deceased cousin and then owned by Mr. Jeannotte at a rental of $150 a month, an amount fixed by the rental she had been paying in Boston. Mr. Jeannotte arranged that Mrs. Langley who had served as housekeeper for the deceased cousins should continue in a like capacity with Miss Beck. Within a few days he became Miss Beck's confidential advisor. He took over the management of her affairs. For example, he did her banking, kept financial records, and prepared checks for her signature. There was ample evidence to satisfy the Court that Mr. Jeannotte acted in a fiduciary capacity with relation to Miss Beck and her affairs.

From 1959 Miss Beck's mind was deteriorating. She was forgetful, easily confused, and did not see well. Her mind was seriously weakened.

In March 1960 Mr. Jeannotte informed

his attorney, Miss Rideout, that Miss Beck wanted to see her. The attorney met with Miss Beck at her home on the housekeeper's "day out." A week later, again on the housekeeper's "day out," the purported will drafted by the attorney was executed. A former will obtained by the attorney was destroyed. . . .

Mr. Jeannotte continued to act as Miss Beck's confidential advisor and trusted friend, plainly in a fiduciary capacity, until her death on September 11, 1961.

Under the purported will Mr. Jeannotte received the entire estate inventoried at about $13,000, apart from a bequest of $1,000 to Mrs. Philbrook, a lifelong friend. He was also named executor without bond. . . .

It will serve no useful purpose to rehearse the facts in more detail. The plain fact is that the confidential and trusted advisor of this elderly spinster with weakened mind from the time of her return to the place of her birth until her death, under a will drawn by his attorney and not by an independent advisor, winds up with the entire estate, except the $1,000 bequest to an old time friend.

We are satisfied that the facts which the Justice was entitled to find with the inferences reasonably drawn therefrom warranted a judgment disallowing the will on the ground of undue influence. The proponent has failed to establish that the findings of fact were "clearly erroneous." The will fails. . . .

The attack is directed against the entire will. There is obviously nothing in itself unusual, improper, or suspicious in a legacy of $1,000 to Mrs. Philbrook, an old friend. We are unable, however, on this record to separate the possibly good from the bad, and so the entire will must fail.

Affirmed.

Watson v. Watson
126 N.E.2d 220 (Ill.) 1955

HERSHEY, J. Carrie D. Watson, plaintiff-appellee, filed her amended complaint in the circuit court of Pope County to cancel a written antenuptial agreement executed by herself and her deceased husband. . . .

Upon hearing, the circuit court found that at the time of the execution of the agreement, plaintiff and her late husband were engaged to be married and as a consequence thereof a fiduciary relationship existed between them requiring the decedent to make a full and complete disclosure of his assets and the value thereof prior to the execution of the antenuptial agreement. The court then found that no such disclosure was made and that the contract was therefore invalid since the consideration received by the plaintiff was so disproportionate to the means of the decedent. . . .

Plaintiff was a spinster sixty-eight years of age at the time of her marriage on December 28, 1944, to one James M. Watson, who was widower seventy-two years of age. At the time of the marriage Watson owned considera-ble property in the city of Golconda, Illinois.

A review of the evidence shows that the plaintiff had lived in and around Golconda, Illinois, all of her life. For almost forty years she had clerked in stores in the town and had known James M. Watson from childhood. Likewise, plaintiff had known and been well acquainted with Watson's first wife, Mary.

On the night of December 26, 1944, two days before their marriage, Watson put an envelope on a table in plaintiff's room containing the antenuptial agreement. She testified that she looked the agreement over that night and signed it the following morning, and, as requested, took it to a Mrs. Ragan for delivery to Watson.

In substance, the antenuptial agreement provided that in contemplation of a marriage between the parties soon to be solemnized, plaintiff for and in consideration of the payment of the sum of $1,000, released, waived and forever renounced all her right, title or claim, or dower in and to all property that would have otherwise accrued to her as the wife of James M. Watson.

The day following the signing of the agreement plaintiff and Watson were married in Bythesville, Arkansas.

The parties in this case agree that where persons, parties to an antenuptial contract, are engaged to be married before the contract is entered into, a confidential relationship exists and if the provision made for the wife is disproportionate to the extent and value of the husband's estate a presumption is raised of an intended concealment by the intended husband. . . .

This presumption, without more, constitutes a *prima facie* case of concealment and casts upon those who would sustain the agreement the burden of showing the absence of concealment and that the intended wife had full knowledge of the nature and extent of the husband's property. . . .

The testimony . . . is sufficient to show an engagement to be married. . . . The provision made for the wife in this case was clearly grossly disproportionate to the value and extent of the husband's estate. There is a presumption of concealment, which the defendants seek to overcome by the following evidence.

Twelve witnesses . . . testified . . . that he was generally regarded as one of the more wealthy persons in Golconda. . . . Examination of plaintiff as a witness indicated that she was not unmindful of the general reputation of Watson as being a person of some wealth. Indeed, she acknowledged that he was known to her as one of the more wealthy persons in Golconda.

While we have held that the information as to the nature and extent of the holdings of the husband need not come directly from him, and that surrounding circumstances may be such as to charge the wife with knowledge of his property . . . it does not follow that general reputation is sufficient to supply that knowledge. . . . To so hold would vitiate the reasoning behind the duty to make a full and fair explanation of the nature and extent of the husband's property. General understanding that a person is relatively wealthy is something less than knowing the exact nature and extent of his wealth. Obviously specific knowledge is required before a prospective wife can intelligently choose to take a small sum in payment for a release of her rights and interest in her prospective husband's property.

The circuit court was correct, therefore, in concluding that a confidential relationship existed between the parties to this antenuptial agreement prior to the execution thereof, in holding that the husband did not make a complete and adequate disclosure to the wife of the nature and extent of his holdings, and in setting aside the antenuptial agreement. . . .

Affirmed.

United Mine Workers of America v. Boyle
418 F.Supp. 406 (1976)

A union sought to attach the beneficial interests of defendant union officers in the union pension trust in order to collect a judgment against the officers. The judgment had been obtained as the result of violations of fiduciary duties owed to the union and for violations of the labor laws. The defendants contended that their interest in the pension plan was not subject to attachment because the pension plan contained a spendthrift clause as follows:

No employee or retired employee shall have any right, title, or interest to any portion of the Pension Fund held by the Trustee, until actual payment to the retired employee by the Trustee. No assignment, anticipation, pledge or encumbrance whatsoever shall be permitted and no attempts on the part of the retired employee to transfer or pledge his right to any payment or portion of the monthly pension herein provided shall be recognized by the Trustee. All pension payments shall be made directly into the hands of the retired employee and to no other person, nor shall any such monthly payments be subject to attachment or other legal process.

CORCORAN, J. . . . . [A] trust which by its terms imposes "a valid restraint on the voluntary and involuntary transfer of the interest of the beneficiary" is a spendthrift trust. . . . We conclude that the settlor did in fact create a valid and enforceable spendthrift trust. . . .

However, where a spendthrift trust has been created, it does not inexorably follow that its terms constitute an absolute bar to the lawful claims of all classes of creditors. . . . Traditionally, in the absence of a statute, several distinct classes of claimants have been permitted to invade the beneficiary's interest.

The UMWA asserts an exception. It contends that . . . considerations of public policy militate against application of [the rule] in the circumstances at hand, *viz.:* (1) "self dealing" by these defendants in the creation and subsequent amendment of the Pension Trust, and (2) the tortious nature of defendants' conduct underlying the Court's final judgment. We address each of those contentions separately.

A. Self-Dealing

Even in those jurisdictions which regard spendthrift trusts as generally enforceable, it is acknowledged that "one cannot settle upon himself a spendthrift or other protective trust, or purchase such a trust from another, which will be effective to protect either the income or the corpus against the claims of his creditors, or to free it from his own power of alienation." This rule has application not only to those "who make a direct conveyance to a trustee in trust for themselves," but also to "persons who procure the creation of trusts for their benefit."

The defendants herein clearly do not fall within the category of direct settlors since they have made no "direct conveyance" to the Trustee. From its inception, the Pension Trust has been non-contributory and a gratuity by the UMWA to its former employees. However, it is the plaintiff's contention that in the creation and amendment of the Trust Indenture, the defendants, as former UMWA employees and/or officers, had it within their power and discretion to exclude themselves as Pension Trust beneficiaries and, in failing to do so, the defendants became indirect settlors of the Trust.

We have some difficulty perceiving the logic of plaintiff's novel arguments in this regard. But assuming *arguendo* that in certain situations tacit ratification through inaction might transform a beneficiary into spendthrift settlor, careful examination of the record before the Court leads to the conclusion that the UMWA's contentions are factually untenable. . . .

B. Public Policy and Tort Creditors

As we have previously noted, in most situations the courts of this jurisdiction have given effect to spendthrift provisions immunizing the beneficiary's interest from claims of his creditors. Nonetheless, on public policy grounds, certain narrowly delineated classes of creditors have been excepted from application of the spendthrift doctrine and permitted to "reach the interest of the beneficiary, notwithstanding an express direction to the contrary in the trust instrument." The commonly recognized public policy exceptions to the spendthrift trust doctrine are set forth at Section 157 of the *Restatement, supra:*

> . . . the interest of the beneficiary can be reached in satisfaction of an enforceable claim against the beneficiary, (a) by the wife or child of the beneficiary for support, or by the wife for alimony; (b) for necessary services rendered to

the beneficiary or necessary supplies furnished to him; (c) for services rendered and materials furnished which preserve or benefit the interest of the beneficiary; (d) by the United States or a State to satisfy a claim against the beneficiary.

The plaintiff has not attempted to characterize any of the present claims as being encompassed within the purview of these "traditional" exceptions—and clearly they are not. Instead, the UMWA has asked the Court to carve out a new and heretofore unrecognized exception for claimants who have become involuntary tort creditors.

While it can scarcely be denied that there is something shocking in the notion that a settlor may be permitted to immune a beneficiary's interest from the lawful claims of third-party tort creditors by the device of a spendthrift trust, we believe that the considerations are different in a case, such as this, in which the tort victim and trust settlor are one and the same person. . . .

A settlor can preserve his rights against the beneficiary's interest in the trust by circumspection in drafting the trust instrument. In anticipation of existing and foreseeable future obligations, the settlor is at liberty to include or exclude from the trust agreement such terms and conditions as he may deem appropriate, even to deleting a spendthrift clause in its entirety. So here . . . the UMWA, as settlor of the Pension Trust, could easily have guaranteed the availability of the defendants' beneficial interests for purposes of satisfying a judgment in its favor based upon a tort committed by the beneficiary against the union and unrelated to duties under the Trust. But the UMWA chose to do otherwise.

In the original Trust Indenture and through its subsequent amendments, the absolute, restrictive language of paragraph 12 was retained. We need look no further than its terms to ascertain the plaintiff's clear intention that no monthly pension payment, or portion thereof, should be "subject to attachment or other legal process," including attachments levied by the UMWA itself. Under such circumstances, the Court is not persuaded that the terms of the Pension Trust Indenture should be subject to *ex post facto* judicial amendment to relieve the plaintiff of its conscious and voluntary commitment thereunder.

It is, accordingly . . .

Ordered that defendants' motion to quash the writs of attachment should be, and the same are hereby, granted.

Estate of Tomlinson
359 N.E.2d 109 (Ill.) 1976

RYAN, J. This case involves the construction of the will of Josie A. Tomlinson which was executed in 1951. She died on February 28, 1973. The will was admitted to probate in the circuit court of Peoria County. Katherine D. Shelton, who is also referred to in these proceedings as Catherine D. Shelton, is the adopted daughter of the decedent. She filed the complaint to construe the will. The primary issue is whether a bequest to a nonexisting charitable beneficiary must fail.

The will provided for certain nominal bequests to the plaintiff and other individuals and for bequests to each of three churches. All of the remainder of her estate was given to the First National Bank of Peoria as trustee with directions to convert it to cash and to erect a suitable monument on decedent's grave and to provide for perpetual care of the burial lot. The will then provided:

> I order and direct that my said Trustee shall then distribute all of the remainder of my said estate to the CANCER RESEARCH FUND absolutely and forever.

Following this provision the testator provided that it was her intent to "generally and specifically disinherit each, any and all persons whomsoever claiming to be or may be determined to be my heirs at law."

The complaint alleges that notice of the petition to admit the will to probate and of the other probate proceedings had been given to her, certain other individuals, the three churches named in the will, the trustee and the American Cancer Society. It alleges that no notice was given to "Cancer Research Fund" because there is not now in existence nor was there in existence at the time of the execution of the will or at the date of decedent's death any organization known as "Cancer Research Fund." . . .

It was stipulated that at the present time, at the time the decedent died and at the time the will was executed there was no organization known as the "Cancer Research Fund." The circuit court of Peoria County construed the questioned clause in the will as intending to bequeath the remainder of the estate to the American Cancer Society, Inc. The plaintiff appealed.

The appellate court found that there was no evidence in the record which establishes that the decedent intended to give the remainder of her estate to the American Cancer Society, Inc., and held that the bequest failed and the property passed as intestate property.

We reverse this holding.

Generally if a bequest is given to a specific entity and the legatee declines to accept the bequest or cannot take or is not capable of taking and holding it the bequest fails. If, however, there is a mistake in the name or description of the legatee, whether an individual or a corporation, or if a latent ambiguity exists as to the identity of the legatee, extrinsic evidence is admissible for the purpose of determining the identity of the intended recipient.

The appellate court found that there was insufficient evidence presented to the trial court to show that the testator intended that the bequest should be given to the American Cancer Society. We agree that the evidence is deficient in this regard. Under the facts of this case, however, this should not invalidate the bequest or cause it to fail.

There can be no doubt that the testator intended to make a bequest to benefit an organization involved in cancer research. The parties stipulated, however, that no organization named "Cancer Research Fund" ever existed. This does not mean that the gift must fail.

It is generally held that if a bequest to a particular charitable entity cannot be carried out and does not manifest a general charitable intent, the doctrine of *cy pres* is not applied. In our case, however, although the bequest to the Cancer Research Fund cannot be carried out, we find in the will evidence that the testator did not intend that the bequest should completely fail under such circumstances. The will contains no provision for the disposition of the remainder of the estate in the event of the failure of the charitable bequest. If the bequest should fail, the property would pass to the heirs as intestate property. Such a disposition would be contrary to the clearly expressed intent of the testator to disinherit her heirs at law. The absence of a gift over or a reversion in case of the failure of a charitable purpose constitutes evidence of a general charitable intent.

Under the circumstances of this case it is appropriate to apply the *cy pres* doctrine to carry out the charitable purpose expressed in the will. Bogert in his treatise states that by the application of *cy pres* "[i]f the failed gift was to or for a charitable institution which never existed, or has ceased to exist, or is too vaguely described to be identified . . . the court will usually either deliver the corpus to another like institution in the same region, to hold outright or in trust, whether a successor, affiliate, parent, or unrelated institution."

It is not necessary that we remand this case to the circuit court of Peoria County for the purpose of ascertaining the manner in which the *cy pres* doctrine should be applied. The record before this court contains sufficient facts for such a determination to be made here.

As indicated above there can be no doubt that the testator intended to make a bequest to benefit an organization engaged in cancer research. The affidavit filed on behalf of the

American Cancer Society's claim to the bequest states that the American Cancer Society, which maintains an office in Peoria, Illinois, is a widely known national organization engaged in raising and distributing funds for cancer research programs. The general charitable purpose expressed in the will of benefiting cancer research will properly be carried out by directing, as the trial court did, that the bequest be given to the American Cancer Society, Inc. . . .

Appellate Court reversed; Circuit Court affirmed.

CHAPTER 45
REVIEW QUESTIONS AND PROBLEMS

1. A created a trust with assets consisting of minority holdings of stock in businesses owned by A's family. A bank was named as trustee. The bank relied on a certified public accountant's report concerning the businesses' financial conditions. One of the beneficiaries sued the bank for negligence, contending the bank should make more detailed investigations of the business activities of these businesses to make sure the ventures were receiving their fair share of income. Is there negligence on the part of the trustee? Explain.

2. X was the administrator of Y's estate. In return for several notes owed the estate, X accepted a deed to some land made out to him. X then sold the land to Z, and the heirs to the estate sued to impress a trust in the land. Should they succeed? Explain.

3. X was one of several legatees to Y's testamentary estate. Y had willed X 300 shares of stock of the 23,614 shares he owned. Later, the stock split 3 for 1. X contends that he should receive 900 shares to get his proportionate share. Is he correct? Explain.

4. A executed a will dated September 22, 1960. He died January 4, 1961. His widow presented for probate a will dated October 14, 1960. B, one of the witnesses to the will, testified that she did not see A sign the will dated October 14, 1960, and that A was not present when she signed as a witness, nor did he acknowledge his signature to her. Was the will of October 14, 1960, properly witnessed? Explain.

5. At A's death, a will executed by her was found with her other papers in a locked closet. Pencil lines had been drawn through every provision of the will and the signature. Was the will entitled to probate? Why?

6. T executed a will when he was 84 years of age. T died 1½ years later, and B, his brother, contested the will, claiming that T was not of sound mind when he made it. At the trial, B introduced evidence showing that T had allowed his person and his property to become filthy and that he was eccentric. Should the will be set aside? Why?

7. T established a trust of certain farmland in which she was trustee and the income beneficiary during her lifetime. The trust agreement provided that upon T's death, the earnings were to go to her brother for his life. T died intestate, and her nieces claimed that the trust arrangement was an attempted substitution for a will, but it was not in compliance with the Statute of Wills and therefore was void. Is the trust valid? Why?

8. T's will established a trust providing that all of T's estate was to be used to construct and maintain an orphans' home under the control of the R Sisterhood. When T's will was admitted to probate, the R Sisterhood declined to accept the trust estate. The heirs of T claimed that the purpose of the trust had failed and the property should be conveyed to them. Are the heirs correct? Why?

9. H and W, husband and wife, owned property in joint tenancy. H died, and his will gave a life estate in the property to W with the remainder going to the children. Has a life estate in the property been conveyed to W by H's will? Why?

10. T executed a will in his hosiptal room, where he was dying from acute alcoholism and cancer. He was under sedation and had been given two ounces of whiskey. The will provided that T's property was to be divided between his wife and daughter. When the will was challenged, witnesses testified that the will had been read to T and he appeared to understand it. Is the will valid? Why?

book eight

APPENDICES

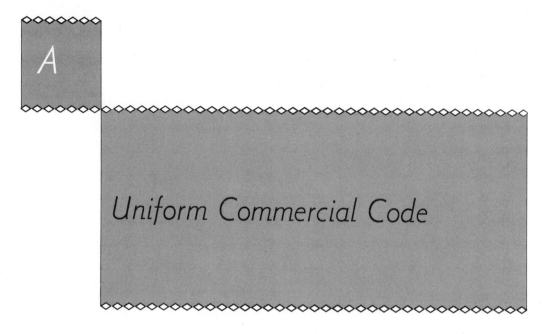

UNIFORM COMMERCIAL CODE

AN ACT

To be known as the Uniform Commercial Code, Relating to Certain Commercial Transactions in or regarding Personal Property and Contracts and other Documents concerning them, including Sales, Commercial Paper, Bank Deposits and Collections, Letters of Credit, Bulk Transfers, Warehouse Receipts, Bills of Lading, other Documents of Title, Investment Securities, and Secured Transactions, including certain Sales of Accounts, Chattel Paper, and Contract Rights, Providing for Public Notice to Third Parties in Certain Circumstances; Regulating Procedure, Evidence and Damages in Certain Court Actions Involving such Transactions, Contracts or Documents; to Make Uniform the Law with Respect Thereto; and Repealing Inconsistent Legislation.

* Please see explanation at the end of this section.

ARTICLE 1

GENERAL PROVISIONS

PART 1

SHORT TITLE, CONSTRUCTION, APPLICATION AND SUBJECT MATTER OF THE ACT

Section 1-101. Short Title. This act shall be known and may be cited as Uniform Commercial Code.

Section 1-102. Purposes; Rules of Construction; Variation by Agreement.

(1) This Act shall be liberally construed and applied to promote its underlying purposes and policies.

(2) Underlying purposes and policies of this Act are

    (a) to simplify, clarify and modernize the law governing commercial transactions;

    (b) to permit the continued expansion

of commercial practices through custom, usage and agreement of the parties;

(c) To make uniform the law among the various jurisdictions.

(3) The effect of provisions of this Act may be varied by agreement, except as otherwise provided in this Act and except that the obligations of good faith, diligence, reasonableness and care prescribed by this Act may not be disclaimed by agreement but the parties may by agreement determine the standards by which the performance of such obligations is to be measured if such standards are not manifestly unreasonable.

(4) The presence in certain provisions of this Act of the words "unless otherwise agreed" or words of similar import does not imply that the effect of other provisions may not be varied by agreement under subsection (3).

(5) In this Act unless the context otherwise requires

(a) words in the singular number include the plural, and in the plural include the singular;

(b) words of the masculine gender include the feminine and the neuter, and when the sense so indicates the words of the neuter gender may refer to any gender.

Section 1-103. Supplementary General Principles of Law Applicable. Unless displaced by the particular provisions of this Act, the principles of law and equity, including the law merchant and the law relative to capacity to contract, principal and agent, estoppel, fraud, misrepresentation, duress, coercion, mistake, bankruptcy, or other validating or invalidating cause shall supplement its provisions.

Section 1-104. Construction Against Implicit Repeal. This Act being a general act intended as a unified coverage of its subject matter, no part of it shall be deemed to be impliedly repealed by subsequent legislation if such construction can reasonable be avoided.

Section 1-105. Territorial Application of the Act; Parties' Power to Choose Applicable Law.

(1) Except as provided hereafter in this section, when a transaction bears a reasonable relation to this state and also to another state or nation the parties may agree that the law either of this state or of such other state or nation shall govern their rights and duties. Failing such agreement this Act applies to transactions bearing an appropriate relation to this state.

(2) Where one of the following provisions of this Act specifies the applicable law, that provision governs and a contrary agreement is effective only to the extent permitted by the law (including the conflict of laws rules) so specified:

Rights of creditors against sold goods. Section 2-402.

Applicability of the Article on Bank Deposits and Collections. Section 4-102.

Bulk transfers subject to the Article on Bulk Transers. Section 6-102.

Applicability of the Article on Investment Securities. Section 8-106.

Policy and scope of the Article on Secured Transactions. Sections 9-102 and 9-103.

Section 1-106. Remedies to be Liberally Administered.

(1) The remedies provided by this Act shall be liberally administered to the end that the aggrieved party may be put in as good a position as if the other party had fully performed but neither consequential or special nor penal damages may be had except as specifically provided in this Act or by other rule of law.

(2) Any right or obligation declared by this Act is enforceable by action unless the provision declaring it specifies a different and limited effect.

Section 1-107. Waiver or Renunciation of Claim or Right After Breach. Any claim or right arising out of an alleged breach can be discharged in whole or in part without consideration by a written waiver or renunciation signed and delivered by the aggrieved party.

Section 1-108. Severability. If any provision or clause of this Act or application thereof to any person or circumstances is held invalid, such invalidity shall not affect other provisions or applications of the Act which can be given effect without the invalid provisions or application, and to this end the provisions of this Act are declared to be severable.

PART 2

GENERAL DEFINITIONS AND PRINCIPLES OF INTERPRETATION

Section 1-201. General Definition. Subject to additional definitions contained in the subsequent Articles of this Act which are applicable to specific Articles or Parts thereof, and unless the context otherwise requires, in this Act:

(1) "Action" in the sense of a judicial proceeding includes recoupment, counterclaim, set-off, suit in equity and any other proceedings in which rights are determined.

(2) "Aggrieved party" means a party entitled to resort to a remedy.

(3) "Agreement" means the bargain of the parties in fact as found in their language or by implication from other circumstances including course of dealing or usage of trade or course of performance as provided in this Act (Sections 1-205 and 2-208). Whether an agreement has legal consequences is determined by the provisions of this Act, if applicable; otherwise by the law of contracts (Section 1-103). (Compare "Contract.")

(4) "Bank" means any person engaged in the business of banking.

(5) "Bearer" means the person in possession of an instrument, document of title, or security payable to bearer or indorsed in blank.

(6) "Bill of lading" means a document evidencing the receipt of goods for shipment issued by a person engaged in the business of transporting or forwarding goods, and includes an airbill. "Airbill" means a document serving for air transportation as a bill of lading does for marine or rail transportation, and includes an air consignment note or air waybill.

(7) "Branch" includes a separately incorporated foreign branch of a bank.

(8) "Burden of establishing" a fact means the burden of persuading the triers of fact that the existence of the fact is more probable than its non-existence.

(9) "Buyer in ordinary course of business" means a person who in good faith and without knowledge that the sale to him is in violation of the ownership rights or security interest of a third party in the goods buys in ordinary course from a person in the business of selling goods of that kind but does not include a pawnbroker. "Buying" may be for cash or by exchange of other property or on secured or unsecured credit and includes receiving goods or documents of title under a pre-existing contract for sale but does not include a transfer in bulk or as security for or in total or partial satisfaction of a money debt.

(10) "Conspicuous": a term or clause is conspicuous when it is so written that a reasonable person against whom it is to operate ought to have noticed it. A printed heading in capitals (as: NON-NEGOTIABLE BILL OF LADING) is conspicuous. Language in the body of a form is "conspicuous" if it is in larger or other contrasting type or color. But in a telegram any stated term is "conspicuous." Whether a term or clause is "conspicuous" or not is for decision by the court.

(11) "Contract" means the total legal obligation which results from the parties' agreement as affected by this Act and any other applicable rules of law. (Compare "Agreement.")

(12) "Creditor" includes a general creditor, a secured creditor, a lien creditor and any representative of creditors, including an assignee for the benefit of creditors, a trustee in bankruptcy, a receiver in equity and an executor or administrator of an insolvent debtor's or assignor's estate.

(13) "Defendant" includes a person in the position of defendant in a cross-action or counterclaim.

(14) "Delivery" with respect to instruments, documents of title, chattel paper or securities means voluntary transfer of possession.

(15) "Document of title" includes bill of lading, dock warrant, dock receipt, warehouse receipt or order for the delivery of goods, and also any other document which

in the regular course of business or financing is treated as adequately evidencing that the person in possession of it is entitled to receive, hold and dispose of the document and the goods it covers. To be a document of title a document must purport to be issued by or addressed to a bailee and purport to cover goods in the bailee's possession which are either identified or are fungible portions of an identified mass.

(16) "Fault" means wrongful act, omission or breach.

(17) "Fungible" with respect to goods or securities means goods or securities of which any unit is, by nature or usage of trade, the equivalent of any other like unit. Goods which are not fungible shall be deemed fungible for the purposes of this Act to the extent that under a particular agreement or document unlike units are treated as equivalents.

(18) "Genuine" means free of forgery or counterfeiting.

(19) "Good faith" means honesty in fact in the conduct or transaction concerned.

(20) "Holder" means a person who is in possession of a document of title or an instrument or an investment security drawn, issued or indorsed to him or to his order or to bearer or in blank.

(21) To "honor" is to pay or to accept and pay, or where a credit so engages to purchase or discount a draft complying with the terms of the credit.

(22) "Insolvency proceedings" includes any assignment for the benefit of creditors or other proceedings intended to liquidate or rehabilitate the estate of the person involved.

(23) A person is "insolvent" who either has ceased to pay his debts in the ordinary course of business or cannot pay his debts as they become due or is insolvent within the meaning of the federal bankruptcy law.

(24) "Money" means a medium of exchange authorized or adopted by a domestic or foreign government as a part of its currency.

(25) A person has "notice" of a fact when

(a)   he has actual knowledge of it; or

(b)   he has received a notice or notification of it; or

(c) from all the facts and circumstances known to him at the time in question he has reason to know that it exists.

A person "knows" or had "knowledge" of a fact when he has actual knowledge of it. "Discover" or "learn" or a word or phrase of similar import refers to knowledge rather than to reason to know. The time and circumstances under which a notice or notification may cease to be effective are not determined by this Act.

(26) A person "notifies" or "gives" a notice or notification to another by taking such steps as may be reasonably required to inform the other person in ordinary course whether or not such other actually comes to know of it. A person "receives" a notice or notification when

(a)   it comes to his attention; or

(b)   it is duly delivered at the place of business through which the contract was made or at any other place held out by him as the place for receipt of such communications.

(27) Notice, knowledge or a notice or notification received by an organization is effective for a particular transaction from the time when it is brought to the attention of the individual conducting that transaction, and in any event from the time when it would have been brought to his attention if the organization had exercised due diligence. An organization exercises due diligence if it maintains reasonable routines for communicating significant information to the person conducting the transaction and there is reasonable compliance with the routines. Due diligence does not require an individual acting for the organization to communicate information unless such communication is part of his regular duties or unless he has reason to know of the transaction and that the transaction would be materially affected by the information.

(28) "Organization" includes a corporation, government or governmental subdivision or agency, business trust, estate, trust, partnership or association, two or more persons having a joint or common interest, or any other legal or commercial entity.

(29) "Party," as distinct from "third party," means a person who has engaged in a transaction or made an agreement within this Act.

(30) "Person" includes an individual or an organization (See Section 1-102).

(31) "Presumption" or "presumed" means that the trier of fact must find the existence of the fact presumed unless and until evi-

dence is introduced which would support a finding of its non-existence.

(32) "Purchase" includes taking by sale, discount, negotiation, mortgage, pledge, lien, issue or re-issue, gift or any other voluntary transaction creating an interest in property.

(33) "Purchaser" means a person who takes by purchase.

(34) "Remedy" means any remedial right to which an aggrieved party is entitled with or without resort to a tribunal.

(35) "Representative" includes an agent, an officer of a corporation or association, and a trustee, executor or administrator of an estate, or any other person empowered to act for another.

(36) "Rights" includes remedies.

(37) "Security interest" means an interest in personal property or fixtures which secures payment or performance of an obligation. The retention or reservation of title by a seller or goods notwithstanding shipment or delivery to the buyer (Section 2-401) is limited in effect to a reservation of a "security interest." The term also includes any interest of a buyer of accounts, chattel paper, or contract rights which is subject to Article 9. The special property interest of a buyer of goods on identification or such goods to a contract for sale under Section 2-401 is not a "security interest," but a buyer may also acquire a "security interest" by complying with Article 9. Unless a lease or consignment is intended as security, reservation of title thereunder is not a "security interest" but a consignment is in any event subject to the provisions on consignment sales (Section 2-326). Whether a lease is intended as security is to be determined by the facts of each case; however (a) the inclusion of an option to purchase does not of itself make the lease one intended for security, and (b) an agreement that upon compliance with the terms of the lease the lessee shall become or has the option to become the owner of the property for no additional consideration or for a nominal consideration does make the lease one intended for security.

(38) "Send" in connection with any writing or notice means to deposit in the mail or deliver for transmission by any other usual means of communication with postage or cost of transmission provided for and properly addressed and in the case of an instrument to an address specified thereon or otherwise agreed, or if there be none to any address reasonable under the circumstances. The receipt of any writing or notice within the time at which it would have arrived if properly sent has the effect of a proper sending.

(39) "Signed" includes any symbol executed or adopted by a party with present intention to authenticate a writing.

(40) "Surety" includes guarantor.

(41) "Telegram" includes a message transmitted by radio, teletype, cable, any mechanical method of transmission, or the like.

(42) "Term" means that portion of an agreement which relates to a particular matter.

(43) "Unauthorized" signature or indorsement means one made without actual, implied or apparent authority and includes a forgery.

(44) "Value." Except as otherwise provided with respect to negotiable instruments and bank collections (Sections 3-303, 4-208 and 4-209) a person gives "value" for rights if he acquires them

(a) in return for a binding commitment to extend credit or for the extension of immediately available credit whether or not drawn upon and whether or not a charge-back is provided for in the event of difficulties in collection; or

(b) as security for or in total or partial satisfaction of a pre-existing claim; or

(c) by accepting delivery pursuant to a pre-existing contract for purchase; or

(d) generally, in return for any consideration sufficient to support a simple contract.

(45) "Warehouse receipt" means a receipt issued by a person engaged in the business of storing goods for hire.

(46) "Written" or "writing" includes printing, typewriting or any other intentional reduction to tangible form.

Section 1-202. Prima Facie Evidence by Third Party Documents. A document in due form purporting to be a bill of lading, policy or certificate of insurance, official weigher's or inspector's certificate, consular invoice, or any other document authorized or required by the contract to be issued by a third party shall be prima facie evidence of its own authenticity and genuineness and of the facts stated in the document by the third party.

Section 1-203. Obligation of Good Faith. Every contract or duty within this Act imposes an obligation of good faith in its performance or enforcement.

Section 1-204. Time; Reasonable Time; "Seasonably."

(1) Whenever this Act requires any action to be taken within a reasonable time, any time which is not manifestly unreasonable may be fixed by agreement.

(2) What is a reasonable time for taking any action depends on the nature, purpose and circumstances of such action.

(3) An action is taken "seasonably" when it is taken at or within the time agreed or if no time is agreed at or within a reasonable time.

Section 1-205. Course of Dealing and Usage of Trade.

(1) A course of dealing in a sequence of previous conduct between the parties to a particular transaction which is fairly to be regarded as establishing a common basis of understanding for interpreting their expressions and other conduct.

(2) A usage of trade is any practice or method of dealing having such regularity of observance in a place, vocation or trade as to justify an expectation that it will be observed with respect to the transaction in question. The existence and scope of such a usage are to be proved as facts. If it is established that such a usage is embodied in a written trade code or similar writing the interpretation of the writing is for the court.

(3) A course of dealing between parties and any usage of trade in the vocation or trade in which they are engaged or of which they are or should be aware give particular meaning to and supplement or qualify terms of an agreement.

(4) The express terms of an agreement and an applicable course of dealing or usage of trade shall be construed wherever reasonable as consistent with each other; but wher such construction is unreasonable express terms control both course of dealing and usage of trade and course of dealing controls usage of trade.

(5) An applicable usage of trade in the place where any part of performance is to occur shall be used in interpreting the agreement as to that part of the performance.

(6) Evidence of a relevant usage of trade offered by one party is not admissible unless and until he has given the other party such notice as the court finds sufficient to prevent unfair surprise to the latter.

Section 1-206. Statute of Frauds for Kinds of Personal Property Not Otherwise Covered.

(1) Except in the cases described in subsection (2) of this section a contract for the sale of personal property is not enforceable by way of action or defense beyond five thousand dollars in amount or value of remedy unless there is some writing which indicates that a contract for sale has been made between the parties at a defined or stated price, reasonably identifies the subject matter, and is signed by the party against whom enforcement is sought or by his authorized agent.

(2) Subsection (1) of this section does not apply to contracts for the sale of goods (Section 2-201) nor of securities (Section 8-319) nor to security agreements (Section 9-203).

Section 1-207. Performance or Acceptance under Reservation of Rights A party who with explicit reservation of rights performs or promises performance or assents to performance in a manner demanded or offered by the other party does not thereby prejudice the rights reserved. Such words as "without prejudice," "under protest" or the like are sufficient.

Section 1-208. Option to Accelerate at Will. A term providing that one party or his successor in interest may accelerate payment of performance or require collateral or additional collateral "at will" or "when he deems himself insecure" or in words of similar import shall be construed to mean that he shall have power to do so only if he in good faith believes that the prospect of payment or performance is impaired. The burden of establishing lack of good faith is on the party against whom the power has been exercised.

ARTICLE 2

SALES

PART 1

SHORT TITLE, GENERAL CONSTRUCTION AND SUBJECT MATTER

Section 2-101. Short Title. This Article shall be known and may be cited as Uniform Commercial Code—Sales.

Section 2-102. Scope; Certain Security and Other Transactions Excluded from this Article. Unless the context otherwise requires, this Article applies to transactions in goods; it does not apply to any transaction which although in the form of an unconditional contract to sell or present sale is intended to operate only as a security transaction nor does this Article impair or repeal any statute regulating sales to consumers, farmers or other specified classes of buyers.

Section 2-103. Definitions and Index of Definitions.

(1) In this Article unless the context otherwise requires

    (a) "Buyer" means a person who buys or contracts to buy goods.

    (b) "Good faith" in the case of a merchant means honesty in fact and the observance of reasonable commercial standards of fair dealing in the trade.

    (c) "Receipt" of goods means taking physical possession of them.

    (d) "Seller" means a person who sells or contracts to sell goods.

(2) Other definitions applying to this Article or to specified parts thereof, and the sections in which they appear are:

"Acceptance." Section 2-606.
"Banker's credit." Section 2-325.
"Between merchants." Section 2-104.
"Cancellation." Section 2-106(4).
"Commercial unit." Section 2-105.
"Confirmed credit." Section 2-325.
"Conforming to contract." Section 2-106.
"Contract for sale." Section 2-106.
"Cover." Section 2-712.

"Entrusting." Section 2-403.
"Financing agency." Section 2-104.
"Future goods." Section 2-105.
"Goods." Section 2-105.
"Identification." Section 2-501.
"Installment contract." Section 2-612.
"Letter of Credit." Section 2-325.
"Lot." Section 2-105.
"Merchant." Section 2-104.
"Overseas." Section 2-323.
"Person on position of seller." Section 2-707.
"Present sale." Section 2-106.
"Sale." Section 2-106.
"Sale on approval." Section 2-326.
"Sale or return." Section 2-326.
"Termination." Section 2-106.

(3) The following definitions in other Articles apply to this Article:

"Check." Section 3-204.
"Consignee." Section 7-102.
"Consignor." Section 7-102.
"Consumer goods." Section 9-109.
"Dishonor." Section 3-507.
"Draft." Section 3-104.

(4) In addition Article 1 contains general definitions and principles of construction and interpretation applicable throughout this Article.

Section 2-104. Definitions: "Merchant"; "Between Merchants"; Financing Agency".

(1) "Merchant" means a person who deals in goods of the kind or otherwise by his occupation holds himself out as having knowledge or skill peculiar to the practices or goods involved in the transaction or to whom such knowledge or skill may be attributed by his employment of an agent or broker or other intermediary who by his occupation holds himself out as having such knowledge or skill.

(2) "Financing agency" means a bank, finance company or other person who in the ordinary course of business makes advances against goods or documents of title or who by arrangement with either the seller or the buyer intervenes in ordinary course to make or collect payment due or claimed under the contract for sale, as by purchasing or paying the seller's draft or making advances against it or by merely taking it for collection whether or not documents of title accompany the draft. "Financing agency" includes also a bank or other person who similarly intervenes between persons who are in the position of seller and buyer in respect to the goods (Section 2-707).

(3) "Between merchants" means in any transaction with respect to which both parties are chargeable with the knowledge or skill of merchants.

Section 2-105. Definitions: Transferability; "Goods"; "Future" Goods; "Lot"; "Commercial Unit."

(1) "Goods" means all things (including specially manufactured goods) which are movable at the time of identification to the contract for sale other than the money in which the price is to be paid, investment securities (Article 8) and things in action. "Goods" also includes the unborn young of animals and growing crops and other identified things attached to realty as described in the section on goods to be severed from realty (Section 2-107).

(2) Goods must be both existing and identified before any interest in them can pass. Goods which are not both existing and identified are "future" goods. A purported present sale of future goods or of any interest therein operates as a contract to sell.

(3) There may be a sale or a part interest in existing identified goods.

(4) An undivided share in an identified bulk of fungible goods is sufficiently identified to be sold although the quantity of the bulk is not determined. Any agreed proportion of such a bulk or any quantity thereof agreed upon by number, weight or other measure may to the extent of the seller's interest in the bulk be sold to the buyer who then becomes an owner in common.

(5) "Lot" means a parcel or a single article which is the subject matter of a separate sale or delivery, whether or not it is usfficient to perform the contract.

(6) "Commercial unit" means such a unit of goods as by commercial usage is a single whole for purposes of sale and division of which materially impairs its character or value on the market or in use. A commercial unit may be a single article (as a machine) or a set of articles (as a suite of furniture or an assortment of sizes) or a quantity (as a bale, gross, or carload) or any other unit treated in use or in the relevant market as a single whole.

Section 2-106. Definitions: "Contract"; "Agreement"; "Contract for Sale"; "Sale"; "Present Sale"; "Conforming" to Contract; "Termination"; "Cancellation."

(1) In this Article unless the context otherwise requires "contract" and "agreement" are limited to those relating to the present or future sale of goods. "Contract for sale" includes both a present sale of goods and a contract to sell goods at a future time. A "sale" consists in the passing of title from the seller to the buyer for a price (Section 2–401). A "present sale" means a sale which is accomplished by the making of the contract.

(2) Goods or conduct including any part of a performance are "conforming" or conform to the contract when they are in accordance with the obligations under the contract.

(3) "Termination" occurs when either party pursuant to a power created by agreement or law puts an end to the contract otherwise than for its breach. On "termination" all obligations which are still executory on both sides are discharged but any right based on prior breach or performance survives.

(4) "Cancellation" occurs when either party puts an end to the contract for breach by the other and its effect is the same as that of "termination" except that the cancelling party also retains any remedy for breach of the whole contract or any unperformed balance.

Section 2-107. Goods to be Severed from Realty: Recording.

(1) A contract for the sale of timber, minerals or the like or a structure or its materials to be removed from realty is a contract for the sale of goods within this Article if they are to be severed by the seller, but until severance a purported present sale thereof which is not effective as

a transfer of an interest in land is effective only as a contract to sell.

(2) A contract for the sale apart from the land of growing crops or other things attached to realty and capable of severance without material harm thereto but not described in subsection (1) is a contract for the sale of goods within this Article whether the subject matter is to be severed by the buyer or by the seller even though it forms part of the realty at the time of contracting, and the parties can by identification effect a present sale before severance.

(3) The provisions of this section are subject to any third party rights provided by the law relating to realty records, and the contract for sale may be executed and recorded as a document transferring an interest in land and shall then constitute notice to third parties of the buyer's rights under the contract for sale.

PART 2

FORM, FORMATION AND READJUSTMENT OF CONTRACT

Section 2-201. Formal Requirements; Statute of Frauds.

(1) Except as otherwise provided in this section a contract for the sale of goods for the price of $500 or more is not enforceable by way of action or defense unless there is some writing sufficient to indicate that a contract for sale has been made between the parties and signed by the party against whom enforcement is sought or by his authorized agent or broker. A writing is not insufficient because it omits or incorrectly states a term agreed upon but the contract is not enforceable under this paragraph beyond the quantity of goods shown in such writing.

(2) Between merchants if within a reasonable time a written confirmation of the contract and sufficient against the sender is received and the party receiving it has reason to know its contents, it satisfies the requirements of subsection (1) against such party unless written notice of objection to its contents is given within ten days after it is received.

(3) A contract which does not satisfy the requirements of subsection (1) but which is valid in other respects is enforceable

(a) if the goods are to be specially manufactured for the buyer and are not suitable for sale to others in the ordinary course of the seller's business and the seller, before notice of repudiation is received and under circumstances which reasonably indicate that the goods are for the buyer, has made either a substantial beginning of their manufacture or commitments for their procurement; or

(b) if the party against whom enforcement is sought admits in his pleading, testimony or otherwise in court that a contract for sale was made, but the contract is not enforceable under this provision beyond the quantity of goods admitted; or

(c) with respect to goods for which payment has been made and accepted or which have been received and accepted (Sec. 2-606).

Section 2-202. Final Written Expression: Parol or Extrinsic Evidence.

Terms with respect to which the confirmatory memoranda of the parties agree or which are otherwise set forth in a writing intended by the parties as a final expression of their agreement with respect to such terms as are included therein may not be contradicted by evidence of any prior agreement or of a contemporaneous oral agreement but may be explained or supplemented.

(a) by course of dealing or usage of trade (Section 1-205) or by course of performance (Section 2-208); and

(b) by evidence of consistent additional terms unless the court finds the writing to have been intended also as a complete and exclusive statement of the terms of the agreement.

Section 2-203. Seals Inoperative.

The affixing of a seal to a writing evidencing a contract for sale or an offer to buy or sell goods does not constitute the writing a sealed instrument and the law with respect to sealed instruments does not apply to such a contract or offer.

Section 2-204. Formation in General.

(1) A contract for sale of goods may be made in any manner sufficient to show agreement, including conduct by both

parties which recognizes the existence of such a contract.

(2) An agreement sufficient to constitute a contract for sale may be found even though the moment of its making is undetermined.

(3) Even though one or more terms are left open a contract for sale does not fail for indefiniteness if the parties have intended to make a contract and there is a reasonably certain basis for giving an appropriate remedy.

Section 2-205. Firm Offers. An offer by a merchant to buy or sell goods in a signed writing which by its terms gives assurance that it will be held open is not revocable, for lack of consideration, during the time stated or if no time is stated for a reasonable time, but in no event may such period of irrevocability exceed three months; but any such term of assurance on a form supplied by the offeree must be separately signed by the offeror.

Section 2-206. Offer and Acceptance in Formation of Contract.

(1) Unless otherwise unambiguously indicated by the language or circumstances

(a) an offer to make a contract shall be construed as inviting acceptance in any manner and by any medium reasonable in the circumstances;

(b) an order or other offer to buy goods for prompt or current shipment shall be construed as inviting acceptance either by a prompt promise to ship or by the prompt or current shipment of conforming or non-conforming goods, but such a shipment of non-conforming goods does not constitute an acceptance if the seller reasonably notifies the buyer that the shipment is offered only as an accommodation to the buyer.

(2) Where the beginning of a requested performance is a reasonable mode of acceptance an offeror who is not notified of acceptance within a reasonable time may treat the offer as having lapsed before acceptance.

Section 2-207. Additional Terms in Acceptance or Confirmation.

(1) A definite and seasonable expression of acceptance or a written confirmation which is sent within a reasonable time operates as an acceptance even though it states terms additional to or different from those offered or agreed upon, unless acceptance is ex-

pressly made conditional on assent to the additional or different terms.

(2) The additional terms are to be construed as proposals for addition to the contract. Between merchants such terms become part of the contract unless:

(a) the offer expressly limits acceptance to the terms of the offer;

(b) they materially alter it; or

(c) notification of objection to them has already been given or is given within a reasonable time after notice of them is received.

(3) Conduct by both parties which recognizes the existence of a contract is sufficient to establish a contract for sale although the writings of the parties do not otherwise establish a contract. In such case the terms of the particular contract consist of those terms on which the writings of the parties agree, together with any supplementary terms incorporated under any other provisions of this Act.

Section 2-208. Course of Performance or Practical Construction.

(1) Where the contract for sale involves repeated occasions for performance by either party with knowledge of the nature of the performance and opportunity for objection to it by the other, any course of performance accepted or acquiesced in without objection shall be relevant to determine the meaning of the agreement.

(2) The express terms of the agreement and any such course of performance, as well as any course of dealing and usage of trade, shall be construed whenever reasonable as consistent with each other; but when such construction is unreasonable, express terms shall control course of performance and course of performance shall control both course of dealing and usage of trade (Section 1-205).

(3) Subject to the provisions of the next section on modification and waiver, such course of performance shall be relevant to show a waiver or modification of any term inconsistent with such course of performance.

Section 2-209. Modification, Rescission and Waiver.

(1) An agreement modifying a contract within this Article needs no consideration to be binding.

(2) A signed agreement which excludes modification or rescission except by a signed writing cannot be otherwise modified or rescinded, but except as between merchants such a requirement on a form supplied by the merchant must be separately signed by the other party.

(3) The requirements of the statute of frauds section of this Article (Section 2-201) must be satisfied if the contract as modified is within its provisions.

(4) Although an attempt at modification or rescission does not satisfy the requirements of subsection (2) or (3) it can operate as a waiver.

(5) A party who has made a waiver affecting an executory portion of the contract may retract the waiver by reasonable notification received by the other party that strict performance will be required of any term waived, unless the retraction would be unjust in view of a material change of position in reliance on the waiver.

Section 2-210. Delegation of Performance; Assignment of Rights.

(1) A party may perform his duty through a delegate unless otherwise agreed or unless the other party has a substantial interest in having his original promisor perform or control the acts required by the contract. No delegation of performance relieves the party delegating of any duty to perform or any liability for breach.

(2) Unless otherwise agreed all rights of either seller or buyer can be assigned except where the assignment would materially change the duty of the other party, or increase materially the burden or risk imposed on him by his contract, or impair materially his chance of obtaining return performance. A right to damages for breach of the whole contract or a right arising out of the assignor's due performance of his entire obligation can be assigned despite agreement otherwise.

(3) Unless the circumstances indicate the contrary a prohibition of assignment of "the contract" is to be construed as barring only the delegation to the assignee of the assignor's performance.

(4) An assignment of "the contract" or of "all my rights under the contract" or an assignment in similar general terms is an assignment of rights and unless the language or the circumstances (as in an assignment for security) indicate the contrary, it is a delegation of performance of the duties of the assignor and its acceptance by the assignee constitutes a promise by him to perform those duties. This promise is enforceable by either the assignor or the other party to the original contract.

(5) The other party may treat any assignment which delegates performance as creating reasonable grounds for insecurity and may without prejudice to his rights against the assignor demand assurances from the assignee (Section 2-609).

PART 3

GENERAL OBLIGATION AND CONSTRUCTION OF CONTRACT

Section 2-301. General Obligations of Parties. The obligation of the seller is to transfer and deliver and that of the buyer is to accept and pay in accordance with the contract.

Section 2-302. Unconscionable Contract or Clause.

(1) If the court as a matter of law finds the contract or any clause of the contract to have been unconscionable at the time it was made the court may refuse to enforce the contract, or it may enforce the remainder of the contract without the unconscionable clause, or it may so limit the application of any unconscionable clause as to avoid any unconscionable result.

(2) When it is claimed or appears to the court that the contract or any clause thereof may be unconscionable the parties shall be afforded a reasonable opportunity to present evidence as to its commercial setting, purpose and effect to aid the court in making the determination.

Section 2-303. Allocation or Division of Risks. Where this Article allocates a risk or a burden as between the parties "unless otherwise agreed," the agreement may not only shift the allocation but may also divide the risk or burden.

Section 2-304. Price Payable in Money, Goods, Realty, or Otherwise.

(1) The price can be made payable in

money or otherwise. If it is payable in whole .or in part in goods each party is a seller of the goods which he is to transfer.

(2) Even though all or part of the price is payable in an interest in realty the transfer of the goods and the seller's obligations with reference to them are subject to this Article, but not the transfer of the interest in realty or the transferor's obligations in connection therewith.

Section 2-305. Open Price Term.

(1) The parties if they so intend can conclude a contract for sale even though the price is not settled. In such a case the price is a reasonable price at the time for delivery if

(a) nothing is said as to price; or

(b) the price is left to be agreed by the parties and they fail to agree; or

(c) the price is to be fixed in terms of some agreed market or other standard as set or recorded by a third person or agency and it is not so set or recorded.

(2) A price to be fixed by the seller or by the buyer means a price for him to fix in good faith.

(3) When a price left to be fixed otherwise than by agreement of the parties fails to be fixed through fault of one party the other may at his option treat the contract as cancelled or himself fix a reasonable price.

(4) Where, however, the parties intend not to be bound unless the price be fixed or agreed and it is not fixed or agreed there is no contract. In such a case the buyer must return any goods already received or if unable to do so must pay their reasonable value at the time of delivery and the seller must return any portion of the price paid on account.

Section 2-306. Output, Requirements and Exclusive Dealings.

(1) A term which measures the quantity by the output of the seller or the requirements of the buyer means such actual output or requirements as may occur in good faith, except that no quantity unreasonably disproportionate to any stated estimate or in the absence of a stated estimate to any normal or otherwise comparable prior output or requirements may be tendered or demanded.

(2) A lawful agreement by either the seller or the buyer for exclusive dealing in the kind of goods concerned imposes unless otherwise agreed an obligation by the seller to use best efforts to supply the goods and by the buyer to use best efforts to promote their sale.

Section 2-307. Delivery in Single Lot or Several Lots.

Unless otherwise agreed all goods called for by a contract for sale must be tendered in a single delivery and payment is due only on such tender but where the circumstances give either party the right to make or demand delivery in lots the price if it can be apportioned may be demanded for each lot.

Section 2-308. Absence of Specified Place for Delivery.

Unless otherwise agreed.

(a) the place for delivery of goods is the seller's place of business or if he has none his residence; but

(b) in a contract for sale of identified goods which to the knowledge of the parties at the time of contracting are in some other place, that place is the place for their delivery; and

(c) documents of title may be delivered through customary banking channels.

Section 2-309. Absence of Specific Time Provisions; Notice of Termination.

(1) The time for shipment or delivery or any other action under a contract if not provided in this Article or agreed upon shall be a reasonable time.

(2) Where the contract provides for successive performances but is indefinite in duration it is valid for a reasonable time but unless otherwise agreed may be terminated at any time by either party.

(3) Termination of a contract by one party except on the happening of an agreed event requires that reasonable notification is invalid if its operation would be unconscionable.

Section 2-310. Open Time for Payment or Running of Credit; Authority to Ship under Reservation.

Unless otherwise agreed

(a) payment is due at the time and place at which the buyer is to receive the goods even though the place of shipment is the place of delivery; and

(b) if the seller is authorized to send the goods he may ship them under reservation, and may tender the documents of title, but the buyer may inspect the goods after their arrival before payment is due unless such inspection is inconsistent with the terms of the contract (Section 2-513); and

(c) if delivery is authorized and made by way of documents of title otherwise than by subsection (b) then payment is due at the time and place at which the buyer is to receive the documents regardless of where the goods are to be received; and

(d) where the seller is required or authorized to ship the goods on credit the credit period runs from the time of shipment but post-dating the invoice or delaying its dispatch will correspondingly delay the starting of the credit period.

Section 2-311. Options and Cooperation Respecting Performance.

(1) An agreement for sale which is otherwise sufficiently definite (subsection (3) of Section 2-204) to be a contract is not made invalid by the fact that it leaves particulars of performance to be specified by one of the parties. Any such specification must be made in good faith and within limits set by commercial reasonableness.

(2) Unless otherwise agreed specifications relating to assortment of the goods are at the buyer's option and except as otherwise provided in subsections (1) (c) and (3) of Section 2-319 specifications or arrangements relating to shipment are at the seller's option.

(3) Where such specification would materially affect the other party's performance but is not seasonably made or where one party's cooperation is necessary to the agreed performance of the other but is not seasonably forthcoming, the other party in addition to all other remedies

(a) is excused for any resulting delay in his own performance; and

(b) may also either proceed to perform in any reasonable manner or after the time for a material part of his own performance treat the failure to specify or to cooperate as a breach by failure to deliver or accept the goods.

Section 2-312. Warranty of Title and Against Infringement; Buyer's Obligation Against Infringement.

(1) Subject to subsection (2) there is in a contract for a sale a warranty by the seller that

(a) the title conveyed shall be good, and its transfer rightful; and

(b) the goods shall be delivered free from any security interest or other lien or encumbrance of which the buyer at the time of contracting has no knowledge.

(2) A warranty under subsection (1) will be excluded or modified only by specific language or by circumstances which give the buyer reason to know that the person selling does not claim title in himself or that he is purporting to sell only such right or title as he or a third person may have.

(3) Unless otherwise agreed a seller who is a merchant regularly dealing in goods of the kind warrants that the goods shall be delivered free of the rightful claim of any third person by way of infringement or the like but a buyer who furnishes specifications to the seller must hold the seller harmless against any such claim which arises out of compliance with the specifications.

Section 2-313. Express Warranties by Affirmation, Promise, Description, Sample.

(1) Express warranties by the seller are created as follows:

(a) Any affirmation of fact or promise made by the seller to the buyer which relates to the goods and becomes part of the basis of the bargain creates an express warranty that the goods shall conform to the affirmation or promise.

(b) Any description of the goods which is made part of the basis of the bargain creates an express warranty that the goods shall conform to the description.

(c) Any sample or model which is made part of the basis of the bargain creates an express warranty that the whole of the goods shall conform to the sample or model.

(2) It is not necessary to the creation of an express warranty that the seller use formal words such as "warrant" or "guarantee" or that he have a specific intention to make a warranty, but an affirmation merely of the value of the goods or a statement purporting to be merely the seller's opinion or commendation of the goods does not create a warranty.

Section 2-314. Implied Warranty: Merchantability; Usage of Trade.

(1) Unless excluded or modified (Section

2-316) a warranty that the goods shall be merchantable is implied in a contract for their sale if the seller is a merchant with respect to goods of that kind. Under this section the serving for value of food or drink to be consumed either on the premises or elsewhere is a sale.

(2) Goods to be merchantable must be at least such as

(a) pass without objection in the trade under the contract description; and

(b) in the case of fungible goods, are of fair average quality within the description; and

(c) are fit for the ordinary purposes for which such goods are used; and

(d) run, within the variations permitted by the agreement, of even kind, quality and quantity within each unit and among all units involved; and

(e) are adequately contained, packaged, and labeled as the agreement may require; and

(f) conform to the promises or affirmations of fact made on the container or label if any.

(3) Unless excluded or modified (Section 2-316) other implied warranties may arise from course of dealing or usage of trade.

Section 2-315. Implied Warranty: Fitness for Particular Purpose. Where the seller at the time of contracting has reason to know any particular purpose for which the goods are required and that the buyer is relying on the seller's skill or judgment to select or furnish suitable goods, there is unless excluded or modified under the next section an implied warranty that the goods shall be fit for such purpose.

Section 2-316. Exclusion or Modification of Warranties.

(1) Words or conduct relevant to the creation of an express warranty and words or conduct tending to negate or limit warranty shall be construed wherever reasonable as consistent with each other; but subject to the provisions of this Article on parol or extrinsic evidence (Section 2-202) negation or limitation is inoperative to the extent that such construction is unreasonable.

(2) Subject to subsection (3), to exclude or modify the implied warranty of merchantability or any part of it the language must mention merchantability and in case of a writing must be conspicuous, and to exclude or modify any implied warranty of fitness the exclusion must be by a writing and conspicuous. Language to exclude all implied warranties of fitness is sufficient if it states, for example, that "There are no warranties which extend beyond the description on the face hereof."

(3) Notwithstanding subsection (2)

(a) unless the circumstances indicate otherwise, all implied warranties are excluded by expressions like "as is," "with all faults" or other language which in common understanding calls the buyer's attention to the exclusion of warranties and makes plain that there is no implied warranty; and

(b) when the buyer before entering into the contract has examined the goods or the sample or model as fully as he desired or has refused to examine the goods there is no implied warranty with regard to defects which an examination ought in the circumstances to have revealed to him; and

(c) an implied warranty can also be excluded or modified by course of dealing or course of performance or usage of trade.

(4) Remedies for breach of warranty can be limited in accordance with the provisions of this Article on liquidation or limitation of damages and on contractual modification of remedy (Sections 2-718 and 2-719).

Section 2-317. Cumulation and Conflict of Warranties Express or Implied. Warranties whether express or implied shall be construed as consistent with each other and as cumulative, but if such construction is unreasonable the intention of the parties shall determine which warranty is dominant. In ascertaining that intention the following rules apply:

(a) Exact or technical specifications displace an inconsistent sample or model or general language of description.

(b) A sample from an existing bulk displaces inconsistent general language of description.

(c) Express warranties displace inconsistent implied warranties other than an implied warranty of fitness for a particular purpose.

Section 2-318. Third Party Beneficiaries or Warranties Express or Implied. A seller's warranty whether express or implied extends to any natural person who is in the family or household of his buyer or who is a guest in his home if it is reasonable to expect that such person may use, consume or be affected by the goods and who is injured in person by breach of the warranty. A seller may not exclude or limit the operation of this section.

Section 2-319. F.O.B. and F.A.S. Terms.

(1) Unless otherwise agreed the term F.O.B. (which means "free on board") at a named place, even though used only in connection with the stated price, is a delivery term under which

(a) when the term is F.O.B. the place of shipment, the seller must at that place ship the goods in the manner provided in this article (Section 2-504) and bear the expense and risk of putting them into the possession of the carrier; or

(b) when the term is F.O.B. the place of destination, the seller must at his own expense and risk transport the goods to that place and there tender delivery of them in the manner provided in this Article (Section 2-503);

(c) when under either (a) or (b) the term is also F.O.B. vessel, car or other vehicle, the seller must in addition at his own expense and risk load the goods on board. If the term is F.O.B. vessel the buyer must name the vessel and in an appropriate case the seller must comply with the provisions of this Article on the form of bill of lading (Section 2-323).

(2) Unless otherwise agreed the term F.A.S. vessel (which means "free alongside") at a named port, even though used only in connection with the stated price, is a delivery term under which the seller must

(a) at his own expense and risk deliver the goods alongside the vessel in the manner usual in that port or on a dock designated and provided by the buyer; and

(b) obtain and tender a receipt for the goods in exchange for which the carrier is under a duty to issue a bill of lading.

(3) Unless otherwise agreed in any case falling within subsection (1)(a) or (c) or subsection (2) the buyer must seasonably give any needed instructions for making delivery, including when the term is F.A.S. or F.O.B. the loading berth of the vessel and in an appropriate case its name and sailing date.

The seller may treat the failure of needed instructions as a failure of cooperation under this Article (Section 2-311). He may also at his option move the goods in any reasonable manner preparatory to delivery or shipment.

(4) Under the term F.O.B. vessel or F.A.S. unless otherwise agreed the buyer must make payment against tender of the required documents and the seller may not tender nor the buyer demand delivery of the goods in substitution for the documents.

Section 2-320. C.I.F. and C. & F. Terms.

(1) The term C.I.F. means that the price includes in a lump sum the cost of the goods and the insurance and freight to the named destination. The term C. & F. or C.F. means that the price so includes cost and freight to the named destination.

(2) Unless otherwise agreed and even though used only in connection with the stated price and destination, the term C.I.F. destination or its equivalent requires the seller at his own expense and risk to

(a) put the goods into the possession of a carrier at the port for shipment and obtain a negotiable bill or bills of lading covering the entire transportation to the named destination; and

(b) load the goods and obtain a receipt from the carrier (which may be contained in the bill of lading) showing that the freight has been paid or provided for; and

(c) obtain a policy or certificate of insurance, including any war risk insurance, of a kind and on terms then current at the port of shipment in the usual amount, in the currency of the contract, shown to cover the same goods covered by the bill of lading and providing for payment of loss to the order of the buyer or for the account of whom it may concern; but the seller may add to the price the amount of the premium for any such war risk insurance; and

(d) prepare an invoice of the goods and procure any other documents required to effect shipment or to comply with the contract; and

(e) forward and tender with commercial promptness all the documents in due form and with any indorsement necessary to perfect the buyer's rights.

(3) Unless otherwise agreed the term C. & F. or its equivalent has the same effect and imposes upon the seller the same obligations and risks as a C.I.F. term except the obligation as to insurance.

(4) Under the term C.I.F. or C. & F. unless otherwise agreed the buyer must make payment against tender of the required documents and the seller may not tender nor the buyer demand delivery of the goods in substitution for the documents.

Section 2-321. C.I.F. or C. & F.: "Net Landed Weights"; "Payment on Arrival"; Warranty of Condition on Arrival. Under a contract containing a term C.I.F. or C. & F.

(1) Where the price is based on or is to be adjusted according to "net landed weights," "delivered weights," "out turn" quantity or quality or the like, unless otherwise agreed the seller must reasonably estimate the price. The payment due on tender of the documents called for by the contract is the amount so estimated, but after final adjustment of the price a settlement must be made with commercial promptness.

(2) An agreement described in subsection (1) or any warranty of quality or condition of the goods on arrival places upon the seller the risk of ordinary deterioration, shrinkage and the like in transportation but has no effect on the place or time of identification to the contract for sale or delivery or on the passing of the risk of loss.

(3) Unless otherwise agreed where the contract provides for payment on or after arrival of the goods the seller must before payment allow such preliminary inspection as is feasible; but if the goods are lost delivery of the documents and payment are due when the goods should have arrived.

Section 2-322. Delivery "Ex-Ship."

(1) Unless otherwise agreed a term for delivery of goods "ex-ship" (which means from the carrying vessel) or in equivalent language is not restricted to a particular ship and requires delivery from a ship which has reached a place at the named port of destination where goods of the kind are usually discharged.

(2) Under such a term unless otherwise agreed

    (a) the seller must discharge all liens arising out of the carriage and furnish

the buyer with a direction which puts the carrier under a duty to deliver the goods; and

    (b) the risk of loss does not pass to the buyer until the goods leave the ship's tackle or are otherwise properly unloaded.

Section 2-323. Form of Bill of Lading Required in Overseas Shipment; "Overseas."

(1) Where the contract contemplates overseas shipment and contains a term C.I.F. or C. & F. or F. O. B. vessel, the seller unless otherwise agreed must obtain a negotiable bill of lading stating that the goods have been loaded on board or, in the case of a term C.I.F. or C. & F., received for shipment.

(2) Where in a case within subsection (1) a bill of lading has been issued in a set of parts, unless otherwise agreed if the documents are not to be sent from abroad the buyer may demand tender of the full set; otherwise only one part of the bill of lading need be tendered. Even if the agreement expressly requires a full set

    (a) due tender of a single part is acceptable within the provisions of this Article on cure of improper delivery (subsection (1) of Section 2-508); and

    (b) even though the full set is demanded, if the documents are sent from abroad the person tendering an incomplete set may nevertheless require payment upon furnishing an indemnity which the buyer in good faith deems adequate.

(3) A shipment by water or by air or a contract contemplating such shipment is "overseas" insofar as by usage of trade or agreement it is subject to the commercial, financing or shipping practices characteristic of international deep water commerce.

Section 2-324. "No Arrival, No Sale" Term. Under a term "no arrival, no sale" or terms of like meaning, unless otherwise agreed.

    (a) the seller must properly ship conforming goods and if they arrive by any means he must tender them on arrival but he assumes no obligation that the goods will arrive unless he has caused the non-arrival; and

    (b) where without fault of the seller the goods are in part lost or have so deteriorated as no longer to conform to the contract or arrive after the contract time, the buyer may proceed as if there had been casualty to identified goods (Section 2-613).

Section 2-325. "Letter of Credit" Term; "Confirmed Credit."

(1) Failure of the buyer seasonably to furnish an agreed letter of credit is a breach of the contract for sale.

(2) The delivery to seller of a proper letter of credit suspends the buyer's obligation to pay. If the letter of credit is dishonored, the seller may on seasonable notification to the buyer require payment directly from him.

(3) Unless otherwise agreed the term "letter of credit" or "banker's credit" in a contract for sale means an irrevocable credit issued by a financing agency of good repute and, where the shipment is overseas, of good international repute. The term "confirmed credit" means that the credit must also carry the direct obligation of such an agency which does business in the seller's financial market.

Section 2-326. Sale on Approval and Sale or Return; Consignment Sales and Rights of Creditors.

(1) Unless otherwise agreed, if delivered goods may be returned by the buyer even though they conform to the contract, the transaction is.

(a) a "sale on approval" if the goods are delivered primarily for use; and

(b) a "sale or return" if the goods are delivered primarily for resale.

(2) Except as provided in subsection (3), goods held on approval are not subject to the claims of the buyer's creditors until acceptance; goods held on sale or return are subject to such claims while in the buyer's possession.

(3) Where goods are delivered to a person for sale and such person maintains a place of business at which he deals in goods of the kind involved, under a name other than the name of the person making delivery, then with respect to claims of creditors of the person conducting the business the goods are deemed to be on sale or return. The provisions of this subsection are applicable even though an agreement purports to reserve title to the person making delivery until payment or resale or uses such words as "on consignment" or "on memoran-

dum." However, this subsection is not applicable if the person making delivery

(a) complies with an applicable law providing for a consignor's interest or the like to be evidenced by a sign, or

(b) establishes that the person conducting the business is generally known by his creditors to be substantially engaged in selling the goods of others, or

(c) complies with the filing provisions of the Article on Secured Transactions (Article 9).

(4) Any "or return" term of a contract for sale is to be treated as a separate contract for sale within the statute of frauds section of this Article (Section 2-201) and as contradicting the sale aspect of the contract within the provisions of this Article on parol or extrinsic evidence (Section 2-202).

Section 2-327. Special Incidents of Sale on Approval and Sale or Return.

(1) Under a sale on approval unless otherwise agreed

(a) although the goods are identified to the contract the risk of loss and the title do not pass to the buyer until acceptance; and

(b) use of the goods consistent with the purpose of trial is not acceptance but failure seasonably to notify the seller of election to return the goods is acceptance, and if the goods conform to the contract acceptance of any part is acceptance of the whole; and

(c) after due notification of election to return, the return is at the seller's risk and expense but a merchant buyer must follow any reasonable instructions.

(2) Under a sale or return unless otherwise agreed

(a) the option to return extends to the whole or any commercial unit of the goods while in substantially their original condition, but must be exercised seasonably; and

(b) the return is at the buyer's risk and expense.

Section 2-328. Sale by Auction.

(1) In a sale by auction if goods are put up in lots each lot is the subject of a separate sale.

(2) A sale by auction is complete when the auctioneer so announces by the fall of the hammer or in other customary manner.

Where a bid is made while the hammer is falling in acceptance of a prior bid the auctioneer may in his discretion reopen the bidding or declare the goods sold under the bid on which the hammer was falling.

(3) Such a sale is with reserve unless the goods are in explicit terms put up without reserve. In an auction with reserve the auctioneer may withdraw the goods at any time until he announces completion of the sale. In an auction without reserve, after the auctioneer calls for bids on an article or lot, that article or lot cannot be withdrawn unless no bid is made within a reasonable time.

In either case a bidder may retract his bid until the auctioneer's announcement of completion of the sale, but a bidder's retraction does not revive any previous bid.

(4) If the auctioneer knowingly receives a bid on the seller's behalf or the seller makes or procures such a bid, and notice has not been given that liberty for such bidding is reserved, the buyer may at his option avoid the sale or take the goods at the price of the last good faith bid prior to the completion of the sale. This subsection shall not apply to any bid at a forced sale.

PART 4

TITLE, CREDITORS AND GOOD FAITH PURCHASERS

Section 2-401. Passing of Title; Reservation for Security; Limited Application of this Section. Each provision of this Article with regard to the rights, obligations and remedies of the seller, the buyer, purchasers or other third parties applies irrespective of title to the goods except where the provision refers to such title. Insofar as situations are not covered by the other provisions of this Article and matters concerning title become material the following rules apply:

(1) Title to goods cannot pass under a contract for sale prior to their identification to the contract (Section 2-501), and unless otherwise explicitly agreed the buyer acquires by their identification a special property as limited by this Act. Any retention or reservation by the seller of the title (property) in goods shipped or delivered to the buyer is limited in effect to a reservation of a security interest. Subject to these provisions and to the provisions of the Article on Secured Transactions (Article 9), title to goods passes from the seller to the buyer in any manner and on any conditions explicitly agreed on by the parties.

(2) Unless otherwise explicitly agreed title passes to the buyer at the time and place at which the seller completes his performance with reference to the physical delivery of the goods, despite any reservation of a security interest and even though a document of title is to be delivered at a different time or place; and in particular and despite any reservation of a security interest by the bill of lading

(a) if the contract requires or authorizes the seller to send the goods to the buyer but does not require him to deliver them at destination, title passes to the buyer at the time and place of shipment; but

(b) if the contract requires delivery at destination, title passes on tender there.

(3) Unless otherwise explicitly agreed where delivery is to be made without moving the goods,

(a) if the seller is to deliver a document of title, title passes at the time when and the place where he delivers such documents; or

(b) if the goods are at the time of contracting already identified and no documents are to be delivered, title passes at the time and place of contracting.

(4) A rejection or other refusal by the buyer to receive or retain the goods, whether or not justified, or a justified revocation of acceptance revests title to the goods in the seller. Such revesting occurs by operation of law and is not a "sale."

Section 2-402. Rights of Seller's Creditors Against Sold Goods.

(1) Except as provided in subsections (2) and (3), rights of unsecured creditors of the seller with respect to goods which have been identified to a contract for sale are subject to the buyer's rights to recover the goods under this Article (Sections 2-502 and 2-716).

(2) A creditor of the seller may treat a sale or an identification of goods to a contract

for sale as void if as against him a retention of possession by the seller is fraudulent under any rule of law of the state where the goods are situated, except that retention of possession in good faith and current course of trade by a merchant-seller for a commercially reasonable time after a sale or identification is not fraudulent.

(3) Nothing in this Article shall be deemed to impair the rights of creditors of the seller

(a) under the provisions of the Article on Secured Transactions (Article 9); or

(b) where identification to the contract or delivery is made not in current course of trade but in satisfaction of or as security for a pre-existing claim for money, security or the like and is made under circumstances which under any rule of law of the state where the goods are situated would apart from this Article constitute the transaction a fraudulent transfer or voidable preference.

Section 2-403. Power to Transfer; Good Faith Purchase of Goods; "Entrusting."

(1) A purchaser of goods acquires all title which his transferor had or had power to transfer except that a purchaser of a limited interest acquires rights only to the extent of the interest purchased. A person with voidable title had power to transfer a good title to a good faith purchaser for value. When goods have been delivered under a transaction of purchase the purchaser has such power even though

(a) the transferor was deceived as to the identity of the purchaser, or

(b) the delivery was in exchange for a check which is later dishonored, or

(c) it was agreed that the transaction was to be a "cash sale," or

(d) the delivery was procured through fraud punishable as larcenous under the criminal law.

(2) Any entrusting of possession of goods to a merchant who deals in goods of that kind gives him power to transfer all rights of the entruster to a buyer in ordinary course of business.

(3) "Entrusting" includes any delivery and any acquiescence in retention of possession regardless of any condition expressed between the parties to the delivery or acquiescence and regardless of whether the procurement of the entrusting or the possessor's disposition of the goods have been such as to be larcenous under the criminal law.

(4) The rights of other purchasers of goods and of lien creditors are governed by the Articles on Secured Transactions (Article 9), Bulk Transfers (Article 6) and Documents of Title (Article 7).

PART 5

PERFORMANCE

Section 2-501. Insurable Interest in Goods; Manner of Identification of Goods.

(1) The buyer obtains a special property and an insurable interest in goods by identification of existing goods as goods to which the contract refers even though the goods so identified are non-conforming and he has an opinion to return or reject them. Such identification can be made at any time and in any manner explicitly agreed to by the parties. In the absence of explicit agreement identification occurs

(a) when the contract is made if it is for the sale of goods already existing and identified;

(b) if the contract is for the sale of future goods other than those described in paragraph (c), when goods are shipped, marked or otherwise designated by the seller as goods to which the contract refers;

(c) when the crops are planted or otherwise become growing crops or the young are conceived if the contract is for the sale of unborn young to be born within twelve months after contracting or for the sale of crops to be harvested within twelve months or the next normal harvest season after contracting whichever is longer.

(2) The seller retains an insurable interest in goods so long as title to or any security interest in the goods remains in him and where the identification is by the seller alone he may until default or insolvency or notification to the buyer that the identification is final substitute other goods for those identified.

(3) Nothing in this section impairs any insurable interest recognized under any other statute or rule of law.

Section 2-502. Buyer's Right to Goods on Seller's Insolvency.

(1) Subject to subsection (2) and even though the goods have not been shipped a buyer who has paid a part or all of the price of the goods in which he has a special property under the provisions of the immediately preceding section may on making and keeping good a tender of any unpaid portion of their price recover them from the seller if the seller becomes insolvent within ten days after receipt of the first installment on their price.

(2) If the identification creating his special property has been made by the buyer he acquires the right to recover the goods only if they conform to the contract for sale.

Section 2-503. Manner of Seller's Tender of Delivery.

(1) Tender of delivery requires that the seller put and hold conforming goods at the buyer's disposition and give the buyer any notification reasonably necessary to enable him to take delivery. The manner, time and place for tender are determined by the agreement and this Article, and in particular

(a) tender must be at a reasonable hour, and if it is of goods they must be kept available for the period reasonably necessary to enable the buyer to take possession; but

(b) unless otherwise agreed the buyer must furnish facilities reasonably suited to the receipt of the goods.

(2) Where the case is within the next section respecting shipment tender requires that the seller comply with its provisions.

(3) Where the seller is required to deliver at a particular destination tender requires that he comply with subsection (1) and also in any appropriate case tender documents as described in subsections (4) and (5) of this section.

(4) Where goods are in the possession of a bailee and are to be delivered without being moved

(a) tender requires that the seller either tender a negotiable document of title covering such goods or procure acknowl-edgment by the bailee of the buyer's right to possession of the goods; but

(b) tender to the buyer of a non-negotiable document of title or of a written direction to the bailee to deliver is sufficient tender unless the buyer seasonably objects, and receipt by the bailee of notification of the buyer's rights fixes those rights as against the bailee and all third persons; but risk of loss of the goods and of any failure by the bailee to honor the non-negotiable document of title or to obey the direction remains on the seller until the buyer has had a reasonable time to present the document or direction, and a refusal by the bailee to honor the document or to obey the direction defeats the tender.

(5) Where the contract requires the seller to deliver documents

(a) he must tender all such documents in correct form, except as provided in this Article with respect to bills of lading in a set (subsection (2) of Section 2-323); and

(b) tender through customary banking channels is sufficient and dishonor of a draft accompanying the documents constitutes non-acceptance or rejection.

Section 2-504. Shipment by Seller. Where the seller is required or authorized to send the goods to the buyer and the contract does not require him to deliver them at a particular destination, then unless otherwise agreed he must

(a) put the goods in the possession of such a carrier and make such a contract for their transportation as may be reasonable having regard to the nature of the goods and other circumstances of the case; and

(b) obtain and promptly deliver or tender in due form any document necessary to enable the buyer to obtain possession of the goods or otherwise required by the agreement or by usage of trade; and

(c) promptly notify the buyer of the shipment.

Failure to notify the buyer under paragraph (c) or to make a proper contract under paragraph (a) is a ground for rejection only if material delay or loss ensued.

Section 2-505. Seller's Shipment Under Reservation.

(1) Where the seller has identified goods to the contract by or before shipment:

(a) his procurement of a negotiable bill of lading to his own order or otherwise reserves in him a security interest in the goods. His procurement of the bill to the order of a financing agency or of the buyer indicates in addition only the seller's expectation of transferring that interest to the person named.

(b) a non-negotiable bill of lading to himself or his nominee reserves possession of the goods as security but except in a case of conditional delivery (subsection (2) of Section 2-507) a non-negotiable bill of lading naming the buyer as consignee reserves no security interest even though the seller retains possession of the bill of lading.

(2) When shipment by the seller with reservation of a security interest is in violation of the contract for sale it constitutes an improper contract for transportation within the preceding section but impairs neither the rights given to the buyer by shipment and identification of the goods to the contract nor the seller's powers as a holder of a negotiable document.

Section 2-506. Rights of Financing Agency.

(1) A financing agency by paying or purchasing for value a draft which relates to a shipment of goods acquires to the extent of the payment or purchase and in addition to its own rights under the draft and any document of title securing it any rights of the shipper in the goods including the right to stop delivery and the shipper's right to have the draft honored by the buyer.

(2) The right to reimbursement of a financing agency which has in good faith honored or purchased the draft under commitment to or authority from the buyer is not impaired by subsequent discovery of defects with reference to any relevant document which was apparently regular on its face.

Section 2-507. Effect of Seller's Tender; Delivery on Condition.

(1) Tender of delivery is a condition to the buyer's duty to accept the goods and, unless otherwise agreed, to his duty to pay for them. Tender entitles the seller to acceptance of the goods and to payment according to the contract.

(2) Where payment is due and demanded on the delivery to the buyer of goods or documents of title, his right as against the seller to retain or dispose of them is conditional upon his making the payment due.

Section 2-508. Cure by Seller of Improper Tender or Delivery; Replacement.

(1) Where any tender or delivery by the seller is rejected because non-conforming and the time for performance has not yet expired, the seller may seasonably notify the buyer of his intention to cure and may then within the contract time make a conforming delivery.

(2) Where the buyer rejects a non-conforming tender which the seller had reasonable grounds to believe would be acceptable with or without money allowance the seller may if he seasonably notifies the buyer have a further reasonable time to substitute a conforming tender.

Section 2-509. Risk of Loss in the Absence of Breach.

(1) Where the contract requires or authorizes the seller to ship the goods by carrier

(a) if it does not require him to deliver them at a particular destination, the risk of loss passes to the buyer when the goods are duly delivered to the carrier even though the shipment is under reservation (Section 2-505); but

(b) if it does require him to deliver them at a particular destination and the goods are there duly tendered while in the possession of the carrier, the risk of loss passes to the buyer when the goods are there duly so tendered as to enable the buyer to take delivery.

(2) Where the goods are held by a bailee to be delivered without being moved, the risk of loss passes to the buyer

(a) on his receipt of a negotiable document of title covering the goods; or

(b) on acknowledgement by the bailee of the buyer's right to possession of the goods; or

(c) after his receipt of a non-negotiable document of title or other written direction to deliver, as provided in subsection (4) (b) of Section 2-503.

(3) In any case not within subsection (1) or (2), the risk of loss passes to the buyer on his receipt of the goods if the seller is a merchant; otherwise the risk passes to the buyer on tender of delivery.

(4) The provisions of this section are subject to contrary agreement of the parties and to the provisions of this Article on sale on approval (Section 2-327) and on effect of breach on risk of loss (Section 2-510).

Section 2-510. Effect of Breach on Risk of Loss

(1) Where a tender or delivery of goods so fails to conform to the contract as to give a right of rejection the risk of their loss remains on the seller until cure or acceptance.

(2) Where the buyer rightfully revokes acceptance he may to the extent of any deficiency in his effective insurance coverage treat the risk of loss as having rested on the seller from the beginning.

(3) Where the buyer as to conforming goods already identified to the contract for sale repudiates or is otherwise in breach before risk of their loss has passed to him the seller may to the extent of any deficiency in his effective insurance coverage treat the risk of loss as resting on the buyer for a commercially reasonable time.

Section 2-511. Tender of Payment by Buyer; Payment by Check.

(1) Unless otherwise agreed tender of payment is a condition to the seller's duty to tender and complete any delivery.

(2) Tender of payment is sufficient when made by any means or in any manner current in the ordinary course of business unless the seller demands payment in legal tender and gives any extension of time reasonably necessary to procure it.

(3) Subject to the provisions of this Act on the effect of an instrument on an obligation (Section 3-802), payment by check is conditional and is defeated as between the parties by dishonor of the check on due presentment.

Section 2-512. Payment by Buyer Before Inspection.

(1) Where the contract requires payment before inspection non-conformity of the goods does not excuse the buyer from so making payment unless

(a) the non-conformity appears without inspection; or

(b) despite tender of the required documents the circumstances would justify injunction against honor under the provisions of this Act (Section 5-114).

(2) Payment pursuant to subsection (1) does not constitute an acceptance of goods or impair the buyer's right to inspect or any of his remedies.

Section 2-513. Buyer's Right to Inspection of Goods.

(1) Unless otherwise agreed and subject to subsection (3), where goods are tendered or delivered or identified to the contract for sale, the buyer has a right before payment or acceptance to inspect them at any reasonable place and time and in any reasonable manner. When the seller is required or authorized to send the goods to the buyer, the inspection may be after their arrival.

(2) Expenses of inspection must be borne by the buyer but may be recovered from the seller if the goods do not conform and are rejected.

(3) Unless otherwise agreed and subject to the provisions of this Article on C.I.F. contracts (subsection (3) of Section 2-321), the buyer is not entitled to inspect the goods before payment of the price when the contract provides

(a) for delivery "C.O.D." or on other like terms; or

(b) for payment against documents of title, except where such payment is due only after the goods are to become available for inspection.

(4) A place or method of inspection fixed by the parties is presumed to be exclusive but unless otherwise expressly agreed it does not postpone identification or shift the place for delivery or for passing the risk of loss. If compliance becomes impossible, inspection shall be as provided in this section unless the place or method fixed was clearly intended as an indispensable condition failure of which avoids the contract.

Section 3-514. When Documents Deliverable on Acceptance; When on Payment.

Unless otherwise agreed documents against which a draft is drawn are to be delivered to the drawee on acceptance of the draft if it is payable more than three days after presentment; otherwise, only on payment.

Section 2-515. Preserving Evidence of Goods in Dispute. In furtherance of the adjustment of any claim or dispute

(a) either party on reasonable notification to the other and for the purpose of ascertaining the facts and preserving evidence has the right to inspect, test and sample the goods including such of them as may be in the possession or control of the other; and

(b) the parties may agree to a third party inspection or survey to determine the conformity or condition of the goods and may agree that the findings shall be binding upon them in any subsequent litigation or adjustment.

PART 6

BREACH, REPUDIATION AND EXCUSE

Section 2-601. Buyer's Rights on Improper Delivery. Subject to the provisions of this Article on breach in installment contracts (Section 2-612) and unless otherwise agreed under the sections on contractual limitations of remedy (Sections 2-718 and 2-719), if the goods or the tender of delivery fail in any respect to conform to the contract, the buyer may may

(a) reject the whole; or

(b) accept the whole; or

(c) accept any commercial unit or units and reject the rest.

Section 2-602. Manner and Effect of Rightful Rejection.

(1) Rejection of goods must be within a reasonable time after their delivery or tender. It is ineffective unless the buyer seasonably notifies the seller.

(2) Subject to the provisions of the two following sections on rejected goods (Sections 2-603 and 2-604),

(a) after rejection any exercise of ownership by the buyer with respect to any commercial unit is wrongful as against the seller; and

(b) if the buyer has before rejection taken physical possession of goods in which he does not have a security interest under the provisions of this Article (subsection (3) of Section 2-711), he is under a duty after rejection to hold them with reasonable care at the seller's disposition for a time sufficient to permit the seller to remove them; but

(c) the buyer has no further obligations with regard to goods rightfully rejected.

(3) The seller's rights with respect to goods wrongfully rejected are governed by the provisions of this Article on Seller's remedies in general (Section 2-703).

Section 2-603. Merchant Buyer's Duties as to Rightfully Rejected Goods.

(1) Subject to any security interest in the buyer (subsection (3) of Section 2-711), when the seller has no agent or place of business at the market of rejection a merchant buyer is under a duty after rejection of goods in his possession or control to follow any reasonable instructions received from the seller with respect to the goods and in the absence of such instructions to make reasonable efforts to sell them for the seller's account if they are perishable or threaten to decline in value speedily. Instructions are not reasonable if on demand indemnity for expenses is not forthcoming.

(2) When the buyer sells goods under subsection (1), he is entitled to reimbursement from the seller or out of the proceeds for reasonable expenses of caring for and selling them, and if the expenses include no selling commission then to such commission as is usual in the trade or if there is none to a reasonable sum not exceeding ten per cent on the gross proceeds.

(3) In complying with this section the buyer is held only to good faith and good faith conduct hereunder is neither acceptance nor conversion nor the basis of an action for damages.

Section 2-604. Buyer's Options as to Salvage of Rightfully Rejected Goods. Subject to the provisions of the immediately preceding section on perishables if the seller gives no instructions within a reasonable time after notifcation of rejection the buyer may store the rejected goods for the seller's account or reship them to him or resell them for the seller's account with reimbursement as provided in the preceding section. Such action is not acceptance or conversion.

Section 2-605. Waiver of Buyer's Objections by Failure to Particularize.

(1) The buyer's failure to state in connection with rejection a particular defect which is ascertainable by reasonable inspection precludes him from relying on the unstated defect to justify rejection or to establish breach

    (a) where the seller could have cured it if stated seasonally; or

    (b) between merchants when the seller has after rejection made a request in writing for a full and final written statement of all defects on which the buyer proposes to rely.

(2) Payment against documents made without reservation of rights precludes recovery of the payment for defects apparent on the fact of the documents.

Section 2-606. What Constitutes Acceptance of Goods.

(1) Acceptance of goods occurs when the buyer

    (a) after a reasonable opportunity to inspect the goods signifies to the seller that the goods are conforming or that he will take or retain them in spite of their non-conformity; or

    (b) fails to make an effective rejection (subsection (1) of Section 2-602), but such acceptance does not occur until the buyer has had a reasonable opportunity to inspect them; or

    (c) does any act inconsistent with the seller's ownership but if such act is wrongful as against the seller it is an acceptance only if ratified by him.

(2) Acceptance of a part of any commercial unit is acceptance of that entire unit.

Section 2-607. Effect of Acceptance; Notice of Breach; Burden of Establishing Breach After Acceptance; Notice of Claim or Litigation to Person Answerable Over.

(1) The buyer must pay at the contract rate for any goods accepted.

(2) Acceptance of goods by the buyer precludes rejection of the goods accepted and if made with knowledge of a non-conformity cannot be revoked because of it unless the acceptance was on the reasonable assumption that the non-conformity would be seasonably cured but acceptance does not of itself impair any other remedy provided by this Article for non-conformity.

(3) Where a tender has been accepted

    (a) the buyer must within a reasonable time after he discovers or should have discovered any breach notify the seller of breach or be barred from any remedy; and

    (b) if the claim is one for infringement or the like (subsection (3) of Section 2-312) and the buyer is sued as a result of such a breach he must so notify the seller within a reasonable time after he receives notice of the litigation or be barred from any remedy over for liability established by the litigation.

(4) The burden is on the buyer to establish any breach with respect to the goods accepted.

(5) Where the buyer is sued for breach of a warranty or other obligation for which his seller is answerable over

    (a) he may give his seller written notice of the litigation. If the notice states that the seller may come in and defend and that if the seller does not do so he will be bound in any action against him by his buyer by any determination of fact common to the two litigations, then unless the seller after seasonable receipt of the notice does come in and defend he is so bound.

    (b) if the claim is one for infringement or the like (subsection (3) of Section 2-312) the original seller may demand in writing that his buyer turn over to him control of the litigation including settlement or else be barred from any remedy over and if he also agrees to bear all expense and to satisfy any adverse judgment, then unless the buyer after seasonable receipt of the demand does turn over control the buyer is so barred.

(6) The provisions of subsections (3), (4) and (5) apply to any obligation of a buyer to hold the seller harmless against infringement or the like (subsection (3) of Section 2-312).

Section 2-608. Revocation of Acceptance in Whole or in Part.

(1) The buyer may revoke his acceptance of a lot or commercial unit whose non-conformity substantially impairs its value to him if he has accepted it

    (a) on the reasonable assumption that

its non-conformity would be cured and it has not been seasonably cured; or

(b) without discovery of such non-conformity if his acceptance was reasonably induced either by the difficulty of discovery before acceptance or by the seller's assurances.

(2) Revocation of acceptance must occur within a reasonable time after the buyer discovers or should have discovered the ground for it and before any substantial change in condition of the goods which is not caused by their own defects. It is not effective until the buyer notifies the seller of it.

(3) A buyer who so revokes has the same rights and duties with regard to the goods involved as if he had rejected them.

Section 2-609. Right to Adequate Assurance of Performance.

(1) A contract for sale imposes an obligation on each party that the other's expectation of receiving due performance will not be impaired. When reasonable grounds for insecurity arise with respect to the performance of either party the other may in writing demand adequate assurance of due performance and until he receives such assurance may if commercially reasonable suspend any performance for which he has not already received the agreed return.

(2) Between merchants the reasonableness of grounds for insecurity and the adequacy of any assurance offered shall be determined according to commercial standards.

(3) Acceptance of any improper delivery or payment does not prejudice the aggrieved party's right to demand adequate assurance of future performance.

(4) After receipt of a justified demand failure to provide within a reasonable time not exceeding thirty days such assurance of due performance as is adequate under the circumstances of the particular case is a repudiation of the contract.

Section 2-610. Anticipatory Repudiation. When

either party repudiates the contract with respect to a performance not yet due the loss of which will substantially impair the value of the contract to the other, the aggrieved party may

(a) for a commercially reasonable time await performance by the repudiating party; or

(b) resort to any remedy for breach (Section 2-703 or Section 2-711), even though he has notified the repudiating party that he would await the latter's performance and has urged retraction; and

(c) in either case suspend his own performance or proceed in accordance with the provisions of this Article on the seller's right to identify goods to the contract notwithstanding breach or to salvage unfinished goods (Section 2-704).

Section 2-611. Retraction of Anticipatory Repudiation.

(1) Until the repudiating party's next performance is due he can retract his repudiation unless the aggrieved party has since the repudiation cancelled or materially changed his position or otherwise indicated that he considers the repudiation final.

(2) Retraction may be by any method which clearly indicates to the aggrieved party that the repudiating party intends to perform, but must include any assurance justifiably demanded under the provisions of this Article (Section 2-609).

(3) Retraction reinstates the repudiating party's rights under the contract with due excuse and allowance to the aggrieved party for any delay occasioned by the repudiation.

Section 2-612. "Installment Contract"; Breach.

(1) An "installment contract" is one which requires or authorizes the delivery of goods in separate lots to be separately accepted, even though the contract contains a clause "each delivery is a separate contract" or its equivalent.

(2) The buyer may reject any installment which is non-conforming if the non-conformity substantially impairs the value of that installment and cannot be cured or if the non-conformity is a defect in the required documents; but if the non-conformity does not fall within subsection (3) and the seller gives adequate assurance of its cure the buyer must accept that installment.

(3) Whenever non-conformity or default with respect to one or more installments substantially impairs the value of the whole contract there is a breach of the whole. But

the aggrieved party reinstates the contract if he accepts a non-conforming installment without seasonably notifying of cancellation or if he brings an action with respect only to past installments or demands performance as to future installments.

Section 2-613. Casualty to Identified Goods. Where the contract requires for its performance goods identified when the contract is made, and the goods suffer casualty without fault of either party before the risk of loss passes to the buyer, or in a proper case under a "no arrival, no sale" term (Section 2-324) then

(a) if the loss is total the contract is avoided; and

(b) if the loss is partial or the goods have so deteriorated as no longer to conform to the contract the buyer may nevertheless demand inspection and at his option either treat the contract as avoided or accept the goods with allowance from the contract price for the deterioration or the deficiency in quantity but without further right against the seller.

Section 2-614. Substituted Performance.

(1) Where without fault of either party the agreed berthing, loading, or unloading facilities fail or an agreed type of carrier becomes unavailable or the agreed manner of delivery otherwise becomes commercially impracticable but a commercially reasonable substitute is available, such substitute performance must be tendered and accepted.

(2) If the agreed means or manner of payment fails because of domestic or foreign governmental regulation, the seller may withhold or stop delivery unless the buyer provides a means or manner of payment which is commercially a substantial equivalent. If delivery has already been taken, payment by the means or in the manner provided by the regulation discharges the buyer's obligation unless the regulation is discriminatory, oppressive or predatory.

Section 2-615. Excuse by Failure of Presupposed Conditions. Except so far as a seller may have assumed a greater obligation and subject to the preceding section on substituted performance:

(a) Delay in delivery or non-delivery in whole or in part by a seller who complies with paragraphs (b) and (c) is not a breach of his duty under a contract for sale if performance as agreed has been made impracticable by the occurrence of a contingency and the non-occurrence of which was a basic assumption on which the contract was made or by compliance in good faith with any applicable foreign or domestic governmental regulation or order whether or not it later proves to be invalid.

(b) Where the causes mentioned in paragraph (a) affect only a part of the seller's capacity to perform, he must allocate production and deliveries among his customers but may at his option include regular customers not then under contract as well as his own requirements for further manufacture. He may so allocate in any manner which is fair and reasonable.

(c) The seller must notify the buyer seasonably that there will be delay or non-delivery and, when allocation is required under paragraph (b), of the estimated quota thus made available for the buyer.

Section 2-616. Procedure on Notice Claiming Excuse.

(1) Where the buyer receives notification of a material or indefinite delay or an allocation justified under the preceding section he may by written notification to the seller as to any delivery concerned, and where the prospective deficiency substantially impairs the value of the whole contract under the provisions of this Article relating to breach of installment contracts (Sections 2-612), then also as to the whole,

(a) terminate and thereby discharge any unexecuted portion of the contract; or

(b) modify the contract by agreeing to take his available quota in substitution.

(2) If after receipt of such notification from the seller the buyer fails so to modify the contract within a reasonable time not exceeding thirty days the contract lapses with respect to any deliveries affected.

(3) The provisions of this section may not be negated by agreement except in so far as the seller has assumed a greater obligation under the preceding section.

PART 7

REMEDIES

Section 2-701. Remedies for Breach of Collateral Contracts Not Impaired. Remedies for breach of any obligation or promise collateral or ancillary to a contract for sale are not impaired by the provisions of this Article.

Section 2-702. Seller's Remedies on Discovery of Buyer's Insolvency.

(1) Where the seller discovers the buyer to be insolvent he may refuse delivery except for cash including payment for all goods theretofore delivered under the contract, and stop delivery under this Article (Section 2-705).

(2) Where the seller discovers that the buyer has received goods on credit while insolvent he may reclaim the goods upon demand made within ten days after receipt, but if misrepresentation of solvency has been made to the particular seller in writing within three months before delivery the ten day limitation does not apply. Except as provided in this subsection the seller may not base a right to reclaim goods on the buyer's fraudulent or innocent misrepresentation of solvency or of intent to pay.

(3) The seller's right to reclaim under subsection (2) is subject to the rights of a buyer in ordinary course or other good faith purchaser or lien creditor under this Article (Section 2-403). Successful reclamation of goods excludes all other remedies with respect to them.

Section 2-703. Seller's Remedies in General. Where the buyer wrongfully rejects or revokes acceptance of goods or fails to make a payment due on or before delivery or repudiates with respect to a part or the whole, then with respect to any goods directly affected and, if the breach is of the whole contract (Section 2-612), then also with respect to the whole undelivered balance, the aggrieved seller may

(a) withhold delivery of such goods;

(b) stop delivery by any bailee as hereafter provided (Section 2-705);

(c) proceed under the next section respecting goods still unidentified to the contract;

(d) resell and recover damages as hereafter provided (Section 2-706);

(e) recover damages for non-acceptance (Section 2-708) or in a proper case the price (Section 2-709);

(f) cancel.

Section 2-704. Seller's Right to Identify Goods to the Contract Notwithstanding Breach or to Salvage Unfinished Goods.

(1) An aggrieved seller under the preceding section may

(a) identify to the contract conforming goods not already identified if at the time he learned of the breach they are in his possession or control;

(b) treat as the subject of resale goods which have demonstrably been intended for the particular contract even though those goods are unfinished.

(2) Where the goods are unfinished an aggrieved seller may in the exercise of reasonable commercial judgment for the purposes of avoiding loss and of effective realization either complete the manufacture and wholly identify the goods to the contract or cease manufacture and resell for scrap or salvage value or proceed in any other reasonable manner.

Section 2-705. Seller's Stoppage of Delivery in Transit or Otherwise.

(1) The seller may stop delivery of goods in the possession of a carrier or other bailee when he discovers the buyer to be insolvent (Section 2-702) and may stop delivery of carload, truckload, planeload or larger shipments of express or freight when the buyer repudiates or fails to make a payment due before delivery or if for any other reason the seller has a right to withhold or reclaim the goods.

(2) As against such buyer the seller may stop delivery until

(a) receipt of the goods by the buyer; or

(b) acknowledgement to the buyer by any bailee of the goods except a carrier that the bailee holds the goods for the buyer; or

(c) such acknowledgement to the buyer by a carrier by reshipment or as warehouseman; or

(d) negotiation to the buyer of any negotiable document of title covering the goods.

(3) (a) To stop delivery the seller must so notify as to enable the bailee by reasonable diligence to prevent delivery of the goods.

(b) After such notification the bailee must hold and deliver the goods according to the directions of the seller but the seller is liable to the bailee for any ensuing charges or damages.

(c) If a negotiable document of title has been issued for goods the bailee is not obliged to obey a notification to stop until surrender of the document.

(d) A carrier who has issued a non-negotiable bill of lading is not obliged to obey a notification to stop received from a person other than the consignor.

Section 2-706. Seller's Resale Including Contract for Resale.

(1) Under the conditions stated in Section 2-703 on seller's remedies, the seller may resell the goods concerned or the undelivered balance thereof. Where the resale is made in good faith and in a commercially reasonable manner the seller may recover the difference between the resale price and the contract price together with any incidental damages allowed under the provisions of this Article (Section 2-710), but less expenses saved in consequence of the buyer's breach.

(2) Except as otherwise provided in subsection (3) or unless otherwise agreed resale may be at public or private sale including sale by way of one or more contracts to sell or of identification to any existing contract of the seller. Sale may be as a unit or in parcels and at any time and place and on any terms but every aspect of the sale including the method, manner, time, place and terms must be commercially reasonable. The resale must be reasonably identified as referring to the broken contract, but it is not necessary that the goods be in existence or that any or all of them have been identified to the contract before the breach.

(3) Where the resale is at private sale the seller must give the buyer reasonable notification of his intention to resell.

(4) Where the resale is at public sale

(a) only identified goods can be sold except where there is a recognized market for a public sale of futures in goods of the kind; and

(b) it must be made at a usual place or market for public sale if one is reasonably available and except in the case of goods which are perishable or threaten to decline in value speedily the seller must give the buyer reasonable notice of the time and place of the resale; and

(c) if the goods are not to be within the view of those attending the sale the notification of sale must state the place where the goods are located and provide for their reasonable inspection by prospective bidders; and

(d) the seller may buy.

(5) A purchaser who buys in good faith at a resale takes the goods free of any rights of the original buyer even though the seller fails to comply with one or more of the requirements of this section.

(6) The seller is not accountable to the buyer for any profit made on any resale. A person in the position of a seller (Section 2-707) or a buyer who has rightfully rejected or justifiably revoked acceptance must account for any excess over the amount of his security interest, as hereinafter defined (subsection (3) of Section 2-711).

Section 2-707. "Person in the Position of a Seller."

(1) A "person in the position of a seller" includes as against a principal an agent who has paid or become responsible for the price of goods on behalf of his principal or anyone who otherwise holds a security interest or other right in goods similar to that of the seller.

(2) A person in the position of a seller may as provided in this Article withhold or stop delivery (Section 2-705) and resell (Section 2-706) and recover incidental damages (Section 2-710).

Section 2-708. Seller's Damages for Non-Acceptance or Repudiation.

(1) Subject to subsection (2) and to the provisions of this Article with respect to

proof of market price (Section 2-723), the measure of damages for non-acceptance or repudiation by the buyer is the difference between the market price at the time and place for tender and the unpaid contract price together with any incidental damages provided in this Article (Section 2-710), but less expenses saved in consequence of the buyer's breach.

(2) If the measure of damages provided in subsection (1) is inadequate to put the seller in as good a position as performance would have done then the measure of damages is the profit (including reasonable overhead) which the seller would have made from full performance by the buyer, together with any incidental damages provided in this Article (Section 2-710), due allowance for costs reasonably incurred and due credit for payments or proceeds of resale.

Section 2-709. Action for the Price.

(1) When the buyer fails to pay the price as it becomes due the seller may recover, together with any incidental damages under the next section, the price

(a) of goods accepted or of conforming goods lost or damaged within a commercially reasonable time after risk of their loss has passed to the buyer; and

(b) of goods identified to the contract if the seller is unable after reasonable effort to resell them at a reasonable price or the circumstances reasonably indicate that such effort will be unavailing.

(2) Where the seller sued for the price he must hold for the buyer any goods which have been identified to the contract and are still in his control except that if resale becomes possible he may resell them at any time prior to the collection of the judgment. The net proceeds of any such resale must be credited to the buyer and payment of the judgment entitles him to any goods not resold.

(3) After the buyer has wrongfully rejected or revoked acceptance of the goods or has failed to make a payment due or has repudiated (Section 2-610), a seller who is held not entitled to the price under this section shall nevertheless be awarded damages for non-acceptance under the preceding section.

Section 2-710. Seller's Incidental Damages. Incidental damages to an aggrieved seller include any commercially reasonable charges, expenses or commissions incurred in stopping delivery, in the transportation, care and custody of goods after the buyer's breach, in connection with return or resale of the goods or otherwise resulting from the breach.

Section 2-711. Buyer's Remedies in General; Buyer's Security Interest in Rejected Goods.

(1) Where the seller fails to make delivery then with respect to any goods involved, and with respect to the whole if the breach goes to the whole contract (Section 2-612), the buyer may cancel and whether or not he has done so may in addition to recovering so much of the price as has been paid

(a) "cover" and have damages under the next section as to all the goods affected whether or not they have been identified to the contract; or

(b) recover damages for non-delivery as provided in this Article (Section 2-713).

(2) Where the seller fails to deliver or repudiates the buyer may also

(a) if the goods have been identified recover them as provided in this Article (Section 2-502); or

(b) in a proper case obtain specific performance or replevy the goods as provided in this Article (Section 2-716).

(3) On rightful rejection or justifiable revocation of acceptance a buyer has a security interest in goods in his possession or control for any payments made on their price and any expenses reasonably incurred in their inspection, receipt, transporation, care and custody and may hold such goods and resell them in like manner as an aggrieved seller (Section 2-706)).

Section 2-712. "Cover"; Buyer's Procurement of Substitute Goods.

(1) After a breach within the preceding section the buyer may "cover" by making in good faith and without unreasonable delay any reasonable purchase of or contract to purchase goods in substitution for those due from the seller.

(2) The buyer may recover from the seller as damages the difference between the cost of cover and the contract price together with any incidental or consequential damages as hereinafter defined (Section 2-715), but less expenses saved in consequence of the seller's breach.

(3) Failure of the buyer to effect cover

within this section does not bar him from any other remedy.

Section 2-713. Buyer's Damages for Non-Delivery or Repudiation.

(1) Subject to the provisions of this Article with respect to proof of market price (Section 2-723), the measure of damages for non-delivery or repudiation by the seller is the difference between the market price at the time when the buyer learned of the breach and the contract price together with any incidental and consequential damages provided in this Article (Section 2-715), but less expenses saved in consequence of the seller's breach.

(2) Market price is to be determined as of the place for tender or, in cases of rejection after arrival or revocation of acceptance, as of the place of arrival.

Section 2-714. Buyer's Damages for Breach in Regard to Accepted Goods.

(1) Where the buyer has accepted goods and given notification (subsection (3) of Section 2-607) he may recover as damages for any non-conformity of tender the loss resulting in the ordinary course of events from the seller's breach as determined in any manner which is reasonable.

(2) The measure of damages for breach of warranty is the difference at the time and place of acceptance between the value of the goods accepted and the value they would have had if they had been as warranted, unless special circumstances show proximate damages of a different amount.

(3) In a proper case any incidental and consequential damages under the next section may also be recovered.

Section 2-715. Buyer's Incidental and Consequential Damages.

(1) Incidental damages resulting from the seller's breach include expenses reasonably incurred in inspection, receipt, transportation and care and custody of goods rightfully rejected, any commercially reasonable charges, expenses or commissions in connection with effecting cover and any other reasonable expense incident to the delay or other breach.

(2) Consequential damages resulting from the seller's breach include

(a) any loss resulting from general or particular requirements and needs of which the seller at the time of contract-ing had reason to know and which could not reasonably be prevented by cover or otherwise; and

(b) injury to person or property proximately resulting from any breach of warranty.

Section 2-716. Buyer's Right to Specific Performance or Replevin.

(1) Specific performance may be decreed where the goods are unique or in other proper circumstances.

(2) The decree for specific performance may include such terms and conditions as to payment of the price, damages, or other relief as the court may deem just.

(3) The buyer has a right of replevin for goods identified to the contract if after reasonable effort he is unable to effect cover for such goods or the circumstances reasonably indicate that such effort will be unavailing or if the goods have been shipped under reservation and satisfaction of the security interest in them has been made or tendered.

Section 2-717. Deduction of Damages from the Price.
The buyer on notifying the seller of his intention to do so may deduct all or any part of the damages resulting from any breach of the contract from any part of the price still due under the same contract.

Section 2-718. Liquidation or Limitation of Damages; Deposits.

(1) Damages for breach by either party may be liquidated in the agreement but only at an amount which is reasonable in the light of the anticipated or actual harm caused by the breach, the difficulties of proof of loss, and the inconvenience or non-feasibility of otherwise obtaining an adequate remedy. A term fixing unreasonably large liquidated damages is void as a penalty.

(2) Where the seller justifiably withholds delivery of goods because of the buyer's breach, the buyer is entitled to restitution of any amount by which the sum of his payments exceeds

(a) the amount to which the seller is entitled by virtue of terms liquidating the seller's damages in accordance with subsection (1), or

(b) in the absence of such terms, twenty per cent of the value of the total performance for which the buyer is obligated under the contract or $500, whichever is smaller.

(3) The buyer's right to restitution under subsection (2) is subject to offset to the extent that the seller establishes

(a) a right to recover damages under the provisions of this Article other than subsection (1), and

(b) the amount or value of any benefits received by the buyer directly or indirectly by reason of the contract.

(4) Where a seller has received payment in goods their reasonable value or the proceeds of their resale shall be treated as payments for the purposes of subsection (2); but if the seller has notice of the buyer's breach before reselling goods received in part performance, his resale is subject to the conditions laid down in this Article on resale by an aggrieved seller (Section 2-706).

Section 2-719. Contractual Modification or Limitation of Remedy.

(1) Subject to the provisions of subsections (2) and (3) of this section and of the preceding section on liquidation and limitation of damages,

(a) the agreement may provide for remedies in addition to or in substitution for those provided in this Article and may limit or alter the measure of damages recoverable under this Article, as by limiting the buyer's remedies to return of the goods and repayment of the price or to repair and replacement of nonconforming goods or parts; and

(b) resort to a remedy as provided is optional unless the remedy is expressly agreed to be exclusive, in which case it is the sole remedy.

(2) Where circumstances cause an exclusive or limited remedy to fail of its essential purpose, remedy may be had as provided in this Act.

(3) Consequential damages may be limited or excluded unless the limitation or exclusion is unconscionable. Limitation of consequential damages for injury to the person in the case of consumer goods is prima facie unconscionable but limitation of damages where the loss is commercial is not.

Section 2-720. Effect of "Cancellation" or "Rescission" on Claims for Antecedent Breach.

Unless the contrary intention clearly appears, expressions of "cancellation" or "rescission" of the contract or the like shall not be construed as a renunciation or discharge of any claim in damages for an antecedent breach.

Section 2-721. Remedies for Fraud.

Remedies for material misrepresentation or fraud include all remedies available under this Article for non-fraudulent breach. Neither rescission or a claim for rescission of the contract for sale nor rejection or return of the goods shall bar or be deemed inconsistent with a claim for damages or other remedy.

Section 2-722. Who can sue Third Parties for Injury to Goods.
Where a third party so deals with goods which have been identified to a contract for sale as to cause actionable injury to a party to that contract

(a) a right of action against the third party is in either party to the contract for sale who has title to or a security interest or a special property or an insurable interest in the goods; and if the goods have been destroyed or converted a right of action is also in the party who either bore the risk of loss under the contract for sale or has since the injury assumed that risk as against the other;

(b) if at the time of the injury the party plaintiff did not bear the risk of loss as against the other party to the contract for sale and there is no arrangement between them for disposition of the recovery, his suit or settlement is, subject to his own interest, as a fiduciary for the other party to the contract;

(c) either party may with the consent of the other sue for the benefit of whom it may concern.

Section 2-723. Proof or Market Price: Time and Place.

(1) If an action based on anticipatory repudiation comes to trial before the time for performance with respect to some or all of the goods, any damages based on market price (Section 2-708 or Section 2-713) shall be determined according to the price of such goods prevailing at the time when the aggrieved party learned of the repudiation.

(2) If evidence of a price prevailing at the times or places described in this Article is not readily available the price prevailing within any reasonable time before or after the time described or at any other place which in commercial judgment or under

usage of trade would serve as a reasonable substitute for the one described may be used, making any proper allowance for the cost of transporting the goods to or from such other place.

(3) Evidence of a relevant price prevailing at a time or place other than the one described in this Article offered by one party is not admissible unless and until he has given the other party such notice as the court finds sufficient to prevent unfair surprise.

Section 2-724. Admissibility of Market Quotations. Whenever the prevailing price or value of any goods regularly bought and sold in any established commodity market is in issue, reports in official publications or trade journals or in newspapers or periodicals of general circulation published as the reports of such market shall be admissible in evidence. The circumstances of the preparation of such a report may be shown to affect its weight but not its admissibility.

Section 2-725. Statute of Limitations in Contracts for Sale.

(1) An action for breach of any contract for sale must be commenced within four years after the cause of action has accrued.

By the original agreement the parties may reduce the period of limitation to not less than one year but may not extend it.

(2) A cause of action accrues when the breach occurs, regardless of the aggrieved party's lack of knowledge of the breach. A breach of warranty occurs when tender of delivery is made, except that where a warranty explicitly extends to future performance of the goods and discovery of the breach must await the time of such performance the cause of action accrues when the breach is or should have been discovered.

(3) Where an action commenced within the time limited by subsection (1) is so terminated as to leave available a remedy by another action from the same breach such other action may be commenced after the expiration of the time limited and within six months after the termination of the first action unless the termination resulted from voluntary discontinuance or from dismissal for failure or neglect to prosecute.

(4) This section does not alter the law on tolling of the statute of limitations nor does it apply to causes of action which have accrued before this Act becomes effective.

ARTICLE 3

COMMERCIAL PAPER

PART 1

SHORT TITLE, FORM AND INTERPRETATION

Section 3-101. Short Title. This article shall be known and may be cited as Uniform Commercial Code—Commercial Paper.

Section 3-102. Definitions and Index of Definitions.

(1) In this Article unless the context otherwise requires

(a) "Issue" means the first delivery of an instrument to a holder or a remitter.

(b) An "order" is a direction to pay and must be more than an authorization or request. It must identify the person to pay with reasonable certainty. It may be addressed to one or more such persons jointly or in the alternative but not in succession.

(c) A "promise" is an undertaking to pay and must be more than an acknowledgment of an obligation.

(d) "Secondary party" means a drawer or endorser.

(e) "Instrument" means a negotiable instrument.

(2) Other definitions applying to this Article and the sections in which they appear are:

"Acceptance." Section 3-410.
"Accommodation party." Section 3-415.
"Alteration." Section 3-407.
"Certificate of deposit." Section 3-104.
"Certification." Section 3-411.
"Check." Section 3-104.
"Definite time." Section 3-109.
"Dishonor." Section 3-507.
"Draft." Section 3-104.
"Holder in due course." Section 3-302.
"Negotiation." Section 3-202.
"Note." Section 3-104.

"Notice of dishonor." Section 3-508.

"On demand." Section 3-108.

"Presentment." Section 3-504.

"Protest." Section 3-509.

"Restrictive Indorsement." Section 3-205.

"Signature." Section 3-401.

(3) The following definitions in other Articles apply to this Article:

"Account." Section 4-104.

"Banking Day." Section 4-104.

"Clearing house." Section 4-104.

"Collecting bank." Section 4-105.

"Customer." Section 4-104.

"Depositary Bank." Section 4-105.

"Documentary Draft." Section 4-104.

"Intermediary Bank." Section 4-105.

"Item." Section 4-104.

"Midnight deadline." Section 4-104.

"Payor bank." Section 4-105.

(4) In addition Article 1 contains general definitions and principles of construction and interpretation applicable throughout this Article.

Section 3-103. Limitations on Scope of Article.

(1) This Article does not apply to money, documents of title or investment securities.

(2) The provisions of this Article are subject to the provisions of the Article on Bank Deposits and Collections (Article 4) and Secured Transactions (Article 9).

Section 3-104. Form of Negotiable Instruments: "Draft"; "Check"; "Certificate of Deposit"; "Note."

(1) Any writing to be a negotiable instrument within this Article must

(a) be signed by the maker or drawer; and

(b) contain an unconditional promise or order to pay a sum certain in money and no other promise, order, obligation or power given by the maker or drawer except as authorized by this Article; and

(c) be payable on demand or at a definite time; and

(d) be payable to order or to bearer.

(2) A writing which complies with the requirements of this section is

(a) a "draft" ("bill of exchange") if it is an order;

(b) a "check" if it is a draft drawn on a bank and payable on demand;

(c) a "certificate of deposit" if it is an acknowledgment by a bank of receipt of money with an engagement to repay it;

(d) a "note" if it is a promise other than a certificate of deposit.

(3) As used in other Articles of this Act, and as the context may require, the terms "draft," "check," "certificate of deposit" and "note" may refer to instruments which are not negotiable within this Article as well as to instruments which are so negotiable.

Section 3-105. When Promise or Order Unconditional.

(1) A promise or order otherwise unconditional is not made conditional by the fact that the instrument

(a) is subject to implied or constructive conditions; or

(b) states its consideration, whether performed or promised, or the transaction which gave rise to the instrument, or that the promise or order is made or the instrument matures in accordance with or "as per" such transaction; or

(c) refers to or states that it arises out of a separate agreement or refers to a separate agreement for rights as to prepayment or acceleration; or

(d) states that it is drawn under a letter of credit; or

(e) states that it is secured, whether by mortgage, reservation of title or otherwise; or

(f) indicates a particular account to be debited or any other fund or source from which reimbursement is expected; or

(g) is limited to payment out of a particular fund or the proceeds of a particular source, if the instrument is issued by a government or governmental agency or unit; or

(h) is limited to payment out of the entire assets of a partnership, unincorporated association, trust or estate by or on behalf of which the instrument is issued.

(2) A promise or order is not unconditional if the instrument

(a) states that it is subject to or governed by any other agreement; or

(b) states that it is to be paid only out of a particular fund or source except as provided in this section.

Section 3-106. Sum Certain.

(1) The sum payable is a sum certain even though it is to be paid

(a) with stated interest or by stated installments; or

(b) with stated different rates of interest before and after default or a specified date; or

(c) with a stated discount or addition if paid before or after the date fixed for payment; or

(d) with exchange or less exchange, whether at a fixed rate or at the current rate; or

(e) with costs of collection or an attorney's fee or both upon default.

(2) Nothing in this section shall validate any term which is otherwise illegal.

Section 3-107. Money.

(1) An instrument is payable in money if the medium of exchange in which it is payable is money at the time the instrument is made. An instrument payable in "currency" or "current funds" is payable in money.

(2) A promise or order to pay a sum stated in a foreign currency is for a sum certain in money and, unless a different medium of payment is specified in the instrument, may be satisfied by payment of that number of dollars which the stated foreign currency will purchase at the buying sight rate for that currency on the day on which the instrument is payable or, if payable on demand, on the day of demand. If such an instrument specifies a foreign currency as the medium of payment the instrument is payable in that currency.

Section 3-108. Payable on Demand.

Instruments payable on demand include those payable at sight or on presentation and those in which no time for payment is stated.

Section 3-109. Definite Time.

(1) An instrument is payable at a definite time if by its terms it is payable

(a) on or before a stated date or at a fixed period after a stated date; or

(b) at a fixed period after sight; or

(c) at a definite time subject to any acceleration; or

(d) at a definite time subject to extension at the option of the holder, or to extension to a further definite time at the option of the maker or acceptor or automatically upon or after a specified act or event.

(2) An instrument which by its terms is otherwise payable only upon an act or event uncertain as to time of occurrence is not payable at a definite time even though the act or event has occurred.

Section 3-110. Payable to Order.

(1) An instrument is payable to order when by its terms it is payable to the order or assigns of any person therein specified with reasonable certainty, or to him or his order, or when it is conspicuously designated on its face as "exchange" or the like and names a payee. It may be payable to the order of

(a) the maker or drawer; or

(b) the drawee; or

(c) a payee who is not maker, drawer or drawee; or

(d) two or more payees together or in the alternative; or

(e) an estate, trust or fund, in which case it is payable to the order of the representative of each estate, trust or fund or his successors; or

(f) an office, or an officer by his title as such in which case it is payable to the principal but the incumbent of the office or his successors may act as if he or they were the holder; or

(g) a partnership or unincorporated association, in which case it is payable to the partnership or association and may be indorsed or transferred by any person thereto authorized.

(2) An instrument not payable to order is not made so payable by such words as "payable upon return of this instrument properly indorsed."

(3) an instrument made payable both to order and to bearer is payable to order unless the bearer words are handwritten or typewritten.

Section 3-111. Payable to Bearer.

An instrument is payable to bearer when by its terms it is payable to

(a) bearer or the order of bearer; or

(b) a specified person or bearer; or

(c) "cash" or the order of "cash," or any other indication which does not purport to designate a specific payee.

Section 3-112. Terms and Omissions Not Affecting Negotiability.

(1) The negotiability of an instrument is not affected by

(a) the omission of a statement of any

consideration or of the place where the instrument is drawn or payable; or

(b) a statement that collateral has been given to secure obligations either on the instrument or otherwise of an obligor on the instrument or that in case of default on those obligations the holder may realize on or dispose of the collateral; or

(c) a promise or power to maintain or protect collateral or to give additional collateral; or

(d) a term authorizing a confession of judgment on the instrument if it is not paid when due; or

(e) a term purporting to waive the benefit of any law intended for the advantage or protection of any obligor; or

(f) a term in a draft providing that the payee by indorsing or cashing it acknowledges full satisfaction of an obligation of the drawer; or

(g) a statement in a draft drawn in a set of parts (Section 3-801) to the effect that the order is effective only if no other part has been honored.

(2) Nothing in this section shall validate any term which is otherwise illegal.

Section 3-113. Seal. An instrument otherwise negotiable is within this Article even though it is under a seal.

Section 3-114. Date, Antedating, Postdating.

(1) The negotiability of an instrument is not affected by the fact that it is undated, antedated or postdated.

(2) Where an instrument is antedated or postdated the time when it is payable is determined by the stated date if the instrument is payable on demand or at a fixed period after date.

(3) Where the instrument or any signature thereon is dated, the date is presumed to be correct.

Section 3-115. Incomplete Instruments.

(1) When a paper whose contents at the time of signing show that it is intended to become an instrument is signed while still incomplete in any necessary respect it cannot be enforced until completed.

(2) If the completion is unauthorized the rules as to material alteration apply (Section 3-407), even though the paper was not delivered by the maker or drawer; but the burden of establishing that any completion is unauthorized is on the party so asserting.

Section 3-116. Instruments Payable to Two or More Persons. An instrument payable to the order of two or more persons

(a) if in the alternative is payable to any one of them and may be negotiated, discharged or enforced by any of them who has possession of it;

(b) if not in the alternative is payable to all of them and may be negotiated, discharged or enforced only by all of them.

Section 3-117. Instruments Payable with Words of Description. An instrument made payable to a named person with the addition of words describing him

(a) as agent or officer of a specified person is payable to his principal but the agent or officer may act as if he were the holder;

(b) as any other fiduciary for a specified person or purpose is payable to the payee and may be negotiated, discharged or enforced by him;

(c) in any other manner is payable to the payee unconditionally and the additional words are without effect on subsequent parties.

Section 3-118. Ambiguous Terms and Rules of Construction. The following rules apply to every instrument:

(a) Where there is doubt whether the instrument is a draft or a note the holder may treat it as either. A draft drawn on the drawer is effective as a note.

(b) Handwritten terms control typewritten and printed terms, and typewritten control printed.

(c) Words control figures except that if the words are ambiguous figures control.

(d) Unless otherwise specified a provision for interest means interest at the judgment rate at the place of payment from the date of the instrument, or if it is undated from the date of issue.

(e) Unless the instrument otherwise specifies two or more persons who sign as maker, acceptor or drawer or indorser and as a part of the same transaction are jointly and severally liable even though the instrument contains such words as "I promise to pay."

(f) Unless otherwise specified consent to extension authorizes a single extension for not longer than the original period. A consent to extension, expressed in the instrument, is binding on secondary parties and accommodation makers. A holder may not exercise his option to extend an instrument over the objection of a maker or acceptor or other party who in accordance with Section 3-604 tenders full payment when the instrument is due.

Section 3-119. Other Writings Affecting Instrument.

(1) As between the obligor and his immediate obligee or any transferee the terms of an instrument may be modified or affected by any other written agreement executed as a part of the same transaction, except that a holder in due course is not affected by any limitation of his rights arising out of the separate written agreement if he had no notice of the limitation when he took the instrument.

(2) A separate agreement does not affect the negotiability of an instrument.

Section 3-120. Instruments "Payable Through" Bank.

An instrument which states that it is "payable through" a bank or the like designates that bank as a collecting bank to make presentment but does not of itself authorize the bank to pay the instrument.

Section 3-121. Instruments Payable at Bank.

NOTE: *If this Act is introduced in the Congress of the United States this section should be omitted.*

(States to select either alternative)

Alternative A—

A note or acceptance which states that it is payable at a bank is the equivalent of a draft drawn on the bank payable when it falls due out of any funds of the maker or acceptor in current account or otherwise available for such payment.

Alternative B—

A note or acceptance which states that it is payable at a bank is not of itself an order or authorization to the bank to pay it.

Section 3-122. Accrual of Cause of Action.

(1) A cause of action against a maker or an acceptor accrues

(a) in the case of a time instrument on the day after maturity;

(b) in the case of a demand instrument upon its date or, if no date is stated, on the date of issue.

(2) A cause of action against the obligor of a demand or time certificate of deposit accrues upon demand, but demand on a time certificate may not be made until on or after the date of maturity.

(3) A cause of action against a drawer of a draft or an indorser of any instrument accrues upon demand following dishonor of the instrument. Notice of dishonor is a demand.

(4) Unless an instrument provides otherwise, interest runs at the rate provided by law for a judgment

(a) in the case of a maker, acceptor or other primary obligor of a demand instrument, from the date of demand;

(b) in all other cases from the date of accrual of the cause of action.

PART 2

TRANSFER AND NEGOTIATION

Section 3-201. Transfer: Right to Indorsement.

(1) Transfer of an instrument vests in the transferee such rights as the transferor has therein, except that a transferee who has himself been a party to any fraud or illegality affecting the instrument or who as a prior holder had notice of a defense or claim against it cannot improve his position by taking from a later holder a due course.

(2) A transfer of a security interest in an instrument vests the foregoing rights in the transferee to the extent of the interest transferred.

(3) Unless otherwise agreed any transfer for value of an instrument not then payable to bearer gives the transferee the specifically enforceable right to have the unqualified indorsement of the transferor. Negotiation takes effect only when the indorsement is made and until that time there is no presumption that the transferee is the owner.

Section 3-202. Negotiation.

(1) Negotiation is the transfer of an instrument in such form that the transferee becomes a holder. If the instrument is payable to order it is negotiated by delivery

with any necessary indorsement; if payable to bearer it is negotiated by delivery.

(2) An indorsement must be writted by or on behalf of the holder and on the instrument or on a paper so firmly affixed thereto as to become a part thereof.

(3) An indorsement is effective for negotiation only when it conveys the entire instrument or any unpaid residue. If it purports to be of less it operates only as a partial assignment.

(4) Words of assignment, condition, waiver, guaranty, limitation or disclaimer of liability and the like accompanying an indorsement do not affect its character as an indorsement.

Section 3-203. Wrong or Misspelled Name. Where an instrument is made payable to a person under a misspelled name or one other than his own he may indorse in that name or his own or both; but signature in both names may be required by a person paying or giving value for the instrument.

Section 3-204. Special Indorsement; Blank Indorsement.

(1) A special indorsement specifies the person to whom or to whose order it makes the instrument payable. Any instrument specially indorsed becomes payable to the order of the special indorsee and may be further negotiated only by his indorsement.

(2) An indorsement in blank specifies no particular indorsee and may consist of a mere signature. An instrument payable to order and indorsed in blank becomes payable to bearer and may be negotiated by delivery alone until specially indorsed.

(3) The holder may convert a blank indorsement into a special indorsement by writing over the signature of the indorser in blank any contract consistent with the character of the indorsement.

Section 3-205. Restrictive Indorsements. An indorsement is restrictive which either

  (a) is conditional; or

  (b) purports to prohibit further transfer of the instrument; or

  (c) includes the words "for collection," "for deposit," "pay any bank" or like terms signifying a purpose of deposit or collection; or

  (d) otherwise states that it is for the benefit or use of the indorser or of another person.

Section 3-206. Effect of Restrictive Indorsement.

(1) No restrictive indorsement presents further transfer or negotiation of the instrument.

(2) An intermediary bank, or a payor bank which is not the depositary bank, is neither given notice nor otherwise affected by a restrictive indorsement of any person except the bank's immediate transferor or the person presenting for payment.

(3) Except for an intermediary bank, any transferee under an indorsement which is conditional or includes the words "for collection," "for deposit," "pay any bank," or like terms (subparagraphs (a) and (c) of Section 3-205) must pay or apply any value given by him for or on the security of the instrument consistently with the indorsement and to the extent that he does so he becomes a holder for value. In addition such transferee is a holder in due course if he otherwise complies with the requirements of Section 3-302 on what constitutes a holder in due course.

(4) The first taker under an indorsement for the benefit of the indorser of another person (subparagraph (d) of Section 3-205) must pay or apply any value given by him for or on the security of the instrument consistently with the indorsement and to the extent that he does so he becomes a holder for value. In addition such taker is a holder in due course if he otherwise complies with the requirements of Section 3-302 on what constitutes a holder in due course. A later holder for value is neither given notice nor otherwise affected by such restrictive indorsement unless he has knowledge that a fiduciary or other person has negotiated the instrument in any transaction for his own benefit or otherwise in breach of duty (subsection (2) of Section 3-304).

Section 3-207. Negotiation Effective Although it may be Rescinded.

(1) Negotiation is effective to transfer the instrument although the negotiation is

  (a) made by an infant, a corporation exceeding its power, or any other person without capacity; or

  (b) obtained by fraud, duress or mistake of any kind; or

  (c) part of an illegal transaction; or

  (d) made in breach of duty.

(2) Except as against a subsequent holder

in due course such negotiation is in an appropriate case subject to rescission, the declaration of a constructive trust or any other remedy permitted by law.

Section 3-208. Reacquisition. Where an instrument is returned to or reacquired by a prior party he may cancel any indorsement which is not necessary to his title and reissue or further negotiate the instrument, but any intervening party is discharged as against the reacquiring party and subsequent holders not in due course and if his indorsement has been cancelled is discharged as against subsequent holders in due course as well.

PART 3

RIGHTS OF A HOLDER

Section 3-301. Rights of a Holder.
The holder of an instrument whether or not he is the owner may transfer or negotiate it and, except as otherwise provided in Section 3-603 on payment or satisfaction, discharge it or enforce payment in his own name.

Section 3-302. Holder in Due Course.
   (1)   A holder in due course is a holder who takes the instrument
      (a)   for value; and
      (b)   in good faith; and
      (c)   without notice that it is overdue or has been dishonored or of any defense against or claim to it on the part of any person.
   (2)   A payee may be a holder in due course.
   (3)   A holder does not become a holder in due course of an instrument:
      (a)   by purchase of it at judicial sale or by taking it under legal process; or
      (b)   by acquiring it in taking over an estate; or
      (c)   by purchasing it as part of a bulk transaction not in regular course of business of the transferor.
   (4)   A purchaser of a limited interest can be a holder in due course only to the extent of the interest purchased.

Section 3-303. Taking for Value. A holder takes the instrument for value
      (a)   to the extent that the agreed consideration has been performed or that he acquires a security interest in or a lien on the instrument otherwise than by legal process; or
      (b)   when he takes the instrument in payment of or as security for an antecedent claim against any person whether or not the claim is due; or
      (c)   when he gives a negotiable instrument for it or makes an irrevocable commitment to a third person.

Section 3-304. Notice to Purchaser.
   (1)   The purchaser has notice of a claim or defense if
      (a)   the instrument is so incomplete, bears such visible evidence of forgery or alteration, or is otherwise so irregular as to call into question its validity, terms or ownership or to create an ambiguity as the party to pay; or
      (b)   the purchaser has notice that the obligation of any party is voidable in whole or in part, or that all parties have been discharged.
   (2)   The purchaser has notice of a claim against the instrument when he has knowledge that a fiduciary has negotiated the instrument in payment of or as security for his own debt or in any transaction for his own benefit or otherwise in breach of duty.
   (3)   The purchaser has notice that an instrument is overdue if he has reason to know
      (a)   that any part of the principal amount is overdue or that there is an uncured default in payment of another instrument of the same series; or
      (b)   that acceleration of the instrument has been made; or
      (c)   that he is taking a demand instrument after demand has been made or more than a reasonable length of time after its issue. A reasonable time for a check drawn and payable within the states and territories of the United States and the District of Columbia is presumed to be thirty days.
   (4)   Knowledge of the following facts does

not of itself give the purchaser notice of a defense of claim

(a) that the instrument is antedated or postdated;

(b) that it was issued or negotiated in return for an executory promise or accompanied by a separate agreement, unless the purchaser has notice that a defense or claim has arisen from the terms thereof;

(c) that any party has signed for accommodation;

(d) that an incomplete instrument has been completed, unless the purchaser has notice of any improper completion;

(e) that any person negotiating the instrument is or was a fiduciary;

(f) that there has been default in payment of interest on the instrument or in payment of any other instrument, except one of the same series.

(5) The filing or recording of a document does not of itself constitute notice within the provisions of this Article to a person who would otherwise be a holder in due course.

(6) To be effective notice must be received at such time and in such manner as to give a reasonable opportunity to act on it.

Section 3-305. Rights of a Holder in Due Course. To the extent that a holder is a holder in due course he takes the instrument free from

(1) all claims to it on the part of any person; and

(2) all defenses of any party to the instrument with whom the holder has not dealt except

(a) infancy, to the extent that it is a defense to a simple contract; and

(b) such other incapacity, or duress, or illegality of the transaction, as renders the obligation of the party a nullity; and

(c) such misrepresentation as has induced the party to sign the instrument with neither knowledge nor reasonable opportunity to obtain knowledge of its character or its essential terms; and

(d) discharge in insolvency proceedings; and

(e) any other discharge of which the holder has notice when he takes the instrument.

Section 3-306. Rights of One Not Holder in Due Course. Unless he has the rights of a holder in due course any person takes the instrument subject to

(a) all valid claims to it on the part of any person; and

(b) all defenses of any party which would be available in an action on a simple contract; and

(c) the defenses of want or failure of consideration, non-performance of any condition precedent, non-delivery, or delivery for a special purpose (Section 3-408); and

(d) the defense that he or a person through whom he holds the instrument acquired it by theft, or that payment or satisfaction to such holder would be inconsistent with the terms of a restrictive indorsement. The claim of any third person to the instrument is not otherwise available as a defense to any party liable thereon unless the third person himself defends the action for such party.

Section 3-307. Burden of Establishing Signatures, Defenses and Due Course.

(1) Unless specifically denied in the pleadings each signature on an instrument is admitted. When the effectiveness of a signature is put in issue

(a) the burden of establishing it is on the party claiming under the signature; but

(b) the signature is presumed to be genuine or authorized except where the action is to enforce the obligation of a purported signer who has died or become incompetent before proof is required.

(2) When signatures are admitted or established, production of the instrument entitles a holder to recover on it unless the defendant establishes a defense.

(3) After it is shown that a defense exists a person claiming the rights of a holder in due course has the burden of establishing that he or some person under whom he claims is in all respects a holder in due course.

PART 4

LIABILITY OF PARTIES

Section 3-401. Signature.

(1) No person is liable on an instrument unless his signature appears thereon.

(2) A signature is made by use of any name, including any trade or assumed name, upon an instrument, or by any word or mark used in lieu of a written signature.

Section 3-402. Signature in Ambiguous Capacity. Unless the instrument clearly indicates that a signature is made in some other capacity it is an indorsement.

Section 3-403. Signature of Authorized Representative.

(1) A signature may be made by an agent or other representative, and his authority to make it may be established as in other cases of representation. No particular form of appointment is necessary to establish such authority.

(2) An authorized representative who signs his own name to an instrument

(a) is personally obligated if the instrument neither names the person represented nor shows that the representative signed in a representative capacity;

(b) except as otherwise established between the immediate parties, is personally obligated if the instrument names the person represented but does not show that the representative signed in a representative capacity, or if the instrument does not name the person represented but does show that the representative signed in a representative capacity.

(3) Except as otherwise established the name of an organization preceded or followed by the name and office of an authorized individual is a signature made in a representative capacity.

Section 3-404. Unauthorized Signatures.

(1) Any unauthorized signature is wholly inoperative as that of the person whose name is signed unless he ratifies it or is precluded from denying it; but it operates as the signature of the unauthorized signer in favor of any person who in good faith pays the instrument or takes it for value.

(2) Any unauthorized signature may be ratified for all purposes of this Article. Such ratification does not of itself affect any rights of the person ratifying against the actual signer.

Section 3-405. Impostors; Signature in Name of Payee.

(1) An indorsement by any person in the name of a named payee is effective if

(a) an impostor by use of the mails or otherwise has induced the maker or drawer to issue the instrument to him or his confederate in the name of the payee; or

(b) a person signing as or on behalf of a maker or drawer intends the payee to have no interest in the instrument; or

(c) an agent or employee of the maker or drawer has supplied him with the name of the payee intending the latter to have no such interest.

(2) Nothing in this section shall affect the criminal or civil liability of the person so indorsing.

Section 3-406. Negligence Contributing to Alteration or Unauthorized Signature. Any person who by his negligence substantially contributes to a material alteration of the instrument or to the making of an unauthorized signature is precluded from asserting the alteration or lack of authority against a holder in due course or against a drawee or other payor who pays the instrument in good faith and in accordance with the reasonable commercial standards of the drawee's or payor's business.

Section 3-407. Alteration.

(1) Any alteration of an instrument is material which changes the contract of any party thereto in any respect, including any such change in

(a) the number or relations of the parties; or

(b) an incomplete instrument, by completing it otherwise than as authorized; or

(c) the writing as signed, by adding to it or by removing any part of it.

(2) As against any person other than a subsequent holder in due course

(a) alteration by the holder which is both fraudulent and material discharges any party whose contract is thereby changed unless that party assents or is precluded from asserting the defense;

(b) no other alteration discharges any party and the instrument may be enforced according to its original tenor, or as to incomplete instruments according to the authority given.

(3) A subsequent holder in due course may in all cases enforce the instrument according to its original tenor, and when an incomplete instrument has been completed, he may enforce it as completed.

Section 3-408. Consideration. Want or failure of consideration is a defense as against any person not having the rights of a holder in due course (Section 3-305), except that no consideration is necessary for an instrument or obligation thereon given in payment of or as security for an antecedent obligation of any kind. Nothing in this section shall be taken to displace any statute outside this Act under which a promise is enforceable notwithstanding lack or failure of consideration. Partial failure of consideration is a defense pro tanto whether or not the failure is in an ascertained or liquidated amount.

Section 3-409. Draft Not an Assignment.

(1) A check or other draft does not of itself operate as an assignment of any funds in the hands of the drawee available for its payment, and the drawee is not liable on the instrument until he accepts it.

(2) Nothing in this section shall affect any liability in contract, tort or otherwise arising from any letter of credit or other obligation or representation which is not an acceptance.

Section 3-410. Definition and Operation of Acceptance.

(1) Acceptance is the drawee's signed engagement to honor the draft as presented. It must be written on the draft, and may consist of his signature alone. It becomes operative when completed by delivery or notification.

(2) A draft may be accepted although it has not been signed by the drawer or is otherwise incomplete or is overdue or has been dishonored.

(3) Where the draft is payable at a fixed period after sight and the acceptor fails to date his acceptance the holder may complete it by supplying a date in good faith.

Section 3-411. Certificate of a Check.

(1) Certification of a check is acceptance.

Where a holder procures certification the drawer and all prior indorsers are discharged.

(2) Unless otherwise agreed a bank has no obligation to certify a check.

(3) A bank may certify a check before returning it for lack of proper indorsement. If it does so the drawer is discharged.

Section 3-412. Acceptance Varying Draft.

(1) Where the drawee's proffered acceptance in any manner varies the draft as presented the holder may refuse the acceptance and treat the draft as dishonored in which case the drawee is entitled to have his acceptance cancelled.

(2) The terms of the draft are not varied by an acceptance to pay at any particular bank or place in the United States, unless the acceptance states that the draft is to be paid only at such bank or place.

(3) Where the holder assents to an acceptance varying the terms of the draft each drawer and indorser who does not affirmatively assent is discharged.

Section 3-413. Contract of Maker, Drawer and Acceptor.

(1) The maker or acceptor engages that he will pay the instrument according to its tenor at the time of his engagement or as completed pursuant to Section 3-115 on incomplete instruments.

(2) The drawer engages that upon dishonor of the draft and any necessary notice of dishonor or protest he will pay the amount of the draft to the holder or to any indorser who takes it up. The drawer may disclaim this liability by drawing without recourse.

(3) By making, drawing or accepting the party admits as against all subsequent parties including the drawee the existence of the payee and his then capacity to indorse.

Section 3-414. Contract of Indorser; Order of Liability.

(1) Unless the indorsement otherwise specifies (as by such words as "without recourse") every indorser engages that upon dishonor and any necessary notice of dishonor and protest he will pay the instrument according to its tenor at the time of his indorsement to the holder or to any subsequent indorser who takes it up, even though the indorser who takes it up was not obligated to do so.

(2) Unless they otherwise agree indorsers

are liable to one another in the order in which they indorse, which is presumed to be the order in which their signatures appear on the instrument.

Section 3-415. Contract of Accommodation Party.

(1) An accommodation party is one who signs the instrument in any capacity for the purpose of lending his name to another party to it.

(2) When the instrument has been taken for value before it is due the accommodation party is liable in the capacity in which he has signed even though the taker knows of the accommodation.

(3) As against a holder in due course and without notice of the accommodation oral proof of the accommodation is not admissible to give the accommodation party the benefit of discharges dependent on his character as such. In other cases the accommodation character may be shown by oral proof.

(4) An indorsement which shows that it is not in the chain of title is notice of its accommodation character.

(5) An accommodation party is not liable to the party accommodated, and if he pays the instrument has a right of recourse on the instrument against such party.

Section 3-416. Contract of Guarantor.

(1) "Payment guaranteed" or equivalent words added to a signature means that the signer engages that if the instrument is not paid when due he will pay it according to its tenor without resort by the holder to any other party.

(2) "Collection guaranteed" or equivalent words added to a signature mean that the signer engages that if the instrument is not paid when due he will pay it according to its tenor, but only after the holder has reduced his claim against the maker or acceptor to judgment and execution has been returned unsatisfied, or after the maker or acceptor has become insolvent or it is otherwise apparent that it is useless to proceed against him.

(3) Words of guaranty which do not otherwise specify guarantee payment.

(4) No words of guaranty added to the signature of a sole maker or acceptor affect his liability on the instrument. Such words added to the signature of one of two or more makers or acceptors create a presumption that the signature is for the accommodation of the others.

(5) When words of guaranty are used presentment, notice of dishonor and protest are not necessary to charge the user.

(6) Any guaranty written on the instrument is enforcible notwithstanding any statute of frauds.

Section 3-417. Warranties on Presentment and Transfer.

(1) Any person who obtains payment or acceptance and any prior transferor warrants to a person who in good faith pays or accepts that

(a) he has a good title to the instrument or is authorized to obtain payment or acceptance on behalf of one who has a good title; and

(b) he has no knowledge that the signature of the maker or drawer is unauthorized, except that this warranty is not given by a holder in due course acting in good faith

(i) to a maker with respect to the maker's own signature; or

(ii) to a drawer with respect to the drawer's own signature, whether or not the drawer is also the drawee; or

(iii) to an acceptor of a draft if the holder in due course took the draft after the acceptance or obtained the acceptance without knowledge that the drawer's signature was unauthorized; and

(c) the instrument has not been materially altered, except that this warranty is not given by a holder in due course acting in good faith

(i) to the maker of a note; or

(ii) to the drawer of a draft whether or not the drawer is also the drawee; or

(iii) to the acceptor of a draft with respect to alteration made prior to the acceptance, even though the acceptance provided "payable as originally drawn" or equivalent terms; or

(iv) to the acceptor of a draft with respect to an alteration made after the acceptance.

(2) Any person who transfers an instrument and receives consideration warrants to

his transferee and if the transfer is by indorsement to any subsequent holder who takes the instrument in good faith that

(a) he has a good title to the instrument or is authorized to obtain payment or acceptance on behalf of one who has a good title and the transfer is otherwise rightful; and

(b) all signatures are genuine or authorized; and

(c) the instrument has not been materially altered; and

(d) no defense of any party is good against him; and

(e) he has no knowledge of any insolvency proceeding instituted with respect to the maker or acceptor or the drawer of an unaccepted instrument.

(3) By transferring "without recourse" the transferor limits the obligation stated in subsection (2) (d) to a warranty that he has no knowledge of such a defense.

(4) A selling agent or broker who does not disclose the fact that he is acting only as such gives the warranties provided in this section, but if he makes such disclosure warrants only his good faith and authority.

Section 3-418. Finality of Payment or Acceptance. Except for recovery of bank payments as provided in the Article on Bank Deposits and Collections (Article 4) and except for liability for breach of warranty on presentment under the preceding section, payment or acceptance of any instrument is final in favor of a holder in due course, or a person who has in good faith changed his position in reliance on the payment.

Section 3-419. Conversion of Instrument; Innocent Representative.

(1) An instrument is converted when

(a) a drawee to whom it is delivered for acceptance refuses to return it on demand; or

(b) any person to whom it is delivered for payment refuses on demand either to pay or to return it; or

(c) it is paid on a forged indorsement.

(2) In an action against a drawee under subsection (1) the measure of the drawee's liability is the face amount of the instrument. In any other action under subsection (1) the measure of liability is presumed to be the face amount of the instrument.

(3) Subject to the provisions of this Act concerning restrictive indorsements a representative, including a depositary or collecting bank, who has in good faith and in accordance with the reasonable commercial standards applicable to the business of such representative dealt with an instrument or its proceeds on behalf of one who was not the true owner is not liable in conversion or otherwise to the true owner beyond the amount of any proceeds remaining in his hands.

(4) An intermediary bank or payor bank which is not a depositary bank is not liable in conversion solely by reason of the fact that proceeds of an item indorsed restrictively (Sections 3-205 and 3-206) are not paid or applied consistently with the restrictive indorsement of an indorser other than its immediate transferor.

PART 5

PRESENTMENT, NOTICE OF DISHONOR AND PROTEST

Section 3-501. When Presentment, Notice of Dishonor, and Protest Necessary or Permissible.

(1) Unless excused (Section 3-511) presentment is necessary to charge secondary parties as follows:

(a) presentment for acceptance is necessary to charge the drawer and indorsers of a draft where the draft so provides, or is payable elsewhere than at the residence or place of business of the drawee, or its date of payment depends upon such presentment. The holder may at his option

present for acceptance any other draft payable at a stated date;

(b) presentment for payment is necessary to charge any indorser;

(c) in the case of any drawer, the acceptor of a draft payable at a bank or the maker of a note payable at a bank, presentment for payment is necessary, but failure to make presentment discharges such drawer, acceptor or maker only as stated in Section 3-502(1) (b).

(2) Unless excused (Section 3-511)

(a) notice of any dishonor is necessary to charge any indorser;

(b) in the case of any drawer, the acceptor of a draft payable at a bank or the maker of a note payable at a bank, notice of any dishonor is necessary, but failure to give such notice discharges such drawer, acceptor or maker only as stated in Section 3-502(1) (b).

(3) Unless excused (Section 3-511) protest of any dishonor is necessary to charge the drawer and indorsers of any draft which on its face appears to be drawn or payable outside of the states and territories of the United States and the District of Columbia. The holder may at his option make protest of any dishonor of any other instrument and in the case of a foreign draft may on insolvency of the acceptor before maturity make protest for a better security.

(4) Notwithstanding any provision of this section, neither presentment nor notice of dishonor nor protest is necessary to charge an indorser who has indorsed an instrument after maturity.

Section 3-502. Unexcused Delay; Discharge.

(1) Where without excuse any necessary presentment or notice of dishonor is delayed beyond the time when it is due

(a) any indorser is discharged; and

(b) any drawer or the acceptor of a draft payable at a bank or the maker of a note payable at a bank who because the drawee or payor bank becomes insolvent during the delay is deprived of funds maintained with the drawee or payor bank to cover the instrument may discharge his liability by written assignment to the holder of his rights against the drawee or payor bank in respect of such funds, but such drawer, acceptor or maker is not otherwise discharged.

(2) Where without excuse a necessary protest is delayed beyond the time when it is due any drawer or indorser is discharged.

Section 3-503. Time of Presentment.

(1) Unless a different time is expressed in the instrument the time for any presentment is determined as follows:

(a) where an instrument is payable at or a fixed period after a stated date any presentment for acceptance must be made on or before the date it is payable;

(b) where an instrument is payable after sight it must either be presented for acceptance or negotiated within a reasonable time after date or issue whichever is later;

(c) where an instrument shows the date on which it is payable presentment for payment is due on that date;

(d) where an instrument is accelerated presentment for payment is due within a reasonable time after the acceleration;

(e) with respect to the liability of any secondary party presentment for acceptance or payment of any other instrument is due within a reasonable time after such party becomes liable thereon.

(2) A reasonable time for presentment is determined by the nature of the instrument, any usage of banking or trade and the facts of the particular case. In the case of an uncertified check which is drawn and payable within the United States and which is not a draft drawn by a bank the following are presumed to be reasonable periods within which to present for payment or to initiate bank collection:

(a) with respect to the liability of the drawer, thirty days after date or issue which ever is later and

(b) with respect to the liability of an indorser, seven days after his indorsement.

(3) Where any presentment is due on a day which is not a full business day for either the person making presentment or the party to pay or accept, presentment is due on the next following day which is a full business day for both parties.

(4) Presentment to be sufficient must be made at a reasonable hour, and if at a bank during its banking day.

Section 3-504. How Presentment Made.

(1) Presentment is a demand for acceptance or payment made upon the maker, acceptor, drawee or other payor by or on behalf of the holder.

(2) Presentment may be made

(a) by mail, in which even the time of presentment is determined by the time or receipt of the mail; or

(b) through a clearing house; or

(c) at the place of acceptance or payment specified in the instrument or if there be none at the place of business or residence of the party to accept or pay. If neither the party to accept or pay nor anyone authorized to act for him is present or accessible at such place presentment is excused.

(3) It may be made

(a) to any one of two or more makers, acceptors, drawees or other payors; or

(b) to any person who has authority to make or refuse the acceptance or payment.

(4) A draft accepted or a note made payable at a bank in the United States must be presented at such bank.

(5) In the cases described in Section 4-210 presentment may be made in the manner and with the result stated in that section.

Section 3-505. Rights of Party to Whom Presentment is Made.

(1) The party to whom presentment is made may without dishonor require

(a) exhibition of the instrument; and

(b) reasonable identification of the person making presentment and evidence of his authority to make it if made for another; and

(c) that the instrument be produced for acceptance or payment at a place specified in it, or if there be none at any place reasonable in the circumstances; and

(d) a signed receipt on the instrument for any partial or full payment and its surrender upon full payment.

(2) Failure to comply with any such requirement invalidates the presentment but the person presenting has a reasonable time in which to comply and the time for acceptance or payment runs from the time of compliance.

Section 3-506. Time Allowed for Acceptance or Payment.

(1) Acceptance may be deferred without dishonor until the close of the next business day following presentment. The holder may also in good faith effort to obtain acceptance and without either dishonor of the instrument or discharge of secondary parties allow postponement of acceptance for an additional business day.

(2) Except as a longer time is allowed in the case of documentary drafts drawn under a letter of credit, and unless an earlier time

is agreed to by the party to pay, payment of an instrument may be deferred without dishonor pending reasonable examination to determine whether it is properly payable, but payment must be made in any event before the close of business on the day of presentment.

Section 3-507. Dishonor; Holder's Right of Recourse; Term Allowing Representment.

(1) An instrument is dishonored when

(a) a necessary or optional presentment is duly made and due acceptance or payment is refused or cannot be obtained within the prescribed time or in case of bank collections the instrument is seasonably returned by the midnight deadline (Section 4-301); or

(b) presentment is excused and the instrument is not duly accepted or paid.

(2) Subject to any necessary notice of dishonor and protest, the holder has upon dishonor an immediate right of recourse against the drawers and indorsers.

(3) Return of an instrument for lack of proper indorsement is not dishonor.

(4) A term in a draft or an indorsement thereof allowing a stated time for representment in the event of any dishonor of the draft by nonacceptance if a time draft or by nonpayment if a sight draft gives the holder as against any secondary party bound by the term an option to waive the dishonor without affecting the liability of the secondary party and he may present again up to the end of the stated time.

Section 3-508. Notice of Dishonor.

(1) Notice of dishonor may be given to any person who may be liable on the instrument by or on behalf of the holder or any party who has himself received notice, or any other party who can be compelled to pay the instrument. In addition an agent or bank in whose hands the instrument is dishonored may give notice to his principal or customer or to another agent or bank from which the instrument was received.

(2) Any necessary notice must be given by a bank before its midnight deadline and by any other person before midnight of the third business day after dishonor or receipt of notice of dishonor.

(3) Notice may be given in any reasonable manner. It may be oral or written and in

any terms which identify the instrument and state that it has been dishonored. A misdescription which does not mislead the party notified does not vitiate the notice. Sending the instrument bearing a stamp, ticket or writing stating that acceptance or payment has been refused or sending a notice of debit with respect to the instrument is sufficient.

(4) Written notice is given when sent although it is not received.

(5) Notice to one partner is notice to each although the firm has been dissolved.

(6) When any party is in insolvency proceedings instituted after the issue of the instrument notice may be given either to the party or to the representative of his estate.

(7) When any party is dead or incompetent notice may be sent to his last known address or given to his personal representative.

(8) Notice operates for the benefit of all parties who have rights on the instrument against the party notified.

Section 3-509. Protest; Noting for Protest.

(1) A protest is a certificate of dishonor made under the hand and seal of a United States consul or vice consul or a notary public or other person authorized to certify dishonor by the law of the place where dishonor occurs. It may be made upon information satisfactory to such person.

(2) The protest must identify the instrument and certify either that due presentment has been made or the reason why it is excused and that the instrument has been dishonored by a nonacceptance or nonpayment.

(3) The protest may also certify that notice of dishonor has been given to all parties or to specified parties.

(4) Subject to subsection (5) any necessary protest is due by the time that notice of dishonor is due.

(5) If, before protest is due, an instrument has been noted for protest by the officer to make protest, the protest may be made at any time thereafter as of the date of the noting.

Section 3-510. Evidence of Dishonor and Notice of Dishonor.

The following are admissible as evidence and create a presumption of dishonor and of any notice or dishonor therein shown:

(a) a document regular in form as provided in the preceding section which purports to be a protest;

(b) the purported stamp or writing of the drawee, payor bank or presenting bank on the instrument or accompanying it stating that acceptance or payment has been refused for reasons consistent with dishonor;

(c) any book or record of the drawee, payor bank, or any collecting bank kept in the usual course of business which shows dishonor, even though there is no evidence of who made the entry.

Section 3-511. Waived or Excused Presentment, Protest or Notice of Dishonor or Delay Therein.

(1) Delay in presentment, protest or notice of dishonor is excused when the party is without notice that it is due or when the delay is caused by circumstances beyond his control and he exercises reasonable diligence after the cause of the delay ceases to operate.

(2) Presentment or notice or protest as the case may be is entirely excused when

(a) the party to be charged has waived it expressly or by implication either before or after it is due; or

(b) such party has himself dishonored the instrument or has countermanded payment or otherwise has no reason to expect or right to require that the instrument be accepted or paid; or

(c) by reasonable diligence the presentment or protest cannot be made or the notice given.

(3) Presentment is also entirely excused when

(a) the maker, acceptor or drawee of any instrument except a documentary draft is dead or in insolvency proceedings instituted after the issue of the instrument; or

(b) acceptance or payment is refused but not for want of proper presentment.

(4) Where a draft has been dishonored by nonacceptance a later presentment for payment and any notice of dishonor and protest for nonpayment are excused unless in the meantime the instrument has been accepted.

(5) A waiver of protest is also a waiver of presentment and of notice of dishonor even though protest is not required.

(6) Where a waiver of presentment or

notice or protest is embodied in the instrument itself it is binding upon all parties; but where it is written above the signature of an indorser it binds him only.

PART 6

DISCHARGE

Section 3-601. Discharge of Parties.

(1) The extent of the discharge of any party from liability on an instrument is governed by the section on

(a) payment or satisfaction (Section 3-603; or

(b) tender of payment (Section 3-604); or

(c) cancellation or renunciation (Section 3-605); or

(d) impairment of right of recourse or of collateral (Section 3-606); or

(e) reacquisition of the instrument by a prior party (Section 3-208); or

(f) fraudulent and material alteration (Section 3-407); or

(g) certification of a check (Section 3-411); or

(h) acceptance varying a draft (Section 3-412); or

(i) unexcused delay in presentment or notice of dishonor or protest (Section 3-502).

(2) Any party is also discharged from his liability on an instrument to another party by any other act or agreement with such party which would discharge his simple contract for the payment of money.

(3) The liability of all parties is discharged when any party who has himself no right of action or recourse on the instrument

(a) reacquires the instrument in his own right; or

(b) is discharged under any provision of this Article, except as otherwise provided with respect to discharge for impairment of recourse or of collateral (Section 3-606).

Section 3-602. Effect of Discharge Against Holder in Due Course.
No discharge of any party provided by this Article is effective against a subsequent holder in due course unless he has notice thereof when he takes the instrument.

Section 3-603. Payment or Satisfaction.

(1) The liability of any party is discharged to the extent of his payment or satisfaction to the holder even though it is made with knowledge of a claim of another person to the instrument unless prior to such payment or satisfaction the person making the claim either supplies indemnity deemed adequate by the party seeking the discharge or enjoins payment or satisfaction by order of a court of competent jurisdiction in an action in which the adverse claimant and the holder are parties. This subsection does not, however, result in the discharge of the liability

(a) of a party who in bad faith pays or satisfies a holder who acquired the instrument, by theft or who (unless having the rights of a holder in due course) holds through one who so acquired it; or

(b) of a party (other than an intermediary bank or a payor bank which is not a depositary bank) who pays or satisfies the holder of an instrument which has been restrictively indorsed in a manner not consistent with the terms of such restrictive indorsement.

(2) Payment or satisfaction may be made with the consent of the holder by any person including a stranger to the instrument. Surrender of the instrument to such a person gives him the rights of a transferee (Section 3-201).

Section 3-604. Tender of Payment.

(1) Any party making tender of full payment to a holder when or after it is due is discharged to the extent of all subsequent liability for interest, costs and attorney's fees.

(2) The holder's refusal of such tender wholly discharges any party who has a right or recourse against the party making the tender.

(3) Where the maker or acceptor of an instrument payable otherwise than on demand is able and ready to pay at every place of payment specified in the instrument when it is due, it is equivalent to tender.

Section 3-605. Cancellation and Renunciation.

(1) The holder of an instrument may even without consideration discharge any party

(a) in any manner apparent on the face of the instrument or the indorsement, as by intentionally cancelling the instrument or the party's signature by destruction or mutilation, or by striking out the party's signature; or

(b) by renouncing his rights by a writing signed and delivered or by surrender of the instrument to the party to be discharged.

(2) Neither cancellation nor renunciation without surrender of the instrument affects the title thereto.

Section 3-606. Impairment of Recourse or of Collateral.

(1) The holder discharges any party to the instrument to the extent that without such party's consent the holder

(a) without express reservation of rights releases or agrees not to sue any person against whom the party has to the knowledge of the holder a right of recourse or agrees to suspend the right to enforce against such person the instrument or collateral or otherwise discharges such person, except that failure or delay in effecting any required presentment, protest or notice of dishonor with respect to any such person does not discharge any party as to whom presentment, protest or notice of dishonor is effective or unnecessary; or

(b) unjustifiably impairs any collateral for the instrument given by or on behalf of the party or any person against whom he has a right of recourse.

(2) By express reservation of rights against a party with a right of recourse the holder preserves

(a) all his rights against such party as of the time when the instrument was originally due; and

(b) the right of the party to pay the instrument as of that time; and

(c) all rights of such party to recourse against others.

PART 7

ADVICE OF INTERNATIONAL SIGHT DRAFT

Section 3-701. Letter of Advice of International Sight Draft.

(1) A "letter of advice" is a drawer's communication to the drawee that a described draft has been drawn.

(2) Unless otherwise agreed when a bank receives from another bank a letter of advice of an international sight draft the drawee bank may immediately debit the drawer's account and stop the running of interest pro tanto. Such a debit and any resulting credit to any account covering outstanding drafts leaves in the drawer full power to stop payment or otherwise dispose of the amount and creates no trust or interest in favor of the holder.

(3) Unless otherwise agreed and except where a draft is drawn under a credit issued by the drawee, the drawee of an international sight draft owes the drawer no duty to pay an unadvised draft but if it does so and the draft is genuine, may appropriately debit the drawer's account.

PART 8

MISCELLANEOUS

Section 3-801. Drafts in a Set.

(1) Where a draft is drawn in a set of parts, each of which is numbered and expressed to be an order only if no other part has been honored, the whole of the parts constitutes one draft but a taker of any part may become a holder in due course of the draft.

(2) Any person who negotiates, indorses or accepts a single part of a draft drawn in a set thereby becomes liable to any holder in due course of that part as if it were the whole set, but as between different holders in due course to whom different parts have been negotiated the holder whose title first accrues has all rights to the draft and its proceeds.

(3) As against the drawee the first presented part of a draft drawn in a set is the part entitled to payment, or if a time draft to acceptance and payment. Acceptance of any subsequently presented part renders the drawee liable thereon under subsection (2). With respect both to a holder and to the drawer payment of a subsequently presented part of a draft payable at sight has the same effect as payment of a check notwithstanding an effective stop order (Section 4-407).

(4) Except as otherwise provided in this section, where any part of a draft in a set is discharged by payment or otherwise the whole draft is discharged.

Section 3-802. Effect of Instrument on Obligation for Which it is Given.

(1) Unless otherwise agreed where an instrument is taken for an underlying obligation

    (a) the obligation is pro tanto discharged if a bank is drawer, maker or acceptor of the instrument and there is no recourse on the instrument against the underlying obligor; and

    (b) in any other case the obligation is suspended pro tanto until the instrument is due or if it is payable on demand until its presentment. If the instrument is dishonored action may be maintained on either the instrument or the obligation; discharge of the underlying obligor on the instrument also discharges him on the obligation.

(2) The taking in good faith of a check which is not postdated does not of itself so extend the time on the original obligation as to discharge a surety.

Section 3-803. Notice to Third Party.

Where a defendant is sued for breach of an obligation for which a third person is answerable over under this Article he may give the third person written notice of the litigation, and the person notified may then give similar notice to any other person who is answerable over to him under this Article. If the notice states that the person notified may come in and defend and that if the person notified does not do so he will in any action against him by the person giving the notice be bound by any determination of fact common to the two litigations, then unless after seasonable receipt of the notice the person notified does come in and defend he is so bound.

Section 3-804. Lost, Destroyed or Stolen Instruments. The owner of an instrument which is lost, whether by destruction, theft or otherwise, may maintain an action in his own name and recover from any party liable thereon upon due proof of his ownership, the facts which prevent his production of the instrument and its terms. The court may require security indemnifying the defendant against loss by reason of further claims on the instrument.

Section 3-805. Instruments Not Payable to Order or to Bearer. This Article applies to any instrument whose terms do not preclude transfer and which is otherwise negotiable within this Article but which is not payable to order to bearer, except that there can be no holder in due course of such an instrument.

ARTICLE 4

BANK DEPOSITS AND COLLECTIONS

PART 1

GENERAL PROVISIONS AND DEFINITIONS

Section 4-101. Short Title. This Article shall be known and may be cited as Uniform Commercial Code—Bank Deposits and Collections.

Section 4-102. Applicability.

(1) To the extent that items within this Article are also within the scope of Articles 3 and 8, they are subject to the provisions of those Articles. In the event of conflict the provisions of this Article govern those of Article 3 but the provisions of Article 8 govern those of this Article.

(2) The liability of a bank for action or non-action with respect to any item handled by it for purposes of presentment, payment or collection is governed by the law of the place where the bank is located. In the case of action or non-action by or at a branch or separate office of a bank, its liability is gov-

erned by the law of the place where the branch or separate office is located.

Section 4-103. Variation by Agreement; Measure of Damages; Certain Action Constituting Ordinary Care.

(1) The effect of the provisions of this Article may be varied by agreement except that no agreement can disclaim a bank's responsibility for its own lack of good faith or failure to exercise ordinary care or can limit the measure of damages for such lack or failure; but the parties may by agreement determine the standards by which such responsibility is to be measured if such standards are not manifestly unreasonable.

(2) Federal Reserve regulations and operating letters, clearing house rules, and the like, have the effect of agreements under subsection (1), whether or not specifically assented to by all parties interested in items handled.

(3) Action or non-action approved by this Article or pursuant to Federal Reserve regulations or operating letters constitutes the exercise of ordinary care and, in the absence of special instructions, action or non-action consistent with clearing house rules and the like or with a general banking usage not disapproved by this Article, prima facie constitutes the exercise of ordinary care.

(4) The specification or approval of certain procedures by this Article does not constitute disapproval of other procedures which may be reasonable under the circumstances.

(5) The measure of damages for failure to exercise ordinary care in handling an item is the amount of the item reduced by an amount which could not have been realized by the use of ordinary care, and where there is bad faith it includes other damages, if any, suffered by the party as a proximate consequence.

Section 4-104. Definitions and Index of Definitions.

(1) In this Article unless the context otherwise requires

(a) "Account" means any account with a bank and includes a checking, time, interest or savings account;

(b) "Afternoon" means the period of a day between noon and midnight;

(c) "Banking day" means that part of any day on which a bank is open to the public for carrying on substantially all of its banking functions;

(d) "Clearing house" means any association of banks or other payors regularly clearing items;

(e) "Customer" means any person having an account with a bank or for whom a bank has agreed to collect items and includes a bank carrying an account with another bank;

(f) "Documentary draft" means any negotiable or non-negotiable draft with accompanying documents, securities or other papers to be delivered against honor of the draft;

(g) "Item" means any instrument for the payment of money even though it is not negotiable but does not include money;

(h) "Midnight deadline" with respect to a bank is midnight on its next banking day following the banking day on which it receives the relevant item or notice or from which the time for taking action commences to run, whichever is later;

(i) "Properly payable" includes the availability of funds for payment at the time of decision to pay or dishonor;

(j) "Settle" means to pay in cash, by clearing house settlement, in a charge or credit or by remittance, or otherwise as instructed. A settlement may be either provisional or final;

(k) "Suspends payments" with respect to a bank means that it has been closed by order of the supervisory authorities, that a public officer has been appointed to take it over or that it ceases or refuses to make payments in the ordinary course of business.

(2) Other definitions applying to this Article and the sections in which they appear are:

"Collecting bank." Section 4-105.
"Depositary bank." Section 4-105.
"Intermediary bank." Section 4-105.
"Payor bank." Section 4-105.
"Presenting bank." Section 4-105.
"Remitting bank." Section 4-105.

(3) The following definitions in other Articles apply to this Article:

"Acceptance." Section 3-410.
"Certificate of deposit." Section 3-104.
"Certification." Section 3-411.
"Check." Section 3-104.
"Draft." Section 3-104.
"Holder in due course." Section 3-302.

"Notice of dishonor." Section 3-508.
"Presentment." Section 3-504.
"Protest." Section 3-509.
"Secondary party." Section 3-102.

(4) In addition Article 1 contains general definitions and principles of construction and interpretation applicable throughout this Article.

Section 4-105. "Depositary Bank"; "Intermediary Bank"; "Collecting Bank"; "Payor Bank"; "Presenting Bank"; "Remitting Bank." In this Article unless the context otherwise requires:

(a) "Depositary bank" means the first bank to which an item is transferred for collection even though it is also the payor bank;

(b) "Payor bank" means a bank by which an item is payable as drawn or accepted;

(c) "Intermediary bank" means any bank to which an item is transferred in course of collection except the depositary or payor bank;

(d) "Collecting bank" means any bank handling the item for collection except the payor bank;

(e) "Presenting bank" means any bank presenting an item except a payor bank;

(f) "Remitting bank" means any payor or intermediary bank remitting for an item.

Section 4-106. Separate Office of a Bank. A branch or separate office of a bank [maintaining its own deposit ledgers] is a separate bank for the purpose of computing the time within which and determining the place at or to which action may be taken or notices or orders shall be given under this Article and under Article 3.

NOTE: *The words in Brackets are optional.*

Section 4-107. Time of Receipt of Items.

(1) For the purpose of allowing time to process items, prove balances and make the necessary entries on its books to determine its position for the day, a bank may fix an afternoon hour of two P.M. or later as a cut-off hour for the handling of money and items and the making of entries on its books.

(2) Any item or deposit of money received on any day after a cut-off hour so fixed or after the close of the banking day may be treated as being received at the opening of the next banking day.

Section 4-108. Delays.

(1) Unless otherwise instructed, a collecting bank in a good faith effort to secure payment may, in the case of specific items and with or without the approval of any person involved, waive, modify or extend time limits imposed or permitted by this Act for a period not in excess of an additional banking day without discharge of secondary parties and without liability to its transferor or any prior party.

(2) Delay by a collecting bank or payor bank beyond time limits prescribed or permitted by this Act or by instructions is excused if caused by interruption of communication facilities, suspension of payments by another bank, war, emergency conditions or other circumstances beyond the control of the bank provided it exercises such diligence as the circumstances require.

Section 4-109. Process of Posting. The "process of posting" means the usual procedure followed by a payor bank in determining to pay an item and in recording the payment including one or more of the following or other steps as determined by the bank:

(a) verification of any signature;

(b) ascertaining that sufficient funds are are available;

(c) affixing a "paid" or other stamp;

(d) entering a charge or entry to a customer's account;

(e) correcting or reversing an entry or erroneous action with respect to the item.

PART 2

COLLECTION OF ITEMS: DEPOSITARY
AND COLLECTING BANKS

Section 4-201. Presumption and Duration of Agency Status of Collecting Banks and Provisional Status of Credits; Applicability of Article; Item Indorsed "Pay any Bank."

(1) Unless a contrary intent clearly appears and prior to the time that a settlement given by a collecting bank for an item is or becomes final (subsection (3) of Section 4-211 and Sections 4-212 and 4-213) the bank is an agent or sub-agent of the owner of the item and any settlement given for the item is provisional. This provision applies regardless of the form of indorsement or lack of indorsement and even though credit given for the item is subject to immediate withdrawal as of right or is in fact withdrawn; but the continuance of ownership of an item by its owner and any rights of the owner to proceeds of the item are subject to rights of a collecting bank such as those resulting from outstanding advances on the item and valid rights of setoff. When an item is handled by banks for purposes of presentment, payment and collection, the relevant provisions of this Article apply even though action of parties clearly establishes that a particular bank has purchased the item and is the owner of it.

(2) After an item has been indorsed with the words "pay any bank" or the like, only a bank may acquire the rights of a holder
    (a) until the item has been returned to the customer initiating collection; or
    (b) until the item has been specially indorsed by a bank to a person who is not a bank.

Section 4-202. Responsibility for Collection; when Action Seasonable.

(1) A collecting bank must use ordinary care in
    (a) presenting an item or sending it for presentment; and
    (b) sending notice of dishonor or non-payment or returning an item other than a documentary draft to the bank's transferor [or directly to the depositary bank under subsection (2) of Section 4-212] *(see note to Section 4-212)* after learning that the item has not been paid or accepted, as the case may be; and

    (c) settling for an item when the bank receives final settlement; and
    (d) making or providing for any necessary protest; and
    (e) notifying its transferor of any loss or delay in transit within a reasonable time after discovery thereof.

(2) A collecting bank taking proper action before its midnight deadline following receipt of an item, notice or payment acts seasonably; taking proper action within a reasonably longer time may be seasonable but the bank has the burden of so establishing.

(3) Subject to subsection (1) (a), a bank is not liable for the insolvency, neglect, misconduct, mistake or default of another bank or person or for loss or destruction of an item in transit or in the possession of others.

Section 4-203. Effect of Instructions. Subject to the provisions of Article 3 concerning conversion of instruments (Section 3-429) and the provisions of both Article 3 and this Article concerning restrictive indorsements only a collecting bank's transferor can give instructions which affect the bank or constitute notice to it and a collecting bank is not liable to prior parties for any action taken pursuant to such instructions or in accordance with any agreement with its transferor.

Section 4-204. Methods of Sending and Presenting; Sending Direct to Payor Bank.

(1) A collecting bank must send items by reasonably prompt method taking into consideration any relevant instructions, the nature of the item, the number of such items on hand, and the cost of collection involved and the method generally used by it or others to present such items.

(2) A collecting bank may send
    (a) any item direct to the payor bank;
    (b) any item to any non-bank payor if authorized by its transferor; and
    (c) any item other than documentary drafts to any non-bank payor, if authorized by Federal Reserve regulation or operating letter. clearing house rule or the like.

(3) Presenting may be made by a presenting bank at a place where the payor bank has requested that presentment be made.

Section 4-205. Supplying Missing Indorsement; No Notice from Prior Indorsement.

(1) A depositary bank which has taken an item for collection may supply any indorsement of the customer which is necessary to title unless the item contains the words "payee's indorsement required" or the like. In the absence of such a requirement a statement placed on the item by the depositary bank to the effect that the item was deposited by a customer or credited to his account is effective as the customer's indorsement.

(2) An intermediary bank, or payor bank which is not a depositary bank, is neither given notice nor otherwise affected by a restrictive indorsement of any person except the bank's immediate transferor.

Section 4-206. Transfer Between Banks. Any agreed method which identifies the transferor bank is sufficient for the item's further transfer to another bank.

Section 4-207. Warranties or Customer and Collecting Bank on Transfer or Presentment of Items; Time for Claims.

(1) Each customer or collecting bank who obtains payment or acceptance of an item and each prior customer and collecting bank warrants to the payor bank or other payor who in good faith pays or accepts the item that

(a) he has a good title to the item or is authorized to obtain payment of acceptance on behalf of one who has a good title and the transfer is otherwise rightful; and

(b) he has no knowledge that the signature of the maker or drawer is unauthorized, except that this warranty is not given by any customer or collecting bank that is a holder in due course and acts in good faith

(i) to a maker with respect to the maker's own signature; or

(ii) to a drawer with respect to the drawer's own signature, whether or not the drawer is also the drawee; or

(iii) to an acceptor of an item if the holder in due course took the item after the acceptance or obtained the acceptance without knowledge that the drawer's signature was unauthorized; and

(c) the time has not been materially altered, except that this warranty is not given by any customer or collecting bank that is a holder in due course and acts in good faith

(i) to the maker of a note; or

(ii) to the drawer of a draft whether or not the drawer is also the drawee; or

(iii) to the acceptor of an item with respect to an alteration made prior to the acceptance if the holder in due course took the item after the acceptance provided "payable as originally drawn" or equivalent terms; or

(iv) to the acceptor of an item with respect to an alteration made after the acceptance.

(2) Each customer and collecting bank who transfers an item and receives a settlement or other consideration for it warrants to his transferee and to any subsequent collecting bank who takes the item in good faith that

(a) he has good title to the item or is authorized to obtain payment or acceptance on behalf of one who has a good title and the transfer is otherwise rightful; and

(b) all signatures are genuine or authorized; and

(c) the item has not been materially altered; and

(d) no defense of any party is good against him; and

(e) he has no knowledge of any insolvency proceeding instituted with respect to the maker or acceptor or the drawer of an unaccepted item.

In addition each customer and collecting bank so transferring an item and receiving a settlement or other consideration engages that upon dishonor and any necessary notice of dishonor and protest he will take up the item.

(3) The warranties and the engagement to honor set forth in the two preceding subsections arise notwithstanding the absence of indorsement or words of guaranty or warranty in the transfer or presentment and a collecting bank remains liable for their breach despite remittance to its transferor. Damages for breach of such warranties or engagement to honor shall not exceed the consideration received by the customer or collecting bank responsible plus finance

charges and expenses related to the item, if any.

(4) Unless a claim for breach of warranty under this section is made within a reasonable time after the person claiming learns of the breach, the person liable is discharged to the extent of any loss caused by the delay in making claim.

Section 4-208. Security Interest of Collecting Bank in Items, Accompanying Documents and Proceeds.

(1) A bank has a security interest in an item and any accompanying documents or the proceeds of either

(a) in case of an item deposited in an account to the extent to which credit given for the item has been withdrawn or applied;

(b) in case of an item for which it has given credit available for withdrawal as of right, to the extent of the credit given whether or not the credit is drawn upon and whether or not there is a right of charge-back; or

(c) if it makes an advance on or against the item.

(2) When credit which has been given for several items received at one time or pursuant to a single agreement is withdrawn or applied in part the security interest remains upon all the items, any accompanying documents or the proceeds of either. For the purpose of this section, credits first given are first withdrawn.

(3) Receipt by a collecting bank of a final settlement for an item is a realization on its security interest in the item, accompanying documents and proceeds. To the extent and so long as the bank does not receive final settlement for the item or give up possession of the item or accompanying documents for purposes other than collection, the security interest continues and is subject to the provisions of Article 9 except that

(a) no security agreement is necessary to make the security interest enforceable (subsection (1) (b) of Section 9-203); and

(b) no filing is required to perfect the security interest; and

(c) the security interest has priority over conflicting perfected security interests in the item, accompanying documents or proceeds.

Section 4-209. When Bank Gives Value for Purposes of Holder in Due Course. For purposes of determining its status as a holder in due course, the bank has given value to the extent that it has a security interest in an item provided that the bank otherwise complies with the requirements of Section 3-302 on what constitutes a holder in due course.

Section 4-210. Presentment by Notice of Item Not Payable by, through or at a Bank; Liability of Secondary Parties.

(1) Unless otherwise instructed, a collecting bank may present an item not payable by, through or at a bank by sending to the party to accept or pay a written notice that the bank holds the item for acceptance or payment. The notice must be sent in time to be received on or before the day when presentment is due and the bank must meet any requirement of the party to accept or pay under Section 3-505 by the close of the bank's next banking day after it knows of the requirement.

(2) Where presentment is made by notice and neither honor nor request for compliance with a requirement under Section 3-505 is received by the close of business on the day after maturity or in the case of demand items by the close of business on the third banking day after notice was sent, the presenting bank may treat the item as dishonored and charge any secondary party by sending him notice of the facts.

Section 4-211. Media or Remittance; Provisional and Final Settlement in Remittance Cases.

(1) A collecting bank may take in settlement of an item

(a) a check of the remitting bank or of another bank on any bank except the remitting bank; or

(b) a cashier's check or similar primary obligation of a remitting bank which is a member of or clears through a member of the same clearing house or group as the collecting bank; or

(c) appropriate authority to charge an account of the remitting bank or of another bank with the collecting bank; or

(d) if the item is drawn upon or payable by a person other than a bank, a cashier's check, certified check or other bank check or obligation.

(2) If before its midnight deadline the collecting bank properly dishonors a remittance check or authorization to charge on itself or presents or forwards for collection a remittance instrument of or on another bank which is of a kind approved by subsection (1) or has not been authorized by it, the collecting bank is not liable to prior parties in the event of the dishonor of such check, instrument or authorization.

(3) A settlement for an item by means of a remittance instrument or authorization to charge is or becomes a final settlement as to both the person making and the person receiving the settlement

(a) if the remittance instrument or authorization to charge is of a kind approved by subsection (1) or has not been authorized by the person receiving the settlement and in either case the person receiving the settlement acts seasonably before its midnight deadline in presenting, forwarding for collection or paying the instrument or authorization is finally paid by the payor by which it is payable;

(b) if the person receiving the settlement has authorized remittance by a non-bank check or obligation or by a cashier's check or similar primary obligation of or a check upon the payor or other remitting bank which is not of a kind approved by subsection (1)(b),—at the time of the receipt of such remittance check or obligation; or

(c) if in case not covered by sub-paragraphs (a) or (b) the person receiving the settlement fails to seasonably present, forward for collection, pay or return a remittance instrument of authorization to it to charge before its midnight deadline,—at such midnight deadline.

Section 4-212. Right of Charge-Back or Refund.

(1) If a collecting bank has made provisional settlement with its customer for an item and itself fails by reason of dishonor, suspension of payments by a bank or otherwise to receive a settlement for the item which is or becomes final, the bank may revoke the settlement given by it, charge back the amount of any credit given for the item to its customer whether or not it is able to return the items if by its midnight deadline or within a longer reasonable time after it learns the facts it returns the item or sends notification of the facts. These rights to revoke, charge-back and obtain refund terminate if and when a settlement for the item received by the bank is or becomes final (subsection (3) of Section 4-211 and subsections (2) and (3) of Section 4-213).

[(2) Within the time and manner prescribed by this section and Section 4-301, an intermediary or payor bank, as the case may be, may return an unpaid item directly to the depositary bank and may send for collection a draft on the depositary bank and obtain reimbursement. In such case, if the depositary bank has received provisional settlement for the item, it must reimburse the bank drawing the draft and any provisional credits for the item between banks shall become and remain final.]

NOTE: *Direct returns is recognized as an innovation that is not yet established bank practice, and therefore, Paragraph 2 has been bracketed. Some lawyers have doubted whether it should be included in legislation or left to development by agreement.*

(3) A depositary bank which is also the payor may charge-back the amount of an item to its customer's account or obtain refund in accordance with the section governing return of an item received by a payor bank for credit on its books (Section 4-301).

(4) The right to charge-back is not affected by

(a) prior use of the credit given for the item; or

(b) failure by any bank to exercise ordinary care with respect to the item but any bank so failing remains liable.

(5) A failure to charge-back or claim refund does not affect other rights of the bank against the customer or any other party.

(6) If credit is given in dollars as the equivalent of the value of an item payable in a foreign currency the dollar amount of any charge-back or refund shall be calculated on the basis of the buying site rate for the foreign currency prevailing on the day when the person entitled to the charge-back or refund learns that it will not receive payment in ordinary course.

Section 4-213. Final Payment of Item by Payor Bank; When Provisional Debits and Credits become Final; When Certain Credits become Available for Withdrawal.

(1) An item is finally paid by a payor bank when the bank has done any of the following whichever happens first:

(a) paid the item in cash; or

(b) settled for the item without reserving a right to revoke the settlement and without having such right under statute, clearing house rule or agreement; or

(c) completed the process of posting the item to the indicated account of the drawer, maker or other person to be charged therewith; or

(d) made a provisional settlement for the item and failed to revoke the settlement in the time and manner permitted by statute, clearing house rule or agreement.

Upon a final payment under subparagraphs (b), (c) or (d) the payor bank shall be accountable for the amount of the item.

(2) If provisional settlement for an item between the presenting and payor banks is made through a clearing house or by debits or credits in an account between them, then to the extent that provisional debits or credits for the item are entered in accounts between the presenting and payor banks or between the presenting and successive prior collecting banks seratim, they become final upon final payment of the item by the payor bank.

(3) If a collecting bank receives a settlement for an item which is or becomes final (subsection (3) of Section 4-211, subsection (2) of Section 4-213) the bank is accountable to its customer for the amount of the item and any provisional credit given for the item in an account with its customer becomes final.

(4) Subject to any right of the bank to apply the credit to an obligation of the customer, credit given by a bank for an item in an account with its customer becomes available for withdrawal as of right

(a) in any case where the bank has received a provisional settlement for the item,—when such settlement becomes final and the bank has had a reasonable time to learn that the settlement is final;

(b) in any case where the bank is both a depositary bank and a payor bank and the item is finally paid,—at the opening of the bank's second banking day following receipt of the item.

(5) A deposit of money in a bank is final when made but, subject to any right of the bank to apply the deposit to an obligation of the customer, the deposit becomes available for withdrawal as of right at the opening of the bank's next banking day following receipt of the deposit.

Section 4-214. Insolvency and Preference.

(1) Any item in or coming into the possession of a payor or collecting bank which suspends payment and which item is not finally paid shall be returned by the receiver, trustee or agent in charge of the closed bank to the presenting bank or the closed bank's customer.

(2) If a payor bank finally pays an item and suspends payments without making a settlement for the item with its customer or the presenting bank which settlement is or becomes final, the owner of the item has a preferred claim against the payor bank.

(3) If a payor bank gives or a collecting bank gives or receives a provisional settlement for an item and thereafter suspends payments, the suspension does not prevent or interfere with the settlement becoming final if such finality occurs automatically upon the lapse of certain time or the happening of certain events (subsection (3) of Section 4-211, subsections (1)(d), (2) and (3) of Section 4-213).

(4) If a collecting bank receives from subsequent parties settlement for an item which settlement is or becomes final and suspends payments without making a settlement for the item with its customer which is or becomes final, the owner of the item has a preferred claim against such collecting bank.

PART 3

COLLECTION OF ITEMS: PAYOR BANKS

Section 4-301. Deferred Posting; Recovery of Payment by Return of Items; Time of Dishonor.

(1) Where an authorized settlement for a demand item (other than a documentary draft) received by a payor bank otherwise than for immediate payment over the counter has been made before midnight of the banking day of receipt the payor bank may revoke the settlement and recover any payment if before it has made final payment (subsection (1) of Section 4-213) and before its midnight deadline it

(a) returns the item; or

(b) sends written notice of dishonor or nonpayment if the item is held for protest or is otherwise unavailable for return.

(2) If a demand item is received by a payor bank for credit on its books it may return such item or send notice of dishonor and may revoke any credit given or recover the amount thereof withdrawn by its customer, if it acts within the time limit and in the manner specified in the preceding subsection.

(3) Unless previous notice of dishonor has been sent an item is dishonored at the time when for purposes of dishonor it is returned or notice sent in accordance with this section.

(4) An item is returned:

(a) as to an item received through a clearing house, when it is delivered to the presenting or last collecting bank or to the clearing house or is sent or delivered in accordance with its rules; or

(b) in all other cases, when it is sent or delivered to the bank's customer or transferor or pursuant to his instructions.

Section 4-302. Payor Bank's Responsibility for Late Return of Item. In the absence of a valid defense such as breach of a presentment warranty (subsection (1) of Section 4-207), settlement effected or the like, of an item is presented on and received by a payor bank the bank is accountable for the amount of

(a) a demand item other than a documentary draft whether properly payable or not if the bank, in any case where it is not also the depositary bank, retains the item beyond midnight of the banking day of receipt without settling for it or, regardless of whether it is also the depositary bank, does not pay or return the item or send notice of dishonor until after its midnight deadline; or

(b) any other properly payable item unless within the time allowed for acceptance or payment of that item the bank either accepts or pays the item or returns it and accompanying documents.

Section 4-303. When Items Subject to Notice, Stop-Order, Legal Process or Setoff; Order in which Items may be Charged or Certified.

(1) Any knowledge, notice or stop-order received by, legal process served upon or setoff exercised by a payor bank, whether or not effective under other rules of law to terminate, suspend or modify the bank's right or duty to pay an item or to charge its customer's account for the item, comes too late to so terminate, suspend or modify such right or duty if the knowledge, notice, stop-order or legal process is received or served and a reasonable time for the bank to act thereon expires or the setoff is exercised after the bank has done any of the following:

(a) accepted or certified the item;

(b) paid the item in cash;

(c) settled for the item without reserving the right to revoke the settlement and without having such right under statute, clearing house rule or agreement;

(d) completed the process of posting the item to the indicated account of the drawer, maker or other person to be charged therewith or otherwise has evidenced by examination of such indicated account and by action its decision to pay the item; or

(e) become accountable for the amount of the item under subsection (1) (d) of Section 4-213 and Section 4-302 dealing with the payor bank's responsibility for late return of items.

(2) Subject to the provisions of subsection (1) items may be accepted, paid, certified or charged to the indicated account of its customer in any order convenient to the bank.

PART 4

RELATIONSHIP BETWEEN PAYOR BANK AND ITS CUSTOMER

Section 4-401. When Bank May Charge Customer's Account.

(1) As against its customer, a bank may charge against his account any item which is otherwise properly payable from that account even though the charge creates an overdraft.

(2) A bank which in good faith makes payment to a holder may charge the indicated account of its customer according to

(a) the original tenor of his altered item; or

(b) the tenor of his completed item, even though the bank knows the item has been completed unless the bank has notice that the completion was improper.

Section 4-402. Bank's Liability to Customer for Wrongful Dishonor. A payor bank is liable to its customer for damages proximately caused by the wrongful dishonor of an item. When the dishonor occurs through mistake liability is limited to actual damages proved. If so proximately caused and proved damages may include damages for an arrest or prosecution of the customer or other consequential damages. Whether any consequential damages are proximately caused by the wrongful dishonor is a question of fact to be determined in each case.

Section 4-403. Customer's Right to Stop Payment; Burden of Proof of Loss.

(1) A customer may by order to his bank stop payment of any item payable for his account but the order must be received at such time and in such manner as to afford the bank a reasonable opportunity to act on it prior to any action by the bank with respect to the item described in Section 4-303.

(2) An oral order is binding upon the bank only for fourteen calendar days unless confirmed in writing within that period. A written order is effective for only six months unless renewed in writing.

(3) The burden of establishing the fact and amount of loss resulting from the payment of an item contrary to a binding stop payment order is on the customer.

Section 4-404. Bank not Obligated to Pay Check more than Six Months old. A bank is under no obligation to a customer having a checking account to pay a check, other than a certified check, which is presented more than six months after its date, but it may charge its customer's account for a payment made thereafter in good faith.

Section 4-405. Death or Incompetence of Customer.

(1) A payor or collecting bank's authority to accept, pay or collect an item or to account for proceeds of its collection if otherwise effective is not rendered ineffective by incompetence of a customer of either bank existing at the time the item is issued or its collection is undertaken if the bank does not know of an adjudication of incompetence. Neither death nor incompetence of a customer revokes such authority to accept, pay, collect or account until the bank knows of the fact of death or of an adjudication of incompetence and has reasonable opportunity to act on it.

(2) Even with knowledge a bank may for ten days after the date of death pay or certify checks drawn on or prior to that date unless ordered to stop payment by a person claiming an interest in the account.

Section 4-406. Customer's Duty to Discover and Report Unauthorized Signature or Alteration.

(1) When a bank sends to its customer a statement of account accompanied by items paid in good faith in support of the debit entries or holds the statement and items

pursuant to a request or instructions of its customer or otherwise in a reasonable manner makes the statement and items available to the customer, the customer must exercise reasonable care and promptness to examine the statement and items to discover his unauthorized signature or any alteration on an item and must notify the bank promptly after discovery thereof.

(2) If the bank establishes that the customer failed with respect to an item to comply with the duties imposed on the customer by subsection (1) the customer is precluded from asserting against the bank

(a) his unauthorized signature or any alteration on the item of the bank also establishes that it suffered a loss by reason of such failure; and

(b) an unauthorized signature or alteration by the same wrongdoer on any other item paid in good faith by the bank after the first item and statement was available to the customer for a reasonable period not exceeding fourteen calendar days and before the bank receives notification from the customer of any such unauthorized signature or alteration.

(3) The preclusion under subsection (2) does not apply if the customer establishes lack of ordinary care on the part of the bank in paying the item(s).

(4) Without regard to care or lack of care of either the customer or the bank a customer who does not within one year from the time the statement and items are made available to the customer (subsection (1))

discover and report his unauthorized signature or any alteration on the fact or back of the item or does not within three years from that time discover and report any unauthorized indorsement is precluded from asserting against the bank such unauthorized signature or indorsement or such alteration.

(5) If under this section a payor bank has a valid defense against a claim of a customer upon or resulting from payment of an item and waives or fails upon request to assert the defense the bank may not assert against any collecting bank or other prior party presenting or transferring the item a claim based upon the unauthorized signature or alteration giving rise to the customer's claim.

Section 4-407. Payor Bank's Right to Subrogation on Improper Payment. If a payor bank has paid an item over the stop payment order of the drawer or maker, or otherwise under circumstances giving a basis for objection by the drawer or maker, to prevent unjust enrichment and only to the extent necessary to prevent loss to the bank by reason of its payment of the item, the payor bank shall be subrogated to the rights

(a) of any holder in due course on the item against the drawer or maker; and

(b) of the payee or any other holder of the item against the drawer or maker either on the item or under the transaction out of which the item arose; and

(c) of the drawer or maker against the payee or any other holder of the item with respect to the transaction out of which the item arose.

PART 5

COLLECTION OF DOCUMENTARY DRAFTS

Section 4-501. Handling of Documentary Drafts; Duty to Send for Presentment and to Notify Customer of Dishonor. A bank which takes a documentary draft for collection must present or send the draft and accompanying documents for presentment and upon learning that the draft has not been paid or accepted in due course must seasonably notify its customer of such fact even though it may have discounted or bought the draft or extended credit available for withdrawal as if right.

Section 4-502. Presentment of "On Arrival" Drafts. When a draft or the relevant instructions require presentment "on arrival," "when goods arrive" or the like, the collecting bank need not present until in its judgment a reasonable time for arrival of the goods has expired. Refusal to pay or accept because the goods have not arrived is not dishonor; the bank must notify its transferor of such refusal but need not present the draft again until it is instructed to do so or learns of the arrival of the goods.

Section 4-503. Responsibility of Presenting Bank for Documents and Goods; Report or Reasons for Dishonor; Referee in Case of Need. Unless otherwise instructed and except as provided in Article 5 a bank presenting a documentary draft

(a) must deliver the documents to the drawee on acceptance of the draft if it is payable more than three days after presentment; otherwise, only on payment; and

(b) upon dishonor, either in the case of presentment for acceptance or presentment for payment, may seek and follow instructions from any referee in case of need designated in the draft or if the presenting bank does not choose to utilize his services it must use diligence and good faith to ascertain the reason for dishonor, must notify its transferor of the dishonor and of the results of its effort to ascertain the reasons therefor and must request instructions.

But the presenting bank is under no obligation with respect to goods represented by the documents except to follow any reasonable instructions seasonably received; it has a right to reimbursement for any expense incurred in following instructions and to prepayment of or indemnity for such expenses.

Section 4-504. Privilege of Presenting Bank to Deal with Goods, Security Interest for Expenses.

(1) A presenting bank which, following the dishonor of a documentary draft, has seasonably requested instructions but does not receive them within a reasonable time may store, sell, or otherwise deal with the goods in any reasonable manner.

(2) For its reasonable expenses incurred by action under subsection (1) the presenting bank has a lien upon the goods or their proceeds, which may be foreclosed in the same manner as an unpaid seller's lien.

ARTICLE 5

LETTERS OF CREDIT

Section 5-101. Short Title. This Article shall be known and may be cited as Uniform Commercial Code—Letters of Credit.

Section 5-102. Scope.

(1) This Article applies

(a) to a credit issued by a bank if the credit requires a documentary draft or a documentary demand for payment; and

(b) to a credit issued by a person other than a bank if the credit requires that the draft or demand for payment be accompanied by a document of title; and

(c) to a credit issued by a bank or other person if the credit is not within subparagraphs (a) or (b) but conspicuously states that it is a letter of credit or is conspicuously so entitled.

(2) Unless the engagement meets the requirements of subsection (1), this Article does not apply to engagements to make advances or to honor drafts or demands for payment, to authorities to pay or purchase, to guarantees or to general agreements.

(3) This Article deals with some but not all of the rules and concepts of letters of credit

as such rules or concepts have developed prior to this act or may hereafter develop. The fact that this Article states a rule does not by itself require, imply or negate application of the same or a converse rule to a situation not provided for or to a person not specified by this Article.

Section 5-103. Definitions.

(1) In this Article unless the context otherwise requires

(a) "credit" or "letter of credit" means an engagement by a bank or other person made at the request of a customer and of a kind within the scope of this Article (Section 5-201) that the issuer will honor drafts or other demands for payment upon compliance with the conditions specified in the credit. A credit may be either revocable or irrevocable. The engagement may be either an agreement to honor or a statement that the bank or other person is authorized to honor.

(b) a "documentary draft" or a "documentary demand for payment" is one honor of which is conditioned upon the presentation of a document or documents. "Document" means any paper including document of title, security, invoice, certificate, notice of default and the like.

(c) an "issuer" is a bank or other person issuing a credit.

(d) a "beneficiary" of a credit is a person who is entitled under its terms to draw or demand payment.

(e) an "advising bank" is a bank which gives notification of the issuance of a credit by another bank.

(f) a "confirming bank" is a bank which engages either that it will itself honor a credit already issued by another bank or that such a credit will be honored by the issuer or a third bank.

(g) a "customer" is a buyer or other person who causes an issuer to issue a credit. The term also includes a bank which procures issuance or confirmation on behalf of that bank's customer.

(2) Other definitions applying to this Article and the sections in which they appear are:

"Notation of Credit." Section 5-108.
"Presenter." Section 5-112(3).

(3) Definitions in other Articles applying to this Article and the sections in which they appear are:

"Accept" or "Acceptance." Section 3-410.
"Contract for sale." Section 2-106.
"Draft." Section 3-104.
"Holder in due course." Section 3-302.
"Midnight deadline." Section 4-104.
"Security." Section 8-102.

(4) In addition, Article 1 contains general definitions and principles of construction and interpretation applicable throughout this Article.

Section 5-104. Formal Requirements; Signing.

(1) Except as otherwise required in subsection (1) (c) of Section 5-102 on scope, no particular form of phrasing is required for a credit. A credit must be in writing and signed by the issuer and a confirmation must be in writing and signed by the confirming bank. A modification of the terms of a credit or confirmation must be signed by the issuer or confirming bank.

(2) A telegram may be a sufficient signed

writing if it identifies its sender by an authorized authentication. The authentication may be in code and the authorized naming of the issuer in an advice of credit is a sufficient signing.

Section 5-106. Time and Effect of Establishment of Credit.

(1) Unless otherwise agreed a credit is established

(a) as regards the customer as soon as a letter of credit is sent to him or the letter of credit or an authorized written advice of its issuance is sent to the beneficiary; and

(b) as regards the beneficiary when he receives a letter of credit or an authorized written advice of its issuance.

(2) Unless otherwise agreed once an irrevocable credit is established as regards the customer it can be modified or revoked only with the consent of the customer and once it is established as regards the beneficiary it can be modified or revoked only with his consent.

(3) Unless otherwise agreed after a revocable credit is established it may be modified or revoked by the issuer without notice to or consent from the customer or beneficiary.

(4) Notwithstanding any modification or revocation of a revocable credit any person authorized to honor or negotiate under the terms of the original credit is entitled to reimbursement for or honor of any draft or demand for payment duly honored or negotiated before receipt of notice of the modification or revocation and the issuer in turn is entitled to reimbursement from its customer.

Section 5-107. Advice of Credit; Confirmation: Error in Statement of Terms.

(1) Unless otherwise specified an advising bank by advising a credit issued by another bank does not assume any obligation to honor drafts drawn or demands for payment made under the credit but it does assume obligation for the accuracy of its own statement.

(2) A confirming bank by confirming a credit becomes directly obligated on the credit to the extent of its confirmation as though it were its issuer and acquires the rights of an issuer.

(3) Even though an advising bank incor-

rectly advises the terms of a credit it has been authorized to advise the credit is established as against the issuer to the extent of its original terms.

(4) Unless otherwise specified the customer bears as against the issuer all risks of transmission and reasonable translation or interpretation of any message relating to a credit.

Section 5-108. "Notation Credit"; Exhaustion of Credit.

(1) A credit which specifies that any person purchasing or paying drafts drawn or demands for payment made under it must note the amount of the draft or demand on the letter or advice of credit is a "notation credit."

(2) Under a notation credit

(a) a person paying the beneficiary or purchasing a draft or demand for payment from him acquires a right to honor only if the appropriate notation is made and by transferring or forwarding for honor the documents under the credit such a person warrants to the issuer that the notation has been made; and

(b) unless the credit or a signed statement that an appropriate notation has been made accompanies the draft or demand for payment the issuer may delay honor until evidence of notation has been procured which is satisfactory to it but its obligation and that of its customer continue for a reasonable time not exceeding thirty days to obtain such evidence.

(3) If the credit is not a notation credit

(a) the issuer may honor complying drafts or demands for payment presented to it in the order in which they are presented and is discharged pro tanto by honor of any such draft or demand;

(b) as between competing good faith purchasers of complying drafts or demands the person first purchasing has priority over a subsequent purchaser even though the later purchased draft or demand has been first honored.

Section 5-109. Issuer's Obligation to its Customer.

(1) An issuer's obligation to its customer includes good faith and observance of any general banking usage but unless otherwise agreed does not include liability or responsibility

(a) for performance of the underlying contract for sale or other transaction between the customer and the beneficiary; or

(b) for any act or omission of any person other than itself or its own branch or for loss or destruction of a draft, demand or document in transit or in the possession of others; or

(c) based on knowledge or lack of knowledge or any usage of any particular trade.

(2) An issuer must examine documents with care so as to ascertain that on their face they appear to comply with the terms of the credit but unless otherwise agreed assumes no liability or responsibility for the genuineness, falsification or effect of any document which appears on such examination to be regular on its face.

(3) A non-bank issuer is not bound by any banking usage of which it has no knowledge.

Section 5-110. Availability of Credit in Portions; Presenter's Reservation of Lien or Claim.

(1) Unless otherwise specified a credit may be used in portions in the discretion of the beneficiary.

(2) Unless otherwise specified a person by presenting a documentary draft or demand for payment under a credit relinquishes upon its honor all claims to the documents and a person by transferring such draft or demand or causing such presentment authorizes such relinquishment. An explicit reservation of claim makes the draft or demand non-complying.

Section 5-111. Warranties on Transfer and Presentment.

(1) Unless otherwise agreed the beneficiary by transferring or presenting a documentary draft or demand for payment warrants to all interested parties that the necessary conditions of the credit have been complied with. This is in addition to any warranties arising under Articles 3, 4, 7 and 8.

(2) Unless otherwise agreed a negotiating, advising, confirming, collecting or issuing bank presenting or transferring a draft or demand for payment under a credit warrants only the matters warranted by a collecting bank under Article 4 and any such bank transferring a document warrants only the matters warranted by an intermediary under Articles 7 and 8.

Section 5-112. Time Allowed for Honor or Rejection; Withholding Honor or Rejection by Consent; Presenter."

(1) A bank to which a documentary draft or demand for payment is presented under a credit may without dishonor of the draft, demand or credit

(a) defer honor until the close of the third banking day following receipt of the documents; and

(b) further defer honor if the presenter has expressly or impliedly consented thereto.

Failure to honor within the time here specified constitutes dishonor of the draft or demand and of the credit [except as otherwise provided in subsection (4) of Section 5-114 on conditional payment].

NOTE: *The bracketed language in the last sentence of subsection (1) should be included only if the optional provisions of Section 5-114(4) and (5) are included.*

(2) Upon dishonor the bank may unless otherwise instructed fulfill its duty to return the draft or demand and the documents by holding them at the disposal of the presenter and sending him an advice to that effect.

(3) "Presenter" means any person presenting a draft or demand for payment for honor under a credit even though that person is a confirming bank or other correspondent which is acting under an issuer's authorization.

Section 5-113. Indemnities.

(1) A bank seeking to obtain (whether for itself or another) honor, negotiation or reimbursement under a credit may give an indemnity to induce such honor, negotiation or reimbursement.

(2) An indemnity agreement inducing honor, negotiation or reimbursement

(a) unless otherwise explicitly agreed applies to defects in the documents but not in the goods; and

(b) unless a longer time is explicitly agreed expires at the end of ten business days following receipt of the documents by the ultimate customer unless notice of objection is sent before such expiration date. The ultimate customer may send notice of objection to the person from whom he received the documents and any bank receiving such notice is under a duty to send notice to its transferor before its midnight deadline.

Section 5-114. Issuer's Duty and Privilege to Honor; Right to Reimbursement.

(1) An issuer must honor a draft or demand for payment which complies with the terms of the relevant credit regardless of whether the goods or documents conform to the underlying contract for sale or other contract between the customer and the beneficiary. The issuer is not excused from honor of such a draft or demand by reason of an additional general term that all documents must be satisfactory to the issuer, but an issuer may require that specified documents must be satisfactory to it.

(2) Unless otherwise agreed when documents appear on their face to comply with the terms of a credit but a required document does not in fact conform to the warranties made on negotiation or transfer of a document of title (Section 7-507) or of a security (Section 8-306) or is forged or fraudulent or there is fraud in the transaction

(a) the issuer must honor the draft or demand for payment if honor is demanded by a negotiating bank or other holder of the draft or demand which has taken the draft or demand under the credit and under circumstances which would make it a holder in due course (Section 3-302) and in an appropriate case would make it a person to whom a document of title has been duly negotiated (Section 7-502) or a bona fide purchaser of a security (Section 8-302); and

(b) in all other cases as against its customer, an issuer acting in good faith may honor the draft or demand for payment despite notification from the customer of fraud, forgery or other defect not apparent on the face of the documents but a court of appropriate jurisdiction may enjoin such honor.

(3) Unless otherwise agreed an issuer which has duly honored a draft or demand for payment is entitled to immediate reimbursement of any payment made under the credit and to be put in effectively available funds not later than the day before maturity of any acceptance made under the credit.

[(4) When a credit provides for payment by the issuer on receipt of notice that the required documents are in the possession of a correspondent or other agent of the issuer

(a) any payment made on receipt of such notice is conditional; and

(b) the issuer may reject documents which do not comply with the credit if it does so within three banking days following its receipt of the documents; and

(c) in the event of such rejection, the issuer is entitled by charge back or otherwise to return of the payment made.]

[(5) In the case covered by subsection (4) failure to reject documents within the time specified in sub-paragraph (b) constitutes acceptance of the documents and makes the payment final in favor of the beneficiary.]

NOTE: *Subsections (4) and (5) are bracketed as optional. If they are included the bracketed language in the last sentence of Section 5-112(1) should also be included.*

Section 5-115. Remedy for Improper Dishonor or Anticipatory Repudiation.

(1) When an issuer wrongfully dishonors a draft or demand for payment under a credit the person entitled to honor has with respect to any documents the rights of a person in the position of a seller (Section 2-707) and may recover from the issuer the face amount of the draft or demand together with incidental damages under Section 2-710 on seller's incidental damages and interest but less any amount realized by resale or other use or disposition of the subject matter of the transaction. In the event no resale or other utilization is made the documents, goods or other subject matter involved in the transaction must be turned over to the issuer on payment of judgment.

(2) When an issuer wrongfully cancels or otherwise repudiates a credit before presentment of a draft or demand for payment drawn under it the beneficiary has the rights of a seller after anticipatory repudiation by the buyer under Section 2-610 if he learns of the repudiation in time reasonably to avoid procurement of the required documents. Otherwise the beneficiary has an immediate right of action for wrongful dishonor.

Section 5-116. Transfer and Assignment.

(1) The right to draw under a credit can be transferred or assigned only when the credit is expressly designated as transferable or assignable.

(2) Even though the credit specifically states that it is nontransferable or nonassignable the beneficiary may before performance of the conditions of the credit assign his right to proceeds. Such an assignment is an assignment of a contract right under Article 9 on Secured Transactions and is governed by that Article except that

(a) the assignment is ineffective until the letter of credit or advice of credit is delivered to the assignee which delivery constitutes perfection of the security interest under Article 9; and

(b) the issuer may honor drafts or demands for payment drawn under the credit until it receives a notification of the assignment signed by the beneficiary which reasonably identifies the credit involved in the assignment and contains a request to pay the assignee; and

(c) after what reasonably appears to be such a notification has been received the issuer may without dishonor refuse to accept or pay even to a person otherwise entitled to honor until the letter of credit or advice of credit is exhibited to the issuer.

(3) Except where the beneficiary has effectively assigned his right to draw or his right to proceeds, nothing in this section limits his right to transfer or negotiate drafts or demands drawn under the credit.

Section 5-117. Insolvency of Bank Holding Funds for Documentary Credit.

(1) Where an issuer or an advising or confirming bank or a bank which has for a customer procured issuance of a credit by another bank becomes insolvent before final payment under the credit and the credit is one to which this Article is made applicable by paragraphs (a) or (b) of Section 5-102(1) on scope, the receipt or allocation of funds or collateral to secure or meet obligations under the credit shall have the following results:

(a) to the extent of any funds or collateral turned over after or before the insolvency as indemnity against or specifically for the purpose of payment of drafts or demand for payment drawn under the designated credit, the drafts or demands are entitled to payment in preference over depositors or other general creditors of the issuer or bank; and

(b) on expiration of the credit or surrender of the beneficiary's rights under it unused any person who has given such funds or collateral is similarly entitled to return thereof; and

(c) a change to a general or current account with a bank if specifically consented to for the purpose of indemnity against or payment of drafts or demands for payment drawn under the designated credit falls under the same rules as if the funds had been drawn out in cash and then turned over with specific instructions.

(2) After honor or reimbursement under this section the customer or other person for whose account the insolvent bank has acted is entitled to receive the documents involved.

ARTICLE 6

BULK TRANSFERS

Section 6-101. Short Title. This Article shall be known and may be cited as Uniform Commercial Code—Bulk Transfers.

Section 6-102. "Bulk Transfers"; Transfers of Equipment; Enterprises Subject to this Article; Bulk Transfers Subject to this Article.

(1) A "bulk transfer" is any transfer in bulk and not in the ordinary course of the transferor's business of a major part of the materials, supplies, merchandise or other inventory (Section 9-109) of an enterprise subject to this Article.

(2) A transfer of a substantial part of the equipment (Section 9-109) of such an enterprise is a bulk transfer if it is made in connection with a bulk transfer of inventory, but not otherwise.

(3) The enterprises subject to this Article are all those whose principal business is the sale of merchandise from stock, including those who manufacture what they sell.

(4) Except as limited by the following section all bulk transfers of goods located within this state are subject to this Article.

Section 6-103. Transfers Excepted from this Article. The following transfers are not subject to this Article:

(1) Those made to give security for the performance of an obligation;

(2) General assignments for the benefit of all the creditors of the transferor, and subsequent transfers by the assignee thereunder;

(3) Transfers in settlement or realization of a lien or other security interest;

(4) Sales by executors, administrators, receivers, trustees in bankruptcy, or any public officer under judicial process;

(5) Sales made in the course of judicial or administrative proceedings for the dissolution or reorganization of a corporation and of which notice is sent to the creditors of the corporation to order of the court or administrative agency;

(6) Transfers to a person maintaining a known place of business in this State who becomes bound to pay the debts of the transferor in full and gives public notice of that fact, and who is solvent after becoming so bound;

(7) A transfer to a new business enterprise organized to take over and continue the business, if public notice of the transaction is given and the new enterprise assumes the debts of the transferor and he receives nothing from the transaction except an interest in the new enterprise junior to the claims of creditors;

(8) Transfers of property which is exempt from execution.

Public notice under subsection (6) or subsection (7) may be given by publishing once a week for two consecutive weeks in a newspaper of general circulation where the transferor had its principal place of business in this state an advertisement including the names and addresses of the transferor and transferee and the effective date of the transfer.

Section 6-104. Schedule of Property, List of Creditors.

(1) Except as provided with respect to auction sales (Section 6-108), a bulk transfer subject to this Article is ineffective against any creditor of the transferor unless:

(a) The transferee requires the transferor to furnish a list of his existing creditors prepared as stated in this section; and

(b) The parties prepare a schedule of the property transferred sufficient to identify it; and

(c) The transferee preserves the list and schedule for six months next following the transfer and permits inspection of either or both and copying therefrom at all reasonable hours by any creditor of the transferor, or files the list and schedule in (a public office to be here identified).

(2) The list of creditors must be signed and sworn to or affirmed by the transferor or his agent. It must contain the names and business addresses of all creditors of the transferor, with the amounts when known, and also the names of all persons who are known to the transferor to assert claims against him even though such claims are disputed. If the transferor is the obligor of an outstanding issue of bonds, debentures or the like as to which there is an indenture trustee, the list of creditors need include only the name and address of the indenture trustee and the aggregate outstanding principal amount of the issue.

(3) Responsibility for the completeness and accuracy of the list of creditors rests on the transferor, and the transfer is not rendered ineffective by errors or omissions therein unless the transferee is shown to have had knowledge.

Section 6-105. Notice to Creditors. In addition to the requirements of the preceding section, any bulk transfer subject to this Article except one made by auction sale (Section 6-108) is ineffective against any creditor of the transferor unless at least ten days before he takes possession of the goods or pays for them, whichever happens first, the transferee gives notice of the transfer in the manner and to the persons hereafter provided (Section 6-107).

Section 6-106. Application of the Proceeds. In addition to the requirements of the two preceding sections:

(1) Upon every bulk transfer subject to this Article for which new consideration becomes payable except those made by sale at auction it is the duty of the transferee to assure that such consideration is applied so far as necessary to pay those debts of the transferor which are either shown on the list

furnished by the transferor (Section 6-104) or filed in writing in the place stated in the notice (Section 6-107) within thirty days after the mailing of such notice. This duty of the transferee runs to all the holders of such debts, and may be enforced by any of them for the benefit of all.

(2) If any of said debts are in dispute the necessary sum may be withheld from distribution until the dispute is settled or adjudicated.

(3) If the consideration payable is not enough to pay all of the said debts in full distribution shall be made pro rata]

NOTE: *This section is bracketed to indicate division of opinion as to whether or not it is a wise provision, and to suggest that this is a point on which state enactments may differ without serious damage to the principle of uniformity.*

In any State where this section is omitted, the following parts of sections also bracketed in the text, should also be omitted, namely:
Section 6-107(2)(e).
6-108(3)(c).
6-109(2).

In any State where this section is enacted, these other provisions should be also.

Optional Subsection (4) [(4) The transferee may within ten days after he takes possession of the goods pay the consideration into the (specify court) in the county where the transferor had its principal place of business in this state and thereafter may discharge his duty under this section by giving notice by registered or certified mail to all the persons to whom the duty runs that the consideration has been paid into that court and that they should file their claims there. On motion of any interested party, the court may order the distribution of the consideration to the persons entitled to it.]

NOTE: *Optional subsection (4) is recommended for those states which do not have a general statute providing for payment of money into court.*

Section 6-107. The Notice.

(1) The notice to creditors (Section 6-105) shall state:

(a) that a bulk transfer is about to be made; and

(b) the names and business addresses of the transferor and transferee, and all other business names and addresses used by the transferor within three years last past so far as known to the transferee; and

(c) whether or not all the debts of the transferor are to be paid in full as they fall due as a result of the transaction, and if so, the address to which creditors should send their bills.

(2) If the debts of the transferor are not to be paid in full as they fall due or if the transferee is in doubt on that point then the notice shall state further:

(a) the location and general description of the property to be transferred and the estimated total of the transferor's debts;

(b) the address where the schedule of property and list of creditors (Section 6-104) may be inspected;

(c) whether the transfer is to pay existing debts and if so the amount of such debts and to whom owing;

(d) whether the transfer is for new consideration and if so the amount of such consideration and the time and place of payment; [and]

[(e) if for new consideration the time and place where creditors of the transferor are to file their claims.]

(3) The notice in any case shall be delivered personally or sent by registered mail to all the persons shown on the list of creditors furnished by the transferor (Section 6-104) and to all other persons who are known to the transferee to hold or assert claims against the transferor.

NOTE: *The words in brackets are optional.*

Section 6-108. Auction Sales; "Auctioneer."

(1) A bulk transfer is subject to this Article even though it is by sale at auction, but only in the manner and with the results stated in this section.

(2) The transferor shall furnish a list of his creditors and assist in the preparation of a schedule of the property to be sold, both prepared as before stated (Section 6-104).

(3) The person or persons other than the transferor who direct, control or are responsible for the auction are collectively called the "auctioneer." The auctioneer shall:

(a) receive and retain the list of creditors and prepare and retain the schedule of property for the period stated in this Article (Section 6-104);

(b) give notice of the auction personally or by registered or certified mail at least ten days before it occurs to all persons shown on the list of creditors and to all other persons who are known to him to hold or assert claims against the transferor; [and]

[(c) assure that the net proceeds of the auction are applied as provided in this Article (Section 6-106).]

(4) Failure of the auctioneer to perform any of these duties does not affect the validity of the sale or the title of the purchasers, but if the auctioneer knows that the auction constitutes a bulk transfer such failure renders the auctioneer liable to the creditors of the transferor as a class for the sums owing to them from the transferor up to but not exceeding the net proceeds of the auction. If the auctioneer consists of several persons their liability is joint and several.

NOTE: *The words in brackets are optional.*

Section 6-109. What Creditors Protected; Credit for Payment to Particular Creditors.

(1) The creditors of the transferor mentioned in this Article are those holding claims based on transactions or events occurring before the bulk transfer, but creditors who become such after notice to creditors is given (Sections 6-105 and 6-107) are not entitled to notice.

[(2) Against the aggregate obligation imposed by the provisions of this Article concerning the application of the proceeds (Section 6-106 and subsection (3) (c) of 6-108) the transferee or auctioneer is entitled to credit for sums paid to particular creditors of the transferor, not exceeding the sums believed in good faith at the time of the payment to be properly payable to such creditors.]

Section 6-110. Subsequent Transfers.

When the title of a transferee to property is subject to a defect by reason of his noncompliance with the requirements of this Article, then:

(1) a purchaser of any of such property from such transferee who pays no value or who takes with notice of such non-compliance takes subject to such defect, but

(2) a purchaser for value in good faith and

without such notice takes free of such defect.

Section 6-111. Limitation of Actions and Levies. No action under this Article shall be brought nor levy made more than six months after the date on which the transferee took possession of the goods unless the transfer has been concealed. If the transfer has been concealed, actions may be brought or levies made within six months after its discovery.

NOTE TO ARTICLE 6: Section 6-106 is bracketed to indicate division of opinion as to whether or not it is a wise provision, and to suggest that this is a point on which State enactments may differ without serious damage to the principle of uniformity.

In any State where Section 6-106 is not enacted, the following parts of sections, also bracketed in the text, should also be omitted, namely:

Sec. 6-107(2)(e)
6-109(3)(c)
6-109(2).

In any State where Section 6-106 is enacted, these other provisions should be also.

ARTICLE 7

WAREHOUSE RECEIPTS, BILLS OF LADING AND OTHER DOCUMENTS OF TITLE

PART 1

GENERAL

Section 7-101. Short Title. This Article shall be known and may be cited as Uniform Commercial Code—Documents of Title.

Section 7-102. Definitions and Index of Definitions.

(1) In this Article, unless the context otherwise requires:

(a) "Bailee" means the person who by a warehouse receipt, bill of lading or other document of title acknowledges possession of goods and contracts to deliver them.

(b) "Consignee" means the person named in a bill to whom or to whose order the bill promises delivery.

(c) "Consignor" means the person named in a bill as the person from whom the goods have been received for shipment.

(d) "Delivery order" means a written order to deliver goods directed to a warehouseman, carrier or other person who in the ordinary course of business issues warehouse receipts of bills of lading.

(e) "Document" means document of title as defined in the general definitions in Article 1 (Section 1-201).

(f) "Goods" means all things which are treated as movable for the purposes of a contract of storage or transportation.

(g) "Issuer" means a bailee who issues a document except that in relation to an unaccepted delivery order it means the person who orders the possessor of goods to deliver. Issuer includes any person for whom an agent or employee purports to act in issuing a document if the agent or employee has real or apparent authority to issue documents, notwithstanding that the issuer received no goods or that the goods were misdescribed or that in any other respect the agent or employee violated his instructions.

(h) "Warehouseman" is a person engaged in the business of storing goods for hire.

(2) Other definitions applying to this Article or to specified Parts thereof, and the sections in which they appear are:

"Duly negotiate." Section 7-501.

"Person entitled under the document." Section 7-403(4).

(3) Definitions in other Articles applying to this Article and the sections in which they appear are:

"Contract for sale." Section 2-106.

"Overseas." Section 2-323.

"Receipt" of goods. Section 2-103.

(4) In addition Article 2 contains general

definitions and principles of construction and interpretation applicable throughout this Article.

Section 7-103. Relation of Article to Treaty, Statute, Tariff, Classification or Regulation. To the extent that any treaty or statute of the United States, regulatory statute of this State or tariff, classification or regulation filed or issued pursuant thereto is applicable, the provisions of this Article are subject thereto.

Section 7-104. Negotiable and Non-Negotiable Warehouse Receipt, Bill of Lading or Other Document of Title.

(1) A warehouse receipt, bill of lading or other document of title is negotiable

(a) if by its terms the goods are to be delivered to bearer or to the order of a named person; or

(b) where recognized in overseas trade, if it runs to a named person or assigns.

(2) Any other document is non-negotiable. A bill of lading in which it is stated that the goods are consigned to a named person is not made negotiable by a provision that the goods are to be delivered only against a written order signed by the same or another named person.

Section 7-105. Construction Against Negative Implication. The omission from either Part 2 or Part 3 of this Article of a provision corresponding to a provision made in the other Part does not imply that a corresponding rule of law is not applicable.

PART 2

WAREHOUSE RECEIPTS: SPECIAL PROVISIONS

Section 7-201. Who may issue a Warehouse Receipt; Storage under Government Bond.

(1) A warehouse receipt may be issued by any warehouseman.

(2) Where goods including distilled spirits and agricultural commodities are stored under a statute requiring a bond against a withdrawal or a license for the issuance of receipts in the nature of warehouse receipts, a receipt for the goods has like effect as a warehouse receipt even though issued by a person who is the owner of the goods and is not a warehouseman.

Section 7-202. Form of Warehouse Receipt; Essential Terms; Optional Terms.

(1) A warehouse receipt need not be in any particular form.

(2) Unless a warehouse receipt embodies within its written or printed terms each of the following, the warehouseman is liable for damages caused by the omission to a person injured thereby:

(a) the location of the warehouse where the goods are stored;

(b) the date of issue of the receipt;

(c) the consecutive number of the receipt;

(d) a statement whether the goods received will be delivered to the bearer, to a specified person, or to a specified person or his order;

(e) the rate of storage and handling charges, except that where goods are stored under a field warehousing arrangement a statement of that fact is sufficient on a non-negotiable receipt;

(f) a description of the goods or of the packages containing them;

(g) the signature of the warehouseman, which may be made by his authorized agent;

(h) if the receipt is issued for goods of which the warehouseman is owner, either solely or jointly or in common with others, the fact of such ownership; and

(i) a statement of the amount of advances made and of liabilities incurred for which the warehouseman claims a lien or security interest (Section 7-209). If the precise amount of such advances made or of such liabilities incurred is, at the time of the issue of the receipt, unknown to the warehouseman or to his agent who issues it, a statement of the fact that advances have been made or liabilities incurred and the purpose thereof is sufficient.

(3) A warehouseman may insert in his receipt any other terms which are not contrary to the provisions of this Act and do not impair his obligation of delivery (Sec-

tion 7-403) or his duty to care (Section 7-204). Any contrary provisions shall be ineffective.

Section 7-203. Liability for Non-Receipt or Misdescription. A party to or purchaser for value in good faith of a document of title other than a bill of lading relying in either case upon the description therein of the goods may recover from the issuer damages caused by the non-receipt or misdescription of the goods, except to the extent that the document conspicuously indicates that the issuer does not know whether any part or all of the goods in fact were received or conform to the description, as where the description is in terms of marks or labels or kind, quantity or condition, or the receipt or description is qualified by "contents, condition and quality unknown," "said to contain" or the like, if such indication be true, or the party or purchaser otherwise has notice.

Section 7-204. Duty of Care: Contractual Limitation of Warehouseman's Liability.

(1) A warehouseman is liable for damages for loss of or injury to the goods caused by his failure to exercise such care in regard to them as a reasonably careful man would exercise under like circumstances but unless otherwise agreed he is not liable for damages which could not have been avoided by the exercise of such care.

(2) Damages may be limited by a term in the warehouse receipt or storage agreement limiting the amount of liability in case of loss or damage, and setting forth a specific liability per article or item, or value per unit of weight, beyond which the warehouseman shall not be liable; provided, however, that such liability may on written request of the bailor at the time of signing such storage agreement or within a reasonable time after receipt of the warehouse receipt be increased on part or all of the goods thereunder, in which event increased rates may be charged based on such increased valuation, but that no such increase shall be permitted contrary to a lawful limitation of liability contained in the warehouseman's tariff, if any. No such limitation is effective with respect to the warehouseman's liability for conversion to his own use.

(3) Reasonable provisions as to the time

and manner of presenting claims and instituting actions based on the bailment may be included in the warehouse receipt or tariff.

(4) This section does not impair or repeal . .

> NOTE: *Insert in subsection (4) a reference to any statute which imposes a higher responsibility upon the warehouseman or invalidates contractual limitations which would be permissible under this Article.*

Section 7-205. Title Under Warehouse Receipt Defeated in Certain Cases. A buyer in the ordinary course of business of fungible goods sold and delivered by a warehouseman who is also in the business of buying and selling such goods takes free of any claim under a warehouse receipt even though it has been duly negotiated.

Section 7-206. Termination of Storage at Warehouseman's Option.

(1) A warehouseman may on notifying the person on whose account the goods are held and any other person known to claim an interest in the goods require payment of any charges and removal of the goods from the warehouse at the termination of the period of storage fixed by the document, or, if no period is fixed, within a stated period not less than thirty days after the notification. If the goods are not removed before the date specified in the notification, the warehouseman may sell them in accordance with the provisions of the section on enforcement of a warehouseman's lien (Section 7-210).

(2) If a warehouseman in good faith believes that the goods are about to deteriorate or decline in value to less than the amount of his lien within the time prescribed in subsection (1) for notification, advertisement and sale, the warehouseman may specify in the notification any reasonable shorter time for removal of the goods and in case the goods are not removed, may sell them at public sale held not less than one week after a single advertisement or posting.

(3) If as a result of a quality or condition of the goods of which the warehouseman had no choice at the time of deposit the goods are a hazard to other property or to the warehouse or to persons, the warehouseman may sell the goods at public or private

sale without advertisement on reasonable notification to all persons known to claim an interest in the goods. If the warehouse man after a reasonable effort is unable to sell the goods he may dispose of them in any lawful manner and shall incur no liability by reason of such disposition.

(4) The warehouseman must deliver the goods to any person entitled to them under this Article upon due demand made at any time prior to the sale or other disposition under this section.

(5) The warehouseman may satisfy his lien from the proceeds of any sale or disposition under this section but must hold the balance for delivery on the demand of any person to whom he would have been bound to deliver the goods.

Section 7-207. Goods Must be Kept Separate; Fungible Goods.

(1) Unless the warehouse receipt otherwise provides, a warehouseman must keep separate the goods covered by each receipt so as to permit at all times identification and delivery of those goods except that different lots of fungible goods may be commingled.

(2) Fungible goods so commingled are owned in common by the persons entitled thereto and the warehouseman is severally liable to each owner for that owner's share. Where because of overissue a mass of fungible goods is insufficient to meet all the receipts which the warehouseman has issued against it, the persons entitled include all holders to whom overissued receipts have been duly negotiated.

Section 7-208. Altered Warehouse Receipts.

Where a blank in a negotiable warehouse receipt has been filled in without authority, a purchaser for value and without notice of the want of authority may treat the insertion as authorized. Any other unauthorized alteration leaves any receipt enforceable against the issuer according to its original tenor.

Section 7-209. Lien of Warehouseman.

(1) A warehouseman has a lien against the bailor on the goods covered by a warehouse receipt or on the proceeds thereof in his possession for charges for storage or transportation (including demurrage and terminal charges), insurance, labor, or charges present

or future in relation to the goods, and for expenses necessary for preservation of the goods or reasonably incurred in their sale pursuant to law. If the person on whose account the goods are held is liable for like charges or expenses in relation to other goods whenever deposited and it is stated in the receipt that a lien is claimed for charges and expenses in relation to other goods, the warehouseman also has a lien against him for such charges and expenses whether or not the other goods have been delivered by the warehouseman. But against a person to whom a negotiable warehouse receipt is duly negotiated a warehouseman's lien is limited to charges in an amount or at a rate specified on the receipt or if no charges are so specified then to a reasonable charge for storage of the goods covered by the receipt subsequent to the date of the receipt.

(2) The warehouseman may also reserve a security interest against the bailor for a maximum amount specified on the receipt for charges other than those specified in subsection (1), such as for money advanced and interest. Such a security interest is governed by the Article on Secured Transactions (Article 9).

(3) A warehouseman's lien for charges and expenses under subsection (1) or a security interest under subsection (2) is also effective against any person who so entrusted the bailor with possession of the goods that a pledge of them by him to a good faith purchaser for value would have been valid but is not effective against a person as to whom the document confers no right in the goods covered by it under Section 7-503.

(4) A warehouseman loses his lien on any goods which he voluntarily delivers or which he unjustifiably refuses to deliver.

Section 7-210. Enforcement of Warehouseman's Lien.

(1) Except as provided in subsection (2), a warehouseman's lien may be enforced by public or private sale of the goods in block or in parcels, at any time or place and on any terms which are commercially reasonable, after notifying all persons known to claim an interest in the goods. Such notification must include a statement of the amount due, the nature of the proposed sale and the

time and place of any public sale. The fact that a better price could have been obtained by a sale at a different time or in a different method from that selected by the warehouseman is not of itself sufficient to establish that the sale was not made in a commercially reasonable manner. If the warehouseman either sells the goods in the usual manner in any recognized market therefore, or if he sells at the price current in such market at the time of his sale, or if he has otherwise sold in conformity with commercially reasonable practices among dealers in the type of goods sold, he has sold in a commercially reasonable manner. A sale of more goods than apparently necessary to be offered to insure satisfaction of the obligation is not commercially reasonable except in cases covered by the preceding sentence.

(2) A warehouseman's lien on goods other than goods stored by a merchant in the course of his business may be enforced only as follows:

(a) All persons known to claim an interest in the goods must be notified.

(b) The notification must be delivered in person or sent by registered or certified letter to the last known address of any person to be notified.

(c) The notification must include an itemized statement of the claim, a description of the goods subject to the lien, a demand for payment within a specified time not less than ten days after receipt of the notification, and a conspicuous statement that unless the claim is paid within that time the goods will be advertised for sale and sold by auction at a specified time and place.

(d) The sale must conform to the terms of the notification.

(e) The sale must be held at the nearest suitable place to that where the goods are held or stored.

(f) After the expiration of the time given in the notification, an advertisement of the sale must be published once a week for two weeks consecutively in a newspaper of general circulation where the sale is to be held. The advertisement must include a description of the goods, the name of the person on whose account they are being held, and the time and place of the sale. The sale must take place at least fifteen days after the first publication. If there is no newspaper of general circulation where the sale is to be held, the advertisement must be posted at least ten days before the sale in not less than six conspicuous places in the neighborhood of the proposed sale.

(3) Before any sale pursuant to this section any person claiming a right in the goods may pay the amount necessary to satisfy the lien and the reasonable expenses incurred under this section. In that event the goods must not be sold, but must be retained by the warehouseman subject to the terms of the receipt and this Article.

(4) The warehouseman may buy at any public sale pursuant to this section.

(5) A purchaser in good faith of goods sold to enforce a warehouseman's lien takes the goods free of any rights of persons against whom the lien was valid, despite noncompliance by the warehouseman with the requirements of this section.

(6) The warehouseman may satisfy his lien from the proceeds of any sale pursuant to this section but must hold the balance, if any, for delivery on demand to any person to whom he would have been bound to deliver the goods.

(7) The rights provided by this section shall be in addition to all other rights allowed by law to a creditor against his debtor.

(8) Where a lien is on goods stored by a merchant in the course of his business the lien may be enforced in accordance with either subsection (1) or (2).

(9) The warehouseman is liable for damages caused by failure to comply with the requirements for sale under this section and in case of willful violation is liable for conversion.

PART 3

BILLS OF LADING: SPECIAL PROVISIONS

Section 7-301. Liability for Non-receipt or Misdescription; "Said to Contain"; "Shipper's Load and Count"; Improper Handling.

(1) A consignee of a non-negotiable bill who has given value in good faith or a holder to whom a negotiable bill has been duly negotiated relying in either case upon the description therein of the goods, or upon the date therein shown, may recover from the issuer damages caused by the misdating of the bill or the nonreceipt or misdescription of the goods, except to the extent that the document indicates that the issuer does not know whether any part or all of the goods in fact were received or conform to the description, as where the description is in terms of marks or labels or kind, quantity, or condition of the receipt or description is qualified by "contents or condition of contents of packages unknown," "said to contain," "shipper's weight, load and count" or the like, if such indication be true.

(2) , When goods are loaded by an issuer who is a common carrier, the issuer must count the packages of goods if package freight and ascertain the kind and quantity if bulk freight. In such cases "shipper's weight, load and count" or other words indicating that the description was made by the shipper are ineffective except as to freight concealed by packages.

(3) When bulk freight is loaded by a shipper who makes available to the issuer adequate facilities for weighing such freight, an issuer who is a common carrier must ascertain the kind and quantity within a reasonable time after receiving the written request of the shipper to do so. In such cases "shipper's weight" or other words of like purport are ineffective.

(4) The issuer may by inserting in the bill the words "shipper's weight, load and count" or other words of like purport indicate that the goods were loaded by the shipper; and if such statement be true the issuer shall not be liable for damages caused by the improper loading. But their omission does not imply liability for such damages.

(5) The shipper shall be deemed to have guaranteed to the issuer the accuracy at the time of shipment of the description, marks, labels, number, kind, quantity, condition and weight, as furnished by him; and the shipper shall indemnify the issuer against damage caused by inaccuracies in such particulars. The right of the issuer to such indemnity shall in no way limit his responsibility and liability under the contract of carriage to any person other than the shipper.

Section 7-302. Through Bills of Lading and Similar Documents.

(1) The issuer of a through bill of lading or other document embodying an undertaking to be performed in part by persons acting as its agents or by connecting carriers is liable to anyone entitled to recover on the document for any breach by such other persons or by a connecting carrier of its obligation under the document but to the extent that the bill covers an undertaking to be performed overseas or in territory not contiguous to the continental United States or an undertaking including matters other than transportation this liability may be varied by agreement of the parties.

(2) Where goods covered by a through bill of lading or other document embodying an undertaking to be performed in part by persons other than the issuer are received by any such person, he is subject with respect to his own performance while the goods are in his possession to the obligation of the issuer. His obligation is discharged by delivery of the goods to another such person pursuant to the document, and does not

include liability for breach by any other such persons or by the issuer.

(3) The issuer of such through bill of lading or other document shall be entitled to recover from the connecting carrier or such other person in possession of the goods when the breach of the obligation under the document occurred, the amount it may be required to pay to anyone entitled to recover on the document therefor, as may be evidenced by any receipt, judgment, or transcript thereof, and the amount of any expense reasonably incurred by it in defending any action brought by anyone entitled to recover on the document therefor.

Section 7-303. Diversion; Reconsignment; Change of Instructions.

(1) Unless the bill of lading otherwise provides, the carrier may deliver the goods to a person or destination other than that stated in the bill or may otherwise dispose of the goods on instructions from

    (a) the holder of a negotiable bill; or

    (b) the consignor on a non-negotiable bill notwithstanding contrary instructions from the consignee; or

    (c) the consignee on a non-negotiable bill in the absence of contrary instructions from the consignor, if the goods have arrived at the billed destination or if the consignee is in possession of the bill; or

    (d) the consignee on a non-negotiable bill if he is entitled as against the consignor to dispose of them.

(2) Unless such instructions are noted on a negotiable bill of lading, a person to whom the bill is duly negotiated can hold the bailee according to the original terms.

Section 7-304. Bills of Lading in a Set.

(1) Except where customary in overseas transportation, a bill of lading must not be issued in a set of parts. The issuer is liable for damages caused by violation of this subsection.

(2) Where a bill of lading is lawfully drawn in a set of parts, each of which is numbered and expressed to be valid only if the goods have not been delivered against any other part, the whole of the parts constitute one bill.

(3) Where a bill of lading is lawfully issued in a set of parts and different parts are negotiated to different persons, the title of the holder to whom the first due negotiation is made prevails as to both the document and the goods even though any later holder may have received the goods from the carrier in good faith and discharged the carrier's obligation by surrender of his part.

(4) Any person who negotiates or transfers a single part of a bill of lading drawn in a set is liable to holders of that part as if it were the whole set.

(5) The bailee is obliged to deliver in accordance with Part 4 of this Article against the first presented part of a bill of lading lawfully drawn in a set. Such delivery discharges the bailee's obligation on the whole bill.

Section 7-305. Destination Bills.

(1) Instead of issuing a bill of lading to the consignor at the place of shipment a carrier may at the request of the consignor procure the bill to be issued at destination or at any other place designated in the request.

(2) Upon request of anyone entitled as against the carrier to control the goods while in transit and on surrender of any outstanding bill of lading or other receipt covering such goods, the issuer may procure a substitute bill to be issued at any place designated in the request.

Section 7-306. Altered Bills of Lading.

An unauthorized alteration or filling of a blank in a bill of lading leaves the bill enforceable according to its original tenor.

Section 7-307. Lien of Carrier.

(1) A carrier has a lien on the goods covered by a bill of lading for charges subsequent to the date of its receipt of the goods for storage or transportation (including demurrage and terminal charges) and for expenses incurred in their sale pursuant to law. But against a purchaser for value of a negotiable bill of lading a carrier's lien is limited to charges stated in the bill or the applicable tariffs, or if no charges are stated then to a reasonable charge.

(2) A lien for charges and expenses under subsection (1) on goods which the carrier was required by law to receive for transportation is effective against the consignor or any person entitled to the goods unless the carrier had notice that the consignor lacked authority to subject the goods to

such charges and expenses. Any other lien under subsection (1) is effective against the consignor and any person who permitted the bailor to have control or possession of the goods unless the carrier had notice that the bailor lacked such authority.

(3) A carrier loses his lien on any goods which he voluntarily delivers or which he unjustifiably refuses to deliver.

Section 7-308. Enforcement of Carrier's Lien.

(1) A carrier's lien may be enforced by public or private sale of the goods, in bloc or in parcels, at any time or place and on any terms which are commercially reasonable, after notifying all persons known to claim an interest in the goods. Such notification must include a statement of the amount due, the nature of the proposed sale and the time and place of any public sale. The fact that a better price could have been obtained by a sale at a different time or in a different method from that selected by the carrier is not of itself sufficient to establish that the sale was not made in a commercially reasonable manner. If the carrier either sells the goods in the usual manner in any recognized market therefor or if he sells at the price current in such market at the time of his sale or if he has otherwise sold in conformity with commercially reasonable practices among dealers in the type of goods sold he has sold in a commercially reasonable manner. A sale of more goods than apparently necessary to be offered to ensure satisfaction of the obligation is not commercially reasonable except in cases covered by the preceding sentence.

(2) Before any sale pursuant to this section any person claiming a right in the goods may pay the amount necessary to satisfy the lien and the reasonable expenses incurred under this section. In that event the goods must not be sold, but must be retained by the carrier subject to the terms of the bill and this Article.

(3) The carrier may buy at any public sale pursuant to this section.

(4) A purchaser in good faith of goods sold to enforce a carrier's lien takes the goods free of any rights of persons against whom the lien was valid, despite non-compliance by the carrier with the requirements of this section.

(5) The carrier may satisfy his lien from the proceeds of any sale pursuant to this section but must hold the balance, if any, for delivery on demand to any person to whom he would have been bound to deliver the goods.

(6) The rights provided by this section shall be in addition to all other rights allowed by law to a creditor against his debtor.

(7) A carrier's lien may be enforced in accordance with either subsection (1) or the procedure set forth in subsection (2) of Section 7-210.

(8) The carrier is liable for damages caused by failure to comply with the requirements for sale under this section and in case of willful violation is liable for conversion.

Section 7-309. Duty of Care; Contractual Limitation of Carrier's Liability.

(1) A carrier who issues a bill of lading whether negotiable or non-negotiable must exercise the degree of care in relation to the goods which a reasonably careful man would exercise under like circumstances. This subsection does not repeal or change any law or rule of law which imposes liability upon a common carrier for damages not caused by its negligence.

(2) Damages may be limited by a provision that the carrier's liability shall not exceed a value stated in the document if the carrier's rates are dependent upon value and the consignor by the carrier's tariff is afforded an opportunity to declare a higher value or a value as lawfully provided in the tariff, or where no tariff is filed he is otherwise advised of such opportunity; but no such limitation is effective with respect to the carrier's liability for conversion to its own use.

(3) Reasonable provisions as to the time and manner of presenting claims and instituting actions based on the shipment may be included in a bill of lading or tariff.

PART 4

WAREHOUSE RECEIPTS AND BILLS OF LADING:
GENERAL OBLIGATIONS

Section 7-401. Irregularities in Issue of Receipt or Bill or Conduct of Issue. The obligations imposed by this Article on an issuer apply to a document of title regardless of the fact that

(a) the document may not comply with the requirements of this Article or of any other law or regulation regarding its issue, form or content; or

(b) the issuer may have violated laws regulating the conduct of his business; or

(c) The goods covered by the document were owned by the bailee at the time the document was issued; or

(d) the person issuing the document does not come within the definition of warehouseman if it purports to be a warehouse receipt.

Section 7-402. Duplicate Receipt or Bill; Overissue. Neither a duplicate nor any other document of title purporting to cover goods already represented by an outstanding document of the same issuer confers any right in the goods, except as provided in the case of bills in a set, overissue of documents for fungible goods and substitutes for lost, stolen or destroyed documents. But the issuer is liable for damages caused by his overissue or failure to identify a duplicate document as such by conspicuous notation on its face.

Section 403. Obligation of Warehouseman or Carrier to Deliver; Excuse.

(1) The bailee must deliver the goods to a person entitled under the document who complies w h subsection (2) and (3), unless and to the extent that the bailee establishes any of the following:

(a) delivery of the goods to a person whose receipt was rightful as against the claimant;

(b) damage to or delay, loss or destruction of the goods for which the bailee is not liable [,but the burden of establishing negligence in such cases is on the person entitled under the document];

NOTE: *The brakets in (1) (b) indicate that State enactments may differ on this point without serious damage to the principle of uniformity.*

(c) previous sale or other disposition of the goods in lawful enforcement of a lien or on warehouseman's lawful termination of storage;

(d) the exercise by a seller of his right to stop delivery pursuant to the provisions of the Article on Sales (Section 2-705);

(e) a diversion, reconsignment or other disposition pursuant to the provisions of this Article (Section 7-303) or tariff regulating such right;

(f) release, satisfaction or any other fact affording a personal defense against the claimant;

(g) any other lawful excuse.

(2) A person claiming goods covered by a document of title must satisfy the bailee's lien where the bailee so requests or where the bailee is prohibited by law from delivering the goods until the charges are paid.

(3) Unless the person claiming is one against whom the document confers no right under Sec. 7-503 (1), he must surrender for cancellation or notation of partial deliveries any outstanding negotiable document covering the goods, and the bailee must cancel the document or conspicuously note the partial delivery thereon or be liable to any person to whom the document is duly negotiated.

(4) "Person entitled under the document" means holder in the case of a negotiable document, or the person to whom delivery is to be made by the terms of or pursuant to written instructions under a non-negotiable document.

Section 7-404. No Liability for Good Faith Delivery Pursuant to Receipt or Bill. A bailee who in good faith including observance of reasonable commercial standards has received goods and delivered or otherwise disposed of them according to the terms of the document of title or pursuant to this Article is not liable therefor. This rule applies even though the person from whom he received the goods had no authority to procure the document or to dispose of the goods and even though the person to whom he delivered the goods had no authority to receive them.

PART 5

WAREHOUSE RECEIPTS AND BILLS OF LADING: NEGOTIATION AND TRANSFER

Section 7-501. Form of Negotiation and Requirements of "Due Negotiation."

(1) A negotiable document of title running to the order of a named person is negotiated by his indorsement and delivery. After his indorsement in blank or to bearer any person can negotiate it by delivery alone.

(2)(a) A negotiable document of title is also negotiated by delivery alone when by its original terms it runs to bearer.

(b) When a document running to the order of a named person is delivered to him the effect is the same as if the document had been negotiated.

(3) Negotiation of a negotiable document of title after it has been indorsed to a specified person requires indorsement by the special indorsee as well as delivery.

(4) A negotiable document of title is "duly negotiated" when it is negotiated in the manner stated in this section to a holder who purchases it in good faith without notice of any defense against or claim to it on the part of any person and for value, unless it is established that the negotiation is not in the regular course of business or financing or involves receiving the document in settlement or payment of a money obligation.

(5) Indorsement of a non-negotiable document neither makes it negotiable nor adds to the transferee's rights.

(6) The naming in a negotiable bill of a person to be notified of the arrival of the goods does not limit the negotiability of the bill nor constitute notice to a purchaser thereof of any interest of such person in the goods.

Section 7-502. Rights Acquired by Due Negotiation.

(1) Subject to the following section and to the provisions of Section 7-205 on fungible goods, a holder to whom a negotiable document of title has been duly negotiated acquires thereby:

(a) title to the document;

(b) title to the goods;

(c) all rights accruing under the law of agency or estoppel, including rights to goods delivered to the bailee after the document was issued; and

(d) the direct obligation of the issuer to hold or deliver the goods according to the terms of the document free of any defense or claim by him except those arising under the terms of the document or under this Article. In the case of a delivery order the bailee's obligation accrued only upon acceptance and the obligation acquired by the holder is that the issuer and any indorser will procure the acceptance of the bailee.

(2) Subject to the following section, title and rights so acquired are not defeated by any stoppage of the goods represented by the document or by surrender of such goods by the bailee, and are not impaired even though the negotiation or any prior negotiation constituted a breach of duty or even though any person has been deprived of possession of the document by misrepresentation, fraud, accident, mistake, duress, loss, theft or conversion, or even though a previous sale or other transfer of the goods has been made to a third person.

Section 7-503. Documents of Title to Goods Defeated in Certain Cases.

(1) A document of title confers no right in goods against a person who before issuance of the document had a legal interest or a perfected security interest in them and who neither

(a) delivered or entrusted them or any document of title covering them to the bailor or his nominee with actual or apparent authority to ship, store or sell or with power to obtain delivery under this Article (Section 7-403) or with power of disposition under this Act (Sections 2-403 and 9-307) or other statute or rule of law; nor

(b) acquiesced in the procurement by the bailor or his nominee of any document of title.

(2) Title to goods based upon an unaccepted delivery order is subject to the rights of anyone to whom a negotiable warehouse receipt or bill of lading covering the goods has been duly negotiated. Such a title may be defeated under the next section to the same extent as the rights of the issuer or a transferee from the issuer.

(3) Title to goods based upon a bill of lading issued to a freight forwarder is subject to the rights of anyone to whom a bill issued by the freight forwarder is duly negotiated; but delivery by the carrier in accordance with Part 4 of this Article pursuant to its own bill of lading discharges the carrier's obligation to deliver.

Section 7-504. Rights Acquired in the Absence of Due Negotiation; Effect of Diversion; Seller's Stoppage of Delivery.

(1) A transferee of a document, whether negotiable or non-negotiable, to whom the document has been delivered but not duly negotiated, acquires the title and rights which his transferor had or had actual authority to convey.

(2) In the case of a non-negotiable document, until but not after the bailee receives notification of the transfer, the rights of the transferee may be defeated

    (a) by those creditors of the transferor who could treat the sale as void under Section 2-402; or

    (b) by a buyer from the transferor in ordinary course of business if the bailee has delivered the goods to the buyer or received notification of his rights; or

    (c) as against the bailee by good faith dealings of the bailee with the transferor.

(3) A diversion or other change of shipping instructions by the consignor in a non-negotiable bill of lading which causes the bailee not to deliver to the consignee defeats the consignee's title to the goods if they have been delivered to a buyer in ordinary course of business and in any event defeats the consignee's rights against the bailee.

(4) Delivery pursuant to a non-negotiable document may be stopped by a seller under Section 2-705, and subject to the requirement of due notification there provided. A bailee honoring the seller's instructions is entitled to be indemnified by the seller against any resulting loss or expense.

Section 7-505. Indorser Not a Guarantor for Other Parties. The indorsement of a document of title issued by a bailee does not make the indorser liable for any default by the bailee or by previous indorsers.

Section 7-506. Delivery Without Indorsement: Right to Compel Indorsement. The transferee of a negotiable document of title has a specifically enforceable right to have his transferor supply any necessary indorsement but the transfer becomes a negotiation only as of the time the indorsement is supplied.

Section 7-507. Warranties on Negotiation or Transfer of Receipt or Bill. Where a person negotiates or transfers a document of title for value otherwise than as a mere intermediary under the next following section, then unless otherwise agreed he warrants to his immediate purchaser only in addition to any warranty made in selling the goods

    (a) that the document is genuine; and

    (b) that he has no knowledge of any fact which would impair its validity or worth; and

    (c) that his negotiation or transfer is rightful and fully effective with respect to the title to the document and the goods it represents.

Section 7-508. Warranties of Collecting Bank as to Documents. A collecting bank or other intermediary known to be entrusted with documents on behalf of another or with collection of a draft or other claim against delivery of documents warrants by such delivery of the documents only its own good faith and authority. This rule applies even though the intermediary has purchased or made advances against the claim or draft to be collected.

Section 7-509. Receipt or Bill: When Adequate Compliance with Commercial Contract. The question whether a document is adequate to fulfill the obligations of a contract for sale or the conditions of a credit is governed by the Articles on Sales (Article 2) and on Letters of Credit (Article 5).

PART 6

WHARHOUSE RECEIPTS AND BILLS OF LADING: MISCELLANEOUS PROVISIONS

Section 7-601. Lost and Missing Documents.

(1) If a document has been lost, stolen or destroyed, a court may order delivery of the goods or issuance of a substitute document and the bailee may without liability to any person comply with such order. If the document was negotiable the claimant must post security approved by the court to indemnify any person who may suffer loss as a result of non-surrender of the document. If the

document was not negotiable, such security may be required at the discretion of the court. The court may also in its discretion order payment of the bailee's reasonable costs and counsel fees.

(2) A bailee who without court order delivers goods to a person claiming under a missing negotiable document is liable to any person injured thereby, and if the delivery is not in good faith becomes liable for conversion. Delivery in good faith is not conversion if made in accordance with a filed classification or tariff or, where no classification or tariff is filed, if the claimant posts security with the bailee in an amount at least double the value of the goods at the time of posting to indemnify any person injured by the delivery who files a notice of claim within one year after the delivery.

Section 7-602. Attachment of Goods Covered by a Negotiable Document. Except where the document was originally issued upon delivery of the goods by a person who had no power to dispose of them, no lien attaches by virtue of any judicial process to goods in the possession of a bailee for which a negotiable document of title is outstanding unless the document be first surrendered to the bailee or its negotiation enjoined, and the bailee shall not be compelled to deliver the goods pursuant to process until the document is surrendered to him or impounded by the court. One who purchases the document for value without notice of the process or injunction takes free of the lien imposed by judicial process.

Section 7-603. Conflicting Claims; Interpleader. If more than one person claims title or possession of the goods, the bailee is excused from delivery until he has had a reasonable time to ascertain the validity of the adverse claims or to bring an action to compel all claimants to interplead and may compel such interpleader, either in defending an action for non-delivery of the goods, or by original action, whichever is appropriate.

ARTICLE 8

INVESTMENT SECURITIES

PART 1

SHORT TITLE AND GENERAL MATTERS

Section 8-101. Short Title. This Article shall be known and may be cited as Uniform Commercial Code—Investment Securities.

Section 8-102. Definitions and Index of Definitions.

(1) In this Article unless the context otherwise requires

  (a) A "security" is an instrument which

    (i) is issued in bearer or registered form; and

    (ii) is of a type commonly dealt in upon securities exchanges or markets or commonly recognized in any area in which it is issued or dealt in as a medium for investment; and

    (iii) is either one of a class or series or by its terms is divisible into a class or series of instruments; and

    (iv) evidences a share, participation or other interest in property or in an enterprise or evidences an obligation of the issuer.

  (b) A writing which is a security is governed by this Article and not by Uniform Commercial Code-Commercial Paper even though it also meets the requirements of that Article. This Article does not apply to money.

  (c) A security is in "registered form" when it specifies a person entitled to the security or to the rights it evidences and when its transfer may be registered upon books maintained for that purpose by or on behalf of an issuer or the security so states.

  (d) A security is in "bearer form" when it runs to bearer according to its terms and not by reason of any indorsement.

(2) A "subsequent purchaser" is a person who takes other than by original issue.

(3) A "clearing corporation" is a corporation all of the capital stock of which is held by or for a national security exchange or association registered under a statute of the United States such as the Securities Exchange Act of 1934.

(4) A "custodian bank" is any bank or trust company which is supervised and examined by state or federal authority having supervision over banks and which is acting as custodian for a clearing corporation.

(5) Other definitions applying to this Article or to specified Parts thereof and the sections in which they appear are:

"Adverse claim." Section 8-301.

"Bona fide purchaser." Section 8-302.

"Broker." Section 8-303.

"Guarantee of
the signature." Section 8-402.

"Intermediary bank." Section 4-105.

"Issuer." Section 8-201.

"Overissue." Section 8-104.

(6) In addition Article 1 contains general definitions and principles of construction and interpretation applicable throughout this Article.

Section 8-103. Issuer's Lien. A lien upon a security in favor of an issuer thereof is valid against a purchaser only if the right of the issuer to such lien is noted conspicuously on the security.

Section 8-104. Effect of Overissue; "Overissue."

(1) The provisions of this Article which validate a security or compel its issue or reissue do not apply to the extent that validation, issue or reissue would result in overissue; but

(a) if an identical secuirty which does not constitute an overissue is reasonably available for purchase, the person entitled to issue or validation may compel the issuer to purchase and deliver such a security to him against surrender of the security, if any, which he holds; or

(b) if a security is not so available for purchase, the person entitled to issue or validation may recover from the issuer the price he or the last purchaser for value paid for it with interest from the date of his demand.

(2) "Overissue" means the issue of securities in excess of the amount which the issuer has corporate power to issue.

Section 8-105. Securities Negotiable; Presumptions.

(1) Securities governed by this Article are negotiable instruments.

(2) In any action on a security

(a) unless specifically denied in the pleadings, each signature on the security or in a necessary indorsement is admitted;

(b) when the effectiveness of a signature is put in issue the burden of establishing it is on the party claiming under the signature but the signature is presumed to be genuine or authorized;

(c) when signatures are admitted or established production of the instrument entitles a holder to recover on it unless the defendant establishes a defense or a defect going to the validity of the security; and

(d) after it is shown that a defense or defect exists the plaintiff has the burden of establishing that he or some person under whom he claims is a person against whom the defense or defect is ineffective (Section 8-202).

Section 8-106. Applicability. The validity of a security and the rights and duties of the issuer with respect to registration of transfer are governed by the law (including the conflict of laws rules) or the jurisdiction of organization or the issuer.

Section 8-107. Securities Deliverable; Action for Price.

(1) Unless otherwise agreed and subject to any applicable law or regulation respecting short sales, a person obligated to deliver securities may deliver any security of the specified issue in bearer form or registered in the name of the transferee or indorsed to him or in blank.

(2) When the buyer fails to pay the price as it comes due under a contract of sale the seller may recover the price

(a) of securities accepted by the buyer; and

(b) of other securities if efforts at their resale would be unduly burdensome or if there is no readily available market for their resale.

PART 2

ISSUE–ISSUER

Section 8-201. "Issuer."

(1) With respect to obligations on or defenses to a security "issuer" includes a person who

(a) places or authorizes the placing of his name on a security (otherwise than as authenticating trustee, registrar, transfer agent or the like) to evidence that it represents a share, participation or other interest in his property or in an enterprise or to evidence his duty to perform an obligation evidenced by the security; or

(b) directly or indirectly creates fractional interests in his rights or property which fractional interests are evidenced by securities; or

(c) becomes responsible for or in place of any other person described as an issuer in this section.

(2) With respect to obligations on or defenses to a security a guarantor is an issuer to the extent of his guaranty whether or not his obligation is noted on the security.

(3) With respect to registration of transfer (Part 4 of this Article) "issuer" means a person on whose behalf transfer books are maintained.

Section 8-202. Issuer's Responsibility and Defenses; Notice of Defect or Defense.

(1) Even against a purchaser for value and without notice, the terms of a security include those stated on the security and those made part of the security by reference to another instrument, indenture or document or to a constitution, statute, ordinance, rule, regulation, order or the like to the extent that the terms so referred to do not conflict with the stated terms. Such a reference does not of itself charge a purchaser for value with notice of a defect going to the validity of the security even though the security expressly states that a person accepting it admits such notice.

(2) (a)   A security other than one issued by a government or governmental agency or unit even though issued with a defect going to its validity is valid in the hands of a purchaser for value and without notice of the particular defect unless the defect involves a violation of constitutional provisions in which case the security is valid in the hands of a subsequent purchaser for value and without notice of the defect.

(b)   The rule of subparagraph (a) applies to an issuer which is a government or governmental agency or unit only if either there has been substantial compliance with the legal requirements governing the issue or the issuer has received a substantial consideration for the issue as a whole or for the particular security and a stated purpose of the issue is one for which the issuer has power to borrow money or issue the security.

(3) Except as otherwise provided in the case of certain unauthorized signatures on issue (Section 8-205), lack of genuineness of a security is a complete defense even against a purchaser for value and without notice.

(4) All other defenses of the issuer including nondelivery and conditional delivery of the security are ineffective against a purchaser for value who has taken without notice of the particular defense.

(5) Nothing in this section shall be construed to affect the right of a party to a "when, as and if issued" or a "when distributed" contract to cancel the contract in the event of a material change in the character of the security which is the subject of the contract or in the plan or arrangement pursuant to which such security is to be issued or distributed.

Section 8-203. Staleness as Notice of Defects or Defenses.

(1) After an act or event which creates a right to immediate performance of the principal obligation evidenced by the security or which sets a date on or after which the security is to be presented or sur-

rendered for redemption or exchange, a purchaser is charged with notice of any defect in its issue or defense of the issuer

(a) if the act or event is one requiring the payment of money or the delivery of securities or both on presentation or surrender of the security and such funds or securities are available on the date set for payment or exchange and he takes the security more than one year after that date; and

(b) if the act or event is not covered by paragraph (a) and he takes the security more than two years after the date set for surrender or presentation or the date on which such performance became due.

(2) A call which has been revoked is not within subsection (1).

Section 8-204. Effect of Issuer's Restrictions on Transfer. Unless noted conspicuously on the security a restriction on transfer imposed by the issuer even though otherwise lawful is ineffective except against a person with actual knowledge of it.

Section 8-205. Effect of Unauthorized Signature on Issue. An unauthorized signature placed on a security prior to or in the course of issue is ineffective except that the signature is effective in favor of a purchaser for value and without notice of the lack of authority if the signing has been done by

(a) an authenticating trustee, registrar, transfer agent or other person entrusted by the issuer with the signing of the security or of similar securities or their immediate preparation for signing; or

(b) an employee of the issuer or of any of the foregoing entrusted with responsible handling of the security.

Section 8-206. Completion or Alteration of Instrument.

(1) Where a security contains the signatures necessary to its issue or transfer but is incomplete in any other respect

(a) any person may complete it by filling in the blanks as authorized; and

(b) even though the blanks are incorrectly filled in, the security as completed is enforceable by a purchaser who took it for value and without notice of such incorrectness.

(2) A complete security which has been improperly altered even though fraudulently remains enforceable but only according to its original terms.

Section 8-207. Rights of Issuer with Respect to Registered Owners.

(1) Prior to due presentment for registration of transfer of a security in registered form the issuer or indenture trustee may treat the registered owner as the person exclusively entitled to vote, to receive notifications and otherwise to exercise all the rights and powers of an owner.

(2) Nothing in this Article shall be construed to affect the liability of the registered owner of a security for calls, assessments or the like.

Section 8-208. Effect of Signature of Authenticating Trustee, Registrar or Transfer Agent.

(1) A person placing his signature upon a security as authenticating trustee, registrar, transfer agent or the like warrants to a purchaser for value without notice of the particular defect that

(a) the security is genuine; and

(b) his own participation in the issue of the security is within his capacity and within the scope of the authorization received by him from the issuer; and

(c) he has reasonable grounds to believe that the security is in the form and within the amount the issuer is authorized to issue.

(2) Unless otherwise agreed, a person by so placing his signature does not assume responsibility for the validity of the security in other respects.

PART 3

PURCHASE

Section 8-301. Rights Acquired by Purchaser; "Adverse Claim"; Title Acquired by Bona Fide Purchaser.

(1) Upon delivery of a security the purchaser acquires the rights in the security which his transferor had or had actual authority to convey except that a purchaser who has himself been a party to any fraud or illegality affecting the security or who as a prior holder had notice of an adverse claim cannot improve his position by taking from a later bona fide purchaser. "Adverse claim"

includes a claim that a transfer was or would be wrongful or that a particular adverse person is the owner of or has an interest in the security.

(2) A bona fide purchaser in addition to acquiring the rights of a purchaser also acquires the security free of any adverse claim.

(3) A purchaser of a limited interest acquires rights only to the extent of the interest purchased.

Section 8-302. "Bona Fide Purchaser." A "bona fide purchaser" is a purchaser for value in good faith and without notice of any adverse claim who takes delivery of a security in bearer form or of one in registered form issued to him or indorsed to him or in blank.

Section 8-303. "Broker." "Broker" means a person engaged for all or part of his time in the business of buying and selling securities, who in the transaction concerned acts for, or buys a security from or sells a security to a customer. Nothing in this Article determines the capacity in which a person acts for purposes of any other statute or rule to which such person is subject.

Section 8-304. Notice to Purchaser of Adverse Claims.

(1) A purchaser (including a broker for the seller or buyer but excluding an intermediary bank) of a security is charged with notice of adverse claims if

(a) the security whether in bearer or registered form has been indorsed "for collection" or "for surrender" or for some other purpose not involving transfer; or

(b) the security is in bearer form and has on it an unambiguous statement that it is the property of a person other than the transferor. The mere writing of a name on a security is not such a statement.

(2) The fact that the purchaser (including a broker for the seller or buyer) has notice that the security is held for a third person or is registered in the name of or indorsed by a fiduciary does not create a duty of inquiry into the rightfulness of the transfer or constitute notice of adverse claims. If, however, the purchaser (excluding an intermediary bank) has knowledge that the proceeds are being used or that the transaction is for the individual benefit of the fiduciary or other-

wise in breach of duty, the purchaser is charged with notice of adverse claims.

Section 8-305. Staleness as Notice of Adverse Claims. An act or event which creates a right to immediate performance of the principal obligation evidenced by the security or which sets a date on or after which the security is to be presented or surrendered for redemption or exchange does not of itself constitute any notice of adverse claims except in the case of a purchase

(a) after one year from any date set for such presentment or surrender for redemption or exchange; or

(b) after six months from any date set for payment of money against presentation or surrender of the security if funds are available for payment on that date.

Section 8-306. Warranties on Presentment and Transfer.

(1) A person who presents a security for registration on transfer or for payment or exchange warrants to the issuer that he is entitled to the registration, payment or exchange. But a purchaser for value without notice of adverse claims who receives a new, reissued or registered security on registration of transfer warrants only that he has no knowledge of any unauthorized signature (Section 8-311) in a necessary indorsement.

(2) A person by transferring a security to a purchaser for value warrants only that

(a) his transfer is effective and rightful; and

(b) the security is genuine and has not been materially altered; and

(c) he knows no fact which might impair the validity of the security.

(3) Where a security is delivered by an intermediary known to be entrusted with delivery of the security on behalf of another or with collection of a draft or other claim against such delivery, the intermediary by such delivery warrants only his own good faith and authority even though he has purchased or made advances against the claim to be collected against the delivery.

(4) A pledgee or other holder for security who redelivers the security received, or after payment and on order of the debtor delivers that security to a third person makes only the warranties of an intermediary under subsection (3).

(5) A broker gives to his customer and to

the issuer and a purchaser the warranties provided in this section and has the rights and privileges of a purchaser under this section. The warranties of and in favor of the broker acting as an agent are in addition to applicable warranties given by and in favor of his customer.

Section 8-307. Effect of Delivery Without Indorsement; Right to Compel Indorsement. Where a security in registered form has been delivered to a purchaser without a necessary indorsement he may become a bona fide purchaser only as of the time the indorsement is supplied, but against the transferor the transfer is complete upon delivery and the purchaser has a specifically enforceable right to have any necessary indorsement supplied.

Section 8-308. Indorsement, How Made; Special Indorsement; Indorser Not a Guarantor; Partial Assignment.

(1) An indorsement of a security in registered form is made when an appropriate person signs on it or on a separate document an assignment or transfer of the security or a power to assign or transfer it or when the signature of such person is written without more upon the back of the security.

(2) An indorsement may be in blank or special. An indorsement in blank includes an indorsement to bearer. A special indorsement specifies the person to whom the security is to be transferred, or who has power to transfer it. A holder may convert a blank indorsement into a special indorsement.

(3) "An appropriate person" in subsection (1) means

(a) the person specified by the security or by special indorsement to be entitled to the security; or

(b) where the person so specified is described as a fiduciary but is no longer serving in the described capacity,—either that person or his successor; or

(c) where the security or indorsement so specifies more than one person as fiduciaries and one or more are no longer serving in the described capacity,—the remaining fiduciary or fiducaries, whether or not a successor has been appointed or qualified; or

(d) where the person so specified is an individual and is without capacity to act by virtue of death, incompetence, in-

fancy or otherwise,—his executor, administrator, guardian or like fiduciary; or

(e) where the security or indorsement so specifies more than one person as tenants by the entirety or with right of survivorship and by reason of death all cannot sign,—the survivor or survivors; or

(f) a person having power to sign under applicable law or controlling instrument; or

(g) to the extent that any of the foregoing persons may act through an agent,—his authorized agent.

(4) Unless otherwise agreed the indorser by his indorsement assumes no obligation that the security will be honored by the issuer.

(5) An indorsement purporting to be only a part of a security representing units intended by the issuer to be separately transferable is effective to the extent of the indorsement.

(6) Whether the person signing is appropriate is determined as of the date of signing and an indorsement by such a person does not become unauthorized for the purposes of this Article by virtue of any subsequent change of circumstances.

(7) Failure of a fiduciary to comply with a controlling instrument or with the law of the state having jurisdiction of the fiduciary relationship, including any law requiring the fiduciary to obtain court approval of the transfer, does not render his indorsement unauthorized for the purposes of this Article.

Section 8-309. Effect of Indorsement Without Delivery. An indorsement of a security whether special or in blank does not constitute a transfer until delivery of the security on which it appears or if the indorsement is on a separate document until delivery of both the document and the security.

Section 8-310. Indorsement of Security in Bearer Form. An indorsement of a security in bearer form may give notice of adverse claims (Section 8-304) but does not otherwise affect any right to registration the holder may possess.

Section 8-311. Effect of Unauthorized Indorsement. Unless the owner has ratified an unauthorizeindorsement or is otherwise precluded from asserting its ineffectiveness

(a) he may assert its ineffectiveness against the issuer or any purchaser other than a purchaser for value and without notice of adverse claims who has in good faith received a new, reissued or re-registered security on registration of transfer; and

(b) an issuer who registers the transfer of a security upon the unauthorized indorsement is subject to liability for improper registration (Section 8-404).

Section 8-312. Effect of Guaranteeing Signature or Indorsement.

(1) Any person guaranteeing a signature of an indorser of a security warrants that at the time of signing

(a) the signature was genuine; and

(b) the signer was an appropriate person to indorse (Section 8-308); and

(c) the signer had legal capacity to sign. But the guarantor does not otherwise warrant the rightfulness of the particular transfer.

(2) Any person may guarantee an indorsement of a security and by so doing warrants not only the signature (subsection 1) but also the rightfulness of the particular transfer in all respects, but no issuer may require a guarantee of indorsement as a condition to registration of transfer.

(3) The foregoing warranties are made to any person taking or dealing with the security in reliance on the guarantee and the guarantor is liable to such person for any loss resulting from breach of the warranties.

Section 8-313. When Delivery to the Purchaser Occurs; Purchaser's Broker as Holder.

(1) Delivery to a purchaser occurs when

(a) he or a person designated by him acquires possession of a security; or

(b) his broker acquires possession of a security specially indorsed to or issued in the name of the purchaser; or

(c) his broker sends him confirmation of the purchase and also by book entry or otherwise identifies a specific security in the broker's possession as belonging to the purchaser; or

(d) with respect to an identified security to be delivered while still in the possession of a third person when that person acknowledges that he holds for the purchaser; or

(e) appropriate entries on the books of a clearing corporation are made under Section 8-320.

(2) The purchaser is the owner of a security held for him by his broker, but is not the holder except as specified in subparagraphs (b), (c) and (e) of subsection (1). Where a security is part of a fungible bulk the purchaser is the owner of a proportionate property interest in the fungible bulk.

(3) Notice of an adverse claim received by the broker or by the purchaser after the broker takes delivery as a holder for value is not effective either as to the broker or as to the purchaser. However, as between the broker and the purchaser the pruchaser may demand delivery of an equivalent security as to which no notice of an adverse claim has been received.

Section 8-314. Duty to Deliver, When Completed.

(1) Unless otherwise agreed where a sale of a security is made on an exchange or otherwise through brokers

(a) the selling customer fulfills his duty to deliver when he places such a security in the possession of the selling broker or of a person designated by the broker or if requested causes an acknowledgement to be made to the selling broker that it is held for him; and

(b) the selling broker including a correspondent broker acting for a selling customer fulfills his duty to deliver by placing the security or a like security in the possession of the buying broker or a person designated by him or by effecting clearance of the sale in accordance with the rules of the exchange on which the transaction took place.

(2) Except as otherwise provided in this section and unless otherwise agreed, a transferor's duty to deliver a security under a contract of purchase is not fulfilled until he places the security in form to be negotiated by the purchaser in the possession of the purchaser or of a person designated by him or at the purchaser's request causes an acknowledgment to be made to the purchaser that it is held for him. Unless made on an exchange a sale to a broker purchasing for his own account is within this subsection and not within subsection (1).

Section 8-315. Action Against Purchaser Based Upon Wrongful Transfer.

(1) Any person against whom the transfer of a security is wrongful for any reason,

including his incapacity, may against anyone except a bona fide purchaser reclaim possession of the security or obtain possession of any new security evidencing all or part of the same rights or have damages.

(2) If the transfer is wrongful because of an unauthorized indorsement, the owner may also reclaim or obtain possession of the security or new security even from a bona fide purchaser if the ineffectiveness of the purported indorsement can be asserted against him under the provisions of this Article on unauthorized indorsements (Section 8-311).

(3) The right to obtain or reclaim possession of a security may be specifically enforced and its transfer enjoined and the security impounded pending the litigation.

Section 8-316. Purchaser's Right to Requisites for Registration of Transfer on Books. Unless otherwise agreed the transferor must on due demand supply his purchaser with any proof of his authority to transfer or with any other requisite which may be necessary to obtain registration of the transfer of the security but if the transfer is not for value a transferor need not do so unless the purchaser furnishes the necessary expenses. Failure to comply with a demand made within a reasonable time gives the purchaser the right to reject or rescind the transfer.

Section 8-317. Attachment or Levy Upon Security.

(1) No attachment or levy upon a security or any share or other interest evidenced thereby which is outstanding shall be valid until the security is actually seized by the officer making the attachment or levy but a security which has been surrendered to the issuer may be attached or levied upon at the source.

(2) A creditor whose debtor is the owner of a security shall be entitled to such aid from courts of appropriate jurisdiction, by injunction or otherwise, in reaching such security or in satisfying the claim by means thereof as is allowed at law or in equity in regard to property which cannot readily be attached or levied upon by ordinary legal process.

Section 8-318. No Conversion by Good Faith Delivery. An agent or bailee who in good faith (including observance of reasonable commercial standards if he is in the business of buying, selling or otherwise dealing with securities) has received securities and sold, pledged or delivered them according to the instructions of his principal is not liable for conversion or for participation in breach of fiduciary duty although the principal had no right to dispose of them.

Section 8-319. Statute of Frauds. A contract for the sale of securities is not enforceable by way of action or defense unless

(a) there is some writing signed by the party against whom enforcement is sought or by his authorized agent or broker sufficient to indicate that a contract has been made for sale of a stated quantity of described securities at a defined or stated price; or

(b) delivery of the security has been accepted or payment has been made but the contract is enforceable under this provision only to the extent of such delivery or payment; or

(c) within a reasonable time a writing in confirmation of the sale or purchase and sufficient against the sender under paragraph (a) has been received by the party against whom enforcement is sought and he has failed to send written objection to its contents within ten days after its receipt; or

(d) the party against whom enforcement is sought admits in his pleading, testimony or otherwise in court that a contract was made for the sale of a stated quantity of described securities at a defined or stated price.

Section 8-320. Transfer or Pledge Within a Central Depository System.

(1) If a security

(a) is in the custody of a clearing corporation or of a custodian bank or a nominee of either subject to the instructions of the clearing corporation; and

(b) is in bearer form or indorsed in blank by an appropriate person or registered in the name of the clearing corporation or custodian bank or a nominee of either; and

(c) is shown on the account of a transferor or pledgor on the books of the clearing corporation;

then, in addition to other methods, a transfer or pledge of the security or any interest therein may be effected by the making of appropriate entries on the books of the clearing corporation reducing the account of the transferor or pledgor and increasing the account of the transferee or pledgee by the amount of the obligation or the number of shares or rights transferred or pledged.

(2) Under this section entries may be with respect to like securities or interests therein as a part of a fungible bulk and may refer merely to a quantity of a particular security without reference to the name of the registered owner, certificate or bond number or the like, and, in appropriate cases, may be on a net basis taking into account other transfers or pledges of the same security.

(3) A transfer or pledge under this section has the effect of a delivery of a security in bearer form or duly indorsed in blank (Section 8-301) representing the amount of the obligation or the number of shares or rights transferred or pledged. If a pledge or the creation of a security interest is intended, the making of entries has the effect of a taking of delivery by the pledgee or a secured party (Sections 9-304 and 9-305). A transferee or pledgee under this section is a holder.

(4) A transfer or pledge under this section does not constitute a registration of transfer under Part 4 of this Article.

(5) That entries made on the books of the clearing corporation as provided in subsection (1) are not appropriate does not affect the validity or effect of the entries nor the liabilities or obligations of the clearing corporation to any person adversely affected thereby.

PART 4

REGISTRATION

Section 8-401. Duty of Issuer to Register Transfer.

(1) Where a security in registered form is presented to the issuer with a request to register transfer, the issuer is under a duty to register the transfer as requested if

(a) the security is indorsed by the appropriate person or persons (Section 8-308); and

(b) reasonable assurance is given that those indorsements are genuine and effective (Section 8-402); and

(c) the issuer has no duty to inquire into adverse claims or has discharged any such duty (Section 8-403); and

(d) any applicable law relating to the collection of taxes has been complied with; and

(e) the transfer is in fact rightful or is to a bona fide purchaser.

(2) Where an issuer is under a duty to register a transfer of a security the issuer is also liable to the person presenting it for registration or his principal for loss resulting from any unreasonable delay in registration or from failure or refusal to register the transfer.

Section 8-402. Assurance that Indorsements are Effective.

(1) The issuer may require the following assurance that each necessary indorsement (Section 8-308) is genuine and effective

(a) in all cases, a guarantee of the signature (subsection (1) of Section 8-312) of the person indorsing; and

(b) where the indorsement is by an agent, appropriate assurance of authority to sign;

(c) where the indorsement is by a fiduciary, appropriate evidence of appointment or incumbency;

(d) where there is more than one fiduciary, reasonable assurance that all who are required to sign have done so;

(e) where the indorsement is by a person not covered by any of the foregoing, assurance appropriate to the case corresponding as nearly as may be to the foregoing.

(2) A "guarantee of the signature" in subsection (1) means a guarantee signed by or on behalf of a person reasonably believed by the issuer to be responsible. The issuer may adopt standards with respect to responsibility provided such standards are not manifestly unreasonable.

(3) "Appropriate evidence of appointment or incumbency" in subsection (1) means

(a) in the case of a fiduciary appointed or qualified by a court, a certificate issued by or under the direction or supervision of that court or an officer thereof and dated within sixty days before the date of presentation for transfer; or

(b) in any other case, a copy of a document showing the appointment or a certificate issued by or on behalf of a person reasonably believed by the issuer to be responsible or, in the absence of such a document or certificate, other evidence reasonably deemed by the issuer to be appropriate. The issuer may adopt standards with respect to such evidence provided such standards are not manifestly unreasonable. The issuer is not charged with notice of the contents of any document obtained pursuant to this paragraph (b) except to the extent that the contents relate directly to the appointment or incumbency.

(4) The issuer may elect to require a reasonable assurance beyond that specified in this section but if it does so and for a purpose other than that specified in subsection (3) (b) both requires and obtains a copy of a will, trust, indenture, articles of co-partnership, by-laws or other controlling instrument it is charged with notice of all matters contained therein affecting the transfer.

Section 8-403. Limited Duty of Inquiry.

(1) An issuer to whom a security is presented for registration is under a duty to inquire into adverse claims if

(a) a written notification of an adverse claim is received at a time and in a manner which affords the issuer a reasonable opportunity to act on it prior to the issuance of a new, reissued or re-registered security and the notification identifies the claimant, the registered owner and the issue of which the security is a part and provides an address for communications directed to the claimant; or

(b) the issuer is charged with notice of an adverse claim from a controlling instrument which it has elected to require under subsection (4) of Section 8-402.

(2) The issuer may discharge any duty of inquiry by any reasonable means, including notifying an adverse claimant by registered or certified mail at the address furnished by him or if there be no such address at his residence or regular place of business that

the security has been presented for registration of transfer by a named person, and that the transfer will be registered unless within thirty days from the date of mailing the notification, either

(a) an appropriate restraining order, injunction or other process issues from a court of competent jurisdiction; or

(b) an indemnity bond sufficient in the issuer's judgment to protect the issuer and any transfer agent, registrar or other agent of the issuer involved, from any loss which it or they may suffer by complying with the adverse claim is filed with the issuer.

(3) Unless an issuer is charged with notice of an adverse claim from a controlling instrument which it has elected to require under subsection (4) of Section 8-402 or receives notification of an adverse claim under subsection (1) of this section, where a security presented for registration is indorsed by the appropriate person or persons the issuer is under no duty to inquire into adverse claims. In particular

(a) an issuer registering a security in the name of a person who is a fiduciary or who is described as a fiduciary is not bound to inquire into the existence, extent, or correct description of the fiduciary relationship and thereafter the issuer may assume without inquiry that the newly registered owner continues to be the fiduciary until the issuer receives written notice that the fiduciary is no longer acting as such with respect to the particular security;

(b) an issuer registering transfer on an indorsement by a fiduciary is not bound to inquire whether the transfer is made in compliance with a controlling instrument or with the law of the state having jurisdiction of the fiduciary relationship, including any law requiring the fiduciary to obtain court approval of the transfer; and

(c) the issuer is not charged with notice of the contents of any court record or file or other recorded or unrecorded documents even though the document is in its possession and even though the transfer is made on the indorsement of a fiduciary to the fiduciary himself or to his nominee.

Section 8-404. Liability and Non-Liability for Registration.

(1) Except as otherwise provided in any law relating to the collection of taxes, the issuer is not liable to the owner or any other person suffering loss as a result of the registration of a transfer of a security if

(a) there were on or with the security the necessary indorsements (Section 8-308); and

(b) the issuer had no duty to inquire into adverse claims or has discharged any such duty (Section 8-403).

(2) Where an issuer has registered a transfer of a security to a person not entitled to it the issuer on demand must deliver a like security to the true owner unless

(a) the registration was pursuant to subsection (1); or

(b) the owner is precluded from asserting any claim for registering the transfer under subsection (1) of the following section; or

(c) such delivery would result in overissue, in which case the issuer's liability is governed by Section 8-104.

Section 8-405. Lost, Destroyed and Stolen Securities.

(1) Where a security has been lost, apparently destroyed or wrongfully taken and the owner fails to notify the issuer of that fact within a reasonable time after he has notice of it and the issuer registerers a transfer of the security before receiving such a notification, the owner is precluded from asserting against the issuer any claim for registering the transfer under the preceding section or any claim to a new security under this section.

(2) Where the owner of a security claims that the security has been lost, destroyed or wrongfully taken, the issuer must issue a new security in place of the original security if the owner

(a) so requests before the issuer has notice that the security has been acquired by a bona fide purchaser; and

(b) files with the issuer a sufficient indemnity bond; and

(c) satisfies any other reasonable requirements imposed by the issuer.

(3) If, after the issue of the new security, a bona fide purchaser of the original security presents it for registration of transfer, the issuer must register the transfer unless registration would result in overissue, in which event the issuer's liability is governed by Section 8-104. In addition to any rights on the indemnity bond, the issuer may recover the new security from the person to whom it was issued or any person taking under him except a bona fide purchaser.

Section 8-406. Duty of Authenticating Grustee, Transfer Agent or Registrar.

(1) Where a person acts as authenticating trustee, transfer agent, registrar, or other agent for an issuer in the registration of transfers of its securities or in the issue of new securities or in the cancellation of surrendered securities

(a) he is under a duty to the issuer to exercise good faith and due diligence in performing his functions; and

(b) he has with regard to the particular functions he performs the same obligation to the holder or owner of the security and has the same rights and privileges as the issuer has in regard to those functions.

(2) Notice to an authenticating trustee, transfer agent, registrar or other such agent is notice to the issuer with respect to the functions performed by the agent.

REVISED ARTICLE 9

SECURED TRANSACTIONS; SALES OF ACCOUNTS AND CHATTEL PAPER

PART 1

SHORT TITLE, APPLICABILITY AND DEFINITIONS

Section 9-101. Short Title. This Article shall be known and may be cited as Uniform Commercial Code—Secured Transactions.

Section 9-102. Policy and Subject Matter of Article.

(1) Except as otherwise provided in Section 9-104 on excluded transactions, this Article applies
    (a) to any transaction (regardless of its form) which is intended to create a security interest in personal property or fixtures including goods, documents, instruments, general intangibles, chattel paper or accounts; and also
    (b) to any sale of accounts or chattel paper.

(2) This Article applies to security interests created by contract including pledge, assignment, chattel mortgage, chattel trust, trust deed, factor's lien, equipment trust, conditional sale, trust receipt, other lien or title retention contract and lease or consignment intended as security. This Article does not apply to statutory liens except as provided in Section 9-310.

(3) The application of this Article to a security interest in a secured obligation is not affected by the fact that the obligation is itself secured by a transaction or interest to which this Article does not apply.

Section 9-103. Perfection of Security Interests in Multiple State Transactions.

(1) Documents, instruments and ordinary goods.
    (a) This subsection applies to documents and instruments and to goods other than those covered by a certificate of title described in subsection (2), mobile goods described in subsection (3), and minerals described in subsection (5).
    (b) Except as otherwise provided in this subsection, perfection and the effect of perfection or non-perfection of a security interest in collateral are governed by the law of the jurisdiction where the collateral is when the last event occurs on which is based the assertion that the security interest is perfected or unperfected.
    (c) If the parties to a transaction creating a purchase money security interest in goods in one jurisdiction understand at the time that the security interest attaches that the goods will be kept in another jurisdiction, then the law of the other jurisdiction governs the perfection and the effect of perfection or non-perfection of the security interest from the time it attaches until thirty days after the debtor receives possession of the goods and thereafter if the goods are taken to the other jurisdiction before the end of the thirty-day period.
    (d) When collateral is brought into and kept in this state while subject to a security interest perfected under the law of the jurisdiction from which the collateral was removed, the security interest remains perfected, but if action is required by Part 3 of this Article to perfect the security interest,
        (i) if the action is not taken before the expiration of the period of perfection in the other jurisdiction or the end of four months after the collateral is brought into this state, whichever period first expires, the security interest becomes unperfected at the end of that period and is thereafter deemed to have been unperfected as against a person who became a purchaser after removal;
        (ii) if the action is taken before the expiration of the period specified in subparagraph (i), the security interest continues perfected thereafter;
        (iii) for the purpose of a priority over a buyer of consumer goods (subsection (2) of Section 9-307), the period of the effectiveness of a filing in the jurisdiction from which the collateral is removed is governed by the rules with respect to perfection in subparagraphs (i) and (ii).

(2) Certificate of title.
    (a) This subsection applies to goods covered by a certificate of title issued under a statute of this state or of another jurisdiction under the law of which indication of a security interest on the certificate is required as a condition of perfection.
    (b) Except as otherwise provided in this subsection, perfection and the effect of perfection or non-perfection of the security interest are governed by the law (including the conflict of laws rules) of the jurisdiction issuing the certificate until four months after the goods are removed from that jurisdiction and thereafter until the goods are registered in an-

other jurisdiction, but in any event not beyond surrender of the certificate. After the expiration of that period, the goods are not covered by the certificate of title within the meaning of this section.

(c) Except with respect to the rights of a buyer described in the next paragraph, a security interest, perfected in another jurisdiction otherwise than by notation on a certificate of title, in goods brought into this state and thereafter covered by a certificate of title issued by this state is subject to the rules stated in paragraph (d) of subsection (1).

(d) If goods are brought into this state while a security interest therein is perfected in any manner under the law of the jurisdiction from which the goods are removed and a certificate of title is issued by this state and the certificate does not show that the goods are subject to the security interest or that they may be subject to security interests not shown on the certificate, the security interest is subordinate to the rights of a buyer of the goods who is not in the business of selling goods of that kind to the extent that he gives value and receives delivery of the goods after issuance of the certificate and without knowledge of the security interest.

(3) Accounts, general intangibles and mobile goods.

(a) This subsection applies to accounts (other than an account described in subsection (5) on minerals) and general intangibles and to goods which are mobile and which are of a type normally used in more than one jurisdiction, such as motor vehicles, trailers, rolling stock, airplanes, shipping containers, road building and construction machinery and commercial harvesting machinery and the like, if the goods are equipment or are inventory leased or held for lease by the debtor to others, and are not covered by a certificate of title described in subsection (2).

(b) The law (including the conflict of laws rules) of the jurisdiction in which the debtor is located governs the perfection or non-perfection of the security interest.

(c) If, however, the debtor is located in a jurisdiction which is not a part of the United States, and which does not provide for perfection of the security interest by filing or recording in that jurisdiction, the law of the jurisdiction in the United States in which the debtor has its major executive office in the United States governs the perfection and the effect of perfection or non-perfection of the security interest through filing. In the alternative, if the debtor is located in a jurisdiction which is not a part of the United States or Canada and the collateral is accounts or general intangibles for money due or to become due, the security interest may be perfected by notification to the account debtor. As used in this paragraph, "United States" includes its territories and possessions and the Commonwealth of Puerto Rico.

(d) A debtor shall be deemed located at his place of business if he has one, at his chief executive office if he has more than one place of business, otherwise at his residence. If, however, the debtor is a foreign air carrier under the Federal Aviation Act of 1958, as amended, it shall be deemed located at the designated office of the agent upon whom service of process may be made on behalf of the foreign air carrier.

(e) A security interest perfected under the law of the jurisdiction of the location of the debtor is perfected until the expiration of four months after a change of the debtor's location to another jurisdiction, or until perfection would have ceased by the law of the first jurisdiction, whichever period first expires. Unless perfected in the new jurisdiction before the end of that period, it becomes unperfected thereafter and is deemed to have been unperfected as against a person who became a purchaser after the change.

(4) Chattel paper.

The rules stated for goods in subsection (1) apply to a possessory security interest in chattel paper. The rules stated for accounts in subsection (3) apply to a non-possessory security interest in chattel paper, but the security interest may not be perfected by notification to the account debtor.

(5) Minerals.

Perfection and the effect of perfection or non-perfection of a security interest which is created by a debtor who has an interest in minerals or the like (including oil and gas) before extraction and which attaches thereto as extracted, or which attaches to an account resulting from the sale thereof at the wellhead or minehead are governed by the law (including the conflict or laws rules) of the jurisdiction wherein the wellhead or minehead is located.

Section 9-104. Transactions Excluded From Article. This Article does not apply

(a) to a security interest subject to any statute of the United States to the extent that such statute governs the rights of parties to and third parties affected by transactions in particular types of property; or

(b) to a landlord's lien; or

(c) to a lien given by statute or other rule of law for services or materials except as provided in Section 9-310 on priority of such liens; or

(d) to a transfer of a claim for wages, salary or other compensation of an employee; or

(e) to a transfer by a government or governmental subdivision or agency; or

(f) to a sale of accounts or chattel paper as part of a sale of the business out of which they arose, or an assignment of accounts or chattel paper which is for the purpose of collection only, or a transfer of a right to payment under a contract to an assignee who is also to do the performance under the contract or a transfer of a single account to an assignee in whole or partial satisfaction of a preexisting indebtedness; or

(g) to a transfer of an interest in or claim in or under any policy of insurance, except as provided with respect to proceeds (Section 9-306) and priorities in proceeds (Section 9-312); or

(h) to a right represented by a judgment (other than a judgment taken on a right to payment which was collateral); or

(i) to any right of set-off; or

(j) except to the extent that provision is made for fixtures in Section 9-313, to the creation or transfer of an interest in or lien on real estate, including a lease or rents thereunder; or

(k) to a transfer in whole or in part of any claim arising out of tort; or

(l) to a transfer of an interest in any deposit account (subsection (1) or Section 9-105), except as provided with respect to proceeds (Section 9-306) and priorities in proceeds (Section 9-312).

Section 9-105. Definitions and Index of Definitions.

(1) In this Article unless the context otherwise requires:

(a) "Account debtor" means the person who is obligated on an account, chattel paper or general intangible,

(b) "Chattel paper" means a writing or writings which evidence both a monetary obligation and a security interest in or a lease of specific goods, but a charter or other contract involving the use or hire of a vessel is not chattel paper. When a transaction is evidenced both by such a security agreement or a lease and by an instrument or a series of instruments, the group of writings taken together constitutes chattel paper;

(c) "Collateral" means the property subject to a security interest, and includes accounts and chattel paper which have been sold;

(d) "Debtor" means the person who owes payment or other performance of the obligation secured, whether or not he owns or has rights in the collateral, and includes the seller of accounts or chattel paper. Where the debtor and the owner of the collateral are not the same person, the term "debtor" means the owner of the collateral in any provision of the Article dealing with the collateral, the obligor in any provision dealing with the obligation, and may include both where the context so requires;

(e) "Deposit account" means a demand, time, savings, passbook or like account maintained with a bank, savings and loan association, credit union or like organization, other than an account evidenced by a certificate of deposit;

(f) "Document" means the document of title as defined in the general definitions of Article 1 (Section 1-201), and a receipt of the kind described in subsection (2) of Section 7-201;

(g) "Encumbrance" includes real estate

mortgages and other liens on real estate and all other rights in real estate that are not ownership interests;

(h) "Goods" includes all things which are movable at the time the security interest attaches or which are fixtures (Section 9-313), but does not include money, documents, instruments, accounts, chattel paper, general intangibles, or minerals or the like (including oil and gas) before extraction. "Goods" also includes standing timber which is to be cut and removed under a conveyance or contract for sale, the unborn young of animals, and growing crops;

(i) "Instrument" means a negotiable instrument (defined in Section 3-104), or a security (defined in Section 8-102) or any other writing which evidences a right to the payment of money and is not itself a security agreement or lease and is of a type which is in ordinary course of business transferred by delivery with any necessary indorsement or assignment;

(j) "Mortgage" means a consensual interest created by a real estate mortgage, a trust deed on real estate, or the like;

(k) An advance is made "pursuant to commitment" if the secured party has bound himself to make it, whether or not a subsequent event of default or other event not within his control has relieved or may relieve him from his obligation;

(l) "Security agreement" means an agreement which creates or provides for a security interest;

(m) "Secured party" means a lender, seller or other person in whose favor there is a security interest, including a person to whom accounts or chattel paper have been sold. When the holders of obligations issued under an indenture of trust, equipment trust agreement or the like are represented by a trustee or other person, the representative is the secured party;

(n) "Transmitting utility" means any person primarily engaged in the railroad, street railway or trolley bus business, the electric or electronics communications transmission business, the transmission of goods by pipeline, or the transmission or the production and transmission of electricity, steam, gas or water, or the provi-

sion of sewer service.

(2) Other definitions applying to this Article and the sections in which they appear are:

"Account". Section 9-106.
"Attach". Section 9-203.
"Construction mortgage". Section 9-313(1).
"Consumer goods". Section 9-109(1).
"Equipment". Section 9-109(2).
"Farm products". Section 9-109(3).
"Fixture". Section 9-313(1).
"Fixture filing". Section 9-313(1).
"General intangibles". Section 9-106.
"Inventory". Section 9-109(4).
"Lien creditor". Section 9-301(3).
"Proceeds". Section 9-306(1).
"Purchase money security interest". Section 9-107.
"United States". Section 9-103.

(3) The following definitions in other Articles apply to this Article:

"Check". Section 3-104.
"Contract for sale". Section 2-106.
"Holder in due course". Section 3-302.
"Note". Section 3-104.
"Sale". Section 2-106.

(4) In addition Article 1 contains general definitions and principles of construction and interpretation applicable throughout this Article.

Section 9-106. Definitions: "Account"; "General Intangibles ." "Account means any right to payment for goods sold or leased or for services rendered which is not evidenced by an instrument or chattel paper, whether or not it has been earned by performance. "General intangibles" means any personal property (including things in action) other than goods, accounts, chattel paper, documents, instruments, and money. All rights to payment earned or unearned under a charter or other contract involving the use or hire of a vessel and all rights incident to the charter or contract are accounts.

Section 9-107. Definitions: "Purchase Money Security Interest." A security interest is a "purchase money security interest" to the extent that it is

(a) taken or retained by the seller of the collateral to secure all or part of its price; or

(b) taken by a person who by making advances or incurring an obligation gives value to enable the debtor to acquire rights in or the use of collateral if such value is in fact so used.

Section 9-108. When After-Acquired Collateral Not Security for Antecedent Debt. Where a secured party makes an advance, incurs an obligation, releases a perfected security interest, or otherwise gives new value which is to be secured in whole or in part by after-acquired property his security interest in the after-acquired collateral shall be deemed to be taken for new value and not as security for an antecedent debt if the debtor acquired his rights in such collateral either in the ordinary course of his business or under a contract of purchase made pursuant to the security agreement within a reasonable time after new value is given.

Section 9-109. Classification of Goods; "Consumer Goods"; "Equipment"; "Farm Products"; "Inventory." Goods are

(1) "consumer goods" if they are used or bought for use primarily for personal, family or household purposes;

(2) "equipment" if they are used or bought for use primarily in business (including farming or a profession) or by a debtor who is a non-profit organization or a governmental subdivision or agency or if the goods are not included in the definitions of inventory, farm products or consumer goods;

(3) "farm products" if they are crops or livestock or supplies used or produced in farming operations or if they are products or crops or livestock in their unmanufactured states (such as ginned cotton, wool-clip, maple syrup, milk and eggs), and if they are in the possession of a debtor engaged in raising, fattening, grazing or other farming operations. If goods are farm products they are neither equipment nor inventory;

(4) "inventory" if they are held by a person who holds them for sale or lease or to be furnished under contracts of service or if he has so furnished them, or if they are raw materials, work in process or materials used or consumed in a business. Inventory of a person is not to be classified as his equipment.

Section 9-110. Sufficiency of Description. For the purposes of this Article any description of personal property or real estate is sufficient whether or not it is specific if it reasonably identifies what is described.

Section 9-111. Applicability of Bulk Transfer Laws. The creation of a security interest is not a bulk transfer under Article 6 (see Section 6-103).

Section 9-112. Where Collateral is Not Owned by Debtor. Unless otherwise agreed, when a secured party knows that collateral is owned by a person who is not the debtor, the owner of the collateral is entitled to receive from the secured party any surplus under Section 9-502(2) or under Section 9-504(1), and is not liable for the debt or for any deficiency after resale, and he has the same right as the debtor

(a) to receive statements under Section 9-208;

(b) to receive notice of and to object to a secured party's proposal to retain the collateral in satisfaction of the indebtedness under Section 9-505;

(c) to redeem the collateral under Section 9-506;

(d) to obtain injunctive or other relief under Section 9-507(1); and

(e) to recover losses caused to him under Section 9-208(2).

Section 9-113. Security Interests Arising Under Article on Sales. A security interest arising solely under the Article on Sales (Article 2) is subject to the provisions of this Article except that to the extent that and so long as the debtor does not have or does not lawfully obtain possession of the goods

(a) no security agreement is necessary to make the security interest enforceable; and

(b) no filing is required to perfect the security interest; and

(c) the rights of the secured party on default by the debtor are governed by the Article on Sales (Article 2).

Section 9-114. Consignment.

(1) A person who delivers goods under a consignment which is not a security interest and who would be required to file under this Article by paragraph (3) (c) of Section 2-326 has priority over a secured party who is or becomes a creditor of the consignee and who would have a perfected security interest in the goods if they were the property of the consignee, and also has priority with respect to identifiable cash proceeds received on or before delivery of the goods to a buyer, if

(a) the consignor complies with the filing provision of the Article on Sales with respect to consignments (paragraph (3) (c) of Section 2-326) before the consignee receives possession of the goods;

and
(b) the consignor gives notification in writing to the holder of the security interest if the holder has filed a financing statement covering the same types of goods before the date of the filing made by the consignor; and
(c) the holder of the security interest receives the notification within five years before the consignee receives possession of the goods; and
(d) the notification states that the con-

signor expects to deliver goods on consignment to the consignee, describing the goods by item or type.
(2) In the case of a consignment which is not a security interest and in which the requirements of the preceding subsection have not been met, a person who delivers goods to another is subordinate to a person who would have a perfected security interest in the goods if they were the property of the debtor.

PART 2

VALIDITY OF SECURITY AGREEMENT AND RIGHTS OF PARTIES THERETO

Section 9-201. General Validity of Security Agreement. Except as otherwise provided by this Act a security agreement is effective according to its terms between the parties, against purchasers of the collateral and against creditors. Nothing in this Article validates any charge or practice illegal under any statute or regulation thereunder governing usury, small loans, retail installment sales, or the like, or extends the application of any such statute or regulation to any transaction not otherwise subject thereto.

Section 9-202. Title to Collateral Immaterial. Each provision of this Article with regard to rights, obligations and remedies applies whether title to collateral is in the secured party or in the debtor.

Section 9-203. Attachment and Enforceability of Security Interest; Proceeds; Formal Requisites.
(1) Subject to the provisions of Section 4-208 on the security interest of a collecting bank and Section 9-113 on a security interest arising under the Article on Sales, a security interest is not enforceable against the debtor or third parties with respect to the collateral and does not attach unless
(a) the collateral is in the possession of the secured party pursuant to agreement, or the debtor has signed a security agreement which contains a description of the collateral and in addition, when the security interest covers crops growing or to be grown or timber to be cut, a description of the land concerned; and
(b) value has been given; and
(c) the debtor has rights in the collateral.
(2) A security interest attaches when it

becomes enforceable against the debtor with respect to the collateral. Attachment occurs as soon as all of the events specified in subsection (1) have taken place unless explicit agreement postpones the time of attaching.
(3) Unless otherwise agreed a security agreement gives the secured party the rights to proceeds provided by Section 9-306.
(4) A transaction, although subject to this Article, is also subject to ....*, and in the case of conflict between the provisions of this Article and any such statute, the provisions of such statute control. Failure to comply with any applicable statute has only the effect which is specified therein.

Section 9-204. After-Acquired Property; Future Advances.
(1) Except as provided in subsection (2), a security agreement may provide that any or all obligations covered by the security agreement are to be secured by after-acquired collateral.
(2) No security interest attaches under an after-acquired property clause to consumer goods other than accessions (Section 9-314) when given as additional security unless the debtor acquires rights in them within ten days after the secured party gives value.
(3) Obligations covered by a security agreement may include future advances or other value whether or not the advances or value are given pursuant to commitment (subsection (1) of Section 9-105).

Section 9-205. Use or Disposition of Collateral Without Accounting Permissible. A security interest is not invalid or fraudulent against creditors by reason of liberty in the debtor to use, commingle or dispose of all or part of the collateral (including returned or repossessed goods) or to collect or compromise accounts or chattel paper, or to accept the return of goods or make repossessions, or to use, commingle or dispose of proceeds, or by reason of the failure of the secured party to require the debtor to account for proceeds or replace collateral. This section does not relax the requirements of possession where perfection of a security interest depends upon possession of the collateral by the secured party or by a bailee.

Section 9-206. Agreement Not to Assert Defenses Against Assignee; Modification of Sales Warranties Where Security Agreement Exists.

(1) Subject to any statute or decision which establishes a different rule for buyers or lessees of consumer goods an agreement by a buyer or lessee that he will not assert against an assignee any claim or defense which he may have against the seller or lessor is enforceable by an assignee who takes his assignment for value, in good faith and without notice of a claim or defense, except as to defenses of a type which may be asserted against a holder in due course of a negotiable instrument under the Article on Commercial Paper (Article 3). A buyer who as part of one transaction signs both a negotiable instrument and a security agreement makes such an agreement.

(2) When a seller retains a purchase money security interest in goods the Article on Sales (Article 2) governs the sale and any disclaimer, limitation or modification of the seller's warranties.

Section 9-207. Rights and Duties When Collateral Is In Secured Party's Possession.

(1) A secured party must use reasonable care in the custody and preservation of collateral in his possession. In the case of an instrument or chattel paper reasonable care includes taking necessary steps to preserve rights against prior parties unless otherwise agreed.

(2) Unless otherwise agreed, when collateral is in the secured party's possession

(a) reasonable expenses (including the cost of any insurance and payment of taxes or other charges) incurred in the custody, preservation, use or operation of the collateral are chargeable to the debtor and are secured by the collateral;

(b) the risk of accidental loss or damage is on the debtor to the extent of any deficiency in any effective insurance coverage;

(c) the secured party may hold as additional security any increase or profits (except money) received from the collateral, but money so received, unless remitted to the debtor, shall be applied in reduction of the secured obligation;

(d) the secured party must keep the collateral identifiable but fungible collateral may be commingled;

(e) the secured party may repledge the collateral upon terms which do not impair the debtor's right to redeem it.

(3) A secured party is liable for any loss caused by his failure to meet any obligation imposed by the preceding subsections but does not lose his security interest.

(4) A secured party may use or operate the collateral for the purpose of preserving the collateral or its value or pursuant to the order of a court of appropriate jurisdiction or, except in the case of consumer goods, in the manner and to the extent provided in the security agreement.

Section 9-208. Request for Statement of Account or List of Collateral .

(1) A debtor may sign a statement indicating what he believes to be the aggregate amount of unpaid indebtedness as of a specified date and may send it to the secured party with a request that the statement be approved or corrected and returned to the debtor. When the security agreement or any other record kept by the secured party identifies the collateral a debtor may similarly request the secured party to approve or correct a list of the collateral.

(2) The secured party must comply with such a request within two weeks after receipt by sending a written correction or approval. If the secured party claims a security interest in all of a particular type of collateral owned by the debtor he may indicate that fact in his reply and need not approve or correct an itemized list of such collateral. If the secured party without reasonable excuse fails to comply he is liable for any loss caused to the debtor thereby; and if the debtor has properly included in his request a good faith statement of the obligation or a list of the collateral or both the secured party may claim a security in-

terest only as shown in the statement against persons misled by his failure to comply. If he no longer has an interest in the obligation or collateral at the time the request is received he must disclose the name and address of any successor in interest known to him and he is liable for any loss caused to the debtor as a result of failure to disclose.

A successor in interest is not subject to this section until a request is received by him. (3) A debtor is entitled to such a statement once every six months without charge. The secured party may require payment of a charge not exceeding $10 for each additional statement furnished.

PART 3

RIGHTS OF THIRD PARTIES; PERFECTED AND UNPERFECTED SECURITY INTERESTS; RULES OF PRIORITY

Section 9-301. Persons Who Take Priority Over Unperfected Security Interests; Rights of "Lien Creditor."

(1) Except as otherwise provided in subsection (2), an unperfected security interest is subordinate to the rights of

(a) persons entitled to priority under Section 9-312;

(b) a person who becomes a lien creditor before the security interest is perfected;

(c) in the case of goods, instruments, documents, and chattel paper, a person who is not a secured party and who is a transferee in bulk or other buyer not in ordinary course of business or is a buyer of farm products in ordinary course of business, to the extent that he gives value and receives delivery of the collateral without knowledge of the security interest and before it is perfected;

(d) in the case of accounts and general intangibles, a person who is not a secured party and who is a transferee to the extent that he gives value without knowledge of the security interest and before it is perfected.

(2) If the secured party files with respect to a purchase money security interest before or within ten days after the debtor receives possession of the collateral, he takes priority over the rights of a transferee in bulk or of a lien creditor which arise between the time the security interest attaches and the time of filing.

(3) A "lien creditor" means a creditor who has acquired a lien on the property involved by attachment, levy or the like and includes an assignee for benefit of creditors from the time of assignment, and a trustee in bankruptcy from the date of filing of the petition

or a receiver in equity from the time of appointment.

(4) A person who becomes a lien creditor while a security interest is perfected takes subject to the security interest only to the extent that it secures advances made before he becomes a lien creditor or within 45 days thereafter or made without knowledge of the lien pursuant to a commitment entered into without knowledge of the lien.

Section 9-302. When Filing is Required to Perfect Security Interest; Security Interests to Which Filing Provisions of This Article Do Not Apply.

(1) A financing statement must be filed to perfect all security interests except the following:

(a) a security interest in collateral in possession of the secured party under Section 9-305;

(b) a security interest temporarily perfected in instruments or documents without delivery under Section 9-304 or in proceeds for a 10 day period under Section 9-306;

(c) a security interest created by an assignment of a beneficial interest in a trust or a decedent's estate;

(d) a purchase money security interest in consumer goods; but filing is required for a motor vehicle required to be registered; and fixture filing is required for priority over conflicting interests in fixtures to the extent provided in Section 9-313;

(e) an assignment of accounts which does not alone or in conjunction with other assignments to the same assignee transfer a significant part of the outstanding accounts of the assignor;

(f) a security interest of a collecting bank

(Section 4-208) or arising under the Article on Sales (see Section 9-113) or covered in subsection (3) of this section; (g) an assignment for the benefit of all the creditors of the transferor, and subsequent transfers by the assignee thereunder.

(2) If a secured party assigns a perfected security interest, no filing under this Article is required in order to continue the perfected status of the security interest against creditors of and transferees from the original debtor.

(3) The filing of a financing statement otherwise required by this Article is not necessary or effective to perfect a security interest in property subject to

(a) a statute or treaty of the United States which provides for a national or international registration or a national or international certificate of title or which specifies a place of filing different from that specified in this Article for filing of the security interest; or

(b) the following statutes of this state; [list any certificate of title statute covering automobiles, trailers, mobile homes, boats, farm tractors, or the like, and any central filing statute*.]; but during any period in which collateral is inventory held for sale by a person who is in the business of selling goods of that kind, the filing provisions of this Article (Part 4) apply to a security interest in that collateral created by him as debtor; or

(c) a certificate of title statute of another jurisdiction under the law of which indication of a security interest on the certificate is required as a condition of perfection (subsection (2) of Section 9-103).

(4) Compliance with a statute or treaty described in subsection (3) is equivalent to the filing of a financing statement under this Article, and a security interest in property subject to the statute or treaty can be perfected only by compliance therewith except as provided in Section 9-103 on multiple state transactions. Duration and renewal of perfection of a security interest perfected by compliance with the statute or treaty are governed by the provisions of the statute or treaty; in other respects the security interest is subject to this Article.

Section 9-303. When Security Interest Is Perfected; Continuity of Perfection.

(1) A security interest is perfected when it has attached and when all of the applicable steps required for perfection have been taken. Such steps are specified in Sections 9-302, 9-304, 9-305 and 9-306. If such steps are taken before the security interest attaches, it is perfected at the time when it attaches.

(2) If a security interest is originally perfected in any way permitted under this Article and is subsequently perfected in some other way under this Article, without an intermediate period when it was unperfected, the security interest shall be deemed to be perfected continuously for the purposes of this Article.

Section 9-304. Perfection of Security Interest in Instruments, Documents, and Goods Covered by Documents; Perfection by Permissive Filing; Temporary Perfection Without Filing or Transfer of Possession.

(1) A security interest in chattel paper or negotiable documents may be perfected by filing. A security interest in money or instruments (other than instruments which constitute part of chattel paper) can be perfected only by the secured party's taking possession, except as provided in subsections (4) and (5) of this section and subsections (2) and (3) of Section 9-306 on proceeds.

(2) During the period that goods are in the possession of the issuer of a negotiable document therefor, a security interest in the goods is perfected by perfecting a security interest in the document, and any security interest in the goods otherwise perfected during such period is subject thereto.

(3) A security interest in goods in the possession of a bailee other than one who has issued a negotiable document therefor is perfected by issuance of a document in the name of the secured party or by the bailee's receipt of notification of the secured party's interest or by filing as to the goods.

(4) A security interest in instruments or negotiable documents is perfected without filing or the taking of possession for a period of 21 days from the time it attaches to the extent that it arises for new value given under a written security agreement.

(5) A security interest remains perfected for

a period of 21 days without filing where a secured party having a perfected security interest in an instrument, a negotiable document or goods in possession of a bailee other than one who has issued a negotiable document therefor

> (a) makes available to the debtor the goods or documents representing the goods for the purpose of ultimate sale or exchange or for the purpose of loading, unloading, storing, shipping, transshipping, manufacturing, processing or otherwise dealing with them in a manner preliminary to their sale or exchange, but priority between conflicting security interests in the goods is subject to subsection (3) of Section 9-312; or
>
> (b) delivers the instrument to the debtor for the purpose of ultimate sale or exchange or of presentation, collection, renewal or registration of transfer.

(6) After the 21 day period in subsections (4) and (5) perfection depends upon compliance with applicable provisions of this Article.

Section 9-305. When Possession by Secured Party Perfects Security Interest Without Filing. A security interest in letters of credit and advices of credit (subsection (2) (a) of Section 5-116), goods, instruments, money, negotiable documents or chattel paper may be perfected by the secured party's taking possession of the collateral. If such collateral other than goods covered by a negotiable document is held by a bailee, the secured party is deemed to have possession from the time the bailee receives notification of the secured party's interest. A security interest is perfected by possession from the time possession is taken without relation back and continues only so long as possession is retained, unless otherwise specified in this Article. The security interest may be otherwise perfected as provided in this Article before or after the period of possession by the secured party.

Section 9-306. "Proceeds"; Secured Party's Rights on Disposition of Collateral.

(1) "Proceeds" includes whatever is received upon the sale, exchange, collection or other disposition of collateral or proceeds. Insurance payable by reason of loss or damage to the collateral is proceeds, except to the extent that it is payable to a person other than a party to the security agreement. Money, checks, deposit accounts, and the like are "cash proceeds". All other proceeds are "non-cash proceeds".

(2) Except where this Article otherwise provides, a security interest continues in collateral notwithstanding sale, exchange or other disposition thereof unless the disposition was authorized by the secured party in the security agreement or otherwise, and also continues in any identifiable proceeds including collections received by the debtor.

(3) The security interest in proceeds in a continuously perfected security interest if the interest in the original collateral was perfected but it ceases to be a perfected security interest and becomes unperfected ten days after receipt of the proceeds by the debtor unless

> (a) a filed financing statement covers the original collateral and the proceeds are collateral in which a security interest may be perfected by filing in the office or offices where the financing statement has been filed and, if the proceeds are acquired with cash proceeds, the description of collateral in the financing statement indicates the types of property constituting the proceeds; or
>
> (b) a filed financing statement covers the original collateral and the proceeds are identifiable cash proceeds; or
>
> (c) the security interest in the proceeds is perfected before the expiration of the ten day period.

Except as provided in this section, a security interest in proceeds can be perfected only by the methods or under the circumstances permitted in this Article for original collateral of the same type.

(4) In the event of insolvency proceedings instituted by or against a debtor, a secured party with a perfected security interest in proceeds has a perfected security interest only in the following proceeds:

> (a) in identifiable non-cash proceeds and in separate deposit accounts containing only proceeds;
>
> (b) in identifiable cash proceeds in the form of money which is neither commingled with other money nor deposited in a deposit account prior to the insolvency proceedings;

(c) in identifiable cash proceeds in the form of checks and the like which are not deposited in a deposit account prior to the insolvency proceedings; and

(d) in all cash and deposit accounts of the debtor in which proceeds have been commingled with other funds, but the perfected security interest under this paragraph (d) is

(i) subject to any right to set-off; and
(ii) limited to an amount not greater than the amount of any cash proceeds received by the debtor within ten days before the institution of the insolvency proceedings less the sum of (I) the payments to the secured party on account of cash proceeds received by the debtor during such period and (II) the cash proceeds received by the debtor during such period to which the secured party is entitled under paragraphs (a) through (c) of this subsection (4).

(5) If a sale of goods results in an account or chattel paper which is transferred by the seller to a secured party, and if the goods are returned to or are repossessed by the seller or the secured party, the following rules determine priorities:

(a) If the goods were collateral at the time of sale, for an indebtedness of the seller which is still unpaid, the original security interest attaches again to the goods and continues as a perfected security interest if it was perfected at the time when the goods were sold. If the security interest was originally perfected by a filing which is still effective, nothing further is required to continue the perfected status; in any other case, the secured party must take possession of the returned or repossessed goods or must file.

(b) An unpaid transferee of the chattel paper has a security interest in the goods against the transferor. Such security interest is prior to a security interest asserted under paragraph (a) to the extent that the transferee of the chattel paper was entitled to priority under Section 9-308.

(c) An unpaid transferee to the account has a security interest in the goods against the transferor. Such security interest is subordinate to a security interest asserted under paragraph (a).

(d) A security interest of an unpaid transferee asserted under paragraph (b) or (c) must be perfected for protection against creditors of the transferor and purchasers of the returned or repossessed goods.

Section 9-307. Protection of Buyers of Goods. (1) A buyer in ordinary course of business (subsection (9) of Section 1-201) other than a person buying farm products from a person engaged in farming operations takes free of a security interest created by his seller even though the security interest is perfected and even though the buyer knows of its existence.

(2) In the case of consumer goods, a buyer takes free of a security interest even though perfected if he buys without knowledge of the security interest, for value and for his own personal, family or household purposes unless prior to the purchase the secured party has filed a financing statement covering such goods.

(3) A buyer other than a buyer in ordinary course of business (subsection (1) of this section) takes free of a security interest to the extent that it secures future advances made after the secured party acquires knowledge of the purchase, or more than 45 days after the purchase, whichever first occurs, unless made pursuant to a commitment entered into without knowledge of the purchase and before the expiration of the 45 day period.

Section 9-308. Purchase of Chattel Paper and Instruments. A purchaser of chattel paper or an instrument who gives new value and takes possession of it in the ordinary course of his business has priority over a security interest in the chattel paper or instrument

(a) which is perfected under Section 9-304 (permissive filing and temporary perfection) or under Section 9-306 (perfection as to proceeds) if he acts without knowledge that the specific paper or instrument is subject to a security interest; or

(b) which is claimed merely as proceeds of inventory subject to a security interest (Section 9-306) even though he knows that the specific paper or instrument is subject to the security interest.

Section 9-309. Protection of Purchasers of Instruments and Documents. Nothing in this Article limits the rights of a holder in due course of a negotiable instrument (Section 3-302) or a holder to whom a negotiable document of title has been duly negotiated (Section 7-501) or a bona fide purchaser of a security (Section 8-301) and such holders or purchasers take priority over an earlier security interest even though perfected. Filing under this Article does not constitute notice of the security interest to such holders or purchasers.

Section 9-310. Priority of Certain Liens Arising by Operation of Law. When a person in the ordinary course of his business furnishes services or materials with respect to goods subject to a security interest, a lien upon goods in the possession of such person given by statute or rule of law for such materials or services takes priority over a perfected security interest unless the lien is statutory and the statute expressly provides otherwise.

Section 9-311. Alienability of Debtor's Rights: Judicial Process. The debtor's rights in collateral may be voluntarily or involuntarily transferred (by way of sale, creation of a security interest, attachment, levy, garnishment or other judicial process) notwithstanding a provision in the security agreement prohibiting any transfer or making the transfer constitute a default.

Section 9-312. Priorities Among Conflicting Security Interests in the Same Collateral.

(1) The rules of priority stated in other sections of this Part and in the following sections shall govern when applicable: Section 4-208 with respect to the security interests of collecting banks in items being collected, accompanying documents and proceeds; Section 9-103 on security interests related to other jurisdictions; Section 9-114 on consignments.

(2) A perfected security interest in crops for new value given to enable the debtor to produce the crops during the production season and given not more than three months before the crops become growing crops by planting or otherwise takes priority over an earlier perfected security interest to the extent that such earlier interest secured obligations due more than six months before the crops become growing crops by planting or otherwise, even though the person giving new value has knowledge of the earlier security interest.

(3) A perfected purchase money security interest in inventory has priority over a conflicting security interest in the same inventory and also has priority in identifiable cash proceeds received on or before the delivery of the inventory to a buyer if

(a) the purchase money security interest is perfected at the time the debtor receives possession of the inventory; and

(b) the purchase money secured party gives notification in writing to the holder of the conflicting security interest if the holder had filed a financing statement covering the same types of inventory (i) before the date of the filing made by the purchase money secured party, or (ii) before the beginning of the 21 day period where the purchase money security interest is temporarily perfected without filing or possession (subsection (5) of Section 9-304); and

(c) the holder of the conflicting security interest receives the notification within five years before the debtor receives possession of the inventory; and

(d) the notification states that the person giving the notice has or expects to acquire a purchase money security interest in inventory of the debtor, describing such inventory by item or type.

(4) A purchase money security interest in collateral other than inventory has priority over a conflicting security interest in the same collateral or its proceeds if the purchase money security interest is perfected at the time the debtor receives possession of the collateral or within ten days thereafter.

(5) In all cases not governed by other rules stated in this section (including cases of purchase money security interests which do not qualify for the special priorities set forth in subsections (3) and (4) of this section), priority between conflicting security interests in the same collateral shall be determined according to the following rules:

(a) Conflicting security interests rank according to priority in time of filing or perfection. Priority dates from the time a filing is first made covering the collateral or the time the security interest is first perfected, whichever is earlier, provided that there is no period thereafter when there is neither filing nor perfection.

(b) So long as conflicting security interests are unperfected, the first to attach has priority.

(6) For the purposes of subsection (5) a date of filing or perfection as to collateral is also a date of filing or perfection as to proceeds.

(7) If future advances are made while a security interest is perfected by filing or the taking of possession, the security interest has the same priority for the purposes of subsection (5) with respect to the future advances as it does with respect to the first advance. If a commitment is made before or while the security interest is so perfected, the security interest has the same priority with respect to advances made pursuant thereto. In other cases a perfected security interest has priority from the date the advance is made.

Section 9-313. Priority of Security Interests in Fixtures.

(1) In this section and in the provisions of Part 4 of this Article referring to fixture filing, unless the context otherwise requires

(a) goods are "fixtures" when they become so related to particular real estate that an interest in them arises under real estate law

(b) a "fixture filing" is the filing in the office where a mortgage on the real estate would be filed or recorded of a financing statement covering goods which are or are to become fixtures and conforming to the requirements of subsection (5) of Section 9-402

(c) a mortgage is a "construction mortgage" to the extent that it secures an obligation incurred for the construction of an improvement on land including the acquisition cost of the land, if the recorded writing so indicates.

(2) A security interest under this Article may be created in goods which are fixtures or may continue in goods which become fixtures, but no security interest exists under this Article in ordinary building materials incorporated into an improvement on land.

(3) This Article does not prevent creation of an encumbrance upon fixtures pursuant to real estate law.

(4) A perfected security interest in fixtures has priority over the conflicting interest of an encumbrancer or owner of the real estate where

(a) the security interest is a purchase money security interest, the interest of the encumbrancer or owner arises before the goods become fixtures, the security interest is perfected by a fixture filing before the goods become fixtures or within ten days thereafter, and the debtor has an interest of record in the real estate or is in possession of the real estate; or

(b) the security interest is perfected by a fixture filing before the interest of the encumbrancer or owner is of record, the security interest has priority over any conflicting interest of a predecessor in title of the encumbrancer or owner, and the debtor has an interest of record in the real estate or is in possession of the real estate; or

(c) the fixtures are readily removable factory or office machines or readily removable replacements of domestic appliances which are consumer goods, and before the goods become fixtures the security interest is perfected by any method permitted by this Article; or

(d) the conflicting interest is a lien on the real estate obtained by legal or equitable proceedings after the security interest was perfected by any method permitted by this Article.

(5) A security interest in fixtures, whether or not perfected, has priority over the conflicting interest of an encumbrancer or owner of the real estate where

(a) the encumbrancer or owner has consented in writing to the security interest or has disclaimed an interest in the goods as fixtures; or

(b) the debtor has a right to remove the goods as against the encumbrancer or owner. If the debtor's right terminates, the priority of the security interest continues for a reasonable time.

(6) Notwithstanding paragraph (a) of subsection (4) but otherwise subject to subsections (4) and (5), a security interest in fixtures is subordinate to a construction

mortgage recorded before the goods become fixtures if the goods become fixtures before the completion of the construction. To the extent that it is given to refinance a construction mortgage, a mortgage has this priority to the same extent as the construction mortgage.

(7) In cases not within the preceding subsections, a security interest in fixtures is subordinate to the conflicting interest of an encumbrancer or owner of the related real estate who is not the debtor.

(8) When the secured party has priority over all owners and encumbrancers of the real estate, he may, on default, subject to the provisions of Part 5, remove his collateral from the real estate but he must reimburse any encumbrancer or owner of the real estate who is not the debtor and who has not otherwise agreed for the cost of repair of any physical injury, but not for any diminution in value of the real estate caused by the absence of the goods removed or by any necessity of replacing them. A person entitled to reimbursement may refuse permission to remove until the secured party gives adequate security for the performance of this obligation.

Section 9-314. Accessions.

(1) A security interest in goods which attaches before they are installed in or affixed to other goods takes priority as to the goods installed or affixed (called in this section "accessions") over the claims of all persons to the whole except as stated in subsection (3) and subject to Section 9-315(1).

(2) A security interest which attaches to goods after they become part of a whole is valid against all persons subsequently acquiring interests in the whole except as stated in subsection (3) but is invalid against any person with an interest in the whole at the time the security interest attaches to the goods who has not in writing consented to the security interest or disclaimed an interest in the goods as part of the whole.

(3) The security interests described in subsections (1) and (2) do not take priority over

(a) a subsequent purchaser for value of any interest in the whole; or

(b) a creditor with a lien on the whole subsequently obtained by judicial proceedings; or

(c) a creditor with a prior perfected security interest in the whole to the extent that he makes subsequent advances

if the subsequent purchase is made, the lien by judicial proceedings obtained or the subsequent advance under the prior perfected security interest is made or contracted for without knowledge of the security interest and before it is perfected. A purchaser of the whole at a foreclosure sale other than the holder of a perfected security interest purchasing at his own foreclosure sale is a subsequent purchaser within this section.

(4) When under subsections (1) or (2) and (3) a secured party has an interest in accessions which has priority over the claims of all persons who have interests in the whole, he may on default subject to the provisions of Part 5 remove his collateral from the whole but he must reimburse any encumbrancer or owner of the whole who is not the debtor and who has not otherwise agreed for the cost of repair of any physical injury but not for any diminution in value of the whole caused by the absence of the goods removed or by any necessity for replacing them. A person entitled to reimbursement may refuse permission to remove until the secured party gives adequate security for the performance of this obligation.

Section 9-315. Priority When Goods Are Commingled or Processed.

(1) If a security interest in goods was perfected and subsequently the goods or a part thereof have become part of a product or mass, the security interest continues in the product or mass if

(a) the goods are so manufactured, processed, assembled or commingled that their identity is lost in the product or mass; or

(b) a financing statement covering the original goods also covers the product into which the goods have been manufactured, processed or assembled.

In a case to which paragraph (b) applies, no separate security interest in that part of the original goods which has been manufactured, processed or assembled into the product may be claimed under Section 9-314.

(2) When under subsection (1) more than

one security interest attaches to the product or mass, they rank equally according to the ratio that the cost of the goods to which each interest originally attached bears to the cost of the total product or mass.

Section 9-316. Priority Subject to Subordination. Nothing in this Article prevents subordination by agreement by any person entitled to priority.

Section 9-317. Secured Party Not Obligated on Contract of Debtor. The mere existence of a security interest or authority given to the debtor to dispose of or use collateral does not impose contract or tort liability upon the secured party for the debtor's acts or omissions.

Section 9-318. Defenses Against Assignee; Modification of Contract After Notification of Assignment; Term Prohibiting Assignment Ineffective; Identification and Proof of Assignment.

(1) Unless an account debtor has made an enforceable agreement not to assert defenses or claims arising out of a sale as provided in Section 9-206 the rights of an assignee are subject to

(a) all the terms of the contract between the account debtor and assignor and any defense or claim arising therefrom; and

(b) any other defense or claim of the account debtor against the assignor which accrues before the account debtor receives notification of the assignment.

(2) So far as the right to payment or a part thereof under an assigned contract has not been fully earned by performance, and notwithstanding notification of the assignment, any modification of or substitution for the contract made in good faith and in accordance with reasonable commercial standards is effective against an assignee unless the account debtor has otherwise agreed but the assignee acquires corresponding rights under the modified or substituted contract. The assignment may provide that such modification or substitution is a breach by the assignor.

(3) The account debtor is authorized to pay the assignor until the account debtor receives notification that the amount due or to become due has been assigned and that payment is to be made to the assignee. A notification which does not reasonably identify the rights assigned is ineffective. If requested by the account debtor, the assignee must seasonably furnish reasonable proof that the assignment has been made and unless he does so the account debtor may pay the assignor.

(4) A term in any contract between an account debtor and an assignor is ineffective if it prohibits assignment of an account or prohibits creation of a security interest in a general intangible for money due or to become due or requires the account debtor's consent to such assignment or security interest.

PART 4

FILING

Section 9-401. Place of Filing; Erroneous Filing; Removal of Collateral.

First Alternative Subsection (1)

(1) The proper place to file in order to perfect a security interest is as follows:

(a) when the collateral is timber to be cut or is minerals or the like (including oil and gas) or accounts subject to subsection (5) of Section 9-103, or when the financing statement is filed as a fixture filing (Section 9-313) and the collateral is goods which are or are to become fixtures, then in the office where a mortgage on the real estate would be filed or recorded;

(b) in all other cases, in the office of the [Secretary of State].

Second Alternative Subsection (1)

(1) The proper place to file in order to perfect a security interest is as follows:

(a) when the collateral is equipment used in farming operations, or farm products, or accounts or general intangibles arising from or relating to the sale of farm products by a farmer, or consumer goods, then in the office of the .... in the county of the debtor's residence or if the debtor is not a resident in this state then in the office of the .... in the county where the goods are kept, and in addition when the collateral is crops growing or to be grown in the office of the .... in the county where the land is located;

(b) when the collateral is timber to be cut or is minerals or the like (including oil and gas) or accounts subject to subsection (5) of Section 9-103, or when the financing statement is filed as a fixture filing (Section 9-313) and the collateral is goods which are or are to become fixtures, then in the office where a mortgage on the real estate would be filed or recorded;

(c) in all other cases, in the office of the [Secretary of State].

Third Alternative Subsection (1)

(1) The proper place to file in order to perfect a security interest is as follows:

(a) when the collateral is equipment used in farming operations, or farm products, or accounts or general intangibles arising from or relating to the sale of farm products by a farmer, or consumer goods, then in the office of the .... in the county of the debtor's residence or if the debtor is not a resident of this state then in the office of the .... in the county where the goods are kept, and in addition when the collateral is crops growing or to be grown in the office of the .... in the county where the land is located;

(b) when the collateral is timber to be cut or is minerals or the like (including oil and gas) or accounts subject to subsection (5) of Section 9-103, or when the financing statement is filed as a fixture filing (Section 9-313) and the collateral is goods which are or are to become fixtures, then in the office where a mortgage on the real estate would be filed or recorded;

(c) in all other cases, in the office of the [Secretary of State] and in addition, if the debtor has a place of business in only

one county of this state, also in the office of .... of such county, or, if the debtor has no place of business in this state, but resides in the state, also in the office of .... of the county in which he resides.

NOTE: *One of the three alternatives should be selected as subsection (1).*

(2) A filing which is made in good faith in an improper place or not in all of the places required by this section is nevertheless effective with regard to any collateral as to which the filing complied with the requirements of this Article and is also effective with regard to collateral covered by the financing statement against any person who has knowledge of the contents of such financing statement.

(3) A filing which is made in the proper place in this state continues effective even though the debtor's residence or place of business or the location of the collateral or its use, whichever controlled the original filing, is thereafter changed.

Alternative Subsection (3)

[(3) A filing which is made in the proper county continues effective for four months after a change to another county of the debtor's residence or place of business or the location of the collateral, whichever controlled the original filing. It becomes ineffective thereafter unless a copy of the financing statement signed by the secured party is filed in the new county within said period. The security interest may also be perfected in the new county after the expiration of the four-month period; in such case perfection dates from the time of perfection in the new county. A change in the use of the collateral does not impair the effectiveness of the original filing.]

(4) The rules stated in Section 9-103 determine whether filing is necessary in this state.

(5) Notwithstanding the preceding subsections, and subject to subsection (3) of Section 9-302, the proper place to file in order to perfect a security interest in collateral, including fixtures, of a transmitting utility is the office of the [Secretary of State]. This filing constitutes a fixture filing (Section 9-313) as to the collateral described

therein which is or is to become fixtures.

(6) For the purposes of this section, the residence of an organization is its place of business if it has one or its chief executive office if it has more than one place of business.

Section 9-402. Formal Requisites of Financing Statement; Amendments; Mortgage as Financing Statement.

(1) A financing statement is sufficient if it gives the names of the debtor and the secured party, is signed by the debtor, gives an address of the secured party from which information concerning the security interest may be obtained, gives a mailing address of the debtor and contains a statement indicating the types, or describing the items, of collateral. A financing statement may be filed before the security agreement is made or a security interest otherwise attaches. When the financing statement covers crops growing or to be grown, the statement must also contain a description of the real estate concerned. When the financing statement covers timber to be cut or covers minerals, or the like, (including oil and gas) or accounts subject to subsection (5) of Section 9-103, or when the financial statement is filed as a fixture filing (Section 9-313) and the collateral is goods which are or are to become fixtures, the statement must also comply with subsection (5). A copy of the security agreement is sufficient as a financing statement if it contains the above information and is signed by the debtor. A carbon, photographic or other reproduction of a security agreement or a financing statement is sufficient as a financing statement if the security agreement so provides or if the original has been filed in this state.

(2) A financing statement which otherwise complies with subsection (1) is sufficient when it is signed by the secured party instead of the debtor if it is filed to perfect a security interest in

(a) collateral already subject to a security interest in another jurisdiction when it is brought into this state, or when the debtor's location is changed to this state. Such a financing statement must state that the collateral was brought into this state or that the debtor's location was changed to this state under such circumstances; or

(b) proceeds under Section 9-306 if the security interest in the original collateral was perfected. Such a financing statement must describe the original collateral; or

(c) collateral as to which the filing has lapsed; or

(d) collateral acquired after a change of name, identity or corporate structure of the debtor (subsection (7)).

(3) A form substantially as follows is sufficient to comply with subsection (1):

Name of debtor (or assignor) . . . .
Address . . . .
Name of secured party (or assignee) . . . .
Address . . . .

1. This financing statement covers the following types (or items) of property:
   (Describe) . . . .
2. (If collateral is crops) The above crops are growing or are to be grown on:
   (Describe Real Estate) . . . .
3. (If applicable) The above goods are to become fixtures on*
   (Describe Real Estate) . . . .
   and this financing statement is to be filed [for record] in the real estate records. (If the debtor does not have an interest of record) The name of a record owner is . . . .
4. (If products of collateral are claimed) Products of the collateral are also covered. Signature of Debtor (or Assignor) . . . .
   Signature of Secured Party (or Assignee). . . . .
(use whichever is applicable)

(4) A financing statement may be amended by filing a writing signed by both the debtor and the secured party. An amendment does not extend the period of effectiveness of a financing statement. If any amendment adds collateral, it is effective as to the added collateral only from the filing date of the amendment. In this Article, unless the context otherwise requires, the term "financial statement" means the original financing statement and any amendments.

(5) A financing statement covering timber

---

*Where appropriate substitute either "The above timber is standing on . . . ." or "The above minerals or the like (including oil and gas) or accounts will be financed at the wellhead or minehead of the well or mine located on . . . ."

to be cut or covering minerals or the like (including oil and gas) or accounts subject to subsection (5) of Section 9-103, or a financing statement filed as a fixture filing (Section 9-313) where the debtor is not a transmitting utility, must show that it covers this type of collateral, must recite that it is to be filed [for record] in the real estate records, and the financing statement must contain a description of the real estate [sufficient if it were contained in a mortgage of the real estate to give constructive notice of the mortgage under the law of this state]. If the debtor does not have an interest of record in the real estate, the financing statement must show the name of a record owner.

(6) A mortgage is effective as a financing statement filed as a fixture filing from the date of its recording if

    (a) the goods are described in the mortgage by item or type; and

    (b) the goods are or are to become fixtures related to the real estate described in the mortgage; and

    (c) the mortgage complies with the requirements for a financing statement in this section other than a recital that it is to be filed in the real estate records; and

    (d) the mortgage is duly recorded.

No fee with reference to the financing statement is required other than the regular recording and satisfaction fees with respect to the mortgage.

(7) A financing statement sufficiently shows the name of the debtor if it gives the individual, partnership or corporate name of the debtor, whether or not it adds other trade names or names of partners. Where the debtor so changes his name or in the case of an organization its name, identity or corporate structure that a filed financing statement becomes seriously misleading, the filing is not effective to perfect a security interest in collateral acquired by the debtor more than four months after the change, unless a new appropriate financing statement is filed before the expiration of that time. A filed financing statement remains effective with respect to collateral transferred by the debtor even though the secured party knows of or consents to the transfer.

(8) A financing statement substantially complying with the requirements of this section is effective even though it contains minor errors which are not seriously misleading.

Section 9-403. What Constitutes Filing; Duration of Filing; Effect of Lapsed Filing; Duties of Filing Officer.

(1) Presentation for filing of a financing statement and tender of the filing fee or acceptance of the statement by the filing officer constitutes filing under this Article.

(2) Except as provided in subsection (6) a filed financing statement is effective for a period of five years from the date of filing. The effectiveness of a filed financing statement lapses on the expiration of the five year period unless a continuation statement is filed prior to the lapse. If a security interest perfected by filing exists at the time insolvency proceedings are commenced by or against the debtor, the security interest remains perfected until termination of the insolvency proceedings and thereafter for a period of sixty days or until the expiration of the five year period, whichever occurs later. Upon lapse the security interest becomes unperfected, unless it is perfected without filing. If the security interest becomes unperfected upon lapse, it is deemed to have been unperfected as against a person who became a purchaser or lien creditor before lapse.

(3) A continuation statement may be filed by the secured party within six months prior to the expiration of the five year period specified in subsection (2). Any such continuation statement must be signed by the secured party, identify the original statement by file number and state that the original statement is still effective. A continuation statement signed by a person other than the secured party of record must be accompanied by a separate written statement of assignment signed by the secured party of record and complying with subsection (2) of Section 9-405, including payment of the required fee. Upon timely filing of the continuation statement, the effectiveness of the original statement is continued for five years after the last date to which the filing was effective whereupon it lapses in the same manner as provided in subsection (2) unless another continuation statement is filed prior to such lapse. Succeeding continuation statements may be filed in the same

manner to continue the effectiveness of the original statement. Unless a statute on disposition of public records provides otherwise, the filing officer may remove a lapsed statement from the files and destroy it immediately if he has retained a microfilm or other photographic record, or in other cases after one year after the lapse. The filing officer shall so arrange matters by physical annexation of financing statements to continuation statements or other related filings, or by other means, that if he physically destroys the financing statements of a period more than five years past, those which have been continued by a continuation statement or which are still effective under subsection (6) shall be retained.

(4) Except as provided in subsection (7) a filing officer shall mark each statement with a file number and with the date and hour of filing and shall hold the statement or a microfilm or other photographic copy thereof for public inspection. In addition the filing officer shall index the statement according to the name of the debtor and shall note in the index the file number and the address of the debtor given in the statement.

(5) The uniform fee for filing and indexing and for stamping a copy furnished by the secured party to show the date and place of filing for an original financing statement or for a continuation statement shall be $ . . . . if the statement is in the standard form prescribed by the [Secretary of State] and otherwise shall be $ . . . . . , plus in each case, if the financing statement is subject to subsection (5) of Section 9-402, $ . . . . . The uniform fee for each name more than one required to be indexed shall be $ . . . . . The secured party may at his option show a trade name for any person and an extra uniform indexing fee of $ . . . . . shall be paid with respect thereto.

(6) If the debtor is a transmitting utility (subsection (5) of Section 9-401) and a filed financing statement so states, it is effective until a termination statement is filed. A real estate mortgage which is effective as a fixture filing under subsection (6) of Section 9-402 remains effective as a fixture filing until the mortgage is released or satisfied of record or its effectiveness otherwise terminates as to the real estate.

(7) When a financing statement covers timber to be cut or covers minerals or the like (including oil and gas) or accounts subject to subsection (5) of Section 9-103, or is filed as a fixture filing, [it shall be filed for record and] the filing officer shall index it under the names of the debtor and any owner of record shown on the financing statement in the same fashion as if they were the mortgagors in a mortgage of the real estate described, and, to the extent that the law of this state provides for indexing of mortgages under the name of the mortgagee, under the name of the secured party as if he were the mortgagee thereunder, or where indexing is by description in the same fashion as if the financing statement were a mortgage of the real estate described.

Section 9-404. Termination Statement.

(1) If a financing statement covering consumer goods is filed on or after . . . . , then within one month or within ten days following written demand by the debtor after there is no outstanding secured obligation and no commitment to make advances, incur obligations or otherwise give value, the secured party must file with each filing officer with whom the financing statement was filed, a termination statement to the effect that he no longer claims a security interest under the financing statement, which shall be identified by file number. In other cases whenever there is no outstanding secured obligation and no commitment to make advances, incur obligations or otherwise give value, the secured party must on written demand by the debtor send the debtor, for each filing officer with whom the financing statement was filed, a termination statement to the effect that he no longer claims a security interest under the financing statement, which shall be identified by file number. A termination statement signed by a person other than the secured party of record must be accompanied by a separate written statement of assignment signed by the secured party of record and complying with subsection (2) of Section 9-405, including payment of the required fee. If the affected secured party fails to file such a termination statement within ten days after proper demand therefor, he shall be liable to the debtor for one hundred dollars, and in

addition for any loss caused to the debtor by such failure.

(2) On presentation to the filing officer of such a termination statement he must note it in the index. If he has received the termination statement in duplicate, he shall return one copy of the termination statement to the secured party stamped to show the time of receipt thereof. If the filing officer has a microfilm or other photographic record of the financing statement, and of any related continuation statement, statement of assignment and statement of release, he may remove the originals from the files at any time after receipt of the termination statement, or if he has no such record, he may remove them from the files at any time after one year after receipt of the termination statement.

(3) If the termination statement is in the standard form prescribed by the [Secretary of State], the uniform fee for filing and indexing the termination statement shall be $. . . . and otherwise shall be $. . . . , plus in each case an additional fee of $. . . . for each name more than one against which the termination statement is required to be indexed.

Section 9-405. Assignment of Security Interest; Duties of Filing Officer; Fees.

(1) A financing statement may disclose an assignment of a security interest in the collateral described in the financing statement by indication in the financing statement of the name and address of the assignee or by an assignment itself or a copy thereof on the face or back of the statement. On presentation to the filing officer of such a financing statement the filing officer shall mark the same as provided in Section 9-403(4). The uniform fee for filing, indexing and furnishing filing data for a financing statement so indicating an assignment shall be $. . . . if the statement is in the standard form prescribed by the [Secretary of State] and otherwise shall be $. . . . , plus in each case an additional fee of $. . . . for each name more than one against which the financing statement is required to be indexed.

(2) A secured party may assign of record all or part of his rights under a financing statement by the filing in the place where the original financing statement was filed of a separate written statement of assignment signed by the secured party of record and setting forth the name of the secured party of record and the debtor, the file number and the date of filing of the financing statement and the name and address of the assignee and containing a description of the collateral assigned. A copy of the assignment is sufficient as a separate statement if it complies with the preceding sentence. On presentation to the filing officer of such a separate statement, the filing officer shall mark such separate statement with the date and hour of the filing. He shall note the assignment on the index of the financing statement, or in the case of a fixture filing, or a filing covering timber to be cut, or covering minerals or the like (including oil and gas) or accounts subject to subsection (5) of Section 9-103, he shall index the assignment under the name of the assignor as grantor and, to the extent that the law of this state provides for indexing the assignment of a mortgage under the name of the assignee, he shall index the assignment of the financing statement under the name of the assignee. The uniform fee for filing, indexing and furnishing filing data about such a separate statement of assignment shall be $. . . . if the statement is in the standard form prescribed by the [Secretary of State] and otherwise shall be $. . . . , plus in each case an additional fee of $. . . . for each name more than one against which the statement of assignment is required to be indexed. Notwithstanding the provisions of this subsection, an assignment of record of a security interest in a fixture contained in a mortgage effective as a fixture filing (subsection (6) of Section 9-402) may be made only by an assignment of the mortgage in the manner provided by the law of the state other than this Act.

(3) After the disclosure of filing of an assignment under this section, the assignee is the secured party of record.

Section 9-406. Release of Collateral; Duties of Filing Officer; Fees. A secured party of record may by his signed statement release all or a part of any collateral described in a filed financing statement. The statement of release is sufficient if it contains a description of the collateral being released, the name and address of the debtor, the name and address of the secured party, and the file number of the financing statement. A statement of release signed by a person other than the secured party of record must be accompanied by a separate written statement of assignment signed by the secured party of record and complying with subsection (2) of Section 9-405, including payment of the required fee. Upon presentation of such a statement of release to the filing officer he shall mark the statement with the hour and date of filing and shall note the same upon the margin of the index of the filing of the financing statement. The uniform fee for filing and noting such a statement of release shall be $. . . . . if the statement is in the standard form prescribed by the [Secretary of State] and otherwise shall be $. . . . . , plus in each case an additional fee of $. . . . . for each name more than one against which the statement of release is required to be indexed.

[Section 9-407. Information From Filing Officer].

[(1) If the person filing any financing statement, termination statement, statement of assignment, or statement of release, furnishes the filing officer a copy thereof, the filing officer shall upon request note upon the copy the file number and date and hour of the filing of the original and deliver or send the copy to such person.]

[(2) Upon request of any person, the filing officer shall issue his certificate showing whether there is on file on the date and hour stated therein, any presently effective financing statement naming a particular debtor and any statement of assignment thereof and if there is, giving the date and hour of filing of each such statement and the names and addresses of each secured party therein. The uniform fee for such a certificate shall be $. . . . . if the request for the certificate is in the standard form prescribed by the [Secretary of State] and otherwise shall be $. . . . . Upon request the filing officer shall furnish a copy of any filed financing statement or statement of assignment for a uniform fee of $. . . . . per page.]

Section 9-408. Financing Statements Covering Consigned or Leased Goods. A consignor or lessor of goods may file a financing statement using the terms "consignor," "consignee," "lessor," "lessee" or the like instead of the terms specified in Section 9-402. The provisions of this Part shall apply as appropriate to such a financing statement but its filing shall not of itself be a factor in determining whether or not the consignment or lease is intended as security (Section 1-201(37)). However, if it is determined for other reasons that the consignment or lease is so intended, a security interest of the consignor or lessor which attaches to the consigned or leased goods is perfected by such filing.

Added in 1972.

PART 5

DEFAULT

Section 9-501. Default; Procedure When Security Agreement Covers Both Real and Personal Property.

(1) When a debtor is in default under a security agreement, a secured party has the rights and remedies provided in this Part and except as limited by subsection (3) those provided in the security agreement. He may reduce his claim to judgment, foreclose or otherwise enforce the security interest by any available judicial procedure. If the collateral is documents the secured party may proceed either as to the documents or as to the goods covered thereby. A secured party in possession has the rights, remedies and duties provided in Section 9-207. The rights and remedies referred to in this subsection are cumulative.

(2) After default, the debtor has the rights and remedies provided in this Part, those provided in the security agreement and those provided in Section 9-207.

(3) To the extent that they give rights to the debtor and impose duties on the secured party, the rules stated in the subsections referred to below may not be waived or varied except as provided with respect to compulsory disposition of collateral (subsection (3) of Section 9-504 and Section 9-505) and with respect to redemption of collateral

(Section 9-506) but the parties may by agreement determine the standards by which the fulfillment of these rights and duties is to be measured if such standards are not manifestly unreasonable:

(a) subsection (2) of Section 9-502 and subsection (2) of Section 9-504 insofar as they require accounting for surplus proceeds of collateral;

(b) subsection (3) of Section 9-504 and subsection (1) of Section 9-505 which deal with disposition of collateral;

(c) subsection (2) of Section 9-505 which deals with acceptance of collateral as discharge of obligation;

(d) Section 9-506 which deals with redemption of collateral; and

(e) subsection (1) of Section 9-507 which deals with the secured party's liability for failure to comply with this Part.

(4) If the security agreement covers both real and personal property, the secured party may proceed under this Part as to the personal property or he may proceed as to both the real and the personal property in accordance with his rights and remedies in respect of the real property in which case the provisions of this Part do not apply.

(5) When a secured party has reduced his claim to judgment the lien of any levy which may be made upon his collateral by virtue of any execution based upon the judgment shall relate back to the date of the perfection of the security interest in such collateral. A judicial sale, pursuant to such execution, is a foreclosure of the security interest by judicial procedure within the meaning of this section, and the secured party may purchase at the sale and thereafter hold the collateral free of any other requirements of this Article.

Section 9-502. Collection Rights of Secured Party.

(1) When so agreed and in any event on default the secured party is entitled to notify an account debtor or the obligor on an instrument to make payment to him whether or not the assignor was theretofore making collections on the collateral, and also to take control of any proceeds to which he is entitled under Section 9-306.

(2) A secured party who by agreement is entitled to charge back uncollected collateral or otherwise to full or limited recourse against the debtor and who undertakes to collect from the account debtors or obligors must proceed in a commercially reasonable manner and may deduct his reasonable expenses of realization from the collections. If the security agreement secures an indebtedness, the secured party must account to the debtor for any surplus, and unless otherwise agreed, the debtor is liable for any deficiency. But, if the underlying transaction was a sale of accounts or chattel paper, the debtor is entitled to any surplus or is liable for any deficiency only if the security agreement so provides.

Section 9-503. Secured Party's Right to Take Possession After Default.

Unless otherwise agreed a secured party has on default the right to take possession of the collateral. In taking possession a secured party may proceed without judicial process if this can be done without breach of the peace or may proceed by action. If the security agreement so provides the secured party may require the debtor to assemble the collateral and make it available to the secured party at a place to be designated by the secured party which is reasonably convenient to both parties. Without removal a secured party may render equipment unusable, and may dispose of collateral on the debtor's premises under Section 9-504.

Section 9-504. Secured Party's Right to Dispose of Collateral After Default; Effect of Disposition.

(1) A secured party after default may sell, lease or otherwise dispose of any or all of the collateral in its then condition or following any commercially reasonable preparation or processing. Any sale of goods is subject to the Article on Sales (Article 2). The proceeds of disposition shall be applied in the order following to

(a) the reasonable expenses of retaking, holding, preparing for sale or lease, selling, leasing and the like and, to the extent provided for in the agreement and not prohibited by law, the reasonable attorneys' fees and legal expenses incurred by the secured party;

(b) the satisfaction of indebtedness secured by the security interest under which the disposition is made;

(c) the satisfaction of indebtedness secured by any subordinate security interest in the collateral if written notification of demand therefor is received before distribution of the proceeds is completed. If requested by the secured party, the holder of a subordinate security interest must seasonably furnish reasonable proof of his interest, and unless he does so, the secured party need not comply with his demand.

(2) If the security interest secured an indebtedness, the secured party must account to the debtor for any surplus, and, unless otherwise agreed, the debtor is liable for any deficiency. But if the underlying transaction was a sale of accounts or chattel paper, the debtor is entitled to any surplus or is liable for any deficiency only if the security agreement so provides.

(3) Disposition of the collateral may be by public or private proceedings and may be made by way of one or more contracts. Sale or other disposition may be as a unit or in parcels and at any time and place and on any terms but every aspect of the disposition including the method, manner, time, place and terms must be commercially reasonable. Unless collateral is perishable or threatens to decline speedily in value or is of a type customarily sold on a recognized market, reasonable notification of the time and place of any public sale or reasonable notification of the time after which any private sale or other intended disposition is to be made shall be sent by the secured party to the debtor, if he has not signed after default a statement renouncing or modifying his right to notification of sale. In the case of consumer goods no other notification need be sent. In other cases notification shall be sent to any other secured party from whom the secured party has received (before sending his notification to the debtor or before the debtor's renunciation of his rights) written notice of a claim of an interest in the collateral. The secured party may buy at any public sale and if the collateral is of a type customarily sold in a recognized market or is of a type which is the subject of widely distributed standard price quotations he may buy at private sale.

(4) When collateral is disposed of by a secured party after default, the disposition transfers to a purchaser for value all of the debtor's rights therein, discharges the security interest under which it is made and any security interest or lien subordinate or lien subordinate thereto. The purchaser takes free of all such rights and interests even though the secured party fails to comply with the requirements of this Part or of any judicial proceedings.

(a) in the case of a public sale, if the purchaser has no knowledge of any defects in the sale and if he does not buy in collusion with the secured party, other bidders or the person conducting the sale; or

(b) in any other case, if the purchaser acts in good faith.

(5) A person who is liable to a secured party under a guaranty, indorsement, repurchase agreement or the like and who receives a transfer of collateral from the secured party or is subrogated to his rights has thereafter the rights and duties of the secured party. Such a transfer of collateral is not a sale or disposition of the collateral under this Article.

Section 9-505. Compulsory Disposition of Collateral; Acceptance of the Collateral as Discharge of Obligation.

(1) If the debtor has paid sixty per cent of the cash price in the case of a purchase money security interest in consumer goods, and has not signed after default at statement renouncing or modifying his rights under this Part a secured party who has taken possession of collateral must dispose of it under Section 9-504 and if he fails to do so within ninety days after he takes possession the debtor at his option may recover in conversion or under Section 9-507(1) on secured party's liability.

(2) In any other case involving consumer goods or any other collateral a secured party in possession may, after default, propose to retain the collateral in satisfaction of the obligation. Written notice of such proposal shall be sent to the debtor if he has not signed after default a statement renouncing or modifying his rights under this subsec-

tion. In the case of consumer goods no other notice need be given. In other cases notice shall be sent to any other secured party from whom the secured party has received (before sending his notice to the debtor or before the debtor's renunciation of his rights) written notice of a claim of an interest in the collateral. If the secured party receives objection in writing from a person entitled to receive notification within twenty-one days after the notice was sent, the secured party must dispose of the collateral under Section 9-504. In the absence of such written objection the secured party may retain the collateral in satisfaction of the debtor's obligation.

Section 9-506. Debtor's Right to Redeem Collateral. At any time before the secured party has disposed of collateral or entered into a contract for its disposition under Section 9-504 or before the obligation has been discharged under Section 9-505(2) the debtor or any other secured party may unless otherwise agreed in writing after default redeem the collateral by tendering fulfillment of all obligations secured by the collateral as well as the expenses reasonably incurred by the secured party in retaking, holding and preparing the collateral for disposition, in arranging for the sale, and to the extent provided in the agreement and not prohibited by law, his reasonable attorneys' fees and legal expenses.

Section 9-507. Secured Party's Liability for Failure to Comply With This Part.

(1) If it is established that the secured party is not proceeding in accordance with the provisions of this Part disposition may be ordered or restrained on appropriate terms and conditions. If the disposition has oc-

curred the debtor or any person entitled to notification or whose security interest has been made known to the secured party prior to the disposition has a right to recover from the secured party any loss caused by a failure to comply with the provisions of this Part. If the collateral is consumer goods, the debtor has a right to recover in any event an amount not less than the credit service charge plus ten per cent of the principal amount of the debt or the time price differential plus ten per cent of the cash price.

(2) The fact that a better price could have been obtained by a sale at a different time or in a different method from that selected by the secured party is not of itself sufficient to establish that the sale was not made in a commercially reasonable manner. If the secured party either sells the collateral in the usual manner in any recognized market therefor or if he sells at the price current in such market at the time of his sale or if he has otherwise sold in conformity with reasonable commercial practices among dealers in the type of property sold he has sold in a commercially reasonable manner. The principles stated in the two preceding sentences with respect to sales also apply as may be appropriate to other types of disposition. A disposition which has been approved in any judicial proceeding or by any bona fide creditors' committee or representative of creditors shall conclusively be deemed to be commercially reasonable, but this sentence does not indicate that any such approval must be obtained in any case nor does it indicate that any disposition not so approved is not commercially reasonable.

ARTICLE 10

EFFECTIVE DATE AND REPEALER

Section 10-101. Effective Date. This Act shall become effective at midnight on December 31st following its enactment. It applies to transactions entered into and events occurring after that date.

Section 10-102. Specific Repealer; Provision for Transition.

(1) The following acts and all other acts and parts of acts inconsistent herewith are hereby repealed:

(Here should follow the acts to be specifically repealed including the following:
Uniform Negotiable Instruments Act
Uniform Warehouse Receipts Act
Uniform Sales Act
Uniform Bills of Lading Act
Uniform Stock Transfer Act
Uniform Trust Receipts Act
Also any acts regulating:
Bank collections

Bulk sales
Chattel mortgages
Conditional sales
Factor's lien acts
Farm storage of grain and similar acts
Assignment of accounts receivable)

(2) Transactions validly entered into before the effective date specified in Section 10-101 and the rights, duties and interests flowing from them remain valid thereafter and may be terminated, completed, consummated or enforced as required or permitted by any statute or other law amended or repealed by this Act as though such repeal or amendment had not occurred.

NOTE: *Subsection (1) should be separately prepared for each state. The foregoing is a list of statutes to be checked.*

Section 10-103. General Repealer.

Except as provided in the following section, all acts and parts of acts inconsistent with this Act are hereby repealed.

Section 10-104. Laws Not Repealed.

(1) The Article on Documents of Title (Article 7) does not repeal or modify any laws prescribing the form or contents of regulating bailees' businesses in respects not specifically dealt with herein; but the fact that such laws are violated does not affect the status of a document of title which otherwise complies with the definition of a document of title (Section 1-201).

[(2) This Act does not repeal . . . .*, cited as the Uniform Act for the Simplification of Fiduciary Security Transfers, and if in any respect there is any inconsistency between that Act and the Article of this Act on investment securities (Article 8) the provisions of the former Act shall control.]

NOTE: *At * in subsection (2) insert the statutory reference to the Uniform Act for the Simplification of Fiduciary Security Transfers if such Act has previously been enacted. If it has not been enacted, omit subsection (2).*

B

Uniform Partnership Act

An Act to make uniform the Law of Partnerships
Be it enacted, etc.:

PART I

PRELIMINARY PROVISIONS

Sec. 1. (Name of Act.) This act may be cited as Uniform Partnership Act.

Sec. 2. (Definition of Terms.) In this act, "Court" includes every court and judge having jurisdiction in the case.

"Business" includes every trade, occupation, or profession.

"Person" includes individuals, partnerships, corporations, and other associations.

"Bankrupt" includes bankrupt under the Federal Bankruptcy Act or insolvent under any state insolvent act.

"Conveyance" includes every assignment, lease, mortgage, or encumbrance.

"Real property" includes land and any interest or estate in land.

Sec. 3. (Interpretation of Knowledge and Notice.) (1) A person has "knowledge" of a fact within the meaning of this act not only when he has actual knowledge thereof, but also when he has knowledge of such other facts as in the circumstances shows bad faith.

(2) A person has "notice" of a fact within the meaning of this act when the person who claims the benefit of the notice

(a) States the fact to such person, or

(b) Delivers through the mail, or by other means of communication, a written statement of the fact to such person or to a proper person at his place of business or residence.

Sec. 4. (Rules of Construction.) (1) The rule that statutes in derogation of the common law are to be strictly construed shall have no application to this act.

(2) The law of estoppel shall apply under this act.

(3) The law of agency shall apply under this act.

(4) This act shall be so interpreted and construed as to effect its general purpose to make uniform the law of those states which enact it.

(5) This act shall not be construed so as to impair the obligations of any contract existing when the act goes into effect, nor to affect any action or proceedings begun or right accrued before this act takes effect.

Sec. 5. (Rules for Cases Not Provided for in this Act.) In any case not provided for in this act the rules of law and equity, including the law merchant, shall govern.

PART II

NATURE OF PARTNERSHIP

Sec. 6. (Partnership Defined.) (1) A partnership is an association of two or more persons to carry on as co-owners a business for profit.

(2) But any association formed under any other statute of this state, or any statute adopted by authority, other than the authority of this state, is not a partnership under this act, unless such association would have been a partnership in this state prior to the adoption of this act; but this act shall apply to limited partnerships except in so far as the statutes relating to such partnerships are inconsistent herewith.

Sec. 7. (Rules for Determining the Existence of a Partnership.) In determining whether a partnership exists, these rules shall apply:

(1) Except as provided by Section 16 persons who are not partners as to each other are not partners as to third persons.

(2) Joint tenancy, tenancy in common, tenancy by the entireties, joint property, common property, or part ownership does not of itself establish a partnership, whether such co-owners do or do not share any profits made by the use of the property.

(3) The sharing of gross returns does not of itself establish a partnership, whether or not the persons sharing them have a joint or common right or interest in any property from which the returns are derived.

(4) The receipt by a person of a share of the profits of a business is prima facie evidence that he is a partner in the business, but no such inference shall be drawn if such profits were received in payment:

(a) As a debt by installments or otherwise,

(b) As wages of an employee or rent to a landlord,

(c) As an annuity to a widow or representative of a deceased partner,

(d) As interest on a loan, though the amount of payment vary with the profits of the business,

(e) As the consideration for the sale of a goodwill of a business or other property by installments or otherwise.

Sec. 8. (Partnership Property.) (1) All property originally brought into the partnership stock or subsequently acquired by purchase or otherwise, on account of the partnership, is partnership property.

(2) Unless the contrary intention appears, property acquired with partnership funds is partnership property.

(3) Any estate in real property may be acquired in the partnership name. Title so acquired can be conveyed only in the partnership name.

(4) A conveyance to a partnership in the partnership name, though without words of inheritance, passes the entire estate of the grantor unless a contrary intent appears.

PART III

RELATIONS OF PARTNERS TO PERSONS DEALING WITH THE PARTNERSHIP

Sec. 9. (Partner Agent of Partnership as to Partnership Business.) (1) Every partner is an agent of the partnership for the purpose of its business, and the act of every partner, including the execution in the partnership name of any instrument, for apparently carrying on in the usual way the business of the partnership of which he is a member binds the partnership, unless the partner so acting has in fact no authority to act for the partnership in the particular matter, and the person with whom he is dealing has knowledge of the fact that he has no such authority.

(2) An act of a partner which is not apparently for the carrying on of the business of the partnership in the usual way does not bind the partnership unless authorized by the other partners.

(3) Unless authorized by the other partners or unless they have abandoned the business, one or more but less than all the partners have no authority to:

(a) Assign the partnership property in trust for creditors or on the assignee's promise to pay the debts of the partnership,

(b) Dispose of the goodwill of the business,

(c) Do any other act which would make it impossible to carry on the ordinary business of a partnership,

(d) Confess a judgment,

(e) Submit a partnership claim or liability to arbitration or reference.

(4) No act of a partner in contravention of a restriction on authority shall bind the partnership to persons having knowledge of the restriction.

Sec. 10. (Conveyance of Real Property of the Partnership.) (1) Where title to real property is in the partnership name, any partner may convey title to such property by a conveyance executed in the partnership name; but the partnership may recover such property unless the partner's act binds the partnership under the provisions of paragraph (1) of section 9 or unless such property has been conveyed by the grantee or a person claiming through such grantee to a holder for value without knowledge that the partner, in making the conveyance, has exceeded his authority.

(2) Where title to real property is in the name of the partnership, a conveyance executed by a partner, in his own name, passes the equitable interest of the partnership, provided the act is one within the authority of the partner under the provisions of paragraph (1) of section 9.

(3) Where title to real property is in the name of one or more but not all the partners, and the record does not disclose the right of the partnership, the partners in whose name the title stands may convey title to such property, but the partnership may recover such property if the partners' act does not bind the partnership under the provisions of paragraph (1) of section 9, unless the purchaser or his assignee, is a holder for value, without knowledge.

(4) Where the title to real property is in the name of one or more or all the partners, or in a third person in trust for the partnership, a conveyance executed by a partner in the partnership name, or in his own name, passes the equitable interest of the partnership, provided the act is one within the authority of the partner under the provisions of paragraph (1) of section 9.

(5) Where the title to real property is in the names of all the partners a conveyance executed by all the partners passes all their rights in such property.

Sec. 11. (Partnership Bound by Admission of Partner.) An admission or representation made by any partner concerning partnership affairs within the scope of his authority as conferred by this act is evidence against the partnership.

Sec. 12. (Partnership Charged with Knowledge of or Notice to Partner.) Notice to any partner of any matter relating to partnership affairs, and the knowledge of the partner acting in the particular matter, acquired while a partner or then present to his mind, and the knowledge of any other partner who reasonably could and should have communicated it to the acting partner, operate as notice to or knowledge of the partnership, except in the case of a fraud on the partnership committed by or with the consent of that partner.

Sec. 13. (Partnership Bound by Partner's Wrongful Act.) Where, by any wrongful act or omission of any partner acting in the ordinary course of the business of the partnership or with the authority of his co-partners, loss or injury is caused to any person, not being a partner in the partnership, or any penalty is incurred, the partnership is liable therefor to the same extent as the partner so acting or omitting to act.

Sec. 14.   (Partnership Bound by Partner's Breach of Trust.)   The partnership is bound to make good the loss:

(a) Where one partner acting within the scope of his apparent authority receives money or property of a third person and misapplies it; and

(b) Where the partnership in the course of its business receives money or property of a third person and the money or property so received is misapplied by any partner while it is in the custody of the partnership.

Sec. 15.   (Nature of Partner's Liability.)
All partners are liable

(a) Jointly and severally for everything chargeable to the partnership under sections 13 and 14.

(b) Jointly for all other debts and obligations of the partnership; but any partner may enter into a separate obligation to perform a partnership contract.

Sec. 16.   (Partner by Estoppel.)   (1) When a person, by words spoken or written or by conduct, represents himself, or consents to another representing him to any one, as a partner in an existing partnership or with one or more persons not actual partners, he is liable to any such person to whom such representation has been made, who has, on the faith of such representation, given credit to the actual or apparent partnership, and if he has made such representation

or consented to its being made in a public manner he is liable to such person, whether the representation has or has not been made or communicated to such person so giving credit by or with the knowledge of the apparent partner making the representation or consenting to its being made.

(a) When a partnership liability results, he is liable as though he were an actual member of the partnership.

(b) When no partnership liability results, he is liable jointly with the other persons, if any, so consenting to the contract or representation as to incur liability, otherwise separately.

(2) When a person has been thus represented to be a partner in an existing partnership, or with one or more persons not actual partners, he is an agent of the persons consenting to such representation to bind them to the same extent and in the same manner as though he were a partner in fact, with respect to persons who rely upon the representation. Where all the members of the existing partnership consent to the representation, a partnership act or obligation results; but in all other cases it is the joint act or obligation of the person acting and the persons consenting to the representation.

Sec. 17.   (Liability of Incoming Partner.)
A person admitted as a partner into an existing partnership is liable for all the obligations of the partnership arising before his admission as though he had been a partner when such obligations were incurred, except that this liability shall be satisfied only out of partnership property.

PART IV

RELATIONS OF PARTNERS TO ONE ANOTHER

Sec. 18.   (Rules Determining Rights and Duties of Partners.)   The rights and duties of the partners in relation to the partnership shall be determined, subject to any agreement between them, by the following rules:

(a) Each partner shall be repaid his contributions, whether by way of capital or advances to the partnership property and share equally in the profits and surplus remaining after all liabilities, including those to partners, are satisfied; and must contribute toward the losses, whether

of capital or otherwise, sustained by the partnership according to his share in the profits.

(b) The partnership must indemnify every partner in respect of payments made and personal liabilities reasonably incurred by him in the ordinary and proper conduct of its business, or for the preservation of its business or property.

(c) A partner, who in aid of the partnership makes any payment or advance beyond the amount of capital which he agreed to contribute, shall be paid interest from the date of the payment or advance.

(d) A partner shall receive interest on the capital contributed by him only from the date when repayment should be made.

(e) All partners have equal rights in the management and conduct of the partnership business.

(f) No partner is entitled to remuneration for acting in the partnership business, except that a surviving partner is entitled to reasonable compensation for his services in winding up the partnership affairs.

(g) No person can become a member of a partnership without the consent of all the partners.

(h) Any difference arising as to ordinary matters connected with the partnership business may be decided by a majority of the partners; but no act in contravention of any agreement between the partners may be done rightfully without the consent of all the partners.

Sec. 19. (Partnership Books.) The partnership books shall be kept, subject to any agreement between the partners, at the principal place of business of the partnership, and every partner shall at all times have access to and may inspect and copy any of them.

Sec. 20. (Duty of Partners to Render Information.) Partners shall render on demand true and full information of all things affecting the partnership to any partner or the legal representative of any deceased partner or partner under legal disability.

Sec. 21. (Partner Accountable as a Fiduciary.) (1) Every partner must account to the partnership for any benefit, and hold as trustee for it any profits derived by him without the consent of the other partners from any transaction connected with the formation, conduct, or liquidation of the partnership or from any use by him of its property.

(2) This section applies also to the representatives of a deceased partner engaged in the liquidation of the affairs of the partnership as the personal representatives of the last surviving partner.

Sec. 22. (Right to an Account.) Any partner shall have the right to a formal account as to partnership affairs:

(a) If he is wrongfully excluded from the partnership business or possession of its property by his co-partners,

(b) If the right exists under the terms of any agreement,

(c) As provided by Section 21,

(d) Whenever other circumstances render it just and reasonable.

Sec. 23. (Continuation of Partnership Beyond Fixed Term.) (1) When a partnership for a fixed term or particular undertaking is continued after the termination of such term or particular undertaking without any express agreement, the rights and duties of the partners remain the same as they were at such termination, so far as is consistent with a partnership at will.

(2) A continuation of the business by the partners or such of them as habitually acted therein during the term, without any settlement or liquidation of the partnership affairs, is prima facie evidence of a continuation of the partnership.

PART V

PROPERTY RIGHTS OF A PARTNER

Sec. 24. (Extent of Property Rights of a Partner.) The property rights of a partner are (1) his rights in specific partnership property, (2) his interest in the partnership, and (3) his right to participate in the management.

Sec. 25. (Nature of a Partner's Right in Specific Partnership Property.) (1) A partner is co-owner with his partners of specific partnership property holding as a tenant in partnership.

(2) The incidents of this tenancy are such that:

(a) A partner, subject to the provisions of this act and to any agreement between the partners, has an equal right with his partners to possess specific partnership property for partnership purposes; but he has no right to possess such property for any other purpose without the consent of his partners.

(b) A partner's right in specific partnership property is not assignable except in connection with the assignment of rights of all the partners in the same property.

(c) A partner's right in specific partnership property is not subject to attachment or execution, except on a claim against the partnership. When partnership property is attached for a partnership debt the partners, or any of them, or the representatives of a deceased partner, cannot claim any right under the homestead or exemption laws.

(d) On the death of a partner his right in specific partnership property vests in the surviving partner or partners, except where the deceased was the last surviving partner, when his right in such property vests in his legal representative. Such surviving partner or partners, or the legal representative of the last surviving partner, has no right to possess the partnership property for any but a partnership purpose.

(e) A partner's right in specific partnership property is not subject to dower, courtesy, or allowances to widows, heirs, or next of kin.

Sec. 26.   (Nature of Partner's Interest in the Partnership.) A partner's interest in the partnership is his share of the profits and surplus, and the same is personal property.

Sec. 27.   (Assignment of Partner's Interest.) (1) A conveyance by a partner of his interest in the partnership does not of itself dissolve the partnership, nor, as against the other partners in the absence of agreement, entitle the assignee, during the continuance of the partnership to interfere in the management or administration of the partnership business or affairs, or to require any information or account of partnership transactions, or to inspect the partnership books; but it merely entitles the assignee to receive in accordance with his contract the profits to which the assigning partner would otherwise be entitled.

(2) In case of a dissolution of the partnership, the assignee is entitled to receive his assignor's interest and may require an account from the date only of the last account agreed to by all the partners.

Sec. 28.   (Partner's Interest Subject to Charging Order.) (1) On due application to a competent court by any judgment creditor of a partner, the court which entered the judgment, order, or decree, or any other court, may charge the interest of the debtor partner with payment of the unsatisfied amount of such judgment debt with interest thereon; and may then or later appoint a receiver of his share of the profits, and of any other money due or to fall due to him in respect of the partnership, and make all other orders, directions, accounts and inquiries which the debtor partner might have made, or which the circumstances of the case may require.

(2) The interest charged may be redeemed at any time before foreclosure, or in case of a sale being directed by the court may be purchased without thereby causing a dissolution:

(a) With separate property, by any one or more of the partners, or

(b) With partnership property, by any one or more of the partners with the consent of all the partners whose interests are not so charged or sold.

(3) Nothing in this act shall be held to deprive a partner of his right, if any, under the exemption laws, as regards his interest in the partnership.

PART VI

DISSOLUTION AND WINDING UP

Sec. 29.   (Dissolution Defined.) The dissolution of a partnership is the change in the relation of the partners caused by any partner ceasing to be associated in the carrying on as distinguished from the winding up of the business.

Sec. 30.   (Partnership Not Terminated by Dissolution.) On dissolution the partnership is not terminated, but continues until the winding up of partnership affairs is completed.

Sec. 31. (Causes of Dissolution.) Dissolution is caused: (1) Without violation of the agreement between the partners,

(a) By the termination of the definite term or particular undertaking specified in the agreement,

(b) By the express will of any partner when no definite term or particular undertaking is specified,

(c) By the express will of all the partners who have not assigned their interests or suffered them to be charged for their separate debts, either before or after the termination of any specified term or particular undertaking,

(d) By the expulsion of any partner from the business bona fide in accordance with such a power conferred by the agreement between the partners;

(2) In contravention of the agreement between the partners, where the circumstances do not permit a dissolution under any other provision of this section, by the express will of any partner at any time;

(3) By any event which makes it unlawful for the business of the partnership to be carried on or for the members to carry it on in partnership;

(4) By the death of any partner;

(5) By the bankruptcy of any partner or the partnership;

(6) By decree of court under Section 32.

Sec. 32. (Dissolution by Decree of Court.) (1) On application by or for a partner the court shall decree a dissolution whenever:

(a) A partner has been declared a lunatic in any judicial proceeding or is shown to be of unsound mind,

(b) A partner becomes in any other way incapable of performing his part of the partnership contract,

(c) A partner has been guilty of such conduct as tends to affect prejudicially the carrying on of the business,

(d) A partner wilfully or persistently commits a breach of the partnership agreement, or otherwise so conducts himself in matters relating to the partnership business that it is

not reasonably practicable to carry on the business in partnership with him,

(e) The business of the partnership can only be carried on at a loss,

(f) Other circumstances render a dissolution equitable.

(2) On the application of the purchaser of a partner's interest under Sections 27 or 28:

(a) After the termination of the specified term or particular undertaking,

(b) At any time if the partnership was a partnership at will when the interest was assigned or when the charging order was issued.

Sec. 33. (General Effect of Dissolution on Authority of Partner.) Except so far as may be necessary to wind up partnership affairs or to complete transactions begun but not then finished, dissolution terminates all authority of any partner to act for the partnership,

(1) With respect to the partners,

(a) When the dissolution is not by the act, bankruptcy or death of a partner; or

(b) When the dissolution is by such act, bankruptcy or death of a partner, in cases where Section 34 so requires.

(2) With respect to persons not partners, as declared in Section 35.

Sec. 34. (Right of Partner to Contribution from Copartners After Dissolution.) Where the dissolution is caused by the act, death or bankruptcy of a partner, each partner is liable to his copartners for his share of any liability created by any partner acting for the partnership as if the partnership had not been dissolved unless

(a) The dissolution being by act of any partner, the partner acting for the partnership had knowledge of the dissolution, or

(b) The dissolution being by the death or bankruptcy of a partner, the partner acting for the partnership had knowledge or notice of the death or bankruptcy.

Sec. 35. (Power of Partner to Bind Partnership to Third Persons After Dissolution.) (1) After dissolution a partner can bind the partnership except as provided in Paragraph (3)

(a) By any act appropriate for winding up partnership affairs or completing transactions unfinished at dissolution;

(b) By any transaction which would bind the partnership if dissolution had not taken place, provided the other party to the transaction

(I) Had extended credit to the partnership prior to dissolution and had no knowledge or notice of the dissolution; or

(II) Though he had not so extended credit, had nevertheless known of the partnership prior to dissolution, and, having no knowledge or notice of dissolution, the fact of dissolution had not been advertised in a newspaper of general circulation in the place (or in each place if more than one) at which the partnership business was regularly carried on.

(2) The liability of a partner under paragraph (1b) shall be satisfied out of partnership assets alone when such partner had been prior to dissolution.

(a) Unknown as a partner to the person with whom the contract is made; and

(b) So far unknown and inactive in partnership affairs that the business reputation of the partnership could not be said to have been in any degree due to his connection with it.

(3) The partnership is in no case bound by any act of a partner after dissolution

(a) Where the partnership is dissolved because it is unlawful to carry on the business, unless the act is appropriate for winding up partnership affairs; or

(b) Where the partner has become bankrupt; or

(c) Where the partner has no authority to wind up partnership affairs; except by a transaction with one who

(I) Had extended credit to the partnership prior to dissolution and had no knowledge or notice of his want of authority; or

(II) Had not extended credit to the partnership prior to dissolution, and, having no knowledge or notice of his want of authority, the fact of his want of authority has not been advertised in the manner provided for advertising the fact of dissolution in paragraph (1bII).

(4) Nothing in this section shall affect the liability under section 16 of any person who after dissolution represents himself or consents to another representing him as a partner in a partnership engaged in carrying on business.

Sec. 36. (Effect of Dissolution on Partner's Existing Liability.) (1) The dissolution of the partnership does not of itself discharge the existing liability of any partner.

(2) A partner is discharged from any existing liability upon dissolution of the partnership by an agreement to that effect between himself, the partnership creditor and the person or partnership continuing the business; and such agreement may be inferred from the course of dealing between the creditor having knowledge of the dissolution and the person or partnership continuing the business.

(3) Where a person agrees to assume the existing obligations of a dissolved partnership, the partners whose obligations have been assumed shall be discharged from any liability to any creditor of the partnership who, knowing of the agreement, consents to a material alteration in the nature or time of payment of such obligations.

(4) The individual property of a deceased partner shall be liable for all obligations of the partnership incurred while he was a partner but subject to the prior payment of his separate debts.

Sec. 37. (Right to Wind Up.) Unless otherwise agreed the partners who have not wrongfully dissolved the partnership or the legal representative of the last surviving partner, not bankrupt, has the right to wind up the partnership affairs; provided, however, that any partner, his legal representative or his assignee, upon cause shown, may obtain winding up by the court.

Sec. 38. (Rights of Partners to Application of Partnership Property.) (1) When dissolution is caused in any way, except in contravention of the partnership agreement, each partner as against his co-partners and all persons claiming through them in respect of their interests in the partnership, unless otherwise agreed, may have the partnership property applied to discharge its liabilities, and the surplus applied to pay in cash the net amount owing to the respective partners. But if dissolution is caused by expulsion of a partner, bona fide under the partnership agreement and if the expelled partner is discharged from all partnership liabilities, either by payment or agreement under Section 36(2), he shall receive in cash only the net amount due him from the partnership.

(2) When dissolution is caused in contravention of the partnership agreement the rights of the partners shall be as follows:

(a) Each partner who has not caused dissolution wrongfully shall have,

(I) All the rights specified in paragraph (1) of this section, and

(II) The right, as against each partner who has caused the dissolution wrongfully, to damages for breach of the agreement.

(b) The partners who have not caused the dissolution wrongfully, if they all desire to continue the business in the same name, either by themselves or jointly with others, may do so, during the agreed term for the partnership and for that purpose may possess the partnership property, provided they secure the payment by bond approved by the court, or pay to any partner who has caused the dissolution wrongfully, the value of his interest in the partnership at the dissolution, less any damages recoverable under clause (2aII) of the section, and in like manner indemnify him against all present or future partnership liabilities.

(c) A partner who has caused the dissolution wrongfully shall have:

(I) If the business is not continued under the provisions of paragraph (2b) all the rights of a partner under paragraph (1), subject to clause (2aII), of this section,

(II) If the business is continued under paragraph (2b) of this section the right as against his co-partners and all claiming through them in respect of their interests in the partnership, to have the value of his interests in the partnership, less any damages caused to his co-partners by the dissolution, ascertained and paid to him in cash, or the payment secured by bond approved by the court, and to be released from all existing liabilities of the partnership; but in ascertaining the value of the partner's interest the value of the goodwill of the business shall not be considered.

Sec. 39. (Rights Where Partnership Is Dissolved for Fraud or Misrepresentation.) Where a partnership contract is rescinded on the ground of the fraud or misrepresentation of one of the parties thereto, the party entitled to rescind is, without prejudice to any other right, entitled,

(a) To a lien on, or right of retention of, the surplus of the partnership property after satisfying the partnership liabilities to third persons for any sum of money paid by him for the purchase of an interest in the partnership and for any capital or advances contributed by him; and

(b) To stand, after all liabilities to third persons have been satisfied, in the place of the creditors of the partnership for any payments made by him in respect of the partnership liabilities; and

(c) To be indemnified by the person guilty of the fraud or making the representation against all debts and liabilities of the partnership.

Sec. 40. (Rules for Distribution.) In settling accounts between the partners after dissolution, the following rules shall be observed, subject to any agreement to the contrary:

(a) The assets of the partnership are;

(I) The partnership property,

(II) The contributions of the partners necessary for the payment of all the liabilities specified in clause (b) of this paragraph.

(b) The liabilities of the partnership shall rank in order of payment, as follows:

(I) Those owing to creditors other than partners,

(II) Those owing to partners other than for capital and profits,

(III) Those owing to partners in respect of capital,

(IV) Those owing to partners in respect of profits.

(c) The assets shall be applied in the order of their declaration in clause (a) of this paragraph to the satisfaction of the liabilities.

(d) The partners shall contribute, as provided by Section 18(a) the amount necessary to satisfy the liabilities; but if any, but not all, of the partners are insolvent, or, not being subject to process, refuse to contribute, the other parties shall contribute their share of the liabilities, and, in the relative proportions in which they share the profits, the additional amount necessary to pay the liabilities.

(e) An assignee for the benefit of creditors or any person appointed by the court shall have the right to enforce the contributions specified in clause (d) of this paragraph.

(f) Any partner or his legal representative shall have the right to enforce the contributions specified in clause (d) of this paragraph, to the extent of the amount which he has paid in excess of his share of the liability.

(g) The individual property of a deceased partner shall be liable for the contributions specified in clause (d) of this paragraph.

(h) When partnership property and the individual properties of the partners are in possession of a court for distribution, partnership creditors shall have priority on partnership property and separate creditors on individual property, saving the rights of lien or secured creditors as heretofore.

(i) Where a partner has become bankrupt or his estate is insolvent the claims against his separate property shall rank in the following order:

(I) Those owing to separate creditors,

(II) Those owing to partnership creditors,

(III) Those owing to partners by way of contribution.

Sec. 41. (Liability of Persons Continuing the Business in Certain Cases.) (1) When any new partner is admitted into an existing partnership, or when any partner retires and assigns (or the representative of the deceased partner assigns) his rights in partnership property to two or more of the partners, or to one or more of the partners and one or more third persons, if the business is continued without liquidation of the partnership affairs, creditors of the first or dissolved partnership are also creditors of the partnership so continuing the business.

(2) When all but one partner retire and assign (or the representative of a deceased partner assigns) their rights in partnership property to the remaining partner, who continues the business without liquidation of partnership affairs, either alone or with others, creditors of the dissolved partnership are also creditors of the person or partnership so continuing the business.

(3) When any partner retires or dies and the business of the dissolved partnership is continued as set forth in paragraphs (1) and (2) of this section, with the consent of the retired partners or the representative of the deceased partner, but without any assignment of his right in partnership property, rights of creditors of the dissolved partnership and of the creditors of the person or partnership continuing the business shall be as if such assignment had been made.

(4) When all the partners or their representatives assign their rights in partnership property to one or more third persons who promise to pay the debts and who continue the business of the dissolved partnership, creditors of the dissolved partnership are also creditors of the person or partnership continuing the business.

(5) When any partner wrongfully causes a dissolution and the remaining partners continue the business under the provisions of section 38(2b), either alone or with others, and without liquidation of the partnership affairs, creditors of the dissolved partnership are also creditors of the person or partnership continuing the business.

(6) When a partner is expelled and the remaining partners continue the business either alone or with others, without liquidation of the partnership affairs, creditors of the dissolved partnership are also creditors of the person or partnership continuing the business.

(7) The liability of a third person becoming a partner in the partnership continuing the business, under this section, to the creditors of the dissolved partnership shall be satisfied out of partnership property only.

(8) When the business of a partnership after dissolution is continued under any conditions set forth in this section the creditors of the dissolved partnership, as against the separate creditors of the retiring or deceased partner or the representative of the deceased partner, have a prior right to any claim of the retired partner or the representative of the deceased partner against the person or partnership continuing the business, on account of the retired or deceased partner's interest in the dissolved partnership or on account of any consideration promised for such interest or for his right in partnership property.

(9) Nothing in this section shall be held to modify any right of creditors to set aside any assignment on the ground of fraud.

(10) The use by the person or partnership continuing the business of the partnership name, or the name of a deceased partner as

part thereof, shall not of itself make the individual property of the deceased partner liable for any debts contracted by such person or partnership.

Sec. 42. (Rights of Retiring or Estate of Deceased Partner When the Business Is Continued.) When any partner retires or dies, and the business is continued under any of the conditions set forth in Section 41(1, 2, 3, 5, 6), or Section 38(2b), without any settlement of accounts as between him or his estate and the person or partnership continuing the business, unless otherwise agreed, he or his legal representative as against such persons or partnership may have the value of his interest at the date of dissolution ascertained, and shall receive as an ordinary creditor an amount equal to the value of his interest in the dissolved partnership with interest, or, at his option or at the option of his legal representative, in lieu of interest, the profits attributable to the use of his right in the property of the dissolved partnership; provided that the creditors of the dissolved partnership as against the separate creditors, or the representative of the retired or deceased partner, shall have priority on any claim arising under this section, as provided by Section 41(8) of this act.

Sec. 43. (Accrual of Actions.) The right to an account of his interest shall accrue to any partner, or his legal representative, as against the winding up partners or the surviving partners or the person or partnership continuing the business, at the date of dissolution, in the absence of any agreement to the contrary.

PART VII

MISCELLANEOUS PROVISIONS

Sec. 44. (When Act Takes Effect.) This act shall take effect on the ———— day of ———— one thousand nine hundred and ————.

Sec. 45. (Legislation Repealed.) All acts or parts of acts inconsistent with this act are hereby repealed.

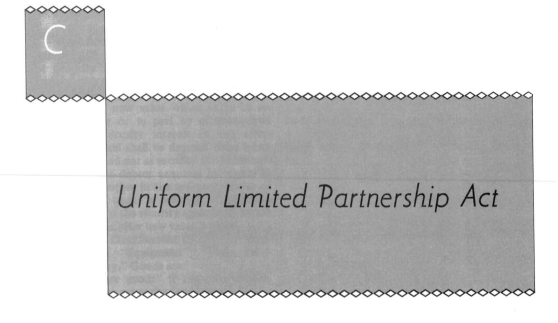

Uniform Limited Partnership Act

Be it enacted, etc., as follows:

Sec. 1. (Limited Partnership Defined.) A limited partnership is a partnership formed by two or more persons under the provisions of Section 2, having as members one or more general partners and one or more limited partners. The limited partners as such shall not be bound by the obligations of the partnership.

Sec. 2. (Formation.) (1) Two or more persons desiring to form a limited partnership shall

(a) Sign and swear to a certificate, which shall state

I. The name of the partnership,

II. The character of the business,

III. The location of the principal place of business,

IV. The name and place of residence of each member; general and limited partners being respectively designated,

V. The term for which the partnership is to exist,

VI. The amount of cash and a description of and the agreed value of the other property contributed by each limited partner,

VII. The additional contributions, if any, agreed to be made by each limited partner and the times at which or events on the happening of which they shall be made,

VIII. The time, if agreed upon, when the contribution of each limited partner is to be returned,

IX. The share of the profits or the other compensation by way of income which each limited partner shall receive by reason of his contribution,

X. The right, if given, of a limited partner to substitute an assignee as contributor in his place, and the terms and conditions of the substitution,

XI. The right, if given, of the partners to admit additional limited partners,

XII. The right, if given, of one or more of the limited partners to priority over other limited partners, as to contributions or as to compensation by way of income, and the nature of such priority,

XIII. The right, if given, of the remaining general partner or partners to continue the business on the death, retirement or insanity of a general partner, and

XIV. The right, if given, of a limited partner to demand and receive property other than cash in return for his contribution.

(b) File for record the certificate in the office of [here designate the proper office].

(2) A limited partnership is formed if there has been substantial compliance in good faith with the requirements of paragraph (1).

Sec. 3. (Business Which may Be Carried On.) A limited partnership may carry on any business which a partnership without limited partners may carry on, except [here designate the business to be prohibited].

Sec. 4. (Character of Limited Partner's Contribution.) The contributions of a limited partner may be cash or other property, but not services.

Sec. 5. (A Name Not to Contain Surname of Limited Partner; Exceptions.) (1) The surname of a limited partner shall not appear in the partnership name, unless

(a) It is also the surname of a general partner, or

(b) Prior to the time when the limited partner became such the business had been carried on under a name in which his surname appeared.

(2) A limited partner whose name appears in a partnership name contrary to the provisions of paragraph (1) is liable as a general partner to partnership creditors who extend credit to the partnership without actual knowledge that he is not a general partner.

Sec. 6. (Liability for False Statements in Certificate.) If the certificate contains a false statement, one who suffers loss by reliance on such statement may hold liable any party to the certificate who knew the statement to be false.

(a) At the time he signed the certificate, or

(b) Subsequently, but within a sufficient time before the statement was relied upon to enable him to cancel or amend the certificate, or to file a petition for its cancellation or amendment as provided in Section 25(3).

Sec. 7. (Limited Partner Not Liable to Creditors.) A limited partner shall not become liable as a general partner unless, in addi-

tion to the exercise of his rights and powers as a limited partner, he takes part in the control of the business.

Sec. 8. (Admission of Additional Limited Partners.) After the formation of a limited partnership, additional limited partners may be admitted upon filing an amendment to the original certificate in accordance with the requirements of Section 25.

Sec. 9. (Rights, Powers and Liabilities of a General Partner.) (1) A general partner shall have all the rights and powers and be subject to all the restrictions and liabilities of a partner in a partnership without limited partners, except that without the written consent or ratification of the specific act by all the limited partners, a general partner or all of the general partners have no authority to

(a) Do any act in contravention of the certificate,

(b) Do any act which would make it impossible to carry on the ordinary business of the partnership,

(c) Confess a judgment against the partnership,

(d) Possess partnership property, or assign their rights in specific partnership property, for other than a partnership purpose,

(e) Admit a person as a general partner,

(f) Admit a person as a limited partner, unless the right to do so is given in the certificate,

(g) Continue the business with partnership property on the death, retirement or insanity of a general partner, unless the right so to do is given in the certificate.

Sec. 10. (Rights of a Limited Partner.) (1) A limited partner shall have the same rights as a general partner to

(a) Have the partnership books kept at the principal place of business of the partnership, and at all times to inspect and copy any of them,

(b) Have on demand true and full information of all things affecting the partnership, and a formal account of partnership affairs, whenever circumstances render it just and reasonable, and

(c) Have dissolution and winding up by decree of court.

(2) A limited partner shall have the right to receive a share of the profits or other compensation by way of income, and to the return of his contribution as provided in Sections 15 and 16.

Sec. 11. (Status of Person Erroneously Believing Himself a Limited Partner.) A person who has contributed to the capital of a business conducted by a person or partnership erroneously believing that he has become a limited partner in a limited partnership, is not, by reason of his exercise of the rights of a limited partner, a general partner with the person or in the partnership carrying on the business, or bound by the obligations of such person or partnership; provided that on ascertaining the mistake he promptly renounces his interest in the profits of the business, or other compensation by way of income.

Sec. 12. (One Person Both General and Limited Partner.) (1) A person may be a general partner and a limited partner in the same partnership at the same time.

(2) A person who is a general, and also at the same time a limited partner, shall have all the rights and powers and be subject to all the restrictions of a general partner; except that, in respect to his contribution, he shall have the rights against the other members which he would have had if he were not also a general partner.

Sec. 13. (Loans and Other Business Transactions with Limited Partner.) (1) A limited partner also may loan money to and transact other business with the partnership, and, unless he is also a general partner, receive on account of resulting claims against the partnership, with general creditors, a pro rata share of the assets. No limited partner shall in respect to any such claim

(a) Receive or hold as collateral security any partnership property, or

(b) Receive from a general partner or the partnership any payment, conveyance, or release from liability, if at the time the assets of the partnership are not sufficient to discharge partnership liabilities to persons not claiming as general or limited partners.

(2) The receiving of collateral security, or a payment, conveyance, or release in violation of the provisions of paragraph (1) is a fraud on the creditors of the partnership.

Sec. 14. (Relation of Limited Partners Inter Se.) Where there are several limited partners the members may agree that one or more of the limited partners shall have a priority over other limited partners as to the return of their contributions, as to their compensation by way of income, or as to any other matter. If such an agreement is made it shall be stated in the certificate, and in the absence of such a statement all the limited partners shall stand upon equal footing.

Sec. 15. (Compensation of Limited Partner.) A limited partner may receive from the partnership the share of the profits or the compensation by way of income stipulated for in the certificate; provided, that after such payment is made, whether from the property of the partnership or that of a general partner, the partnership assets are in excess of all liabilities of the partnership except liabilities to limited partners on account of their contributions and to general partners.

Sec. 16. (Withdrawal or Reduction of Limited Partner's Contribution.) (1) A limited partner shall not receive from a general partner or out of partnership property any part of his contribution until

(a) All liabilities of the partnership, except liabilities to general partners and to limited partners on account of their contributions, have been paid or there remains property of the partnership sufficient to pay them,

(b) The consent of all members is had, unless the return of the contribution may be rightfully demanded under the provisions of paragraph (2), and

(c) The certificate is cancelled or so amended as to set forth the withdrawal or reduction.

(2) Subject to the provisions of paragraph (1) a limited partner may rightfully demand the return of his contribution

(a) On the dissolution of a partnership, or

(b) When the date specified in the certificate for its return has arrived, or

(c) After he has given six months' notice in writing to all other members, if no time is specified in the certificate either for the return of the contribution or for the dissolution of the partnership,

(3) In the absence of any statement in the certificate to the contrary or the consent of all members, a limited partner, irrespective of the nature of his contribution, has only the right to demand and receive cash in return for his contribution.

(4) A limited partner may have the partnership dissolved and its affairs wound up when

(a) He rightfully but unsuccessfully demands the return of his contribution, or

(b) The other liabilities of the partnership have not been paid, or the partnership property is insufficient for their payment as required by paragraph (1a) and the limited partner would otherwise be entitled to the return of his contribution.

Sec. 17.   (Liability of Limited Partner to Partnership.)   (1) A limited partner is liable to the partnership

(a) For the difference between his contribution as actually made and that stated in the certificate as having been made, and

(b) For any unpaid contribution which he agreed in the certificate to make in the future at the time and on the conditions stated in the certificate.

(2) A limited partner holds as trustee for the partnership

(a) Specific property stated in the certificate as contributed by him, but which was not contributed or which has been wrongfully returned, and

(b) Money or other property wrongfully paid or conveyed to him on account of his contribution.

(3) The liabilities of a limited partner as set forth in this section can be waived or compromised only by the consent of all members; but a waiver or compromise shall not affect the right of a creditor of a partnership, who extended credit or whose claim arose after the filing and before a cancellation or amendment of the certificate, to enforce such liabilities.

(4) When a contributor has rightfully received the return in whole or in part of the capital of his contribution, he is nevertheless liable to the partnership for any sum, not in excess of such return with interest, necessary to discharge its liabilities to all creditors who extended credit or whose claims arose before such return.

Sec. 18.   (Nature of Limited Partner's Interest in Partnership.)   A limited partner's interest in the partnership is personal property.

Sec. 19.   (Assignment of Limited Partner's Interest.)   (1) A limited partner's interest is assignable.

(2) A substituted limited partner is a person admitted to all the rights of a limited partner who has died or has assigned his interest in a partnership.

(3) An assignee, who does not become a substituted limited partner, has no right to require any information or account of the partnership transactions or to inspect the partnership books; he is only entitled to receive the share of the profits or other compensation by way of income, or the return of his contribution, to which his assignor would otherwise be entitled.

(4) An assignee shall have the right to become a substituted limited partner if all the members (except the assignor) consent thereto or if the assignor, being thereunto empowered by the certificate, gives the assignee that right.

(5) An assignee becomes a substituted limited partner when the certificate is appropriately amended in accordance with Section 25.

(6) The substituted limited partner has all the rights and powers, and is subject to all the restrictions and liabilities of his assignor, except those liabilities of which he was ignorant at the time he became a limited partner and which could not be ascertained from the certificate.

(7) The substitution of the assignee as a limited partner does not release the assignor from liability to the partnership under Sections 6 and 17.

Sec. 20.   (Effect of Retirement, Death or Insanity of a General Partner.)   The retirement, death or insanity of a general partner dissolves the partnership, unless the business is continued by the remaining general partners

(a) Under a right so to do stated in the certificate, or

(b) With the consent of all members.

Sec. 21. (Death of Limited Partner.) (1) On the death of a limited partner his executor or administrator shall have all the rights of a limited partner for the purpose of settling his estate, and such power as the deceased had to constitute his assignee a substituted limited partner.

(2) The estate of a deceased limited partner shall be liable for all his liabilities as a limited partner.

Sec. 22. (Rights of Creditors of Limited Partner.) (1) On due application to a court of competent jurisdiction by any judgment creditor of a limited partner, the court may charge the interest of the indebted limited partner with payment of the unsatisfied amount of the judgment debt; and may appoint a receiver, and make all other orders, directions, and inquiries which the circumstances of the case may require.

In those states where a creditor on beginning an action can attach debts due the defendant before he has obtained a judgment against the defendant it is recommended that paragraph (1) of this section read as follows:

On due application to a court of competent jurisdiction by any creditor of a limited partner, the court may charge the interest of the indebted limited partner with payment of the unsatisfied amount of such claim; and may appoint a receiver, and make all other orders, directions, and inquiries which the circumstances of the case may require.

(2) The interest may be redeemed with the separate property of any general partner, but may not be redeemed with partnership property.

(3) The remedies conferred by paragraph (1) shall not be deemed exclusive of others which may exist.

(4) Nothing in this act shall be held to deprive a limited partner of his statutory exemption.

Sec. 23. (Distribution of Assets.) (1) In settling accounts after dissolution the liabilities of the partnership shall be entitled to payment in the following order:

(a) Those to creditors, in the order of priority as provided by law, except those to limited partners on account of their contributions, and to general partners,

(b) Those to limited partners in respect to their share of the profits and other compensa-

tion by way of income on their contributions,

(c) Those to limited partners in respect to the capital of their contributions,

(d) Those to general partners other than for capital and profits,

(e) Those to general partners in respect to profits,

(f) Those to general partners in respect to capital.

(2) Subject to any statement in the certificate or to subsequent agreement, limited partners share in the partnership assets in respect to their claims for capital, and in respect to their claims for profits or for compensation by way of income on their contributions respectively, in proportion to the respective amounts of such claims.

Sec. 24. (When Certificate Shall Be Cancelled or Amended.) (1) The certificate shall be cancelled when the partnership is dissolved or all limited partners cease to be such.

(2) A certificate shall be amended when

(a) There is a change in the name of the partnership or in the amount or character of the contribution of any limited partner,

(b) A person is substituted as a limited partner,

(c) An additional limited partner is admitted,

(d) A person is admitted as a general partner,

(e) A general partner retires, dies or becomes insane, and the business is continued under Section 20,

(f) There is a change in the character of the business of the partnership,

(g) There is a false or erroneous statement in the certificate,

(h) There is a change in the time as stated in the certificate for the dissolution of the partnership or for the return of a contribution,

(i) A time is fixed for the dissolution of the partnership, or the return of a contribution, no time having been specified in the certificate, or

(j) The members desire to make a change in any other statement in the certificate in order that it shall accurately represent the agreement between them.

Sec. 25. (Requirements for Amendment and for Cancellation of Certificate.) (1) The writing to amend a certificate shall

(a) Conform to the requirements of Section 2(1a) as far as necessary to set forth clearly the change in the certificate which it is desired to make, and

(b) Be signed and sworn to by all members, and an amendment substituting a limited partner or adding a limited or general partner shall be signed also by the member to be substituted or added, and when a limited partner is to be substituted, the amendment shall also be signed by the assigning limited partner.

(2) The writing to cancel a certificate shall be signed by all members.

(3) A person desiring the cancellation or amendment of a certificate, if any person designated in paragraphs (1) and (2) as a person who must execute the writing refuses to do so, may petition the [here designate the proper court] to direct a cancellation or amendment thereof.

(4) If the court finds that the petitioner has a right to have the writing executed by a person who refuses to do so, it shall order the [here designate the responsible official in the office designated in Section 2] in the office where the certificate is recorded to record the cancellation or amendment of the certificate; and where the certificate is to be amended, the court also cause to be filed for record in said office a certified copy of its decree setting forth the amendment.

(5) A certificate is amended or cancelled when there is filed for record in the office [here designate the office designated in Section 2] where the certificate is recorded

(a) A writing in accordance with the provisions of paragraph (1), or (2) or

(b) A certified copy of the order of court in accordance with the provisions of paragraph (4).

(6) After the certificate is duly amended in accordance with this section, the amended certificate shall thereafter be for all purposes the certificate provided for by this act.

Sec. 26.   (Parties to Actions.)   A contributor, unless he is a general partner, is not a proper party to proceedings by or against a partnership, except where the object is to enforce a limited partner's right against or liability to the partnership.

Sec. 27.   (Name of Act.)   This act may be cited as The Uniform Limited Partnership Act.

Sec. 28.   (Rules of Construction.)   (1) The rule that statutes in derogation of the common law are to be strictly construed shall have no application to this act.

(2) This act shall be so interpreted and construed as to effect its general purpose to make uniform the law of those states which enact it.

(3) This act shall not be so construed as to impair the obligations of any contract existing when the act goes into effect, nor to affect any action on proceedings begun or right accrued before this act takes effect.

Sec. 29.   (Rules for Cases Not Provided for in this Act.)   In any case not provided for in this act the rules of law and equity, including the law merchant, shall govern.

Sec. 30.[1]   (Provisions for Existing Limited Partnerships.)   (1) A limited partnership formed under any statute of this state prior to the adoption of this act, may become a limited partnership under this act by complying with the provisions of Section 2; provided the certificate sets forth

(a) The amount of the original contribution of each limited partner, and the time when the contribution was made, and

(b) That the property of the partnership exceeds the amount sufficient to discharge its liabilities to persons not claiming as general or limited partners by an amount greater than the sum of the contributions of its limited partners.

(2) A limited partnership formed under any statute of this state prior to the adoption of this act, until or unless it becomes a limited partnership under this act, shall continue to be governed by the provisions of [here insert proper reference to the existing limited partnership act or acts], except that such partnership shall not be renewed unless so provided in the original agreement.

Sec. 31.[1]   (Act [Acts] Repealed.)   Except as affecting existing limited partnerships to the extent set forth in Section 30, the act (acts) of [here designate the existing limited partnership act or acts] is (are) hereby repealed.

[1] Sections 30, 31, will be omitted in any state which has not a limited partnership act.

Revised Uniform Limited Partnership Act

ARTICLE 1

GENERAL PROVISIONS

Sec. 101. (Definitions.) As used in this Act:

(1) "Certificate of limited partnership" means the certificate referred to in Section 201, as that certificate is amended from time to time.

(2) "Contribution" means any cash, property, or services rendered, or a promissory note or other binding obligation to contribute cash or property or to perform services, which a partner contributes to a limited partnership in his capacity as a partner.

(3) "Event of withdrawal of a general partner" means an event that causes a person to cease to be a general partner as provided in Section 402.

(4) "Foreign limited partnership" means a partnership formed under the laws of any state other than this State and having as partners one or more general partners and one or more limited partners.

(5) "General partner" means a person who has been admitted to a limited partnership as a general partner in accordance with the partnership agreement and who is named in the certificate of limited partnership as a general partner.

(6) "Limited partner" means a person who has been admitted to a limited partnership as a limited partner in accordance with the partnership agreement and who is named in the certificate of limited partnership as a limited partner in accordance with the partnership agreement and who is named in the certi-

(7) "Limited partnership" and "domestic limited partnership" mean a partnership formed by 2 or more persons under the laws of this State and having one or more general partners and one or more limited partners.

(8) "Partner" means any limited partner or general partner.

(9) "Partnership agreement" means the agreement, written or, to the extent not prohibited by law, oral or both, of the partners as to the affairs of a limited partnership and the conduct of its business.

(10) "Partnership interest" has the meaning specified in Section 701.

(11) "Person" means a natural person, partnership, limited partnership (domestic or foreign), trust, estate, association, or corporation.

A134

(12) "State" means a state, territory, or possession of the United States, the District of Columbia, or the Commonwealth of Puerto Rico.

Sec. 102. (Name.) The name of each limited partnership as set forth in its certificate of limited partnership:

(1) shall contain the words "limited partnership" in full;

(2) may not contain the name of a limited partner unless (i) it is also the name of a general partner or (ii) the business of the limited partnership had been carried on under that name before the admission of that limited partner;

(3) may not contain any word or phrase indicating or implying that it is organized other than for a purpose stated in its certificate of limited partnership;

(4) may not be the same as, or deceptively similar to, the name of any corporation or limited partnership organized under the laws of this State or licensed or registered as a foreign corporation or limited partnership in this State; and

(5) may not contain the following words [here insert prohibited words].

Sec. 103. (Reservation of Name.)

(a) The exclusive right to the use of a name may be reserved by:

(1) any person intending to organize a limited partnership under this Act and to adopt that name;

(2) any domestic limited partnership or any foreign limited partnership registered in this State which, in either case, intends to adopt that name;

(3) any foreign limited partnership intending to register in this State and to adopt that name; and

(4) any person intending to organize a foreign limited partnership and intending to have it registered in this State and to adopt that name.

(b) The reservation shall be made by filing with the Secretary of State an application, executed by the applicant, to reserve a specified name. If the Secretary of State finds that the name is available for use by a domestic or foreign limited partnership, he shall reserve the name for the exclusive use of the applicant for a period of 120 days. Once having reserved a name, the same applicant may not again reserve the same name until more than 60 days after the expiration of the last 120-day period for which that applicant had reserved that name. The right to the exclusive use of a name so reserved may be transferred to any other person by filing in the office of the Secretary of State a notice of the transfer, executed by the applicant for whom the name was reserved and specifying the name and address of the transferee.

Sec. 104. (Specified Office and Agent.) Each limited partnership shall continuously maintain in this State:

(1) an office, which may but need not be a place of its business in this State, at which shall be kept the records required to be maintained by Section 105; and

(2) an agent for service of process on the limited partnership, which agent must be an individual resident of this State, a domestic corporation, or a foreign corporation authorized to do business in this State.

Sec. 105. (Records to Be Kept.) Each limited partnership shall keep at the office referred to in Section 104(1) the following: (1) a current list of the full name and last-known business address of each partner set forth in alphabetical order, (2) a copy of the certificate of limited partnership and all certificates of amendment thereto, together with executed copies of any powers of attorney pursuant to which any certificate has been executed, (3) copies of the limited partnership's federal, state, and local income tax returns and reports, if any, for the 3 most recent years, and (4) copies of any then effective written partnership agreements and of any financial statements of the limited partnership for the 3 most recent years. These records shall be available for inspection and copying at the reasonable request, and at the expense, of any partner during ordinary business hours.

Sec. 106. (Nature of Business.) A limited partnership may carry on any business that a partnership without limited partners may carry on except [here designate prohibited activities].

Sec. 107. (Business Transactions of Partner with the Partnership.) Except as otherwise provided in the partnership agreement, a partner may lend money to and transact other business with the limited partnership and, subject to other applicable provisions of law, has the same rights and obligations with respect thereto as a person who is not a partner.

ARTICLE 2

FORMATION; CERTIFICATE OF LIMITED PARTNERSHIP

Sec. 201. (Certificate of Limited Partnership.)

(a) Two or more persons desiring to form a limited partnership shall execute a certificate of limited partnership. The certificate shall be filed in the office of the Secretary of State and shall set forth:

(1) the name of the limited partnership;

(2) the general character of its business;

(3) the address of the office and the name and address of the agent for service of process required to be maintained by Section 104;

(4) the name and the business address of each partner (specifying the general partners and limited partners separately);

(5) the amount of cash and a description and statement of the agreed value of the other property or services contributed by each partner and which each partner has agreed to contribute in the future;

(6) the times at which or events on the happening of which any additional contributions agreed to be made by each partner are to be made;

(7) any power of a limited partner to grant an assignee of any part of his partnership interest the right to become a limited partner, and the terms and conditions of the power;

(8) if agreed upon, the time at which or the events on the happening of which a partner may terminate his membership in the limited partnership and the amount of, or the method of determining, the distribution to which he may be entitled respecting his partnership interest, and the terms and conditions of the termination and distribution;

(9) any right of a partner to receive distributions of property including cash from the limited partnership;

(10) any right of a partner to receive, or of a general partner to make, distributions to a partner which include a return of all or any part of the partner's contribution;

(11) any time at which or events upon the happening of which the limited partnership is to be dissolved and its affairs wound up;

(12) any right of the remaining general partners to continue the business on the happening of an event of withdrawal of a general partner; and

(13) any other matters the partners, in their sole discretion, determine to include therein.

(b) A limited partnership is formed at the time of the filing of the certificate of limited partnership in the office of the Secretary of State or at any later time specified in the certificate of limited partnership if, in each case, there has been substantial compliance with the requirements of this section.

Sec. 202. (Amendments to Certificate.)

(a) A certificate of limited partnership is amended by filing a certificate of amendment thereto in the office of the Secretary of State. The certificate shall set forth:

(1) the name of the limited partnership;

(2) the date of filing of the certificate; and

(3) the amendments to the certificate.

(b) Within 30 days after the happening of any of the following events an amendment to a certificate of limited partnership reflecting the occurrence of the event or events shall be filed:

(1) a change in the amount or character of the contribution of any partner, or in any partner's obligation to make a contribution;

(2) the admission of a new partner;

(3) the withdrawal of a partner; and

(4) the continuation of the business under Section 801 after an event of withdrawal of a general partner.

(c) A certificate of limited partnership must be amended promptly by any general partner upon becoming aware that any statement therein was false when made or that any arrangements or other facts described have changed, making the certificate inaccurate in any respect, but amendments to show changes of addresses of limited partners need be filed only once every 12 months.

(d) A certificate of limited partnership may be amended at any time for any other proper purpose the general partners may determine.

(e) No person shall have any liability because an amendment to a certificate of limited partnership has not been filed to reflect the occurrence of any event referred to in subsection (b) of this section if the amendment is filed within the 30-day period specified in subsection (b).

Sec. 203. (Cancellation of Certificate.) A certificate of limited partnership shall be cancelled upon the dissolution and the commencement of winding up of the limited partnership and at any other time there are no remaining limited partners. A certificate of cancellation shall be filed in the office of the Secretary of State and shall set forth:

(1) the name of the limited partnership;

(2) the date of filing of its certificate of limited partnership;

(3) the reason for filing the certificate of cancellation;

(4) the effective date (which shall be a date certain) of cancellation if it is not to be effective upon the filing of the certificate; and

(5) any other information the general partners filing the certificate may determine.

Sec. 204. (Execution of Certificates.)

(a) Each certificate required by this Article to be filed in the office of the Secretary of State shall be executed in the following manner:

(1) each original certificate of limited partnership must be signed by each partner named therein;

(2) each certificate of amendment must be signed by at least one general partner and by each other partner who is designated in the certificate as a new partner or whose contribution is described as having been increased; and

(3) each certificate of cancellation must be signed by each general partner.

(b) Any person may sign a certificate by an attorney-in-fact, but any power of attorney to sign a certificate relating to the admission or increased contribution of a partner must specifically describe the admission or increase.

(c) The execution of a certificate by a general partner constitutes an affirmation under the penalties of perjury that the facts stated therein are true.

Sec. 205. (Amendment or Cancellation by Judicial Act.) If the persons required by Section 204 to execute any certificate of amendment or cancellation fail or refuse to do so, any other partner, and any assignee of a partnership interest, who is adversely affected by the failure or refusal, may petition the [here designate the proper court] to direct the amendment or cancellation. If the court finds that the amendment or cancellation is proper and that the persons so designated have failed or refused to execute the certificate, it shall order the Secretary of State to record an appropriate certificate of amendment or cancellation.

Sec. 206. (Filing in the Office of the Secretary of State.)

(a) Two signed copies of the certificate of limited partnership and of any certificates of amendment or cancellation (or of any judicial decree of amendment or cancellation) shall be delivered to the Secretary of State. A person who executes a certificate as an agent or fiduciary need not exhibit evidence of his authority as a prerequisite to filing. Unless the Secretary of State finds that any certificate does not conform to law, upon receipt of all filing fees required by law the Secretary of State shall:

(1) endorse on each duplicate original the word "Filed" and the day, month, and year of the filing thereof;

(2) file one duplicate original in his office; and

(3) return the other duplicate original to the person who filed it or his representative.

(b) Upon the filing of a certificate of amendment (or judicial decree of amendment) in the office of the Secretary of State, the certificate of limited partnership shall be amended as set forth therein, and upon the effective date of a certificate of cancellation (or a judicial decree thereof), the certificate of limited partnership shall be cancelled.

Sec. 207. (Liability for False Statement in Certificate.) If any certificate of limited partnership or certificate of amendment or cancellation contains a false statement, one who suffers loss by reliance on the statement may recover damages for the loss from:

(1) any person actually executing, or causing another to execute on his behalf, the certificate who knew, and any general partner who knew or should have known, the statement to be false at the time the certificate was executed; and

(2) any general partner who thereafter knew or should have known that any arrangements or other facts described in the certificate have changed, making the statement inaccurate in any respect, within a sufficient time before the statement was relied upon to have reasonably enabled that general partner to cancel or amend the certificate, or to file a petition for its cancellation or amendment under Section 205.

Sec. 208. **(Constructive Notice.)** The fact that a certificate of limited partnership is on file in the office of the Secretary of State is constructive notice that the partnership is a limited partnership and that the persons designated therein as limited partners are limited partners, but is not constructive notice of any other fact.

Sec. 209. **(Delivery of Certificates to Limited Partners.)** Upon the return by the Secretary of State pursuant to Section 206 of any certificate marked "Filed," the general partners shall promptly deliver or mail a copy of the certificate to each limited partner unless the partnership agreement provides otherwise.

ARTICLE 3

LIMITED PARTNERS

Sec. 301 (Admission of Additional Limited Partners.)

(a) After the filing of a limited partnership's original certificate of limited partnership, a person may be admitted as a new limited partner:

(1) in the case of a person acquiring a partnership interest directly from the limited partnership, upon compliance with the partnership agreement or, if the partnership agreement does not so provide, upon the written consent of all partners; and

(2) in the case of an assignee of a partnership interest of a partner who has the power, as provided in Section 704, to grant the assignee the right to become a limited partner, upon the exercise of that power and compliance with any conditions limiting the grant or exercise of the power.

(b) In each case under subsection (a), the person acquiring the partnership interest becomes a limited partner only upon amendment of the certificate of limited partnership reflecting that fact.

Sec. 302. **(Voting.)** Subject to the provisions of Section 303, the partnership agreement may grant to all or a specified group of the limited partners the right to vote (on a per capita or any other basis) upon any matter.

Sec. 303. **(Liability to Third Parties.)**

(a) Except as provided in subsection (d), a limited partner as such is not liable for the obligations of a limited partnership unless, in addition to the exercise of his rights and powers as a limited partner, he takes part in the control of the business. But the limited partner's participation in the control of the business is not substantially the same as the exercise of the powers of a general partner, he is liable only to persons who transact business with the limited partnership with actual knowledge of his participation in control.

(b) A limited partner does not participate in the control of the business within the meaning of subsection (a) solely by doing one or more of the following:

(1) being a contractor for or an agent or employee of a limited partnership or of a general partner;

(2) consulting with and advising a general partner with respect to the business of the limited partnership;

(3) acting as surety for the limited partnership;

(4) approving or disapproving an amendment to the partnership agreement; and

(5) voting on one or more of the following matters:

(i) the dissolution and winding up of the limited partnership;

(ii) the sale, exchange, lease, mortgage, pledge, or other transfer of all or substantially all of the assets of the limited partnership other than in the ordinary course of its business;

(iii) the incurrence of indebtedness by the limited partnership other than in the ordinary course of its business;

(iv) a change in the nature of the business; or

(v) the removal of a general partner.

(c) The enumeration in subsection (b) shall not be construed to mean that the possession or exercise of any other powers by a limited partner constitutes participation by him in the business of the limited partnership.

(d) A limited partner who knowingly permits his name to be used in the name of the limited partnership, except under circumstances permitted by Section 102(2)(i), is liable to creditors who extend credit to the limited partnership without actual knowledge that the limited partner is not a general partner.

Sec. 304. (Person Erroneously Believing Himself a Limited Partner.)

(a) Except as provided in subsection (b) a person who makes a contribution to a business enterprise and erroneously and in good faith believes that he has become a limited partner in the enterprise is not a general partner in the enterprise and is not bound by its obligations by reason of making the contribution, receiving distributions from the enterprise, or exercising any rights of a limited partner, if, on ascertaining the mistake, he:

(1) causes an appropriate certificate of limited partnership or a certificate of amendment to be executed and filed; or

(2) withdraws from future equity participation in the enterprise.

(b) Any person who makes a contribution of the kind described in subsection (a) is liable as a general partner to any third party who transacts business with the enterprise (i) before the person withdraws and an appropriate certificate if any is filed to show the withdrawal, or (ii) before an appropriate certificate is filed to show his status as a limited partner and, in the case of an amendment, after expiration of the 30-day period for filing an amendment relating to the person as a limited partner under Section 202, but in each case only if the third party actually believed in good faith that the person was a general partner at the time of the transaction.

Sec. 305. (Information.) Each limited partner has the right to:

(1) inspect and copy any of the partnership records required to be maintained by Section 105; and

(2) obtain from the general partners from time to time upon reasonable demand (i) true and full information regarding the state of the business and financial condition of the limited partnership, (ii) promptly after becoming available, a copy of the limited partnership's federal, state, and local income tax return for each year, and (iii) any other information regarding the affairs of the limited partnership as is just and reasonable.

ARTICLE 4

GENERAL PARTNERS

Sec. 401. (Admission.)
After the filing of a limited partnership's original certificate of limited partnership, new general partners may be admitted only with the specific written consent of each partner.

Sec. 402. (Events of Withdrawal.)
Except as otherwise approved by the specific written consent at the time of all partners, a person ceases to be a general partner of a limited partnership upon the happening of any of the following events:

(1) the general partner withdraws from the limited partnership as provided in Section 602;

(2) the general partner ceases to be a member of the limited partnership as provided in Section 702;

(3) the general partner is removed as a gen-

eral partner in accordance with the partnership agreement;

(4) unless otherwise provided in the certificate of limited partnership, the general partner: makes an assignment for the benefit of creditors; files a voluntary petition in bankruptcy; is adjudicated a bankrupt or insolvent; files any petition or answer seeking for himself any reorganization, arrangement, composition, readjustment, liquidation, dissolution, or similar relief under any statute, law, or regulation; files any answer or other pleading admitting or failing to contest the material allegations of a petition filed against him in any proceeding of this nature; or seeks, consents to, or acquiesces in the appointment of any trustee, receiver, or liquidator of the general partner or of all or any substantial part of his properties;

(5) unless otherwise provided in the certificate of limited partnership, [120] days after the commencement of any proceeding against the general partner seeking any reorganization, arrangement, composition, readjustment, liquidation, dissolution, or similar relief under any statute, law, or regulation, the proceeding has not been dismissed, or if, within [90] days after the appointment without his consent or acquiescence of any trustee, receiver, or liquidator of the general partner or of all or any substantial part of his properties, the appointment is not vacated or stayed, or if, within [90] days after the expiration of any stay, the appointment is not vacated;

(6) in the case of a general partner who is a natural person

(i) his death; or

(ii) the entry by a court of competent jurisdiction adjudicating him incompetent to manage his person or his property;

(7) in the case of a general partner who is acting as such in the capacity of a trustee of a trust, the termination of the trust (but not merely the substitution of a new trustee);

(8) in the case of a general partner that is a partnership, the dissolution and commencement of winding up of the partnership;

(9) in the case of a general partner that is a corporation, the filing of a certificate of dissolution, or its equivalent, for the corporation or the revocation of its charter; and

(10) in the case of an estate, the distribution by the fiduciary of all of the estate's interest in the partnership.

Sec. 403.   (General Powers and Liabilities.) Except as otherwise provided in this Act and in the partnership agreement, a general partner of a limited partnership has all the rights and powers and is subject to all the restrictions and liabilities of a partner in a partnership without limited partners.

Sec. 404.   (Contributions by a General Partner.)   A general partner may make contributions to a limited partnership and share in the profits and losses of, and in distributions from, the limited partnership as a general partner. A general partner may also make contributions to and share in profits, losses, and distributions as a limited partner. A person who is both a general partner and a limited partner has all the rights and powers, and is subject to all the restrictions and liabilities, of a general partner and also has, except as otherwise provided in the partnership agreement, all powers, and is subject to the restrictions, of a limited partner to the extent he is participating in the partnership as a limited partner.

Sec. 405.   (Voting.) The partnership agreement may grant to all or a specified group of general partners the right to vote (on a per capita or any other basis), separately or with all or any class of the limited partners, on any matter.

ARTICLE 5

FINANCE

Sec. 501.   (Form of Contributions.) The contribution of a partner may be in cash, property, or services rendered, or a promissory note or other obligation to contribute cash or property or to perform services.

Sec. 502. (Liability for Contributions.)

(a) Except as otherwise provided in the certificate of limited partnership, a partner is obligated to the limited partnership to perform any promise to contribute cash or property or to perform services regardless of whether he is unable to perform because of death, disability or any other reason. If a partner does not make the required contribution of property or services, he is obligated at the option of the limited partnership to contribute cash equal to that portion of the value (as stated in the certificate of limited partnership) of the stated contribution that has not been made.

(b) Unless otherwise provided in the partnership agreement, the obligation of a partner to make a contribution or return money or other property paid or distributed in violation of this Act may be compromised only by consent of all of the partners. Notwithstanding a compromise so authorized, a creditor of a limited partnership who extends credit, or whose claim arises, after the filing of the certificate of limited partnership or an amendment thereto which, in either case, reflects the obligation and before the amendment or cancellation thereof to reflect the compromise may enforce the precompromise obligation.

Sec. 503. (Sharing of Profits and Losses.) The profits and losses of a limited partnership shall be allocated among the partners, and among classes of partners, in the manner provided in the partnership agreement. If the partnership agreement does not so provide, profits and losses shall be allocated on the basis of the value (as stated in the certificate of limited partnership) of the contributions actually made by each partner to the extent they have not been returned.

Sec. 504. (Sharing of Distributions.) Distributions of cash or other assets of a limited partnership shall be allocated among the partners, and among classes of partners, in the manner provided in the partnership agreement. If the partnership agreement does not so provide, distributions shall be made on the basis of the value (as stated in the certificate of limited partnership) of the contributions actually made by each partner to the extent they have not been returned.

ARTICLE 6

DISTRIBUTIONS AND WITHDRAWAL

Sec. 601. (Interim Distributions.) Except as otherwise provided in this Article, a partner is entitled to receive distributions from a limited partnership before his withdrawal from the limited partnership and before the dissolution and winding up thereof:

(1) to the extent and at the times or upon the happening of the events specified in the partnership agreement; and

(2) if any distribution constitutes a return of any part of his contribution under Section 608(b), to the extent and at the times or upon the happening of the events specified in the certificate of limited partnership.

Sec. 602. (Withdrawal of General Partner.) A general partner may withdraw from a limited partnership at any time by giving written notice to the other partners, but if the withdrawal violates the partnership agreement, the limited partnership may recover from the withdrawing general partner damages for breach of the partnership agreement and offset the damages against the amount otherwise distributable to him.

Sec. 603. (Withdrawal of Limited Partner.) A limited partner may withdraw from a limited partnership at the time or upon the happening of the events specified in the certificate of limited partnership and in accordance with any procedures provided in the partnership agreement. If the certificate of limited partnership does not specify the time or the events upon the happening of which a limited partner may withdraw from the limited partnership or a definite time for the dissolution and winding up of the limited partnership, a limited partner may withdraw from the limited partnership upon not less than 6 months' prior written notice to each general partner at his address on the books of the limited partnership at its office in this State.

Sec. 604. (Distributions Upon Withdrawal.) Except as provided in this Article, upon withdrawal any withdrawing partner is entitled to receive any distributions to which he is entitled under the partnership agreement and, if not provided, he is entitled to receive, within a reasonable time after withdrawal, the fair value of his interest in the limited partnership as of the date of withdrawal, based upon his right to share in distributions from the limited partnership.

Sec. 605. (Distributions in Kind.) Except as provided in the certificate of limited partnership, a partner, regardless of the nature of his contribution, has no right to demand and receive any distribution from a limited partnership in any form other than cash. Except as provided in the partnership agreement, a partner may not be compelled to accept a distribution of any asset in kind from a limited partnership to the extent that the percentage of the asset distributed to him exceeds a percentage of that asset which is equal to the percentage in which he shares in distributions from the limited partnership.

Sec. 606. (Right to Distributions.) At the time a partner becomes entitled to receive a distribution, he has the status of, and is entitled to all of the remedies available to, a creditor of the limited partnership with respect to the distribution.

Sec. 607. (Limitations on Distributions.) A partner may not receive a distribution from a limited partnership to the extent that, after giving effect to the distribution, all liabilities of the limited partnership other than liabilities to partners on account of their partnership interests, exceed the fair value of the partnership's assets.

Sec. 608. (Liability Upon Return of Contributions.)

(a) If a partner has received the return of any part of his contribution without violation of the partnership agreement or this Act, for a period of one year thereafter he is liable to the limited partnership for the amount of his contribution returned, but only to the extent necessary to discharge the limited partnership's liabilities to creditors who extended credit to the limited partnership during the period the contribution was held by the partnership.

(b) If a partner has received the return of any part of his contribution in violation of the partnership agreement or this Act, for a period of 6 years thereafter he is liable to the limited partnership for the amount of the contribution wrongfully returned.

(c) A partner has received a return of his contribution to the extent that a distribution to him reduces his share of the fair value of the net assets of the limited partnership below the value (as set forth in the certificate of limited partnership) of his contributions which have not theretofore been distributed to him.

ARTICLE 7

ASSIGNMENT OF PARTNERSHIP INTERESTS

Sec. 701. (Nature of Partnership Interest.) A partnership interest is a partner's share of the profits and losses of a limited partnership and the right to receive distributions of partnership assets. A partnership interest is personal property.

Sec. 702. (Assignment of Partnership Interest.) Except as otherwise provided in the partnership agreement, a partnership interest is assignable in whole or in part. An assignment of a partnership interest does not dissolve a limited partnership nor entitle the assignee to become a partner or to exercise any of the rights thereof. An assignment only entitles the assignee to receive, to the extent assigned, any distributions to which the assignor would be entitled. Except as otherwise provided in the partnership agreement, a partner ceases to be a partner upon assignment of all his partnership interest.

Sec. 703. (Rights of Creditors.) On due application to a court of competent jurisdiction by any judgment creditor of a partner, the court may charge the partnership interest of the partner with payment of the unsatisfied amount of the judgment debt with interest thereon. To the extent so charged, the judgment creditor has only the rights of an assignee of the partnership interest. This Act shall not be construed to deprive any partner of the benefit of any exemption laws applicable to his partnership interest.

Sec. 704. (Right of Assignee to Become Limited Partner.)

(a) An assignee of a partnership interest, including an assignee of a general partner, may become a limited partner if and to the extent that (1) the assignor gives the assignee that right in accordance with authority described in the certificate of limited partnership or, (2) in the absence of that authority, all other partners consent.

(b) An assignee who has become a limited partner has, to the extent assigned, all the rights and powers, and is subject to all the restrictions and liabilities, of a limited partner under the partnership agreement and this Act. An assignee who becomes a limited partner is also liable for the obligations of his assignor to make and return contributions as provided in Article 6, but the assignee is not obligated for liabilities unknown to the assignee at the time he became a limited partner and which could not be ascertained from the certificate of limited partnership.

(c) If an assignee of a partnership interest becomes a limited partner, the assignor is not released from the liability to the limited partnership under Sections 207 and 502.

Sec. 705. (Power of Estate of Deceased or Incompetent Partner.) If a partner who is a natural person dies or a court of competent jurisdiction adjudges him to be incompetent to manage his person or his property, the partner's executor, administrator, guardian, conservator, or other legal representative may exercise all of the partner's rights for the purpose of settling his estate or administering his property, including any power the partner had to give an assignee the right to become a limited partner. If a partner that is a corporation, trust, or other entity other than a natural person is dissolved or terminated, those powers may be exercised by the legal representative or successor of the partner.

ARTICLE 8

DISSOLUTION

Sec. 801. (Nonjudicial Dissolution.) A limited partnership is dissolved and its affairs shall be wound up upon the happening of the first to occur of the following:

(1) at the time or upon the happening of the events specified in the certificate of limited partnership;

(2) upon the unanimous written consent of all partners;

(3) upon the happening of an event of withdrawal of a general partner unless at the time there is at least one other general partner and the certificate of limited partnership permits the business of the limited partnership to be carried on by the remaining general partner and he does so, but the limited partnership shall not be dissolved or wound up by reason of any event of withdrawal if, within 90 days after the withdrawal, all partners agree in writing to continue the business of the limited partnership and to the appointment of one or more new general partners if necessary or desired; or

(4) upon entry of a decree of judicial dissolution in accordance with Section 802.

Sec. 802. (Dissolution by Decree of Court.) On application by or for a partner the [here designate the proper court] court may decree a dissolution of a limited partnership whenever it is not reasonably practicable to carry on the business in conformity with the partnership agreement.

Sec. 803. (Winding Up.) Unless otherwise provided in the partnership agreement, the general partners who have not wrongfully dissolved the limited partnership or, if none, the limited partners, may wind up the limited partnership's affairs; but any partner, his legal representative or his assignee, upon cause shown, may obtain winding up by the [here designate the proper court] court.

Sec. 804. (Distribution of Assets.) Upon the winding up of a limited partnership, the assets shall be distributed as follows:

(1) to creditors, including partners who are creditors (to the extent otherwise permitted by law), in satisfaction of liabilities of the limited partnership other than liabilities for distribu-tions to partners pursuant to Section 601 or 604;

(2) except as otherwise provided in the partnership agreement, to partners and ex-partners in satisfaction of liabilities for distri-butions pursuant to Section 601 or 604; and

(3) except as otherwise provided in the partnership agreement, to partners *first* for the return of their contributions and *second* re-specting their partnership interests, in the proportions in which the partners share in dis-tributions.

ARTICLE 9

FOREIGN LIMITED PARTNERSHIPS

Sec. 901. (Law Governing.) Subject to the constitution and public policy of this State, the laws of the state under which a foreign limited partnership is organized govern its organization and internal affairs and the lia-bility of its limited partners, and a foreign limited partnership may not be denied registra-tion by reason of any difference betwen those laws and the laws of this state.

Sec. 902. (Registration.) Before transact-ing business in this State, a foreign limited partnership shall register with the Secretary of State. In order to register, a foreign limited partnership shall submit to the Secretary of State in duplicate an application for registra-tion as a foreign limited partnership, signed and sworn to by a general partner and setting forth:

(1) the name of the foreign limited partner-ship and, if different, the name under which it proposes to transact business and register in this State;

(2) the state and date of its formation;

(3) the general character of the business it proposes to transact in this State;

(4) the name and address of any agent for service of process on the foreign limited part-nership whom the foreign limited partnership desires to appoint, which agent must be an individual resident of this State, a domestic corporation, or a foreign corporation author-ized to do business in this State; and with a place of business in this State;

(5) a statement that the Secretary of State is appointed the agent of the foreign limited partnership for service of process if no agent has been appointed pursuant to paragraph (4) or, if appointed the agent's authority has been revoked or the agent cannot be found or served with the exercise of reasonable diligence;

(6) the address of the office required to be maintained in the state of its organization by the laws of that state or, if not so required, of the principal office of the foreign limited part-nership; and

(7) if the certificate of limited partnership filed in the foreign limited partnerships' state of organization is not required to include the names and business addresses of the partners, or list of the names and addresses.

Sec. 903. (Issuance of Registration.)

(a) If the Secretary of State finds that an application for registration conforms to law and all requisite fees have been paid, he shall:

(1) endorse on the application the word "Filed," and the month, day, and year of the filing thereof;

(2) file in his office one of the duplicate originals of the application; and

(3) issue a certificate of registration to transact business in this State.

(b) The certificate of registration, together with one duplicate original of the application, shall be returned to the person who filed the application or his representative.

Sec. 904. (Name.) A foreign limited part-nership may register with the Secretary of State under any name (whether or not it is the name under which it is registered in its state of organization) that includes the words "limited partnership" and that could be registered by a domestic limited partnership.

Sec. 905. (Changes and Amendments.) If any statement in a foreign limited partnership's application for registration was false when made or any arrangements or other facts described have changed, making the application inaccurate in any respect, the foreign limited partnership shall promptly file in the office of the Secretary of State a certificate, signed and sworn to by a general partner, correcting the statement.

Sec. 906. (Cancellation of Registration.) A foreign limited partnership may cancel its registration by filing with the Secretary of State a certificate of cancellation signed and sworn to by a general partner. A cancellation does not terminate the authority of the Secretary of State to accept service of process on the foreign limited partnership with respect to [claims for relief] [causes of action] arising out of the transaction of business in this State.

Sec. 907. (Transaction of Business Without Registration.) (a) A foreign limited partnership transacting business in this State without registration may not maintain any action, suit, or proceeding in any court of this State until it has registered.

(b) The failure of a foreign limited partnership to register in this State does not impair the validity of any contract or act of the foreign limited partnership, and does not prevent the foreign limited partnership from defending any action, suit, or proceeding in any court of this State.

(c) A limited partner of a foreign limited partnership is not liable as a general partner of the foreign limited partnership solely by reason of the foreign limited partnership's transacting business in this State without registration.

(d) A foreign limited partnership, by transacting business in this State without registration, appoints the Secretary of State as its agent for service of process with respect to [claims for relief] [causes of action] arising out of the transaction of business in this State.

Sec. 908. (Action by [Appropriate Official].) The [appropriate official] may bring an action to restrain a foreign limited partnership from transacting business in this State in violation of this Article.

ARTICLE 10

DERIVATIVE ACTIONS

Sec. 1001. (Right of Action.) A limited partner may bring an action in the right of a limited partnership to recover a judgment in its favor if the general partners having authority to do so have refused to bring the action or an effort to cause those general partners to bring the action is not likely to succeed.

Sec. 1002. (Proper Plaintiff.) In a derivative action, the plaintiff must be a partner at (1) the time of bringing the action, and (2) at the time of the transaction of which he complains or his status as a partner must have devolved upon him by operation of law or pursuant to the terms of the partnership agreement from a person who was a partner at the time of the transaction.

Sec. 1003. (Pleading.) In any derivative action, the complaint shall set forth with particularity the effort of the plaintiff to secure initiation of the action by a general partner having authority to do so or the reasons for not making the effort.

Sec. 1004. (Expenses.) If a derivative action is successful, in whole or in part, or anything is received by the plaintiff as a result of a judgment, compromise, or settlement of an action or claim, the court may award the plaintiff reasonable expenses, including reasonable attorney's fees, and shall direct him to account to the limited partnership for the remainder of the proceeds so received by him.

ARTICLE 11

MISCELLANEOUS

Sec. 1101.   (Savings Clause.)

Sec. 1102.   (Name of Act.)   This Act may be cited as the Uniform Limited Partnership Act.

Sec. 1103.   (Construction and Application.) This Act shall be so construed and applied to effect its general purpose to make uniform the law with respect to the subject of this Act among states enacting it.

Sec. 1104.   (Rules for Cases Not Provided for in This Act.)   In any case not provided for in this Act the provisions of the Uniform Partnership Act govern.

Sec. 1105.   (Act   Repealed.) Except as affecting existing limited partnerships to the extent set forth in Section ——, the Act of [here designate the existing limited partnership act or acts] is hereby repealed.

E

Model Business Corporation Act

1. Short Title

This Act shall be known and may be cited as the " . . . . . . * Business Corporation Act."

2. Definitions

As used in this Act, unless the context otherwise requires, the term:

(a) "Corporation" or "domestic corporation" means a corporation for profit subject to the provisions of this Act, except a foreign corporation.

(b) "Foreign corporation" means a corporation for profit organized under laws other than the laws of this State for a purpose or purposes for which a corporation may be organized under this Act.

(c) "Articles of incorporation" means the original or restated articles of incorporation or articles of consolidation and all amendments thereto including articles of merger.

(d) "Shares" means the units into which the proprietary interests in a corporation are divided.

(e) "Subscriber" means one who subscribes for shares in a corporation, whether before or after incorporation.

(f) "Shareholder" means one who is a holder of record of shares in a corporation. If the articles of incorporation or the by-laws so provide, the board of directors may adopt by resolution a procedure whereby a shareholder of the corporation may certify in writing to the corporation that all or a portion of the shares registered in the name of such shareholder are held for the account of a specified person or persons. The resolution shall set forth (1) the classification of shareholders who may certify, (2) the purpose or purposes for which the certification may be made, (3) the form of certification and information to be contained therein, (4) if the certification is with respect to a record date or closing of the stock transfer books, the time after the record date or closing of the stock transfer books within which the certification must be received by the corporation and (5) such other provisions with respect to the procedure as are deemed necessary or desirable. Upon receipt by the corporation of a certification complying with the procedure, the persons specified in the certification shall be deemed, for the purpose or purposes set forth in the certification, to be the holders of record

A147

of the number of shares specified in place of the shareholder making the certification.

(g) "Authorized shares" means the shares of all classes which the corporation is authorized to issue.

(h) "Treasury shares" means shares of a corporation which have been issued, have been subsequently acquired by and belong to the corporation, and have not, either by reason of the acquisition or thereafter, been cancelled or restored to the status of authorized but unissued shares. Treasury shares shall be deemed to be "issued" shares, but not "outstanding" shares.

(i) "Net assets" means the amount by which the total assets of a corporation exceed the total debts of the corporation.

(j) "Stated capital" means, at any particular time, the sum of (1) the par value of all shares of the corporation having a par value that have been issued, (2) the amount of the consideration received by the corporation for all shares of the corporation without par value that have been issued, except such part of the consideration therefor as may have been allocated to capital surplus in a manner permitted by law, and (3) such amounts not included in clauses (1) and (2) of this paragraph as have been transferred to stated capital of the corporation, whether upon the issue of shares as a share dividend or otherwise, minus all reductions from such sum as have been effected in a manner permitted by law. Irrespective of the manner of designation thereof by the laws under which a foreign corporation is organized, the stated capital of a foreign corporation shall be determined on the same basis and in the same manner as the stated capital of a domestic corporation, for the purpose of computing fees, franchise taxes and other charges imposed by this Act.

(k) "Surplus" means the excess of the net assets of a corporation over its stated capital.

(l) "Earned surplus" means the portion of the surplus of a corporation equal to the balance of its net profits, income, gains and losses from the date of incorporation, or from the latest date when a deficit was eliminated by an application of its capital surplus or stated capital or otherwise, after deducting subsequent distributions to shareholders and transfers to stated capital and capital surplus to the extent such distributions and transfers are made out of earned surplus. Earned surplus shall include also any portion of surplus allocated to earned surplus in mergers, consolidations or acquisitions of all or substantially all of the outstanding shares or of the property and assets of another corporation, domestic or foreign.

(m) "Capital surplus" means the entire surplus of a corporation other than its earned surplus.

(n) "Insolvent" means inability of a corporation to pay its debts as they become due in the usual course of its business.

(o) "Employee" includes officers but not directors. A director may accept duties which make him also an employee.

3. Purposes

Corporations may be organized under this Act for any lawful purpose or purposes, except for the purpose of banking or insurance.

4. General Powers

Each corporation shall have power:

(a) To have perpetual succession by its corporate name unless a limited period of duration is stated in its articles of incorporation.

(b) To sue and be sued, complain and defend, in its corporate name.

(c) To have a corporate seal which may be altered at pleasure, and to use the same by causing it, or a facsimile thereof, to be impressed or affixed or in any other manner reproduced.

(d) To purchase, take, receive, lease, or otherwise acquire, own, hold, improve, use and otherwise deal in and with, real or personal property, or any interest therein, wherever situated.

(e) To sell, convey, mortgage, pledge, lease, exchange, transfer and otherwise dispose of all or any part of its property and assets.

(f) To lend money and use its credit to assist its employees.

(g) To purchase, take, receive, subscribe for, or otherwise acquire, own, hold, vote, use, employ, sell, mortgage, lend, pledge, or otherwise dispose of, and otherwise use and deal in and with, shares or other interests in, or obligations of, other domestic or foreign corporations, associations, partnerships or individuals, or direct or indirect obligations of the United States or of any other government, state, territory, governmental district or municipality or of any instrumentality thereof.

(h) To make contracts and guarantees and incur liabilities, borrow money at such rates of interest as the corporation may determine, issue its notes, bonds, and other obligations, and secure any of its obligations by mortgage or pledge of all or any of its property, franchises and income.

(i) To lend money for its corporate purposes, invest and reinvest its funds, and take and hold real and personal property as security for the payment of funds so loaned or invested.

(j) To conduct its business, carry on its operations and have offices and exercise the powers granted by this Act, within or without this State.

(k) To elect or appoint officers and agents of the corporation, and define their duties and fix their compensation.

(l) To make and alter by-laws, not inconsistent with its articles of incorporation or with the laws of this State, for the administration and regulation of the affairs of the corporation.

(m) To make donations for the public welfare or for charitable, scientific or educational purposes.

(n) To transact any lawful business which the board of directors shall find will be in aid of governmental policy.

(o) To pay pensions and establish pension plans, pension trusts, profit sharing plans, stock bonus plans, stock option plans and other incentive plans for any or all of its directors, officers and employees.

(p) To be a promoter, partner, member, associate, or manager of any partnership, joint venture, trust or other enterprise.

(q) To have and exercise all powers necessary or convenient to effect its purposes.

5. Indemnification of Officers, Directors, Employees, and Agents

(a) A corporation shall have power to indemnify any person who was or is a party or is threatened to be made a party to any threatened, pending or completed action, suit or proceeding, whether civil, criminal, administrative or investigative (other than an action by or in the right of the corporation) by reason of the fact that he is or was a director, officer, employee or agent of the corporation, or is or was serving at the request of the corporation as a director, officer, employee or agent of another corporation, partnership, joint venture, trust or other enterprise, against expenses (including attorneys' fees), judgments, fines and amounts paid in settlement actually and reasonably incurred by him in connection with such action, suit or proceeding if he acted in good faith and in a manner he reasonably believed to be in or not opposed to the best interests of the corporation, and, with respect to any criminal action or proceeding, had no reasonable cause to believe his conduct was unlawful. The termination of any action, suit or proceeding by judgment, order, settlement, conviction, or upon a plea of nolo contendere or its equivalent, shall not, of itself, create a presumption that the person did not act in good faith and in a manner which he reasonably believed to be in or not opposed to the best interests of the corporation, and, with respect to any criminal action or proceeding, had reasonable cause to believe that his conduct was unlawful.

(b) A corporation shall have power to indemnify any person who was or is a party or is threatened to be made a party to any threatened, pending or completed action or suit by or in the right of the corporation to procure a judgment in its favor by reason of the fact that he is or was a director, officer, employee or agent of the corporation, or is or was serving at the request of the corporation as a director, officer, employee or agent of another corporation, partnership, joint venture, trust or other enterprise against expenses (including attorneys' fees) actually and reasonably incurred by him in connection with the defense or settlement of such action or suit if he acted in good faith and in a manner he reasonably believed to be in or not opposed to the best interests of the corporation and except that no indemnification shall be made in respect of any claim, issue or matter as to which such person shall have been adjudged to be liable for negligence or misconduct in the performance of his duty to the corporation unless and only to the extent that the court in which such action or suit was brought shall determine upon application that, despite the adjudication of liability but in view of all circumstances of the case, such person is fairly and reasonably entitled to indemnity for such expenses which such court shall deem proper.

(c) To the extent that a director, officer, employee or agent of a corporation has been successful on the merits or otherwise in defense of any action, suit or proceeding referred to in subsections (a) or (b), or in defense of any claim, issue or matter therein, he shall be indemnified against expenses (including attorneys' fees) actually and reasonably incurred by him in connection therewith.

(d) Any indemnification under subsections (a) or (b) (unless ordered by a court) shall be made by the corporation only as authorized in the specific case upon a determination that indemnification of the director, officer, employee or agent is proper in the circumstances because he has met the applicable standard of conduct set forth in subsections (a) or (b). Such determination shall be made (1) by the board of directors by a majority vote of a quorum consisting of directors who were not parties to such action, suit or proceeding, or (2) if such a quorum is not obtainable, or, even if obtainable a quorum of disinterested directors so directs, by independent legal counsel in a written opinion, or (3) by the shareholders.

(e) Expenses (including attorneys' fees) incurred in defending a civil or criminal action, suit or proceeding may be paid by the corporation in advance of the final disposition of such action, suit or proceeding as authorized in the manner provided in subsection (d) upon receipt of an undertaking by or on behalf of the directors, officers, employee or agent to repay such amount unless it shall ultimately be determined that he is entitled to be indemnified by the corporation as authorized in this section.

(f) The indemnification provided by this section shall not be deemed exclusive of any other rights to which those indemnified may be entitled under any by-law, agreement, vote of shareholders or disinterested directors or otherwise, both as to action in his official capacity and as to action in another capacity while holding such office, and shall continue as to a person who has ceased to be a director, officer, employee or agent and shall inure to the benefit of the heirs, executors and administrators of such a person.

(g) A corporation shall have power to purchase and maintain insurance on behalf of any person who is or was a director, officer, employee or agent of the corporation, or is or was serving at the request of the corporation as a director, officer, employee or agent of another corporation, partnership, joint venture, trust or other enterprise against any liability asserted against him and incurred by him in any such capacity or arising out of his status as such, whether or not the corporation would have the power to indemnify him against such liability under the provisions of this section.

6. Right of Corporation to Acquire and Dispose of Its Own Shares

A corporation shall have the right to purchase, take, receive or otherwise acquire, hold, own, pledge, transfer or otherwise dispose of its own shares, but purchases of its own shares, whether direct or indirect, shall be made only to the extent of unreserved and unrestricted earned surplus available therefor, and, if the articles of incorporation so permit or with the affirmative vote of the holders of a majority of all shares entitled to vote thereon, to the extent of unreserved and unrestricted capital surplus available therefor.

To the extent that earned surplus or capital surplus is used as the measure of the corporation's right to purchase its own shares, such surplus shall be restricted so long as such shares are held as treasury shares, and upon the disposition or cancellation of any such shares the restriction shall be removed pro tanto.

Notwithstanding the foregoing limitation, a corporation may purchase or otherwise acquire its own shares for the purpose of:

(a) Eliminating fractional shares.

(b) Collecting or compromising indebtedness to the corporation.

(c) Paying dissenting shareholders entitled to payment for their shares under the provisions of this Act.

(d) Effecting, subject to the other provisions of this Act, the retirement of its redeemable shares by redemption or by purchase at not to exceed the redemption price.

No purchase of or payment for its own shares shall be made at a time when the corporation is insolvent or when such purchase or payment would make it insolvent.

7. Defense of Ultra Vires

No act of a corporation and no conveyance or transfer of real or personal property to or by a corporation shall be invalid by reason of the fact that the corporation was without capacity or power to do such act or to make or receive such conveyance or transfer, but such lack of capacity or power may be asserted:

(a) In a proceeding by a shareholder against the corporation to enjoin the doing of any act or the transfer of real or personal property by or to the corporation. If the unauthorized act or transfer sought to be enjoined is being, or is to be, performed or made pursuant to a contract to which the corporation is a party, the court may, if all of the parties to the contract are parties to the proceeding and if it deems the same to be equitable, set aside and enjoin the performance of such contract, and in so doing may allow to the corporation or to the other parties to the contract, as the case may be, compensation for the loss or damage sustained by either of them which may result from the action of the court in setting aside and enjoining the performance of such contract, but anticipated profits to be derived from the performance of the contract shall not be awarded by the court as a loss or damage sustained.

(b) In a proceeding by the corporation, whether acting directly or through a receiver, trustee, or other legal representative, or through shareholders in a representative suit, against the incumbent or former officers or directors of the corporation.

(c) In a proceeding by the Attorney General, as provided in this Act, to dissolve the corporation, or in a proceeding by the Attorney General to enjoin the corporation from the transaction of unauthorized business.

8. Corporate Name

The corporate name:

(a) Shall contain the word "corporation," "company," "incorporated" or "limited," or shall contain an abbreviation of one of such words.

(b) Shall not contain any word or phrase which indicates or implies that it is organized for any purpose other than one or more of the purposes contained in its articles of incorporation.

(c) Shall not be the same as, or deceptively similar to, the name of any domestic corporation existing under the laws of this State or any foreign corporation authorized to transact business in this State, or a name the exclusive right to which is, at the time, reserved in the manner provided in this Act, or the name of a corporation which has in effect a registration of its corporate name as provided in this Act, except that this provision shall not apply if the applicant files with the Secretary of State either of the following: (1) the written consent of such other corporation or holder of a reserved or registered name to use the same or deceptively similar name and one or more words are added to make such name distinguishable from such other name, or (2) a certified copy of a final decree of a court of competent jurisdiction establishing the prior right of the applicant to the use of such name in this State.

A corporation with which another corporation, domestic or foreign, is merged, or which is formed by the reorganization or consolidation of one or more domestic or foreign corporations or upon a sale, lease or other disposition to or exchange with, a domestic corporation of all or substantially all the assets of another corporation, domestic or foreign, including its name, may have the same name as that used in this State by any of such corporations if such other corporation was organized under the laws of, or is authorized to transact business in, this State.

9. Reserved Name

The exclusive right to the use of a corporate name may be reserved by:

(a) Any person intending to organize a corporation under this Act.

(b) Any domestic corporation intending to change its name.

(c) Any foreign corporation intending to make application for a certificate of authority to transact business in this State.

(d) Any foreign corporation authorized to transact business in this State and intending to change its name.

(e) Any person intending to organize a foreign corporation and intending to have such corporation make application for a ceritficate of authority to transact busines in this State.

The reservation shall be made by filing with the Secretary of State an application to reserve a specified corporate name, executed by the applicant. If the Secretary of State finds that the name is available for corporate use, he shall reserve the same for the exclusive use of the applicant for a period of one hundred and twenty days.

The right to the exclusive use of a specified corporate name so reserved may be transferred to any other person or corporation by filing in the office of the Secretary of State a notice of such transfer, executed by the applicant for whom the name was reserved, and specifying the name and address of the transferee.

10. Registered Name

Any corporation organized and existing under the laws of any state or territory of the United States may register its corporate name under this Act, provided its corporate name is not the same as, or deceptively similar to, the name of any domestic corporation existing under the laws of this State, or the name of any foreign corporation authorized to transact business in this State, or any corporate name reserved or registered under this Act.

Such registration shall be made by:

(a) Filing with the Secretary of State (1) an application for registration executed by the corporation by an officer thereof, setting forth the name of the corporation, the state or territory under the laws of which it is incorporated, the date of its incorporation, a statement that it is carrying on or doing business, and a brief statement of the business in which it is engaged, and (2) a certificate setting forth that such corporation is in good standing under the laws of the state or territory wherein it is organized, executed by the Secretary of State of such state or territory or by such other official as may have custody of the records pertaining to corporations, and

(b) Paying to the Secretary of State a registration fee in the amount of .... for each month, or fraction thereof, between the date of filing such application and December 31st of the calender year in which such application is filed.

Such registration shall be effective until the close of the calendar year in which the application for registration is filed.

11. Renewal of Registered Name

A corporation which has in effect a registration of its corporate name, may renew such registration from year to year by annually filing an application for renewal setting forth the facts required to be set forth in an original application for registration and a certificate of good standing as required for the original registration and by paying a fee of .... A renewal application may be filed between the first day of October and the thirty-first day of December in each year, and shall extend the registration for the following calendar year.

12. Registered Office and Registered Agent

Each corporation shall have and continuously maintain in this State:

(a) A registered office which may be, but need not be, the same as its place of business.

(b) A registered agent, which agent may be either an individual resident in this State whose business office is identical with such registered office, or a domestic corporation, or a foreign corporation authorized to transact business in this State, having a business office identical with such registered office.

13. Change of Registered Office or Registered Agent

A corporation may change its registered office or change its registered agent, or both, upon filing in the office of the Secretary of State a statement setting forth:

(a) The name of the corporation.

(b) The address of its then registered office.

(c) If the address of its registered office is to be changed, the address to which the registered office is to be changed.

(d) The name of its then registered agent.

(e) If its registered agent is to be changed, the name of its successor registered agent.

(f) That the address of its registered office and the address of the business office of its registered agent, as changed, will be identical.

(g) That such change was authorized by resolution duly adopted by its board of directors.

Such statement shall be executed by the corporation by its president, or a vice president, and verified by him, and delivered to the Secretary of State. If the Secretary of State finds that such statement conforms to the provisions of this Act, he shall file such statement in his office, and upon such filing the change of address of the registered office, or the appointment of a new registered agent, or both, as the case may be, shall become effective.

Any registered agent of a corporation may resign as such agent upon filing a written notice thereof, executed in duplicate, with the Secretary of State, who shall forthwith mail a copy thereof to the corporation at its registered office. The appointment of such agent shall terminate upon the expiration of thirty days after receipt of such notice by the Secretary of State.

If a registered agent changes his or its business address to another place within the same ......,* he or it may change such address and the address of the registered office of any corporation of which he or it is registered agent by filing a statement as required above except that it need be signed only by the registered agent and need not be responsive to (e) or (g) and must recite that a copy of the statement has been mailed to the corporation.

14. Service of Process on Corporation

The registered agent so appointed by a corporation shall be an agent of such corporation upon whom any process, notice or demand required or permitted by law to be served upon the corporation may be served.

Whenever a corporation shall fail to appoint or maintain a registered agent in this State, or whenever its registered agent cannot with reasonable diligence be found at the registered office, then the Secretary of State shall be an agent of such corporation upon whom any such process, notice, or demand may be served. Service on the Secretary of State of any such process, notice, or demand shall be made by delivering to and leaving with him, or with any clerk having charge of the corporation department of his office, duplicate copies of such process, notice or demand. In the event any such process, notice or demand is served on the Secretary of State, he shall immediately cause one of the copies thereof to be forwarded by registered mail, addressed to the corporation at its registered office. Any service so had on the Secretary of State shall be returnable in not less than thirty days.

The Secretary of State shall keep a record of

* Supply designation of jurisdiction, such as county, etc., in accordance with local practice.

all processes, notices and demands served upon him under this section, and shall record therein the time of such service and his action with reference thereto.

Nothing herein contained shall limit or affect the right to serve any process, notice or demand required or permitted by law to be served upon a corporation in any other manner now or hereafter permitted by law.

15. Authorized Shares

Each corporation shall have power to create and issue the number of shares stated in its articles of incorporation. Such shares may be divided into one or more classes, any or all of which classes may consist of shares with par value or shares without par value, with such designations, preferences, limitations, and relative rights as shall be stated in the articles of incorporation. The articles of incorporation may limit or deny the voting rights of or provide special voting rights for the shares of any class to the extent not inconsistent with the provisions of this Act.

Without limiting the authority herein contained, a corporation, when so provided in its articles of incorporation, may issue shares of preferred or special classes:

(a) Subject to the right of the corporation to redeem any of such shares at the price fixed by the articles of incorporation for the redemption thereof.

(b) Entitling the holders thereof to cumulative, noncumulative or partially cumulative dividends.

(c) Having preference over any other class or classes of shares as to the payment of dividends.

(d) Having preference in the assets of the corporation over any other class or classes of shares upon the voluntary or involuntary liquidation of the corporation.

(e) Convertible into shares of any other class or into shares of any series of the same or any other class, except a class having prior or superior rights and preferences as to dividends or distribution of assets upon liquidation, but shares without par value shall not be converted into shares with par value unless that part of the stated capital of the corporation represented by such shares without par value is, at the time of conversion, at least equal to the aggregate par value of the shares into which the shares without par value are to be converted or the amount of any such deficiency is transferred from surplus to stated capital.

16. Issuance of Shares of Preferred or Special Classes in Series

If the articles of incorporation so provide, the share of any preferred or special class may be divided into and issued in series. If the shares of any such class are to be issued in series, then each series shall be so designated as to distinguish the shares thereof from the shares of all other series and classes. Any or all of the series of any such class and the variations in the relative rights and preferences as between different series may be fixed and determined by the articles of incorporation, but all shares of the same class shall be identical except as to the following relative rights and preferences, as to which there may be variations between different series:

(A) The rate of dividend.

(B) Whether shares may be redeemed and, if so, the redemption price and the terms and conditions of redemption.

(C) The amount payable upon shares in event of voluntary and involuntary liquidation.

(D) Sinking fund provisions, if any, for the redemption or purchase of shares.

(E) The terms and conditions, if any, on which shares may be converted.

(F) Voting rights, if any.

If the articles of incorporation shall expressly vest authority in the board of directors, then, to the extent that the articles of incorporation shall not have established series and fixed and determined the variations in the relative rights and preferences as between series, the board of directors shall have authority to divide any or all of such classes into series and, within the limitations set forth in this section and in the articles of incorporation, fix and determine the relative rights and preferences of the shares of any series so established.

In order for the board of directors to establish a series, where authority so to do is contained in the articles of incorporation, the board of directors shall adopt a resolution setting forth the designation of the series and fixing and determining the relative rights and preferences

thereof, or so much thereof as shall not be fixed and determined by the articles of incorporation.

Prior to the issue of any shares of a series established by resolution adopted by the board of directors, the corporation shall file in the office of the Secretary of State a statement setting forth:

(a) The name of the corporation.

(b) A copy of the resolution establishing and designating the series, and fixing and determining the relative rights and preferences thereof.

(c) The date of adoption of such resolution.

(d) That such resolution was duly adopted by the board of directors.

Such statement shall be executed in duplicate by the corporation by its president or a vice president and by its secretary or an assistant secretary, and verified by one of the officers signing such statement, and shall be delivered to the Secretary of State. If the Secretary of State finds that such statement conforms to law, he shall, when all franchise taxes and fees have been paid as in this Act prescribed:

(1) Endorse on each or such duplicate originals the word "Filed," and the month, day, and year of the filing thereof.

(2) File one of such duplicate originals in his office.

(3) Return the other duplicate original to the corporation or its representative.

Upon the filing of such statement by the Secretary of State, the resolution establishing and designating the series and fixing and determining the relative rights and preferences thereof shall become effective and shall constitute an amendment of the articles of incorporation.

17. Subscriptions for Shares

A subscription for shares of a corporation to be organized shall be irrevocable for a period of six months, unless otherwise provided by the terms of the subscription agreement or unless all of the subscribers consent to the revocation of such subscription.

Unless otherwise provided in the subscription agreement, subscriptions for shares, whether made before or after the organization of a corporation, shall be paid in full at such times, or in such installments and at such times, as shall be determined by the board of directors. Any call made by the board of directors for payment on subscriptions shall be uniform as to all shares of the same class or as to all shares of the same series, as the case may be. In case of default in the payment of any installment or call when such payment is due, the corporation may proceed to collect the amount due in the same manner as any debt due the corporation. The by-laws may prescribe other penalties for failure to pay installments or calls that may become due, but no penalty working a forfeiture of a subscription, or of the amounts paid thereon, shall be declared as against any subscriber unless the amount due thereon shall remain unpaid for a period of twenty days after written demand has been made therefor. If mailed, such written demand shall be deemed to be made when deposited in the United States mail in a sealed envelope addressed to the subscriber at his last post-office address known to the corporation, with postage thereon prepaid. In the event of the sale of any shares by reason of any forfeiture, the excess of proceeds realized over the amount due and unpaid on such shares shall be paid to the delinquent subscriber or to his legal representative.

18. Consideration for Shares

Shares having a par value may be issued for such consideration expressed in dollars, not less than the par value thereof, as shall be fixed from time to time by the board of directors.

Shares without par value may be issued for such consideration expressed in dollars as may be fixed from time to time by the board of directors unless the articles of incorporation reserve to the shareholders the right to fix the consideration. In the event that such right be reserved as to any shares, the shareholders shall, prior to the issuance of such shares, fix the consideration to be received for such shares, by a vote of the holders of a majority of all shares entitled to vote thereon.

Treasury shares may be disposed of by the corporation for such consideration expressed in dollars as may be fixed from time to time by the board of directors.

That part of the surplus of a corporation which is transferred to stated capital upon the issuance of shares as a share dividend shall be deemed to be the consideration for the issuance of such shares.

In the event of the issuance of shares upon the conversion or exchange of indebtedness or shares, the consideration for the shares so issued shall be (1) the principal sum of, and accrued interest on, the indebtedness so exchanged or converted, or the stated capital then represented by the shares so exchanged or converted, and (2) that part of surplus, if any, transferred to stated capital upon the issuance of shares for the shares so exchanged or converted, and (3) any additional consideration paid to the corporation upon the issuance of shares for the indebtedness or shares so exchanged or converted.

19. Payment for Shares

The consideration for the issuance of shares may be paid, in whole or in part, in money, in other property, tangible or intangible, or in labor or services actually performed for the corporation. When payment of the consideration for which shares are to be issued shall have been received by the corporation, such shares shall be deemed to be fully paid and nonassessable.

Neither promissory notes nor future services shall constitute payment or part payment for the issuance of shares of a corporation.

In the absence of fraud in the transaction, the judgment of the board of directors or the shareholders, as the case may be, as to the value of consideration received for shares shall be conclusive.

20. Stock Rights and Options

Subject to any provisions in respect thereof set forth in its articles of incorporation, a corporation may create and issue, whether or not in connection with the issuance and sale of any of its shares or other securities, rights or options entitling the holders thereof to purchase from the corporation shares of any class or classes. Such rights or options shall be evidenced in such manner as the board of directors shall approve and, subject to the provisions of the articles of incorporation, shall set forth the terms upon which the time or times within which and the price or prices at which such shares may be purchased from the corporation upon the exercise of any such right or option.

If such rights or options are to be issued to directors, officers or employees as such of the corporation or of any subsidiary thereof, and not to the shareholders generally, their issuance shall be approved by the affirmative vote of the holders of a majority of the shares entitled to vote there on or shall be authorized by and consistent with a plan approved or ratified by such a vote of shareholders. In the absence of fraud in the transaction, the judgment of the board of directors as to the adequacy of the consideration received for such rights or options shall be conclusive. The price or prices to be received for any shares having a par value, other than treasury shares to be issued upon the exercise of such rights or options, shall not be less than the par value thereof.

21. Determination of Amount of Stated Capital

In case of the issuance by a corporation of shares having a par value, the consideration received therefor shall constitute stated capital to the extent of the par value of such shares, and the excess, if any, of such consideration shall constitute capital surplus.

In case of the issuance by a corporation of shares without par value, the entire consideration received therefor shall constitute stated capital unless the corporation shall determine as provided in this section that only a part thereof shall be stated capital. Within a period of sixty days after the issuance of any shares without par value, the board of directors may allocate to capital surplus any portion of the consideration received for the issuance of such shares. No such allocation shall be made of any portion of the consideration received for shares without par value having a preference in the assets of the corporation in the event of involuntary liquidation except the amount, if any, of such consideration in excess of such preference.

If shares have been or shall be issued by a corporation in merger or consolidation or in acquisition of all or substantially all of the outstanding shares or of the property and assets of another corporation, whether domestic or foreign, any amount that would otherwise constitute capital surplus under the foregoing provisions of this section may instead be allocated to earned surplus by the board of directors of the issuing corporation except that its aggregate earned surplus shall not exceed the sum of the earned surpluses as defined in this Act of the issuing corporation and of all other corporations, domestic or foreign, that were merged or consolidated or of which the shares or assets were acquired.

The stated capital of a corporation may be increased from time to time by resolution of the board of directors directing that all or a part of the surplus of the corporation be transferred to stated capital. The board of directors may direct that the amount of the surplus so transferred shall be deemed to be stated capital in respect of any designated class of shares.

22. Expenses of Organization, Reorganization, and Financing

The reasonable charges and expenses of organization or reorganization of a corporation, and the reasonable expenses of and compensation for the sale or underwriting of its shares, may be paid or allowed by such corporation out of the consideration received by it in payment for its shares without thereby rendering such shares not fully paid or assessable.

23. Certificates Representing Shares

The shares of a corporation shall be represented by certificates signed by the president or a vice president and the secretary or an assistant secretary of the corporation, and may be sealed with the seal of the corporation or a facsimile thereof. The signatures of the president or vice president and the secretary or assistant secretary upon a certificate may be facsimiles if the certificate is manually signed on behalf of a transfer agent or a registrar, other than the corporation itself or an employee of the corporation. In case any officer who has signed or whose facsimile signature had been placed upon such certificate shall have ceased to be such officer before such certificate is issued, it may be issued by the corporation with the same effect as if he were such officer at the date of its issue.

Every certificate representing shares issued by a corporation which is authorized to issue shares of more than one class shall set forth upon the face or back of the certificate, or shall state that the corporation will furnish to any shareholder upon request and without charge, a full statement of the designations, preferences, limitations, and relative rights of the shares of each class authorized to be issued, and if the corporation is authorized to issue any preferred or special class in series, the variations in the relative rights and preferences between the shares of each such series so far as the same have been fixed and determined and the authority of the board of directors to fix and determine the relative rights and preferences of subsequent series.

Each certificate representing shares shall state upon the face thereof:

(a) That the corporation is organized under the laws of this State.

(b) The name of the person to whom issued.

(c) The number and class of shares, and the designation of the series, if any, which such certificate represents.

(d) The par value of each share represented by such certificate, or a statement that the shares are without par value.

No certificate shall be issued for any share until such share is fully paid.

24. Fractional Shares

A corporation may (1) issue fractions of a share, (2) arrange for the disposition of fractional interests by those entitled thereto, (3) pay in cash the fair value of fractions of a share as of the time when those entitled to receive such fractions are determined, or (4) issue scrip in registered or bearer form which shall entitle the holder to receive a certificate for a full share upon the surrender of such scrip aggregating a full share. A certificate for a fractional share shall, but scrip shall not unless otherwise provided therein, entitle the holder to exercise voting rights, to receive dividends thereon, and to participate in any of the assets of the corporation in the event of liquidation. The board of directors may cause scrip to be issued subject to the condition that it shall become void if not exchanged for certificates representing full shares before a specified date, or subject to the condition that the shares for which scrip is exchangeable may be sold by the corporation and the proceeds thereof distributed to the holders of scrip, or subject to any other conditions which the board of directors may deem advisable.

25. Liability of Subscribers and Shareholders

A holder of or subscriber to shares of a corporation shall be under no obligation to the corporation or its creditors with respect to such shares other than the obligation to pay to the corporation the full consideration for which such shares were issued or to be issued.

Any person becoming an assignee or transferee of shares or of a subscription for shares in good faith and without knowledge or notice that the full consideration therefor has not been paid shall not be personally liable to the corporation or its creditors for any unpaid portion of such consideration.

An executor, administrator, conservator, guardian, trustee, assignee for the benefit of creditors, or receiver shall not be personally liable to the corporation as a holder of or subscriber to shares of a corporation but the estate and funds in his hands shall be so liable.

No pledgee or other holder of shares as collateral security shall be personally liable as a shareholder.

26. Shareholders' Preemptive Rights

The shareholders of a corporation shall have no preemptive right to acquire unissued or treasury shares of the corporation, or securities of the corporation convertible into or carrying a right to subscribe to or acquire shares, except to the extent, if any, that such right is provided in the articles of incorporation.

26A. Shareholders' Preemptive Rights [Alternative]

Except to the extent limited or denied by this section or by the articles of incorporation, shareholders shall have a preemptive right to acquire unissued or treasury shares or securities convertible into such shares or carrying a right to subscribe to or acquire shares.

Unless otherwise provided in the articles of incorporation.

(a) No preemptive right shall exist

(1) to acquire any shares issued to directors, officers or employees pursuant to approval by the affirmative vote of the holders of a majority of the shares entitled to vote thereon or when authorized by and consistent with a plan theretofore approved by such a vote of shareholders; or

(2) to acquire any shares sold otherwise than for cash.

(b) Holders of shares of any class that is preferred or limited as to dividends or assets shall not be entitled to any preemptive right.

(c) Holders of shares of common stock shall not be entitled to any preemptive right to shares of any class that is preferred or limited as to dividends or assets or to any obligations, unless convertible into shares of common stock or carrying a right to subscribe to or acquire shares of common stock.

(d) Holders of common stock without voting power shall have no preemptive right to shares of common stock with voting power.

(e) The preemptive right shall be only an opportunity to acquire shares or other securities under such terms and conditions as the board of directors may fix for the purpose of providing a fair and reasonable opportunity for the exercise of such right.

27. By-Laws

The initial by-laws of a corporation shall be adopted by its board of directors. The power to alter, amend or repeal the by-laws or adopt new by-laws, subject to repeal or change by action of the shareholders, shall be vested in the board of directors unless reserved to the shareholders by the articles of incorporation. The by-laws may contain any provisions for the regulation and management of the affairs of the corporation not inconsistent with law or the articles of incorporation.

27A. By-Laws and Other Powers in Emergency [Optional]

The board of directors of any corporation may adopt emergency by-laws, subject to repeal or change by action of the shareholders, which shall, notwithstanding any different provision elsewhere in this Act or in the articles of incorporation or by-laws, be operative during any emergency in the conduct of the business of the corporation resulting from an attack on the United States or any nuclear or atomic disaster. The emergency by-laws may make any provision that may be practical and necessary for the circumstances of the emergency, including provisions that:

(a) A meeting of the board of directors may be called by any officer or director in such manner and under such conditions as shall be prescribed in the emergency by-laws;

(b) The director or directors in attendance at the meeting, or any greater number fixed by the emergency by-laws, shall constitute a quorum; and

(c) The officers or other persons designated on a list approved by the board of directors before the emergency, all in such order of priority and subject to such conditions, and for such period of time (not longer than reasonably necessary after the termination of the emergency) as may be provided in the emergency by-laws or in the resolution approving the list shall, to the extent required to provide a quorum at any meeting of the board of directors, be deemed directors for such meeting.

The board of directors, either before or during any such emergency, may provide, and from time to time modify, lines of succession in the event that during such an emergency any or all officers or agents of the corporation shall for any reason be rendered incapable of discharging their duties.

The board of directors, either before or during any such emergency, may, effective in the emergency, change the head office or designate several alternative head offices or regional offices, or authorize the officers so to do.

To the extent not inconsistent with any emergency by-laws so adopted, the by-laws of the corporation shall remain in effect during any such emergency and upon its termination the emergency by-laws shall cease to be operative.

Unless otherwise provided in emergency by-laws, notice of any meeting of the board of directors during any such emergency may be given only to such of the directors as it may be feasible to reach at the time and by such means as may be feasible at the time, including publication or radio.

To the extent required to constitute a quorum at any meeting of the board of directors during any such emergency, the officers of the corporation who are present shall, unless otherwise provided in emergency by-laws, be deemed, in order of rank and within the same rank in order of seniority, directors for such meeting.

No officer, director or employee acting in accordance with any emergency by-laws shall be liable except for willful misconduct. No officer, director or employee shall be liable for any action taken by him in good faith in such an emergency in furtherance of the ordinary business affairs of the corporation even though not authorized by the by-laws then in effect.

28. Meetings of Shareholders

Meetings of shareholders may be held at such place within or without this State as may be stated in or fixed in accordance with the by-laws. If no other place is stated or so fixed, meetings shall be held at the registered office of the corporation.

An annual meeting of the shareholders shall be held at such time as may be stated in or fixed in accordance with the by-laws. If the annual meeting is not held within any thirteen-month period the Court of . . . . may, on the application of any shareholder, summarily order a meeting to be held.

Special meetings of the shareholders may be called by the board of directors, the holders of not less than one-tenth of all the shares entitled to vote at the meeting, or such other persons as may be authorized in the articles of incorporation or the by-laws.

29. Notice of Shareholders' Meetings

Written notice stating the place, day and hour of the meeting and, in case of a special meeting, the purpose or purposes for which the meeting is called, shall be delivered not less than ten nor more than fifty days before the date of the meeting, either personally or by mail, by or at the direction of the president, the secretary or the officer or persons calling the meeting, to each shareholder of record entitled to vote at such meeting. If mailed, such notice shall be deemed to be delivered when deposited in the United States mail addressed to the shareholder at his address as it appears on the stock transfer books of the corporation, with postage thereon prepaid.

30. Closing of Transfer Books and Fixing Record Date

For the purpose of determining shareholders entitled to notice of or to vote at any meeting of shareholders or any adjournment thereof, or entitled to receive payment of any dividend, or in order to make a determination of shareholders for any other proper purpose, the board of directors of a corporation may provide that the stock transfer books shall be closed for a stated period but not to exceed, in any case, fifty days. If the stock transfer books shall be closed for the purpose of determining shareholders entitled to notice of or to vote at a meeting of shareholders, such books shall be closed for at least ten days immediately preceding such meeting. In lieu of closing the stock transfer books, the by-laws, or in the absence of an applicable by-law the board of directors, may fix in advance a date as the record date for any such determination of shareholders, such date in any case to be not more than fifty days and, in case of a meeting of shareholders, not less than ten days prior to the date on which the particular action, requiring such determination of shareholders, is to be taken. If the stock transfer books are not closed and no record date is fixed for the determination of shareholders entitled to notice of or to vote at a meeting of shareholders, or shareholders entitled to receive payment of a dividend, the date on which notice of the meeting is mailed or the date on which the resolution of the board of directors declaring such dividend is adopted, as the case may be, shall be the record date for such determination of shareholders. When a determination of shareholders entitled to vote at any meeting of shareholders has been made as provided in this section, such determination shall apply to any adjournment thereof.

31. Voting Record

The officer or agent having charge of the stock transfer books for shares of a corporation shall make a complete record of the shareholders entitled to vote at such meeting or any adjournment thereof, arranged in alphabetical order, with the address of and the number of shares held by each. Such record shall be produced and kept open at the time and place of the meeting and shall be subject to the inspection of any shareholder during the whole time of the meeting for the purposes thereof.

Failure to comply with the requirements of this section shall not affect the validity of any action taken at such meeting.

An officer or agent having charge of the stock transfer books who shall fail to prepare the record of shareholders, or produce and keep it open for inspection at the meeting, as provided in this section, shall be liable to any shareholder suffering damage on account of such failure, to the extent of such damage.

32. Quorum of Shareholders

Unless otherwise provided in the articles of incorporation, a majority of the shares entitled to vote, represented in person or by proxy, shall constitute a quorum at a meeting of shareholders, but in no event shall a quorum consist of less than one-third of the shares entitled to vote at the meeting. If a quorum is present, the affirmative vote of the majority of the shares represented at the meeting and entitled to vote on the subject matter shall be the act of the shareholders, unless the vote of a greater number or voting by classes is required by this Act or the articles of incorporation or by-laws.

33. Voting of Shares

Each outstanding share, regardless of class, shall be entitled to one vote on each matter submitted to a vote at a meeting of shareholders, except as may be otherwise provided in the articles of incorporation. If the articles of incorporation provide for more or less than one vote for any share, on any matter, every reference in this Act to a majority or other proportion of shares shall refer to such a majority or other proportion of votes entitled to be cast.

Neither treasury shares, nor shares held by another corporation if a majority of the shares entitled to vote for the election of directors of such other corporation is held by the corporation, shall be voted at any meeting or counted in determining the total number of outstanding shares at any given time.

A shareholder may vote either in person or by proxy executed in writing by the shareholder or by his duly authorized attorney-in-fact. No proxy shall be valid after eleven months from the date of its execution, unless otherwise provided in the proxy.

[Either of the following prefatory phrases may be inserted here: "The articles of incorporation may provide that" or "Unless the articles of incorporation otherwise provide"] . . . at each election for directors every shareholder entitled to vote at such election shall have the right to vote, in person or by proxy, the number of shares owned by him for as many persons as there are directors to be elected and for whose election he has a right to vote, or to cumulate his votes by giving one candidate as many votes as the number of such directors multiplied by the number of his shares shall equal, or by distributing such votes on the same principle among any number of such candidates.

Shares standing in the name of another corporation, domestic or foreign, may be voted by such officer, agent or proxy as the by-laws of such other corporation may prescribe, or, in the absence of such provision, as the board of directors of such other corporation may determine.

Shares held by an administrator, executor, guardian or conservator may be voted by him, either in person or by proxy, without a transfer of such shares into his name. Shares standing in the name of a trustee may be voted by him, either in person or by proxy, but no trustee shall be entitled to vote shares held by him without a transfer of such shares into his name.

Shares standing in the name of a receiver may be voted by such receiver, and shares held by or under the control of a receiver may be voted by such receiver without the transfer thereof into his name if authority so to do be contained in an appropriate order of the court by which such receiver was appointed.

A shareholder whose shares are pledged shall be entitled to vote such shares until the shares have been transferred into the name of the pledgee, and thereafter the pledgee shall be entitled to vote the shares so transferred.

On and after the date on which written notice of redemption of redeemable shares has been mailed to the holders thereof and a sum sufficient to redeem such shares has been deposited with a bank or trust company with irrevocable instruction and authority to pay the redemption price to the holders thereof upon surrender of certificates therefor, such shares shall not be entitled to vote on any manner and shall not be deemed to be outstanding shares.

34. Voting Trusts and Agreements Among Shareholders

Any number of shareholders of a corporation may create a voting trust for the purpose of conferring upon a trustee or trustees the right to vote or otherwise represent their shares, for a period of not to exceed ten years, by entering into a written voting trust agreement specifying the terms and conditions of the voting trust, by depositing a counterpart of the agreement with the corporation at its registered office, and by transferring their shares to such trustee or trustees for the purposes of the agreement. Such trustee or trustees shall keep a record of the holders of voting trust certificates evidencing a beneficial interest in the voting trust, giving the names and addresses of all such holders and the number and class of the shares in respect of which the voting trust certificates held by each are issued, and shall deposit a copy of such record with the corporation at its registered office. The counterpart of the voting trust agreement and the copy of such record so deposited with the corporation shall be subject to the same right of examination by a shareholder of the corporation, in person or by agent or attorney, as are the books and records of the corporation, and such counterpart and such copy of such record shall be subject to examination by any holder of record of voting trust certificates, either in person or by agent or attorney, at any reasonable time for any proper purpose.

Agreements among shareholders regarding the voting of their shares shall be valid and enforceable in accordance with their terms. Such agreements shall not be subject to the provisions of this section regarding voting trusts.

35. Board of Directors

All corporate powers shall be exercised by or under authority of, and the business and affairs of a corporation shall be managed under the direction of, a board of directors except as may be otherwise provided in this Act or the articles of incorporation. If any such provision is made in the articles of incorporation, the powers and duties conferred or imposed upon the board of directors by this Act shall be exercised or performed to such extent and by such person or persons as shall be provided in the articles of incorporation. Directors need not be residents of this State or shareholders of the corporation unless the articles of incorporation or by-laws so require. The articles of incorporation or by-laws may prescribe other qualifications for directors. The board of directors shall have authority to fix the compensation of directors unless otherwise provided in the articles of incorporation.

A director shall perform his duties as a director, including his duties as a member of any committee of the board upon which he may serve, in good faith, in a manner he reasonably believes to be in the best interests of the corporation, and with such care as an ordinarily prudent person in a like position would use under similar circumstances. In performing his duties, a director shall be entitled to rely on information, opinions, reports or statements, including financial statements and other financial data, in each case prepared or presented by:

(a) one or more officers or employees of the corporation whom the director reasonably believes to be reliable and competent in the matters presented,

(b) counsel, public accountants or other persons as to matters which the director reasonably believes to be within such person's professional or expert competence, or

(c) a committee of the board upon which he does not serve, duly designated in accordance with a provision of the articles of incorporation or the by-laws, as to matters within its designated authority, which committee the director reasonably believes to merit confidence,

but he shall not be considered to be acting in good faith if he has knowledge concerning the matter in question that would cause such reliance to be unwarranted. A person who so performs his duties shall have no liability by reason of being or having been a director of the corporation.

A director of a corporation who is present at a meeting of its board of directors at which action on any corporate matter is taken shall be presumed to have assented to the action taken unless his dissent shall be entered in the minutes of the meeting or unless he shall file his written dissent to such action with the secretary of the meeting before the adjournment thereof or shall forward such dissent by registered mail to the secretary of the corporation immediately after the adjournment of the meeting. Such right to dissent shall not apply to a director who voted in favor of such action.

36. Number and Election of Directors

The board of directors of a corporation shall consist of one or more members. The number of directors shall be fixed by, or in the manner provided in, the articles of incorporation or the by-laws, except as to the number constituting the initial board of directors, which number shall be fixed by the articles of incorporation. The number of directors may be increased or decreased from time to time by amendment to, or in the manner provided in, the articles of incorporation or the by-laws, but no decrease shall have the effect of shortening the term of any incumbent director. In the absence of a by-law providing for the number of directors, the number shall be the same as that provided for in the articles of incorporation. The names and addresses of the members of the first board of directors shall be stated in the articles of incorporation. Such persons shall hold office until the first annual meeting of shareholders, and until their successors shall have been elected and qualified. At the first annual meeting of shareholders and at each annual meeting thereafter the shareholders shall elect directors to hold office until the next succeeding annual meeting, except in case of the classification of directors as permitted by this Act. Each director shall hold office for the term for which he is elected and until his successor shall have been elected and qualified.

37. Classification of Directors

When the board of directors shall consist of nine or more members, in lieu of electing the whole number of directors annually, the articles of incorporation may provide that the directors be divided into either two or three classes, each class to be as nearly equal in number as possible, the term of office of directors of the first class to expire at the first annual meeting of shareholders after their election, that of the second class to expire at the second annual meeting after their election, and that of the third class, if any, to expire at the third annual meeting after their election. At each annual meeting after such classification the number of directors equal to the number of the class whose term expires at the time of such meeting shall be elected to hold office until the second succeeding annual meeting, if there be two classes, or until the third succeeding annual meeting, if there be three classes. No classification of directors shall be effective prior to the first annual meeting of shareholders.

38. Vacancies

Any vacancy occurring in the board of directors may be filled by the affirmative vote of a majority of the remaining directors though less than a quorum of the board of directors. A director elected to fill a vacancy shall be elected for the unexpired term of his predecessor in office. Any directorship to be filled by reason of an increase in the number of directors may be filled by the board of directors for a term of office continuing only until the next election of directors by the shareholders.

39. Removal of Directors

At a meeting of shareholders called expressly for that purpose, directors may be removed in the manner provided in this section. Any director or the entire board of directors may be removed, with or without cause, by a vote of the holders of a majority of the shares then entitled to vote at an election of directors.

In the case of a corporation having cumulative voting, if less than the entire board is to be removed, no one of the directors may be removed if the votes cast against his removal would be sufficient to elect him if then cumulatively voted at an election of the entire board of directors, or, if there be classes of directors, at an election of the class of directors of which he is a part.

Whenever the holders of the shares of any class are entitled to elect one or more directors by the provisions of the articles of incorporation, the provisions of this section shall apply, in respect to the removal of a director or directors so elected, to the vote of the holders of the outstanding shares of that class and not to the vote of the outstanding shares as a whole.

40. Quorum of Directors

A majority of the number of directors fixed by or in the manner provided in the by-laws or in the absence of a by-law fixing or providing for the number of directors, then of the number stated in the articles of incorporation, shall constitute a quorum for the transaction of business unless a greater number is required by the articles of incorporation or the by-laws. The act of the majority of the directors present at a meeting at which a quorum is present shall be the act of the board of directors, unless the act of a greater number is required by the articles of incorporation or the by-laws.

41. Director Conflicts of Interest

No contract or other transaction between a corporation and one or more of its directors or any other corporation, firm, association or entity in which one or more of its directors are directors or officers or are financially interested, shall be either void or voidable because of such relationship or interest or because such director or directors are present at the meeting of the board of directors or a committee thereof which authorizes, approves or ratifies such contract or transaction or because his or their votes are counted for such purpose, if:

(a) the fact of such relationship or interest is disclosed or known to the board of directors or committee which authorizes, approves or ratifies the contract or transaction by a vote or consent sufficient for the purpose without counting the votes or consents of such interested directors; or

(b) the fact of such relationship or interest is disclosed or known to the shareholders entitled to vote and they authorize, approve or ratify such contract or transaction by vote or written consent; or

(c) the contract or transaction is fair and reasonable to the corporation.

Common or interested directors may be counted in determining the presence of a quorum at a meeting of the board of directors or a committee thereof which authorizes, approves or ratifies such contract or transaction.

42. Executive and Other Committees

If the articles of incorporation or the by-laws so provide, the board of directors, by resolution adopted by a majority of the full board of directors, may designate from among its members an executive committee and one or more other committees each of which, to the extent provided in such resolution or in the articles of incorporation or the by-laws of the corporation, shall have and may exercise all the authority of the board of directors, except that no such committee shall have authority to (i) declare dividends or distributions, (ii) approve or recommend to shareholders actions or proposals required by this Act to be approved by shareholders, (iii) designate candidates for the office of director, for purposes of proxy

solicitation or otherwise, or fill vacancies on the board of directors or any committee thereof, (iv) amend the by-laws, (v) approve a plan of merger not requiring shareholder approval, (vi) reduce earned or capital surplus, (vii) authorize or approve the reacquisition of shares unless pursuant to a general formula or method specified by the board of directors, or (viii) authorize or approve the issuance or sale of, or any contract to issue or sell, shares or designate the terms of a series of a class of shares, provided that the board of directors, having acted regarding general authorization for the issuance or sale of shares, or any contract therefor, and, in the case of a series, the designation thereof, may, pursuant to a general formula or method specified by the board by resolution or by adoption of a stock option or other plan, authorize a committee to fix the terms of any contract for the sale of the shares and to fix the terms upon which such shares may be issued or sold, including, without limitation, the price, the dividend rate, provisions for redemption, sinking fund, conversion, voting or preferential rights, and provisions for other features of a class of shares, or a series of a class of shares, with full power in such committee to adopt any final resolution setting forth all the terms thereof and to authorize the statement of the terms of a series for filing with the Secretary of State under this Act.

Neither the designation of any such committee, the delegation thereto of authority, nor action by such committee pursuant to such authority shall alone constitute compliance by any member of the board of directors, not a member of the committee in question, with his responsibility to act in good faith, in a manner he reasonably believes to be in the best interests of the corporation, and with such care as an ordinarily prudent person in a like position would use under similar circumstances.

43. Place and Notice of Directors' Meetings; Committee Meetings

Meetings of the board of directors, regular or special, may be held either within or without this State.

Regular meetings of the board of directors or any committee designated thereby may be held with or without notice as prescribed in the by-laws. Special meetings of the board of directors or any committee designated thereby shall be held upon such notice as is prescribed in the by-laws. Attendance of a director at a meeting shall constitute a waiver of notice of such meeting, except where a director attends a meeting for the express purpose of objecting to the transaction of any business because the meeting is not lawfully called or convened. Neither the business to be transacted at, nor the purpose of, any regular or special meeting of the board of directors or any committee designated thereby need be specified in the notice or waiver of notice of such meeting unless required by the by-laws.

Except as may be otherwise restricted by the articles of incorporation or by-laws, members of the board of directors or any committee designated thereby may participate in a meeting of such board or committee by means of a conference telephone or similar communications equipment by means of which all persons participating in the meeting can hear each other at the same time and participation by such means shall constitute presence in person at a meeting.

44. Action by Directors Without a Meeting

Unless otherwise provided by the articles of incorporation or by-laws, any action required by this Act to be taken at a meeting of the directors of a corporation, or any action which may be taken at a meeting of the directors or of a committee, may be taken without a meeting if a consent in writing, setting forth the action so taken, shall be signed by all of the directors, or all of the members of the committee, as the case may be. Such consent shall have the same effect as a unanimous vote.

45. Dividends

The board of directors of a corporation may, from time to time, declare and the corporation may pay dividends in cash, property, or its own shares, except when the corporation is insolvent or when the payment thereof would render the corporation insolvent or when the declaration or payment thereof would be contrary to any restriction contained in the articles of incorporation, subject to the following provisions:

(a) Dividends may be declared and paid in cash or property only out of the unreserved and unrestricted earned surplus of the corporation, except as otherwise provided in this section.

[Alternative] (a) Dividends may be declared and paid in cash or property only out of the unreserved and unrestricted earned surplus of the corporation, or out of the unreserved and unrestricted net earnings of the current fiscal year and the next preceding fiscal year taken as a single period, except as otherwise provided in this section.

(b) If the articles of incorporation of a corporation engaged in the business of exploiting natural resources so provide, dividends may be declared and paid in cash out of the depletion reserves, but each such dividend shall be identified as a distribution of such reserves and the amount per share paid from such reserves shall be disclosed to the shareholders receiving the same concurrently with the distribution thereof.

(c) Dividends may be declared and paid in its own treasury shares.

(d) Dividends may be declared and paid in its own authorized but unissued shares out of any unreserved and unrestricted surplus of the corporation upon the following conditions:

(1) If a dividend is payable in its own shares having a par value, such shares shall be issued at not less than the par value thereof and there shall be transferred to stated capital at the time such dividend is paid an amount of surplus equal to the aggregate par value of the shares to be issued as a dividend.

(2) If a dividend is payable in its own shares without par value, such shares shall be issued at such stated value as shall be fixed by the board of directors by resolution adopted at the time such dividend is declared, and there shall be transferred to stated capital at the time such dividend is paid an amount of surplus equal to the aggregate stated value so fixed in respect of such shares; and the amount per share so transferred to stated capital shall be disclosed to the shareholders receiving such dividend concurrently with the payment thereof.

(e) No dividend payable in shares of any class shall be paid to the holders of shares of any other class unless the articles of incorporation so provide or such payment is authorized by the affirmative vote or the written consent of the holders of at least a majority of the outstanding shares of the class in which the payment is to be made.

A split-up or division of the issued shares of any class into a greater number of shares of the same class without increasing the stated capital of the corporation shall not be construed to be a share dividend within the meaning of this section.

46. Distributions from Capital Surplus

The board of directors of a corporation may, from time to time, distribute to its shareholders out of capital surplus of the corporation a portion of its assets, in cash or property, subject to the following provisions:

(a) No such distribution shall be made at a time when the corporation is insolvent or when such distribution would render the corporation insolvent.

(b) No such distribution shall be made unless the articles of incorporation so provide or such distribution is authorized by the affirmative vote of the holders of a majority of the outstanding shares of each class whether or not entitled to vote thereon by the provisions of the articles of incorporation of the corporation.

(c) No such distribution shall be made to the holders of any class of shares unless all cumulative dividends accrued on all preferred or special classes of shares entitled to preferential dividends shall have been fully paid.

(d) No such distribution shall be made to the holders of any class of shares which would reduce the remaining net assets of the corporation below the aggregate preferential amount payable in event of involuntary liquidation to the holders of shares having preferential rights to the assets of the corporation in the event of liquidation.

(e) Each such distribution, when made, shall be identified as a distribution from capital surplus and the amount per share disclosed to the shareholders receiving the same concurrently with the distribution thereof.

The board of directors of a corporation may also, from time to time, distribute to the holders of its outstanding shares having a cumulative preferential right to receive dividends, in discharge of their cumulative dividend rights, dividends payable in cash out of the capital surplus of the corporation, if at the time the corporation has no earned surplus and is not insolvent and would not thereby be rendered insolvent. Each such distribution when made, shall be identified as a payment of cumulative dividends out of capital surplus.

47. Loans to Employees and Directors

A corporation shall not lend money to or use its credit to assist its directors without authorization in the particular case by its shareholders, but may lend money to and use its credit to assist any employee of the corporation or of a subsidiary, including any such employee who is a director of the corporation, if the board of directors decides that such loan or assistance may benefit the corporation.

48. Liability of Directors in Certain Cases

In addition to any other liabilities, a director shall be liable in the following circumstances unless he complies with the standard provided in this Act for the performance of the duties of directors:

(a) A director who votes for or assents to the declaration of any dividend or other distribution of the assets of a corporation to its shareholders contrary to the provisions of this Act or contrary to any restrictions contained in the articles of incorporation, shall be liable to the corporation, jointly or severally with all other directors so voting or assenting, for the amount of such dividend which is paid or the value of such assets which are distributed in excess of the amount of such dividend or distribution which could have been paid or distributed without a violation of the provisions of this Act or the restrictions in the articles of incorporation.

(b) A director who votes for or assents to the purchase of the corporation's own shares contrary to the provisions of this Act shall be liable to the corporation, jointly and severally with all other directors so voting or assenting, for the amount of consideration paid for such shares which is in excess of the maximum amount which could have been paid therefor without a violation of the provisions of this Act.

(c) A director who votes for or assents to any distribution of assets of a corporation to its shareholders during the liquidation of the corporation without the payment and discharge of, or making adequate provision for, all known debts, obligations, and liabilities of the corporation shall be liable to the corporation, jointly and severally with all other directors so voting or assenting, for the value of such assets which are distributed, to the extent that such debts, obligations and liabilities of the corporation are not thereafter paid and discharged.

Any director against whom a claim shall be asserted under or pursuant to this section for the payment of a dividend or other distribution of assets of a corporation and who shall be held liable thereon, shall be entitled to contribution from the shareholders who accepted or received any such dividend or assets, knowing such dividend or distribution to have been made in violation of this Act, in proportion to the amounts received by them.

Any director against whom a claim shall be asserted under or pursuant to this section shall be entitled to contribution from the other directors who voted for or assented to the action upon which the claim is asserted.

49. Provisions Relating to Actions by Shareholders

No action shall be brought in this State by a shareholder in the right of a domestic or foreign corporation unless the plaintiff was a holder of record of shares or of voting trust certificates thereof at the time of the transaction of which he complains, or his shares or voting trust certificates thereafter devolved upon him by operation of law from a person who was a holder of record at such time.

In any action hereafter instituted in the right of any domestic or foreign corporation by the holder or holders of record of shares of such corporation or of voting trust certificates therefor, the court having jurisdiction, upon final judgment and a finding that the action was brought without reasonable cause, may require the plaintiff or plaintiffs to pay to the parties named as defendant the reasonable expenses, including fees of attorneys, incurred by them in the defense of such action.

In any action now pending or hereafter instituted or maintained in the right of any domestic or foreign corporation by the holder or holders of record of less than five per cent of the outstanding shares of any class of such corporation or of voting trust certificates therefor, unless the shares or voting trust certificates so held have a market value in excess of twenty-five thousand dollars, the corporation in whose right such action is brought shall be entitled at any time before final judgment to require the plaintiff or plaintiffs to give security for the reasonable expenses, including fees of attorneys, that may be insurred by it in connection with such action or may be incurred by other parties named as defendant for which it may become legally liable. Market value shall be determined as of the date that the plaintiff institutes the action or, in the case of an intervenor, as of the date that he becomes a party to the action. The amount of such security may from time to time be increased or decreased, in the discretion of the court, upon showing that the security provided has or may become inadequate or is excessive. The corporation shall have recourse to such security in such amount as the court having jurisdiction shall determine upon the termination of such action, whether or not the court finds the action was brought without reasonable cause.

50. Officers

The officers of a corporation shall consist of a president, one or more vice presidents as may be prescribed by the by-laws, a secretary, and a treasurer, each of whom shall be elected by the board of directors at such time and in such manner as may be prescribed by the by-laws. Such other officers and assistant officers and agents as may be deemed necessary may be elected or appointed by the board of directors or chosen in such other manner as may be prescribed by the by-laws. Any two or more officers may be held by the same person, except the offices of president and secretary.

All officers and agents of the corporation, as between themselves and the corporation, shall have such authority and perform such duties in the management of the corporation as may be provided in the by-laws, or as may be determined by resolution of the board of directors not inconsistent with the by-laws.

51. Removal of Officers

Any officer or agent may be removed by the board of directors whenever in its judgment the best interests of the corporation will be served thereby, but such removal shall be without prejudice to the contract rights, if any, of the person so removed. Election or appointment of an officer or agent shall not of itself create contract rights.

52. Books and Records

Each corporation shall keep correct and complete books and records of account and shall keep minutes of the proceedings of its shareholders and board of directors and shall keep at its registered office or principal place of business, or at the office of its transfer agent or registrar, a record of its shareholders, giving the names and addresses of all shareholders and the number and class of the shares held by each. Any books, records and minutes may be in written form or in any other form capable of being converted into written form within a reasonable time.

Any person who shall have been a holder of record of shares or of voting trust certificates therefor at least six months immediately preceding his demand or shall be the holder of record of, or the holder of record of voting trust certificates for, at least five per cent of all the outstanding shares of the corporation, upon written demand stating the purpose thereof, shall have the right to examine, in person, or by agent or attorney, at any reasonable time or times, for any proper purpose its relevant books and records of account, minutes, and record of shareholders and to make extracts therefrom.

Any officer or agent who, or a corporation which, shall refuse to allow any such shareholder or holder of voting trust certificates, or his agent or attorney, so to examine and make extracts from its books and records of account, minutes, and record of shareholders, for any proper purpose, shall be liable to such shareholder or holder of voting trust certificates in a penalty of ten per cent of the value of the shares owned by such shareholder, or in respect of which such voting trust certificates are issued, in addition to any other damages or remedy afforded him by law. It shall be a defense to any action for penalties under this section that the person suing therefor has within two years sold or offered for sale any list of shareholders or of holders of voting trust certificates for shares of such corporation or any other corporation or has aided or abetted any person in procuring any list of shareholders or of holders of voting trust certificates for any such purpose, or has improperly used any information secured through any prior examination of the books and records of account, or minutes, or record of shareholders or of holders of voting trust certificates for shares of such corporation or any other corporation, or was not acting in good faith or for a proper purpose in making his demand.

Nothing herein contained shall impair the power of any court of competent jurisdiction, upon proof by a shareholder or holder of voting trust certificates of proper purpose, irrespective of the period of time during which such shareholder or holder of voting trust certificates shall have been a shareholder of record or a holder of record of voting trust certificates, and irrespective of the number of shares held by him or represented by voting trust certificates held by him, to compel the production for examination by such shareholder or holder of voting trust certificates of the books and records of account, minutes and record of shareholders of a corporation.

Upon the written request of any shareholder or holder of voting trust certificates for shares of a corporation, the corporation shall mail to such shareholder or holder of voting trust certificates its most recent financial statements showing in reasonable detail its assets and liabilities and the results of its operations.

53. Incorporators

One or more persons, or a domestic or foreign corporation, may act as incorporator or incorporators of a corporation by signing and delivering in duplicate to the Secretary of State articles of incorporation for such corporation.

54. Articles of Incorporation

The articles of incorporation shall set forth:

(a) The name of the corporation.

(b) The period of duration, which may be perpetual.

(c) The purpose or purposes for which the corporation is organized which may be stated to be, or to include, the transaction of any or all lawful business for which corporations may be incorporated under this Act.

(d) The aggregate number of shares which the corporation shall have authority to issue; if such shares are to consist of one class only, the par value of each of such shares, or a statement that all of such shares are without par value; or, if such shares are to be divided into classes, the number of shares of each class, and a statement of the par value of the shares of each such class or that such shares are to be without par value.

(e) If the shares are to be divided into classes, the designation of each class and a statement of the preferences, limitations and relative rights in respect of the shares of each class.

(f) If the corporation is to issue the shares of any preferred or special class in series, then the designation of each series and a statement of the variations in the relative rights and preferences as between series insofar as the same are to be fixed in the articles of incorporation, and a statement of any authority to be vested in the board of directors to establish series and fix and determine the variations in the relative rights and preferences as between series.

(g) If any preemptive right is to be granted to shareholders, the provisions therefor.

(h) Any provision, not inconsistent with law, which the incorporators elect to set forth in the articles of incorporation for the regulation of the internal affairs of the corporation, including any provision restricting the transfer of shares and any provision which under this Act is required or permitted to be set forth in the by-laws.

(i) The address of its initial registered office, and the name of its initial registered agent at such address.

(j) The number of directors constituting the initial board of directors and the names and addresses of the persons who are to serve as directors until the first annual meeting of shareholders or until their successors be elected and qualify.

(k) The name and address of each incorporator.

It shall not be necessary to set forth in the articles of incorporation any of the corporate powers enumerated in this Act.

55. Filing of Articles of Incorporation

Duplicate originals of the articles of incorporation shall be delivered to the Secretary of State. If the Secretary of State finds that the articles of incorporation conform to law, he shall, when all fees have been paid as in this Act prescribed:

(a) Endorse on each of such duplicate originals the word "Filed," and the month, day and year of the filing thereof.

(b) File one of such duplicate originals in his office.

(c) Issue a certificate of incorporation to which he shall affix the other duplicate original.

The certificate of incorporation, together with the duplicate original of the articles of incorporation affixed thereto by the Secretary of State, shall be returned to the incorporators or their representative.

56. Effect of Issuance of Certificate of Incorporation

Upon the issuance of the certificate of incorporation, the corporate existence shall begin, and such certificate of incorporation shall be conclusive evidence that all conditions precedent required to be performed by the incorporators have been complied with and that the corporation has been incorporated under this Act, except as against this State in a proceeding to cancel or revoke the certificate of incorporation or for involuntary dissolution of the corporation.

57. Organization Meeting of Directors

After the issuance of the certificate of incorporation an organization meeting of the board of directors named in the articles of incorporation shall be held, either within or without this State, at the call of a majority of the directors named in the articles of incorporation, for the purpose of adopting by-laws, electing officers and transacting such other business as may come before the meeting. The directors calling the meeting shall give at least three days' notice thereof by mail to each director so named, stating the time and place of the meeting.

58. Right to Amend Articles of Incorporation

A corporation may amend its articles of incorporation, from time to time, in any and as many respects as may be desired, so long as its articles of incorporation as amended contain only such provisions as might be lawfully contained in original articles of incorporation at the time of making such amendment, and, if a change in shares or the rights of shareholders, or an exchange, reclassification or cancellation of shares or rights of shareholders is to be made, such provisions as may be necessary to effect such change, exchange, reclassification or cancellation.

In particular, and without limitation upon such general power of amendment, a corporation may amend its articles of incorporation, from time to time, so as:

(a) To change its corporate name.

(b) To change its period of duration.

(c) To change, enlarge or diminish its corporate purposes.

(d) To increase or decrease the aggregate number of shares, or shares of any class, which the corporation has authority to issue.

(e) To increase or decrease the par value of the authorized shares of any class having a par value, whether issued or unissued.

(f) To exchange, classify, reclassify or cancel all or any part of its shares, whether issued or unissued.

(g) To change the designation of all or any part of its shares, whether issued or unissued, and to change the preferences, limitations, and the relative rights in respect of all or any part of its shares, whether issued or unissued.

(h) To change shares having the par value, whether issued or unissued, into the same or a different number of shares without par value, and to change shares without par value, whether issued or unissued, into the same or a different number of shares having a par value.

(i) To change the shares of any class, whether issued or unissued and whether with or without par value, into a different number of shares of the same class or into the same or a different number of shares, either with or without par value, of other classes.

(j) To create new classes of shares having rights and preferences either prior and superior or subordinate and inferior to the shares of any class then authorized, whether issued or unissued.

(k) To cancel or otherwise affect the right of the holders of the shares of any class to receive dividends which have accrued but have not been declared.

(l) To divide any preferred or special class of shares, whether issued or unissued, into series and fix and determine the designations of such series and the variations in the relative rights and preferences as between the shares of such series.

(m) To authorize the board of directors to establish, out of authorized but unissued shares, series of any preferred or special class of shares and fix and determine the relative rights and preferences of the shares of any series so established.

(n) To authorize the board of directors to fix and determine the relative rights and preferences of the authorized but unissued shares of series theretofore established in respect to which either the relative rights and preferences have not been fixed and determined or the relative rights and preferences therefore fixed and determined are to be changed.

(o) To revoke, diminish, or enlarge the authority of the board of directors to establish series out of authorized but unissued shares of any preferred or special class and fix and determine the relative rights and preferences of the shares of any series so established.

(p) To limit, deny or grant to shareholders of any class the preemptive right to acquire additional or treasury shares of the corporation, whether then or thereafter authorized.

59. Procedure to Amend Articles of Incorporation

Amendments to the articles of incorporation shall be made in the following manner:

(a) The board of directors shall adopt a resolution setting forth the proposed amendment and, if shares have been issued, directing that it be submitted to a vote at a meeting of shareholders, which may be either the annual or a special meeting. If no shares have been issued, the amendment shall be adopted by resolution of the board of directors and the provisions for adoption by shareholders shall not apply. The resolution may incorporate the proposed amendment in restated articles of incorporation which contain a statement that except for the designated amendment the restated articles of incorporation correctly set forth without change the corresponding provisions of the articles of incorporation as theretofore amended, and that the restated articles of incorporation together with the designated amendment supersede the original articles of incorporation and all amendments thereto.

(b) Written notice setting forth the proposed amendment or a summary of the changes to be effected thereby shall be given to each shareholder of record entitled to vote thereon within the time and in the manner provided in this Act for the giving of notice of meetings of shareholders. If the meeting be an annual meeting, the proposed amendment of such summary may be included in the notice of such annual meeting.

(c) At such meeting a vote of the shareholders entitled to vote thereon shall be taken on the proposed amendment. The proposed amendment shall be adopted upon receiving the affirmative vote of the holders of a majority of the shares entitled to vote thereon, unless any class of shares is entitled to vote thereon as a class, in which event the proposed amendment shall be adopted upon receiving the affirmative vote of the holders of a majority of the shares of each class of shares entitled to vote thereon as a class and of the total shares entitled to vote thereon.

Any number of amendments may be submitted to the shareholders, and voted upon by them, at one meeting.

60. Class Voting on Amendments

The holders of the outstanding shares of a class shall be entitled to vote as a class upon a proposed amendment, whether or not entitled to vote thereon by the provisions of the articles of incorporation, if the amendment would:

(a) Increase or decrease the aggregate number of authorized shares of such class.

(b) Increase or decrease the par value of the shares of such class.

(c) Effect an exchange, reclassification or cancellation of all or part of the shares of such class.

(d) Effect an exchange, or create a right of exchange, of all or any part of the shares of another class into the shares of such class.

(e) Change the designations, preferences, limitations or relative rights of the shares of such class.

(f) Change the shares of such class, whether with or without par value, into the same or a different number of shares, either with or without par value, of the same class or another class or classes.

(g) Create a new class of shares having rights and preferences prior and superior to the shares of such class, or increase the rights and preferences or the number of authorized shares, of any class having rights and preferences prior or superior to the shares of such class.

(h) In the case of a preferred or special class of shares, divide the shares of such class into series and fix and determine the designation of such series and the variations in the relative rights and preferences between the shares of such series, or authorize the board of directors to do so.

(i) Limit or deny any existing preemptive rights of the shares of such class.

(j) Cancel or otherwise affect dividends on the shares of such class which have accrued but have not been declared.

61. Articles of Amendment

The articles of amendment shall be executed in duplicate by the corporation by its president or a vice president and by its secretary or an assistant secretary, and verified by one of the officers signing such articles, and shall set forth:

(a) The name of the corporation.

(b) The amendments so adopted.

(c) The date of the adoption of the amendment by the shareholders, or by the board of directors where no shares have been issued.

(d) The number of shares outstanding, and the number of shares entitled to vote thereon, and if the shares of any class are entitled to vote thereon as a class, the designation and number of outstanding shares entitled to vote thereon each such class.

(e) The number of shares voted for and against such amendment, respectively, and, if the shares of any class are entitled to vote thereon as a class, the number of shares of each such class voted for and against such amendment, respectively, or if no shares have been issued, a statement to that effect.

(f) If such amendment provides for an exchange, reclassification or cancellation of issued shares, and if the manner in which the same shall be effected is not set forth in the amendment, then a statement of the manner in which the same shall be effected.

(g) If such amendment effects a change in the amount of stated capital, then a statement of the manner in which the same is effected and a statement, expressed in dollars, of the amount of stated capital as changed by such amendment.

62. Filing of Articles of Amendment

Duplicate originals of the articles of amendment shall be delivered to the Secretary of State. If the Secretary of State finds that the articles of amendment conform to law, he shall, when all fees and franchise taxes have been paid as in this Act prescribed:

(a) Endorse on each of such duplicate originals the word "Filed," and the month, day and year of the filing thereof.

(b) File one of such duplicate originals in his office.

(c) Issue a certificate of amendment to which he shall affix the other duplicate original.

The certificate of amendment, together with the duplicate original of the articles of amendment affixed thereto by the Secretary of State, shall be returned to the corporation or its representative.

63. Effect of Certificate of Amendment

Upon the issuance of the certificate of amendment by the Secretary of State, the amendment shall become effective and the articles of incorporation shall be deemed to be amended accordingly.

No amendment shall affect any existing cause of action in favor of or against such corporation, or any pending suit to which such corporation shall be a party, or the existing rights of persons other than shareholders; and, in the event the corporate name shall be changed by amendment, no suit brought by or against such corporation under its former name shall abate for that reason.

64. Restated Articles of Incorporation

A domestic corporation may at any time restate its articles of incorporation as theretofore amended, by a resolution adopted by the board of directors.

Upon the adoption of such resolution, restated articles of incorporation shall be executed in duplicate by the corporation by its president or a vice president and by its secretary or assistant secretary and verified by one of the officers signing such articles and shall set forth all of the operative provisions of the articles of incorporation as theretofore amended together with a statement that the restated articles of incorporation correctly set forth without change the corresponding provisions of the articles of incorporation as theretofore amended and that the restated articles of incorporation supersede the original articles of incorporation and all amendments thereto.

Duplicate originals of the restated articles of incorporation shall be delivered to the Secretary of State. If the Secretary of State finds that such restated articles of incorporation conform to law, he shall, when all fees and franchise taxes have been paid as in this Act prescribed:

(1) Endorse on each of such duplicate originals the word "Filed," and the month, day and year of the filing thereof.

(2) File one of such duplicate originals in his office.

(3) Issue a restated certificate of incorporation, to which he shall affix the other duplicate original.

The restated certificate of incorporation, together with the duplicate original of the restated articles of incorporation affixed thereto by the Secretary of State, shall be returned to the corporation or its representative.

Upon the issuance of the restated certificate of incorporation by the Secretary of State, the restated articles of incorporation shall become effective and shall supersede the original articles of incorporation and all amendments thereto.

65. Amendment of Articles of Incorporation in Reorganization Proceedings

Whenever a plan of reorganization of a corporation has been confirmed by decree or order of a court of competent jurisdiction in proceedings for the reorganization of such corporation, pursuant to the provisions of any applicable statute of the United States relating to reorganizations of corporations, the articles of incorporation of the corporation may be amended, in the manner provided in this section, in as many respects as may be necessary to carry out the plan and put it into effect, so long as the articles of incorporation as amended contain only such provisions as might be lawfully contained in original articles of incorporation at the time of making such amendment.

In particular and without limitation upon such general power of amendment, the articles of incorporation may be amended for such purpose so as to:

(A) Change the corporate name, period of duration or corporate purposes of the corporation;

(B) Repeal, alter or amend the by-laws of the corporation;

(C) Change the aggregate number of shares or shares of any class, which the corporation has authority to issue;

(D) Change the preferences, limitations and relative rights in respect of all or any part of the shares of the corporation, and classify, reclassify or cancel all or any part thereof, whether issued or unissued;

(E) Authorize the issuance of bonds, debentures or other obligations of the corporation, whether or not convertible into shares of any class or bearing warrants or other evidences of optional rights to purchase or subscribe for shares of any class, and fix the terms and conditions thereof; and

(F) Constitute or reconstitute and classify or reclassify the board of directors of the corporation, and appoint directors and officers in place of or in addition to all or any of the directors or officers then in office.

Amendments to the articles of incorporation pursuant to this section shall be made in the following manner:

(a) Articles of amendment approved by decree or order of such court shall be executed and verified in duplicate by such person or persons as the court shall designate or appoint for the purpose, and shall set forth the name of the corporation, the amendments of the articles of incorporation approved by the court, the date of the decree or order approving the articles of amendment, the title of the proceedings in which the decree or order was entered, and a statement that such decree or order was entered by a court having jurisdiction of the proceedings for the reorganization of the corporation pursuant to the provisions of an applicable statute of the United States.

(b) Duplicate originals of the articles of amendment shall be delivered to the Secretary of State. If the Secretary of State finds that the articles of amendment conform to law, he shall, when all fees and franchise taxes have been paid as in this Act prescribed:

(1) Endorse on each of such duplicate originals the word "Filed," and the month, day and year of the filing thereof.

(2) File one of such duplicate originals in his office.

(3) Issue a certificate of amendment to which he shall affix the other duplicate original.

The certificate of amendment, together with the duplicate original of the articles of amendment affixed thereto by the Secretary of State, shall be returned to the corporation or its representative.

Upon the issuance of the certificate of amendment by the Secretary of State, the amendment shall become effective and the articles of incorporation shall be deemed to be amended accordingly, without any action thereon by the directors or shareholders of the corporation and with the same effect as if the amendments had been adopted by unanimous action of the directors and shareholders of the corporation.

66. Restriction on Redemption or Purchase of Redeemable Shares

No redemption or purchase of redeemable shares shall be made by a corporation when it is insolvent or when such redemption or purchase would render it insolvent, or which would reduce the net assets below the aggregate amount payable to the holders of shares having prior or equal rights to the assets of the corporation upon involuntary dissolution.

67. Cancellation of Redeemable Shares by Redemption or Purchase

When redeemable shares of a corporation are redeemed or purchased by the corporation, the redemption or purchase shall effect a cancellation of such shares, and a statement of cancellation shall be filed as provided in this section. Thereupon such shares shall be restored to the status of authorized but unissued shares, unless the articles of incorporation provide that such shares when redeemed or purchased shall not be reissued, in which case the filing of the statement of cancellation shall constitute an amendment to the articles of incorporation and shall reduce the number of shares of the class so cancelled which the corporation is authorized to issue by the number of shares so cancelled.

The statement of cancellation shall be executed in duplicate by the corporation by its president or a vice president and by its secretary or an assistant secretary, and verified by one of the officers signing such statement, and shall set forth:

(a) The name of the corporation.

(b) The number of redeemable shares cancelled through redemption or purchase, itemized by classes and series.

(c) The aggregate number of issued shares, itemized by classes and series, after giving effect to such cancellation.

(d) The amount, expressed in dollars, of the stated capital of the corporation after giving effect to such cancellation.

(e) If the articles of incorporation provide that the cancelled shares shall not be reissued, the number of shares which the corporation will have authority to issue itemized by classes and series, after giving effect to such cancellation.

Duplicate originals of such statement shall be delivered to the Secretary of State. If the Secretary of State finds that such statement conforms to law, he shall, when all fees and franchise taxes have been paid as in this Act prescribed:

(1) Endorse on each of such duplicate originals the word "Filed," and the month, day and year of the filing thereof.

(2) File one of such duplicate originals in his office.

(3) Return the other duplicate original to the corporation or its representative.

Upon the filing of such statement of cancellation, the stated capital of the corporation shall be deemed to be reduced by that part of the stated capital which was, at the time of such cancellation, represented by the shares so cancelled.

Nothing contained in this section shall be construed to forbid a cancellation of shares or a reduction of stated capital in any other manner permitted by this Act.

68. Cancellation of Other Reacquired Shares

A corporation may at any time, by resolution of its board of directors, cancel all or any part of the shares of the corporation of any class reacquired by it, other than redeemable shares redeemed or purchased, and in such event a statement of cancellation shall be filed as provided in this section.

The statement of cancellation shall be executed in duplicate by the corporation by its president or a vice president and by its secretary or an assistant secretary, and verified by one of the officers signing such statement, and shall set forth:

(a) The name of the corporation.

(b) The number of reacquired shares cancelled by resolution duly adopted by the board of directors, itemized by classes and series, and the date of its adoption.

(c) The aggregate number of issued shares, itemized by classes and series, after giving effect to such cancellation.

(d) The amount, expressed in dollars, of the stated capital of the corporation after giving effect to such cancellation.

Duplicate originals of such statement shall be delivered to the Secretary of State. If the Secretary of State finds that such statement conforms to law, he shall, when all fees and franchise taxes have been paid as in this Act prescribed:

(1) Endorse on each of such duplicate originals the word "Filed," and the month, day and year of the filing thereof.

(2) File one of such duplicate originals in his office.

(3) Return the other duplicate original to the corporation or its representative.

Upon the filing of such statement of cancellation, the stated capital of the corporation shall be deemed to be reduced by that part of the stated capital which was, at the time of such cancellation, represented by the shares so cancelled, and the shares so cancelled shall be restored to the status of authorized but unissued shares.

Nothing contained in this section shall be construed to forbid a cancellation of shares or a reduction of stated capital in any other manner permitted by this Act.

69. Reduction of Stated Capital in Certain Cases

A reduction of the stated capital of a corporation, where such reduction is not accompanied by any action requiring an amendment of the articles of incorporation and not accompanied by a cancellation of shares, may be made in the following manner:

(A) The board of directors shall adopt a resolution setting forth the amount of the proposed reduction and the manner in which the reduction shall be effected, and directing that the question of such reduction be submitted to a vote at a meeting of shareholders, which may be either an annual or a special meeting.

(B) Written notice, stating that the purpose or one of the purposes of such meeting is to consider the question of reducing the stated capital of the corporation in the amount and manner proposed by the board of directors, shall be given to each shareholder of record entitled to vote thereon within the time and in the manner provided in this Act for the giving of notice of meetings of shareholders.

(C) At such meeting a vote of the shareholders entitled to vote thereon shall be taken on the question of approving the proposed reduction of stated capital, which shall require for its adoption the affirmative vote of the holders of a majority of the shares entitled to vote thereon.

When a reduction of the stated capital of a corporation has been approved as provided in this section, a statement shall be executed in duplicate by the corporation by its president or a vice president and by its secretary or an assistant secretary, and verified by one of the officers signing such statement, and shall set forth:

(a) The name of the corporation.

(b) A copy of the resolution of the shareholders approving such reduction, and the date of its adoption.

(c) The number of shares outstanding, and the number of shares entitled to vote thereon.

(d) The number of shares voted for and against such reduction, respectively.

(e) A statement of the manner in which such reduction is effected, and a statement, expressed in dollars, of the amount of stated capital of the corporation after giving effect to such reduction.

Duplicate originals of such statement shall be delivered to the Secretary of State. If the Secretary of State finds that such statement conforms to law, he shall, when all fees and franchise taxes have been paid as in this Act prescribed:

(1) Endorse on each of such duplicate originals the word "Filed," and the month, day and year of the filing thereof.

(2) File one of such duplicate originals in his office.

(3) Return the other duplicate original to the corporation or its representative.

Upon the filing of such statement, the stated capital of the corporation shall be reduced as therein set forth.

No reduction of stated capital shall be made under the provisions of this section which would reduce the amount of the aggregate stated capital of the corporation to an amount equal to or less than the aggregate preferential amounts payable upon all issued shares having a preferential right in the assets of the corporation in the event of involuntary liquidation, plus the aggregate par value of all issued shares having a par value but no preferential right in the assets of the corporation in the event of involuntary liquidation.

70. Special Provisions Relating to Surplus and Reserves

The surplus, if any, created by or arising out of a reduction of the stated capital of a corporation shall be capital surplus.

The capital surplus of a corporation may be increased from time to time by resolution of the board of directors directing that all or a part of the earned surplus of the corporation be transferred to capital surplus.

A corporation may, by resolution of its board of directors, apply any part or all of its capital surplus to the reduction or elimination of any deficit arising from losses, however incurred, but only after first eliminating the earned surplus, if any, of the corporation by applying such losses against earned surplus and only to the extent that such losses exceed the earned surplus, if any. Each such application of capital surplus shall, to the extent thereof, effect a reduction of capital surplus.

A corporation may, by resolution of its board of directors, create a reserve or reserves out of its earned surplus for any proper purpose or purposes, and may abolish any such reserve in the same manner. Earned surplus of the corporation to the extent so reserved shall not be available for the payment of dividends or other distributions by the corporation except as expressly permitted by this Act.

71. Procedure for Merger

Any two or more domestic corporations may merge into one of such corporations pursuant to a plan of merger approved in the manner provided in this Act.

The board of directors of each corporation shall, by resolution adopted by each such board, approve a plan of merger setting forth:

(a) The names of the corporations proposing to merge, and the name of the corporation into which they propose to merge, which is hereinafter designated as the surviving corporation.

(b) The terms and conditions of the proposed merger.

(c) The manner and basis of converting the shares of each corporation into shares, obligations or other securities of the surviving corporation or of any other corporation or, in whole or in part, into cash or other property.

(d) A statement of any changes in the articles of incorporation of the surviving corporation to be effected by such merger.

(e) Such other provisions with respect to the proposed merger as are deemed necessary or desirable.

72. Procedure for Consolidation

Any two or more domestic corporations may consolidate into a new corporation pursuant to a plan of consolidation approved in the manner provided in this Act.

The board of directors of each corporation shall, by a resolution adopted by each such board, approve a plan of consolidation setting forth:

(a) The names of the corporations proposing to consolidate, and the name of the new corporation into which they propose to consolidate, which is hereinafter designated as the new corporation.

(b) The terms and conditions of the proposed consolidation.

(c) The manner and basis of converting the shares of each corporation into shares, obligations or other securities of the new corporation or of any other corporation or, in whole or in part, into cash or other property.

(d) With respect to the new corporation, all of the statements required to be set forth in articles of incorporation for corporations organized under this Act.

(e) Such other provisions with respect to the proposed consolidation as are deemed necessary or desirable.

73. Approval by Shareholders

The board of directors of each corporation, upon approving such plan of merger or plan of consolidation, shall, by resolution, direct that the plan be submitted to a vote at a meeting of shareholders, which may be either an annual or a special meeting. Written notice shall be given to each shareholder of record, whether or not entitled to vote at such meeting, not less than twenty days before such meeting, in the manner provided in this Act for the giving of notice of meetings of shareholders, and, whether the meeting be an annual or a special meeting, shall state that the purpose or one of the purposes is to consider the proposed plan of merger or consolidation. A copy or a summary of the plan of merger or plan of consolidation, as the case may be, shall be included in or enclosed with such notice.

At each such meeting, a vote of the shareholders shall be taken on the proposed plan of merger or consolidation. The plan of merger or consolidation shall be approved upon receiving the affirmative vote of the holders of a majority of the shares entitled to vote thereon of each such corporation, unless any class of shares of any such corporation is entitled to vote thereon as a class, in which event, as to such corporation, the plan of merger, or consolidation shall be approved upon receiving the affirmative vote of the holders of a majority of the shares of each class of shares entitled to vote thereon as a class and of the total shares entitled to vote thereon. Any class of shares or any such corporation shall be entitled to vote as a class if the plan of merger or consolidation, as the case may be, contains any provision which, if contained in a proposed amendment to articles of incorporation, would entitle such class of shares to vote as a class.

After such approval by a vote of the shareholders of each corporation, and at any time prior to the filing of the articles of merger or consolidation, the merger or consolidation may be abandoned pursuant to provisions therefor, if any, set forth in the plan of merger or consolidation.

74. Articles of Merger or Consolidation

Upon such approval, articles of merger or articles of consolidation shall be executed in duplicate by each corporation by its president or a vice president and by its secretary or an assistant secretary, and verified by one of the officers of each corporation signing such articles, and shall set forth:

(a) The plan of merger or the plan of consolidation.

(b) As to each corporation, the number of shares outstanding, and, if the shares of any class are entitled to vote as a class, the designation and number of outstanding shares of each such class.

(c) As to each corporation, the number of shares voted for and against such plan, respectively, and, if the shares of any class are entitled to vote as a class, the number of shares of each such class voted for and against such plan, respectively.

Duplicate originals of the articles of merger or articles of consolidation shall be delivered to the Secretary of State. If the Secretary of State finds that such articles conform to law, he shall, when all fees and franchise taxes have been paid as in this Act prescribed:

(1) Endorse on each of such duplicate originals the word "Filed," and the month, day and year of the filing thereof.

(2) File one of such duplicate originals in his office.

(3) Issue a certificate of merger or a certificate of consolidation to which he shall affix the other duplicate original.

The certificate of merger or certificate of consolidation, together with the duplicate original of the articles of merger or articles of consolidation affixed thereto by the Secretary of State, shall be returned to the surviving or new corporation, as the case may be, or its representative.

75. Merger of Subsidiary Corporation

Any corporation owning at least ninety per cent of the outstanding shares of each class of another corporation may merge such other corporation into itself without approval by a vote of the shareholders of either corporation. Its board of directors shall, by resolution, approve a plan of merger setting forth:

(A) The name of the subsidiary corporation and the name of the corporation owning at least ninety per cent of its shares, which is hereinafter designated as the surviving corporation.

(B) The manner and basis of converting the shares of the subsidiary corporation into shares, obligations or other securities of the surviving corporation or of any other corporation or, in whole or in part, into cash or other property.

A copy of such plan of merger shall be mailed to each shareholder of record of the subsidiary corporation.

Articles of merger shall be executed in duplicate by the surviving corporation by its president or a vice president and by its secretary or an assistant secretary, and verified by one of its officers signing such articles, and shall set forth:

(a) The plan of merger;

(b) The number of outstanding shares of each class of the subsidiary corporation and the number of such shares of each class owned by the surviving corporation; and

(c) The date of the mailing to shareholders of the subsidiary corporation of a copy of the plan of merger.

On and after the thirtieth day after the mailing of a copy of the plan of merger to shareholders of the subsidiary corporation or upon the waiver thereof by the holders of all outstanding shares duplicate originals of the articles of merger shall be delivered to the Secretary of State. If the Secretary of State finds that such articles conform to law, he shall, when all fees and franchise taxes have been paid as in this Act prescribed:

(1) Endorse on each of such duplicate originals the word "Filed," and the month, day and year of the filing thereof,

(2) File one of such duplicate originals in his office, and

(3) Issue a certificate of merger to which he shall affix the other duplicate original.

The certificate of merger, together with the duplicate original of the articles of merger affixed thereto by the Secretary of State, shall be returned to the surviving corporation or its representative.

76. Effect of Merger or Consolidation

Upon the issuance of the certificate of merger or the certificate of consolidation by the Secretary of State, the merger or consolidation shall be effected.

When such merger or consolidation has been effected:

(a) The several corporations parties to the plan of merger or consolidation shall be a single corporation, which, in the case of a merger, shall be that corporation designated in the plan of merger as the surviving corporation, and, in the case of a consolidation, shall be the new corporation provided for in the plan of consolidation.

(b) The separate existence of all corporations parties to the plan of merger or consolidation, except the surviving or new corporation, shall cease.

(c) Such surviving or new corporation shall have all the rights, privileges, immunities and powers and shall be subject to all the duties and liabilities of a corporation organized under this Act.

(d) Such surviving or new corporation shall thereupon and thereafter possess all the rights, privileges, immunities, and franchises, of a public as well as of a private nature, of each of the merging or consolidating corporations; and all property, real, personal and mixed, and all debts due on whatever account, including subscriptions to shares, and all other choses in action, and all and every other interest of or belonging to or due to each of the corporations so merged or consolidated, shall be taken and deemed to be transferred to and vested in such single corporation without further act or deed; and the title to any real estate, or any interest therein, vested in any of such corporations shall not revert or be in any way impaired by reason of such merger or consolidation.

(e) Such surviving or new corporation shall thenceforth be responsible and liable for all the liabilities and obligations of each of the corporations so merged or consolidated; and any claim existing or action or proceeding pending by or against any of such corporations may be prosecuted as if such merger or consolidation had not taken place, or such surviving or new corporation may be substituted in its place. Neither the rights of creditors nor any liens upon the property of any such corporation shall be impaired by such merger or consolidation.

(f) In the case of a merger, the articles of incorporation of the surviving corporation shall be deemed to be amended to the extent, if any, that changes in its articles of incorporation are stated in the plan of merger; and, in the case of a consolidation, the statements set forth in the articles of consolidation and which are required or permitted to be set forth in the articles of incorporation of corporations organized under this Act shall be deemed to be the original articles of incorporation of the new corporation.

77. Merger or Consolidation of Domestic and Foreign Corporations

One or more foreign corporations and one or more domestic corporations may be merged or consolidated in the following manner, if such merger or consolidation is permitted by the laws of the state under which each such foreign corporation is organized:

(a) Each domestic corporation shall comply with the provisions of this Act with respect to the merger or consolidation, as the case may be, of domestic corporations and each foreign corporation shall comply with the applicable provisions of the laws of the state under which it is organized.

(b) If the surviving or new corporation, as the case may be, is to be governed by the laws of any state other than this State, it shall comply with the provisions of this Act with respect to foreign corporations if it is to transact business in this State, and in every case it shall file with the Secretary of State of this State:

(1) An agreement that it may be served with process in this State in any proceeding for the enforcement of any obligation of any domestic corporation which is a party to such merger or consolidation and in any proceeding for the enforcement of the rights of a dissenting shareholder of any such domestic corporation against the surviving or new corporation;

(2) An irrevocable appointment of the Secretary of State of this State as its agent to accept service of process in any such proceeding; and

(3) An agreement that it will promptly pay to the dissenting shareholders of any such domestic corporation the amount, if any, to which they shall be entitled under the provisions of this Act with respect to the rights of dissenting shareholders.

The effect of such merger or consolidation shall be the same as in the case of the merger or consolidation of domestic corporations, if the surviving or new corporation is to be governed by the laws of this State. If the surviving or new corporation is to be governed by the laws of any state other than this State, the effect of such merger or consolidation shall be the same as in the case of the merger or consolidation of domestic corporations except insofar as the laws of such other state provide otherwise.

At any time prior to the filing of the articles of merger or consolidation, the merger or consolidation may be abandoned pursuant to provisions therefor, if any, set forth in the plan of merger or consolidation.

78. Sale of Assets in Regular Course of Business and Mortgage or Pledge of Assets

The sale, lease, exchange, or other disposition of all, or substantially all, the property and assets of a corporation in the usual and regular course of its business and the mortgage or pledge of any or all property and assets of a corporation whether or not in the usual and regular course of business may be made upon such terms and conditions and for such consideration, which may consist in whole or in part of cash or other property, including shares, obligations or other securities of any other corporation, domestic or foreign, as shall be authorized by its board of directors; and in any such case no authorization or consent of the shareholders shall be required.

79. Sale of Assets Other Than in Regular Course of Business

A sale, lease, exchange, or other disposition of all, or substantially all, the property and assets, with or without the good will, of a corporation, if not in the usual and regular course of its business, may be made upon such terms and conditions and for such consideration, which may consist in whole or in part of cash or other property, including shares, obligations or other securities of any other corporation, domestic or foreign, as may be authorized in the following manner:

(a) The board of directors shall adopt a resolution recommending such sale, lease, exchange, or other disposition and directing the submission thereof to a vote at a meeting of shareholders, which may be either an annual or a special meeting.

(b) Written notice shall be given to each shareholder of record, whether or not entitled to vote at such meeting, not less than twenty days before such meeting, in the manner provided in this Act for the giving of notice of meetings of shareholders, and, whether the meeting be an annual or a special meeting, shall state that the purpose, or one of the purposes is to consider the proposed sale, lease, exchange, or other disposition.

(c) At such meeting the shareholders may authorize such sale, lease, exchange, or other disposition and may fix, or may authorize the board of directors to fix, any or all of the terms and conditions thereof and the consideration to be received by the corporation therefor. Such authorization shall require the affirmative vote of the holders of a majority of the shares of the corporation entitled to vote thereon, unless any class of shares is entitled to vote thereon as a class, in which event such authorization shall require the affirmative vote of the holders of a majority of the shares of each class of shares entitled to vote as a class thereon and of the total shares entitled to vote thereon.

(d) After such authorization by a vote of shareholders, the board of directors nevertheless, in its discretion, may abandon such sale, lease, exchange, or other disposition of assets, subject to the rights of third parties under any contracts relating thereto, without further action or approval by shareholders.

80. Right of Shareholders to Dissent

Any shareholder of a corporation shall have the right to dissent from any of the following corporate actions:

(a) Any plan of merger or consolidation to which the corporation is a party; or

(b) Any sale or exchange of all or substantially all of the property and assets of the corporation not made in the usual and regular course of its business, including a sale in dissolution, but not including a sale pursuant to an order of a court having jurisdiction in the premises or a sale for cash on terms requiring that all or substantially all of the net proceeds of sale be distributed to the shareholders in accordance with their respective interests within one year after the date of sale.

A shareholder may dissent as to less than all of the shares registered in his name. In that event, his rights shall be determined as if the shares as to which he has dissented and his other shares were registered in the names of different shareholders.

This section shall not apply to the shareholders of the surviving corporation in a merger if a vote of the shareholders of such corporation is not necessary to authorize such merger. Nor shall it apply to the holders of shares of any class or series if the shares of such class or series were registered on a national securities exchange on the date fixed to determine the shareholders entitled to vote at the meeting of shareholders at which a plan of merger or consolidation or a proposed sale or exchange of property and assets is to be acted upon unless the articles of incorporation of the corporation shall otherwise provide.

81. Rights of Dissenting Shareholders

Any shareholder electing to exercise such right of dissent shall file with the corporation, prior to or at the meeting of shareholders at which such proposed corporate action is submitted to a vote, a written objection to such proposed corporate action. If such proposed corporate action be approved by the required vote and such shareholder shall not have voted in favor thereof, such shareholder may, within ten days after the date on which the vote was taken or if a corporation is to be merged without a vote of its shareholders into another corporation, any of its shareholders may, within fifteen days after the plan of such merger shall have been mailed to such shareholders, make written demand on the corporation, or, in the case of a merger or consolidation, on the surviving or new corporation, domestic or foreign, for payment of the fair value of such shareholder's shares, and, if such proposed corporate action is effected, such corporation shall pay to such shareholder, upon surrender of the certificate or certificates representing such shares, the fair value thereof as of the day prior to the date on which the vote was taken approving the proposed corporate action, excluding any appreciation or depreciation in anticipation of such corporate action. Any shareholder failing to make demand within the applicable ten-day or fifteen-day period shall be bound by the terms of the proposed corporate action. Any shareholder making such demand shall thereafter be entitled only to payment as in

this section provided and shall not be entitled to vote or to exercise any other rights of a shareholder.

No such demand may be withdrawn unless the corporation shall consent thereto. If, however, such demand shall be withdrawn upon consent, or if the proposed corporate action shall be abandoned or rescinded or the shareholders shall revoke the authority to effect such action, or if, in the case of a merger, on the date of the filing of the articles of merger the surviving corporation is the owner of all the outstanding shares of the other corporations, domestic and foreign, that are parties to the merger, or if no demand or petition for the determination of fair value by a court shall have been made or filed within the time provided in this section, or if a court of competent jurisdiction shall determine that such shareholder is not entitled to the relief provided by this section, then the right of such shareholder to be paid the fair value of his shares shall cease and his status as a shareholder shall be restored, without prejudice to any corporate proceedings which may have been taken during the interim.

Within ten days after such corporate action is effected, the corporation, or, in the case of a merger or consolidation, the surviving or new corporation, domestic or foreign, shall give written notice thereof to each dissenting shareholder who has made demand as herein provided, and shall make a written offer to each such shareholder to pay for such shares at a specified price deemed by such corporation to be the fair value thereof. Such notice and offer shall be accompanied by a balance sheet of the corporation the shares of which the dissenting shareholder holds, as of the latest available date and not more than twelve months prior to the making of such offer, and a profit and loss statement of such corporation for the twelve months' period ended on the date of such balance sheet.

If within thirty days after the date on which such corporate action was effected the fair value of such shares is agreed upon between any such dissenting shareholder and the corporation, payment therefore shall be made within ninety days after the date on which such corporate action was effected, upon surrender of the certificate or certificates representing such shares. Upon payment of the agreed value the dissenting shareholder shall cease to have any interst in such shares.

If within such period of thirty days a dissenting shareholder and the corporation do not so agree, then the corporation, within thirty days after receipt of written demand from any dissenting shareholder given within sixty days after the date on which such corporate action was effected, shall, or at its election at any time within such period of sixty days may, file a petition in any court of competent jurisdiction in the county in this State where the registered office of the corporation is located requesting that the fair value of such shares be found and determined. If, in the case of a merger or consolidation, the surviving or new corporation is a foreign corporation without a registered office in this State, such petition shall be filed in the county where the registered office of the domestic corporation was last located. If the corporation shall fail to institute the proceeding as herein provided, any dissenting shareholder may do so in the name of the corporation. All dissenting shareholders, wherever residing, shall be made parties to the proceeding as an action against their shares quasi in rem. A copy of the petition shall be served on each dissenting shareholder who is a resident of this State and shall be served by registered or certified mail on each dissenting shareholder who is a nonresident. Service on nonresidents shall also be made by publication as provided by law. The jurisdiction of the court shall be plenary and exclusive. All shareholders who are parties to the proceeding shall be entitled to judgment against the corporation for the amount of the fair value of their shares. The court may, if it so elects, appoint one or more persons as appraisers to receive evidence and recommend a decision on the question of fair value. The appraisers shall have such power and authority as shall be specified in the order of their appointment or an amendment thereof. The judgment shall be payable only upon and concurrently with the surrender to the corporation of the certificate or certificates representing such shares. Upon payment of the judgment, the dissenting shareholder shall cease to have any interest in such shares.

The judgment shall include an allowance for interest at such rate as the court may find to be fair and equitable in all the circumstances, from the date on which the vote was taken on the proposed corporate action to the date of payment.

The costs and expenses of any such proceeding shall be determined by the court and shall be assessed against the corporation, but all or any part of such costs and expenses may be apportioned and assessed as the court may deem equitable against any or all of the dissenting shareholders who are parties to the proceeding to whom the corporation shall have made an offer to pay for the shares if the court shall find that the action of such shareholders in failing to accept such offer was arbitrary or vexatious or not in good faith. Such expenses shall include reasonable compensation for and reasonable expenses of the appraisers, but shall exclude the fees and expenses of counsel for and experts employed by any party; but if the fair value of the shares as determined materially exceeds the amount which the corporation offered to pay therefor, or if no offer was made, the court in its discretion may award to any shareholder who is a party to the proceeding such sum as the court may determine to be reasonable compensation to any expert or experts employed by the shareholder in the proceeding.

Within twenty days after demanding payment for his shares, each shareholder demanding payment shall submit the certificate or certificates representing his shares to the corporation for notation thereon that such demand has been made. His failure to do so shall, at the option of the corporation, terminate his rights under this section unless a court of competent jurisdiction, for good and sufficient cause shown, shall otherwise direct. If shares represented by a certificate on which notation has been so made shall be transferred, each new certificate issued therefor shall bear similar notation, together with the name of the original dissenting holder of such shares, and a transferee of such shares shall acquire by such transfer no rights in the corporation other than those which the original dissenting shareholder had after making demand for payment of the fair value thereof.

Shares acquired by a corporation pursuant to payment of the agreed value therefor or to payment of the judgment entered therefor, as in this section provided, may be held and disposed of by such corporation as in the case of other treasury shares, except that, in the case of a merger or consolidation, they may be held and disposed of as the plan of merger or consolidation may otherwise provide.

82. Voluntary Dissolution by Incorporators

A corporation which has not commenced business and which has not issued any shares, may be voluntarily dissolved by its incorporators at any time in the following manner:

(a) Articles of dissolution shall be executed in duplicate by a majority of the incorporators, and verified by them, and shall set forth:

(1) The name of the corporation.

(2) The date of issuance of its certificate of incorporation.

(3) That none of its shares has been issued.

(4) That the corporation has not commenced business.

(5) That the amount, if any, actually paid in on subscriptions for its shares, less any part thereof disbursed for necessary expenses, has been returned to those entitled thereto.

(6) That no debts of the corporation remain unpaid.

(7) That a majority of the incorporators elect that the corporation be dissolved.

(b) Duplicate originals of the articles of dissolution shall be delivered to the Secretary of State. If the Secretary of State finds that the articles of dissolution conform to law, he shall, when all fees and franchise taxes have been paid as in this Act prescribed:

(1) Endorse on each of such duplicate originals the word "Filed," and the month, day and year of the filing thereof.

(2) File one of such duplicate originals in his office.

(3) Issue a certificate of dissolution to which he shall affix the other duplicate original.

The certificate of dissolution, together with the duplicate original of the articles of dissolution affixed thereto by the Secretary of State, shall be returned to the incorporators or their representative. Upon the issuance of such certificate of dissolution by the Secretary of State, the existence of the corporation shall cease.

83. Voluntary Dissolution by Consent of Shareholders

A corporation may be voluntarily dissolved by the written consent of all of its shareholders.

Upon the execution of such written consent, a statement of intent to dissolve shall be executed in duplicate by the corporation by its president or a vice president and by its secretary or an assistant secretary, and verified by one of the officers signing such statement, which statement shall set forth:

(a) The name of the corporation.

(b) The names and respective addresses of its officers.

(c) The names and respective addresses of its directors.

(d) A copy of the written consent signed by all shareholders of the corporation.

(e) A statement that such written consent has been signed by all shareholders of the corporation or signed in their names by their attorneys thereunto duly authorized.

84. Voluntary Dissolution by Act of Corporation

A corporation may be dissolved by the act of the corporation, when authorized in the following manner:

(a) The board of directors shall adopt a resolution recommending that the corporation be dissolved, and directing that the question of such dissolution be submitted to a vote at a meeting of shareholders, which may be either an annual or a special meeting.

(b) Written notice shall be given to each shareholder of record entitled to vote at such meeting within the time and in the manner provided in this Act for the giving of notice of meetings of shareholders, and, whether the meeting be an annual or special meeting, shall state that the purpose, or one of the purposes, of such meeting is to consider the advisability of dissolving the corporation.

(c) At such meeting a vote of shareholders entitled to vote thereat shall be taken on a resolution to dissolve the corporation. Such resolution shall be adopted upon receiving the affirmative vote of the holders of a majority of the shares of the corporation entitled to vote thereon, unless any class of shares is entitled to vote thereon as a class, in which event the resolution shall be adopted upon receiving the affirmative vote of the holders of a majority of the shares of each class of shares entitled to vote thereon as a class and of the total shares entitled to vote thereon.

(d) Upon the adoption of such resolution, a statement of intent to dissolve shall be executed in duplicate by the corporation by its president or a vice president and by its secretary or an assistant secretary, and verified by one of the officers signing such statement, which statement shall set forth:

(1) The name of the corporation.

(2) The names and respective addresses of its officers.

(3) The names and respective addresses of its directors.

(4) A copy of the resolution adopted by the shareholders authorizing the dissolution of the corporation.

(5) The number of shares outstanding, and, if the shares of any class are entitled to vote as a class, the designation and number of outstanding shares of each such class.

(6) The number of shares voted for and against the resolution, respectively, and, if the shares of any class are entitled to vote as a class, the number of shares of each such class voted for and against the resolution, respectively.

85. Filing of Statement of Intent to Dissolve

Duplicate originals of the statement of intent to dissolve, whether by consent of shareholders or by act of the corporation, shall be delivered to the Secretary of State. If the Secretary of State finds that such statement conforms to law, he shall, when all fees and franchise taxes have been paid as in this Act prescribed:

(a) Endorse on each of such duplicate originals the word "Filed," and the month, day and year of the filing thereof.

(b) File one of such duplicate originals in his office.

(c) Return the other duplicate original to the corporation or its representative.

86. Effect of Statement of Intent to Dissolve

Upon the filing by the Secretary of State of a statement of intent to dissolve, whether by consent of shareholders or by act of the corporation, the corporation shall cease to carry on its business, except insofar as may be necessary for the winding up thereof, but its corporate existence shall continue until a certificate of dissolution has been issued by the Secretary of State or until a decree dissolving the corporation has

been entered by a court of competent jurisdiction as in this Act provided.

87. Procedure after Filing of Statement of Intent to Dissolve

After the filing by the Secretary of State of a statement of intent to dissolve:

(a) The corporation shall immediately cause notice thereof to be mailed to each known creditor of the corporation.

(b) The corporation shall proceed to collect its assets, convey and dispose of such of its properties as are not to be distributed in kind to its shareholders, pay, satisfy and discharge its liabilities and obligations and do all other acts required to liquidate its business and affairs, and, after paying or adequately providing for the payment of all its obligations, distribute the remainder of its assets, either in cash or in kind, among its shareholders according to their respective rights and interests.

(c) The corporation, at any time during the liquidation of its business and affairs, may make application to a court of competent jurisdiction within the state and judicial subdivision in which the registered office or principal place of business of the corporation is situated, to have the liquidation continued under the supervision of the court as provided in this Act.

88. Revocation of Voluntary Dissolution Proceedings by Consent of Shareholders

By the written consent of all of its shareholders, a corporation may, at any time prior to the issuance of a certificate of dissolution by the Secretary of State, revoke voluntary dissolution proceedings theretofore taken, in the following manner:

Upon the execution of such written consent, a statement of revocation of voluntary dissolution proceedings shall be executed in duplicate by the corporation by its president or a vice president and by its secretary or an assistant secretary, and verified by one of the officers signing such statement, which statement shall set forth:

(a) The name of the corporation.

(b) The names and respective addresses of its officers.

(c) The names and respective addresses of its directors.

(d) A copy of the written consent signed by all shareholders of the corporation revoking such voluntary dissolution proceedings.

(e) That such written consent has been signed by all shareholders of the corporation or signed in their names by their attorneys thereunto duly authorized.

89. Revocation of Voluntary Dissolution Proceedings by Act of Corporation

By the act of the corporation, a corporation may, at any time prior to the issuance of a certificate of dissolution by the Secretary of State, revoke voluntary dissolution proceedings theretofore taken, in the following manner:

(a) The board of directors shall adopt a resolution recommending that the voluntary dissolution proceedings be revoked, and directing that the question of such revocation be submitted to a vote at a special meeting of shareholders.

(b) Written notice, stating that the purpose or one of the purposes of such meeting is to consider the advisability of revoking the voluntary dissolution proceedings, shall be given to each shareholder of record entitled to vote at such meeting within the time and in the manner provided in this Act for the giving of notice of special meetings of shareholders.

(c) At such meeting a vote of the shareholders entitled to vote thereat shall be taken on a resolution to revoke the voluntary dissolution proceedings, which shall require for its adoption the affirmative vote of the holders of a majority of the shares entitled to vote thereon.

(d) Upon the adoption of such resolution, a statement of revocation of voluntary dissolution proceedings shall be executed in duplicate by the corporation by its president or a vice president and by its secretary or an assistant secretary, and verified by one of the officers signing such statement, which statement shall set forth:

(1) The name of the corporation.

(2) The names and respective addresses of its officers.

(3) The names and respective addresses of its directors.

(4) A copy of the resolution adopted by the shareholders revoking the voluntary dissolution proceedings.

(5) The number of shares outstanding.

(6) The number of shares voted for and against the resolution, respectively.

90. Filing of Statement of Revocation of Voluntary Dissolution Proceedings

Duplicate originals of the statement of revocation of voluntary dissolution proceedings, whether by consent of shareholders or by act of the corporation, shall be delivered to the Secretary of State. If the Secretary of State finds that such statement conforms to law, he shall, when all fees and franchise taxes have been paid as in this Act prescribed:

(a) Endorse on each of such duplicate originals the word "Filed," and the month, day and year of the filing thereof.

(b) File one of such duplicate originals in his office.

(c) Return the other duplicate original to the corporation or its representative.

91. Effect of Statement of Revocation of Voluntary Dissolution Proceedings

Upon the filing by the Secretary of State of a statement of revocation of voluntary dissolution proceedings, whether by consent of shareholders or by act of the corporation, the revocation of the voluntary dissolution proceedings shall become effective and the corporation may again carry on its business.

92. Articles of Dissolution

If voluntary dissolution proceedings have not been revoked, then when all debts, liabilities and obligations of the corporation have been paid and discharged, or adequate provision has been made therefor, and all of the remaining property and assets of the corporation have been distributed to its shareholders, articles of dissolution shall be executed in duplicate by the corporation by its president or a vice president and by its secretary or an assistant secretary, and verified by one of the officers signing such statement, which statement shall set forth:

(a) The name of the corporation.

(b) That the Secretary of State has theretofore filed a statement of intent to dissolve the corporation, and the date on which such statement was filed.

(c) That all debts, obligations and liabilities of the corporation have been paid and discharged or that adequate provision has been made therefor.

(d) That all the remaining property and assets of the corporation have been distributed among its shareholders in accordance with their respective rights and interests.

(e) That there are no suits pending against the corporation in any court, or that adequate provision has been made for the satisfaction of any judgment, order or decree which may be entered against it in any pending suit.

93. Filing of Articles of Dissolution

Duplicate originals of such articles of dissolution shall be delivered to the Secretary of State. If the Secretary of State finds that such articles of dissolution conform to law, he shall, when all fees and franchise taxes have been paid as in this Act prescribed:

(a) Endorse on each of such duplicate originals the word "Filed," and the month, day and year of the filing thereof.

(b) File one of such duplicate originals in his office.

(c) Issue a certificate of dissolution to which he shall affix the other duplicate original.

The certificate of dissolution, together with the duplicate original of the articles of dissolution affixed thereto by the Secretary of State, shall be returned to the representative of the dissolved corporation. Upon the issuance of such certificate of dissolution the existence of the corporation shall cease, except for the purpose of suits, other proceedings and appropriate corporate action by shareholders, directors and officers as provided in this Act.

94. Involuntary Dissolution

A corporation may be dissolved involuntarily by a decree of the .... court in an action filed by the Attorney General when it is established that:

(a) The corporation has failed to file its annual report within the time required by this Act, or has failed to pay its franchise tax on or before the first day of August of the year in which such franchise tax becomes due and payable; or

(b) The corporation procured its articles of incorporation through fraud; or

(c) The corporation has continued to exceed or abuse the authority conferred upon it by law; or

(d) The corporation has failed for thirty days to appoint and maintain a registered agent in this State; or

(e) The corporation has failed for thirty days after change of its registered office or registered agent to file in the office of the Secretary of State a statement of such change.

95. Notification to Attorney General

The Secretary of State, on or before the last day of December of each year, shall certify to the Attorney General the names of all corporations which have failed to file their annual reports or to pay franchise taxes in accordance with the provisions of this Act, together with the facts pertinent thereto. He shall also certify, from time to time, the names of all corporations which have given other cause for dissolution as provided in this Act, together with the facts pertinent thereto. Whenever the Secretary of State shall certify the name of a corporation to the Attorney General as having given any cause for dissolution, the Secretary of State shall concurrently mail to the corporation at its registered office a notice that such certification has been made. Upon the receipt of such certification, the Attorney General shall file an action in the name of the State against such corporation for its dissolution. Every such certificate from the Secretary of State to the Attorney General pertaining to the failure of a corporation to file an annual report or pay a franchise tax shall be taken and received in all courts as prima facie evidence of the facts therein stated. If, before action is filed, the corporation shall file its annual report or pay its franchise tax, together with all penalties thereon, or shall appoint or maintain a registered agent as provided in this Act, or shall file with the Secretary of State the required statement of change of registered office or registered agent, such fact shall be forthwith certified by the Secretary of State to the Attorney General and he shall not file an action against such corporation for such cause. If, after action is filed, the corporation shall file its annual report or pay its franchise tax, together with all penalties thereon, or shall appoint or maintain a registered agent as provided in this Act, or shall file with the Secretary of State the required statement of change of registered office or registered agent, and shall pay the costs of such action, the action for such cause shall abate.

96.   Venue and Process

Every action for the involuntary dissolution of a corporation shall be commenced by the Attorney General either in the . . . . . . court of the county in which the registered office of the corporation is situated, or in the . . . . court of . . . . county. Summons shall issue and be served as in other civil actions. If process is returned not found, the Attorney General shall cause publication to be made as in other civil cases in some newspaper published in the county where the registered office of the corporation is situated, containing a notice of the pendency of such action, the title of the court, the title of the action, and the date on or after which default may be entered. The Attorney General may include in one notice the names of any number of corporations against which actions are then pending in the same court. The Attorney General shall cause a copy of such notice to be mailed to the corporation at its registered office within ten days after the first publication thereof. The certificate of the Attorney General of the mailing of such notice shall be prima facie evidence thereof. Such notice shall be published at least once each week for two successive weeks, and the first publication thereof may begin at any time after the summons has been returned. Unless a corporation shall have been served with summons, no default shall be taken against it earlier than thirty days after the first publication of such notice.

97.   Jurisdiction of Court to Liquidate Assets and Business of Corporation

The . . . . courts shall have full power to liquidate the assets and business of a corporation:

(a) In an action by a shareholder when it is established:

(1) That the directors are deadlocked in the management of the corporate affairs and the shareholders are unable to break the deadlock, and that irreparable injury to the corporation is being suffered or is threatened by reason thereof; or

(2) That the acts of the directors or those in control of the corporation are illegal, oppressive or fraudulent; or

(3) That the shareholders are deadlocked in voting power, and have failed, for a period which includes at least two consecutive annual meeting dates, to elect successors to directors whose terms have expired or would have expired upon the election of their successors; or

(4) That the corporate assets are being misapplied or wasted.

(b) In an action by a creditor:

(1) When the claim of the creditor has been reduced to judgment and an execution thereon returned unsatisfied and it is established that the corporation is insolvent; or

(2) When the corporation has admitted in writing that the claim of the creditor is due and owing and it is established that the corporation is insolvent.

(c) Upon application by a corporation which has filed a statement of intent to dissolve, as provided in this Act, to have its liquidation continued under the supervision of the court.

(d) When an action has been filed by the Attorney General to dissolve a corporation and it is established that liquidation of its business and affairs should precede the entry of a decree of dissolution.

Proceedings under clause (a), (b) or (c) of this section shall be brought in the county in which the registered office or the principal office of the corporation is situated.

It shall not be necessary to make shareholders parties to any such action or proceeding unless relief is sought aagainst them personally.

98.   Procedure in Liquidation of Corporation by Court

In proceedings to liquidate the assets and business of a corporation the court shall have power to issue injunctions, to appoint a receiver or receivers pendente lite, with such powers and duties as the court, from time to time, may direct, and to take such other proceedings as may be requisite to preserve the corporate assets wherever situated, and carry on the business of the corporation until a full hearing can be had.

After a hearing had upon such notice as the court may direct to be given to all parties to the proceedings and to any other parties in interest designated by the court, the court may appoint a liquidating receiver or receivers with authority to collect the assets of the corporation, including all amounts owing to the corporation by subscribers on account of any unpaid portion of the consideration for the issuance of shares. Such liquidating receiver or receivers shall have authority, subject to the order of the court, to sell, to convey and dispose of all or any part of the assets of the corporation wherever situated, either at public or private sale. The assets of the corporation or the proceeds resulting from a sale, conveyance or other disposition thereof shall be applied to the expenses of such liquidation and to the payment of the liabilities and obligations of the corporation, and any remaining assets or proceeds shall be distributed among its shareholders according to their respective rights and interests. The order appointing such liquidating receiver or receivers shall state their powers and duties. Such powers and duties may be increased or diminished at any time during the proceedings.

The court shall have power to allow from time to time as expenses of the liquidation compensation to the receiver or receivers and to attorneys in the proceeding, and to direct the payment thereof out of the assets of the corporation or the proceeds of any sale or disposition of such assets.

A receiver of a corporation appointed under the provisions of this section shall have authority to sue and defend in all courts in his own name as receiver of such corporation. The court appointing such receiver shall have exclusive jurisdiction of the corporation and its property, wherever situated.

99. Qualifications of Receivers

A receiver shall in all cases be a natural person or a corporation authorized to act as receiver, which corporation may be a domestic corporation or a foreign corporation authorized to transact business in this State, and shall in all cases give such bond as the court may direct with such sureties as the court may require.

100. Filing of Claims in Liquidation Proceedings

In proceedings to liquidate the assets and business of a corporation the court may require all creditors of the corporation to file with the clerk of the court or with the receiver, in such form as the court may prescribe, proofs under oath of their respective claims. If the court requires the filing of claims it shall fix a date, which shall be not less than four months from the date of the order, as the last day for the filing of claims, and shall prescribe the notice that shall be given to creditors and claimants of the date so fixed. Prior to the date so fixed, the court may extend the time for the filing of claims. Creditors and claimants failing to file proofs of claim on or before the date so fixed may be barred, by order of court, from participating in the distribution of the assets of the corporation.

101. Discontinuance of Liquidation Proceedings

The liquidation of the assets and business of a corporation may be discontinued at any time during the liquidation proceedings when it is established that cause for liquidation no longer exists. In such event the court shall dismiss the proceedings and direct the receiver to redeliver to the corporation all its remaining property and assets.

102. Decree of Involuntary Dissolution

In proceedings to liquidate the assets and business of a corporation, when the costs and expenses of such proceedings and all debts, obligations and liabilities of the corporation shall have been paid and discharged and all of its remaining property and assets distributed to its shareholders, or in case its property and assets are not sufficient to satisfy and discharge such costs, expenses, debts and obligations, all the property and assets have been applied so far as they will go to their payment, the court shall enter a decree dissolving the corporation, whereupon the existence of the corporation shall cease.

103. Filing of Decree of Dissolution

In case the court shall enter a decree dissolving a corporation, it shall be the duty of the clerk of such court to cause a certified copy of the decree to be filed with the Secretary of State. No fee shall be charged by the Secretary of State for the filing thereof.

104. Deposit with State Treasurer of Amount Due Certain Shareholders

Upon the voluntary or involuntary dissolution of a corporation, the portion of the assets distributable to a creditor or shareholder who is unknown or cannot be found, or who is under disability and there is no person legally competent to receive such distributive portion, shall be reduced to cash and deposited with the State Treasurer and shall be paid over to such creditor or shareholder or to his legal representative upon proof satisfactory to the State Treasurer of his right thereto.

105. Survival of Remedy after Dissolution

The dissolution of a corporation either (1) by the issuance of a certificate of dissolution by the Secretary of State, or (2) by a decree of court when the court has not liquidated the assets and business of the corporation as provided in this Act, or (3) by expiration of its period of duration, shall not take away or impair any remedy available to or against such corporation, its directors, officers, or shareholders, for any right or claim existing, or any liability incurred, prior to such dissolution if action or other proceeding thereon is commenced within two years after the date of such dissolution. Any such action or proceeding by or against the corporation may be prosecuted or defended by the corporation in its corporate name. The shareholders, directors and officers shall have power to take such corporate or other action as shall be appropriate to protect such remedy, right or claim. If such corporation was dissolved by the expiration of its period of duration, such corporation may amend its articles of incorporation at any time during such period of two years so as to extend its period of duration.

106. Admission of Foreign Corporation

No foreign corporation shall have the right to transact business in this State until it shall have procured a certificate of authority so to do from the Secretary of State. No foreign corporation shall be entitled to procure a certificate of authority under this Act to transact in this State any business which a corporation organized under this Act is not permitted to transact. A foreign corporation shall not be denied a certificate of authority by reason of the fact that the laws of the state or country under which such corporation is organized governing its organization and internal affairs differ from the laws of this State, and nothing

in this Act contained shall be construed to authorize this State to regulate the organization or the internal affairs of such corporation.

Without excluding other activities which may not constitute transacting business in this State, a foreign corporation shall not be considered to be transacting business in this State, for the purposes of this Act, by reason of carrying on in this State any one or more of the following activities:

(a) Maintaining or defending any action or suit or any administrative or arbitration proceeding, or effecting the settlement thereof or the settlement of claims or disputes.

(b) Holding meetings of its directors or shareholders or carrying on other activities concerning its internal affairs.

(c) Maintaining bank accounts.

(d) Maintaining offices or agencies for the transfer, exchange and registration of its securities, or appointing and maintaining trustees or depositaries with relation to its securities.

(e) Effecting sales through independent contractors.

(f) Soliciting or procuring orders, whether by mail or through employees or agents or otherwise, where such orders require acceptance without this State before becoming binding contracts.

(g) Creating evidences of debt, mortgages or liens on real or personal property.

(h) Securing or collecting debts or enforcing any rights in property securing the same.

(i) Transacting any business in interstate commerce.

(j) Conducting an isolated transaction completed within a period of thirty days and not in the course of a number of repeated transactions of like nature.

107. Powers of Foreign Corporation

A foreign corporation which shall have received a certificate of authority under this Act shall, until a certificate of revocation or of withdrawal shall have been issued as provided in this Act, enjoy the same, but no greater, rights and privileges as a domestic corporation organized for the purposes set forth in the application pursuant to which such certificate of authority is issued; and, except as in this Act otherwise provided, shall be subject to the same duties, restrictions, penalties and liabilities now or hereafter imposed upon a domestic corporation of like character.

108. Corporate Name of Foreign Corporation

No certificate of authority shall be issued to a foreign corporation unless the corporate name of such corporation:

(a) Shall contain the word "corporation," "company," "incorporated," or "limited," or shall contain an abbreviation of one of such words, or such corporation shall, for use in this State, add at the end of its name one of such words or an abbreviation thereof.

(b) Shall not contain any word or phrase which indicates or implies that it is organized for any purpose other than one or more of the purposes contained in its articles of incorporation or that it is authorized or empowered to conduct the business of banking or insurance.

(c) Shall not be the same as, or deceptively similar to, the name of any domestic corporation existing under the laws of this State or any foreign corporation authorized to transact business in this State, or a name the exclusive right to which is, at the time, reserved in the manner provided in this Act, or the name of a corporation which has in effect a registration of its name as provided in this Act, except that this provision shall not apply if the foreign corporation applying for a certificate of authority files with the Secretary of State any one of the following:

(1) a resolution of its board of directors adopting a fictitious name for use in transacting business in this State which fictitious name is not deceptively similar to the name of any domestic corporation or of any foreign corporation authorized to transact business in this State or to any name reserved or registered as provided in this Act, or

(2) the written consent of such other corporation or holder of a reserved or registered name to use the same or deceptively similar name and one or more words are added to make such name distinguishable from such other name, or

(3) a certified copy of a final decree of a court of competent jurisdiction establishing the prior right of such foreign corporation to the use of such name in this State.

109. Change of Name by Foreign Corporation

Whenever a foreign corporation which is authorized to transact business in this State shall change its name to one under which a certificate of authority would not be granted to it on application therefor, the certificate of authority of such corporation shall be suspended and it shall not thereafter transact any business in this State until it has changed its name to a name which is available to it under the laws of this State or has otherwise complied with the provisions of this Act.

110. Application for Certificate of Authority

A foreign corporation, in order to procure a certificate of authority to transact business in this State, shall make application therefor to the Secretary of State, which application shall set forth:

(a) The name of the corporation and the state or country under the laws of which it is incorporated.

(b) If the name of the corporation does not contain the word "corporation," "company," "incorporated," or "limited," or does not contain an abbreviation of one of such words, then the name of the corporation with the word or abbreviation which it elects to add thereto for use in this State.

(c) The date of incorporation and the period of duration of the corporation.

(d) The address of the principal office of the corporation in the state or country under the laws of which it is incorporated.

(e) The address of the proposed registered office of the corporation in this State, and the name of its proposed registered agent in this State at such address.

(f) The purpose or purposes of the corporation which it proposes to pursue in the transaction of business in this State.

(g) The names and respective addresses of the directors and officers of the corporation.

(h) A statement of the aggregate number of shares which the corporation has authority to issue, itemized by classes, par value of shares, shares without par value, and series, if any, within a class.

(i) A statement of the aggregate number of issued shares itemized by classes, par value of shares, shares without par value, and series, if any, within a class.

(j) A statement, expressed in dollars, of the amount of stated capital of the corporation, as defined in this Act.

(k) An estimate, expressed in dollars, of the value of all property to be owned by the corporation for the following year, wherever located, and an estimate of the value of the property of the corporation to be located within this State during such year, and an estimate, expressed in dollars, of the gross amount of business which will be transacted by the corporation during such year, and an estimate of the gross amount thereof which will be transacted by the corporation at or from places of business in this State during such year.

(l) Such additional information as may be necessary or appropriate in order to enable the Secretary of State to determine whether such corporation is entitled to a certificate of authority to transact business in this State and to determine and assess the fees and franchise taxes payable as in this Act prescribed.

Such application shall be made on forms prescribed and furnished by the Secretary of State and shall be executed in duplicate by the corporation by its president or a vice president and by its secretary or an assistant secretary, and verified by one of the officers signing such application.

111. Filing of Application for Certificate of Authority

Duplicate originals of the application of the corporation for a certificate of authority shall be delivered to the Secretary of State, together with a copy of its articles of incorporation and all amendments thereto, duly authenticated by the proper officer of the state or country under the laws of which it is incorporated.

If the Secretary of State finds that such application conforms to law, he shall, when all fees and franchise taxes have been paid as in this Act prescribed:

(a) Endorse on each of such documents the word "Filed," and the month, day and year of the filing thereof.

(b) File in his office one of such duplicate originals of the application and the copy of the articles of incorporation and amendments thereto.

(c) Issue a certificate of authority to trans-

act business in this State to which he shall affix the other duplicate original application.

The certificate of authority, together with the duplicate original of the application affixed thereto by the Secretary of State, shall be returned to the corporation or its representative.

112. Effect of Certificate of Authority

Upon the issuance of a certificate of authority by the Secretary of State, the corporation shall be authorized to transact business in this State for those purposes set forth in its application, subject, however, to the right of this State to suspend or to revoke such authority as provided in this Act.

113. Registered Office and Registered Agent of Foreign Corporation

Each foreign corporation authorized to transact business in this State shall have and continuously maintain in this State:

(a) A registered office which may be, but need not be, the same as its place of business in this State.

(b) A registered agent, which agent may be either an individual resident in this State whose business office is identical with such registered office, or a domestic corporation, or a foreign corporation authorized to transact business in this State, having a business office identical with such registered office.

114. Change of Registered Office or Registered Agent of Foreign Corporation

A foreign corporation authorized to transact business in this State may change its registered office or change its registered agent, or both, upon filing in the office of the Secretary of State a statement setting forth:

(a) The name of the corporation.

(b) The address of its then registered office.

(c) If the address of its registered office be changed, the address to which the registered office is to be changed.

(d) The name of its then registered agent.

(e) If its registered agent be changed, the name of its successor registered agent.

(f) That the address of its registered office and the address of the business office of its registered agent, as changed, will be identical.

(g) That such change was authorized by resolution duly adopted by its board of directors.

Such statement shall be executed by the corporation by its president or a vice president, and verified by him, and delivered to the Secretary of State. If the Secretary of State finds that such statement conforms to the provisions of this Act, he shall file such statement in his office, and upon such filing the change of address of the registered office, or the appointment of a new registered agent, or both, as the case may be, shall become effective.

Any registered agent of a foreign corporation may resign as such agent upon filing a written notice thereof, executed in duplicate, with the Secretary of State, who shall forthwith mail a copy thereof to the corporation at its principal office in the state or country under the laws of which it is incorporated. The appointment of such agent shall terminate upon the expiration of thirty days after receipt of such notice by the Secretary of State.

If a registered agent changes his or its business address to another place within the same ....,* he or it may change such address and the address of the registered office of any corporation of which he or it is registered agent by filing a statement as required above except that it need be signed only by the registered agent and need not be responsive to (e) or (g) and must recite that a copy of the statement has been mailed to the corporation.

115.   Service of Process on Foreign Corporation

The registered agent so appointed by a foreign corporation authorized to transact business in this State shall be an agent of such corporation upon whom any process, notice or demand required or permitted by law to be served upon the corporation may be served.

Whenever a foreign corporation authorized to transact business in this State shall fail to appoint or maintain a registered agent in this State, or whenever any such registered agent cannot with reasonable diligence be found at the registered office, or whenever the certificate

---

* Supply designation of jurisdiction, such as county, etc., in accordance with local practice.

of authority of a foreign corporation shall be suspended or revoked, then the Secretary of State shall be an agent of such corporation upon whom any such process, notice, or demand may be served. Service on the Secretary of State of any such process, notice or demand shall be made by delivering to and leaving with him, or any clerk having charge of the corporation department of his office, duplicate copies of such process, notice or demand. In the event any such process, notice or demand is served on the Secretary of State, he shall immediately cause one of such copies thereof to be forwarded by registered mail, addressed to the corporation at its principal office in the state or country under the laws of which it is incorporated. Any service so had on the Secretary of State shall be returnable in not less than thirty days.

The Secretary of State shall keep a record of all processes, notices and demands served upon him under this section, and shall record therein the time of such service and his action with reference thereto.

Nothing herein contained shall limit or affect the right to serve any process, notice or demand, required or permitted by law to be served upon a foreign corporation in any other manner now or hereafter permitted by law.

116.   Amendment to Articles of Incorporation of Foreign Corporation

Whenever the articles of incorporation of a foreign corporation authorized to transact business in this State are amended, such foreign corporation shall, within thirty days after such amendment becomes effective, file in the office of the Secretary of State a copy of such amendment duly authenticated by the proper officer of the state or country under the laws of which it is incorporated; but the filing thereof shall not of itself enlarge or alter the purpose or purposes which such corporation is authorized to pursue in the transaction of business in this State, nor authorize such corporation to transact business in this State under any other name than the name set forth in its certificate of authority.

117.   Merger of Foreign Corporation Authorized to Transact Business in This State

Whenever a foreign corporation authorized to transact business in this State shall be a party to a statutory merger permitted by the laws of the state or country under the laws of which it is incorporated, and such corporation shall be the surviving corporation, it shall, within thirty days after such merger becomes effective, file with the Secretary of State a copy of the articles of merger duly authenticated by the proper officer of the state or country under the laws of which such statutory merger was effected; and it shall not be necessary for such corporation to procure either a new or amended certificate of authority to transact business in this State unless the name of such corporation be changed thereby or unless the corporation desires to pursue in this State other or additional purposes than those which it is then authorized to transact in this State.

118. Amended Certificate of Authority

A foreign corporation authorized to transact business in this State shall procure an amended certificate of authority in the event it changes its corporate name, or desires to pursue in this State other or additional purposes than those set forth in its prior application for a certificate of authority, by making application therefor to the Secretary of State.

The requirements in respect to the form and contents of such application, the manner of its execution, the filing of duplicate originals thereof with the Secretary of State, the issuance of an amended certificate of authority and the effect thereof, shall be the same as in the case of an original application for a certificate of authority.

119. Withdrawal of Foreign Corporation

A foreign corporation authorized to transact business in this State may withdraw from this State upon procuring from the Secretary of State a certificate of withdrawal. In order to procure such certificate of withdrawal, such foreign corporation shall deliver to the Secretary of State an application for withdrawal, which shall set forth:

(a) The name of the corporation and the state or country under the laws of which it is incorporated.

(b) That the corporation is not transacting business in this State.

(c) That the corporation surrenders its authority to transact business in this State.

(d) That the corporation revokes the authority of its registered agent in this State to accept service of process and consents that service of process in any action, suit or proceeding based upon any cause of action arising in this State during the time the corporation was authorized to transact business in this State may thereafter be made on such corporation by service thereof on the Secretary of State.

(e) A post-office address to which the Secretary of State may mail a copy of any process against the corporation that may be served on him.

(f) A statement of the aggregate number of shares which the corporation has authority to issue, itemized by classes, par value of shares, shares without par value, and series, if any, within a class, as of the date of such application.

(g) A statement of the aggregate number of issued shares, itemized by classes, par value of shares, shares without par value, and series, if any, within a class, as of the date of such application.

(h) A statement, expressed in dollars, of the amount of stated capital of the corporation, as of the date of such application.

(i) Such additional information as may be necessary or appropriate in order to enable the Secretary of State to determine and assess any unpaid fees or franchise taxes payable by such foreign corporation as in this Act prescribed.

The application for withdrawal shall be made on forms prescribed and furnished by the Secretary of State and shall be executed by the corporation by its president or a vice president and by its secretary or an assistant secretary, and verified by one of the officers signing the application, or, if the corporation is in the hands of a receiver or trustee, shall be executed on behalf of the corporation by such receiver or trustee and verified by him.

120. Filing of Application for Withdrawal

Duplicate originals of such application for withdrawal shall be delivered to the Secretary of State. If the Secretary of State finds that such application conforms to the provisions of this Act, he shall, when all fees and franchise taxes have been paid as in this Act prescribed:

(a) Endorse on each of such duplicate originals the word "Filed," and the month, day and year of the filing thereof.

(b) File one of such duplicate originals in his office.

(c) Issue a certificate of withdrawal to which he shall affix the other duplicate original.

The certificate of withdrawal, together with the duplicate original of the application for withdrawal affixed thereto by the Secretary of State, shall be returned to the corporation or its representative. Upon the issuance of such certificate of withdrawal, the authority of the corporation to transact business in this State shall cease.

121. Revocation of Certificate of Authority

The certificate of authority of a foreign corporation to transact business in this State may be revoked by the Secretary of State upon the conditions prescribed in this section when:

(a) The corporation has failed to file its annual report within the time required by this Act, or has failed to pay any fees, franchise taxes or penalties prescribed by this Act when they have become due and payable; or

(b) The corporation has failed to appoint and maintain a registered agent in this State as required by this Act; or

(c) The corporation has failed, after change of its registered office or registered agent, to file in the office of the Secretary of State a statement of such change as required by this Act; or

(d) The corporation has failed to file in the office of the Secretary of State any amendment to its articles of incorporation or any articles of merger within the time prescribed by this Act; or

(e) A misrepresentation has been made of any material matter in any application, report, affidavit, or other document submitted by such corporation pursuant to this Act.

No certificate of authority of a foreign corporation shall be revoked by the Secretary of State unless (1) he shall have given the corporation not less than sixty days' notice thereof by mail addressed to its registered office in this State, and (2) the corporation shall fail prior to revocation to file such annual report, or pay such fees, franchise taxes or penalties, or file the required statement of change of registered agent or registered office, or file such articles of amendment or articles of merger, or correct such misrepresentation.

122. Issuance of Certificate of Revocation

Upon revoking any such certificate of authority, the Secretary of State shall:

(a) Issue a certificate of revocation in duplicate.

(b) File one of such certificates in his office.

(c) Mail to such corporation at its registered office in this State a notice of such revocation accompanied by one of such certificates.

Upon the issuance of such certificate of revocation, the authority of the corporation to transact business in this State shall cease.

123. Application to Corporations Heretofore Authorized to Transact Business in this State

Foreign corporations which are duly authorized to transact business in this State at the time this Act takes effect, for a purpose or purposes for which a corporation might secure such authority under this Act, shall, subject to the limitations set forth in their respective certificates of authority, be entitled to all the rights and privileges applicable to foreign corporations procuring certificates of authority to transact business in this State under this Act, and from the time this Act takes effect such corporations shall be subject to all the limitations, restrictions, liabilities, and duties prescribed herein for foreign corporations procuring certificates of authority to transact business in this State under this Act.

124. Transacting Business Without Certificate of Authority

No foreign corporation transacting business in this State without a certificate of authority shall be permitted to maintain any action, suit or proceeding in any court of this State, until such corporation shall have obtained a certificate of authority. Nor shall any action, suit or proceeding be maintained in any court of this State by any successor or assignee of such corporation on any right, claim or demand arising out of the transaction of business by such corporation in this State, until a certificate of authority shall have been obtained by such corporation or by a corporation which has acquired all or substantially all of its assets.

The failure of a foreign corporation to obtain a certificate of authority to transact business in this State shall not impair the validity of any contract or act of such corporation, and shall not prevent such corporation from defending any action, suit or proceeding in any court of this State.

A foreign corporation which transacts business in this State without a certificate of authority shall be liable to this State, for the years or parts thereof during which it transacted business in this State without a certificate of authority, in an amount equal to all fees and franchise taxes which would have been imposed by this Act upon such corporation had it duly applied for and received a certificate of authority to transact business in this State as required by this Act and thereafter filed all reports required by this Act, plus all penalties imposed by this Act for failure to pay such fees and franchise taxes. The Attorney General shall bring proceedings to recover all amounts due this State under the provisions of this Section.

125. Annual Report of Domestic and Foreign Corporations

Each domestic corporation, and each foreign corporation authorized to transact business in this State, shall file, within the time prescribed by this Act, an annual report setting forth:

(a) The name of the corporation and the state or country under the laws of which it is incorporated.

(b) The address of the registered office of the corporation in this State, and the name of its registered agent in this State at such address, and, in case of a foreign corporation, the address of its principal office in the state or country under the laws of which it is incorporated.

(c) A brief statement of the character of the business in which the corporation is actually engaged in this State.

(d) The names and respective addresses of the directors and officers of the corporation.

(e) A statement of the aggregate number of shares which the corporation has authority to issue, itemized by classes, par value of shares, shares without par value, and series, if any, within a class.

(f) A statement of the aggregate number of issued shares, itemized by classes, par value of shares, shares without par value, and series, if any, within a class.

(g) A statement, expressed in dollars, of the amount of stated capital of the corporation, as defined in this Act.

(h) A statement, expressed in dollars, of the value of all the property owned by the corporation, wherever located, and the value of the property of the corporation located within this State, and a statement, expressed in dollars, of the gross amount of business transacted by the corporation for the twelve months ended on the thirty-first day of December preceding the date herein provided for the filing of such report and the gross amount thereof transacted by the corporation at or from places of business in this State. If, on the thirty-first day of December preceding the time herein provided for the filing of such report, the corporation had not been in existence for a period of twelve months, or in the case of a foreign corporation had not been authorized to transact business in this State for a period of twelve months, the statement with respect to business transacted shall be furnished for the period between the date of incorporation or the date of its authorization to transact business in this State, as the case may be, and such thirty-first day of December. If all the property of the corporation is located in this State and all of its business is transacted at or from places of business in this State, or if the corporation elects to pay the annual franchise tax on the basis of its entire stated capital, then the information required by this subparagraph need not be set forth in such report.

(i) Such additional information as may be necessary or appropriate in order to enable the Secretary of State to determine and assess the proper amount of franchise taxes payable by such corporation.

Such annual report shall be made on forms prescribed and furnished by the Secretary of State, and the information therein contained shall be given as of the date of the execution of the report, except as to the information required by subparagraphs (g), (h) and (i) which shall be given as of the close of business on the thirty-first day of December next preceding the date herein provided for the filing of such report. It shall be executed by the corporation by its president, a vice president, secretary, an assistant secretary, or treasurer, and verified by the officer executing the report, or, if the corporation is in the hands of a receiver or trustee, it shall be executed on behalf of the corporation and verified by such receiver or trustee.

126. Filing of Annual Report of Domestic and Foreign Corporations

Such annual report of a domestic or foreign corporation shall be delivered to the Secretary of State between the first day of January and the first day of March of each year, except that the first annual report of a domestic or foreign corporation shall be filed between the first day of January and the first day of March of the year next succeeding the calendar year in which its certificate of incorporation or its certificate of authority, as the case may be, was issued by the Secretary of State. Proof to the satisfaction of the Secretary of State that prior to the first day of March such report was deposited in the United States mail in a sealed envelope, properly addressed, with postage prepaid, shall be deemed a compliance with this requirement. If the Secretary of State finds that such report conforms to the requirements of this Act, he shall file the same. If he finds that it does not so conform, he shall promptly return the same to the corporation for any necessary corrections, in which event the penalties hereinafter prescribed for failure to file such report within the time hereinabove provided shall not apply, if such report is corrected to conform to the requirements of this Act and returned to the Secretary of State within thirty days from the date on which it was mailed to the corporation by the Secretary of State.

127. Fees, Franchise Taxes and Charges to be Collected by Secretary of State
[Text omitted.]

128. Fees for Filing Documents and Issuing Certificates
[Text omitted.]

129. Miscellaneous Charges
[Text omitted.]

130. License Fees Payable by Domestic Corporations
[Text omitted.]

131. License Fees Payable by Foreign Corporations
[Text omitted.]

132. Franchise Taxes Payable by Domestic Corporations
[Text omitted.]

133. Franchise Taxes Payable by Foreign Corporations
[Text omitted.]

134. Assessment and Collection of Annual Franchise Taxes
[Text omitted.]

135. Penalties Imposed upon Corporations

Each corporation, domestic or foreign, that fails or refuses to file its annual report for any year within the time prescribed by this Act shall be subject to a penalty of ten per cent of the amount of the franchise tax assessed against it for the period beginning July 1 of the year in which such report should have been filed. Such penalty shall be assessed by the Secretary of State at the time of the assessment of the franchise tax. If the amount of the franchise tax as originally assessed against such corporation be thereafter adjusted in accordance with the provisions of this Act, the amount of the penalty shall be likewise adjusted to ten per cent of the amount of the adjusted franchise tax. The amount of the franchise tax and the amount of the penalty shall be separately stated in any notice to the corporation with respect thereto.

If the franchise tax assessed in accordance with the provisions of this Act shall not be paid on or before the thirty-first day of July, it shall be deemed to be delinquent, and there shall be added a penalty of one per cent for each month or part of month that the same is delinquent, commencing with the month of August.

Each corporation, domestic or foreign, that fails or refuses to answer truthfully and fully within the time prescribed by this Act interrogatories propounded by the Secretary of State in accordance with the provisions of this Act, shall be deemed to be guilty of a misdemeanor and upon conviction thereof may be fined in any amount not exceeding five hundred dollars.

136. Penalties Imposed upon Officers and Directors

Each officer and director of a corporation, domestic or foreign, who fails or refuses within the time prescribed by this Act to answer truthfully and fully interrogatories propounded to him by the Secretary of State in accordance with the provisions of this Act, or who signs any articles, statement, report, application or other document filed with the Secretary of State which is known to such officer or director to be false in any material respect, shall be deemed to be guilty of a misdemeanor, and upon conviction thereof may be fined in any amount not exceeding . . . . dollars.

137. Interrogatories by Secretary of State

The Secretary of State may propound to any corporation, domestic or foreign, subject to the provisions of this Act, and to any officer or director thereof, such interrogatories as may be reasonably necessary and proper to enable him to ascertain whether such corporation has complied with all the provisions of this Act applicable to such corporation. Such interrogatories shall be answered within thirty days after the mailing thereof, or within such additional time as shall be fixed by the Secretary of State, and the answers thereto shall be full and complete and shall be made in writing and under oath. If such interrogatories be directed to an individual they shall be answered by him, and if directed to a corporation they shall be answered by the president, vice president, secretary or assistant secretary thereof. The Secretary of State need not file any document to which such interrogatories relate until such interrogatories be answered as herein provided, and not then if the answers thereto disclose that such document is not in conformity with the provisions of this Act. The Secretary of State shall certify to the Attorney General, for such action as the Attorney General may deem appropriate, all interrogatories and answers thereto which disclose a violation of any of the provisions of this Act.

138. Information Disclosed by Interrogatories

Interrogatories propounded by the Secretary of State and the answers thereto shall not be open to public inspection nor shall the Secretary of State disclose any facts or information obtained therefrom except insofar as his official duty may require the same to be made public or in the event such interrogatories or the answers thereto are required for evidence in any criminal proceedings or in any other action by this State.

139. Powers of Secretary of State

The Secretary of State shall have the power and authority reasonably necessary to enable him to administer this Act efficiently and to perform the duties therein imposed upon him.

140. Appeal from Secretary of State
[Text omitted.]

141. Certificates and Certified Copies to Be Received in Evidence
[Text omitted.]

142. Forms to Be Furnished by Secretary of State
[Text omitted.]

143. Greater Voting Requirements

Whenever, with respect to any action to be taken by the shareholders of a corporation, the articles of incorporation require the vote or concurrence of the holders of a greater proportion of the shares, or of any class or series thereof, than required by this Act with respect to such action, the provisions of the articles of incorporation shall control.

144. Waiver of Notice

Whenever any notice is required to be given to any shareholder or director of a corporation under the provisions of this Act or under the provisions of the articles of incorporation or by-laws of the corporation, a waiver thereof in writing signed by the person or persons entitled to such notice, whether before or after the time stated therein, shall be equivalent to the giving of such notice.

145. Action by Shareholders Without a Meeting

Any action required by this Act to be taken at a meeting of the shareholders of a corporation, or any action which may be taken at a meeting of the shareholders, may be taken without a meeting if a consent in writing, setting forth the action so taken, shall be signed by all of the shareholders entitled to vote with respect to the subject matter thereof.

Such consent shall have the same effect as a unanimous vote of shareholders, and may be stated as such in any articles or document filed with the Secretary of State under this Act.

146. Unauthorized Assumption of Corporate Powers

All persons who assume to act as a corporation without authority so to do shall be jointly and severally liable for all debts and liabilities incurred or arising as a result thereof.

147. Application to Existing Corporations
[Text omitted.]

148. Application to Foreign and Interstate Commerce
[Text omitted.]

149. Reservation of Power

The .... * shall at all times have power to prescribe such regulations, provisions and limitations as it may deem advisable, which regulations, provisions and limitations shall be binding upon any and all corporations subject to the provisions of this Act, and the ...... * shall have power to amend, repeal or modify this Act at pleasure.

150. Effect of Repeal of Prior Acts
[Text omitted.]

151. Effect of Invalidity of Part of this Act
[Text omitted.]

152. Repeal of Prior Acts
(Insert appropriate provisions) ......

* Insert name of legislative body.

The above Sections 1–152 of the Model Business Corporation Act were prepared by the Committee on Corporate Laws (Section of Corporation Banking and Business Law) of the American Bar Association.

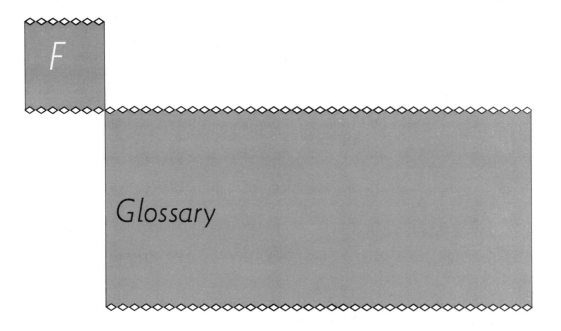

Glossary

Abandonment: The term applies to many situations. Abandonment of property is the giving up of the dominion and control over it with the intention to relinquish all claim to the same. Losing property is an involuntary act; abandonment is voluntary.

When used with duty, the word *abandonment* is synonymous with *repudiation.*

Abatement of a nuisance: An action to end any act detrimental to the public, such as a suit to enjoin a plant from permitting the escape of noxious vapors.

Acceptance:* Under Article 3—Commercial Paper, this is the drawee's signed engagement to honor a draft as presented. It must be written on the draft and may consist of his signature alone. It becomes operative when completed by delivery or notification.

Accord and satisfaction: An agreement between two persons, one of whom has a right of action against the other, that the latter should do or give, and the former accept, something in satisfaction of the right of action different from, and usually less than, what might legally be enforced.

Account:* Any right to payment for goods sold or leased or for services rendered which is not evidenced by an instrument or chattel paper.

Account:* Under Article 4—Bank Deposits and Collections, this means any account with a bank and includes a checking, time, interest, or savings account.

Account debtor: The person who is obligated on an account, chattel paper, contract right, or general intangible.

Accretion: The gradual and imperceptible accumulation of land by natural causes, usually next to a stream or river.

Action ex contractu: An action at law to recover damages for the breach of a duty arising out of contract. There are two types of causes of action: those arising out of contract, ex contractu, and those arising out of tort, ex delicto.

Action ex delicto: An action at law to recover damages for the breach of a duty existing by reason of a general law. An action to recover damages for an injury caused by the negligent use of an automobile is an ex delicto

---

*The terms followed by an asterisk are defined in the Uniform Commercial Code, and therefore these terms have significance in connection with Code materials. They are often given a particular meaning as related to the Code, and the definitions are therefore not necessarily in conformity with meanings outside the framework of the Code.

action. Tort or wrong is the basis of the action. See *Action ex contractu.*

Adjudicate: The exercise of judicial power by hearing, trying, and determining the claims of litigants before the court.

Administrator: A person to whom letters of administration have been issued by a probate court, giving such person authority to administer, manage, and close the estate of a deceased person.

Adverse possession: To acquire, by adverse possession, the legal title to another's land, the claimant must be in continuous possession during the period prescribed in the statute. This possession must be actual, visible, known to the world, with an intention by the possessor to claim the title as owner as against the rights of the true owner. The claimant usually must pay the taxes and liens lawfully charged against the property. Cutting timber or grass from time to time on the land of another is not such adverse possession as to confer title.

Advising Bank:* A bank that gives notification of the issuance of a credit by another bank.

Affidavit: A voluntary statement of facts formally reduced to writing, sworn to, or affirmed before, some officer authorized to administer oaths. Such officer is usually a notary public.

A fortiori: Latin words meaning "by a stronger reason." The phrase is often used in judicial opinions to say that, since specific proven facts lead to a certain conclusion, there are for this reason other facts that logically follow which make stronger the argument for the conclusion.

Agency coupled with an interest: When an agent has possession or control over the property of his principal and has a right of action against interference by third parties, an agency with an interest has been created. A, an agent, advances freight for goods sent him by his principal. He thus has an interest in the goods.

Agent: An agent is a person authorized to act for another (principal). The term may apply to a person in the service of another, but in the strict sense an agent is one who stands in place of his principal. A works for B as a gardener and is thus a servant; but he may be an agent. If A sells goods for B he becomes more than a servant. He acts in the place of B.

Agreement:* This means the bargain of the parties in fact as found in their language or by implication from other circumstances, including course of dealing or usage of trade or course of performance as provided in the Uniform Commercial Code.

Annuity: A sum of money paid yearly to a person during his lifetime, which sum arises out of a contract by which the recipient or another had previously deposited sums in whole or in part with the grantor—the grantor to return a designated portion of the principal and interest in periodic payments upon the arrival of the beneficiary at a designated age.

Appellant: The party who takes an appeal from one court or jurisdiction to another.

Appellee: The party in a cause against whom an appeal is taken.

A priori: A generalization resting on presuppositions and not upon proven facts.

Arbitration: The submission for determination of disputed matter to private unofficial persons selected in a manner provided by law or agreement.

Architect's certificate: A formal statement signed by an architect that a contractor has performed under his contract and is entitled to be paid. The construction contract provides when and how such certificates shall be issued.

Artisan's lien: One who has expended labor upon or added to another's property is entitled to the possession of such property as security until reimbursed for the value of labor or material. A repairs B's watch. A may keep the watch in his possession until paid by B for such repairs.

Assignee: An assign or assignee is one to whom an assignment has been made.

Assignment: An assignment is the transfer by one person to another of a right that usually arises out of a contract. Such rights are called choses in action. A sells and assigns his contract right to purchase B's house to C. A is an assignor. C is an assignee. The transfer is an assignment.

Assignment:* A transfer of the "contract" or of "all my rights under the contract" or an assignment in similar general terms is an assignment of rights, and unless the language or the circumstances (as in an assignment for security) indicate the contrary, it is a delegation of performance of the duties of the assignor, and its acceptance by the assignee constitutes a promise by him to perform those duties. This promise is enforceable by either the assignor or the other party to the original contract.

Assignment for the benefit of creditors: A, a debtor, has many creditors. An assignment of his property to X, a third party, with directions to make distribution of his property to his creditors is called an assignment for the benefit of creditors. See *Composition of creditors*.

Assignor: An assignor is one who makes an assignment.

Attachment: A legal proceeding accompanying an action in court by which a plaintiff may acquire a lien on a defendant's property as a security for the payment of any judgment that the plaintiff may recover. It is provisional and independent of the court action and is usually provided for by statute. A sues B. Before judgment, A attaches B's automobile in order to make sure of the payment of any judgment that A may secure.

Attorney at law: A person who has been granted a license by the state giving him the privilege of practicing law.

Attorney in fact: A person acting for another under a grant of special power created by an instrument in writing. B, in writing, grants special power to A to execute and deliver for B a conveyance of B's land to X.

Bad faith: The term means "actual intent" to mislead or deceive another. It does not mean misleading by an honest, inadvertent, or careless misstatement.

Bail (verb): To set at liberty an arrested or imprisoned person upon security's being given to the state by himself or at least two other persons that will appear at the proper time and place for trial.

Bailee: A person into whose possession personal property is delivered.

Bailee:* The person who by a warehouse receipt, bill of lading, or other document of title acknowledges possession of goods and contracts to deliver them.

Bailment: A bailment is the delivery of personal property to another for a special purpose. Such delivery is made under a contract, either expressed or implied, that upon the completion of the special purpose, the property shall be redelivered to the bailor or placed at his disposal. A loans B his truck. A places his watch with B for repair. A places his furniture in B's warehouse. A places his securities in B bank's safety deposit vault. In each case, A is a bailor and B is a bailee.

Bailor: One who delivers personal property into the possession of another.

Banking day:* Under Article 4—Bank Deposits and Collections, this means that part of any day on which a bank is open to the public for carrying on substantially all of its banking functions.

Bearer:* The person in possession of an instrument, document of title, or security payable to bearer or indorsed in blank.

Bearer form:* A security is in bearer form when it runs to bearer according to its terms and not by reason of any indorsement.

Beneficiary: A person (not a promisee) for whose benefit a trust, an insurance policy, a will, or a contract promise is made.

Beneficiary:* A person who is entitled under a letter of credit to draw or demand payment.

Bequest: A term used in a will to designate a gift of personal property.

Bid: An offering of money in exchange for property placed for sale. At an ordinary auction sale, a bid is an offer to purchase. It may be withdrawn before acceptance is indicated by the fall of the hammer.

Bilateral contract: One containing mutual promises, with each party being both a promisor and a promisee.

Bill of lading:* A document evidencing the receipt of goods for shipment issued by a person engaged in the business of transporting or forwarding goods, and includes an airbill. "Airbill" means a document serving for air transportation as a bill of lading does for marine or rail transportation, and includes an air consignment note or air way-bill.

Bill of sale: A written evidence that the title to personal property has been transferred from one person to another. It must contain words of transfer and be more than a receipt.

Blue-sky laws: Popular name for acts providing for the regulation and supervision of investment securities.

Bona fide purchaser:* A purchaser of a security for value in good faith and without notice of any adverse claim who takes delivery of a security in bearer form or of one in registered form issued to him or indorsed to him or in blank.

Bond: A promise under seal to pay money. The term is generally used to designate the promise made by a corporation, either public or private, to pay money to bearer. U.S. government bonds; Illinois Central Railroad bonds.

The term also describes an obligation by which one person promises to answer for the debt or default of another—a surety bond.

Broker: A person employed to make contracts with third persons on behalf of his principal. Such contracts involve trade, commerce, buying and selling for a fee (called brokerage or commission).

Broker:* A person engaged for all or part of his time in the business of buying and selling securities, who in the transaction concerned acts for, or buys a security from, or sells a security to a customer. Nothing in this Article determines the capacity in which a person acts for purposes of any other statute or rule to which such person is subject.

Bulk Transfer:* Any transfer in bulk and not in the ordinary course of the transferor's business of a major part of the materials, supplies, merchandise or other inventory of an enterprise subject to this Article.

Buyer:* A person who buys or contracts to buy goods.

Buyer in ordinary course of business:* A person who in good faith and without knowledge that the sale to him is in violation of the ownership rights or security interest of a third party in the goods buys in ordinary course from a person in the bus-iness of selling goods of that kind but does not include a pawnbroker. "Buying" may be for cash or by exchange of other property or on secured or unsecured credit and includes receiving goods or documents of title under a preexisting contract for sale but does not include a transfer in bulk or as security for or in total or partial satisfaction of a money debt.

Bylaws: The rules adopted by the members or the board of directors of a corporation or other organization for its government. These rules must not be contrary to the law of the land, and they affect only the rights and duties of the members of the corporation or organization. They are not applicable to third persons.

Call: An assessment upon a subscriber for partial or full payment on shares of unpaid stock of a corporation. The term may also mean the power of a corporation to make an assessment, notice of an assessment, or the time when the assessment is to be paid.

Cancellation:* When either party puts an end to the contract for breach by the other. Its effect is the same as that of "termination" except that the canceling party also retains any remedy for breach of the whole contract or any unperformed balance.

Capital: The net assets of an individual enterprise, partnership, joint stock company, corporation, or business institution, including not only the original investment but also all gains and profits realized from the continued conduct of the business.

Carrier: A natural person or a corporation who receives goods under a contract to transport for a consideration from one place to another. A railroad, a truckline, a busline, an airline.

Cashier's check: A bill of exchange drawn by the cashier of a bank, for the bank, upon the bank. After the check is delivered or issued to the payee or holder, the drawer bank cannot put a "stop order" against itself. By delivery of the check, the drawer bank has accepted, and thus becomes the primary obligor.

Cause of action: When one's legal rights have been invaded either by a breach of a contract or by a breach of a legal duty toward one's person or property, a cause of action has been created.

Caveat: Literally this means "let him beware." It is used generally to mean a warning.

Caveat emptor: These words express an old idea at common law—"let the buyer beware"—and mean that when goods are sold without an express warranty by the vendor as to their quality and capacity for a particular use and purpose, the buyer must take the risk of loss as to all defects in the goods.

Caveat venditor: These words mean "let the seller beware" (In contradistinction to caveat emptor—"let the buyer beware"). Caveat venditor means that unless the seller by express language disclaims any responsibility, he shall be liable to the buyer if the goods delivered are different in kind, quality, use, and purpose from those described in the contract of sale.

Certiorari: An order issuing out of an appellate court to a lower court, at the request of an appellant directing that the record of a case pending in the lower court be transmitted to the upper court for review.

Cestui que trust: A person who is the real or beneficial owner of property held in trust. The trustee holds the legal title to the property for the benefit of the cestui que trust.

Charter: As to a private corporation, the word *charter* includes the contract between the created corporation and the state, the act creating the corporation, and the articles of association granted to the corporation by authority of the legislative act.

As to municipal corporations, charter does not mean a contract between the legislature and the city created. A city charter is a delegation of powers by a state legislature to the governing body of the city. The term includes the creative act, the powers enumerated, and the organization authorized.

Chattel: The word *chattel* is derived from the word *cattle*. It is a very broad term and includes every kind of property that is not real property. Movable properties, such as horses, automobiles, choses in action, stock certificates, bills of lading, and all "good wares, and merchandise," are chattels personal. Chattels real concern real property such as a lease for years—in which case the lessee owns a chattel real.

Chattel paper:* A writing or writings that evidence both a monetary obligation and a security interest in or a lease of specific goods. When a transaction is evidenced both by such a security agreement or a lease and by an instrument or a series of instruments, the group of writings taken together constitutes chattel paper.

Chose in action: Words used to define the "right" one person has to recover money or property from another by a judicial proceeding. Such right arises out of contract, claims for money, debts, and rights against property. Notes, drafts, stock certificates, bills of lading, warehouse receipts, and insurance policies are illustrations of choses in action. They are called tangible choses. Book accounts, simple debts, and obligations not evidenced by formal writing are called intangible choses. Choses in action are transferred by assignment.

Circumstantial evidence: If from certain facts and circumstances, according to the experience of mankind, an ordinary, intelligent person may infer that other connected facts and circumstances must necessarily exist, the latter facts and circumstances are considered proven by circumstantial evidence. Proof of fact *A* from which fact *B* may be inferred is proof of fact *B* by circumstantial evidence.

Civil action: A proceeding in a law court or a suit in equity by one person against another for the enforcement or protection of a private right or the prevention of a wrong. It includes actions on contract, ex delicto, and all suits in equity. Civil action is in contradistinction to criminal action in which the state prosecutes a person for breach of a duty.

Clearinghouse:* Under Article 4—Bank Deposits and Collections, this means any association of banks or other payors regularly clearing items.

Cloud on title: Words used to express the idea that there is some evidence of record that shows a third person has some prima facie interest in another's property.

Code: A collection or compilation of the statutes passed by the legislative body of a state. Such codes are often annotated with citations of cases decided by the state supreme courts. These decisions construe the statutes. Example—Oregon Compiled Laws Annotated, United States Code Annotated.

Codicil: An addition to or a change in an executed last will and testament. It is a part of the original will and must be executed with the same formality as the original will.

Coinsurer: A term in a fire insurance policy that requires the insured to bear a certain portion of the loss when he fails to carry complete coverage. For example, unless the insured carries insurance that totals 80 percent of the value of the property, the insurer shall be liable for only that portion of the loss that the total insurance carried bears to 80 percent of the value of the property.

Collateral: With reference to debts or other obligations, the term *collateral* means security placed with a creditor to assure the performance of the obligator. If the obligator performs, the collateral is returned by the creditor. A owes B $1,000. To secure the payment, A places with B a $500 certificate of stock in X company. The $500 certificate is called collateral security.

Collateral:* The property subject to a security interest, and includes accounts, contract rights, and chattel paper which have been sold.

Collecting bank:* Under Article 4—Bank Deposits and Collections, is any bank handling the item for collection except the payor bank.

Commercial unit:* Such a unit of goods as by commercial usage is a single whole for purposes of sale and division of which materially impairs its character or value on the market or in use. A commercial unit may be a single article (as a machine) or a set of articles (as a suite of furniture or an assortment of sizes) or a quantity (as a bale, gross, or carload) or any other unit treated in use or in the relevant market as a single whole.

Commission: The sum of money, interest, brokerage, compensation, or allowance given to a factor or broker for carrying on the business of his principal.

Commission merchant: An agent or factor employed to sell "goods, wares, and mer-

chandise" consigned or delivered to him by his principal.

Common carrier: One who is engaged in the business of transporting personal property from one place to another for a compensation. Such person is bound to carry for all who tender their goods and the price for transportation. A common carrier operates as a public utility and is subject to state and federal regulations.

Community property: All property acquired after marriage by husband and wife other than separate property acquired by devise, bequest, or from the proceeds of noncommunity property. Community property is a concept of property ownership by husband and wife inherited from the civil law. The husband and wife are somewhat like partners in their ownership of property acquired during marriage.

Complaint: The first paper a plaintiff files in a court in a lawsuit. It is called a pleading. It is a statement of the facts upon which the plaintiff rests his cause of action.

Composition of creditors: An agreement between creditors and their debtors by which they agree that the creditors will take a lesser amount in complete satisfaction of the total debt due. A owes B and C $500 each. A agrees to pay B and C $250 each in complete satisfaction of the $500 due each. B and C agree to take $250 in satisfaction. Such agreement is called a composition of creditors.

Compromise: An agreement between two or more persons, usually opposing parties in a lawsuit, to settle the matters of the controversy without further resort to hostile litigation. An adjustment of issues in dispute by mutual concessions before resorting to a lawsuit.

Condemnation proceedings: An action or proceeding in court authorized by legislation (federal or state) for the purpose of taking private property for public use. It is the exercise by the judiciary of the sovereign power of eminent domain.

Condition: A clause in a contract, either expressed or implied, that has the effect of investing or divesting the legal rights and duties of the parties to the contract. In a deed, a condition is a qualification or restriction providing for the happening or non-happening of events that on occurrence will destroy, commence, or enlarge an estate. "A grants Blackacre to B so long as said land shall be used for church purposes." If it ceases to be used for church purposes, the title to Blackacre will revert to the grantor

Condition precedent: A clause in a contract providing that immediate rights and duties shall vest only upon the happening of some event. Securing an architect's certificate by a contractor before he (the contractor) is entitled to payment is a condition precedent.

A condition is not a promise; hence, its breach will not give rise to a cause of action for damages. A breach of a condition is the basis for a defense. In the above illustration, if the contractor sues the owner without securing the architect's certificate, the owner has a defense.

Conditions concurrent: Conditions concurrent are conditions that are mutually dependent and must be performed at the same time by the parties to the contract. Payment of money and delivery of goods in a cash sale are conditions concurrent. Failure to perform by one party permits a cause of action upon tender by the other party. If S refuses to deliver goods in a cash sale, B, upon tender but not delivery of the money, places S in default and thus may sue S. B does not part with his money without getting the goods. If S sued B, B would have a defense.

Condition subsequent: A clause in a contract providing for the happening of an event that divests legal rights and duties. A clause in a fire insurance policy providing that the policy shall be null and void if combustible material is stored within ten feet of the building is a condition subsequent. If a fire occurs and combustible material was within ten feet of the building, the insurance company is excused from its duty to pay for the loss.

Confirming bank: A bank that engages either that it will itself honor a credit already issued by another bank or that such a credit will be honored by the issuer or a third bank.

Conforming:* Goods or conduct including any part of a performance are "conforming" or conform to the contract when they are in accordance with the obligations under contract.

Consideration: An essential element in the creation of contract obligation. A detriment to the promisee and a benefit to the promisor. One promise is consideration for another promise. The creates a bilateral contract. An act is consideration for a promise. This creates a unilateral contract. Performance of the act asked for by the promisee is a legal detriment to the promisee and a benefit to the promisor.

Consignee: A person to whom a shipper usually directs a carrier to deliver goods. Such person is generally the buyer of goods and is called a consignee on a bill of lading.

Consignee:* The person named in a bill to whom or to whose order the bill promises delivery.

Consignment: The delivery, sending, or transferring of property, "goods, wares, and merchandise" into the possession of another, usually for the purpose of sale. Consignment may be a bailment or an agency for sale.

Consignor: The person who delivers freight to a carrier for shipment and who directs the bill of lading to be executed by the carrier is called a consignor or shipper. Such person may be the consignor-consignee if the bill of lading is made to his own order.

Consignor:* The person named in a bill as the person from whom the goods have been received for shipment.

Conspicuous:* A term or clause is conspicuous when it is so written that a reasonable person against whom it is to operate ought to have noticed it. A printed heading in capitals (as: NONNEGOTIABLE BILL OF LADING) is conspicuous. Language in the body of a form is "conspicuous" if it is in larger or other contrasting type or color. But in a telegram any stated term is "conspicuous." Whether a term or clause is "conspicuous" or not is for decision by the court.

Constitution: The Constitution of the United States constitutes the rules of organization of the United States and enumerates the powers and duties of the federal government thereby created. The constitutions of the several states prescribe the organization of each of the states and in general enumerate those powers not delegated to the federal government.

Constructive delivery: Although physical delivery of personal property has not occurred, yet by the conduct of the parties it may be inferred that as between them possession and title has passed. A sells large and bulky goods to B. Title and possession may pass by the act and conduct of the parties.

Consumer goods:* Goods that are used or bought for use primarily for personal, family, or household purposes.

Contract:* The total obligation that results from the parties' agreement as affected by the Code and any other applicable rules of law.

Contract right:* Any right to payment under a contract not yet earned by performance and not evidenced by an instrument or chattel paper.

Conversion:* Under Article 3—Commercial Paper, an instrument is converted when a drawee to whom it is delivered for acceptance refuses to return it on demand; or any person to whom it is delivered for payment refuses on demand either to pay or to return it; or it is paid on a forged indorsement.

Conveyance: A formal written instrument usually called a deed by which the title or other interests in land (real property) is transferred from one person to another. The word expresses also the fact that the title to real property has been transferred from one person to another.

Corporation: A collection of individuals created by statute as a legal person, vested with powers and capacity to contract, own, control, convey property, and transact business within the limits of the powers granted.

Corporation de facto: If persons have attempted in good faith to organize a corporation under a valid law (statute) and have failed in some minor particular, but have thereafter exercised corporate powers, such is a corporation de facto. Failure to have incorporators' signatures on applications for charter notarized is an illustration of noncompliance with statutory requirements.

Corporation de jure: A corporation that has been formed by complying with the mandatory requirements of the law authorizing such a corporation.

Corporeal: Physical things that are susceptible to the senses are corporeal. Automobiles, grain, fruit, and horses are corporeal and tangible and are called "chattels." The word corporeal is used in contradistinction to incorporeal or intangible. A chose in action (such as a check) is corporeal and tangible, or a chose in action may be a simple debt, incorporeal and intangible.

Costs: Costs, in litigation, are an allowance authorized by statute to a party for the expenses incurred in prosecuting or defending a lawsuit. The word *costs*, unless specifically designated by statute or contract, does not include attorney's fees.

Counterclaims: A claim by the defendant by way of cross-action that the defendant is entitled to recover from the plaintiff. It must arise out of the same transaction set forth in the plaintiff's complaint, and be connected with the same subject matter. S sues B for the purchase price. B counterclaims that the goods were defective, and that he thereby suffered damages.

Course of dealing: This 'is a sequence of previous conduct between the parties to a particular transaction which is fairly to be regarded as establishing a common basis of understanding for interpreting their expressions and other conduct.

Covenant: A promise in writing under seal. It is often used as a substitute for the word contract. There are convenants (promises) in deeds, leases, mortgages, and other instruments under seal. The word is used sometimes to name promises in unsealed instruments such as insurance policies.

Cover:* After a breach by a seller, the buyer may "cover" by making in good faith and without unreasonable delay any reasonable purchase of or contract to purchase goods in substitution for those due from the seller.

Credit:* ("Letter of credit") This means an engagement by a bank or other person made at the request of a customer and of a kind within the scope of Article 5—Letters of Credit that the issuer will honor drafts or

other demands for payment upon compliance with the conditions specified in the
credit. A credit may be either revocable or
irrevocable. The engagement may be either
an agreement to honor or a statement that
the bank or other person is authorized to
honor.

Creditor:* This includes a general creditor, a
secured creditor, a lien creditor, and any
representative of creditors, including an assignee for the benefit of creditors, a trustee
in bankruptcy, a receiver in equity, and an
executor or administrator of an insolvent
debtor's or assignor's estate.

Creditor beneficiary: If a promisee is under a
duty to a third party and, for a consideration, secures a promise from a promisor
which promise, if performed, discharges the
promisee's duty to the third party, such
third party is a creditor beneficiary. A owes
C $100. B, for a consideration, promises A
to pay A's debt to C. C is a creditor
beneficiary.

Cumulative voting: A stockholder in voting
for a director may cast as many votes for
one candidate for given office as there are
offices to be filled multiplied by the number
of shares of his stock, or he may distribute
this same number of votes among the other
candidates as he sees fit.

Custodian bank:* Any bank or trust company
that is supervised and examined by state or
federal authority having supervision over
banks and which is acting as custodian for a
clearing corporation.

Custody (personal property): The words *custody* and *possession* are not synonymous.
Custody means in charge of, to keep and
care for under the direction of the true
owner, without any interest therein adverse
to the true owner. A servant is in custody of
his master's goods. See *Possession.*

Customer:* Under Article 4—Bank Deposits
and Collections, this means any person
having an account with a bank or for whom
a bank has agreed to collect items and
includes a bank carrying an account with
another bank.

Customer:* As used in Letters of Credit, a
customer is a buyer or other person who
causes an issuer to issue a credit. The term

also includes a bank that procures issuance
or confirmation on behalf of that bank's
customer.

Damages: A sum of money the court imposes
upon a defendant as compensation for the
plaintiff because the defendant has injured
the plaintiff by breach of a legal duty.

d.b.a.: An abbreviation of "doing business as."
A person who conducts his business under
an assumed name is designated "John Doe
d.b.a. Excelsior Co."

Debenture: A term used to name corporate
obligations that are sold as investments. It is
similar to a corporate bond. However, it is
not secured by a trust deed. It is not like
corporate stock.

Debtor:* The person who owes payment or
other performance of the obligation secured,
whether or not he owns or has rights in the
collateral, and includes the seller of accounts, contract rights, or chattel paper.
Where the debtor and the owner of the
collateral are not the same person, the term
debtor means the owner of the collateral in
any provision of the Article dealing with the
obligation, and may include both where the
context so requires.

Deceit: A term to define that conduct in a
business transaction by which one man,
through fraudulent representations, misleads
another who has a right to rely on such
representations as the truth, or, who by
reason of an unequal station in life, has no
means of detecting such fraud.

Declaratory judgment: A determination by a
court on a question of law which simply
declares the rights of the parties without
ordering anything to be done.

Decree: The judgment of the chancellor
(judge) in a suit in equity. Like a judgment
at law, it is the determination of the rights
between the parties and is in the form of an
order that requires the decree to be carried
out. An order that a contract be specifically
enforced is an example of a decree.

Deed: A written instrument in a special form
signed, sealed, and delivered, that is used to
pass the legal title of real property from one
person to another. See *Conveyance.*
In order that the public may know about the
title to real property, deeds are recorded in

the Deed Record office of the county where the land is situated.

Deed of trust: An instrument by which title to real property is conveyed to a trustee to hold as security for the holder of notes or bonds. It is like a mortgage except the security title is held by a person other than the mortgagee-creditor. Most corporate bonds are secured by a deed of trust.

De facto: Arising out of, or founded upon, fact, although merely apparent or colorable. A de facto officer is one who assumes to be an officer under some color of right, acts as an officer, but in point of law is not a real officer. See *Corporation de facto.*

Defendant: A person who has been sued in a court of law; the person who answers the plaintiff's complaint. The word is applied to the defending party in civil actions. In criminal actions, the defending party is referred to as the accused.

Deficiency judgment: If, upon the foreclosure of a mortgage, the mortgaged property does not sell for a sufficient amount to pay the mortgage indebtedness, such difference is called a "deficiency" and is chargeable to the mortgagor or to any person who has purchased the property and assumed and agreed to pay the mortgage. Illus.: M borrows $10,000 from B and as security gives a mortgage on Blackacre. At maturity M does not pay the debt. B forecloses, and at public sale Blackacre sells for $8,000. There is a deficiency of $2,000, chargeable against M. If M had sold Blackacre to C and C had assumed and agreed to pay the mortgage, he would also be liable for the deficiency.

Defraud: To deprive one of some right by deceitful means. To cheat or withhold wrongfully that which belongs to another. Conveying one's property for the purpose of avoiding payment of debts is a transfer to "hinder, delay, or defraud creditors."

Del credere agency: When an agent, factor, or broker undertakes to guarantee to his principal the payment of a debt due from a buyer of goods, such agent, factor, or broker is operating under a del credere commission or agency.

Delivery: A voluntary transfer of the possession of property, actual or constructive, from one person to another with the intention that title vests in the transferee. In the law of sales, delivery contemplates the absolute giving up of control and dominion over the property by the vendor, and the assumption of the same by the vendee.

Delivery:* With respect to instruments, documents of title, chattel paper, or securities, this means voluntary transfer of possession.

Delivery order:* A written order to deliver goods directed to a warehouseman, carrier, or other person who in the ordinary course of business issues warehouse receipts or bills of lading.

Demand: A request by a party entitled, under a claim of right, that a particular act be performed. In order to bind an indorser on a negotiable instrument, a demand must first be made by the holder on the primary party and such person must dishonor the instrument. Demand notes mean "due when demanded." The word *demand* is also used to mean a claim or legal obligation.

Demurrage: Demurrage is a sum, provided for in a contract of shipment, to be paid for the delay or detention of vessels or railroad cars beyond the time agreed upon for loading or unloading.

Demurrer: A common-law procedural method by which the defendant admits all the facts alleged in the plaintiff's complaint but denies that such facts state a cause of action. It raises a question of law on the facts, which must be decided by the court.

Dependent covenants (promises): In contracts, covenants are either concurrent or mutual, dependent or independent. Dependent covenants mean the performance of one promise must occur before the performance of the other promise. In a cash sale, the buyer must pay the money before the seller is under a duty to deliver the goods.

Depositary bank:* Under Article 4—Bank Deposits and Collections, this means the first bank to which an item is transferred for collection even though it is also the payor bank.

Descent: The transfer of the title of property to the heirs upon the death of the ancestor, heredity; succession. If a person dies without making a will, his property will "descend" according to the Statute of Descent of the state wherein the property is located.

Detriment: Legal detriment that is sufficient consideration constitutes change of position or acts of forbearance by a promisee at the request of a promisor. See *Consideration.*

Devise: A gift, usually of real property, by a last will and testament.

Devisee: The person who receives title to real property by will.

Dictum: An expression of an idea, argument, or rule in the written opinion of a judge that is not essential for the determination of the issues. It lacks the force of a decision in a judgment.

Directed verdict: If it is apparent to reasonable men and the court that the plaintiff by his evidence has not made out his case, the court may instruct the jury to bring in a verdict for the defendant. If, however, different inferences may be drawn from the evidence by reasonable men, then the court cannot direct a verdict.

Discharge: The word has many meanings. A servant or laborer upon being released from his employment is discharged. A guardian or trustee, upon termination of his trust, is discharged by the court. A debtor released from his debts is discharged in bankruptcy. A person who is released from any legal obligation is discharged.

Discovery practice: The disclosure by one party of facts, titles, documents, and other things which are in his knowledge or possession and which are necessary to the party seeking the discovery as a part of a cause of action pending.

Dishonor: A negotiable instrument is dishonored when it is presented for acceptance or payment, and acceptance or payment is refused or cannot be obtained.

Distress for rent: The taking of personal property of a tenant in payment of rent on real estate.

Dividend: A dividend is a stockholder's pro rata share in the profits of a corporation. Dividends are declared by the board of directors of a corporation. Dividends are cash, script, property, and stock.

Documentary draft: * Under Article 4—Bank Deposits and Collections, this means any negotiable or nonnegotiable draft with accompanying documents, securities, or other papers to be delivered against honor of the draft.

Documentary draft: * ("Documentary demand for payment.") A draft the honor of which is conditioned upon the presentation of a document or documents. "Document" means any paper including document of title, security, invoice, certificate, notice of default, and the like.

Document of title: * This term includes bill of lading, dock warrant, dock receipt, warehouse receipt, or order for the delivery of goods, and also any other document that in the regular course of business or financing is treated as adequately evidencing that the person in possession of it is entitled to receive, hold, and dispose of the document and the goods it covers. To be a document of title, a document must purport to be issued by or addressed to a bailee and purport to cover goods in the bailee's possession which are either identified or are fungible portions of an identified mass.

Domicile: That place that a person intends as his fixed and permanent home and establishment and to which, if he is absent, he intends to return. A person can have but one domicile. The old one continues until the acquisition of a new one. One can have more than one residence at a time, but only one domicile. The word is not synonymous with *residence.*

Dominion: As applied to the delivery of property by one person to another, the word means the separation by the transferor or donor from all control over the possession and ownership of the property and the endowing of the transferee or donee with such control of possession and ownership. See *Gift.*

Donee: A recipient of a gift.

Donee beneficiary: If a promisee is under no duty to a third party, but for a consideration secures a promise from a promisor for the purpose of making a gift to a third party, such third party is a donee beneficiary. A, promisee for a premium paid, secures a promise from the insurance company, the promisor, to pay A's wife $10,000 upon A's death. A's wife is a donee beneficiary.

Donor: One that gives, donates, or presents.

Dormant partner: A partner who is not known to third persons but is entitled to share in the profits and is subject to the losses. Since credit is not extended upon the strength of such partner's name, he may withdraw without notice and is not subject to debts contracted after his withdrawal.

Duress (of person): Duress means a threat of bodily injury, criminal prosecution, or imprisonment of a contracting party or his near relative to such extent that the threatened party is unable to exercise freely his will at the time of entering into or discharging a legal obligation.

Duress (of property): The seizure by force or the withholding of goods by one not entitled, and the demanding by such person of something as a condition for the release of the goods.

Duty (in law): A legal obligation imposed by general law or voluntarily imposed by the creation of a binding promise. For every legal duty there is a corresponding legal right. By general law, A is under a legal duty not to injure B's person or property. B has a right that A not injure his person or property. X may voluntarily create a duty in himself to Y by a promise to sell Y a horse for $100. If Y accepts, X is under a legal duty to perform his promise. See *Right.*

Earnest money: A term used to describe money that one contracting party gives to another at the time of entering into the contract in order to "bind the bargain" and which will be forfeited by the donor if he fails to carry out the contract. Generally, in real estate contracts such money is used as part payment of the purchase price.

Easement: An easement is an interest in land —a right that one person has to some profit, benefit, or use in or over the land of another. Such right is created by a deed, or it may be acquired by prescription (the continued use of another's land for a statutory period).

Ejectment: An action to recover the possession of real property. It is now generally defined by statute and is a statutory action. See *Forcible entry and detainer.*

Ejusdem generis: Of the same class. General words taking their meaning from specific words which precede the general words. General words have the same meaning as specific words mentioned.

Embezzelment: The fraudulent appropriation by one person, acting in a fiduciary capacity, of the money or property of another. See *Conversion.*

Eminent domain: The right that resides in the United States, state, county, city, school, or other public body, to take private property for public use, upon payment of just compensation.

Entirety (Tenancy by): Property acquired by husband and wife whereby upon the death of one, the survivor takes the whole property. The tenancy exists in only a few states. The husband and wife are both vested with the whole estate so that the survivor takes no new title upon death of the other but remains in possession of the whole as originally granted. For the legal effect of such estate, the state statute should be consulted. See *Joint tenants.*

Entity: The word means "in being" or "existing." The artificial person created when a corporation is organized is "in being" or "existing" for legal purposes; thus, an entity. It is separate from the stockholders. The estate of a deceased person while in administration is an entity. A partnership for many legal purposes is an entity.

Equipment:* Goods that are used or bought for use primarily in business (including farming or a profession) or by a debtor who is a non-profit organization or a governmental subdivision or agency, or if the goods are not included in the definitions of inventory, farm products or consumer goods.

Equitable action: In Anglo-American law there have developed two types of courts and procedures for the administration of justice: law courts and equity courts. Law courts give as a remedy money damages only, whereas equity courts give the plaintiff what he bargains for. A suit for specific performance of a contract is an equitable action. In many states these two courts are now merged.

Equitable conversion: An equitable principle that, for certain purposes, permits real property to be converted into personalty. Thus real property owned by a partnership is, for the purpose of the partnership, personal property because to ascertain a partner's interest, the real property must be reduced to cash. This is an application of the equitable maxim, "Equity considers that done which ought to be done."

Equitable mortgage: A written agreement to make certain property security for a debt, and upon the faith of which the parties have acted in making advances, loans, and thus creating a debt. Example: an improperly executed mortgage, one without seal where a seal is required. An absolute deed made to the mortgagee and intended for security only is an equitable mortgage.

Equity: Because the law courts in early English law did not always give an adequate remedy, an aggrieved party sought redress from the king. Since this appeal was to the king's conscience, he referred the case to his spiritual adviser, the chancellor. The chancellor decided the case according to rules of fairness, honesty, right, and natural justice. From this there developed the rules in equity. The laws of trusts, divorce, rescission of contracts for fraud, injunction, and specific performance are enforced in courts of equity.

Equity of redemption: The right a mortgagor has to redeem or get back his property after it has been forfeited for nonpayment of the debt it secured. By statute, within a certain time before final foreclosure decree, a mortgagor has the privilege, by paying the amount of the debt, interest, and costs, of redeeming his property.

Escrow: An agreement under which a grantor, promisor, or obligor places the instrument upon which he is bound with a third person called escrow holder, until the performance of a condition or the happening of an event stated in the agreement permits the escrow holder to make delivery or performance to the grantee, promisee, or obligee. A (grantor) places a deed to C (grantee) accompanied by the contract of conveyance with B bank, conditioned upon B bank delivering the deed to C (grantee) when C pays all moneys due under contract. The contract and deed have been placed in "escrow."

Estate: A word used to name all the property of a living, deceased, bankrupt, or insane person. It is also applied to the property of a ward. In the law of taxation, wills, and inheritance, the word has a broad meaning. Historically, the word was limited to an interest in land: i.e., estate in fee simple, estate for years, estate for life, and so forth.

Estoppel: When one ought to speak the truth, but does not, and by one's acts, representations, or silence intentionally or through negligence induces another to believe certain facts exist, and such person acts to his detriment on the belief that such facts are true, the first person is estopped to deny the truth of the facts. B, knowingly having kept and used defective goods delivered by S under a contract of sale, is estopped to deny the goods are defective. X holds out Y as his agent. X is estopped to deny Y is not his agent. Persons are estopped to deny the legal effect of written instruments such as deeds, contracts, bills and notes, court records, and judgments. A man's own acts speak louder than his words.

Et al.: Literally translated means "and other persons." Words used in pleadings and cases to indicate that persons other than those specifically named are parties to a lawsuit.

Eviction: An action to expel a tenant from the estate of the landlord. Interfering with the tenant's right of possession or enjoyment amounts to an eviction. Eviction may be actual or constructive. Premises made uninhabitable because the landlord maintains a nuisance is constructive eviction.

Evidence: In law the word has two meanings. First, that testimony of witnesses and facts presented to the court and jury by way of writings and exhibits, which impress the minds of the court and jury, to the extent that an allegation has been proven. *Testimony* and *evidence* are not synonymous Testimony is a broader word and includes all the witness says. *Proof* is distinguished from *evidence* in that proof is the legal consequence of evidence. Second, the rules of law, called the law of evidence, that deter what evidence shall be introduced at a trial and what shall not; also what importance shall be placed upon the evidence.

Ex contractu: See *Action ex contractu.*

Ex delicto: See *Action ex delicto.*

Executed: As applied to contracts or other written instruments, means signed, sealed, and delivered. Effective legal obligations have thus been created. The term is also used to mean that the performances of a contract have been completed. The contract is then at an end. All is done that is to be done.

Execution: Execution of a judgment is the process by which the court through the sheriff enforces the payment of the judgment received by the successful party. The sheriff by a "writ" levies upon the unsuccessful party's property and sells it to pay the judgment creditor.

Executor (of an estate): The person, named or appointed in a will by a testator (the one who makes the will), who by authority of the will has the power to administer the estate upon the death of the testator and to dispose of it according to the intention of the testator. The terms *executor* and *administrator* are not synonymous. An executor is appointed by the deceased to administer an estate. An administrator is appointed by the court to administer the estate of a person who dies without having made a will. See *Intestate.*

Executory (contract): Until the performance required in a contract is completed, it is said to be executory as to that part not executed. See *Executed.*

Exemplary damages: A sum assessed by the jury in a tort action (over and above the compensatory damages) as punishment in order to make an example of the wrongdoer and to deter like conduct by others. Injuries caused by willful, malicious, wanton, and reckless conduct will subject the wrongdoers to exemplary damages.

Exemption: The condition of a person who is free or excused from a duty imposed by some rule of law, statutory or otherwise.

Express warranty: When a seller makes some positive representation concerning the nature, quality, character, use, and purpose of goods, which induces the buyer to buy, and the seller intends the buyer to rely thereon, the seller has made an express warranty.

Factor: A factor is an agent for the sale of merchandise. He may hold possession of the goods in his own name or in the name of his principal. He is authorized to sell and to receive payment for the goods. See *Agent.*

Factor's lien: A lien or right that a factor has to keep the possession of goods consigned to him for the purpose of reimbursing himself for all advances previously made to the consignor.

Farm products: * Goods that are crops or livestock or supplies used or produced in farming operations or if they are products of crops or livestock in their unmanufactured states (such as ginned cotton, wool-clip, maple syrup, milk and eggs), and if they are in the possession of a debtor engaged in raising, fattening, grazing, or other farming operations. If goods are farm products, they are neither equipment nor inventory.

Featherbedding: A term used in labor relations to describe the situation in which demand is made for the payment of wages for a particular service not actually rendered.

Fee simple estate: A term describing the total interest a person may have in land. Such an estate is not qualified by any other interest and passes upon the death of the owners to the heirs free from any conditions.

Felony: A term including all those criminal offenses that are punishable by death or imprisonment in a penitentiary.

Fiduciary: In general, a person is a fiduciary when he occupies a position of trust or confidence in relation to another person or his property. Trustees, guardians, and executors are illustrations of persons occupying fiduciary positions.

Financing agency: * A bank, finance company, or other person who in the ordinary course of business makes advances against goods or documents of title or who by arrangement with either the seller or the buyer intervenes in ordinary course to make or collect payment due or claimed under the contract for sale, as by purchasing or paying the seller's draft or making advances against it or by merely taking it for collection whether or not documents of title accompany the draft. "Financing agency" includes also a bank or other person who similarly intervenes between persons who are in the position of seller and buyer in respect to the goods.

Fine: A sum of money collected by a court from a person guilty of some criminal offense. The amount may be fixed by statute or left to the discretion of the court.

Firm offers:* An offer by a merchant to buy or sell goods in a signed writing which by its terms gives assurance that it will be held open.

Forbearance: Giving up the right to enforce what one honestly believes to be a valid claim in return for a promise is called forbearance and is sufficient "consideration" to make binding a promise.

Forcible entry and detainer: A remedy given to a landowner to evict persons unlawfully in possession of his land. A landlord may use such remedy to evict a tenant in default.

Forfeiture: Loss of money or property by way of compensation and punishment for injury or damage to the person or property of another or to the state. One may forfeit interest earnings for charging a usurious rate.

Forgery: Forgery is the false writing or alteration of an instrument with the fraudulent intent of deceiving and injuring another. Writing, without his consent, another's name upon a check for the purpose of securing money, is a forgery.

Franchise: A right conferred or granted by a legislative body. It is a contract right and cannot be revoked without cause. A franchise is more than a license. A license is only a privilege and may be revoked. A corporation exists by virtue of a "franchise." A corporation secures a franchise from the city council to operate a waterworks within the city. See *License.*

Franchise tax: A tax on the right of a corporation to do business under its corporate name.

Fraud: An intentional misrepresentation of the truth for the purpose of deceiving another person. The elements of fraud are (1) false representation of fact, not opinion, intentionally made; (2) intent that the deceived person act thereon; (3) knowledge that such statements would naturally deceive; and (4) that the deceived person acted to his injury.

Fraudulent conveyance: A conveyance of property by a debtor for the intent and purpose of defrauding his creditors. Such conveyance is of no effect, and such property may be reached by the creditors through appropriate legal proceedings.

Freehold: An estate in fee or one for life is a "freehold." A freeholder is usually a person who has a property right in the title to real estate amounting to an estate of inheritance (in fee), or one who has title for life, or for an indeterminate period.

Fungible:* With respect to goods or securities this means goods and securities of which any unit is, by nature or usage of trade, the equivalent of any other like unit. Goods which are not fungible shall be deemed fungible for the purposes of this Act to the extent that under a particular agreement or document unlike units are treated as equivalents.

Fungible goods: Fungible goods are those "of which any unit is from its nature of mercantile usage treated as the equivalent of any other unit." Grain, wine, and similar items are examples.

Future goods:* Goods that are not both existing and identified.

Futures: Contracts for the sale and delivery of commodities in the future, made with the intention that no commodity be delivered or received immediately.

Garnishee: A person upon whom a garnishment is served. He is a debtor of a defendant and has money or property that the plaintiff is trying to reach in order to satisfy a debt due from the defendant.

Garnishment: A proceeding by which a plaintiff seeks to reach the credits of the defendant that are in the hands of a third party, the garnishee. A garnishment is distinguished from an attachment in that by an attachment an officer of the court takes actual possession of property by virtue of his writ. In a garnishment, the property or money is left with the garnishee until final adjudication.

General agent: An agent authorized to do all the acts connected with carrying on a particular trade, business, or profession.

General intangibles:* Any personal property (including things in action) other than goods, accounts, contract rights, chattel paper, documents, and instruments.

Gift: A gift is made when a donor delivers the subject matter of the gift into the donee's hands, or places in the donee the means of obtaining possession of the subject matter, accompanied by such acts as show clearly that the donor intends to divest himself of all dominion and control over the property.

Gift causa mortis: A gift made in anticipation of death. The donor must have been in sickness and have died as expected; otherwise no effective gift has been made. If the donor survives, the gift is revocable.

Gift inter vivos: A gift inter vivos is an effective gift made during the life of the donor. By a gift inter vivos, property vests immediately in the donee at the time of delivery; whereas a gift causa mortis is made in contemplation of death and is effective only upon the donor's death.

Good faith:* In the case of a merchant this means honesty in fact and the observance of reasonable commercial standards of fair dealing in the trade.

Good faith:* Honesty in fact in the conduct or transaction concerned.

Goods:* All things (including specially manufactured goods) that are movable at the time of identification to the contract for sale other than the money in which the price is to be paid, investment securities, and things in action. "Goods" also includes the unborn young animals and growing crops and other identified things attached to realty as described in the section on goods to be severed from realty.

Grant: A term used in deeds for the transfer of the title to real property. The words *convey*, *transfer*, and *grant* as operative words in a deed to pass title are equivalent. The words *grant*, *bargain*, and *sell* in a deed, in absence of statute, mean the grantor promises he has good title to transfer free from incumbrances and warrants it to be such.

Grantee: A grantee is a person to whom a grant is made; one named in a deed to receive title.

Grantor: A grantor is a person who makes a grant. The grantor executes the deed by which he divests himself of title.

Gross negligence: The lack of even slight or ordinary care.

Guarantor: One who by contract undertakes "to answer for the debt, default, and miscarriage of another." In general, a guarantor undertakes to pay if the principal debtor does not; a surety, on the other hand, joins in the contract of the principal and becomes an original party with the principal.

Guardian: A person appointed by the court to look after the property rights and person of minors, the insane, and other incompetents or legally incapacitated persons.

Guardian ad litem: A special guardian appointed for the sole purpose of carrying on litigation and preserving the interests of a ward. He exercises no control or power over property.

Habeas corpus: A writ issued to a sheriff, warden, or official having custody of a person, directing the official to return the person, alleged to be unlawfully held, before a court in order to determine the legality of the imprisonment.

Hearsay evidence: Evidence that is learned from someone else. It does not derive its value from the credit of the witness testifying but rests upon the veracity of another person. It is not good evidence because there is no opportunity to cross-examine the person who is the source of the testimony.

Hedging contract: A contract of purchase or sale of an equal amount of commodities in the future by which brokers, dealers, or manufacturers protect themselves against the fluctuations of the market. It is a type of insurance against changing prices. A grain dealer, to protect himself, may contract to sell for future delivery the same amount of grain he has purchased in the present market.

Heirs: Those persons upon whom the statute of descent casts the title to real property upon the death of the ancestor. See statutes of descent for the particular state. See *Descent.*

Holder:* A person who is in possession of a document of title or an instrument or an investment security drawn, issued, or indorsed to him or to his order or to bearer or in blank.

Holding company: A corporation organized for the purpose of owning and holding the stock of other corporations. Shareholders of underlying corporations receive in exchange for their stock, upon an agreed value, the shares in the holding corporation.

Homestead: A parcel of land upon which a family dwells or resides, and which to them is home. The statute of the state or federal governments should be consulted to determine the meaning of the term as applied to debtor's exemptions, federal land grants, and so forth.

Honor:* This means to pay or to accept and pay, or where a creditor so engages to purchase or discount a draft complying with the terms of the instrument.

Illegal: Conduct that is contrary to public policy and the fundamental principles of law is illegal. Such conduct includes not only violations of criminal statutes but also the creation of agreements that are prohibited by statute and the common law.

Illusory: That which has a false appearance. If that which appears to be a promise is not a promise, it is said to be illusory. For example: "A promises to buy B's horse, if A wants to," is no promise. Such equivocal statement would not justify reliance; thus, it is not a promise.

Immunity: Freedom from the legal duties and penalties imposed upon others. The "privileges and immunities" clause of the United States Constitution means no state can deny to the citizens of another state the same rights granted to its own citizens. This does not apply to office holding. See *Exemption.*

Implied: The finding of a legal right or duty by inference from facts or circumstances. See *Warranty.*

Imputed negligence: Negligence that is not directly attributable to the person himself, but which is the negligence of a person who is in privity with him and with whose fault he is chargeable.

Incidental beneficiary: If the performance of a promise would indirectly benefit a person not a party to a contract, such person is an incidental beneficiary. A promises B, for a consideration, to plant a valuable nut orchard on B's land. Such improvement would increase the value of the adjacent land. C, the owner of the adjacent land, is an incidental beneficiary. He has no remedy if A breaches his promise with B.

Incumbrance: A burden on either the title to land or thing, or upon the land or thing itself. A mortgage or other lien is an incumbrance upon the title. A right of way over the land is an incumbrance upon the land and affects its physical condition.

Indemnify: Literally it means "to save harmless." Thus one person agrees to protect another against loss.

Indenture: A deed executed by both parties, as distinguished from a deed poll that is executed only by the grantor.

Independent contractor: The following elements are essential to establish the relation of independent contractor in contradistinction to principal and agent. An independent contractor must (1) exercise his independent judgment as to the means used to accomplish the result; (2) be free from control or orders from any other person; (3) be responsible only under his contract for the result obtained.

Indictment: An indictment is a finding by a grand jury that it has reason to believe the accused is guilty as charged. It informs the accused of the offense with which he is charged in order that he may prepare its defense. It is a pleading in a criminal action.

Indorsement: Writing one's name upon paper for the purpose of transferring the title. When a payee of a negotiable instrument writes his name on the back of the instrument, such writing is an indorsement.

Infringement: Infringement of a patent on a machine is the manufacturing of a machine that produces the same result by the same means and operation as the patented machine. Infringement of a trademark consists in the reproduction of a registered trademark and its use upon goods in order to mislead the public to believe that the goods are the genuine, original product.

Inherit: The word is used in contradistinction to acquiring property by will. See *Descent*.

Inheritance: An inheritance denotes an estate that descends to heirs. See *Descent*.

Injunction: A writ of judicial process issued by a court of equity by which a party is required to do a particular thing or to refrain from doing a particular thing.

In personam: A legal proceeding, the judgment of which binds the defeated party to a personal liability.

In rem: A legal proceeding, the judgment of which binds, affects, or determines the status of property.

Insolvent:* Refers to a person who either has ceased to pay his debts in the ordinary course of business or cannot pay his debts as they become due or is insolvent within the meaning of the federal bankruptcy law.

Installment contract:* One which requires or authorizes the delivery of goods in separate lots to be separately accepted, even though the contract contains a clause "each delivery is a separate contract" or its equivalent.

Instrument:* This means a negotiable instrument or a security or any other writing that evidences a right to the payment of money and is not itself a security agreement or lease and is of a type that is in ordinary course of business transferred by delivery with any necessary indorsement or assignment.

Insurable interest: A person has an insurable interest in a person or property if he will be directly and financially affected by the death of the person or the loss of the property.

Insurance: By an insurance contract, one party, for an agreed premium, binds himself to another, called the insured, to pay the insured a sum of money conditioned upon the loss of life or property of the insured.

Intent: A state of mind that exists prior to or contemporaneous with an act. A purpose or design to do or forbear to do an act. It cannot be directly proven but is inferred from known facts.

Interlocutory decree: A decree of a court of equity that does not settle the complete issue but settles only some intervening part, awaiting a final decree.

Intermediary bank:* Under Article 4—Bank Deposits and Collections, is a bank to which an item is transferred in course of collection except the depositary or payor bank.

Interpleader: A procedure whereby a person who has an obligation, e.g., to pay money, and does not know which of two or more claimants are entitled to performance, can bring a suit that requires the contesting parties to litigate between themselves.

Intestate: The intestate laws are the laws of descent or distribution of the estate of a deceased person. A person dies intestate who has not made a will.

Inventory:* Goods that are held by a person who holds them for sale or lease or to be furnished under contracts of service or if he has so furnished them, or if they are raw materials, work in process or materials used or consumed in a business. Inventory of a person is not to be classified as his equipment.

Irreparable damage or injury: Irreparable does not mean such injury as is beyond the possibility of repair, but it does mean that it is so constant and frequent in occurrence that no fair or reasonable redress can be had in a court of law. Thus the plaintiff must seek a remedy in equity by way of an injunction.

Issue:* Under Article 3—Commercial Paper, "issue" means the first delivery of an instrument to a holder or a remitter.

Issuer:* A bailee who issues a document except that in relation to an unaccepted delivery order it means the person who orders the possessor of goods to deliver. Issuer includes any person for whom an agent or employee purports to act in issuing a document if the agent or employee has real or apparent authority to issue documents, notwithstanding that the issuer received no goods or that the goods were misdescribed or that in any other respect the agent or employee violated his instructions.

Item:* Under Article 4—Bank Deposits and Collections, this means any instrument for the payment of money even though it is not negotiable but does not include money.

Jeopardy: A person is in jeopardy when he is regularly charged with a crime before a court properly organized and competent to try him. If acquitted, he cannot be tried again for the same offense.

Joint and several: Two or more persons have an obligation which binds them individually as well as jointly. The obligation can be enforced either by joint action against all of them or by separate actions against one or more.

Joint ownership: The interest that two or more parties have in property. See *Joint tenants.*

Joint tenants: Two or more persons to whom is deeded land in such manner that they have "one and the same interest, accruing by one and the same conveyance, commencing at one and the same time, and held by one and the same undivided possession." Upon the death of one joint tenant, his property passes to the survivor or survivors.

Joint tortfeasors: When two persons commit an injury with a common intent, they are joint tortfeasors.

Judgment (in law): A judgment is the decision, pronouncement, or sentence rendered by a court upon an issue in which it has jurisdiction.

Judgment in personam: A judgment against a person directing the defendant to do or not to do something, is a judgment in personam. See *In personam.*

Judgment in rem: A judgment against a thing, as distinguished from a judgment against a person. See *In rem.*

Judicial sale: A judicial sale is a sale authorized by a court that has jurisdiction to grant such authority. Such sales are conducted by an officer of the court.

Jurisdiction: The authority conferred upon a court by the Constitution to try cases and determine causes.

Jury: A group of persons, usually twelve, sworn to declare the facts of a case as they are proved from the evidence presented to them and, upon instructions from the court, to find a verdict in the cause before them.

Laches: Laches is a term used in equity to name that conduct that is neglect to assert one's rights or to do what by the law a person should have done and did not do. Such failure on the part of one to assert a right will give an equitable defense to another party.

Latent defect: A defect in materials not discernible by examination. Used in contradistinction to patent defect, which is discernible.

Lease: A contract by which one person divests himself of possession of lands or chattels and grants such possession to another for a period of time. The relationship were land is involved is called landlord and tenant.

Leasehold: The land held by a tenant under a lease.

Legacy: Personal property disposed of by a will. Sometimes the term is synonymous with *bequest.* The word *devise* is used in connection with real property distributed by will. See *Bequest, Devise.*

Legatee: A person to whom a legacy is given by will.

Liability: In its broadest legal sense, the word means any obligation one may be under by reason of some rule of law. It includes debt, duty, and responsibility.

Libel: The malicious publication of a defamation of a person by printing, writing, signs, or pictures, for the purpose of injuring the reputation and good name of such person. "The exposing of a person to public hatred, contempt, or ridicule."

License (governmental regulation): A license is a privilege granted by a state or city upon the payment of a fee, which confers authority upon the licensee to do some act or series of acts, which otherwise would be illegal. A license is not a contract and may be revoked for cause. It is a method of governmental regulation exercised under the police power.

License (privilege): A license is a mere personal privilege given by the owner to another to do designated acts upon the land of the owner. It is revocable at will, creates no estate in the land, and such licensee is not in possession. "It is a mere excuse for what otherwise would be a trespass."

Lien: A right one person, usually a creditor, has, to keep possession of or control the property of another for the purpose of satisfying a debt. There are many kinds of liens: judgment liens, attorney's liens, innkeeper's liens, logger's liens, vendor's liens. Consult statute of state for type of liens. See *Judgment.*

Lien creditor:* A creditor who has acquired a lien on the property involved by attachment, levy, or the like and includes an assignee for benefit of creditors from the time of assignment, and a trustee in bankruptcy from the date of the filing of the petition or a receiver in equity from the time of appointment. Unless all the creditors represented had knowledge of the security interest, such a representative of creditors is a lien creditor without knowledge even though he personally has knowledge of the security interest.

Limitation of actions: Statutes of limitations exist for the purpose of bringing to an end old claims. Because witnesses die, memory fails, papers are lost, and the evidence becomes inadequate, stale claims are barred. Such statutes are called statutes of repose. Within a certain period of time, action on claims must be brought; otherwise, they are barred. The period varies from six months to twenty years.

Liquidated: A claim is liquidated when it has been made fixed and certain by the parties concerned.

Liquidated damages: A fixed sum agreed upon between the parties to a contract, to be paid as ascertained damages by that party who breaches the contract. If the sum is excessive, the courts will declare it to be a penalty and unenforceable.

Liquidation: The process of winding up the affairs of a corporation or firm for the purpose of paying its debts and disposing of its assets. May be done voluntarily or under the orders of a court.

Lis pendens: The words mean "pending the suit nothing should be changed." The court, having control of the property involved in the suit, issues notice "lis pendens," that persons dealing with the defendant regarding the subject matter of the suit, do so subject to final determination of the action.

Lot:* A parcel or a single article that is the subject matter of a separate sale or delivery, whether or not it is sufficient to perform the contract.

Magistrate: A public officer, usually a judge, "who has power to issue a warrant for the arrest of a person charged with a public offense." The word has wide application and includes justices of the peace, notaries public, recorders, and other public officers who have power to issue executive orders.

Malice: Malice is a term to define a wrongful act done intentionally without excuse. It does not necessarily mean ill will, but it indicates a state of mind that is reckless concerning the law and the rights of others. Malice is distinguished from negligence in that in *malice* there is always a purpose to injure, whereas such is not true of the word *negligence.*

Malicious prosecution: The prosecution of another at law with malice and without probable cause to believe that such legal action will be successful.

Mandamus: A writ issued by a court of law, in the name of the state, directed to some inferior court, officer, corporation, or person commanding them to do a particular thing that appertains to their office or duty.

Mandatory injunction: An injunctive order issued by a court of equity that compels affirmative action by the defendant.

Marketable title: A title of such character that no apprehension as to its validity would occur to the mind of a reasonable and intelligent person. The title to goods in litigation, subject to incumbrances, in doubt as to a third party's right, or subject to lien, is not marketable.

Marshaling assets: A principle in equity for a fair distribution of a debtor's assets among his creditors. For example, when a creditor of A, by reason of prior right, has two funds X and Y belonging to A out of which he may satisfy his debt, but B, also a creditor of A, has a right to X fund, the first creditor will be compelled to exhaust Y fund before he will be permitted to participate in X fund.

Master in chancery: An officer appointed by the court to assist the court of equity in taking testimony, computing interest, auditing accounts, estimating damages, ascertaining liens, and doing such other tasks incidental to a suit, as the court may require. The power of a master is merely advisory and his tasks largely fact finding.

Maxim: A proposition of law that because of its universal approval needs no proof or argument, and the mere statement of which gives it authority. Example: "A principal is bound by the acts of his agent, when the agent is acting within the scope of his authority."

Mechanic's lien: A mechanic's lien is created by statute to assist suppliers and laborers in collecting their accounts and wages. Such lien has for its purpose to subject the land of an owner to a lien for material and labor expended in the construction of buildings and other improvements.

Merchant: A person who deals in goods of the kind or otherwise by his occupation holds himself out as having knowledge or skill peculiar to the practices or goods involved in the transaction or to whom such knowledge or skill may be attributed by his employment of an agent or broker or other intermediary who by his occupation holds himself out as having such knowledge or skill.

Merger: Two corporations are merged when one corporation continues in existence and the other loses its identity by its absorption into the first. *Merger* must be distinguished from *consolidation*, in which case both corporations are dissolved and a new one is created, which takes over the assets of the dissolved corporations.

Metes and bounds: The description of the boundaries of real property.

Midnight deadline:* Under Article 4—Bank Deposits and Collections, with respect to a bank this is midnight on its next banking day following the banking day on which it receives the relevant item or notice or from which the time for taking action commences to run, whichever is later.

Ministerial duty: The performance of a prescribed duty that requires the exercise of little judgment or discretion. A sheriff performs ministerial duties.

Minutes: The record of a court or the written transactions of the members or board of directors of a corporation. Under the certificate of the clerk of a court or the secretary of a corporation, the minutes are the official evidence of court or corporate action.

Misdemeanor: A criminal offense, less than a felony, that is not punishable by death or imprisonment. Consult the local statute.

Misrepresentation: The affirmative statement or affirmation of a fact that is not true; the term does not include concealment of true facts or nondisclosure or the mere expression of opinion.

Mistake of fact: The unconscious ignorance or forgetfulness of the existence or nonexistence of a fact, past or present, which is material and important to the creation of a legal obligation.

Mistake or law: An erroneous conclusion of the legal effect of known facts.

Mitigation of damages: A plaintiff is entitled to recover damages caused by the defendant's breach, but the plaintiff is also under a duty to avoid increasing or enhancing such damages. Such is called a duty to mitigate damages. If a seller fails to deliver the proper goods on time, the buyer, where possible, must buy other goods, thus mitigating damages.

Monopoly: The exclusive control of the supply and price of a commodity that may be acquired by a franchise or patent from the government; or, the ownership of the source of a commodity or the control of its distribution.

Mortgage: A conveyance or transfer of an interest in property for the purpose of creating a security for a debt. The mortgage becomes void upon payment of the debt, although the recording of a release is necessary to clear the title of the mortgaged property.

Mutual assent: In every contract each party must agree to the same thing. Each must know what the other intends; they must mutually assent or be in agreement.

Mutuality: A word used to describe the situation in every contract that it must be binding on both parties. Each party to the contract must be bound to the other party to do something by virtue of the legal duty created.

Negligence: The failure to do that which an ordinary, reasonable, prudent man would do, or the doing of some act that an ordinary, prudent man would not do. Reference must always be made to the situation, the circumstances, and the knowledge of the parties.

Negotiation:* Under Article 3—Commercial Paper, this is the transfer of an instrument in such form that the transferee becomes a holder. If the instrument is payable to order it is negotiated by delivery with any necessary indorsement; if payable to bearer it is negotiated by delivery.

Net assets: The property or effects of a firm, corporation, institution, or estate, remaining after all its obligations have been paid.

Nexus: Connection, tie, or link used in the law of taxation to establish a connection between a tax and the activity or person being taxed.

Nolo contendere: A plea by an accused in a criminal action. It does not admit guilt of the offense charged, but does equal a plea of guilty for purpose of sentencing.

Nominal damages: A small sum assessed as sufficient to award the case and cover the costs. In such case, no actual damages have been proven.

Nonsuit: A judgment given against the plaintiff when he is unable to prove his case or fails to proceed with the trial after the case is at issue.

Noscitur a sociis: The meaning of a word is or may be known from the accompanying words.

Notary: A public officer authorized to administer oaths by way of affidavits and depositions; also to attest deeds and other formal papers in order that such papers may be used as evidence and be qualified for recording.

Notice:* A person has "notice" of a fact when (a) he has actual knowledge of it; or (b) he has received a notice or notification of it; or (c) from all the facts and circumstances known to him at the time in question he has reason to know that it exists.
A person "knows" or has "knowledge" of a fact when he has actual knowledge of it. "Discover" or "learn" or a word or phrase of similar import refers to knowledge rather than to reason to know.

Novation: The substitution of one obligation for another. When debtor A is substituted for debtor B, and by agreement with the creditor C, debtor B is discharged, a novation has occurred.

Nudum pactum: A naked promise—one for which no consideration has been given.

Nuisance: The word *nuisance* is generally applied to any continuous or continued conduct that causes annoyance, inconvenience, and damage to person or property. It usually applies to the unreasonable and wrongful use of property that produces material discomfort, hurt, and damage to the person or property of another. Example: Fumes from a factory.

Obligee: A creditor or promisee.

Obligor: A debtor or promisor.

Option: A right secured by a contract to accept or reject an offer to purchase property at a fixed price within a fixed time. It is an irrevocable offer sometimes called a "paid-for offer."

Order:* Under Article 3—Commercial Paper, this means a direction to pay and must be more than an authorization or request. It must identify the person to pay with reasonable certainty. It may be addressed to one or more such persons jointly or in the alternative but not in succession.

Ordinance: An ordinance is, generally speaking, the legislative act of a municipality. A city council is a legislative body and passes ordinances that are the laws of the city.

Ordinary care: That care that a prudent man would take under the circumstances of the particular case.

Par value: The words mean "face value." The par value of stocks and bonds on the date of issuance is the principal. At a later date, the par value is the principal plus interest.

Pari delicto: The fault or blame is shared equally.

Pari materia: Latin words that mean "related to the same matter or subject." Statutes and covenants concerning the same subject matter are in pari materia, and as a general rule, for the purpose of ascertaining their meaning, are construed together.

Partition: Court proceedings brought at the request of a party in interest, that real property be taken by the court and divided among the respective owners as their interests appear. If the property is incapable of division in kind, then the property is to be sold and the money divided as each interest appears.

Party:* A person who has engaged in a transaction or made an agreement within the Uniform Commercial Code.

Patent ambiguity: An uncertainty in a written instrument that is obvious upon reading.

Payor bank:* Under Article 4—Bank Deposits and Collections, a bank by which an item is payable as drawn or accepted.

Penal bond: A bond given by an accused, or by another person in his behalf, for the payment of money if the accused fails to appear in court on a certain day.

Pendente lite: A Latin phrase that means "pending during the progress of a suit at law."

Per curiam: A decision by the full court without indicating the author of the decision.

Peremptory challenge: An objection, by a party to a lawsuit, to a person serving as a juror, for which no reason need be given.

Perjury: False swearing upon an oath properly administered in some judicial proceedings.

Per se: Literally it means "by itself." Thus a contract clause may be inherently unconscionable—unconscionable per se.

Personal property: The rights, powers, and privileges a person has in movable things such as chattels, and choses in action. Personal property is used in contradistinction to real property.

Personal representative: The administrator or executor of a deceased person or the guardian of a child or the conservator of an incompetent.

Personal service: The term means that the sheriff actually delivered to the defendant in person a service of process.

Plaintiff: In an action at law, the complaining party or the one who commences the action is called the plaintiff. He is the person who seeks a remedy in court.

Plea: An allegation or answer in a court proceeding.

Pleading: The process by which the parties in a lawsuit arrive at an issue.

Pledge: The deposit or placing of personal property as security for a debt or other obligation with a person called a pledgee. The pledgee has the implied power to sell the property if the debt is not paid. If the debt is paid, the right to possession returns to the pledgor.

Polling jury: To poll the jury is to call the name of each juror and inquire what his verdict is before such is made a matter of record.

Possession: The method, recognized by law, of holding, detaining, or controlling by one's self or by another, property, either personal or real, which will exclude others from holding, detaining, or controlling such property.

Power of attorney: An instrument authorizing another to act as one's agent or attorney in fact.

Precedent: A previously decided case that can serve as an authority to help decide a present controversy. The use of such case is called the doctrine of *stare decisis*, which means to adhere to decided cases and settled principles. Literally, "to stand as decided."

Preference: The term is used most generally in bankruptcy law. Where a bankrupt makes payment of money to certain creditors enabling them to obtain a greater percentage of their debts than other creditors in the same class, and the payment is made within four months prior to the filing of a bankruptcy petition, such payment constitutes illegal and voidable preference. An intention to prefer such creditors must be shown. An insolvent person may lawfully prefer one creditor to another, if done in good faith and without intent to defraud others.

Preferred stock: Stock that entitles the holder to dividends from earnings before the owners of common stock can receive a dividend.

Preponderance: Preponderance of the evidence means that evidence that in the judgment of the jurors is entitled to the greatest weight, which appears to be more credible, has greater force, and overcomes not only the opposing presumptions but also the opposing evidence.

Presenting bank:* Under Article 4—Bank Deposits and Collections, this is any bank presenting an item except a payor bank.

Presentment:* Under Article 3—Commercial Paper, "Presentment" is a demand for acceptance or payment made upon the maker, acceptor, drawee, or other payor by or on behalf of the holder.

Presumption:* "Presumed" means that the trier of fact must find the existence of the fact presumed unless and until evidence is introduced which would support a finding of its nonexistence.

Prima facie: The words literally mean "at first view." Thus, that which first appears seems to be true. A prima facie case is one that stands until contrary evidence is produced.

Privilege: A legal idea or concept of lesser significance than a right. An invitee has only a privilege to walk on another's land because such privilege may be revoked at will; whereas a person who has an easement to go on another's land has a right, created by a grant, which is an interest in land and cannot be revoked at will. To be exempt from jury service is a privilege.

Privity: Mutual and successive relationship to the same interest. Offeror and offeree, assignor and assignee, grantor and grantee are in privity. Privity of estate means that one takes title from another. In contract law, privity denotes parties in mutual legal relationship to each other by virtue of being promisees and promisors. At early common law, third-party beneficiaries and assignees were said to be not in "privity."

Probate: A court that handles the settlement of estates.

Proceeds:* Whatever is received when collateral or proceeds are sold, exchanged, collected or otherwise disposed of. The term also includes the account arising when the right to payment is earned under a contract right. Money, checks, and the like are "cash proceeds." All other proceeds are "non-cash proceeds."

Process: In a court proceeding, a process is an instrument issued by the court in the name of the state before or during the progress of the trial, under the seal of the court, directing an officer of the court to do, act, or cause some act to be done incidental to the trial.

Promise:* Under Article 3—Commercial Paper, it is an undertaking to pay, and must be more than an acknowledgment of an obligation.

Property: All those rights, powers, privileges, and immunities that one has concerning tangibles and intangibles. The term includes everything of value subject to ownership.

Proximate cause: The cause that sets other causes in operation. The responsible cause of an injury.

Proxy: Authority to act for another, used by absent stockholders or members of legislative bodies to have their votes cast by others.

Punitive damages: Damages by way of punishment allowed for an injury caused by a wrong that is willful and malicious.

Purchase:* This includes taking by sale, discount, negotiation, mortgage, pledge, lien, issue or re-issue, gift or any other voluntary transaction creating an interest in property.

Purchase-money security interest:* A security interest that is taken or retained by the seller of the collateral to secure all or part of its price; or taken by a person who by making advances or incurring an obligation gives value to enable the debtor to acquire rights in or the use of collateral if such value is in fact so used.

Quasi contract: The term *quasi contract* is used to define a situation where a legal duty arises that does not rest upon a promise but does involve the payment of money. In order to do justice by a legal fiction, the court enforces the duty as if a promise in fact exists. Thus, if A gives B money by mistake, A can compel B to return the money by an action in quasi contract.

Quiet title: A suit brought by the owner of real property for the purpose of bringing into court any person who claims an adverse interest in the property and requiring him to either establish his claim or be barred from asserting it thereafter. It may be said that the purpose is to remove "clouds" from the title.

Quitclaim: A deed that releases a right or interest in land but does not include any covenants of warranty. The grantor transfers only that which he has.

Quo warranto: A proceeding in court by which a governmental body tests or inquires into the authority or legality of the claim of any person to a public office, franchise, or privilege.

Ratification: The confirmation of one's own previous act or act of another: e.g., a principal may ratify the previous unauthorized act of his agent. B's agent, without authority, buys goods. B, by keeping the goods and receiving the benefits of the agent's act, ratifies the agency.

Real property: The term means land with all its buildings, appurtenances, equitable and legal interests therein. The word is used in contradistinction to personal property, which refers to movables or chattels.

Reasonable care: The care that prudent persons would exercise under the same circumstances.

Receiver: An officer of the court appointed on behalf of all parties to the litigation to take possession of, hold, and control the property involved in the suit, for the benefit of the party who will be determined to be entitled thereto.

Recoupment: A right to deduct from the plaintiff's claim any payment or loss that the defendant has suffered by reason of the plaintiff's wrongful act. The word means "a cutting back."

Redemption: To buy back, a debtor buys back or redeems his mortgaged property when he pays the debt.

Referee: A person to whom a cause pending in a court is referred by the court, to take testimony, hear the parties, and report thereon to the court.

Registered form:* A security is in registered form when it specifies a person entitled to the security or to the rights it evidences and when its transfer may be registered upon books maintained for that purpose by or on behalf of an issuer as security so states.

Reinsurance: In a contract of reinsurance, one insurance company agrees to indemnify another insurance company in whole or in part against risks that the first company has assumed. The original contract of insurance and the reinsurance contract are distinct contracts. There is no privity between the original insured and the reinsurer.

Release: The voluntary relinquishing of a right, lien, or any other obligation. A release need not be under seal, nor does it necessarily require consideration. The words *release, remise, and discharge* are often used together to mean the same thing.

Remand: To send back a cause for the appellate court to the lower court in order that the lower court may comply with the instructions of the appellate court. Also to return a prisoner to jail.

Remedy: The word is used to signify the judicial means or court procedures by which legal and equitable rights are enforced.

Remitting bank:* Under Article 4—Bank Deposits and Collections, is any payor or intermediary bank remitting for an item.

Replevin: A remedy given by statute for the recovery of the possession of a chattel. Only the right to possession can be tried in such action.

Res: A Latin word that means "thing."

Res judicata: The doctrine of *res judicata*

means that a controversy once having been decided or adjudged upon its merits is forever settled so far as the particular parties involved are concerned. Such a doctrine avoids vexatious lawsuits.

Rescission: (From *rescissio*) Rescission is where an act, valid in appearance, nevertheless conceals a defect, which may make it null and void, if demanded by any of the parties.

Respondent: One who answers another's bill or pleading, particularly in an equity case. Quite similar, in many instances, to defendant in law cases.

Respondeat superior: Latin words that mean the master is liable for the acts of his agent.

Responsible bidder: The word *responsible*, as used by most statutes concerning public works in the phrase "lowest responsible bidder," means that such bidder has the requisite skill, judgment, and integrity necessary to perform the contract involved and has the financial resources and ability to carry the task to completion.

Restraining order: An order issued by a court of equity in aid of a suit to hold matters in abeyance until parties may be heard. A temporary injunction is a restraining order.

Restraint of trade: Monopolies, combinations, and contracts that impede free competition are in restraint of trade.

Right: The phrase "legal right" is a correlative of the phrase "legal duty." One has a legal right if, upon the breach of the correlative legal duty, he can secure a remedy in a court of law.

Right of action: The words are synonymous with *cause of action*: a right to enforce a claim in a court.

Riparian: A person is a riparian owner if his land is situated beside a stream of water, either flowing over or along the border of the land.

Satisfaction: The term *satisfaction* in legal phraseology means the release and discharge of a legal obligation. Such satisfaction may be partial or full performance of the obligation. The word is used with *accord*. Accord means a promise to give a substituted performance for a contract obligation; satisfaction

means the acceptance by the obligee of such performance.

Scienter: Knowledge by a defrauding party of the falsity of a representation. In a tort action of deceit, knowledge that a representation is false must be proved.

Seal: A seal is to show that an instrument was executed in a formal manner. At early common law, sealing legal documents was of great legal significance. A promise under seal was binding by virtue of the seal. Today under most statutes any stamp, wafer, mark, scroll, or impression made, adopted, and affixed, is adequate. The printed word "seal" or the letters "L.S." is sufficient.

Seasonably:* An action is taken "seasonably" when it is taken at or within the time agreed or if no time is agreed at or within a reasonable time.

Secondary party:* Under Article 3—Commercial Paper, this means a drawer or indorser.

Secured party:* A lender, seller, or other person in whose favor there is a security interest, including a person to whom accounts, contract rights, or chattel paper have been sold. When the holders of obligations issued under an indenture of trust, equipment trust agreement, or the like are represented by a trustee or other person, the representative is the secured party.

Security: Security may be bonds, stocks, and other property placed by a debtor with a creditor, with power to sell if the debt is not paid. The plural of the term, *securities*, is used broadly to mean tangible choses in action, such as promissory notes, bonds, stocks, and other vendible obligations.

Security:* An instrument that is issued in bearer form or registered form; and is of a type commonly dealt in upon securities exchanges or markets or commonly recognized in any area in which it is issued or dealt in as a medium for investment; and is either one of a class or series or by its terms is divisible into a class or series of instruments; and evidences a share, a participation or other interest in property or in an enterprise or evidences an obligation of the issuer.

Security agreement:* An agreement that creates or provides for a security interest.

Security interest:* This means an interest in personal property or fixtures that secures payment or performance of an obligation.

Sell: The words *to sell* mean to negotiate or make arrangement for a sale. A sale is an executed contract *Sell* is the name of the process in executing the contract.

Servant: A person employed by another and subject to the direction and control of the employer in performance of his duties.

Setoff: A matter of defense, called a cross-complaint, used by the defendant for the purpose of making a demand on the plaintiff and which arises out of contract but is independent and unconnected with the cause of action set out in the complaint. See *Counterclaims* and *Recoupment.*

Settle:* Under Article 4—Bank Deposits and Collections, this means to pay in cash, by clearinghouse settlement, in a charge or credit or by remittance, or otherwise as instructed. A settlement may be either provisional or final.

Severable contract: A contract in which the performance is divisible. Two or more parts may be set over against each other. Items and prices may be apportioned to each other without relation to the full performance of all of its parts.

Share of stock: A proportional part of the rights in the management and assets of a corporation. It is a chose in action. The certificate is the evidence of the share.

Situs: Situs means "place, situation." The place where a thing is located. The "situs" of personal property is the domicile of the owner. The "situs" of land is the state or county where it is located.

Slander: Slander is an oral utterance that tends to injure the reputation of another. See *Libel.*

Special appearance: The appearance in court of a person through his attorney for a limited purpose only. A court does not get jurisdiction over a person by special appearance.

Special verdict: A special verdict is one in which the jury finds the facts only, leaving it to the court to apply the law and draw the conclusion as to the proper disposition of the case.

Specific performance: A remedy in personam in equity that compels such substantial performance of a contract as will do justice among the parties. A person who fails to obey a writ for specific performance may be put in jail by the equity judge for contempt of court. Such remedy applies to contracts involving real property. In absence of unique goods or peculiar circumstances, damages generally are an adequate remedy for the breach of contracts involving personal property.

Stare decisis: Translated, the term means "stand by the decision." The law should adhere to decided cases. See *Precedent.*

Statute: A law passed by the legislative body of a state is a statute.

Stock dividend: The issue by a corporation of new shares of its own stock to its shareholders as dividends in order to transfer retained earnings to capital stock.

Stockholders: Those persons whose names appear on the books of a corporation as the owners of the shares of stock and who are entitled to participate in the management and control of the corporation.

Stock split: A readjustment of the financial plan of a corporation whereby each existing share of stock is split into new shares, usually with a lowering of par value.

Stock warrant: A certificate that gives to the holder thereof the right to subscribe for and purchase a given number of shares of stock in a corporation at a stated price.

Stoppage in transitu: The right of a seller of goods, which have not been paid for, upon learning of the insolvency of the buyer, to stop the goods in transit and hold the same as security for the purchase price. It is an extension of the unpaid seller's lien.

Subordinate: In the case of a mortgage or other security interest, the mortgagee may agree to make his mortgage inferior to another mortgage or interest.

Subpoena: A process issued out of a court requiring the attendance of a witness at a trial.

Subrogation: The substitution of one person in another's place, whether as a creditor or as the possessor of any lawful right, so that the substituted person may succeed to the rights, remedies, or proceeds of the claim. It rests in equity on the theory that, where a party is compelled to pay a debt for which another is liable, such payment should vest the paying party with all the rights the creditor has against the debtor. For example: X insurance company pays Y for an injury to Y's car by reason of X's negligent act. X insurance company will be subrogated to Y's cause of action against Z.

Subsequent purchaser:* A person who takes a security other than by original issue.

Substantial performance: The complete performance of all the essential elements of a contract. The only permissible omissions or derivations are those that are trivial, inadvertent, and inconsequential. Such performance will not justify repudiation. Compensation for defects may be substituted for actual performance.

Substantive law: A word applied to that law that regulates and controls the rights and duties of all persons in society. It is used in contradistinction to the term *adjective law*, which means the rules of court procedure or remedial law which prescribe the methods by which substantive law is enforced.

Succession: The word means the transfer by operation of law of all the rights and obligations of a deceased person to those who are entitled to take.

Summons: A writ issued by a court to the sheriff directing him to notify the defendant that the plaintiff claims to have a cause of action against the defendant and that he is required to answer. If the defendant does not answer, judgment will be taken by default.

Suspends payments:* Under Article 4—Bank Deposits and Collections, with respect to a bank this means that it has been closed by order of the supervisory authorities, that a public officer has been appointed to take it over, or that it ceases or refuses to make payments in the ordinary course of business.

Tangible: Tangible is a word used to describe property that is physical in character and capable of being moved. A debt is intangible, but a promissory note evidencing such debt is tangible. See *Chose in action, Chattel.*

Tenancy: The interest in property that a tenant acquired from a landlord by a lease is called a tenancy. It may be at will or for a term. It is an interest in land.

Tenant: The person to whom a lease is made. A lessee.

Tender: To offer money in satisfaction of a debt or obligation by producing the same and expressing to the creditor a willingness to pay.

Tender of delivery:* This means that the seller must put and hold conforming goods at the buyer's disposition and give the buyer any notification reasonably necessary to enable him to take delivery.

Testamentary capacity: A person is said to have testamentary capacity when he understands the nature of his business, the value of his property, knows those persons who are natural objects of his bounty, and comprehends the manner in which he has provided for the distribution of his property.

Testator: A male person who has died leaving a will. A female person is called a testatrix.

Testimony: Those statements made by a witness under oath or affirmation in a legal proceeding.

Title: This word has different meanings. It may be limited or broad in its meaning. When a person has the exclusive rights, powers, privileges, and immunities to property, real and personal, tangible and intangible, against all other persons, he may be said to have the complete title thereto. The aggregate of legal relations concerning property is the title. The term is used to describe the means by which a person exercises control and dominion over property. A trustee has a limited title. See *Possession.*

Tort: A wrongful act committed by one person against another person or his property. It is the breach of a legal duty imposed by law other than by contract. The word *tort* means "twisted" or "wrong." A assaults B, thus committing a tort. See *Right, Duty.*

Tortfeasor: One who commits a tort.

Trade fixtures: Personal property placed upon or annexed to leased land by a tenant for the purpose of carrying on a trade or business during the term of the lease. Such property is generally to be removed at the end of the term, providing it can be so removed without destruction or injury to the premises. Trade fixtures include showcases, shelving, racks, machinery, and the like.

Trademark: No complete definition can be given for a trademark. Generally it is any sign, symbol, mark, word, or arrangement of words in the form of a label adopted and used by a manufacturer or distributor to designate his particular goods, and which no other person has the legal right to use. Originally, the design or trademark indicated origin, but today it is used more as an advertising mechanism.

Transfer: In its broadest sense, the word means the act by which an owner sets over or delivers his right, title, and interest in property to another person. A "bill of sale" to personal property is evidence of a transfer.

Treason: The offense of attempting by overt acts to overthrow the government of the state to which the offender owes allegiance; or of betraying the state into the hands of a foreign power.

Treasury stock: Stock or a corporation that has been issued by the corporation for value but is later returned to the corporation by way of gift or purchase or otherwise. It may be returned to the trustees of a corporation for the purpose of sale.

Trespass: An injury to the person, property, or rights of another person committed by actual force and violence, or under such circumstances that the law will imply that the injury was caused by force or violence.

Trust: A relationship between persons by which one holds property for the use and benefit of another. The relationship is called fiduciary. Such rights are enforced in a court of equity. The person trusted is called a trustee. The person for whose benefit the property is held is called a beneficiary or "cestui que trust."

Trustee in bankruptcy: An agent of the court authorized to liquidate the assets of the bankrupt, protect them, and bring them to the court for final distribution for the benefit of the bankrupt and all the creditors.

Trustee (generally): A person who is entrusted with the management and control of another's property and estate. A person occupying a fiduciary position. An executor, an administrator, a guardian.

Ultra vires: Literally the words mean "beyond power." The acts of a corporation are ultra vires when they are beyond the power or capacity of the corporation as granted by the state in its charter.

Unauthorized:* Refers to a signature or indorsement made without actual, implied, or apparent authority and includes a forgery.

Unfair competition: The imitation by design of the goods of another for the purpose of palming them off on the public, thus misleading the public by inducing it to buy goods made by the imitator. It includes misrepresentation and deceit; thus, such conduct is fraudulent not only as to competitors but as to the public.

Unilateral contract: A promise for an act or an act for a promise, a single enforceable promise. A promises B $10 if B will mow A's lawn. B mows the lawn. A's promise now binding is a unilateral contract. See *Bilateral contract.*

Usage of trade:* Any practice or method of dealing having such regularity of observance in a place, vocation, or trade as to justify an expectation that it will be observed with respect to the transaction in question. The existence and scope of such a usage are to be proved as facts. If it is established that such a usage is embodied in a written trade code or similar writing, the interpretation of the writing is for the court.

Usurious: A contract is usurious if made for a loan of money at a rate of interest in excess of that permitted by statute.

Utter: The word means to "put out" or "pass off." Tos utter a check is to offer it to another in payment of a debt. The words *utter a forged writing* mean to put such writing in circulation, knowing of the falsity of the instrument with the intent to injure another.

Value:* Except as otherwise provided with respect to negotiable instruments and bank collections, a person gives "value" for rights if he acquires them (a) in return for a binding commitment to extend credit or for the extension of immediately available credit whether or not drawn upon and whether or not a chargeback is provided for in the event of difficulties in collection; or (b) as security for or in total or partial satisfaction of a preexisting claim; or (c) by accepting delivery pursuant to a preexisting contract for purchase; or (d) generally, in return for any consideration sufficient to support a simple contract.

Vendee: A purchaser of property. The term is generally applied to the purchaser of real property. The word *buyer* is usually applied to the purchaser of chattels.

Vendor: The seller of property. The term is usually applied to the seller of real property. The word *seller* is applied to the seller of personal property.

Vendor's lien: An unpaid seller's right to hold possession of property until he has recovered the purchase price.

Venire: To come into court, a writ used to summon potential jurors.

Venue: The geographical area over which a court presides. Venue designates the county in which the action is tried. Change of venue means a move to another county.

Verdict: The decision of a jury, reported to the court, on matters properly submitted to it for its consideration.

Void: That which has no legal effect. A contract that is void is a nullity and confers no rights or duties.

Voidable: That which is valid until one party, who has the power of avoidance, exercises such power. An infant has the power of avoidance of his contract. A defrauded party has the power to avoid his contract. Such contract is voidable.

Voir dire: This phrase denotes the preliminary examination of a prospective juror.

Voting trust: A device whereby two or more persons, owning stock, with voting powers, divorce voting rights thereof from ownership, retaining to all intents and purposes the latter in themselves and transferring the former to trustees in whom voting rights of all depositors in the trust are pooled.

Wager: A relationship between persons by which they agree that a certain sum of money or thing owned by one of them will be paid or delivered to the other upon the happening of an uncertain event, which event is not within the control of the parties and rests upon chance.

Waive (verb): To "waive" at law is to relinquish or give up intentionally a known right or to do an act that is inconsistent with the claiming of a known right.

Waiver (noun): The intentional relinquishment or giving up of a known right. It may be done by express words or conduct that involves any acts inconsistent with an intention to claim the right. Such conduct creates an estoppel on the part of the claimant. See *Estoppel.*

Warehouseman:* A person engaged in the business of storing goods for hire.

Warehouse receipt:* A receipt issued by a person engaged in the business of storing goods for hire.

Warehouse receipt: An instrument showing that the signer has in his possession certain described goods for storage, and which obligates the signer, the warehouseman, to deliver the goods to a specified person or to his order or bearer upon the return of the instrument. Consult Uniform Warehouse Receipts Act.

Warrant (noun): An order in writing in the name of the state and signed by a magistrate directed to an officer commanding him to arrest a person.

Warrant (verb): To guarantee, to answer for, to assure that a state of facts exists.

Warranty: An undertaking, either expressed or implied, that a certain fact regarding the subject matter of a contract is presently true or will be true. The word has particular application in the law of sales of chattels. The word relates to title and quality. The word should be distinguished from *guaranty,* which means a contract or promise by one person to answer for the performance of another.

Waste: Damage to the real property so that its value as security is impaired.

Watered stock: Corporate stock issued by a corporation for property at an overvaluation, or stock issued for which the corporation receives nothing in payment therefor.

Will (testament): The formal instrument by which a person makes disposition of his property to take effect upon his death.

Working capital: The amount of cash necessary for the convenient and safe transaction of present business.

Writ: An instrument in writing under seal in the name of the state, issued out of a court of justice the commencement of, or during a legal proceeding, directed to an officer of the court commanding him to do some act, or requiring some person to do or refrain from doing some act pertinent or relative to the cause being tried.

Zoning ordinance: An ordinance passed by a city council by virtue of the police power which regulates and prescribes the kind of buildings, residences, or businesses that shall be built and used in different parts of a city.

Index